The Sporting News
NBA REGISTER
1992-93 EDITION

Editors/NBA Register

ALEX SACHARE
MARK SHIMABUKURO

Contributing Editors/NBA Register

SANDI BITTLER
JOHN DUXBURY
DAVE SLOAN

─PUBLISHING CO.─

Thomas G. Osenton, President and Chief Operating Officer; **Kathy Kinkeade**, Vice President/Production; **William N. Topaz**, Director/Information Development; **Gary Levy**, Editor; **Mike Nahrstedt**, Managing Editor; **Joe Hoppel**, Senior Editor; **Craig Carter and Tom Dienhart**, Associate Editors; **Kyle Barry, Lee Hart, Craig Mulcahy, Michelle Poston, George Puro, David Ressner and Terry Shea**, Editorial Assistants; **Bill Perry**, Director of Graphic Presentation; **Mike Bruner**, Art Director/Yearbooks and Books; **Gary Brinker**, Director of Information Systems.

A Times Mirror
Company

NBA statistics compiled by Elias Sports Bureau, New York.

ISBN: 0-89204-437-3   10 9 8 7 6 5 4 3 2 1

CONTENTS

EXPLANATION OF FOOTNOTES AND ABBREVIATIONS

*   Led league.
†   Tied for league lead.
‡   College freshman or junior varsity statistics; not counted toward totals.
... Statistic unavailable, unofficial or mathematically impossible to calculate.
—   Statistic not applicable.

POSITIONS: C: center. F: forward. G: guard.

STATISTICS: Ast.: assists. **Avg.:** average. **Blk.:** Blocked shots. **Def.:** Defensive rebounds. **Dq.:** Disqualifications. **FGA:** Field goals attempted. **FGM:** Field goals made. **FTA:** Free throws attempted. **FTM:** Free throws made. **G:** Games. **L:** Losses. **Min.:** Minutes. **Off.:** Offensive rebounds. **Pct.:** Percentage. **PF:** Personal fouls. **Pts.:** Points. **Reb.:** Rebounds. **Stl.:** Steals. **TO:** Turnovers. **Tot.:** Total. **W:** Wins.

LEAGUES/ORGANIZATIONS: AABA: All-America Basketball Alliance. **ABA:** American Basketball Association. **ABL:** American Basketball League. **BAA:** Basketball Association of America. **CBA:** Continental Basketball Association. **EBL:** Eastern Basketball League. **IL:** Inter-State League. **MBL:** Metropolitan Basketball League. **NAIA:** National Association of Intercollegiate Athletics. **NBA:** National Basketball Association. **NBL:** National Basketball League or National League. **NCAA:** National Collegiate Athletic Association. **NIT:** National Invitation Tournament. **NYSL:** New York State League. **PBLA:** Professional Basketball League of America. **WBA:** Western Basketball Association.

TEAMS: Al., Alb.: Albany. **Anch.:** Anchorage. **Atl.:** Atlanta. **Bak.:** Bakersfield. **Balt., Blt.:** Baltimore. **Bay St.:** Bay State. **Birm.:** Birmingham. **Bos., Bost.:** Boston. **Bu., Buff.:** Buffalo. **Char.:** Charlotte. **Ch., Chi.:** Chicago. **Cin.:** Cincinnati. **Cl., Clev.:** Cleveland. **Col.:** Columbus. **C.R.:** Cedar Rapids. **Da., Dal.:** Dallas. **Den.:** Denver. **Det.:** Detroit. **Evans.:** Evansville. **F.W.:** Fort Wayne. **Gold. St., Golden St., G. St., G.S.:** Golden State. **G.R., Gr. Rap.:** Grand Rapids. **Ho., Hou.:** Houston. **Ind.:** Indiana. **K.C.:** Kansas City. **KCO, K.C./Om.:** Kansas City/Omaha. **L.A., Los Ang.:** Los Angeles. **L.A.C., L.A. Clip.:** Los Angeles Clippers. **La Cr., La Cros.:** La Crosse. **L.A.L., L.A. Lak.:** Los Angeles Lakers. **Mia.:** Miami. **Mil.:** Milwaukee. **Min., Minn.:** Minnesota. **Miss.:** Mississippi. **Mont.:** Montana. **N.J.:** New Jersey. **N.O.:** New Orleans. **N.Y.:** New York. **Ok. City:** Oklahoma City. **Orl.:** Orlando. **Pens.:** Pensacola. **Phil.:** Philadelphia. **Phoe.:** Phoenix. **Port.:** Portland. **Q.C.:** Quad City. **R.C.:** Rapid City. **Rock.:** Rockford. **Roch.:** Rochester. **S.A., S. Ant., San. Ant.:** San Antonio. **Sac.:** Sacramento. **San Fran.:** San Francisco. **Sav.:** Savannah. **S.B.:** Santa Barbara. **Sea.:** Seattle. **S.F.:** San Francisco or Sioux Falls. **St.L.:** St. Louis. **Syr.:** Syracuse. **Tul.:** Tulsa. **Va.:** Virginia. **Was., Wash.:** Washington. **W.F., W. Falls:** Wichita Falls. **Wisc.:** Wisconsin. **Yak.:** Yakima.

BASEBALL STATISTICS: A: Assists. **AB:** At-bats. **A.L.:** American League. **Am. Assoc.:** American Association. **Avg.:** Average. **BB:** Bases on balls. **E:** Errors. **East.:** Eastern League. **ER:** Earned runs. **ERA:** Earned-run average. **G:** Games. **H:** Hits. **HR:** Home runs. **IP:** Innings pitched. **L:** Losses. **N.L.:** National League. **OF:** Outfield. **Pct.:** Winning percentage. **PO:** Putouts. **Pos.:** Position. **R:** Runs. **RBI:** Runs batted in. **SB:** Stolen bases. **SO:** Strikeouts. **Southern Assoc.:** Southern Association. **SS:** Shortstop. **Sv.:** Saves. **W:** Wins. **1B:** First base. **2B:** Doubles or second base. **3B:** Triples or third base.

ON THE COVER: Golden State forward Chris Mullin, who helped the U.S. Olympic team win gold medals as a collegian in 1984 and as a pro in 1992, averaged 25.6 points per game and was named to the All-NBA first team last season. (Photo by Andrew D. Bernstein/NBA Photos)

VETERAN PLAYERS

ABDELNABY, ALAA
F, BUCKS

PERSONAL: Born June 24, 1968, in Cairo, Egypt. . . . 6-10/240. . . . Name pronounced ALL-ah Ab-del-NOB-ee.
HIGH SCHOOL: Bloomfield Senior (N.J.).
COLLEGE: Duke.
TRANSACTIONS/CAREER NOTES: Selected by Portland Trail Blazers in first round (25th pick overall) of 1990 NBA Draft. . . . Traded by Trail Blazers to Milwaukee Bucks for rights to Tracy Murray (July 1, 1992).

COLLEGIATE RECORD

Season Team	G	Min.	FGM	FGA	Pct.	FTM	FTA	Pct.	Reb.	Pts.	Avg.
86-87 —Duke	29	192	47	81	.580	12	23	.522	50	106	3.7
87-88 —Duke	34	320	61	123	.496	44	63	.698	67	166	4.9
88-89 —Duke	33	530	123	194	.634	47	67	.701	125	293	8.9
89-90 —Duke	38	947	217	350	.620	138	178	.775	252	572	15.1
Totals	134	1989	448	748	.599	241	331	.728	494	1137	8.5

NBA REGULAR-SEASON RECORD

Season Team	G	Min.	FGM	FGA	Pct.	FTM	FTA	Pct.	REBOUNDS Off.	Def.	Tot.	Ast.	PF	Dq.	Stl.	Blk.	TO	Pts.	Avg.
90-91 —Portland	43	290	55	116	.474	25	44	.568	27	62	89	12	39	0	4	12	22	135	3.1
91-92 —Portland	71	934	178	361	.493	76	101	.752	81	179	260	30	132	1	25	16	66	432	6.1
Totals	114	1224	233	477	.488	101	145	.697	108	241	349	42	171	1	29	28	88	567	5.0

NBA PLAYOFF RECORD

Season Team	G	Min.	FGM	FGA	Pct.	FTM	FTA	Pct.	REBOUNDS Off.	Def.	Tot.	Ast.	PF	Dq.	Stl.	Blk.	TO	Pts.	Avg.
90-91 —Portland	5	13	2	6	.333	0	0	...	1	2	3	0	0	0	0	0	0	4	0.8
91-92 —Portland	8	25	5	10	.500	2	4	.500	0	4	4	2	4	0	0	0	2	12	1.5
Totals	13	38	7	16	.438	2	4	.500	1	6	7	2	4	0	0	0	2	16	1.2

ACRES, MARK
F/C

PERSONAL: Born November 15, 1962, in Inglewood, Calif. . . . 6-11/225. . . . Full name: Mark Richard Acres. . . . Name pronounced A-kers.
HIGH SCHOOL: Palos Verdes Estates (Palos Verdes, Calif.).
COLLEGE: Oral Roberts.
TRANSACTIONS/CAREER NOTES: Selected by Dallas Mavericks in second round (40th pick overall) of 1985 NBA Draft. . . . Played in Italy (1985-86) . . . Played in Belgium (1986-87). . . . Draft rights relinquished by Mavericks (July 31, 1986). . . . Signed as free agent by Boston Celtics (May 7, 1987). . . . Selected by Orlando Magic from Celtics in NBA expansion draft (June 15, 1989).

COLLEGIATE RECORD

Season Team	G	Min.	FGM	FGA	Pct.	FTM	FTA	Pct.	Reb.	Pts.	Avg.
81-82 —Oral Roberts	22	702	109	186	.586	104	143	.727	178	322	14.6
82-83 —Oral Roberts	28	976	203	368	.552	120	167	.719	269	526	18.8
83-84 —Oral Roberts	31	...	266	482	.552	114	159	.717	324	646	20.8
84-85 —Oral Roberts	29	959	221	380	.582	102	163	.626	280	544	18.8
Totals	110	...	799	1416	.564	440	632	.696	1051	2038	18.5

ITALIAN LEAGUE RECORD

Season Team	G	Min.	FGM	FGA	Pct.	FTM	FTA	Pct.	Reb.	Pts.	Avg.
85-86 —Pall. Varese	5	135	17	41	.415	17	20	.850	41	51	10.2

NBA REGULAR-SEASON RECORD

Season Team	G	Min.	FGM	FGA	Pct.	FTM	FTA	Pct.	REBOUNDS Off.	Def.	Tot.	Ast.	PF	Dq.	Stl.	Blk.	TO	Pts.	Avg.
87-88 —Boston	79	1151	108	203	.532	71	111	.640	105	165	270	42	198	2	29	27	54	287	3.6
88-89 —Boston	62	632	55	114	.482	26	48	.542	59	87	146	19	94	0	19	6	23	137	2.2
89-90 —Orlando	80	1691	138	285	.484	83	120	.692	154	277	431	67	248	4	36	25	70	362	4.5
90-91 —Orlando	68	1313	109	214	.509	66	101	.653	140	219	359	25	218	4	25	25	42	285	4.2
91-92 —Orlando	68	926	78	151	.517	51	67	.761	97	155	252	22	140	1	25	15	33	208	3.1
Totals	357	5713	488	967	.505	297	447	.664	555	903	1458	175	898	11	134	98	222	1279	3.6

Three-point field goals: 1988-89, 1-for-1. 1989-90, 3-for-4 (.750). 1990-91, 1-for-3 (.333). 1991-92, 1-for-3 (.333). Totals, 6-for-11 (.545).

NBA PLAYOFF RECORD

Season Team	G	Min.	FGM	FGA	Pct.	FTM	FTA	Pct.	REBOUNDS Off.	Def.	Tot.	Ast.	PF	Dq.	Stl.	Blk.	TO	Pts.	Avg.
87-88 —Boston	17	158	14	26	.538	9	18	.500	14	22	36	2	33	0	1	1	6	37	2.2
88-89 —Boston	2	2	0	1	.000	0	0	...	0	1	1	0	0	0	0	0	0	0	0.0
Totals	19	160	14	27	.519	9	18	.500	14	23	37	2	33	0	1	1	6	37	1.9

Three-point field goals: 1987-88, 0-for-1. 1988-89, 0-for-1. Totals, 0-for-2.

DID YOU KNOW. . .

. . . that Michael Jordan is the only player to be named MVP of the NBA Finals in consecutive seasons?

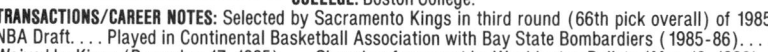

ADAMS, MICHAEL
G, BULLETS

PERSONAL: Born January 19, 1963, in Hartford, Conn. . . . 5-10/175.
HIGH SCHOOL: Hartford Public (Conn.).
COLLEGE: Boston College.

TRANSACTIONS/CAREER NOTES: Selected by Sacramento Kings in third round (66th pick overall) of 1985 NBA Draft. . . . Played in Continental Basketball Association with Bay State Bombardiers (1985-86). . . . Waived by Kings (December 17, 1985). . . . Signed as free agent by Washington Bullets (May 13, 1986). . . . Waived by Bullets (September 25, 1986). . . . Re-signed as free agent by Bullets (September 29, 1986). . . . Waived by Bullets (October 28, 1986). . . . Re-signed as free agent by Bullets (November 21, 1986). . . . Traded by Bullets with Jay Vincent to Denver Nuggets for Mark Alarie and Darrell Walker (November 2, 1987). . . . Traded by Nuggets with 1991 first-round draft choice and future considerations to Bullets for 1991 first-round draft choice (June 11, 1991).

COLLEGIATE RECORD

Season Team	G	Min.	FGM	FGA	Pct.	FTM	FTA	Pct.	Reb.	Pts.	Avg.
81-82 —Boston College	26	379	51	103	.495	36	61	.590	30	138	5.3
82-83 —Boston College	32	1075	195	405	.481	127	157	.809	86	517	16.2
83-84 —Boston College	30	1026	195	429	.455	130	172	.756	102	520	17.3
84-85 —Boston College	31	1044	193	413	.467	89	119	.748	102	475	15.3
Totals	119	3524	634	1350	.470	382	509	.750	320	1650	13.9

CBA REGULAR-SEASON RECORD

NOTES: CBA Rookie of the Year (1986). . . . CBA All-Star second team (1986). . . . CBA All-Defensive second team (1986).

Season Team	G	Min.	2-POINT FGM	FGA	Pct.	3-POINT FGM	FGA	Pct.	FTM	FTA	Pct.	Reb.	Ast.	Pts.	Avg.
85-86 —Bay State	38	1526	241	487	.495	21	71	.296	125	164	.762	149	320	670	17.6

NBA REGULAR-SEASON RECORD

RECORDS: Holds career records for most three-point field goals made—783; and most three-point field goals attempted—2,332. . . . Holds single-season record for most three-point field goals attempted—564 (1991). . . . Holds single-game records for most three-point field goals attempted—20; and most three-point field goals attempted in one half—13 (April 12, 1991, vs. Los Angeles Clippers). . . . Shares single-game record for most three-point field goals made—9 (April 12, 1991, vs. Los Angeles Clippers).

Season Team	G	Min.	FGM	FGA	Pct.	FTM	FTA	Pct.	Off.	Def.	Tot.	Ast.	PF	Dq.	Stl.	Blk.	TO	Pts.	Avg.
85-86 —Sacramento	18	139	16	44	.364	8	12	.667	2	4	6	22	9	0	9	1	11	40	2.2
86-87 —Washington	63	1303	160	393	.407	105	124	.847	38	85	123	244	88	0	85	6	81	453	7.2
87-88 —Denver	82	2778	416	927	.449	166	199	.834	40	183	223	503	138	0	168	16	144	1137	13.9
88-89 —Denver	77	2787	468	1082	.433	322	393	.819	71	212	283	490	149	0	166	11	180	1424	18.5
89-90 —Denver	79	2690	398	989	.402	267	314	.850	49	176	225	495	133	0	121	3	141	1221	15.5
90-91 —Denver	66	2346	560	1421	.394	465	529	.879	58	198	256	693	162	1	147	6	240	1752	26.5
91-92 —Washington	78	2795	485	1233	.393	313	360	.869	58	252	310	594	162	1	145	9	212	1408	18.1
Totals	463	14838	2503	6089	.411	1646	1931	.852	316	1110	1426	3041	841	2	841	52	1009	7435	16.1

Three-point field goals: 1985-86, 0-for-3. 1986-87, 28-for-102 (.275). 1987-88, 139-for-379 (.367). 1988-89, 166-for-466 (.356). 1989-90, 158-for-432 (.366). 1990-91, 167-for-564 (.296). 1991-92, 125-for-386 (.324). Totals, 783-for-2332 (.336).

NBA PLAYOFF RECORD

Season Team	G	Min.	FGM	FGA	Pct.	FTM	FTA	Pct.	Off.	Def.	Tot.	Ast.	PF	Dq.	Stl.	Blk.	TO	Pts.	Avg.
86-87 —Washington	3	82	8	25	.320	1	3	.333	0	7	7	10	6	0	7	0	5	19	6.3
87-88 —Denver	11	406	47	130	.362	36	41	.878	9	27	36	64	19	0	18	2	23	147	13.4
88-89 —Denver	2	75	15	36	.417	7	8	.875	5	12	17	9	6	0	3	0	8	47	23.5
89-90 —Denver	3	105	13	34	.382	7	8	.875	0	6	6	18	10	0	4	0	8	39	13.0
Totals	19	668	83	225	.369	51	60	.850	14	52	66	101	41	0	32	2	44	252	13.3

Three-point field goals: 1986-87, 2-for-9 (.222). 1987-88, 17-for-54 (.315). 1988-89, 10-for-22 (.455). 1989-90, 6-for-20 (.300). Totals, 35-for-105 (.333).

NBA ALL-STAR GAME RECORD

Season Team	Min.	FGM	FGA	Pct.	FTM	FTA	Pct.	Off.	Def.	Tot.	Ast.	PF	Dq.	Stl.	Blk.	TO	Pts.
1992 —Washington	14	4	8	.500	0	0	. . .	1	0	1	1	1	0	4	0	1	9

Three-point field goals: 1992, 1-for-3 (.333).

ADDISON, RAFAEL
F/G, NETS

PERSONAL: Born July 22, 1964, in Jersey City, N.J. . . . 6-7/226.
HIGH SCHOOL: Snyder (Jersey City, N.J.).
COLLEGE: Syracuse.
TRANSACTIONS/CAREER NOTES: Selected by Phoenix Suns in second round (39th pick overall) of 1986 NBA Draft. . . . Played in Italy (1987-88 through 1990-91). . . . Signed as free agent by New Jersey Nets (October 4, 1991).

COLLEGIATE RECORD

Season Team	G	Min.	FGM	FGA	Pct.	FTM	FTA	Pct.	Reb.	Pts.	Avg.
82-83 —Syracuse	31	572	110	211	.521	41	63	.651	98	261	8.4
83-84 —Syracuse	32	1104	229	410	.559	107	128	.836	192	565	17.7
84-85 —Syracuse	31	1110	235	452	.520	101	139	.727	180	571	18.4
85-86 —Syracuse	32	1012	205	385	.532	69	87	.793	179	479	15.0
Totals	126	3798	779	1458	.534	318	417	.763	649	1876	14.9

NBA REGULAR-SEASON RECORD

Season	Team	G	Min.	FGM	FGA	Pct.	FTM	FTA	Pct.	REBOUNDS Off.	Def.	Tot.	Ast.	PF	Dq.	Stl.	Blk.	TO	Pts.	Avg.
86-87	—Phoenix	62	711	146	331	.441	51	64	.797	41	65	106	45	75	1	27	7	54	359	5.8
91-92	—New Jersey	76	1175	187	432	.433	56	76	.737	65	100	165	68	109	1	28	28	46	444	5.8
Totals		138	1886	333	763	.436	107	140	.764	106	165	271	113	184	2	55	35	100	803	5.8

Three-point field goals: 1986-87, 16-for-50 (.320). 1991-92, 14-for-49 (.286). Totals, 30-for-99 (.303).

NBA PLAYOFF RECORD

Season	Team	G	Min.	FGM	FGA	Pct.	FTM	FTA	Pct.	REBOUNDS Off.	Def.	Tot.	Ast.	PF	Dq.	Stl.	Blk.	TO	Pts.	Avg.
91-92	—New Jersey	1	9	2	7	.286	0	0	...	0	0	0	1	0	0	0	0	0	5	5.0

Three-point field goals: 1991-92, 1-for-2 (.500).

ITALIAN LEAGUE RECORD

Season	Team	G	Min.	FGM	FGA	Pct.	FTM	FTA	Pct.	Reb.	Pts.	Avg.
87-88	—Livorno	36	1398	368	722	.510	130	170	.765	214	949	26.4
88-89	—Livorno	40	1517	405	790	.513	189	240	.788	235	1056	26.4
89-90	—Livorno	40	1569	434	778	.558	199	235	.847	261	1157	28.9
90-91	—Livorno	30	1142	287	508	.565	121	149	.812	201	771	25.7
Totals		146	5626	1494	2798	.534	639	794	.805	911	3933	26.9

AGUIRRE, MARK
F, PISTONS

PERSONAL: Born December 10, 1959, in Chicago.... 6-6/232.... Full name: Mark Anthony Aguirre.... Name pronounced a-GWI-er.
HIGH SCHOOL: Austin (Chicago), then Westinghouse Vocational (Chicago).
COLLEGE: DePaul.
TRANSACTIONS/CAREER NOTES: Selected by Dallas Mavericks in first round (first pick overall) of 1981 NBA Draft.... Traded by Mavericks to Detroit Pistons for Adrian Dantley and 1991 first-round draft choice (February 15, 1989).
MISCELLANEOUS: Member of NBA championship teams (1989, 1990).... Member of U.S. Olympic team (1980).

COLLEGIATE RECORD

NOTES: THE SPORTING NEWS College Player of the Year (1981).... THE SPORTING NEWS All-America first team (1980, 1981).

Season	Team	G	Min.	FGM	FGA	Pct.	FTM	FTA	Pct.	Reb.	Pts.	Avg.
78-79	—DePaul	32	...	302	581	.520	163	213	.765	244	767	24.0
79-80	—DePaul	28	...	281	520	.540	187	244	.766	213	749	26.8
80-81	—DePaul	29	1069	280	481	.582	106	137	.774	249	666	23.0
Totals		89	...	863	1582	.546	456	594	.768	706	2182	24.5

NBA REGULAR-SEASON RECORD

Season	Team	G	Min.	FGM	FGA	Pct.	FTM	FTA	Pct.	REBOUNDS Off.	Def.	Tot.	Ast.	PF	Dq.	Stl.	Blk.	TO	Pts.	Avg.
81-82	—Dallas	51	1468	381	820	.465	168	247	.680	89	160	249	164	152	0	37	22	135	955	18.7
82-83	—Dallas	81	2784	767	1589	.483	429	589	.728	191	317	508	332	247	5	80	26	261	1979	24.4
83-84	—Dallas	79	2900	*925	*1765	.524	465	621	.749	161	308	469	358	246	5	80	22	285	2330	29.5
84-85	—Dallas	80	2699	794	1569	.506	440	580	.759	188	289	477	249	256	3	60	24	253	2055	25.7
85-86	—Dallas	74	2501	668	1327	.503	318	451	.705	177	268	445	339	229	6	62	14	252	1670	22.6
86-87	—Dallas	80	2663	787	1590	.495	429	557	.770	181	246	427	254	243	4	84	30	217	2056	25.7
87-88	—Dallas	77	2610	746	1571	.475	388	504	.770	182	252	434	278	223	1	70	57	203	1932	25.1
88-89	—Dallas-Det.	80	2597	586	1270	.461	288	393	.733	146	240	386	278	229	2	45	36	208	1511	18.9
89-90	—Detroit	78	2005	438	898	.488	192	254	.756	117	188	305	145	201	2	34	19	121	1099	14.1
90-91	—Detroit	78	2006	420	909	.462	240	317	.757	134	240	374	139	200	2	47	20	128	1104	14.2
91-92	—Detroit	75	1582	339	787	.431	158	230	.687	67	169	236	126	171	0	51	11	105	851	11.3
Totals		833	25815	6851	14095	.486	3515	4743	.741	1633	2677	4310	2662	2400	30	650	281	2168	17542	21.1

Three-point field goals: 1981-82, 25-for-71 (.352). 1982-83, 16-for-76 (.211). 1983-84, 15-for-56 (.268). 1984-85, 27-for-85 (.318). 1985-86, 16-for-56 (.286). 1986-87, 53-for-150 (.353). 1987-88, 52-for-172 (.302). 1988-89, 51-for-174 (.293). 1989-90, 31-for-93 (.333). 1990-91, 24-for-78 (.308). 1991-92, 15-for-71 (.211). Totals, 325-for-1082 (.300).

NBA PLAYOFF RECORD

Season	Team	G	Min.	FGM	FGA	Pct.	FTM	FTA	Pct.	REBOUNDS Off.	Def.	Tot.	Ast.	PF	Dq.	Stl.	Blk.	TO	Pts.	Avg.
83-84	—Dallas	10	350	88	184	.478	44	57	.772	21	55	76	32	34	2	5	5	27	220	22.0
84-85	—Dallas	4	164	44	89	.494	27	32	.844	16	14	30	16	16	1	3	0	15	116	29.0
85-86	—Dallas	10	345	105	214	.491	35	55	.636	21	50	71	54	28	1	9	0	23	247	24.7
86-87	—Dallas	4	130	31	62	.500	23	30	.767	11	13	24	8	15	1	8	0	9	85	21.3
87-88	—Dallas	17	558	147	294	.500	60	86	.698	34	66	100	56	49	0	14	9	41	367	21.6
88-89	—Detroit	17	462	89	182	.489	28	38	.737	26	49	75	28	38	0	8	3	20	214	12.6
89-90	—Detroit	20	439	86	184	.467	39	52	.750	31	60	91	27	51	0	10	3	30	219	11.0
90-91	—Detroit	15	397	90	178	.506	42	51	.824	17	44	61	29	41	0	12	1	20	234	15.6
91-92	—Detroit	5	113	16	48	.333	12	16	.750	4	5	9	12	9	0	2	1	13	45	9.0
Totals		102	2958	696	1435	.485	310	417	.743	181	356	537	262	281	5	71	22	198	1747	17.1

Three-point field goals: 1983-84, 0-for-5. 1984-85, 1-for-2 (.500). 1985-86, 2-for-6 (.333). 1986-87, 0-for-4. 1987-88, 13-for-34 (.382). 1988-89, 8-for-29 (.276). 1989-90, 8-for-24 (.333). 1990-91, 12-for-33 (.364). 1991-92, 1-for-5 (.200). Totals, 45-for-142 (.317).

NBA ALL-STAR GAME RECORD

Season	Team	Min.	FGM	FGA	Pct.	FTM	FTA	Pct.	REBOUNDS Off.	Def.	Tot.	Ast.	PF	Dq.	Stl.	Blk.	TO	Pts.
1984	—Dallas	13	5	8	.625	3	4	.750	1	0	1	2	1	0	1	1	2	13
1987	—Dallas	17	3	6	.500	2	3	.667	1	1	2	1	1	0	0	0	2	9
1988	—Dallas	12	5	10	.500	3	3	1.000	0	1	1	1	3	0	1	0	3	14
Totals		42	13	24	.542	8	10	.800	2	2	4	4	5	0	2	1	7	36

Three-point field goals: 1987, 1-for-2 (.500). 1988, 1-for-3 (.333). Totals, 2-for-5 (.400).

AINGE, DANNY

G, SUNS

PERSONAL: Born March 17, 1959, in Eugene, Ore. . . . 6-5/185. . . . Full name: Daniel Ray Ainge.
HIGH SCHOOL: North Eugene (Eugene, Ore.).
COLLEGE: Brigham Young.
TRANSACTIONS/CAREER NOTES: Selected by Boston Celtics in second round (31st pick overall) of 1981 NBA Draft. . . . Traded by Celtics with Brad Lohaus to Sacramento Kings for Ed Pinckney and Joe Kleine (February 23, 1989). . . . Traded by Kings to Portland Trail Blazers for Byron Irvin, 1991 first-round draft choice and 1992 second-round draft choice (August 1, 1990). . . . Signed as free agent by Phoenix Suns (July 3, 1992).
MISCELLANEOUS: Member of NBA championship teams (1984, 1986).

COLLEGIATE RECORD

NOTES: THE SPORTING NEWS All-America first team (1981).

Season Team	G	Min.	FGM	FGA	Pct.	FTM	FTA	Pct.	Reb.	Pts.	Avg.
77-78 — Brigham Young	30	. . .	243	473	.514	146	169	.864	173	632	21.1
78-79 — Brigham Young	27	922	206	376	.548	86	112	.768	102	498	18.4
79-80 — Brigham Young	29	984	229	430	.533	97	124	.782	114	555	19.1
80-81 — Brigham Young	32	1212	309	596	.518	164	199	.824	152	782	24.4
Totals	118	. . .	987	1875	.526	493	604	.816	541	2467	20.9

NBA REGULAR-SEASON RECORD

Season Team	G	Min.	FGM	FGA	Pct.	FTM	FTA	Pct.	REBOUNDS Off.	Def.	Tot.	Ast.	PF	Dq.	Stl.	Blk.	TO	Pts.	Avg.
81-82 — Boston	53	564	79	221	.357	56	65	.862	25	31	56	87	86	1	37	3	53	219	4.1
82-83 — Boston	80	2048	357	720	.496	72	97	.742	83	131	214	251	259	2	109	6	98	791	9.9
83-84 — Boston	71	1154	166	361	.460	46	56	.821	29	87	116	162	143	2	41	4	70	384	5.4
84-85 — Boston	75	2564	419	792	.529	118	136	.868	76	192	268	399	228	4	122	6	149	971	12.9
85-86 — Boston	80	2407	353	701	.504	123	136	.904	47	188	235	405	204	4	94	7	129	855	10.7
86-87 — Boston	71	2499	410	844	.486	148	165	.897	49	193	242	400	189	3	101	14	141	1053	14.8
87-88 — Boston	81	3018	482	982	.491	158	180	.878	59	190	249	503	203	1	115	17	153	1270	15.7
88-89 — Boston-Sac.	73	2377	480	1051	.457	205	240	.854	71	184	255	402	186	1	93	8	145	1281	17.5
89-90 — Sacramento .	75	2727	506	1154	.438	222	267	.831	69	257	326	453	238	2	113	18	185	1342	17.9
90-91 — Portland	80	1710	337	714	.472	114	138	.826	45	160	205	285	195	2	63	13	100	890	11.1
91-92 — Portland	81	1595	299	676	.442	108	131	.824	40	108	148	202	148	0	73	13	70	784	9.7
Totals	820	22663	3888	8216	.473	1370	1611	.850	593	1721	2314	3549	2079	22	961	109	1293	9840	12.0

Three-point field goals: 1981-82, 5-for-17 (.294). 1982-83, 5-for-29 (.172). 1983-84, 6-for-22 (.273). 1984-85, 15-for-56 (.268). 1985-86, 26-for-73 (.356). 1986-87, 85-for-192 (.443). 1987-88, 148-for-357 (.415). 1988-89, 116-for-305 (.380). 1989-90, 108-for-289 (.374). 1990-91, 102-for-251 (.406). 1991-92, 78-for-230 (.339). Totals, 694-for-1821 (.381).

NBA PLAYOFF RECORD

NOTES: Shares NBA Finals single-game record for most points in an overtime period—9 (June 5, 1992, vs. Chicago).

Season Team	G	Min.	FGM	FGA	Pct.	FTM	FTA	Pct.	REBOUNDS Off.	Def.	Tot.	Ast.	PF	Dq.	Stl.	Blk.	TO	Pts.	Avg.
81-82 — Boston	10	129	19	45	.422	10	13	.769	6	7	13	11	21	0	2	1	11	50	5.0
82-83 — Boston	7	201	28	72	.389	8	11	.727	2	12	14	25	24	0	5	1	6	66	9.4
83-84 — Boston	19	253	41	90	.456	7	10	.700	4	12	16	38	36	0	9	2	13	91	4.8
84-85 — Boston	21	687	97	208	.466	30	39	.769	20	38	58	121	76	1	32	1	32	231	11.0
85-86 — Boston	18	652	107	193	.554	52	60	.867	22	54	76	93	57	0	41	1	31	280	15.6
86-87 — Boston	20	762	116	238	.487	31	36	.861	13	39	52	92	62	0	24	4	41	295	14.8
87-88 — Boston	17	670	71	184	.386	37	42	.881	15	38	53	109	64	2	9	1	41	198	11.6
90-91 — Portland	16	277	47	105	.448	23	28	.821	1	27	28	31	33	0	12	4	24	128	8.0
91-92 — Portland	21	449	81	169	.479	39	47	.830	8	32	40	49	58	1	15	1	25	222	10.6
Totals	149	4080	607	1304	.465	237	286	.829	91	259	350	569	431	4	149	16	224	1561	10.5

Three-point field goals: 1981-82, 2-for-4 (.500). 1982-83, 2-for-5 (.400). 1983-84, 2-for-9 (.222). 1984-85, 7-for-16 (.438). 1985-86, 14-for-34 (.412). 1986-87, 32-for-73 (.438). 1987-88, 19-for-57 (.333). 1990-91, 11-for-36 (.306). 1991-92, 21-for-52 (.404). Totals, 110-for-286 (.385).

NBA ALL-STAR GAME RECORD

Season Team	Min.	FGM	FGA	Pct.	FTM	FTA	Pct.	REBOUNDS Off.	Def.	Tot.	Ast.	PF	Dq.	Stl.	Blk.	TO	Pts.
1988 — Boston	19	4	11	.364	1	2	.500	1	2	3	2	1	0	1	0	1	12

Three-point field goals: 1988, 3-for-4 (.750).

RECORD AS BASEBALL PLAYER

TRANSACTIONS/CAREER NOTES: Selected by Toronto Blue Jays organization in 15th round of free-agent draft (June 7, 1977). . . . On restricted list (September 3-October 3, 1979 and September 9-October 8, 1980). . . . Placed on voluntary retired list (November 30, 1981).

Year Team (League)	Pos.	G	AB	R	H	BATTING 2B	3B	HR	RBI	Avg.	SB	FIELDING PO	A	E	Avg.
1978 — Syracuse (International)	SS-2B	119	389	33	89	10	1	4	30	.229	4	206	328	29	.948
1979 — Syracuse (International)	2B	27	101	10	25	4	2	0	8	.248	0	56	77	4	.971
— Toronto (A.L.)	2B	87	308	26	73	7	1	2	19	.237	1	198	261	11	.977
1980 — Syracuse (International)	3-0-SS	80	295	37	72	9	1	2	17	.244	14	111	140	3	.988
— Toronto (A.L.)	OF-3-2	38	111	11	27	6	1	0	4	.243	3	69	12	1	.988
1981 — Toronto (A.L.)	3-S-0-2	86	246	20	46	6	2	0	14	.187	8	88	146	12	.951
Major league totals (3 years)		211	665	57	146	19	4	2	37	.220	12	355	419	24	.970

DID YOU KNOW. . .

. . . that the Lakers have made the playoffs a league-high 16 straight years?

ALARIE, MARK
F, BULLETS

PERSONAL: Born December 11, 1963, in Phoenix. . . . 6-8/225. . . . Full name: Mark Steven Alarie. . . . Name pronounced AL-er-ee.
HIGH SCHOOL: Brophy Prep School (Phoenix).
COLLEGE: Duke.
TRANSACTIONS/CAREER NOTES: Selected by Denver Nuggets in first round (18th pick overall) of 1986 NBA Draft. . . . Traded by Nuggets with Darrell Walker to Washington Bullets for Michael Adams and Jay Vincent (November 2, 1987).

COLLEGIATE RECORD

Season Team	G	Min.	FGM	FGA	Pct.	FTM	FTA	Pct.	Reb.	Pts.	Avg.
82-83 — Duke	28	785	130	263	.494	104	128	.813	181	364	13.0
83-84 — Duke	34	1129	230	400	.575	134	176	.761	245	594	17.5
84-85 — Duke	31	935	206	352	.585	80	101	.792	158	492	15.9
85-86 — Duke	40	1193	262	490	.535	162	197	.822	249	686	17.2
Totals	133	4042	828	1505	.550	480	602	.797	833	2136	16.1

Three-point field goals: 1982-83, 0-for-2.

NBA REGULAR-SEASON RECORD

Season Team	G	Min.	FGM	FGA	Pct.	FTM	FTA	Pct.	REBOUNDS Off.	Def.	Tot.	Ast.	PF	Dq.	Stl.	Blk.	TO	Pts.	Avg.
86-87 — Denver	64	1110	217	443	.490	67	101	.663	73	141	214	74	138	1	22	28	56	503	7.9
87-88 — Washington	63	769	144	300	.480	35	49	.714	70	90	160	39	107	1	10	12	50	327	5.2
88-89 — Washington	74	1141	206	431	.478	73	87	.839	103	152	255	63	160	1	25	22	62	498	6.7
89-90 — Washington	82	1893	371	785	.473	108	133	.812	151	223	374	142	219	2	60	39	101	860	10.5
90-91 — Washington	42	587	99	225	.440	41	48	.854	41	76	117	45	88	1	15	8	40	244	5.8
Totals	325	5500	1037	2184	.475	324	418	.775	438	682	1120	363	712	6	132	109	309	2432	7.5

Three-point field goals: 1986-87, 2-for-9 (.222). 1987-88, 4-for-18 (.222). 1988-89, 13-for-38 (.342). 1989-90, 10-for-49 (.204). 1990-91, 5-for-21 (.238). Totals, 34-for-135 (.252).

NBA PLAYOFF RECORD

Season Team	G	Min.	FGM	FGA	Pct.	FTM	FTA	Pct.	REBOUNDS Off.	Def.	Tot.	Ast.	PF	Dq.	Stl.	Blk.	TO	Pts.	Avg.
86-87 — Denver	3	41	9	15	.600	2	2	1.000	0	5	5	1	9	0	2	2	4	20	6.7
87-88 — Washington	1	4	1	2	.500	0	0	...	0	1	1	0	0	0	0	0	0	3	3.0
Totals	4	45	10	17	.588	2	2	1.000	0	6	6	1	9	0	2	2	4	23	5.8

Three-point field goals: 1987-88, 1-for-2 (.500).

ALEXANDER, VICTOR
F/C, WARRIORS

PERSONAL: Born August 31, 1969, in Detroit. . . . 6-9/265. . . . Full name: Victor Joe Alexander.
HIGH SCHOOL: Denby (Detroit).
COLLEGE: Iowa State.
TRANSACTIONS/CAREER NOTES: Selected by Golden State Warriors in first round (17th pick overall) of 1991 NBA Draft.

COLLEGIATE RECORD

Season Team	G	Min.	FGM	FGA	Pct.	FTM	FTA	Pct.	Reb.	Pts.	Avg.
87-88 — Iowa State	23	120	18	30	.600	3	6	.500	17	39	1.7
88-89 — Iowa State	29	923	240	412	.583	97	149	.651	255	577	19.9
89-90 — Iowa State	28	887	226	386	.585	100	173	.578	243	552	19.7
90-91 — Iowa State	31	1020	294	446	.659	136	201	.677	280	724	23.4
Totals	111	2950	778	1274	.611	336	529	.635	795	1892	17.0

Three-point field goals: 1989-90, 0-for-1.

NBA REGULAR-SEASON RECORD

Season Team	G	Min.	FGM	FGA	Pct.	FTM	FTA	Pct.	REBOUNDS Off.	Def.	Tot.	Ast.	PF	Dq.	Stl.	Blk.	TO	Pts.	Avg.
91-92 — Golden State	80	1350	243	459	.529	103	149	.691	106	230	336	32	176	0	45	62	91	589	7.4

Three-point field goals: 1991-92, 0-for-1.

NBA PLAYOFF RECORD

Season Team	G	Min.	FGM	FGA	Pct.	FTM	FTA	Pct.	REBOUNDS Off.	Def.	Tot.	Ast.	PF	Dq.	Stl.	Blk.	TO	Pts.	Avg.
91-92 — Golden State	4	24	3	5	.600	1	1	1.000	1	5	6	1	8	0	2	0	2	7	1.8

ANDERSON, GREG
F/C, NUGGETS

PERSONAL: Born June 22, 1964, in Houston. . . . 6-10/230. . . . Full name: Gregory Wayne Anderson. . . . Nickname: Cadillac.
HIGH SCHOOL: E.E. Worthing (Houston).
COLLEGE: Houston.
TRANSACTIONS/CAREER NOTES: Selected by San Antonio Spurs in first round (23rd pick overall) of 1987 NBA Draft. . . . Traded by Spurs with Alvin Robertson and future considerations to Milwaukee Bucks for Terry Cummings and future considerations (May 28, 1989). . . . Traded by Bucks to New Jersey Nets for Lester Conner (January 11, 1991). . . . Traded by Nets to Denver Nuggets in three-way deal in which Nuggets sent Terry Mills to Nets and Walter Davis to Portland Trail Blazers, and Trail Blazers sent Drazen Petrovic to Nets (January 23, 1991); Nuggets also received 1992 first-round draft choice from Nets and 1993 second-round draft choice from Trail Blazers, and Trail Blazers also received 1992 second-round draft choice from Nuggets.

COLLEGIATE RECORD

Season	Team	G	Min.	FGM	FGA	Pct.	FTM	FTA	Pct.	Reb.	Pts.	Avg.
83-84	—Houston	35	414	49	101	.485	19	36	.528	123	117	3.3
84-85	—Houston	30	931	197	344	.573	69	129	.535	244	463	15.4
85-86	—Houston	28	1055	215	376	.572	106	181	.586	360	536	19.1
86-87	—Houston	30	1057	215	409	.526	116	192	.604	318	546	18.2
	Totals	123	3457	676	1230	.550	310	538	.576	1045	1662	13.5

HONORS: NBA All-Rookie team (1988).

NBA REGULAR-SEASON RECORD

Season	Team	G	Min.	FGM	FGA	Pct.	FTM	FTA	Pct.	Off. Reb.	Def.	Tot.	Ast.	PF	Dq.	Stl.	Blk.	TO	Pts.	Avg.
87-88	—San Antonio.	82	1984	379	756	.501	198	328	.604	161	352	513	79	228	1	54	122	143	957	11.7
88-89	—San Antonio.	82	2401	460	914	.503	207	403	.514	255	421	676	61	221	2	102	103	180	1127	13.7
89-90	—Milwaukee ...	60	1291	219	432	.507	91	170	.535	112	261	373	24	176	3	32	54	80	529	8.8
90-91	—Mil-NJ-Den .	68	924	116	270	.430	60	115	.522	97	221	318	16	140	3	35	45	84	292	4.3
91-92	—Denver	82	2793	389	854	.456	167	268	.623	337	604	941	78	263	3	88	65	201	945	11.5
	Totals	374	9393	1563	3226	.485	723	1284	.563	962	1859	2821	258	1028	12	311	389	688	3850	10.3

Three-point field goals: 1987-88, 1-for-5 (.200). 1988-89, 0-for-3. 1990-91, 0-for-1. 1991-92, 0-for-4. Totals, 1-for-13 (.077).

NBA PLAYOFF RECORD

Season	Team	G	Min.	FGM	FGA	Pct.	FTM	FTA	Pct.	Off. Reb.	Def.	Tot.	Ast.	PF	Dq.	Stl.	Blk.	TO	Pts.	Avg.
87-88	—San Antonio.	3	95	17	36	.472	4	9	.444	6	15	21	3	10	1	2	4	10	38	12.7
89-90	—Milwaukee ...	4	101	13	19	.684	7	14	.500	6	18	24	0	19	2	1	4	4	33	8.3
	Totals	7	196	30	55	.545	11	23	.478	12	33	45	3	29	3	3	8	14	71	10.1

ANDERSON, KENNY
G, NETS

PERSONAL: Born October 9, 1970, in Queens, N.Y. . . . 6-1/168. . . . Full name: Kenneth Anderson.
HIGH SCHOOL: Archbishop Molloy (Queens, N.Y.).
COLLEGE: Georgia Tech.
TRANSACTIONS/CAREER NOTES: Selected by New Jersey Nets as undergraduate in first round (second pick overall) of 1991 NBA Draft.

COLLEGIATE RECORD

NOTES: THE SPORTING NEWS All-America second team (1990, 1991).

Season	Team	G	Min.	FGM	FGA	Pct.	FTM	FTA	Pct.	Reb.	Pts.	Avg.
89-90	—Georgia Tech	35	1321	283	549	.515	107	146	.733	193	721	20.6
90-91	—Georgia Tech	30	1167	278	636	.437	155	187	.829	171	776	25.9
	Totals	65	2488	561	1185	.473	262	333	.787	364	1497	23.0

Three-point field goals: 1989-90, 48-for-117 (.410). 1990-91, 65-for-185 (.351). Totals, 113-for-302 (.374).

NBA REGULAR-SEASON RECORD

Season	Team	G	Min.	FGM	FGA	Pct.	FTM	FTA	Pct.	Off. Reb.	Def.	Tot.	Ast.	PF	Dq.	Stl.	Blk.	TO	Pts.	Avg.
91-92	—New Jersey ..	64	1086	187	480	.390	73	98	.745	38	89	127	203	68	0	67	9	97	450	7.0

Three-point field goals: 1991-92, 3-for-13 (.231).

NBA PLAYOFF RECORD

Season	Team	G	Min.	FGM	FGA	Pct.	FTM	FTA	Pct.	Off. Reb.	Def.	Tot.	Ast.	PF	Dq.	Stl.	Blk.	TO	Pts.	Avg.
91-92	—New Jersey ..	3	24	3	9	.333	2	2	1.000	1	2	3	3	1	0	1	0	1	8	2.7

ANDERSON, NICK
G/F, MAGIC

PERSONAL: Born January 20, 1968, in Chicago. . . . 6-6/205. . . . Full name: Nelison Anderson.
HIGH SCHOOL: Prosser Vocational (Chicago), then Neal F. Simeon (Chicago).
COLLEGE: Illinois.
TRANSACTIONS/CAREER NOTES: Selected as undergraduate by Orlando Magic in first round (11th pick overall) of 1989 NBA Draft.

COLLEGIATE RECORD

Season	Team	G	Min.	FGM	FGA	Pct.	FTM	FTA	Pct.	Reb.	Pts.	Avg.
86-87	—Illinois				Did not play—Proposition 48.							
87-88	—Illinois	33	909	223	390	.572	77	120	.642	217	525	15.9
88-89	—Illinois	36	1125	262	487	.538	99	148	.669	285	647	18.0
	Totals	69	2034	485	877	.553	176	268	.657	502	1172	17.0

Three-point field goals: 1987-88, 2-for-6 (.333). 1988-89, 24-for-66 (.364). Totals, 26-for-72 (.361).

NBA REGULAR-SEASON RECORD

Season	Team	G	Min.	FGM	FGA	Pct.	FTM	FTA	Pct.	Off. Reb.	Def.	Tot.	Ast.	PF	Dq.	Stl.	Blk.	TO	Pts.	Avg.
89-90	—Orlando	81	1785	372	753	.494	186	264	.705	107	209	316	124	140	0	69	34	138	931	11.5
90-91	—Orlando	70	1971	400	857	.467	173	259	.668	92	294	386	106	145	0	74	44	113	990	14.1
91-92	—Orlando	60	2203	482	1042	.463	202	303	.667	98	286	384	163	132	0	97	33	125	1196	19.9
	Totals	211	5959	1254	2652	.473	561	826	.679	297	789	1086	393	417	0	240	111	376	3117	14.8

Three-point field goals: 1989-90, 1-for-17 (.059). 1990-91, 17-for-58 (.293). 1991-92, 30-for-85 (.353). Totals, 48-for-160 (.300).

— 9 —

ANDERSON, RON
F, 76ERS

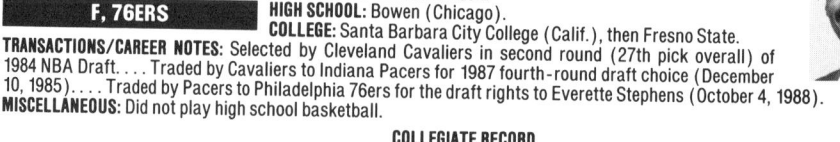

PERSONAL: Born October 15, 1958, in Chicago. . . . 6-7/215. . . . Full name: Ronald Gene Anderson.
HIGH SCHOOL: Bowen (Chicago).
COLLEGE: Santa Barbara City College (Calif.), then Fresno State.
TRANSACTIONS/CAREER NOTES: Selected by Cleveland Cavaliers in second round (27th pick overall) of 1984 NBA Draft. . . . Traded by Cavaliers to Indiana Pacers for 1987 fourth-round draft choice (December 10, 1985). . . . Traded by Pacers to Philadelphia 76ers for the draft rights to Everette Stephens (October 4, 1988).
MISCELLANEOUS: Did not play high school basketball.

COLLEGIATE RECORD

Season Team	G	Min.	FGM	FGA	Pct.	FTM	FTA	Pct.	Reb.	Pts.	Avg.
80-81—Santa Barbara City College.....	33	. . .	167	333	.502	56	75	.747	328	390	11.8
81-82—Santa Barbara City College.....	32	. . .	292	448	.652	66	84	.786	340	650	20.3
82-83—Fresno State	35	1303	234	426	.549	104	128	.813	204	572	16.3
83-84—Fresno State	33	1197	249	437	.570	82	104	.788	200	580	17.6
Junior college totals	65	. . .	459	781	.588	122	159	.767	668	1040	16.0
Four-year-college totals	68	2500	483	863	.560	186	232	.802	404	1152	16.9

NBA REGULAR-SEASON RECORD

Season Team	G	Min.	FGM	FGA	Pct.	FTM	FTA	Pct.	REBOUNDS Off.	Def.	Tot.	Ast.	PF	Dq.	Stl.	Blk.	TO	Pts.	Avg.
84-85—Cleveland.....	36	520	84	195	.431	41	50	.820	39	49	88	34	40	0	9	7	34	210	5.8
85-86—Clev.-Ind.....	77	1676	310	628	.494	85	127	.669	130	144	274	144	125	0	56	6	82	707	9.2
86-87—Indiana.........	63	721	139	294	.473	85	108	.787	73	78	151	54	65	0	31	3	55	363	5.8
87-88—Indiana.........	74	1097	217	436	.498	108	141	.766	89	127	216	78	98	0	41	6	73	542	7.3
88-89—Philadelphia..	82	2618	566	1152	.491	196	229	.856	167	239	406	139	166	1	71	23	126	1330	16.2
89-90—Philadelphia..	78	2089	379	841	.451	165	197	.838	81	214	295	143	147	0	72	13	78	926	11.9
90-91—Philadelphia..	82	2340	512	1055	.485	165	198	.833	103	264	367	115	163	1	65	13	100	1198	14.6
91-92—Philadelphia..	82	2432	469	1008	.465	143	163	.877	96	182	278	135	128	0	86	11	109	1123	13.7
Totals	574	13493	2676	5609	.477	988	1213	.815	778	1297	2075	842	928	2	431	82	657	6399	11.1

Three-point field goals: 1984-85, 1-for-2 (.500). 1985-86, 2-for-9 (.222). 1986-87, 0-for-5. 1987-88, 0-for-2. 1988-89, 2-for-11 (.182). 1989-90, 3-for-21 (.143). 1990-91, 9-for-43 (.209). 1991-92, 42-for-127 (.331). Totals, 59-for-220 (.268).

NBA PLAYOFF RECORD

Season Team	G	Min.	FGM	FGA	Pct.	FTM	FTA	Pct.	REBOUNDS Off.	Def.	Tot.	Ast.	PF	Dq.	Stl.	Blk.	TO	Pts.	Avg.
84-85—Cleveland.....	2	9	0	3	.000	0	0	. . .	1	2	3	0	0	0	0	0	0	0	0.0
86-87—Indiana.........	4	24	2	4	.500	0	0	. . .	2	1	3	0	2	0	0	0	4	4	1.0
88-89—Philadelphia..	3	109	29	51	.569	4	5	.800	7	9	16	13	10	0	1	2	2	62	20.7
89-90—Philadelphia..	10	256	40	93	.430	29	30	.967	6	31	37	14	22	0	4	0	15	112	11.2
90-91—Philadelphia..	8	223	35	88	.398	17	19	.895	9	12	21	19	24	0	6	0	12	88	11.0
Totals	27	621	106	239	.444	50	54	.926	25	55	80	46	58	0	11	2	29	266	9.9

Three-point field goals: 1988-89, 0-for-1. 1989-90, 3-for-5 (.600). 1990-91, 1-for-5 (.200). Totals, 4-for-11 (.364).

ANDERSON, WILLIE
G/F, SPURS

PERSONAL: Born January 8, 1967, in Greenville, S.C. . . . 6-8/202. . . . Full name: Willie Lloyd Anderson.
HIGH SCHOOL: East Atlanta (Atlanta).
COLLEGE: Georgia.
TRANSACTIONS/CAREER NOTES: Selected by San Antonio Spurs in first round (10th pick overall) of 1988 NBA Draft.
MISCELLANEOUS: Member of bronze-medal-winning U.S. Olympic team (1988).

COLLEGIATE RECORD

Season Team	G	Min.	FGM	FGA	Pct.	FTM	FTA	Pct.	Reb.	Pts.	Avg.
84-85—Georgia	13	80	19	39	.487	5	8	.625	19	43	3.3
85-86—Georgia	29	493	99	197	.503	48	61	.787	98	246	8.5
86-87—Georgia	30	1047	187	374	.500	77	97	.794	123	476	15.9
87-88—Georgia	35	1161	241	482	.500	91	116	.784	177	583	16.7
Totals	107	2781	546	1092	.500	221	282	.784	417	1348	12.6

Three-point field goals: 1986-87, 25-for-64 (.391). 1987-88, 10-for-44 (.227). Totals, 35-for-108 (.324).

NBA REGULAR-SEASON RECORD

HONORS: NBA All-Rookie first team (1989).

Season Team	G	Min.	FGM	FGA	Pct.	FTM	FTA	Pct.	REBOUNDS Off.	Def.	Tot.	Ast.	PF	Dq.	Stl.	Blk.	TO	Pts.	Avg.
88-89—San Antonio.	81	2738	640	1285	.498	224	289	.775	152	265	417	372	295	8	150	62	261	1508	18.6
89-90—San Antonio.	82	2788	532	1082	.492	217	290	.748	115	257	372	364	252	3	111	58	198	1288	15.7
90-91—San Antonio.	75	2592	453	991	.457	170	213	.798	68	283	351	358	226	4	79	46	167	1083	14.4
91-92—San Antonio.	57	1889	312	685	.455	107	138	.775	62	238	300	302	151	2	54	51	140	744	13.1
Totals	295	10007	1937	4043	.479	718	930	.772	397	1043	1440	1396	924	17	394	217	766	4623	15.7

Three-point field goals: 1988-89, 4-for-21 (.190). 1989-90, 7-for-26 (.269). 1990-91, 7-for-35 (.200). 1991-92, 13-for-56 (.232). Totals, 31-for-138 (.225).

NBA PLAYOFF RECORD

Season Team	G	Min.	FGM	FGA	Pct.	FTM	FTA	Pct.	REBOUNDS Off.	Def.	Tot.	Ast.	PF	Dq.	Stl.	Blk.	TO	Pts.	Avg.
89-90—San Antonio.	10	375	87	168	.518	29	36	.806	16	38	54	52	40	2	9	4	26	205	20.5
90-91—San Antonio.	4	159	33	68	.485	8	13	.615	2	17	19	19	16	0	6	2	13	76	19.0
Totals	14	534	120	236	.508	37	49	.755	18	55	73	71	56	2	15	6	39	281	20.1

Three-point field goals: 1989-90, 2-for-5 (.400). 1990-91, 2-for-10 (.200). Totals, 4-for-15 (.267).

ANSLEY, MICHAEL

F

PERSONAL: Born February 8, 1967, in Birmingham, Ala.... 6-7/ 225.... Full name: Michael Antonio Ansley.
HIGH SCHOOL: Jackson-Olin (Birmingham, Ala.).
COLLEGE: Alabama.

TRANSACTIONS/CAREER NOTES: Selected by Orlando Magic in second round (37th pick overall) of 1989 NBA Draft.... Rights renounced by Magic (June 28, 1991).... Signed as free agent by Milwaukee Bucks (September 20, 1991).... Waived by Bucks (October 28, 1991).... Signed as free agent by Philadelphia 76ers (December 3, 1991).... Waived by 76ers (January 6, 1992).... Signed by Charlotte Hornets to 10-day contract (January 10, 1992).... Played in Continental Basketball Association with Birmingham Bandits (1991-92).

COLLEGIATE RECORD

Season Team	G	Min.	FGM	FGA	Pct.	FTM	FTA	Pct.	Reb.	Pts.	Avg.
85-86 — Alabama	33	594	87	144	.604	21	39	.538	140	195	5.9
86-87 — Alabama	33	1009	145	243	.597	73	109	.670	259	363	11.0
87-88 — Alabama	31	1085	218	389	.560	125	171	.731	285	561	18.1
88-89 — Alabama	31	1053	255	446	.572	119	155	.768	284	630	20.3
Totals	128	3741	705	1222	.577	338	474	.713	968	1749	13.7

Three-point field goals: 1987-88, 0-for-1. 1988-89, 1-for-4 (.250). Totals, 1-for-5 (.200).

NBA REGULAR-SEASON RECORD

Season Team	G	Min.	FGM	FGA	Pct.	FTM	FTA	Pct.	Off.	Def.	Tot.	Ast.	PF	Dq.	Stl.	Blk.	TO	Pts.	Avg.
89-90 — Orlando	72	1221	231	465	.497	164	227	.722	187	175	362	40	152	0	24	17	50	626	8.7
90-91 — Orlando	67	877	144	263	.548	91	127	.717	122	131	253	25	125	0	27	7	32	379	5.7
91-92 — Phil.-Char.	10	45	8	18	.444	5	6	.833	2	4	6	2	7	0	0	0	3	21	2.1
Totals	149	2143	383	746	.513	260	360	.722	311	310	621	67	284	0	51	24	85	1026	6.9

CBA REGULAR-SEASON RECORD

Season Team	G	Min.	2-POINT FGM	2-POINT FGA	Pct.	3-POINT FGM	3-POINT FGA	Pct.	FTM	FTA	Pct.	Reb.	Ast.	Pts.	Avg.
91-92 — Birmingham	12	500	163	298	.547	0	1	.000	93	109	.853	133	31	419	34.9

ANTHONY, GREG

G, KNICKS

PERSONAL: Born November 15, 1967, in Las Vegas.... 6-2/185.... Full name: Gregory C. Anthony.
HIGH SCHOOL: Rancho (North Las Vegas, Nev.).
COLLEGE: Portland, then UNLV.

TRANSACTIONS/CAREER NOTES: Selected by New York Knicks in first round (12th pick overall) of 1991 NBA Draft.

COLLEGIATE RECORD

NOTES: Member of NCAA Division I championship team (1990).

Season Team	G	Min.	FGM	FGA	Pct.	FTM	FTA	Pct.	Reb.	Pts.	Avg.
86-87 — Portland	28	923	147	369	.398	100	144	.694	121	429	15.3
87-88 — UNLV					Did not play—transfer student.						
88-89 — UNLV	36	1025	155	350	.443	107	153	.699	102	464	12.9
89-90 — UNLV	39	1160	145	317	.457	101	148	.682	116	436	11.2
90-91 — UNLV	35	1100	141	309	.456	79	102	.775	89	406	11.6
Totals	138	4208	588	1345	.437	387	547	.707	428	1735	12.6

Three-point field goals: 1986-87, 35-for-95 (.368). 1988-89, 47-for-125 (.376). 1989-90, 45-for-120 (.375). 1990-91, 45-for-114 (.395). Totals, 172-for-454 (.379).

NBA REGULAR-SEASON RECORD

Season Team	G	Min.	FGM	FGA	Pct.	FTM	FTA	Pct.	Off.	Def.	Tot.	Ast.	PF	Dq.	Stl.	Blk.	TO	Pts.	Avg.
91-92 — New York	82	1510	161	435	.370	117	158	.741	33	103	136	314	170	0	59	9	98	447	5.5

Three-point field goals: 1991-92, 8-for-55 (.145).

NBA PLAYOFF RECORD

Season Team	G	Min.	FGM	FGA	Pct.	FTM	FTA	Pct.	Off.	Def.	Tot.	Ast.	PF	Dq.	Stl.	Blk.	TO	Pts.	Avg.
91-92 — New York	12	213	19	46	.413	20	33	.606	4	13	17	41	28	0	16	1	13	63	5.3

Three-point field goals: 1991-92, 5-for-12 (.417).

ARMSTRONG, B.J.

G, BULLS

PERSONAL: Born September 9, 1967, in Detroit.... 6-2/175.... Full name: Benjamin Roy Armstrong Jr.
HIGH SCHOOL: Brother Rice (Birmingham, Mich.).
COLLEGE: Iowa.

TRANSACTIONS/CAREER NOTES: Selected by Chicago Bulls in first round (18th pick overall) of 1989 NBA Draft.
MISCELLANEOUS: Member of NBA championship teams (1991, 1992).

COLLEGIATE RECORD

Season Team	G	Min.	FGM	FGA	Pct.	FTM	FTA	Pct.	Reb.	Pts.	Avg.
85-86 — Iowa	29	232	32	66	.485	19	21	.905	16	83	2.9
86-87 — Iowa	35	995	153	295	.519	100	126	.794	89	434	12.4

Season Team	G	Min.	FGM	FGA	Pct.	FTM	FTA	Pct.	Reb.	Pts.	Avg.
87-88 —Iowa	34	1023	203	421	.482	124	146	.849	74	592	17.4
88-89 —Iowa	32	1015	195	403	.484	160	192	.833	79	596	18.6
Totals	130	3265	583	1185	.492	403	485	.831	258	1705	13.1

Three-point field goals: 1986-87, 28-for-54 (.519). 1987-88, 62-for-137 (.453). 1988-89, 46-for-116 (.397). Totals, 136-for-307 (.443).

NBA REGULAR-SEASON RECORD

Season Team	G	Min.	FGM	FGA	Pct.	FTM	FTA	Pct.	REBOUNDS Off.	Def.	Tot.	Ast.	PF	Dq.	Stl.	Blk.	TO	Pts.	Avg.
89-90 —Chicago	81	1291	190	392	.485	69	78	.885	19	83	102	199	105	0	46	6	83	452	5.6
90-91 —Chicago	82	1731	304	632	.481	97	111	.874	25	124	149	301	118	0	70	4	107	720	8.8
91-92 —Chicago	82	1875	335	697	.481	104	129	.806	19	126	145	266	88	0	46	5	94	809	9.9
Totals	245	4897	829	1721	.482	270	318	.849	63	333	396	766	311	0	162	15	284	1981	8.1

Three-point field goals: 1989-90, 3-for-6 (.500). 1990-91, 15-for-30 (.500). 1991-92, 35-for-87 (.402). Totals, 53-for-123 (.431).

NBA PLAYOFF RECORD

Season Team	G	Min.	FGM	FGA	Pct.	FTM	FTA	Pct.	REBOUNDS Off.	Def.	Tot.	Ast.	PF	Dq.	Stl.	Blk.	TO	Pts.	Avg.
89-90 —Chicago	16	217	21	62	.339	22	24	.917	3	17	20	29	22	0	10	0	12	64	4.0
90-91 —Chicago	17	273	35	70	.500	20	25	.800	5	22	27	43	13	0	19	1	13	93	5.5
91-92 —Chicago	22	434	63	139	.453	30	38	.789	2	22	24	47	33	0	14	0	18	161	7.3
Totals	55	924	119	271	.439	72	87	.828	10	61	71	119	68	0	43	1	43	318	5.8

Three-point field goals: 1989-90, 0-for-4. 1990-91, 3-for-5 (.600). 1991-92, 5-for-17 (.294). Totals, 8-for-26 (.308).

ASKEW, VINCENT
G

PERSONAL: Born February 28, 1966, in Memphis, Tenn. . . . 6-6/ 226. . . . Full name: Vincent Jerome Askew.
HIGH SCHOOL: Frayser (Memphis, Tenn.)
COLLEGE: Memphis State.

TRANSACTIONS/CAREER NOTES: Selected as undergraduate by Philadelphia 76ers in second round (39th pick overall) of 1987 NBA Draft. . . . Waived by 76ers (December 22, 1987). . . . Played in Continental Basketball Association with Savannah Spirits (1987-88) and Albany Patroons (1988-89, 1989-90 and 1990-91). . . . Signed as free agent by Washington Bullets (September 23, 1988). . . . Waived by Bullets (October 12, 1988). . . . Played in Italy (1988-89). . . . Signed as free agent by Golden State Warriors (April 6, 1991). . . . Granted free agency (July 1992).

COLLEGIATE RECORD

Season Team	G	Min.	FGM	FGA	Pct.	FTM	FTA	Pct.	Reb.	Pts.	Avg.
84-85 —Memphis State	35	1177	115	225	.511	59	93	.634	117	289	8.3
85-86 —Memphis State	34	1094	150	306	.490	70	86	.814	228	370	10.9
86-87 —Memphis State	34	1164	187	387	.483	122	155	.787	170	512	15.1
Totals	103	3435	452	918	.492	251	334	.751	515	1171	11.4

Three-point field goals: 1986-87, 16-for-42 (.381).

NBA REGULAR-SEASON RECORD

Season Team	G	Min.	FGM	FGA	Pct.	FTM	FTA	Pct.	REBOUNDS Off.	Def.	Tot.	Ast.	PF	Dq.	Stl.	Blk.	TO	Pts.	Avg.
87-88 —Philadelphia	14	234	22	74	.297	8	11	.727	6	16	22	33	12	0	10	6	12	52	3.7
90-91 —Golden State	7	85	12	25	.480	9	11	.818	7	4	11	13	21	1	2	0	6	33	4.7
91-92 —Golden State	80	1496	193	379	.509	111	160	.694	89	144	233	188	128	1	47	23	84	498	6.2
Totals	101	1815	227	478	.475	128	182	.703	102	164	266	234	161	2	59	29	102	583	5.8

Three-point field goals: 1991-92, 1-for-10 (.100).

NBA PLAYOFF RECORD

Season Team	G	Min.	FGM	FGA	Pct.	FTM	FTA	Pct.	REBOUNDS Off.	Def.	Tot.	Ast.	PF	Dq.	Stl.	Blk.	TO	Pts.	Avg.
90-91 —Golden State	6	41	6	15	.400	3	6	.500	5	6	11	2	6	0	2	0	6	15	2.5
91-92 —Golden State	4	30	1	8	.125	0	0	. . .	3	1	4	5	3	0	0	0	2	2	0.5
Totals	10	71	7	23	.304	3	6	.500	8	7	15	7	9	0	2	0	2	17	1.7

CBA REGULAR-SEASON RECORD

NOTES: CBA Most Valuable Player (1990, 1991). . . . CBA All-Star first team (1990, 1991). . . . CBA All-Defensive team (1991).

Season Team	G	Min.	2-POINT FGM	FGA	Pct.	3-POINT FGM	FGA	Pct.	FTM	FTA	Pct.	Reb.	Ast.	Pts.	Avg.
87-88 —Savannah	5	35	5	10	.500	0	0	. . .	0	0	. . .	4	0	10	2.0
88-89 —Albany	29	989	196	368	.533	0	4	.000	152	225	.676	267	76	544	18.8
89-90 —Albany	56	2271	587	1134	.518	3	9	.333	301	402	.749	435	247	*1484	26.5
90-91 —Albany	53	2017	441	827	.533	0	5	.000	293	392	.747	494	301	1175	22.2
Totals	143	5312	1229	2339	.525	3	18	.167	746	1019	.732	1200	624	3213	22.5

ITALIAN LEAGUE RECORD

Season Team	G	Min.	FGM	FGA	Pct.	FTM	FTA	Pct.	Reb.	Pts.	Avg.
88-89 —Bologna Arimo	20	703	142	258	.550	93	122	.762	138	380	19.0

ASKINS, KEITH
G/F, HEAT

PERSONAL: Born December 15, 1967, in Athens, Ala. . . . 6-8/205. . . . Full name: Keith Bernard Askins.
HIGH SCHOOL: Athens (Ala.).
COLLEGE: Alabama.

TRANSACTIONS/CAREER NOTES: Never drafted by an NBA franchise. . . . Signed as free agent by Miami Heat (September 7, 1990).

COLLEGIATE RECORD

Season Team	G	Min.	FGM	FGA	Pct.	FTM	FTA	Pct.	Reb.	Pts.	Avg.
86-87 —Alabama	32	432	38	80	.475	16	29	.552	95	94	2.9
87-88 —Alabama	30	805	58	139	.417	43	62	.694	147	171	5.7
88-89 —Alabama	31	741	87	175	.497	24	35	.686	131	241	7.8
89-90 —Alabama	35	978	117	268	.437	61	93	.656	180	346	9.9
Totals	128	2956	300	662	.453	144	219	.658	553	852	6.7

Three-point field goals: 1986-87, 2-for-7 (.286). 1987-88, 12-for-27 (.444). 1988-89, 43-for-96 (.448). 1989-90, 51-for-140 (.364). Totals, 108-for-270 (.400).

NBA REGULAR-SEASON RECORD

Season Team	G	Min.	FGM	FGA	Pct.	FTM	FTA	Pct.	REBOUNDS Off.	Def.	Tot.	Ast.	PF	Dq.	Stl.	Blk.	TO	Pts.	Avg.
90-91 —Miami	39	266	34	81	.420	12	25	.480	30	38	68	19	46	0	16	13	11	86	2.2
91-92 —Miami	59	843	84	205	.410	26	37	.703	65	77	142	38	109	0	40	15	47	219	3.7
Totals	98	1109	118	286	.413	38	62	.613	95	115	210	57	155	0	56	28	58	305	3.1

Three-point field goals: 1990-91, 6-for-25 (.240). 1991-92, 25-for-73 (.342). Totals, 31-for-98 (.316).

NBA PLAYOFF RECORD

Season Team	G	Min.	FGM	FGA	Pct.	FTM	FTA	Pct.	REBOUNDS Off.	Def.	Tot.	Ast.	PF	Dq.	Stl.	Blk.	TO	Pts.	Avg.
91-92 —Miami	3	48	5	11	.455	0	2	.000	4	5	9	3	7	0	1	0	1	13	4.3

Three-point field goals: 1991-92, 3-for-5 (.600).

AUGMON, STACEY
G/F, HAWKS

PERSONAL: Born August 1, 1968, in Pasadena, Calif. . . . 6-8/205. . . . Full name: Stacey Orlando Augmon. . . . Name pronounced AUGH-mon.
HIGH SCHOOL: John Muir (Pasadena, Calif.).
COLLEGE: UNLV.
TRANSACTIONS/CAREER NOTES: Selected by Atlanta Hawks in first round (ninth pick overall) of 1991 NBA Draft.
MISCELLANEOUS: Member of bronze-medal-winning U.S. Olympic team (1988).

COLLEGIATE RECORD

NOTES: THE SPORTING NEWS All-America first team (1991).

Season Team	G	Min.	FGM	FGA	Pct.	FTM	FTA	Pct.	Reb.	Pts.	Avg.
86-87 —UNLV					Did not play—ineligible.						
87-88 —UNLV	34	884	117	204	.574	75	116	.647	206	311	9.1
88-89 —UNLV	37	1091	210	405	.519	106	160	.663	274	567	15.3
89-90 —UNLV	39	1246	210	380	.553	118	176	.670	270	554	14.2
90-91 —UNLV	35	1062	220	375	.587	101	139	.727	255	579	16.5
Totals	145	4283	757	1364	.555	400	591	.677	1005	2011	13.9

Three-point field goals: 1987-88, 2-for-2. 1988-89, 41-for-98 (.418). 1989-90, 16-for-50 (.320). 1990-91, 38-for-81 (.469). Totals, 97-for-231 (.420).

NBA REGULAR-SEASON RECORD

HONORS: NBA All-Rookie first team (1992).

Season Team	G	Min.	FGM	FGA	Pct.	FTM	FTA	Pct.	REBOUNDS Off.	Def.	Tot.	Ast.	PF	Dq.	Stl.	Blk.	TO	Pts.	Avg.
91-92 —Atlanta	82	2505	440	899	.489	213	320	.666	191	229	420	201	161	0	124	27	181	1094	13.3

Three-point field goals: 1991-92, 1-for-6 (.167).

AUSTIN, ISAAC
C, JAZZ

PERSONAL: Born August 18, 1969, in Gridley, Calif. . . . 6-10/260. . . . Full name: Isaac Edward Austin.
HIGH SCHOOL: Las Plumas (Oroville, Calif.).
COLLEGE: Kings River (Calif.), then Arizona State.
TRANSACTIONS/CAREER NOTES: Selected by Utah Jazz in second round (48th pick overall) of 1991 NBA Draft.

COLLEGIATE RECORD

Season Team	G	Min.	FGM	FGA	Pct.	FTM	FTA	Pct.	Reb.	Pts.	Avg.
87-88 —Kings River	32	. . .	113	231	.489	62	87	.713	182	288	9.0
88-89 —Kings River	31	. . .	215	405	.531	131	182	.720	279	561	18.1
89-90 —Arizona State	31	848	164	300	.547	97	150	.647	192	425	13.7
90-91 —Arizona State	30	906	189	331	.571	112	178	.629	262	490	16.3
Junior college totals	63	. . .	328	636	.516	193	269	.717	461	849	13.5
Four-year-college totals	61	1754	353	631	.559	209	328	.637	454	915	15.0

Three-point field goals: 1989-90, 0-for-1. 1990-91, 0-for-1. Totals, 0-for-2.

NBA REGULAR-SEASON RECORD

Season Team	G	Min.	FGM	FGA	Pct.	FTM	FTA	Pct.	REBOUNDS Off.	Def.	Tot.	Ast.	PF	Dq.	Stl.	Blk.	TO	Pts.	Avg.
91-92 —Utah	31	112	21	46	.457	19	30	.633	11	24	35	5	20	0	2	2	8	61	2.0

DID YOU KNOW. . .

. . . that the Chicago Bulls' 67 wins last season tied for the third-highest total in NBA history?

BABIC, MILOS
F/C

PERSONAL: Born November 23, 1968, in Kraljevo, Yugoslavia. . . . 7-0/240. . . . Name pronounced Me-losh Bob-itch.
COLLEGE: Tennessee Tech.
TRANSACTIONS/CAREER NOTES: Selected by Phoenix Suns in second round (50th pick overall) of 1990 NBA Draft. . . . Draft rights traded by Suns to Cleveland Cavaliers for draft rights to Stefano Rusconi (June 27, 1990). . . . Rights renounced by Cavaliers (August 22, 1991). . . . Signed as free agent by Miami Heat (October 4, 1991). . . . Waived by Heat (October 29, 1991). . . . Re-signed by Heat (November 19, 1991). . . . Waived by Heat (December 31, 1991).

COLLEGIATE RECORD

Season Team	G	Min.	FGM	FGA	Pct.	FTM	FTA	Pct.	Reb.	Pts.	Avg.
86-87 — Tennessee Tech					Did not play — ineligible.						
87-88 — Tennessee Tech	25	650	103	224	.460	64	97	.660	170	270	10.8
88-89 — Tennessee Tech	30	899	161	322	.500	75	114	.658	244	399	13.3
89-90 — Tennessee Tech	25	591	122	259	.471	65	95	.684	183	309	12.4
Totals	80	2140	386	805	.480	204	306	.667	597	978	12.2

Three-point field goals: 1988-89, 2-for-7 (.286).

NBA REGULAR-SEASON RECORD

Season Team	G	Min.	FGM	FGA	Pct.	FTM	FTA	Pct.	Off.	Def.	Tot.	Ast.	PF	Dq.	Stl.	Blk.	TO	Pts.	Avg.
90-91 — Cleveland	12	52	6	19	.316	7	12	.583	6	3	9	4	7	0	1	1	5	19	1.6
91-92 — Miami	9	35	6	13	.462	6	8	.750	2	9	11	6	0	0	1	0	5	18	2.0
Totals	21	87	12	32	.375	13	20	.650	8	12	20	10	7	0	2	1	10	37	1.8

BAGLEY, JOHN
G, CELTICS

PERSONAL: Born April 23, 1960, in Bridgeport, Conn. . . . 6-0/205. . . . Full name: John Edward Bagley.
HIGH SCHOOL: Warren Harding (Bridgeport, Conn.).
COLLEGE: Boston College.
TRANSACTIONS/CAREER NOTES: Selected as undergraduate by Cleveland Cavaliers in first round (12th pick overall) of 1982 NBA Draft. . . . Traded by Cavaliers with Keith Lee to New Jersey Nets for Darryl Dawkins and James Bailey (October 8, 1987). . . . Traded by Nets to Boston Celtics for 1991 and 1993 second-round draft choices (October 5, 1989).

COLLEGIATE RECORD

Season Team	G	Min.	FGM	FGA	Pct.	FTM	FTA	Pct.	Reb.	Pts.	Avg.
79-80 — Boston College	29	. . .	130	270	.481	83	115	.722	91	343	11.8
80-81 — Boston College	30	965	209	418	.500	193	245	.788	115	611	20.4
81-82 — Boston College	32	1065	257	513	.501	161	202	.797	122	675	21.1
Totals	91	. . .	596	1201	.496	437	562	.778	328	1629	17.9

NBA REGULAR-SEASON RECORD

Season Team	G	Min.	FGM	FGA	Pct.	FTM	FTA	Pct.	Off.	Def.	Tot.	Ast.	PF	Dq.	Stl.	Blk.	TO	Pts.	Avg.
82-83 — Cleveland	68	990	161	373	.432	64	84	.762	17	79	96	167	74	0	54	5	118	386	5.7
83-84 — Cleveland	76	1712	257	607	.423	157	198	.793	49	107	156	333	113	1	78	4	170	673	8.9
84-85 — Cleveland	81	2401	338	693	.488	125	167	.749	54	237	291	697	132	0	129	5	207	804	9.9
85-86 — Cleveland	78	2472	366	865	.423	170	215	.791	76	199	275	735	165	1	122	10	239	911	11.7
86-87 — Cleveland	72	2182	312	732	.426	113	136	.831	55	197	252	379	114	0	91	7	163	768	10.7
87-88 — New Jersey	82	2774	393	896	.439	148	180	.822	61	196	257	479	162	0	110	10	201	981	12.0
88-89 — New Jersey	68	1642	200	481	.416	89	123	.724	36	108	144	391	117	0	72	5	159	500	7.4
89-90 — Boston	54	1095	100	218	.459	29	39	.744	26	63	89	296	77	0	40	4	90	230	4.3
90-91 — Boston								Did not play — injured.										
91-92 — Boston	73	1742	223	506	.441	68	95	.716	38	123	161	480	123	1	57	4	148	524	7.2
Totals	652	17010	2350	5371	.438	963	1237	.778	412	1309	1721	3957	1077	3	753	54	1495	5777	8.9

Three-point field goals: 1982-83, 0-for-14. 1983-84, 2-for-17 (.118). 1984-85, 3-for-26 (.115). 1985-86, 9-for-37 (.243). 1986-87, 31-for-103 (.301). 1987-88, 47-for-161 (.292). 1988-89, 11-for-54 (.204). 1989-90, 1-for-18 (.056). 1991-92, 10-for-42 (.238). Totals, 114-for-472 (.242).

NBA PLAYOFF RECORD

Season Team	G	Min.	FGM	FGA	Pct.	FTM	FTA	Pct.	Off.	Def.	Tot.	Ast.	PF	Dq.	Stl.	Blk.	TO	Pts.	Avg.
84-85 — Cleveland	4	168	22	56	.393	7	10	.700	1	15	16	40	7	0	10	0	17	51	12.8
89-90 — Boston	5	70	8	15	.533	3	4	.750	3	1	4	17	9	0	4	1	9	19	3.8
91-92 — Boston	10	308	42	95	.442	26	37	.703	8	19	27	85	17	0	9	1	35	111	11.1
Totals	19	546	72	166	.434	36	51	.706	12	35	47	142	33	0	23	2	61	181	9.5

Three-point field goals: 1984-85, 0-for-3. 1989-90, 0-for-1. 1991-92, 1-for-4 (.250). Totals, 1-for-8 (.125).

BAILEY, THURL
F, TIMBERWOLVES

PERSONAL: Born April 7, 1961, in Washington, D.C. . . . 6-11/232. . . . Full name: Thurl Lee Bailey.
HIGH SCHOOL: Bladensburg School (Md.).
COLLEGE: North Carolina State.
TRANSACTIONS/CAREER NOTES: Selected by Utah Jazz in first round (seventh pick overall) of 1983 NBA Draft. . . . Traded by Jazz with 1992 second-round draft choice to Minnesota Timberwolves for Tyrone Corbin (November 25, 1991).

COLLEGIATE RECORD

NOTES: Member of NCAA Division I championship team (1983).

Season	Team	G	Min.	FGM	FGA	Pct.	FTM	FTA	Pct.	Reb.	Pts.	Avg.
79-80	—North Carolina State	28	...	44	101	.436	37	55	.673	102	125	4.5
80-81	—North Carolina State	27	...	146	278	.525	39	53	.736	165	331	12.3
81-82	—North Carolina State	32	...	171	312	.548	96	118	.814	216	438	13.7
82-83	—North Carolina State	36	...	250	499	.501	91	127	.717	276	601	16.7
	Totals	123	...	611	1190	.513	263	353	.745	759	1495	12.2

Three-point field goals: 1982-83, 10-for-15 (.667).

NBA REGULAR-SEASON RECORD

HONORS: NBA All-Rookie team (1984).

Season	Team	G	Min.	FGM	FGA	Pct.	FTM	FTA	Pct.	Off.	Def.	Tot.	Ast.	PF	Dq.	Stl.	Blk.	TO	Pts.	Avg.
83-84	—Utah	81	2009	302	590	.512	88	117	.752	115	349	464	129	193	1	38	122	105	692	8.5
84-85	—Utah	80	2481	507	1034	.490	197	234	.842	153	372	525	138	215	2	51	105	152	1212	15.2
85-86	—Utah	82	2358	483	1077	.448	230	277	.830	148	345	493	153	160	0	42	114	144	1196	14.6
86-87	—Utah	81	2155	463	1036	.447	190	236	.805	145	287	432	102	150	0	38	88	123	1116	13.8
87-88	—Utah	82	2804	633	1286	.492	337	408	.826	134	397	531	158	186	1	49	125	190	1604	19.6
88-89	—Utah	82	2777	615	1272	.483	363	440	.825	115	332	447	138	185	0	48	91	208	1595	19.5
89-90	—Utah	82	2583	470	977	.481	222	285	.779	116	294	410	137	175	2	32	100	139	1162	14.2
90-91	—Utah	82	2486	399	872	.458	219	271	.808	101	306	407	124	160	0	53	91	130	1017	12.4
91-92	—Utah-Min.	84	2104	368	836	.440	215	270	.796	122	363	485	78	160	1	35	117	108	951	11.3
	Totals	736	21757	4240	8980	.472	2061	2538	.812	1149	3045	4194	1157	1584	7	386	953	1299	10545	14.3

Three-point field goals: 1984-85, 1-for-1. 1985-86, 0-for-7. 1986-87, 0-for-2. 1987-88, 1-for-3 (.333). 1988-89, 2-for-5 (.400). 1989-90, 0-for-8. 1990-91, 0-for-3. 1991-92, 0-for-2. Totals, 4-for-31 (.129).

NBA PLAYOFF RECORD

Season	Team	G	Min.	FGM	FGA	Pct.	FTM	FTA	Pct.	Off.	Def.	Tot.	Ast.	PF	Dq.	Stl.	Blk.	TO	Pts.	Avg.
83-84	—Utah	11	340	50	97	.515	17	21	.810	15	46	61	10	33	0	2	11	16	117	10.6
84-85	—Utah	10	375	62	152	.408	45	55	.818	21	71	92	27	30	0	5	18	21	169	16.9
85-86	—Utah	4	147	28	77	.364	8	11	.727	11	21	32	13	13	0	2	2	5	64	16.0
86-87	—Utah	5	151	30	63	.476	18	18	1.000	14	16	30	9	12	1	3	6	12	78	15.6
87-88	—Utah	11	449	99	203	.488	57	68	.838	21	42	63	18	32	0	6	23	21	255	23.2
88-89	—Utah	3	122	12	34	.353	12	15	.800	10	15	25	3	11	0	1	4	9	36	12.0
89-90	—Utah	5	190	43	88	.489	19	24	.792	8	24	32	7	19	1	5	6	5	105	21.0
90-91	—Utah	9	228	23	64	.359	22	25	.880	11	21	32	9	27	1	3	6	12	68	7.6
	Totals	58	2002	347	778	.446	198	237	.835	111	256	367	96	177	3	27	76	101	892	15.4

Three-point field goals: 1983-84, 0-for-2. 1985-86, 0-for-1. 1987-88, 0-for-1. Totals, 0-for-4.

BARDO, STEVE
G

PERSONAL: Born April 5, 1968, in Henderson, Ky. ... 6-6/200. ... Full name: Stephen Dean Bardo.
HIGH SCHOOL: Carbondale (Ill.).
COLLEGE: Illinois.

TRANSACTIONS/CAREER NOTES: Selected by Atlanta Hawks in second round (41st pick overall) of 1991 NBA Draft. ... Played in Continental Basketball Association with Quad City Thunder (1990-91 and 1991-92) and Wichita Falls Texans (1991-92). ... Signed as free agent by San Antonio Spurs (September 5, 1991). ... Waived by Spurs (November 12, 1991). ... Signed by Spurs to 10-day contract (February 19, 1992). ... Released by Spurs (February 27, 1992).

COLLEGIATE RECORD

Season	Team	G	Min.	FGM	FGA	Pct.	FTM	FTA	Pct.	Reb.	Pts.	Avg.
86-87	—Illinois	31	630	42	102	.412	34	50	.680	92	119	3.8
87-88	—Illinois	33	820	80	178	.449	53	87	.609	138	216	6.5
88-89	—Illinois	36	1000	94	212	.443	76	96	.792	144	293	8.1
89-90	—Illinois	29	944	99	225	.440	55	78	.705	178	281	9.7
	Totals	129	3394	315	717	.439	218	311	.701	552	909	7.0

Three-point field goals: 1986-87, 1-for-3 (.333). 1987-88, 3-for-8 (.375). 1988-89, 29-for-59 (.492). 1989-90, 28-for-64 (.438). Totals, 61-for-134 (.455).

CBA REGULAR-SEASON RECORD

Season	Team	G	Min.	2-POINT			3-POINT			FTM	FTA	Pct.	Reb.	Ast.	Pts.	Avg.
				FGM	FGA	Pct.	FGM	FGA	Pct.							
90-91	—Quad City	56	1847	298	642	.464	12	43	.279	191	243	.786	266	277	823	14.7
91-92	—Quad C.-W.F.	38	1393	229	483	.474	15	43	.349	166	210	.790	235	229	669	17.6
	Totals	94	3240	527	1125	.468	27	86	.314	357	453	.788	501	506	1492	15.9

NBA REGULAR-SEASON RECORD

Season	Team	G	Min.	FGM	FGA	Pct.	FTM	FTA	Pct.	Off.	Def.	Tot.	Ast.	PF	Dq.	Stl.	Blk.	TO	Pts.	Avg.
91-92	—San Antonio	1	1	0	0	...	0	0	...	1	0	1	0	0	0	0	0	0	0	0.0

BARKLEY, CHARLES
F, SUNS

PERSONAL: Born February 20, 1963, in Leeds, Ala. ... 6-6/252. ... Full name: Charles Wade Barkley.
HIGH SCHOOL: Leeds (Ala.).
COLLEGE: Auburn.

TRANSACTIONS/CAREER NOTES: Selected as undergraduate by Philadelphia 76ers in first round (fifth pick overall) of 1984 NBA Draft. ... Traded by 76ers to Phoenix Suns for Jeff Hornacek, Tim Perry and Andrew

Lang (June 17, 1992).
MISCELLANEOUS: Member of gold-medal-winning U.S. Olympic team (1992).

COLLEGIATE RECORD

Season Team	G	Min.	FGM	FGA	Pct.	FTM	FTA	Pct.	Reb.	Pts.	Avg.
81-82 — Auburn	28	746	144	242	.595	68	107	.636	275	356	12.7
82-83 — Auburn	28	782	161	250	.644	82	130	.631	266	404	14.4
83-84 — Auburn	28	794	162	254	.638	99	145	.683	265	423	15.1
Totals	84	2322	467	746	.626	249	382	.652	806	1183	14.1

NBA REGULAR-SEASON RECORD

HONORS: Schick Award, for all-around contributions to team's success (1986, 1987, 1988).... All-NBA first team (1988, 1989, 1990, 1991).... All-NBA second team (1986, 1987, 1992).... NBA All-Rookie team (1985).
NOTES: Led NBA with 14.6 rebounds per game (1987).

Season Team	G	Min.	FGM	FGA	Pct.	FTM	FTA	Pct.	REBOUNDS Off.	Def.	Tot.	Ast.	PF	Dq.	Stl.	Blk.	TO	Pts.	Avg.
84-85 — Philadelphia.	82	2347	427	783	.545	293	400	.733	266	437	703	155	301	5	95	80	209	1148	14.0
85-86 — Philadelphia.	80	2952	595	1041	.572	396	578	.685	354	672	1026	312	*333	8	173	125	*350	1603	20.0
86-87 — Philadelphia.	68	2740	557	937	.594	429	564	.761	*390	604	994	331	262	5	119	104	322	1564	23.0
87-88 — Philadelphia.	80	3170	753	1283	.587	714	*951	.751	*385	566	951	254	278	6	100	103	304	2264	28.3
88-89 — Philadelphia.	79	3088	700	1208	.579	602	799	.753	*403	583	986	325	262	3	126	67	254	2037	25.8
89-90 — Philadelphia.	79	3085	706	1177	.600	557	744	.749	361	548	909	307	250	2	148	50	243	1989	25.2
90-91 — Philadelphia.	67	2498	665	1167	.570	475	658	.722	258	422	680	284	173	2	110	33	210	1849	27.6
91-92 — Philadelphia.	75	2881	622	1126	.552	454	653	.695	271	559	830	308	196	2	136	44	235	1730	23.1
Totals	610	22761	5025	8722	.576	3920	5347	.733	2688	4391	7079	2276	2045	33	1007	606	2127	14184	23.3

Three-point field goals: 1984-85, 1-for-6 (.167). 1985-86, 17-for-75 (.227). 1986-87, 21-for-104 (.202). 1987-88, 44-for-157 (.280). 1988-89, 35-for-162 (.216). 1989-90, 20-for-92 (.217). 1990-91, 44-for-155 (.284). 1991-92, 32-for-137 (.234). Totals, 214-for-888 (.241).

NBA PLAYOFF RECORD

Season Team	G	Min.	FGM	FGA	Pct.	FTM	FTA	Pct.	REBOUNDS Off.	Def.	Tot.	Ast.	PF	Dq.	Stl.	Blk.	TO	Pts.	Avg.
84-85 — Philadelphia.	13	408	75	139	.540	40	63	.635	52	92	144	26	49	0	23	15	35	194	14.9
85-86 — Philadelphia.	12	497	104	180	.578	91	131	.695	60	129	189	67	52	2	27	15	65	300	25.0
86-87 — Philadelphia.	5	210	43	75	.573	36	45	.800	27	36	63	12	21	0	4	8	22	123	24.6
88-89 — Philadelphia.	3	135	29	45	.644	22	31	.710	8	27	35	16	9	0	5	2	11	81	27.0
89-90 — Philadelphia.	10	419	88	162	.543	65	108	.602	66	89	155	43	36	0	8	7	30	247	24.7
90-91 — Philadelphia.	8	326	74	125	.592	49	75	.653	31	53	84	48	23	0	15	3	25	199	24.9
Totals	51	1995	413	726	.569	303	453	.669	244	426	670	212	190	2	82	50	188	1144	22.4

Three-point field goals: 1984-85, 4-for-6 (.667). 1985-86, 1-for-15 (.067). 1988-89, 1-for-5 (.200). 1989-90, 6-for-18 (.333). 1990-91, 2-for-20 (.100). Totals, 14-for-64 (.219).

NBA ALL-STAR GAME RECORD

NOTES: NBA All-Star Game Most Valuable Player (1991).

Season Team	Min.	FGM	FGA	Pct.	FTM	FTA	Pct.	REBOUNDS Off.	Def.	Tot.	Ast.	PF	Dq.	Stl.	Blk.	TO	Pts.
1987 — Philadelphia	16	2	6	.333	3	6	.500	1	3	4	1	2	0	1	0	0	7
1988 — Philadelphia	15	1	4	.250	2	2	1.000	1	2	3	0	2	0	1	1	3	4
1989 — Philadelphia	20	6	11	.545	5	8	.625	3	2	5	0	0	0	2	1	1	17
1990 — Philadelphia	22	7	12	.583	3	3	.667	2	2	4	0	1	0	1	1	2	17
1991 — Philadelphia	35	7	15	.467	3	6	.500	8	14	22	4	5	0	1	1	3	17
1992 — Philadelphia	28	6	14	.429	0	0	...	2	7	9	1	3	0	0	0	3	12
Totals	136	29	62	.468	15	25	.600	17	30	47	6	13	0	6	4	12	74

Three-point field goals: 1987, 0-for-2. 1988, 0-for-1. 1990, 1-for-1. 1992, 0-for-2. Totals, 1-for-6 (.167).

BARROS, DANA
G, SUPERSONICS

PERSONAL: Born April 13, 1967, in Boston.... 5-11/165.... Full name: Dana Bruce Barros.
HIGH SCHOOL: Xaverian Brothers (Westwood, Mass.).
COLLEGE: Boston College.
TRANSACTIONS/CAREER NOTES: Selected by Seattle SuperSonics in first round (16th pick overall) of 1989 NBA Draft.

COLLEGIATE RECORD

Season Team	G	Min.	FGM	FGA	Pct.	FTM	FTA	Pct.	Reb.	Pts.	Avg.
85-86 — Boston College	28	971	158	330	.479	68	86	.791	78	384	13.7
86-87 — Boston College	29	1145	194	424	.458	85	100	.850	85	543	18.7
87-88 — Boston College	33	1223	242	504	.480	130	153	.850	113	723	21.9
88-89 — Boston College	29	1096	230	484	.475	120	140	.857	103	692	23.9
Totals	119	4435	824	1742	.473	403	479	.841	379	2342	19.7

Three-point field goals: 1986-87, 70-for-173 (.405). 1987-88, 109-for-240 (.454). 1988-89, 112-for-261 (.429). Totals, 291-for-674 (.432).

NBA REGULAR-SEASON RECORD

NOTES: Led NBA with .446 three-point field-goal percentage (1992).

Season Team	G	Min.	FGM	FGA	Pct.	FTM	FTA	Pct.	REBOUNDS Off.	Def.	Tot.	Ast.	PF	Dq.	Stl.	Blk.	TO	Pts.	Avg.
89-90 — Seattle	81	1630	299	738	.405	89	110	.809	35	97	132	205	97	0	53	1	123	782	9.7
90-91 — Seattle	66	750	154	311	.495	78	85	.918	17	54	71	111	40	0	23	1	54	418	6.3
91-92 — Seattle	75	1331	238	493	.483	60	79	.759	17	64	81	125	84	0	51	4	56	619	8.3
Totals	222	3711	691	1542	.448	227	274	.828	69	215	284	441	221	0	127	6	233	1819	8.2

Three-point field goals: 1989-90, 95-for-238 (.399). 1990-91, 32-for-81 (.395). 1991-92, 83-for-186 (.446). Totals, 210-for-505 (.416).

NBA PLAYOFF RECORD

Season	Team	G	Min.	FGM	FGA	Pct.	FTM	FTA	Pct.	Off.	Def.	Tot.	Ast.	PF	Dq.	Stl.	Blk.	TO	Pts.	Avg.
90-91	—Seattle.........	3	25	9	13	.692	3	4	.750	1	3	4	5	1	0	3	0	3	23	7.7
91-92	—Seattle.........	7	96	21	40	.525	0	0	...	1	6	7	8	11	0	4	0	6	52	7.4
	Totals	10	121	30	53	.566	3	4	.750	2	9	11	13	12	0	7	0	9	75	7.5

(Under REBOUNDS: Off., Def., Tot.)

Three-point field goals: 1990-91, 2-for-5 (.400). 1991-92, 10-for-17 (.588). Totals, 12-for-22 (.545).

BATTLE, JOHN
G, CAVALIERS

PERSONAL: Born November 9, 1962, in Washington, D.C.... 6-2/190.... Full name: John Sidney Battle.
HIGH SCHOOL: McKinley Technical (Washington, D.C.).
COLLEGE: Rutgers.
TRANSACTIONS/CAREER NOTES: Selected by Atlanta Hawks in fourth round (84th pick overall) of 1985 NBA Draft.... Signed as unrestricted free agent by Cleveland Cavaliers (July 16, 1991).

COLLEGIATE RECORD

Season	Team	G	Min.	FGM	FGA	Pct.	FTM	FTA	Pct.	Reb.	Pts.	Avg.
81-82	—Rutgers..............................	29	373	29	67	.433	12	28	.429	29	70	2.4
82-83	—Rutgers..............................	31	443	68	139	.489	37	51	.725	48	182	5.9
83-84	—Rutgers..............................	25	814	207	420	.493	111	153	.725	78	525	21.0
84-85	—Rutgers..............................	29	1017	231	470	.491	129	177	.729	115	608	21.0
	Totals	114	2647	535	1096	.488	289	409	.707	270	1385	12.1

Three-point field goals: 1982-83, 9-for-18 (.500). 1984-85, 17-for-58 (.293). Totals, 26-for-76 (.342).

NBA REGULAR-SEASON RECORD

Season	Team	G	Min.	FGM	FGA	Pct.	FTM	FTA	Pct.	Off.	Def.	Tot.	Ast.	PF	Dq.	Stl.	Blk.	TO	Pts.	Avg.
85-86	—Atlanta........	64	639	101	222	.455	75	103	.728	12	50	62	74	80	0	23	3	47	277	4.3
86-87	—Atlanta........	64	804	144	315	.457	93	126	.738	16	44	60	124	76	0	29	5	60	381	6.0
87-88	—Atlanta........	67	1227	278	613	.454	141	188	.750	26	87	113	158	84	0	31	5	75	713	10.6
88-89	—Atlanta........	82	1672	287	628	.457	194	238	.815	30	110	140	197	125	0	42	9	104	779	9.5
89-90	—Atlanta........	60	1477	275	544	.506	102	135	.756	27	72	99	154	115	0	28	3	89	654	10.9
90-91	—Atlanta........	79	1863	397	862	.461	270	316	.854	34	125	159	217	145	0	45	6	113	1078	13.6
91-92	—Cleveland	76	1637	316	659	.480	145	171	.848	19	93	112	159	116	0	36	5	91	779	10.3
	Totals	492	9319	1798	3843	.468	1020	1277	.799	164	581	745	1083	741	0	234	36	579	4661	9.5

Three-point field goals: 1985-86, 0-for-7. 1986-87, 0-for-10. 1987-88, 16-for-41 (.390). 1988-89, 11-for-34 (.324). 1989-90, 2-for-13 (.154). 1990-91, 14-for-49 (.286). 1991-92, 2-for-17 (.118). Totals, 45-for-171 (.263).

NBA PLAYOFF RECORD

Season	Team	G	Min.	FGM	FGA	Pct.	FTM	FTA	Pct.	Off.	Def.	Tot.	Ast.	PF	Dq.	Stl.	Blk.	TO	Pts.	Avg.
85-86	—Atlanta........	6	27	4	11	.364	3	4	.750	0	4	4	2	5	0	2	0	3	11	1.8
86-87	—Atlanta........	8	78	15	34	.441	21	23	.913	2	8	10	8	13	0	1	0	7	53	6.6
87-88	—Atlanta........	12	166	32	67	.478	17	25	.680	2	18	20	26	14	0	2	0	11	81	6.8
88-89	—Atlanta........	5	118	20	46	.435	9	12	.750	5	8	13	16	13	0	2	0	5	49	9.8
90-91	—Atlanta........	5	107	16	44	.364	24	25	.960	4	6	10	11	11	0	1	0	9	58	11.6
91-92	—Cleveland	15	202	34	82	.415	21	23	.913	4	8	12	15	11	0	5	1	18	89	5.9
	Totals	51	698	121	284	.426	95	112	.848	17	52	69	78	67	0	13	1	53	341	6.7

Three-point field goals: 1985-86, 0-for-1. 1986-87, 2-for-5 (.400). 1987-88, 0-for-2. 1988-89, 0-for-6. 1990-91, 2-for-5 (.400). 1991-92, 0-for-2. Totals, 4-for-21 (.190).

BATTLE, KENNY
F

PERSONAL: Born October 10, 1964, in Aurora, Ill.... 6-6/210.... Full name: Kenneth R. Battle.
HIGH SCHOOL: Aurora West (Ill.).
COLLEGE: Northern Illinois, then Illinois.
TRANSACTIONS/CAREER NOTES: Selected by Detroit Pistons in first round (27th pick overall) of 1989 NBA Draft.... Draft rights traded by Pistons with Micheal Williams to Phoenix Suns for draft rights to Anthony Cook (June 27, 1989).... Waived by Suns (January 23, 1991).... Claimed off waivers by Denver Nuggets (January 25, 1991).... Rights renounced by Nuggets (October 31, 1991).... Signed by Boston Celtics to first of two consecutive 10-day contracts (January 18, 1992).... Signed by Golden State Warriors to first of two consecutive 10-day contracts (February 10, 1992).... Played in Continental Basketball Association with La Crosse Catbirds (1991-92).

COLLEGIATE RECORD

Season	Team	G	Min.	FGM	FGA	Pct.	FTM	FTA	Pct.	Reb.	Pts.	Avg.
84-85	—Northern Illinois......................	27	...	195	369	.528	154	234	.658	167	544	20.1
85-86	—Northern Illinois......................	27	...	201	354	.568	126	193	.653	175	528	19.6
86-87	—Illinois.................................					Did not play—transfer student.						
87-88	—Illinois.................................	33	1027	197	341	.578	122	179	.682	183	516	15.6
88-89	—Illinois.................................	36	1105	218	361	.604	151	200	.755	174	596	16.6
	Totals	123	...	811	1425	.569	553	806	.686	699	2184	17.8

Three-point field goals: 1987-88, 0-for-1. 1988-89, 9-for-17 (.529). Totals, 9-for-18 (.500).

NBA REGULAR-SEASON RECORD

Season	Team	G	Min.	FGM	FGA	Pct.	FTM	FTA	Pct.	Off.	Def.	Tot.	Ast.	PF	Dq.	Stl.	Blk.	TO	Pts.	Avg.
89-90	—Phoenix........	59	729	93	170	.547	55	82	.671	44	80	124	38	94	2	35	11	32	242	4.1
90-91	—Phoe.-Den. ..	56	945	133	282	.472	70	93	.753	83	93	176	62	108	0	60	18	53	339	6.1
91-92	—Boston-G.S..	16	92	11	17	.647	10	12	.833	4	12	16	4	10	0	2	2	4	32	2.0
	Totals	131	1766	237	469	.505	135	187	.722	131	185	316	104	212	2	97	31	89	613	4.7

Three-point field goals: 1989-90, 1-for-4 (.250). 1990-91, 3-for-24 (.125). 1991-92, 0-for-1. Totals, 4-for-29 (.138).

NBA PLAYOFF RECORD

Season Team	G	Min.	FGM	FGA	Pct.	FTM	FTA	Pct.	Off.	Def.	Tot.	Ast.	PF	Dq.	Stl.	Blk.	TO	Pts.	Avg.
89-90 —Phoenix........	8	34	4	13	.308	1	1	1.000	1	4	5	0	5	0	0	0	2	9	1.1

CBA REGULAR-SEASON RECORD

NOTES: Led CBA with 3.0 steals per game (1992).

Season Team	G	Min.	2-POINT FGM	FGA	Pct.	3-POINT FGM	FGA	Pct.	FTM	FTA	Pct.	Reb.	Ast.	Pts.	Avg.
91-92 —La Crosse........	32	1269	192	367	.523	6	16	.375	167	221	.756	276	81	569	17.8

BEDFORD, WILLIAM
C, CLIPPERS

PERSONAL: Born December 3, 1963, in Memphis, Tenn. . . . 7-1/252.
HIGH SCHOOL: Melrose (Memphis, Tenn.).
COLLEGE: Memphis State.

TRANSACTIONS/CAREER NOTES: Selected as undergraduate by Phoenix Suns in first round (sixth pick overall) of 1986 NBA Draft. . . . Traded by Suns to Detroit Pistons for 1989 first-round draft choice (June 21, 1987). . . . Traded by Pistons with rights to Don MacLean to Los Angeles Clippers for Olden Polynice and 1996 and 1997 second-round draft choices (June 24, 1992).
MISCELLANEOUS: Member of NBA championship team (1990).

COLLEGIATE RECORD

Season Team	G	Min.	FGM	FGA	Pct.	FTM	FTA	Pct.	Reb.	Pts.	Avg.
83-84 —Memphis State.....................	26	684	108	187	.578	30	56	.536	137	246	9.5
84-85 —Memphis State.....................	35	1099	179	330	.542	68	101	.673	265	426	12.2
85-86 —Memphis State.....................	32	1038	227	389	.584	98	156	.628	273	552	17.3
Totals	93	2821	514	906	.567	196	313	.626	675	1224	13.2

NBA REGULAR-SEASON RECORD

Season Team	G	Min.	FGM	FGA	Pct.	FTM	FTA	Pct.	Off.	Def.	Tot.	Ast.	PF	Dq.	Stl.	Blk.	TO	Pts.	Avg.
86-87 —Phoenix.....	50	979	142	358	.397	50	86	.581	79	167	246	57	125	1	18	37	85	334	6.7
87-88 —Detroit.........	38	298	44	101	.436	13	23	.565	27	38	65	4	47	0	8	17	19	101	2.7
88-89 —Detroit.........								Did not play.											
89-90 —Detroit.........	42	246	54	125	.432	9	22	.409	15	43	58	4	39	0	3	17	21	118	2.8
90-91 —Detroit.........	60	562	106	242	.438	55	78	.705	55	76	131	32	76	0	2	36	32	272	4.5
91-92 —Detroit.........	32	363	50	121	.413	14	22	.636	24	39	63	12	56	0	6	18	15	114	3.6
Totals	222	2448	396	947	.418	141	231	.610	200	363	563	109	343	1	37	125	172	939	4.2

Three-point field goals: 1986-87, 0-for-1. 1989-90, 1-for-6 (.167). 1990-91, 5-for-13 (.385). 1991-92, 0-for-1. Totals, 6-for-21 (.286).

NBA PLAYOFF RECORD

Season Team	G	Min.	FGM	FGA	Pct.	FTM	FTA	Pct.	Off.	Def.	Tot.	Ast.	PF	Dq.	Stl.	Blk.	TO	Pts.	Avg.
89-90 —Detroit.........	5	19	1	6	.167	2	2	1.000	0	2	2	0	4	0	0	1	0	4	0.8
90-91 —Detroit.........	8	65	5	24	.208	9	14	.643	9	13	22	4	14	0	2	4	4	19	2.4
91-92 —Detroit.........	1	9	3	6	.500	0	0	...	0	2	2	0	1	0	1	0	0	6	6.0
Totals	14	93	9	36	.250	11	16	.688	9	17	26	4	19	0	3	5	4	29	2.1

Three-point field goals: 1990-91, 0-for-2.

BENJAMIN, BENOIT
C, SUPERSONICS

PERSONAL: Born November 22, 1964, in Monroe, La. . . . 7-0/265. . . . Full name: Lenard Benoit Benjamin.
HIGH SCHOOL: Carroll (Monroe, La.).
COLLEGE: Creighton.

TRANSACTIONS/CAREER NOTES: Selected by Los Angeles Clippers in first round (third pick overall) of 1985 NBA Draft. . . . Traded by Clippers to Seattle SuperSonics for Olden Polynice, 1991 first-round draft choice and 1993 or 1994 first-round draft choice (February 20, 1991).

COLLEGIATE RECORD

Season Team	G	Min.	FGM	FGA	Pct.	FTM	FTA	Pct.	Reb.	Pts.	Avg.
82-83 —Creighton................................	27	871	162	292	.555	76	116	.655	259	400	14.8
83-84 —Creighton................................	30	1112	190	350	.543	107	144	.743	295	487	16.2
84-85 —Creighton................................	32	1193	258	443	.582	172	233	.738	451	688	21.5
Totals	89	3176	610	1085	.562	355	493	.720	1005	1575	17.7

NBA REGULAR-SEASON RECORD

Season Team	G	Min.	FGM	FGA	Pct.	FTM	FTA	Pct.	Off.	Def.	Tot.	Ast.	PF	Dq.	Stl.	Blk.	TO	Pts.	Avg.
85-86 —L.A. Clippers	79	2088	324	661	.490	229	307	.746	161	439	600	79	286	5	64	206	145	878	11.1
86-87 —L.A. Clippers	72	2230	320	713	.449	188	263	.715	134	452	586	135	251	7	60	187	184	828	11.5
87-88 —L.A. Clippers	66	2171	340	693	.491	180	255	.706	112	418	530	172	203	2	50	225	223	860	13.0
88-89 —L.A. Clippers	79	2585	491	907	.541	317	426	.744	164	532	696	157	221	4	57	221	237	1299	16.4
89-90 —L.A. Clippers	71	2313	362	688	.526	235	321	.732	156	501	657	159	217	3	59	187	187	959	13.5
90-91 —LAC-Seattle..	70	2236	386	778	.496	210	295	.712	157	566	723	119	184	1	54	145	175	982	14.0
91-92 —Seattle.........	63	1941	354	740	.478	171	249	.687	130	383	513	76	185	1	39	118	175	879	14.0
Totals	500	15564	2577	5180	.497	1530	2116	.723	1014	3291	4305	897	1547	23	383	1289	1386	6685	13.4

Three-point field goals: 1985-86, 1-for-3 (.333). 1986-87, 0-for-2. 1987-88, 0-for-8. 1988-89, 0-for-2. 1989-90, 0-for-1. 1991-92, 0-for-2. Totals, 1-for-18 (.056).

NBA PLAYOFF RECORD

Season Team	G	Min.	FGM	FGA	Pct.	FTM	FTA	Pct.	REBOUNDS Off.	Def.	Tot.	Ast.	PF	Dq.	Stl.	Blk.	TO	Pts.	Avg.
90-91 —Seattle	5	163	20	41	.488	29	32	.906	7	26	33	1	17	1	3	13	11	69	13.8
91-92 —Seattle	9	161	23	41	.561	9	18	.500	10	36	46	5	20	0	5	13	8	55	6.1
Totals	14	324	43	82	.524	38	50	.760	17	62	79	6	37	1	8	26	19	124	8.9

Three-point field goals: 1991-92, 0-for-1.

BENNETT, WINSTON
F

PERSONAL: Born February 9, 1965, in Louisville, Ky. . . . 6-7/220. . . . Full name: Winston George Bennett III.
HIGH SCHOOL: Louisville Male (Ky.).
COLLEGE: Kentucky.
TRANSACTIONS/CAREER NOTES: Selected by Cleveland Cavaliers in third round (64th pick overall) of 1988 NBA Draft. . . . Played in Continental Basketball Association with Pensacola Tornados (1988-89). . . . Played in Italy (1988-89). . . . Waived by Cavaliers (March 27, 1992). . . . Signed by Miami Heat to 10-day contract (April 10, 1992).

COLLEGIATE RECORD

Season Team	G	Min.	FGM	FGA	Pct.	FTM	FTA	Pct.	Reb.	Pts.	Avg.
83-84 —Kentucky	34	642	67	156	.429	88	126	.698	129	222	6.5
84-85 —Kentucky	30	851	82	191	.429	52	77	.675	160	216	7.2
85-86 —Kentucky	36	1129	171	338	.506	115	158	.728	252	457	12.7
86-87 —Kentucky				Did not play—knee injury.							
87-88 —Kentucky	33	1091	195	380	.513	113	155	.729	258	504	15.3
Totals	133	3713	515	1065	.484	368	516	.713	799	1399	10.5

Three-point field goals: 1987-88, 1-for-2 (.500).

CBA REGULAR-SEASON RECORD

Season Team	G	Min.	2-POINT FGM	FGA	Pct.	3-POINT FGM	FGA	Pct.	FTM	FTA	Pct.	Reb.	Ast.	Pts.	Avg.
88-89 —Pensacola	26	793	130	265	.491	0	0	. . .	99	138	.717	288	28	359	13.8

ITALIAN LEAGUE RECORD

Season Team	G	Min.	FGM	FGA	Pct.	FTM	FTA	Pct.	Reb.	Pts.	Avg.
88-89 —Teo. Arese	7	253	55	131	.420	38	55	.691	54	148	21.1

NBA REGULAR-SEASON RECORD

Season Team	G	Min.	FGM	FGA	Pct.	FTM	FTA	Pct.	REBOUNDS Off.	Def.	Tot.	Ast.	PF	Dq.	Stl.	Blk.	TO	Pts.	Avg.
89-90 —Cleveland	55	990	137	286	.479	64	96	.667	84	104	188	54	133	1	23	10	62	338	6.1
90-91 —Cleveland	27	334	40	107	.374	35	47	.745	30	34	64	28	50	0	8	2	20	115	4.3
91-92 —Clev.-Miami	54	833	80	211	.379	35	50	.700	63	99	162	38	122	1	19	9	33	195	3.6
Totals	136	2157	257	604	.425	134	193	.694	177	237	414	120	305	2	50	21	115	648	4.8

Three-point field goals: 1991-92, 0-for-1.

NBA PLAYOFF RECORD

Season Team	G	Min.	FGM	FGA	Pct.	FTM	FTA	Pct.	REBOUNDS Off.	Def.	Tot.	Ast.	PF	Dq.	Stl.	Blk.	TO	Pts.	Avg.
89-90 —Cleveland	5	135	23	47	.489	4	6	.667	14	7	21	5	11	0	3	1	4	50	10.0

BENOIT, DAVID
F, JAZZ

PERSONAL: Born May 9, 1968, in Lafayette, La. . . . 6-8/225. . . . Name pronounced BEN-wa.
HIGH SCHOOL: Lafayette (La.).
COLLEGE: Tyler Junior College (Tex.), then Alabama.
TRANSACTIONS/CAREER NOTES: Never drafted by an NBA franchise. . . . Played in Spain (1990-91). . . . Signed as free agent by Utah Jazz (August 7, 1991).

COLLEGIATE RECORD

Season Team	G	Min.	FGM	FGA	Pct.	FTM	FTA	Pct.	Reb.	Pts.	Avg.
86-87 —Tyler Junior College					Statistics unavailable.						
87-88 —Tyler Junior College					Statistics unavailable.						
88-89 —Alabama	31	913	136	268	.507	62	84	.738	248	335	10.8
89-90 —Alabama	35	920	156	303	.515	46	60	.767	212	367	10.5
Totals	66	1833	292	571	.511	108	144	.750	460	702	10.6

Three-point field goals: 1988-89, 1-for-3 (.333). 1989-90, 9-for-20 (.450). Totals, 10-for-23 (.435).

SPANISH LEAGUE RECORD

Season Team	G	Min.	FGM	FGA	Pct.	FTM	FTA	Pct.	Reb.	Pts.	Avg.
90-91 —Malaga	34	1235	302	609	.496	128	165	.776	349	749	22.0

NBA REGULAR-SEASON RECORD

Season Team	G	Min.	FGM	FGA	Pct.	FTM	FTA	Pct.	REBOUNDS Off.	Def.	Tot.	Ast.	PF	Dq.	Stl.	Blk.	TO	Pts.	Avg.
91-92 —Utah	77	1161	175	375	.467	81	100	.810	105	191	296	34	124	0	19	44	71	434	5.6

Three-point field goals: 1991-92, 3-for-14 (.214).

NBA PLAYOFF RECORD

Season Team	G	Min.	FGM	FGA	Pct.	FTM	FTA	Pct.	REBOUNDS Off.	Def.	Tot.	Ast.	PF	Dq.	Stl.	Blk.	TO	Pts.	Avg.
91-92 —Utah	13	257	36	84	.429	11	11	1.000	18	32	50	6	30	0	6	5	10	89	6.8

Three-point field goals: 1991-92, 6-for-13 (.462).

BLACKMAN, ROLANDO
G, KNICKS

PERSONAL: Born February 26, 1959, in Panama City, Panama. . . . 6-6/206. . . . Full name: Rolando Antonio Blackman. . . . Name pronounced Roll-ON-doe.
HIGH SCHOOL: William E. Grady Vocational Technical School (Brooklyn, N.Y.).
COLLEGE: Kansas State.
TRANSACTIONS/CAREER NOTES: Selected by Dallas Mavericks in first round (ninth pick overall) of 1981 NBA Draft. . . . Traded by Mavericks to New York Knicks for 1995 first-round draft choice (June 24, 1992).
MISCELLANEOUS: Member of U.S. Olympic team (1980).

COLLEGIATE RECORD

NOTES: THE SPORTING NEWS All-America first team (1981).

Season Team	G	Min.	FGM	FGA	Pct.	FTM	FTA	Pct.	Reb.	Pts.	Avg.
77-78 —Kansas State	29	...	127	269	.472	61	93	.656	187	315	10.9
78-79 —Kansas State	28	...	200	392	.510	83	113	.735	110	483	17.3
79-80 —Kansas State	31	...	226	419	.539	100	145	.690	145	552	17.8
80-81 —Kansas State	33	...	202	380	.532	90	115	.783	165	494	15.0
Totals	121	...	755	1460	.517	334	466	.717	607	1844	15.2

NBA REGULAR-SEASON RECORD

									— REBOUNDS —									
Season Team	G	Min.	FGM	FGA	Pct.	FTM	FTA	Pct.	Off.	Def.	Tot.	Ast.	PF	Dq.	Stl.	Blk.	TO	Pts.	Avg.
81-82 —Dallas	82	1979	439	855	.513	212	276	.768	97	157	254	105	122	0	46	30	113	1091	13.3
82-83 —Dallas	75	2349	513	1042	.492	297	381	.780	108	185	293	185	116	0	37	29	118	1326	17.7
83-84 —Dallas	81	3025	721	1320	.546	372	458	.812	124	249	373	288	127	0	56	37	169	1815	22.4
84-85 —Dallas	81	2834	625	1230	.508	342	413	.828	107	193	300	289	96	0	61	16	162	1598	19.7
85-86 —Dallas	82	2787	677	1318	.514	404	483	.836	88	203	291	271	138	0	79	25	189	1762	21.5
86-87 —Dallas	80	2758	626	1264	.495	419	474	.884	96	182	278	266	142	0	64	21	174	1676	21.0
87-88 —Dallas	71	2580	497	1050	.473	331	379	.873	82	164	246	262	112	0	64	18	144	1325	18.7
88-89 —Dallas	78	2946	594	1249	.476	316	370	.854	70	203	273	288	137	0	65	20	165	1534	19.7
89-90 —Dallas	80	2934	626	1256	.498	287	340	.844	88	192	280	289	128	0	77	21	174	1552	19.4
90-91 —Dallas	80	2965	634	1316	.482	282	326	.865	63	193	256	301	153	0	69	19	159	1590	19.9
91-92 —Dallas	75	2527	535	1161	.461	239	266	.899	78	161	239	204	134	0	50	22	153	1374	18.3
Totals	865	29684	6487	13061	.497	3501	4166	.840	1001	2082	3083	2748	1405	0	668	258	1720	16643	19.2

Three-point field goals: 1981-82, 1-for-4 (.250). 1982-83, 3-for-15 (.200). 1983-84, 1-for-11 (.091). 1984-85, 6-for-20 (.300). 1985-86, 4-for-29 (.138). 1986-87, 5-for-15 (.333). 1987-88, 0-for-5. 1988-89, 30-for-85 (.353). 1989-90, 13-for-43 (.302). 1990-91, 40-for-114 (.351). 1991-92, 65-for-169 (.385). Totals, 168-for-510 (.329).

NBA PLAYOFF RECORD

									— REBOUNDS —									
Season Team	G	Min.	FGM	FGA	Pct.	FTM	FTA	Pct.	Off.	Def.	Tot.	Ast.	PF	Dq.	Stl.	Blk.	TO	Pts.	Avg.
83-84 —Dallas	10	397	93	175	.531	53	63	.841	15	26	41	40	15	0	6	4	24	239	23.9
84-85 —Dallas	4	169	47	92	.511	36	38	.947	11	15	26	19	8	0	2	2	14	131	32.8
85-86 —Dallas	10	371	83	167	.497	42	53	.792	15	20	35	32	26	1	8	1	20	208	20.8
86-87 —Dallas	4	153	36	73	.493	22	24	.917	4	10	14	17	7	0	2	0	8	94	23.5
87-88 —Dallas	17	672	126	261	.483	55	62	.887	26	29	55	77	28	0	15	3	25	307	18.1
89-90 —Dallas	3	127	24	54	.444	10	10	1.000	2	7	9	13	7	0	6	2	13	60	20.0
Totals	48	1889	409	822	.498	218	250	.872	73	107	180	198	91	1	39	12	104	1039	21.6

Three-point field goals: 1984-85, 1-for-2 (.500). 1985-86, 0-for-1. 1986-87, 0-for-1. 1987-88, 0-for-3. 1989-90, 2-for-5 (.400). Totals, 3-for-12 (.250).

NBA ALL-STAR GAME RECORD

								— REBOUNDS —								
Season Team	Min.	FGM	FGA	Pct.	FTM	FTA	Pct.	Off.	Def.	Tot.	Ast.	PF	Dq.	Stl.	Blk.	TO	Pts.
1985 —Dallas	23	7	14	.500	1	2	.500	1	2	3	2	1	0	1	1	0	15
1986 —Dallas	22	6	11	.545	0	0	...	1	3	4	8	1	0	2	1	1	12
1987 —Dallas	22	9	15	.600	11	13	.846	1	3	4	1	2	0	0	0	2	29
1990 —Dallas	21	7	9	.778	1	1	1.000	1	1	2	2	1	0	2	0	2	15
Totals	88	29	49	.592	13	16	.813	4	9	13	13	5	0	5	2	5	71

BLANKS, LANCE
G, PISTONS

PERSONAL: Born September 9, 1966, in Del Rio, Tex. . . . 6-4/195. . . . Son of Sid Blanks, running back with Houston Oilers and Boston Patriots (1964, 1966-70); and cousin of Larvell Blanks, infielder with Atlanta Braves, Cleveland Indians and Texas Rangers (1972-80).
HIGH SCHOOL: McCullough (The Woodlands, Tex.).
COLLEGE: Virginia, then Texas.
TRANSACTIONS/CAREER NOTES: Selected by Detroit Pistons in first round (26th pick overall) of 1990 NBA Draft.

COLLEGIATE RECORD

Season Team	G	Min.	FGM	FGA	Pct.	FTM	FTA	Pct.	Reb.	Pts.	Avg.
85-86 —Virginia	14	103	14	32	.438	6	12	.500	15	34	2.4
86-87 —Virginia	24	145	13	25	.520	2	7	.286	18	29	1.2
87-88 —Texas					Did not play—transfer student.						
88-89 —Texas	34	1295	237	527	.450	119	174	.684	191	671	19.7
89-90 —Texas	32	1157	206	512	.402	161	202	.797	136	651	20.3
Totals	104	2700	470	1096	.429	288	395	.729	360	1385	13.3

Three-point field goals: 1986-87, 1-for-4 (.250). 1988-89, 78-for-218 (.358). 1989-90, 78-for-214 (.364). Totals, 157-for-436 (.360).

NBA REGULAR-SEASON RECORD

Season — Team	G	Min.	FGM	FGA	Pct.	FTM	FTA	Pct.	Off.	Def.	Tot.	Ast.	PF	Dq.	Stl.	Blk.	TO	Pts.	Avg.
90-91 — Detroit	38	214	26	61	.426	10	14	.714	4	16	20	26	35	0	9	2	18	64	1.7
91-92 — Detroit	43	189	25	55	.455	8	11	.727	9	13	22	19	26	0	14	1	14	64	1.5
Totals	81	403	51	116	.440	18	25	.720	13	29	42	45	61	0	23	3	32	128	1.6

Three-point field goals: 1990-91, 2-for-16 (.125). 1991-92, 6-for-16 (.375). Totals, 8-for-32 (.250).

NBA PLAYOFF RECORD

Season — Team	G	Min.	FGM	FGA	Pct.	FTM	FTA	Pct.	Off.	Def.	Tot.	Ast.	PF	Dq.	Stl.	Blk.	TO	Pts.	Avg.
91-92 — Detroit	1	10	1	2	.500	0	0	...	0	1	1	3	2	0	3	0	1	2	2.0

BLAYLOCK, MOOKIE
G, NETS

PERSONAL: Born March 20, 1967, in Garland, Tex. . . . 6-1/185. . . . Full name: Daron Oshay Blaylock.
HIGH SCHOOL: Garland (Tex.).
COLLEGE: Midland (Tex.), then Oklahoma.

TRANSACTIONS/CAREER NOTES: Selected by New Jersey Nets in first round (12th pick overall) of 1989 NBA Draft.

COLLEGIATE RECORD

NOTES: THE SPORTING NEWS All-America second team (1989).

Season — Team	G	Min.	FGM	FGA	Pct.	FTM	FTA	Pct.	Reb.	Pts.	Avg.
85-86 — Midland	34	. . .	254	449	.566	62	84	.738	109	570	16.8
86-87 — Midland	33	. . .	258	500	.516	60	83	.723	138	647	19.6
87-88 — Oklahoma	39	1347	241	524	.460	78	114	.684	162	638	16.4
88-89 — Oklahoma	35	1359	272	598	.455	65	100	.650	164	700	20.0
Junior college totals	67	. . .	512	949	.540	122	167	.731	247	1217	18.2
Four-year-college totals	74	2706	513	1122	.457	143	214	.668	326	1338	18.1

Three-point field goals: 1987-88, 78-for-201 (.388). 1988-89, 91-for-245 (.371). Totals, 169-for-446 (.379).

NBA REGULAR-SEASON RECORD

Season — Team	G	Min.	FGM	FGA	Pct.	FTM	FTA	Pct.	Off.	Def.	Tot.	Ast.	PF	Dq.	Stl.	Blk.	TO	Pts.	Avg.
89-90 — New Jersey	50	1267	212	571	.371	63	81	.778	42	98	140	210	110	0	82	14	111	505	10.1
90-91 — New Jersey	72	2585	432	1039	.416	139	176	.790	67	182	249	441	180	0	169	40	207	1017	14.1
91-92 — New Jersey	72	2548	429	993	.432	126	177	.712	101	168	269	492	182	1	170	40	152	996	13.8
Totals	194	6400	1073	2603	.412	328	434	.756	210	448	658	1143	472	1	421	94	470	2518	13.0

Three-point field goals: 1989-90, 18-for-80 (.225). 1990-91, 14-for-91 (.154). 1991-92, 12-for-54 (.222). Totals, 44-for-225 (.196).

NBA PLAYOFF RECORD

Season — Team	G	Min.	FGM	FGA	Pct.	FTM	FTA	Pct.	Off.	Def.	Tot.	Ast.	PF	Dq.	Stl.	Blk.	TO	Pts.	Avg.
91-92 — New Jersey	4	148	17	55	.309	3	4	.750	5	11	16	31	16	0	15	2	7	38	9.5

Three-point field goals: 1991-92, 1-for-6 (.167).

BOGUES, TYRONE
G, HORNETS

PERSONAL: Born January 9, 1965, in Baltimore. . . . 5-3/140. . . . Name pronounced Boags. . . . Nickname: Muggsy.
HIGH SCHOOL: Dunbar (Baltimore).
COLLEGE: Wake Forest.

TRANSACTIONS/CAREER NOTES: Selected by Washington Bullets in first round (12th pick overall) of 1987 NBA Draft. . . . Selected by Charlotte Hornets from Bullets in NBA expansion draft (June 23, 1988).

COLLEGIATE RECORD

Season — Team	G	Min.	FGM	FGA	Pct.	FTM	FTA	Pct.	Reb.	Pts.	Avg.
83-84 — Wake Forest	32	312	14	46	.304	9	13	.692	21	37	1.2
84-85 — Wake Forest	29	1025	81	162	.500	30	44	.682	69	192	6.6
85-86 — Wake Forest	29	1101	132	290	.455	65	89	.730	90	329	11.3
86-87 — Wake Forest	29	1130	159	318	.500	75	93	.806	110	428	14.8
Totals	119	3568	386	816	.473	179	239	.749	290	986	8.3

Three-point field goals: 1986-87, 35-for-79 (.443).

NBA REGULAR-SEASON RECORD

Season — Team	G	Min.	FGM	FGA	Pct.	FTM	FTA	Pct.	Off.	Def.	Tot.	Ast.	PF	Dq.	Stl.	Blk.	TO	Pts.	Avg.
87-88 — Washington	79	1628	166	426	.390	58	74	.784	35	101	136	404	138	1	127	3	101	393	5.0
88-89 — Charlotte	79	1755	178	418	.426	66	88	.750	53	112	165	620	141	1	111	7	124	423	5.4
89-90 — Charlotte	81	2743	326	664	.491	106	134	.791	48	159	207	867	168	1	166	3	146	763	9.4
90-91 — Charlotte	81	2299	241	524	.460	86	108	.796	58	158	216	669	160	2	137	3	120	568	7.0
91-92 — Charlotte	82	2790	317	671	.472	94	120	.783	58	177	235	743	156	0	170	6	156	730	8.9
Totals	402	11215	1228	2703	.454	410	524	.782	252	707	959	3303	763	5	711	22	647	2877	7.2

Three-point field goals: 1987-88, 3-for-16 (.188). 1988-89, 1-for-13 (.077). 1989-90, 5-for-26 (.192). 1990-91, 0-for-12. 1991-92, 2-for-27 (.074). Totals, 11-for-94 (.117).

NBA PLAYOFF RECORD

Season — Team	G	Min.	FGM	FGA	Pct.	FTM	FTA	Pct.	Off.	Def.	Tot.	Ast.	PF	Dq.	Stl.	Blk.	TO	Pts.	Avg.
87-88 — Washington	1	2	0	0	...	0	0	...	0	0	0	2	0	0	0	0	1	0	0.0

BOL, MANUTE
C, 76ERS

PERSONAL: Born October 16, 1962, in Gogrial, Sudan. . . . 7-7/225. . . . Name pronounced Muh-NOOT Bowl.
HIGH SCHOOL: Case Western Reserve English Language School (Cleveland).
COLLEGE: Bridgeport (Conn.).
TRANSACTIONS/CAREER NOTES: Selected by San Diego Clippers in fifth round (97th pick overall) of 1983 NBA Draft. . . . Declared ineligible for 1983 NBA draft. . . . Selected as undergraduate by Washington Bullets in second round (31st pick overall) of 1985 NBA Draft. . . . Traded by Bullets to Golden State Warriors for Dave Feitl and 1989 second-round draft choice (June 8, 1988). . . . Traded by Warriors to Philadelphia 76ers for 1991 first-round draft choice (August 1, 1990).

COLLEGIATE RECORD

Season Team	G	Min.	FGM	FGA	Pct.	FTM	FTA	Pct.	Reb.	Pts.	Avg.
84-85 — Bridgeport	31	...	303	496	.611	91	153	.595	419	697	22.5

NBA REGULAR-SEASON RECORD

RECORDS: Holds single-season record for most blocked shots by a rookie—397; and highest blocked shots-per-game average by a rookie—4.96 (1986).
HONORS: NBA All-Defensive second team (1986).
NOTES: Led NBA with 4.96 blocked shots per game (1986) and 4.31 blocked shots per game (1989).

Season Team	G	Min.	FGM	FGA	Pct.	FTM	FTA	Pct.	Off.	Def.	Tot.	Ast.	PF	Dq.	Stl.	Blk.	TO	Pts.	Avg.
85-86 — Washington	80	2090	128	278	.460	42	86	.488	123	354	477	23	255	5	28	*397	65	298	3.7
86-87 — Washington	82	1552	103	231	.446	45	67	.672	84	278	362	11	189	1	20	302	61	251	3.1
87-88 — Washington	77	1136	75	165	.455	26	49	.531	72	203	275	13	160	0	11	208	35	176	2.3
88-89 — Golden State	80	1769	127	344	.369	40	66	.606	116	346	462	27	226	2	11	*345	79	314	3.9
89-90 — Golden State	75	1310	56	169	.331	25	49	.510	33	243	276	36	194	3	13	238	51	146	1.9
90-91 — Philadelphia	82	1522	65	164	.396	24	41	.585	66	284	350	20	184	0	16	247	63	155	1.9
91-92 — Philadelphia	71	1267	49	128	.383	12	26	.462	54	168	222	22	139	1	11	205	41	110	1.5
Totals	547	10646	603	1479	.408	214	384	.557	548	1876	2424	152	1347	12	110	1942	395	1450	2.7

Three-point field goals: 1985-86, 0-for-1. 1986-87, 0-for-1. 1987-88, 0-for-1. 1988-89, 20-for-91 (.220). 1989-90, 9-for-48 (.188). 1990-91, 1-for-14 (.071). 1991-92, 0-for-9. Totals, 30-for-165 (.182).

NBA PLAYOFF RECORD

Season Team	G	Min.	FGM	FGA	Pct.	FTM	FTA	Pct.	Off.	Def.	Tot.	Ast.	PF	Dq.	Stl.	Blk.	TO	Pts.	Avg.
85-86 — Washington	5	152	10	17	.588	3	8	.375	16	22	38	1	15	0	3	29	4	23	4.6
86-87 — Washington	3	43	4	10	.400	0	2	.000	5	4	9	0	6	0	0	5	0	8	2.7
87-88 — Washington	5	44	4	7	.571	1	1	1.000	7	5	12	0	5	0	0	2	1	9	1.8
88-89 — Golden State	8	148	7	36	.194	2	7	.286	5	26	31	1	21	0	2	29	3	18	2.3
90-91 — Philadelphia	8	109	9	18	.500	6	9	.667	4	15	19	1	14	0	1	12	5	24	3.0
Totals	29	496	34	88	.386	12	27	.444	37	72	109	3	61	0	6	77	13	82	2.8

Three-point field goals: 1986-87, 0-for-1. 1988-89, 2-for-22 (.091). Totals, 2-for-23 (.087).

BONNER, ANTHONY
F, KINGS

PERSONAL: Born June 8, 1968, in St. Louis. . . . 6-8/225.
HIGH SCHOOL: Vashon (St. Louis).
COLLEGE: St. Louis.
TRANSACTIONS/CAREER NOTES: Selected by Sacramento Kings in first round (23rd pick overall) of 1990 NBA Draft.

COLLEGIATE RECORD

NOTES: Led NCAA Division I with 13.8 rebounds per game (1990).

Season Team	G	Min.	FGM	FGA	Pct.	FTM	FTA	Pct.	Reb.	Pts.	Avg.
86-87 — St. Louis	35	1066	138	233	.592	84	127	.661	337	360	10.3
87-88 — St. Louis	28	942	154	287	.537	77	129	.597	245	385	13.8
88-89 — St. Louis	37	1246	228	407	.560	117	201	.582	386	573	15.5
89-90 — St. Louis	33	...	254	508	.500	142	205	.693	456	654	19.8
Totals	133	...	774	1435	.539	420	662	.634	1424	1972	14.8

Three-point field goals: 1989-90, 4-for-12 (.333).

NBA REGULAR-SEASON RECORD

Season Team	G	Min.	FGM	FGA	Pct.	FTM	FTA	Pct.	Off.	Def.	Tot.	Ast.	PF	Dq.	Stl.	Blk.	TO	Pts.	Avg.
90-91 — Sacramento	34	750	103	230	.448	44	76	.579	59	102	161	49	62	0	39	5	41	250	7.4
91-92 — Sacramento	79	2287	294	658	.447	151	241	.627	192	293	485	125	194	0	94	26	133	740	9.4
Totals	113	3037	397	888	.447	195	317	.615	251	395	646	174	256	0	133	31	174	990	8.8

Three-point field goals: 1991-92, 1-for-4 (.250).

BOWIE, ANTHONY
G, MAGIC

PERSONAL: Born November 9, 1963, in Tulsa, Okla. . . . 6-6/190. . . . Full name: Anthony Lee Bowie.
HIGH SCHOOL: East Central (Tulsa, Okla.).
COLLEGE: Oklahoma.
TRANSACTIONS/CAREER NOTES: Selected by Houston Rockets in third round (66th overall) of 1986 NBA draft. . . . Waived by Rockets (November 4, 1986). . . . Re-signed as free agent by Rockets (June 11, 1987). . . . Waived by Rockets (November 5, 1987). . . . Played in Continental Basketball Association with Quad City Thunder (1987-88, 1988-89 and 1991-92). . . . Signed as free agent by New Jersey Nets (July 19, 1988). . . . Waived by Nets (Novem-

ber 1, 1988).... Signed by San Antonio Spurs to first of two consecutive 10-day contracts (March 20, 1989).... Re-signed by Spurs for remainder of season (April 9, 1989). ... Traded by Spurs to Rockets for cash (August 15, 1989).... Waived by Rockets (July 5, 1990).... Played in Italy (1990-91).... Signed as free agent by Chicago Bulls (October 2, 1991).... Waived by Bulls (October 30, 1991).... Signed as free agent by Orlando Magic (December 31, 1991).

COLLEGIATE RECORD

Season	Team	G	Min.	FGM	FGA	Pct.	FTM	FTA	Pct.	Reb.	Pts.	Avg.
82-83	Seminole Junior College	40	...	...	...	.525	...	...	.770	...	712	17.8
83-84	Seminole Junior College	38	...	...	...	.542	...	...	.793	...	707	18.6
84-85	Oklahoma	37	1282	202	392	.515	92	119	.773	215	496	13.4
85-86	Oklahoma	35	1170	202	402	.502	63	78	.808	161	467	13.3
	Junior college totals	78	...	...	...	...	...	...	...	...	1419	18.2
	Four-year-college totals	72	2452	404	794	.509	155	197	.787	376	963	13.4

CBA REGULAR-SEASON RECORD

NOTES: CBA Most Valuable Player (1989).... CBA All-Star first team (1989).

				2-POINT			3-POINT								
Season	Team	G	Min.	FGM	FGA	Pct.	FGM	FGA	Pct.	FTM	FTA	Pct.	Reb.	Ast.	Pts.	Avg.
87-88	Quad City	37	1028	198	365	.542	7	23	.304	75	83	.904	163	105	492	13.3
88-89	Quad City	53	1959	442	878	.503	14	58	.241	171	213	.803	363	238	1097	20.7
91-92	Quad City	23	841	191	371	.515	6	13	.462	75	86	.872	174	77	475	20.7
	Totals	113	3828	831	1614	.515	27	94	.287	321	382	.840	700	420	2064	18.3

NBA REGULAR-SEASON RECORD

											REBOUNDS									
Season	Team	G	Min.	FGM	FGA	Pct.	FTM	FTA	Pct.	Off.	Def.	Tot.	Ast.	PF	Dq.	Stl.	Blk.	TO	Pts.	Avg.
88-89	San Antonio	18	438	72	144	.500	10	15	.667	25	31	56	29	43	1	18	4	22	155	8.6
89-90	Houston	66	918	119	293	.406	40	54	.741	36	82	118	96	80	0	42	5	59	284	4.3
91-92	Orlando	52	1721	312	633	.493	117	136	.860	70	175	245	163	101	1	55	38	107	758	14.6
	Totals	136	3077	503	1070	.470	167	205	.815	131	288	419	288	224	2	115	47	188	1197	8.8

Three-point field goals: 1988-89, 1-for-5 (.200). 1989-90, 6-for-21 (.286). 1991-92, 17-for-44 (.386). Totals, 24-for-70 (.343).

NBA PLAYOFF RECORD

											REBOUNDS									
Season	Team	G	Min.	FGM	FGA	Pct.	FTM	FTA	Pct.	Off.	Def.	Tot.	Ast.	PF	Dq.	Stl.	Blk.	TO	Pts.	Avg.
89-90	Houston	2	4	0	1	.000	0	0	...	0	0	0	0	1	0	0	0	0	0	0.0

BOWIE, SAM
C, NETS

PERSONAL: Born March 17, 1961, in Lebanon, Pa.... 7-1/240.... Full name: Samuel Paul Bowie.
HIGH SCHOOL: Lebanon (Pa.).
COLLEGE: Kentucky.
TRANSACTIONS/CAREER NOTES: Selected by Portland Trail Blazers in first round (second pick overall) of 1984 NBA Draft.... Traded by Trail Blazers with 1989 first-round draft choice to New Jersey Nets for Buck Williams (June 24, 1989).
MISCELLANEOUS: Member of U.S. Olympic team (1980).

COLLEGIATE RECORD

NOTES: THE SPORTING NEWS All-America second team (1984).

Season	Team	G	Min.	FGM	FGA	Pct.	FTM	FTA	Pct.	Reb.	Pts.	Avg.
79-80	Kentucky	34	886	165	311	.531	110	144	.764	276	440	12.9
80-81	Kentucky	28	895	185	356	.520	118	164	.720	254	488	17.4
81-82	Kentucky				Did not play—injured.							
82-83	Kentucky				Did not play—injured.							
83-84	Kentucky	34	980	133	258	.516	91	126	.722	313	357	10.5
	Totals	96	2761	483	925	.522	319	434	.735	843	1285	13.4

NBA REGULAR-SEASON RECORD

HONORS: NBA All-Rookie team (1985).

											REBOUNDS									
Season	Team	G	Min.	FGM	FGA	Pct.	FTM	FTA	Pct.	Off.	Def.	Tot.	Ast.	PF	Dq.	Stl.	Blk.	TO	Pts.	Avg.
84-85	Portland	76	2216	299	557	.537	160	225	.711	207	449	656	215	278	9	55	203	172	758	10.0
85-86	Portland	38	1132	167	345	.484	114	161	.708	93	234	327	99	142	4	21	96	88	448	11.8
86-87	Portland	5	163	30	66	.455	20	30	.667	14	19	33	9	19	0	1	10	15	80	16.0
87-88	Portland					Did not play—injured.														
88-89	Portland	20	412	69	153	.451	28	49	.571	36	70	106	36	43	0	7	33	33	171	8.6
89-90	New Jersey	68	2207	347	834	.416	294	379	.776	206	484	690	91	211	5	38	121	125	998	14.7
90-91	New Jersey	62	1916	314	723	.434	169	231	.732	176	304	480	147	175	4	43	90	141	801	12.9
91-92	New Jersey	71	2179	421	947	.445	212	280	.757	203	375	578	186	212	2	41	120	150	1062	15.0
	Totals	340	10225	1647	3625	.454	997	1355	.736	935	1935	2870	783	1080	24	206	673	724	4318	12.7

Three-point field goals: 1988-89, 5-for-7 (.714). 1989-90, 10-for-31 (.323). 1990-91, 4-for-22 (.182). 1991-92, 8-for-25 (.320). Totals, 27-for-85 (.318).

NBA PLAYOFF RECORD

											REBOUNDS									
Season	Team	G	Min.	FGM	FGA	Pct.	FTM	FTA	Pct.	Off.	Def.	Tot.	Ast.	PF	Dq.	Stl.	Blk.	TO	Pts.	Avg.
84-85	Portland	9	259	26	59	.441	14	25	.560	16	60	76	21	36	2	4	21	12	66	7.3
88-89	Portland	3	67	12	28	.429	6	8	.750	10	10	20	3	8	0	0	7	3	31	10.3
91-92	New Jersey	4	112	14	33	.424	8	12	.667	8	11	19	9	19	0	3	3	5	37	9.3
	Totals	16	438	52	120	.433	28	45	.622	34	81	115	33	63	2	7	31	20	134	8.4

Three-point field goals: 1988-89, 1-for-2 (.500). 1991-92, 1-for-2 (.500). Totals, 2-for-4 (.500).

BRANDON, TERRELL

PERSONAL: Born May 20, 1970, in Portland, Ore. . . . 6-0/180. . . . Full name: Thomas Terrell Brandon. . . . Name pronounced Tur-RELL.
HIGH SCHOOL: Grant (Portland, Ore.).
COLLEGE: Oregon.
TRANSACTIONS/CAREER NOTES: Selected as undergraduate by Cleveland Cavaliers in first round (11th pick overall) of 1991 NBA Draft.

COLLEGIATE RECORD

Season Team	G	Min.	FGM	FGA	Pct.	FTM	FTA	Pct.	Reb.	Pts.	Avg.
88-89 — Oregon					Did not play — ineligible.						
89-90 — Oregon	29	1067	190	401	.474	97	129	.752	106	518	17.9
90-91 — Oregon	28	1108	273	556	.491	159	187	.850	101	745	26.6
Totals	57	2175	463	957	.484	256	316	.810	207	1263	22.2

Three-point field goals: 1989-90, 41-for-94 (.436). 1990-91, 40-for-119 (.336). Totals, 81-for-213 (.380).

HONORS: NBA All-Rookie second team (1992).

NBA REGULAR-SEASON RECORD

Season Team	G	Min.	FGM	FGA	Pct.	FTM	FTA	Pct.	Off.	Def.	Tot.	Ast.	PF	Dq.	Stl.	Blk.	TO	Pts.	Avg.
91-92 — Cleveland	82	1605	252	601	.419	100	124	.806	49	113	162	316	107	0	81	22	136	605	7.4

Three-point field goals: 1991-92, 1-for-23 (.043).

NBA PLAYOFF RECORD

Season Team	G	Min.	FGM	FGA	Pct.	FTM	FTA	Pct.	Off.	Def.	Tot.	Ast.	PF	Dq.	Stl.	Blk.	TO	Pts.	Avg.
91-92 — Cleveland	12	157	22	55	.400	3	4	.750	4	18	22	30	17	0	3	1	11	47	3.9

Three-point field goals: 1991-92, 0-for-3.

BREUER, RANDY

PERSONAL: Born October 11, 1960, in Lake City, Minn. . . . 7-3/258. . . . Full name: Randall W. Breuer. . . . Name pronounced Brewer.
HIGH SCHOOL: Lincoln (Lake City, Minn.).
COLLEGE: Minnesota.
TRANSACTIONS/CAREER NOTES: Selected by Milwaukee Bucks in first round (18th pick overall) of 1983 NBA Draft. . . . Traded by Bucks with a conditional exchange of 1991 or 1992 second-round draft choices to Minnesota Timberwolves for Brad Lohaus (January 4, 1990).

COLLEGIATE RECORD

Season Team	G	Min.	FGM	FGA	Pct.	FTM	FTA	Pct.	Reb.	Pts.	Avg.
79-80 — Minnesota	31	. . .	96	172	.558	48	74	.649	98	240	7.7
80-81 — Minnesota	30	. . .	180	313	.575	97	141	.688	166	457	15.2
81-82 — Minnesota	29	. . .	180	325	.554	127	168	.756	209	487	16.8
82-83 — Minnesota	29	. . .	225	384	.586	143	186	.769	257	593	20.4
Totals	119	. . .	681	1194	.570	415	569	.729	730	1777	14.9

NBA REGULAR-SEASON RECORD

Season Team	G	Min.	FGM	FGA	Pct.	FTM	FTA	Pct.	Off.	Def.	Tot.	Ast.	PF	Dq.	Stl.	Blk.	TO	Pts.	Avg.
83-84 — Milwaukee	57	472	68	177	.384	32	46	.696	48	61	109	17	98	1	11	38	35	168	2.9
84-85 — Milwaukee	78	1083	162	317	.511	89	127	.701	92	164	256	40	179	4	21	82	63	413	5.3
85-86 — Milwaukee	82	1792	272	570	.477	141	198	.712	159	299	458	114	214	2	50	116	122	685	8.4
86-87 — Milwaukee	76	1467	241	497	.485	118	202	.584	129	221	350	47	229	9	56	61	100	600	7.9
87-88 — Milwaukee	81	2258	390	788	.495	188	286	.657	191	360	551	103	198	3	46	107	107	968	12.0
88-89 — Milwaukee	48	513	86	179	.480	28	51	.549	51	84	135	22	59	0	9	37	29	200	4.2
89-90 — Mil.-Min.	81	1879	298	696	.428	126	193	.653	154	263	417	97	196	2	42	108	96	722	8.9
90-91 — Minnesota	73	1505	197	435	.453	35	79	.443	114	231	345	73	132	1	35	80	69	429	5.9
91-92 — Minnesota	67	1176	161	344	.468	41	77	.532	98	183	281	89	117	0	27	99	41	363	5.4
Totals	643	12145	1875	4003	.468	798	1259	.634	1036	1866	2902	602	1422	22	297	728	662	4548	7.1

Three-point field goals: 1985-86, 0-for-1. 1989-90, 0-for-1. 1991-92, 0-for-1. Totals, 0-for-3.

NBA PLAYOFF RECORD

Season Team	G	Min.	FGM	FGA	Pct.	FTM	FTA	Pct.	Off.	Def.	Tot.	Ast.	PF	Dq.	Stl.	Blk.	TO	Pts.	Avg.
83-84 — Milwaukee	12	66	11	26	.423	3	5	.600	6	11	17	4	18	0	0	6	2	25	2.1
84-85 — Milwaukee	8	104	15	26	.577	14	21	.667	9	15	24	0	15	0	2	2	8	44	5.5
85-86 — Milwaukee	14	318	46	86	.535	26	38	.684	20	40	60	11	38	1	11	18	13	118	8.4
86-87 — Milwaukee	12	156	16	33	.485	8	12	.667	9	22	31	4	32	1	7	9	4	40	3.3
87-88 — Milwaukee	4	47	9	16	.563	1	6	.167	2	10	12	1	7	0	1	2	1	19	4.8
88-89 — Milwaukee	9	162	17	32	.531	5	13	.385	9	31	40	5	17	0	2	6	2	39	4.3
Totals	59	853	114	219	.521	57	95	.600	55	129	184	25	127	2	23	43	30	285	4.8

BRICKOWSKI, FRANK

PERSONAL: Born August 15, 1959, in Bayville, N.Y. . . . 6-10/248. . . . Full name: Francis Anthony Brickowski. . . . Name pronounced Brick-COW-skee.
HIGH SCHOOL: Locust Valley (N.Y.).
COLLEGE: Penn State.
TRANSACTIONS/CAREER NOTES: Selected by New York Knicks in third round (57th pick overall) of 1981

NBA Draft. . . . Played in Italy (1981-82). . . . Draft rights relinquished by Knicks (June 30, 1983). . . . Played in France (1982-83). . . . Played in Israel (1983-84). . . . Signed as free agent by Seattle SuperSonics (September 23, 1984). . . . Signed as veteran free agent by Los Angeles Lakers (October 8, 1986); SuperSonics agreed not to exercise their right of first refusal in exchange for 1988 third-round draft choice and cash. . . . Traded by Lakers with Petur Gudmundsson, 1987 first-round draft choice, 1990 second-round draft choice and cash to San Antonio Spurs for Mychal Thompson (February 13, 1987). . . . Traded by Spurs to Milwaukee Bucks for Paul Pressey (August 1, 1990).

COLLEGIATE RECORD

Season	Team	G	Min.	FGM	FGA	Pct.	FTM	FTA	Pct.	Reb.	Pts.	Avg.
77-78	Penn State	25	266	37	81	.457	21	25	.840	64	95	3.8
78-79	Penn State	24	349	49	99	.495	38	48	.792	109	136	5.7
79-80	Penn State	27	692	111	213	.521	82	105	.781	202	304	11.3
80-81	Penn State	24	615	131	218	.601	49	63	.778	150	311	13.0
	Totals	100	1922	328	611	.537	190	241	.788	525	846	8.5

NBA REGULAR-SEASON RECORD

Season	Team	G	Min.	FGM	FGA	Pct.	FTM	FTA	Pct.	Off.	Def.	Tot.	Ast.	PF	Dq.	Stl.	Blk.	TO	Pts.	Avg.
84-85	Seattle	78	1115	150	305	.492	85	127	.669	76	184	260	100	171	1	34	15	100	385	4.9
85-86	Seattle	40	311	30	58	.517	18	27	.667	16	38	54	21	74	2	11	7	23	78	2.0
86-87	L.A.L.-S.A.	44	487	63	124	.508	50	70	.714	48	68	116	17	118	4	20	6	32	176	4.0
87-88	San Antonio	70	2227	425	805	.528	268	349	.768	167	316	483	266	275	11	74	36	207	1119	16.0
88-89	San Antonio	64	1822	337	654	.515	201	281	.715	148	258	406	131	252	10	102	35	165	875	13.7
89-90	San Antonio	78	1438	211	387	.545	95	141	.674	89	238	327	105	226	4	66	37	93	517	6.6
90-91	Milwaukee	75	1912	372	706	.527	198	248	.798	129	297	426	131	255	4	86	43	160	942	12.6
91-92	Milwaukee	65	1556	306	584	.524	125	163	.767	97	247	344	122	223	11	60	23	112	740	11.4
	Totals	514	10868	1894	3623	.523	1040	1406	.740	770	1646	2416	893	1594	47	453	202	892	4832	9.4

Three-point field goals: 1984-85, 0-for-4. 1986-87, 0-for-4. 1987-88, 1-for-5 (.200). 1988-89, 0-for-2. 1989-90, 0-for-2. 1990-91, 0-for-2. 1991-92, 3-for-6 (.500). Totals, 4-for-25 (.160).

NBA PLAYOFF RECORD

Season	Team	G	Min.	FGM	FGA	Pct.	FTM	FTA	Pct.	Off.	Def.	Tot.	Ast.	PF	Dq.	Stl.	Blk.	TO	Pts.	Avg.
87-88	San Antonio	3	113	22	44	.500	13	19	.684	7	15	22	14	12	0	6	2	9	58	19.3
89-90	San Antonio	10	161	31	54	.574	17	26	.654	16	28	44	11	31	0	8	1	15	79	7.9
90-91	Milwaukee	3	110	24	45	.533	7	14	.500	5	21	26	3	16	1	1	2	6	55	18.3
	Totals	16	384	77	143	.538	37	59	.627	28	64	92	28	59	1	15	5	30	192	12.0

Three-point field goals: 1987-88, 1-for-1. 1990-91, 0-for-2. Totals, 1-for-3 (.333).

BROOKS, KEVIN
F, NUGGETS

PERSONAL: Born October 12, 1969, in Beaufort, S.C. . . . 6-8/200.
HIGH SCHOOL: White Castle (La.).
COLLEGE: Southwestern Louisiana.
TRANSACTIONS/CAREER NOTES: Selected by Milwaukee Bucks in first round (18th pick overall) of 1991 NBA Draft. . . . Draft rights traded by Bucks to Denver Nuggets in three-way deal in which Nuggets sent Blair Rasmussen to Atlanta Hawks and Hawks sent draft rights to Anthony Avent to Bucks (July 1, 1991); Nuggets also received Bucks' 1994 second-round draft choice and other considerations.

COLLEGIATE RECORD

Season	Team	G	Min.	FGM	FGA	Pct.	FTM	FTA	Pct.	Reb.	Pts.	Avg.
87-88	Southwestern Louisiana	27	998	179	317	.565	83	109	.761	170	453	16.8
88-89	Southwestern Louisiana	29	1097	218	418	.522	128	170	.753	158	600	20.7
89-90	Southwestern Louisiana	29	1117	225	451	.499	93	114	.816	204	583	20.1
90-91	Southwestern Louisiana	31	1121	261	507	.515	77	99	.778	187	658	21.2
	Totals	116	4333	883	1693	.522	381	492	.774	719	2294	19.8

Three-point field goals: 1987-88, 12-for-34 (.353). 1988-89, 36-for-94 (.383). 1989-90, 40-for-99 (.404). 1990-91, 59-for-132 (.447). Totals, 147-for-359 (.409).

NBA REGULAR-SEASON RECORD

Season	Team	G	Min.	FGM	FGA	Pct.	FTM	FTA	Pct.	Off.	Def.	Tot.	Ast.	PF	Dq.	Stl.	Blk.	TO	Pts.	Avg.
91-92	Denver	37	270	43	97	.443	17	21	.810	13	26	39	11	19	0	8	2	18	105	2.8

Three-point field goals: 1991-92, 2-for-11 (.182).

BROOKS, SCOTT
G, TIMBERWOLVES

PERSONAL: Born July 31, 1965, in French Camp, Calif. . . . 5-11/165. . . . Full name: Scott William Brooks.
HIGH SCHOOL: East Union (Manteca, Calif.).
COLLEGE: Texas Christian, then San Joaquin Delta College (Calif.), then UC Irvine.
TRANSACTIONS/CAREER NOTES: Never drafted by an NBA franchise. . . . Played in Continental Basketball Association with Albany Patroons (1987-88). . . . Signed as free agent by Philadelphia 76ers (September 23, 1988). . . . Traded by 76ers to Minnesota Timberwolves for 1990 second-round draft choice (June 25, 1990).

COLLEGIATE RECORD

Season	Team	G	Min.	FGM	FGA	Pct.	FTM	FTA	Pct.	Reb.	Pts.	Avg.
83-84	Texas Christian	27	. . .	46	87	.529	10	14	.714	32	102	3.8
84-85	San Joaquin Delta	31	. . .	158	301	.525	90	102	.882	45	406	13.1
85-86	UC Irvine	30	945	100	223	.448	78	88	.886	70	308	10.3
86-87	UC Irvine	28	1027	206	431	.478	142	168	.845	50	665	23.8
	Junior college totals	31	. . .	158	301	.525	90	102	.882	45	406	13.1
	Four-year-college totals	85	. . .	352	741	.475	230	270	.852	152	1075	12.6

Three-point field goals: 1985-86, 30-for-80 (.375). 1986-87, 111-for-257 (.432). Totals, 141-for-337 (.418).

NOTES: CBA All-Rookie team (1988).

CBA REGULAR-SEASON RECORD

Season Team	G	Min.	FGM	2-POINT FGA	Pct.	FGM	3-POINT FGA	Pct.	FTM	FTA	Pct.	Reb.	Ast.	Pts.	Avg.
87-88 — Albany	52	1155	135	289	.467	25	76	.329	106	132	.803	94	116	451	8.7

NBA REGULAR-SEASON RECORD

Season Team	G	Min.	FGM	FGA	Pct.	FTM	FTA	Pct.	REBOUNDS Off.	Def.	Tot.	Ast.	PF	Dq.	Stl.	Blk.	TO	Pts.	Avg.
88-89 — Philadelphia.	82	1372	156	371	.420	61	69	.884	19	75	94	306	116	0	69	3	65	428	5.2
89-90 — Philadelphia.	72	975	119	276	.431	50	57	.877	15	49	64	207	105	0	47	0	38	319	4.4
90-91 — Minnesota....	80	980	159	370	.430	61	72	.847	28	44	72	204	122	1	53	5	51	424	5.3
91-92 — Minnesota....	82	1082	167	374	.447	51	63	.810	27	72	99	205	82	0	66	7	51	417	5.1
Totals	316	4409	601	1391	.432	223	261	.854	89	240	329	922	425	1	235	15	205	1588	5.0

Three-point field goals: 1988-89, 55-for-153 (.359). 1989-90, 31-for-79 (.392). 1990-91, 45-for-135 (.333). 1991-92, 32-for-90 (.356). Totals, 163-for-457 (.357).

NBA PLAYOFF RECORD

Season Team	G	Min.	FGM	FGA	Pct.	FTM	FTA	Pct.	REBOUNDS Off.	Def.	Tot.	Ast.	PF	Dq.	Stl.	Blk.	TO	Pts.	Avg.
88-89 — Philadelphia.	3	21	1	6	.167	2	2	1.000	0	4	4	5	4	0	0	0	1	5	1.7
89-90 — Philadelphia.	9	99	6	19	.316	6	9	.667	2	6	8	16	13	0	3	0	7	21	2.3
Totals	12	120	7	25	.280	8	11	.727	2	10	12	21	17	0	3	0	8	26	2.2

Three-point field goals: 1988-89, 1-for-2 (.500). 1989-90, 3-for-7 (.429). Totals, 4-for-9 (.444).

BROWN, CHUCKY
F, LAKERS

PERSONAL: Born February 29, 1968, in New York. . . . 6-8/214. . . . Full name: Clarence Brown.
HIGH SCHOOL: North Brunswick (Leland, N.C.).
COLLEGE: North Carolina State.

TRANSACTIONS/CAREER NOTES: Selected by Cleveland Cavaliers in second round (43rd pick overall) of 1989 NBA Draft. . . . Waived by Cavaliers (December 2, 1991). . . . Signed as free agent by Los Angeles Lakers (December 5, 1991).

COLLEGIATE RECORD

Season Team	G	Min.	FGM	FGA	Pct.	FTM	FTA	Pct.	Reb.	Pts.	Avg.
85-86 — North Carolina State...............	31	310	38	80	.475	21	34	.618	67	97	3.1
86-87 — North Carolina State...............	34	629	81	138	.587	61	80	.763	145	223	6.6
87-88 — North Carolina State...............	32	1024	226	395	.572	77	121	.636	193	530	16.6
88-89 — North Carolina State...............	31	1051	210	383	.548	81	125	.648	274	507	16.4
Totals	128	3014	555	996	.557	240	360	.667	679	1357	10.6

Three-point field goals: 1986-87, 0-for-1. 1987-88, 1-for-6 (.167). 1988-89, 6-for-21 (.286). Totals, 7-for-28 (.250).

NBA REGULAR-SEASON RECORD

Season Team	G	Min.	FGM	FGA	Pct.	FTM	FTA	Pct.	REBOUNDS Off.	Def.	Tot.	Ast.	PF	Dq.	Stl.	Blk.	TO	Pts.	Avg.
89-90 — Cleveland.....	75	1339	210	447	.470	125	164	.762	83	148	231	50	148	0	33	26	69	545	7.3
90-91 — Cleveland.....	74	1485	263	502	.524	101	144	.701	78	135	213	80	130	0	26	24	94	627	8.5
91-92 — Clev.-L.A.L..	42	431	60	128	.469	30	49	.612	31	51	82	26	48	0	12	7	29	150	3.6
Totals	191	3255	533	1077	.495	256	357	.717	192	334	526	156	326	0	71	57	192	1322	6.9

Three-point field goals: 1989-90, 0-for-7. 1990-91, 0-for-4. 1991-92, 0-for-3. Totals, 0-for-14.

NBA PLAYOFF RECORD

Season Team	G	Min.	FGM	FGA	Pct.	FTM	FTA	Pct.	REBOUNDS Off.	Def.	Tot.	Ast.	PF	Dq.	Stl.	Blk.	TO	Pts.	Avg.
91-92 — L.A. Lakers ..	3	44	8	19	.421	3	6	.500	3	8	11	2	3	0	2	1	19	6.3	

Three-point field goals: 1991-92, 0-for-1.

BROWN, DEE
G, CELTICS

PERSONAL: Born November 29, 1968, in Jacksonville, Fla. . . . 6-1/161. . . . Full name: DeCovan Kadell Brown.
HIGH SCHOOL: The Bolles School (Jacksonville, Fla.).
COLLEGE: Jacksonville.

TRANSACTIONS/CAREER NOTES: Selected by Boston Celtics in first round (19th pick overall) of 1990 NBA Draft.

COLLEGIATE RECORD

Season Team	G	Min.	FGM	FGA	Pct.	FTM	FTA	Pct.	Reb.	Pts.	Avg.
86-87 — Jacksonville........................	21	186	28	65	.431	13	22	.591	28	71	3.4
87-88 — Jacksonville........................	28	764	108	239	.452	54	66	.818	125	282	10.1
88-89 — Jacksonville........................	30	1133	219	447	.490	108	131	.824	228	589	19.6
89-90 — Jacksonville........................	29	1052	231	466	.496	69	101	.683	192	561	19.3
Totals	108	3135	586	1217	.482	244	320	.763	573	1503	13.9

Three-point field goals: 1986-87, 2-for-12 (.167). 1987-88, 12-for-45 (.267). 1988-89, 43-for-101 (.426). 1989-90, 30-for-80 (.375). Totals, 87-for-238 (.366).

NBA REGULAR-SEASON RECORD

HONORS: NBA All-Rookie first team (1991).

Season	Team	G	Min.	FGM	FGA	Pct.	FTM	FTA	Pct.	REBOUNDS Off.	Def.	Tot.	Ast.	PF	Dq.	Stl.	Blk.	TO	Pts.	Avg.
90-91 —Boston	....	82	1945	284	612	.464	137	157	.873	41	141	182	344	161	0	83	14	137	712	8.7
91-92 —Boston	....	31	883	149	350	.426	60	78	.769	15	64	79	164	74	0	33	7	59	363	11.7
Totals	....	113	2828	433	962	.450	197	235	.838	56	205	261	508	235	0	116	21	196	1075	9.5

Three-point field goals: 1990-91, 7-for-34 (.206). 1991-92, 5-for-22 (.227). Totals, 12-for-56 (.214).

NBA PLAYOFF RECORD

Season	Team	G	Min.	FGM	FGA	Pct.	FTM	FTA	Pct.	REBOUNDS Off.	Def.	Tot.	Ast.	PF	Dq.	Stl.	Blk.	TO	Pts.	Avg.
90-91 —Boston	....	11	284	53	108	.491	28	34	.824	9	36	45	41	32	0	11	6	22	134	12.2
91-92 —Boston	....	6	120	22	44	.500	4	6	.667	3	9	12	31	16	2	1	4	7	48	8.0
Totals	....	17	404	75	152	.493	32	40	.800	12	45	57	72	48	2	12	10	29	182	10.7

Three-point field goals: 1990-91, 0-for-5. 1991-92, 0-for-3. Totals, 0-for-8.

BROWN, MIKE
F, JAZZ

PERSONAL: Born July 19, 1963, in Newark, N.J. . . . 6-10/260. . . . Full name: Michael Brown.
HIGH SCHOOL: Clifford J. Scott (East Orange, N.J.).
COLLEGE: George Washington.

TRANSACTIONS/CAREER NOTES: Selected by Chicago Bulls in third round (69th pick overall) of 1985 NBA Draft. . . . Played in Italy (1985-86). . . . Selected by Charlotte Hornets from Bulls in NBA expansion draft (June 23, 1988). . . . Traded by Hornets to Utah Jazz for Kelly Tripucka (June 23, 1988). . . . Signed as unrestricted free agent by Jazz (July 18, 1991).

COLLEGIATE RECORD

Season	Team	G	Min.	FGM	FGA	Pct.	FTM	FTA	Pct.	Reb.	Pts.	Avg.
81-82 —George Washington	....	27	926	174	350	.497	73	141	.518	230	421	15.6
82-83 —George Washington	....	29	1058	192	369	.520	112	171	.655	298	496	17.1
83-84 —George Washington	....	29	1049	190	355	.535	187	256	.730	351	567	19.6
84-85 —George Washington	....	26	937	154	321	.480	124	191	.649	287	432	16.6
Totals	....	111	3970	710	1395	.509	496	759	.653	1166	1916	17.3

ITALIAN LEAGUE RECORD

Season	Team	G	Min.	FGM	FGA	Pct.	FTM	FTA	Pct.	Reb.	Pts.	Avg.
85-86 —Filanto Desio	....	30	1080	255	415	.614	142	185	.768	362	655	21.8

NBA REGULAR-SEASON RECORD

Season	Team	G	Min.	FGM	FGA	Pct.	FTM	FTA	Pct.	REBOUNDS Off.	Def.	Tot.	Ast.	PF	Dq.	Stl.	Blk.	TO	Pts.	Avg.
86-87 —Chicago	......	62	818	106	201	.527	46	72	.639	71	143	214	24	129	2	20	7	59	258	4.2
87-88 —Chicago	......	46	591	78	174	.448	41	71	.577	66	93	159	28	85	0	11	4	38	197	4.3
88-89 —Utah	....	66	1051	104	248	.419	92	130	.708	92	166	258	41	133	0	25	17	77	300	4.5
89-90 —Utah	....	82	1397	157	344	.515	157	199	.789	111	262	373	47	187	0	32	28	88	512	6.2
90-91 —Utah	....	82	1391	129	284	.454	132	178	.742	109	228	337	49	166	0	29	24	82	390	4.8
91-92 —Utah	....	82	1783	221	488	.453	190	285	.667	187	289	476	81	196	1	42	34	105	632	7.7
Totals	....	420	7031	815	1739	.469	658	935	.704	636	1181	1817	270	896	3	159	114	449	2289	5.5

Three-point field goals: 1987-88, 0-for-1. 1989-90, 1-for-2 (.500). 1991-92, 0-for-1. Totals, 1-for-4 (.250).

NBA PLAYOFF RECORD

Season	Team	G	Min.	FGM	FGA	Pct.	FTM	FTA	Pct.	REBOUNDS Off.	Def.	Tot.	Ast.	PF	Dq.	Stl.	Blk.	TO	Pts.	Avg.
86-87 —Chicago	....	1	3	0	1	.000	0	0	...	0	0	0	0	1	0	1	0	1	0	0.0
87-88 —Chicago	....	1	4	0	0	...	1	2	.500	0	0	0	1	0	0	1	0	1	1	1.0
88-89 —Utah	....	2	11	0	2	.000	0	0	...	0	2	2	0	3	0	0	0	0	0	0.0
89-90 —Utah	....	5	67	7	15	.467	4	5	.800	5	5	10	3	11	0	1	1	5	18	3.6
90-91 —Utah	....	9	223	27	56	.482	32	38	.842	20	46	66	5	36	1	3	1	12	86	9.6
91-92 —Utah	....	16	274	30	75	.400	32	41	.780	22	43	65	11	43	0	2	2	16	92	5.8
Totals	....	34	582	64	149	.430	69	86	.802	47	96	143	20	94	1	8	4	34	197	5.8

BROWN, MYRON
G

PERSONAL: Born November 3, 1969, in McKees Rocks, Pa. . . . 6-3/180. . . . Full name: Julian Myron Brown.
HIGH SCHOOL: Sto-Rox (McKees Rocks, Pa.).
COLLEGE: Slippery Rock (Pa.).

TRANSACTIONS/CAREER NOTES: Selected by Minnesota Timberwolves in second round (34th pick overall) of 1991 NBA Draft. . . . Waived by Timberwolves (December 18, 1991). . . . Played in Continental Basketball Association with Fort Wayne Fury (1991-92).

COLLEGIATE RECORD

Season	Team	G	Min.	FGM	FGA	Pct.	FTM	FTA	Pct.	Reb.	Pts.	Avg.
87-88 —Slippery Rock	....	28	. . .	196	395	.496	89	110	.809	150	516	18.4
88-89 —Slippery Rock	....	28	. . .	192	395	.486	131	159	.824	189	568	20.3
89-90 —Slippery Rock	....	29	1016	246	522	.471	167	197	.848	189	709	24.4
90-91 —Slippery Rock	....	31	1128	253	533	.475	251	306	.820	232	826	26.6
Totals	....	116	. . .	887	1845	.481	638	772	.826	760	2619	22.6

Three-point field goals: 1987-88, 35-for-96 (.365). 1988-89, 53-for-126 (.421). 1989-90, 50-for-127 (.394). 1990-91, 69-for-189 (.365). Totals, 207-for-538 (.385).

NBA REGULAR-SEASON RECORD

Season Team	G	Min.	FGM	FGA	Pct.	FTM	FTA	Pct.	— REBOUNDS — Off.	Def.	Tot.	Ast.	PF	Dq.	Stl.	Blk.	TO	Pts.	Avg.
91-92 — Minnesota....	4	23	4	6	.667	0	0	...	0	3	3	6	2	0	1	0	4	9	2.3

Three-point field goals: 1991-92, 1-for-3 (.333).

CBA REGULAR-SEASON RECORD

Season Team	G	Min.	2-POINT FGM	FGA	Pct.	3-POINT FGM	FGA	Pct.	FTM	FTA	Pct.	Reb.	Ast.	Pts.	Avg.
91-92 — Fort Wayne......	31	773	93	191	.487	11	35	.314	57	77	.740	78	88	276	8.9

BROWN, RANDY
G, KINGS
B

PERSONAL: Born May 22, 1968, in Chicago.... 6-3/190.
HIGH SCHOOL: Collins (Chicago).
COLLEGE: Houston, then Howard County (Tex.), then New Mexico State.
TRANSACTIONS/CAREER NOTES: Selected by Sacramento Kings in second round (31st pick overall) of 1991 NBA Draft.

COLLEGIATE RECORD

Season Team	G	Min.	FGM	FGA	Pct.	FTM	FTA	Pct.	Reb.	Pts.	Avg.
86-87 — Houston	28	578	42	83	.506	21	36	.583	75	105	3.8
87-88 — Houston	29	998	64	142	.451	75	100	.750	83	203	7.0
88-89 — Howard County					Did not play.						
89-90 — New Mexico State	31	907	131	294	.446	131	184	.712	106	409	13.2
90-91 — New Mexico State	29	917	110	276	.399	121	175	.691	116	351	12.1
Four-year-college totals	117	3400	347	795	.436	348	495	.703	380	1068	9.1

Three-point field goals: 1986-87, 0-for-2. 1987-88, 0-for-4. 1989-90, 16-for-42 (.381). 1990-91, 10-for-36 (.278). Totals, 26-for-84 (.310).

NBA REGULAR-SEASON RECORD

Season Team	G	Min.	FGM	FGA	Pct.	FTM	FTA	Pct.	— REBOUNDS — Off.	Def.	Tot.	Ast.	PF	Dq.	Stl.	Blk.	TO	Pts.	Avg.
91-92 — Sacramento .	56	535	77	169	.456	38	58	.655	26	43	69	59	68	0	35	12	42	192	3.4

Three-point field goals: 1991-92, 0-for-6.

BROWN, TONY
F, SUPERSONICS

PERSONAL: Born July 29, 1960, in Chicago.... 6-6/195.... Full name: Anthony William Brown.
HIGH SCHOOL: Farragut (Chicago).
COLLEGE: Arkansas.
TRANSACTIONS/CAREER NOTES: Selected by New Jersey Nets in fourth round (82nd pick overall) of 1982 NBA Draft.... Waived by Nets (October 25, 1982).... Played in Continental Basketball Association with Ohio Mixers (1982-83), Kansas City Sizzlers (1985-86), Grand Rapids Hoops (1989-90) and Albany Patroons (1990-91).... Signed as free agent by Detroit Pistons (May 7, 1983).... Waived by Pistons (August 19, 1983).... Signed as free agent by Indiana Pacers (September 28, 1984).... Waived by Pacers (October 22, 1985).... Signed by Chicago Bulls to first of two consecutive 10-day contracts (February 22, 1986).... Signed as free agent by Nets (September 3, 1986).... Traded by Nets with Frank Johnson, Tim McCormick and Lorenzo Romar to Houston Rockets for Joe Barry Carroll and Lester Conner (November 2, 1988).... Waived by Rockets (February 2, 1989).... Signed as free agent by Milwaukee Bucks for remainder of season (February 7, 1989).... Signed as unrestricted free agent by Los Angeles Lakers (October 2, 1990).... Waived by Lakers (December 6, 1990).... Signed by Utah Jazz to 10-day contract (March 1, 1991).... Re-signed by Jazz for remainder of season (April 1, 1991).... Signed as free agent by Los Angeles Clippers (September 20, 1991).... Waived by Clippers (January 2, 1992).... Signed by Dallas Mavericks to first of two consecutive 10-day contracts (January 27, 1992).... Signed as free agent by Seattle SuperSonics for remainder of season (February 20, 1992).

COLLEGIATE RECORD

Season Team	G	Min.	FGM	FGA	Pct.	FTM	FTA	Pct.	Reb.	Pts.	Avg.
78-79 — Arkansas	23	354	38	66	.576	11	14	.786	29	87	3.8
79-80 — Arkansas	28	299	37	68	.544	13	23	.565	39	87	3.1
80-81 — Arkansas	32	654	63	113	.558	29	46	.630	88	155	4.8
81-82 — Arkansas	27	826	109	185	.589	52	68	.765	87	270	10.0
Totals	110	2133	247	432	.572	105	151	.695	243	599	5.4

CBA REGULAR-SEASON RECORD

NOTES: CBA All-Defensive second team (1983).

Season Team	G	Min.	2-POINT FGM	FGA	Pct.	3-POINT FGM	FGA	Pct.	FTM	FTA	Pct.	Reb.	Ast.	Pts.	Avg.
82-83 — Ohio.................	44	1584	371	745	.498	0	5	.000	223	321	.695	304	115	965	21.9
85-86 — Kansas City	23	767	181	370	.489	3	15	.200	130	178	.730	135	144	501	21.8
89-90 — Grand Rapids...	49	970	117	221	.529	0	1	.000	73	119	.613	380	30	307	6.3
90-91 — Albany	3	87	16	36	.444	1	2	.500	11	15	.733	14	10	46	15.3
Totals	119	3408	685	1372	.499	4	23	.174	437	633	.690	833	299	1819	15.3

NBA REGULAR-SEASON RECORD

Season Team	G	Min.	FGM	FGA	Pct.	FTM	FTA	Pct.	— REBOUNDS — Off.	Def.	Tot.	Ast.	PF	Dq.	Stl.	Blk.	TO	Pts.	Avg.
84-85 — Indiana........	82	1586	214	465	.460	116	171	.678	146	142	288	159	212	3	59	12	116	544	6.6
85-86 — Chicago........	10	132	18	41	.439	9	13	.692	5	11	16	14	16	0	5	1	4	45	4.5
86-87 — New Jersey ..	77	2339	358	810	.442	152	206	.738	84	135	219	259	273	12	89	14	153	873	11.3
87-88 — New Jersey ..							Did not play — injured.												
88-89 — Hou.-Mil.	43	365	50	118	.424	24	31	.774	22	22	44	26	42	0	15	4	17	128	3.0

Season Team	G	Min.	FGM	FGA	Pct.	FTM	FTA	Pct.	Off.	Def.	Tot.	Ast.	PF	Dq.	Stl.	Blk.	TO	Pts.	Avg.
89-90 —Milwaukee ...	61	635	88	206	.427	38	56	.679	39	33	72	41	79	0	32	4	51	219	3.6
90-91 —LAL-Utah	30	294	30	80	.375	20	23	.870	24	19	43	16	47	0	4	0	16	83	2.8
91-92 —LAC-Seattle.	57	655	102	249	.410	48	66	.727	32	52	84	48	82	0	30	5	35	271	4.8
Totals	360	6006	860	1969	.437	407	566	.719	352	414	766	563	751	15	234	40	392	2163	6.0

Three-point field goals: 1984-85, 0-for-6. 1985-86, 0-for-2. 1986-87, 5-for-20 (.250). 1988-89, 4-for-16 (.250). 1989-90, 5-for-20 (.250). 1990-91, 3-for-12 (.250). 1991-92, 19-for-63 (.302). Totals, 36-for-139 (.259).

NBA PLAYOFF RECORD

Season Team	G	Min.	FGM	FGA	Pct.	FTM	FTA	Pct.	Off.	Def.	Tot.	Ast.	PF	Dq.	Stl.	Blk.	TO	Pts.	Avg.
88-89 —Milwaukee ...	6	69	4	11	.364	3	4	.750	2	5	7	6	9	1	2	0	1	11	1.8
89-90 —Milwaukee ...	2	13	1	3	.333	0	0	...	0	0	0	0	3	0	2	0	0	3	1.5
90-91 —Utah	4	29	4	8	.500	0	0	...	2	1	3	1	2	0	0	1	9	2.3
91-92 —Seattle.........	5	22	2	6	.333	4	7	.571	0	2	2	2	3	0	0	0	0	9	1.8
Totals	17	133	11	28	.393	7	11	.636	4	8	12	9	17	1	4	0	2	32	1.9

Three-point field goals: 1988-89, 0-for-1. 1989-90, 1-for-1. 1990-91, 1-for-2 (.500). 1991-92, 1-for-4 (.250). Totals, 3-for-8 (.375).

BRYANT, MARK
F, TRAIL BLAZERS

PERSONAL: Born April 25, 1965, in Glen Ridge, N.J.... 6-9/245.... Full name: Mark Craig Bryant.
HIGH SCHOOL: Columbia (Maplewood, N.J.).
COLLEGE: Seton Hall.
TRANSACTIONS/CAREER NOTES: Selected by Portland Trail Blazers in first round (21st pick overall) of 1988 NBA Draft.

COLLEGIATE RECORD

Season Team	G	Min.	FGM	FGA	Pct.	FTM	FTA	Pct.	Reb.	Pts.	Avg.
84-85 —Seton Hall	26	774	122	257	.475	74	114	.649	177	318	12.2
85-86 —Seton Hall	30	901	169	323	.523	82	121	.678	226	420	14.0
86-87 —Seton Hall	28	891	171	345	.496	127	180	.706	198	470	16.8
87-88 —Seton Hall	34	1105	267	473	.564	163	218	.748	311	698	20.5
Totals	118	3671	729	1398	.521	446	633	.705	912	1906	16.2

Three-point field goals: 1986-87, 1-for-1. 1987-88, 1-for-2 (.500). Totals, 2-for-3 (.667).

NBA REGULAR-SEASON RECORD

Season Team	G	Min.	FGM	FGA	Pct.	FTM	FTA	Pct.	Off.	Def.	Tot.	Ast.	PF	Dq.	Stl.	Blk.	TO	Pts.	Avg.
88-89 —Portland	56	803	120	247	.486	40	69	.580	65	114	179	33	144	3	20	7	41	280	5.0
89-90 —Portland	58	562	70	153	.458	28	50	.560	54	92	146	13	93	0	18	9	25	168	2.9
90-91 —Portland	53	781	99	203	.488	74	101	.733	65	125	190	27	120	0	15	12	33	272	5.1
91-92 —Portland	56	800	95	198	.480	40	60	.667	87	114	201	41	105	0	26	8	30	230	4.1
Totals	223	2946	384	801	.479	182	280	.650	271	445	716	114	462	3	79	36	129	950	4.3

Three-point field goals: 1990-91, 0-for-1. 1991-92, 0-for-3. Totals, 0-for-4.

NBA PLAYOFF RECORD

Season Team	G	Min.	FGM	FGA	Pct.	FTM	FTA	Pct.	Off.	Def.	Tot.	Ast.	PF	Dq.	Stl.	Blk.	TO	Pts.	Avg.
89-90 —Portland	13	160	18	33	.545	6	8	.750	9	20	29	3	27	1	3	2	12	42	3.2
90-91 —Portland	14	137	10	22	.455	14	16	.875	14	18	32	2	25	0	2	1	4	34	2.4
91-92 —Portland	12	116	10	29	.345	3	4	.750	11	18	29	1	22	0	3	0	9	23	1.9
Totals	39	413	38	84	.452	23	28	.821	34	56	90	6	74	1	8	3	25	99	2.5

BUECHLER, JUD
F, WARRIORS

PERSONAL: Born June 19, 1968, in San Diego.... 6-6/220.... Full name: Judson Donald Buechler.... Name pronounced BUSH-ler.
HIGH SCHOOL: Poway (Calif.).
COLLEGE: Arizona.
TRANSACTIONS/CAREER NOTES: Selected by Seattle SuperSonics in second round (38th pick overall) of 1990 NBA Draft.... Draft rights traded by SuperSonics to New Jersey Nets in exchange for Nets agreement not to select Dennis Scott in the 1990 draft (June 27, 1990).... Waived by Nets (November 8, 1991).... Claimed off waivers by San Antonio Spurs (November 12, 1991).... Waived by Spurs (December 17, 1991).... Signed as free agent by Golden State Warriors (December 22, 1991).

COLLEGIATE RECORD

Season Team	G	Min.	FGM	FGA	Pct.	FTM	FTA	Pct.	Reb.	Pts.	Avg.
86-87 —Arizona	30	474	54	111	.486	16	28	.571	68	134	4.5
87-88 —Arizona	36	422	64	124	.516	38	58	.655	87	170	4.7
88-89 —Arizona	33	962	139	229	.607	84	103	.816	219	363	11.0
89-90 —Arizona	32	1072	182	338	.538	88	115	.765	264	477	14.9
Totals	131	2930	439	802	.547	226	304	.743	638	1144	8.7

Three-point field goals: 1986-87, 10-for-25 (.400). 1987-88, 4-for-9 (.444). 1988-89, 1-for-5 (.200). 1989-90, 25-for-66 (.379). Totals, 40-for-105 (.381).

NBA REGULAR-SEASON RECORD

Season Team	G	Min.	FGM	FGA	Pct.	FTM	FTA	Pct.	Off.	Def.	Tot.	Ast.	PF	Dq.	Stl.	Blk.	TO	Pts.	Avg.
90-91 —New Jersey ..	74	859	94	226	.416	43	66	.652	61	80	141	51	79	0	33	15	26	232	3.1
91-92 —NJ-SA-GS ...	28	290	29	71	.408	12	21	.571	18	34	52	23	31	0	19	7	13	70	2.5
Totals	102	1149	123	297	.414	55	87	.632	79	114	193	74	110	0	52	22	39	302	3.0

Three-point field goals: 1990-91, 1-for-4 (.250). 1991-92, 0-for-1. Totals, 1-for-5 (.200).

BULLARD, MATT

F, ROCKETS

PERSONAL: Born June 5, 1967, in West Des Moines, Ia.... 6-10/225. ... Full name: Matthew Gordon Bullard. ... Name pronounced BULL-ard.
HIGH SCHOOL: Valley (West Des Moines, Ia.).
COLLEGE: Colorado, then Iowa.
TRANSACTIONS/CAREER NOTES: Never drafted by an NBA franchise.... Signed as free agent by Houston Rockets (August 22, 1990).

COLLEGIATE RECORD

Season Team	G	Min.	FGM	FGA	Pct.	FTM	FTA	Pct.	Reb.	Pts.	Avg.
85-86 —Colorado	28	869	142	235	.604	72	88	.818	179	356	12.7
86-87 —Colorado	28	938	182	349	.521	95	128	.742	280	464	16.6
87-88 —Iowa					Did not play—transfer student.						
88-89 —Iowa	20	498	66	117	.564	32	40	.800	123	181	9.1
89-90 —Iowa	18	366	72	166	.434	36	50	.720	53	205	11.4
Totals	94	2671	462	867	.533	235	306	.768	635	1206	12.8

Three-point field goals: 1986-87, 5-for-26 (.192). 1988-89, 17-for-43 (.395). 1989-90, 25-for-71 (.352). Totals, 47-for-140 (.336).

NBA REGULAR-SEASON RECORD

Season Team	G	Min.	FGM	FGA	Pct.	FTM	FTA	Pct.	Off.	Def.	Tot.	Ast.	PF	Dq.	Stl.	Blk.	TO	Pts.	Avg.
90-91 —Houston	18	63	14	31	.452	11	17	.647	6	8	14	2	10	0	3	0	3	39	2.2
91-92 —Houston	80	1278	205	447	.459	38	50	.760	73	150	223	75	129	1	26	21	56	512	6.4
Totals	98	1341	219	478	.458	49	67	.731	79	158	237	77	139	1	29	21	59	551	5.6

Three-point field goals: 1990-91, 0-for-3. 1991-92, 64-for-166 (.386). Totals, 64-for-169 (.379).

BURTON, WILLIE

G/F, HEAT

PERSONAL: Born May 26, 1968, in Detroit.... 6-8/219.... Full name: Willie Ricardo Burton.
HIGH SCHOOL: St. Martin DePorres (Detroit).
COLLEGE: Minnesota.
TRANSACTIONS/CAREER NOTES: Selected by Miami Heat in first round (ninth pick overall) of 1990 NBA Draft.

COLLEGIATE RECORD

Season Team	G	Min.	FGM	FGA	Pct.	FTM	FTA	Pct.	Reb.	Pts.	Avg.
86-87 —Minnesota	28	674	96	211	.455	48	74	.649	118	243	8.7
87-88 —Minnesota	28	751	142	275	.516	97	136	.713	158	384	13.7
88-89 —Minnesota	30	922	198	374	.529	137	172	.797	224	557	18.6
89-90 —Minnesota	32	1001	210	405	.519	144	187	.770	205	616	19.3
Totals	118	3348	646	1265	.511	426	569	.749	705	1800	15.3

Three-point field goals: 1986-87, 3-for-11 (.273). 1987-88, 3-for-10 (.300). 1988-89, 24-for-60 (.400). 1989-90, 52-for-136 (.382). Totals, 82-for-217 (.378).

NBA REGULAR-SEASON RECORD

HONORS: NBA All-Rookie second team (1991).

Season Team	G	Min.	FGM	FGA	Pct.	FTM	FTA	Pct.	Off.	Def.	Tot.	Ast.	PF	Dq.	Stl.	Blk.	TO	Pts.	Avg.
90-91 —Miami	76	1928	341	773	.441	229	293	.782	111	151	262	107	275	6	72	24	144	915	12.0
91-92 —Miami	68	1585	280	622	.450	196	245	.800	76	168	244	123	186	2	46	37	119	762	11.2
Totals	144	3513	621	1395	.445	425	538	.790	187	319	506	230	461	8	118	61	263	1677	11.6

Three-point field goals: 1990-91, 4-for-30 (.133). 1991-92, 6-for-15 (.400). Totals, 10-for-45 (.222).

BURTT, STEVE

G

PERSONAL: Born November 5, 1962, in New York.... 6-2/195.... Full name: Steven Dwayne Burtt.
HIGH SCHOOL: Charles Evans Hughes (New York).
COLLEGE: Iona.
TRANSACTIONS/CAREER NOTES: Selected by Golden State Warriors in second round (30th pick overall) of 1984 NBA Draft.... Played in Continental Basketball Association with Albany Patroons (1984-85 and 1989-90), Savannah Spirits (1987-88) and Oklahoma City Cavalry (1990-91).... Right of first refusal relinquished by Warriors (September 26, 1985).... Signed by Los Angeles Clippers to first of two consecutive 10-day contracts (March 18, 1988). ... Re-signed by Clippers for remainder of season (April 7, 1988).... Signed by Phoenix Suns to first of two consecutive 10-day contracts (February 14, 1992).... Signed by Suns for remainder of season (March 5, 1992).... Waived by Suns (June 17, 1992).

COLLEGIATE RECORD

Season Team	G	Min.	FGM	FGA	Pct.	FTM	FTA	Pct.	Reb.	Pts.	Avg.
80-81 —Iona	28	800	149	309	.482	83	126	.659	73	381	13.6
81-82 —Iona	31	1148	251	496	.506	182	251	.725	108	684	22.1
82-83 —Iona	31	1139	294	544	.540	132	171	.772	129	720	23.2
83-84 —Iona	31	1065	309	574	.538	131	179	.732	109	749	24.2
Totals	121	4152	1003	1923	.522	528	727	.726	419	2534	20.9

NBA REGULAR-SEASON RECORD

Season Team	G	Min.	FGM	FGA	Pct.	FTM	FTA	Pct.	Off.	Def.	Tot.	Ast.	PF	Dq.	Stl.	Blk.	TO	Pts.	Avg.
84-85 —Golden State	47	418	72	188	.383	53	77	.688	10	18	28	20	76	0	21	4	33	197	4.2
87-88 —L.A. Clippers	19	312	62	138	.449	47	69	.681	6	21	27	38	56	0	10	5	40	171	9.0

Season Team	G	Min.	FGM	FGA	Pct.	FTM	FTA	Pct.	REBOUNDS Off.	Def.	Tot.	Ast.	PF	Dq.	Stl.	Blk.	TO	Pts.	Avg.
91-92 —Phoenix	31	356	74	160	.463	38	54	.704	10	24	34	59	58	0	16	4	33	187	6.0
Totals	97	1086	208	486	.428	138	200	.690	26	63	89	117	190	0	47	13	106	555	5.7

Three-point field goals: 1984-85, 0-for-1. 1987-88, 0-for-4. 1991-92, 1-for-6 (.167). Totals, 1-for-11 (.091).

NBA PLAYOFF RECORD

Season Team	G	Min.	FGM	FGA	Pct.	FTM	FTA	Pct.	REBOUNDS Off.	Def.	Tot.	Ast.	PF	Dq.	Stl.	Blk.	TO	Pts.	Avg.
91-92 —Phoenix	8	104	16	38	.421	18	21	.857	3	9	12	14	18	0	5	0	8	50	6.3

Three-point field goals: 1991-92, 0-for-2.

CBA REGULAR-SEASON RECORD

Season Team	G	Min.	2-POINT FGM	FGA	Pct.	3-POINT FGM	FGA	Pct.	FTM	FTA	Pct.	Reb.	Ast.	Pts.	Avg.
85-86 —Albany	6	86	21	53	.396	0	0	...	11	16	.688	6	4	53	8.8
87-88 —Savannah	45	1449	368	717	.513	4	19	.211	299	399	.749	117	138	1047	23.3
89-90 —Albany	19	407	92	184	.500	3	3	1.000	86	102	.843	41	28	279	14.7
90-91 —Oklahoma City	25	955	246	472	.521	1	22	.045	195	239	.816	79	97	690	27.6
Totals	95	2897	727	1426	.510	8	44	.182	591	756	.782	243	267	2069	21.8

CAGE, MICHAEL
C/F, SUPERSONICS

PERSONAL: Born January 28, 1962, in West Memphis, Ark. ... 6-9/230. ... Full name: Michael Jerome Cage.
HIGH SCHOOL: West Memphis (Ark.).
COLLEGE: San Diego State.
TRANSACTIONS/CAREER NOTES: Selected by Los Angeles Clippers in first round (14th pick overall) of 1984 NBA Draft. ... Traded by Clippers to Seattle SuperSonics for draft rights to Gary Grant and 1989 first-round draft choice (June 28, 1988).

COLLEGIATE RECORD

Season Team	G	Min.	FGM	FGA	Pct.	FTM	FTA	Pct.	Reb.	Pts.	Avg.
80-81 —San Diego State	27	1031	115	206	.558	65	86	.756	355	295	10.9
81-82 —San Diego State	29	1076	123	252	.488	72	109	.661	256	318	11.0
82-83 —San Diego State	28	1070	191	335	.570	165	221	.747	354	547	19.5
83-84 —San Diego State	28	1085	250	445	.562	186	251	.741	352	686	24.5
Totals	112	4262	679	1238	.548	488	667	.732	1317	1846	16.5

NBA REGULAR-SEASON RECORD

NOTES: Led NBA with 13.03 rebounds per game (1988).

Season Team	G	Min.	FGM	FGA	Pct.	FTM	FTA	Pct.	REBOUNDS Off.	Def.	Tot.	Ast.	PF	Dq.	Stl.	Blk.	TO	Pts.	Avg.
84-85 —L.A. Clippers	75	1610	216	398	.543	101	137	.737	126	266	392	51	164	1	41	32	81	533	7.1
85-86 —L.A. Clippers	78	1566	204	426	.479	113	174	.649	168	249	417	81	176	1	62	34	106	521	6.7
86-87 —L.A. Clippers	80	2922	457	878	.521	341	467	.730	354	568	922	131	221	1	99	67	171	1255	15.7
87-88 —L.A. Clippers	72	2660	360	766	.470	326	474	.688	371	567	938	110	194	1	91	58	160	1046	14.5
88-89 —Seattle	80	2536	314	630	.498	197	265	.743	276	489	765	126	184	1	92	52	124	825	10.3
89-90 —Seattle	82	2595	325	645	.504	148	212	.698	306	515	821	70	232	1	79	45	94	798	9.7
90-91 —Seattle	82	2141	226	445	.508	70	112	.625	177	381	558	89	194	0	85	58	83	522	6.4
91-92 —Seattle	82	2461	307	542	.566	106	171	.620	266	462	728	92	237	0	99	55	78	720	8.8
Totals	631	18491	2409	4730	.509	1402	2012	.697	2044	3497	5541	750	1602	6	648	401	897	6220	9.9

Three-point field goals: 1985-86, 0-for-3. 1986-87, 0-for-3. 1987-88, 0-for-1. 1988-89, 0-for-4. 1991-92, 0-for-5. Totals, 0-for-16.

NBA PLAYOFF RECORD

Season Team	G	Min.	FGM	FGA	Pct.	FTM	FTA	Pct.	REBOUNDS Off.	Def.	Tot.	Ast.	PF	Dq.	Stl.	Blk.	TO	Pts.	Avg.
88-89 —Seattle	8	175	24	40	.600	9	22	.409	22	24	46	5	14	0	7	3	8	57	7.1
90-91 —Seattle	5	80	6	14	.429	13	17	.765	9	12	21	2	12	0	3	2	3	25	5.0
91-92 —Seattle	9	197	19	34	.559	1	1	1.000	18	33	51	4	22	0	6	8	8	39	4.3
Totals	22	452	49	88	.557	23	40	.575	49	69	118	11	48	0	16	13	19	121	5.5

Three-point field goals: 1988-89, 0-for-1.

CALIP, DEMETRIUS
G

PERSONAL: Born November 18, 1969, in Flint, Mich. ... 6-1/165. ... Name pronounced Dem-ee-TREE-us CAL-ip.
HIGH SCHOOL: Northern (Flint, Mich.).
COLLEGE: Michigan.
TRANSACTIONS/CAREER NOTES: Never drafted by an NBA franchise. ... Signed as free agent by Los Angeles Lakers (September 30, 1991). ... Waived by Lakers (October 24, 1991). ... Re-signed by Lakers (October 29, 1991). ... Waived by Lakers (November 14, 1991). ... Re-signed by Lakers (November 19, 1991). ... Waived by Lakers (December 6, 1991). ... Played in Continental Basketball Association with Rapid City Thrillers and Yakima Sun Kings (1991-92).

COLLEGIATE RECORD

Season Team	G	Min.	FGM	FGA	Pct.	FTM	FTA	Pct.	Reb.	Pts.	Avg.
87-88 —Michigan	6	...	3	8	.375	1	2	.500	4	7	1.2
88-89 —Michigan	30	...	22	50	.440	14	17	.824	19	60	2.0
89-90 —Michigan	31	...	101	193	.523	41	61	.672	49	263	8.5
90-91 —Michigan	29	...	214	487	.439	91	123	.740	112	594	20.5
Totals	96	...	340	738	.461	147	203	.724	184	924	9.6

Three-point field goals: 1987-88, 0-for-1. 1988-89, 2-for-9 (.222). 1989-90, 20-for-46 (.435). 1990-91, 75-for-188 (.399). Totals, 97-for-244 (.398).

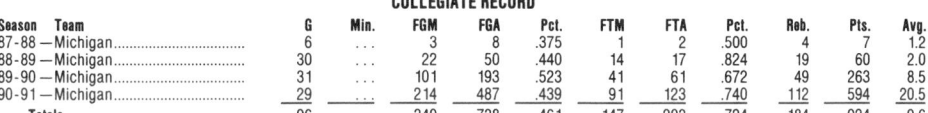

NBA REGULAR-SEASON RECORD

									— REBOUNDS —									
Season Team	G	Min.	FGM	FGA	Pct.	FTM	FTA	Pct.	Off.	Def.	Tot.	Ast.	PF	Dq.	Stl.	Blk.	TO	Pts.	Avg.
91-92 —L.A. Lakers ..	7	58	4	18	.222	2	3	.667	1	4	5	12	8	0	1	0	5	11	1.6

Three-point field goals: 1991-92, 1-for-5 (.200).

CBA REGULAR-SEASON RECORD

			2-POINT			3-POINT								
Season Team	G	Min.	FGM	FGA	Pct.	FGM	FGA	Pct.	FTM	FTA	Pct.	Reb.	Ast.	Pts.	Avg.
91-92 —R.C.-Yak.	15	209	27	64	.422	7	21	.333	14	21	.667	31	21	89	5.9

CAMPBELL, ELDEN
F/C, LAKERS

PERSONAL: Born July 23, 1968, in Los Angeles. . . . 6-11/230. . . . Full name: Elden Jerome Campbell.
HIGH SCHOOL: Morningside (Inglewood, Calif.).
COLLEGE: Clemson.
TRANSACTIONS/CAREER NOTES: Selected by Los Angeles Lakers in first round (27th pick overall) of 1990 NBA Draft.

COLLEGIATE RECORD

Season Team	G	Min.	FGM	FGA	Pct.	FTM	FTA	Pct.	Reb.	Pts.	Avg.
86-87 —Clemson	31	534	107	193	.554	59	84	.702	126	273	8.8
87-88 —Clemson	28	808	217	345	.629	91	147	.619	207	525	18.8
88-89 —Clemson	29	814	205	373	.550	95	138	.688	222	507	17.5
89-90 —Clemson	35	1038	225	431	.522	124	207	.599	281	575	16.4
Totals	123	3194	754	1342	.562	369	576	.641	836	1880	15.3

Three-point field goals: 1987-88, 0-for-4. 1988-89, 2-for-5 (.400). 1989-90, 1-for-1. Totals, 3-for-10 (.300).

NBA REGULAR-SEASON RECORD

									— REBOUNDS —									
Season Team	G	Min.	FGM	FGA	Pct.	FTM	FTA	Pct.	Off.	Def.	Tot.	Ast.	PF	Dq.	Stl.	Blk.	TO	Pts.	Avg.
90-91 —L.A. Lakers ..	52	380	56	123	.455	32	49	.653	40	56	96	10	71	1	11	38	16	144	2.8
91-92 —L.A. Lakers ..	81	1876	220	491	.448	138	223	.619	155	268	423	59	203	1	53	159	73	578	7.1
Totals	133	2256	276	614	.450	170	272	.625	195	324	519	69	274	2	64	197	89	722	5.4

Three-point field goals: 1991-92, 0-for-2.

NBA PLAYOFF RECORD

									— REBOUNDS —									
Season Team	G	Min.	FGM	FGA	Pct.	FTM	FTA	Pct.	Off.	Def.	Tot.	Ast.	PF	Dq.	Stl.	Blk.	TO	Pts.	Avg.
90-91 —L.A. Lakers ..	14	138	25	38	.658	7	15	.467	8	21	29	3	23	1	6	8	6	57	4.1
91-92 —L.A. Lakers ..	4	117	14	37	.378	12	18	.667	9	16	25	6	14	0	3	6	4	40	10.0
Totals	18	255	39	75	.520	19	33	.576	17	37	54	9	37	1	9	14	10	97	5.4

CAMPBELL, TONY
G/F, TIMBERWOLVES

PERSONAL: Born May 7, 1962, in Teaneck, N.J. . . . 6-7/215. . . . Full name: Anthony Campbell.
HIGH SCHOOL: Teaneck (N.J.).
COLLEGE: Ohio State.
TRANSACTIONS/CAREER NOTES: Selected by Detroit Pistons in first round (20th pick overall) of 1984 NBA Draft. . . . Signed as veteran free agent by Washington Bullets (October 8, 1987); Pistons agreed not to exercise their right of first refusal in exchange for 1989 second-round draft choice. . . . Waived by Bullets (November 3, 1987). . . . Played in Continental Basketball Association with Albany Patroons (1987-88). . . . Signed as free agent by Los Angeles Lakers (March 30, 1988). . . . Signed as unrestricted free agent by Minnesota Timberwolves (September 13, 1989).
MISCELLANEOUS: Member of NBA championship team (1988).

COLLEGIATE RECORD

Season Team	G	Min.	FGM	FGA	Pct.	FTM	FTA	Pct.	Reb.	Pts.	Avg.
80-81 —Ohio State	14	55	10	24	.417	3	6	.500	9	23	1.6
81-82 —Ohio State	31	986	151	356	.424	95	119	.798	154	397	12.8
82-83 —Ohio State	30	1122	227	451	.503	115	144	.799	250	569	19.0
83-84 —Ohio State	29	1095	201	392	.513	138	171	.807	215	540	18.6
Totals	104	3258	589	1223	.482	351	440	.798	628	1529	14.7

Three-point field goals: 1982-83, 0-for-2.

NBA REGULAR-SEASON RECORD

RECORDS: Shares single-game record for most free throws attempted in one half—22 (March 8, 1990, vs. Los Angeles Clippers).

									— REBOUNDS —									
Season Team	G	Min.	FGM	FGA	Pct.	FTM	FTA	Pct.	Off.	Def.	Tot.	Ast.	PF	Dq.	Stl.	Blk.	TO	Pts.	Avg.
84-85 —Detroit	56	625	130	262	.496	56	70	.800	41	48	89	24	107	1	28	3	69	316	5.6
85-86 —Detroit	82	1292	294	608	.484	58	73	.795	83	153	236	45	164	0	62	7	86	648	7.9
86-87 —Detroit	40	332	57	145	.393	24	39	.615	21	37	58	19	40	0	12	1	34	138	3.5
87-88 —L.A. Lakers ...	13	242	57	101	.564	28	39	.718	8	19	27	15	41	0	11	2	26	143	11.0
88-89 —L.A. Lakers ...	63	787	158	345	.458	70	83	.843	53	77	130	47	108	0	37	6	62	388	6.2
89-90 —Minnesota	82	3164	723	1581	.457	448	569	.787	209	242	451	213	260	7	111	31	251	1903	23.2
90-91 —Minnesota	77	2893	652	1502	.434	358	446	.803	161	185	346	214	204	0	121	48	190	1678	21.8
91-92 —Minnesota	78	2441	527	1137	.464	240	299	.803	141	145	286	229	206	1	84	31	165	1307	16.8
Totals	491	11776	2598	5681	.457	1282	1618	.792	717	906	1623	806	1130	9	466	129	883	6521	13.3

Three-point field goals: 1984-85, 0-for-1. 1985-86, 2-for-9 (.222). 1986-87, 0-for-3. 1987-88, 1-for-3 (.333). 1988-89, 2-for-21 (.095). 1989-90, 9-for-54 (.167). 1990-91, 16-for-61 (.262). 1991-92, 13-for-37 (.351). Totals, 43-for-189 (.228).

C

NBA PLAYOFF RECORD

Season	Team	G	Min.	FGM	FGA	Pct.	FTM	FTA	Pct.	Off.	Def.	Tot.	Ast.	PF	Dq.	Stl.	Blk.	TO	Pts.	Avg.
84-85	—Detroit.........	2	9	1	3	.333	0	0	...	0	2	2	1	1	0	0	0	0	2	1.0
85-86	—Detroit.........	2	16	4	10	.400	1	2	.500	0	2	2	0	5	0	0	0	1	9	4.5
86-87	—Detroit.........	4	13	3	6	.500	2	2	1.000	0	5	5	0	1	0	0	0	0	9	2.3
87-88	—L.A. Lakers ..	15	94	18	42	.429	11	16	.688	4	6	10	5	16	0	3	0	5	47	3.1
88-89	—L.A. Lakers ..	9	106	19	31	.613	16	22	.727	4	8	12	6	26	1	3	0	9	56	6.2
	Totals	32	238	45	92	.489	30	42	.714	8	23	31	12	49	1	6	0	15	123	3.8

Three-point field goals: 1986-87, 1-for-1. 1987-88, 0-for-1. 1988-89, 2-for-4 (.500). Totals, 3-for-6 (.500).

CBA REGULAR-SEASON RECORD

NOTES: CBA Newcomer of the Year (1988).... CBA All-Star first team (1988).

Season	Team	G	Min.	2-POINT FGM	2-POINT FGA	2-POINT Pct.	3-POINT FGM	3-POINT FGA	3-POINT Pct.	FTM	FTA	Pct.	Reb.	Ast.	Pts.	Avg.
87-88	—Albany	38	1133	332	513	*.647	3	8	.375	229	266	*.861	251	51	902	23.7

CARR, ANTOINE
F, SPURS

PERSONAL: Born July 23, 1961, in Oklahoma City.... 6-9/265.... Full name: Antoine Labotte Carr.
HIGH SCHOOL: Wichita Heights (Wichita, Kan.).
COLLEGE: Wichita State.

TRANSACTIONS/CAREER NOTES: Selected by Detroit Pistons in first round (eighth pick overall) of 1983 NBA Draft.... Played in Italy (1983-84).... Draft rights traded by Pistons with Cliff Levingston and 1986 and 1987 second-round draft choices to Atlanta Hawks for Dan Roundfield (June 18, 1984).... Traded by Hawks with Sedric Toney and future considerations to Sacramento Kings for Kenny Smith and Mike Williams (February 13, 1990).... Traded by Kings to San Antonio Spurs for Dwayne Schintzius and 1994 second-round draft choice (September 23, 1991).

COLLEGIATE RECORD

NOTES: THE SPORTING NEWS All-America first team (1983).

Season	Team	G	Min.	FGM	FGA	Pct.	FTM	FTA	Pct.	Reb.	Pts.	Avg.
79-80	—Wichita State..........................	29	818	178	355	.501	86	129	.667	171	442	15.2
80-81	—Wichita State..........................	33	1030	211	360	.586	101	132	.765	241	523	15.8
81-82	—Wichita State..........................	28	785	179	316	.566	91	115	.791	196	449	16.0
82-83	—Wichita State..........................	22	727	195	339	.575	104	136	.765	168	497	22.6
	Totals	112	3360	763	1370	.557	382	512	.746	776	1911	17.1

Three-point field goals: 1982-83, 3-for-5 (.600).

ITALIAN LEAGUE RECORD

Season	Team	G	Min.	FGM	FGA	Pct.	FTM	FTA	Pct.	Reb.	Pts.	Avg.
83-84	—Milan.....................................	27	956	242	434	.558	86	137	.628	237	570	21.1

NBA REGULAR-SEASON RECORD

Season	Team	G	Min.	FGM	FGA	Pct.	FTM	FTA	Pct.	Off.	Def.	Tot.	Ast.	PF	Dq.	Stl.	Blk.	TO	Pts.	Avg.
84-85	—Atlanta........	62	1195	198	375	.528	101	128	.789	79	153	232	80	219	4	29	78	108	499	8.0
85-86	—Atlanta........	17	258	49	93	.527	18	27	.667	16	36	52	14	51	1	7	15	14	116	6.8
86-87	—Atlanta........	65	695	134	265	.506	73	103	.709	60	96	156	34	146	1	14	48	40	342	5.3
87-88	—Atlanta........	80	1483	281	517	.544	142	182	.780	94	195	289	103	272	7	38	83	116	705	8.8
88-89	—Atlanta........	78	1488	226	471	.480	130	152	.855	106	168	274	91	221	0	31	62	82	582	7.5
89-90	—Atlanta-Sac.	77	1727	356	721	.494	237	298	.795	115	207	322	119	247	6	30	68	125	949	12.3
90-91	—Sacramento .	77	2527	628	1228	.511	295	389	.758	163	257	420	191	315	14	45	101	171	1551	20.1
91-92	—San Antonio.	81	1867	359	732	.490	162	212	.764	128	218	346	63	264	5	32	96	114	881	10.9
	Totals	537	11240	2231	4402	.507	1158	1491	.777	761	1330	2091	695	1735	38	226	551	770	5625	10.5

Three-point field goals: 1984-85, 2-for-6 (.333). 1986-87, 1-for-3 (.333). 1987-88, 1-for-4 (.250). 1988-89, 0-for-1. 1989-90, 0-for-7. 1990-91, 0-for-3. 1991-92, 1-for-5 (.200). Totals, 5-for-29 (.172).

NBA PLAYOFF RECORD

Season	Team	G	Min.	FGM	FGA	Pct.	FTM	FTA	Pct.	Off.	Def.	Tot.	Ast.	PF	Dq.	Stl.	Blk.	TO	Pts.	Avg.
86-87	—Atlanta........	9	162	39	56	.696	26	32	.813	11	16	27	13	36	1	3	8	10	104	11.6
87-88	—Atlanta........	12	210	36	68	.529	9	14	.643	12	29	41	15	47	2	4	17	10	81	6.8
88-89	—Atlanta........	5	81	13	21	.619	8	11	.727	5	3	8	7	13	0	0	4	4	34	6.8
91-92	—San Antonio.	3	109	24	44	.545	10	16	.625	8	15	23	3	14	1	2	11	4	59	19.7
	Totals	29	562	112	189	.593	53	73	.726	36	63	99	38	110	4	9	40	28	278	9.6

Three-point field goals: 1988-89, 0-for-1. 1991-92, 1-for-2 (.500). Totals, 1-for-3 (.333).

CARTWRIGHT, BILL
C, BULLS

PERSONAL: Born July 30, 1957, in Lodi, Calif.... 7-1/245.... Full name: James William Cartwright.
HIGH SCHOOL: Elk Grove (Calif.).
COLLEGE: San Francisco.

TRANSACTIONS/CAREER NOTES: Selected by New York Knicks in first round (third pick overall) of 1979 NBA Draft.... Traded by Knicks with 1988 first- and third-round draft choices to Chicago Bulls for Charles Oakley and 1988 first- and third-round draft choices (June 27, 1988).... Signed as unrestricted free agent by Bulls (August 12, 1991).
MISCELLANEOUS: Member of NBA championship teams (1991, 1992).

COLLEGIATE RECORD

NOTES: THE SPORTING NEWS All-America first team (1979).

Season	Team	G	Min.	FGM	FGA	Pct.	FTM	FTA	Pct.	Reb.	Pts.	Avg.
75-76	—San Francisco	30	845	151	285	.530	72	98	.735	207	374	12.5
76-77	—San Francisco	31	969	241	426	.566	118	161	.733	262	600	19.4
77-78	—San Francisco	21	712	168	252	.667	96	131	.733	213	432	20.6
78-79	—San Francisco	29	1020	268	443	.605	174	237	.734	455	710	24.5
Totals		111	3546	828	1406	.589	460	627	.734	1137	2116	19.1

HONORS: NBA All-Rookie team (1980).

NBA REGULAR-SEASON RECORD

Season	Team	G	Min.	FGM	FGA	Pct.	FTM	FTA	Pct.	Off.	Def.	Tot.	Ast.	PF	Dq.	Stl.	Blk.	TO	Pts.	Avg.
79-80	—New York	82	3150	665	1215	.547	451	566	.797	194	532	726	165	279	2	48	101	222	1781	21.7
80-81	—New York	82	2925	619	1118	.554	408	518	.788	161	452	613	111	259	2	48	83	200	1646	20.1
81-82	—New York	72	2060	390	694	.562	257	337	.763	116	305	421	87	208	2	48	65	166	1037	14.4
82-83	—New York	82	2468	455	804	.566	380	511	.744	185	405	590	136	315	7	41	127	204	1290	15.7
83-84	—New York	77	2487	453	808	.561	404	502	.805	195	454	649	107	262	4	44	97	200	1310	17.0
84-85	—New York							Did not play—injured.												
85-86	—New York	2	36	3	7	.429	6	10	.600	2	8	10	5	6	0	1	1	6	12	6.0
86-87	—New York	58	1989	335	631	.531	346	438	.790	132	313	445	96	188	2	40	26	128	1016	17.5
87-88	—New York	82	1676	287	528	.544	340	426	.798	127	257	384	85	234	4	43	43	135	914	11.1
88-89	—Chicago	78	2333	365	768	.475	236	308	.766	152	369	521	90	234	2	21	41	190	966	12.4
89-90	—Chicago	71	2160	292	598	.488	227	280	.811	137	328	465	145	243	6	38	34	123	811	11.4
90-91	—Chicago	79	2273	318	649	.490	124	178	.697	167	319	486	126	167	0	32	15	113	760	9.6
91-92	—Chicago	64	1471	208	445	.467	96	159	.604	93	231	324	87	131	0	22	14	75	512	8.0
Totals		829	25028	4390	8265	.531	3275	4233	.774	1661	3973	5634	1240	2526	31	426	647	1762	12055	14.5

Three-point field goals: 1980-81, 0-for-1. 1983-84, 0-for-1. Totals, 0-for-2.

NBA PLAYOFF RECORD

Season	Team	G	Min.	FGM	FGA	Pct.	FTM	FTA	Pct.	Off.	Def.	Tot.	Ast.	PF	Dq.	Stl.	Blk.	TO	Pts.	Avg.
80-81	—New York	2	49	6	17	.353	8	12	.667	4	9	13	1	7	0	1	1	6	20	10.0
82-83	—New York	6	172	25	43	.581	17	22	.773	9	25	34	4	25	0	3	7	19	67	11.2
83-84	—New York	12	398	70	126	.556	69	80	.863	27	72	99	5	44	0	2	14	26	209	17.4
87-88	—New York	4	76	9	18	.500	11	15	.733	8	11	19	6	12	0	0	3	8	29	7.3
88-89	—Chicago	17	583	72	148	.486	56	80	.700	33	88	121	20	70	1	9	12	41	200	11.8
89-90	—Chicago	16	462	50	121	.413	29	43	.674	25	50	75	16	52	0	5	4	25	129	8.1
90-91	—Chicago	17	511	70	135	.519	22	32	.688	25	55	80	32	55	0	9	7	21	162	9.5
91-92	—Chicago	22	612	55	116	.474	13	31	.419	29	69	98	38	70	1	11	4	27	123	5.6
Totals		96	2863	357	724	.493	225	315	.714	160	379	539	122	335	2	40	52	173	939	9.8

NBA ALL-STAR GAME RECORD

Season	Team	Min.	FGM	FGA	Pct.	FTM	FTA	Pct.	Off.	Def.	Tot.	Ast.	PF	Dq.	Stl.	Blk.	TO	Pts.
1980	—New York	14	4	8	.500	0	0	...	1	2	3	1	1	0	0	0	2	8

CATLEDGE, TERRY
F, MAGIC

PERSONAL: Born August 22, 1963, in Houston, Miss. . . . 6-8/230. . . . Full name: Terry DeWayne Catledge.
HIGH SCHOOL: Houston (Miss.).
COLLEGE: Itawamba Junior College (Miss.), then South Alabama.
TRANSACTIONS/CAREER NOTES: Selected by Philadelphia 76ers in first round (21st pick overall) of 1985 NBA Draft. . . . Traded by 76ers with Moses Malone and 1986 and 1988 first-round draft choices to Washington Bullets for Jeff Ruland and Cliff Robinson (June 16, 1986). . . . Selected by Orlando Magic from Bullets in NBA expansion draft (June 15, 1989).

COLLEGIATE RECORD

NOTES: Left Itawamba Junior College before 1981-82 season.

Season	Team	G	Min.	FGM	FGA	Pct.	FTM	FTA	Pct.	Reb.	Pts.	Avg.
81-82	—South Alabama					Did not play—transfer student.						
82-83	—South Alabama	28	911	216	387	.558	119	171	.696	278	551	19.7
83-84	—South Alabama	30	1032	220	373	.590	157	219	.717	332	597	19.9
84-85	—South Alabama	28	1038	285	536	.532	148	250	.592	322	718	25.6
Totals		86	2981	721	1296	.556	424	640	.663	932	1866	21.7

NBA REGULAR-SEASON RECORD

Season	Team	G	Min.	FGM	FGA	Pct.	FTM	FTA	Pct.	Off.	Def.	Tot.	Ast.	PF	Dq.	Stl.	Blk.	TO	Pts.	Avg.
85-86	—Philadelphia	64	1092	202	431	.469	90	139	.647	107	165	272	21	127	0	31	8	69	494	7.7
86-87	—Washington	78	2149	413	835	.495	199	335	.594	248	312	560	56	195	1	43	14	145	1025	13.1
87-88	—Washington	70	1610	296	585	.506	154	235	.655	180	217	397	63	172	0	33	9	101	746	10.7
88-89	—Washington	79	2077	334	681	.490	153	254	.602	230	342	572	75	250	5	46	25	120	822	10.4
89-90	—Orlando	74	2462	546	1152	.474	341	486	.702	271	292	563	72	201	0	36	17	181	1435	19.4
90-91	—Orlando	51	1459	292	632	.462	161	258	.624	168	187	355	58	113	2	34	9	107	745	14.6
91-92	—Orlando	78	2430	457	922	.496	240	346	.694	257	292	549	109	196	2	58	16	138	1154	14.8
Totals		494	13279	2540	5238	.485	1338	2053	.652	1461	1807	3268	454	1254	10	281	98	861	6421	13.0

Three-point field goals: 1985-86, 0-for-4. 1986-87, 0-for-4. 1987-88, 0-for-2. 1988-89, 1-for-5 (.200). 1989-90, 2-for-8 (.250). 1990-91, 0-for-5. 1991-92, 0-for-4. Totals, 3-for-32 (.094).

NBA PLAYOFF RECORD

Season	Team	G	Min.	FGM	FGA	Pct.	FTM	FTA	Pct.	Off.	Def.	Tot.	Ast.	PF	Dq.	Stl.	Blk.	TO	Pts.	Avg.
85-86	—Philadelphia	11	293	46	117	.393	22	38	.579	37	38	75	5	34	0	6	8	14	114	10.4
86-87	—Washington	3	98	23	41	.561	9	17	.529	7	18	25	0	5	0	3	1	7	55	18.3
87-88	—Washington	5	45	4	11	.364	3	4	.750	2	4	6	2	9	0	0	0	2	11	2.2
Totals		19	436	73	169	.432	34	59	.576	46	60	106	7	48	0	9	9	23	180	9.5

Three-point field goals: 1987-88, 0-for-1.

CAUSWELL, DUANE
C, KINGS

PERSONAL: Born May 31, 1968, in Queens Village, N.Y. . . . 7-0/240.
HIGH SCHOOL: Benjamin Cardozo (Bayside, N.Y.).
COLLEGE: Temple.
TRANSACTIONS/CAREER NOTES: Selected by Sacramento Kings in first round (18th pick overall) of 1990 NBA Draft.

COLLEGIATE RECORD

Season Team	G	Min.	FGM	FGA	Pct.	FTM	FTA	Pct.	Reb.	Pts.	Avg.
86-87 — Temple					Did not play—redshirted.						
87-88 — Temple	33	399	27	55	.491	13	30	.433	85	67	2.0
88-89 — Temple	30	1081	128	249	.514	84	123	.683	267	340	11.3
89-90 — Temple	12	416	52	107	.486	31	52	.596	99	135	11.3
Totals	75	1896	207	411	.504	128	205	.624	451	542	7.2

Three-point field goals: 1988-89, 0-for-1.

NBA REGULAR-SEASON RECORD

Season Team	G	Min.	FGM	FGA	Pct.	FTM	FTA	Pct.	Off.	Def.	Tot.	Ast.	PF	Dq.	Stl.	Blk.	TO	Pts.	Avg.
										REBOUNDS									
90-91—Sacramento	76	1719	210	413	.508	105	165	.636	141	250	391	69	225	4	49	148	96	525	6.9
91-92—Sacramento	80	2291	250	455	.549	136	222	.613	196	384	580	59	281	4	47	215	124	636	8.0
Totals	156	4010	460	868	.530	241	387	.623	337	634	971	128	506	8	96	363	220	1161	7.4

Three-point field goals: 1991-92, 0-for-1.

CEBALLOS, CEDRIC
F, SUNS

PERSONAL: Born August 2, 1969, in Maui, Hawaii. . . . 6-6/210. . . . Full name: Cedric Z. Ceballos. . . . Name pronounced Sed-rick Se-BAL-ose.
HIGH SCHOOL: Dominquez (Compton, Calif.).
COLLEGE: Ventura (Calif.), then Cal State Fullerton.
TRANSACTIONS/CAREER NOTES: Selected by Phoenix Suns in second round (48th pick overall) of 1990 NBA Draft.

COLLEGIATE RECORD

Season Team	G	Min.	FGM	FGA	Pct.	FTM	FTA	Pct.	Reb.	Pts.	Avg.
86-87 — Ventura					Statistics unavailable.						
87-88 — Ventura					Statistics unavailable.						
88-89 — Cal State Fullerton	29	986	241	545	.442	117	174	.672	256	615	21.2
89-90 — Cal State Fullerton	29	1071	247	509	.485	144	215	.670	362	669	23.1
Four-year-college totals	58	2057	488	1054	.463	261	389	.671	618	1284	22.1

Three-point field goals: 1988-89, 16-for-58 (.276). 1989-90, 31-for-96 (.323). Totals, 47-for-154 (.305).

NBA REGULAR-SEASON RECORD

Season Team	G	Min.	FGM	FGA	Pct.	FTM	FTA	Pct.	Off.	Def.	Tot.	Ast.	PF	Dq.	Stl.	Blk.	TO	Pts.	Avg.
										REBOUNDS									
90-91—Phoenix	63	730	204	419	.487	110	166	.663	77	73	150	37	70	0	22	5	69	519	8.2
91-92—Phoenix	64	725	176	365	.482	109	148	.736	60	92	152	50	52	0	16	11	71	462	7.2
Totals	127	1455	380	784	.485	219	314	.697	137	165	302	85	122	0	38	16	140	981	7.7

Three-point field goals: 1990-91, 1-for-6 (.167). 1991-92, 1-for-6 (.167). Totals, 2-for-12 (.167).

NBA PLAYOFF RECORD

Season Team	G	Min.	FGM	FGA	Pct.	FTM	FTA	Pct.	Off.	Def.	Tot.	Ast.	PF	Dq.	Stl.	Blk.	TO	Pts.	Avg.
										REBOUNDS									
90-91—Phoenix	3	24	7	12	.583	2	6	.333	3	2	5	2	0	0	2	0	1	16	5.3
91-92—Phoenix	8	188	44	80	.550	20	30	.667	20	31	51	12	14	0	6	6	11	108	13.5
Totals	11	212	51	92	.554	22	36	.611	23	33	56	14	14	0	8	6	12	124	11.3

CHAMBERS, TOM
F, SUNS

PERSONAL: Born June 21, 1959, in Ogden, Utah. . . . 6-10/230. . . . Full name: Thomas Doane Chambers.
HIGH SCHOOL: Fairview (Boulder, Colo.).
COLLEGE: Utah.
TRANSACTIONS/CAREER NOTES: Selected by San Diego Clippers in first round (eighth pick overall) of 1981 NBA Draft. . . . Traded by Clippers with Al Wood, 1987 second-round draft choice and future third-round draft choice to Seattle SuperSonics for James Donaldson, Greg Kelser, Mark Radford, 1984 first-round draft choice and 1985 second-round draft choice (August 18, 1983). . . . Signed as unrestricted free agent by Phoenix Suns (July 5, 1988).

COLLEGIATE RECORD

Season Team	G	Min.	FGM	FGA	Pct.	FTM	FTA	Pct.	Reb.	Pts.	Avg.
77-78 — Utah	28	355	69	139	.496	40	64	.625	104	178	6.4
78-79 — Utah	30	853	206	379	.544	69	127	.543	266	481	16.0
79-80 — Utah	28	792	195	359	.543	92	129	.713	244	482	17.2
80-81 — Utah	30	959	221	372	.594	115	155	.742	262	557	18.6
Totals	116	2959	691	1249	.553	316	475	.665	876	1698	14.6

NBA REGULAR-SEASON RECORD

HONORS: All-NBA second team (1989, 1990).

Season	Team	G	Min.	FGM	FGA	Pct.	FTM	FTA	Pct.	Off.	Def.	Tot.	Ast.	PF	Dq.	Stl.	Blk.	TO	Pts.	Avg.
81-82	—San Diego.....	81	2682	554	1056	.525	284	458	.620	211	350	561	146	341	17	58	46	220	1392	17.2
82-83	—San Diego.....	79	2665	519	1099	.472	353	488	.723	218	301	519	192	333	15	79	57	234	1391	17.6
83-84	—Seattle.........	82	2570	554	1110	.499	375	469	.800	219	313	532	133	309	8	47	51	192	1483	18.1
84-85	—Seattle.........	81	2923	629	1302	.483	475	571	.832	164	415	579	209	312	4	70	57	260	1739	21.5
85-86	—Seattle.........	66	2019	432	928	.466	346	414	.836	126	305	431	132	248	6	55	37	194	1223	18.5
86-87	—Seattle.........	82	3018	660	1446	.456	535	630	.849	163	382	545	245	307	9	81	50	268	1674	23.3
87-88	—Seattle.........	82	2680	611	1364	.448	419	519	.807	135	355	490	212	297	4	87	53	209	1674	20.4
88-89	—Phoenix.......	81	3002	774	1643	.471	509	598	.851	143	541	684	231	271	2	87	55	231	2085	25.7
89-90	—Phoenix.......	81	3046	810	1617	.501	557	647	.861	121	450	571	190	260	1	88	47	218	2201	27.2
90-91	—Phoenix.......	76	2475	556	1271	.437	379	459	.826	104	386	490	194	235	3	65	52	177	1511	19.9
91-92	—Phoenix.......	69	1948	426	989	.431	258	311	.830	86	315	401	142	196	1	57	37	103	1128	16.3
Totals	....	860	29028	6525	13825	.472	4490	5564	.807	1690	4113	5803	2026	3109	70	774	542	2306	17736	20.6

Three-point field goals: 1981-82, 0-for-2. 1982-83, 0-for-8. 1983-84, 0-for-12. 1984-85, 6-for-22 (.273). 1985-86, 13-for-48 (.271). 1986-87, 54-for-145 (.372). 1987-88, 33-for-109 (.303). 1988-89, 28-for-86 (.326). 1989-90, 24-for-86 (.279). 1990-91, 20-for-73 (.274). 1991-92, 18-for-49 (.367). Totals, 196-for-640 (.306).

NBA PLAYOFF RECORD

Season	Team	G	Min.	FGM	FGA	Pct.	FTM	FTA	Pct.	Off.	Def.	Tot.	Ast.	PF	Dq.	Stl.	Blk.	TO	Pts.	Avg.
83-84	—Seattle.........	5	191	28	59	.475	12	18	.667	4	29	33	8	23	0	5	3	9	68	13.6
86-87	—Seattle.........	14	498	118	263	.449	80	99	.808	32	58	90	32	51	0	12	13	34	322	23.0
87-88	—Seattle.........	5	168	50	91	.549	29	35	.829	8	23	31	11	24	1	3	1	13	129	25.8
88-89	—Phoenix.......	12	495	118	257	.459	67	78	.859	22	109	131	46	44	0	13	15	39	312	26.0
89-90	—Phoenix.......	16	612	117	275	.425	116	132	.879	20	87	107	31	54	0	7	7	49	355	22.2
90-91	—Phoenix.......	4	142	27	66	.409	14	19	.737	2	21	23	10	12	1	7	5	12	68	17.0
91-92	—Phoenix.......	7	194	39	85	.459	27	32	.844	8	23	31	19	25	1	2	5	15	109	15.6
Totals	....	63	2300	497	1096	.453	345	413	.835	96	350	446	157	233	3	49	49	171	1363	21.6

Three-point field goals: 1983-84, 0-for-1. 1986-87, 6-for-17 (.353). 1987-88, 0-for-2. 1988-89, 9-for-22 (.409). 1989-90, 5-for-19 (.263). 1990-91, 0-for-5. 1991-92, 4-for-7 (.571). Totals, 24-for-73 (.329).

NBA ALL-STAR GAME RECORD

NOTES: NBA All-Star Game Most Valuable Player (1987).

Season	Team	Min.	FGM	FGA	Pct.	FTM	FTA	Pct.	Off.	Def.	Tot.	Ast.	PF	Dq.	Stl.	Blk.	TO	Pts.
1987	—Seattle..............	29	13	25	.520	6	9	.667	3	1	4	2	5	0	4	0	3	34
1989	—Phoenix..............	16	4	8	.500	6	6	1.000	2	3	5	1	3	0	0	0	2	14
1990	—Phoenix..............	21	8	12	.667	5	7	.714	2	1	3	1	0	0	1	0	3	21
1991	—Phoenix..............	18	4	11	.364	0	0	....	2	2	4	1	3	0	1	0	4	8
Totals	....	84	29	56	.518	17	22	.773	9	7	16	5	11	0	6	0	12	77

Three-point field goals: 1987, 2-for-3 (.667). 1990, 0-for-1. 1991, 0-for-1. Totals, 2-for-5 (.400).

CHAPMAN, REX
G, BULLETS

PERSONAL: Born October 5, 1967, in Bowling Green, Ky.... 6-4/205.... Full name: Rex Everett Chapman.... Son of Wayne Chapman, guard with Kentucky Colonels, Denver Rockets and Indiana Pacers of American Basketball Association (1968-69 through 1971-72).

HIGH SCHOOL: Apollo (Owensboro, Ky.).

COLLEGE: Kentucky.

TRANSACTIONS/CAREER NOTES: Selected as undergraduate by Charlotte Hornets in first round (eighth pick overall) of 1988 NBA Draft.... Traded by Hornets to Washington Bullets for Tom Hammonds (February 19, 1992).

COLLEGIATE RECORD

Season	Team	G	Min.	FGM	FGA	Pct.	FTM	FTA	Pct.	Reb.	Pts.	Avg.
86-87	—Kentucky	29	962	173	390	.444	50	68	.735	66	464	16.0
87-88	—Kentucky	32	1108	231	461	.501	81	102	.794	93	609	19.0
Totals	....	61	2070	404	851	.475	131	170	.771	159	1073	17.6

Three-point field goals: 1986-87, 68-for-176 (.386). 1987-88, 66-for-159 (.415). Totals, 134-for-335 (.400).

NBA REGULAR-SEASON RECORD

HONORS: NBA All-Rookie second team (1989).

Season	Team	G	Min.	FGM	FGA	Pct.	FTM	FTA	Pct.	Off.	Def.	Tot.	Ast.	PF	Dq.	Stl.	Blk.	TO	Pts.	Avg.
88-89	—Charlotte......	75	2219	526	1271	.414	155	195	.795	74	113	187	176	167	1	70	25	113	1267	16.9
89-90	—Charlotte......	54	1762	377	924	.408	144	192	.750	52	127	179	132	113	0	46	6	100	945	17.5
90-91	—Charlotte......	70	2100	410	922	.445	234	282	.830	45	146	191	250	167	1	73	16	131	1102	15.7
91-92	—Char.-Wash.	22	567	113	252	.448	36	53	.679	10	48	58	89	51	0	15	8	45	270	12.3
Totals	....	221	6648	1426	3369	.423	569	722	.788	181	434	615	647	498	2	204	55	389	3584	16.2

Three-point field goals: 1988-89, 60-for-191 (.314). 1989-90, 47-for-142 (.331). 1990-91, 48-for-148 (.324). 1991-92, 8-for-29 (.276). Totals, 163-for-510 (.320).

CHEEKS, MAURICE
G, HAWKS

PERSONAL: Born September 8, 1956, in Chicago.... 6-1/180.... Full name: Maurice Edward Cheeks.

HIGH SCHOOL: Du Sable (Chicago).

COLLEGE: West Texas State.

TRANSACTIONS/CAREER NOTES: Selected by Philadelphia 76ers in second round (36th pick overall) of 1978 NBA Draft.... Traded by 76ers with Christian Welp and David Wingate to San Antonio Spurs for Johnny Dawkins and Jay Vincent (August 28, 1989).... Traded by Spurs to New York Knicks for Rod Strickland (February 21, 1990).

... Traded by Knicks to Atlanta Hawks for Tim McCormick (October 3, 1991).
MISCELLANEOUS: Member of NBA championship team (1983).

COLLEGIATE RECORD

Season Team	G	Min.	FGM	FGA	Pct.	FTM	FTA	Pct.	Reb.	Pts.	Avg.
74-75 — West Texas State	26	...	35	75	.467	31	53	.585	56	101	3.9
75-76 — West Texas State	23	767	102	170	.600	52	84	.619	91	256	11.1
76-77 — West Texas State	30	1095	149	246	.606	119	169	.704	119	417	13.9
77-78 — West Texas State	27	941	174	319	.545	105	147	.714	152	453	16.8
Totals	106	...	460	810	.568	307	453	.678	418	1227	11.6

NBA REGULAR-SEASON RECORD

RECORDS: Holds career record for most steals—2,277.
HONORS: NBA All-Defensive first team (1983, 1984, 1985, 1986).... NBA All-Defensive second team (1987).

Season Team	G	Min.	FGM	FGA	Pct.	FTM	FTA	Pct.	Off.	Def.	Tot.	Ast.	PF	Dq.	Stl.	Blk.	TO	Pts.	Avg.
78-79 — Philadelphia.	82	2409	292	572	.510	101	140	.721	63	191	254	431	198	2	174	12	193	685	8.4
79-80 — Philadelphia.	79	2623	357	661	.540	180	231	.779	75	199	274	556	197	1	183	32	216	898	11.4
80-81 — Philadelphia.	81	2415	310	581	.534	140	178	.787	67	178	245	560	231	1	193	39	174	763	9.4
81-82 — Philadelphia.	79	2498	352	676	.521	171	220	.777	51	197	248	667	247	0	209	33	184	881	11.2
82-83 — Philadelphia.	79	2465	404	745	.542	181	240	.754	53	156	209	543	182	0	184	31	179	990	12.5
83-84 — Philadelphia.	75	2494	386	702	.550	170	232	.733	44	161	205	478	196	1	171	20	182	950	12.7
84-85 — Philadelphia.	78	2616	422	741	.570	175	199	.879	54	163	217	497	184	0	169	24	155	1025	13.1
85-86 — Philadelphia.	82	*3270	490	913	.537	282	335	.842	55	180	235	753	160	0	207	27	238	1266	15.4
86-87 — Philadelphia.	68	2624	415	788	.527	227	292	.777	47	168	215	538	109	0	180	15	173	1061	15.6
87-88 — Philadelphia.	79	2871	428	865	.495	227	275	.825	59	194	253	635	116	0	167	22	160	1086	13.7
88-89 — Philadelphia.	71	2298	336	696	.483	151	195	.774	39	144	183	554	114	0	105	17	116	824	11.6
89-90 — S.A.-N.Y.	81	2519	307	609	.504	171	202	.847	50	190	240	453	78	0	124	10	121	789	9.7
90-91 — New York	76	2147	241	483	.499	105	129	.814	22	151	173	435	138	0	128	10	108	592	7.8
91-92 — Atlanta.........	56	1086	115	249	.462	26	43	.605	29	66	95	185	73	0	83	0	36	259	4.6
Totals	1066	34335	4855	9281	.523	2307	2911	.793	708	2338	3046	7285	2223	5	2277	292	2235	12069	11.3

Three-point field goals: 1979-80, 4-for-9 (.444). 1980-81, 3-for-8 (.375). 1981-82, 6-for-22 (.273). 1982-83, 1-for-6 (.167). 1983-84, 8-for-20 (.400). 1984-85, 6-for-26 (.231). 1985-86, 4-for-17 (.235). 1986-87, 4-for-17 (.235). 1987-88, 3-for-22 (.136). 1988-89, 1-for-13 (.077). 1989-90, 4-for-16 (.250). 1990-91, 5-for-20 (.250). 1991-92, 3-for-6 (.500). Totals, 52-for-202 (.257).

NBA PLAYOFF RECORD

NOTES: Shares NBA Finals single-game record for most steals—6 (May 7, 1980, vs. Los Angeles Lakers).... Shares single-game record for most steals—8 (April 11, 1979, vs. New Jersey).

Season Team	G	Min.	FGM	FGA	Pct.	FTM	FTA	Pct.	Off.	Def.	Tot.	Ast.	PF	Dq.	Stl.	Blk.	TO	Pts.	Avg.
78-79 — Philadelphia.	9	330	66	121	.545	37	56	.661	13	22	35	63	29	0	37	4	29	169	18.8
79-80 — Philadelphia.	18	675	89	174	.511	29	41	.707	22	52	74	111	43	0	45	4	45	208	11.6
80-81 — Philadelphia.	16	513	68	125	.544	32	42	.762	4	47	51	116	55	1	40	12	36	168	10.5
81-82 — Philadelphia.	21	765	125	265	.472	50	65	.769	15	47	62	172	58	0	48	6	49	301	14.3
82-83 — Philadelphia.	13	483	83	165	.503	45	64	.703	11	28	39	91	23	0	26	2	34	212	16.3
83-84 — Philadelphia.	5	171	35	67	.522	13	15	.867	2	10	12	19	18	0	13	0	10	83	16.6
84-85 — Philadelphia.	13	483	81	153	.529	36	42	.857	12	34	46	67	29	0	31	5	34	198	15.2
85-86 — Philadelphia.	12	519	94	182	.516	62	73	.849	13	43	56	85	18	0	13	3	32	250	20.8
86-87 — Philadelphia.	5	210	35	66	.530	18	21	.857	1	12	13	44	14	0	9	4	12	88	17.6
88-89 — Philadelphia.	3	128	21	41	.512	11	13	.846	3	8	11	39	4	0	7	1	3	53	17.7
89-90 — New York	10	388	50	104	.481	28	31	.903	12	27	39	85	21	0	17	2	19	128	12.8
90-91 — New York	3	101	14	23	.609	1	2	.500	3	6	9	16	9	0	3	1	8	30	10.0
Totals	128	4766	761	1486	.512	362	465	.778	111	336	447	908	321	1	289	44	311	1888	14.8

Three-point field goals: 1979-80, 1-for-5 (.200). 1980-81, 0-for-3. 1981-82, 1-for-9 (.111). 1982-83, 1-for-2 (.500). 1983-84, 0-for-1. 1984-85, 0-for-5. 1985-86, 0-for-7. 1986-87, 0-for-1. 1988-89, 0-for-1. 1989-90, 0-for-4. 1990-91, 1-for-3 (.333). Totals, 4-for-41 (.098).

NBA ALL-STAR GAME RECORD

Season Team	Min.	FGM	FGA	Pct.	FTM	FTA	Pct.	Off.	Def.	Tot.	Ast.	PF	Dq.	Stl.	Blk.	TO	Pts.
1983 — Philadelphia........	18	3	8	.375	0	0	...	0	1	1	1	0	0	0	0	0	6
1986 — Philadelphia........	14	3	6	.500	0	0	...	0	0	0	2	0	0	2	0	3	6
1987 — Philadelphia........	8	1	2	.500	2	2	1.000	0	0	0	0	1	0	1	0	1	4
1988 — Philadelphia........	4	0	0	...	0	0	...	0	2	2	1	1	0	0	0	0	0
Totals	44	7	16	.438	2	2	1.000	0	3	3	4	2	0	3	0	4	16

CHILCUTT, PETE
F/C, KINGS

PERSONAL: Born September 14, 1968, in Sumter, S.C. .... 6-10/232. ... Full name: Peter Shawn Chilcutt.
HIGH SCHOOL: Tuscaloosa Academy (Eutaw, Ala.).
COLLEGE: North Carolina.
TRANSACTIONS/CAREER NOTES: Selected by Sacramento Kings in first round (27th pick overall) of 1991 NBA Draft.

COLLEGIATE RECORD

Season Team	G	Min.	FGM	FGA	Pct.	FTM	FTA	Pct.	Reb.	Pts.	Avg.
86-87 — North Carolina				Did not play—redshirted.							
87-88 — North Carolina	34	573	66	117	.564	36	51	.706	110	168	4.9
88-89 — North Carolina	37	750	110	205	.537	33	53	.623	200	256	6.9
89-90 — North Carolina	34	917	132	257	.514	30	42	.714	225	306	9.0
90-91 — North Carolina	35	937	175	325	.538	65	85	.765	231	420	12.0
Totals	140	3177	483	904	.534	164	231	.710	766	1150	8.2

Three-point field goals: 1987-88, 0-for-1. 1988-89, 3-for-8 (.375). 1989-90, 12-for-30 (.400). 1990-91, 5-for-19 (.263). Totals, 20-for-58 (.345).

NBA REGULAR-SEASON RECORD

Season Team	G	Min.	FGM	FGA	Pct.	FTM	FTA	Pct.	Reb. Off.	Def.	Tot.	Ast.	PF	Dq.	Stl.	Blk.	TO	Pts.	Avg.
91-92 —Sacramento .	69	817	113	250	.452	23	28	.821	78	109	187	38	70	0	32	17	41	251	3.6

Three-point field goals: 1991-92, 2-for-2.

COLEMAN, DERRICK
F, NETS

PERSONAL: Born June 21, 1967, in Mobile, Ala. . . . 6-10/230. . . . Full name: Derrick D. Coleman.
HIGH SCHOOL: Northern (Detroit).
COLLEGE: Syracuse.
TRANSACTIONS/CAREER NOTES: Selected by New Jersey Nets in first round (first pick overall) of 1990 NBA Draft.

COLLEGIATE RECORD

NOTES: THE SPORTING NEWS All-America first team (1990). . . . 1986-87 minutes played totals are missing one game.

Season Team	G	Min.	FGM	FGA	Pct.	FTM	FTA	Pct.	Reb.	Pts.	Avg.
86-87 —Syracuse..............................	38	1163	173	309	.560	107	156	.686	333	453	11.9
87-88 —Syracuse..............................	35	1133	176	300	.587	121	192	.630	384	474	13.5
88-89 —Syracuse..............................	37	1226	227	395	.575	171	247	.692	422	625	16.9
89-90 —Syracuse..............................	33	1166	194	352	.551	188	263	.715	398	591	17.9
Totals	143	4688	770	1356	.568	587	858	.684	1537	2143	15.0

Three-point field goals: 1987-88, 1-for-6 (.167). 1988-89, 0-for-8. 1989-90, 15-for-41 (.366). Totals, 16-for-55 (.291).

NBA REGULAR-SEASON RECORD

HONORS: NBA Rookie of the Year (1991). . . . NBA All-Rookie first team (1991).

Season Team	G	Min.	FGM	FGA	Pct.	FTM	FTA	Pct.	Reb. Off.	Def.	Tot.	Ast.	PF	Dq.	Stl.	Blk.	TO	Pts.	Avg.
90-91 —New Jersey ..	74	2602	514	1100	.467	323	442	.731	269	490	759	163	217	3	71	99	217	1364	18.4
91-92 —New Jersey ..	65	2207	483	958	.504	300	393	.763	203	415	618	205	168	2	54	98	248	1289	19.8
Totals	139	4809	997	2058	.484	623	835	.746	472	905	1377	368	385	5	125	197	465	2653	19.1

Three-point field goals: 1990-91, 13-for-38 (.342). 1991-92, 23-for-76 (.303). Totals, 36-for-114 (.316).

NBA PLAYOFF RECORD

Season Team	G	Min.	FGM	FGA	Pct.	FTM	FTA	Pct.	Reb. Off.	Def.	Tot.	Ast.	PF	Dq.	Stl.	Blk.	TO	Pts.	Avg.
91-92 —New Jersey ..	4	162	36	74	.486	16	21	.762	13	32	45	21	12	0	7	4	11	89	22.3

Three-point field goals: 1991-92, 1-for-6 (.167).

COLES, BIMBO
G, HEAT

PERSONAL: Born April 22, 1968, in Covington, Va. . . . 6-2/182. . . . Full name: Vernell E. Coles.
HIGH SCHOOL: Greenbriar East (Lewisburg, W. Va.).
COLLEGE: Virginia Tech.
TRANSACTIONS/CAREER NOTES: Selected by Sacramento Kings in second round (40th pick overall) of 1990 NBA Draft. . . . Draft rights traded by Kings to Miami Heat for Rory Sparrow (June 27, 1990).
MISCELLANEOUS: Member of bronze-medal-winning U.S. Olympic team (1988).

COLLEGIATE RECORD

Season Team	G	Min.	FGM	FGA	Pct.	FTM	FTA	Pct.	Reb.	Pts.	Avg.
86-87 —Virginia Tech	28	752	101	245	.412	78	109	.716	85	280	10.0
87-88 —Virginia Tech	29	990	241	544	.443	200	270	.741	103	702	24.2
88-89 —Virginia Tech	27	924	249	547	.455	157	200	.785	111	717	26.6
89-90 —Virginia Tech	31	1147	280	693	.404	158	214	.738	147	785	25.3
Totals	115	3813	871	2029	.429	593	793	.748	446	2484	21.6

Three-point field goals: 1986-87, 0-for-14. 1987-88, 20-for-62 (.323). 1988-89, 62-for-166 (.373). 1989-90, 67-for-218 (.307). Totals, 149-for-460 (.324).

NBA REGULAR-SEASON RECORD

Season Team	G	Min.	FGM	FGA	Pct.	FTM	FTA	Pct.	Reb. Off.	Def.	Tot.	Ast.	PF	Dq.	Stl.	Blk.	TO	Pts.	Avg.
90-91 —Miami..........	82	1355	162	393	.412	71	95	.747	56	97	153	232	149	0	65	12	98	401	4.9
91-92 —Miami..........	81	1976	295	649	.455	216	262	.824	69	120	189	366	151	2	73	13	167	816	10.1
Totals	163	3331	457	1042	.439	287	357	.804	125	217	342	598	300	3	138	25	265	1217	7.5

Three-point field goals: 1990-91, 6-for-34 (.176). 1991-92, 10-for-52 (.192). Totals, 16-for-86 (.186).

NBA PLAYOFF RECORD

Season Team	G	Min.	FGM	FGA	Pct.	FTM	FTA	Pct.	Reb. Off.	Def.	Tot.	Ast.	PF	Dq.	Stl.	Blk.	TO	Pts.	Avg.
91-92 —Miami..........	3	45	7	10	.700	8	10	.800	2	5	7	6	5	0	3	0	5	23	7.7

Three-point field goals: 1991-92, 1-for-1.

CONLON, MARTY
F, SUPERSONICS

PERSONAL: Born January 19, 1968, in Bronx, N.Y. . . . 6-10/224. . . . Full name: Martin McBride Conlon.
HIGH SCHOOL: Archbishop Stepinac (White Plains, N.Y.).
COLLEGE: Providence.
TRANSACTIONS/CAREER NOTES: Never drafted by an NBA franchise. . . . Played in Continental Basketball Association with Rockford Lightning (1990-91). . . . Signed as free agent by Seattle SuperSonics (October 1, 1991).

COLLEGIATE RECORD

Season	Team	G	Min.	FGM	FGA	Pct.	FTM	FTA	Pct.	Reb.	Pts.	Avg.
86-87	Providence	34	487	43	96	.448	64	77	.831	100	150	4.4
87-88	Providence	11	282	45	88	.511	55	66	.833	62	145	13.2
88-89	Providence	29	885	154	294	.524	91	125	.728	202	415	14.3
89-90	Providence	29	866	136	271	.502	138	187	.738	220	425	14.7
	Totals	103	2520	378	749	.505	348	455	.765	584	1135	11.0

Three-point field goals: 1987-88, 0-for-3. 1988-89, 16-for-42 (.381). 1989-90, 15-for-48 (.313). Totals, 31-for-93 (.333).

CBA REGULAR-SEASON RECORD

Season	Team	G	Min.	2-POINT FGM	2-POINT FGA	Pct.	3-POINT FGM	3-POINT FGA	Pct.	FTM	FTA	Pct.	Reb.	Ast.	Pts.	Avg.
90-91	Rockford	41	1104	215	339	.634	0	3	.000	118	157	.752	286	72	548	13.4

NBA REGULAR-SEASON RECORD

Season	Team	G	Min.	FGM	FGA	Pct.	FTM	FTA	Pct.	REBOUNDS Off.	REBOUNDS Def.	REBOUNDS Tot.	Ast.	PF	Dq.	Stl.	Blk.	TO	Pts.	Avg.
91-92	Seattle	45	381	48	101	.475	24	32	.750	33	36	69	12	40	0	9	7	27	120	2.7

NBA PLAYOFF RECORD

Season	Team	G	Min.	FGM	FGA	Pct.	FTM	FTA	Pct.	REBOUNDS Off.	REBOUNDS Def.	REBOUNDS Tot.	Ast.	PF	Dq.	Stl.	Blk.	TO	Pts.	Avg.
91-92	Seattle	1	1	0	1	.000	2	2	1.000	0	1	1	0	0	0	0	0	0	2	2.0

CONNER, LESTER
G, MAGIC

PERSONAL: Born September 17, 1959, in Memphis, Tenn. . . . 6-4/180. . . . Full name: Lester Allen Conner.
HIGH SCHOOL: Fremont (Oakland, Calif.).
COLLEGE: Los Medanos (Calif.), then Chabot (Calif.), then Oregon State.

TRANSACTIONS/CAREER NOTES: Selected by Golden State Warriors in first round (14th pick overall) of 1982 NBA Draft. . . . Signed as veteran free agent by Houston Rockets (October 9, 1987); Warriors agreed not to exercise their right of first refusal in exchange for 1988 second-round draft choice. . . . Traded by Rockets with Joe Barry Carroll to New Jersey Nets for Tony Brown, Frank Johnson, Tim McCormick and Lorenzo Romar (November 2, 1988). . . . Traded by Nets to Milwaukee Bucks for Greg Anderson (January 11, 1991). . . . Traded by Bucks to Orlando Magic for Sam Vincent and 1994 second-round draft choice (August 4, 1992).

COLLEGIATE RECORD

Season	Team	G	Min.	FGM	FGA	Pct.	FTM	FTA	Pct.	Reb.	Pts.	Avg.
78-79	Los Medanos	31	. . .	. . .	. . .	. . .	. . .	. . .	. . .	. . .	781	25.2
79-80	Chabot	35	1179	319	549	.581	158	217	.728	215	796	22.7
80-81	Oregon State	28	790	68	141	.482	61	91	.670	119	197	7.0
81-82	Oregon State	30	1106	151	292	.517	146	196	.745	163	448	14.9
	Junior college totals	66	. . .	. . .	. . .	. . .	. . .	. . .	. . .	. . .	1577	23.9
	Four-year-college totals	58	1896	219	433	.506	207	287	.721	282	645	11.1

NBA REGULAR-SEASON RECORD

Season	Team	G	Min.	FGM	FGA	Pct.	FTM	FTA	Pct.	REBOUNDS Off.	REBOUNDS Def.	REBOUNDS Tot.	Ast.	PF	Dq.	Stl.	Blk.	TO	Pts.	Avg.
82-83	Golden State	75	1416	145	303	.479	79	113	.699	69	152	221	253	141	1	116	7	99	369	4.9
83-84	Golden State	82	2573	360	730	.493	186	259	.718	132	173	305	401	176	1	162	12	143	907	11.1
84-85	Golden State	79	2258	246	546	.451	144	192	.750	87	159	246	369	136	1	161	13	138	640	8.1
85-86	Golden State	36	413	51	136	.375	40	54	.741	25	37	62	43	23	0	24	1	15	144	4.0
86-87	Golden State									Did not play.										
87-88	Houston	52	399	50	108	.463	32	41	.780	20	18	38	59	31	0	38	1	33	132	2.5
88-89	New Jersey	82	2532	309	676	.457	212	269	.788	100	255	355	604	132	1	181	5	181	843	10.3
89-90	New Jersey	82	2355	237	573	.414	172	214	.804	90	175	265	385	182	0	172	8	138	648	7.9
90-91	N.J.-Mil.	74	1008	96	207	.464	68	94	.723	21	91	112	165	75	0	85	2	58	260	3.5
91-92	Milwaukee	81	1420	103	239	.431	81	115	.704	63	121	184	294	86	0	97	10	79	287	3.5
	Totals	643	14374	1597	3518	.454	1014	1351	.751	607	1181	1788	2573	982	4	1036	59	884	4230	6.6

Three-point field goals: 1982-83, 0-for-4. 1983-84, 1-for-6 (.167). 1984-85, 4-for-20 (.200). 1985-86, 2-for-7 (.286). 1987-88, 0-for-7. 1988-89, 13-for-37 (.351). 1989-90, 2-for-13 (.154). 1990-91, 0-for-5. 1991-92, 0-for-7. Totals, 22-for-106 (.208).

NBA PLAYOFF RECORD

Season	Team	G	Min.	FGM	FGA	Pct.	FTM	FTA	Pct.	REBOUNDS Off.	REBOUNDS Def.	REBOUNDS Tot.	Ast.	PF	Dq.	Stl.	Blk.	TO	Pts.	Avg.
87-88	Houston	1	1	0	0	. . .	2	2	1.000	0	1	1	1	0	0	1	0	0	2	2.0
90-91	Milwaukee	1	7	1	1	1.000	0	1	.000	1	0	1	2	1	0	0	0	1	2	2.0
	Totals	2	8	1	1	1.000	2	3	.667	1	1	2	3	1	0	1	0	1	4	2.0

COOK, ANTHONY
F/C, NUGGETS

PERSONAL: Born March 19, 1967, in Los Angeles. . . . 6-9/215. . . . Full name: Anthony Lacquise Cook.
HIGH SCHOOL: Van Nuys (Calif.).
COLLEGE: Arizona.

TRANSACTIONS/CAREER NOTES: Selected by Phoenix Suns in first round (24th pick overall) of 1989 NBA Draft. . . . Played in Greece (1989-90). . . . Draft rights traded by Suns to Detroit Pistons for Michael Williams and draft rights to Kenny Battle (June 27, 1989). . . . Traded by Pistons to Denver Nuggets for future second-round draft choice (September 28, 1990).

Season Team	G	Min.	FGM	FGA	Pct.	FTM	FTA	Pct.	Reb.	Pts.	Avg.
COLLEGIATE RECORD											
85-86 — Arizona	32	833	73	146	.500	48	73	.658	137	194	6.1
86-87 — Arizona	30	969	118	246	.480	54	100	.540	217	290	9.7
87-88 — Arizona	38	1169	201	325	.618	126	176	.716	269	528	13.9
88-89 — Arizona	33	1066	237	377	.629	104	166	.627	238	578	17.5
Totals	133	4037	629	1094	.575	332	515	.645	861	1590	12.0

Three-point field goals: 1987-88, 0-for-1.

NBA REGULAR-SEASON RECORD

Season Team	G	Min.	FGM	FGA	Pct.	FTM	FTA	Pct.	Off.	Def.	Tot.	Ast.	PF	Dq.	Stl.	Blk.	TO	Pts.	Avg.
									— REBOUNDS —										
90-91 — Denver	58	1121	118	283	.417	71	129	.550	134	192	326	26	100	1	35	72	50	307	5.3
91-92 — Denver	22	115	15	25	.600	4	6	.667	13	21	34	2	10	0	5	4	3	34	1.5
Totals	80	1236	133	308	.432	75	135	.556	147	213	360	28	110	1	40	76	53	341	4.3

Three-point field goals: 1990-91, 0-for-3.

COOPER, WAYNE
C, TRAIL BLAZERS

PERSONAL: Born November 16, 1956, in Milan, Ga. . . . 6-10/220. . . . Full name: Artis Wayne Cooper.
HIGH SCHOOL: Telfair County (McRae, Ga.).
COLLEGE: New Orleans.
TRANSACTIONS/CAREER NOTES: Selected by Golden State Warriors in second round (40th pick overall) of 1978 NBA Draft. . . . Traded by Warriors with 1981 second-round draft choice to Utah Jazz for Bernard King (September 11, 1980). . . . Traded by Jazz with Allan Bristow to Dallas Mavericks for Bill Robinzine (August 20, 1981). . . . Traded by Mavericks with 1985 first-round draft choice to Portland Trail Blazers for Kelvin Ransey (June 28, 1982). . . . Traded by Trail Blazers with Fat Lever, Calvin Natt, 1984 second-round draft choice and 1985 first-round draft choice to Denver Nuggets for Kiki Vandeweghe (June 7, 1984). . . . Signed as unrestricted free agent by Trail Blazers (July 24, 1989).

COLLEGIATE RECORD

Season Team	G	Min.	FGM	FGA	Pct.	FTM	FTA	Pct.	Reb.	Pts.	Avg.
74-75 — New Orleans	17	. . .	16	33	.485	3	4	.750	52	35	2.1
75-76 — New Orleans	26	. . .	140	278	.504	34	47	.723	244	314	12.1
76-77 — New Orleans	28	. . .	166	368	.451	38	55	.691	284	370	13.2
77-78 — New Orleans	27	. . .	202	377	.536	86	111	.775	343	490	18.1
Totals	98	. . .	524	1056	.496	161	217	.742	923	1209	12.3

NBA REGULAR-SEASON RECORD

Season Team	G	Min.	FGM	FGA	Pct.	FTM	FTA	Pct.	Off.	Def.	Tot.	Ast.	PF	Dq.	Stl.	Blk.	TO	Pts.	Avg.
									— REBOUNDS —										
78-79 — Golden State	65	795	128	293	.437	41	61	.672	90	190	280	21	118	0	7	44	52	297	4.6
79-80 — Golden State	79	1781	367	750	.489	136	181	.751	202	305	507	42	246	5	20	79	140	871	11.0
80-81 — Utah	71	1420	213	471	.452	62	90	.689	166	274	440	52	219	8	18	51	77	489	6.9
81-82 — Dallas	76	1818	281	669	.420	119	160	.744	200	350	550	115	285	10	37	106	88	682	9.0
82-83 — Portland	80	2099	320	723	.443	135	197	.685	214	397	611	116	318	5	27	136	162	775	9.7
83-84 — Portland	81	1662	304	663	.459	185	230	.804	176	300	476	76	247	2	26	106	110	793	9.8
84-85 — Denver	80	2031	404	856	.472	161	235	.685	229	402	631	86	304	2	28	197	149	969	12.1
85-86 — Denver	78	2112	422	906	.466	174	219	.795	190	420	610	81	315	6	42	227	117	1021	13.1
86-87 — Denver	69	1561	235	524	.448	79	109	.725	162	311	473	68	257	5	13	101	78	549	8.0
87-88 — Denver	45	865	118	270	.437	50	67	.746	98	172	270	30	145	3	12	94	59	286	6.4
88-89 — Denver	79	1864	220	444	.496	79	106	.745	212	407	619	78	302	7	36	211	73	520	6.6
89-90 — Portland	79	1176	138	304	.454	25	39	.641	118	221	339	44	211	2	18	95	39	301	3.8
90-91 — Portland	67	746	57	145	.393	33	42	.786	54	134	188	22	120	0	7	61	22	147	2.2
91-92 — Portland	35	344	35	82	.427	7	11	.636	38	63	101	21	57	0	4	27	15	77	2.2
Totals	984	20274	3242	7100	.457	1286	1747	.736	2149	3946	6095	852	3144	55	295	1535	1181	7777	7.9

Three-point field goals: 1979-80, 1-for-4 (.250). 1980-81, 1-for-3 (.333). 1981-82, 1-for-8 (.125). 1982-83, 0-for-5. 1983-84, 0-for-7. 1984-85, 0-for-2. 1985-86, 3-for-7 (.429). 1986-87, 0-for-3. 1987-88, 0-for-1. 1988-89, 1-for-4 (.250). 1989-90, 0-for-3. 1990-91, 0-for-1. Totals, 7-for-48 (.146).

NBA PLAYOFF RECORD

Season Team	G	Min.	FGM	FGA	Pct.	FTM	FTA	Pct.	Off.	Def.	Tot.	Ast.	PF	Dq.	Stl.	Blk.	TO	Pts.	Avg.
									— REBOUNDS —										
82-83 — Portland	7	228	36	74	.486	15	17	.882	24	32	56	9	33	3	2	8	17	87	12.4
83-84 — Portland	5	104	10	27	.370	4	8	.500	11	9	20	4	14	0	1	4	5	24	4.8
84-85 — Denver	15	321	67	143	.469	30	40	.750	34	59	93	20	52	0	8	36	19	164	10.9
85-86 — Denver	8	154	24	56	.429	15	22	.682	11	29	40	7	31	2	2	5	11	63	7.9
86-87 — Denver	3	41	5	12	.417	2	2	1.000	6	11	17	2	9	0	0	1	1	12	4.0
87-88 — Denver	9	96	8	23	.348	2	2	1.000	16	17	33	6	19	0	3	8	4	18	2.0
88-89 — Denver	3	44	6	12	.500	0	0	. . .	4	9	13	2	10	0	1	2	0	12	4.0
89-90 — Portland	18	248	19	47	.404	10	19	.526	25	46	71	5	40	0	5	29	5	48	2.7
90-91 — Portland	3	13	1	2	.500	0	0	. . .	1	4	5	1	2	0	0	0	1	2	0.7
91-92 — Portland	3	27	2	4	.500	0	0	. . .	1	7	8	0	4	0	0	3	1	4	1.3
Totals	74	1276	178	400	.445	78	110	.709	133	223	356	56	214	5	22	96	64	434	5.9

Three-point field goals: 1985-86, 0-for-1.

COPA, TOM
F

PERSONAL: Born October 30, 1964, in Robbinsdale, Minn. . . . 6-10/275. . . . Full name: Thomas James Copa.
HIGH SCHOOL: Coon Rapids (Minn.).
COLLEGE: Marquette.
TRANSACTIONS/CAREER NOTES: Never drafted by an NBA franchise. . . . Did not play basketball (1987-88). . . . Played in Belgium (1988-89 through 1990-91). . . . Signed as free agent by San Antonio Spurs (August 8, 1991).

COLLEGIATE RECORD

Season	Team	G	Min.	FGM	FGA	Pct.	FTM	FTA	Pct.	Reb.	Pts.	Avg.
83-84 —Marquette		30	...	101	201	.502	54	83	.651	134	256	8.5
84-85 —Marquette		31	...	107	208	.514	49	85	.576	171	263	8.5
85-86 —Marquette		30	543	89	185	.481	61	89	.685	121	239	8.0
86-87 —Marquette		29	661	98	194	.505	29	51	.569	136	225	7.8
Totals		120	...	395	788	.501	193	308	.627	562	983	8.2

NBA REGULAR-SEASON RECORD

										— REBOUNDS —								
Season	Team	G	Min.	FGM	FGA	Pct.	FTM	FTA	Pct.	Off.	Def.	Tot.	Ast.	PF	Dq.	Stl.	Blk.	TO	Pts.	Avg.
91-92 —San Antonio.	33	132	22	40	.550	4	13	.308	14	22	36	3	29	0	2	6	8	48	1.5

COPELAND, LANARD
G

PERSONAL: Born July 16, 1965, in Atlanta. . . . 6-6/210. . . .
Name pronounced La-NARD.
HIGH SCHOOL: Booker T. Washington (Atlanta).
COLLEGE: Georgia State.

TRANSACTIONS/CAREER NOTES: Never drafted by an NBA franchise. . . . Signed as free agent by Philadelphia 76ers (August 11, 1989). . . . Played in Continental Basketball Association with Tulsa Zone and Rapid City Thrillers (1990-91). . . . Signed as unrestricted free agent by Los Angeles Clippers (August 30, 1991). . . . Waived by Clippers (December 3, 1991).

COLLEGIATE RECORD

Season	Team	G	Min.	FGM	FGA	Pct.	FTM	FTA	Pct.	Reb.	Pts.	Avg.
85-86 —Georgia State		6	42	7	15	.467	8	11	.727	9	22	3.7
86-87 —Georgia State		27	563	99	217	.456	25	39	.641	108	226	8.4
87-88 —Georgia State		28	654	119	290	.410	25	35	.714	116	307	11.0
88-89 —Georgia State		28	779	171	398	.430	51	75	.680	113	428	15.3
Totals		89	2038	396	920	.430	109	160	.681	346	983	11.0

Three-point field goals: 1986-87, 3-for-9 (.333). 1987-88, 44-for-111 (.396). 1988-89, 35-for-111 (.315). Totals, 82-for-231 (.355).

NBA REGULAR-SEASON RECORD

										— REBOUNDS —								
Season	Team	G	Min.	FGM	FGA	Pct.	FTM	FTA	Pct.	Off.	Def.	Tot.	Ast.	PF	Dq.	Stl.	Blk.	TO	Pts.	Avg.
89-90 —Philadelphia.	23	110	31	68	.456	11	14	.786	4	6	10	9	12	0	1	1	...	74	3.2
91-92 —L.A. Clippers	10	48	7	23	.304	2	2	1.000	1	6	7	5	5	0	2	0	4	16	1.6
Totals	33	158	38	91	.418	13	16	.813	5	12	17	14	17	0	3	1	4	90	2.7

Three-point field goals: 1989-90, 1-for-5 (.200). 1991-92, 0-for-2. Totals, 1-for-7 (.143).

NBA PLAYOFF RECORD

										— REBOUNDS —								
Season	Team	G	Min.	FGM	FGA	Pct.	FTM	FTA	Pct.	Off.	Def.	Tot.	Ast.	PF	Dq.	Stl.	Blk.	TO	Pts.	Avg.
89-90 —Philadelphia.	4	9	2	6	.333	0	0	...	0	1	1	0	1	0	0	0	1	4	1.0

CBA REGULAR-SEASON RECORD

				2-POINT			3-POINT								
Season	Team	G	Min.	FGM	FGA	Pct.	FGM	FGA	Pct.	FTM	FTA	Pct.	Reb.	Ast.	Pts.	Avg.
90-91 —Tulsa-R.C.	16	332	57	134	.425	2	5	.400	24	34	.706	37	18	144	9.0

CORBIN, TYRONE
F, JAZZ

PERSONAL: Born December 31, 1962, in Columbia, S.C. . . . 6-6/222.
. . . Full name: Tyrone Kennedy Corbin.
HIGH SCHOOL: A. C. Flora (Columbia, S.C.).
COLLEGE: DePaul.

TRANSACTIONS/CAREER NOTES: Selected by San Antonio Spurs in second round (35th pick overall) of 1985 NBA Draft. . . . Waived by Spurs (January 21, 1987). . . . Signed as free agent by Cleveland Cavaliers (January 24, 1987). . . . Traded by Cavaliers with Kevin Johnson, Mark West, 1988 first- and second-round draft choices and 1989 second-round draft choice to Phoenix Suns for Larry Nance, Mike Sanders and 1988 first-round draft choice (February 25, 1988). . . . Selected by Minnesota Timberwolves from Suns in NBA expansion draft (June 15, 1989). . . . Traded by Timberwolves to Utah Jazz for Thurl Bailey and 1992 second-round draft choice (November 25, 1991).

COLLEGIATE RECORD

Season	Team	G	Min.	FGM	FGA	Pct.	FTM	FTA	Pct.	Reb.	Pts.	Avg.
81-82 —DePaul		28	602	43	103	.417	56	78	.718	172	142	5.1
82-83 —DePaul		33	1060	124	263	.471	102	132	.773	262	350	10.6
83-84 —DePaul		30	1070	166	316	.525	93	125	.744	223	425	14.2
84-85 —DePaul		29	1004	189	354	.534	83	102	.814	236	461	15.9
Totals		120	3736	522	1036	.504	334	437	.764	893	1378	11.5

NBA REGULAR-SEASON RECORD

										— REBOUNDS —								
Season	Team	G	Min.	FGM	FGA	Pct.	FTM	FTA	Pct.	Off.	Def.	Tot.	Ast.	PF	Dq.	Stl.	Blk.	TO	Pts.	Avg.
85-86 —San Antonio.	16	174	27	64	.422	10	14	.714	11	14	25	11	21	0	11	2	12	64	4.0
86-87 —S.A.-Clev.	63	1170	156	381	.409	91	124	.734	88	127	215	97	129	0	55	5	66	404	6.4
87-88 —Clev.-Phoe.	84	1739	257	525	.490	110	138	.797	127	223	350	115	181	2	72	18	104	625	7.4
88-89 —Phoenix	77	1655	245	454	.540	141	179	.788	176	222	398	118	222	2	82	13	92	631	8.2
89-90 —Minnesota	82	3011	521	1083	.481	161	209	.770	219	385	604	216	288	5	175	41	143	1203	14.7
90-91 —Minnesota	82	3196	587	1311	.448	296	371	.798	185	404	589	347	257	3	162	53	209	1472	18.0
91-92 —Min.-Utah	80	2207	303	630	.481	174	201	.866	163	309	472	140	193	1	82	20	97	780	9.8
Totals	484	13152	2096	4448	.471	983	1236	.795	969	1684	2653	1044	1291	13	639	152	723	5179	10.7

Three-point field goals: 1985-86, 0-for-1. 1986-87, 1-for-4 (.250). 1987-88, 1-for-6 (.167). 1988-89, 0-for-2. 1989-90, 0-for-11. 1990-91, 2-for-10 (.200). 1991-92, 0-for-4. Totals, 4-for-38 (.105).

— 41 —

NBA PLAYOFF RECORD

Season Team	G	Min.	FGM	FGA	Pct.	FTM	FTA	Pct.	Off.	Def.	Tot.	Ast.	PF	Dq.	Stl.	Blk.	TO	Pts.	Avg.
									— REBOUNDS —										
85-86 —San Antonio .	1	14	0	4	.000	0	0	. . .	0	1	1	1	0	0	0	0	0	0	0.0
88-89 —Phoenix	12	310	45	86	.523	19	25	.760	43	42	85	26	37	0	24	4	14	109	9.1
91-92 —Utah	16	447	69	137	.504	42	54	.778	39	49	88	17	45	0	12	3	17	180	11.3
Totals	29	771	114	227	.502	61	79	.772	82	92	174	44	82	0	36	7	31	289	10.0

Three-point field goals: 1991-92, 0-for-2.

CORCHIANI, CHRIS
G, MAGIC

PERSONAL: Born March 28, 1968, in Coral Gables, Fla. . . . 6-1/186. . . . Full name: Christopher Corchiani.
HIGH SCHOOL: Hialeah Miami Lakes (Hialeah, Fla.).
COLLEGE: North Carolina State.

TRANSACTIONS/CAREER NOTES: Selected by Orlando Magic in second round (36th pick overall) of 1991 NBA Draft. . . . Waived by Magic (October 28, 1991). . . . Re-signed by Magic (January 4, 1992).

COLLEGIATE RECORD

NOTES: Led NCAA Division I with 9.65 assists per game (1991).

Season Team	G	Min.	FGM	FGA	Pct.	FTM	FTA	Pct.	Reb.	Pts.	Avg.
87-88 —North Carolina State...............	32	788	61	120	.508	60	72	.833	44	202	6.3
88-89 —North Carolina State...............	31	1015	101	204	.495	99	123	.805	78	324	10.5
89-90 —North Carolina State...............	30	1125	131	311	.421	99	119	.832	63	394	13.1
90-91 —North Carolina State...............	31	1169	160	343	.466	134	163	.822	78	505	16.3
Totals	124	4097	453	978	.463	392	477	.822	263	1425	11.5

Three-point field goals: 1987-88, 20-for-40 (.500). 1988-89, 23-for-54 (.426). 1989-90, 33-for-82 (.402). 1990-91, 51-for-135 (.378). Totals, 127-for-311 (.408).

NBA REGULAR-SEASON RECORD

Season Team	G	Min.	FGM	FGA	Pct.	FTM	FTA	Pct.	Off.	Def.	Tot.	Ast.	PF	Dq.	Stl.	Blk.	TO	Pts.	Avg.
									— REBOUNDS —										
91-92 —Orlando	51	741	77	193	.399	91	104	.875	18	60	78	141	94	0	45	2	74	255	5.0

Three-point field goals: 1991-92, 10-for-37 (.270).

CROWDER, COREY
G/F, JAZZ

PERSONAL: Born April 13, 1969, in Carrollton, Ga. . . . 6-5/214. . . . Full name: Jonathan Corey Crowder.
HIGH SCHOOL: Carrollton (Ga.).
COLLEGE: Kentucky Wesleyan.

TRANSACTIONS/CAREER NOTES: Never drafted by an NBA franchise. . . . Signed as free agent by Utah Jazz (October 3, 1991).

COLLEGIATE RECORD

NOTES: Member of NCAA Division II championship team (1990).

Season Team	G	Min.	FGM	FGA	Pct.	FTM	FTA	Pct.	Reb.	Pts.	Avg.
87-88 —Kentucky Wesleyan................	24	635	137	296	.463	61	82	.744	129	398	16.6
88-89 —Kentucky Wesleyan................	31	924	213	469	.454	103	151	.682	194	592	19.1
89-90 —Kentucky Wesleyan................	33	864	217	376	.577	135	183	.738	239	613	18.6
90-91 —Kentucky Wesleyan................	30	899	237	451	.525	130	193	.674	244	679	22.6
Totals	118	3322	804	1592	.505	429	609	.704	806	2282	19.3

Three-point field goals: 1987-88, 63-for-153 (.412). 1988-89, 63-for-186 (.339). 1989-90, 44-for-94 (.468). 1990-91, 75-for-171 (.439). Totals, 245-for-604 (.406).

NBA REGULAR-SEASON RECORD

Season Team	G	Min.	FGM	FGA	Pct.	FTM	FTA	Pct.	Off.	Def.	Tot.	Ast.	PF	Dq.	Stl.	Blk.	TO	Pts.	Avg.
									— REBOUNDS —										
91-92 —Utah	51	328	43	112	.384	15	18	.833	16	25	41	17	35	0	7	2	13	114	2.2

Three-point field goals: 1991-92, 13-for-30 (.433).

NBA PLAYOFF RECORD

Season Team	G	Min.	FGM	FGA	Pct.	FTM	FTA	Pct.	Off.	Def.	Tot.	Ast.	PF	Dq.	Stl.	Blk.	TO	Pts.	Avg.
									— REBOUNDS —										
91-92 —Utah	4	12	5	9	.556	0	1	.000	1	1	2	1	1	0	1	0	2	10	2.5

Three-point field goals: 1991-92, 0-for-2.

CUMMINGS, TERRY
F, SPURS

PERSONAL: Born March 15, 1961, in Chicago. . . . 6-9/235. . . . Full name: Robert Terrell Cummings.
HIGH SCHOOL: Carver (Chicago).
COLLEGE: DePaul.

TRANSACTIONS/CAREER NOTES: Selected as undergraduate by San Diego Clippers in first round (second pick overall) of 1982 NBA Draft. . . . Clippers franchise moved from San Diego to Los Angeles for 1984-85 season. . . . Traded by Clippers with Craig Hodges and Ricky Pierce to Milwaukee Bucks for Marques Johnson, Harvey Catchings, Junior Bridgeman and cash (September 29, 1984). . . . Traded by Bucks with future considerations to San Antonio Spurs for Alvin Robertson, Greg Anderson and future considerations (May 28, 1989).

COLLEGIATE RECORD

NOTES: THE SPORTING NEWS All-America first team (1982).

Season	Team	G	Min.	FGM	FGA	Pct.	FTM	FTA	Pct.	Reb.	Pts.	Avg.
79-80	—DePaul	28	...	154	303	.508	89	107	.832	263	397	14.2
80-81	—DePaul	29	994	151	303	.498	75	100	.750	260	377	13.0
81-82	—DePaul	28	1031	244	430	.567	136	180	.756	334	624	22.3
Totals		85		549	1036	.530	300	387	.775	857	1398	16.4

NBA REGULAR-SEASON RECORD

HONORS: NBA Rookie of the Year (1983).... All-NBA second team (1985).... All-NBA third team (1989).... NBA All-Rookie team (1983).

										— REBOUNDS —										
Season	Team	G	Min.	FGM	FGA	Pct.	FTM	FTA	Pct.	Off.	Def.	Tot.	Ast.	PF	Dq.	Stl.	Blk.	TO	Pts.	Avg.
82-83	—San Diego	70	2531	684	1309	.523	292	412	.709	303	441	744	177	294	10	129	62	204	1660	23.7
83-84	—San Diego	81	2907	737	1491	.494	380	528	.720	323	454	777	139	298	6	92	57	218	1854	22.9
84-85	—Milwaukee	79	2722	759	1532	.495	343	463	.741	244	472	716	228	264	4	117	67	190	1861	23.6
85-86	—Milwaukee	82	2669	681	1438	.474	265	404	.656	222	472	694	193	283	4	121	51	191	1627	19.8
86-87	—Milwaukee	82	2770	729	1426	.511	249	376	.662	214	486	700	229	296	3	129	81	172	1707	20.8
87-88	—Milwaukee	76	2629	675	1392	.485	270	406	.665	184	369	553	181	274	6	78	46	170	1621	21.3
88-89	—Milwaukee	80	2824	730	1563	.467	362	460	.787	281	369	650	198	265	5	106	72	201	1829	22.9
89-90	—San Antonio	81	2821	728	1532	.475	343	440	.780	226	451	677	219	286	1	110	52	202	1818	22.4
90-91	—San Antonio	67	2195	503	1039	.484	164	240	.683	194	327	521	157	225	5	61	30	131	1177	17.6
91-92	—San Antonio	70	2149	514	1053	.488	177	247	.711	247	384	631	102	210	4	58	34	115	1210	17.3
Totals		768	26217	6740	13775	.489	2845	3978	.715	2438	4225	6663	1823	2695	48	1001	552	1794	16364	21.3

Three-point field goals: 1982-83, 0-for-1. 1983-84, 0-for-3. 1984-85, 0-for-1. 1985-86, 0-for-2. 1986-87, 0-for-3. 1987-88, 1-for-3 (.333). 1988-89, 7-for-15 (.467). 1989-90, 19-for-59 (.322). 1990-91, 7-for-33 (.212). 1991-92, 5-for-13 (.385). Totals, 39-for-133 (.293).

NBA PLAYOFF RECORD

										— REBOUNDS —										
Season	Team	G	Min.	FGM	FGA	Pct.	FTM	FTA	Pct.	Off.	Def.	Tot.	Ast.	PF	Dq.	Stl.	Blk.	TO	Pts.	Avg.
84-85	—Milwaukee	8	311	86	149	.577	48	58	.828	21	49	70	20	33	1	12	7	26	220	27.5
85-86	—Milwaukee	14	510	130	253	.514	43	62	.694	33	105	138	42	52	0	20	16	39	303	21.6
86-87	—Milwaukee	12	443	105	215	.488	57	83	.687	29	66	95	28	51	1	12	13	15	267	22.3
87-88	—Milwaukee	5	193	50	89	.562	29	44	.659	12	27	39	13	16	0	9	3	12	129	25.8
88-89	—Milwaukee	5	124	25	69	.362	14	16	.875	19	14	33	7	16	0	3	0	4	64	12.8
89-90	—San Antonio	10	375	103	195	.528	42	52	.808	31	63	94	22	39	0	7	4	19	249	24.9
90-91	—San Antonio	4	124	25	49	.510	9	18	.500	14	23	37	4	13	0	3	2	9	59	14.8
91-92	—San Antonio	3	122	34	66	.515	10	20	.500	15	19	34	7	9	0	4	4	7	78	26.0
Totals		61	2202	558	1085	.514	252	353	.714	174	366	540	143	229	2	70	49	131	1369	22.4

Three-point field goals: 1984-85, 0-for-1. 1988-89, 0-for-1. 1989-90, 1-for-5 (.200). 1990-91, 0-for-1. 1991-92, 0-for-1. Totals, 1-for-9 (.111).

NBA ALL-STAR GAME RECORD

									— REBOUNDS —								
Season	Team	Min.	FGM	FGA	Pct.	FTM	FTA	Pct.	Off.	Def.	Tot.	Ast.	PF	Dq.	Stl.	Blk.	TO	Pts.
1985	—Milwaukee	16	7	17	.412	3	4	.750	4	3	7	0	1	0	0	1	0	17
1989	—Milwaukee	19	4	9	.444	2	2	1.000	2	3	5	1	4	0	3	1	0	10
Totals		35	11	26	.423	5	6	.833	6	6	12	1	5	0	3	2	0	27

CURRY, DELL
G, HORNETS

PERSONAL: Born June 25, 1964, in Harrisonburg, Va.... 6-5/200.... Full name: Wardell Stephen Curry.
HIGH SCHOOL: Fort Defiance (Va.).
COLLEGE: Virginia Tech.
TRANSACTIONS/CAREER NOTES: Selected by Utah Jazz in first round (15th pick overall) of 1986 NBA Draft. ... Traded by Jazz with Kent Benson and future second-round draft considerations to Cleveland Cavaliers for Darryl Dawkins, Mel Turpin and future second-round draft considerations (October 8, 1987).... Selected by Charlotte Hornets from Cavaliers in NBA expansion draft (June 23, 1988).

COLLEGIATE RECORD

NOTES: THE SPORTING NEWS All-America second team (1986).

Season	Team	G	Min.	FGM	FGA	Pct.	FTM	FTA	Pct.	Reb.	Pts.	Avg.
82-83	—Virginia Tech	32	1024	198	417	.475	68	80	.850	95	464	14.5
83-84	—Virginia Tech	35	1166	293	561	.522	88	116	.759	143	674	19.3
84-85	—Virginia Tech	29	968	225	467	.482	75	99	.758	169	529	18.2
85-86	—Virginia Tech	30	1117	305	577	.529	112	142	.789	203	722	24.1
Totals		126	4275	1021	2022	.505	343	437	.785	610	2389	19.0

Three-point field goals: 1984-85, 4-for-7 (.571).

NBA REGULAR-SEASON RECORD

										— REBOUNDS —										
Season	Team	G	Min.	FGM	FGA	Pct.	FTM	FTA	Pct.	Off.	Def.	Tot.	Ast.	PF	Dq.	Stl.	Blk.	TO	Pts.	Avg.
86-87	—Utah	67	636	139	326	.426	30	38	.789	30	48	78	58	86	0	27	4	44	325	4.9
87-88	—Cleveland	79	1499	340	742	.458	79	101	.782	43	123	166	149	128	0	94	22	108	787	10.0
88-89	—Charlotte	48	813	256	521	.491	40	46	.870	26	78	104	50	68	0	42	4	44	571	11.9
89-90	—Charlotte	67	1860	461	990	.466	96	104	.923	31	137	168	159	148	0	98	26	100	1070	16.0
90-91	—Charlotte	76	1515	337	715	.471	96	114	.842	47	152	199	166	125	0	75	25	80	802	10.6
91-92	—Charlotte	77	2020	504	1038	.486	127	152	.836	57	202	259	177	156	1	93	20	134	1209	15.7
Totals		414	8343	2037	4332	.470	468	555	.843	234	740	974	759	711	1	429	101	510	4764	11.5

Three-point field goals: 1986-87, 17-for-60 (.283). 1987-88, 28-for-81 (.346). 1988-89, 19-for-55 (.345). 1989-90, 52-for-147 (.354). 1990-91, 32-for-86 (.372). 1991-92, 74-for-183 (.404). Totals, 222-for-612 (.363).

Season	Team	G	Min.	FGM	FGA	Pct.	FTM	FTA	Pct.	Off.	Def.	Tot.	Ast.	PF	Dq.	Stl.	Blk.	TO	Pts.	Avg.
86-87	—Utah.............	2	4	0	3	.000	0	1	.000	0	0	0	0	1	0	0	0	0	0	0.0
87-88	—Cleveland.....	2	17	1	4	.250	0	0	...	1	0	1	2	1	0	0	1	0	2	1.0
Totals	....	4	21	1	7	.143	0	1	.000	1	0	1	2	2	0	0	1	0	2	0.5

Three-point field goals: 1986-87, 0-for-1. 1987-88, 0-for-1. Totals, 0-for-2.

DAILEY, QUINTIN
G

PERSONAL: Born January 22, 1961, in Baltimore.... 6-3/180.
HIGH SCHOOL: Cardinal Gibbons (Baltimore).
COLLEGE: San Francisco.
TRANSACTIONS/CAREER NOTES: Selected as undergraduate by Chicago Bulls in first round (seventh pick overall) of 1982 NBA Draft.... Signed as free agent by Los Angeles Clippers (December 29, 1986); Bulls waived their right of first refusal.... Played in Continental Basketball Association with Mississippi Jets (1986-87), Sioux Falls Skyforce (1989-90) and Yakima Sun Kings (1991-92).... Signed as unrestricted free agent by Los Angeles Lakers (September 12, 1989).... Waived by Lakers (October 13, 1989).... Signed by Seattle SuperSonics to first of two consecutive 10-day contracts (February 2, 1990).... Re-signed by SuperSonics for remainder of season (February 22, 1990).... Signed as unrestricted free agent by SuperSonics (October 1, 1990).... Waived by SuperSonics (December 10, 1991).

COLLEGIATE RECORD

NOTES: THE SPORTING NEWS All-America first team (1982).

Season	Team	G	Min.	FGM	FGA	Pct.	FTM	FTA	Pct.	Reb.	Pts.	Avg.
79-80	—San Francisco........................	29	...	154	292	.527	85	134	.634	107	393	13.6
80-81	—San Francisco........................	31	...	267	467	.572	159	206	.772	170	693	22.4
81-82	—San Francisco........................	30	1138	286	524	.546	183	232	.789	156	755	25.2
Totals	....	90	...	707	1283	.551	427	572	.747	433	1841	20.5

NBA REGULAR-SEASON RECORD

HONORS: NBA All-Rookie team (1983).

Season	Team	G	Min.	FGM	FGA	Pct.	FTM	FTA	Pct.	Off.	Def.	Tot.	Ast.	PF	Dq.	Stl.	Blk.	TO	Pts.	Avg.
82-83	—Chicago.......	76	2081	470	1008	.466	206	282	.731	87	173	260	280	248	7	72	10	205	1151	15.1
83-84	—Chicago.......	82	2449	583	1229	.474	321	396	.811	61	174	235	254	218	4	109	11	220	1491	18.2
84-85	—Chicago.......	79	2101	525	1111	.473	205	251	.817	57	151	208	191	192	0	71	5	154	1262	16.0
85-86	—Chicago.......	35	723	203	470	.432	163	198	.823	20	48	68	67	86	0	22	5	67	569	16.3
86-87	—L.A. Clippers	49	924	200	491	.407	119	155	.768	34	49	83	79	113	4	43	8	71	520	10.6
87-88	—L.A. Clippers	67	1282	328	755	.434	243	313	.776	62	92	154	109	128	1	69	4	123	901	13.4
88-89	—L.A. Clippers	69	1722	448	964	.465	217	286	.759	69	135	204	154	152	0	90	6	122	1114	16.1
89-90	—Seattle........	30	491	97	240	.404	52	66	.788	18	33	51	34	63	0	12	0	34	247	8.2
90-91	—Seattle........	30	299	73	155	.471	38	62	.613	11	21	32	16	25	0	7	1	19	184	6.1
91-92	—Seattle.........	11	98	9	37	.243	13	16	.813	2	10	12	4	6	0	5	1	10	31	2.8
Totals	....	528	12170	2936	6460	.454	1577	2025	.779	421	886	1307	1188	1231	16	500	51	1025	7470	14.1

Three-point field goals: 1982-83, 5-for-25 (.200). 1983-84, 4-for-32 (.125). 1984-85, 7-for-30 (.233). 1985-86, 0-for-8. 1986-87, 1-for-10 (.100). 1987-88, 2-for-12 (.167). 1988-89, 1-for-9 (.111). 1989-90, 1-for-5 (.200). 1990-91, 0-for-1. 1991-92, 0-for-1. Totals, 21-for-133 (.158).

NBA PLAYOFF RECORD

Season	Team	G	Min.	FGM	FGA	Pct.	FTM	FTA	Pct.	Off.	Def.	Tot.	Ast.	PF	Dq.	Stl.	Blk.	TO	Pts.	Avg.
84-85	—Chicago.......	4	129	26	62	.419	8	11	.727	5	8	13	11	9	0	4	0	5	61	15.3

Three-point field goals: 1984-85, 1-for-7 (.143).

CBA REGULAR-SEASON RECORD

Season	Team	G	Min.	2-POINT			3-POINT			FTM	FTA	Pct.	Reb.	Ast.	Pts.	Avg.
				FGM	FGA	Pct.	FGM	FGA	Pct.							
86-87	—Mississippi.......	8	220	54	99	.545	0	2	.000	35	47	.745	17	11	143	17.9
89-90	—Sioux Falls.......	25	578	147	336	.438	2	6	.333	89	119	.748	80	71	389	15.6
91-92	—Yakima............	10	175	40	95	.421	0	1	.000	19	24	.792	18	11	99	9.9
Totals	....	43	973	241	530	.455	2	9	.222	143	190	.753	115	93	631	14.7

DAUGHERTY, BRAD
C, CAVALIERS

PERSONAL: Born October 19, 1965, in Black Mountain, N.C.... 7-0/263.... Full name: Bradley Lee Daugherty.
HIGH SCHOOL: Charles D. Owen (Swannanoa, N.C.).
COLLEGE: North Carolina.
TRANSACTIONS/CAREER NOTES: Selected by Cleveland Cavaliers in first round (first pick overall) of 1986 NBA Draft.

COLLEGIATE RECORD

NOTES: THE SPORTING NEWS All-America second team (1986).... Led NCAA Division I with .648 field-goal percentage (1986).

Season	Team	G	Min.	FGM	FGA	Pct.	FTM	FTA	Pct.	Reb.	Pts.	Avg.
82-83	—North Carolina	35	815	110	197	.558	67	101	.663	181	287	8.2
83-84	—North Carolina	30	821	128	210	.610	59	87	.678	167	315	10.5
84-85	—North Carolina	36	1250	238	381	.625	147	198	.742	349	623	17.3
85-86	—North Carolina	34	1087	284	438	.648	119	174	.684	306	687	20.2
Totals	....	135	3973	760	1226	.620	392	560	.700	1003	1912	14.2

Three-point field goals: 1982-83, 0-for-1.

NBA REGULAR-SEASON RECORD

HONORS: NBA All-Rookie team (1987).... All-NBA third team (1992).

Season Team	G	Min.	FGM	FGA	Pct.	FTM	FTA	Pct.	Off.	Def.	Tot.	Ast.	PF	Dq.	Stl.	Blk.	TO	Pts.	Avg.
										— REBOUNDS —									
86-87 —Cleveland.....	80	2695	487	905	.538	279	401	.696	152	495	647	304	248	3	49	63	248	1253	15.7
87-88 —Cleveland.....	79	2957	551	1081	.510	378	528	.716	151	514	665	333	235	2	48	56	267	1480	18.7
88-89 —Cleveland.....	78	2821	544	1012	.538	386	524	.737	167	551	718	285	175	1	63	40	230	1475	18.9
89-90 —Cleveland.....	41	1438	244	509	.479	202	287	.704	77	296	373	130	108	1	29	22	110	690	16.8
90-91 —Cleveland.....	76	2946	605	1155	.524	435	579	.751	177	653	830	253	191	2	74	46	211	1645	21.6
91-92 —Cleveland.....	73	2643	576	1010	.570	414	533	.777	191	569	760	262	190	1	65	78	185	1566	21.5
Totals	427	15500	3007	5672	.530	2094	2852	.734	915	3078	3993	1567	1147	10	328	305	1251	8109	19.0

Three-point field goals: 1987-88, 0-for-2. 1988-89, 1-for-3 (.333). 1989-90, 0-for-2. 1990-91, 0-for-3. 1991-92, 0-for-2. Totals, 1-for-12 (.083).

NBA PLAYOFF RECORD

Season Team	G	Min.	FGM	FGA	Pct.	FTM	FTA	Pct.	Off.	Def.	Tot.	Ast.	PF	Dq.	Stl.	Blk.	TO	Pts.	Avg.
										— REBOUNDS —									
87-88 —Cleveland.....	5	204	29	63	.460	21	31	.677	10	36	46	16	11	0	2	7	16	79	15.8
88-89 —Cleveland.....	5	167	17	47	.362	21	35	.600	12	34	46	12	18	0	6	5	6	55	11.0
89-90 —Cleveland.....	5	186	41	70	.586	32	46	.696	4	44	48	20	12	0	2	4	13	114	22.8
91-92 —Cleveland.....	17	687	124	235	.528	118	145	.814	37	137	174	58	47	0	11	17	37	366	21.5
Totals	32	1244	211	415	.508	192	257	.747	63	251	314	106	88	0	21	33	72	614	19.2

Three-point field goals: 1988-89, 0-for-1. 1991-92, 0-for-1. Totals, 0-for-2.

NBA ALL-STAR GAME RECORD

Season Team	Min.	FGM	FGA	Pct.	FTM	FTA	Pct.	Off.	Def.	Tot.	Ast.	PF	Dq.	Stl.	Blk.	TO	Pts.
									— REBOUNDS —								
1988 —Cleveland	15	6	7	.857	0	0	...	0	3	3	1	4	0	0	1	0	12
1989 —Cleveland	15	0	3	.000	0	0	...	2	1	3	0	1	0	1	0	1	0
1991 —Cleveland	12	3	7	.429	2	3	.667	3	2	5	1	3	0	0	0	0	8
1992 —Cleveland	15	3	8	.375	0	0	...	3	3	6	1	0	0	1	0	3	6
Totals	57	12	25	.480	2	3	.667	8	9	17	3	7	0	2	1	4	26

DAVIS, BRAD
G

PERSONAL: Born December 17, 1955, in Monaca, Pa.... 6-3/180.... Full name: Bradley Ernest Davis.
HIGH SCHOOL: Monaca Senior (Pa.).
COLLEGE: Maryland.
TRANSACTIONS/CAREER NOTES: Selected as undergraduate by Los Angeles Lakers in first round (15th pick overall) of 1977 NBA Draft.... Waived by Lakers (October 27, 1978).... Played in Western Basketball Association with Montana Sky (1978-79).... Signed as free agent by Indiana Pacers (February 14, 1979).... Waived by Pacers (October 22, 1979).... Played in Continental Basketball Association with Anchorage Northern Knights (1979-80 and 1980-81).... Signed by Utah Jazz to first of two consecutive 10-day contracts (February 29, 1980).... Signed as free agent by Detroit Pistons (July 9, 1980).... Waived by Pistons (October 8, 1980).... Signed as free agent by Dallas Mavericks (December 2, 1980).... Signed as unrestricted free agent by Mavericks (August 2, 1991).

COLLEGIATE RECORD

Season Team	G	Min.	FGM	FGA	Pct.	FTM	FTA	Pct.	Reb.	Pts.	Avg.
74-75 —Maryland	29	...	141	243	.580	82	100	.820	95	364	12.6
75-76 —Maryland	28	...	117	228	.513	92	116	.793	73	326	11.6
76-77 —Maryland	27	...	128	250	.512	80	102	.784	94	336	12.4
Totals	84	...	386	721	.535	254	318	.799	262	1026	12.2

NBA REGULAR-SEASON RECORD

Season Team	G	Min.	FGM	FGA	Pct.	FTM	FTA	Pct.	Off.	Def.	Tot.	Ast.	PF	Dq.	Stl.	Blk.	TO	Pts.	Avg.
										— REBOUNDS —									
77-78 —Los Angeles .	33	334	30	72	.417	22	29	.759	4	31	35	83	39	1	15	2	35	82	2.5
78-79 —L.A.-Ind.	27	298	31	55	.564	16	23	.696	1	16	17	52	32	0	16	2	17	78	2.9
79-80 —Ind.-Utah	18	268	35	63	.556	13	16	.813	4	13	17	50	28	0	13	1	14	83	4.6
80-81 —Dallas..........	56	1686	230	410	.561	163	204	.799	29	122	151	385	156	2	52	11	123	626	11.2
81-82 —Dallas..........	82	2614	397	771	.515	185	230	.804	35	191	226	509	218	5	73	6	159	993	12.1
82-83 —Dallas..........	79	2323	359	628	.572	186	220	.845	34	164	198	565	176	2	80	11	143	915	11.6
83-84 —Dallas..........	81	2665	345	651	.530	199	238	.836	41	146	187	561	218	4	94	13	166	896	11.1
84-85 —Dallas..........	82	2539	310	614	.505	158	178	.888	39	154	193	581	219	1	91	10	123	825	10.1
85-86 —Dallas..........	82	1971	267	502	.532	198	228	.868	26	120	146	467	174	2	57	15	110	764	9.3
86-87 —Dallas..........	82	1582	199	436	.456	147	171	.860	27	87	114	373	159	0	63	10	114	537	7.0
87-88 —Dallas..........	75	1480	208	415	.501	91	108	.843	18	84	102	303	149	0	51	18	91	537	7.2
88-89 —Dallas..........	78	1395	183	379	.483	99	123	.805	14	94	108	242	151	0	48	18	92	497	6.4
89-90 —Dallas..........	73	1292	179	365	.490	77	100	.770	12	81	93	242	151	2	47	9	86	470	6.4
90-91 —Dallas..........	80	1426	159	373	.426	91	118	.771	13	105	118	230	212	1	45	17	77	431	5.4
91-92 —Dallas..........	33	429	38	86	.442	11	15	.733	4	29	33	66	57	0	11	3	27	92	2.8
Totals	961	22302	2970	5820	.510	1656	2001	.828	301	1437	1738	4709	2139	20	756	146	1377	7866	8.2

Three-point field goals: 1979-80, 0-for-1. 1980-81, 3-for-17 (.176). 1981-82, 14-for-49 (.286). 1982-83, 11-for-43 (.256). 1983-84, 7-for-38 (.184). 1984-85, 47-for-115 (.409). 1985-86, 32-for-89 (.360). 1986-87, 32-for-106 (.302). 1987-88, 30-for-74 (.405). 1988-89, 32-for-102 (.314). 1989-90, 35-for-104 (.337). 1990-91, 22-for-85 (.259). 1991-92, 5-for-18 (.278). Totals, 270-for-841 (.321).

NBA PLAYOFF RECORD

Season Team	G	Min.	FGM	FGA	Pct.	FTM	FTA	Pct.	Off.	Def.	Tot.	Ast.	PF	Dq.	Stl.	Blk.	TO	Pts.	Avg.
										— REBOUNDS —									
83-84 —Dallas..........	10	304	33	73	.452	15	19	.789	6	13	19	50	18	0	6	0	18	81	8.1
84-85 —Dallas..........	4	113	13	26	.500	12	13	.923	1	7	8	22	11	0	4	1	6	41	10.3
85-86 —Dallas..........	10	163	24	44	.545	19	24	.792	1	18	19	23	22	0	3	0	15	77	7.7

Season Team	G	Min.	FGM	FGA	Pct.	FTM	FTA	Pct.	Off.	Def.	Tot.	Ast.	PF	Dq.	Stl.	Blk.	TO	Pts.	Avg.
86-87 —Dallas..........	4	75	13	23	.565	7	9	.778	2	7	9	17	4	0	0	0	6	33	8.3
87-88 —Dallas..........	17	295	42	70	.600	24	26	.923	1	19	20	55	34	0	3	5	29	109	6.4
Totals	45	950	125	236	.530	77	91	.846	11	64	75	167	89	0	16	6	74	341	7.6

Three-point field goals: 1983-84, 0-for-2. 1984-85, 3-for-8 (.375). 1985-86, 10-for-15 (.667). 1986-87, 0-for-2. 1987-88, 1-for-5 (.200). Totals, 14-for-32 (.438).

WBA AND CBA REGULAR-SEASON RECORD

NOTES: CBA co-Newcomer of the Year (1980).... CBA All-Star second team (1980).... Member of CBA championship team (1980).

Season Team	G	Min.	2-POINT FGM	FGA	Pct.	3-POINT FGM	FGA	Pct.	FTM	FTA	Pct.	Reb.	Ast.	Pts.	Avg.
78-79 —Mont. (WBA)...	34	1395	194	362	.536	3	16	.188	105	133	.789	119	224	502	14.8
79-80 —Anchorage.......	40	955	206	361	.571	0	8	.000	120	139	.863	158	291	532	13.3
80-81 —Anchorage.......	5	165	18	43	.419	0	5	.000	12	16	.750	18	41	48	9.6
Totals	79	2515	418	766	.546	3	29	.103	237	288	.823	295	556	1082	13.7

DAVIS, DALE
F, PACERS

PERSONAL: Born March 25, 1969, in Toccoa, Ga.... 6-11/230.... Full name: Elliott Lydell Davis.
HIGH SCHOOL: Stephens County (Toccoa, Ga.).
COLLEGE: Clemson.
TRANSACTIONS/CAREER NOTES: Selected by Indiana Pacers in first round (13th pick overall) of 1991 NBA Draft.

COLLEGIATE RECORD

Season Team	G	Min.	FGM	FGA	Pct.	FTM	FTA	Pct.	Reb.	Pts.	Avg.
87-88 —Clemson	29	714	91	171	.532	45	89	.506	223	227	7.8
88-89 —Clemson	29	736	146	218	.670	93	144	.646	258	385	13.3
89-90 —Clemson	35	1077	205	328	.625	127	213	.596	395	537	15.3
90-91 —Clemson	28	971	191	359	.532	119	205	.580	340	501	17.9
Totals	121	3498	633	1076	.588	384	651	.590	1216	1650	13.6

Three-point field goals: 1989-90, 0-for-1. 1990-91, 0-for-2. Totals, 0-for-3.

NBA REGULAR-SEASON RECORD

Season Team	G	Min.	FGM	FGA	Pct.	FTM	FTA	Pct.	Off.	Def.	Tot.	Ast.	PF	Dq.	Stl.	Blk.	TO	Pts.	Avg.
91-92 —Indiana.........	64	1301	154	279	.552	87	152	.572	158	252	410	30	191	2	27	74	49	395	6.2

Three-point field goals: 1991-92, 0-for-1.

NBA PLAYOFF RECORD

Season Team	G	Min.	FGM	FGA	Pct.	FTM	FTA	Pct.	Off.	Def.	Tot.	Ast.	PF	Dq.	Stl.	Blk.	TO	Pts.	Avg.
91-92 —Indiana.........	3	69	4	10	.400	0	0	...	5	14	19	2	8	0	0	5	1	8	2.7

DAVIS, TERRY
F/C, MAVERICKS

PERSONAL: Born June 17, 1967, in Danville, Va.... 6-10/246.... Full name: Terry Raymond Davis.
HIGH SCHOOL: George Washington (Danville, Va.).
COLLEGE: Virginia Union.
TRANSACTIONS/CAREER NOTES: Never drafted by an NBA franchise.... Signed as free agent by Miami Heat (September 28, 1989).... Signed as unrestricted free agent by Dallas Mavericks (August 6, 1991).

COLLEGIATE RECORD

Season Team	G	Min.	FGM	FGA	Pct.	FTM	FTA	Pct.	Reb.	Pts.	Avg.
85-86 —Virginia Union.........................	27	...	42	91	.462	26	43	.605	116	110	4.1
86-87 —Virginia Union.........................	32	...	135	259	.521	98	142	.690	360	368	11.5
87-88 —Virginia Union.........................	31	...	257	454	.566	191	267	.715	338	705	22.7
88-89 —Virginia Union.........................	31	1034	272	442	.615	148	217	.682	369	692	22.3
Totals	121	...	706	1246	.567	463	669	.692	1183	1875	15.5

Three-point field goals: 1988-89, 0-for-1.

NBA REGULAR-SEASON RECORD

Season Team	G	Min.	FGM	FGA	Pct.	FTM	FTA	Pct.	Off.	Def.	Tot.	Ast.	PF	Dq.	Stl.	Blk.	TO	Pts.	Avg.
89-90 —Miami..........	63	884	122	262	.466	54	87	.621	93	136	229	25	171	2	25	28	68	298	4.7
90-91 —Miami..........	55	996	115	236	.487	69	124	.556	107	159	266	39	129	2	18	28	36	300	5.5
91-92 —Dallas..........	68	2149	256	531	.482	181	285	.635	228	444	672	57	202	1	26	29	117	693	10.2
Totals	186	4029	493	1029	.479	304	496	.613	428	739	1167	121	502	5	69	85	221	1291	6.9

Three-point field goals: 1989-90, 0-for-1. 1990-91, 1-for-2 (.500). 1991-92, 0-for-5. Totals, 1-for-8 (.125).

DAVIS, WALTER
G, NUGGETS

PERSONAL: Born September 9, 1954, in Pineville, N.C.... 6-6/200.... Full name: Walter Paul Davis.... Uncle of Hubert Davis, guard with New York Knicks.
HIGH SCHOOL: South Mecklenburg (Charlotte, N.C.).
COLLEGE: North Carolina.
TRANSACTIONS/CAREER NOTES: Selected by Phoenix Suns in first round (fifth pick overall) of 1977 NBA Draft.... Signed as unrestricted free agent by Denver Nuggets (July 6, 1988).... Traded by Nuggets to Portland Trail Blazers

in three-way deal in which Trail Blazers sent Drazen Petrovic to New Jersey Nets, Nets sent Greg Anderson to Nuggets, and Nuggets sent Terry Mills to Nets (January 23, 1991); Nuggets also received 1992 first-round draft choice from Nets and 1993 second-round draft choice from Trail Blazers, and Trail Blazers also received 1992 second-round draft choice from Nuggets. . . . Waived by Trail Blazers (October 29, 1991). . . . Signed as free agent by Nuggets (November 1, 1991).
MISCELLANEOUS: Member of gold-medal-winning U.S. Olympic team (1976).

COLLEGIATE RECORD

Season Team	G	Min.	FGM	FGA	Pct.	FTM	FTA	Pct.	Reb.	Pts.	Avg.
73-74 —North Carolina	27	...	161	322	.500	65	82	.793	126	387	14.3
74-75 —North Carolina	31	...	200	396	.505	98	130	.754	195	498	16.1
75-76 —North Carolina	29	...	190	351	.541	101	130	.777	166	481	16.6
76-77 —North Carolina	32	...	203	351	.578	91	117	.778	183	497	15.5
Totals	119	...	754	1420	.531	355	459	.773	670	1863	15.7

NBA REGULAR-SEASON RECORD

HONORS: NBA Rookie of the Year (1978). . . . All-NBA second team (1978, 1979). . . . NBA All-Rookie team (1978).

Season Team	G	Min.	FGM	FGA	Pct.	FTM	FTA	Pct.	Off. REBOUNDS	Def.	Tot.	Ast.	PF	Dq.	Stl.	Blk.	TO	Pts.	Avg.
77-78 —Phoenix	81	2590	786	1494	.526	387	466	.830	158	326	484	273	242	2	113	20	283	1959	24.2
78-79 —Phoenix	79	2437	764	1362	.561	340	409	.831	111	262	373	339	250	5	147	26	293	1868	23.6
79-80 —Phoenix	75	2309	657	1166	.563	299	365	.819	75	197	272	337	202	2	114	19	242	1613	21.5
80-81 —Phoenix	78	2182	593	1101	.539	209	250	.836	63	137	200	302	192	3	97	12	222	1402	18.0
81-82 —Phoenix	55	1182	350	669	.523	91	111	.820	21	82	103	162	104	1	46	3	112	794	14.4
82-83 —Phoenix	80	2491	665	1289	.516	184	225	.818	63	134	197	397	186	2	117	12	188	1521	19.0
83-84 —Phoenix	78	2546	652	1274	.512	233	270	.863	38	164	202	429	202	0	107	12	213	1557	20.0
84-85 —Phoenix	23	570	139	309	.450	64	73	.877	6	29	35	98	42	0	18	0	50	345	15.0
85-86 —Phoenix	70	2239	624	1287	.485	257	305	.843	54	149	203	361	153	1	99	3	219	1523	21.8
86-87 —Phoenix	79	2646	779	1515	.514	288	334	.862	90	154	244	364	184	1	96	5	226	1867	23.6
87-88 —Phoenix	68	1951	488	1031	.473	205	231	.887	32	127	159	278	131	0	86	3	126	1217	17.9
88-89 —Denver	81	1857	536	1076	.498	175	199	.879	41	110	151	190	187	1	72	5	132	1267	15.6
89-90 —Denver	69	1635	497	1033	.481	207	227	.912	46	133	179	155	160	1	59	9	102	1207	17.5
90-91 —Den.-Port.	71	1483	403	862	.468	107	117	.915	71	110	181	125	150	2	80	3	88	924	13.0
91-92 —Denver	46	741	185	403	.459	82	94	.872	20	50	70	68	69	0	29	1	45	457	9.9
Totals	1033	28859	8118	15871	.511	3128	3676	.851	889	2164	3053	3878	2454	21	1280	133	2541	19521	18.9

Three-point field goals: 1979-80, 0-for-4. 1980-81, 7-for-17 (.412). 1981-82, 3-for-16 (.188). 1982-83, 7-for-23 (.304). 1983-84, 20-for-87 (.230). 1984-85, 3-for-10 (.300). 1985-86, 18-for-76 (.237). 1986-87, 21-for-81 (.259). 1987-88, 36-for-96 (.375). 1988-89, 20-for-69 (.290). 1989-90, 6-for-46 (.130). 1990-91, 11-for-36 (.306). 1991-92, 5-for-16 (.313). Totals, 157-for-577 (.272).

NBA PLAYOFF RECORD

Season Team	G	Min.	FGM	FGA	Pct.	FTM	FTA	Pct.	Off. REBOUNDS	Def.	Tot.	Ast.	PF	Dq.	Stl.	Blk.	TO	Pts.	Avg.
77-78 —Phoenix	2	66	19	40	.475	12	16	.750	4	13	17	8	8	0	3	0	6	50	25.0
78-79 —Phoenix	15	490	127	244	.520	78	96	.813	24	45	69	79	41	0	26	5	66	332	22.1
79-80 —Phoenix	8	245	69	137	.504	28	38	.737	9	14	23	35	20	0	4	1	20	166	20.8
80-81 —Phoenix	7	199	51	106	.481	10	17	.588	7	12	19	22	17	0	7	1	17	112	16.0
81-82 —Phoenix	7	173	52	116	.448	22	24	.917	5	17	22	30	19	0	5	1	12	127	18.1
82-83 —Phoenix	3	113	30	69	.435	17	21	.810	5	10	15	13	6	0	6	5	5	78	26.0
83-84 —Phoenix	17	623	175	327	.535	70	78	.897	15	31	46	109	55	0	29	3	43	423	24.9
88-89 —Denver	3	94	31	60	.517	15	15	1.000	2	3	5	4	11	0	3	0	8	77	25.7
89-90 —Denver	3	70	18	45	.400	6	6	1.000	4	5	9	6	4	0	1	0	5	42	14.0
90-91 —Portland	13	111	19	48	.396	5	6	.833	7	8	15	6	5	0	4	0	7	43	3.3
Totals	78	2184	591	1192	.496	263	317	.830	82	158	240	312	186	0	88	16	189	1450	18.6

Three-point field goals: 1979-80, 0-for-3. 1980-81, 0-for-1. 1981-82, 1-for-3 (.333). 1982-83, 1-for-2 (.500). 1983-84, 3-for-11 (.273). 1988-89, 0-for-4. 1989-90, 0-for-1. 1990-91, 0-for-1. Totals, 5-for-26 (.192).

NBA ALL-STAR GAME RECORD

Season Team	Min.	FGM	FGA	Pct.	FTM	FTA	Pct.	Off. REBOUNDS	Def.	Tot.	Ast.	PF	Dq.	Stl.	Blk.	TO	Pts.
1978 —Phoenix	15	3	6	.500	4	4	1.000	0	1	1	6	1	0	1	0	0	10
1979 —Phoenix	19	4	9	.444	0	0	...	1	3	4	4	0	0	1	0	2	8
1980 —Phoenix	23	5	10	.500	2	2	1.000	2	2	4	2	2	0	4	0	3	12
1981 —Phoenix	22	5	9	.556	2	2	1.000	1	6	7	1	2	0	0	0	1	12
1984 —Phoenix	15	5	9	.556	0	0	...	0	2	2	1	0	0	1	0	0	10
1987 —Phoenix	15	3	12	.250	0	0	...	2	0	2	1	0	0	0	0	0	7
Totals	109	25	55	.455	8	8	1.000	6	14	20	15	5	0	7	0	6	59

Three-point field goals: 1987, 1-for-1.

DAWKINS, JOHNNY
G, 76ERS

PERSONAL: Born September 28, 1963, in Washington, D.C. . . . 6-2/170. . . . Full name: Johnny Earl Dawkins Jr.
HIGH SCHOOL: Mackin (Washington, D.C.).
COLLEGE: Duke.

TRANSACTIONS/CAREER NOTES: Selected by San Antonio Spurs in first round (10th pick overall) of 1986 NBA Draft. . . . Traded by Spurs with Jay Vincent to Philadelphia 76ers for Maurice Cheeks, Christian Welp and David Wingate (August 28, 1989).

COLLEGIATE RECORD

NOTES: THE SPORTING NEWS All-America first team (1986). . . . THE SPORTING NEWS All-America second team (1985).

Season Team	G	Min.	FGM	FGA	Pct.	FTM	FTA	Pct.	Reb.	Pts.	Avg.
82-83 —Duke	28	1002	207	414	.500	73	107	.682	115	506	18.1
83-84 —Duke	34	1306	263	547	.481	133	160	.831	138	659	19.4

Season Team	G	Min.	FGM	FGA	Pct.	FTM	FTA	Pct.	Reb.	Pts.	Avg.
84-85 —Duke	31	1117	225	455	.495	132	166	.795	141	582	18.8
85-86 —Duke	40	1324	331	603	.549	147	181	.812	142	809	20.2
Totals	133	4749	1026	2019	.508	485	614	.790	536	2556	19.2

Three-point field goals: 1982-83, 19-for-54 (.352).

NBA REGULAR-SEASON RECORD

Season Team	G	Min.	FGM	FGA	Pct.	FTM	FTA	Pct.	Off.	Def.	Tot.	Ast.	PF	Dq.	Stl.	Blk.	TO	Pts.	Avg.
									REBOUNDS										
86-87 —San Antonio	81	1682	334	764	.437	153	191	.801	56	113	169	290	118	0	67	3	120	835	10.3
87-88 —San Antonio	65	2179	405	835	.485	198	221	.896	66	138	204	480	95	0	88	2	154	1027	15.8
88-89 —San Antonio	32	1083	177	400	.443	100	112	.893	32	69	101	224	64	0	55	0	111	454	14.2
89-90 —Philadelphia	81	2865	465	950	.489	210	244	.861	48	199	247	601	159	1	121	9	214	1162	14.3
90-91 —Philadelphia	4	124	26	41	.634	10	11	.909	0	16	16	28	4	0	3	0	8	63	15.8
91-92 —Philadelphia	82	2815	394	902	.437	164	186	.882	42	185	227	567	158	0	89	5	183	988	12.0
Totals	345	10748	1801	3892	.463	835	965	.865	244	720	964	2190	598	1	423	19	790	4529	13.1

Three-point field goals: 1986-87, 14-for-47 (.298). 1987-88, 19-for-61 (.311). 1988-89, 0-for-4. 1989-90, 22-for-66 (.333). 1990-91, 1-for-4 (.250). 1991-92, 36-for-101 (.356). Totals, 92-for-283 (.325).

NBA PLAYOFF RECORD

Season Team	G	Min.	FGM	FGA	Pct.	FTM	FTA	Pct.	Off.	Def.	Tot.	Ast.	PF	Dq.	Stl.	Blk.	TO	Pts.	Avg.
									REBOUNDS										
87-88 —San Antonio	3	53	6	23	.261	3	4	.750	1	2	3	5	2	0	2	0	1	15	5.0
89-90 —Philadelphia	10	386	53	115	.461	36	43	.837	5	17	22	93	22	0	17	2	29	142	14.2
Totals	13	439	59	138	.428	39	47	.830	6	19	25	98	24	0	19	2	30	157	12.1

Three-point field goals: 1987-88, 0-for-2. 1989-90, 0-for-7. Totals, 0-for-9.

DEL NEGRO, VINNY
G, SPURS

PERSONAL: Born August 9, 1966, in Springfield, Mass. . . . 6-5/ 185. . . . Full name: Vincent Joseph Del Negro.
HIGH SCHOOL: Suffield Academy (Conn.).
COLLEGE: North Carolina State.
TRANSACTIONS/CAREER NOTES: Selected by Sacramento Kings in second round (29th pick overall) of 1988 NBA Draft. . . . Played in Italy (1990-91 and 1991-92). . . . Signed as free agent by San Antonio Spurs (July 30, 1992).

COLLEGIATE RECORD

Season Team	G	Min.	FGM	FGA	Pct.	FTM	FTA	Pct.	Reb.	Pts.	Avg.
84-85 —North Carolina State	19	125	12	21	.571	15	23	.652	14	39	2.1
85-86 —North Carolina State	17	139	11	30	.367	7	11	.636	14	29	1.7
86-87 —North Carolina State	35	918	133	269	.494	63	71	.887	115	265	7.6
87-88 —North Carolina State	32	1093	187	363	.515	104	124	.839	158	509	15.9
Totals	103	2275	343	683	.502	189	229	.825	301	842	8.2

Three-point field goals: 1986-87, 36-for-72 (.500). 1987-88, 31-for-78 (.397). Totals, 67-for-150 (.447).

NBA REGULAR-SEASON RECORD

Season Team	G	Min.	FGM	FGA	Pct.	FTM	FTA	Pct.	Off.	Def.	Tot.	Ast.	PF	Dq.	Stl.	Blk.	TO	Pts.	Avg.
									REBOUNDS										
88-89 —Sacramento	80	1556	239	503	.475	85	100	.850	48	123	171	206	160	2	65	14	77	569	7.1
89-90 —Sacramento	76	1858	297	643	.462	135	155	.871	39	159	198	250	182	2	64	10	111	739	9.7
Totals	156	3414	536	1146	.468	220	255	.863	87	282	369	456	342	4	129	24	188	1308	8.4

Three-point field goals: 1988-89, 6-for-20 (.300). 1989-90, 10-for-32 (.313). Totals, 16-for-52 (.308).

ITALIAN LEAGUE RECORD

Season Team	G	Min.	FGM	FGA	Pct.	FTM	FTA	Pct.	Reb.	Pts.	Avg.
90-91 —Benetton Treviso	35	1345	271	455	.596	214	263	.814	146	894	25.5
91-92 —Benetton Treviso	27	1038	261	453	.576	161	177	.910	131	703	26.0

DIVAC, VLADE
C, LAKERS

PERSONAL: Born February 3, 1968, in Prijepolje, Yugoslavia. . . . 7-1/250. . . . Name pronounced VLA-day DEE-vatz.
HIGH SCHOOL: Belgrade (Yugoslavia).
TRANSACTIONS/CAREER NOTES: Did not attend college. . . . Selected by Los Angeles Lakers in first round (26th pick overall) of 1989 NBA Draft.
MISCELLANEOUS: Member of silver-medal-winning Yugoslavian Olympic team (1988).

NBA REGULAR-SEASON RECORD

HONORS: NBA All-Rookie first team (1990).

Season Team	G	Min.	FGM	FGA	Pct.	FTM	FTA	Pct.	Off.	Def.	Tot.	Ast.	PF	Dq.	Stl.	Blk.	TO	Pts.	Avg.
									REBOUNDS										
89-90 —L.A. Lakers	82	1611	274	549	.499	153	216	.708	167	345	512	75	240	2	79	114	110	701	8.5
90-91 —L.A. Lakers	82	2310	360	637	.565	196	279	.703	205	461	666	92	247	3	106	127	146	921	11.2
91-92 —L.A. Lakers	36	979	157	317	.495	86	112	.768	87	160	247	60	114	3	55	35	88	405	11.3
Totals	200	4900	791	1503	.526	435	607	.717	459	966	1425	227	601	8	240	276	344	2027	10.1

Three-point field goals: 1989-90, 0-for-5. 1990-91, 5-for-14 (.357). 1991-92, 5-for-19 (.263). Totals, 10-for-38 (.263).

NBA PLAYOFF RECORD

Season Team	G	Min.	FGM	FGA	Pct.	FTM	FTA	Pct.	Off.	Def.	Tot.	Ast.	PF	Dq.	Stl.	Blk.	TO	Pts.	Avg.
									REBOUNDS										
89-90 —L.A. Lakers	9	175	32	44	.727	17	19	.895	16	32	48	10	27	1	8	15	13	82	9.1
90-91 —L.A. Lakers	19	609	97	172	.564	57	71	.803	49	78	127	21	65	2	27	41	41	252	13.3
91-92 —L.A. Lakers	4	143	15	43	.349	9	10	.900	6	16	22	15	17	1	5	3	18	39	9.8
Totals	32	927	144	259	.556	83	100	.830	71	126	197	46	109	4	40	59	72	373	11.7

Three-point field goals: 1989-90, 1-for-2 (.500). 1990-91, 1-for-6 (.167). 1991-92, 0-for-2. Totals, 2-for-10 (.200).

DONALDSON, JAMES
C

PERSONAL: Born August 16, 1957, in Heacham, England. . . . 7-2/278. . . . Full name: James Lee Donaldson III.
HIGH SCHOOL: Luther Burbank Senior (Sacramento, Calif.).
COLLEGE: Washington State.

TRANSACTIONS/CAREER NOTES: Selected by Seattle SuperSonics in fourth round (73rd pick overall) of 1979 NBA Draft. . . . Played in Europe (1979-80). . . . Traded by SuperSonics with Greg Kelser, Mark Radford, 1984 first-round draft choice and 1985 second-round draft choice to San Diego Clippers for Tom Chambers, Al Wood, 1987 second-round draft choice and 1984 third-round draft choice (August 18, 1983). . . . Clippers franchise moved from San Diego to Los Angeles for 1984-85 season. . . . Traded by Clippers to Dallas Mavericks for Kurt Nimphius (November 25, 1985). . . . Traded by Mavericks to New York Knicks for Brian Quinnett (February 20, 1992).

COLLEGIATE RECORD

Season Team	G	Min.	FGM	FGA	Pct.	FTM	FTA	Pct.	Reb.	Pts.	Avg.
75-76 — Washington State	9	36	4	7	.571	2	3	.667	17	10	1.1
76-77 — Washington State	22	297	34	59	.576	6	19	.316	74	74	3.4
77-78 — Washington State	27	999	131	251	.522	79	121	.653	305	341	12.6
78-79 — Washington State	26	946	120	216	.556	53	98	.541	281	293	11.3
Totals	84	2278	289	533	.542	140	241	.581	677	718	8.5

NBA REGULAR-SEASON RECORD

Season Team	G	Min.	FGM	FGA	Pct.	FTM	FTA	Pct.	Off.	Def.	Tot.	Ast.	PF	Dq.	Stl.	Blk.	TO	Pts.	Avg.
									— REBOUNDS —										
80-81 — Seattle	68	980	129	238	.542	101	170	.594	107	202	309	42	79	0	8	74	68	359	5.3
81-82 — Seattle	82	1710	255	419	.609	151	240	.629	138	352	490	51	186	2	27	139	132	661	8.1
82-83 — Seattle	82	1789	289	496	.583	150	218	.688	131	370	501	97	171	1	19	101	132	728	8.9
83-84 — San Diego	82	2525	360	604	.596	249	327	.761	165	484	649	90	214	1	40	139	171	969	11.8
84-85 — L.A. Clippers	82	2392	351	551 *.637		227	303	.749	168	500	668	48	217	1	28	130	206	929	11.3
85-86 — L.A.C.-Dal.	83	2682	256	459	.558	204	254	.803	171	624	795	96	189	0	28	139	123	716	8.6
86-87 — Dallas	82	3028	311	531	.586	267	329	.812	295	678	973	63	191	0	51	136	104	889	10.8
87-88 — Dallas	81	2523	212	380	.558	147	189	.778	247	508	755	66	175	2	40	104	113	571	7.0
88-89 — Dallas	53	1746	193	337	.573	95	124	.766	158	412	570	38	111	0	24	81	83	481	9.1
89-90 — Dallas	73	2265	258	479	.539	149	213	.700	155	475	630	57	129	0	22	47	119	665	9.1
90-91 — Dallas	82	2800	327	615	.532	165	229	.721	201	526	727	69	181	0	34	93	146	819	10.0
91-92 — Dallas-N.Y.	58	1075	112	245	.457	61	86	.709	99	190	289	33	103	0	8	49	48	285	4.9
Totals	908	25515	3053	5354	.570	1966	2682	.733	2035	5321	7356	750	1946	7	329	1232	1428	8072	8.9

NBA PLAYOFF RECORD

Season Team	G	Min.	FGM	FGA	Pct.	FTM	FTA	Pct.	Off.	Def.	Tot.	Ast.	PF	Dq.	Stl.	Blk.	TO	Pts.	Avg.
									— REBOUNDS —										
81-82 — Seattle	8	189	18	43	.419	18	24	.750	25	49	74	7	16	0	2	5	10	54	6.8
82-83 — Seattle	2	47	11	22	.500	2	3	.667	5	12	17	2	4	0	0	3	0	24	12.0
85-86 — Dallas	10	410	36	48	.750	37	40	.925	30	87	117	10	26	0	6	12	10	109	10.9
86-87 — Dallas	3	68	4	5	.800	8	9	.889	2	15	17	2	6	0	1	3	2	16	5.3
87-88 — Dallas	17	499	68	104	.654	22	37	.595	47	99	146	12	41	0	7	15	29	158	9.3
89-90 — Dallas	3	74	9	13	.692	4	5	.800	6	10	16	2	8	0	2	0	4	22	7.3
91-92 — New York	2	11	2	2	1.000	0	0	. . .	0	4	4	0	2	0	0	1	2	4	2.0
Totals	45	1298	148	237	.624	91	118	.771	115	276	391	35	103	0	18	39	57	387	8.6

NBA ALL-STAR GAME RECORD

Season Team	Min.	FGM	FGA	Pct.	FTM	FTA	Pct.	Off.	Def.	Tot.	Ast.	PF	Dq.	Stl.	Blk.	TO	Pts.
								— REBOUNDS —									
1988 — Dallas	8	0	0	. . .	2	2	1.000	1	5	6	1	2	0	0	2	0	2

DOUGLAS, SHERMAN
G, CELTICS

PERSONAL: Born September 15, 1966, in Washington, D.C. . . . 6-1/180.
HIGH SCHOOL: Spingarn (Washington, D.C.).
COLLEGE: Syracuse.

TRANSACTIONS/CAREER NOTES: Selected by Miami Heat in second round (28th pick overall) of 1989 NBA Draft. . . . Traded by Heat to Boston Celtics for Brian Shaw (January 10, 1992).

COLLEGIATE RECORD

NOTES: 1986-87 minutes played totals are missing one game.

Season Team	G	Min.	FGM	FGA	Pct.	FTM	FTA	Pct.	Reb.	Pts.	Avg.
85-86 — Syracuse	27	307	57	93	.613	32	44	.727	33	146	5.4
86-87 — Syracuse	38	1240	246	463	.531	151	203	.744	97	659	17.3
87-88 — Syracuse	35	1195	222	428	.519	104	150	.693	76	562	16.1
88-89 — Syracuse	38	1348	272	498	.546	110	174	.632	93	693	18.2
Totals	138	4090	797	1482	.538	397	571	.695	299	2060	14.9

Three-point field goals: 1986-87, 16-for-49 (.327). 1987-88, 14-for-53 (.264). 1988-89, 39-for-106 (.368). Totals, 69-for-208 (.332).

HONORS: NBA All-Rookie first team (1990).

NBA REGULAR-SEASON RECORD

Season Team	G	Min.	FGM	FGA	Pct.	FTM	FTA	Pct.	Off.	Def.	Tot.	Ast.	PF	Dq.	Stl.	Blk.	TO	Pts.	Avg.
									— REBOUNDS —										
89-90 — Miami	81	2470	463	938	.494	224	326	.687	70	136	206	619	187	0	145	10	246	1155	14.3
90-91 — Miami	73	2562	532	1055	.504	284	414	.686	78	131	209	624	178	2	121	5	270	1352	18.5
91-92 — Miami-Bos.	42	752	117	253	.462	73	107	.682	13	50	63	172	78	0	25	9	68	308	7.3
Totals	196	5784	1112	2246	.495	581	847	.686	161	317	478	1415	443	2	291	24	584	2815	14.4

Three-point field goals: 1989-90, 5-for-31 (.161). 1990-91, 4-for-31 (.129). 1991-92, 1-for-10 (.100). Totals, 10-for-72 (.139).

| | | | | | | | | | — REBOUNDS — | | | | | | | | |
Season	Team	G	Min.	FGM	FGA	Pct.	FTM	FTA	Pct.	Off.	Def.	Tot.	Ast.	PF	Dq.	Stl.	Blk.	TO	Pts.	Avg.
91-92 —Boston		6	65	9	25	.360	1	2	.500	1	3	4	10	8	0	0	0	4	19	3.2

Three-point field goals: 1991-92, 0-for-2.

DREILING, GREG
C, PACERS

PERSONAL: Born November 7, 1963, in Wichita, Kan. . . . 7-1/250. . . . Full name: Gregory Alan Dreiling. . . . Name pronounced DRY-ling.
HIGH SCHOOL: Kapaun Mt. Carmel (Wichita, Kan).
COLLEGE: Wichita State, then Kansas.
TRANSACTIONS/CAREER NOTES: Selected by Indiana Pacers in second round (26th pick overall) of 1986 NBA Draft.

COLLEGIATE RECORD

Season	Team	G	Min.	FGM	FGA	Pct.	FTM	FTA	Pct.	Reb.	Pts.	Avg.
81-82 —Wichita State.........................		29	534	82	151	.543	70	93	.753	121	234	8.1
82-83 —Kansas.................................						Did not play—transfer student.						
83-84 —Kansas.................................		32	742	121	228	.531	69	93	.742	153	311	9.7
84-85 —Kansas.................................		34	987	173	300	.577	101	139	.727	235	447	13.1
85-86 —Kansas.................................		39	1031	180	300	.600	91	128	.711	262	451	11.6
Totals		134	3294	556	979	.568	331	453	.731	771	1443	10.8

NBA REGULAR-SEASON RECORD

| | | | | | | | | | — REBOUNDS — | | | | | | | | |
Season	Team	G	Min.	FGM	FGA	Pct.	FTM	FTA	Pct.	Off.	Def.	Tot.	Ast.	PF	Dq.	Stl.	Blk.	TO	Pts.	Avg.
86-87 —Indiana.........		24	128	16	37	.432	10	12	.833	12	31	43	7	42	0	2	2	7	42	1.8
87-88 —Indiana.........		20	74	8	17	.471	18	26	.692	3	14	17	5	19	0	2	4	11	34	1.7
88-89 —Indiana.........		53	396	43	77	.558	43	64	.672	39	53	92	18	100	0	5	11	39	129	2.4
89-90 —Indiana.........		49	307	20	53	.377	25	34	.735	21	66	87	8	69	0	4	14	19	65	1.3
90-91 —Indiana.........		73	1031	98	194	.505	63	105	.600	66	189	255	51	178	1	24	29	57	259	3.5
91-92 —Indiana.........		60	509	43	87	.494	30	40	.750	22	74	96	25	123	1	10	16	31	117	2.0
Totals		279	2445	228	465	.490	189	281	.673	163	427	590	114	531	2	47	76	164	646	2.3

Three-point field goals: 1990-91, 0-for-2. 1991-92, 1-for-1. Totals, 1-for-3 (.333).

NBA PLAYOFF RECORD

| | | | | | | | | | — REBOUNDS — | | | | | | | | |
Season	Team	G	Min.	FGM	FGA	Pct.	FTM	FTA	Pct.	Off.	Def.	Tot.	Ast.	PF	Dq.	Stl.	Blk.	TO	Pts.	Avg.
90-91 —Indiana.........		5	75	5	15	.333	4	6	.667	8	10	18	0	17	0	0	0	3	14	2.8
91-92 —Indiana.........		1	3	0	0	...	0	0	...	0	0	0	0	2	0	0	0	0	0	0.0
Totals		6	78	5	15	.333	4	6	.667	8	10	18	0	19	0	0	0	3	14	2.3

DREXLER, CLYDE
G, TRAIL BLAZERS

PERSONAL: Born June 22, 1962, in New Orleans. . . . 6-7/222.
HIGH SCHOOL: Sterling (Houston).
COLLEGE: Houston.
TRANSACTIONS/CAREER NOTES: Selected as undergraduate by Portland Trail Blazers in first round (14th pick overall) of 1983 NBA Draft.
MISCELLANEOUS: Member of gold-medal-winning U.S. Olympic team (1992).

COLLEGIATE RECORD

Season	Team	G	Min.	FGM	FGA	Pct.	FTM	FTA	Pct.	Reb.	Pts.	Avg.
80-81 —Houston		30	992	153	303	.505	50	85	.588	314	356	11.9
81-82 —Houston		32	1077	206	362	.569	73	120	.608	336	485	15.2
82-83 —Houston		34	1186	236	440	.536	70	95	.737	298	542	15.9
Totals		96	3255	595	1105	.538	193	300	.643	948	1383	14.4

NBA REGULAR-SEASON RECORD

HONORS: All-NBA first team (1992). . . . All-NBA second team (1988, 1991). . . . All-NBA third team (1990).

| | | | | | | | | | — REBOUNDS — | | | | | | | | |
Season	Team	G	Min.	FGM	FGA	Pct.	FTM	FTA	Pct.	Off.	Def.	Tot.	Ast.	PF	Dq.	Stl.	Blk.	TO	Pts.	Avg.
83-84 —Portland		82	1408	252	559	.451	123	169	.728	112	123	235	153	209	2	107	29	123	628	7.7
84-85 —Portland		80	2555	573	1161	.494	223	294	.759	217	259	476	441	265	3	177	68	223	1377	17.2
85-86 —Portland		75	2576	542	1142	.475	293	381	.769	171	250	421	600	270	6	197	46	282	1389	18.5
86-87 —Portland		82	3114	707	1408	.502	357	470	.760	227	291	518	566	281	7	204	71	253	1782	21.7
87-88 —Portland		81	3060	849	1679	.506	476	587	.811	261	272	533	467	250	2	203	52	236	2185	27.0
88-89 —Portland		78	3064	829	1672	.496	438	548	.799	289	326	615	450	269	2	213	54	250	2123	27.2
89-90 —Portland		73	2683	670	1357	.494	333	430	.774	208	299	507	432	222	1	145	51	191	1703	23.3
90-91 —Portland		82	2852	645	1338	.482	416	524	.794	212	334	546	493	226	2	144	60	232	1767	21.5
91-92 —Portland		76	2751	694	1476	.470	401	505	.794	166	334	500	512	229	2	138	70	240	1903	25.0
Totals		709	24063	5761	11792	.489	3060	3908	.783	1863	2488	4351	4114	2221	29	1528	501	2030	14857	21.0

Three-point field goals: 1983-84, 1-for-4 (.250). 1984-85, 8-for-37 (.216). 1985-86, 12-for-60 (.200). 1986-87, 11-for-47 (.234). 1987-88, 11-for-52 (.212). 1988-89, 27-for-104 (.260). 1989-90, 30-for-106 (.283). 1990-91, 61-for-191 (.319). 1991-92, 114-for-338 (.337). Totals, 275-for-939 (.293).

NBA PLAYOFF RECORD

NOTES: Holds single-game record for most points in an overtime period— 13 (April 29, 1992, vs. Los Angeles Lakers).

| | | | | | | | | | — REBOUNDS — | | | | | | | | |
Season	Team	G	Min.	FGM	FGA	Pct.	FTM	FTA	Pct.	Off.	Def.	Tot.	Ast.	PF	Dq.	Stl.	Blk.	TO	Pts.	Avg.
83-84 —Portland		5	85	15	35	.429	6	7	.857	7	10	17	8	11	0	5	1	7	36	7.2
84-85 —Portland		9	339	55	134	.410	38	45	.844	27	28	55	83	37	0	23	9	29	150	16.7

Season Team	G	Min.	FGM	FGA	Pct.	FTM	FTA	Pct.	REBOUNDS Off.	Def.	Tot.	Ast.	PF	Dq.	Stl.	Blk.	TO	Pts.	Avg.
85-86—Portland	4	145	26	57	.456	18	23	.783	9	16	25	26	19	1	6	3	19	72	18.0
86-87—Portland	4	153	36	79	.456	23	29	.793	16	14	30	15	16	1	7	3	6	96	24.0
87-88—Portland	4	170	32	83	.386	21	29	.724	12	16	28	21	14	0	12	2	12	88	22.0
88-89—Portland	3	128	35	71	.493	13	17	.765	13	7	20	25	11	0	6	2	12	83	27.7
89-90—Portland	21	853	172	390	.441	96	124	.774	63	88	151	150	72	2	53	18	67	449	21.4
90-91—Portland	16	633	128	269	.476	76	98	.776	40	89	129	129	56	0	34	16	61	347	21.7
91-92—Portland	21	847	198	425	.466	138	171	.807	60	95	155	147	77	2	31	20	58	553	26.3
Totals	87	3353	697	1543	.452	429	543	.790	247	363	610	604	313	6	177	74	271	1874	21.5

Three-point field goals: 1983-84, 0-for-1. 1984-85, 2-for-7 (.286). 1985-86, 2-for-5 (.400). 1986-87, 1-for-4 (.250). 1987-88, 3-for-6 (.500). 1988-89, 0-for-2. 1989-90, 9-for-41 (.220). 1990-91, 15-for-56 (.268). 1991-92, 19-for-81 (.235). Totals, 51-for-203 (.251).

NBA ALL-STAR GAME RECORD

Season Team	Min.	FGM	FGA	Pct.	FTM	FTA	Pct.	REBOUNDS Off.	Def.	Tot.	Ast.	PF	Dq.	Stl.	Blk.	TO	Pts.
1986—Portland	15	5	7	.714	0	0	...	0	4	4	4	3	0	3	1	3	10
1988—Portland	15	3	5	.600	6	6	1.000	2	3	5	0	3	0	1	0	1	12
1989—Portland	25	7	19	.368	0	0	...	6	6	12	4	3	0	2	0	6	14
1990—Portland	19	2	6	.333	2	2	1.000	4	0	4	2	1	0	1	1	0	7
1991—Portland	19	4	9	.444	4	4	1.000	2	2	4	2	3	0	1	1	0	12
1992—Portland	28	10	15	.667	0	0	...	2	7	9	6	2	0	0	2	1	22
Totals	121	31	61	.508	12	12	1.000	16	22	38	18	15	0	8	5	12	77

Three-point field goals: 1986, 0-for-1. 1988, 0-for-1. 1990, 1-for-1. 1992, 2-for-4 (.500). Totals, 3-for-7 (.429).

DUCKWORTH, KEVIN
C, TRAIL BLAZERS

PERSONAL: Born April 1, 1964, in Harvey, Ill. . . . 7-0/280. . . . Full name: Kevin Jerome Duckworth. **HIGH SCHOOL:** Thornridge (Dolton, Ill.). **COLLEGE:** Eastern Illinois.

TRANSACTIONS/CAREER NOTES: Selected by San Antonio Spurs in second round (33rd pick overall) of 1986 NBA Draft. . . . Traded by Spurs to Portland Trail Blazers for Walter Berry (December 18, 1986).

COLLEGIATE RECORD

Season Team	G	Min.	FGM	FGA	Pct.	FTM	FTA	Pct.	Reb.	Pts.	Avg.
82-83—Eastern Illinois	30	669	112	212	.528	64	95	.674	181	288	9.6
83-84—Eastern Illinois	28	642	132	221	.597	61	89	.685	191	325	11.6
84-85—Eastern Illinois	28	733	133	258	.516	65	99	.657	205	331	11.8
85-86—Eastern Illinois	32	1023	250	396	.631	125	164	.762	290	625	19.5
Totals	118	3067	627	1087	.577	315	447	.705	867	1569	13.3

NBA REGULAR-SEASON RECORD

HONORS: NBA Most Improved Player (1988).

Season Team	G	Min.	FGM	FGA	Pct.	FTM	FTA	Pct.	REBOUNDS Off.	Def.	Tot.	Ast.	PF	Dq.	Stl.	Blk.	TO	Pts.	Avg.
86-87—S.A.-Port.	65	875	130	273	.476	92	134	.687	76	147	223	29	192	3	21	21	78	352	5.4
87-88—Portland	78	2223	450	907	.496	331	430	.770	224	352	576	66	280	5	31	32	177	1231	15.8
88-89—Portland	79	2662	554	1161	.477	324	428	.757	246	389	635	60	300	6	56	49	200	1432	18.1
89-90—Portland	82	2462	548	1146	.478	231	312	.740	184	325	509	91	271	2	36	34	171	1327	16.2
90-91—Portland	81	2511	521	1084	.481	240	311	.772	177	354	531	89	251	5	33	34	186	1282	15.8
91-92—Portland	82	2222	362	786	.461	156	226	.690	151	346	497	99	264	5	38	37	143	880	10.7
Totals	467	12955	2565	5357	.479	1374	1841	.746	1058	1913	2971	434	1558	26	215	207	955	6504	13.9

Three-point field goals: 1986-87, 0-for-1. 1988-89, 0-for-2. 1990-91, 0-for-2. 1991-92, 0-for-3. Totals, 0-for-8.

NBA PLAYOFF RECORD

Season Team	G	Min.	FGM	FGA	Pct.	FTM	FTA	Pct.	REBOUNDS Off.	Def.	Tot.	Ast.	PF	Dq.	Stl.	Blk.	TO	Pts.	Avg.
86-87—Portland	4	53	6	12	.500	2	5	.400	3	5	8	1	14	0	4	1	6	14	3.5
87-88—Portland	4	151	34	70	.486	18	23	.783	20	24	44	7	14	0	1	2	21	86	21.5
88-89—Portland	3	83	14	35	.400	6	11	.545	8	9	17	2	17	2	1	1	5	34	11.3
89-90—Portland	15	453	82	187	.439	33	46	.717	28	59	87	16	60	2	5	9	33	197	13.1
90-91—Portland	16	511	73	182	.401	41	56	.732	40	67	107	14	53	1	8	8	39	187	11.7
91-92—Portland	21	647	107	216	.495	35	53	.660	40	77	117	41	76	1	11	12	45	249	11.9
Totals	63	1898	316	702	.450	135	194	.696	139	241	380	81	234	6	30	33	149	767	12.2

Three-point field goals: 1987-88, 0-for-1.

NBA ALL-STAR GAME RECORD

Season Team	Min.	FGM	FGA	Pct.	FTM	FTA	Pct.	REBOUNDS Off.	Def.	Tot.	Ast.	PF	Dq.	Stl.	Blk.	TO	Pts.
1989—Portland	7	2	5	.400	1	2	.500	1	0	1	0	2	0	0	0	0	5
1991—Portland	19	2	3	.667	2	2	1.000	2	2	4	0	3	0	1	0	2	6
Totals	26	4	8	.500	3	4	.750	3	2	5	0	5	0	1	0	2	11

DUDLEY, CHRIS
C, NETS

PERSONAL: Born February 22, 1965, in Stamford, Conn. . . . 6-11/240. . . . Full name: Christen Guilford Dudley. **HIGH SCHOOL:** Torrey Pines (Encinitas, Calif.). **COLLEGE:** Yale.

TRANSACTIONS/CAREER NOTES: Selected by Cleveland Cavaliers in fourth round (75th pick overall) of 1987 NBA Draft. . . . Traded by Cavaliers to New Jersey Nets for 1991 and 1993 second-round draft choices (February 21, 1990).

Season Team	G	Min.	FGM	FGA	Pct.	FTM	FTA	Pct.	Reb.	Pts.	Avg.
83-84 —Yale	26	498	45	97	.464	28	60	.467	132	118	4.5
84-85 —Yale	26	795	131	294	.446	65	122	.533	266	327	12.6
85-86 —Yale	26	756	171	317	.539	80	166	.482	256	422	16.2
86-87 —Yale	24	749	165	290	.569	96	177	.542	320	426	17.8
Totals	102	2798	512	998	.513	269	525	.512	974	1293	12.7

NBA REGULAR-SEASON RECORD

Season Team	G	Min	FGM	FGA	Pct.	FTM	FTA	Pct.	Off.	Def.	Tot.	Ast.	PF	Dq.	Stl.	Blk.	TO	Pts.	Avg.
87-88 —Cleveland	55	513	65	137	.474	40	71	.563	74	70	144	23	87	2	13	19	31	170	3.1
88-89 —Cleveland	61	544	73	168	.435	39	107	.364	72	85	157	21	82	0	9	23	44	185	3.0
89-90 —Clev.-N.J.	64	1356	146	355	.411	58	182	.319	174	249	423	39	164	2	41	72	84	350	5.5
90-91 —New Jersey	61	1560	170	417	.408	94	176	.534	229	282	511	37	217	6	39	153	80	434	7.1
91-92 —New Jersey	82	1902	190	472	.403	80	171	.468	343	396	739	58	275	5	38	179	79	460	5.6
Totals	323	5875	644	1549	.416	311	707	.440	892	1082	1974	178	825	15	140	446	318	1599	5.0

Three-point field goals: 1988-89, 0-for-1.

NBA PLAYOFF RECORD

Season Team	G	Min.	FGM	FGA	Pct.	FTM	FTA	Pct.	Off.	Def.	Tot.	Ast.	PF	Dq.	Stl.	Blk.	TO	Pts.	Avg.
87-88 —Cleveland	4	24	2	4	.500	1	2	.500	4	2	6	2	3	0	0	0	1	5	1.3
88-89 —Cleveland	1	4	0	1	.000	0	0	...	0	0	0	0	1	0	0	0	1	0	0.0
91-92 —New Jersey	4	77	5	14	.357	4	8	.500	13	12	25	3	14	1	2	10	1	14	3.5
Totals	9	105	7	19	.368	5	10	.500	17	14	31	5	18	1	2	10	3	19	2.1

DUMARS, JOE

G, PISTONS

PERSONAL: Born May 24, 1963, in Shreveport, La. ... 6-3/195. ... Full name: Joe Dumars III.
HIGH SCHOOL: Natchitoches Central (La.).
COLLEGE: McNeese State.
TRANSACTIONS/CAREER NOTES: Selected by Detroit Pistons in first round (18th pick overall) of 1985 NBA Draft.
MISCELLANEOUS: Member of NBA championship teams (1989, 1990).

COLLEGIATE RECORD

NOTES: THE SPORTING NEWS All-America second team (1985).

Season Team	G	Min.	FGM	FGA	Pct.	FTM	FTA	Pct.	Reb.	Pts.	Avg.
81-82 —McNeese State	29	...	206	464	.444	115	160	.719	64	527	18.2
82-83 —McNeese State	29	...	212	487	.435	140	197	.711	128	569	19.6
83-84 —McNeese State	31	...	276	586	.471	267	324	.824	164	819	26.4
84-85 —McNeese State	27	...	248	501	.495	201	236	.852	132	697	25.8
Totals	116	...	942	2038	.462	723	917	.788	488	2612	22.5

Three-point field goals: 1982-83, 5-for-8 (.625).

NBA REGULAR-SEASON RECORD

HONORS: All-NBA third team (1990, 1991). ... NBA All-Defensive first team (1989, 1990, 1992). ... NBA All-Defensive second team (1991). ... NBA All-Rookie team (1986).

Season Team	G	Min.	FGM	FGA	Pct.	FTM	FTA	Pct.	Off.	Def.	Tot.	Ast.	PF	Dq.	Stl.	Blk.	TO	Pts.	Avg.
85-86 —Detroit	82	1957	287	597	.481	190	238	.798	60	59	119	390	200	1	66	11	158	769	9.4
86-87 —Detroit	79	2439	369	749	.493	184	246	.748	50	117	167	352	194	1	83	5	171	931	11.8
87-88 —Detroit	82	2732	453	960	.472	251	308	.815	63	137	200	387	155	1	87	15	172	1161	14.2
88-89 —Detroit	69	2408	456	903	.505	260	306	.850	57	115	172	390	103	1	63	5	178	1186	17.2
89-90 —Detroit	75	2578	508	1058	.480	297	330	.900	60	152	212	368	129	1	63	2	145	1335	17.8
90-91 —Detroit	80	3046	622	1292	.481	371	417	.890	62	125	187	443	135	0	89	7	189	1629	20.4
91-92 —Detroit	82	3192	587	1311	.448	412	475	.867	82	106	188	375	145	0	71	12	193	1635	19.9
Totals	549	18352	3282	6870	.478	1965	2320	.847	434	811	1245	2705	1061	5	522	57	1206	8646	15.7

Three-point field goals: 1985-86, 5-for-16 (.313). 1986-87, 9-for-22 (.409). 1987-88, 4-for-19 (.211). 1988-89, 14-for-29 (.483). 1989-90, 22-for-55 (.400). 1990-91, 14-for-45 (.311). 1991-92, 49-for-120 (.408). Totals, 117-for-306 (.382).

NBA PLAYOFF RECORD

NOTES: NBA Finals Most Valuable Player (1989).

Season Team	G	Min.	FGM	FGA	Pct.	FTM	FTA	Pct.	Off.	Def.	Tot.	Ast.	PF	Dq.	Stl.	Blk.	TO	Pts.	Avg.
85-86 —Detroit	4	147	25	41	.610	10	15	.667	6	7	13	25	16	0	4	0	7	60	15.0
86-87 —Detroit	15	473	78	145	.538	32	41	.780	8	11	19	72	26	0	12	1	27	190	12.7
87-88 —Detroit	23	804	113	247	.457	56	63	.889	18	32	50	112	50	1	13	2	40	284	12.3
88-89 —Detroit	17	620	106	233	.455	87	101	.861	11	33	44	96	31	0	12	1	31	300	17.6
89-90 —Detroit	20	754	130	284	.458	99	113	.876	18	26	44	95	37	0	22	0	54	364	18.2
90-91 —Detroit	15	588	105	245	.429	82	97	.845	21	29	50	62	33	1	16	1	17	309	20.6
91-92 —Detroit	5	221	32	68	.471	15	19	.789	5	3	8	16	11	0	5	1	7	84	16.8
Totals	99	3607	589	1263	.466	381	449	.849	87	141	228	478	204	2	84	6	183	1591	16.1

Three-point field goals: 1986-87, 2-for-3 (.667). 1987-88, 2-for-6 (.333). 1988-89, 1-for-12 (.083). 1989-90, 5-for-19 (.263). 1990-91, 17-for-42 (.405). 1991-92, 5-for-10 (.500). Totals, 32-for-92 (.348).

NBA ALL-STAR GAME RECORD

Season Team	Min.	FGM	FGA	Pct.	FTM	FTA	Pct.	Off.	Def.	Tot.	Ast.	PF	Dq.	Stl.	Blk.	TO	Pts.
1990 —Detroit	18	3	4	.750	1	2	.500	0	1	1	5	0	0	0	0	3	9

Season	Team	Min.	FGM	FGA	Pct.	FTM	FTA	Pct.	REBOUNDS Off.	Def.	Tot.	Ast.	PF	Dq.	Stl.	Blk.	TO	Pts.
1991	—Detroit	15	1	4	.250	0	0	...	1	1	2	1	1	0	0	0	4	2
1992	—Detroit	17	2	7	.286	0	0	...	0	1	1	3	0	0	0	0	2	4
	Totals	50	6	15	.400	1	2	.500	1	3	4	9	1	0	0	0	9	15

Three-point field goals: 1990, 2-for-2. 1991, 0-for-1. 1992, 0-for-2. Totals, 2-for-5 (.400).

EACKLES, LEDELL
G, BULLETS

PERSONAL: Born November 24, 1966, in Baton Rouge, La. . . . 6-5/225. . . . Name pronounced Le-DELL ECK-uls.
HIGH SCHOOL: Broadmoor (Baton Rouge, La.).
COLLEGE: San Jacinto (Tex.), then New Orleans.
TRANSACTIONS/CAREER NOTES: Selected by Washington Bullets in second round (36th pick overall) of 1988 NBA Draft.

COLLEGIATE RECORD

Season	Team	G	Min.	FGM	FGA	Pct.	FTM	FTA	Pct.	Reb.	Pts.	Avg.
84-85	—San Jacinto	29	...	...	...	...	...	...	...	156	552	19.0
85-86	—San Jacinto	37	...	417	715	.583	173	229	.755	238	1007	27.2
86-87	—New Orleans	28	902	239	554	.431	84	116	.724	114	632	22.6
87-88	—New Orleans	31	982	260	512	.508	186	232	.802	153	726	23.4
	Junior college totals	66	...	...	...	...	...	...	...	394	1559	23.6
	Four-year-college totals	59	1884	499	1066	.468	270	348	.776	267	1358	23.0

Three-point field goals: 1986-87, 70-for-172 (.407). 1987-88, 20-for-84 (.238). Totals, 90-for-256 (.352).

NBA REGULAR-SEASON RECORD

Season	Team	G	Min.	FGM	FGA	Pct.	FTM	FTA	Pct.	REBOUNDS Off.	Def.	Tot.	Ast.	PF	Dq.	Stl.	Blk.	TO	Pts.	Avg.
88-89	—Washington	80	1459	318	732	.434	272	346	.786	100	80	180	123	156	1	41	5	128	917	11.5
89-90	—Washington	78	1696	413	940	.439	210	280	.750	74	101	175	182	157	0	50	4	143	1055	13.5
90-91	—Washington	67	1616	345	762	.453	164	222	.739	47	81	128	136	121	0	47	10	115	868	13.0
91-92	—Washington	65	1463	355	759	.468	139	187	.743	39	139	178	125	145	1	47	7	75	856	13.2
	Totals	290	6234	1431	3193	.448	785	1035	.758	260	401	661	566	579	2	185	26	461	3696	12.7

Three-point field goals: 1988-89, 9-for-40 (.225). 1989-90, 19-for-59 (.322). 1990-91, 14-for-59 (.237). 1991-92, 7-for-35 (.200). Totals, 49-for-193 (.254).

EATON, MARK
C, JAZZ

PERSONAL: Born January 24, 1957, in Westminster, Calif. . . . 7-4/290. . . . Full name: Mark E. Eaton.
HIGH SCHOOL: Westminster (Calif.).
COLLEGE: Cypress (Calif.), then UCLA.
TRANSACTIONS/CAREER NOTES: Selected by Phoenix Suns in fifth round (107th pick overall) of 1979 NBA Draft (eligible for NBA draft because he was out of school three seasons between high school and college and his college class graduated in 1979). . . . Selected by Utah Jazz in fourth round (72nd pick overall) of 1982 NBA Draft.

COLLEGIATE RECORD

Season	Team	G	Min.	FGM	FGA	Pct.	FTM	FTA	Pct.	Reb.	Pts.	Avg.
78-79	—Cypress	35	...	202	319	.633	78	117	.667	381	482	13.8
79-80	—Cypress	25	...	167	289	.578	40	83	.482	218	374	15.0
80-81	—UCLA	19	155	17	37	.459	5	17	.294	49	39	2.1
81-82	—UCLA	11	41	5	12	.417	4	5	.800	22	14	1.3
	Junior college totals	60	...	369	608	.607	118	200	.590	599	856	14.3
	Four-year-college totals	30	196	22	49	.449	9	22	.409	71	53	1.8

NBA REGULAR-SEASON RECORD

RECORDS: Holds career record for highest blocked shots-per-game average (minimum 400 games)—3.68. . . . Holds single-season records for most blocked shots—456; and highest blocked shots-per-game average—5.56 (1985).
HONORS: NBA Defensive Player of the Year (1985, 1989). . . . NBA All-Defensive first team (1985, 1986, 1989). . . . NBA All-Defensive second team (1987, 1988).
NOTES: Led NBA with 4.28 blocked shots per game (1984), 5.56 blocked shots per game (1985), 4.06 blocked shots per game (1987) and 3.71 blocked shots per game (1988).

Season	Team	G	Min.	FGM	FGA	Pct.	FTM	FTA	Pct.	REBOUNDS Off.	Def.	Tot.	Ast.	PF	Dq.	Stl.	Blk.	TO	Pts.	Avg.
82-83	—Utah	81	1528	146	353	.414	59	90	.656	86	376	462	112	257	6	24	275	140	351	4.3
83-84	—Utah	82	2139	194	416	.466	73	123	.594	148	447	595	113	303	4	25	*351	98	461	5.6
84-85	—Utah	82	2813	302	673	.449	190	267	.712	207	*720	927	124	312	5	36	*456	206	794	9.7
85-86	—Utah	80	2551	277	589	.470	122	202	.604	172	503	675	101	282	5	33	369	157	676	8.5
86-87	—Utah	79	2505	234	585	.400	140	213	.657	211	486	697	105	273	5	43	*321	142	608	7.7
87-88	—Utah	82	2731	226	541	.418	119	191	.623	230	487	717	55	320	8	41	*304	131	571	7.0
88-89	—Utah	82	2914	188	407	.462	132	200	.660	227	616	843	83	290	6	40	315	142	508	6.2
89-90	—Utah	82	2281	158	300	.527	79	118	.669	171	430	601	39	238	3	33	201	75	395	4.8
90-91	—Utah	80	2580	169	292	.579	71	112	.634	182	485	667	51	298	6	39	188	99	409	5.1
91-92	—Utah	81	2023	107	240	.446	52	87	.598	150	341	491	40	239	2	36	205	60	266	3.3
	Totals	811	24065	2001	4396	.455	1037	1603	.647	1784	4891	6675	823	2812	50	350	2985	1250	5039	6.2

Three-point field goals: 1982-83, 0-for-1. 1983-84, 0-for-1. Totals, 0-for-2.

NBA PLAYOFF RECORD

NOTES: Shares single-game record for most blocked shots—10 (April 26, 1985, vs. Houston).

Season Team	G	Min.	FGM	FGA	Pct.	FTM	FTA	Pct.	Off.	Def.	Tot.	Ast.	PF	Dq.	Stl.	Blk.	TO	Pts.	Avg.
										— REBOUNDS —									
83-84 —Utah............	11	254	21	41	.512	8	17	.471	19	57	76	9	33	1	5	34	16	50	4.5
84-85 —Utah............	5	158	12	34	.353	5	7	.714	11	34	45	5	19	0	4	29	12	29	5.8
85-86 —Utah............	4	157	28	57	.491	2	3	.667	13	23	36	10	12	0	1	18	4	58	14.5
86-87 —Utah............	5	193	19	41	.463	16	25	.640	16	39	55	3	18	0	1	21	4	54	10.8
87-88 —Utah............	11	461	31	65	.477	23	36	.639	28	75	103	13	48	3	12	34	14	85	7.7
88-89 —Utah............	3	99	8	17	.471	9	11	.818	11	22	33	1	6	0	1	2	7	25	8.3
89-90 —Utah............	5	128	9	17	.529	1	5	.200	8	22	30	0	17	0	3	14	4	19	3.8
90-91 —Utah............	9	255	16	31	.516	7	12	.583	17	39	56	5	41	1	1	13	7	39	4.3
91-92 —Utah............	16	473	26	46	.565	21	27	.778	30	60	90	4	47	0	7	36	11	73	4.6
Totals	69	2178	170	349	.487	92	143	.643	153	371	524	50	241	5	35	201	79	432	6.3

NBA ALL-STAR GAME RECORD

Season Team	Min.	FGM	FGA	Pct.	FTM	FTA	Pct.	Off.	Def.	Tot.	Ast.	PF	Dq.	Stl.	Blk.	TO	Pts.
									— REBOUNDS —								
1989 —Utah..................	9	0	0	...	0	0	...	0	5	5	0	1	0	0	2	0	0

EDDIE, PATRICK
C

PERSONAL: Born December 27, 1967, in Milwaukee.... 6-11/240.
HIGH SCHOOL: Milwaukee Trade and Technical.
COLLEGE: Arkansas State, then Mississippi.
TRANSACTIONS/CAREER NOTES: Signed as free agent by New York Knicks (August 14, 1991).

COLLEGIATE RECORD

Season Team	G	Min.	FGM	FGA	Pct.	FTM	FTA	Pct.	Reb.	Pts.	Avg.
86-87 —Arkansas State......................					Did not play—redshirted.						
87-88 —Arkansas State......................	26	160	24	47	.511	14	20	.700	36	62	2.4
88-89 —Arkansas State......................	5	47	8	18	.444	1	6	.167	21	17	3.4
89-90 —Mississippi	24	482	73	169	.432	26	52	.500	145	173	7.2
90-91 —Mississippi	28	558	95	217	.438	52	83	.627	152	242	8.6
Totals	83	1247	200	451	.443	93	161	.578	354	494	6.0

Three-point field goals: 1989-90, 1-for-1.

NBA REGULAR-SEASON RECORD

Season Team	G	Min.	FGM	FGA	Pct.	FTM	FTA	Pct.	Off.	Def.	Tot.	Ast.	PF	Dq.	Stl.	Blk.	TO	Pts.	Avg.
										— REBOUNDS —									
91-92 —New York	4	13	2	9	.222	0	0	...	0	1	1	0	3	0	0	0	4	4	1.0

EDWARDS, BLUE
G/F, BUCKS

E

PERSONAL: Born October 31, 1965, in Washington, D.C.... 6-5/200.
... Full name: Theodore Edwards.
HIGH SCHOOL: Greene Central (Snow Hill, N.C.).
COLLEGE: Louisburg (N.C.), then East Carolina.
TRANSACTIONS/CAREER NOTES: Selected by Utah Jazz in first round (21st pick overall) of 1989 NBA Draft. ... Traded by Jazz with Eric Murdock and 1992 first-round draft choice to Milwaukee Bucks for Jay Humphries and Larry Krystkowiak (June 24, 1992).

COLLEGIATE RECORD

Season Team	G	Min.	FGM	FGA	Pct.	FTM	FTA	Pct.	Reb.	Pts.	Avg.
84-85 —Louisburg	29	...	...	...	...	...	...	...	177	515	17.8
85-86 —Louisburg	31	...	...	...	...	...	...	...	187	690	22.3
86-87 —East Carolina	28	876	169	301	.561	65	88	.739	158	404	14.4
87-88 —East Carolina					Did not play—disciplinary reasons.						
88-89 —East Carolina	29	987	297	539	.551	154	204	.755	201	773	26.7
Junior college totals	60	...	...	...	...	...	...	...	364	1205	20.1
Four-year-college totals	57	1863	466	840	.555	219	292	.750	359	1177	20.6

Three-point field goals: 1986-87, 1-for-4 (.250). 1988-89, 25-for-51 (.490). Totals, 26-for-55 (.473).

NBA REGULAR-SEASON RECORD

HONORS: NBA All-Rookie second team (1990).

Season Team	G	Min.	FGM	FGA	Pct.	FTM	FTA	Pct.	Off.	Def.	Tot.	Ast.	PF	Dq.	Stl.	Blk.	TO	Pts.	Avg.
										— REBOUNDS —									
89-90 —Utah............	82	1889	286	564	.507	146	203	.719	69	182	251	145	280	2	76	36	152	727	8.9
90-91 —Utah............	62	1611	244	464	.526	82	117	.701	51	150	201	108	203	4	57	29	105	576	9.3
91-92 —Utah............	81	2283	433	830	.522	113	146	.774	86	212	298	137	236	1	81	46	122	1018	12.6
Totals	225	5783	963	1858	.518	341	466	.732	206	544	750	390	719	7	214	111	379	2321	10.3

Three-point field goals: 1989-90, 9-for-30 (.300). 1990-91, 6-for-24 (.250). 1991-92, 39-for-103 (.379). Totals, 54-for-157 (.344).

NBA PLAYOFF RECORD

Season Team	G	Min.	FGM	FGA	Pct.	FTM	FTA	Pct.	Off.	Def.	Tot.	Ast.	PF	Dq.	Stl.	Blk.	TO	Pts.	Avg.
										— REBOUNDS —									
89-90 —Utah............	5	94	14	26	.538	7	8	.875	8	10	18	8	16	0	7	2	12	36	7.2
90-91 —Utah............	9	241	37	77	.481	16	20	.800	7	21	28	16	37	0	8	1	15	91	10.1
91-92 —Utah............	16	354	52	111	.468	23	32	.719	22	29	51	17	45	0	23	3	25	129	8.1
Totals	30	689	103	214	.481	46	60	.767	37	60	97	41	98	0	38	6	52	256	8.5

Three-point field goals: 1989-90, 1-for-3 (.333). 1990-91, 1-for-2 (.500). 1991-92, 2-for-10 (.200). Totals, 4-for-15 (.267).

EDWARDS, JAMES
C, LAKERS

PERSONAL: Born November 22, 1955, in Seattle.... 7-1/252.... Full name: James Franklin Edwards. **HIGH SCHOOL:** Roosevelt (Seattle). **COLLEGE:** Washington.

TRANSACTIONS/CAREER NOTES: Selected by Los Angeles Lakers in third round (46th pick overall) of 1977 NBA Draft.... Traded by Lakers with Earl Tatum and cash to Indiana Pacers for Adrian Dantley and Dave Robisch (December 13, 1977).... Signed as veteran free agent by Cleveland Cavaliers (May 25, 1981); Pacers agreed not to exercise their right of first refusal in exchange for 1981 and 1982 second-round draft choices (June 8, 1981).... Traded by Cavaliers to Phoenix Suns for Jeff Cook, 1983 third-round draft choice and cash (February 7, 1983).... Traded by Suns to Detroit Pistons for Ron Moore and 1991 second-round draft choice (February 24, 1988).... Traded by Pistons to Los Angeles Clippers for Jeff Martin and 1995 second-round draft pick (August 13, 1991).... Signed as unrestricted free agent by Los Angeles Lakers (August 13, 1992).
MISCELLANEOUS: Member of NBA championship teams (1989, 1990).

COLLEGIATE RECORD

Season	Team	G	Min.	FGM	FGA	Pct.	FTM	FTA	Pct.	Reb.	Pts.	Avg.
73-74	Washington	25	...	68	160	.425	34	62	.548	115	170	6.8
74-75	Washington	26	575	125	264	.473	70	129	.543	198	320	12.3
75-76	Washington	28	811	205	392	.523	83	137	.606	200	493	17.6
76-77	Washington	27	940	223	404	.552	119	184	.647	282	565	20.9
	Totals	106	...	621	1220	.509	306	512	.598	795	1548	14.6

NBA REGULAR-SEASON RECORD

										— REBOUNDS —										
Season	Team	G	Min.	FGM	FGA	Pct.	FTM	FTA	Pct.	Off.	Def.	Tot.	Ast.	PF	Dq.	Stl.	Blk.	TO	Pts.	Avg.
77-78	L.A.-Ind.	83	2405	495	1093	.453	272	421	.646	197	418	615	85	322	12	53	78	169	1262	15.2
78-79	Indiana	82	2546	534	1065	.501	298	441	.676	179	514	693	92	363	16	60	109	162	1366	16.7
79-80	Indiana	82	2314	528	1032	.512	231	339	.681	179	399	578	127	324	12	55	104	131	1287	15.7
80-81	Indiana	81	2375	511	1004	.509	244	347	.703	191	380	571	212	304	7	32	128	154	1266	15.6
81-82	Cleveland	77	2539	528	1033	.511	232	339	.684	189	392	581	123	347	17	24	117	162	1288	16.7
82-83	Clev.-Phoe.	31	667	128	263	.487	69	108	.639	56	99	155	40	110	5	12	19	49	325	10.5
83-84	Phoenix	72	1897	438	817	.536	183	254	.720	108	240	348	184	254	3	23	30	140	1059	14.7
84-85	Phoenix	70	1787	384	766	.501	276	370	.746	95	292	387	153	237	5	26	52	162	1044	14.9
85-86	Phoenix	52	1314	318	587	.542	212	302	.702	79	222	301	74	200	5	23	29	128	848	16.3
86-87	Phoenix	14	304	57	110	.518	54	70	.771	20	40	60	19	42	1	6	7	15	168	12.0
87-88	Phoe.-Det.	69	1705	302	643	.470	210	321	.654	119	293	412	78	216	2	16	37	130	814	11.8
88-89	Detroit	76	1254	211	422	.500	133	194	.686	68	163	231	49	226	1	11	31	72	555	7.3
89-90	Detroit	82	2283	462	928	.498	265	354	.749	112	233	345	63	295	4	23	37	133	1189	14.5
90-91	Detroit	72	1903	383	792	.484	215	295	.729	91	186	277	65	249	4	12	30	126	982	13.6
91-92	L.A. Clippers	72	1437	250	538	.465	198	271	.731	55	147	202	53	236	1	24	33	72	698	9.7
	Totals	1015	26730	5529	11093	.498	3092	4426	.699	1738	4018	5756	1417	3725	95	400	841	1815	14151	13.9

Three-point field goals: 1979-80, 0-for-1. 1980-81, 0-for-3. 1981-82, 0-for-4. 1983-84, 0-for-1. 1984-85, 0-for-3. 1987-88, 0-for-1. 1988-89, 0-for-2. 1989-90, 0-for-3. 1990-91, 1-for-2 (.500). 1991-92, 0-for-1. Totals, 1-for-21 (.048).

NBA PLAYOFF RECORD

										— REBOUNDS —										
Season	Team	G	Min.	FGM	FGA	Pct.	FTM	FTA	Pct.	Off.	Def.	Tot.	Ast.	PF	Dq.	Stl.	Blk.	TO	Pts.	Avg.
80-81	Indiana	2	56	7	24	.292	0	0	...	4	10	14	5	8	0	1	1	4	14	7.0
82-83	Phoenix	3	54	11	26	.423	6	6	1.000	6	12	18	4	7	0	1	1	5	28	9.3
83-84	Phoenix	17	463	93	189	.492	48	68	.706	22	69	91	27	62	3	4	11	31	234	13.8
87-88	Detroit	22	308	56	110	.509	27	41	.659	23	45	68	11	55	0	2	10	10	139	6.3
88-89	Detroit	17	317	40	85	.471	40	51	.784	11	25	36	12	53	0	1	8	15	120	7.1
89-90	Detroit	20	536	114	231	.494	58	96	.604	24	47	71	13	74	0	5	11	31	286	14.3
90-91	Detroit	15	345	61	150	.407	38	55	.691	15	22	37	9	43	0	2	3	24	160	10.7
91-92	L.A. Clippers	5	87	10	24	.417	12	19	.632	5	8	13	3	11	0	1	1	4	32	6.4
	Totals	101	2166	392	839	.467	229	336	.682	110	238	348	84	313	3	17	46	124	1013	10.0

Three-point field goals: 1987-88, 0-for-1. 1988-89, 0-for-1. 1989-90, 0-for-1. Totals, 0-for-3.

EDWARDS, KEVIN
G, HEAT

PERSONAL: Born October 30, 1965, in Cleveland Heights, O.... 6-3/197.... Full name: Kevin Durell Edwards. **HIGH SCHOOL:** St. Joseph Academy (Cleveland). **COLLEGE:** Lakeland Community College (O.), then DePaul.

TRANSACTIONS/CAREER NOTES: Selected by Miami Heat in first round (20th pick overall) of 1988 NBA Draft.

COLLEGIATE RECORD

Season	Team	G	Min.	FGM	FGA	Pct.	FTM	FTA	Pct.	Reb.	Pts.	Avg.
84-85	Lakeland Community College	33	...	256	435	.589	103	144	.715	178	615	18.6
85-86	Lakeland Community College	32	...	325	519	.626	121	159	.761	239	771	24.1
86-87	DePaul	31	1060	184	343	.536	63	78	.808	156	447	14.4
87-88	DePaul	30	999	220	413	.533	83	106	.783	158	548	18.3
	Junior college totals	65	...	581	954	.609	224	303	.739	417	1386	21.3
	Four-year-college totals	61	2059	404	756	.534	146	184	.793	314	995	16.3

Three-point field goals: 1986-87, 16-for-36 (.444). 1987-88, 25-for-56 (.446). Totals, 41-for-92 (.446).

NBA REGULAR-SEASON RECORD

HONORS: NBA All-Rookie Second team (1989).

Season Team	G	Min.	FGM	FGA	Pct.	FTM	FTA	Pct.	Off.	Def.	Tot.	Ast.	PF	Dq.	Stl.	Blk.	TO	Pts.	Avg.
88-89 —Miami..........	79	2349	470	1105	.425	144	193	.746	85	177	262	349	154	0	139	27	246	1094	13.8
89-90 —Miami..........	78	2211	395	959	.412	139	183	.760	77	205	282	252	149	1	125	33	180	938	12.0
90-91 —Miami..........	79	2000	380	927	.410	171	213	.803	80	125	205	240	151	2	129	46	163	955	12.1
91-92 —Miami..........	81	1840	325	716	.454	162	191	.848	56	155	211	170	138	1	99	20	120	819	10.1
Totals	317	8400	1570	3707	.424	616	780	.790	298	662	960	1011	592	4	492	126	709	3806	12.0

Three-point field goals: 1988-89, 10-for-37 (.270). 1989-90, 9-for-30 (.300). 1990-91, 24-for-84 (.286). 1991-92, 7-for-32 (.219). Totals, 50-for-183 (.273).

NBA PLAYOFF RECORD

Season Team	G	Min.	FGM	FGA	Pct.	FTM	FTA	Pct.	Off.	Def.	Tot.	Ast.	PF	Dq.	Stl.	Blk.	TO	Pts.	Avg.
91-92 —Miami..........	3	55	5	13	.385	5	8	.625	1	6	7	7	3	0	2	0	5	15	5.0

EHLO, CRAIG
G/F, CAVALIERS

PERSONAL: Born August 11, 1961, in Lubbock, Tex. ... 6-7/205. ... Full name: Joel Craig Ehlo.... Name pronounced EE-low.
HIGH SCHOOL: Monterey (Lubbock, Tex.).
COLLEGE: Odessa (Tex.), then Washington State.
TRANSACTIONS/CAREER NOTES: Selected by Houston Rockets in third round (48th pick overall) of 1983 NBA Draft.... Waived by Rockets (October 30, 1986).... Played in Continental Basketball Association with Mississippi Jets (1986-87).... Signed as free agent by Cleveland Cavaliers (January 13, 1987).

COLLEGIATE RECORD

Season Team	G	Min.	FGM	FGA	Pct.	FTM	FTA	Pct.	Reb.	Pts.	Avg.
79-80 —Odessa.................................	28	. . .	146	300	.487	60	84	.714	142	352	12.6
80-81 —Odessa.................................	30	. . .	241	482	.500	139	180	.772	204	621	20.7
81-82 —Washington State..................	30	592	57	119	.479	39	65	.600	65	153	5.1
82-83 —Washington State..................	30	911	145	265	.547	69	109	.633	97	359	12.0
Junior college totals........................	58	. . .	387	782	.495	199	264	.754	346	973	16.8
Four-year-college totals	60	1503	202	384	.526	108	174	.621	162	512	8.5

NBA REGULAR-SEASON RECORD

Season Team	G	Min.	FGM	FGA	Pct.	FTM	FTA	Pct.	Off.	Def.	Tot.	Ast.	PF	Dq.	Stl.	Blk.	TO	Pts.	Avg.
83-84 —Houston	7	63	11	27	.407	1	1	1.000	4	5	9	6	13	0	3	0	3	23	3.3
84-85 —Houston	45	189	34	69	.493	19	30	.633	8	17	25	26	26	0	11	3	22	87	1.9
85-86 —Houston	36	199	36	84	.429	23	29	.793	17	29	46	29	22	0	11	4	15	98	2.7
86-87 —Cleveland	44	890	99	239	.414	70	99	.707	55	106	161	92	80	0	40	30	61	273	6.2
87-88 —Cleveland	79	1709	226	485	.466	89	132	.674	86	188	274	206	182	0	82	30	107	563	7.1
88-89 —Cleveland	82	1867	249	524	.475	71	117	.607	100	195	295	266	161	0	110	19	116	608	7.4
89-90 —Cleveland	81	2894	436	940	.464	126	185	.681	147	292	439	371	226	2	126	23	161	1102	13.6
90-91 —Cleveland	82	2766	344	773	.445	95	140	.679	142	246	388	376	209	0	121	34	160	832	10.1
91-92 —Cleveland	63	2016	310	684	.453	87	123	.707	94	213	307	238	150	0	78	22	104	776	12.3
Totals	519	12593	1745	3825	.456	581	856	.679	653	1291	1944	1610	1069	2	582	165	749	4362	8.4

Three-point field goals: 1984-85, 0-for-3. 1985-86, 3-for-9 (.333). 1986-87, 5-for-29 (.172). 1987-88, 22-for-64 (.344). 1988-89, 39-for-100 (.390). 1989-90, 104-for-248 (.419). 1990-91, 49-for-149 (.329). 1991-92, 69-for-167 (.413). Totals, 291-for-769 (.378).

NBA PLAYOFF RECORD

Season Team	G	Min.	FGM	FGA	Pct.	FTM	FTA	Pct.	Off.	Def.	Tot.	Ast.	PF	Dq.	Stl.	Blk.	TO	Pts.	Avg.
84-85 —Houston	3	6	1	1	1.000	2	2	1.000	0	0	0	0	3	0	4	0	0	4	1.3
85-86 —Houston	10	38	8	16	.500	4	5	.800	1	2	3	6	4	0	4	1	3	20	2.0
87-88 —Cleveland	5	128	17	40	.425	10	16	.625	3	15	18	17	14	0	5	0	12	44	8.8
88-89 —Cleveland	4	97	17	39	.436	9	11	.818	2	4	6	13	10	0	3	1	5	48	12.0
89-90 —Cleveland	5	196	26	62	.419	12	19	.632	7	25	32	32	18	0	6	0	12	69	13.8
91-92 —Cleveland	17	552	63	152	.414	16	21	.762	22	55	77	77	40	0	21	5	18	163	9.6
Totals	44	1017	132	310	.426	53	74	.716	35	101	136	145	89	0	43	7	50	348	7.9

Three-point field goals: 1985-86, 0-for-1. 1987-88, 0-for-8. 1988-89, 5-for-13 (.385). 1989-90, 5-for-15 (.333). 1991-92, 21-for-51 (.412). Totals, 31-for-88 (.352).

CBA REGULAR-SEASON RECORD

Season Team	G	Min.	2-POINT			3-POINT			FTM	FTA	Pct.	Reb.	Ast.	Pts.	Avg.
			FGM	FGA	Pct.	FGM	FGA	Pct.							
86-87 —Mississippi......	6	144	20	31	.645	1	1	1.000	20	30	.667	22	20	63	10.5

ELIE, MARIO
G, TRAIL BLAZERS

PERSONAL: Born November 26, 1963, in New York.... 6-5/210.... Full name: Mario Antoine Elie.... Name pronounced Ehl-LEE.
HIGH SCHOOL: Power Memorial (New York).
COLLEGE: American International (Mass.).
TRANSACTIONS/CAREER NOTES: Selected by Milwaukee Bucks in seventh round (160th pick overall) of 1985 NBA Draft.... Waived by Bucks (July 25, 1985).... Played in Continental Basketball Association with Albany Patroons (1989-90 and 1990-91).... Signed as free agent by Los Angeles Lakers (October 2, 1990).... Waived by Lakers (October 15, 1990).... Signed by Philadelphia 76ers to 10-day contract (December 28, 1990).... Signed by Golden State Warriors to 10-day contract (February 23, 1991).... Re-signed by Warriors for remainder of season (March 5, 1991). ... Signed as free agent by Portland Trail Blazers (August 4, 1992); Warriors waived their right of first refusal.

COLLEGIATE RECORD

Season Team	G	Min.	FGM	FGA	Pct.	FTM	FTA	Pct.	Reb.	Pts.	Avg.
81-82 —American International	25	754	157	268	.586	72	97	.742	207	386	15.4
82-83 —American International	31	1060	188	357	.527	116	157	.739	239	492	15.9

Season Team	G	Min.	FGM	FGA	Pct.	FTM	FTA	Pct.	Reb.	Pts.	Avg.
83-84 — American International	31	1174	225	398	.565	135	170	.794	256	585	18.9
84-85 — American International	33	1208	252	459	.549	157	202	.777	299	661	20.0
Totals	120	4196	822	1482	.555	480	626	.767	1001	2124	17.7

CBA REGULAR-SEASON RECORD

NOTES: CBA All-Star first team (1991).

				2-POINT			3-POINT						
Season Team	G	Min.	FGM	FGA	Pct.	FGM	FGA	Pct.	FTM	FTA	Pct.	Reb.	Ast.	Pts.	Avg.
89-90 — Albany	56	1772	338	578	.585	29	76	.382	259	295	.878	339	193	1022	18.3
90-91 — Albany	41	1451	324	571	.567	28	87	.322	270	302	.894	235	197	1002	24.4
Totals	97	3223	662	1149	.576	57	163	.350	529	597	.886	574	390	2024	20.9

NBA REGULAR-SEASON RECORD

									— REBOUNDS —								
Season Team	G	Min.	FGM	FGA	Pct.	FTM	FTA	Pct.	Off.	Def.	Tot.	Ast.	PF	Dq.	Stl.	Blk.	TO	Pts.	Avg.
90-91 — Phil.-G.S.	33	644	79	159	.497	75	89	.843	46	64	110	45	85	1	19	10	30	237	7.2
91-92 — Golden State	79	1677	221	424	.521	155	182	.852	69	158	227	174	159	3	68	15	83	620	7.8
Totals	112	2321	300	583	.515	230	271	.849	115	222	337	219	244	4	87	25	113	857	7.7

Three-point field goals: 1990-91, 4-for-10 (.400). 1991-92, 23-for-70 (.329). Totals, 27-for-80 (.338).

NBA PLAYOFF RECORD

									— REBOUNDS —								
Season Team	G	Min.	FGM	FGA	Pct.	FTM	FTA	Pct.	Off.	Def.	Tot.	Ast.	PF	Dq.	Stl.	Blk.	TO	Pts.	Avg.
90-91 — Golden State	9	197	28	56	.500	27	32	.844	17	15	32	13	32	0	5	1	10	84	9.3
91-92 — Golden State	4	80	23	36	.639	2	3	.667	11	11	22	10	11	1	5	0	6	50	12.5
Totals	13	277	51	92	.554	29	35	.829	28	26	54	23	43	1	10	1	16	134	10.3

Three-point field goals: 1990-91, 1-for-1. 1991-92, 2-for-2. Totals, 3-for-3.

ELLIOTT, SEAN
F, SPURS

PERSONAL: Born February 2, 1968, in Tucson, Ariz. . . . 6-8/210. . . . Full name: Sean Michael Elliott.
HIGH SCHOOL: Cholla (Tucson, Ariz.).
COLLEGE: Arizona.
TRANSACTIONS/CAREER NOTES: Selected by San Antonio Spurs in first round (third pick overall) of 1989 NBA Draft.

COLLEGIATE RECORD

NOTES: THE SPORTING NEWS All-America first team (1988, 1989).

Season Team	G	Min.	FGM	FGA	Pct.	FTM	FTA	Pct.	Reb.	Pts.	Avg.
85-86 — Arizona	32	1079	187	385	.486	125	167	.749	171	499	15.6
86-87 — Arizona	30	1046	209	410	.510	127	165	.770	181	578	19.3
87-88 — Arizona	38	1249	263	461	.571	176	222	.793	219	743	19.6
88-89 — Arizona	33	1125	237	494	.480	195	232	.841	237	735	22.3
Totals	133	4499	896	1750	.512	623	786	.793	808	2555	19.2

Three-point field goals: 1986-87, 33-for-89 (.371). 1987-88, 41-for-87 (.471). 1988-89, 66-for-151 (.437). Totals, 140-for-327 (.428).

NBA REGULAR-SEASON RECORD

HONORS: NBA All-Rookie second team (1990).

									— REBOUNDS —								
Season Team	G	Min.	FGM	FGA	Pct.	FTM	FTA	Pct.	Off.	Def.	Tot.	Ast.	PF	Dq.	Stl.	Blk.	TO	Pts.	Avg.
89-90 — San Antonio.	81	2032	311	647	.481	187	216	.866	127	170	297	154	172	0	45	14	112	810	10.0
90-91 — San Antonio.	82	3044	478	976	.490	325	402	.808	142	314	456	238	190	2	69	33	147	1301	15.9
91-92 — San Antonio.	82	3120	514	1040	.494	285	331	.861	143	296	439	214	149	0	84	29	152	1338	16.3
Totals	245	8196	1303	2663	.489	797	949	.840	412	780	1192	606	511	2	198	76	411	3449	14.1

Three-point field goals: 1989-90, 1-for-9 (.111). 1990-91, 20-for-64 (.313). 1991-92, 25-for-82 (.305). Totals, 46-for-155 (.297).

NBA PLAYOFF RECORD

									— REBOUNDS —								
Season Team	G	Min.	FGM	FGA	Pct.	FTM	FTA	Pct.	Off.	Def.	Tot.	Ast.	PF	Dq.	Stl.	Blk.	TO	Pts.	Avg.
89-90 — San Antonio.	10	291	53	96	.552	21	29	.724	11	30	41	18	37	0	9	6	15	127	12.7
90-91 — San Antonio.	4	132	17	40	.425	25	32	.781	8	14	22	16	9	0	4	1	9	59	14.8
91-92 — San Antonio.	3	137	19	40	.475	16	18	.889	4	9	13	8	6	0	3	4	6	59	19.7
Totals	17	560	89	176	.506	62	79	.785	23	53	76	42	52	0	16	11	30	245	14.4

Three-point field goals: 1989-90, 0-for-1. 1990-91, 0-for-3. 1991-92, 5-for-8 (.625). Totals, 5-for-12 (.417).

ELLIS, DALE
G/F, SPURS

PERSONAL: Born August 6, 1960, in Marietta, Ga. . . . 6-7/215.
HIGH SCHOOL: Marietta (Ga.).
COLLEGE: Tennessee.
TRANSACTIONS/CAREER NOTES: Selected by Dallas Mavericks in first round (ninth pick overall) of 1983 NBA Draft. . . . Traded by Mavericks to Seattle SuperSonics for Al Wood (July 23, 1986). . . . Traded by SuperSonics to Milwaukee Bucks for Ricky Pierce (February 15, 1991). . . . Traded by Bucks to San Antonio Spurs for rights to Tracy Murray (July 1, 1992).

COLLEGIATE RECORD

NOTES: THE SPORTING NEWS All-America first team (1983).

Season Team	G	Min.	FGM	FGA	Pct.	FTM	FTA	Pct.	Reb.	Pts.	Avg.
79-80 — Tennessee..............................	27	573	81	182	.445	31	40	.775	96	193	7.1
80-81 — Tennessee..............................	29	1057	215	360	.597	83	111	.748	185	513	17.7

Season Team	G	Min.	FGM	FGA	Pct.	FTM	FTA	Pct.	Reb.	Pts.	Avg.
81-82 —Tennessee	30	1134	257	393	.654	121	152	.796	189	635	21.2
82-83 —Tennessee	32	1179	279	464	.601	166	221	.751	209	724	22.6
Totals	118	3943	832	1399	.595	401	524	.765	679	2065	17.5

NBA REGULAR-SEASON RECORD

RECORDS: Holds single-game record for most minutes played—69 (November 9, 1989, vs. Milwaukee).... Shares single-game record for most three-point field goals made—9 (April 20, 1990, vs. Los Angeles Clippers).
HONORS: NBA Most Improved Player (1987).... All-NBA third team (1989).

Season Team	G	Min.	FGM	FGA	Pct.	FTM	FTA	Pct.	Off.	Def.	Tot.	Ast.	PF	Dq.	Stl.	Blk.	TO	Pts.	Avg.
83-84 —Dallas	67	1059	225	493	.456	87	121	.719	106	144	250	56	118	0	41	9	78	549	8.2
84-85 —Dallas	72	1314	274	603	.454	77	104	.740	100	138	238	56	131	1	46	7	58	667	9.3
85-86 —Dallas	72	1086	193	470	.411	59	82	.720	86	82	168	37	78	0	40	9	38	508	7.1
86-87 —Seattle	82	3073	785	1520	.516	385	489	.787	187	260	447	238	267	2	104	32	238	2041	24.9
87-88 —Seattle	75	2790	764	1519	.503	303	395	.767	167	173	340	197	221	1	74	11	172	1938	25.8
88-89 —Seattle	82	3190	857	1710	.501	377	462	.816	156	186	342	164	197	0	108	22	218	2253	27.5
89-90 —Seattle	55	2033	502	1011	.497	193	236	.818	90	148	238	110	124	3	59	7	119	1293	23.5
90-91 —Seattle-Mil.	51	1424	340	718	.474	120	166	.723	66	107	173	95	112	1	49	8	81	857	16.8
91-92 —Milwaukee	81	2191	485	1034	.469	164	212	.774	92	161	253	104	151	0	57	18	119	1272	15.7
Totals	637	18160	4425	9078	.487	1765	2267	.779	1050	1399	2449	1057	1399	8	578	123	1121	11378	17.9

Three-point field goals: 1983-84, 12-for-29 (.414). 1984-85, 42-for-109 (.385). 1985-86, 63-for-173 (.364). 1986-87, 86-for-240 (.358). 1987-88, 107-for-259 (.413). 1988-89, 162-for-339 (.478). 1989-90, 96-for-256 (.375). 1990-91, 57-for-157 (.363). 1991-92, 138-for-329 (.419). Totals, 763-for-1891 (.403).

NBA PLAYOFF RECORD

Season Team	G	Min.	FGM	FGA	Pct.	FTM	FTA	Pct.	Off.	Def.	Tot.	Ast.	PF	Dq.	Stl.	Blk.	TO	Pts.	Avg.
83-84 —Dallas	8	178	26	80	.325	6	8	.750	19	23	42	4	17	0	10	2	5	59	7.4
84-85 —Dallas	4	68	10	23	.435	1	2	.500	4	3	7	3	3	0	4	0	4	23	5.8
85-86 —Dallas	7	67	9	22	.409	5	5	1.000	3	4	7	2	6	0	2	2	4	30	4.3
86-87 —Seattle	14	530	148	304	.487	44	54	.815	37	53	90	37	54	1	10	6	33	353	25.2
87-88 —Seattle	5	172	40	83	.482	21	29	.724	11	12	23	15	17	0	3	2	12	104	20.8
88-89 —Seattle	8	304	72	160	.450	24	33	.727	14	18	32	10	19	1	11	1	21	183	22.9
Totals	46	1319	305	672	.454	101	131	.771	88	113	201	71	116	2	40	13	79	752	16.3

Three-point field goals: 1983-84, 1-for-12 (.083). 1984-85, 2-for-5 (.400). 1985-86, 7-for-12 (.583). 1986-87, 13-for-36 (.361). 1987-88, 3-for-12 (.250). 1988-89, 15-for-37 (.405). Totals, 41-for-114 (.360).

NBA ALL-STAR GAME RECORD

Season Team	Min.	FGM	FGA	Pct.	FTM	FTA	Pct.	Off.	Def.	Tot.	Ast.	PF	Dq.	Stl.	Blk.	TO	Pts.
1989 —Seattle	26	12	16	.750	2	2	1.000	3	3	6	2	2	0	0	0	2	27

Three-point field goals: 1989, 1-for-1.

ELLIS, LeRON
C/F, CLIPPERS

PERSONAL: Born April 28, 1969, in Los Angeles.... 6-10/240.... Full name: LeRon Perry Ellis.... Name pronounced La-RON.... Son of Leroy Ellis, center/forward with five NBA teams (1962-63 through 1975-76). **HIGH SCHOOL:** Mater Dei (Santa Ana, Calif.).
COLLEGE: Kentucky, then Syracuse.
TRANSACTIONS/CAREER NOTES: Selected by Los Angeles Clippers in first round (22nd pick overall) of 1991 NBA Draft.

COLLEGIATE RECORD

Season Team	G	Min.	FGM	FGA	Pct.	FTM	FTA	Pct.	Reb.	Pts.	Avg.
87-88 —Kentucky	28	386	49	106	.462	22	42	.524	83	120	4.3
88-89 —Kentucky	32	1006	200	385	.519	111	164	.677	177	511	16.0
89-90 —Syracuse	32	682	79	175	.451	28	54	.519	129	192	6.0
90-91 —Syracuse	32	929	142	280	.507	72	119	.605	246	356	11.1
Totals	124	3003	470	946	.497	233	379	.615	635	1179	9.5

Three-point field goals: 1988-89, 0-for-2. 1989-90, 6-for-15 (.400). 1990-91, 0-for-4. Totals, 6-for-21 (.286).

NBA REGULAR-SEASON RECORD

Season Team	G	Min.	FGM	FGA	Pct.	FTM	FTA	Pct.	Off.	Def.	Tot.	Ast.	PF	Dq.	Stl.	Blk.	TO	Pts.	Avg.
91-92 —L.A. Clippers	29	103	17	50	.340	9	19	.474	12	12	24	1	11	0	6	9	11	43	1.5

NBA PLAYOFF RECORD

Season Team	G	Min.	FGM	FGA	Pct.	FTM	FTA	Pct.	Off.	Def.	Tot.	Ast.	PF	Dq.	Stl.	Blk.	TO	Pts.	Avg.
91-92 —L.A. Clippers	1	2	0	0	...	0	0	...	0	0	0	0	0	0	0	0	0	0	0.0

ELLISON, PERVIS
F/C, BULLETS

PERSONAL: Born April 3, 1967, in Savannah, Ga.... 6-10/225. **HIGH SCHOOL:** Savannah (Ga.).
COLLEGE: Louisville.
TRANSACTIONS/CAREER NOTES: Selected by Sacramento Kings in first round (first pick overall) of 1989 NBA Draft.... Traded by Kings to Washington Bullets in three-way deal in which Bullets sent Jeff Malone to Utah Jazz and Jazz sent Bobby Hansen, Eric Leckner and 1990 first- and second-round draft choices to Kings (June 25, 1990); Jazz also received 1990 second-round draft choice and Kings also received 1991 second-round draft choice.

COLLEGIATE RECORD

NOTES: THE SPORTING NEWS All-America second team (1989).... Most Outstanding Player in NCAA Division I tournament (1986).... Member of NCAA Division I championship team (1986).

Season Team	G	Min.	FGM	FGA	Pct.	FTM	FTA	Pct.	Reb.	Pts.	Avg.
85-86 —Louisville	39	1194	210	379	.554	90	132	.682	318	510	13.1
86-87 —Louisville	31	952	185	347	.533	100	139	.719	270	470	15.2
87-88 —Louisville	35	1175	235	391	.601	146	211	.692	291	617	17.6
88-89 —Louisville	31	1014	227	369	.615	92	141	.652	270	546	17.6
Totals	136	4335	857	1486	.577	428	623	.687	1149	2143	15.8

Three-point field goals: 1987-88, 1-for-2 (.500). 1988-89, 0-for-1. Totals, 1-for-3 (.333).

NBA REGULAR-SEASON RECORD

HONORS: NBA Most Improved Player (1992).

Season Team	G	Min.	FGM	FGA	Pct.	FTM	FTA	Pct.	Off.	Def.	Tot.	Ast.	PF	Dq.	Stl.	Blk.	TO	Pts.	Avg.
89-90 —Sacramento	34	866	111	251	.442	49	78	.628	64	132	196	65	132	4	16	57	62	271	8.0
90-91 —Washington	76	1942	326	636	.513	139	214	.650	224	361	585	102	268	6	49	157	146	791	10.4
91-92 —Washington	66	2511	547	1014	.539	227	312	.728	217	523	740	190	222	2	62	177	196	1322	20.0
Totals	176	5319	984	1901	.518	415	604	.687	505	1016	1521	357	622	12	127	391	404	2384	13.5

Three-point field goals: 1989-90, 0-for-2. 1990-91, 0-for-6. 1991-92, 1-for-3 (.333). Totals, 1-for-11 (.091).

ENGLISH, A.J.
G, BULLETS

PERSONAL: Born July 11, 1967, in Wilmington, Del.... 6-3/180.... Full name: Albert Jay English.
HIGH SCHOOL: Howard Career Center (Wilmington, Del.).
COLLEGE: Virginia Union.
TRANSACTIONS/CAREER NOTES: Selected by Washington Bullets in second round (37th pick overall) of 1990 NBA Draft.

COLLEGIATE RECORD

NOTES: Led NCAA Division II with 33.4 points per game (1990).

Season Team	G	Min.	FGM	FGA	Pct.	FTM	FTA	Pct.	Reb.	Pts.	Avg.
86-87 —Virginia Union	31	...	105	235	.447	72	95	.758	90	305	9.8
87-88 —Virginia Union	29	...	172	365	.471	95	133	.714	137	474	16.3
88-89 —Virginia Union	30	...	210	417	.504	138	170	.812	120	616	20.5
89-90 —Virginia Union	30	...	333	672	.496	270	341	.792	154	1001	33.4
Totals	120	...	820	1689	.485	575	739	.778	501	2396	20.0

Three-point field goals: 1986-87, 23-for-50 (.460). 1987-88, 35-for-79 (.443). 1988-89, 58-for-123 (.472). 1989-90, 65-for-144 (.451). Totals, 181-for-396 (.457).

NBA REGULAR-SEASON RECORD

Season Team	G	Min.	FGM	FGA	Pct.	FTM	FTA	Pct.	Off.	Def.	Tot.	Ast.	PF	Dq.	Stl.	Blk.	TO	Pts.	Avg.
90-91 —Washington	70	1443	251	572	.439	111	157	.707	66	81	147	177	127	1	25	15	114	616	8.8
91-92 —Washington	81	1665	366	846	.433	148	176	.841	74	94	168	143	160	1	32	9	89	886	10.9
Totals	151	3108	617	1418	.435	259	333	.778	140	175	315	320	287	2	57	24	203	1502	9.9

Three-point field goals: 1990-91, 3-for-31 (.097). 1991-92, 6-for-34 (.176). Totals, 9-for-65 (.138).

EWING, PATRICK
C, KNICKS

PERSONAL: Born August 5, 1962, in Kingston, Jamaica.... 7-0/240. ...Full name: Patrick Aloysius Ewing.
HIGH SCHOOL: Cambridge Rindge & Latin School (Mass.).
COLLEGE: Georgetown.
TRANSACTIONS/CAREER NOTES: Selected by New York Knicks in first round (first pick overall) of 1985 NBA Draft.
MISCELLANEOUS: Member of gold-medal-winning U.S. Olympic teams (1984, 1992).

COLLEGIATE RECORD

NOTES: THE SPORTING NEWS College Player of the Year (1985).... THE SPORTING NEWS All-America first team (1985).... THE SPORTING NEWS All-America second team (1983, 1984).... NCAA Division I Tournament Most Outstanding Player (1984).... Member of NCAA Division I championship team (1984).

Season Team	G	Min.	FGM	FGA	Pct.	FTM	FTA	Pct.	Reb.	Pts.	Avg.
81-82 —Georgetown	37	1064	183	290	.631	103	167	.617	279	469	12.7
82-83 —Georgetown	32	1024	212	372	.570	141	224	.629	325	565	17.7
83-84 —Georgetown	37	1179	242	368	.658	124	189	.656	371	608	16.4
84-85 —Georgetown	37	1132	220	352	.625	102	160	.638	341	542	14.6
Totals	143	4399	857	1382	.620	470	740	.635	1316	2184	15.3

NBA REGULAR-SEASON RECORD

HONORS: NBA Rookie of the Year (1986).... All-NBA first team (1990).... All-NBA second team (1988, 1989, 1991, 1992). ...NBA All-Defensive second team (1988, 1989, 1992).... NBA All-Rookie team (1986).

Season Team	G	Min.	FGM	FGA	Pct.	FTM	FTA	Pct.	Off.	Def.	Tot.	Ast.	PF	Dq.	Stl.	Blk.	TO	Pts.	Avg.
85-86 —New York	50	1771	386	814	.474	226	306	.739	124	327	451	102	191	7	54	103	172	998	20.0
86-87 —New York	63	2206	530	1053	.503	296	415	.713	157	398	555	104	248	5	89	147	229	1356	21.5
87-88 —New York	82	2546	656	1183	.555	341	476	.716	245	431	676	125	*332	5	104	245	287	1653	20.2
88-89 —New York	80	2896	727	1282	.567	361	484	.746	213	527	740	188	311	5	117	281	266	1815	22.7
89-90 —New York	82	3165	922	1673	.551	502	648	.775	235	658	893	182	325	7	78	327	278	2347	28.6

Season Team	G	Min.	FGM	FGA	Pct.	FTM	FTA	Pct.	Off.	Def.	Tot.	Ast.	PF	Dq.	Stl.	Blk.	TO	Pts.	Avg.
90-91—New York	81	3104	845	1645	.514	464	623	.745	194	711	905	244	287	3	80	258	291	2154	26.6
91-92—New York	82	3150	796	1525	.522	377	511	.738	228	693	921	156	277	2	88	245	209	1970	24.0
Totals	520	18838	4862	9175	.530	2567	3463	.741	1396	3745	5141	1101	1971	34	610	1606	1732	12293	23.6

Three-point field goals: 1985-86, 0-for-5. 1986-87, 0-for-7. 1987-88, 0-for-3. 1988-89, 0-for-6. 1989-90, 1-for-4 (.250). 1990-91, 0-for-6. 1991-92, 1-for-6 (.167). Totals, 2-for-37 (.054).

NBA PLAYOFF RECORD

Season Team	G	Min.	FGM	FGA	Pct.	FTM	FTA	Pct.	Off.	Def.	Tot.	Ast.	PF	Dq.	Stl.	Blk.	TO	Pts.	Avg.
87-88—New York	4	153	28	57	.491	19	22	.864	16	35	51	10	17	0	6	13	11	75	18.8
88-89—New York	9	340	70	144	.486	39	52	.750	23	67	90	20	35	0	9	18	15	179	19.9
89-90—New York	10	395	114	219	.521	65	79	.823	21	84	105	31	41	0	13	20	27	294	29.4
90-91—New York	3	110	18	45	.400	14	18	.778	2	28	30	6	12	0	1	5	11	50	16.7
91-92—New York	12	482	109	239	.456	54	73	.740	33	100	133	27	49	1	7	31	23	272	22.7
Totals	38	1480	339	704	.482	191	244	.783	95	314	409	94	154	1	36	87	87	870	22.9

Three-point field goals: 1987-88, 0-for-1. 1989-90, 1-for-2 (.500). 1991-92, 0-for-1. Totals, 1-for-4 (.250).

NBA ALL-STAR GAME RECORD

Season Team	Min.	FGM	FGA	Pct.	FTM	FTA	Pct.	Off.	Def.	Tot.	Ast.	PF	Dq.	Stl.	Blk.	TO	Pts.
1986 —New York							Did not play—injured.										
1988 —New York	16	4	8	.500	1	1	1.000	1	5	6	0	1	0	0	1	1	9
1989 —New York	17	2	8	.250	0	4	.000	1	5	6	2	2	0	1	2	3	4
1990 —New York	27	5	9	.556	2	2	1.000	1	9	10	1	5	0	1	5	5	12
1991 —New York	30	8	10	.800	2	2	1.000	2	8	10	0	5	0	1	4	2	18
1992 —New York	17	4	7	.571	2	5	.400	2	2	4	0	3	0	2	1	2	10
Totals	107	23	42	.548	7	14	.500	7	29	36	3	16	0	5	13	13	53

FEITL, DAVE

C

PERSONAL: Born June 8, 1962, in Butler, Pa. . . . 7-0/250. . . . Full name: Dave Scott Feitl.
HIGH SCHOOL: Santa Rita (Tucson, Ariz.).
COLLEGE: Texas-El Paso.
TRANSACTIONS/CAREER NOTES: Selected by Houston Rockets in second round (43rd pick overall) of 1986 NBA Draft. . . . Traded by Rockets with 1989 first-round draft choice to Golden State Warriors for Purvis Short (November 5, 1987). . . . Traded by Warriors with 1989 second-round draft choice to Washington Bullets for Manute Bol (June 8, 1988). . . . Played in Italy (1989-90). . . . Signed as unrestricted free agent by Rockets (October 6, 1990). . . . Rights renounced by Rockets (August 23, 1991). . . . Signed as free agent by New Jersey Nets (October 7, 1991). . . . Waived by Nets (November 8, 1991). . . . Re-signed as free agent by Nets (November 13, 1991).

COLLEGIATE RECORD

Season Team	G	Min.	FGM	FGA	Pct.	FTM	FTA	Pct.	Reb.	Pts.	Avg.
81-82—Texas-El Paso........................					Did not play—back injury.						
82-83—Texas-El Paso........................	29	641	95	191	.497	67	89	.753	141	257	8.9
83-84—Texas-El Paso........................	31	575	82	176	.466	40	60	.667	132	204	6.6
84-85—Texas-El Paso........................	32	911	158	305	.518	117	156	.750	227	433	13.5
85-86—Texas-El Paso........................	33	1017	208	412	.505	132	182	.725	226	548	16.6
Totals	125	3144	543	1084	.501	356	487	.731	726	1442	11.5

NBA REGULAR-SEASON RECORD

Season Team	G	Min.	FGM	FGA	Pct.	FTM	FTA	Pct.	Off.	Def.	Tot.	Ast.	PF	Dq.	Stl.	Blk.	TO	Pts.	Avg.
86-87—Houston	62	498	88	202	.436	53	71	.746	39	78	117	22	83	0	9	4	38	229	3.7
87-88—Golden State	70	1128	182	404	.451	94	134	.701	83	252	335	53	146	1	15	9	87	458	6.5
88-89—Washington .	57	828	116	266	.436	54	65	.831	69	133	202	36	136	0	17	18	65	286	5.0
90-91—Houston	52	372	52	140	.371	33	44	.750	29	71	100	8	52	0	3	12	25	137	2.6
91-92—New Jersey ..	34	175	33	77	.429	16	19	.842	21	40	61	6	22	0	2	3	19	82	2.4
Totals	275	3001	471	1089	.433	250	333	.751	241	574	815	125	439	1	46	46	234	1192	4.3

Three-point field goals: 1986-87, 0-for-1. 1987-88, 0-for-4. 1988-89, 0-for-1. 1990-91, 0-for-3. Totals, 0-for-9.

NBA PLAYOFF RECORD

Season Team	G	Min.	FGM	FGA	Pct.	FTM	FTA	Pct.	Off.	Def.	Tot.	Ast.	PF	Dq.	Stl.	Blk.	TO	Pts.	Avg.
86-87—Houston	6	8	0	0	...	2	2	1.000	0	1	1	0	0	0	0	0	0	2	0.3
91-92—New Jersey ..	1	3	1	2	.500	0	0	...	0	1	1	0	0	0	0	0	1	2	2.0
Totals	7	11	1	2	.500	2	2	1.000	0	2	2	0	0	0	0	0	1	4	0.6

FERRELL, DUANE

F, HAWKS

PERSONAL: Born February 28, 1965, in Baltimore. . . . 6-7/215.
HIGH SCHOOL: Calvert Hall (Towson, Md.).
COLLEGE: Georgia Tech.
TRANSACTIONS/CAREER NOTES: Never drafted by an NBA franchise. . . . Signed as free agent by Atlanta Hawks (October 6, 1988). . . . Waived by Hawks (November 2, 1989). . . . Played in Continental Basketball Association with Topeka Sizzlers (1989-90). . . . Re-signed by Hawks to first of two consecutive 10-day contracts (February 23, 1990). . . . Re-signed by Hawks for remainder of season (March 15, 1990). . . . Re-signed as free agent by Hawks (June 29, 1990). . . . Waived by Hawks (September 18, 1990). . . . Re-signed as free agent by Hawks (November 2, 1990).

EF

COLLEGIATE RECORD

Season Team	G	Min.	FGM	FGA	Pct.	FTM	FTA	Pct.	Reb.	Pts.	Avg.
84-85 — Georgia Tech	32	802	117	232	.504	56	98	.571	131	290	9.1
85-86 — Georgia Tech	34	1068	172	289	.595	69	91	.758	168	413	12.1
86-87 — Georgia Tech	29	1058	201	387	.519	112	138	.812	170	520	17.9
87-88 — Georgia Tech	32	1051	230	432	.532	131	175	.749	211	595	18.6
Totals	127	3979	720	1340	.537	368	502	.733	680	1818	14.3

Three-point field goals: 1986-87, 6-for-15 (.400). 1987-88, 4-for-14 (.286). Totals, 10-for-29 (.345).

NBA REGULAR-SEASON RECORD

Season Team	G	Min.	FGM	FGA	Pct.	FTM	FTA	Pct.	— REBOUNDS — Off.	Def.	Tot.	Ast.	PF	Dq.	Stl.	Blk.	TO	Pts.	Avg.
88-89 — Atlanta	41	231	35	83	.422	30	44	.682	19	22	41	10	33	0	7	6	12	100	2.4
89-90 — Atlanta	14	29	5	14	.357	2	6	.333	3	4	7	2	3	0	1	0	2	12	0.9
90-91 — Atlanta	78	1165	174	356	.489	125	156	.801	97	82	179	55	151	3	33	27	78	475	6.1
91-92 — Atlanta	66	1598	331	632	.524	166	218	.761	105	105	210	92	134	0	49	17	99	839	12.7
Totals	199	3023	545	1085	.502	323	424	.762	224	213	437	159	321	3	90	50	191	1426	7.2

Three-point field goals: 1989-90, 0-for-1. 1990-91, 2-for-3 (.667). 1991-92, 11-for-33 (.333). Totals, 13-for-37 (.351).

NBA PLAYOFF RECORD

Season Team	G	Min.	FGM	FGA	Pct.	FTM	FTA	Pct.	— REBOUNDS — Off.	Def.	Tot.	Ast.	PF	Dq.	Stl.	Blk.	TO	Pts.	Avg.
90-91 — Atlanta	5	73	8	18	.444	8	12	.667	6	11	17	3	10	0	0	0	2	24	4.8

CBA REGULAR-SEASON RECORD

Season Team	G	Min.	2-POINT FGM	FGA	Pct.	3-POINT FGM	FGA	Pct.	FTM	FTA	Pct.	Reb.	Ast.	Pts.	Avg.
89-90 — Topeka	40	1546	372	683	.545	5	16	.313	212	276	.768	252	95	971	24.3

FERRY, DANNY
F, CAVALIERS

PERSONAL: Born October 17, 1966, in Hyattsville, Md. . . . 6-10/245. . . . Full name: Daniel John Willard Ferry. . . . Son of Bob Ferry, center/forward with St. Louis Hawks, Detroit Pistons and Baltimore Bullets (1959-60 through 1968-69).

HIGH SCHOOL: DeMatha Catholic (Hyattsville, Md.).

COLLEGE: Duke.

TRANSACTIONS/CAREER NOTES: Selected by Los Angeles Clippers in first round (second pick overall) of 1989 NBA Draft. . . . Draft rights traded by Clippers with Reggie Williams to Cleveland Cavaliers for Ron Harper, 1990 and 1992 first-round draft choices and 1991 second-round draft choice (November 16, 1989). . . . Played in Italy (1989-90).

COLLEGIATE RECORD

NOTES: THE SPORTING NEWS All-America first team (1988, 1989).

Season Team	G	Min.	FGM	FGA	Pct.	FTM	FTA	Pct.	Reb.	Pts.	Avg.
85-86 — Duke	40	912	91	198	.460	54	86	.628	221	236	5.9
86-87 — Duke	33	1094	172	383	.449	92	109	.844	256	461	14.0
87-88 — Duke	35	1138	247	519	.476	135	163	.828	266	667	19.1
88-89 — Duke	35	1163	300	575	.522	146	193	.756	260	791	22.6
Totals	143	4307	810	1675	.484	427	551	.775	1003	2155	15.1

Three-point field goals: 1986-87, 25-for-63 (.397). 1987-88, 38-for-109 (.349). 1988-89, 45-for-106 (.425). Totals, 108-for-278 (.388).

ITALIAN LEAGUE RECORD

Season Team	G	Min.	FGM	FGA	Pct.	FTM	FTA	Pct.	Reb.	Pts.	Avg.
89-90 — Il Messaggero	30	1090	203	370	.549	125	168	.744	195	878	29.3

NBA REGULAR-SEASON RECORD

Season Team	G	Min.	FGM	FGA	Pct.	FTM	FTA	Pct.	— REBOUNDS — Off.	Def.	Tot.	Ast.	PF	Dq.	Stl.	Blk.	TO	Pts.	Avg.
90-91 — Cleveland	81	1661	275	643	.428	124	152	.816	99	187	286	142	230	1	43	25	120	697	8.6
91-92 — Cleveland	68	937	134	328	.409	61	73	.836	53	160	213	75	135	0	22	15	46	346	5.1
Totals	149	2598	409	971	.421	185	225	.822	152	347	499	217	365	1	65	40	166	1043	7.0

Three-point field goals: 1990-91, 23-for-77 (.299). 1991-92, 17-for-48 (.354). Totals, 40-for-125 (.320).

NBA PLAYOFF RECORD

Season Team	G	Min.	FGM	FGA	Pct.	FTM	FTA	Pct.	— REBOUNDS — Off.	Def.	Tot.	Ast.	PF	Dq.	Stl.	Blk.	TO	Pts.	Avg.
91-92 — Cleveland	9	55	7	15	.467	4	4	1.000	7	9	16	1	7	0	1	1	2	19	2.1

Three-point field goals: 1991-92, 1-for-3 (.333).

FLEMING, VERN
G, PACERS

PERSONAL: Born February 4, 1962, in New York. . . . 6-5/185.

HIGH SCHOOL: Mater Christi (Long Island, N.Y.).

COLLEGE: Georgia.

TRANSACTIONS/CAREER NOTES: Selected by Indiana Pacers in first round (18th pick overall) of 1984 NBA Draft.

MISCELLANEOUS: Member of gold-medal-winning U.S. Olympic team (1984).

COLLEGIATE RECORD

Season Team	G	Min.	FGM	FGA	Pct.	FTM	FTA	Pct.	Reb.	Pts.	Avg.
80-81 — Georgia	30	1082	108	225	.480	85	122	.697	80	301	10.0
81-82 — Georgia	31	1079	117	236	.496	73	114	.640	120	307	9.9

F

Season Team	G	Min.	FGM	FGA	Pct.	FTM	FTA	Pct.	Reb.	Pts.	Avg.
82-83 — Georgia	34	1130	227	424	.535	121	169	.716	158	575	16.9
83-84 — Georgia	30	1030	248	493	.503	98	130	.754	120	594	19.8
Totals	125	4321	700	1378	.508	377	535	.705	478	1777	14.2

NBA REGULAR-SEASON RECORD

Season Team	G	Min.	FGM	FGA	Pct.	FTM	FTA	Pct.	— REBOUNDS —			Ast.	PF	Dq.	Stl.	Blk.	TO	Pts.	Avg.
									Off.	Def.	Tot.								
84-85 — Indiana	80	2486	433	922	.470	260	339	.767	148	175	323	247	232	4	99	8	197	1126	14.1
85-86 — Indiana	80	2870	436	862	.506	263	353	.745	102	284	386	505	230	3	131	5	208	1136	14.2
86-87 — Indiana	82	2549	370	727	.509	238	302	.788	109	225	334	473	222	3	109	18	167	980	12.0
87-88 — Indiana	80	2733	442	845	.523	227	283	.802	106	258	364	568	225	0	115	11	175	1111	13.9
88-89 — Indiana	76	2552	419	814	.515	243	304	.799	85	225	310	494	212	4	77	12	192	1084	14.3
89-90 — Indiana	82	2876	467	919	.508	230	294	.782	118	204	322	610	213	1	92	10	206	1176	14.3
90-91 — Indiana	69	1929	356	671	.531	161	221	.729	83	131	214	369	116	0	76	13	137	877	12.7
91-92 — Indiana	82	1737	294	610	.482	132	179	.737	69	140	209	266	134	0	56	7	140	726	8.9
Totals	631	19732	3217	6370	.505	1754	2275	.771	820	1642	2462	3532	1584	15	755	84	1422	8216	13.0

Three-point field goals: 1984-85, 0-for-4. 1985-86, 1-for-6 (.167). 1986-87, 2-for-10 (.200). 1987-88, 0-for-13. 1988-89, 3-for-23 (.130). 1989-90, 12-for-34 (.353). 1990-91, 4-for-18 (.222). 1991-92, 6-for-27 (.222). Totals, 28-for-135 (.207).

NBA PLAYOFF RECORD

Season Team	G	Min.	FGM	FGA	Pct.	FTM	FTA	Pct.	— REBOUNDS —			Ast.	PF	Dq.	Stl.	Blk.	TO	Pts.	Avg.
									Off.	Def.	Tot.								
86-87 — Indiana	4	141	13	36	.361	23	30	.767	9	17	26	24	15	1	4	1	10	49	12.3
89-90 — Indiana	3	113	16	34	.471	8	9	.889	4	9	13	18	6	0	2	1	8	40	13.3
90-91 — Indiana	5	115	18	40	.450	11	14	.786	10	7	17	23	10	0	1	3	8	47	9.4
91-92 — Indiana	3	51	10	18	.556	1	3	.333	0	2	2	6	5	0	3	0	4	21	7.0
Totals	15	420	57	128	.445	43	56	.768	23	35	58	71	36	1	10	5	30	157	10.5

Three-point field goals: 1986-87, 0-for-1. 1989-90, 0-for-2. 1990-91, 0-for-1. Totals, 0-for-4.

FLOYD, SLEEPY

G, ROCKETS

PERSONAL: Born March 6, 1960, in Gastonia, N.C. . . . 6-3/183. . . . Full name: Eric Augustus Floyd.
HIGH SCHOOL: Hunter Huss (Gastonia, N.C.).
COLLEGE: Georgetown.
TRANSACTIONS/CAREER NOTES: Selected by New Jersey Nets in first round (13th pick overall) of 1982 NBA Draft. . . . Traded by Nets with Mickey Johnson to Golden State Warriors for Michael Ray Richardson (February 6, 1983). . . . Traded by Warriors with Joe Barry Carroll to Houston Rockets for Ralph Sampson and Steve Harris (December 12, 1987).

COLLEGIATE RECORD

NOTES: THE SPORTING NEWS All-America second team (1982).

Season Team	G	Min.	FGM	FGA	Pct.	FTM	FTA	Pct.	Reb.	Pts.	Avg.
78-79 — Georgetown	29	975	177	388	.456	126	155	.813	119	480	16.6
79-80 — Georgetown	32	1052	246	444	.554	106	140	.757	98	598	18.7
80-81 — Georgetown	32	1115	237	508	.467	133	165	.806	133	60	1.9
81-82 — Georgetown	37	1200	249	494	.504	121	168	.720	127	619	16.7
Totals	130	4342	909	1834	.496	486	628	.774	477	1757	13.5

NBA REGULAR-SEASON RECORD

Season Team	G	Min.	FGM	FGA	Pct.	FTM	FTA	Pct.	— REBOUNDS —			Ast.	PF	Dq.	Stl.	Blk.	TO	Pts.	Avg.
									Off.	Def.	Tot.								
82-83 — N.J.-G.S.	76	1248	226	527	.429	150	180	.833	56	81	137	138	134	3	58	17	106	612	8.1
83-84 — Golden State	77	2555	484	1045	.463	315	386	.816	87	184	271	269	216	0	103	31	196	1291	16.8
84-85 — Golden State	82	2873	610	1372	.445	336	415	.810	62	140	202	406	226	1	134	41	251	1598	19.5
85-86 — Golden State	82	2764	510	1007	.506	351	441	.796	76	22	98	746	199	2	157	16	290	1410	17.2
86-87 — Golden State	82	3064	503	1030	.488	462	537	.860	56	212	268	848	199	1	146	18	280	1541	18.8
87-88 — G.S.-Hou.	77	2514	420	969	.433	301	354	.850	77	219	296	544	190	1	95	12	223	1155	15.0
88-89 — Houston	82	2788	396	893	.443	261	309	.845	48	258	306	709	196	1	124	11	253	1162	14.2
89-90 — Houston	82	2630	362	803	.451	187	232	.806	46	152	198	600	159	0	94	11	204	1000	12.2
90-91 — Houston	82	1850	386	939	.411	185	246	.752	52	107	159	317	122	0	95	17	140	1005	12.3
91-92 — Houston	82	1662	286	704	.406	135	170	.794	34	116	150	239	128	0	57	21	128	744	9.1
Totals	804	23948	4183	9289	.450	2683	3270	.820	594	1491	2085	4816	1769	9	1063	195	2071	11518	14.3

Three-point field goals: 1982-83, 10-for-25 (.400). 1983-84, 8-for-45 (.178). 1984-85, 39-for-143 (.294). 1985-86, 39-for-119 (.328). 1986-87, 73-for-190 (.384). 1987-88, 14-for-72 (.194). 1988-89, 109-for-292 (.373). 1989-90, 89-for-234 (.380). 1990-91, 48-for-176 (.273). 1991-92, 37-for-123 (.301). Totals, 469-for-1419 (.331).

NBA PLAYOFF RECORD

NOTES: Holds single-game records for most field goals made in one half—15; most field goals made in one quarter—12; most points in one half—39; and most points in one quarter—29 (May 10, 1987, vs. Los Angeles Lakers).

Season Team	G	Min.	FGM	FGA	Pct.	FTM	FTA	Pct.	— REBOUNDS —			Ast.	PF	Dq.	Stl.	Blk.	TO	Pts.	Avg.
									Off.	Def.	Tot.								
86-87 — Golden State	10	414	77	152	.507	47	51	.922	9	21	30	102	24	0	18	2	35	214	21.4
87-88 — Houston	4	154	26	61	.426	19	22	.864	3	4	7	34	10	0	8	0	12	75	18.8
88-89 — Houston	4	160	22	46	.478	10	14	.714	3	15	18	26	10	0	8	1	10	62	15.5
89-90 — Houston	4	172	30	64	.469	11	17	.647	7	8	15	41	5	0	5	1	15	74	18.5
90-91 — Houston	3	41	8	24	.333	0	0		0	2	2	7	4	0	2	1	7	16	5.3
Totals	25	941	163	347	.470	87	104	.837	22	50	72	210	53	0	41	5	79	441	17.6

Three-point field goals: 1986-87, 13-for-28 (.464). 1987-88, 4-for-8 (.500). 1988-89, 8-for-15 (.533). 1989-90, 3-for-12 (.250). 1990-91, 0-for-4. Totals, 28-for-67 (.418).

NBA ALL-STAR GAME RECORD

								— REBOUNDS —									
Season	Team	Min.	FGM	FGA	Pct.	FTM	FTA	Pct.	Off.	Def.	Tot.	Ast.	PF	Dq.	Stl.	Blk.	TO	Pts.
1987	—Golden State	19	4	7	.571	5	7	.714	2	3	5	1	2	0	1	0	2	14

Three-point field goals: 1987, 1-for-3 (.333).

FOSTER, GREG
F/C, BULLETS

PERSONAL: Born October 3, 1968, in Oakland, Calif.... 6-11/240.... Full name: Gregory Clinton Foster.
HIGH SCHOOL: Skyline (Oakland, Calif.).
COLLEGE: UCLA, then Texas-El Paso.
TRANSACTIONS/CAREER NOTES: Selected by Washington Bullets in second round (35th pick overall) of 1990 NBA Draft.

COLLEGIATE RECORD

Season	Team	G	Min.	FGM	FGA	Pct.	FTM	FTA	Pct.	Reb.	Pts.	Avg.
86-87	—UCLA..	31	441	44	88	.500	13	26	.500	76	101	3.3
87-88	—UCLA..	11	292	39	74	.527	16	37	.432	61	94	8.5
88-89	—Texas-El Paso......................	26	728	117	242	.483	54	83	.651	189	288	11.1
89-90	—Texas-El Paso......................	32	837	133	286	.465	73	90	.811	198	339	10.6
	Totals....................................	100	2298	333	690	.483	156	236	.661	524	822	8.2

Three-point field goals: 1988-89, 0-for-1. 1989-90, 0-for-2. Totals, 0-for-3.

NBA REGULAR-SEASON RECORD

									— REBOUNDS —										
Season	Team	G	Min.	FGM	FGA	Pct.	FTM	FTA	Pct.	Off.	Def.	Tot.	Ast.	PF	Dq.	Stl.	Blk.	TO	Pts.	Avg.
90-91	—Washington .	54	606	97	211	.460	42	61	.689	52	99	151	37	112	1	12	22	45	236	4.4
91-92	—Washington .	49	548	89	193	.461	35	49	.714	43	102	145	35	83	0	6	12	36	213	4.3
	Totals	103	1154	186	404	.460	77	110	.700	95	201	296	72	195	1	18	34	81	449	4.4

Three-point field goals: 1990-91, 0-for-5. 1991-92, 0-for-1. Totals, 0-for-6.

FOX, RICK
G/F, CELTICS

PERSONAL: Born July 24, 1969, in Toronto.... 6-7/231.... Full name: Ulrich A. Fox.
HIGH SCHOOL: Warsaw Community (Ind.).
COLLEGE: North Carolina.
TRANSACTIONS/CAREER NOTES: Selected by Boston Celtics in first round (24th pick overall) of 1991 NBA Draft.

COLLEGIATE RECORD

NOTES: THE SPORTING NEWS All-America third team (1991).

Season	Team	G	Min.	FGM	FGA	Pct.	FTM	FTA	Pct.	Reb.	Pts.	Avg.
87-88	—North Carolina	34	371	59	94	.628	15	30	.500	63	136	4.0
88-89	—North Carolina	37	829	165	283	.583	83	105	.790	142	426	11.5
89-90	—North Carolina	34	981	203	389	.522	75	102	.735	157	551	16.2
90-91	—North Carolina	35	999	206	455	.453	111	138	.804	232	590	16.9
	Totals	140	3180	633	1221	.518	284	375	.757	594	1703	12.2

Three-point field goals: 1987-88, 3-for-9 (.333). 1988-89, 13-for-29 (.448). 1989-90, 70-for-160 (.438). 1990-91, 67-for-196 (.342). Totals, 153-for-394 (.388).

NBA REGULAR-SEASON RECORD

HONORS: NBA All-Rookie second team (1992).

									— REBOUNDS —										
Season	Team	G	Min.	FGM	FGA	Pct.	FTM	FTA	Pct.	Off.	Def.	Tot.	Ast.	PF	Dq.	Stl.	Blk.	TO	Pts.	Avg.
91-92	—Boston	81	1535	241	525	.459	139	184	.755	73	147	220	126	230	3	78	30	123	644	8.0

Three-point field goals: 1991-92, 23-for-70 (.329).

NBA PLAYOFF RECORD

								— REBOUNDS —									
Season	Team	G	Min.	FGM	FGA	Pct.	FTM	FTA	Pct.	Off.	Def.	Tot.	Ast.	PF	Dq.	Stl.	Blk.	TO	Pts.	Avg.
91-92	—Boston	8	67	11	23	.478	4	4	1.000	3	3	6	4	11	0	2	2	2	29	3.6

Three-point field goals: 1991-92, 3-for-6 (.500).

FRANK, TELLIS
F

PERSONAL: Born April 26, 1965, in Gary, Ind.... 6-10/240.... Full name: Tellis Joseph Frank Jr.
HIGH SCHOOL: Lew Wallace (Gary, Ind.).
COLLEGE: Western Kentucky.
TRANSACTIONS/CAREER NOTES: Selected by Golden State Warriors in first round (14th pick overall) of 1987 NBA Draft.... Traded by Warriors to Miami Heat for 1992 second-round draft choice (October 2, 1989). ... Heat relinquished right-of-first-refusal (July 1, 1990).... Played in Italy (1990-91).... Signed as free agent by Minnesota Timberwolves (October 3, 1991).... Waived by Timberwolves (November 29, 1991).

COLLEGIATE RECORD

Season	Team	G	Min.	FGM	FGA	Pct.	FTM	FTA	Pct.	Reb.	Pts.	Avg.
83-84	—Western Kentucky..................	27	...	42	121	.347	22	36	.611	92	106	3.9
84-85	—Western Kentucky..................	27	...	93	213	.437	41	62	.661	134	227	8.4
85-86	—Western Kentucky..................	30	...	109	212	.514	88	111	.793	157	306	10.2
86-87	—Western Kentucky..................	38	...	281	542	.518	122	175	.697	281	684	18.0
	Totals	122	...	525	1088	.483	273	384	.711	664	1323	10.8

NBA REGULAR-SEASON RECORD

										REBOUNDS									
Season Team	G	Min.	FGM	FGA	Pct.	FTM	FTA	Pct.	Off.	Def.	Tot.	Ast.	PF	Dq.	Stl.	Blk.	TO	Pts.	Avg.
87-88 —Golden State	78	1597	242	565	.428	150	207	.725	95	235	330	111	267	5	53	23	109	634	8.1
88-89 —Golden State	32	245	34	91	.374	39	51	.765	26	35	61	15	59	1	14	6	29	107	3.3
89-90 —Miami	77	1762	278	607	.458	179	234	.765	151	234	385	85	282	6	51	27	134	735	9.5
91-92 —Minnesota....	10	140	18	33	.545	10	15	.667	8	18	26	8	24	0	5	4	5	46	4.6
Totals	197	3744	572	1296	.441	378	507	.746	280	522	802	219	632	12	123	60	177	1522	7.7

Three-point field goals: 1987-88, 0-for-1. 1988-89, 0-for-1. Totals, 0-for-2.

FREDERICK, ANTHONY
F, HORNETS

PERSONAL: Born December 7, 1964, in Los Angeles. . . . 6-7/205.
HIGH SCHOOL: Gardena (Calif.).
COLLEGE: Santa Monica (Calif.), then Pepperdine.
TRANSACTIONS/CAREER NOTES: Selected by Denver Nuggets in sixth round (133rd pick overall) of 1986 NBA Draft. . . . Waived by Nuggets (July 1986). . . . Played in Continental Basketball Association with La Crosse Catbirds (1986-87), Mississippi Jets (1987-88) and Oklahoma City Cavalry (1990-91). . . . Signed as free agent by Indiana Pacers (October 5, 1987). . . . Waived by Pacers (October 19, 1987). . . . Re-signed as free agent by Pacers (August 5, 1988). . . . Waived by Pacers (October 31, 1989). . . . Played in Spain (1989-90). . . . Signed by Sacramento Kings to first of two consecutive 10-day contracts (January 14, 1991). . . . Re-signed by Kings for remainder of season (February 28, 1991). . . . Signed as free agent by Charlotte Hornets (September 4, 1991).

COLLEGIATE RECORD

Season Team	G	Min.	FGM	FGA	Pct.	FTM	FTA	Pct.	Reb.	Pts.	Avg.
82-83 —Santa Monica					Statistics unavailable.						
83-84 —Santa Monica					Statistics unavailable.						
84-85 —Pepperdine.............................	32	1027	152	302	.503	73	137	.533	230	377	11.8
85-86 —Pepperdine.............................	30	936	123	225	.547	36	58	.621	207	282	9.4
Four-year-college totals	62	1963	275	527	.522	109	195	.559	437	659	10.6

CBA REGULAR-SEASON RECORD

NOTES: CBA All-Star second team (1991).

			2-POINT			3-POINT								
Season Team	G	Min.	FGM	FGA	Pct.	FGM	FGA	Pct.	FTM	FTA	Pct.	Reb.	Ast.	Pts.	Avg.
86-87 —La Crosse........	48	1350	275	546	.504	0	6	.000	109	164	.665	271	117	659	13.7
87-88 —Mississippi.......	54	1989	440	864	.509	10	63	.159	234	301	.777	396	172	1144	21.2
90-91 —Oklahoma City .	38	1483	336	691	.486	15	50	.300	200	276	.725	278	190	917	24.1
Totals	140	4822	1051	2101	.500	25	119	.210	543	741	.733	945	479	2720	19.4

NBA REGULAR-SEASON RECORD

										REBOUNDS									
Season Team	G	Min.	FGM	FGA	Pct.	FTM	FTA	Pct.	Off.	Def.	Tot.	Ast.	PF	Dq.	Stl.	Blk.	TO	Pts.	Avg.
88-89 —Indiana.........	46	313	63	125	.504	24	34	.706	26	26	52	20	59	0	14	6	34	152	3.3
90-91 —Sacramento .	35	475	67	168	.399	43	60	.717	36	48	84	44	50	0	22	13	40	177	5.1
91-92 —Charlotte......	66	852	161	370	.435	63	92	.685	75	69	144	71	91	0	40	26	58	389	5.9
Totals	147	1640	291	663	.439	130	186	.699	137	143	280	135	200	0	76	45	132	718	4.9

Three-point field goals: 1988-89, 2-for-5 (.400). 1991-92, 4-for-17 (.235). Totals, 6-for-22 (.273).

GAMBLE, KEVIN
G/F, CELTICS

PERSONAL: Born November 13, 1965, in Springfield, Ill. . . . 6-5/210. . . . Full name: Kevin Douglas Gamble.
HIGH SCHOOL: Lanphier (Springfield, Ill.).
COLLEGE: Lincoln (Ill.), then Iowa.
TRANSACTIONS/CAREER NOTES: Selected by Portland Trail Blazers in third round (63rd pick overall) of 1987 NBA Draft. . . . Waived by Trail Blazers (December 9, 1987). . . . Played in Continental Basketball Association with Quad City Thunder (1987-88, 1988-89). . . . Signed as free agent by Boston Celtics (December 15, 1988).

FG

COLLEGIATE RECORD

Season Team	G	Min.	FGM	FGA	Pct.	FTM	FTA	Pct.	Reb.	Pts.	Avg.
83-84 —Lincoln	30	. . .	262	469	.559	115	148	.777	276	639	21.3
84-85 —Lincoln	31	. . .	267	461	.579	103	126	.817	301	637	20.5
85-86 —Iowa	30	260	36	76	.474	7	10	.700	52	79	2.6
86-87 —Iowa	35	867	162	298	.544	69	99	.697	158	418	11.9
Junior college totals	61	. . .	529	930	.569	218	274	.796	577	1276	20.9
Four-year-college totals	65	1127	198	374	.529	76	109	.697	210	497	7.6

Three-point field goals: 1986-87, 35-for-76 (.461).

CBA REGULAR-SEASON RECORD

			2-POINT			3-POINT								
Season Team	G	Min.	FGM	FGA	Pct.	FGM	FGA	Pct.	FTM	FTA	Pct.	Reb.	Ast.	Pts.	Avg.
87-88 —Quad City	40	1450	299	565	.529	31	75	.413	151	184	.821	237	149	842	21.1
88-89 —Quad City	12	490	107	203	.527	3	20	.150	110	129	.853	66	48	333	27.8
Totals	52	1940	406	768	.529	34	95	.358	261	313	.834	303	197	1175	22.6

NBA REGULAR-SEASON RECORD

										REBOUNDS									
Season Team	G	Min.	FGM	FGA	Pct.	FTM	FTA	Pct.	Off.	Def.	Tot.	Ast.	PF	Dq.	Stl.	Blk.	TO	Pts.	Avg.
87-88 —Portland.......	9	19	0	3	.000	0	0	. . .	2	1	3	1	2	0	2	0	2	0	0.0
88-89 —Boston	44	375	75	136	.551	35	55	.636	11	31	42	34	40	0	14	3	19	187	4.3

Season Team	G	Min.	FGM	FGA	Pct.	FTM	FTA	Pct.	Off.	Def.	Tot.	Ast.	PF	Dq.	Stl.	Blk.	TO	Pts.	Avg.
89-90—Boston	71	990	137	301	.455	85	107	.794	42	70	112	119	77	1	28	8	44	362	5.1
90-91—Boston	82	2706	548	933	.587	185	227	.815	85	182	267	256	237	6	100	34	148	1281	15.6
91-92—Boston	82	2496	480	908	.529	139	157	.885	80	206	286	219	200	2	75	37	97	1108	13.5
Totals	288	6586	1240	2281	.544	444	546	.813	220	490	710	629	556	9	219	82	310	2938	10.2

Three-point field goals: 1987-88, 0-for-1. 1988-89, 2-for-11 (.182). 1989-90, 3-for-18 (.167). 1990-91, 0-for-7. 1991-92, 9-for-31 (.290). Totals, 14-for-68 (.206).

NBA PLAYOFF RECORD

Season Team	G	Min.	FGM	FGA	Pct.	FTM	FTA	Pct.	Off.	Def.	Tot.	Ast.	PF	Dq.	Stl.	Blk.	TO	Pts.	Avg.
88-89—Boston	1	29	4	11	.364	0	2	.000	1	0	1	2	1	0	1	0	0	8	8.0
89-90—Boston	3	8	3	5	.600	0	0		1	0	1	2	1	0	0	0	1	6	2.0
90-91—Boston	11	238	29	60	.483	8	12	.667	3	10	13	19	24	0	4	2	7	66	6.0
91-92—Boston	10	335	62	131	.473	12	15	.800	13	29	42	23	26	0	12	6	10	136	13.6
Totals	25	610	98	207	.473	20	29	.690	18	39	57	46	52	0	17	8	18	216	8.6

Three-point field goals: 1988-89, 0-for-1. 1991-92, 0-for-2. Totals, 0-for-3.

GARLAND, WINSTON
G, NUGGETS

PERSONAL: Born December 19, 1964, in Gary, Ind. . . . 6-2/175. . . . Full name: Winston Kinnard Garland.
HIGH SCHOOL: Roosevelt (Gary, Ind.).
COLLEGE: Southeastern Community College (Ia.), then Southwest Missouri State.
TRANSACTIONS/CAREER NOTES: Selected by Milwaukee Bucks in second round (40th pick overall) of 1987 NBA Draft. . . . Waived by Bucks (November 4, 1987). . . . Played in Continental Basketball Association with Pensacola Tornados (1987-88). . . . Signed as free agent by Golden State Warriors (November 25, 1987). . . . Waived by Warriors (December 9, 1987). . . . Re-signed by Warriors (December 14, 1987). . . . Traded by Warriors to Los Angeles Clippers for two future second-round draft choices (February 22, 1990). . . . Traded by Clippers to Denver Nuggets for 1996 or 1997 second-round draft choice (June 26, 1991).

COLLEGIATE RECORD

Season Team	G	Min.	FGM	FGA	Pct.	FTM	FTA	Pct.	Reb.	Pts.	Avg.
83-84—Southeastern C.C.	34	1053	233	450	.518	112	134	.836	150	578	17.0
84-85—Southeastern C.C.	30	1006	207	401	.516	133	156	.853	107	547	18.2
85-86—Southwest Missouri State	32	1006	205	445	.461	118	153	.771	116	528	16.5
86-87—Southwest Missouri State	34	1119	274	545	.503	115	153	.752	85	720	21.2
Junior college totals	64	2059	440	851	.517	245	290	.845	257	1125	17.6
Four-year-college totals	66	2125	479	990	.484	233	306	.761	201	1248	18.9

Three-point field goals: 1986-87, 57-for-113 (.504).

CBA REGULAR-SEASON RECORD

Season Team	G	Min.	FGM	2-POINT FGA	Pct.	FGM	3-POINT FGA	Pct.	FTM	FTA	Pct.	Reb.	Ast.	Pts.	Avg.
87-88—Pensaola	4	60	17	34	.500	0	1	.000	10	11	.909	7	5	44	11.0

NBA REGULAR-SEASON RECORD

Season Team	G	Min.	FGM	FGA	Pct.	FTM	FTA	Pct.	Off.	Def.	Tot.	Ast.	PF	Dq.	Stl.	Blk.	TO	Pts.	Avg.
87-88—Golden State	67	2122	340	775	.439	138	157	.879	68	159	227	429	188	2	116	7	167	831	12.4
88-89—Golden State	79	2661	466	1074	.434	203	251	.809	101	227	328	505	216	2	175	14	187	1145	14.5
89-90—G.S.-L.A.C. ..	79	1762	230	573	.401	102	122	.836	51	163	214	303	152	1	78	10	158	574	7.3
90-91—L.A. Clippers	69	1702	221	519	.426	118	157	.752	46	152	198	317	189	3	97	10	116	564	8.2
91-92—Denver	78	2209	333	750	.444	171	199	.859	67	123	190	411	206	1	98	22	175	846	10.8
Totals	372	10456	1590	3691	.431	732	886	.826	333	824	1157	1965	951	9	564	63	803	3960	10.6

Three-point field goals: 1987-88, 13-for-39 (.333). 1988-89, 10-for-43 (.233). 1989-90, 12-for-36 (.333). 1990-91, 4-for-26 (.154). 1991-92, 9-for-28 (.321). Totals, 48-for-172 (.279).

NBA PLAYOFF RECORD

Season Team	G	Min.	FGM	FGA	Pct.	FTM	FTA	Pct.	Off.	Def.	Tot.	Ast.	PF	Dq.	Stl.	Blk.	TO	Pts.	Avg.
88-89—Golden State	8	270	41	98	.418	24	28	.857	14	19	33	29	31	1	13	2	15	107	13.4

Three-point field goals: 1988-89, 1-for-3 (.333).

GARRICK, TOM
G

PERSONAL: Born July 7, 1966, in West Warwick, R.I. . . . 6-2/185. . . . Full name: Thomas S. Garrick.
HIGH SCHOOL: West Warwick (R.I.).
COLLEGE: Rhode Island.
TRANSACTIONS/CAREER NOTES: Selected by Los Angeles Clippers in second round (45th pick overall) of 1988 NBA Draft. . . . Waived by Clippers (November 14, 1988). . . . Re-signed as free agent by Clippers (November 17, 1988). . . . Rights renounced by Clippers (June 26, 1991). . . . Signed as free agent by San Antonio Spurs (October 3, 1991). . . . Waived by Spurs (December 12, 1991). . . . Claimed off waivers by Minnesota Timberwolves (December 16, 1991). . . . Waived by Timberwolves (March 6, 1992). . . . Signed by Dallas Mavericks to first of two consecutive 10-day contracts (March 22, 1992).

COLLEGIATE RECORD

Season Team	G	Min.	FGM	FGA	Pct.	FTM	FTA	Pct.	Reb.	Pts.	Avg.
84-85—Rhode Island	28	739	54	114	.474	58	78	.744	102	166	5.9
85-86—Rhode Island	27	623	65	135	.481	49	66	.742	76	179	6.6

G

Season Team	G	Min.	FGM	FGA	Pct.	FTM	FTA	Pct.	Reb.	Pts.	Avg.
86-87 —Rhode Island	30	1037	192	421	.456	108	132	.818	129	510	17.0
87-88 —Rhode Island	35	1241	273	561	.487	138	174	.793	143	718	20.5
Totals	120	3640	584	1231	.474	353	450	.784	450	1573	13.1

Three-point field goals: 1986-87, 18-for-55 (.327). 1987-88, 34-for-62 (.548). Totals, 52-for-117 (.444).

NBA REGULAR-SEASON RECORD

Season Team	G	Min.	FGM	FGA	Pct.	FTM	FTA	Pct.	REBOUNDS Off.	Def.	Tot.	Ast.	PF	Dq.	Stl.	Blk.	TO	Pts.	Avg.
88-89 —L.A. Clippers	71	1499	176	359	.490	102	127	.803	37	119	156	243	141	1	78	9	116	454	6.4
89-90 —L.A. Clippers	73	1721	208	421	.494	88	114	.772	34	128	162	289	151	4	90	7	117	508	7.0
90-91 —L.A. Clippers	67	949	100	236	.424	60	79	.759	40	87	127	223	101	0	62	2	66	260	3.9
91-92 —SA-Min-Dal.	40	549	59	143	.413	18	26	.692	12	44	56	98	54	0	36	4	44	137	3.4
Totals	251	4718	543	1159	.469	268	346	.775	123	378	501	853	447	5	266	22	343	1359	5.4

Three-point field goals: 1988-89, 0-for-13. 1989-90, 4-for-21 (.190). 1990-91, 0-for-22. 1991-92, 1-for-4 (.250). Totals, 5-for-60 (.083).

GATLING, CHRIS
F, WARRIORS

PERSONAL: Born September 3, 1967, in Elizabeth, N.J. . . . 6-10/220. . . . Full name: Chris Raymond Gatling.
HIGH SCHOOL: Elizabeth (N.J.).
COLLEGE: Pittsburgh, then Old Dominion.
TRANSACTIONS/CAREER NOTES: Selected by Golden State Warriors in first round (16th pick overall) of 1991 NBA Draft.

COLLEGIATE RECORD

Season Team	G	Min.	FGM	FGA	Pct.	FTM	FTA	Pct.	Reb.	Pts.	Avg.
86-87 —Pittsburgh					Did not play.						
87-88 —Old Dominion					Did not play—transfer student.						
88-89 —Old Dominion	27	839	239	388	.616	126	179	.704	244	604	22.4
89-90 —Old Dominion	26	822	207	357	.580	120	179	.670	259	534	20.5
90-91 —Old Dominion	32	1002	251	405	.620	171	247	.692	356	673	21.0
Totals	85	2663	697	1150	.606	417	605	.689	859	1811	21.3

Three-point field goals: 1990-91, 0-for-1.

NBA REGULAR-SEASON RECORD

Season Team	G	Min.	FGM	FGA	Pct.	FTM	FTA	Pct.	REBOUNDS Off.	Def.	Tot.	Ast.	PF	Dq.	Stl.	Blk.	TO	Pts.	Avg.
91-92 —Golden State	54	612	117	206	.568	72	109	.661	75	107	182	16	101	0	31	36	44	306	5.7

Three-point field goals: 1991-92, 0-for-4.

NBA PLAYOFF RECORD

Season Team	G	Min.	FGM	FGA	Pct.	FTM	FTA	Pct.	REBOUNDS Off.	Def.	Tot.	Ast.	PF	Dq.	Stl.	Blk.	TO	Pts.	Avg.
91-92 —Golden State	4	81	18	29	.621	14	22	.636	9	16	25	0	14	0	2	10	1	50	12.5

GATTISON, KENNY
F, HORNETS

PERSONAL: Born May 23, 1964, in Wilmington, N.C. . . . 6-8/252. . . . Full name: Kenneth Clay Gattison.
HIGH SCHOOL: New Hanover (Wilmington, N.C.).
COLLEGE: Old Dominion.
TRANSACTIONS/CAREER NOTES: Selected by Phoenix Suns in third round (55th pick overall) of 1986 NBA Draft. . . . Played in Italy (1988-89). . . . Waived by Suns (September 21, 1989). . . . Signed as free agent by Charlotte Hornets (September 26, 1989). . . . Waived by Hornets (October 18, 1989). . . . Re-signed as free agent by Hornets (December 2, 1989). . . . Played in Continental Basketball Association with Quad City Thunder (1989-90).

COLLEGIATE RECORD

Season Team	G	Min.	FGM	FGA	Pct.	FTM	FTA	Pct.	Reb.	Pts.	Avg.
82-83 —Old Dominion	29	705	94	187	.503	55	78	.705	218	243	8.4
83-84 —Old Dominion	31	916	127	257	.494	89	137	.650	219	343	11.1
84-85 —Old Dominion	31	890	192	357	.538	114	187	.610	285	498	16.1
85-86 —Old Dominion	31	1008	218	342	.637	103	153	.673	241	539	17.4
Totals	122	3519	631	1143	.552	361	555	.650	963	1623	13.3

NBA REGULAR-SEASON RECORD

Season Team	G	Min.	FGM	FGA	Pct.	FTM	FTA	Pct.	REBOUNDS Off.	Def.	Tot.	Ast.	PF	Dq.	Stl.	Blk.	TO	Pts.	Avg.
86-87 —Phoenix	77	1104	148	311	.476	108	171	.632	87	183	270	36	178	1	24	33	88	404	5.2
87-88 —Phoenix						Did not play—injured.													
88-89 —Phoenix	2	9	0	1	.000	1	2	.500	0	1	1	0	2	0	0	0	0	1	0.5
89-90 —Charlotte	63	941	148	269	.550	75	110	.682	75	122	197	39	150	1	35	31	67	372	5.9
90-91 —Charlotte	72	1552	243	457	.532	164	248	.661	136	243	379	44	211	3	48	67	102	650	9.0
91-92 —Charlotte	82	2223	423	799	.529	196	285	.688	177	403	580	131	273	4	59	69	140	1042	12.7
Totals	296	5829	962	1837	.524	544	816	.667	475	952	1427	250	814	9	166	200	397	2469	8.3

Three-point field goals: 1988-89, 0-for-3. 1989-90, 1-for-1. 1990-91, 0-for-2. 1991-92, 0-for-2. Totals, 1-for-8 (.125).

ITALIAN LEAGUE RECORD

Season Team	G	Min.	FGM	FGA	Pct.	FTM	FTA	Pct.	Reb.	Pts.	Avg.
88-89 —Jolly	21	769	147	235	.626	73	109	.670	202	367	17.5

CBA REGULAR-SEASON RECORD

Season Team	G	Min.	2-POINT FGM	FGA	Pct.	3-POINT FGM	FGA	Pct.	FTM	FTA	Pct.	Reb.	Ast.	Pts.	Avg.
89-90 —Quad City	7	277	55	99	.556	0	1	.000	51	61	.836	81	15	161	23.0

G

GEORGE, TATE
G, NETS

PERSONAL: Born May 29, 1968, in Newark, N.J. . . . 6-5/190. . . . Full name: Tate Claude George.
HIGH SCHOOL: Union Catholic (N.J.).
COLLEGE: Connecticut.
TRANSACTIONS/CAREER NOTES: Selected by New Jersey Nets in first round (22nd pick overall) of 1990 NBA Draft.

COLLEGIATE RECORD

Season Team	G	Min.	FGM	FGA	Pct.	FTM	FTA	Pct.	Reb.	Pts.	Avg.
86-87 — Connecticut	26	962	91	247	.368	69	89	.775	93	261	10.0
87-88 — Connecticut	34	1111	115	230	.500	98	118	.831	99	337	9.9
88-89 — Connecticut	31	863	77	178	.433	69	91	.758	104	225	7.3
89-90 — Connecticut	37	1090	160	334	.479	88	121	.727	131	424	11.5
Totals	128	4026	443	989	.448	324	419	.773	427	1247	9.7

Three-point field goals: 1986-87, 10-for-29 (.345). 1987-88, 9-for-23 (.391). 1988-89, 2-for-10 (.200). 1989-90, 16-for-53 (.302). Totals, 37-for-115 (.322).

NBA REGULAR-SEASON RECORD

									— REBOUNDS —									
Season Team	G	Min.	FGM	FGA	Pct.	FTM	FTA	Pct.	Off.	Def.	Tot.	Ast.	PF	Dq.	Stl.	Blk.	TO	Pts.	Avg.
90-91 — New Jersey	56	594	80	193	.415	32	40	.800	19	28	47	104	58	0	25	5	42	192	3.4
91-92 — New Jersey	70	1037	165	386	.427	87	106	.821	36	69	105	162	98	0	41	3	82	418	6.0
Totals	126	1631	245	579	.423	119	146	.815	55	97	152	266	156	0	66	8	124	610	4.8

Three-point field goals: 1990-91, 0-for-2. 1991-92, 1-for-6 (.167). Totals, 1-for-8 (.125).

NBA PLAYOFF RECORD

									— REBOUNDS —									
Season Team	G	Min.	FGM	FGA	Pct.	FTM	FTA	Pct.	Off.	Def.	Tot.	Ast.	PF	Dq.	Stl.	Blk.	TO	Pts.	Avg.
91-92 — New Jersey	4	44	7	23	.304	1	3	.333	0	0	0	8	8	0	3	1	4	15	3.8

GILL, KENDALL
G, HORNETS

PERSONAL: Born May 25, 1968, in Chicago. . . . 6-5/200. . . . Full name: Kendall Cedric Gill.
HIGH SCHOOL: Rich Central (Olympia Fields, Ill.).
COLLEGE: Illinois.
TRANSACTIONS/CAREER NOTES: Selected by Charlotte Hornets in first round (fifth pick overall) of 1990 NBA Draft.

COLLEGIATE RECORD

NOTES: THE SPORTING NEWS All-America third team (1990).

Season Team	G	Min.	FGM	FGA	Pct.	FTM	FTA	Pct.	Reb.	Pts.	Avg.
86-87 — Illinois	31	345	40	83	.482	34	53	.642	42	114	3.7
87-88 — Illinois	33	946	128	272	.471	67	89	.753	73	344	10.4
88-89 — Illinois	24	681	143	264	.542	46	58	.793	70	370	15.4
89-90 — Illinois	29	1000	211	422	.500	136	175	.777	143	581	20.0
Totals	117	2972	522	1041	.501	283	375	.755	328	1409	12.0

Three-point field goals: 1986-87, 0-for-1. 1987-88, 21-for-69 (.304). 1988-89, 38-for-83 (.458). 1989-90, 23-for-66 (.348). Totals, 82-for-219 (.374).

NBA REGULAR-SEASON RECORD

HONORS: NBA All-Rookie first team (1991).

									— REBOUNDS —									
Season Team	G	Min.	FGM	FGA	Pct.	FTM	FTA	Pct.	Off.	Def.	Tot.	Ast.	PF	Dq.	Stl.	Blk.	TO	Pts.	Avg.
90-91 — Charlotte	82	1944	376	836	.450	152	182	.835	105	158	263	303	186	0	104	39	163	906	11.0
91-92 — Charlotte	79	2906	666	1427	.467	284	381	.745	165	237	402	329	237	1	154	46	180	1622	20.5
Totals	161	4850	1042	2263	.460	436	563	.774	270	395	665	632	423	1	258	85	343	2528	15.7

Three-point field goals: 1990-91, 2-for-14 (.143). 1991-92, 6-for-25 (.240). Totals, 8-for-39 (.205).

GILLIAM, ARMON
F, 76ERS

G

PERSONAL: Born May 28, 1964, in Pittsburgh. . . . 6-9/245. . . . Full name: Armon Louis Gilliam.
HIGH SCHOOL: Bethel Park Senior (Pa.).
COLLEGE: Independence Junior College (Kan.), then UNLV.
TRANSACTIONS/CAREER NOTES: Selected by Phoenix Suns in first round (second pick overall) of 1987 NBA Draft. . . . Traded by Suns to Charlotte Hornets for Kurt Rambis and two future second-round draft choices (December 13, 1989). . . . Traded by Hornets with Dave Hoppen to Philadelphia 76ers for Mike Gminski (January 4, 1991).

COLLEGIATE RECORD

NOTES: THE SPORTING NEWS All-America second team (1987).

Season Team	G	Min.	FGM	FGA	Pct.	FTM	FTA	Pct.	Reb.	Pts.	Avg.
82-83 — Independence Junior College	38	. . .	262	422	.621	117	185	.632	314	641	16.9
83-84 — UNLV					Did not play — redshirted.						
84-85 — UNLV	31	800	136	219	.621	98	150	.653	212	370	11.9
85-86 — UNLV	37	1243	221	418	.529	140	190	.737	315	582	15.7
86-87 — UNLV	39	1259	359	598	.600	185	254	.728	363	903	23.2
Junior college totals	38	. . .	262	422	.621	117	185	.632	314	641	16.9
Four-year-college totals	107	3302	716	1235	.580	423	594	.712	890	1855	17.3

HONORS: NBA All-Rookie team (1988).

NBA REGULAR-SEASON RECORD

Season Team	G	Min.	FGM	FGA	Pct.	FTM	FTA	Pct.	Off.	Def.	Tot.	Ast.	PF	Dq.	Stl.	Blk.	TO	Pts.	Avg.
87-88 —Phoenix........	55	1807	342	720	.475	131	193	.679	134	300	434	72	143	1	58	29	123	815	14.8
88-89 —Phoenix........	74	2120	468	930	.503	240	323	.743	165	376	541	52	176	2	54	27	140	1176	15.9
89-90 —Phoe.-Char..	76	2426	484	940	.515	303	419	.723	211	388	599	99	212	4	69	51	183	1271	16.7
90-91 —Char.-Phil....	75	2644	487	1001	.487	268	329	.815	220	378	598	105	185	2	69	53	174	1242	16.6
91-92 —Philadelphia.	81	2771	512	1001	.511	343	425	.807	234	426	660	118	176	1	51	85	166	1367	16.9
Totals	361	11768	2293	4592	.499	1285	1689	.761	964	1868	2832	446	892	10	301	245	786	5871	16.3

Three-point field goals: 1989-90, 0-for-2. 1990-91, 0-for-2. 1991-92, 0-for-2. Totals, 0-for-6.

NBA PLAYOFF RECORD

Season Team	G	Min.	FGM	FGA	Pct.	FTM	FTA	Pct.	Off.	Def.	Tot.	Ast.	PF	Dq.	Stl.	Blk.	TO	Pts.	Avg.
88-89 —Phoenix........	9	126	27	51	.529	19	22	.864	18	27	45	2	11	0	1	2	10	73	8.1
90-91 —Philadelphia.	8	287	48	104	.462	39	46	.848	14	38	52	10	16	0	5	6	15	135	16.9
Totals	17	413	75	155	.484	58	68	.853	32	65	97	12	27	0	6	8	25	208	12.2

GLASS, GERALD
G/F, TIMBERWOLVES

PERSONAL: Born November 12, 1967, in Greenwood, Miss. . . . 6-6/ 221. . . . Full name: Gerald Damon Glass.
HIGH SCHOOL: Amanda Elzy (Greenwood, Miss.).
COLLEGE: Delta State (Miss.), then Mississippi.
TRANSACTIONS/CAREER NOTES: Selected by Minnesota Timberwolves in first round (20th pick overall) of 1990 NBA Draft.

COLLEGIATE RECORD

Season Team	G	Min.	FGM	FGA	Pct.	FTM	FTA	Pct.	Reb.	Pts.	Avg.
85-86 —Delta State..............................	31	. . .	168	303	.554	52	72	.722	203	388	12.5
86-87 —Delta State..............................	33	. . .	360	595	.605	134	191	.702	414	861	26.1
87-88 —Mississippi..............................					Did not play—transfer student.						
88-89 —Mississippi..............................	30	1070	326	613	.532	148	201	.736	255	841	28.0
89-90 —Mississippi..............................	30	1108	284	580	.490	109	148	.736	229	723	24.1
Totals	124		1138	2091	.544	443	612	.724	1101	2813	22.7

Three-point field goals: 1986-87, 7-for-27 (.259). 1988-89, 41-for-109 (.376). 1989-90, 46-for-122 (.377). Totals, 94-for-258 (.364).

NBA REGULAR-SEASON RECORD

Season Team	G	Min.	FGM	FGA	Pct.	FTM	FTA	Pct.	Off.	Def.	Tot.	Ast.	PF	Dq.	Stl.	Blk.	TO	Pts.	Avg.
90-91 —Minnesota....	51	606	149	340	.438	52	76	.684	54	48	102	42	76	2	28	9	41	352	6.9
91-92 —Minnesota....	75	1822	383	871	.440	77	125	.616	107	153	260	175	171	0	66	30	103	859	11.5
Totals	126	2428	532	1211	.439	129	201	.642	161	201	362	217	247	2	94	39	144	1211	9.6

Three-point field goals: 1990-91, 2-for-17 (.118). 1991-92, 16-for-54 (.296). Totals, 18-for-71 (.254).

GMINSKI, MIKE
C, HORNETS

PERSONAL: Born August 3, 1959, in Monroe, Conn. . . . 6-11/260. . . . Full name: Michael Thomas Gminski. . . . Name pronounced Juh-MIN-skee.
HIGH SCHOOL: Masuk (Monroe, Conn.).
COLLEGE: Duke.
TRANSACTIONS/CAREER NOTES: Selected by New Jersey Nets in first round (seventh pick overall) of 1980 NBA Draft. . . . Traded by Nets with Ben Coleman to Philadelphia 76ers for Roy Hinson, Tim McCormick and 1989 second-round draft choice (January 16, 1988). . . . Traded by 76ers to Charlotte Hornets for Armon Gilliam and Dave Hoppen (January 4, 1991).

NOTES: THE SPORTING NEWS All-America second team (1979, 1980).

COLLEGIATE RECORD

Season Team	G	Min.	FGM	FGA	Pct.	FTM	FTA	Pct.	Reb.	Pts.	Avg.
76-77 —Duke............................	27	. . .	175	340	.515	64	91	.703	289	414	15.3
77-78 —Duke............................	32	. . .	246	450	.547	148	176	.841	319	640	20.0
78-79 —Duke............................	30	. . .	218	420	.519	129	177	.729	275	565	18.8
79-80 —Duke............................	33	1192	262	487	.538	180	214	.841	359	704	21.3
Totals	122	. . .	901	1697	.531	521	658	.792	1242	2323	19.0

NBA REGULAR-SEASON RECORD

Season Team	G	Min.	FGM	FGA	Pct.	FTM	FTA	Pct.	Off.	Def.	Tot.	Ast.	PF	Dq.	Stl.	Blk.	TO	Pts.	Avg.
80-81 —New Jersey ..	56	1579	291	688	.423	155	202	.767	137	282	419	72	127	1	54	100	128	737	13.2
81-82 —New Jersey ..	64	740	119	270	.441	97	118	.822	70	116	186	41	69	0	17	48	56	335	5.2
82-83 —New Jersey ..	80	1255	213	426	.500	175	225	.778	154	228	382	61	118	0	35	116	126	601	7.5
83-84 —New Jersey ..	82	1655	237	462	.513	147	184	.799	161	272	433	92	162	0	37	70	120	621	7.6
84-85 —New Jersey ..	81	2418	380	818	.465	276	328	.841	229	404	633	158	135	0	38	92	136	1036	12.8
85-86 —New Jersey ..	81	2525	491	949	.517	351	393	.893	206	462	668	133	163	0	56	71	140	1333	16.5
86-87 —New Jersey ..	72	2272	433	947	.457	313	370	.846	192	438	630	99	159	0	52	69	129	1179	16.4
87-88 —N.J.-Phil.	81	2961	505	1126	.448	355	392	.906	245	569	814	139	176	0	64	118	177	1365	16.9
88-89 —Philadelphia.	82	2739	556	1166	.477	297	341	.871	213	556	769	138	142	0	46	106	129	1409	17.2
89-90 —Philadelphia.	81	2659	458	1002	.457	193	235	.821	196	491	687	128	136	0	43	102	98	1112	13.7
90-91 —Phil.-Char.	80	2196	357	808	.442	128	158	.810	186	396	582	93	99	0	40	56	85	844	10.6
91-92 —Charlotte......	35	499	90	199	.452	21	28	.750	37	81	118	31	37	0	11	16	20	202	5.8
Totals	875	23498	4130	8861	.466	2508	2974	.843	2026	4295	6321	1185	1523	1	493	964	1344	10774	12.3

G

Three-point field goals: 1980-81, 0-for-1. 1982-83, 0-for-1. 1983-84, 0-for-3. 1984-85, 0-for-1. 1985-86, 0-for-1. 1987-88, 0-for-2. 1988-89, 0-for-6. 1989-90, 3-for-17 (.176). 1990-91, 2-for-14 (.143). 1991-92, 1-for-3 (.333). Totals, 6-for-49 (.122).

NBA PLAYOFF RECORD

Season Team	G	Min.	FGM	FGA	Pct.	FTM	FTA	Pct.	Off.	Def.	Tot.	Ast.	PF	Dq.	Stl.	Blk.	TO	Pts.	Avg.
81-82 —New Jersey ..	1	10	2	3	.667	1	2	.500	0	2	2	0	2	0	0	0	0	5	5.0
82-83 —New Jersey ..	2	29	6	9	.667	3	4	.750	4	5	9	1	2	0	0	4	1	15	7.5
83-84 —New Jersey ..	11	223	29	50	.580	36	52	.692	22	33	55	6	17	0	7	15	9	94	8.5
84-85 —New Jersey ..	3	81	18	33	.545	6	6	1.000	4	15	19	4	5	0	3	5	10	42	14.0
85-86 —New Jersey ..	3	109	16	43	.372	26	27	.963	11	19	30	5	11	0	4	2	9	58	19.3
88-89 —Philadelphia.	3	118	19	48	.396	11	16	.688	6	17	23	2	8	0	0	8	2	49	16.3
89-90 —Philadelphia.	10	342	57	117	.487	14	15	.933	8	46	54	11	27	0	8	23	17	128	12.8
Totals	33	912	147	303	.485	97	122	.795	55	137	192	29	72	0	22	57	48	391	11.8

Three-point field goals: 1989-90, 0-for-5.

GODFREAD, DAN
F/C

PERSONAL: Born June 14, 1967, in Fort Wayne, Ind.... 6-10/250.... Full name: Daniel Joseph Godfread.
HIGH SCHOOL: Stillman Valley (Ill.).
COLLEGE: Evansville.
TRANSACTIONS/CAREER NOTES: Never drafted by an NBA franchise.... Signed as free agent by New Jersey Nets (August 16, 1990).... Waived by Nets (October 29, 1990).... Played in Continental Basketball Association with Rockford Lightning (1990-91 and 1991-92).... Signed by Minnesota Timberwolves to first of two consecutive 10-day contracts (December 29, 1990).... Re-signed by Timberwolves for remainder of season (January 18, 1991).... Signed as restricted free agent by Timberwolves (July 15, 1991).... Waived by Timberwolves (October 28, 1991).... Signed as free agent by Houston Rockets (November 28, 1991).... Waived by Rockets (December 9, 1991).

COLLEGIATE RECORD

NOTES: Suffered back ailment during 1985-86 season; granted extra year of eligibility.

Season Team	G	Min.	FGM	FGA	Pct.	FTM	FTA	Pct.	Reb.	Pts.	Avg.
85-86 —Evansville	2	16	2	7	.286	0	1	.000	1	4	2.0
86-87 —Evansville	23	440	59	109	.541	15	25	.600	101	133	5.8
87-88 —Evansville	29	849	176	290	.607	68	100	.680	246	420	14.5
88-89 —Evansville	31	909	201	320	.628	89	127	.701	248	491	15.8
89-90 —Evansville	17	546	134	227	.590	69	94	.734	141	338	19.9
Totals	102	2760	572	953	.600	241	347	.695	737	1386	13.6

Three-point field goals: 1989-90, 1-for-2 (.500).

CBA REGULAR-SEASON RECORD

Season Team	G	Min.	2-POINT FGM	2-POINT FGA	2-POINT Pct.	3-POINT FGM	3-POINT FGA	3-POINT Pct.	FTM	FTA	Pct.	Reb.	Ast.	Pts.	Avg.
90-91 —Rockford	21	691	165	307	.537	0	0	...	58	75	.773	192	21	388	18.5
91-92 —Rockford	30	1130	249	467	.533	0	3	.000	116	133	.872	250	37	614	20.5
Totals	51	1821	414	774	.535	0	3	.000	174	208	.837	442	58	1002	19.6

NBA REGULAR-SEASON RECORD

Season Team	G	Min.	FGM	FGA	Pct.	FTM	FTA	Pct.	Off.	Def.	Tot.	Ast.	PF	Dq.	Stl.	Blk.	TO	Pts.	Avg.
90-91 —Minnesota	10	20	5	12	.417	3	4	.750	0	2	2	0	5	0	1	4	0	13	1.3
91-92 —Houston	1	2	0	0	...	0	0	...	0	0	0	0	0	0	0	0	0	0	0.0
Totals	11	22	5	12	.417	3	4	.750	0	2	2	0	5	0	1	4	0	13	1.2

Three-point field goals: 1990-91, 0-for-1.

GRAHAM, PAUL
F, HAWKS

PERSONAL: Born November 28, 1967, in Philadelphia.... 6-6/200.
HIGH SCHOOL: Ben Franklin (Philadelphia).
COLLEGE: Ohio University.
TRANSACTIONS/CAREER NOTES: Never drafted by an NBA franchise.... Played in Australia (1989-90).... Played in Continental Basketball Association with Albany Patroons (1990-91).... Signed as free agent by Atlanta Hawks (October 3, 1991).... Waived by Hawks (October 31, 1991).... Signed as free agent by Hawks (November 8, 1991).

COLLEGIATE RECORD

Season Team	G	Min.	FGM	FGA	Pct.	FTM	FTA	Pct.	Reb.	Pts.	Avg.
85-86 —Ohio University	29	757	181	377	.480	99	128	.773	136	461	15.9
86-87 —Ohio University	22	664	187	391	.478	81	109	.743	118	465	21.1
87-88 —Ohio University	30	860	227	413	.550	141	183	.770	153	599	20.0
88-89 —Ohio University	29	943	224	431	.520	176	217	.811	203	645	22.2
Totals	110	3224	819	1612	.508	497	637	.780	610	2170	19.7

Three-point field goals: 1986-87, 10-for-39 (.256). 1987-88, 4-for-9 (.444). 1988-89, 21-for-46 (.457). Totals, 35-for-94 (.372).

CBA REGULAR-SEASON RECORD

Season Team	G	Min.	2-POINT FGM	2-POINT FGA	2-POINT Pct.	3-POINT FGM	3-POINT FGA	3-POINT Pct.	FTM	FTA	Pct.	Reb.	Ast.	Pts.	Avg.
90-91 —Albany	53	1210	271	521	.520	20	62	.323	123	155	.794	198	94	725	13.7

NBA REGULAR-SEASON RECORD

Season Team	G	Min.	FGM	FGA	Pct.	FTM	FTA	Pct.	Off.	Def.	Tot.	Ast.	PF	Dq.	Stl.	Blk.	TO	Pts.	Avg.
91-92 —Atlanta	78	1718	305	682	.447	126	170	.741	72	159	231	175	193	3	96	21	91	791	10.1

Three-point field goals: 1991-92, 55-for-141 (.390).

GRANDISON, RON
F

PERSONAL: Born July 9, 1964, in Los Angeles. . . . 6-6/220. **HIGH SCHOOL:** St. Bernard (Playa del Ray, Calif.). **COLLEGE:** UC Irvine, then Tulane, then New Orleans. **TRANSACTIONS/CAREER NOTES:** Selected by Denver Nuggets in fifth round (100th overall) of 1987 NBA draft. . . . Waived by Nuggets (October 29, 1987). . . . Played in Continental Basketball Association with Rochester Flyers (1987-88) and Omaha Racers (1991-92). . . . Signed as free agent by Boston Celtics (September 27, 1988). . . . Sat out 1989-90 season. . . . Played with Athletes in Action (1990-91). . . . Signed as free agent by Miami Heat (October 1, 1991). . . . Waived by Heat (October 22, 1991). . . . Signed as free agent by Charlotte Hornets (December 30, 1991). . . . Waived by Hornets (January 7, 1992). . . . Signed by Hornets to first of two consecutive 10-day contracts (January 10, 1992).

COLLEGIATE RECORD

Season	Team	G	Min.	FGM	FGA	Pct.	FTM	FTA	Pct.	Reb.	Pts.	Avg.
82-83	UC Irvine	28	464	66	128	.516	40	66	.606	100	172	6.1
83-84	UC Irvine	29	394	49	91	.538	29	50	.580	89	127	4.4
84-85	Tulane					Did not play—transfer student.						
85-86	New Orleans	28	934	186	363	.512	93	162	.574	271	465	16.6
86-87	New Orleans	30	1059	179	339	.528	155	231	.671	292	513	17.1
	Totals	115	2851	480	921	.521	317	509	.623	752	1277	11.1

Three-point field goals: 1986-87, 0-for-1.

CBA REGULAR-SEASON RECORD

Season	Team	G	Min.	2-POINT FGM	2-POINT FGA	2-POINT Pct.	3-POINT FGM	3-POINT FGA	3-POINT Pct.	FTM	FTA	Pct.	Reb.	Ast.	Pts.	Avg.
87-88	Rochester	31	1082	166	317	.524	1	4	.250	104	148	.703	295	40	439	14.2
91-92	Omaha	43	1488	263	499	.527	2	12	.167	242	295	.820	432	85	774	18.0
	Totals	74	2570	429	816	.526	3	16	.188	346	443	.781	727	125	1213	16.4

NBA REGULAR-SEASON RECORD

Season	Team	G	Min.	FGM	FGA	Pct.	FTM	FTA	Pct.	REBOUNDS Off.	REBOUNDS Def.	REBOUNDS Tot.	Ast.	PF	Dq.	Stl.	Blk.	TO	Pts.	Avg.
88-89	Boston	72	528	59	142	.415	59	80	.738	47	45	92	42	71	0	18	3	36	177	2.5
91-92	Charlotte	3	25	2	4	.500	6	10	.600	3	8	11	1	4	0	1	1	3	10	3.3
	Totals	75	553	61	146	.418	65	90	.722	50	53	103	43	75	0	19	4	39	187	2.5

Three-point field goals: 1988-89, 0-for-10.

GRANT, GARY
G, CLIPPERS

PERSONAL: Born April 21, 1965, in Canton, O. . . . 6-3/195. **HIGH SCHOOL:** McKinley (Canton, O.). **COLLEGE:** Michigan. **TRANSACTIONS/CAREER NOTES:** Selected by Seattle SuperSonics in first round (15th pick overall) of 1988 NBA Draft. . . . Draft rights traded by SuperSonics with 1989 first-round draft choice to Los Angeles Clippers for Michael Cage (June 28, 1988).

COLLEGIATE RECORD

NOTES: THE SPORTING NEWS All-America second team (1988).

Season	Team	G	Min.	FGM	FGA	Pct.	FTM	FTA	Pct.	Reb.	Pts.	Avg.
84-85	Michigan	30	950	169	307	.550	49	60	.817	76	387	12.9
85-86	Michigan	33	1010	172	348	.494	58	78	.744	104	402	12.2
86-87	Michigan	32	...	286	533	.537	111	142	.782	116	716	22.4
87-88	Michigan	34	1190	269	508	.530	135	167	.808	116	717	21.1
	Totals	129	...	896	1696	.528	353	447	.790	455	2222	17.2

Three-point field goals: 1986-87, 33-for-68 (.485). 1987-88, 44-for-99 (.444). Totals, 77-for-167 (.461).

NBA REGULAR-SEASON RECORD

Season	Team	G	Min.	FGM	FGA	Pct.	FTM	FTA	Pct.	REBOUNDS Off.	REBOUNDS Def.	REBOUNDS Tot.	Ast.	PF	Dq.	Stl.	Blk.	TO	Pts.	Avg.
88-89	L.A. Clippers	71	1924	361	830	.435	119	162	.735	80	158	238	506	170	1	144	9	258	846	11.9
89-90	L.A. Clippers	44	1529	241	517	.466	88	113	.779	59	136	195	442	120	1	108	5	206	575	13.1
90-91	L.A. Clippers	68	2105	265	587	.451	51	74	.689	69	140	209	587	192	4	103	12	210	590	8.7
91-92	L.A. Clippers	78	2049	275	595	.462	44	54	.815	34	150	184	538	181	4	138	14	187	609	7.8
	Totals	261	7607	1142	2529	.452	302	403	.749	242	584	826	2073	663	10	493	40	861	2620	10.0

Three-point field goals: 1988-89, 5-for-22 (.227). 1989-90, 5-for-21 (.238). 1990-91, 9-for-39 (.231). 1991-92, 15-for-51 (.294). Totals, 34-for-133 (.256).

NBA PLAYOFF RECORD

Season	Team	G	Min.	FGM	FGA	Pct.	FTM	FTA	Pct.	REBOUNDS Off.	REBOUNDS Def.	REBOUNDS Tot.	Ast.	PF	Dq.	Stl.	Blk.	TO	Pts.	Avg.
91-92	L.A. Clippers	5	77	10	21	.476	2	2	1.000	0	4	4	18	10	0	3	2	8	22	4.4

Three-point field goals: 1991-92, 0-for-2.

GRANT, GREG
G, 76ERS

PERSONAL: Born August 29, 1966, in Trenton, N.J. . . . 5-7/140. . . . Full name: Gregory Alan Grant. **HIGH SCHOOL:** Central (Trenton, N.J.). **COLLEGE:** Morris Brown (Ga.), then Trenton State (N.J.). **TRANSACTIONS/CAREER NOTES:** Selected by Phoenix Suns in second round (52nd pick overall) of 1989 NBA Draft. . . . Signed as unrestricted free agent by New York Knicks (October 1, 1990). . . . Signed as free agent by Indiana Pacers (September 6, 1991).... Waived by Pacers (October 29, 1991).... Claimed off waivers by Charlotte Hornets (October 31, 1991).... Waived by Hornets (December 9, 1991).... Signed as free agent by Philadelphia 76ers (December 22, 1991).

COLLEGIATE RECORD

NOTES: Outstanding Player in NCAA Division III Tournament (1989).... Led NCAA Division III with 32.6 points per game (1989).

Season	Team	G	Min.	FGM	FGA	Pct.	FTM	FTA	Pct.	Reb.	Pts.	Avg.
85-86	—Morris Brown					Statistics unavailable.						
86-87	—Trenton State	26	...	263	543	.484	171	220	.777	104	740	28.5
87-88	—Trenton State	27	912	302	537	.562	171	204	.838	69	827	30.6
88-89	—Trenton State	32	1077	387	742	.522	194	239	.812	75	1044	32.6
	Totals	85	...	952	1822	.523	536	663	.808	248	2611	30.7

Three-point field goals: 1986-87, 43-for-83 (.518). 1987-88, 52-for-105 (.495). 1988-89, 76-for-186 (.409). Totals, 171-for-374 (.457).

NBA REGULAR-SEASON RECORD

Season	Team	G	Min.	FGM	FGA	Pct.	FTM	FTA	Pct.	REBOUNDS Off.	Def.	Tot.	Ast.	PF	Dq.	Stl.	Blk.	TO	Pts.	Avg.
89-90	—Phoenix	67	678	83	216	.384	39	59	.661	16	43	59	168	58	0	36	1	77	208	3.1
90-91	—New York	22	107	10	27	.370	5	6	.833	1	9	10	20	12	0	9	0	10	26	1.2
91-92	—Char.-Phil.	68	891	99	225	.440	20	24	.833	14	55	69	217	76	0	45	2	46	225	3.3
	Totals	157	1676	192	468	.410	64	89	.719	31	107	138	405	146	0	90	3	133	459	2.9

Three-point field goals: 1989-90, 3-for-16 (.188). 1990-91, 1-for-3 (.333). 1991-92, 7-for-18 (.389). Totals, 11-for-37 (.297).

NBA PLAYOFF RECORD

Season	Team	G	Min.	FGM	FGA	Pct.	FTM	FTA	Pct.	REBOUNDS Off.	Def.	Tot.	Ast.	PF	Dq.	Stl.	Blk.	TO	Pts.	Avg.
89-90	—Phoenix	7	47	9	20	.450	0	0	...	2	4	6	10	2	0	2	0	...	19	2.7

Three-point field goals: 1989-90, 1-for-3 (.333).

GRANT, HARVEY
F, BULLETS

PERSONAL: Born July 4, 1965, in Augusta, Ga.... 6-9/235.... Twin brother of Horace Grant, forward with Chicago Bulls.
HIGH SCHOOL: Hancock Central (Sparta, Ga.).
COLLEGE: Clemson, then Independence Junior College (Kan.), then Oklahoma.
TRANSACTIONS/CAREER NOTES: Selected by Washington Bullets in first round (12th pick overall) of 1988 NBA Draft.

COLLEGIATE RECORD

Season	Team	G	Min.	FGM	FGA	Pct.	FTM	FTA	Pct.	Reb.	Pts.	Avg.
83-84	—Clemson					Did not play—redshirted.						
84-85	—Clemson	28	418	60	121	.496	24	41	.585	126	144	5.1
85-86	—Independence Junior College	33	...	340	580	.586	58	82	.707	388	738	22.4
86-87	—Oklahoma	34	1165	228	427	.534	119	163	.730	338	575	16.9
87-88	—Oklahoma	39	1339	350	640	.547	113	155	.729	365	816	20.9
	Junior college totals	33	...	340	580	.586	58	82	.707	388	738	22.4
	Four-year-college totals	101	2922	638	1188	.537	256	359	.713	829	1535	15.2

Three-point field goals: 1986-87, 0-for-1. 1987-88, 3-for-14 (.214). Totals, 3-for-15 (.200).

NBA REGULAR-SEASON RECORD

Season	Team	G	Min.	FGM	FGA	Pct.	FTM	FTA	Pct.	REBOUNDS Off.	Def.	Tot.	Ast.	PF	Dq.	Stl.	Blk.	TO	Pts.	Avg.
88-89	—Washington	71	1193	181	390	.464	34	57	.596	75	88	163	79	147	2	35	29	28	396	5.6
89-90	—Washington	81	1846	284	601	.473	96	137	.701	138	204	342	131	194	1	52	43	85	664	8.2
90-91	—Washington	77	2842	609	1224	.498	185	249	.743	179	378	557	204	232	0	91	61	125	1405	18.2
91-92	—Washington	64	2388	489	1022	.478	176	220	.800	157	275	432	170	178	1	74	27	109	1155	18.0
	Totals	293	8269	1563	3237	.483	491	663	.741	549	945	1494	584	751	6	252	160	347	3620	12.4

Three-point field goals: 1988-89, 0-for-1. 1989-90, 0-for-8. 1990-91, 2-for-15 (.133). 1991-92, 1-for-8 (.125). Totals, 3-for-32 (.094).

GRANT, HORACE
F, BULLS

PERSONAL: Born July 4, 1965, in Augusta, Ga.... 6-10/220.... Full name: Horace Junior Grant.... Twin brother of Harvey Grant, forward with Washington Bullets.
HIGH SCHOOL: Hancock Central (Sparta, Ga.).
COLLEGE: Clemson.
TRANSACTIONS/CAREER NOTES: Selected by Chicago Bulls in first round (10th pick overall) of 1987 NBA Draft.
MISCELLANEOUS: Member of NBA championship teams (1991, 1992).

COLLEGIATE RECORD

Season	Team	G	Min.	FGM	FGA	Pct.	FTM	FTA	Pct.	Reb.	Pts.	Avg.
83-84	—Clemson	28	551	64	120	.533	32	43	.744	129	160	5.7
84-85	—Clemson	29	703	132	238	.555	65	102	.637	196	329	11.3
85-86	—Clemson	34	1099	208	356	.584	140	193	.725	357	556	16.4
86-87	—Clemson	31	1010	256	390	.656	138	195	.708	299	651	21.0
	Totals	122	3363	660	1104	.598	375	533	.704	981	1696	13.9

Three-point field goals: 1986-87, 1-for-2 (.500).

G

Season	Team	G	Min.	FGM	FGA	Pct.	FTM	FTA	Pct.	REBOUNDS Off.	REBOUNDS Def.	REBOUNDS Tot.	Ast.	PF	Dq.	Stl.	Blk.	TO	Pts.	Avg.
87-88	—Chicago	81	1827	254	507	.501	114	182	.626	155	292	447	89	221	3	51	53	86	622	7.7
88-89	—Chicago	79	2809	405	781	.519	140	199	.704	240	441	681	168	251	1	86	62	128	950	12.0
89-90	—Chicago	80	2753	446	853	.523	179	256	.699	236	393	629	227	230	1	92	84	110	1071	13.4
90-91	—Chicago	78	2641	401	733	.547	197	277	.711	266	393	659	178	203	2	95	69	92	1000	12.8
91-92	—Chicago	81	2859	457	790	.578	235	317	.741	344	463	807	217	196	0	100	131	98	1149	14.2
	Totals	399	12889	1963	3664	.536	865	1231	.703	1241	1982	3223	879	1101	7	424	399	514	4792	12.0

Three-point field goals: 1987-88, 0-for-2. 1988-89, 0-for-5. 1990-91, 1-for-6 (.167). 1991-92, 0-for-2. Totals, 1-for-15 (.067).

NBA PLAYOFF RECORD

Season	Team	G	Min.	FGM	FGA	Pct.	FTM	FTA	Pct.	REBOUNDS Off.	REBOUNDS Def.	REBOUNDS Tot.	Ast.	PF	Dq.	Stl.	Blk.	TO	Pts.	Avg.
87-88	—Chicago	10	299	46	81	.568	9	15	.600	25	45	70	16	35	2	14	2	7	101	10.1
88-89	—Chicago	17	625	72	139	.518	40	50	.800	53	114	167	35	68	2	11	16	31	184	10.8
89-90	—Chicago	16	616	81	159	.509	33	53	.623	73	86	159	40	51	1	18	18	26	195	12.2
90-91	—Chicago	17	666	91	156	.583	44	60	.733	56	82	138	38	45	0	15	6	20	226	13.3
91-92	—Chicago	22	856	99	183	.541	51	76	.671	76	118	194	66	68	1	24	39	21	249	11.3
	Totals	82	3062	389	718	.542	177	254	.697	283	445	728	195	267	6	82	81	105	955	11.6

Three-point field goals: 1987-88, 0-for-1. 1989-90, 0-for-2. 1991-92, 0-for-2. Totals, 0-for-5.

GRAYER, JEFF
F/G, WARRIORS

PERSONAL: Born December 17, 1965, in Flint, Mich. . . . 6-5/210. . . . Full name: Jeffrey Grayer.
HIGH SCHOOL: Northwestern Community (Flint, Mich.).
COLLEGE: Iowa State.
TRANSACTIONS/CAREER NOTES: Selected by Milwaukee Bucks in first round (13th pick overall) of 1988 NBA Draft. . . . Signed as unrestricted free agent by Golden State Warriors (July 31, 1992).
MISCELLANEOUS: Member of bronze-medal-winning U.S. Olympic team (1988).

COLLEGIATE RECORD

Season	Team	G	Min.	FGM	FGA	Pct.	FTM	FTA	Pct.	Reb.	Pts.	Avg.
84-85	—Iowa State	33	1119	153	289	.529	96	147	.653	213	402	12.2
85-86	—Iowa State	33	1159	281	514	.547	122	194	.629	208	684	20.7
86-87	—Iowa State	27	995	228	452	.504	142	192	.740	189	605	22.4
87-88	—Iowa State	32	1165	312	597	.523	167	235	.711	300	811	25.3
	Totals	125	4438	974	1852	.526	527	768	.686	910	2502	20.0

Three-point field goals: 1986-87, 7-for-21 (.333). 1987-88, 20-for-61 (.328). Totals, 27-for-82 (.329).

NBA REGULAR-SEASON RECORD

Season	Team	G	Min.	FGM	FGA	Pct.	FTM	FTA	Pct.	REBOUNDS Off.	REBOUNDS Def.	REBOUNDS Tot.	Ast.	PF	Dq.	Stl.	Blk.	TO	Pts.	Avg.
88-89	—Milwaukee	11	20	32	73	.438	17	20	.850	14	21	35	22	15	0	10	1	19	81	7.4
89-90	—Milwaukee	71	1427	224	487	.460	99	152	.651	94	123	217	107	125	0	48	10	82	548	7.7
90-91	—Milwaukee	82	1422	210	485	.433	101	147	.687	111	135	246	123	98	0	48	9	86	521	6.4
91-92	—Milwaukee	82	1659	309	689	.448	102	153	.667	129	128	257	150	142	0	64	13	105	739	9.0
	Totals	246	4528	775	1734	.447	319	472	.676	348	407	755	402	380	0	170	33	292	1889	7.7

Three-point field goals: 1988-89, 0-for-2. 1989-90, 1-for-8 (.125). 1990-91, 0-for-3. 1991-92, 19-for-66 (.288). Totals, 20-for-79 (.253).

NBA PLAYOFF RECORD

Season	Team	G	Min.	FGM	FGA	Pct.	FTM	FTA	Pct.	REBOUNDS Off.	REBOUNDS Def.	REBOUNDS Tot.	Ast.	PF	Dq.	Stl.	Blk.	TO	Pts.	Avg.
89-90	—Milwaukee	4	12	0	0	...	0	0	...	0	2	2	1	1	0	0	0	1	0	0.0
90-91	—Milwaukee	3	37	5	13	.385	5	6	.833	3	3	6	6	2	0	1	0	3	15	5.0
	Totals	7	49	5	13	.385	5	6	.833	3	5	8	7	3	0	1	0	4	15	2.1

GREEN, A.C.
F, LAKERS

PERSONAL: Born October 4, 1963, in Portland, Ore. . . . 6-9/225. . . . Full name: A.C. Green Jr.
HIGH SCHOOL: Benson Polytechnic (Portland, Ore.).
COLLEGE: Oregon State.
TRANSACTIONS/CAREER NOTES: Selected by Los Angeles Lakers in first round (23rd pick overall) of 1985 NBA Draft.
MISCELLANEOUS: Member of NBA championship teams (1987, 1988).

G

COLLEGIATE RECORD

Season	Team	G	Min.	FGM	FGA	Pct.	FTM	FTA	Pct.	Reb.	Pts.	Avg.
81-82	—Oregon State	30	895	99	161	.615	61	100	.610	158	259	8.6
82-83	—Oregon State	31	1113	162	290	.559	111	161	.689	235	435	14.0
83-84	—Oregon State	23	853	134	204	.657	141	183	.770	201	409	17.8
84-85	—Oregon State	31	1191	217	362	.599	157	231	.680	286	591	19.1
	Totals	115	4052	612	1017	.602	470	675	.696	880	1694	14.7

NBA REGULAR-SEASON RECORD

HONORS: NBA All-Defensive second team (1989).

Season	Team	G	Min.	FGM	FGA	Pct.	FTM	FTA	Pct.	REBOUNDS Off.	REBOUNDS Def.	REBOUNDS Tot.	Ast.	PF	Dq.	Stl.	Blk.	TO	Pts.	Avg.
85-86	—L.A. Lakers	82	1542	209	388	.539	102	167	.611	160	221	381	54	229	2	49	49	99	521	6.4
86-87	—L.A. Lakers	79	2240	316	587	.538	220	282	.780	210	405	615	84	171	0	70	80	102	852	10.8
87-88	—L.A. Lakers	82	2636	322	640	.503	293	379	.773	245	465	710	93	204	0	87	45	120	937	11.4

Season Team	G	Min.	FGM	FGA	Pct.	FTM	FTA	Pct.	REBOUNDS Off.	Def.	Tot.	Ast.	PF	Dq.	Stl.	Blk.	TO	Pts.	Avg.
88-89 —L.A. Lakers..	82	2510	401	758	.529	282	359	.786	258	481	739	103	172	0	94	55	119	1088	13.3
89-90 —L.A. Lakers..	82	2709	385	806	.478	278	370	.751	262	450	712	90	207	0	66	50	116	1061	12.9
90-91 —L.A. Lakers..	82	2164	258	542	.476	223	302	.738	201	315	516	71	117	0	59	23	99	750	9.1
91-92 —L.A. Lakers..	82	2902	382	803	.476	340	457	.744	306	456	762	117	141	0	91	36	111	1116	13.6
Totals	571	16703	2273	4524	.502	1738	2316	.750	1642	2793	4435	612	1241	2	516	338	766	6325	11.1

Three-point field goals: 1985-86, 1-for-6 (.167). 1986-87, 0-for-5. 1987-88, 0-for-2. 1988-89, 4-for-17 (.235). 1989-90, 13-for-46 (.283). 1990-91, 11-for-55 (.200). 1991-92, 12-for-56 (.214). Totals, 41-for-187 (.219).

NBA PLAYOFF RECORD

Season Team	G	Min.	FGM	FGA	Pct.	FTM	FTA	Pct.	REBOUNDS Off.	Def.	Tot.	Ast.	PF	Dq.	Stl.	Blk.	TO	Pts.	Avg.
85-86 —L.A. Lakers..	9	106	9	17	.529	4	9	.444	3	13	16	0	13	0	1	3	4	22	2.4
86-87 —L.A. Lakers..	18	505	71	130	.546	65	87	.747	54	88	142	11	47	0	9	8	17	207	11.5
87-88 —L.A. Lakers..	24	726	92	169	.544	55	73	.753	57	118	175	20	61	0	11	12	26	239	10.0
88-89 —L.A. Lakers..	15	502	47	114	.412	58	76	.763	38	99	137	18	37	1	16	6	23	152	10.1
89-90 —L.A. Lakers..	9	252	41	79	.519	24	32	.750	34	47	81	9	22	0	5	4	14	106	11.8
90-91 —L.A. Lakers..	19	400	41	97	.423	38	54	.704	46	56	102	9	37	0	12	3	19	124	6.5
91-92 —L.A. Lakers..	4	153	16	39	.410	19	23	.826	15	21	36	7	10	0	7	0	5	51	12.8
Totals	98	2644	317	645	.491	263	354	.743	247	442	689	74	227	1	61	36	108	901	9.2

Three-point field goals: 1988-89, 0-for-3. 1990-91, 4-for-8 (.500). Totals, 4-for-11 (.364).

NBA ALL-STAR GAME RECORD

Season Team	Min.	FGM	FGA	Pct.	FTM	FTA	Pct.	REBOUNDS Off.	Def.	Tot.	Ast.	PF	Dq.	Stl.	Blk.	TO	Pts.
1990 —L.A. Lakers	12	0	3	.000	0	0	...	0	3	3	1	1	0	1	0	1	0

GREEN, RICKEY

G

PERSONAL: Born August 18, 1954, in Chicago. . . . 6-0/172.
HIGH SCHOOL: Hirsch Metro (Ill.).
COLLEGE: Vincennes (Ind.), then Michigan.
TRANSACTIONS/CAREER NOTES: Selected by Golden State Warriors in first round (16th pick overall) of 1977 NBA Draft. . . . Traded by Warriors to Detroit Pistons for 1980 second-round draft choice (October 9, 1978). . . . Waived by Pistons (December 11, 1978). . . . Played in Continental Basketball Association with Hawaii Volcanos and Billings Volcanos (1979-80 and 1980-81). . . . Signed as free agent by Chicago Bulls (August 12, 1980). . . . Waived by Bulls (October 8, 1980). . . . Signed as free agent by Utah Jazz (December 2, 1980). . . . Selected by Charlotte Hornets from Jazz in NBA expansion draft (June 23, 1988). . . . Waived by Hornets (February 22, 1989). . . . Signed as free agent by Milwaukee Bucks (March 1, 1989). . . . Signed as unrestricted free agent by Indiana Pacers (October 3, 1989). . . . Signed as unrestricted free agent by Philadelphia 76ers (October 3, 1990). . . . Waived by 76ers (October 31, 1991). . . . Signed as free agent by Boston Celtics (November 6, 1991). . . . Waived by Celtics (March 23, 1992).

COLLEGIATE RECORD

NOTES: THE SPORTING NEWS All-America first team (1977).

Season Team	G	Min.	FGM	FGA	Pct.	FTM	FTA	Pct.	Reb.	Pts.	Avg.
73-74 —Vincennes...............	36	...	254	633	.401	114	163	.699	237	622	17.3
74-75 —Vincennes...............	32	...	302	600	.503	69	105	.657	208	673	21.0
75-76 —Michigan...............	32	...	266	542	.491	106	135	.785	117	638	19.9
76-77 —Michigan...............	28	...	224	464	.483	98	128	.766	81	546	19.5
Junior college totals...............	68	...	556	1233	.451	183	268	.683	445	1295	19.0
Four-year-college totals...............	60	...	490	1006	.487	204	263	.776	198	1184	19.7

NBA REGULAR-SEASON RECORD

NOTES: Led NBA with 2.65 steals per game (1984).

Season Team	G	Min.	FGM	FGA	Pct.	FTM	FTA	Pct.	REBOUNDS Off.	Def.	Tot.	Ast.	PF	Dq.	Stl.	Blk.	TO	Pts.	Avg.
77-78 —Golden State	76	1098	143	375	.381	54	90	.600	49	67	116	149	95	0	58	1	79	340	4.5
78-79 —Detroit.........	27	431	67	177	.379	45	67	.672	15	25	40	63	37	0	25	1	44	179	6.6
80-81 —Utah.............	47	1307	176	366	.481	70	97	.722	30	86	116	235	123	2	75	1	83	422	9.0
81-82 —Utah.............	81	2822	500	1015	.493	202	264	.765	85	158	243	630	183	0	185	9	198	1202	14.8
82-83 —Utah.............	78	2783	464	942	.493	185	232	.797	62	161	223	697	154	0	*220	4	222	1115	14.3
83-84 —Utah.............	81	2768	439	904	.486	192	234	.821	56	174	230	748	155	1	*215	13	172	1072	13.2
84-85 —Utah.............	77	2431	381	798	.477	232	267	.869	37	152	189	597	131	0	132	3	177	1000	13.0
85-86 —Utah.............	80	2012	357	758	.471	213	250	.852	32	103	135	411	130	0	106	6	132	932	11.7
86-87 —Utah.............	81	2090	301	644	.467	172	208	.827	38	125	163	541	108	0	110	2	133	781	9.6
87-88 —Utah.............	81	1116	157	370	.424	75	83	.904	14	66	80	300	83	0	57	1	94	393	4.9
88-89 —Char.-Mil......	63	871	129	264	.489	30	33	.909	11	58	69	187	35	0	40	2	61	291	4.6
89-90 —Indiana..........	69	927	100	231	.433	43	51	.843	9	45	54	182	60	0	51	1	62	244	3.5
90-91 —Philadelphia.	79	2248	334	722	.463	117	141	.830	33	104	137	413	130	0	57	6	108	793	10.0
91-92 —Boston	26	367	46	103	.447	13	18	.722	3	21	24	68	28	0	17	1	18	106	4.1
Totals	946	23271	3594	7669	.469	1643	2035	.807	474	1345	1819	5221	1452	3	1348	51	1583	8870	9.4

Three-point field goals: 1980-81, 0-for-1. 1981-82, 0-for-8. 1982-83, 2-for-13 (.154). 1983-84, 2-for-17 (.118). 1984-85, 6-for-20 (.300). 1985-86, 5-for-29 (.172). 1986-87, 7-for-19 (.368). 1987-88, 4-for-19 (.211). 1988-89, 3-for-11 (.273). 1989-90, 1-for-11 (.091). 1990-91, 8-for-36 (.222). 1991-92, 1-for-4 (.250). Totals, 39-for-188 (.207).

NBA PLAYOFF RECORD

Season Team	G	Min.	FGM	FGA	Pct.	FTM	FTA	Pct.	REBOUNDS Off.	Def.	Tot.	Ast.	PF	Dq.	Stl.	Blk.	TO	Pts.	Avg.
83-84 —Utah.............	11	404	64	151	.424	32	43	.744	9	25	34	104	17	0	19	4	29	161	14.6
84-85 —Utah.............	10	302	57	106	.538	35	38	.921	10	20	30	75	23	0	12	0	20	150	15.0
85-86 —Utah.............	4	119	21	43	.488	10	11	.909	0	9	9	38	1	0	2	0	5	53	13.3
86-87 —Utah.............	4	72	11	23	.478	5	6	.833	1	7	8	25	5	0	2	0	7	27	6.8
87-88 —Utah.............	7	38	2	8	.250	0	0	...	0	1	1	9	2	0	2	0	3	4	0.6

G

Season Team	G	Min.	FGM	FGA	Pct.	FTM	FTA	Pct.	REBOUNDS Off.	Def.	Tot.	Ast.	PF	Dq.	Stl.	Blk.	TO	Pts.	Avg.
88-89—Milwaukee ...	8	110	12	29	.414	4	4	1.000	3	10	13	18	9	0	5	0	4	29	3.6
89-90—Indiana........	3	31	1	7	.143	0	0	...	0	1	1	3	5	0	1	0	2	2	0.7
90-91—Philadelphia.	8	199	24	55	.436	8	9	.889	1	8	9	22	9	0	7	0	13	59	7.4
Totals	55	1275	192	422	.455	94	111	.847	24	81	105	294	71	0	50	4	83	485	8.8

Three-point field goals: 1983-84, 1-for-4 (.250). 1984-85, 1-for-7 (.143). 1985-86, 1-for-2 (.500). 1986-87, 0-for-1. 1988-89, 1-for-2 (.500). 1990-91, 3-for-4 (.750). Totals, 7-for-20 (.350).

NBA ALL-STAR GAME RECORD

Season Team	Min.	FGM	FGA	Pct.	FTM	FTA	Pct.	REBOUNDS Off.	Def.	Tot.	Ast.	PF	Dq.	Stl.	Blk.	TO	Pts.
1984 —Utah	19	3	8	.375	0	0	...	0	0	0	11	1	0	1	0	4	6

CBA REGULAR-SEASON RECORD

Season Team	G	Min.	2-POINT FGM	FGA	Pct.	3-POINT FGM	FGA	Pct.	FTM	FTA	Pct.	Reb.	Ast.	Pts.	Avg.
79-80—Hawaii.............	44	1753	408	824	.495	3	17	.176	155	205	.756	188	*345	980	22.3
80-81—Billings............	5	197	47	95	.495	0	1	.000	19	24	.792	22	32	113	22.6
Totals	49	1950	455	919	.495	3	18	.167	174	229	.760	210	377	1093	22.3

GREEN, SEAN
G, PACERS

PERSONAL: Born February 2, 1970, in Santa Monica, Calif. ... 6-5/210. ... Full name: Sean Curtis Green.
HIGH SCHOOL: August Martin (Queens, N.Y.), then Oak Hill Academy (Mouth of Wilson, Va.).
COLLEGE: North Carolina State, then Iona.
TRANSACTIONS/CAREER NOTES: Selected by Indiana Pacers in second round (41st pick overall) of 1991 NBA Draft.

COLLEGIATE RECORD

Season Team	G	Min.	FGM	FGA	Pct.	FTM	FTA	Pct.	Reb.	Pts.	Avg.
87-88—North Carolina State...............	7	89	12	32	.375	2	3	.667	7	33	4.7
88-89—Iona...	23	570	119	291	.409	37	55	.673	93	301	13.1
89-90—Iona...	28	1012	215	508	.423	71	104	.683	139	553	19.8
90-91—Iona...	30	1069	265	550	.482	113	149	.758	155	696	23.2
Totals	88	2740	611	1381	.442	223	311	.717	394	1583	18.0

Three-point field goals: 1987-88, 7-for-17 (.412). 1988-89, 26-for-87 (.299). 1989-90, 52-for-158 (.329). 1990-91, 53-for-155 (.342). Totals, 138-for-417 (.331).

NBA REGULAR-SEASON RECORD

Season Team	G	Min.	FGM	FGA	Pct.	FTM	FTA	Pct.	REBOUNDS Off.	Def.	Tot.	Ast.	PF	Dq.	Stl.	Blk.	TO	Pts.	Avg.
91-92—Indiana.........	35	256	62	158	.392	15	28	.536	22	20	42	22	31	0	13	6	27	141	4.0

Three-point field goals: 1991-92, 2-for-10 (.200).

NBA PLAYOFF RECORD

Season Team	G	Min.	FGM	FGA	Pct.	FTM	FTA	Pct.	REBOUNDS Off.	Def.	Tot.	Ast.	PF	Dq.	Stl.	Blk.	TO	Pts.	Avg.
91-92—Indiana.........	1	3	0	0	...	0	0	...	0	0	0	0	0	0	0	0	0	0	0.0

GREEN, SIDNEY
F, SPURS

PERSONAL: Born January 4, 1961, in Brooklyn, N.Y. ... 6-9/240.
HIGH SCHOOL: Thomas Jefferson (Brooklyn, N.Y.).
COLLEGE: UNLV.
TRANSACTIONS/CAREER NOTES: Selected by Chicago Bulls in first round (fifth pick overall) of 1983 NBA Draft. ... Traded by Bulls to Detroit Pistons for Earl Cureton and 1987 second-round draft choice (August 21, 1986). ... Traded by Pistons to New York Knicks for Ron Moore and 1988 second-round draft choice (October 29, 1987). ... Selected by Orlando Magic from Knicks in NBA expansion draft (June 15, 1989). ... Traded by Magic to San Antonio Spurs for Mark McNamara and 1991 first-round draft choice (October 30, 1990).

COLLEGIATE RECORD

NOTES: THE SPORTING NEWS All-America second team (1983).

Season Team	G	Min.	FGM	FGA	Pct.	FTM	FTA	Pct.	Reb.	Pts.	Avg.
79-80—UNLV	32	1024	201	388	.518	96	132	.727	354	498	15.6
80-81—UNLV	26	817	153	297	.515	85	120	.708	284	391	15.0
81-82—UNLV	30	963	200	374	.535	100	130	.769	270	500	16.7
82-83—UNLV	31	1120	269	491	.548	142	203	.700	368	684	22.1
Totals	119	3924	823	1550	.531	423	585	.723	1276	2073	17.4

Three-point field goals: 1982-83, 4-for-12 (.333).

NBA REGULAR-SEASON RECORD

Season Team	G	Min.	FGM	FGA	Pct.	FTM	FTA	Pct.	REBOUNDS Off.	Def.	Tot.	Ast.	PF	Dq.	Stl.	Blk.	TO	Pts.	Avg.
83-84—Chicago.......	49	667	100	228	.439	55	77	.714	58	116	174	25	128		18	17	60	255	5.2
84-85—Chicago.......	48	740	108	250	.432	79	98	.806	72	174	246	29	102	0	11	11	68	295	6.1
85-86—Chicago.......	80	2307	407	875	.465	262	335	.782	208	450	658	139	292	5	70	37	220	1076	13.5
86-87—Detroit.........	80	1792	256	542	.472	119	177	.672	196	457	653	62	197	0	41	50	127	631	7.9
87-88—New York	82	2049	258	585	.441	126	190	.663	221	421	642	93	318	9	65	32	148	642	7.8
88-89—New York	82	1277	194	422	.460	129	170	.759	157	237	394	76	172	0	47	18	125	517	6.3

G

Season Team	G	Min.	FGM	FGA	Pct.	FTM	FTA	Pct.	Off.	Def.	Tot.	Ast.	PF	Dq.	Stl.	Blk.	TO	Pts.	Avg.
89-90 —Orlando.......	73	1860	312	667	.468	136	209	.651	166	422	588	99	231	4	50	26	119	761	10.4
90-91 —San Antonio.......	66	1099	177	384	.461	89	105	.848	98	215	313	52	172	0	32	13	89	443	6.7
91-92 —San Antonio.	80	1127	147	344	.427	73	89	.820	92	250	342	36	148	0	29	11	62	367	4.6
Totals	640	12918	1959	4297	.456	1068	1450	.737	1268	2742	4010	611	1760	19	363	215	1018	4987	7.8

Three-point field goals: 1984-85, 0-for-4. 1985-86, 0-for-8. 1986-87, 0-for-2. 1987-88, 0-for-2. 1988-89, 0-for-3. 1989-90, 1-for-3 (.333). 1990-91, 0-for-3. Totals, 1-for-25 (.040).

NBA PLAYOFF RECORD

Season Team	G	Min.	FGM	FGA	Pct.	FTM	FTA	Pct.	Off.	Def.	Tot.	Ast.	PF	Dq.	Stl.	Blk.	TO	Pts.	Avg.
84-85 —Chicago.......	3	54	12	24	.500	7	11	.636	10	5	15	2	8	0	0	1	1	31	10.3
85-86 —Chicago.......	3	53	6	20	.300	6	12	.500	7	5	12	0	9	0	1	1	3	18	6.0
86-87 —Detroit.......	9	42	6	10	.600	5	6	.833	3	6	9	1	2	0	1	2	3	17	1.9
87-88 —New York	4	93	8	17	.471	0	0	...	8	25	33	7	14	0	0	1	9	16	4.0
88-89 —New York	9	128	13	30	.433	10	14	.714	14	22	36	5	23	0	2	1	7	36	4.0
90-91 —San Antonio.	3	11	3	6	.500	2	2	1.000	1	3	4	0	3	0	0	1	1	8	2.7
91-92 —San Antonio.	3	47	3	10	.300	3	4	.750	5	6	11	2	6	0	0	0	2	9	3.0
Totals	34	428	51	117	.436	33	49	.673	48	72	120	17	65	0	4	6	26	135	4.0

HALEY, JACK
F/C, LACERS

PERSONAL: Born January 27, 1964, in Long Beach, Calif.... 6-10/250....
Full name: Jack Kevin Haley.
HIGH SCHOOL: Huntington Beach (Calif.).
COLLEGE: Golden West (Calif.), then UCLA.
TRANSACTIONS/CAREER NOTES: Selected by Chicago Bulls in fourth round (79th pick overall) of 1987 NBA Draft.... Played in Spain (1987-88).... Waived by Bulls (December 18, 1989).... Claimed off waivers by New Jersey Nets (December 20, 1989).... Signed as unrestricted free agent by Los Angeles Lakers (October 4, 1991).

COLLEGIATE RECORD

Season Team	G	Min.	FGM	FGA	Pct.	FTM	FTA	Pct.	Reb.	Pts.	Avg.
82-83 —Golden West...............................					Did not play.						
83-84 —Golden West...............................					Statistics unavailable.						
84-85 —UCLA................................	25	125	9	22	.409	7	17	.412	42	25	1.0
85-86 —UCLA................................	29	709	41	108	.380	44	61	.721	183	126	4.3
86-87 —UCLA................................	32	740	57	122	.467	52	84	.619	151	166	5.2
Four-year-college totals	86	1574	107	252	.425	103	162	.636	376	317	3.7

SPANISH LEAGUE RECORD

Season Team	G	Min.	FGM	FGA	Pct.	FTM	FTA	Pct.	Reb.	Pts.	Avg.
87-88 —Grupo Ifa Espanol's	...	...	...	...	...	...	...	...	...	...	20.2

NBA REGULAR-SEASON RECORD

Season Team	G	Min.	FGM	FGA	Pct.	FTM	FTA	Pct.	Off.	Def.	Tot.	Ast.	PF	Dq.	Stl.	Blk.	TO	Pts.	Avg.
88-89 —Chicago.......	51	289	37	78	.474	36	46	.783	21	50	71	10	56	0	11	0	26	110	2.2
89-90 —Chi.-N.J.......	67	1084	138	347	.398	85	125	.680	115	185	300	26	170	1	18	12	72	361	5.4
90-91 —New Jersey ..	78	1178	161	343	.469	112	181	.619	140	216	356	31	199	0	20	21	63	434	5.6
91-92 —L.A. Lakers ..	49	394	31	84	.369	14	29	.483	31	64	95	7	75	0	7	8	25	76	1.6
Totals	245	2945	367	852	.431	247	381	.648	307	515	822	74	500	1	56	41	186	981	4.0

Three-point field goals: 1989-90, 0-for-1.

NBA PLAYOFF RECORD

Season Team	G	Min.	FGM	FGA	Pct.	FTM	FTA	Pct.	Off.	Def.	Tot.	Ast.	PF	Dq.	Stl.	Blk.	TO	Pts.	Avg.
88-89 —Chicago.......	5	7	2	3	.667	1	2	.500	0	1	1	1	2	0	0	0	0	5	1.0
91-92 —L.A. Lakers ..	2	12	1	4	.250	0	0	...	1	0	1	1	3	0	0	0	2	2	1.0
Totals	7	19	3	7	.429	1	2	.500	1	1	2	2	5	0	0	0	0	7	1.0

HAMMONDS, TOM
F, HORNETS

PERSONAL: Born March 27, 1967, in Fort Walton, Fla.... 6-9/225.... Full name: Tom Edward Hammonds.
HIGH SCHOOL: Crestview (Fla.).
COLLEGE: Georgia Tech.
TRANSACTIONS/CAREER NOTES: Selected by Washington Bullets in first round (ninth pick overall) of 1989 NBA Draft.... Traded by Bullets to Charlotte Hornets for Rex Chapman (February 19, 1992).

COLLEGIATE RECORD

Season Team	G	Min.	FGM	FGA	Pct.	FTM	FTA	Pct.	Reb.	Pts.	Avg.
85-86 —Georgia Tech	34	1112	168	276	.609	80	98	.816	219	416	12.2
86-87 —Georgia Tech	29	1088	206	362	.569	59	74	.797	208	471	16.2
87-88 —Georgia Tech	30	1076	229	403	.568	109	132	.826	216	567	18.9
88-89 —Georgia Tech	30	1111	250	465	.538	126	163	.773	242	627	20.9
Totals	123	4387	853	1506	.566	374	467	.801	885	2081	16.9

Three-point field goals: 1988-89, 1-for-3 (.333).

NBA REGULAR-SEASON RECORD

Season Team	G	Min.	FGM	FGA	Pct.	FTM	FTA	Pct.	Off.	Def.	Tot.	Ast.	PF	Dq.	Stl.	Blk.	TO	Pts.	Avg.
89-90 —Washington .	61	805	129	295	.437	63	98	.643	61	107	168	51	98	0	11	14	46	321	5.3
90-91 —Washington .	70	1023	155	336	.461	57	79	.722	58	148	206	43	108	0	15	7	54	367	5.2

Season Team	G	Min.	FGM	FGA	Pct.	FTM	FTA	Pct.	Off.	Def.	Tot.	Ast.	PF	Dq.	Stl.	Blk.	TO	Pts.	Avg.
								— REBOUNDS —											
91-92—Washington.	37	984	195	400	.488	50	82	.610	49	136	185	36	118	1	22	13	58	440	11.9
Totals	168	2812	479	1031	.465	170	259	.656	168	391	559	130	324	1	48	34	158	1128	6.7

Three-point field goals: 1989-90, 0-for-1. 1990-91, 0-for-4. 1991-92, 0-for-1. Totals, 0-for-6.

HANSEN, BOBBY

G, BULLS

PERSONAL: Born January 18, 1961, in Des Moines, Ia. . . . 6-6/195. . . . Full name: Robert Louis Hansen II.
HIGH SCHOOL: Dowling (West Des Moines, Ia.).
COLLEGE: Iowa.

TRANSACTIONS/CAREER NOTES: Selected by Utah Jazz in third round (54th pick overall) of 1983 NBA Draft. . . . Traded by Jazz with Eric Leckner and 1990 first- and second-round draft choices to Sacramento Kings in three-way deal in which Washington Bullets sent Jeff Malone to Jazz and Kings sent Pervis Ellison to Bullets (June 25, 1990); Jazz also received 1990 second-round draft choice and Kings also received 1991 second-round draft choice. . . . Traded by Kings with 1992 second-round draft choice to Chicago Bulls for Dennis Hopson (November 4, 1991).
MISCELLANEOUS: Member of NBA championship team (1992).

COLLEGIATE RECORD

Season Team	G	Min.	FGM	FGA	Pct.	FTM	FTA	Pct.	Reb.	Pts.	Avg.
79-80—Iowa	33	. . .	71	167	.425	43	73	.589	67	185	5.6
80-81—Iowa	22	. . .	70	156	.449	45	53	.849	75	185	8.4
81-82—Iowa	25	. . .	117	237	.494	65	93	.699	102	299	12.0
82-83—Iowa	31	. . .	184	378	.487	98	129	.760	166	476	15.4
Totals	111	. . .	442	938	.471	251	348	.721	410	1145	10.3

Three-point field goals: 1982-83, 10-for-20 (.500).

NBA REGULAR-SEASON RECORD

Season Team	G	Min.	FGM	FGA	Pct.	FTM	FTA	Pct.	Off.	Def.	Tot.	Ast.	PF	Dq.	Stl.	Blk.	TO	Pts.	Avg.
									— REBOUNDS —										
83-84—Utah	55	419	65	145	.448	18	28	.643	13	35	48	44	62	0	15	4	35	148	2.7
84-85—Utah	54	646	110	225	.489	40	72	.556	20	50	70	75	88	0	25	1	49	261	4.8
85-86—Utah	82	2032	299	628	.476	95	132	.720	82	162	244	193	205	1	74	9	126	710	8.7
86-87—Utah	72	1453	272	601	.453	136	179	.760	84	119	203	102	146	0	44	6	77	696	9.7
87-88—Utah	81	1796	316	611	.517	113	152	.743	64	123	187	175	193	2	65	5	91	777	9.6
88-89—Utah	46	964	140	300	.467	42	75	.560	29	99	128	50	105	0	37	6	43	341	7.4
89-90—Utah	81	2174	265	568	.467	33	64	.516	66	163	229	149	194	2	52	11	79	617	7.6
90-91—Sacramento .	36	811	96	256	.375	18	36	.500	33	63	96	90	72	1	20	5	34	229	6.4
91-92—Sac.-Chi.	68	809	79	178	.444	8	22	.364	17	60	77	69	134	0	27	3	28	173	2.5
Totals	575	11104	1642	3512	.468	503	760	.662	408	874	1282	947	1199	6	359	50	562	3952	6.9

Three-point field goals: 1983-84, 0-for-8. 1984-85, 1-for-7 (.143). 1985-86, 17-for-50 (.340). 1986-87, 16-for-45 (.356). 1987-88, 32-for-97 (.330). 1988-89, 19-for-54 (.352). 1989-90, 54-for-154 (.351). 1990-91, 19-for-69 (.275). 1991-92, 7-for-27 (.259). Totals, 165-for-511 (.323).

NBA PLAYOFF RECORD

NOTES: Holds career record for highest three-point field goal percentage (minimum 15 made)—.500.

Season Team	G	Min.	FGM	FGA	Pct.	FTM	FTA	Pct.	Off.	Def.	Tot.	Ast.	PF	Dq.	Stl.	Blk.	TO	Pts.	Avg.
									— REBOUNDS —										
83-84—Utah	4	18	2	7	.286	1	2	.500	2	5	7	2	4	0	0	0	2	7	1.8
84-85—Utah	8	34	2	8	.250	5	8	.625	1	3	4	6	6	0	3	0	3	9	1.1
85-86—Utah	4	140	27	37	.730	8	9	.889	10	8	18	11	16	0	3	1	7	64	16.0
86-87—Utah	5	142	21	49	.429	17	20	.850	3	12	15	11	14	0	1	1	7	61	12.2
87-88—Utah	11	408	67	135	.496	16	22	.727	8	31	39	32	42	1	7	0	27	169	15.4
88-89—Utah	3	123	11	35	.314	8	10	.800	5	12	17	4	15	0	1	2	6	33	11.0
89-90—Utah	5	145	21	43	.488	1	4	.250	7	7	14	5	14	0	3	0	4	50	10.0
91-92—Chicago........	9	69	9	22	.409	1	3	.333	4	5	9	10	10	0	1	0	2	22	2.4
Totals	49	1079	160	336	.476	57	78	.731	40	83	123	81	121	1	19	4	58	415	8.5

Three-point field goals: 1983-84, 2-for-3 (.667). 1985-86, 2-for-3 (.667). 1986-87, 2-for-5 (.400). 1987-88, 19-for-36 (.528). 1988-89, 3-for-9 (.333). 1989-90, 7-for-14 (.500). 1991-92, 3-for-6 (.500). Totals, 38-for-76 (.500).

HARDAWAY, TIM

G, WARRIORS

PERSONAL: Born September 1, 1966, in Chicago. . . . 6-0/195. . . . Full name: Timothy Duane Hardaway.
HIGH SCHOOL: Carver (Chicago).
COLLEGE: Texas-El Paso.

TRANSACTIONS/CAREER NOTES: Selected by Golden State Warriors in first round (14th pick overall) of 1989 NBA Draft.

COLLEGIATE RECORD

Season Team	G	Min.	FGM	FGA	Pct.	FTM	FTA	Pct.	Reb.	Pts.	Avg.
85-86—Texas-El Paso	28	435	37	71	.521	41	63	.651	35	115	4.1
86-87—Texas-El Paso	31	922	120	245	.490	67	101	.663	62	310	10.0
87-88—Texas-El Paso	32	1036	159	354	.449	98	130	.754	93	434	13.6
88-89—Texas-El Paso	33	1182	255	509	.501	169	228	.741	131	727	22.0
Totals	124	3575	571	1179	.484	375	522	.718	321	1586	12.8

Three-point field goals: 1986-87, 3-for-12 (.250). 1987-88, 18-for-53 (.340). 1988-89, 48-for-131 (.366). Totals, 69-for-196 (.352).

NBA REGULAR-SEASON RECORD

HONORS: NBA All-Rookie first team (1990). . . . All-NBA second team (1992).

H

Season Team	G	Min.	FGM	FGA	Pct.	FTM	FTA	Pct.	Off.	Def.	Tot.	Ast.	PF	Dq.	Stl.	Blk.	TO	Pts.	Avg.
									— REBOUNDS —										
89-90—Golden State	79	2663	464	985	.471	211	276	.764	57	253	310	689	232	6	165	12	260	1162	14.7
90-91—Golden State	82	3215	739	1551	.476	306	381	.803	87	245	332	793	228	7	214	12	270	1881	22.9
91-92—Golden State	81	3332	734	1592	.461	298	389	.766	81	229	310	807	208	1	164	13	267	1893	23.4
Totals	242	9210	1937	4128	.469	815	1046	.779	225	727	952	2289	668	14	543	37	797	4936	20.4

Three-point field goals: 1989-90, 23-for-84 (.274). 1990-91, 97-for-252 (.385). 1991-92, 127-for-376 (.338). Totals, 247-for-712 (.347).

NBA PLAYOFF RECORD

NOTES: Shares single-game record for most steals—8 (May 8, 1991, vs. Los Angles Lakers; and April 30, 1992, vs. Seattle).

Season Team	G	Min.	FGM	FGA	Pct.	FTM	FTA	Pct.	Off.	Def.	Tot.	Ast.	PF	Dq.	Stl.	Blk.	TO	Pts.	Avg.
									— REBOUNDS —										
90-91—Golden State	9	396	90	185	.486	30	38	.789	5	28	33	101	22	0	28	7	25	227	25.2
91-92—Golden State	4	176	32	80	.400	24	37	.649	6	9	15	29	14	0	13	0	14	98	24.5
Totals	13	572	122	265	.460	54	75	.720	11	37	48	130	36	0	41	7	39	325	25.0

Three-point field goals: 1990-91, 17-for-48 (.354). 1991-92, 10-for-29 (.345). Totals, 27-for-77 (.351).

NBA ALL-STAR GAME RECORD

Season Team	Min.	FGM	FGA	Pct.	FTM	FTA	Pct.	Off.	Def.	Tot.	Ast.	PF	Dq.	Stl.	Blk.	TO	Pts.
								— REBOUNDS —									
1991—Golden State	12	2	7	.286	0	0	...	2	1	3	4	1	0	2	0	0	5
1992—Golden State	20	5	10	.500	2	2	1.000	0	0	0	7	2	0	1	0	2	14
Totals	32	7	17	.412	2	2	1.000	2	1	3	11	3	0	3	0	2	19

Three-point field goals: 1991, 1-for-2 (.500). 1992, 2-for-5 (.400). Totals, 3-for-7 (.429).

HARPER, DEREK
G, MAVERICKS

PERSONAL: Born October 13, 1961, in Elberton, Ga. . . . 6-4/206. . . . Full name: Derek Ricardo Harper.
HIGH SCHOOL: North Shore (West Palm Beach, Fla.).
COLLEGE: Illinois.
TRANSACTIONS/CAREER NOTES: Selected by Dallas Mavericks in first round (11th pick overall) of 1983 NBA Draft.

COLLEGIATE RECORD

Season Team	G	Min.	FGM	FGA	Pct.	FTM	FTA	Pct.	Reb.	Pts.	Avg.
80-81—Illinois	29	934	104	252	.413	33	46	.717	75	241	8.3
81-82—Illinois	29	1059	105	230	.457	34	45	.756	133	244	8.4
82-83—Illinois	32	1182	198	369	.537	83	123	.675	112	492	15.4
Totals	90	3175	407	851	.478	150	214	.701	320	977	10.9

Three-point field goals: 1982-83, 13-for-24 (.542).

NBA REGULAR-SEASON RECORD

HONORS: NBA All-Defensive second team (1987, 1990).

Season Team	G	Min.	FGM	FGA	Pct.	FTM	FTA	Pct.	Off.	Def.	Tot.	Ast.	PF	Dq.	Stl.	Blk.	TO	Pts.	Avg.
									— REBOUNDS —										
83-84—Dallas..........	82	1712	200	451	.443	66	98	.673	53	119	172	239	143	0	95	21	111	469	5.7
84-85—Dallas..........	82	2218	329	633	.520	111	154	.721	47	152	199	360	194	1	144	37	123	790	9.6
85-86—Dallas..........	79	2150	390	730	.534	171	229	.747	75	151	226	416	166	1	153	23	144	963	12.2
86-87—Dallas..........	77	2556	497	993	.501	160	234	.684	51	148	199	609	195	0	167	25	138	1230	16.0
87-88—Dallas..........	82	3032	536	1167	.459	261	344	.759	71	175	246	634	164	0	168	35	190	1393	17.0
88-89—Dallas..........	81	2968	538	1127	.477	229	284	.806	46	182	228	570	219	3	172	41	205	1404	17.3
89-90—Dallas..........	82	3007	567	1161	.488	250	315	.794	54	190	244	609	224	1	187	26	207	1473	18.0
90-91—Dallas..........	77	2879	572	1226	.467	286	391	.731	59	174	233	548	222	1	147	14	177	1519	19.7
91-92—Dallas..........	65	2252	448	1011	.443	198	261	.759	49	121	170	373	150	0	101	17	154	1152	17.7
Totals	707	22774	4077	8499	.480	1732	2310	.750	505	1412	1917	4358	1677	7	1334	239	1449	10393	14.7

Three-point field goals: 1983-84, 3-for-26 (.115). 1984-85, 21-for-61 (.344). 1985-86, 12-for-51 (.235). 1986-87, 76-for-212 (.358). 1987-88, 60-for-192 (.313). 1988-89, 99-for-278 (.356). 1989-90, 89-for-240 (.371). 1990-91, 89-for-246 (.362). 1991-92, 58-for-186 (.312). Totals, 507-for-1492 (.340).

NBA PLAYOFF RECORD

Season Team	G	Min.	FGM	FGA	Pct.	FTM	FTA	Pct.	Off.	Def.	Tot.	Ast.	PF	Dq.	Stl.	Blk.	TO	Pts.	Avg.
									— REBOUNDS —										
83-84—Dallas..........	10	226	21	54	.389	5	7	.714	8	12	20	28	16	0	11	2	6	50	5.0
84-85—Dallas..........	4	132	10	21	.476	5	7	.714	1	11	12	20	12	0	6	1	4	26	6.5
85-86—Dallas..........	10	348	57	107	.533	12	16	.750	13	6	19	76	27	0	23	0	23	134	13.4
86-87—Dallas..........	4	123	20	40	.500	24	30	.800	2	10	12	27	7	0	7	0	5	66	16.5
87-88—Dallas..........	17	602	89	202	.441	43	59	.729	11	32	43	121	44	0	32	5	32	230	13.5
89-90—Dallas..........	3	119	21	48	.438	11	16	.688	2	6	8	23	13	0	4	0	12	58	19.3
Totals	48	1550	218	472	.462	100	135	.741	37	77	114	295	119	0	83	8	82	564	11.8

Three-point field goals: 1983-84, 3-for-8 (.375). 1984-85, 1-for-3 (.333). 1985-86, 8-for-14 (.571). 1986-87, 2-for-9 (.222). 1987-88, 9-for-36 (.250). 1989-90, 5-for-16 (.313). Totals, 28-for-86 (.326).

HARPER, RON
G, CLIPPERS

PERSONAL: Born January 20, 1964, in Dayton, O. . . . 6-6/198. . . . Full name: Ronald Harper.
HIGH SCHOOL: Kiser (Dayton, O.).
COLLEGE: Miami of Ohio.
TRANSACTIONS/CAREER NOTES: Selected by Cleveland Cavaliers in first round (eighth pick overall) of 1986 NBA Draft. . . . Traded by Cavaliers with 1990 and 1992 first-round draft choices and 1991 second-round draft choice to Los Angeles Clippers for Reggie Williams and draft rights to Danny Ferry (November 16, 1989).

H

COLLEGIATE RECORD

NOTES: The Sporting News All-America second team (1986).

Season	Team	G	Min.	FGM	FGA	Pct.	FTM	FTA	Pct.	Reb.	Pts.	Avg.
82-83	Miami of Ohio	28	887	148	298	.497	64	95	.674	195	360	12.9
83-84	Miami of Ohio	30	989	197	367	.537	94	165	.570	229	488	16.3
84-85	Miami of Ohio	31	1144	312	577	.541	148	224	.661	333	772	24.9
85-86	Miami of Ohio	31	1144	312	572	.545	133	200	.665	362	757	24.4
	Totals	120	4164	969	1814	.534	439	684	.642	1119	2377	19.8

NBA REGULAR-SEASON RECORD

HONORS: NBA All-Rookie team (1987).

Season	Team	G	Min.	FGM	FGA	Pct.	FTM	FTA	Pct.	Off. Reb.	Def.	Tot.	Ast.	PF	Dq.	Stl.	Blk.	TO	Pts.	Avg.
86-87	Cleveland	82	3064	734	1614	.455	386	564	.684	169	223	392	394	247	3	209	84	*345	1874	22.9
87-88	Cleveland	57	1830	340	732	.464	196	278	.705	64	159	223	281	157	3	122	52	158	879	15.4
88-89	Cleveland	82	2851	587	1149	.511	323	430	.751	122	287	409	434	224	1	185	74	230	1526	18.6
89-90	Clev.-L.A.C.	35	1367	301	637	.473	182	231	.788	74	132	206	182	105	1	81	41	100	798	22.8
90-91	L.A. Clippers	39	1383	285	729	.391	145	217	.668	58	130	188	209	111	0	66	35	129	763	19.6
91-92	L.A. Clippers	82	3144	569	1292	.440	293	398	.736	120	327	447	417	199	0	152	72	252	1495	18.2
	Totals	377	13639	2816	6153	.458	1525	2118	.720	607	1258	1865	1917	1043	8	815	358	1214	7335	19.5

Three-point field goals: 1986-87, 20-for-94 (.213). 1987-88, 3-for-20 (.150). 1988-89, 29-for-116 (.250). 1989-90, 14-for-51 (.275). 1990-91, 48-for-148 (.324). 1991-92, 64-for-211 (.303). Totals, 178-for-640 (.278).

NBA PLAYOFF RECORD

Season	Team	G	Min.	FGM	FGA	Pct.	FTM	FTA	Pct.	Off. Reb.	Def.	Tot.	Ast.	PF	Dq.	Stl.	Blk.	TO	Pts.	Avg.
87-88	Cleveland	4	134	30	63	.476	11	16	.688	4	16	20	15	9	0	11	4	11	71	17.8
88-89	Cleveland	5	189	39	69	.565	20	26	.769	7	14	21	20	20	1	11	4	7	98	19.6
91-92	L.A. Clippers	5	206	39	87	.448	11	14	.786	10	22	32	23	13	0	5	4	15	90	18.0
	Totals	14	529	108	219	.493	42	56	.750	21	52	73	58	42	1	27	12	33	259	18.5

Three-point field goals: 1987-88, 0-for-2. 1988-89, 0-for-2. 1991-92, 1-for-9 (.111). Totals, 1-for-13 (.077).

HASTINGS, SCOTT

F/C, NUGGETS

PERSONAL: Born June 3, 1960, in Independence, Kan. . . . 6-11/ 245. . . . Full name: Scott Alan Hastings.
HIGH SCHOOL: Independence (Kan.).
COLLEGE: Arkansas.
TRANSACTIONS/CAREER NOTES: Selected by New York Knicks in second round (29th pick overall) of 1982 NBA Draft. . . . Traded by Knicks with cash to Atlanta Hawks for Rory Sparrow (February 12, 1983). . . . Selected by Miami Heat from Hawks in NBA expansion draft (June 23, 1988). . . . Signed as unrestricted free agent by Detroit Pistons (July 15, 1989). . . . Traded by Pistons with 1992 second-round draft choice to Denver Nuggets for Orlando Woolridge (August 13, 1991).
MISCELLANEOUS: Member of NBA championship team (1990).

COLLEGIATE RECORD

Season	Team	G	Min.	FGM	FGA	Pct.	FTM	FTA	Pct.	Reb.	Pts.	Avg.
78-79	Arkansas	30	753	97	191	.508	54	74	.730	138	248	8.3
79-80	Arkansas	29	1033	172	322	.534	125	160	.781	194	469	16.2
80-81	Arkansas	32	1054	192	341	.563	139	189	.735	173	523	16.3
81-82	Arkansas	29	1040	204	369	.553	131	177	.740	175	539	18.6
	Totals	120	3880	665	1223	.544	449	600	.748	680	1779	14.8

NBA REGULAR-SEASON RECORD

Season	Team	G	Min.	FGM	FGA	Pct.	FTM	FTA	Pct.	Off. Reb.	Def.	Tot.	Ast.	PF	Dq.	Stl.	Blk.	TO	Pts.	Avg.
82-83	N.Y.-Atl.	31	140	13	38	.342	11	20	.550	15	26	41	3	34	0	6	1	9	37	1.2
83-84	Atlanta	68	1135	111	237	.468	82	104	.788	96	174	270	46	220	7	40	36	66	305	4.5
84-85	Atlanta	64	825	89	188	.473	63	81	.778	59	100	159	46	135	1	24	23	50	241	3.8
85-86	Atlanta	62	650	65	159	.409	60	70	.857	44	80	124	26	118	2	14	8	40	193	3.1
86-87	Atlanta	40	256	23	68	.338	23	29	.793	16	54	70	13	35	0	10	7	13	71	1.8
87-88	Atlanta	55	403	40	82	.488	25	27	.926	27	70	97	16	67	1	8	10	14	110	2.0
88-89	Miami	75	1206	143	328	.436	91	107	.850	72	159	231	59	203	5	32	42	68	386	5.1
89-90	Detroit	40	166	10	33	.303	19	22	.864	7	25	32	8	31	0	3	3	7	42	1.1
90-91	Detroit	27	113	16	28	.571	13	13	1.000	14	14	28	7	23	0	0	0	7	48	1.8
91-92	Denver	40	421	17	50	.340	24	28	.857	30	68	98	26	56	0	10	15	22	58	1.5
	Totals	502	5315	527	1211	.435	411	501	.820	380	770	1150	250	922	16	147	145	296	1491	3.0

Three-point field goals: 1982-83, 0-for-3. 1983-84, 1-for-4 (.250). 1985-86, 3-for-4 (.750). 1986-87, 2-for-12 (.167). 1987-88, 5-for-12 (.417). 1988-89, 9-for-28 (.321). 1989-90, 3-for-12 (.250). 1990-91, 3-for-4 (.750). 1991-92, 0-for-9. Totals, 26-for-88 (.295).

NBA PLAYOFF RECORD

Season	Team	G	Min.	FGM	FGA	Pct.	FTM	FTA	Pct.	Off. Reb.	Def.	Tot.	Ast.	PF	Dq.	Stl.	Blk.	TO	Pts.	Avg.
83-84	Atlanta	5	32	2	9	.222	3	4	.750	2	6	8	1	4	0	1	0	2	7	1.4
85-86	Atlanta	9	49	11	14	.786	5	11	.455	3	7	10	2	11	0	2	0	5	28	3.1
86-87	Atlanta	4	21	2	3	.667	2	2	1.000	1	5	6	0	5	0	1	1	0	6	1.5
87-88	Atlanta	11	103	9	14	.643	8	8	1.000	7	10	17	3	21	1	3	1	5	26	2.4
89-90	Detroit	5	16	1	4	.250	0	0	. . .	0	0	0	0	4	0	0	0	0	2	0.4
90-91	Detroit	10	35	3	6	.500	0	0	. . .	2	4	6	3	6	0	1	1	1	8	0.8
	Totals	44	256	28	50	.560	18	25	.720	15	32	47	9	51	1	8	3	13	77	1.8

Three-point field goals: 1985-86, 1-for-4 (.250). 1987-88, 0-for-1. 1989-90, 0-for-3. 1990-91, 2-for-4 (.500). Totals, 3-for-12 (.250).

HAWKINS, HERSEY

G, 76ERS

PERSONAL: Born September 29, 1965, in Chicago. . . . 6-3/190. . . . Full name: Hersey R. Hawkins Jr.
HIGH SCHOOL: Westinghouse Vocational (Chicago).
COLLEGE: Bradley.

TRANSACTIONS/CAREER NOTES: Selected by Los Angeles Clippers in first round (sixth pick overall) of 1988 NBA Draft. . . . Draft rights traded with 1989 first-round draft choice by Clippers to Philadelphia 76ers for draft rights to Charles Smith (June 28, 1988).
MISCELLANEOUS: Member of bronze-medal-winning U.S. Olympic team (1988).

COLLEGIATE RECORD

NOTES: THE SPORTING NEWS College Player of the Year (1988). . . . THE SPORTING NEWS All-America first team (1988). . . . Led NCAA Division I with 36.3 points per game (1988).

Season Team	G	Min.	FGM	FGA	Pct.	FTM	FTA	Pct.	Reb.	Pts.	Avg.
84-85—Bradley	30	1121	179	308	.581	81	105	.771	182	439	14.6
85-86—Bradley	35	1291	250	461	.542	156	203	.768	200	656	18.7
86-87—Bradley	29	1102	294	552	.533	169	213	.793	195	788	27.2
87-88—Bradley	31	1202	377	720	.524	284	335	.848	241	1125	36.3
Totals	125	4716	1100	2041	.539	690	856	.806	818	3008	24.1

Three-point field goals: 1986-87, 31-for-108 (.287). 1987-88, 87-for-221 (.394). Totals, 118-for-329 (.359).

NBA REGULAR-SEASON RECORD

HONORS: NBA All-Rookie first team (1989).

										— REBOUNDS —								
Season Team	G	Min.	FGM	FGA	Pct.	FTM	FTA	Pct.	Off.	Def.	Tot.	Ast.	PF	Dq.	Stl.	Blk.	TO	Pts.	Avg.
88-89—Philadelphia	79	2577	442	971	.455	241	290	.831	51	174	225	239	184	0	120	37	158	1196	15.1
89-90—Philadelphia	82	2856	522	1136	.460	387	436	.888	85	219	304	261	217	2	130	28	185	1515	18.5
90-91—Philadelphia	80	3110	590	1251	.472	479	550	.871	48	262	310	299	182	0	178	39	213	1767	22.1
91-92—Philadelphia	81	3013	521	1127	.462	403	461	.874	53	218	271	248	174	0	157	43	189	1536	19.0
Totals	322	11556	2075	4485	.463	1510	1737	.869	237	873	1110	1047	757	2	585	147	745	6014	18.7

Three-point field goals: 1988-89, 71-for-166 (.428). 1989-90, 84-for-200 (.420). 1990-91, 108-for-270 (.400). 1991-92, 91-for-229 (.397). Totals, 354-for-865 (.409).

NBA PLAYOFF RECORD

NOTES: Holds career record for highest free-throw percentage (minimum 100 made)—.938.

										— REBOUNDS —								
Season Team	G	Min.	FGM	FGA	Pct.	FTM	FTA	Pct.	Off.	Def.	Tot.	Ast.	PF	Dq.	Stl.	Blk.	TO	Pts.	Avg.
88-89—Philadelphia	3	72	3	24	.125	2	2	1.000	1	4	5	4	6	0	3	1	3	8	2.7
89-90—Philadelphia	10	415	81	163	.497	59	63	.937	8	23	31	36	25	0	12	7	31	235	23.5
90-91—Philadelphia	8	329	47	101	.465	59	63	.937	8	38	46	27	29	1	20	10	16	167	20.9
Totals	21	816	131	288	.455	120	128	.938	17	65	82	67	60	1	35	18	50	410	19.5

Three-point field goals: 1988-89, 0-for-5. 1989-90, 14-for-36 (.389). 1990-91, 14-for-26 (.538). Totals, 28-for-67 (.418).

NBA ALL-STAR GAME RECORD

							— REBOUNDS —								
Season Team	Min.	FGM	FGA	Pct.	FTM	FTA	Pct.	Off.	Def.	Tot.	Ast.	PF	Dq.	Stl.	Blk.	TO	Pts.
1991—Philadelphia	14	3	5	.600	0	0	...	0	0	0	1	1	0	0	0	1	6

Three-point field goals: 1991, 0-for-1.

HENDERSON, GERALD

G

PERSONAL: Born January 16, 1956, in Richmond, Va. . . . 6-2/180. . . . Full name: Jerome McKinley Henderson.
HIGH SCHOOL: Huguenot (Richmond, Va.).
COLLEGE: Virginia Commonwealth.

TRANSACTIONS/CAREER NOTES: Selected by San Antonio Spurs in third round (64th pick overall) of 1978 NBA Draft. . . . Waived by Spurs (September 20, 1978). . . . Played in Western Basketball Association with Tucson Gunners (1978-79). . . . Signed as free agent by Boston Celtics (June 25, 1979). . . . Traded by Celtics to Seattle SuperSonics for 1986 first-round draft choice (October 16, 1984). . . . Traded by SuperSonics to New York Knicks for 1990 second-round draft choice and right to exchange 1987 first-round draft choices (November 12, 1986). . . . Waived by Knicks (November 14, 1987). . . . Signed as free agent by Philadelphia 76ers (December 3, 1987). . . . Signed as unrestricted free agent by Milwaukee Bucks (October 6, 1989). . . . Waived by Bucks (November 27, 1989). . . . Signed as unrestricted free agent by Detroit Pistons (December 6, 1989). . . . Rights renounced by Pistons (November 11, 1990). . . . Re-signed by Pistons to first of two consecutive 10-day contracts (February 24, 1991). . . . Re-signed by Pistons for remainder of season (March 15, 1991). . . . Rights renounced by Pistons (July 10, 1991). . . . Signed as free agent by Houston Rockets (October 4, 1991). . . . Waived by Rockets (October 28, 1991). . . . Re-signed by Rockets (November 25, 1991). . . . Waived by Rockets (January 7, 1992). . . . Signed by Pistons to first of two consecutive 10-day contracts (January 21, 1992).
MISCELLANEOUS: Member of NBA championship teams (1981, 1984, 1990).

COLLEGIATE RECORD

Season Team	G	Min.	FGM	FGA	Pct.	FTM	FTA	Pct.	Reb.	Pts.	Avg.
74-75—Virginia Commonwealth	25	...	73	182	.401	21	39	.538	64	167	6.7
75-76—Virginia Commonwealth	25	...	196	395	.496	27	43	.628	71	419	16.8
76-77—Virginia Commonwealth	25	903	228	465	.490	50	81	.617	102	506	20.2
77-78—Virginia Commonwealth	28	939	185	377	.491	80	121	.661	94	450	16.1
Totals	103		682	1419	.481	178	284	.627	331	1542	15.0

WBA REGULAR-SEASON RECORD

			2-POINT			3-POINT								
Season Team	G	Min.	FGM	FGA	Pct.	FGM	FGA	Pct.	FTM	FTA	Pct.	Reb.	Ast.	Pts.	Avg.
78-79—Tucson	48	1288	239	447	.535	1	7	.143	124	173	.717	138	140	605	12.6

H

NBA REGULAR-SEASON RECORD

Season Team	G	Min.	FGM	FGA	Pct.	FTM	FTA	Pct.	— REBOUNDS — Off.	Def.	Tot.	Ast.	PF	Dq.	Stl.	Blk.	TO	Pts.	Avg.
79-80—Boston	76	1061	191	382	.500	89	129	.690	37	46	83	147	96	0	45	15	109	473	6.2
80-81—Boston	82	1608	261	579	.451	113	157	.720	43	89	132	213	177	0	79	12	160	636	7.8
81-82—Boston	82	1844	353	705	.501	125	172	.727	47	105	152	252	199	3	82	11	150	833	10.2
82-83—Boston	82	1551	286	618	.463	96	133	.722	57	67	124	195	190	6	95	3	128	671	8.2
83-84—Boston	78	2088	376	718	.524	136	177	.768	68	79	147	300	209	1	117	14	161	908	11.6
84-85—Seattle........	79	2648	427	891	.479	199	255	.780	71	119	190	559	196	1	140	9	231	1062	13.4
85-86—Seattle........	82	2568	434	900	.482	185	223	.830	89	98	187	487	230	2	138	12	184	1071	13.1
86-87—Seattle-N.Y..	74	2045	298	674	.442	190	230	.826	50	125	175	471	208	1	101	11	172	805	10.9
87-88—N.Y.-Phil.....	75	1505	194	453	.428	138	170	.812	27	80	107	231	187	0	69	5	133	595	7.9
88-89—Philadelphia.	65	986	144	348	.414	104	127	.819	17	51	68	140	121	1	42	3	73	425	6.5
89-90—Mil.-Detroit..	57	464	53	109	.486	12	15	.800	11	32	43	74	50	0	16	2	24	135	2.4
90-91—Detroit........	23	392	50	117	.427	16	21	.762	8	29	37	62	43	0	12	2	28	123	5.3
91-92—Hou.-Det.....	16	96	12	32	.375	9	11	.818	1	7	8	10	12	0	3	0	8	36	2.3
Totals	871	18856	3079	6526	.472	1412	1820	.776	526	927	1453	3141	1918	15	939	99	1561	7773	8.9

Three-point field goals: 1979-80, 2-for-6 (.333). 1980-81, 1-for-16 (.063). 1981-82, 2-for-12 (.167). 1982-83, 3-for-16 (.188). 1983-84, 20-for-57 (.351). 1984-85, 9-for-38 (.237). 1985-86, 18-for-52 (.346). 1986-87, 19-for-77 (.247). 1987-88, 69-for-163 (.423). 1988-89, 33-for-107 (.308). 1989-90, 17-for-38 (.447). 1990-91, 7-for-21 (.333). 1991-92, 3-for-8 (.375). Totals, 203-for-611 (.332).

NBA PLAYOFF RECORD

Season Team	G	Min.	FGM	FGA	Pct.	FTM	FTA	Pct.	— REBOUNDS — Off.	Def.	Tot.	Ast.	PF	Dq.	Stl.	Blk.	TO	Pts.	Avg.
79-80—Boston	9	101	15	37	.405	12	20	.600	4	6	10	12	8	0	4	0	7	42	4.7
80-81—Boston	16	228	41	86	.477	10	12	.833	10	15	25	26	24	0	10	3	12	92	5.8
81-82—Boston	12	310	38	93	.409	24	35	.686	12	13	25	48	30	0	14	2	25	100	8.3
82-83—Boston	7	187	35	85	.412	6	7	.857	8	6	14	31	25	1	11	1	14	76	10.9
83-84—Boston	23	616	115	237	.485	54	75	.720	23	29	52	97	78	0	34	1	41	287	12.5
88-89—Philadelphia.	3	69	10	25	.400	2	6	.333	3	4	7	5	10	0	2	0	5	24	8.0
89-90—Detroit.........	8	19	1	5	.200	0	0	...	2	1	3	4	3	0	2	0	1	2	0.3
90-91—Detroit.........	10	40	4	16	.250	0	0	...	1	0	1	6	4	0	1	0	0	8	0.8
Totals	88	1570	259	584	.443	108	155	.697	63	74	137	229	182	1	78	7	105	631	7.2

Three-point field goals: 1979-80, 0-for-2. 1980-81, 0-for-1. 1981-82, 0-for-2. 1982-83, 0-for-3. 1983-84, 3-for-11 (.273). 1988-89, 2-for-7 (.286). 1989-90, 0-for-3. 1990-91, 0-for-3. Totals, 5-for-32 (.156).

HENSON, STEVE
G

PERSONAL: Born February 2, 1968, in Junction City, Kan.... 6-1/180. ... Full name: Steven Michael Henson.
HIGH SCHOOL: McPherson (Kan.).
COLLEGE: Kansas State.
TRANSACTIONS/CAREER NOTES: Selected by Milwaukee Bucks in second round (44th pick overall) of 1990 NBA Draft.

COLLEGIATE RECORD

NOTES: Led NCAA Division I with .925 free-throw percentage (1988).

Season Team	G	Min.	FGM	FGA	Pct.	FTM	FTA	Pct.	Reb.	Pts.	Avg.
86-87—Kansas State	31	950	75	190	.395	57	69	.826	63	233	7.5
87-88—Kansas State	34	1243	79	184	.429	111	120	.925	81	311	9.1
88-89—Kansas State	30	1123	192	413	.465	92	100	.920	81	555	18.5
89-90—Kansas State	32	1158	181	406	.446	101	112	.902	85	556	17.4
Totals	127	4474	527	1193	.442	361	401	.900	310	1655	13.0

Three-point field goals: 1986-87, 26-for-64 (.406). 1987-88, 42-for-83 (.506). 1988-89, 79-for-177 (.446). 1989-90, 93-for-213 (.437). Totals, 240-for-537 (.447).

NBA REGULAR-SEASON RECORD

Season Team	G	Min.	FGA	FGA	Pct.	FTM	FTA	Pct.	— REBOUNDS — Off.	Def.	Tot.	Ast.	PF	Dq.	Stl.	Blk.	TO	Pts.	Avg.
90-91—Milwaukee ...	68	690	79	189	.418	38	42	.905	14	37	51	131	83	0	32	0	43	214	3.1
91-92—Milwaukee ...	50	386	52	144	.361	23	29	.793	17	24	41	82	50	0	15	1	40	150	3.0
Totals	118	1076	131	333	.393	61	71	.859	31	61	92	213	133	0	47	1	83	364	3.1

Three-point field goals: 1990-91, 18-for-54 (.333). 1991-92, 23-for-48 (.479). Totals, 41-for-102 (.402).

NBA PLAYOFF RECORD

Season Team	G	Min.	FGM	FGA	Pct.	FTM	FTA	Pct.	— REBOUNDS — Off.	Def.	Tot.	Ast.	PF	Dq.	Stl.	Blk.	TO	Pts.	Avg.
90-91—Milwaukee ...	3	40	6	12	.500	3	4	.750	0	3	3	3	3	0	1	0	6	17	5.7

Three-point field goals: 1990-91, 2-for-3 (.667).

HERRERA, CARL
F, ROCKETS

PERSONAL: Born December 14, 1966, in Trinidad.... 6-9/215.... Full name: Carl Victor Herrera.
HIGH SCHOOL: Simon Bolivar (Caracas, Venezuela).
COLLEGE: Jacksonville (Tex.), then Houston.
TRANSACTIONS/CAREER NOTES: Selected by Miami Heat in second round (30th pick overall) of 1990 NBA Draft.... Draft rights traded by Heat with draft rights to Dave Jamerson to Houston Rockets for draft rights to Alec Kessler (June 27, 1990).... Played in Spain (1990-91).
MISCELLANEOUS: Member of Venezuelan Olympic team (1992).

COLLEGIATE RECORD

Season	Team	G	Min.	FGM	FGA	Pct.	FTM	FTA	Pct.	Reb.	Pts.	Avg.
87-88	—Jacksonville					Statistics unavailable.						
88-89	—Jacksonville	28	...	261	459	.569	180	238	.756	...	713	25.5
89-90	—Houston	33	...	188	333	.565	172	214	.804	302	551	16.7
	Junior college totals	28	...	261	459	.569	180	238	.756	...	713	25.5
	Four-year-college totals	33	...	188	333	.565	172	214	.804	302	551	16.7

Three-point field goals: 1989-90, 3-for-8 (.375).

NBA REGULAR-SEASON RECORD

										— REBOUNDS —									
Season	Team	G	Min.	FGM	FGA	Pct.	FTM	FTA	Pct.	Off.	Def.	Tot.	Ast.	PF	Dq.	Stl.	Blk.	TO	Pts.	Avg.
91-92	—Houston	43	566	83	161	.516	25	44	.568	33	66	99	27	60	0	16	25	37	191	4.4

Three-point field goals: 1991-92, 0-for-1.

HIGGINS, ROD

F

PERSONAL: Born January 31, 1960, in Monroe, La. ... 6-7/215. ... Full name: Roderick Dwayne Higgins. **HIGH SCHOOL:** Thornton Township (Harvey, Ill.). **COLLEGE:** Fresno State.

TRANSACTIONS/CAREER NOTES: Selected by Chicago Bulls in second round (31st pick overall) of 1982 NBA Draft. ... Waived by Bulls (October 24, 1985). ... Signed as free agent by Seattle SuperSonics (November 4, 1985). ... Waived by SuperSonics (December 17, 1985). ... Signed by San Antonio Spurs to first of two consecutive 10-day contracts (January 15, 1986). ... Played in Continental Basketball Association with Tampa Bay Thrillers (1985-86). ... Signed by New Jersey Nets to 10-day contract (February 21, 1986). ... Signed by Bulls to 10-day contract (March 14, 1986). ... Re-signed by Bulls (March 24, 1986). ... Released by Bulls (March 27, 1986). ... Signed as free agent by Golden State Warriors (October 2, 1986).

COLLEGIATE RECORD

Season	Team	G	Min.	FGM	FGA	Pct.	FTM	FTA	Pct.	Reb.	Pts.	Avg.
78-79	—Fresno State	22	...	79	153	.516	49	66	.742	127	207	9.4
79-80	—Fresno State	24	...	119	235	.506	72	86	.837	136	310	12.9
80-81	—Fresno State	29	941	178	319	.558	92	108	.852	158	448	15.4
81-82	—Fresno State	29	1025	178	335	.531	81	105	.771	182	437	15.1
	Totals	104	...	554	1042	.532	294	365	.805	603	1402	13.5

NBA REGULAR-SEASON RECORD

										— REBOUNDS —									
Season	Team	G	Min.	FGM	FGA	Pct.	FTM	FTA	Pct.	Off.	Def.	Tot.	Ast.	PF	Dq.	Stl.	Blk.	TO	Pts.	Avg.
82-83	—Chicago	82	2196	313	698	.448	209	264	.792	159	207	366	175	248	3	66	65	127	848	10.3
83-84	—Chicago	78	1577	193	432	.447	113	156	.724	87	119	206	116	161	0	49	29	76	500	6.4
84-85	—Chicago	68	942	119	270	.441	60	90	.667	55	92	147	73	91	0	21	13	49	308	4.5
85-86	—S-SA-NJ-C	30	332	39	106	.368	19	27	.704	14	37	51	24	49	0	9	11	13	98	3.3
86-87	—Golden State	73	1497	214	412	.519	200	240	.833	72	165	237	96	145	0	40	21	76	631	8.6
87-88	—Golden State	68	2188	381	725	.526	273	322	.848	94	199	293	188	188	2	70	31	111	1054	15.5
88-89	—Golden State	81	1887	301	633	.476	188	229	.821	111	265	376	160	172	2	39	42	76	856	10.6
89-90	—Golden State	82	1993	304	632	.481	234	285	.821	120	302	422	129	184	0	47	53	93	909	11.1
90-91	—Golden State	82	2024	259	559	.463	185	226	.819	109	245	354	113	198	2	52	37	65	776	9.5
91-92	—Golden State	25	535	87	211	.412	48	59	.814	30	55	85	22	75	2	15	13	15	255	10.2
	Totals	669	15171	2210	4678	.472	1529	1898	.806	851	1686	2537	1096	1511	11	408	315	701	6235	9.3

Three-point field goals: 1982-83, 13-for-41 (.317). 1983-84, 1-for-22 (.045). 1984-85, 10-for-37 (.270). 1985-86, 1-for-9 (.111). 1986-87, 3-for-17 (.176). 1987-88, 19-for-39 (.487). 1988-89, 66-for-168 (.393). 1989-90, 67-for-193 (.347). 1990-91, 73-for-220 (.332). 1991-92, 33-for-95 (.347). Totals, 286-for-841 (.340).

NBA PLAYOFF RECORD

										— REBOUNDS —									
Season	Team	G	Min.	FGM	FGA	Pct.	FTM	FTA	Pct.	Off.	Def.	Tot.	Ast.	PF	Dq.	Stl.	Blk.	TO	Pts.	Avg.
84-85	—Chicago	1	1	0	0	...	0	0	...	0	0	0	0	0	0	0	0	0	0	0.0
86-87	—Golden State	10	177	18	46	.391	6	9	.667	5	16	21	12	20	0	11	6	2	43	4.3
88-89	—Golden State	8	267	40	82	.488	29	34	.853	23	36	59	20	19	0	13	7	11	119	14.9
90-91	—Golden State	9	214	26	61	.426	23	28	.821	9	20	29	18	28	0	2	8	7	83	9.2
91-92	—Golden State	2	17	2	5	.400	2	2	1.000	0	0	0	1	1	0	1	0	0	6	3.0
	Totals	30	676	86	194	.443	60	73	.822	37	72	109	51	68	0	27	21	20	251	8.4

Three-point field goals: 1986-87, 1-for-1. 1988-89, 10-for-35 (.286). 1990-91, 8-for-26 (.308). 1991-92, 0-for-2. Totals, 19-for-64 (.297).

CBA REGULAR-SEASON RECORD

NOTES: CBA Playoff Most Valuable Player (1986). ... Member of CBA championship team (1986).

				— 2-POINT —			— 3-POINT —								
Season	Team	G	Min.	FGM	FGA	Pct.	FGM	FGA	Pct.	FTM	FTA	Pct.	Reb.	Ast.	Pts.	Avg.
85-86	—Tampa Bay	11	422	105	190	.553	4	10	.400	92	115	.800	85	30	314	28.5

HIGGINS, SEAN

G/F, LAKERS

PERSONAL: Born December 30, 1968, in Los Angeles. ... 6-9/215. ... Full name: Sean Marielle Higgins. ... Son of Earle Higgins, forward with Indiana Pacers of American Basketball Association (1970-71). **HIGH SCHOOL:** Fairfax (Los Angeles).

COLLEGE: Michigan.

TRANSACTIONS/CAREER NOTES: Selected as undergraduate by San Antonio Spurs in second round (54th pick overall) of 1990 NBA Draft. ... Waived by Spurs (December 13, 1991). ... Signed by Orlando Magic to first of two consecutive 10-day contracts (January 10, 1992). ... Signed by Magic for the remainder of season (January 30, 1992). ... Signed as unrestricted free agent by Los Angeles Lakers (August 13, 1992).

H

COLLEGIATE RECORD

NOTES: Member of NCAA Division I championship team (1989).

Season Team	G	Min.	FGM	FGA	Pct.	FTM	FTA	Pct.	Reb.	Pts.	Avg.
87-88 —Michigan	12	228	48	96	.500	11	14	.786	38	117	9.8
88-89 —Michigan	34	782	158	312	.506	54	70	.771	107	421	12.4
89-90 —Michigan	26	728	142	302	.470	37	46	.804	93	364	14.0
Totals	72	1738	348	710	.490	102	130	.785	238	902	12.5

Three-point field goals: 1987-88, 10-for-20 (.500). 1988-89, 51-for-110 (.464). 1989-90, 43-for-102 (.422). Totals, 104-for-232 (.448).

NBA REGULAR-SEASON RECORD

Season Team	G	Min.	FGM	FGA	Pct.	FTM	FTA	Pct.	Off.	Def.	Tot.	Ast.	PF	Dq.	Stl.	Blk.	TO	Pts.	Avg.
90-91 —San Antonio.	50	464	97	212	.458	28	33	.848	18	45	63	35	53	0	8	1	49	225	4.5
91-92 —S.A.-Orl.	38	616	127	277	.458	31	36	.861	29	73	102	41	58	0	16	6	41	291	7.7
Totals	88	1080	224	489	.458	59	69	.855	47	118	165	76	111	0	24	7	90	516	5.9

Three-point field goals: 1990-91, 3-for-19 (.158). 1991-92, 6-for-25 (.240). Totals, 9-for-44 (.205).

NBA PLAYOFF RECORD

Season Team	G	Min.	FGM	FGA	Pct.	FTM	FTA	Pct.	Off.	Def.	Tot.	Ast.	PF	Dq.	Stl.	Blk.	TO	Pts.	Avg.
90-91 —San Antonio.	3	13	0	2	.000	0	0	...	0	0	0	1	1	0	0	0	0	0	0.0

HILL, TYRONE
F, WARRIORS

PERSONAL: Born March 17, 1968, in Cincinnati. . . . 6-9/243.
HIGH SCHOOL: Withrow (Cincinnati).
COLLEGE: Xavier.
TRANSACTIONS/CAREER NOTES: Selected by Golden State Warriors in first round (11th pick overall) of 1990 NBA Draft.

COLLEGIATE RECORD

Season Team	G	Min.	FGM	FGA	Pct.	FTM	FTA	Pct.	Reb.	Pts.	Avg.
86-87 —Xavier	31	881	95	172	.552	84	125	.672	261	274	8.8
87-88 —Xavier	30	858	172	309	.557	114	153	.745	314	458	15.3
88-89 —Xavier	33	1094	235	388	.606	155	221	.701	403	625	18.9
89-90 —Xavier	32	1063	250	430	.581	146	222	.658	402	646	20.2
Totals	126	3896	752	1299	.579	499	721	.692	1380	2003	15.9

Three-point field goals: 1989-90, 0-for-2.

NBA REGULAR-SEASON RECORD

Season Team	G	Min.	FGM	FGA	Pct.	FTM	FTA	Pct.	Off.	Def.	Tot.	Ast.	PF	Dq.	Stl.	Blk.	TO	Pts.	Avg.
90-91 —Golden State	74	1192	147	299	.492	96	152	.632	157	226	383	19	264	8	33	30	72	390	5.3
91-92 —Golden State	82	1886	254	487	.522	163	235	.694	182	411	593	47	*315	7	73	43	106	671	8.2
Totals	156	3078	401	786	.510	259	387	.669	339	637	976	66	579	15	106	73	178	1061	6.8

Three-point field goals: 1991-92, 0-for-1.

NBA PLAYOFF RECORD

Season Team	G	Min.	FGM	FGA	Pct.	FTM	FTA	Pct.	Off.	Def.	Tot.	Ast.	PF	Dq.	Stl.	Blk.	TO	Pts.	Avg.
90-91 —Golden State	9	80	9	14	.643	4	6	.667	7	16	23	2	25	2	3	4	2	22	2.4
91-92 —Golden State	4	47	3	7	.429	0	2	.000	3	5	8	1	12	0	2	0	3	6	1.5
Totals	13	127	12	21	.571	4	8	.500	10	21	31	3	37	2	5	4	5	28	2.2

Three-point field goals: 1990-91, 0-for-1.

HODGE, DONALD
C, MAVERICKS

PERSONAL: Born February 25, 1969, in Washington, D.C. . . . 7-0/233. . . . Full name: Donald Jerome Hodge.
HIGH SCHOOL: Coolidge (Washington, D.C.).
COLLEGE: Temple.
TRANSACTIONS/CAREER NOTES: Selected by Dallas Mavericks in second round (33rd pick overall) of 1991 NBA Draft.

COLLEGIATE RECORD

Season Team	G	Min.	FGM	FGA	Pct.	FTM	FTA	Pct.	Reb.	Pts.	Avg.
88-89 —Temple					Did not play—ineligible.						
89-90 —Temple	31	1118	164	303	.541	139	195	.713	253	467	15.1
90-91 —Temple	34	1187	147	275	.535	101	141	.716	234	395	11.6
Totals	65	2305	311	578	.538	240	336	.714	487	862	13.3

NBA REGULAR-SEASON RECORD

Season Team	G	Min.	FGM	FGA	Pct.	FTM	FTA	Pct.	Off.	Def.	Tot.	Ast.	PF	Dq.	Stl.	Blk.	TO	Pts.	Avg.
91-92 —Dallas	51	1058	163	328	.497	100	150	.667	118	157	275	39	128	2	25	23	75	426	8.4

HODGES, CRAIG
G

PERSONAL: Born June 27, 1960, in Park Forest, Ill. . . . 6-2/190. . . . Full name: Craig Anthony Hodges.
HIGH SCHOOL: Rich East (Park Forest, Ill.).
COLLEGE: Long Beach State.
TRANSACTIONS/CAREER NOTES: Selected by San Diego Clippers in third round (48th pick overall) of 1982 NBA Draft. . . . Clippers franchise moved from San Diego to Los Angeles for 1984-85 season. . . . Traded by

Clippers with Terry Cummings and Ricky Pierce to Milwaukee Bucks for Marques Johnson, Harvey Catchings, Junior Bridgeman and cash (September 29, 1984).... Traded by Bucks with 1988 second-round draft choice to Phoenix Suns for Jay Humphries (February 25, 1988).... Traded by Suns to Chicago Bulls for Ed Nealy and 1989 second-round draft choice (December 14, 1988).... Waived by Bulls (July 10, 1992).
MISCELLANEOUS: Member of NBA championship teams (1991, 1992).

COLLEGIATE RECORD

Season Team	G	Min.	FGM	FGA	Pct.	FTM	FTA	Pct.	Reb.	Pts.	Avg.
78-79 — Long Beach State	28	801	122	234	.521	38	49	.776	56	282	10.1
79-80 — Long Beach State	33	1148	180	361	.499	57	68	.838	70	417	12.6
80-81 — Long Beach State	26	755	127	275	.462	33	55	.600	67	287	11.0
81-82 — Long Beach State	28	1005	211	444	.475	68	92	.739	89	490	17.5
Totals	115	3709	640	1314	.487	196	264	.742	282	1476	12.8

NBA REGULAR-SEASON RECORD

NOTES: Led NBA with .4506 three-point field-goal percentage (1986) and .491 three-point field-goal percentage (1988).

Season Team	G	Min.	FGM	FGA	Pct.	FTM	FTA	Pct.	REBOUNDS Off.	Def.	Tot.	Ast.	PF	Dq.	Stl.	Blk.	TO	Pts.	Avg.
82-83 — San Diego	76	2022	318	704	.452	94	130	.723	53	69	122	275	192	3	82	4	161	750	9.9
83-84 — San Diego	76	1571	258	573	.450	66	88	.750	22	64	86	116	166	2	58	1	85	592	7.8
84-85 — Milwaukee	82	2496	359	733	.490	106	130	.815	74	112	186	349	262	8	96	1	135	871	10.6
85-86 — Milwaukee	66	1739	284	568	.500	75	86	.872	39	78	117	229	157	3	74	2	89	716	10.8
86-87 — Milwaukee	78	2147	315	682	.462	131	147	.891	48	92	140	240	189	3	76	7	124	846	10.8
87-88 — Mil.-Phoe.	66	1445	242	523	.463	59	71	.831	19	59	78	153	118	1	46	2	77	629	9.5
88-89 — Phoe.-Chi.	59	1204	203	430	.472	48	57	.842	23	66	89	146	90	0	43	4	57	529	9.0
89-90 — Chicago	63	1055	145	331	.438	30	33	.909	11	42	53	110	87	1	30	2	30	407	6.5
90-91 — Chicago	73	843	146	334	.424	26	27	.963	10	32	42	97	74	0	34	2	35	362	5.0
91-92 — Chicago	56	555	93	242	.384	16	17	.941	7	17	24	54	33	0	14	1	22	238	4.3
Totals	695	15077	2363	5130	.461	651	786	.828	306	631	937	1769	1368	21	553	26	815	5940	8.5

Three-point field goals: 1982-83, 20-for-90 (.222). 1983-84, 10-for-46 (.217). 1984-85, 47-for-135 (.348). 1985-86, 73-for-162 (.451). 1986-87, 85-for-228 (.373). 1987-88, 86-for-175 (.491). 1988-89, 75-for-180 (.417). 1989-90, 87-for-181 (.481). 1990-91, 44-for-115 (.383). 1991-92, 36-for-96 (.375). Totals, 563-for-1408 (.400).

NBA PLAYOFF RECORD

NOTES: Shares single-game record for most steals — 8 (May 9, 1986, vs. Philadelphia).

Season Team	G	Min.	FGM	FGA	Pct.	FTM	FTA	Pct.	REBOUNDS Off.	Def.	Tot.	Ast.	PF	Dq.	Stl.	Blk.	TO	Pts.	Avg.
84-85 — Milwaukee	8	216	28	77	.364	4	5	.800	2	11	13	26	29	2	12	1	18	64	8.0
85-86 — Milwaukee	14	460	74	145	.510	27	34	.794	9	16	25	63	44	1	32	2	24	189	13.5
86-87 — Milwaukee	12	226	40	77	.519	10	11	.909	11	11	22	20	16	0	9	2	3	95	7.9
88-89 — Chicago	17	554	73	177	.412	10	14	.714	8	17	25	62	55	1	22	3	24	191	11.2
89-90 — Chicago	16	254	28	74	.378	3	4	.750	6	12	18	17	31	1	4	0	14	71	4.4
90-91 — Chicago	17	209	33	78	.423	3	4	.750	0	4	4	10	21	0	11	0	11	80	4.7
91-92 — Chicago	17	137	16	41	.390	1	2	.500	3	1	4	5	10	0	5	0	8	42	2.5
Totals	101	2056	292	669	.436	58	74	.784	39	72	111	203	206	5	95	8	102	732	7.2

Three-point field goals: 1984-85, 4-for-23 (.174). 1985-86, 14-for-31 (.452). 1986-87, 5-for-17 (.294). 1988-89, 35-for-88 (.398). 1989-90, 12-for-41 (.293). 1990-91, 11-for-28 (.393). 1991-92, 9-for-20 (.450). Totals, 90-for-248 (.363).

HOPPEN, DAVE
C, SPURS

PERSONAL: Born March 13, 1964, in Omaha, Neb. ... 6-11/240. ... Full name: David Dirk Hoppen.
HIGH SCHOOL: Benson (Omaha, Neb.).
COLLEGE: Nebraska.
TRANSACTIONS/CAREER NOTES: Selected by Atlanta Hawks in third round (65th pick overall) of 1986 NBA Draft. ... Waived by Hawks (December 29, 1987). ... Played in Continental Basketball Association with Topeka Sizzlers (1987-88). ... Played in Italy (1987-88). ... Signed by Milwaukee Bucks to 10-day contract (January 12, 1988). ... Signed as free agent by Golden State Warriors (January 22, 1988). ... Selected by Charlotte Hornets from Warriors in NBA expansion draft (June 23, 1988). ... Traded by Hornets with Armon Gilliam to Philadelphia 76ers for Mike Gminski (January 4, 1991). ... Signed as unrestricted free agent by San Antonio Spurs (September 3, 1992).

COLLEGIATE RECORD

Season Team	G	Min.	FGM	FGA	Pct.	FTM	FTA	Pct.	Reb.	Pts.	Avg.
82-83 — Nebraska	32	829	163	311	.524	119	159	.748	161	445	13.9
83-84 — Nebraska	30	1058	220	367	.599	158	208	.760	207	598	19.9
84-85 — Nebraska	30	1155	270	418	.646	164	210	.781	258	704	23.5
85-86 — Nebraska	19	669	151	245	.616	118	147	.803	147	420	22.1
Totals	111	3711	804	1341	.600	559	724	.772	773	2167	19.5

NBA REGULAR-SEASON RECORD

Season Team	G	Min.	FGM	FGA	Pct.	FTM	FTA	Pct.	REBOUNDS Off.	Def.	Tot.	Ast.	PF	Dq.	Stl.	Blk.	TO	Pts.	Avg.
86-87 — Atlanta							Did not play — injured.												
87-88 — Mil.-G.S.	39	642	84	183	.459	54	62	.871	58	116	174	32	87	1	13	6	37	222	5.7
88-89 — Charlotte	77	1419	199	353	.564	101	139	.727	123	261	384	57	239	4	25	21	77	500	6.5
89-90 — Charlotte	10	135	16	41	.390	8	10	.800	19	17	36	6	26	0	2	1	8	40	4.0
90-91 — Char.-Phil.	30	155	24	44	.545	16	22	.727	18	21	39	3	29	0	3	1	13	64	2.1
91-92 — Philadelphia	11	40	2	7	.286	5	10	.500	1	9	10	2	6	0	0	0	3	9	0.8
Totals	167	2391	325	628	.518	184	243	.757	219	424	643	100	387	5	43	29	138	835	5.0

Three-point field goals: 1987-88, 0-for-1. 1988-89, 1-for-2 (.500). 1990-91, 0-for-2. Totals, 1-for-5 (.200).

NBA PLAYOFF RECORD

Season Team	G	Min.	FGM	FGA	Pct.	FTM	FTA	Pct.	REBOUNDS Off.	Def.	Tot.	Ast.	PF	Dq.	Stl.	Blk.	TO	Pts.	Avg.
90-91 — Philadelphia	3	9	3	3	1.000	0	2	.000	0	3	3	0	1	0	0	0	0	6	2.0

H

CBA REGULAR-SEASON RECORD

Season	Team	G	Min.	2-POINT FGM	FGA	Pct.	3-POINT FGM	FGA	Pct.	FTM	FTA	Pct.	Reb.	Ast.	Pts.	Avg.
87-88 — Topeka		6	204	33	51	.647	0	0	...	26	33	.788	65	11	92	15.3

ITALIAN LEAGUE RECORD

Season	Team	G	Min.	FGM	FGA	Pct.	FTM	FTA	Pct.	Reb.	Pts.	Avg.
87-88 — Biklim Rimini		2	73	9	20	.450	6	10	.600	18	24	12.0

HOPSON, DENNIS
G

PERSONAL: Born April 22, 1965, in Toledo, O. . . . 6-5/200.
HIGH SCHOOL: E.L. Bowsher (Toledo, O.).
COLLEGE: Ohio State.
TRANSACTIONS/CAREER NOTES: Selected by New Jersey Nets in first round (third pick overall) of 1987 NBA Draft. . . . Traded by Nets to Chicago Bulls for 1990 first-round draft choice and 1991 and 1992 second-round draft choices (June 26, 1990). . . . Traded by Bulls to Sacramento Kings for Bobby Hansen and 1992 second-round draft choice (November 4, 1991).
MISCELLANEOUS: Member of NBA championship team (1991).

COLLEGIATE RECORD

NOTES: THE SPORTING NEWS All-America first team (1987).

Season	Team	G	Min.	FGM	FGA	Pct.	FTM	FTA	Pct.	Reb.	Pts.	Avg.
83-84 — Ohio State		29	541	63	133	.474	29	35	.829	108	155	5.3
84-85 — Ohio State		30	764	120	243	.494	53	72	.736	142	293	9.8
85-86 — Ohio State		33	1148	275	505	.545	140	180	.778	193	690	20.9
86-87 — Ohio State		33	1158	338	653	.518	215	264	.814	269	958	29.0
Totals		125	3611	796	1534	.519	437	551	.793	712	2096	16.8

Three-point field goals: 1986-87, 67-for-160 (.419).

NBA REGULAR-SEASON RECORD

Season	Team	G	Min.	FGM	FGA	Pct.	FTM	FTA	Pct.	REBOUNDS Off.	Def.	Tot.	Ast.	PF	Dq.	Stl.	Blk.	TO	Pts.	Avg.
87-88 — New Jersey		61	1365	222	549	.404	131	177	.740	63	80	143	118	145	0	57	25	119	587	9.6
88-89 — New Jersey		62	1551	299	714	.419	186	219	.849	91	111	202	103	150	0	70	30	102	788	12.7
89-90 — New Jersey		79	2551	474	1093	.434	271	342	.792	113	166	279	151	183	1	100	51	168	1251	15.8
90-91 — Chicago		61	728	104	244	.426	55	83	.663	49	60	109	65	79	0	25	14	59	264	4.3
91-92 — Chi.-Sac.		71	1314	276	593	.465	179	253	.708	105	101	206	102	115	0	67	39	100	743	10.5
Totals		334	7509	1375	3193	.431	822	1074	.765	421	518	939	539	672	1	319	159	548	3633	10.9

Three-point field goals: 1987-88, 12-for-45 (.267). 1988-89, 4-for-27 (.148). 1989-90, 32-for-101 (.317). 1990-91, 1-for-5 (.200). 1991-92, 12-for-47 (.255). Totals, 61-for-225 (.271).

NBA PLAYOFF RECORD

Season	Team	G	Min.	FGM	FGA	Pct.	FTM	FTA	Pct.	REBOUNDS Off.	Def.	Tot.	Ast.	PF	Dq.	Stl.	Blk.	TO	Pts.	Avg.
90-91 — Chicago		5	18	2	6	.333	4	9	.444	2	2	4	1	2	0	0	1	1	8	1.6

HORNACEK, JEFF
G, 76ERS

PERSONAL: Born May 3, 1963, in Elmhurst, Ill. . . . 6-4/190. . . . Full name: Jeffrey John Hornacek. . . . Name pronounced HORN-a-seck.
HIGH SCHOOL: Lyons Township (La Grange, Ill.).
COLLEGE: Iowa State.
TRANSACTIONS/CAREER NOTES: Selected by Phoenix Suns in second round (46th pick overall) of 1986 NBA Draft. . . . Traded by Suns with Andrew Lang and Tim Perry to Philadelphia 76ers for Charles Barkley (June 17, 1992).

COLLEGIATE RECORD

Season	Team	G	Min.	FGM	FGA	Pct.	FTM	FTA	Pct.	Reb.	Pts.	Avg.
81-82 — Iowa State						Did not play—redshirted.						
82-83 — Iowa State		27	583	57	135	.422	32	45	.711	62	146	5.4
83-84 — Iowa State		29	1065	104	208	.500	83	105	.790	101	291	10.0
84-85 — Iowa State		34	1224	172	330	.521	81	96	.844	122	425	12.5
85-86 — Iowa State		33	1229	177	370	.478	97	125	.776	127	451	13.7
Totals		123	4101	510	1043	.489	293	371	.790	412	1313	10.7

NBA REGULAR-SEASON RECORD

Season	Team	G	Min.	FGM	FGA	Pct.	FTM	FTA	Pct.	REBOUNDS Off.	Def.	Tot.	Ast.	PF	Dq.	Stl.	Blk.	TO	Pts.	Avg.
86-87 — Phoenix		80	1561	159	350	.454	94	121	.777	41	143	184	361	130	0	70	5	153	424	5.3
87-88 — Phoenix		82	2243	306	605	.506	152	185	.822	71	191	262	540	151	0	107	10	156	781	9.5
88-89 — Phoenix		78	2487	440	889	.495	147	178	.826	75	191	266	465	188	0	129	8	111	1054	13.5
89-90 — Phoenix		67	2278	483	901	.536	173	202	.856	86	227	313	337	144	2	117	14	125	1179	17.6
90-91 — Phoenix		80	2733	544	1051	.518	201	224	.897	74	247	321	409	185	1	111	16	130	1350	16.9
91-92 — Phoenix		81	3078	635	1240	.512	279	315	.886	106	301	407	411	218	1	158	31	170	1632	20.1
Totals		468	14380	2567	5036	.510	1046	1225	.854	453	1300	1753	2523	1016	4	692	84	845	6420	13.7

Three-point field goals: 1986-87, 12-for-43 (.279). 1987-88, 17-for-58 (.293). 1988-89, 27-for-81 (.333). 1989-90, 40-for-98 (.408). 1990-91, 61-for-146 (.418). 1991-92, 83-for-189 (.439). Totals, 240-for-615 (.390).

NBA PLAYOFF RECORD

Season	Team	G	Min.	FGM	FGA	Pct.	FTM	FTA	Pct.	REBOUNDS Off.	Def.	Tot.	Ast.	PF	Dq.	Stl.	Blk.	TO	Pts.	Avg.
88-89 — Phoenix		12	374	74	149	.497	21	25	.840	25	44	69	62	34	0	16	3	18	169	14.1
89-90 — Phoenix		16	583	112	219	.511	68	73	.932	13	49	62	73	43	1	24	0	34	298	18.6

H

Season Team	G	Min.	FGM	FGA	Pct.	FTM	FTA	Pct.	REBOUNDS Off.	Def.	Tot.	Ast.	PF	Dq.	Stl.	Blk.	TO	Pts.	Avg.
90-91 —Phoenix.......	4	145	22	51	.431	26	28	.929	3	22	25	8	13	0	3	2	3	73	18.3
91-92 —Phoenix.......	8	343	62	128	.484	31	34	.912	12	39	51	42	23	0	14	2	19	163	20.4
Totals	40	1445	270	547	.494	146	160	.913	53	154	207	185	113	1	57	7	74	703	17.6

Three-point field goals: 1988-89, 0-for-7. 1989-90, 6-for-24 (.250). 1990-91, 3-for-6 (.500). 1991-92, 8-for-17 (.471). Totals, 17-for-54 (.315).

NBA ALL-STAR GAME RECORD

Season Team	Min.	FGM	FGA	Pct.	FTM	FTA	Pct.	REBOUNDS Off.	Def.	Tot.	Ast.	PF	Dq.	Stl.	Blk.	TO	Pts.
1992 —Phoenix..............	24	5	7	.714	0	0	...	1	1	2	3	0	0	1	0	0	11

Three-point field goals: 1992, 1-for-2 (.500).

HOWARD, BRIAN
F, MAVERICKS

PERSONAL: Born October 19, 1967, in Winston Salem, N.C. . . . 6-7/ 215.
HIGH SCHOOL: North Forsyth (Winston Salem, N.C.).
COLLEGE: North Carolina State.
TRANSACTIONS/CAREER NOTES: Never drafted by an NBA franchise. . . . Played in Continental Basketball Association with Omaha Racers (1990-91 and 1991-92). . . . Signed by Dallas Mavericks to first of two consecutive 10-day contracts (February 3, 1992). . . . Signed by Mavericks for remainder of season (February 23, 1992).

COLLEGIATE RECORD

Season Team	G	Min.	FGM	FGA	Pct.	FTM	FTA	Pct.	Reb.	Pts.	Avg.
86-87 —North Carolina State...............	18	73	5	14	.357	3	4	.750	9	13	0.7
87-88 —North Carolina State...............	32	783	93	189	.492	53	69	.768	110	244	7.6
88-89 —North Carolina State...............	31	976	160	306	.523	53	74	.716	166	389	12.5
89-90 —North Carolina State...............	30	1003	152	330	.461	55	77	.714	154	389	13.0
Totals	111	2835	410	839	.489	164	224	.732	439	1035	9.3

Three-point field goals: 1987-88, 5-for-10 (.500). 1988-89, 16-for-49 (.327). 1989-90, 30-for-78 (.385). Totals, 51-for-137 (.372).

CBA REGULAR-SEASON RECORD

NOTES: CBA All-Rookie team (1991).

Season Team	G	Min.	2-POINT FGM	FGA	Pct.	3-POINT FGM	FGA	Pct.	FTM	FTA	Pct.	Reb.	Ast.	Pts.	Avg.
90-91 —Omaha	56	1865	493	894	.551	1	2	.500	175	239	.732	381	105	1164	20.8
91-92 —Omaha	37	1246	276	538	.513	2	5	.400	128	164	.780	240	94	686	18.5
Totals	93	3111	769	1432	.537	3	7	.429	303	403	.752	621	199	1850	19.9

NBA REGULAR-SEASON RECORD

Season Team	G	Min.	FGM	FGA	Pct.	FTM	FTA	Pct.	REBOUNDS Off.	Def.	Tot.	Ast.	PF	Dq.	Stl.	Blk.	TO	Pts.	Avg.
91-92 —Dallas...........	27	318	54	104	.519	22	31	.710	17	34	51	14	55	2	11	8	15	131	4.9

Three-point field goals: 1991-92, 1-for-2 (.500).

HUMPHRIES, JAY
G, JAZZ

PERSONAL: Born October 17, 1962, in Los Angeles. . . . 6-3/185. . . . Full name: John Jay Humphries.
HIGH SCHOOL: Inglewood (Calif.).
COLLEGE: Colorado.
TRANSACTIONS/CAREER NOTES: Selected by Phoenix Suns in first round (13th pick overall) of 1984 NBA Draft. . . . Traded by Suns to Milwaukee Bucks for Craig Hodges and 1988 second-round draft choice (February 25, 1988). . . . Traded by Bucks with Larry Krystkowiak to Utah Jazz for Blue Edwards, Eric Murdock and 1992 first-round draft choice (June 24, 1992).

COLLEGIATE RECORD

Season Team	G	Min.	FGM	FGA	Pct.	FTM	FTA	Pct.	Reb.	Pts.	Avg.
80-81 —Colorado	28	762	74	143	.517	31	47	.660	59	179	6.4
81-82 —Colorado	27	948	113	242	.467	53	83	.639	71	279	10.3
82-83 —Colorado	28	1034	170	339	.501	60	95	.632	91	400	14.3
83-84 —Colorado	29	1120	170	334	.509	108	137	.788	94	448	15.4
Totals	112	3864	527	1058	.498	252	362	.696	315	1306	11.7

NBA REGULAR-SEASON RECORD

Season Team	G	Min.	FGM	FGA	Pct.	FTM	FTA	Pct.	REBOUNDS Off.	Def.	Tot.	Ast.	PF	Dq.	Stl.	Blk.	TO	Pts.	Avg.
84-85 —Phoenix.......	80	2062	279	626	.446	141	170	.829	32	132	164	350	209	2	107	8	167	703	8.8
85-86 —Phoenix.......	82	2733	352	753	.479	197	257	.767	56	204	260	526	222	1	132	9	190	905	11.0
86-87 —Phoenix.......	82	2579	359	753	.477	200	260	.769	62	198	260	632	239	1	112	9	195	923	11.3
87-88 —Phoe.-Mil.....	68	1809	284	538	.528	112	153	.732	49	125	174	395	177	1	81	5	127	683	10.0
88-89 —Milwaukee ...	73	2220	345	714	.483	129	158	.816	70	119	189	405	187	1	142	5	160	844	11.6
89-90 —Milwaukee ...	81	2818	496	1005	.494	224	285	.786	80	189	269	472	253	2	156	11	151	1237	15.3
90-91 —Milwaukee ...	80	2726	482	960	.502	191	239	.799	51	163	220	538	237	2	129	7	151	1215	15.2
91-92 —Milwaukee ...	71	2261	377	803	.469	195	249	.783	44	140	184	466	210	2	119	13	148	991	14.0
Totals	617	19208	2974	6134	.485	1389	1771	.784	450	1270	1720	3784	1734	12	978	67	1289	7501	12.2

Three-point field goals: 1984-85, 4-for-20 (.200). 1985-86, 4-for-29 (.138). 1986-87, 5-for-27 (.185). 1987-88, 3-for-18 (.167). 1988-89, 25-for-94 (.266). 1989-90, 21-for-70 (.300). 1990-91, 60-for-161 (.373). 1991-92, 42-for-144 (.292). Totals, 164-for-563 (.291).

H

NBA PLAYOFF RECORD

Season	Team	G	Min.	FGM	FGA	Pct.	FTM	FTA	Pct.	Reb. Off.	Reb. Def.	Tot.	Ast.	PF	Dq.	Stl.	Blk.	TO	Pts.	Avg.
84-85	Phoenix	3	90	20	31	.645	9	12	.750	1	4	5	16	12	0	2	0	8	49	16.3
87-88	Milwaukee	2	18	0	5	.000	0	0	...	1	2	3	1	6	0	1	0	1	0	0.0
88-89	Milwaukee	9	323	49	99	.495	30	34	.882	8	19	27	70	29	0	8	0	12	131	14.6
89-90	Milwaukee	3	79	8	15	.533	10	13	.769	1	4	5	19	6	0	3	0	8	27	9.0
90-91	Milwaukee	3	123	17	32	.531	9	10	.900	2	4	6	25	17	2	2	0	6	45	15.0
Totals		20	633	94	182	.516	58	69	.841	13	33	46	131	70	2	16	0	35	252	12.6

Three-point field goals: 1988-89, 3-for-18 (.167). 1989-90, 1-for-3 (.333). 1990-91, 2-for-5 (.400). Totals, 6-for-26 (.231).

HUNTER, CEDRIC
G

PERSONAL: Born January 16, 1965, in Omaha, Neb. . . . 6-0/180.
HIGH SCHOOL: South (Omaha, Neb.).
COLLEGE: Kansas.
TRANSACTIONS/CAREER NOTES: Never drafted by an NBA franchise. . . . Played in Continental Basketball Association with Topeka Sizzlers (1987-88 through 1989-90), Tulsa Fast Breakers (1988-89), Santa Barbara Islanders (1989-90) and Omaha Racers (1990-91 and 1991-92). . . . Signed by Charlotte Hornets to 10-day contract (February 15, 1992). . . . Released by Hornets (February 20, 1992).

COLLEGIATE RECORD

Season	Team	G	Min.	FGM	FGA	Pct.	FTM	FTA	Pct.	Reb.	Pts.	Avg.
83-84	Kansas	11	290	18	41	.439	10	23	.435	21	46	4.2
84-85	Kansas	34	887	92	167	.551	43	83	.518	82	227	6.7
85-86	Kansas	39	1217	140	249	.562	74	137	.540	141	354	9.1
86-87	Kansas	34	1167	166	321	.517	62	120	.517	173	395	11.6
Totals		118	3561	416	778	.535	189	363	.521	417	1022	8.7

Three-point field goals: 1986-87, 1-for-7 (.143).

CBA REGULAR-SEASON RECORD

NOTES: CBA All-Star second team (1990).

Season	Team	G	Min.	2-POINT FGM	2-POINT FGA	2-POINT Pct.	3-POINT FGM	3-POINT FGA	3-POINT Pct.	FTM	FTA	Pct.	Reb.	Ast.	Pts.	Avg.
87-88	Topeka	53	1720	242	442	.548	4	19	.211	117	154	.760	167	394	613	11.6
88-89	Tulsa-Topeka	53	2021	268	555	.483	8	24	.333	170	229	.742	177	430	730	13.8
89-90	Topeka-S.B.	55	2241	329	580	.567	2	11	.182	198	243	.815	188	605	862	15.7
90-91	Omaha	56	1980	352	648	.543	2	13	.154	253	315	.803	231	466	963	17.2
91-92	Omaha	50	1724	248	426	.582	0	8	.000	153	189	.810	181	406	649	13.0
Totals		267	9686	1439	2651	.543	16	75	.213	891	1130	.788	944	2301	3817	14.3

NBA REGULAR-SEASON RECORD

Season	Team	G	Min.	FGM	FGA	Pct.	FTM	FTA	Pct.	Reb. Off.	Reb. Def.	Tot.	Ast.	PF	Dq.	Stl.	Blk.	TO	Pts.	Avg.
91-92	Charlotte	1	1	0	0	...	0	0	...	0	0	0	0	0	0	0	0	0	0	0.0

IUZZOLINO, MIKE
G, MAVERICKS

PERSONAL: Born January 22, 1968, in Altoona, Pa. . . . 5-11/175. . . . Full name: Michael Alan Iuzzolino. . . . Name pronounced Izz-a-LEE-no.
HIGH SCHOOL: Altoona Area (Pa.).
COLLEGE: Penn State, then St. Francis (Pa.).
TRANSACTIONS/CAREER NOTES: Selected by Dallas Mavericks in second round (35th pick overall) of 1991 NBA Draft.

COLLEGIATE RECORD

Season	Team	G	Min.	FGM	FGA	Pct.	FTM	FTA	Pct.	Reb.	Pts.	Avg.
86-87	Penn State	27	292	13	46	.283	35	41	.854	32	64	2.4
87-88	Penn State	26	272	26	55	.473	17	19	.895	15	83	3.2
88-89	St. Francis (Pa.)					Did not play—transfer student.						
89-90	St. Francis (Pa.)	27	982	180	326	.552	135	155	.871	67	574	21.3
90-91	St. Francis (Pa.)	32	1169	227	419	.542	215	243	.885	97	772	24.1
Totals		112	2715	446	846	.527	402	458	.878	211	1493	13.3

Three-point field goals: 1986-87, 3-for-12 (.250). 1987-88, 14-for-29 (.483). 1989-90, 79-for-153 (.516). 1990-91, 103-for-195 (.528). Totals, 199-for-389 (.512).

NBA REGULAR-SEASON RECORD

Season	Team	G	Min.	FGM	FGA	Pct.	FTM	FTA	Pct.	Reb. Off.	Reb. Def.	Tot.	Ast.	PF	Dq.	Stl.	Blk.	TO	Pts.	Avg.
91-92	Dallas	52	1280	160	355	.451	107	128	.836	27	71	98	194	79	0	33	1	92	486	9.3

Three-point field goals: 1991-92, 59-for-136 (.434).

JACKSON, CHRIS
G, NUGGETS

PERSONAL: Born March 9, 1969, in Gulfport, Miss. . . . 6-1/170. . . . Full name: Chris Wayne Jackson.
HIGH SCHOOL: Gulfport (Miss.).
COLLEGE: Louisiana State.
TRANSACTIONS/CAREER NOTES: Selected as undergraduate by Denver Nuggets in first round (third pick overall) of 1990 NBA Draft.

COLLEGIATE RECORD

NOTES: THE SPORTING NEWS All-America first team (1989).... THE SPORTING NEWS All-America second team (1990).

Season Team	G	Min.	FGM	FGA	Pct.	FTM	FTA	Pct.	Reb.	Pts.	Avg.
88-89—Louisiana State	32	1180	359	739	.486	163	200	.815	108	965	30.2
89-90—Louisiana State	32	1202	305	662	.461	191	210	.910	81	889	27.8
Totals	64	2382	664	1401	.474	354	410	.863	189	1854	29.0

Three-point field goals: 1988-89, 84-for-216 (.389). 1989-90, 88-for-246 (.358). Totals, 172-for-462 (.372).

NBA REGULAR-SEASON RECORD

HONORS: NBA All-Rookie second team (1991).

Season Team	G	Min.	FGM	FGA	Pct.	FTM	FTA	Pct.	Off.	Def.	Tot.	Ast.	PF	Dq.	Stl.	Blk.	TO	Pts.	Avg.
90-91—Denver	67	1505	417	1009	.413	84	98	.857	34	87	121	206	149	2	55	4	110	942	14.1
91-92—Denver	81	1538	356	845	.421	94	108	.870	22	92	114	192	130	0	44	4	117	837	10.3
Totals	148	3043	773	1854	.417	178	206	.864	56	179	235	398	279	2	99	8	227	1779	12.0

Three-point field goals: 1990-91, 24-for-100 (.240). 1991-92, 31-for-94 (.330). Totals, 55-for-194 (.284).

JACKSON, JAREN
G

PERSONAL: Born October 27, 1967, in New Orleans.... 6-6/200.
HIGH SCHOOL: Walter Cohen (New Orleans).
COLLEGE: Georgetown.
TRANSACTIONS/CAREER NOTES: Never drafted by an NBA franchise.
... Signed as free agent by New Jersey Nets (October 3, 1989).... Waived by Nets (February 27, 1990).
... Played in Continental Basketball Association with Wichita Falls Texans (1990-91) and La Crosse Catbirds (1991-92).... Signed by Golden State Warriors to first of two consecutive 10-day contracts (January 24, 1992).

COLLEGIATE RECORD

Season Team	G	Min.	FGM	FGA	Pct.	FTM	FTA	Pct.	Reb.	Pts.	Avg
85-86—Georgetown	32	283	42	97	.433	18	22	.818	49	102	3.2
86-87—Georgetown	34	387	68	148	.459	37	52	.712	69	193	5.7
87-88—Georgetown	30	558	100	243	.412	42	56	.750	88	262	8.7
88-89—Georgetown	34	923	161	357	.451	59	90	.656	176	417	12.3
Totals	130	2151	371	845	.439	156	220	.709	382	974	7.5

Three-point field goals: 1986-87, 20-for-48 (.417). 1987-88, 20-for-73 (.274). 1988-89, 36-for-87 (.414). Totals, 76-for-208 (.365).

NBA REGULAR-SEASON RECORD

Season Team	G	Min.	FGM	FGA	Pct.	FTM	FTA	Pct.	Off.	Def.	Tot.	Ast.	PF	Dq.	Stl.	Blk.	TO	Pts.	Avg.
89-90—New Jersey	28	160	25	69	.362	17	21	.810	16	8	24	13	16	0	13	1	18	67	2.4
91-92—Golden State	5	54	11	23	.478	4	6	.667	5	5	10	3	7	1	2	0	4	26	5.2
Totals	33	214	36	92	.391	21	27	.778	21	13	34	16	23	1	15	1	22	93	2.8

Three-point field goals: 1989-90, 0-for-3.

CBA REGULAR-SEASON RECORD

			2-POINT			3-POINT								
Season Team	G	Min.	FGM	FGA	Pct.	FGM	FGA	Pct.	FTM	FTA	Pct.	Reb.	Ast.	Pts.	Avg.
90-91—Wichita Falls	51	1099	215	470	.457	18	55	.327	113	165	.685	214	74	597	11.7
91-92—La Crosse	43	1596	304	637	.477	10	37	.270	147	184	.799	215	157	785	18.3
Totals	94	2695	519	1107	.469	28	92	.304	260	349	.745	429	231	1382	14.7

JACKSON, MARK
G, KNICKS

PERSONAL: Born April 1, 1965, in Brooklyn, N.Y.... 6-3/192....
Full name: Mark A. Jackson.
HIGH SCHOOL: Bishop Loughlin Memorial (Brooklyn, N.Y.).
COLLEGE: St. John's.
TRANSACTIONS/CAREER NOTES: Selected by New York Knicks in first round (18th pick overall) of 1987 NBA Draft.

COLLEGIATE RECORD

NOTES: THE SPORTING NEWS All-America second team (1987).... Led NCAA Division I with 9.11 assists per game (1986).

Season Team	G	Min.	FGM	FGA	Pct.	FTM	FTA	Pct.	Reb.	Pts.	Avg.
83-84—St. John's	30	855	61	106	.575	53	77	.688	59	175	5.8
84-85—St. John's	35	601	57	101	.564	66	91	.725	44	180	5.1
85-86—St. John's	36	1340	151	316	.478	105	142	.739	125	407	11.3
86-87—St. John's	30	1184	196	389	.504	125	155	.806	110	566	18.9
Totals	131	3980	465	912	.510	349	465	.751	338	1328	10.1

Three-point field goals: 1986-87, 49-for-117 (.419).

NBA REGULAR-SEASON RECORD

RECORDS: Holds single-season record for most assists by a rookie—868 (1988).
HONORS: NBA Rookie of the Year (1988).... NBA All-Rookie team (1988).

Season Team	G	Min.	FGM	FGA	Pct.	FTM	FTA	Pct.	Off.	Def.	Tot.	Ast.	PF	Dq.	Stl.	Blk.	TO	Pts.	Avg.
87-88—New York	82	3249	438	1013	.432	206	266	.774	120	276	396	868	244	2	205	6	258	1114	13.6
88-89—New York	72	2477	479	1025	.467	180	258	.698	106	235	341	619	163	1	139	7	226	1219	16.9
89-90—New York	82	2428	327	749	.437	120	165	.727	106	212	318	604	121	0	109	4	211	809	9.9
90-91—New York	72	1595	250	508	.492	117	160	.731	62	135	197	452	81	0	60	9	135	630	8.8
91-92—New York	81	2461	367	747	.491	171	222	.770	95	210	305	694	153	0	112	13	211	916	11.3
Totals	389	12210	1861	4042	.460	794	1071	.741	489	1068	1557	3237	762	3	625	39	1041	4688	12.1

Three-point field goals: 1987-88, 32-for-126 (.254). 1988-89, 81-for-240 (.338). 1989-90, 35-for-131 (.267). 1990-91, 13-for-51 (.255). 1991-92, 11-for-43 (.256). Totals, 172-for-591 (.291).

NBA PLAYOFF RECORD

| | | | | | | | | — REBOUNDS — | | | | | | | | |
Season Team	G	Min.	FGM	FGA	Pct.	FTM	FTA	Pct.	Off.	Def.	Tot.	Ast.	PF	Dq.	Stl.	Blk.	TO	Pts.	Avg.
87-88 — New York	4	171	22	60	.367	8	11	.727	6	13	19	39	13	0	10	0	14	57	14.3
88-89 — New York	9	336	51	100	.510	19	28	.679	7	24	31	91	9	0	10	3	28	132	14.7
89-90 — New York	9	81	13	31	.419	8	11	.727	1	4	5	21	5	0	2	0	7	34	3.8
90-91 — New York	3	36	1	3	.333	0	0	...	0	0	0	8	1	0	1	1	5	2	0.7
91-92 — New York	12	368	37	92	.402	22	27	.815	12	15	27	86	26	0	10	0	30	100	8.3
Totals	37	992	124	286	.434	57	77	.740	26	56	82	245	54	0	33	4	84	325	8.8

Three-point field goals: 1987-88, 5-for-12 (.417). 1988-89, 11-for-28 (.393). 1989-90, 0-for-2. 1991-92, 4-for-21 (.190). Totals, 20-for-63 (.317).

NBA ALL-STAR GAME RECORD

| | | | | | | | — REBOUNDS — | | | | | | | | |
Season Team	Min.	FGM	FGA	Pct.	FTM	FTA	Pct.	Off.	Def.	Tot.	Ast.	PF	Dq.	Stl.	Blk.	TO	Pts.
1989 — New York	16	3	5	.600	2	4	.500	1	1	2	4	1	0	1	1	2	9

Three-point field goals: 1989, 1-for-1.

JAMERSON, DAVE
G, ROCKETS

PERSONAL: Born August 13, 1967, in Clarksburg, W. Va. . . . 6-5/192. . . . Full name: John David Jamerson.
HIGH SCHOOL: Stow (O.).
COLLEGE: Ohio University.
TRANSACTIONS/CAREER NOTES: Selected by Miami Heat in first round (15th pick overall) of 1990 NBA Draft. . . . Draft rights traded by Heat with draft rights to Carl Herrera to Houston Rockets for draft rights to Alec Kessler (June 27, 1990).

COLLEGIATE RECORD

NOTES: Led NCAA Division I with 4.68 three-point field-goals made per game (1990).

Season Team	G	Min.	FGM	FGA	Pct.	FTM	FTA	Pct.	Reb.	Pts.	Avg.
85-86 — Ohio University	28	668	169	294	.575	54	65	.831	85	392	14.0
86-87 — Ohio University					Did not play — knee injury.						
87-88 — Ohio University	30	948	198	416	.476	74	87	.851	115	519	17.3
88-89 — Ohio University	29	1034	200	413	.484	92	107	.860	136	551	19.0
89-90 — Ohio University	28	1072	297	647	.459	149	177	.842	179	874	31.2
Totals	115	3722	864	1770	.488	369	436	.846	515	2336	20.3

Three-point field goals: 1987-88, 49-for-122 (.402). 1988-89, 59-for-145 (.407). 1989-90, 131-for-303 (.432). Totals, 239-for-570 (.419).

NBA REGULAR-SEASON RECORD

| | | | | | | | | — REBOUNDS — | | | | | | | | |
Season Team	G	Min.	FGM	FGA	Pct.	FTM	FTA	Pct.	Off.	Def.	Tot.	Ast.	PF	Dq.	Stl.	Blk.	TO	Pts.	Avg.
90-91 — Houston	37	202	43	113	.381	22	27	.815	9	21	30	27	24	0	6	1	20	113	3.1
91-92 — Houston	48	378	79	191	.414	25	27	.926	22	21	43	33	39	0	17	0	24	191	4.0
Totals	85	580	122	304	.401	47	54	.870	31	42	73	60	63	0	23	1	44	304	3.6

Three-point field goals: 1990-91, 5-for-19 (.263). 1991-92, 8-for-28 (.286). Totals, 13-for-47 (.277).

NBA PLAYOFF RECORD

| | | | | | | | | — REBOUNDS — | | | | | | | | |
Season Team	G	Min.	FGM	FGA	Pct.	FTM	FTA	Pct.	Off.	Def.	Tot.	Ast.	PF	Dq.	Stl.	Blk.	TO	Pts.	Avg.
90-91 — Houston	2	21	5	13	.385	6	6	1.000	1	2	3	4	4	0	1	0	1	16	8.0

Three-point field goals: 1990-91, 0-for-1.

JAMES, HENRY
F

PERSONAL: Born July 29, 1965, in Centreville, Ala. . . . 6-8/220. . . . Full name: Henry Charles James.
HIGH SCHOOL: North Side (Fort Wayne, Ind.).
COLLEGE: South Plains (Tex.), then St. Mary's (Tex.).
TRANSACTIONS/CAREER NOTES: Never drafted by an NBA franchise. . . . Played in Spain (1988-89). . . . Played in Continental Basketball Association with Wichita Falls Texans (1988-89 and 1990-91). . . . Played in Belgium (1989-90). . . . Signed as free agent by Cleveland Cavaliers (July 30, 1990). . . . Waived by Cavaliers (November 2, 1990). . . . Re-signed by Cavaliers to first of two consecutive 10-day contracts (December 31, 1990). . . . Re-signed by Cavaliers for remainder of season (January 21, 1991). . . . Signed as restricted free agent by Cavaliers (August 14, 1991).

COLLEGIATE RECORD

Season Team	G	Min.	FGM	FGA	Pct.	FTM	FTA	Pct.	Reb.	Pts.	Avg.
84-85 — South Plains	28	...	85	190	.447	21	29	.724	72	191	6.8
85-86 — South Plains	28	...	119	236	.504	72	98	.735	234	310	11.1
86-87 — St. Mary's (Tex.)	23	...	143	279	.513	41	57	.719	140	328	14.3
87-88 — St. Mary's (Tex.)	26	...	218	396	.551	136	158	.861	198	606	23.3
Junior college totals	56	...	204	426	.479	93	127	.732	306	501	8.9
Four-year-college totals	49	...	361	675	.535	177	215	.823	338	934	19.1

Three-point field goals: 1986-87, 1-for-2 (.500). 1987-88, 34-for-61 (.557). Totals, 35-for-63 (.556).

CBA REGULAR-SEASON RECORD

| | | | 2-POINT | | | 3-POINT | | | | | | | | |
Season Team	G	Min.	FGM	FGA	Pct.	FGM	FGA	Pct.	FTM	FTA	Pct.	Reb.	Ast.	Pts.	Avg.
88-89 — Wichita Falls ...	12	182	31	73	.425	9	23	.391	22	26	.846	40	5	111	9.3
90-91 — Wichita Falls ...	23	826	156	308	.506	31	92	.337	96	110	.873	179	35	501	21.8
Totals	35	1008	187	381	.491	40	115	.348	118	136	.868	219	40	612	17.5

Season Team	G	Min.	FGM	FGA	Pct.	FTM	FTA	Pct.	REBOUNDS Off.	Def.	Tot.	Ast.	PF	Dq.	Stl.	Blk.	TO	Pts.	Avg.
90-91 —Cleveland.....	37	505	112	254	.441	52	72	.722	26	53	79	32	59	1	15	5	37	300	8.1
91-92 —Cleveland.....	65	866	164	403	.407	61	76	.803	35	77	112	25	94	1	16	11	43	418	6.4
Totals	102	1371	276	657	.420	113	148	.764	61	130	191	57	153	2	31	16	80	718	7.0

Three-point field goals: 1990-91, 24-for-60 (.400). 1991-92, 29-for-90 (.322). Totals, 53-for-150 (.353).

NBA PLAYOFF RECORD

Season Team	G	Min.	FGM	FGA	Pct.	FTM	FTA	Pct.	REBOUNDS Off.	Def.	Tot.	Ast.	PF	Dq.	Stl.	Blk.	TO	Pts.	Avg.
91-92 —Cleveland.....	8	22	1	10	.100	2	4	.500	1	1	2	2	2	0	1	0	1	4	0.5

Three-point field goals: 1991-92, 0-for-3.

JEPSEN, LES

C, KINGS

PERSCNAL: Born June 24, 1967, in Bowbells, N.D. . . . 7-0/237. . . . Full name: Leslie Burnell Jepsen. **HIGH SCHOOL:** Bowbells (N.D.). **COLLEGE:** Iowa.

TRANSACTIONS/CAREER NOTES: Selected by Golden State Warriors in second round (28th pick overall) of 1990 NBA Draft. . . . Traded by Warriors with Mitch Richmond to Sacramento Kings for Billy Owens (November 1, 1991).

COLLEGIATE RECORD

Season Team	G	Min.	FGM	FGA	Pct.	FTM	FTA	Pct.	Reb.	Pts.	Avg.
85-86 —Iowa					Did not play—redshirted.						
86-87 —Iowa	15	46	5	11	.455	5	9	.556	16	15	1.0
87-88 —Iowa	26	114	10	27	.370	14	30	.467	39	35	1.3
88-89 —Iowa	33	666	53	94	.564	33	53	.623	175	139	4.2
89-90 —Iowa	28	818	155	249	.622	107	173	.619	281	417	14.9
Totals	102	1644	223	381	.585	159	265	.600	511	606	5.9

Three-point field goals: 1987-88, 1-for-1. 1988-89, 0-for-2. 1989-90, 0-for-1. Totals, 1-for-4 (.250).

NBA REGULAR-SEASON RECORD

Season Team	G	Min.	FGM	FGA	Pct.	FTM	FTA	Pct.	REBOUNDS Off.	Def.	Tot.	Ast.	PF	Dq.	Stl.	Blk.	TO	Pts.	Avg.
90-91 —Golden State	21	105	11	36	.306	6	9	.667	17	20	37	1	16	0	1	3	3	28	1.3
91-92 —Sacramento .	31	87	9	24	.375	7	11	.636	12	18	30	1	17	0	1	5	3	25	0.8
Totals	52	192	20	60	.333	13	20	.650	29	38	67	2	33	0	2	8	6	53	1.0

Three-point field goals: 1990-91, 0-for-1. 1991-92, 0-for-1. Totals, 0-for-2.

JOHNSON, AVERY

G, ROCKETS

PERSONAL: Born March 25, 1965, in New Orleans. . . . 5-11/175. **HIGH SCHOOL:** St. Augustine (New Orleans). **COLLEGE:** New Mexico Junior College, then Cameron (Okla.), then Southern (La.).

TRANSACTIONS/CAREER NOTES: Never drafted by an NBA franchise. . . . Signed as free agent by Seattle SuperSonics (August 2, 1988). . . . Traded by SuperSonics to Denver Nuggets for 1997 second-round draft choice (October 24, 1990). . . . Waived by Nuggets (December 24, 1990). . . . Signed as free agent by San Antonio Spurs (January 17, 1991). . . . Waived by Spurs (December 17, 1988). . . . Signed by Houston Rockets to first of two consecutive 10-day contracts (January 10, 1992). . . . Signed by Rockets for remainder of season (January 31, 1992).

COLLEGIATE RECORD

NOTES: Led NCAA Division I with 10.74 assists per game (1987) and 13.30 assists per game (1988).

Season Team	G	Min.	FGM	FGA	Pct.	FTM	FTA	Pct.	Reb.	Pts.	Avg.
83-84 —New Mexico Junior College......					Statistics unavailable.						
84-85 —Cameron	33	. . .		54	106	.509	34	55	.618	31	142	4.3
85-86 —Southern					Did not play—transfer student.						
86-87 —Southern	31	1111	86	196	.439	40	65	.615	73	219	7.1
87-88 —Southern	30	1145	138	257	.537	44	64	.688	84	342	11.4
Four-year-college totals	94	. . .	278	559	.497	118	184	.641	188	703	7.5

Three-point field goals: 1986-87, 7-for-24 (.292). 1987-88, 22-for-47 (.468). Totals, 29-for-71 (.408).

NBA REGULAR-SEASON RECORD

Season Team	G	Min.	FGM	FGA	Pct.	FTM	FTA	Pct.	REBOUNDS Off.	Def.	Tot.	Ast.	PF	Dq.	Stl.	Blk.	TO	Pts.	Avg.
88-89 —Seattle.........	43	291	29	83	.349	9	16	.563	11	13	24	73	34	0	21	3	18	68	1.6
89-90 —Seattle.........	53	575	55	142	.387	29	40	.725	21	22	43	162	55	0	26	1	48	140	2.6
90-91 —Denver-S.A...	68	959	130	277	.469	59	87	.678	22	55	77	230	62	0	47	4	74	320	4.7
91-92 —S.A.-Hou.....	69	1235	158	330	.479	66	101	.653	13	67	80	266	89	1	61	9	110	386	5.6
Totals	233	3060	372	832	.447	163	244	.668	67	157	224	731	240	1	155	17	250	914	3.9

Three-point field goals: 1988-89, 1-for-9 (.111). 1989-90, 1-for-4 (.250). 1990-91, 1-for-9 (.111). 1991-92, 4-for-15 (.267). Totals, 7-for-37 (.189).

NBA PLAYOFF RECORD

Season Team	G	Min.	FGM	FGA	Pct.	FTM	FTA	Pct.	REBOUNDS Off.	Def.	Tot.	Ast.	PF	Dq.	Stl.	Blk.	TO	Pts.	Avg.
88-89 —Seattle.........	6	31	5	12	.417	1	2	.500	2	2	4	5	1	0	4	0	0	11	1.8
90-91 —San Antonio .	3	19	0	5	.000	2	2	1.000	0	0	0	4	3	0	1	0	0	2	0.7
Totals	9	50	5	17	.294	3	4	.750	2	2	4	9	4	0	5	0	0	13	1.4

Three-point field goals: 1988-89, 0-for-4. 1990-91, 0-for-1. Totals, 0-for-5.

JOHNSON, BUCK

F

PERSONAL: Born January 3, 1964, in Birmingham, Ala. . . . 6-7/212. . . . Full name: Alfonso Johnson Jr.
HIGH SCHOOL: Hayes (Birmingham, Ala.).
COLLEGE: Alabama.
TRANSACTIONS/CAREER NOTES: Selected by Houston Rockets in first round (20th pick overall) of 1986 NBA Draft.

COLLEGIATE RECORD

Season Team	G	Min.	FGM	FGA	Pct.	FTM	FTA	Pct.	Reb.	Pts.	Avg.
82-83 — Alabama	32	834	104	217	.479	56	88	.636	144	264	8.3
83-84 — Alabama	28	1042	183	356	.514	111	152	.730	237	477	17.0
84-85 — Alabama	33	1172	209	373	.560	111	156	.712	310	529	16.0
85-86 — Alabama	29	1082	235	407	.577	129	155	.832	242	599	20.7
Totals	122	4130	731	1353	.540	407	551	.739	933	1869	15.3

NBA REGULAR-SEASON RECORD

Season Team	G	Min.	FGM	FGA	Pct.	FTM	FTA	Pct.	REBOUNDS Off.	REBOUNDS Def.	REBOUNDS Tot.	Ast.	PF	Dq.	Stl.	Blk.	TO	Pts.	Avg.
86-87 — Houston	60	520	94	201	.468	40	58	.690	38	50	88	40	81	0	17	15	37	228	3.8
87-88 — Houston	70	879	155	298	.520	67	91	.736	77	91	168	49	127	0	30	26	54	378	5.4
88-89 — Houston	67	1850	270	515	.524	101	134	.754	114	172	286	126	213	4	64	35	110	642	9.6
89-90 — Houston	82	2832	504	1019	.495	205	270	.759	113	268	381	252	321	8	104	62	167	1215	14.8
90-91 — Houston	73	2279	416	873	.477	157	216	.727	108	222	330	142	240	5	81	47	122	991	13.6
91-92 — Houston	80	2202	290	633	.458	104	143	.727	95	217	312	158	234	2	72	49	104	685	8.6
Totals	432	10562	1729	3539	.489	674	912	.739	545	1020	1565	767	1216	19	368	234	594	4139	9.6

Three-point field goals: 1986-87, 0-for-1. 1987-88, 1-for-8 (.125). 1988-89, 1-for-9 (.111). 1989-90, 2-for-17 (.118). 1990-91, 2-for-15 (.133). 1991-92, 1-for-9 (.111). Totals, 7-for-59 (.119).

NBA PLAYOFF RECORD

Season Team	G	Min.	FGM	FGA	Pct.	FTM	FTA	Pct.	REBOUNDS Off.	REBOUNDS Def.	REBOUNDS Tot.	Ast.	PF	Dq.	Stl.	Blk.	TO	Pts.	Avg.
86-87 — Houston	5	10	2	6	.333	0	0	...	0	0	0	0	1	0	0	0	2	4	0.8
87-88 — Houston	4	20	2	3	.667	1	2	.500	2	2	4	0	1	0	1	0	4	5	1.3
88-89 — Houston	4	118	19	40	.475	8	14	.571	6	8	14	12	15	0	3	2	6	46	11.5
89-90 — Houston	4	148	20	48	.417	11	13	.846	8	8	16	9	16	0	6	2	4	51	12.8
90-91 — Houston	3	86	10	28	.357	4	4	1.000	4	10	14	8	13	0	2	1	5	24	8.0
Totals	20	382	53	125	.424	24	33	.727	20	28	48	29	46	0	12	5	21	130	6.5

Three-point field goals: 1988-89, 0-for-1. 1989-90, 0-for-1. Totals, 0-for-2.

JOHNSON, EDDIE

F, SUPERSONICS

PERSONAL: Born May 1, 1959, in Chicago. . . . 6-7/215. . . . Full name: Edward A. Johnson.
HIGH SCHOOL: Westinghouse Vocational (Chicago).
COLLEGE: Illinois.
TRANSACTIONS/CAREER NOTES: Selected by Kansas City Kings in second round (29th pick overall) of 1981 NBA Draft. . . . Kings franchise moved from Kansas City to Sacramento for 1985-86 season. . . . Traded by Kings to Phoenix Suns for Ed Pinckney and 1988 second-round draft choice (June 21, 1987). . . . Traded by Suns with 1991 first-round draft choice and 1993 or 1994 first-round draft choice to Seattle SuperSonics for Xavier McDaniel (December 7, 1990).

COLLEGIATE RECORD

Season Team	G	Min.	FGM	FGA	Pct.	FTM	FTA	Pct.	Reb.	Pts.	Avg.
77-78 — Illinois	27	469	100	234	.427	20	27	.741	84	220	8.1
78-79 — Illinois	30	786	168	405	.415	26	49	.531	170	362	12.1
79-80 — Illinois	35	1215	266	576	.462	78	119	.655	310	610	17.4
80-81 — Illinois	29	1009	219	443	.494	62	82	.756	267	500	17.2
Totals	121	3479	753	1658	.454	186	277	.671	831	1692	14.0

NBA REGULAR-SEASON RECORD

HONORS: NBA Sixth Man Award (1989).

Season Team	G	Min.	FGM	FGA	Pct.	FTM	FTA	Pct.	REBOUNDS Off.	REBOUNDS Def.	REBOUNDS Tot.	Ast.	PF	Dq.	Stl.	Blk.	TO	Pts.	Avg.
81-82 — Kansas City	74	1517	295	643	.459	99	149	.664	128	194	322	109	210	6	50	14	97	690	9.3
82-83 — Kansas City	82	2933	677	1370	.494	247	317	.779	191	310	501	216	259	3	70	20	181	1621	19.8
83-84 — Kansas City	82	2920	753	1552	.485	268	331	.810	165	290	455	296	266	4	76	21	213	1794	21.9
84-85 — Kansas City	82	3029	769	1565	.491	325	373	.871	151	256	407	273	237	2	83	22	225	1876	22.9
85-86 — Sacramento	82	2514	623	1311	.475	280	343	.816	173	246	419	214	237	0	54	17	191	1530	18.7
86-87 — Sacramento	81	2457	606	1309	.463	267	322	.829	146	207	353	251	218	4	42	19	163	1516	18.7
87-88 — Phoenix	73	2177	533	1110	.480	204	240	.850	121	197	318	180	190	0	33	9	139	1294	17.7
88-89 — Phoenix	70	2043	608	1224	.497	217	250	.868	91	215	306	162	198	0	47	7	122	1504	21.5
89-90 — Phoenix	64	1811	411	907	.453	188	205	.917	69	177	246	107	174	4	32	10	108	1080	16.9
90-91 — Phoe.-Sea.	81	2085	543	1122	.484	229	257	.891	107	164	271	111	181	0	58	9	122	1354	16.7
91-92 — Seattle	81	2366	534	1164	.459	291	338	.861	118	174	292	161	199	0	55	11	130	1386	17.1
Totals	852	25852	6352	13277	.478	2615	3125	.837	1460	2430	3890	2080	2369	23	600	159	1691	15645	18.4

Three-point field goals: 1981-82, 1-for-11 (.091). 1982-83, 20-for-71 (.282). 1983-84, 20-for-64 (.313). 1984-85, 13-for-54 (.241). 1985-86, 4-for-20 (.200). 1986-87, 37-for-118 (.314). 1987-88, 24-for-94 (.255). 1988-89, 71-for-172 (.413). 1989-90, 70-for-184 (.380). 1990-91, 39-for-120 (.325). 1991-92, 27-for-107 (.252). Totals, 326-for-1015 (.321).

NBA PLAYOFF RECORD

								— REBOUNDS —										
Season	Team	G	Min.	FGM	FGA	Pct.	FTM	FTA	Pct.	Off.	Def.	Tot.	Ast.	PF	Dq.	Stl.	Blk.	TO	Pts.	Avg.
83-84—Kansas City .		3	107	21	48	.438	7	7	1.000	4	6	10	12	8	0	3	1	2	51	17.0
85-86—Sacramento .		3	96	24	55	.436	8	9	.889	10	11	21	4	7	0	3	1	6	56	18.7
88-89—Phoenix.......		12	392	85	206	.413	30	39	.769	28	59	87	25	41	1	12	2	18	213	17.8
89-90—Phoenix.......		16	337	72	160	.450	37	47	.787	15	42	57	17	40	0	10	4	20	196	12.3
90-91—Seattle.........		5	171	46	89	.517	24	29	.828	12	9	21	7	13	0	7	1	8	120	24.0
91-92—Seattle.........		9	247	65	137	.474	32	34	.941	8	19	27	8	19	0	3	3	15	166	18.4
Totals		48	1350	313	695	.450	138	165	.836	77	146	223	73	128	1	38	12	69	802	16.7

Three-point field goals: 1983-84, 2-for-5 (.400). 1985-86, 0-for-3. 1988-89, 13-for-38 (.342). 1989-90, 15-for-38 (.395). 1990-91, 4-for-15 (.267). 1991-92, 4-for-22 (.182). Totals, 38-for-121 (.314).

JOHNSON, KEVIN
G, SUNS

PERSONAL: Born March 4, 1966, in Sacramento, Calif. . . . 6-1/190. . . . Full name: Kevin Maurice Johnson. **HIGH SCHOOL:** Sacramento (Calif.). **COLLEGE:** California.

TRANSACTIONS/CAREER NOTES: Selected by Cleveland Cavaliers in first round (seventh pick overall) of 1987 NBA Draft. . . . Traded by Cavaliers with Tyrone Corbin, Mark West, 1988 first- and second-round draft choices and 1989 second-round draft choice to Phoenix Suns for Larry Nance, Mike Sanders and 1988 second-round draft choice (February 25, 1988).

COLLEGIATE RECORD

Season	Team	G	Min.	FGM	FGA	Pct.	FTM	FTA	Pct.	Reb.	Pts.	Avg.
83-84—California.............................		28	...	98	192	.510	75	104	.721	83	271	9.7
84-85—California.............................		27	...	127	282	.450	94	142	.662	104	348	12.9
85-86—California.............................		29	...	164	335	.490	123	151	.815	104	451	15.6
86-87—California.............................		34	...	212	450	.471	113	138	.819	132	585	17.2
Totals		118	...	601	1259	.477	405	535	.757	423	1655	14.0

Three-point field goals: 1986-87, 48-for-124 (.387).

NBA REGULAR-SEASON RECORD

HONORS: NBA Most Improved Player (1989). . . . All-NBA second team (1989, 1990, 1991). . . . All-NBA third team (1992).

								— REBOUNDS —										
Season	Team	G	Min.	FGM	FGA	Pct.	FTM	FTA	Pct.	Off.	Def.	Tot.	Ast.	PF	Dq.	Stl.	Blk.	TO	Pts.	Avg.
87-88—Clev.-Phoe...		80	1917	275	596	.461	177	211	.839	36	155	191	437	155	1	103	24	146	732	9.2
88-89—Phoenix........		81	3179	570	1128	.505	508	576	.882	46	294	340	991	226	1	135	24	*322	1650	20.4
89-90—Phoenix........		74	2782	578	1159	.499	501	598	.838	42	228	270	846	143	0	95	14	263	1665	22.5
90-91—Phoenix........		77	2772	591	1145	.516	519	616	.843	54	217	271	781	174	0	163	11	269	1710	22.2
91-92—Phoenix........		78	2899	539	1125	.479	448	555	.807	61	.231	292	836	180	0	116	23	272	1536	19.7
Totals		390	13549	2553	5153	.495	2153	2556	.842	239	1125	1364	3891	878	2	612	96	1272	7293	18.7

Three-point field goals: 1987-88, 5-for-24 (.208). 1988-89, 2-for-22 (.091). 1989-90, 8-for-41 (.195). 1990-91, 9-for-44 (.205). 1991-92, 10-for-46 (.217). Totals, 34-for-177 (.192).

NBA PLAYOFF RECORD

								— REBOUNDS —										
Season	Team	G	Min.	FGM	FGA	Pct.	FTM	FTA	Pct.	Off.	Def.	Tot.	Ast.	PF	Dq.	Stl.	Blk.	TO	Pts.	Avg.
88-89—Phoenix........		12	494	90	182	.495	102	110	.927	12	39	51	147	28	0	19	5	55	285	23.8
89-90—Phoenix........		16	582	123	257	.479	92	112	.821	9	44	53	170	28	0	25	0	62	340	21.3
90-91—Phoenix........		4	146	16	53	.302	18	30	.600	2	11	13	39	9	0	2	1	12	51	12.8
91-92—Phoenix........		8	335	62	128	.484	62	72	.861	8	25	33	93	24	1	12	2	25	189	23.6
Totals		40	1557	291	620	.469	274	324	.846	31	119	150	449	89	1	58	8	154	865	21.6

Three-point field goals: 1988-89, 3-for-10 (.300). 1989-90, 2-for-11 (.182). 1990-91, 1-for-7 (.143). 1991-92, 3-for-6 (.500). Totals, 9-for-34 (.265).

NBA ALL-STAR GAME RECORD

								— REBOUNDS —							
Season	Team	Min.	FGM	FGA	Pct.	FTM	FTA	Pct.	Off.	Def.	Tot.	Ast.	PF	Dq.	Stl.	Blk.	TO	Pts.
1990 —Phoenix..............		14	1	1	1.000	0	0	...	0	0	0	4	2	0	0	0	3	2
1991 —Phoenix..............		23	2	5	.400	1	2	.500	1	1	2	7	2	0	3	1	3	5
Totals		37	3	6	.500	1	2	.500	1	1	2	11	4	0	3	1	6	7

RECORD AS BASEBALL PLAYER

TRANSACTIONS/CAREER NOTES: Selected by Oakland Athletics organization in 23rd round of free-agent draft (June 2, 1986).

						—BATTING								—FIELDING			
Year	Team (League)	Pos.	G	AB	R	H	2B	3B	HR	RBI	Avg.	SB	PO	A	E	Avg.
1986 —Modesto (California)		SS	2	2	1	0	0	0	0	0	.000	0	1	2	1	.750

JOHNSON, LARRY
F, HORNETS

PERSONAL: Born March 14, 1969, in Tyler, Tex. . . . 6-7/250. . . . Full name: Larry Demetric Johnson. **HIGH SCHOOL:** Skyline (Dallas). **COLLEGE:** Odessa Junior College (Tex.), then UNLV.

TRANSACTIONS/CAREER NOTES: Selected by Charlotte Hornets in first round (first pick overall) of 1991 NBA Draft.

COLLEGIATE RECORD

NOTES: The Sporting News College Player of the Year (1991). . . . The Sporting News All-America first team (1990, 1991). . . . Member of NCAA Division I championship team (1990).

Season Team	G	Min.	FGM	FGA	Pct.	FTM	FTA	Pct.	Reb.	Pts.	Avg.
87-88 — Odessa Junior College	35	...	324	499	.649	131	167	.784	430	779	22.3
88-89 — Odessa Junior College	35	...	422	646	.653	196	258	.760	380	1043	29.8
89-90 — UNLV	40	1259	304	487	.624	201	262	.767	457	822	20.6
90-91 — UNLV	35	1113	308	465	.662	162	198	.818	380	795	22.7
Junior college totals	70		746	1145	.652	327	425	.769	810	1822	26.0
Four-year-college totals	75	2372	612	952	.643	363	460	.789	837	1617	21.6

Three-point field goals: 1989-90, 13-for-38 (.342). 1990-91, 17-for-48 (.354). Totals, 30-for-86 (.349).

NBA REGULAR-SEASON RECORD

HONORS: NBA Rookie of the Year (1992).... NBA All-Rookie first team (1992).

Season Team	G	Min.	FGM	FGA	Pct.	FTM	FTA	Pct.	— REBOUNDS — Off.	Def.	Tot.	Ast.	PF	Dq.	Stl.	Blk.	TO	Pts.	Avg.
91-92 — Charlotte......	82	3047	616	1258	.490	339	409	.829	323	576	899	292	225	3	81	51	160	1576	19.2

Three-point field goals: 1991-92, 5-for-22 (.227).

JOHNSON, MAGIC

G, LAKERS

PERSONAL: Born August 14, 1959, in Lansing, Mich. ... 6-9/225. ... Full name: Earvin Johnson Jr.
HIGH SCHOOL: Everett (Lansing, Mich.).
COLLEGE: Michigan State.
TRANSACTIONS/CAREER NOTES: Selected as undergraduate by Los Angeles Lakers in first round (first pick overall) of 1979 NBA Draft.
MISCELLANEOUS: Member of NBA championship teams (1980, 1982, 1985, 1987, 1988).... Member of gold-medal-winning U.S. Olympic team (1992).

COLLEGIATE RECORD

NOTES: THE SPORTING NEWS All-America first team (1979). ... NCAA Division I Tournament Most Outstanding Player (1979). ... Member of NCAA championship team (1979).

Season Team	G	Min.	FGM	FGA	Pct.	FTM	FTA	Pct.	Reb.	Pts.	Avg.
77-78 — Michigan State	30	...	175	382	.458	161	205	.785	237	511	17.0
78-79 — Michigan State	32	1159	173	370	.468	202	240	.842	234	548	17.1
Totals	62	...	348	752	.463	363	445	.816	471	1059	17.1

NBA REGULAR-SEASON RECORD

RECORDS: Holds career records for most assists—9,921; and highest assists-per-game average (minimum 400 games)—11.4.
HONORS: NBA Most Valuable Player (1987, 1989, 1990). ... Schick Award, for all-around contributions to team's success (1984).... Citizenship Award (1992).... All-NBA first team (1983, 1984, 1985, 1986, 1987, 1988, 1989, 1990, 1991).... All-NBA second team (1982).... NBA All-Rookie team (1980).
NOTES: Led NBA with 10.5 assists per game (1983), 13.1 assists per game (1984), 12.6 assists per game (1986) and 12.2 assists per game (1987).... Led NBA with 3.43 steals per game (1981) and 2.67 steals per game (1982).

Season Team	G	Min.	FGM	FGA	Pct.	FTM	FTA	Pct.	— REBOUNDS — Off.	Def.	Tot.	Ast.	PF	Dq.	Stl.	Blk.	TO	Pts.	Avg.
79-80 — Los Angeles ..	77	2795	503	949	.530	374	462	.810	166	430	596	563	218	1	187	41	305	1387	18.0
80-81 — Los Angeles ..	37	1371	312	587	.532	171	225	.760	101	219	320	317	100	0	127	27	143	798	21.6
81-82 — Los Angeles ..	78	2991	556	1036	.537	329	433	.760	252	499	751	743	223	1	208	34	286	1447	18.6
82-83 — Los Angeles ..	79	2907	511	933	.548	304	380	.800	214	469	683	*829	200	1	176	47	301	1326	16.8
83-84 — Los Angeles ..	67	2567	441	780	.565	290	358	.810	99	392	491	875	169	1	150	49	306	1178	17.6
84-85 — L.A. Lakers ..	77	2781	504	899	.561	391	464	.843	90	386	476	968	155	0	113	25	305	1406	18.3
85-86 — L.A. Lakers ..	72	2578	483	918	.526	378	434	.871	85	341	426	*907	133	0	113	16	273	1354	18.8
86-87 — L.A. Lakers ..	80	2904	683	1308	.522	535	631	.848	122	382	504	*977	168	0	138	36	300	1909	23.9
87-88 — L.A. Lakers ..	72	2637	490	996	.492	417	489	.853	88	361	449	858	147	0	114	13	269	1408	19.6
88-89 — L.A. Lakers ..	77	2886	579	1137	.509	513	563	*.911	111	496	607	988	172	0	138	22	312	1730	22.5
89-90 — L.A. Lakers ..	79	2937	546	1138	.480	567	637	.890	128	394	522	907	167	1	132	34	289	1765	22.3
90-91 — L.A. Lakers ..	79	2933	466	976	.477	519	573	.906	105	446	551	989	150	0	102	17	*314	1531	19.4
91-92 — L.A. Lakers ..								Did not play—medical reasons.											
Totals	874	32287	6074	11657	.521	4788	5649	.848	1561	4815	6376	9921	2002	5	1698	361	3403	17239	19.7

Three-point field goals: 1979-80, 7-for-31 (.226). 1980-81, 3-for-17 (.176). 1981-82, 6-for-29 (.207). 1982-83, 0-for-21. 1983-84, 6-for-29 (.207). 1984-85, 7-for-37 (.189). 1985-86, 10-for-43 (.233). 1986-87, 8-for-39 (.205). 1987-88, 11-for-56 (.196). 1988-89, 59-for-188 (.314). 1989-90, 106-for-276 (.384). 1990-91, 80-for-250 (.320). Totals, 303-for-1016 (.298).

NBA PLAYOFF RECORD

NOTES: NBA Finals Most Valuable Player (1980, 1982, 1987). ... Holds career record for most assists—2,320; and most steals—358. ... Holds NBA Finals records for highest assists-per-game average—14.0 (1985); and highest assists-per-game average by a rookie—8.7 (1980). ... Holds NBA Finals single-game records for most points by a rookie—42 (May 16, 1980, vs. Philadelphia); most assists—21 (June 3, 1984, vs. Boston); most assists by a rookie—11 (May 7, 1980, vs. Philadelphia); and most assists in one half—14 (June 19, 1988, vs. Detroit); ... Shares NBA Finals single-game record for most assists in one quarter—8 (four times). ... Holds single-series record for highest assists-per-game average—17.0 (1985). ... Holds single-game records for most free throws attempted in one half—21 (May 8, 1991, vs. Golden State); and most assists in one quarter—10 (May 22, 1985, vs. Denver; April 27, 1991, vs. Houston; and May 18, 1991, vs. Portland). ... Shares single-game record for most free throws made in one half—19 (May 8, 1991, vs. Golden State); most assists—24 (May 15, 1984, vs. Phoenix); and most assists in one half—15 (May 3, 1985, vs. Portland).

Season Team	G	Min.	FGM	FGA	Pct.	FTM	FTA	Pct.	— REBOUNDS — Off.	Def.	Tot.	Ast.	PF	Dq.	Stl.	Blk.	TO	Pts.	Avg.
79-80 — Los Angeles .	16	658	103	199	.518	85	106	.802	52	116	168	151	47	1	49	6	65	293	18.3
80-81 — Los Angeles .	3	127	19	49	.388	13	20	.650	8	33	41	21	14	1	8	3	11	51	17.0
81-82 — Los Angeles .	14	562	83	157	.529	77	93	.828	54	104	158	130	50	0	40	3	44	243	17.4
82-83 — Los Angeles .	15	643	100	206	.485	68	81	.840	51	77	128	192	49	0	34	12	64	268	17.9
83-84 — Los Angeles .	21	837	151	274	.551	80	100	.800	26	113	139	284	71	0	42	20	79	382	18.2
84-85 — L.A. Lakers ..	19	687	116	226	.513	100	118	.847	19	115	134	289	48	0	32	4	76	333	17.5

Season Team	G	Min.	FGM	FGA	Pct.	FTM	FTA	Pct.	Off.	Def.	Tot.	Ast.	PF	Dq.	Stl.	Blk.	TO	Pts.	Avg.
85-86 —L.A. Lakers ..	14	541	110	205	.537	82	107	.766	21	79	100	211	43	0	27	1	45	302	21.6
86-87 —L.A. Lakers ..	18	666	146	271	.539	98	118	.831	28	111	139	219	37	0	31	7	51	392	21.8
87-88 —L.A. Lakers ..	24	965	169	329	.514	132	155	.852	32	98	130	303	61	0	34	4	83	477	19.9
88-89 —L.A. Lakers ..	14	518	85	174	.489	78	86	.907	15	68	83	165	30	1	27	3	53	258	18.4
89-90 —L.A. Lakers ..	9	376	76	155	.490	70	79	.886	12	45	57	115	28	0	11	1	36	227	25.2
90-91 —L.A. Lakers ..	19	823	118	268	.440	157	178	.882	23	131	154	240	43	0	23	0	77	414	21.8
Totals	186	7403	1276	2513	.508	1040	1241	.838	341	1090	1431	2320	521	3	358	64	684	3640	19.6

Three-point field goals: 1979-80, 2-for-8 (.250). 1981-82, 0-for-4. 1982-83, 0-for-11. 1983-84, 0-for-7. 1984-85, 1-for-7 (.143). 1985-86, 0-for-11. 1986-87, 2-for-10 (.200). 1987-88, 7-for-14 (.500). 1988-89, 10-for-35 (.286). 1989-90, 5-for-25 (.200). 1990-91, 21-for-71 (.296). Totals, 48-for-203 (.236).

NBA ALL-STAR GAME RECORD

NOTES: NBA All-Star Game Most Valuable Player (1990, 1992). . . . Holds career record for most assists—127; most three-point field goals made—10; and most three-point field goals attempted—22. . . . Holds single-game record for most assists—22 (1984).

Season Team	Min.	FGM	FGA	Pct.	FTM	FTA	Pct.	Off.	Def.	Tot.	Ast.	PF	Dq.	Stl.	Blk.	TO	Pts.
1980 —Los Angeles	24	5	8	.625	2	2	1.000	2	0	2	4	3	0	3	2	2	12
1982 —Los Angeles	23	5	9	.556	6	7	.857	3	1	4	7	5	0	0	0	1	16
1983 —Los Angeles	33	7	16	.438	3	4	.750	3	2	5	16	2	0	5	0	7	17
1984 —Los Angeles	37	6	13	.462	2	2	1.000	4	5	9	22	3	0	3	2	4	15
1985 —L.A. Lakers	31	7	14	.500	7	8	.875	2	3	5	15	2	0	1	0	3	21
1986 —L.A. Lakers	28	1	3	.333	4	4	1.000	0	4	4	15	4	0	1	0	9	6
1987 —L.A. Lakers	34	4	10	.400	1	2	.500	1	6	7	13	2	0	4	0	1	9
1988 —L.A. Lakers	39	4	15	.267	9	9	1.000	1	5	6	19	2	0	2	2	8	17
1989 —L.A. Lakers						Did not play—injured.											
1990 —L.A. Lakers	25	9	15	.600	0	0	. . .	1	5	6	4	1	0	0	1	3	22
1991 —L.A. Lakers	28	7	16	.438	0	0	. . .	1	3	4	3	1	0	0	0	3	16
1992 —L.A. Lakers	29	9	12	.750	4	4	1.000	3	2	5	9	0	0	2	0	7	25
Totals	331	64	131	.489	38	42	.905	21	36	57	127	25	0	21	7	48	176

Three-point field goals: 1980, 0-for-1. 1983, 0-for-2. 1984, 1-for-3 (.333). 1986, 0-for-1. 1988, 0-for-1. 1990, 4-for-6 (.667). 1991, 2-for-5 (.400). 1992, 3-for-3. Totals, 10-for-22 (.455).

JOHNSON, VINNIE
G

PERSONAL: Born September 1, 1956, in Brooklyn, N.Y. . . . 6-2/200. . . . Full name: Vincent Johnson. . . . Brother of Eric Johnson, guard with Utah Jazz (1989-90).
HIGH SCHOOL: Franklin D. Roosevelt (Brooklyn, N.Y.).
COLLEGE: McLennan Community College (Tex.), then Baylor.
TRANSACTIONS/CAREER NOTES: Selected by Seattle SuperSonics in first round (seventh pick overall) of 1979 NBA Draft. . . . Traded by SuperSonics to Detroit Pistons for Greg Kelser (November 23, 1981). . . . Waived by Pistons (September 4, 1991). . . . Signed as free agent by San Antonio Spurs (December 12, 1991).
MISCELLANEOUS: Member of NBA championship teams (1989, 1990).

COLLEGIATE RECORD

Season Team	G	Min.	FGM	FGA	Pct.	FTM	FTA	Pct.	Reb.	Pts.	Avg.
75-76 —McLennan C.C.	35	...	398	...	...	169	...	...	...	965	27.6
76-77 —McLennan C.C.	31	...	382	...	...	152	...	...	...	916	29.5
77-78 —Baylor	25	...	241	481	.501	93	141	.660	140	575	23.0
78-79 —Baylor	26	...	262	502	.522	132	170	.776	128	656	25.2
Junior college totals	66	...	780	...	...	321	...	...	...	1881	28.5
Four-year-college totals	51	...	503	983	.512	225	311	.723	268	1231	24.1

NBA REGULAR-SEASON RECORD

Season Team	G	Min.	FGM	FGA	Pct.	FTM	FTA	Pct.	Off.	Def.	Tot.	Ast.	PF	Dq.	Stl.	Blk.	TO	Pts.	Avg.
79-80 —Seattle.........	38	325	45	115	.391	31	39	.795	19	36	55	54	40	0	19	4	42	121	3.2
80-81 —Seattle.........	81	2311	419	785	.534	214	270	.793	193	173	366	341	198	0	78	20	216	1053	13.0
81-82 —Seattle-Det...	74	1295	217	444	.489	107	142	.754	82	77	159	171	101	0	56	25	96	544	7.4
82-83 —Detroit.........	82	2511	520	1013	.513	245	315	.778	167	186	353	301	263	2	93	49	152	1296	15.8
83-84 —Detroit.........	82	1909	426	901	.473	207	275	.753	130	107	237	271	196	1	44	19	135	1063	13.0
84-85 —Detroit.........	82	2093	428	942	.454	190	247	.769	134	118	252	325	205	0	71	20	135	1051	12.8
85-86 —Detroit.........	79	1978	465	946	.467	165	214	.771	119	107	226	269	180	2	80	23	88	1097	13.9
86-87 —Detroit.........	78	2166	533	1154	.462	158	201	.786	123	134	257	300	159	0	92	16	133	1228	15.7
87-88 —Detroit.........	82	1935	425	959	.443	147	217	.677	90	141	231	267	164	0	58	18	152	1002	12.2
88-89 —Detroit.........	82	2073	462	996	.464	193	263	.734	109	146	255	242	155	0	74	17	105	1130	13.8
89-90 —Detroit.........	82	1972	334	775	.431	131	196	.668	108	148	256	255	143	0	71	13	123	804	9.8
90-91 —Detroit.........	82	2390	406	936	.434	135	209	.646	110	170	280	271	166	0	75	15	118	958	11.7
91-92 —San Antonio.	60	1350	202	499	.405	55	85	.647	67	115	182	145	93	0	41	14	74	478	8.0
Totals	984	24308	4882	10515	.464	1978	2673	.740	1451	1658	3109	3212	2063	7	852	253	1569	11825	12.0

Three-point field goals: 1979-80, 0-for-1. 1980-81, 1-for-5 (.200). 1981-82, 3-for-12 (.250). 1982-83, 11-for-40 (.275). 1983-84, 4-for-19 (.211). 1984-85, 5-for-27 (.185). 1985-86, 2-for-13 (.154). 1986-87, 4-for-14 (.286). 1987-88, 5-for-24 (.208). 1988-89, 13-for-44 (.295). 1989-90, 5-for-34 (.147). 1990-91, 11-for-34 (.324). 1991-92, 19-for-60 (.317). Totals, 83-for-327 (.254).

NBA PLAYOFF RECORD

Season Team	G	Min.	FGM	FGA	Pct.	FTM	FTA	Pct.	Off.	Def.	Tot.	Ast.	PF	Dq.	Stl.	Blk.	TO	Pts.	Avg.
79-80 —Seattle.........	5	12	1	3	.333	0	0	. . .	0	2	2	2	1	0	1	0	0	2	0.4
83-84 —Detroit.........	5	132	17	46	.370	17	19	.895	5	9	14	12	9	0	1	1	4	51	10.2
84-85 —Detroit.........	9	235	53	103	.515	22	28	.786	15	12	27	29	24	0	6	1	15	128	14.2
85-86 —Detroit.........	4	85	22	49	.449	7	13	.538	8	9	17	11	9	0	3	0	5	51	12.8

Season Team	G	Min.	FGM	FGA	Pct.	FTM	FTA	Pct.	— REBOUNDS — Off.	Def.	Tot.	Ast.	PF	Dq.	Stl.	Blk.	TO	Pts.	Avg.
86-87—Detroit.........	15	388	95	207	.459	31	36	.861	20	24	44	62	33	0	9	4	23	221	14.7
87-88—Detroit.........	23	477	101	239	.423	33	50	.660	35	40	75	43	48	0	17	4	21	236	10.3
88-89—Detroit.........	17	372	91	200	.455	47	62	.758	16	29	45	43	32	0	4	3	21	239	14.1
89-90—Detroit.........	20	463	85	184	.462	34	43	.791	28	28	56	54	38	0	8	4	31	206	10.3
90-91—Detroit.........	15	438	102	220	.464	22	31	.710	37	39	76	43	33	0	11	4	17	228	15.2
91-92—San Antonio.	3	69	11	24	.458	1	2	.500	3	5	8	7	7	0	5	1	5	25	8.3
Totals	116	2671	578	1275	.453	214	284	.754	167	197	364	306	234	0	65	22	142	1387	12.0

Three-point field goals: 1983-84, 0-for-1. 1984-85, 0-for-3. 1985-86, 0-for-1. 1986-87, 0-for-2. 1987-88, 1-for-7 (.143). 1988-89, 10-for-24 (.417). 1989-90, 2-for-7 (.286). 1991-92, 2-for-4 (.500). Totals, 15-for-49 (.306).

J

JONES, CHARLES
F/C, BULLETS

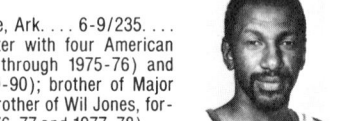

PERSONAL: Born April 3, 1957, in McGehee, Ark. . . . 6-9/235. . . . Brother of Caldwell Jones, forward/center with four American Basketball Association teams (1973-74 through 1975-76) and four NBA teams (1976-77 through 1989-90); brother of Major Jones, forward/center with two NBA teams (1979-80 through 1984-85); and brother of Wil Jones, forward with three ABA teams (1969-70 through 1975-76) and two NBA teams (1976-77 and 1977-78).
HIGH SCHOOL: Delta (Rohwer, Ark.).
COLLEGE: Albany State (Ga.).
TRANSACTIONS/CAREER NOTES: Selected by Phoenix Suns in eighth round (165th pick overall) of 1979 NBA Draft. . . . Waived by Suns (October 1, 1979). . . . Played in Continental Basketball Association with Maine Lumberjacks (1979-80 and 1982-83), Bay State Bombardiers (1983-84), and Tampa Bay Thrillers (1984-85). . . . Signed as free agent by Portland Trail Blazers (April 14, 1980). . . . Waived by Trail Blazers (July 21, 1980). . . . Played in France (1980-81). . . . Played in Italy (1981-82). . . . Signed as free agent by New York Knicks (September 30, 1983). . . . Waived by Knicks (October 24, 1983). . . . Signed by Philadelphia 76ers to first of two consecutive 10-day contracts (February 1984). . . . Signed as free agent by San Antonio Spurs (May 2, 1984). . . . Waived by Spurs (September 11, 1984). . . . Signed as free agent by Chicago Bulls (September 20, 1984). . . . Waived by Bulls (November 16, 1984). . . . Signed as free agent by Washington Bullets (February 14, 1985).

COLLEGIATE RECORD

Season Team	G	Min.	FGM	FGA	Pct.	FTM	FTA	Pct.	Reb.	Pts.	Avg.
75-76—Albany State............................	24	. . .	106	206	.515	16	35	.457	198	228	9.5
76-77—Albany State............................	27	. . .	136	284	.479	39	84	.464	374	311	11.5
77-78—Albany State............................	27	. . .	148	276	.536	68	100	.680	368	364	13.5
78-79—Albany State............................	29	. . .	182	352	.517	66	97	.680	438	430	14.8
Totals	107	. . .	572	1118	.512	189	316	.598	1378	1333	12.5

CBA REGULAR-SEASON RECORD

NOTES: Led CBA with 185 blocked shots (1980) and 130 blocked shots (1984). . . . Led CBA with 4.7 blocked shots per game (1980), 4.0 blocked shots per game (1983) and 3.5 blocked shots per game (1984). . . . CBA All-Star second team (1984). . . . CBA All-Defensive first team (1983, 1984). . . . CBA All-Defensive second team (1985).

Season Team	G	Min.	2-POINT FGM	FGA	Pct.	3-POINT FGM	FGA	Pct.	FTM	FTA	Pct.	Reb.	Ast.	Pts.	Avg.
79-80—Maine	39	1606	222	459	.484	0	2	.000	60	94	.638	506	70	504	12.9
82-83—Maine	24	914	105	215	.488	0	1	.000	70	89	.787	223	35	280	11.7
83-84—Bay State	37	1365	149	297	.502	0	1	.000	94	139	.676	293	73	392	10.6
84-85—Tampa Bay	24	802	80	154	.519	0	1	.000	38	53	.717	227	38	198	8.3
Totals	124	4687	556	1125	.494	0	5	.000	262	375	.699	1249	216	1374	11.1

ITALIAN LEAGUE RECORD

Season Team	G	Min.	FGM	FGA	Pct.	FTM	FTA	Pct.	Reb.	Pts.	Avg.
81-82—S. Benedetto................	38	1458	215	398	.540	73	114	.640	429	503	13.2

NBA REGULAR-SEASON RECORD

Season Team	G	Min.	FGM	FGA	Pct.	FTM	FTA	Pct.	— REBOUNDS — Off.	Def.	Tot.	Ast.	PF	Dq.	Stl.	Blk.	TO	Pts.	Avg.
83-84—Philadelphia.	1	3	0	1	.000	1	4	.250	0	0	0	0	1	0	0	0	0	1	1.0
84-85—Chi.-Wash...	31	667	67	127	.528	40	58	.690	71	113	184	26	107	3	22	79	25	174	5.6
85-86—Washington	81	1609	129	254	.508	54	86	.628	122	199	321	76	235	2	57	133	71	312	3.9
86-87—Washington	79	1609	118	249	.474	48	76	.632	144	212	356	80	252	2	67	165	77	284	3.6
87-88—Washington	69	1313	72	177	.407	53	75	.707	106	219	325	59	226	5	53	113	57	197	2.9
88-89—Washington	53	1154	60	125	.480	16	25	.640	77	180	257	42	187	4	39	76	39	136	2.6
89-90—Washington	81	2240	94	185	.508	68	105	.648	145	359	504	139	296	10	50	197	76	256	3.2
90-91—Washington	62	1499	67	124	.540	29	50	.580	119	240	359	48	199	2	51	124	46	163	2.6
91-92—Washington	75	1365	33	90	.367	20	40	.500	105	212	317	62	214	0	43	92	39	86	1.1
Totals	532	11459	640	1332	.480	329	519	.634	889	1734	2623	532	1717	28	382	979	430	1609	3.0

Three-point field goals: 1985-86, 0-for-2. 1986-87, 0-for-1. 1987-88, 0-for-1. 1988-89, 0-for-1. Totals, 0-for-5.

NBA PLAYOFF RECORD

Season Team	G	Min.	FGM	FGA	Pct.	FTM	FTA	Pct.	— REBOUNDS — Off.	Def.	Tot.	Ast.	PF	Dq.	Stl.	Blk.	TO	Pts.	Avg.
84-85—Washington .	4	110	10	19	.526	9	16	.563	11	15	26	3	16	0	3	10	6	29	7.3
85-86—Washington .	5	72	4	11	.364	4	4	1.000	6	3	9	3	13	0	2	2	5	12	2.4
86-87—Washington .	3	56	3	5	.600	0	0	. . .	1	7	8	3	9	0	2	5	1	6	2.0
87-88—Washington .	5	95	1	5	.200	1	2	.500	5	12	17	2	18	0	2	4	0	3	0.6
Totals	17	333	18	40	.450	14	22	.636	23	37	60	11	56	0	9	21	12	50	2.9

DID YOU KNOW. . .

. . . that Moses Malone has not fouled out of a game since January 7, 1978?

JORDAN, MICHAEL
G, BULLS

PERSONAL: Born February 17, 1963, in Brooklyn, N.Y. . . . 6-6/ 198. . . . Full name: Michael Jeffrey Jordan.
HIGH SCHOOL: Emsley A. Laney (Wilmington, N.C.).
COLLEGE: North Carolina.
TRANSACTIONS/CAREER NOTES: Selected by Chicago Bulls in first round (third pick overall) of 1984 NBA Draft.
MISCELLANEOUS: Member of NBA championship teams (1991, 1992). . . . Member of gold-medal-winning U.S. Olympic teams (1984, 1992).

COLLEGIATE RECORD

NOTES: THE SPORTING NEWS College Player of the Year (1983, 1984). . . . THE SPORTING NEWS All-America first team (1983, 1984). . . . Member of NCAA Division I championship team (1982).

Season Team	G	Min.	FGM	FGA	Pct.	FTM	FTA	Pct.	Reb.	Pts.	Avg.
81-82 —North Carolina	34	. . .	191	358	.534	78	108	.722	149	460	13.5
82-83 —North Carolina	36	. . .	282	527	.535	123	167	.737	197	721	20.0
83-84 —North Carolina	31	. . .	247	448	.551	113	145	.779	163	607	19.6
Totals	101	. . .	720	1333	.540	314	420	.748	509	1788	17.7

Three-point field goals: 1982-83, 34-for-76 (.447).

NBA REGULAR-SEASON RECORD

RECORDS: Holds career record for highest points-per-game average (minimum 400 games or 10,000 points)—32.3. . . . Shares single-game record for most free throws made in one quarter—14 (November 15, 1989, vs. Utah).
HONORS: NBA Most Valuable Player (1988, 1991, 1992). . . . NBA Defensive Player of the Year (1988). . . . NBA Rookie of the Year (1985). . . . Schick Award, for all-around contributions to team's success (1985, 1989). . . . All-NBA first team (1987, 1988, 1989, 1990, 1991, 1992). . . . All-NBA second team (1985). . . . NBA All-Defensive first team (1988, 1989, 1990, 1991, 1992). . . . NBA All-Rookie team (1985).
NOTES: Led NBA with 3.16 steals per game (1988) and 2.77 steals per game (1990).

| | | | | | | | | | | REBOUNDS | | | | | | | | |
Season Team	G	Min.	FGM	FGA	Pct.	FTM	FTA	Pct.	Off.	Def.	Tot.	Ast.	PF	Dq.	Stl.	Blk.	TO	Pts.	Avg.
84-85 —Chicago	82	3144	837	1625	.515	630	746	.845	167	367	534	481	285	4	196	69	291	*2313	28.2
85-86 —Chicago	18	451	150	328	.457	105	125	.840	23	41	64	53	46	0	37	21	45	408	22.7
86-87 —Chicago	82	*3281	*1098	*2279	.482	*833	*972	.857	166	264	430	377	237	0	236	125	272	*3041	*37.1
87-88 —Chicago	82	*3311	*1069	*1998	.535	*723	860	.841	139	310	449	485	270	2	*259	131	252	*2868	*35.0
88-89 —Chicago	81	*3255	*966	*1795	.538	674	793	.850	149	503	652	650	247	2	234	65	290	*2633	*32.5
89-90 —Chicago	82	*3197	*1034	*1964	.526	593	699	.848	143	422	565	519	241	0	*227	54	247	*2753	*33.6
90-91 —Chicago	82	3034	*990	*1837	.539	571	671	.851	118	374	492	453	229	1	223	83	202	*2580	*31.5
91-92 —Chicago	80	3102	*943	*1818	.519	491	590	.832	91	420	511	489	201	1	182	75	200	*2404	*30.1
Totals	589	22775	7087	13644	.519	4620	5456	.847	996	2701	3697	3507	1756	10	1594	623	1799	19000	32.3

Three-point field goals: 1984-85, 9-for-52 (.173). 1985-86, 3-for-18 (.167). 1986-87, 12-for-66 (.182). 1987-88, 7-for-53 (.132). 1988-89, 27-for-98 (.276). 1989-90, 92-for-245 (.376). 1990-91, 29-for-93 (.312). 1991-92, 27-for-100 (.270). Totals, 206-for-725 (.284).

NBA PLAYOFF RECORD

NOTES: NBA Finals Most Valuable Player (1991, 1992). . . . Holds career record for highest points-per-game average (minimum 25 games or 625 points)—34.6. . . . Holds NBA Finals single-game record for most points in one half—35; and most three-point field goals attempted—10 (June 3, 1992, vs. Portland). . . . Shares NBA Finals single-game record for most three-point field goals—6; and most field goals in one half—14 (June 3, 1992, vs. Portland). . . . Holds single-game records for most points—63 (April 20, 1986, vs. Boston); most free throws made in one quarter—13; and most free throws attempted in one quarter—14 (May 21, 1991, vs. Detroit). . . . Shares single-game records for most field goals made—24 (May 1, 1988, vs. Cleveland); and most field goals attempted in one half—25 (May 1, 1988, vs. Cleveland).

| | | | | | | | | | | REBOUNDS | | | | | | | | |
Season Team	G	Min.	FGM	FGA	Pct.	FTM	FTA	Pct.	Off.	Def.	Tot.	Ast.	PF	Dq.	Stl.	Blk.	TO	Pts.	Avg.
84-85 —Chicago	4	171	34	78	.436	48	58	.828	7	16	23	34	15	0	11	4	15	117	29.3
85-86 —Chicago	3	135	48	95	.505	34	39	.872	5	14	19	17	13	1	7	4	14	131	43.7
86-87 —Chicago	3	128	35	84	.417	35	39	.897	7	14	21	18	11	0	6	7	8	107	35.7
87-88 —Chicago	10	427	138	260	.531	86	99	.869	23	48	71	47	38	1	24	11	39	363	36.3
88-89 —Chicago	17	718	199	390	.510	183	229	.799	26	93	119	130	65	1	42	13	68	591	34.8
89-90 —Chicago	16	674	219	426	.514	133	159	.836	24	91	115	109	54	0	45	14	56	587	36.7
90-91 —Chicago	17	689	197	376	.524	125	148	.845	18	90	108	142	53	0	40	23	43	529	31.1
91-92 —Chicago	22	920	290	581	.499	162	189	.857	37	100	137	127	62	0	44	16	81	759	34.5
Totals	92	3862	1160	2290	.507	806	960	.840	147	466	613	624	311	3	219	92	324	3184	34.6

Three-point field goals: 1984-85, 1-for-8 (.125). 1985-86, 1-for-1. 1986-87, 2-for-5 (.400). 1987-88, 1-for-3 (.333). 1988-89, 10-for-35 (.286). 1989-90, 16-for-50 (.320). 1990-91, 10-for-26 (.385). 1991-92, 17-for-44 (.386). Totals, 58-for-172 (.337).

NBA ALL-STAR GAME RECORD

NOTES: NBA All-Star Game Most Valuable Player (1988). . . . Holds career record for highest points-per-game average—21.0.

| | | | | | | | | | REBOUNDS | | | | | | | | |
Season Team	Min.	FGM	FGA	Pct.	FTM	FTA	Pct.	Off.	Def.	Tot.	Ast.	PF	Dq.	Stl.	Blk.	TO	Pts.
1985 —Chicago	22	2	9	.222	3	4	.750	3	3	6	2	4	0	3	1	1	7
1986 —Chicago							Selected, did not play—injured.										
1987 —Chicago	28	5	12	.417	1	2	.500	0	0	0	4	2	0	2	0	5	11
1988 —Chicago	29	17	23	.739	6	6	1.000	3	5	8	3	5	0	4	4	2	40
1989 —Chicago	33	13	23	.565	2	4	.500	1	1	2	3	1	0	5	0	4	28
1990 —Chicago	29	8	17	.471	0	0	. . .	1	4	5	2	1	0	5	1	5	17
1991 —Chicago	36	10	25	.400	6	7	.857	3	2	5	5	2	0	2	0	10	26
1992 —Chicago	31	9	17	.529	0	0	. . .	1	0	1	5	2	0	2	0	1	18
Totals	208	64	126	.508	18	23	.783	12	15	27	24	17	0	23	6	28	147

Three-point field goals: 1985, 0-for-1. 1987, 0-for-1. 1989, 0-for-1. 1990, 1-for-1. 1991, 0-for-2. Totals, 1-for-6 (.167).

KEMP, SHAWN
F, SUPERSONICS

PERSONAL: Born November 26, 1969, in Elkhart, Ind. . . . 6-10/245. . . . Full name: Shawn T. Kemp.
HIGH SCHOOL: Concord (Elkhart, Ind.).
COLLEGE: Kentucky, then Trinity Valley Community College (Tex.).
TRANSACTIONS/CAREER NOTES: Selected as undergraduate by Seattle SuperSonics in first round (17th pick overall) of 1989 NBA Draft.

COLLEGIATE RECORD

Season Team	G	Min.	FGM	FGA	Pct.	FTM	FTA	Pct.	Reb.	Pts.	Avg.
88-89 — Kentucky						Did not play—left school before basketball season.					
88-89 — Trinity Valley Community College						Did not play.					

NBA REGULAR-SEASON RECORD

Season Team	G	Min.	FGM	FGA	Pct.	FTM	FTA	Pct.	REBOUNDS Off.	Def.	Tot.	Ast.	PF	Dq.	Stl.	Blk.	TO	Pts.	Avg.
89-90 — Seattle	81	1120	203	424	.479	117	159	.736	146	200	346	26	204	5	47	70	107	525	6.5
90-91 — Seattle	81	2442	462	909	.508	288	436	.661	267	412	679	144	319	11	77	123	202	1214	15.0
91-92 — Seattle	64	1808	362	718	.504	270	361	.748	264	401	665	86	261	*13	70	124	156	994	15.5
Totals	226	5370	1027	2051	.501	675	956	.706	677	1013	1690	256	784	29	194	317	465	2733	12.1

Three-point field goals: 1989-90, 2-for-12 (.167). 1990-91, 2-for-12 (.167). 1991-92, 0-for-3. Totals, 4-for-27 (.148).

NBA PLAYOFF RECORD

Season Team	G	Min.	FGM	FGA	Pct.	FTM	FTA	Pct.	REBOUNDS Off.	Def.	Tot.	Ast.	PF	Dq.	Stl.	Blk.	TO	Pts.	Avg.
90-91 — Seattle	5	149	22	57	.386	22	27	.815	13	23	36	6	20	1	3	4	16	66	13.2
91-92 — Seattle	9	338	48	101	.475	61	80	.763	47	63	110	4	41	0	5	14	27	157	17.4
Totals	14	487	70	158	.443	83	107	.776	60	86	146	10	61	1	8	18	43	223	15.9

Three-point field goals: 1990-91, 0-for-1.

KEMPTON, TIM
C, SUNS

PERSONAL: Born January 25, 1964, in Jamaica, N.Y. . . . 6-10/245. . . . Full name: Timothy Joseph Kempton.
HIGH SCHOOL: St. Dominic (Oyster Bay, N.Y.).
COLLEGE: Notre Dame.
TRANSACTIONS/CAREER NOTES: Selected by Los Angeles Clippers in sixth round (124th pick overall) of 1986 NBA Draft. . . . Played in Italy (1987-88, 1990-91 and 1991-92). . . . Granted free agency (July 1, 1988). . . . Signed as free agent by Charlotte Hornets (August 17, 1988). . . . Traded by Hornets to Denver Nuggets for 1991 second-round draft choice (September 11, 1989). . . . Signed as unrestricted free agent by Phoenix Suns (August 18, 1992).

COLLEGIATE RECORD

Season Team	G	Min.	FGM	FGA	Pct.	FTM	FTA	Pct.	Reb.	Pts.	Avg.
82-83 — Notre Dame	27	739	101	168	.601	83	113	.735	159	285	10.6
83-84 — Notre Dame	26	775	78	165	.473	113	148	.764	165	269	10.3
84-85 — Notre Dame	27	671	62	141	.440	68	87	.782	130	192	7.1
85-86 — Notre Dame	27	617	69	127	.543	43	58	.741	143	181	6.7
Totals	107	2802	310	601	.516	307	406	.756	597	927	8.7

NBA REGULAR-SEASON RECORD

Season Team	G	Min.	FGM	FGA	Pct.	FTM	FTA	Pct.	REBOUNDS Off.	Def.	Tot.	Ast.	PF	Dq.	Stl.	Blk.	TO	Pts.	Avg.
86-87 — L.A. Clippers	66	936	97	206	.471	95	137	.693	70	124	194	53	162	6	38	12	49	289	4.4
88-89 — Charlotte	79	1341	171	335	.510	142	207	.686	91	213	304	102	215	3	41	14	121	484	6.1
89-90 — Denver	71	1061	153	312	.490	77	114	.675	51	167	218	118	144	2	30	9	80	383	5.4
Totals	216	3338	421	853	.494	314	458	.686	212	504	716	273	521	11	109	35	250	1156	5.4

Three-point field goals: 1986-87, 0-for-1. 1988-89, 0-for-1. 1989-90, 0-for-1. Totals, 0-for-3.

NBA PLAYOFF RECORD

Season Team	G	Min.	FGM	FGA	Pct.	FTM	FTA	Pct.	REBOUNDS Off.	Def.	Tot.	Ast.	PF	Dq.	Stl.	Blk.	TO	Pts.	Avg.
89-90 — Denver	3	32	7	9	.778	4	4	1.000	1	4	5	4	8	0	0	0	2	18	6.0

ITALIAN LEAGUE RECORD

Season Team	G	Min.	FGM	FGA	Pct.	FTM	FTA	Pct.	Reb.	Pts.	Avg.
87-88 — Wuber	33	1229	252	462	.545	127	188	.676	298	631	19.1
90-91 — Glaxo Verona	24	779	126	222	.568	136	169	.805	195	388	16.2
91-92 — Glaxo Verona	27	909	142	270	.526	156	186	.839	257	441	16.3
Totals	84	2917	520	954	.545	419	543	.772	750	1460	17.4

KERR, STEVE
G, CAVALIERS

PERSONAL: Born September 27, 1965, in Beirut, Lebanon. . . . 6-3/180. . . . Full name: Stephen Douglas Kerr.
HIGH SCHOOL: Pacific Palisades (Calif.).
COLLEGE: Arizona.
TRANSACTIONS/CAREER NOTES: Selected by Phoenix Suns in second round (50th pick overall) of 1988 NBA Draft. . . . Traded by Suns to Cleveland Cavaliers for 1993 second-round draft choice (September 5, 1989).

COLLEGIATE RECORD

Season Team	G	Min.	FGM	FGA	Pct.	FTM	FTA	Pct.	Reb.	Pts.	Avg.
83-84 — Arizona	28	633	81	157	.516	36	52	.692	33	198	7.1
84-85 — Arizona	31	1036	126	222	.568	57	71	.803	73	309	10.0
85-86 — Arizona	32	1228	195	361	.540	71	79	.899	101	461	14.4
86-87 — Arizona					Did not play — knee injury.						
87-88 — Arizona	38	1239	151	270	.559	61	74	.824	76	477	12.6
Totals	129	4136	553	1010	.548	225	276	.815	283	1445	11.2

Three-point field goals: 1987-88, 114-for-199 (.573).

NBA REGULAR-SEASON RECORD

RECORDS: Holds career record for highest three-point field-goal percentage (minimum 100 made) —.475.
NOTES: Led NBA with .507 three-point field-goal percentage (1990).

Season Team	G	Min.	FGM	FGA	Pct.	FTM	FTA	Pct.	Off.	Def.	Tot.	Ast.	PF	Dq.	Stl.	Blk.	TO	Pts.	Avg.
88-89 — Phoenix	26	157	20	46	.435	6	9	.667	3	14	17	24	12	0	7	0	6	54	2.1
89-90 — Cleveland	78	1664	192	432	.444	63	73	.863	12	86	98	248	59	0	45	7	74	520	6.7
90-91 — Cleveland	57	905	99	223	.444	45	53	.849	5	32	37	131	52	0	29	4	40	271	4.8
91-92 — Cleveland	48	847	121	237	.511	45	54	.833	14	64	78	110	29	0	27	10	31	319	6.6
Totals	209	3573	432	938	.461	159	189	.841	34	196	230	513	152	0	108	21	151	1164	5.6

Three-point field goals: 1988-89, 8-for-17 (.471). 1989-90, 73-for-144 (.507). 1990-91, 28-for-62 (.452). 1991-92, 32-for-74 (.432). Totals, 141-for-297 (.475).

NBA PLAYOFF RECORD

Season Team	G	Min.	FGM	FGA	Pct.	FTM	FTA	Pct.	Off.	Def.	Tot.	Ast.	PF	Dq.	Stl.	Blk.	TO	Pts.	Avg.
89-90 — Cleveland	5	73	4	14	.286	0	0	...	1	5	6	10	6	0	4	0	2	8	1.6
91-92 — Cleveland	12	149	18	41	.439	5	5	1.000	1	5	6	10	12	0	5	0	4	44	3.7
Totals	17	222	22	55	.400	5	5	1.000	2	10	12	20	18	0	9	0	6	52	3.1

Three-point field goals: 1989-90, 0-for-3. 1991-92, 3-for-11 (.273). Totals, 3-for-14 (.214).

KERSEY, JEROME
F, TRAIL BLAZERS

PERSONAL: Born June 26, 1962, in Clarksville, Va. . . . 6-7/225.
HIGH SCHOOL: Bluestone Senior (Skipwith, Va.).
COLLEGE: Longwood (Va.).
TRANSACTIONS/CAREER NOTES: Selected by Portland Trail Blazers in second round (46th pick overall) of 1984 NBA Draft.

COLLEGIATE RECORD

NOTES: Led NCAA Division II with 14.2 rebounds per game (1984).

Season Team	G	Min.	FGM	FGA	Pct.	FTM	FTA	Pct.	Reb.	Pts.	Avg.
80-81 — Longwood	28	...	197	313	.629	78	133	.586	249	472	16.9
81-82 — Longwood	23	...	165	282	.585	62	98	.633	260	392	17.0
82-83 — Longwood	25	...	144	257	.560	76	125	.608	270	364	14.6
83-84 — Longwood	27	...	214	411	.521	100	165	.606	383	528	19.6
Totals	103	...	720	1263	.570	316	521	.607	1162	1756	17.0

NBA REGULAR-SEASON RECORD

Season Team	G	Min.	FGM	FGA	Pct.	FTM	FTA	Pct.	Off.	Def.	Tot.	Ast.	PF	Dq.	Stl.	Blk.	TO	Pts.	Avg.
84-85 — Portland	77	958	178	372	.478	117	181	.646	95	111	206	63	147	1	49	29	66	473	6.1
85-86 — Portland	79	1217	258	470	.549	156	229	.681	137	156	293	83	208	2	85	32	113	672	8.5
86-87 — Portland	82	2088	373	733	.509	262	364	.720	201	295	496	194	328	5	122	77	149	1009	12.3
87-88 — Portland	79	2888	611	1225	.499	291	396	.735	211	446	657	243	302	8	127	65	161	1516	19.2
88-89 — Portland	76	2716	533	1137	.469	258	372	.694	246	383	629	243	277	6	137	84	167	1330	17.5
89-90 — Portland	82	2843	519	1085	.478	269	390	.690	251	439	690	188	304	7	121	63	144	1310	16.0
90-91 — Portland	73	2359	424	887	.478	232	327	.709	169	312	481	227	251	4	101	76	149	1084	14.8
91-92 — Portland	77	2553	398	852	.467	174	262	.664	241	392	633	243	254	1	114	71	151	971	12.6
Totals	625	17622	3294	6761	.487	1759	2521	.698	1551	2534	4085	1484	2071	34	856	497	1100	8365	13.4

Three-point field goals: 1984-85, 0-for-3. 1985-86, 0-for-6. 1986-87, 1-for-23 (.043). 1987-88, 3-for-15 (.200). 1988-89, 6-for-21 (.286). 1989-90, 3-for-20 (.150). 1990-91, 4-for-13 (.308). 1991-92, 1-for-8 (.125). Totals, 18-for-109 (.165).

NBA PLAYOFF RECORD

Season Team	G	Min.	FGM	FGA	Pct.	FTM	FTA	Pct.	Off.	Def.	Tot.	Ast.	PF	Dq.	Stl.	Blk.	TO	Pts.	Avg.
84-85 — Portland	8	60	16	31	.516	6	8	.750	5	4	9	6	11	0	7	2	2	38	4.8
85-86 — Portland	4	56	9	22	.409	4	4	1.000	7	8	15	4	13	0	1	4	6	22	5.5
86-87 — Portland	4	60	10	25	.400	4	4	1.000	6	13	19	3	13	0	5	1	6	24	6.0
87-88 — Portland	4	127	32	65	.492	15	21	.714	17	13	30	9	17	1	7	4	5	79	19.8
88-89 — Portland	3	117	23	47	.489	15	19	.789	11	13	24	7	12	0	10	1	4	61	20.3
89-90 — Portland	21	831	166	361	.460	103	144	.715	66	108	174	45	87	2	34	20	45	435	20.7
90-91 — Portland	16	588	105	226	.465	76	101	.752	52	59	111	49	68	2	28	7	17	286	17.9
91-92 — Portland	21	756	131	257	.510	79	114	.693	59	103	162	75	85	2	41	19	53	341	16.2
Totals	81	2595	492	1034	.476	302	415	.728	223	321	544	198	306	7	133	58	138	1286	15.9

Three-point field goals: 1985-86, 0-for-1. 1987-88, 0-for-1. 1988-89, 0-for-2. 1989-90, 0-for-3. 1991-92, 0-for-3. Totals, 0-for-10.

DID YOU KNOW. . .

. . . that in 1991-92, Larry Brown became the first coach in NBA history to coach two teams in the same season? Brown coached the Spurs for 38 games, the Clippers for 35.

KESSLER, ALEC
F/C, HEAT

PERSONAL: Born January 13, 1967, in Minneapolis. . . . 6-11/241. . . . Full name: Alec Christopher Kessler.
HIGH SCHOOL: Roswell (Ga.).
COLLEGE: Georgia.

TRANSACTIONS/CAREER NOTES: Selected by Houston Rockets in first round (12th pick overall) of 1990 NBA Draft. . . . Draft rights traded by Rockets to Miami Heat for draft rights to Dave Jamerson and Carl Herrera (June 27, 1990).

COLLEGIATE RECORD

Season Team	G	Min.	FGM	FGA	Pct.	FTM	FTA	Pct.	Reb.	Pts.	Avg.
85-86 —Georgia					Did not play—redshirted.						
86-87 —Georgia	28	421	55	89	.618	30	42	.714	95	140	5.0
87-88 —Georgia	35	1077	149	303	.492	144	183	.787	197	442	12.6
88-89 —Georgia	31	984	210	431	.487	176	232	.759	301	596	19.2
89-90 —Georgia	29	970	198	403	.491	199	263	.757	300	610	21.0
Totals	123	3452	612	1226	.499	549	720	.763	893	1788	14.5

Three-point field goals: 1988-89, 0-for-1. 1989-90, 14-for-35 (.400). Totals, 14-for-36 (.389).

NBA REGULAR-SEASON RECORD

Season Team	G	Min.	FGM	FGA	Pct.	FTM	FTA	Pct.	Off.	Def.	Tot.	Ast.	PF	Dq.	Stl.	Blk.	TO	Pts.	Avg.
90-91 —Miami	78	1259	199	468	.425	88	131	.672	115	221	336	31	189	1	17	26	108	486	6.2
91-92 —Miami	77	1197	158	383	.413	94	115	.817	114	200	314	34	185	3	17	32	58	410	5.3
Totals	155	2456	357	851	.420	182	246	.740	229	421	650	65	374	4	34	58	166	896	5.8

Three-point field goals: 1990-91, 0-for-4.

NBA PLAYOFF RECORD

Season Team	G	Min.	FGM	FGA	Pct.	FTM	FTA	Pct.	Off.	Def.	Tot.	Ast.	PF	Dq.	Stl.	Blk.	TO	Pts.	Avg.
91-92 —Miami	2	12	0	2	.000	2	2	1.000	0	1	1	0	1	0	0	0	1	2	1.0

KIMBLE, BO
G, CLIPPERS

PERSONAL: Born April 9, 1966, in Philadelphia. . . . 6-4/190. . . . Full name: Greg Kimble.
HIGH SCHOOL: Dobbins Area Vocational Technical School (Philadelphia).
COLLEGE: Southern California, then Loyola Marymount.

TRANSACTIONS/CAREER NOTES: Selected by Los Angeles Clippers in first round (eighth pick overall) of 1990 NBA Draft.

COLLEGIATE RECORD

NOTES: THE SPORTING NEWS All-America third team (1990). . . . Led NCAA Division I with 35.3 points per game (1990).

Season Team	G	Min.	FGM	FGA	Pct.	FTM	FTA	Pct.	Reb.	Pts.	Avg.
85-86 —Southern California	28	694	138	297	.465	64	83	.771	101	340	12.1
86-87 —Loyola Marymount					Did not play—transfer student.						
87-88 —Loyola Marymount	26	683	211	481	.439	81	103	.786	81	577	22.2
88-89 —Loyola Marymount	18	421	119	259	.459	31	41	.756	76	302	16.8
89-90 —Loyola Marymount	32	1053	404	763	.529	231	268	.862	247	1131	35.3
Totals	104	2851	872	1800	.484	407	495	.822	505	2350	22.6

Three-point field goals: 1987-88, 74-for-195 (.379). 1988-89, 33-for-94 (.351). 1989-90, 92-for-200 (.460). Totals, 199-for-489 (.407).

NBA REGULAR-SEASON RECORD

Season Team	G	Min.	FGM	FGA	Pct.	FTM	FTA	Pct.	Off.	Def.	Tot.	Ast.	PF	Dq.	Stl.	Blk.	TO	Pts.	Avg.
90-91 —L.A. Clippers	62	1004	159	418	.380	92	119	.773	42	77	119	76	158	2	30	8	77	429	6.9
91-92 —L.A. Clippers	34	277	44	111	.396	20	31	.645	13	19	32	17	37	0	10	6	15	112	3.3
Totals	96	1281	203	529	.384	112	150	.747	55	96	151	93	195	2	40	14	92	541	5.6

Three-point field goals: 1990-91, 19-for-65 (.292). 1991-92, 4-for-13 (.308). Totals, 23-for-78 (.295).

NBA PLAYOFF RECORD

Season Team	G	Min.	FGM	FGA	Pct.	FTM	FTA	Pct.	Off.	Def.	Tot.	Ast.	PF	Dq.	Stl.	Blk.	TO	Pts.	Avg.
91-92 —L.A. Clippers	3	5	0	1	.000	0	0	...	0	0	0	1	2	0	0	0	1	0	0.0

KING, ALBERT
G/F

PERSONAL: Born December 17, 1959, in Brooklyn, N.Y. . . . 6-6/215. . . . Brother of Bernard King, forward with Washington Bullets.
HIGH SCHOOL: Fort Hamilton (Brooklyn, N.Y.).
COLLEGE: Maryland.

TRANSACTIONS/CAREER NOTES: Selected by New Jersey Nets in first round (10th pick overall) of 1981 NBA Draft. . . . Signed as free agent by Philadelphia 76ers (November 24, 1987). . . . Nets agreed not to exercise their right of first refusal in exchange for 1988 second-round draft choice. . . . Traded by 76ers to San Antonio Spurs for Pete Myers (August 24, 1988). . . . Waived by Spurs (March 6, 1989). . . . Played in Israel (1989-90). . . . Played in Continental Basketball Association with Albany Patroons (1990-91). . . . Signed as free agent by Washington Bullets (September 30, 1991). . . . Waived by Bullets (November 19, 1991).

COLLEGIATE RECORD

NOTES: THE SPORTING NEWS All-America first team (1981).

Season	Team	G	Min.	FGM	FGA	Pct.	FTM	FTA	Pct.	Reb.	Pts.	Avg.
77-78	Maryland	28	...	164	327	.502	53	82	.646	187	381	13.6
78-79	Maryland	28	...	191	387	.494	62	81	.765	144	444	15.9
79-80	Maryland	31	...	275	497	.553	124	151	.821	207	674	21.7
80-81	Maryland	31	1075	232	462	.502	95	117	.812	177	559	18.0
	Totals	118		862	1673	.515	334	431	.775	715	2058	17.4

NBA REGULAR-SEASON RECORD

Season	Team	G	Min.	FGM	FGA	Pct.	FTM	FTA	Pct.	REBOUNDS Off.	Def.	Tot.	Ast.	PF	Dq.	Stl.	Blk.	TO	Pts.	Avg.
81-82	New Jersey ..	76	1694	391	812	.482	133	171	.778	105	207	312	142	261	4	64	36	180	918	12.1
82-83	New Jersey ..	79	2447	582	1226	.475	176	227	.775	157	299	456	291	278	5	95	41	245	1346	17.0
83-84	New Jersey ..	79	2103	465	946	.492	232	295	.786	125	263	388	203	258	6	91	33	208	1165	14.7
84-85	New Jersey ..	42	860	226	460	.491	85	104	.817	70	89	159	58	110	0	41	9	65	537	12.8
85-86	New Jersey ..	73	1998	438	961	.456	167	203	.823	116	250	366	181	205	4	58	24	181	1047	14.3
86-87	New Jersey ..	61	1291	244	573	.426	81	100	.810	82	132	214	103	177	5	34	28	103	582	9.5
87-88	Philadelphia.	72	1593	211	540	.391	78	103	.757	71	145	216	103	177	4	39	18	93	517	7.2
88-89	San Antonio .	46	791	141	327	.431	37	48	.771	33	107	140	79	97	2	27	7	74	327	7.1
91-92	Washington .	6	59	11	30	.367	7	8	.875	1	10	11	5	7	0	3	0	2	31	5.2
	Totals	534	12836	2709	5875	.461	996	1259	.791	760	1502	2262	1165	1570	30	452	196	1151	6470	12.1

Three-point field goals: 1981-82, 3-for-13 (.231). 1982-83, 6-for-23 (.261). 1983-84, 3-for-22 (.136). 1984-85, 0-for-8. 1985-86, 4-for-23 (.174). 1986-87, 13-for-32 (.406). 1987-88, 17-for-49 (.347). 1988-89, 8-for-32 (.250). 1991-92, 2-for-7 (.286). Totals, 56-for-209 (.268).

NBA PLAYOFF RECORD

Season	Team	G	Min.	FGM	FGA	Pct.	FTM	FTA	Pct.	REBOUNDS Off.	Def.	Tot.	Ast.	PF	Dq.	Stl.	Blk.	TO	Pts.	Avg.
81-82	New Jersey ..	2	58	18	33	.545	4	5	.800	3	5	8	6	8	0	5	1	5	40	20.0
82-83	New Jersey ..	2	68	18	38	.474	5	6	.833	4	4	8	3	12	2	2	0	4	42	21.0
83-84	New Jersey ..	11	295	53	128	.414	32	46	.696	25	33	58	25	32	0	10	4	23	138	12.5
84-85	New Jersey ..	3	105	28	57	.491	9	13	.692	4	19	23	5	14	0	7	2	10	66	22.0
85-86	New Jersey ..	3	98	18	42	.429	4	4	1.000	8	5	13	10	15	1	2	1	5	41	13.7
	Totals	21	624	135	298	.453	54	74	.730	44	66	110	49	81	3	26	8	47	327	15.6

Three-point field goals: 1982-83, 1-for-2 (.500). 1983-84, 0-for-2. 1984-85, 1-for-1. 1985-86, 1-for-4 (.250). Totals, 3-for-9 (.333).

CBA REGULAR-SEASON RECORD

NOTES: CBA Newcomer of the Year (1991).

Season	Team	G	Min.	2-POINT FGM	FGA	Pct.	3-POINT FGM	FGA	Pct.	FTM	FTA	Pct.	Reb.	Ast.	Pts.	Avg.
90-91	Albany	47	1060	244	506	.482	27	69	.391	89	103	.864	261	85	658	14.0

KING, BERNARD
F, BULLETS

PERSONAL: Born December 4, 1956, in Brooklyn, N.Y.... 6-7/205.... Brother of Albert King, guard/forward with four NBA teams (1981-82 through 1988-89 and 1991-92).
HIGH SCHOOL: Fort Hamilton (Brooklyn, N.Y.).
COLLEGE: Tennessee.
TRANSACTIONS/CAREER NOTES: Selected as undergraduate by New Jersey Nets in first round (seventh pick overall) of 1977 NBA Draft.... Traded by Nets with John Gianelli and Jim Boylan to Utah Jazz for Rich Kelley (October 2, 1979).... Traded by Jazz to Golden State Warriors for Wayne Cooper and 1981 second-round draft choice (September 11, 1980).... Signed as veteran free agent by New York Knicks (September 28, 1982); Warriors matched offer and traded King to Knicks for Micheal Ray Richardson and 1984 fifth-round draft choice (October 22, 1982).... Rights renounced by Knicks (1987).... Signed as free agent by Washington Bullets (October 16, 1987).

COLLEGIATE RECORD

NOTES: THE SPORTING NEWS All-America second team (1977).... Led NCAA Division I with .622 field-goal percentage (1975).

Season	Team	G	Min.	FGM	FGA	Pct.	FTM	FTA	Pct.	Reb.	Pts.	Avg.
74-75	Tennessee	25	...	273	439	.622	115	147	.782	308	661	26.4
75-76	Tennessee	25	...	260	454	.573	109	163	.669	325	629	25.2
76-77	Tennessee	26	...	278	481	.578	116	163	.712	371	672	25.8
	Totals	76		811	1374	.590	340	473	.719	1004	1962	25.8

NBA REGULAR-SEASON RECORD

HONORS: All-NBA first team (1984, 1985).... All-NBA second team (1982).... All-NBA third team (1991).... NBA All-Rookie team (1978).... NBA Comeback Player of the Year (1981).

Season	Team	G	Min.	FGM	FGA	Pct.	FTM	FTA	Pct.	REBOUNDS Off.	Def.	Tot.	Ast.	PF	Dq.	Stl.	Blk.	TO	Pts.	Avg.
77-78	New Jersey ..	79	3092	798	1665	.479	313	462	.677	265	486	751	193	302	5	122	36	311	1909	24.2
78-79	New Jersey ..	82	2859	710	1359	.522	349	619	.564	251	418	669	295	326	10	118	39	323	1769	21.6
79-80	Utah	19	419	71	137	.518	34	63	.540	24	64	88	52	66	3	7	4	50	176	9.3
80-81	Golden State	81	2914	731	1244	.588	307	437	.703	178	373	551	287	304	5	72	34	265	1771	21.9
81-82	Golden State	79	2861	740	1307	.566	352	499	.705	140	329	469	282	285	6	78	23	267	1833	23.2
82-83	New York	68	2207	603	1142	.528	280	388	.722	99	227	326	195	233	5	90	13	197	1486	21.9
83-84	New York	77	2667	795	1391	.572	437	561	.779	123	271	394	164	273	2	75	17	197	2027	26.3
84-85	New York	55	2063	691	1303	.530	426	552	.772	114	203	317	204	191	3	71	15	204	1809	*32.9
85-86	New York							Did not play—injured.												
86-87	New York	6	214	52	105	.495	32	43	.744	13	19	32	19	14	0	2	0	15	136	22.7
87-88	Washington .	69	2044	470	938	.501	247	324	.762	86	194	280	192	202	3	49	10	211	1188	17.2
88-89	Washington .	81	2559	654	1371	.477	361	441	.819	133	251	384	294	219	1	64	13	227	1674	20.7
89-90	Washington .	82	2687	711	1459	.487	412	513	.803	129	275	404	376	230	1	51	7	248	1837	22.4
90-91	Washington .	64	2401	713	1511	.472	383	485	.790	114	205	319	292	187	1	56	16	255	1817	28.4
91-92	Washington .							Did not play—injured.												
	Totals	842	28987	7739	14932	.518	3933	5387	.730	1669	3315	4984	2845	2832	45	855	227	2770	19432	23.1

Three-point field goals: 1980-81, 2-for-6 (.333). 1981-82, 1-for-5 (.200). 1982-83, 0-for-6. 1983-84, 0-for-4. 1984-85, 1-for-10 (.100). 1987-88, 1-for-6 (.167). 1988-89, 5-for-30 (.167). 1989-90, 3-for-23 (.130). 1990-91, 8-for-37 (.216). Totals, 21-for-127 (.165).

NBA PLAYOFF RECORD

Season Team	G	Min.	FGM	FGA	Pct.	FTM	FTA	Pct.	REBOUNDS Off.	Def.	Tot.	Ast.	PF	Dq.	Stl.	Blk.	TO	Pts.	Avg.
78-79—New Jersey ..	2	81	21	42	.500	10	24	.417	5	6	11	7	10	0	4	0	6	52	26.0
82-83—New York	6	184	56	97	.577	28	35	.800	8	16	24	13	16	0	2	0	10	141	23.5
83-84—New York	12	477	162	282	.574	93	123	.756	28	46	74	36	48	0	14	6	31	417	34.8
87-88—Washington .	5	168	26	53	.491	17	21	.810	3	8	11	9	17	0	3	0	14	69	13.8
Totals	25	910	265	474	.559	148	203	.729	44	76	120	65	91	0	23	6	61	679	27.2

Three-point field goals: 1982-83, 1-for-3 (.333). 1983-84, 0-for-1. Totals, 1-for-4 (.250).

NBA ALL-STAR GAME RECORD

Season Team	Min.	FGM	FGA	Pct.	FTM	FTA	Pct.	REBOUNDS Off.	Def.	Tot.	Ast.	PF	Dq.	Stl.	Blk.	TO	Pts.
1982 —Golden State	14	2	7	.286	2	2	1.000	0	4	4	1	2	0	3	1	2	6
1984 —New York	22	8	13	.615	2	5	.400	2	1	3	4	2	0	0	0	0	18
1985 —New York	22	6	10	.600	1	2	.500	4	3	7	1	5	0	0	0	1	13
1991 —Washington	26	2	8	.250	4	4	1.000	2	1	3	3	1	0	0	1	1	8
Totals	84	18	38	.474	9	13	.692	8	9	17	9	10	0	3	2	4	45

KING, RICH
C, SUPERSONICS

PERSONAL: Born April 4, 1969, in Lincoln, Neb. . . . 7-2/265. . . . Full name: Richard Thomas King.
HIGH SCHOOL: Harry A. Burke (Omaha, Neb.).
COLLEGE: Nebraska.
TRANSACTIONS/CAREER NOTES: Selected by Seattle SuperSonics in first round (14th pick overall) of 1991 NBA Draft.

COLLEGIATE RECORD

Season Team	G	Min.	FGM	FGA	Pct.	FTM	FTA	Pct.	Reb.	Pts.	Avg.
87-88—Nebraska	29	420	56	108	.519	24	34	.706	84	136	4.7
88-89—Nebraska	33	771	136	235	.579	91	139	.655	195	363	11.0
89-90—Nebraska	28	809	170	305	.557	110	158	.696	208	450	16.1
90-91—Nebraska	34	928	202	352	.574	120	179	.670	274	526	15.5
Totals	124	2928	564	1000	.564	345	510	.676	761	1475	11.9

Three-point field goals: 1990-91, 2-for-5 (.400).

NBA REGULAR-SEASON RECORD

Season Team	G	Min.	FGM	FGA	Pct.	FTM	FTA	Pct.	REBOUNDS Off.	Def.	Tot.	Ast.	PF	Dq.	Stl.	Blk.	TO	Pts.	Avg.
91-92—Seattle..........	40	213	27	71	.380	34	45	.756	20	29	49	12	42	0	4	5	18	88	2.2

Three-point field goals: 1991-92, 0-for-1.

KING, STACEY
F/C, BULLS

PERSONAL: Born January 29, 1967, in Lawton, Okla. . . . 6-11/230. . . . Full name: Ronald Stacey King.
HIGH SCHOOL: Lawton (Okla.).
COLLEGE: Oklahoma.
TRANSACTIONS/CAREER NOTES: Selected by Chicago Bulls in first round (sixth pick overall) of 1989 NBA Draft.
MISCELLANEOUS: Member of NBA championship teams (1991, 1992).

COLLEGIATE RECORD

NOTES: THE SPORTING NEWS College Player of the Year (1989). . . . THE SPORTING NEWS All-America first team (1989). . . . THE SPORTING NEWS All-America second team (1988).

Season Team	G	Min.	FGM	FGA	Pct.	FTM	FTA	Pct.	Reb.	Pts.	Avg.
85-86—Oklahoma...............................	14	230	26	67	.388	32	43	.744	53	84	6.0
86-87—Oklahoma...............................	28	441	71	162	.438	54	87	.621	108	196	7.0
87-88—Oklahoma...............................	39	1212	337	621	.543	195	289	.675	332	869	22.3
88-89—Oklahoma...............................	33	1142	324	618	.524	211	294	.718	332	859	26.0
Totals	114	3025	758	1468	.516	492	713	.690	825	2008	17.6

Three-point field goals: 1986-87, 0-for-1. 1987-88, 0-for-1. Totals, 0-for-2.

NBA REGULAR-SEASON RECORD

HONORS: NBA All-Rookie second team (1990).

Season Team	G	Min.	FGM	FGA	Pct.	FTM	FTA	Pct.	REBOUNDS Off.	Def.	Tot.	Ast.	PF	Dq.	Stl.	Blk.	TO	Pts.	Avg.
89-90—Chicago........	82	1777	267	530	.504	194	267	.727	169	215	384	87	215	0	38	58	119	728	8.9
90-91—Chicago........	76	1198	156	334	.467	107	152	.704	72	136	208	65	134	0	24	42	91	419	5.5
91-92—Chicago........	79	1268	215	425	.506	119	158	.753	87	118	205	77	129	0	21	25	76	551	7.0
Totals	237	4243	638	1289	.495	420	577	.728	328	469	797	229	478	0	83	125	286	1698	7.2

Three-point field goals: 1989-90, 0-for-1. 1990-91, 0-for-2. 1991-92, 2-for-5 (.400). Totals, 2-for-8 (.250).

NBA PLAYOFF RECORD

Season Team	G	Min.	FGM	FGA	Pct.	FTM	FTA	Pct.	REBOUNDS Off.	Def.	Tot.	Ast.	PF	Dq.	Stl.	Blk.	TO	Pts.	Avg.
89-90—Chicago........	16	281	37	91	.407	36	47	.766	17	34	51	9	32	0	6	8	17	110	6.9
90-91—Chicago........	11	86	8	27	.296	7	11	.636	9	13	22	2	15	0	1	1	9	23	2.1

Season Team	G	Min.	FGM	FGA	Pct.	FTM	FTA	Pct.	Off.	Def.	Tot.	Ast.	PF	Dq.	Stl.	Blk.	TO	Pts.	Avg.
91-92 —Chicago........	14	111	18	40	.450	15	23	.652	7	13	20	5	12	0	5	2	10	53	3.8
Totals	41	478	63	158	.399	58	81	.716	33	60	93	16	59	0	12	11	36	186	4.5

Three-point field goals: 1989-90, 0-for-1. 1990-91, 0-for-1. 1991-92, 2-for-2. Totals, 2-for-4 (.500).

KITE, GREG
C, MAGIC

PERSONAL: Born August 5, 1961, in Houston. . . . 6-11/270. . . . Full name: Gregory Fuller Kite.
HIGH SCHOOL: James Madison (Houston).
COLLEGE: Brigham Young.
TRANSACTIONS/CAREER NOTES: Selected by Boston Celtics in first round (21st pick overall) of 1983 NBA Draft. . . . Waived by Celtics (February 1, 1988). . . . Claimed off waivers by Los Angeles Clippers (February 3, 1988). . . . Waived by Clippers (March 27, 1989). . . . Signed as free agent by Charlotte Hornets (March 29, 1989). . . . Signed as unrestricted free agent by Sacramento Kings (November 25, 1989). . . . Signed as unrestricted free agent by Orlando Magic (August 16, 1990). . . . Re-signed as unrestricted free agent by Magic (July 1, 1991)
MISCELLANEOUS: Member of NBA championship teams (1984, 1986).

COLLEGIATE RECORD

Season Team	G	Min.	FGM	FGA	Pct.	FTM	FTA	Pct.	Reb.	Pts.	Avg.
79-80 —Brigham Young......................	21	192	14	48	.292	12	25	.480	86	40	1.9
80-81 —Brigham Young......................	32	1002	108	221	.489	50	101	.495	272	266	8.3
81-82 —Brigham Young......................	30	853	79	169	.467	29	65	.446	234	187	6.2
82-83 —Brigham Young......................	29	896	90	206	.437	44	77	.571	255	224	7.7
Totals	112	2943	291	644	.452	135	268	.504	847	717	6.4

NBA REGULAR-SEASON RECORD

Season Team	G	Min	FGM	FGA	Pct.	FTM	FTA	Pct.	Off.	Def.	Tot.	Ast.	PF	Dq.	Stl.	Blk.	TO	Pts.	Avg.
83-84 —Boston	35	197	30	66	.455	5	16	.313	27	35	62	7	42	0	1	5	20	65	1.9
84-85 —Boston	55	424	33	88	.375	22	32	.688	38	51	89	17	84	3	3	10	29	88	1.6
85-86 —Boston	64	464	34	91	.374	15	39	.385	35	93	128	17	81	1	3	28	32	83	1.3
86-87 —Boston	74	745	47	110	.427	29	76	.382	61	108	169	27	148	2	17	46	34	123	1.7
87-88 —Bos.-L.A.C..	53	1063	92	205	.449	40	79	.506	85	179	264	47	153	1	19	58	73	224	4.2
88-89 —LAC-Char	70	942	65	151	.430	20	41	.488	81	162	243	36	161	1	27	54	58	150	2.1
89-90 —Sacramento .	71	1515	101	234	.432	27	54	.500	131	246	377	76	201	2	31	51	76	230	3.2
90-91 —Orlando	82	2225	166	338	.491	63	123	.512	189	399	588	59	298	4	25	81	102	395	4.8
91-92 —Orlando	72	1479	94	215	.437	40	68	.588	156	246	402	44	212	2	30	57	61	228	3.2
Totals	576	9054	662	1498	.442	261	528	.494	803	1519	2322	330	1380	16	156	390	485	1586	2.8

Three-point field goals: 1985-86, 0-for-1. 1986-87, 0-for-1. 1987-88, 0-for-1. 1989-90, 1-for-1. 1991-92, 0-for-1. Totals, 1-for-5 (.200).

NBA PLAYOFF RECORD

Season Team	G	Min.	FGM	FGA	Pct.	FTM	FTA	Pct.	Off.	Def.	Tot.	Ast.	PF	Dq.	Stl.	Blk.	TO	Pts.	Avg.
83-84 —Boston	11	38	1	8	.125	5	6	.833	5	4	9	3	9	0	0	1	3	7	0.6
84-85 —Boston	9	63	5	12	.417	1	2	.500	5	11	16	3	13	0	1	0	2	11	1.2
85-86 —Boston	13	78	7	10	.700	4	7	.571	5	14	19	3	20	0	2	4	3	18	1.4
86-87 —Boston	20	172	7	20	.350	3	7	.429	15	31	46	8	43	1	2	8	7	17	0.9
Totals	53	351	20	50	.400	13	22	.591	30	60	90	17	85	1	5	13	15	53	1.0

KLEINE, JOE
C, CELTICS

PERSONAL: Born January 4, 1962, in Colorado Springs, Colo. . . . 7-0/271. . . . Full name: Joseph William Kleine.
HIGH SCHOOL: Slater (Mo.).
COLLEGE: Notre Dame, then Arkansas.
TRANSACTIONS/CAREER NOTES: Selected by Sacramento Kings in first round (sixth pick overall) of 1985 NBA Draft. . . . Traded by Kings with Ed Pinckney to Boston Celtics for Brad Lohaus and Danny Ainge (February 23, 1989).
MISCELLANEOUS: Member of gold-medal-winning U.S. Olympic team (1984).

COLLEGIATE RECORD

Season Team	G	Min.	FGM	FGA	Pct.	FTM	FTA	Pct.	Reb.	Pts.	Avg.
80-81 —Notre Dame.............................	29	291	32	50	.640	12	16	.750	71	76	2.6
81-82 —Arkansas				Did not play—transfer student.							
82-83 —Arkansas	30	950	165	307	.537	69	109	.633	219	399	13.3
83-84 —Arkansas	32	1173	209	351	.595	163	211	.773	293	581	18.2
84-85 —Arkansas	35	1289	294	484	.607	185	257	.720	294	773	22.1
Totals	126	3703	700	1192	.587	429	593	.723	877	1829	14.5

NBA REGULAR-SEASON RECORD

Season Team	G	Min.	FGM	FGA	Pct.	FTM	FTA	Pct.	Off.	Def.	Tot.	Ast.	PF	Dq.	Stl.	Blk.	TO	Pts.	Avg.
85-86 —Sacramento .	80	1180	160	344	.465	94	130	.723	113	260	373	46	224	1	24	34	107	414	5.2
86-87 —Sacramento .	79	1658	256	543	.471	110	140	.786	173	310	483	71	213	2	35	30	90	622	7.9
87-88 —Sacramento .	82	1999	324	686	.472	153	188	.814	179	400	579	93	228	1	28	59	107	801	9.8
88-89 —Sac.-Boston .	75	1411	175	432	.405	134	152	.882	124	254	378	67	192	2	33	23	104	484	6.5
89-90 —Boston	81	1365	176	367	.480	83	100	.830	117	238	355	46	170	0	15	27	64	435	5.4
90-91 —Boston	72	850	102	218	.468	54	69	.783	71	173	244	21	108	0	15	14	53	258	3.6
91-92 —Boston	70	991	144	293	.491	34	48	.708	94	202	296	32	99	0	23	14	27	326	4.7
Totals	539	9454	1337	2883	.464	662	827	.800	871	1837	2708	376	1234	6	173	201	552	3340	6.2

Three-point field goals: 1986-87, 0-for-1. 1988-89, 0-for-2. 1989-90, 0-for-4. 1990-91, 0-for-2. 1991-92, 4-for-8 (.500). Totals, 4-for-17 (.235).

K

NBA PLAYOFF RECORD

Season Team	G	Min.	FGM	FGA	Pct.	FTM	FTA	Pct.	REBOUNDS Off.	Def.	Tot.	Ast.	PF	Dq.	Stl.	Blk.	TO	Pts.	Avg.
85-86 —Sacramento .	3	45	5	13	.385	5	6	.833	8	6	14	1	8	0	1	1	2	15	5.0
88-89 —Boston	3	65	6	11	.545	7	9	.778	4	13	17	2	9	0	0	1	6	19	6.3
89-90 —Boston	5	79	13	17	.765	5	6	.833	3	11	14	2	12	0	2	3	4	31	6.2
90-91 —Boston	5	31	4	9	.444	0	0	. . .	5	6	11	1	7	0	0	0	2	8	1.6
91-92 —Boston	9	82	9	22	.409	2	2	1.000	6	16	22	1	11	0	0	1	3	20	2.2
Totals	25	302	37	72	.514	19	23	.826	26	52	78	7	47	0	3	6	17	93	3.7

Three-point field goals: 1988-89, 0-for-1. 1989-90, 0-for-1. 1991-92, 0-for-1. Totals, 0-for-3.

KNIGHT, NEGELE
G, SUNS

PERSONAL: Born March 6, 1967, in Detroit. . . . 6-1/182. . . . Full name: Negele Oscar Knight. . . . Name pronounced Na-GELL. **HIGH SCHOOL:** St. Martin De Porres (Detroit). **COLLEGE:** Dayton.

TRANSACTIONS/CAREER NOTES: Selected by Phoenix Suns in second round (31st pick overall) of 1990 NBA Draft.

COLLEGIATE RECORD

Season Team	G	Min.	FGM	FGA	Pct.	FTM	FTA	Pct.	Reb.	Pts.	Avg.
85-86 —Dayton	30	801	75	198	.379	63	94	.670	63	213	7.1
86-87 —Dayton					Did not play—ankle surgery.						
87-88 —Dayton	31	1169	176	373	.472	97	136	.713	98	459	14.8
88-89 —Dayton	29	1024	145	306	.474	100	136	.735	96	403	13.9
89-90 —Dayton	32	1072	234	465	.503	192	240	.800	123	731	22.8
Totals	122	4066	630	1342	.469	452	606	.746	380	1806	14.8

Three-point field goals: 1987-88, 10-for-36 (.278). 1988-89, 13-for-41 (.317). 1989-90, 71-for-144 (.493). Totals, 94-for-221 (.425).

NBA REGULAR-SEASON RECORD

Season Team	G	Min.	FGM	FGA	Pct.	FTM	FTA	Pct.	REBOUNDS Off.	Def.	Tot.	Ast.	PF	Dq.	Stl.	Blk.	TO	Pts.	Avg.
90-91 —Phoenix.......	64	792	131	308	.425	71	118	.602	20	51	71	191	83	0	20	7	76	339	5.3
91-92 —Phoenix.......	42	631	103	217	.475	33	48	.688	16	30	46	112	58	0	24	3	58	243	5.8
Totals	106	1423	234	525	.446	104	166	.627	36	81	117	303	141	0	44	10	134	582	5.5

Three-point field goals: 1990-91, 6-for-25 (.240). 1991-92, 4-for-13 (.308). Totals, 10-for-38 (.263).

NBA PLAYOFF RECORD

Season Team	G	Min.	FGM	FGA	Pct.	FTM	FTA	Pct.	REBOUNDS Off.	Def.	Tot.	Ast.	PF	Dq.	Stl.	Blk.	TO	Pts.	Avg.
90-91 —Phoenix........	4	56	13	26	.500	5	7	.714	1	3	4	9	7	0	1	0	4	32	8.0

Three-point field goals: 1990-91, 1-for-3 (.333).

KOFOED, BART
G, SUPERSONICS

PERSONAL: Born March 24, 1964, in Omaha, Neb. . . . 6-4/210. . . . Name pronounced KO-fode. **HIGH SCHOOL:** Westside (Omaha, Neb.). **COLLEGE:** Hastings (Neb.), then Kearney State (Neb.).

TRANSACTIONS/CAREER NOTES: Selected by Utah Jazz in fifth round (107th pick overall) of 1987 NBA Draft. . . . Played in Continental Basketball Association with Rochester Flyers (1988-1989) and La Crosse Catbirds and Yakima Sun Kings (1990-91). . . . Waived by Jazz (January 4, 1989). . . . Signed as free agent by Golden State Warriors (October 3, 1990). . . . Waived by Warriors (November 26, 1990). . . . Signed as free agent by Seattle SuperSonics (August 23, 1991).

COLLEGIATE RECORD

Season Team	G	Min.	FGM	FGA	Pct.	FTM	FTA	Pct.	Reb.	Pts.	Avg.
82-83 —Hastings	28	. . .	55	116	.474	18	31	.581	75	128	4.6
83-84 —Hastings				Statistics unavailable.							
84-85 —Kearney State.........................				Did not play—transfer student.							
85-86 —Kearney State	32	. . .	288	566	.509	102	146	.699	186	678	21.2
86-87 —Kearney State.........................	34	. . .	358	747	.479	148	203	.729	184	902	26.5
Totals	94	. . .	701	1429	.491	268	380	.705	445	1708	18.2

Three-point field goals: 1986-87, 38-for-114 (.333).

NBA REGULAR-SEASON RECORD

Season Team	G	Min.	FGM	FGA	Pct.	FTM	FTA	Pct.	REBOUNDS Off.	Def.	Tot.	Ast.	PF	Dq.	Stl.	Blk.	TO	Pts.	Avg.
87-88 —Utah	36	225	18	48	.375	8	13	.615	4	11	15	23	42	0	6	1	18	46	1.3
88-89 —Utah	19	176	12	33	.364	6	11	.545	4	7	11	20	22	0	9	0	13	30	1.6
90-91 —Golden State	5	21	0	3	.000	3	6	.500	2	1	3	4	4	0	0	0	2	3	0.6
91-92 —Seattle.........	44	239	25	53	.472	15	26	.577	6	20	26	51	26	0	2	2	20	66	1.5
Totals	104	661	55	137	.401	32	56	.571	16	39	55	98	94	0	17	3	53	145	1.4

Three-point field goals: 1987-88, 2-for-7 (.286). 1988-89, 1-for-7. 1991-92, 1-for-7 (.143). Totals, 3-for-15 (.200).

NBA PLAYOFF RECORD

Season Team	G	Min.	FGM	FGA	Pct.	FTM	FTA	Pct.	REBOUNDS Off.	Def.	Tot.	Ast.	PF	Dq.	Stl.	Blk.	TO	Pts.	Avg.
87-88 —Utah	10	109	9	23	.391	2	2	1.000	3	11	14	11	18	0	1	0	9	21	2.1

Three-point field goals: 1987-88, 1-for-5 (.200).

CBA REGULAR-SEASON RECORD

Season Team	G	Min.	2-POINT FGM	FGA	Pct.	3-POINT FGM	FGA	Pct.	FTM	FTA	Pct.	Reb.	Ast.	Pts.	Avg.
88-89 —Rochester	17	413	42	100	.420	3	11	.273	32	39	.821	53	61	125	7.4
90-91 —La Cros.-Yak. ...	47	1908	255	497	.513	25	68	.368	134	171	.784	218	357	719	15.3
Totals	64	2321	297	597	.497	28	79	.354	166	210	.790	271	418	844	13.2

KONCAK, JON
C, HAWKS

PERSONAL: Born May 17, 1963, in Cedar Rapids, Ia. . . . 7-0/250. . . . Full name: Jon Francis Koncak. . . . Name pronounced KON-kak.
HIGH SCHOOL: Center (Kansas City, Mo.).
COLLEGE: Southern Methodist.
TRANSACTIONS/CAREER NOTES: Selected by Atlanta Hawks in first round (fifth pick overall) of 1985 NBA Draft.
MISCELLANEOUS: Member of gold-medal-winning U.S. Olympic team (1984).

COLLEGIATE RECORD

NOTES: THE SPORTING NEWS All-America second team (1985).

Season Team	G	Min.	FGM	FGA	Pct.	FTM	FTA	Pct.	Reb.	Pts.	Avg.
81-82 —Southern Methodist	27	745	107	232	.461	57	92	.620	155	271	10.0
82-83 —Southern Methodist	30	980	176	334	.527	85	123	.691	282	437	14.6
83-84 —Southern Methodist	33	1162	211	340	.621	88	145	.607	378	510	15.5
84-85 —Southern Methodist	33	1084	219	370	.592	128	192	.667	354	566	17.2
Totals	123	3971	713	1276	.559	358	552	.649	1169	1784	14.5

NBA REGULAR-SEASON RECORD

Season Team	G	Min.	FGM	FGA	Pct.	FTM	FTA	Pct.	REBOUNDS Off.	Def.	Tot.	Ast.	PF	Dq.	Stl.	Blk.	TO	Pts.	Avg.
85-86 —Atlanta........	82	1695	263	519	.507	156	257	.607	171	296	467	55	296	10	37	69	111	682	8.3
86-87 —Atlanta........	82	1684	169	352	.480	125	191	.654	153	340	493	31	262	2	52	76	92	463	5.6
87-88 —Atlanta........	49	1073	98	203	.483	83	136	.610	103	230	333	19	161	1	36	56	53	279	5.7
88-89 —Atlanta........	74	1531	141	269	.524	63	114	.553	147	306	453	56	238	4	54	98	60	345	4.7
89-90 —Atlanta........	54	977	78	127	.614	42	79	.532	58	168	226	23	182	4	38	34	47	198	3.7
90-91 —Atlanta........	77	1931	140	321	.436	32	54	.593	101	274	375	124	265	6	74	76	50	313	4.1
91-92 —Atlanta........	77	1489	111	284	.391	19	29	.655	62	199	261	132	207	2	50	67	54	241	3.1
Totals	495	10380	1000	2075	.482	520	860	.605	795	1813	2608	440	1611	29	341	476	467	2521	5.1

Three-point field goals: 1985-86, 0-for-1. 1986-87, 0-for-1. 1987-88, 0-for-2. 1988-89, 0-for-3. 1989-90, 0-for-1. 1990-91, 1-for-8 (.125). 1991-92, 0-for-12. Totals, 1-for-28 (.036).

NBA PLAYOFF RECORD

Season Team	G	Min.	FGM	FGA	Pct.	FTM	FTA	Pct.	REBOUNDS Off.	Def.	Tot.	Ast.	PF	Dq.	Stl.	Blk.	TO	Pts.	Avg.
85-86 —Atlanta........	9	193	14	29	.483	26	46	.565	11	23	34	5	27	2	6	10	7	54	6.0
86-87 —Atlanta........	8	86	7	13	.538	6	8	.750	5	20	25	3	24	0	3	4	0	20	2.5
88-89 —Atlanta........	5	192	18	29	.621	28	33	.848	16	32	48	4	23	1	2	8	8	64	12.8
90-91 —Atlanta........	5	133	4	14	.286	2	2	1.000	4	19	23	7	17	0	2	4	3	10	2.0
Totals	27	604	43	85	.506	62	89	.697	36	94	130	19	91	3	13	26	18	148	5.5

KRYSTKOWIAK, LARRY
F/C, JAZZ

PERSONAL: Born September 23, 1964, in Missoula, Mont. . . . 6-9/240. . . . Full name: Larry Brett Krystkowiak. . . . Name pronounced Crist-KO-vee-ak.
HIGH SCHOOL: Big Sky (Missoula, Mont.).
COLLEGE: Montana.
TRANSACTIONS/CAREER NOTES: Selected by Chicago Bulls in second round (28th pick overall) of 1986 NBA Draft. . . . Draft rights traded by Bulls with 1987 and 1992 second-round draft choices to Portland Trail Blazers for Steve Colter (June 17, 1986). . . . Draft rights traded by Trail Blazers with Mychal Thompson to San Antonio Spurs for Steve Johnson (June 20, 1986). . . . Traded by Spurs to Milwaukee Bucks for Charles Davis and 1989 second-round draft choice (November 18, 1987). . . . Played in Italy (1987-88). . . . Traded by Bucks with Jay Humphries to Utah Jazz for Blue Edwards, Eric Murdock and 1992 first-round draft choice (June 24, 1992).

COLLEGIATE RECORD

Season Team	G	Min.	FGM	FGA	Pct.	FTM	FTA	Pct.	Reb.	Pts.	Avg.
82-83 —Montana	28	396	42	97	.433	53	77	.688	120	137	4.9
83-84 —Montana	30	1068	185	338	.547	169	210	.805	315	539	18.0
84-85 —Montana	30	1079	214	366	.585	204	243	.840	306	632	21.1
85-86 —Montana	32	1118	258	446	.578	193	254	.760	364	709	22.2
Totals	120	3661	699	1247	.561	619	784	.790	1105	2017	16.8

NBA REGULAR-SEASON RECORD

Season Team	G	Min.	FGM	FGA	Pct.	FTM	FTA	Pct.	REBOUNDS Off.	Def.	Tot.	Ast.	PF	Dq.	Stl.	Blk.	TO	Pts.	Avg.
86-87 —San Antonio .	68	1004	170	373	.456	110	148	.743	77	162	239	85	141	1	22	12	67	451	6.6
87-88 —Milwaukee ...	50	1050	128	266	.481	103	127	.811	88	143	231	50	137	0	18	8	57	359	7.2
88-89 —Milwaukee ...	80	2472	362	766	.473	289	351	.823	198	412	610	107	219	0	93	9	147	1017	12.7
89-90 —Milwaukee ...	16	381	43	118	.364	26	33	.788	16	60	76	25	41	0	10	2	19	112	7.0
90-91 —Milwaukee ...								Did not play—injured.											
91-92 —Milwaukee ...	79	1848	293	660	.444	128	169	.757	131	298	429	114	218	2	54	12	115	714	9.0
Totals	293	6755	996	2183	.456	656	828	.792	510	1075	1585	381	756	3	197	43	405	2653	9.1

Three-point field goals: 1986-87, 1-for-12 (.083). 1987-88, 0-for-3. 1988-89, 4-for-12 (.333). 1989-90, 0-for-2. 1991-92, 0-for-5. Totals, 5-for-34 (.147).

NBA PLAYOFF RECORD

| | | | | | | | | — REBOUNDS — | | | | | | | | | | |
Season	Team	G	Min.	FGM	FGA	Pct.	FTM	FTA	Pct.	Off.	Def.	Tot.	Ast.	PF	Dq.	Stl.	Blk.	TO	Pts.	Avg.
87-88	—Milwaukee ...	5	163	13	29	.448	16	18	.889	13	21	34	7	17	0	4	0	5	42	8.4
88-89	—Milwaukee ...	8	239	29	68	.426	27	31	.871	14	31	45	12	22	0	2	1	16	85	10.6
90-91	—Milwaukee ...	3	25	1	6	.167	0	0	...	0	3	3	2	3	0	1	0	0	2	0.7
	Totals	16	427	43	103	.417	43	49	.878	27	55	82	21	42	0	7	1	21	129	8.1

Three-point field goals: 1988-89, 0-for-2.

ITALIAN LEAGUE RECORD

Season	Team	G	Min.	FGM	FGA	Pct.	FTM	FTA	Pct.	Reb.	Pts.	Avg.
87-88	—Roberts	8	291	70	129	.543	46	52	.885	84	186	23.3

LAIMBEER, BILL
C, PISTONS

PERSONAL: Born May 19, 1957, in Boston. .... 6-11/260. .... Full name: William Laimbeer Jr.... Name pronounced LAM-beer.
HIGH SCHOOL: Palos Verdes (Calif.).
COLLEGE: Owens Technical (O.), then Notre Dame.
TRANSACTIONS/CAREER NOTES: Selected by Cleveland Cavaliers in third round (65th pick overall) of 1979 NBA Draft.... Played in Italy (1979-80).... Traded by Cavaliers with Kenny Carr to Detroit Pistons for Phil Hubbard, Paul Mokeski and 1982 first- and second round-draft choices (February 16, 1982).
MISCELLANEOUS: Member of NBA championship teams (1989, 1990).

COLLEGIATE RECORD

Season	Team	G	Min.	FGM	FGA	Pct.	FTM	FTA	Pct.	Reb.	Pts.	Avg.
76-77	—Owens Technical College.........						Did not play.					
75-76	—Notre Dame............................	10	190	32	65	.492	18	23	.783	79	82	8.2
77-78	—Notre Dame............................	29	654	97	175	.554	42	62	.677	190	236	8.1
78-79	—Notre Dame............................	30	614	78	145	.538	35	50	.700	164	191	6.4
	Four-year-college totals	69	1458	207	385	.538	95	135	.704	433	509	7.4

ITALIAN LEAGUE RECORD

Season	Team	G	Min.	FGM	FGA	Pct.	FTM	FTA	Pct.	Reb.	Pts.	Avg.
79-80	—Brescia	29	...	258	465	.555	97	124	.782	363	613	21.1

NBA REGULAR-SEASON RECORD

NOTES: Led NBA with 13.1 rebounds per game (1986).

| | | | | | | | | — REBOUNDS — | | | | | | | | | | |
Season	Team	G	Min.	FGM	FGA	Pct.	FTM	FTA	Pct.	Off.	Def.	Tot.	Ast.	PF	Dq.	Stl.	Blk.	TO	Pts.	Avg.
80-81	—Cleveland.....	81	2460	337	670	.503	117	153	.765	266	427	693	216	332	14	56	78	132	791	9.8
81-82	—Clev.-Det.	80	1829	265	536	.494	184	232	.793	234	383	617	100	296	5	39	64	121	718	9.0
82-83	—Detroit........	82	2871	436	877	.497	245	310	.790	282	711	993	263	320	9	51	118	176	1119	13.6
83-84	—Detroit........	82	2864	553	1044	.530	316	365	.866	329	674	*1003	149	273	4	49	84	151	1422	17.3
84-85	—Detroit........	82	2892	595	1177	.506	244	306	.797	295	718	1013	154	308	4	69	71	129	1438	17.5
85-86	—Detroit........	82	2891	545	1107	.492	266	319	.834	305	*770	*1075	146	291	4	59	65	133	1360	16.6
86-87	—Detroit........	82	2854	506	1010	.501	245	274	.894	243	712	955	151	283	4	72	69	120	1263	15.4
87-88	—Detroit........	82	2897	455	923	.493	187	214	.874	165	667	832	199	284	6	66	78	136	1110	13.5
88-89	—Detroit........	81	2640	449	900	.499	178	212	.840	138	638	776	177	259	2	51	100	129	1106	13.7
89-90	—Detroit........	81	2675	380	785	.484	164	192	.854	166	614	780	171	278	4	57	84	98	981	12.1
90-91	—Detroit........	82	2668	372	778	.478	123	147	.837	173	564	737	157	242	3	38	56	98	904	11.0
91-92	—Detroit........	81	2234	342	727	.470	67	75	.893	104	347	451	160	225	0	51	54	102	783	9.7
	Totals	978	31775	5235	10534	.497	2336	2799	.835	2700	7225	9925	2043	3391	59	658	921	1525	12995	13.3

Three-point field goals: 1981-82, 4-for-13 (.308). 1982-83, 2-for-13 (.154). 1983-84, 0-for-11. 1984-85, 4-for-18 (.222). 1985-86, 4-for-14 (.286). 1986-87, 6-for-21 (.286). 1987-88, 13-for-39 (.333). 1988-89, 30-for-86 (.349). 1989-90, 57-for-158 (.361). 1990-91, 37-for-125 (.296). 1991-92, 32-for-85 (.376). Totals, 189-for-583 (.324).

NBA PLAYOFF RECORD

NOTES: Shares NBA Finals single-game records for most three-point field goals made—6; and most points in an overtime period—9 (June 7, 1990, vs. Portland).

| | | | | | | | | — REBOUNDS — | | | | | | | | | | |
Season	Team	G	Min.	FGM	FGA	Pct.	FTM	FTA	Pct.	Off.	Def.	Tot.	Ast.	PF	Dq.	Stl.	Blk.	TO	Pts.	Avg.
83-84	—Detroit.........	5	165	29	51	.569	18	20	.900	14	48	62	12	23	2	4	3	12	76	15.2
84-85	—Detroit.........	9	325	48	107	.449	36	51	.706	36	60	96	15	32	1	7	7	16	132	14.7
85-86	—Detroit.........	4	168	34	68	.500	21	23	.913	20	36	56	1	19	1	2	3	8	90	22.5
86-87	—Detroit.........	15	543	84	163	.515	15	24	.625	30	126	156	37	53	2	15	12	20	184	12.3
87-88	—Detroit.........	23	779	114	250	.456	40	45	.889	43	178	221	44	77	2	18	19	30	273	11.9
88-89	—Detroit.........	17	497	66	142	.465	25	31	.806	26	114	140	31	55	1	6	8	19	172	10.1
89-90	—Detroit.........	20	667	91	199	.457	25	29	.862	41	170	211	28	77	3	23	18	16	222	11.1
90-91	—Detroit.........	15	446	66	148	.446	27	31	.871	42	80	122	19	54	0	5	12	17	164	10.9
91-92	—Detroit.........	5	145	17	46	.370	5	5	1.000	5	28	33	8	18	1	4	1	5	41	8.2
	Totals	113	3735	549	1174	.468	212	259	.819	257	840	1097	195	408	13	84	83	143	1354	12.0

Three-point field goals: 1984-85, 0-for-2. 1985-86, 1-for-1. 1986-87, 1-for-5 (.200). 1987-88, 5-for-17 (.294). 1988-89, 15-for-42 (.357). 1989-90, 15-for-43 (.349). 1990-91, 5-for-17 (.294). 1991-92, 2-for-10 (.200). Totals, 44-for-137 (.321).

NBA ALL-STAR GAME RECORD

| | | | | | | | | — REBOUNDS — | | | | | | | |
Season	Team	Min.	FGM	FGA	Pct.	FTM	FTA	Pct.	Off.	Def.	Tot.	Ast.	PF	Dq.	Stl.	Blk.	TO	Pts.
1983	—Detroit...............	6	1	1	1.000	0	0	...	1	0	1	0	1	0	0	0	1	2
1984	—Detroit...............	17	6	8	.750	1	1	1.000	1	4	5	0	3	0	1	2	0	13
1985	—Detroit...............	11	2	4	.500	1	2	.500	1	2	3	1	1	0	0	0	0	5
1987	—Detroit...............	11	4	7	.571	0	0	...	0	2	2	1	2	0	1	0	0	8
	Totals	45	13	20	.650	2	3	.667	3	8	11	2	7	0	2	2	1	28

KL

LANE, JEROME
F, CAVALIERS

PERSONAL: Born December 4, 1966, in Akron, O. . . . 6-6/230.
HIGH SCHOOL: St. Vincent-St. Mary (Akron, O.).
COLLEGE: Pittsburgh.
TRANSACTIONS/CAREER NOTES: Selected as undergraduate by Denver Nuggets in first round (23rd pick overall) of 1988 NBA Draft. . . . Waived by Nuggets (November 25, 1991) . . . Signed by Indiana Pacers to first of two consecutive 10-day contracts (January 24, 1992). . . . Released by Pacers (February 13, 1992). . . . Signed by Milwaukee Bucks to first of two consecutive 10-day contracts (February 13, 1992). . . . Signed as free agent by Cleveland Cavaliers (August 31, 1992).

COLLEGIATE RECORD

NOTES: Led NCAA Division I with 13.5 rebounds per game (1987).

Season Team	G	Min.	FGM	FGA	Pct.	FTM	FTA	Pct.	Reb.	Pts.	Avg.
85-86—Pittsburgh	29	711	95	202	.470	74	113	.655	148	264	9.1
86-87—Pittsburgh	33	1169	187	329	.568	114	230	.496	444	522	15.8
87-88—Pittsburgh	31	1090	154	300	.513	123	200	.615	378	431	13.9
Totals	93	2970	436	831	.525	311	543	.573	970	1217	13.1

Three-point field goals: 1986-87, 4-for-8 (.500). 1987-88, 0-for-7. Totals, 4-for-15 (.267).

NBA REGULAR-SEASON RECORD

Season Team	G	Min.	FGM	FGA	Pct.	FTM	FTA	Pct.	Off.	Def.	Tot.	Ast.	PF	Dq.	Stl.	Blk.	TO	Pts.	Avg.
88-89—Denver	54	550	109	256	.426	43	112	.384	87	113	200	60	105	1	20	4	50	261	4.8
89-90—Denver	67	956	145	309	.469	44	120	.367	144	217	361	105	189	1	53	17	85	334	5.0
90-91—Denver	62	1383	202	461	.438	58	141	.411	280	298	578	123	192	1	51	14	105	463	7.5
91-92—Den-Ind-Mil	14	177	14	46	.304	9	27	.333	32	34	66	17	28	0	2	1	14	37	2.6
Totals	197	3066	470	1072	.438	154	400	.385	543	662	1205	305	514	3	126	36	254	1095	5.6

Three-point field goals: 1988-89, 0-for-7. 1989-90, 0-for-5. 1990-91, 1-for-4 (.250). Totals, 1-for-16 (.063).

NBA PLAYOFF RECORD

Season Team	G	Min.	FGM	FGA	Pct.	FTM	FTA	Pct.	Off.	Def.	Tot.	Ast.	PF	Dq.	Stl.	Blk.	TO	Pts.	Avg.
88-89—Denver	2	21	2	7	.286	2	2	1.000	1	5	6	2	4	0	0	0	6	6	3.0
89-90—Denver	2	14	0	3	.000	1	2	.500	0	1	1	2	4	0	0	0	2	1	0.5
Totals	4	35	2	10	.200	3	4	.750	1	6	7	4	8	0	0	0	2	7	1.8

Three-point field goals: 1988-89, 0-for-1.

LANG, ANDREW
C, 76ERS

PERSONAL: Born June 28, 1966, in Pine Bluff, Ark. . . . 6-11/250. . . . Full name: Andrew Charles Lang Jr.
HIGH SCHOOL: Dollarway (Pine Bluff, Ark.).
COLLEGE: Arkansas.
TRANSACTIONS/CAREER NOTES: Selected by Phoenix Suns in second round (28th pick overall) of 1988 NBA Draft. . . . Traded by Suns with Jeff Hornacek and Tim Perry to Philadelphia 76ers for Charles Barkley (June 17, 1992).

COLLEGIATE RECORD

Season Team	G	Min.	FGM	FGA	Pct.	FTM	FTA	Pct.	Reb.	Pts.	Avg.
84-85—Arkansas	33	467	34	84	.405	18	32	.563	67	86	2.6
85-86—Arkansas	26	694	88	189	.466	37	61	.607	168	213	8.2
86-87—Arkansas	32	722	102	204	.500	56	87	.644	240	260	8.1
87-88—Arkansas	30	743	126	239	.527	27	60	.450	218	279	9.3
Totals	121	2626	350	716	.489	138	240	.575	693	838	6.9

NBA REGULAR-SEASON RECORD

Season Team	G	Min.	FGM	FGA	Pct.	FTM	FTA	Pct.	Off.	Def.	Tot.	Ast.	PF	Dq.	Stl.	Blk.	TO	Pts.	Avg.
88-89—Phoenix	62	526	60	117	.513	39	60	.650	54	93	147	9	112	1	17	48	28	159	2.6
89-90—Phoenix	74	1011	97	174	.557	64	98	.653	83	188	271	21	171	1	22	133	41	258	3.5
90-91—Phoenix	63	1152	109	189	.577	93	130	.715	113	190	303	27	168	2	17	127	45	311	4.9
91-92—Phoenix	81	1965	248	475	.522	126	164	.768	170	376	546	43	306	8	48	201	87	622	7.7
Totals	280	4654	514	955	.538	322	452	.712	420	847	1267	100	757	12	104	509	201	1350	4.8

Three-point field goals: 1990-91, 0-for-1. 1991-92, 0-for-1. Totals, 0-for-2.

NBA PLAYOFF RECORD

Season Team	G	Min.	FGM	FGA	Pct.	FTM	FTA	Pct.	Off.	Def.	Tot.	Ast.	PF	Dq.	Stl.	Blk.	TO	Pts.	Avg.
88-89—Phoenix	4	8	0	2	.000	0	0	...	3	3	6	1	3	0	0	0	3	0	0.0
89-90—Phoenix	12	93	6	9	.667	4	7	.571	4	16	20	2	17	0	3	10	5	16	1.3
90-91—Phoenix	4	55	6	11	.545	14	17	.824	4	14	18	1	12	0	1	3	2	26	6.5
91-92—Phoenix	8	192	15	40	.375	15	19	.789	15	17	32	2	33	2	3	15	8	45	5.6
Totals	28	348	27	62	.435	33	43	.767	26	50	76	6	65	2	7	28	18	87	3.1

LECKNER, ERIC
C, HORNETS

PERSONAL: Born May 27, 1966, in Inglewood, Calif. . . . 6-11/265. . . . Full name: Eric Charles Leckner.
HIGH SCHOOL: Mira Costa (Manhattan Beach, Calif.).
COLLEGE: Wyoming.
TRANSACTIONS/CAREER NOTES: Selected by Utah Jazz in first round (17th pick overall) of 1988 NBA Draft. . . . Traded by Jazz with Bob Hansen and 1990 first- and second-round draft choices to Sacramento Kings

in three-way deal in which Washington Bullets sent Jeff Malone to Jazz and Kings sent Pervis Ellison to Bullets (June 25, 1990); Jazz also received 1990 second-round draft choice and Kings also received 1991 second-round draft choice. . . . Traded by Kings to Charlotte Hornets for 1995 second-round draft choice and other draft considerations (January 29, 1991).

COLLEGIATE RECORD

Season Team	G	Min.	FGM	FGA	Pct.	FTM	FTA	Pct.	Reb.	Pts.	Avg.
84-85 —Wyoming	29	600	98	168	.583	48	78	.615	112	244	8.4
85-86 —Wyoming	36	1113	228	392	.582	112	183	.612	207	568	15.8
86-87 —Wyoming	34	1123	246	390	.631	142	201	.706	245	634	18.6
87-88 —Wyoming	32	972	181	281	.644	130	172	.756	210	492	15.4
Totals	131	3808	753	1231	.612	432	634	.681	774	1938	14.8

NBA REGULAR-SEASON RECORD

Season Team	G	Min.	FGM	FGA	Pct.	FTM	FTA	Pct.	REBOUNDS Off.	Def.	Tot.	Ast.	PF	Dq.	Stl.	Blk.	TO	Pts.	Avg.
88-89 —Utah	75	779	120	220	.545	79	113	.699	48	151	199	16	174	1	8	22	69	319	4.3
89-90 —Utah	77	764	125	222	.563	81	109	.743	48	144	192	19	157	0	15	23	63	331	4.3
90-91 —Sac.-Char.	72	1122	131	294	.446	62	111	.559	82	213	295	39	192	4	14	22	69	324	4.5
91-92 —Charlotte	59	716	79	154	.513	38	51	.745	49	157	206	31	114	1	9	18	39	196	3.3
Totals	283	3381	455	890	.511	260	384	.677	227	665	892	105	637	6	46	85	240	1170	4.1

Three-point field goals: 1991-92, 0-for-1.

NBA PLAYOFF RECORD

Season Team	G	Min.	FGM	FGA	Pct.	FTM	FTA	Pct.	REBOUNDS Off.	Def.	Tot.	Ast.	PF	Dq.	Stl.	Blk.	TO	Pts.	Avg.
88-89 —Utah	3	10	1	4	.250	0	0	...	1	1	2	0	2	0	0	0	3	2	0.7
89-90 —Utah	3	28	6	10	.600	5	9	.556	2	6	8	2	8	0	0	0	1	18	6.0
Totals	6	38	7	14	.500	5	9	.556	3	7	10	2	10	0	0	0	4	20	3.3

Three-point field goals: 1989-90, 1-for-1.

LEE, DOUG
G, NETS

PERSONAL: Born October 24, 1964, in Washington, Ill. . . . 6-6/200. . . . Full name: Douglas E. Lee.
HIGH SCHOOL: Washington (Ill.).
COLLEGE: Texas A&M, then Purdue.
TRANSACTIONS/CAREER NOTES: Selected by Houston Rockets in second round (35th pick overall) of 1987 NBA Draft. . . . Played in Continental Basketball Association with Albany Patroons (1988-89) and Rockford Lightning and Grand Rapids Hoops (1990-91). . . . Played in France (1989-90). . . . Played in Israel (1990-91). . . . Signed as free agent by New Jersey Nets (October 1, 1991).

COLLEGIATE RECORD

Season Team	G	Min.	FGM	FGA	Pct.	FTM	FTA	Pct.	Reb.	Pts.	Avg.
82-83 —Texas A&M	30	348	63	124	.508	22	45	.489	50	148	4.9
83-84 —Texas A&M	24	332	48	116	.414	26	36	.722	56	122	5.1
84-85 —Purdue					Did not play—transfer student.						
85-86 —Purdue	32	975	129	256	.504	41	60	.683	170	299	9.3
86-87 —Purdue	30	917	113	236	.479	50	69	.725	141	312	10.4
Totals	116	2572	353	732	.482	139	210	.662	417	881	7.6

Three-point field goals: 1986-87, 36-for-94 (.383).

CBA REGULAR-SEASON RECORD

Season Team	G	Min.	2-POINT FGM	FGA	Pct.	3-POINT FGM	FGA	Pct.	FTM	FTA	Pct.	Reb.	Ast.	Pts.	Avg.
88-89 —Albany	53	1682	220	482	.456	*95	220	.432	245	285	.860	174	138	970	18.3
90-91 —Rock-Gr. Rap...	14	348	51	102	.500	9	31	.290	34	41	.829	36	30	163	11.6
Totals	67	2030	271	584	.464	104	251	.414	279	326	.856	210	168	1133	16.9

NBA REGULAR-SEASON RECORD

Season Team	G	Min.	FGM	FGA	Pct.	FTM	FTA	Pct.	REBOUNDS Off.	Def.	Tot.	Ast.	PF	Dq.	Stl.	Blk.	TO	Pts.	Avg.
91-92 —New Jersey	46	307	50	116	.431	10	19	.526	17	18	35	22	39	0	11	1	12	120	2.6

Three-point field goals: 1991-92, 10-for-37 (.270).

NBA PLAYOFF RECORD

Season Team	G	Min.	FGM	FGA	Pct.	FTM	FTA	Pct.	REBOUNDS Off.	Def.	Tot.	Ast.	PF	Dq.	Stl.	Blk.	TO	Pts.	Avg.
91-92 —New Jersey	2	6	0	3	.000	0	0	...	0	0	0	1	1	0	0	1	0	0	0.0

Three-point field goals: 1991-92, 0-for-2.

LEONARD, GARY
C

PERSONAL: Born February 16, 1967, in Belleville, Ill. . . . 7-1/265. . . . Full name: Gary Francis Leonard.
HIGH SCHOOL: Belleville East (Ill.).
COLLEGE: Missouri.
TRANSACTIONS/CAREER NOTES: Selected by Minnesota Timberwolves in second round (34th pick overall) of 1989 NBA Draft. . . . Waived by Timberwolves (November 1, 1990). . . . Played in Continental Basketball Association with Cedar Rapids Silver Bullets and Sioux Falls Skyforce (1990-91). . . . Signed as free agent by Atlanta Hawks (March 1, 1991). . . . Waived by Hawks (October 3, 1991). . . . Re-signed as free agent by Hawks (October 7, 1991). . . . Waived by Hawks (January 2, 1991).

COLLEGIATE RECORD

Season Team	G	Min.	FGM	FGA	Pct.	FTM	FTA	Pct.	Reb.	Pts.	Avg.
85-86 — Missouri	34	685	67	141	.475	35	80	.438	123	169	5.0
86-87 — Missouri	32	416	60	113	.531	22	35	.629	99	142	4.4
87-88 — Missouri	29	339	59	94	.628	35	76	.461	100	153	5.3
88-89 — Missouri	37	776	160	270	.593	65	113	.575	205	385	10.4
Totals	132	2216	346	618	.560	157	304	.516	527	849	6.4

NBA REGULAR-SEASON RECORD

Season Team	G	Min.	FGM	FGA	Pct.	FTM	FTA	Pct.	Off.	Def.	Tot.	Ast.	PF	Dq.	Stl.	Blk.	TO	Pts.	Avg.
89-90 — Minnesota	22	127	13	31	.419	6	14	.429	10	17	27	1	26	0	3	9	8	32	1.5
90-91 — Atlanta	4	9	0	0	...	2	4	.500	0	2	2	0	2	0	1	0	1	2	0.5
91-92 — Atlanta	5	13	4	6	.667	2	2	1.000	3	2	5	1	3	0	1	0	1	10	2.0
Totals	31	149	17	37	.459	10	20	.500	13	21	34	2	31	0	4	10	9	44	1.4

Three-point field goals: 1989-90, 0-for-1.

NBA PLAYOFF RECORD

Season Team	G	Min.	FGM	FGA	Pct.	FTM	FTA	Pct.	Off.	Def.	Tot.	Ast.	PF	Dq.	Stl.	Blk.	TO	Pts.	Avg.
90-91 — Atlanta	2	5	2	2	1.000	0	0	...	0	2	2	0	0	0	0	0	0	4	2.0

CBA REGULAR-SEASON RECORD

Season Team	G	Min.	FGM (2-POINT)	FGA (2-POINT)	Pct. (2-POINT)	FGM (3-POINT)	FGA (3-POINT)	Pct. (3-POINT)	FTM	FTA	Pct.	Reb.	Ast.	Pts.	Avg.
90-91 — C.R.-S.F.	19	244	26	55	.473	0	0	...	9	21	.429	72	3	61	3.2

LES, JIM
G, KINGS

PERSONAL: Born August 18, 1963, in Niles, Ill. . . . 5-11/165. . . . Full name: James Allen Les.
HIGH SCHOOL: Notre Dame (Niles, Ill.).
COLLEGE: Cleveland State, then Bradley.
TRANSACTIONS/CAREER NOTES: Selected by Atlanta Hawks in third round (70th pick overall) of 1986 NBA Draft. . . . Waived by Hawks (July, 1986). . . . Signed as free agent by Philadelphia 76ers (September 9, 1986). . . . Waived by 76ers (December 8, 1986). . . . Missed entire 1986-87 season due to injury. . . . Re-signed as free agent by 76ers (June 1, 1987). . . . Waived by 76ers (December 3, 1987). . . . Played in Continental Basketball Association with Rochester Flyers (1987-88), Santa Barbara Islanders (1989-90) and Omaha Racers (1990-91). . . . Signed as free agent by Milwaukee Bucks (October 19, 1988). . . . Waived by Bucks (October 20, 1988). . . . Signed as free agent by Utah Jazz (October 25, 1988). . . . Waived by Jazz (November 6, 1989). . . . Signed by Los Angeles Clippers to first of two consecutive 10-day contracts (February 6, 1990). . . . Signed as free agent by Charlotte Hornets (August 29, 1990). . . . Waived by Hornets (October 24, 1990). . . . Signed by Sacramento Kings to first of two consecutive 10-day contracts (December 31, 1990). . . . Re-signed by Kings for remainder of season (January 20, 1991). . . . Signed as unrestricted free agent by Kings (July 3, 1991).

COLLEGIATE RECORD

Season Team	G	Min.	FGM	FGA	Pct.	FTM	FTA	Pct.	Reb.	Pts.	Avg.
81-82 — Cleveland State	27	...	71	152	.467	51	66	.773	67	193	7.1
82-83 — Bradley					Did not play—transfer student.						
83-84 — Bradley	22	800	49	119	.412	41	58	.707	46	139	6.3
84-85 — Bradley	30	1126	107	215	.498	71	83	.855	100	285	9.5
85-86 — Bradley	35	1278	198	408	.485	102	135	.756	120	498	14.2
Totals	114		425	894	.475	265	342	.775	333	1115	9.8

CBA REGULAR-SEASON RECORD

Season Team	G	Min.	FGM (2-POINT)	FGA (2-POINT)	Pct. (2-POINT)	FGM (3-POINT)	FGA (3-POINT)	Pct. (3-POINT)	FTM	FTA	Pct.	Reb.	Ast.	Pts.	Avg.
87-88 — Rochester	12	334	25	59	.424	10	25	.400	26	39	.667	25	81	106	8.8
89-90 — Santa Barbara	20	594	89	187	.476	24	49	.490	89	100	.890	82	229	339	17.0
90-91 — Omaha	25	964	133	276	.482	46	108	.426	94	113	.832	121	281	498	19.9
Totals	57	1892	247	522	.473	80	182	.440	209	252	.829	228	591	943	16.5

NBA REGULAR-SEASON RECORD

NOTES: Led NBA with .461 three-point field-goal percentage (1991).

Season Team	G	Min.	FGM	FGA	Pct.	FTM	FTA	Pct.	Off.	Def.	Tot.	Ast.	PF	Dq.	Stl.	Blk.	TO	Pts.	Avg.
88-89 — Utah	82	781	40	133	.301	57	73	.781	23	64	87	215	88	0	27	5	88	138	1.7
89-90 — Utah-L.A.C.	7	92	5	14	.357	13	17	.765	3	4	7	21	9	0	3	0	10	23	3.3
90-91 — Sacramento	55	1399	119	268	.444	86	103	.835	18	93	111	299	141	0	57	4	75	395	7.2
91-92 — Sacramento	62	712	74	192	.385	38	47	.809	11	52	63	143	58	0	31	3	42	231	3.7
Totals	206	2984	238	607	.392	194	240	.808	55	213	268	678	296	0	118	12	215	787	3.8

Three-point field goals: 1988-89, 1-for-14 (.071). 1989-90, 0-for-1. 1990-91, 71-for-154 (.461). 1991-92, 45-for-131 (.344). Totals, 117-for-300 (.390).

NBA PLAYOFF RECORD

Season Team	G	Min.	FGM	FGA	Pct.	FTM	FTA	Pct.	Off.	Def.	Tot.	Ast.	PF	Dq.	Stl.	Blk.	TO	Pts.	Avg.
88-89 — Utah	3	5	0	0	...	0	0	...	0	0	0	1	2	0	0	1	0	0	0.0

LEVER, FAT
G, MAVERICKS

PERSONAL: Born August 18, 1960, in Pine Bluff, Ark. . . . 6-3/182. . . . Full name: Lafayette Lever.
HIGH SCHOOL: Pueblo (Tucson, Ariz.).
COLLEGE: Arizona State.
TRANSACTIONS/CAREER NOTES: Selected by Portland Trail Blazers in first round (11th pick overall) of 1982 NBA Draft. . . . Traded by Trail Blazers with Calvin Natt, Wayne Cooper, 1984 second-round draft choice

and 1985 first-round draft choice to Denver Nuggets for Kiki Vandeweghe (June 7, 1984). . . . Traded by Nuggets to Dallas Mavericks for 1990 and 1991 first-round draft choices (June 21, 1990).

COLLEGIATE RECORD

Season Team	G	Min.	FGM	FGA	Pct.	FTM	FTA	Pct.	Reb.	Pts.	Avg.
78-79 — Arizona State	29	377	38	92	.413	28	38	.737	44	104	3.6
79-80 — Arizona State	29	974	98	220	.445	72	103	.699	125	268	9.2
80-81 — Arizona State	28	1038	120	259	.463	84	116	.724	138	324	11.6
81-82 — Arizona State	27	1032	162	357	.454	117	143	.818	146	441	16.3
Totals	113	3421	418	928	.450	301	400	.753	453	1137	10.1

NBA REGULAR-SEASON RECORD

HONORS: All-NBA second team (1987). . . . NBA All-Defensive second team (1988).

Season Team	G	Min.	FGM	FGA	Pct.	FTM	FTA	Pct.	Off.	Def.	Tot.	Ast.	PF	Dq.	Stl.	Blk.	TO	Pts.	Avg.
82-83 — Portland	81	2020	256	594	.431	116	159	.730	85	140	225	426	179	2	153	15	137	633	7.8
83-84 — Portland	81	2010	313	701	.447	159	214	.743	96	122	218	372	178	1	135	31	125	788	9.7
84-85 — Denver	82	2559	424	985	.430	197	256	.770	147	264	411	613	226	1	202	30	203	1051	12.8
85-86 — Denver	78	2616	468	1061	.441	132	182	.725	136	284	420	584	204	3	178	15	210	1080	13.8
86-87 — Denver	82	3054	643	1370	.469	244	312	.782	216	513	729	654	219	1	201	34	167	1552	18.9
87-88 — Denver	82	3061	643	1360	.473	248	316	.785	203	462	665	639	214	0	223	21	182	1546	18.9
88-89 — Denver	71	2745	558	1221	.457	270	344	.785	187	475	662	559	178	1	195	20	157	1409	19.8
89-90 — Denver	79	2832	568	1283	.443	271	337	.804	230	504	734	517	172	1	168	13	156	1443	18.3
90-91 — Dallas	4	86	9	23	.391	11	14	.786	3	12	15	12	5	0	6	3	10	29	7.3
91-92 — Dallas	31	884	135	349	.387	60	80	.750	56	105	161	107	73	0	46	12	36	347	11.2
Totals	671	21867	4017	8947	.449	1708	2214	.771	1359	2881	4240	4483	1648	10	1507	194	1383	9878	14.7

Three-point field goals: 1982-83, 5-for-15 (.333). 1983-84, 3-for-15 (.200). 1984-85, 6-for-24 (.250). 1985-86, 12-for-38 (.316). 1986-87, 22-for-92 (.239). 1987-88, 12-for-57 (.211). 1988-89, 23-for-66 (.348). 1989-90, 36-for-87 (.414). 1990-91, 0-for-3. 1991-92, 17-for-52 (.327). Totals, 136-for-449 (.303).

NBA PLAYOFF RECORD

Season Team	G	Min.	FGM	FGA	Pct.	FTM	FTA	Pct.	Off.	Def.	Tot.	Ast.	PF	Dq.	Stl.	Blk.	TO	Pts.	Avg.
82-83 — Portland	7	134	19	42	.452	4	5	.800	3	11	14	31	13	0	7	0	42	6.0
83-84 — Portland	5	75	8	30	.267	8	10	.800	10	5	15	9	6	0	4	0	3	26	5.2
84-85 — Denver	11	342	49	122	.402	48	63	.762	23	48	71	93	33	0	26	2	34	146	13.3
85-86 — Denver	10	347	59	131	.450	17	24	.708	15	33	48	53	33	0	20	2	23	143	14.3
86-87 — Denver	3	99	19	50	.380	6	9	.667	5	13	18	22	7	0	7	0	2	46	15.3
87-88 — Denver	7	273	45	98	.459	26	33	.788	16	49	65	49	15	0	13	4	4	119	17.0
88-89 — Denver	2	58	9	24	.375	2	2	1.000	2	11	13	19	4	0	4	0	6	22	11.0
89-90 — Denver	3	113	19	51	.373	13	14	.929	11	21	32	21	7	0	8	1	5	52	17.3
Totals	48	1441	227	548	.414	124	160	.775	85	191	276	297	118	0	89	9	81	596	12.4

Three-point field goals: 1983-84, 2-for-3 (.667). 1984-85, 0-for-1. 1985-86, 8-for-14 (.571). 1986-87, 2-for-8 (.250). 1987-88, 3-for-7 (.429). 1988-89, 2-for-3 (.667). 1989-90, 1-for-7 (.143). Totals, 18-for-44 (.409).

NBA ALL-STAR GAME RECORD

Season Team	Min.	FGM	FGA	Pct.	FTM	FTA	Pct.	Off.	Def.	Tot.	Ast.	PF	Dq.	Stl.	Blk.	TO	Pts.
1988 — Denver	31	7	14	.500	3	4	.750	0	4	4	3	4	0	0	0	0	17
1990 — Denver	22	7	13	.538	2	2	1.000	0	3	3	2	0	0	2	0	0	16
Totals	53	14	27	.519	5	6	.833	0	7	7	5	4	0	2	0	0	33

Three-point field goals: 1990, 0-for-2.

LEVINGSTON, CLIFF
F, BULLS

PERSONAL: Born January 4, 1961, in San Diego. . . . 6-8/220. . . . Full name: Clifford Eugene Levingston.
HIGH SCHOOL: Samuel F.B. Morse (San Diego).
COLLEGE: Wichita State.
TRANSACTIONS/CAREER NOTES: Selected as undergraduate by Detroit Pistons in first round (ninth pick overall) of 1982 NBA Draft. . . . Traded by Pistons with draft rights to Antoine Carr and 1986 and 1987 second-round draft choices to Atlanta Hawks for Dan Roundfield (June 18, 1984). . . . Signed as unrestricted free agent by Chicago Bulls (October 3, 1990).
MISCELLANEOUS: Member of NBA championship teams (1991, 1992).

COLLEGIATE RECORD

Season Team	G	Min.	FGM	FGA	Pct.	FTM	FTA	Pct.	Reb.	Pts.	Avg.
79-80 — Wichita State	29	914	189	346	.546	79	127	.622	294	457	15.8
80-81 — Wichita State	33	1108	246	452	.544	120	194	.619	376	612	18.5
81-82 — Wichita State	29	902	162	312	.519	78	125	.624	295	402	13.9
Totals	91	2924	597	1110	.538	277	446	.621	965	1471	16.2

NBA REGULAR-SEASON RECORD

Season Team	G	Min.	FGM	FGA	Pct.	FTM	FTA	Pct.	Off.	Def.	Tot.	Ast.	PF	Dq.	Stl.	Blk.	TO	Pts.	Avg.
82-83 — Detroit	62	879	131	270	.485	84	147	.571	104	128	232	52	125	2	23	36	73	346	5.6
83-84 — Detroit	80	1746	229	436	.525	125	186	.672	234	311	545	109	281	7	44	78	77	583	7.3
84-85 — Atlanta	74	2017	291	552	.527	145	222	.653	230	336	566	104	231	3	70	69	133	727	9.8
85-86 — Atlanta	81	1945	294	551	.534	164	242	.678	193	341	534	72	260	5	76	39	113	752	9.3
86-87 — Atlanta	82	1848	251	496	.506	155	212	.731	219	314	533	40	261	4	68	72	657	8.0
87-88 — Atlanta	82	2135	314	564	.557	190	246	.772	228	276	504	71	287	5	52	84	94	819	10.0
88-89 — Atlanta	80	2184	300	568	.528	133	191	.696	194	304	498	75	270	4	97	70	105	734	9.2
89-90 — Atlanta	75	1706	216	424	.509	83	122	.680	113	206	319	80	216	2	55	41	49	516	6.9
90-91 — Chicago	78	1013	127	282	.450	59	91	.648	99	126	225	56	143	0	29	43	50	314	4.0
91-92 — Chicago	79	1020	125	251	.498	60	96	.625	109	118	227	66	134	0	27	45	42	311	3.9
Totals	773	16493	2278	4394	.518	1198	1755	.683	1723	2460	4183	725	2208	32	521	573	808	5759	7.5

Three-point field goals: 1982-83, 0-for-1. 1983-84, 0-for-3. 1984-85, 0-for-2. 1985-86, 0-for-1. 1986-87, 0-for-3. 1987-88, 1-for-2 (.500). 1988-89, 1-for-5 (.200). 1989-90, 1-for-4 (.250). 1991-92, 1-for-6 (.167). Totals, 4-for-27 (.148).

NBA PLAYOFF RECORD

Season Team	G	Min.	FGM	FGA	Pct.	FTM	FTA	Pct.	REBOUNDS Off.	Def.	Tot.	Ast.	PF	Dq.	Stl.	Blk.	TO	Pts.	Avg.
83-84 —Detroit.........	5	101	15	19	.789	10	16	.625	11	13	24	1	15	0	1	2	3	40	8.0
85-86 —Atlanta.........	9	180	22	37	.595	7	9	.778	15	26	41	3	23	0	4	9	9	52	5.8
86-87 —Atlanta.........	9	108	7	18	.389	14	18	.778	12	22	34	3	21	0	0	3	4	28	3.1
87-88 —Atlanta.........	12	163	24	50	.480	12	16	.750	14	12	26	7	25	0	5	5	8	60	5.0
88-89 —Atlanta.........	5	77	3	11	.273	9	10	.900	6	11	17	2	15	0	0	3	3	16	3.2
90-91 —Chicago.......	17	192	21	41	.512	3	6	.500	22	19	41	7	28	0	10	7	2	45	2.6
91-92 —Chicago.......	22	191	25	57	.439	14	28	.500	17	24	41	9	31	0	4	6	11	64	2.9
Totals	79	1012	117	233	.502	69	103	.670	97	127	224	32	158	0	24	35	40	305	3.9

Three-point field goals: 1985-86, 1-for-1. 1986-87, 0-for-1. 1988-89, 1-for-1. 1991-92, 0-for-1. Totals, 2-for-4 (.500).

LEWIS, REGGIE

G/F, CELTICS

PERSONAL: Born November 21, 1965, in Baltimore.... 6-7/195. **HIGH SCHOOL:** Dunbar (Baltimore). **COLLEGE:** Northeastern. **TRANSACTIONS/CAREER NOTES:** Selected by Boston Celtics in first round (22nd pick overall) of 1987 NBA Draft.

COLLEGIATE RECORD

Season Team	G	Min.	FGM	FGA	Pct.	FTM	FTA	Pct.	Reb.	Pts.	Avg.
83-84 —Northeastern	32	1030	236	447	.528	99	144	.688	198	571	17.8
84-85 —Northeastern	31	1082	294	585	.503	159	213	.746	241	747	24.1
85-86 —Northeastern	30	1118	265	559	.474	184	229	.803	279	714	23.8
86-87 —Northeastern	29	957	248	507	.489	150	197	.761	246	676	23.3
Totals	122	4187	1043	2098	.497	592	783	.756	964	2708	22.2

Three-point field goals: 1986-87, 30-for-91 (.330).

NBA REGULAR-SEASON RECORD

Season Team	G	Min.	FGM	FGA	Pct.	FTM	FTA	Pct.	REBOUNDS Off.	Def.	Tot.	Ast.	PF	Dq.	Stl.	Blk.	TO	Pts.	Avg.
87-88 —Boston	49	405	90	193	.466	40	57	.702	28	35	63	26	54	0	16	15	30	220	4.5
88-89 —Boston	81	2657	604	1242	.486	284	361	.787	116	261	377	218	258	5	124	72	142	1495	18.5
89-90 —Boston	79	2522	540	1089	.496	256	317	.808	109	238	347	225	216	2	88	63	120	1340	17.0
90-91 —Boston	79	2878	598	1219	.491	281	340	.826	119	291	410	201	234	1	98	85	147	1478	18.7
91-92 —Boston	82	3070	703	1397	.503	292	343	.851	117	277	394	185	258	4	125	105	136	1703	20.8
Totals	370	11532	2535	5140	.493	1153	1418	.813	489	1102	1591	855	1020	12	451	340	575	6236	16.9

Three-point field goals: 1987-88, 0-for-4. 1988-89, 3-for-22 (.136). 1989-90, 4-for-15 (.267). 1990-91, 1-for-13 (.077). 1991-92, 5-for-21 (.238). Totals, 13-for-75 (.173).

NBA PLAYOFF RECORD

Season Team	G	Min.	FGM	FGA	Pct.	FTM	FTA	Pct.	REBOUNDS Off.	Def.	Tot.	Ast.	PF	Dq.	Stl.	Blk.	TO	Pts.	Avg.
87-88 —Boston	12	70	13	34	.382	3	5	.600	9	7	16	4	13	0	3	2	0	29	2.4
88-89 —Boston	3	125	26	55	.473	9	13	.692	5	16	21	11	11	0	5	0	8	61	20.3
89-90 —Boston	5	200	37	62	.597	27	35	.771	9	16	25	22	14	0	7	2	12	101	20.2
90-91 —Boston	11	462	95	195	.487	56	68	.824	18	50	68	32	33	1	12	6	20	246	22.4
91-92 —Boston	10	408	115	218	.528	48	63	.762	11	32	43	39	38	2	24	8	16	280	28.0
Totals	41	1265	286	564	.507	143	184	.777	52	121	173	108	109	3	51	18	56	717	17.5

Three-point field goals: 1987-88, 0-for-1. 1988-89, 0-for-2. 1989-90, 0-for-1. 1990-91, 0-for-4. 1991-92, 2-for-6 (.333). Totals, 2-for-14 (.143).

NBA ALL-STAR GAME RECORD

Season Team	Min.	FGM	FGA	Pct.	FTM	FTA	Pct.	REBOUNDS Off.	Def.	Tot.	Ast.	PF	Dq.	Stl.	Blk.	TO	Pts.
1992 —Boston	15	3	7	.429	1	2	.500	4	0	4	2	3	0	0	1	1	7

LIBERTY, MARCUS
F, NUGGETS

PERSONAL: Born October 27, 1968, in Chicago.... 6-8/205. **HIGH SCHOOL:** King (Chicago). **COLLEGE:** Illinois. **TRANSACTIONS/CAREER NOTES:** Selected as undergraduate by Denver Nuggets in second round (42nd pick overall) of 1990 NBA Draft.

COLLEGIATE RECORD

Season Team	G	Min.	FGM	FGA	Pct.	FTM	FTA	Pct.	Reb.	Pts.	Avg.
87-88 —Illinois					Did not play—ineligible.						
88-89 —Illinois	36	748	120	252	.476	57	73	.781	141	303	8.4
89-90 —Illinois	29	958	203	400	.508	103	135	.763	206	517	17.8
Totals	65	1706	323	652	.495	160	208	.769	347	820	12.6

Three-point field goals: 1988-89, 6-for-12 (.500). 1989-90, 8-for-21 (.381). Totals, 14-for-33 (.424).

NBA REGULAR-SEASON RECORD

Season Team	G	Min.	FGM	FGA	Pct.	FTM	FTA	Pct.	REBOUNDS Off.	Def.	Tot.	Ast.	PF	Dq.	Stl.	Blk.	TO	Pts.	Avg.
90-91 —Denver	76	1171	216	513	.421	58	92	.630	117	104	221	64	153	2	48	19	71	507	6.7
91-92 —Denver	75	1527	275	621	.443	131	180	.728	144	164	308	58	165	3	66	29	90	698	9.3
Totals	151	2698	491	1134	.433	189	272	.695	261	268	529	122	318	5	114	48	161	1205	8.0

Three-point field goals: 1990-91, 17-for-57 (.298). 1991-92, 17-for-50 (.340). Totals, 34-for-107 (.318).

LICHTI, TODD
G, NUGGETS

PERSONAL: Born January 8, 1967, in Walnut Creek, Calif. . . . 6-4/205. . . . Full name: Todd Samuel Lichti. . . . Name pronounced LICK-tee.
HIGH SCHOOL: Mt. Diablo (Concord, Calif.).
COLLEGE: Stanford.
TRANSACTIONS/CAREER NOTES: Selected by Denver Nuggets in first round (15th pick overall) of 1989 NBA Draft.

COLLEGIATE RECORD

Season Team	G	Min.	FGM	FGA	Pct.	FTM	FTA	Pct.	Reb.	Pts.	Avg.
85-86 —Stanford	30	876	188	353	.533	140	172	.814	142	516	17.2
86-87 —Stanford	28	974	170	329	.517	123	152	.809	160	493	17.6
87-88 —Stanford	33	1140	222	406	.547	174	198	.879	184	664	20.1
88-89 —Stanford	33	1117	240	437	.549	147	173	.850	166	663	20.1
Totals	124	4107	820	1525	.538	584	695	.840	652	2336	18.8

Three-point field goals: 1986-87, 30-for-63 (.476). 1987-88, 46-for-89 (.517). 1988-89, 36-for-83 (.434). Totals, 112-for-235 (.477).

NBA REGULAR-SEASON RECORD

Season Team	G	Min.	FGM	FGA	Pct.	FTM	FTA	Pct.	Off.	Def.	Tot.	Ast.	PF	Dq.	Stl.	Blk.	TO	Pts.	Avg.
89-90 —Denver	79	1326	250	514	.486	130	174	.747	49	102	151	116	145	1	55	13	95	630	8.0
90-91 —Denver	29	860	166	378	.439	59	69	.855	49	63	112	72	65	1	46	8	33	405	14.0
91-92 —Denver	68	1176	173	376	.460	99	118	.839	36	82	118	74	131	0	43	12	72	446	6.6
Totals	176	3362	589	1268	.465	288	361	.798	134	247	381	262	341	2	144	33	200	1481	8.4

Three-point field goals: 1989-90, 0-for-14. 1990-91, 14-for-47 (.298). 1991-92, 1-for-9 (.111). Totals, 15-for-70 (.214).

NBA PLAYOFF RECORD

Season Team	G	Min.	FGM	FGA	Pct.	FTM	FTA	Pct.	Off.	Def.	Tot.	Ast.	PF	Dq.	Stl.	Blk.	TO	Pts.	Avg.
89-90 —Denver	3	70	15	29	.517	14	19	.737	5	13	18	9	6	0	1	0	8	44	14.7

Three-point field goals: 1989-90, 0-for-1.

LISTER, ALTON
C/F, WARRIORS

PERSONAL: Born October 1, 1958, in Dallas. . . . 7-0/245. . . . Full name: Alton Lavelle Lister. . . . Name pronounced ALL-ton.
HIGH SCHOOL: Woodrow Wilson (Dallas).
COLLEGE: San Jacinto (Tex.), then Arizona State.
TRANSACTIONS/CAREER NOTES: Selected by Milwaukee Bucks in first round (21st pick overall) of 1981 NBA Draft. . . . Traded by Bucks with 1987 and 1989 first-round draft choices to Seattle SuperSonics for Jack Sikma and 1987 and 1989 second-round draft choices (July 1, 1986). . . . Traded by SuperSonics to Golden State Warriors for 1990 first-round draft choice (August 7, 1989).
MISCELLANEOUS: Member of U.S. Olympic team (1980).

COLLEGIATE RECORD

Season Team	G	Min.	FGM	FGA	Pct.	FTM	FTA	Pct.	Reb.	Pts.	Avg.
76-77 —San Jacinto	40	...	...	...	...	...	...	...	640	680	17.0
77-78 —San Jacinto					Did not play—redshirted.						
78-79 —Arizona State	29	584	104	209	.498	47	84	.560	194	255	8.8
79-80 —Arizona State	27	793	133	264	.504	58	104	.558	231	324	12.0
80-81 —Arizona State	26	845	158	282	.560	85	123	.691	251	401	15.4
Junior college totals	40	...	...	...	...	...	...	...	640	680	17.0
Four-year-college totals	82	2222	395	755	.523	190	311	.611	676	980	12.0

Three-point field goals: 1984-85, 0-for-1. 1985-86, 0-for-2. 1986-87, 0-for-1. 1987-88, 1-for-2 (.500). 1989-90, 0-for-1. 1990-91, 0-for-1. Totals, 1-for-8 (.125).

NBA REGULAR-SEASON RECORD

Season Team	G	Min.	FGM	FGA	Pct.	FTM	FTA	Pct.	Off.	Def.	Tot.	Ast.	PF	Dq.	Stl.	Blk.	TO	Pts.	Avg.
81-82 —Milwaukee	80	1186	149	287	.519	64	123	.520	108	279	387	84	239	4	18	118	129	362	4.5
82-83 —Milwaukee	80	1885	272	514	.529	130	242	.537	168	400	568	111	328	18	50	177	186	674	8.4
83-84 —Milwaukee	82	1955	256	512	.500	114	182	.626	156	447	603	110	327	11	41	140	153	626	7.6
84-85 —Milwaukee	81	2091	322	600	.538	154	262	.588	219	428	647	127	287	5	49	167	183	798	9.9
85-86 —Milwaukee	81	1812	318	577	.551	160	266	.602	199	393	592	101	300	8	49	142	161	796	9.8
86-87 —Seattle	75	2288	346	687	.504	179	265	.675	223	482	705	110	289	11	32	180	169	871	11.6
87-88 —Seattle	82	1812	173	343	.504	114	188	.606	200	427	627	58	319	8	27	140	90	461	5.6
88-89 —Seattle	82	1806	271	543	.499	115	178	.646	207	338	545	54	310	3	28	180	117	657	8.0
89-90 —Golden State	3	40	4	8	.500	4	7	.571	5	3	8	2	8	0	1	0	0	12	4.0
90-91 —Golden State	77	1552	188	393	.478	115	202	.569	121	362	483	93	282	4	20	90	106	491	6.4
91-92 —Golden State	26	293	44	79	.557	14	33	.424	21	71	92	14	61	0	5	16	20	102	3.9
Totals	749	16720	2343	4541	.516	1163	1948	.597	1627	3630	5257	864	2750	72	320	1350	1314	5850	7.8

Three-point field goals: 1984-85, 0-for-1. 1985-86, 0-for-2. 1986-87, 0-for-1. 1987-88, 1-for-2 (.500). 1989-90, 0-for-1. 1990-91, 0-for-1. Totals, 1-for-8 (.125).

NBA PLAYOFF RECORD

Season Team	G	Min.	FGM	FGA	Pct.	FTM	FTA	Pct.	Off.	Def.	Tot.	Ast.	PF	Dq.	Stl.	Blk.	TO	Pts.	Avg.
81-82 —Milwaukee	6	112	14	24	.583	5	7	.714	6	21	27	5	23	0	2	15	9	33	5.5
82-83 —Milwaukee	9	206	27	63	.429	4	5	.800	21	40	61	11	30	1	9	15	17	58	6.4
83-84 —Milwaukee	16	368	39	78	.500	30	48	.625	26	70	96	10	63	2	5	24	27	108	6.8
84-85 —Milwaukee	8	203	27	60	.450	15	32	.469	27	35	62	15	36	1	6	15	16	69	8.6
85-86 —Milwaukee	14	335	66	103	.641	35	58	.603	37	59	96	12	56	3	7	22	21	167	11.9
86-87 —Seattle	9	206	20	50	.400	14	20	.700	29	27	56	7	37	3	7	13	10	54	6.0
87-88 —Seattle	5	77	12	17	.706	4	5	.800	9	20	29	5	17	0	1	5	4	28	5.6

Season Team	G	Min.	FGM	FGA	Pct.	FTM	FTA	Pct.	Off.	Def.	Tot.	Ast.	PF	Dq.	Stl.	Blk.	TO	Pts.	Avg.
88-89 —Seattle.........	8	160	17	39	.436	22	26	.846	13	25	38	2	28	0	2	21	9	56	7.0
90-91 —Golden State	6	72	12	25	.480	2	5	.400	7	21	28	2	15	0	0	7	8	26	4.3
91-92 —Golden State	4	47	6	15	.400	4	5	.800	3	8	11	1	9	0	0	4	3	16	4.0
Totals	85	1786	240	474	.506	135	211	.640	178	326	504	70	314	10	39	141	124	615	7.2

Three-point field goals: 1982-83, 0-for-1. 1985-86, 0-for-1. Totals, 0-for-2.

LOHAUS, BRAD
C/F

PERSONAL: Born September 29, 1964, in New Ulm, Minn. . . . 7-0/235. . . . Full name: Brad Allen Lohaus. . . . Name pronounced LOW-haas.
HIGH SCHOOL: Greenway (Phoenix).
COLLEGE: Iowa.
TRANSACTIONS/CAREER NOTES: Selected by Boston Celtics in second round (45th pick overall) of 1987 NBA Draft. . . . Traded by Celtics with Danny Ainge to Sacramento Kings for Joe Kleine and Ed Pinckney (February 23, 1989). . . . Selected by Minnesota Timberwolves from Kings in NBA expansion draft (June 15, 1989). . . . Traded by Timberwolves to Milwaukee Bucks for Randy Breuer and conditional exchange of 1991 or 1992 second-round draft choices (January 4, 1990).

COLLEGIATE RECORD

Season Team	G	Min.	FGM	FGA	Pct.	FTM	FTA	Pct.	Reb.	Pts.	Avg.
82-83 —Iowa	20	...	9	29	.310	7	13	.538	11	26	1.3
83-84 —Iowa	28	626	78	193	.404	35	52	.673	146	191	6.8
84-85 —Iowa					Did not play—redshirted.						
85-86 —Iowa	32	407	44	102	.431	27	34	.794	101	115	3.6
86-87 —Iowa	35	943	149	276	.540	72	104	.692	268	395	11.3
Totals	115	...	280	600	.467	141	203	.695	526	727	6.3

Three-point field goals: 1982-83, 1-for-1. 1986-87, 25-for-72 (.347). Totals, 26-for-73 (.356).

NBA REGULAR-SEASON RECORD

Season Team	G	Min.	FGM	FGA	Pct.	FTM	FTA	Pct.	Off.	Def.	Tot.	Ast.	PF	Dq.	Stl.	Blk.	TO	Pts.	Avg.
87-88 —Boston	70	718	122	246	.496	50	62	.806	46	92	138	49	123	1	20	41	59	297	4.2
88-89 —Boston-Sac.	77	1214	210	486	.432	81	103	.786	84	172	256	66	161	1	30	56	77	502	6.5
89-90 —Min.-Mil.....	80	1943	305	663	.460	75	103	.728	98	300	398	168	211	3	58	88	109	732	9.2
90-91 —Milwaukee ...	81	1219	179	415	.431	37	54	.685	59	158	217	75	170	3	50	74	60	428	5.3
91-92 —Milwaukee ...	70	1081	162	360	.450	27	41	.659	65	184	249	74	144	5	40	71	46	408	5.8
Totals	378	6175	978	2170	.451	270	363	.744	352	906	1258	432	809	13	198	330	351	2367	6.3

Three-point field goals: 1987-88, 3-for-13 (.231). 1988-89, 1-for-11 (.091). 1989-90, 47-for-137 (.343). 1990-91, 33-for-119 (.277). 1991-92, 57-for-144 (.396). Totals, 141-for-424 (.333).

NBA PLAYOFF RECORD

Season Team	G	Min.	FGM	FGA	Pct.	FTM	FTA	Pct.	Off.	Def.	Tot.	Ast.	PF	Dq.	Stl.	Blk.	TO	Pts.	Avg.
87-88 —Boston	9	26	8	11	.727	0	0	...	1	3	4	0	4	0	0	1	1	16	1.8
89-90 —Milwaukee ...	4	147	16	40	.400	0	0	...	4	23	27	5	17	1	8	9	9	38	9.5
90-91 —Milwaukee ...	3	41	5	16	.313	1	2	.500	4	5	9	1	6	0	0	0	3	14	4.7
Totals	16	214	29	67	.433	1	2	.500	9	31	40	6	27	1	8	10	13	68	4.3

Three-point field goals: 1987-88, 0-for-2. 1989-90, 6-for-16 (.375). 1990-91, 3-for-8 (.375). Totals, 9-for-26 (.346).

L

LONG, GRANT
F, HEAT

PERSONAL: Born March 12, 1966, in Wayne, Mich. . . . 6-9/230. . . . Full name: Grant Andrew Long. . . . Nephew of John Long, guard with Detroit Pistons, Indiana Pacers and Atlanta Hawks (1978-79 through 1990-91).
HIGH SCHOOL: Romulus (Mich.).
COLLEGE: Eastern Michigan.
TRANSACTIONS/CAREER NOTES: Selected by Miami Heat in second round (33rd pick overall) of 1988 NBA Draft.

COLLEGIATE RECORD

Season Team	G	Min.	FGM	FGA	Pct.	FTM	FTA	Pct.	Reb.	Pts.	Avg.
84-85 —Eastern Michigan	28	551	44	78	.564	28	46	.609	112	116	4.1
85-86 —Eastern Michigan	27	803	92	175	.526	47	73	.644	178	231	8.6
86-87 —Eastern Michigan	29	879	169	308	.549	95	131	.725	260	433	14.9
87-88 —Eastern Michigan	30	1026	237	427	.555	215	281	.765	313	689	23.0
Totals	114	3259	542	988	.549	385	531	.725	863	1469	12.9

NBA REGULAR-SEASON RECORD

Season Team	G	Min.	FGM	FGA	Pct.	FTM	FTA	Pct.	Off.	Def.	Tot.	Ast.	PF	Dq.	Stl.	Blk.	TO	Pts.	Avg.
88-89 —Miami..........	82	2435	336	692	.486	304	406	.749	240	306	546	149	*337	13	122	48	201	976	11.9
89-90 —Miami..........	81	1856	257	532	.483	172	241	.714	156	246	402	96	300	11	91	38	139	686	8.5
90-91 —Miami..........	80	2514	276	561	.492	181	230	.787	225	343	568	176	295	10	119	43	156	734	9.2
91-92 —Miami..........	82	3063	440	890	.494	326	404	.807	259	432	691	225	248	2	139	40	185	1212	14.8
Totals	325	9868	1309	2675	.489	983	1281	.767	880	1327	2207	646	1180	36	471	169	681	3608	11.1

Three-point field goals: 1988-89, 0-for-5. 1989-90, 0-for-3. 1990-91, 1-for-6 (.167). 1991-92, 6-for-22 (.273). Totals, 7-for-36 (.194).

NBA PLAYOFF RECORD

Season Team	G	Min.	FGM	FGA	Pct.	FTM	FTA	Pct.	Off.	Def.	Tot.	Ast.	PF	Dq.	Stl.	Blk.	TO	Pts.	Avg.
91-92 —Miami..........	3	120	15	36	.417	7	10	.700	7	8	15	8	11	0	5	0	5	37	12.3

Three-point field goals: 1991-92, 0-for-4.

LONGLEY, LUC

C, TIMBERWOLVES

PERSONAL: Born January 19, 1969, in Melbourne, Australia.... 7-2/265. ... Full name: Lucien James Longley.
HIGH SCHOOL: Scotch College (Perth, Australia).
COLLEGE: New Mexico.
TRANSACTIONS/CAREER NOTES: Selected by Minnesota Timberwolves in first round (seventh pick overall) of 1991 NBA Draft.
MISCELLANEOUS: Member of Australian Olympic team (1988, 1992).

COLLEGIATE RECORD

Season Team	G	Min.	FGM	FGA	Pct.	FTM	FTA	Pct.	Reb.	Pts.	Avg.
87-88 — New Mexico	35	424	60	120	.500	20	51	.392	94	140	4.0
88-89 — New Mexico	33	966	174	301	.578	80	104	.769	223	428	13.0
89-90 — New Mexico	34	1192	233	417	.559	161	196	.821	330	627	18.4
90-91 — New Mexico	30	1067	229	349	.656	116	162	.716	275	574	19.1
Totals	132	3649	696	1187	.586	377	513	.735	922	1769	13.4

Three-point field goals: 1990-91, 0-for-2.

NBA REGULAR-SEASON RECORD

Season Team	G	Min.	FGM	FGA	Pct.	FTM	FTA	Pct.	REBOUNDS Off.	Def.	Tot.	Ast.	PF	Dq.	Stl.	Blk.	TO	Pts.	Avg.
91-92 — Minnesota....	66	991	114	249	.458	53	80	.663	67	190	257	53	157	0	35	64	83	281	4.3

LYNCH, KEVIN

G/F, HORNETS

PERSONAL: Born December 24, 1968, in Bloomington, Minn.... 6-5/197. ... Full name: Kevin Joseph Lynch.
HIGH SCHOOL: Thomas Jefferson (Bloomington, Minn.).
COLLEGE: Minnesota.
TRANSACTIONS/CAREER NOTES: Selected by Charlotte Hornets in second round (28th pick overall) of 1991 NBA Draft.

COLLEGIATE RECORD

Season Team	G	Min.	FGM	FGA	Pct.	FTM	FTA	Pct.	Reb.	Pts.	Avg.
87-88 — Minnesota	28	445	39	101	.386	15	19	.789	31	103	3.7
88-89 — Minnesota	31	854	123	262	.469	48	64	.750	131	318	10.3
89-90 — Minnesota	32	943	167	330	.506	53	71	.746	91	428	13.4
90-91 — Minnesota	28	952	190	413	.460	84	101	.832	121	506	18.1
Totals	119	3194	519	1106	.469	200	255	.784	374	1355	11.4

Three-point field goals: 1987-88, 10-for-22 (.455). 1988-89, 24-for-66 (.364). 1989-90, 41-for-103 (.398). 1990-91, 42-for-107 (.393). Totals, 117-for-298 (.393).

NBA REGULAR-SEASON RECORD

Season Team	G	Min.	FGM	FGA	Pct.	FTM	FTA	Pct.	REBOUNDS Off.	Def.	Tot.	Ast.	PF	Dq.	Stl.	Blk.	TO	Pts.	Avg.
91-92 — Charlotte......	55	819	93	223	.417	35	46	.761	30	55	85	83	107	0	37	9	44	224	4.1

Three-point field goals: 1991-92, 3-for-8 (.375).

MACON, MARK

G, NUGGETS

PERSONAL: Born April 14, 1969, in Saginaw, Mich.... 6-5/185.... Full name: Mark L. Macon.
HIGH SCHOOL: Buena Vista (Saginaw, Mich.).
COLLEGE: Temple.
TRANSACTIONS/CAREER NOTES: Selected by Denver Nuggets in first round (eighth pick overall) of 1991 NBA Draft.

COLLEGIATE RECORD

Season Team	G	Min.	FGM	FGA	Pct.	FTM	FTA	Pct.	Reb.	Pts.	Avg.
87-88 — Temple	34	1203	280	617	.454	74	96	.771	192	699	20.6
88-89 — Temple	30	1137	204	501	.407	97	125	.776	168	548	18.3
89-90 — Temple	31	1192	242	622	.389	134	168	.798	187	679	21.9
90-91 — Temple	31	1190	254	578	.439	98	128	.766	153	683	22.0
Totals	126	4722	980	2318	.423	403	517	.779	700	2609	20.7

Three-point field goals: 1987-88, 65-for-154 (.422). 1988-89, 43-for-134 (.321). 1989-90, 61-for-185 (.330). 1990-91, 77-for-184 (.418). Totals, 246-for-657 (.374).

NBA REGULAR-SEASON RECORD

HONORS: NBA All-Rookie second team (1992).

Season Team	G	Min.	FGM	FGA	Pct.	FTM	FTA	Pct.	REBOUNDS Off.	Def.	Tot.	Ast.	PF	Dq.	Stl.	Blk.	TO	Pts.	Avg.
91-92 — Denver	76	2304	333	889	.375	135	185	.730	80	140	220	168	242	4	154	14	155	805	10.6

Three-point field goals: 1991-92, 4-for-30 (.133).

MAJERLE, DAN

G/F, SUNS

PERSONAL: Born September 9, 1965, in Traverse City, Mich.... 6-6/220.... Full name: Daniel Lewis Majerle.... Name pronounced MAR-lee.
HIGH SCHOOL: Traverse City Senior (Mich.).
COLLEGE: Central Michigan.
TRANSACTIONS/CAREER NOTES: Selected by Phoenix Suns in first round (14th pick overall) of 1988 NBA

Draft.
MISCELLANEOUS: Member of bronze-medal-winning U.S. Olympic team (1988).

COLLEGIATE RECORD

Season Team	G	Min.	FGM	FGA	Pct.	FTM	FTA	Pct.	Reb.	Pts.	Avg.
83-84 — Central Michigan					Did not play—back injury.						
84-85 — Central Michigan	12	360	92	162	.568	39	67	.582	80	223	18.6
85-86 — Central Michigan	27	1002	228	433	.527	122	170	.718	212	578	21.4
86-87 — Central Michigan	23	824	191	344	.555	101	183	.552	196	485	21.1
87-88 — Central Michigan	32	1197	279	535	.522	156	242	.645	346	759	23.7
Totals	94	3383	790	1474	.536	418	662	.631	834	2045	21.8

Three-point field goals: 1986-87, 2-for-8 (.250). 1987-88, 45-for-101 (.446). Totals, 47-for-109 (.431).

NBA REGULAR-SEASON RECORD

HONORS: NBA All-Defensive second team (1991).

Season Team	G	Min.	FGM	FGA	Pct.	FTM	FTA	Pct.	Off.	Def.	Tot.	Ast.	PF	Dq.	Stl.	Blk.	TO	Pts.	Avg.
88-89 — Phoenix	54	1354	181	432	.419	78	127	.614	62	147	209	130	139	1	63	14	48	467	8.6
89-90 — Phoenix	73	2244	296	698	.424	198	260	.762	144	286	430	188	177	5	100	32	82	809	11.1
90-91 — Phoenix	77	2281	397	821	.484	227	298	.762	168	250	418	216	162	0	106	40	114	1051	13.6
91-92 — Phoenix	82	2853	551	1153	.478	229	303	.756	148	335	483	274	158	0	131	43	101	1418	17.3
Totals	286	8732	1425	3104	.459	732	988	.741	522	1018	1540	808	636	6	400	129	345	3745	13.1

Three-point field goals: 1988-89, 27-for-82 (.329). 1989-90, 19-for-80 (.238). 1990-91, 30-for-86 (.349). 1991-92, 87-for-228 (.382). Totals, 163-for-476 (.342).

NBA PLAYOFF RECORD

Season Team	G	Min.	FGM	FGA	Pct.	FTM	FTA	Pct.	Off.	Def.	Tot.	Ast.	PF	Dq.	Stl.	Blk.	TO	Pts.	Avg.
88-89 — Phoenix	12	352	63	144	.438	38	48	.792	22	35	57	14	28	0	13	4	15	172	14.3
89-90 — Phoenix	16	479	73	150	.487	51	65	.785	30	51	81	34	34	0	20	2	18	201	12.6
90-91 — Phoenix	4	110	12	32	.375	14	19	.737	6	9	15	7	12	0	5	1	2	42	10.5
91-92 — Phoenix	7	266	48	111	.432	25	26	.962	13	31	44	20	11	0	10	0	9	130	18.6
Totals	39	1207	196	437	.449	128	158	.810	71	126	197	75	85	0	48	7	44	545	14.0

Three-point field goals: 1988-89, 8-for-28 (.286). 1989-90, 4-for-12 (.333). 1990-91, 4-for-11 (.364). 1991-92, 9-for-33 (.273). Totals, 25-for-84 (.298).

NBA ALL-STAR GAME RECORD

Season Team	Min.	FGM	FGA	Pct.	FTM	FTA	Pct.	Off.	Def.	Tot.	Ast.	PF	Dq.	Stl.	Blk.	TO	Pts.
1992 — Phoenix	12	2	5	.400	0	0	...	0	3	3	2	0	0	0	0	1	4

Three-point field goals: 1992, 0-for-2.

MALONE, JEFF
G, JAZZ

PERSONAL: Born June 28, 1961, in Mobile, Ala.... 6-4/205.... Full name: Jeffrey Nigel Malone.
HIGH SCHOOL: Southwest (Macon, Ga.).
COLLEGE: Mississippi State.
TRANSACTIONS/CAREER NOTES: Selected by Washington Bullets in first round (10th pick overall) of 1983 NBA Draft.... Traded by Bullets to Utah Jazz in three-way deal in which Sacramento Kings sent Pervis Ellison to Bullets and Jazz sent Bob Hansen, Eric Leckner and 1990 first- and second-round draft choices to Kings (June 25, 1990); Jazz also received 1990 second-round draft choice and Kings also received 1991 second-round draft choice.

COLLEGIATE RECORD

NOTES: THE SPORTING NEWS All-America first team (1983).

Season Team	G	Min.	FGM	FGA	Pct.	FTM	FTA	Pct.	Reb.	Pts.	Avg.
79-80 — Mississippi State	27	781	139	303	.459	42	51	.824	90	320	11.9
80-81 — Mississippi State	27	999	219	447	.490	105	128	.820	113	543	20.1
81-82 — Mississippi State	27	1001	225	410	.549	52	70	.743	111	502	18.6
82-83 — Mississippi State	29	1070	323	608	.531	131	159	.824	106	777	26.8
Totals	110	3851	906	1768	.512	330	408	.809	420	2142	19.5

NBA REGULAR-SEASON RECORD

HONORS: NBA All-Rookie team (1984).

Season Team	G	Min.	FGM	FGA	Pct.	FTM	FTA	Pct.	Off.	Def.	Tot.	Ast.	PF	Dq.	Stl.	Blk.	TO	Pts.	Avg.
83-84 — Washington	81	1976	408	918	.444	142	172	.826	57	98	155	151	162	1	23	13	110	982	12.1
84-85 — Washington	76	2613	605	1213	.499	211	250	.844	60	146	206	184	176	1	52	9	107	1436	18.9
85-86 — Washington	80	2992	735	1522	.483	322	371	.868	66	222	288	191	180	2	70	12	168	1795	22.4
86-87 — Washington	80	2763	689	1509	.457	376	425	.885	50	168	218	298	154	0	75	13	182	1758	22.0
87-88 — Washington	80	2655	648	1360	.476	335	380	.882	44	162	206	237	198	1	51	13	172	1641	20.5
88-89 — Washington	76	2418	677	1410	.480	296	340	.871	55	124	179	219	155	0	39	14	165	1651	21.7
89-90 — Washington	75	2567	781	1592	.491	257	293	.877	54	152	206	243	116	1	48	6	125	1820	24.3
90-91 — Utah	69	2466	525	1034	.508	231	252	.917	36	170	206	143	128	0	50	6	108	1282	18.6
91-92 — Utah	81	2922	691	1353	.511	256	285	.898	49	184	233	180	126	1	56	5	140	1639	20.2
Totals	698	23372	5759	11911	.484	2426	2768	.876	471	1426	1897	1846	1395	7	464	91	1277	14004	20.1

Three-point field goals: 1983-84, 24-for-74 (.324). 1984-85, 15-for-72 (.208). 1985-86, 3-for-17 (.176). 1986-87, 4-for-26 (.154). 1987-88, 10-for-24 (.417). 1988-89, 1-for-19 (.053). 1989-90, 1-for-6 (.167). 1990-91, 1-for-6 (.167). 1991-92, 1-for-12 (.083). Totals, 60-for-256 (.234).

NBA PLAYOFF RECORD

Season Team	G	Min.	FGM	FGA	Pct.	FTM	FTA	Pct.	Off.	Def.	Tot.	Ast.	PF	Dq.	Stl.	Blk.	TO	Pts.	Avg.
83-84 — Washington	4	71	12	26	.462	0	0	...	2	3	5	2	6	0	1	0	3	24	6.0

Season Team	G	Min.	FGM	FGA	Pct.	FTM	FTA	Pct.	Off.	Def.	Tot.	Ast.	PF	Dq.	Stl.	Blk.	TO	Pts.	Avg.
84-85—Washington .	4	126	27	56	.482	10	13	.769	3	3	6	8	14	1	5	0	4	65	16.3
85-86—Washington .	5	197	42	103	.408	26	29	.897	4	12	16	17	13	0	7	3	11	110	22.0
86-87—Washington .	3	105	17	46	.370	11	11	1.000	1	6	7	9	8	0	1	0	11	45	15.0
87-88—Washington .	5	199	50	97	.515	28	37	.757	3	14	17	11	16	0	5	5	14	128	25.6
90-91—Utah	9	351	71	144	.493	44	48	.917	7	28	35	29	22	0	9	1	12	186	20.7
91-92—Utah	16	610	134	275	.487	62	72	.861	12	27	39	31	33	0	8	2	26	331	20.7
Totals	46	1659	353	747	.473	181	210	.862	32	93	125	107	112	1	36	11	81	889	19.3

Three-point field goals: 1983-84, 0-for-1. 1984-85, 1-for-3 (.333). 1985-86, 0-for-2. 1987-88, 0-for-1. 1990-91, 0-for-2. 1991-92, 1-for-3 (.333). Totals, 2-for-12 (.167).

NBA ALL-STAR GAME RECORD

Season Team	Min.	FGM	FGA	Pct.	FTM	FTA	Pct.	Off.	Def.	Tot.	Ast.	PF	Dq.	Stl.	Blk.	TO	Pts.
1986—Washington	12	3	5	.600	0	0	...	0	1	1	4	0	0	1	0	0	6
1987—Washington	13	3	5	.600	0	0	...	1	1	2	2	1	0	0	0	1	6
Totals	25	6	10	.600	0	0	...	1	2	3	6	1	0	1	0	1	12

Three-point field goals: 1987, 0-for-1.

MALONE, KARL
F, JAZZ

PERSONAL: Born July 24, 1963, in Summerfield, La. . . . 6-9/256. . . . Nickname: The Mailman.
HIGH SCHOOL: Summerfield (La.).
COLLEGE: Louisiana Tech.
TRANSACTIONS/CAREER NOTES: Selected by Utah Jazz in first round (13th pick overall) of 1985 NBA Draft.
MISCELLANEOUS: Member of gold-medal-winning U.S. Olympic team (1992).

COLLEGIATE RECORD

Season Team	G	Min.	FGM	FGA	Pct.	FTM	FTA	Pct.	Reb.	Pts.	Avg.
81-82—Louisiana Tech				Did not play—academically ineligible.							
82-83—Louisiana Tech	28	...	217	373	.582	152	244	.623	289	586	20.9
83-84—Louisiana Tech	32	...	220	382	.576	161	236	.682	282	601	18.8
84-85—Louisiana Tech	32	...	216	399	.541	97	170	.571	288	529	16.5
Totals	92	...	653	1154	.566	410	650	.631	859	1716	18.7

NBA REGULAR-SEASON RECORD

HONORS: All-NBA first team (1989, 1990, 1991, 1992). . . . All-NBA second team (1988). . . . NBA All-Defensive second team (1988). . . . NBA All-Rookie team (1986).

Season Team	G	Min.	FGM	FGA	Pct.	FTM	FTA	Pct.	Off.	Def.	Tot.	Ast.	PF	Dq.	Stl.	Blk.	TO	Pts.	Avg.
85-86—Utah	81	2475	504	1016	.496	195	405	.481	174	544	718	236	295	2	105	44	279	1203	14.9
86-87—Utah	82	2857	728	1422	.512	323	540	.598	278	577	855	158	323	6	104	60	237	1779	21.7
87-88—Utah	82	3198	858	1650	.520	552	789	.700	277	709	986	199	296	2	117	50	*325	2268	27.7
88-89—Utah	80	3126	809	1559	.519	*703	*918	.766	259	594	853	219	286	3	144	70	285	2326	29.1
89-90—Utah	82	3122	914	1627	.562	*696	*913	.762	232	679	911	226	259	1	121	50	304	2540	31.0
90-91—Utah	82	3302	847	1608	.527	*684	*888	.770	236	*731	967	270	268	2	89	79	244	2382	29.0
91-92—Utah	81	3054	798	1516	.526	*673	*865	.778	225	684	909	241	226	2	108	51	248	2272	28.0
Totals	570	21134	5458	10398	.525	3826	5318	.719	1681	4518	6199	1549	1953	18	788	404	1922	14770	25.9

Three-point field goals: 1985-86, 0-for-2. 1986-87, 0-for-7. 1987-88, 0-for-5. 1988-89, 5-for-16 (.313). 1989-90, 16-for-43 (.372). 1990-91, 4-for-14 (.286). 1991-92, 3-for-17 (.176). Totals, 28-for-104 (.269).

NBA PLAYOFF RECORD

NOTES: Shares single-game record for most free throws made in one half—19 (May 9, 1991, vs. Portland).

Season Team	G	Min.	FGM	FGA	Pct.	FTM	FTA	Pct.	Off.	Def.	Tot.	Ast.	PF	Dq.	Stl.	Blk.	TO	Pts.	Avg.
85-86—Utah	4	144	38	72	.528	11	26	.423	6	24	30	4	18	1	8	0	6	87	21.8
86-87—Utah	5	200	37	88	.420	26	36	.722	15	33	48	6	20	1	11	4	17	100	20.0
87-88—Utah	11	494	123	255	.482	81	112	.723	33	97	130	17	35	0	13	7	39	327	29.7
88-89—Utah	3	136	33	66	.500	26	32	.813	22	27	49	4	16	1	3	1	13	92	30.7
89-90—Utah	5	203	46	105	.438	34	45	.756	16	35	51	11	22	1	11	5	12	126	25.2
90-91—Utah	9	383	95	209	.455	77	91	.846	23	97	120	29	35	0	9	11	26	267	29.7
91-92—Utah	16	688	148	284	.521	169	210	.805	43	138	181	42	57	0	22	19	46	465	29.1
Totals	53	2248	520	1079	.482	424	552	.768	158	451	609	113	203	4	77	47	159	1464	27.6

Three-point field goals: 1987-88, 0-for-1. 1989-90, 0-for-1. 1990-91, 0-for-8. 1991-92, 0-for-2. Totals, 0-for-12.

NBA ALL-STAR GAME RECORD

NOTES: NBA All-Star Game Most Valuable Player (1989).

Season Team	Min.	FGM	FGA	Pct.	FTM	FTA	Pct.	Off.	Def.	Tot.	Ast.	PF	Dq.	Stl.	Blk.	TO	Pts.
1988—Utah	33	9	19	.474	4	5	.800	4	6	10	2	4	0	2	0	3	22
1989—Utah	26	12	17	.706	4	6	.667	4	5	9	3	3	0	2	0	2	28
1990—Utah						Selected, did not play—injured.											
1991—Utah	31	6	11	.545	4	6	.667	4	7	11	4	1	0	1	1	3	16
1992—Utah	19	5	7	.714	1	2	.500	0	7	7	3	1	0	1	1	1	11
Totals	109	32	54	.593	13	19	.684	12	25	37	12	9	0	6	2	9	77

DID YOU KNOW. . .

. . . that Michael Jordan has scored exactly 19,000 points in regular-season play?

MALONE, MOSES
C, BUCKS

PERSONAL: Born March 23, 1955, in Petersburg, Va. . . . 6-10/255. . . . Full name: Moses Eugene Malone.
HIGH SCHOOL: Petersburg (Va.).
COLLEGE: Did not attend college.

TRANSACTIONS/CAREER NOTES: Selected as undergraduate by Utah Stars in third round of 1974 American Basketball Association Draft. . . . Sold by Stars to Spirits of St. Louis (December 2, 1975). . . . Selected by Portland Trail Blazers of NBA from Spirits in ABA dispersal draft (August 5, 1976). . . . Traded by Trail Blazers to Buffalo Braves for 1978 first-round draft choice (October 18, 1976). . . . Traded by Braves to Houston Rockets for 1977 and 1978 first-round draft choices (October 24, 1976). . . . Signed as veteran free agent by Philadelphia 76ers (September 2, 1982); Rockets matched offer and traded Malone to 76ers for Caldwell Jones and 1983 first-round draft choice (September 15, 1982). . . . Traded by 76ers with Terry Catledge and 1986 and 1988 first-round draft choices to Washington Bullets for Jeff Ruland and Cliff Robinson (June 16, 1986). . . . Signed as unrestricted free agent by Atlanta Hawks (August 16, 1988). . . . Signed as unrestricted free agent by Milwaukee Bucks (July 10, 1991).
MISCELLANEOUS: Member of NBA championship team (1983).

ABA REGULAR-SEASON RECORD

NOTES: ABA All-Rookie team (1975).

Season Team	G	Min.	FGM	2-POINT FGA	Pct.	FGM	3-POINT FGA	Pct.	FTM	FTA	Pct.	Reb.	Ast.	Pts.	Avg.
74-75—Utah	83	3205	591	1034	.572	0	1	.000	375	591	.635	1209	82	1557	18.8
75-76—St. Louis	43	1168	251	488	.514	0	2	.000	112	183	.612	413	58	614	14.3
Totals	126	4373	842	1522	.553	0	3	.000	487	774	.629	1622	140	2171	17.2

ABA PLAYOFF RECORD

Season Team	G	Min.	FGM	2-POINT FGA	Pct.	FGM	3-POINT FGA	Pct.	FTM	FTA	Pct.	Reb.	Ast.	Pts.	Avg.
74-75—Utah	6	235	51	80	.638	0	0	. . .	34	51	.667	105	9	136	22.7

ABA ALL-STAR GAME RECORD

Season Team	Min.	FGM	2-POINT FGA	Pct.	FGM	3-POINT FGA	Pct.	FTM	FTA	Pct.	Reb.	Ast.	Pts.
1975—Utah	20	2	3	.667	0	0	. . .	2	5	.400	10	0	6

NBA REGULAR-SEASON RECORD

RECORDS: Holds career records for most free throws made—8,395; and most offensive rebounds—6,583. . . . Holds single-season record for most offensive rebounds—587 (1979). . . . Holds single-game record for most offensive rebounds—21 (February 11, 1982, vs. Seattle).
HONORS: NBA Most Valuable Player (1979, 1982, 1983). . . . All-NBA first team (1979, 1982, 1983, 1985). . . . All-NBA second team (1980, 1981, 1984, 1987). . . . NBA All-Defensive first team (1983). . . . NBA All-Defensive second team (1979).
NOTES: Led NBA with 17.6 rebounds per game (1979), 14.8 rebounds per game (1981), 14.7 rebounds per game (1982), 15.3 rebounds per game (1983), 13.4 rebounds per game (1984) and 13.1 rebounds per game (1985).

Season Team	G	Min.	FGM	FGA	Pct.	FTM	FTA	Pct.	REBOUNDS Off.	Def.	Tot.	Ast.	PF	Dq.	Stl.	Blk.	TO	Pts.	Avg.
76-77—Buff.-Hou	82	2506	389	810	.480	305	440	.693	*437	635	1072	89	275	3	67	181	0	1083	13.2
77-78—Houston	59	2107	413	828	.499	318	443	.718	*380	506	886	31	179	2	48	76	220	1144	19.4
78-79—Houston	82	*3390	716	1325	.540	599	811	.739	*587	*857	*1444	147	223	0	79	159	326	2031	24.8
79-80—Houston	82	3140	778	1549	.502	563	*783	.719	*573	617	1190	147	210	0	80	107	300	2119	25.8
80-81—Houston	80	3245	806	1545	.522	609	*804	.757	*474	706	*1180	141	223	0	83	150	*308	2222	27.8
81-82—Houston	81	*3398	945	1822	.519	630	*827	.762	*558	630	*1188	142	208	0	76	125	294	2520	31.1
82-83—Philadelphia	78	2922	654	1305	.501	*600	*788	.761	*445	*749	*1194	101	206	0	89	157	264	1908	24.5
83-84—Philadelphia	71	2613	532	1101	.483	545	727	.750	352	598	950	96	188	0	71	110	250	1609	22.7
84-85—Philadelphia	79	2957	602	1284	.469	*737	*904	.815	385	646	*1031	130	216	0	67	123	286	1941	24.6
85-86—Philadelphia	74	2706	571	1246	.458	*617	*784	.787	339	533	872	90	194	0	67	71	261	1759	23.8
86-87—Washington	73	2488	595	1311	.454	570	692	.824	340	484	824	120	139	0	59	92	202	1760	24.1
87-88—Washington	79	2692	531	1090	.487	543	689	.788	372	512	884	112	160	0	59	72	249	1607	20.3
88-89—Atlanta	81	2878	538	1096	.491	561	711	.789	386	570	956	112	154	0	79	100	245	1637	20.2
89-90—Atlanta	81	2735	517	1077	.480	493	631	.781	*364	448	812	130	158	0	47	84	232	1528	18.9
90-91—Atlanta	82	1912	280	598	.468	309	372	.831	271	396	667	68	134	0	30	74	137	869	10.6
91-92—Milwaukee	82	2511	440	929	.474	396	504	.786	320	424	744	93	136	0	74	64	150	1279	15.6
Totals	1246	44200	9307	18916	.492	8395	10910	.769	6583	9311	15894	1749	3003	5	1075	1705	3724	27016	21.7

Three-point field goals: 1979-80, 0-for-6. 1980-81, 1-for-3 (.333). 1981-82, 0-for-6. 1982-83, 0-for-1. 1983-84, 0-for-4. 1984-85, 0-for-2. 1985-86, 0-for-1. 1986-87, 0-for-11. 1987-88, 2-for-7 (.286). 1988-89, 0-for-12. 1989-90, 1-for-9 (.111). 1990-91, 0-for-7. 1991-92, 3-for-8 (.375). Totals, 7-for-77 (.091).

NBA PLAYOFF RECORD

NOTES: NBA Finals Most Valuable Player (1983). . . . Holds single-game record for most offensive rebounds—15 (April 21, 1977, vs. Washington).

Season Team	G	Min.	FGM	FGA	Pct.	FTM	FTA	Pct.	REBOUNDS Off.	Def.	Tot.	Ast.	PF	Dq.	Stl.	Blk.	TO	Pts.	Avg.
76-77—Houston	12	518	81	162	.500	63	91	.692	84	119	203	7	42	0	13	21	. . .	225	18.8
78-79—Houston	2	78	18	41	.439	13	18	.722	25	16	41	2	5	0	1	8	8	49	24.5
79-80—Houston	7	275	74	138	.536	33	43	.767	42	55	97	7	18	0	4	16	22	181	25.9
80-81—Houston	21	955	207	432	.479	148	208	.712	125	180	305	35	54	0	13	34	59	562	26.8
81-82—Houston	3	136	29	67	.433	14	15	.933	28	23	51	10	8	0	2	2	6	72	24.0
82-83—Philadelphia	13	524	126	235	.536	86	120	.717	70	136	206	20	40	0	19	25	40	338	26.0
83-84—Philadelphia	5	212	38	83	.458	31	32	.969	20	49	69	7	15	0	3	11	21	107	21.4
84-85—Philadelphia	13	505	90	212	.425	82	103	.796	36	102	138	24	39	0	17	22	23	262	20.2
86-87—Washington	3	114	21	47	.447	20	21	.952	15	23	38	5	5	0	0	3	8	62	20.7
87-88—Washington	5	198	30	65	.462	33	40	.825	22	34	56	7	9	0	3	4	15	93	18.6

Season Team	G	Min.	FGM	FGA	Pct.	FTM	FTA	Pct.	REBOUNDS Off.	Def.	Tot.	Ast.	PF	Dq.	Stl.	Blk.	TO	Pts.	Avg.
88-89—Atlanta	5	197	32	64	.500	40	51	.784	27	33	60	9	5	0	7	4	11	105	21.0
90-91—Atlanta	5	84	4	20	.200	13	14	.929	16	15	31	3	4	0	2	1	2	21	4.2
Totals	94	3796	750	1566	.479	576	756	.762	510	785	1295	136	244	0	84	151	215	2077	22.1

Three-point field goals: 1979-80, 0-for-1. 1980-81, 0-for-2. 1982-83, 0-for-1. 1984-85, 0-for-1. 1987-88, 0-for-1. 1988-89, 1-for-1. Totals, 1-for-7 (.143).

NBA ALL-STAR GAME RECORD

Season Team	Min.	FGM	FGA	Pct.	FTM	FTA	Pct.	REBOUNDS Off.	Def.	Tot.	Ast.	PF	Dq.	Stl.	Blk.	TO	Pts.
1978 —Houston	14	1	1	1.000	2	4	.500	1	3	4	1	1	0	1	0	0	4
1979 —Houston	17	2	2	1.000	4	5	.800	2	5	7	1	0	0	1	0	1	8
1980 —Houston	31	7	12	.583	6	12	.500	6	6	12	2	4	0	1	2	5	20
1981 —Houston	22	3	8	.375	2	4	.500	2	4	6	3	3	0	1	0	1	8
1982 —Houston	20	5	11	.455	2	6	.333	5	6	11	0	2	0	1	1	3	12
1983 —Philadelphia	24	3	8	.375	4	6	.667	2	6	8	3	1	0	0	1	1	10
1984 —Philadelphia							Selected, did not play—injured.										
1985 —Philadelphia	33	2	10	.200	3	6	.500	5	7	12	1	4	0	0	0	3	7
1986 —Philadelphia	34	5	12	.417	6	9	.667	5	8	13	0	4	0	1	0	1	16
1987 —Washington	35	11	19	.579	5	6	.833	7	11	18	2	4	0	2	1	1	27
1988 —Washington	22	2	6	.333	3	6	.500	5	4	9	2	2	0	0	0	2	7
1989 —Atlanta	19	3	9	.333	3	3	1.000	4	4	8	0	1	0	1	1	1	9
Totals	271	44	98	.449	40	67	.597	44	64	108	15	26	0	9	6	19	128

MANNING, DANNY
F, CLIPPERS

PERSONAL: Born May 17, 1966, in Hattiesburg, Miss. . . . 6-10/234. . . . Full name: Daniel Ricardo Manning. . . . Son of Ed Manning, current assistant coach with San Antonio Spurs and forward with Baltimore Bullets, Chicago Bulls and Portland Trail Blazers of NBA (1967-68 through 1970-71) and Carolina Cougars, New York Nets, and Indiana Pacers of American Basketball Association (1971-72 through 1975-76).
HIGH SCHOOL: Page (Greensboro, N.C.), then Lawrence (Kan.).
COLLEGE: Kansas.
TRANSACTIONS/CAREER NOTES: Selected by Los Angeles Clippers in first round (first pick overall) of 1988 NBA Draft.
MISCELLANEOUS: Member of bronze-medal-winning U.S. Olympic team (1988).

COLLEGIATE RECORD

NOTES: THE SPORTING NEWS All-America first team (1987, 1988). . . . Most Outstanding Player in NCAA Division I tournament (1988). . . . Member of NCAA Division I championship team (1988).

Season Team	G	Min.	FGM	FGA	Pct.	FTM	FTA	Pct.	Reb.	Pts.	Avg.
84-85 —Kansas	34	1120	209	369	.566	78	102	.765	258	496	14.6
85-86 —Kansas	39	1256	279	465	.600	95	127	.748	245	653	16.7
86-87 —Kansas	36	1249	347	562	.617	165	226	.730	342	860	23.9
87-88 —Kansas	38	1336	381	653	.583	171	233	.734	342	942	24.8
Totals	147	4961	1216	2049	.593	509	688	.740	1187	2951	20.1

Three-point field goals: 1986-87, 1-for-3 (.333). 1987-88, 9-for-26 (.346). Totals, 10-for-29 (.345).

NBA REGULAR-SEASON RECORD

Season Team	G	Min.	FGM	FGA	Pct.	FTM	FTA	Pct.	REBOUNDS Off.	Def.	Tot.	Ast.	PF	Dq.	Stl.	Blk.	TO	Pts.	Avg.
88-89—L.A. Clippers	26	950	177	358	.494	79	103	.767	70	101	171	81	89	1	44	25	93	434	16.7
89-90—L.A. Clippers	71	2269	440	826	.533	274	370	.741	142	280	422	187	261	4	91	39	188	1154	16.3
90-91—L.A. Clippers	73	2197	470	905	.519	219	306	.716	169	257	426	196	281	5	117	62	188	1159	15.9
91-92—L.A. Clippers	82	2904	650	1199	.542	279	385	.725	229	335	564	285	293	5	135	122	210	1579	19.3
Totals	252	8320	1737	3288	.528	851	1164	.731	610	973	1583	749	924	15	387	248	679	4326	17.2

Three-point field goals: 1988-89, 1-for-5 (.200). 1989-90, 0-for-5. 1990-91, 0-for-3. 1991-92, 0-for-5. Totals, 1-for-18 (.056).

NBA PLAYOFF RECORD

Season Team	G	Min.	FGM	FGA	Pct.	FTM	FTA	Pct.	REBOUNDS Off.	Def.	Tot.	Ast.	PF	Dq.	Stl.	Blk.	TO	Pts.	Avg.
91-92 —L.A. Clippers	5	194	46	81	.568	20	31	.645	15	13	28	14	21	1	5	4	13	113	22.6

Three-point field goals: 1991-92, 1-for-3 (.333).

MARCIULIONIS, SARUNAS
G, WARRIORS

PERSONAL: Born June 13, 1964, in Kaunas, U.S.S.R. . . . 6-5/215. . . . Full name: Raimondas Sarunas Marciulionis. . . . Name pronounced Shaw-ROON-iss Marsh-a-LOAN-iss.
COLLEGE: State University of Vilnius (Lithuania, U.S.S.R.).
TRANSACTIONS/CAREER NOTES: Selected by Golden State Warriors in sixth round (127th pick overall) of 1987 NBA Draft; pick was later disallowed by NBA officials who found Marciulionis to be eight days too old to have been eligible for the draft. . . . Played in Lithuania, U.S.S.R., for Statbe and Zalgiris clubs. . . . Signed as free agent by Warriors (June 23, 1989).
MISCELLANEOUS: Member of gold-medal-winning Soviet Olympic team (1988). . . . Member of bronze-medal-winning Lithuanian Olympic team (1992).

NBA REGULAR-SEASON RECORD

Season Team	G	Min.	FGM	FGA	Pct.	FTM	FTA	Pct.	REBOUNDS Off.	Def.	Tot.	Ast.	PF	Dq.	Stl.	Blk.	TO	Pts.	Avg.
89-90 —Golden State	75	1695	289	557	.519	317	403	.787	84	137	221	121	230	5	94	7	137	905	12.1

Season Team	G	Min.	FGM	FGA	Pct.	FTM	FTA	Pct.	Off.	Def.	Tot.	Ast.	PF	Dq.	Stl.	Blk.	TO	Pts.	Avg.
										— REBOUNDS —									
90-91 —Golden State	50	987	183	365	.501	178	246	.724	51	67	118	85	136	4	62	4	75	545	10.9
91-92 —Golden State	72	2117	491	912	.538	376	477	.788	68	140	208	243	237	4	116	10	193	1361	18.9
Totals	197	4799	963	1834	.525	871	1126	.774	203	344	547	449	603	13	272	21	405	2811	14.3

Three-point field goals: 1989-90, 10-for-39 (.256). 1990-91, 1-for-6 (.167). 1991-92, 3-for-10 (.300). Totals, 14-for-55 (.255).

NBA PLAYOFF RECORD

Season Team	G	Min.	FGM	FGA	Pct.	FTM	FTA	Pct.	Off.	Def.	Tot.	Ast.	PF	Dq.	Stl.	Blk.	TO	Pts.	Avg.
										— REBOUNDS —									
90-91 —Golden State	9	206	42	84	.500	35	39	.897	8	15	23	27	21	1	11	1	14	119	13.2
91-92 —Golden State	4	133	25	47	.532	34	41	.829	3	6	9	20	15	0	3	1	4	85	21.3
Totals	13	339	67	131	.511	69	80	.863	11	21	32	47	36	1	14	2	18	204	15.7

Three-point field goals: 1990-91, 0-for-1. 1991-92, 1-for-2 (.500). Totals, 1-for-3 (.333).

MARTIN, JEFF
G

PERSONAL: Born January 14, 1967, in Cherry Valley, Ark. . . . 6-5/195. . . . Full name: Jeffery Allen Martin.
HIGH SCHOOL: Cross Country (Cherry Valley, Ark.).
COLLEGE: Murray State.
TRANSACTIONS/CAREER NOTES: Selected by Los Angeles Clippers in second round (31st pick overall) of 1989 NBA Draft. . . . Traded by Clippers with 1995 second-round draft choice to Detroit Pistons for James Edwards (August 13, 1991). . . . Waived by Pistons (October 29, 1991). . . . Played in Continental Basketball Association with Grand Rapids Hoops (1991-92).

COLLEGIATE RECORD

Season Team	G	Min.	FGM	FGA	Pct.	FTM	FTA	Pct.	Reb.	Pts.	Avg.
85-86 —Murray State	29	918	128	271	.472	83	123	.675	157	339	11.7
86-87 —Murray State	28	1041	228	436	.523	123	158	.778	158	594	21.2
87-88 —Murray State	31	1162	304	545	.558	181	231	.784	204	806	26.0
88-89 —Murray State	29	1056	266	522	.510	148	186	.796	150	745	25.7
Totals	117	4177	926	1774	.522	535	698	.766	669	2484	21.2

Three-point field goals: 1986-87, 15-for-37 (.405). 1987-88, 17-for-48 (.354). 1988-89, 65-for-131 (.496). Totals, 97-for-216 (.449).

NBA REGULAR-SEASON RECORD

Season Team	G	Min.	FGM	FGA	Pct.	FTM	FTA	Pct.	Off.	Def.	Tot.	Ast.	PF	Dq.	Stl.	Blk.	TO	Pts.	Avg.
										— REBOUNDS —									
89-90 —L.A. Clippers	69	1351	170	414	.411	91	129	.705	78	81	159	44	97	0	41	16	47	433	6.3
90-91 —L.A. Clippers	74	1334	214	507	.422	68	100	.680	53	78	131	65	104	0	37	31	49	523	7.1
Totals	143	2685	384	921	.417	159	229	.694	131	159	290	109	201	0	78	47	96	956	6.7

Three-point field goals: 1989-90, 2-for-15 (.133). 1990-91, 27-for-88 (.307). Totals, 29-for-103 (.282).

CBA REGULAR-SEASON RECORD

NOTES: CBA All-Star second team (1992).

Season Team	G	Min.	2-POINT FGM	FGA	Pct.	3-POINT FGM	FGA	Pct.	FTM	FTA	Pct.	Reb.	Ast.	Pts.	Avg.
91-92 —Grand Rapids ...	56	2362	462	1038	.445	37	116	.319	342	435	.786	288	169	1377	24.6

MASON, ANTHONY
F, KNICKS

PERSONAL: Born December 14, 1966, in Miami. . . . 6-7/250. . . . Full name: Anthony George Douglas Mason.
HIGH SCHOOL: Springfield Gardens (N.Y.).
COLLEGE: Tennessee State.
TRANSACTIONS/CAREER NOTES: Selected by Portland Trail Blazers in third round (53rd pick overall) of 1988 NBA Draft. . . . Played in Turkey (1988-89). . . . Draft rights relinquished by Trail Blazers (June 30, 1989). . . . Signed as free agent by New Jersey Nets (September 19, 1989). . . . Waived by Nets (October 30, 1990). . . . Played in Continental Basketball Association with Tulsa Fast Breakers (1990-91). . . . Signed by Denver Nuggets to first of two consecutive 10-day contracts (December 28, 1990). . . . Signed as free agent by New York Knicks (July 30, 1991).

COLLEGIATE RECORD

Season Team	G	Min.	FGM	FGA	Pct.	FTM	FTA	Pct.	Reb.	Pts.	Avg.
84-85 —Tennessee State	28	801	100	213	.469	79	122	.648	148	279	10.0
85-86 —Tennessee State	28	913	206	427	.482	93	130	.715	192	505	18.0
86-87 —Tennessee State	27	951	201	449	.448	89	135	.659	262	508	18.8
87-88 —Tennessee State	28	1064	276	608	.454	191	247	.773	292	783	28.0
Totals	111	3729	783	1697	.461	452	634	.713	894	2075	18.7

Three-point field goals: 1986-87, 17-for-49 (.347). 1987-88, 40-for-81 (.494). Totals, 57-for-130 (.438).

NBA REGULAR-SEASON RECORD

Season Team	G	Min.	FGM	FGA	Pct.	FTM	FTA	Pct.	Off.	Def.	Tot.	Ast.	PF	Dq.	Stl.	Blk.	TO	Pts.	Avg.
										— REBOUNDS —									
89-90 —New Jersey ..	21	108	14	40	.350	9	15	.600	11	23	34	7	20	0	2	2	11	37	1.8
90-91 —Denver	3	21	2	4	.500	6	8	.750	3	2	5	0	6	0	1	0	0	10	3.3
91-92 —New York	82	2198	203	399	.509	167	260	.642	216	357	573	106	229	0	46	20	101	573	7.0
Totals	106	2327	219	443	.494	182	283	.643	230	382	612	113	255	0	49	22	112	620	5.8

NBA PLAYOFF RECORD

Season Team	G	Min.	FGM	FGA	Pct.	FTM	FTA	Pct.	Off.	Def.	Tot.	Ast.	PF	Dq.	Stl.	Blk.	TO	Pts.	Avg.
										— REBOUNDS —									
91-92 —New York	12	288	19	43	.442	22	28	.786	28	48	76	10	34	0	2	8	11	60	5.0

Season Team	G	Min.	2-POINT FGM	FGA	Pct.	3-POINT FGM	FGA	Pct.	FTM	FTA	Pct.	Reb.	Ast.	Pts.	Avg.
90-91—Tulsa	26	1074	256	456	.561	0	0	...	266	370	.719	384	102	778	29.9

MASSENBURG, TONY
F

PERSONAL: Born July 31, 1967, in Sussex, Va. . . . 6-9/220.
. . . Full name: Tony Arnel Massenburg.
HIGH SCHOOL: Sussex Central (Va.).
COLLEGE: Maryland.

TRANSACTIONS/CAREER NOTES: Selected by San Antonio Spurs in second round (43rd pick overall) of 1990 NBA Draft. . . . Waived by Spurs (December 2, 1991). . . . Signed as free agent by Charlotte Hornets (December 11, 1991). . . . Waived by Hornets (January 7, 1992). . . . Signed by Boston Celtics to first of two consecutive 10-day contracts (January 10, 1992). . . . Signed by Golden State Warriors to first of two consecutive 10-day contracts (February 13, 1992).

COLLEGIATE RECORD

Season Team	G	Min.	FGM	FGA	Pct.	FTM	FTA	Pct.	Reb.	Pts.	Avg.
85-86—Maryland	29	349	28	56	.500	27	48	.563	60	83	2.9
86-87—Maryland					Did not play.						
87-88—Maryland	23	616	93	179	.520	47	82	.573	122	233	10.1
88-89—Maryland	29	1001	197	358	.550	87	145	.600	226	481	16.6
89-90—Maryland	31	973	206	408	.505	145	201	.721	314	557	18.0
Totals	112	2939	524	1001	.523	306	476	.643	722	1354	12.1

Three-point field goals: 1988-89, 0-for-1. 1989-90, 0-for-2. Totals, 0-for-3.

NBA REGULAR-SEASON RECORD

Season Team	G	Min.	FGM	FGA	Pct.	FTM	FTA	Pct.	REBOUNDS Off.	Def.	Tot.	Ast.	PF	Dq.	Stl.	Blk.	TO	Pts.	Avg.
90-91—San Antonio	35	161	27	60	.450	28	45	.622	23	35	58	4	26	0	4	9	13	82	2.3
91-92—SA-C-B-GS	18	90	10	25	.400	9	15	.600	7	18	25	0	21	0	1	1	9	29	1.6
Totals	53	251	37	85	.435	37	60	.617	30	53	83	4	47	0	5	10	22	111	2.1

NBA PLAYOFF RECORD

Season Team	G	Min.	FGM	FGA	Pct.	FTM	FTA	Pct.	REBOUNDS Off.	Def.	Tot.	Ast.	PF	Dq.	Stl.	Blk.	TO	Pts.	Avg.
90-91—San Antonio	1	1	0	0	...	0	0	...	0	0	0	0	0	0	0	0	0	0	0.0

MAXWELL, VERNON
G, ROCKETS

M

PERSONAL: Born September 12, 1965, in Gainesville, Fla. . . . 6-4/190.
HIGH SCHOOL: Buchholz (Gainesville, Fla.).
COLLEGE: Florida.

TRANSACTIONS/CAREER NOTES: Selected by Denver Nuggets in second round (47th pick overall) of 1988 NBA Draft. . . . Draft rights traded by Nuggets to San Antonio Spurs for 1989 second-round draft choice (June 28, 1988). . . . Traded by Spurs to Houston Rockets for cash (February 21, 1990).

COLLEGIATE RECORD

Season Team	G	Min.	FGM	FGA	Pct.	FTM	FTA	Pct.	Reb.	Pts.	Avg.
84-85—Florida	30	752	163	366	.445	72	105	.686	72	398	13.3
85-86—Florida	33	1142	262	566	.463	124	177	.701	147	648	19.6
86-87—Florida	34	1086	266	548	.485	161	217	.742	125	738	21.7
87-88—Florida	33	1214	230	515	.447	148	207	.715	138	666	20.2
Totals	130	4194	921	1995	.462	505	706	.715	482	2450	18.8

Three-point field goals: 1986-87, 45-for-128 (.352). 1987-88, 58-for-147 (.395). Totals, 103-for-275 (.375).

NBA REGULAR-SEASON RECORD

RECORDS: Holds single-season record for most three-point field goals made—172 (1991).

Season Team	G	Min.	FGM	FGA	Pct.	FTM	FTA	Pct.	REBOUNDS Off.	Def.	Tot.	Ast.	PF	Dq.	Stl.	Blk.	TO	Pts.	Avg.
88-89—San Antonio	79	2065	357	827	.432	181	243	.745	49	153	202	301	136	0	86	8	178	927	11.7
89-90—S.A.-Hou.	79	1987	275	627	.439	136	211	.645	50	178	228	296	148	0	84	10	143	714	9.0
90-91—Houston	82	2870	504	1247	.404	217	296	.733	41	197	238	303	179	2	127	15	171	1397	17.0
91-92—Houston	80	2700	502	1216	.413	206	267	.772	37	206	243	326	200	3	104	28	178	1372	17.2
Totals	320	9622	1638	3917	.418	740	1017	.728	177	734	911	1226	663	5	401	61	670	4410	13.8

Three-point field goals: 1988-89, 32-for-129 (.248). 1989-90, 28-for-105 (.267). 1990-91, 172-for-510 (.337). 1991-92, 162-for-473 (.342). Totals, 394-for-1217 (.324).

NBA PLAYOFF RECORD

NOTES: Holds single-game record for most three-point field goals attempted—13 (April 27, 1991, vs. Los Angeles Lakers).

Season Team	G	Min.	FGM	FGA	Pct.	FTM	FTA	Pct.	REBOUNDS Off.	Def.	Tot.	Ast.	PF	Dq.	Stl.	Blk.	TO	Pts.	Avg.
89-90—Houston	4	159	30	81	.370	11	21	.524	5	7	12	17	12	0	5	0	6	79	19.8
90-91—Houston	3	113	23	56	.411	1	2	.500	1	7	8	9	8	0	2	1	7	56	18.7
Totals	7	272	53	137	.387	12	23	.522	6	14	20	26	20	0	7	1	13	135	19.3

Three-point field goals: 1989-90, 8-for-26 (.308). 1990-91, 9-for-27 (.333). Totals, 17-for-53 (.321).

MAYES, THARON
G

PERSONAL: Born September 9, 1968, in New Haven, Conn. . . . 6-3/ 175. . . . Name pronounced Tha-RON.
HIGH SCHOOL: Hillhouse (New Haven, Conn.).
COLLEGE: Florida State.

TRANSACTIONS/CAREER NOTES: Never drafted by an NBA franchise. . . . Played in Continental Basketball Association with Sioux Falls Skyforce (1990-91 and 1991-92). . . . Signed as free agent by Philadelphia 76ers (August 12, 1991). . . . Waived by 76ers (December 23, 1991). . . . Signed by Los Angeles Clippers to 10-day contract (March 3, 1992). . . . Released by Clippers (March 9, 1992).

COLLEGIATE RECORD

Season Team	G	Min.	FGM	FGA	Pct.	FTM	FTA	Pct.	Reb.	Pts.	Avg.
86-87 —Florida State					Did not play—ineligible.						
87-88 —Florida State	30	780	142	299	.475	66	90	.733	83	396	13.2
88-89 —Florida State	23	645	126	229	.550	29	39	.744	53	305	13.3
89-90 —Florida State	24	874	198	414	.478	105	126	.833	81	559	23.3
Totals	77	2299	466	942	.495	200	255	.784	217	1260	16.4

Three-point field goals: 1987-88, 46-for-100 (.460). 1988-89, 24-for-76 (.316). 1989-90, 58-for-161 (.360). Totals, 128-for-337 (.380).

CBA REGULAR-SEASON RECORD

Season Team	G	Min.	FGM	2-POINT FGA	Pct.	FGM	3-POINT FGA	Pct.	FTM	FTA	Pct.	Reb.	Ast.	Pts.	Avg.
90-91 —Sioux Falls	54	1878	371	734	.505	96	277	.347	324	390	.831	197	245	1354	25.1
91-92 —Sioux Falls	13	362	55	123	.447	19	54	.352	50	65	.769	38	38	217	16.7
Totals	67	2240	426	857	.497	115	331	.347	374	455	.822	235	283	1571	23.4

NBA REGULAR-SEASON RECORD

Season Team	G	Min.	FGM	FGA	Pct.	FTM	FTA	Pct.	Off.	REBOUNDS Def.	Tot.	Ast.	PF	Dq.	Stl.	Blk.	TO	Pts.	Avg.
91-92 —Phil.-L.A.C...	24	255	30	99	.303	24	36	.667	3	13	16	35	41	0	16	2	31	99	4.1

Three-point field goals: 1991-92, 15-for-41 (.366).

MAYS, TRAVIS
G, HAWKS

PERSONAL: Born June 19, 1968, in Ocala, Fla. . . . 6-2/190. . . . Full name: Travis Cortez Mays.
HIGH SCHOOL: Vanguard (Ocala, Fla.).
COLLEGE: Texas.

TRANSACTIONS/CAREER NOTES: Selected by Sacramento Kings in first round (14th pick overall) of 1990 NBA Draft. . . . Traded by Kings to Atlanta Hawks for Spud Webb and 1994 second-round draft choice (July 1, 1991).

COLLEGIATE RECORD

Season Team	G	Min.	FGM	FGA	Pct.	FTM	FTA	Pct.	Reb.	Pts.	Avg.
86-87 —Texas	30	890	101	239	.423	50	84	.595	112	258	8.6
87-88 —Texas	28	1055	164	357	.459	128	166	.771	153	506	18.1
88-89 —Texas	34	1210	253	564	.449	142	200	.710	161	743	21.9
89-90 —Texas	32	1186	240	554	.433	197	243	.811	164	772	24.1
Totals	124	4341	758	1714	.442	517	693	.746	590	2279	18.4

Three-point field goals: 1986-87, 6-for-26 (.231). 1987-88, 50-for-129 (.388). 1988-89, 95-for-257 (.370). 1989-90, 95-for-252 (.377). Totals, 246-for-664 (.370).

NBA REGULAR-SEASON RECORD

HONORS: NBA All-Rookie second team (1991).

Season Team	G	Min.	FGM	FGA	Pct.	FTM	FTA	Pct.	Off.	REBOUNDS Def.	Tot.	Ast.	PF	Dq.	Stl.	Blk.	TO	Pts.	Avg.
90-91 —Sacramento .	64	2145	294	724	.406	255	331	.770	54	124	178	253	169	1	81	11	159	915	14.3
91-92 —Atlanta	2	32	6	14	.429	2	2	1.000	1	1	2	1	4	0	0	0	3	17	8.5
Totals	66	2177	300	738	.407	257	333	.772	55	125	180	254	173	1	81	11	162	932	14.1

Three-point field goals: 1990-91, 72-for-197 (.365). 1991-92, 3-for-6 (.500). Totals, 75-for-203 (.369).

McCANN, BOB
F, TIMBERWOLVES

PERSONAL: Born April 22, 1964, in Morristown, N.J. . . . 6-7/248. . . . Full name: Robert McCann.
HIGH SCHOOL: Morristown (N.J.).
COLLEGE: Upsala (N.J.), then Morehead State.

TRANSACTIONS/CAREER NOTES: Selected by Milwaukee Bucks in second round (32nd pick overall) of 1987 NBA Draft. . . . Waived by Bucks (November 4, 1987). . . . Signed as free agent by Dallas Mavericks (October 5, 1988). . . . Waived by Mavericks (November 1, 1988). . . . Played in Continental Basketball Association with Charleston Gunners (1988-89) and Pensacola Tornados (1988-89, 1989-90 and 1990-91). . . . Re-signed by Mavericks to first of two consecutive 10-day contracts (February 12, 1990). . . . Re-signed by Mavericks for remainder of season (March 5, 1990). . . . Re-signed by Mavericks (October 2, 1991). . . . Released by Mavericks (October 27, 1991). . . . Signed by Detroit Pistons (November 2, 1991). . . . Signed as free agent by Minnesota Timberwolves (August 5, 1992).

COLLEGIATE RECORD

Season Team	G	Min.	FGM	FGA	Pct.	FTM	FTA	Pct.	Reb.	Pts.	Avg.
82-83 —Upsala	26	. . .	112	236	.475	34	64	.531	208	258	9.9
83-84 —Morehead State					Did not play—transfer student.						
84-85 —Morehead State	27	911	188	383	.491	85	152	.559	263	461	17.1

M

Season Team	G	Min.	FGM	FGA	Pct.	FTM	FTA	Pct.	Reb.	Pts.	Avg.
85-86 —Morehead State	27	803	171	320	.534	113	173	.653	282	455	16.9
86-87 —Morehead State	28	872	206	376	.548	107	170	.629	317	520	18.6
Totals	108	...	677	1315	.515	339	559	.606	1070	1694	15.7

Three-point field goals: 1986-87, 1-for-3 (.333).

CBA REGULAR-SEASON RECORD

Season Team	G	Min.	2-POINT			3-POINT			FTM	FTA	Pct.	Reb.	Ast.	Pts.	Avg.
			FGM	FGA	Pct.	FGM	FGA	Pct.							
88-89 —Char.-Pens.	43	1555	327	636	.514	0	5	.000	143	213	.671	356	97	797	18.5
89-90 —Pensacola	43	1879	388	735	.528	1	7	.143	203	296	.686	374	138	982	22.8
90-91 —Pensacola	8	265	52	109	.477	2	3	.667	17	30	.567	58	6	127	15.9
Totals	94	3699	767	1480	.518	3	15	.200	363	539	.673	788	241	1906	20.3

NBA REGULAR-SEASON RECORD

Season Team	G	Min.	FGM	FGA	Pct.	FTM	FTA	Pct.	REBOUNDS Off.	Def.	Tot.	Ast.	PF	Dq.	Stl.	Blk.	TO	Pts.	Avg.
89-90 —Dallas	10	62	7	21	.333	12	14	.857	4	8	12	6	7	0	2	2	6	26	2.6
91-92 —Detroit	26	129	13	33	.394	4	13	.308	12	18	30	6	23	0	6	4	7	30	1.2
Totals	36	191	20	54	.370	16	27	.593	16	26	42	12	30	0	8	6	13	56	1.6

Three-point field goals: 1991-92, 0-for-1.

NBA PLAYOFF RECORD

Season Team	G	Min.	FGM	FGA	Pct.	FTM	FTA	Pct.	REBOUNDS Off.	Def.	Tot.	Ast.	PF	Dq.	Stl.	Blk.	TO	Pts.	Avg.
91-92 —Detroit	1	13	3	6	.500	0	0	...	1	1	2	0	2	0	0	1	2	6	6.0

McCLOUD, GEORGE
G/F, PACERS

PERSONAL: Born May 27, 1967, in Daytona Beach, Fla.... 6-8/215.... Full name: George Aaron McCloud.
HIGH SCHOOL: Mainland (Daytona Beach, Fla.).
COLLEGE: Florida State.
TRANSACTIONS/CAREER NOTES: Selected by Indiana Pacers in first round (seventh pick overall) of 1989 NBA Draft.

COLLEGIATE RECORD

Season Team	G	Min.	FGM	FGA	Pct.	FTM	FTA	Pct.	Reb.	Pts.	Avg.
85-86 —Florida State	27	283	42	87	.483	31	49	.633	49	115	4.3
86-87 —Florida State	30	590	87	197	.442	42	68	.618	126	230	7.7
87-88 —Florida State	30	902	193	403	.479	88	112	.786	111	546	18.2
88-89 —Florida State	30	1067	207	462	.448	154	176	.875	109	683	22.8
Totals	117	2842	529	1149	.460	315	405	.778	395	1574	13.5

Three-point field goals: 1986-87, 14-for-47 (.298). 1987-88, 72-for-159 (.453). 1988-89, 115-for-262 (.439). Totals, 201-for-468 (.429).

NBA REGULAR-SEASON RECORD

Season Team	G	Min.	FGM	FGA	Pct.	FTM	FTA	Pct.	REBOUNDS Off.	Def.	Tot.	Ast.	PF	Dq.	Stl.	Blk.	TO	Pts.	Avg.
89-90 —Indiana	44	413	45	144	.313	15	19	.789	12	30	42	45	56	0	19	3	36	118	2.7
90-91 —Indiana	74	1070	131	351	.373	38	49	.776	35	83	118	150	141	1	40	11	91	343	4.6
91-92 —Indiana	51	892	128	313	.409	50	64	.781	45	87	132	116	95	1	26	11	62	338	6.6
Totals	169	2375	304	808	.376	103	132	.780	92	200	292	311	292	2	85	25	189	799	4.7

Three-point field goals: 1989-90, 13-for-40 (.325). 1990-91, 43-for-124 (.347). 1991-92, 32-for-94 (.340). Totals, 88-for-258 (.341).

NBA PLAYOFF RECORD

Season Team	G	Min.	FGM	FGA	Pct.	FTM	FTA	Pct.	REBOUNDS Off.	Def.	Tot.	Ast.	PF	Dq.	Stl.	Blk.	TO	Pts.	Avg.
89-90 —Indiana	1	4	1	2	.500	0	0	...	1	0	1	0	2	0	0	0	1	2	2.0
91-92 —Indiana	2	53	6	12	.500	8	11	.727	0	2	2	6	5	0	2	1	3	23	11.5
Totals	3	57	7	14	.500	8	11	.727	1	2	3	6	7	0	2	1	4	25	8.3

Three-point field goals: 1991-92, 3-for-6 (.500).

McCORMICK, TIM
C, KNICKS

PERSONAL: Born March 10, 1962, in Detroit.... 7-0/240.... Full name: Timothy Daniel McCormick.
HIGH SCHOOL: Clarkston (Mich.).
COLLEGE: Michigan.
TRANSACTIONS/CAREER NOTES: Selected as undergraduate by Cleveland Cavaliers in first round (12th pick overall) of 1984 NBA Draft.... Draft rights traded by Cavaliers with Cliff Robinson and cash to Washington Bullets for draft rights to Melvin Turpin (June 19, 1984).... Draft rights traded by Bullets with Ricky Sobers to Seattle SuperSonics for Gus Williams (June 19, 1984).... Traded by SuperSonics with Danny Vranes to Philadelphia 76ers for Clemon Johnson and 1989 first-round draft choice (September 29, 1986).... Traded by 76ers with Roy Hinson and 1989 second-round draft choice to New Jersey Nets for Mike Gminski and Ben Coleman (January 16, 1988).... Traded by Nets with Tony Brown, Frank Johnson and Lorenzo Romar to Houston Rockets for Joe Barry Carroll and Lester Conner (November 2, 1988).... Traded by Rockets with John Lucas to Atlanta Hawks for Kenny Smith and Roy Marble (September 27, 1990).... Traded by Hawks to New York Knicks for Maurice Cheeks (October 3, 1991).

COLLEGIATE RECORD

Season Team	G	Min.	FGM	FGA	Pct.	FTM	FTA	Pct.	Reb.	Pts.	Avg.
80-81 —Michigan	30	524	54	106	.509	47	60	.783	106	155	5.2
81-82 —Michigan					Did not play—knee surgery.						

Season Team	G	Min.	FGM	FGA	Pct.	FTM	FTA	Pct.	Reb.	Pts.	Avg.
82-83 —Michigan	28	...	122	220	.555	109	134	.813	180	353	12.6
83-84 —Michigan	32	960	131	226	.580	124	186	.667	189	386	12.1
Totals	90		307	552	.556	280	380	.737	475	894	9.9

NBA REGULAR-SEASON RECORD

Season Team	G	Min.	FGM	FGA	Pct.	FTM	FTA	Pct.	Off.	Def.	Tot.	Ast.	PF	Dq.	Stl.	Blk.	TO	Pts.	Avg.
84-85 —Seattle	78	1584	269	483	.557	188	263	.715	146	252	398	78	207	2	18	33	114	726	9.3
85-86 —Seattle	77	1705	253	444	.570	174	244	.713	140	263	403	83	219	4	19	28	110	681	8.8
86-87 —Philadelphia	81	2817	391	718	.545	251	349	.719	180	431	611	114	270	4	36	64	153	1033	12.8
87-88 —Phil.-N.J.	70	2114	348	648	.537	145	215	.674	146	321	467	118	234	3	32	23	111	841	12.0
88-89 —Houston	81	1257	169	351	.481	87	129	.674	87	174	261	54	193	0	18	24	68	425	5.2
89-90 —Houston	18	116	10	29	.345	10	19	.526	8	19	27	3	24	0	3	1	10	30	1.7
90-91 —Atlanta	56	689	93	187	.497	66	90	.733	56	109	165	32	91	1	11	14	45	252	4.5
91-92 —New York	22	108	14	33	.424	14	21	.667	14	20	34	9	18	0	2	0	8	42	1.9
Totals	483	10390	1547	2893	.535	935	1330	.703	777	1589	2366	491	1256	14	139	187	619	4030	8.3

Three-point field goals: 1984-85, 0-for-1. 1985-86, 1-for-2 (.500). 1986-87, 0-for-4. 1987-88, 0-for-2. 1988-89, 0-for-4. 1990-91, 0-for-3. Totals, 1-for-16 (.063).

NBA PLAYOFF RECORD

Season Team	G	Min.	FGM	FGA	Pct.	FTM	FTA	Pct.	Off.	Def.	Tot.	Ast.	PF	Dq.	Stl.	Blk.	TO	Pts.	Avg.
86-87 —Philadelphia	5	121	12	24	.500	4	4	1.000	7	24	31	6	19	0	1	2	7	28	5.6
88-89 —Houston	4	53	7	13	.538	8	9	.889	2	11	13	0	9	0	3	2	0	22	5.5
89-90 —Houston	3	21	1	3	.333	1	2	.500	1	7	8	0	5	0	0	0	0	3	1.0
90-91 —Atlanta	2	13	2	7	.286	2	3	.667	1	1	2	0	1	0	0	0	0	6	3.0
91-92 —New York	1	6	0	2	.000	0	0	...	0	3	3	0	1	0	0	0	0	0	0.0
Totals	15	214	22	49	.449	15	18	.833	11	46	57	6	35	0	4	4	7	59	3.9

Three-point field goals: 1988-89, 0-for-1.

McCRAY, RODNEY
F, MAVERICKS

PERSONAL: Born August 29, 1961, in Mt. Vernon, N.Y.... 6-8/248. ... Full name: Rodney Earl McCray. ... Brother of Carlton (Scooter) McCray, forward with Seattle SuperSonics and Cleveland Cavaliers (1983-84, 1984-85 and 1986-87).
HIGH SCHOOL: Mt. Vernon (N.Y.).
COLLEGE: Louisville.
TRANSACTIONS/CAREER NOTES: Selected by Houston Rockets in first round (third pick overall) of 1983 NBA Draft.... Traded by Rockets with Jim Petersen to Sacramento Kings for Otis Thorpe (October 11, 1988).... Traded by Kings with 1990 and 1991 second-round draft choices to Dallas Mavericks for Bill Wennington and two 1990 first-round draft choices (June 26, 1990).
MISCELLANEOUS: Member of U.S. Olympic team (1980).

COLLEGIATE RECORD

NOTES: Member of NCAA Division I championship team (1980).

Season Team	G	Min.	FGM	FGA	Pct.	FTM	FTA	Pct.	Reb.	Pts.	Avg.
79-80 —Louisville	36	1178	107	197	.543	66	102	.647	269	280	7.8
80-81 —Louisville	30	917	114	194	.588	60	90	.667	222	288	9.6
81-82 —Louisville	33	961	112	196	.571	59	84	.702	234	283	8.6
82-83 —Louisville	36	1197	152	259	.587	92	124	.742	304	396	11.0
Totals	135	4253	485	846	.573	277	400	.693	1029	1247	9.2

NBA REGULAR-SEASON RECORD

HONORS: NBA All-Defensive first team (1988).... NBA All-Defensive second team (1987).

Season Team	G	Min.	FGM	FGA	Pct.	FTM	FTA	Pct.	Off.	Def.	Tot.	Ast.	PF	Dq.	Stl.	Blk.	TO	Pts.	Avg.
83-84 —Houston	79	2081	335	672	.499	182	249	.731	173	277	450	176	205	1	53	54	120	853	10.8
84-85 —Houston	82	3001	476	890	.535	231	313	.738	201	338	539	355	215	2	90	75	178	1183	14.4
85-86 —Houston	82	2610	338	629	.537	171	222	.770	159	361	520	292	197	2	50	58	130	847	10.3
86-87 —Houston	81	3136	432	783	.552	306	393	.779	190	388	578	434	172	2	88	53	208	1170	14.4
87-88 —Houston	81	2689	359	746	.481	288	367	.785	232	399	631	264	166	2	57	51	144	1006	12.4
88-89 —Sacramento	68	2435	340	729	.466	169	234	.722	143	371	514	293	121	0	57	36	168	854	12.6
89-90 —Sacramento	82	3238	537	1043	.515	273	348	.784	192	477	669	377	176	0	60	70	174	1358	16.6
90-91 —Dallas	74	2561	336	679	.495	159	198	.803	153	407	560	259	203	3	70	51	129	844	11.4
91-92 —Dallas	75	2106	271	622	.436	110	153	.719	149	319	468	219	180	2	48	30	115	677	9.0
Totals	704	23857	3424	6793	.504	1889	2477	.763	1592	3337	4929	2669	1635	14	573	478	1366	8792	12.5

Three-point field goals: 1983-84, 1-for-4 (.250). 1984-85, 0-for-6. 1985-86, 0-for-3. 1986-87, 0-for-9. 1987-88, 0-for-4. 1988-89, 5-for-22 (.227). 1989-90, 11-for-42 (.262). 1990-91, 13-for-39 (.333). 1991-92, 25-for-85 (.294). Totals, 55-for-214 (.257).

NBA PLAYOFF RECORD

Season Team	G	Min.	FGM	FGA	Pct.	FTM	FTA	Pct.	Off.	Def.	Tot.	Ast.	PF	Dq.	Stl.	Blk.	TO	Pts.	Avg.
84-85 —Houston	5	181	19	34	.559	15	23	.652	9	21	30	11	17	0	6	1	13	53	10.6
85-86 —Houston	20	835	108	202	.535	43	58	.741	23	95	118	125	45	0	18	19	37	259	13.0
86-87 —Houston	10	436	57	101	.564	43	54	.796	32	51	83	56	21	0	5	9	26	157	15.7
87-88 —Houston	4	159	12	31	.387	8	12	.667	15	12	27	9	12	0	4	3	7	32	8.0
Totals	39	1611	196	368	.533	109	147	.741	79	179	258	201	95	0	33	32	83	501	12.8

Three-point field goals: 1985-86, 0-for-3. 1986-87, 0-for-2. 1987-88, 0-for-1. Totals, 0-for-6.

M

DID YOU KNOW. . .

... that the Atlanta Hawks were a combined 0-10 against Chicago and Cleveland in 1991-92?

McDANIEL, XAVIER

F, KNICKS

PERSONAL: Born June 4, 1963, in Columbia, S.C. . . . 6-8/205.
. . . Full name: Xavier Maurice McDaniel.
HIGH SCHOOL: A.C. Flora (Columbia, S.C.).
COLLEGE: Wichita State.

TRANSACTIONS/CAREER NOTES: Selected by Seattle SuperSonics in first round (fourth pick overall) of 1985 NBA Draft. . . . Traded by SuperSonics to Phoenix Suns for Eddie Johnson, 1991 first-round draft choice and 1993 or 1994 first-round draft choice (December 7, 1990). . . . Traded by Suns to New York Knicks for Trent Tucker, Jerrod Mustaf and 1992 and 1994 second-round draft choices (October 1, 1991).

COLLEGIATE RECORD

NOTES: Led NCAA Division I with 14.4 rebounds per game (1983) and 14.8 rebounds per game (1985). . . . Led NCAA Division I with 27.2 points per game (1985). . . . One of only two players in NCAA history to lead nation in both scoring and rebounding in same season (1985).

Season Team	G	Min.	FGM	FGA	Pct.	FTM	FTA	Pct.	Reb.	Pts.	Avg.
81-82 — Wichita State	28	378	68	135	.504	27	43	.628	103	163	5.8
82-83 — Wichita State	28	987	223	376	.593	80	148	.541	403	526	18.8
83-84 — Wichita State	30	1130	251	445	.564	117	172	.680	393	619	20.6
84-85 — Wichita State	31	1143	351	628	.559	142	224	.634	460	844	27.2
Totals	117	3638	893	1584	.564	366	587	.624	1359	2152	18.4

NBA REGULAR-SEASON RECORD

HONORS: NBA All-Rookie team (1986).

Season Team	G	Min.	FGM	FGA	Pct.	FTM	FTA	Pct.	Off.	Def.	Tot.	Ast.	PF	Dq.	Stl.	Blk.	TO	Pts.	Avg.
85-86 — Seattle	82	2706	576	1176	.490	250	364	.687	307	348	655	193	305	8	101	37	248	1404	17.1
86-87 — Seattle	82	3031	806	1583	.509	275	395	.696	338	367	705	207	300	4	115	52	234	1890	23.0
87-88 — Seattle	78	2703	687	1407	.488	281	393	.715	206	312	518	263	230	2	96	52	223	1669	21.4
88-89 — Seattle	82	2385	677	1385	.489	312	426	.732	177	256	433	134	231	0	84	40	210	1677	20.5
89-90 — Seattle	69	2432	611	1233	.496	244	333	.733	165	282	447	171	231	2	73	36	187	1471	21.3
90-91 — Sea.-Phoe.	81	2634	590	1186	.497	193	267	.723	173	384	557	187	264	2	76	46	184	1373	17.0
91-92 — New York	82	2344	488	1021	.478	137	192	.714	176	284	460	149	241	3	57	24	147	1125	13.7
Totals	556	18235	4435	8991	.493	1692	2370	.714	1542	2233	3775	1304	1802	21	602	287	1433	10609	19.1

Three-point field goals: 1985-86, 2-for-10 (.200). 1986-87, 3-for-14 (.214). 1987-88, 14-for-50 (.280). 1988-89, 11-for-36 (.306). 1989-90, 5-for-17 (.294). 1990-91, 0-for-8. 1991-92, 12-for-39 (.308). Totals, 47-for-174 (.270).

NBA PLAYOFF RECORD

Season Team	G	Min.	FGM	FGA	Pct.	FTM	FTA	Pct.	Off.	Def.	Tot.	Ast.	PF	Dq.	Stl.	Blk.	TO	Pts.	Avg.
86-87 — Seattle	14	528	124	254	.488	34	56	.607	52	65	117	42	63	2	21	9	42	284	20.3
87-88 — Seattle	5	180	45	81	.556	12	24	.500	14	34	48	25	15	0	3	1	11	106	21.2
88-89 — Seattle	8	281	58	144	.403	31	41	.756	24	43	67	22	30	0	2	5	22	150	18.8
90-91 — Phoenix	4	101	17	41	.415	4	6	.667	4	11	15	5	10	0	0	2	10	38	9.5
91-92 — New York	12	458	94	197	.477	36	49	.735	43	43	86	23	34	1	9	2	27	226	18.8
Totals	43	1548	338	717	.471	117	176	.665	137	196	333	117	152	3	35	19	112	804	18.7

Three-point field goals: 1986-87, 2-for-10 (.200). 1987-88, 4-for-8 (.500). 1988-89, 3-for-9 (.333). 1990-91, 0-for-1. 1991-92, 2-for-8 (.250). Totals, 11-for-36 (.306).

NBA ALL-STAR GAME RECORD

Season Team	Min.	FGM	FGA	Pct.	FTM	FTA	Pct.	Off.	Def.	Tot.	Ast.	PF	Dq.	Stl.	Blk.	TO	Pts.
1988 — Seattle	13	1	9	.111	0	0	. . .	1	1	2	0	1	0	0	0	1	2

McHALE, KEVIN

F/C, CELTICS

PERSONAL: Born December 19, 1957, in Hibbing, Minn. . . . 6-10/225.
. . . Full name: Kevin Edward McHale.
HIGH SCHOOL: Hibbing (Minn.).
COLLEGE: Minnesota.

TRANSACTIONS/CAREER NOTES: Selected by Boston Celtics in first round (third pick overall) of 1980 NBA Draft.
MISCELLANEOUS: Member of NBA championship teams (1981, 1984, 1986).

COLLEGIATE RECORD

Season Team	G	Min.	FGM	FGA	Pct.	FTM	FTA	Pct.	Reb.	Pts.	Avg.
76-77 — Minnesota	27	. . .	133	241	.552	58	77	.753	218	324	12.0
77-78 — Minnesota	26	. . .	143	242	.591	54	77	.701	192	340	13.1
78-79 — Minnesota	27	. . .	202	391	.517	79	96	.823	259	483	17.9
79-80 — Minnesota	32	. . .	236	416	.567	85	107	.794	281	557	17.4
Totals	112	. . .	714	1290	.553	276	357	.773	950	1704	15.2

NBA REGULAR-SEASON RECORD

HONORS: NBA Sixth Man Award (1984, 1985). . . . All-NBA first team (1987). . . . NBA All-Defensive first team (1986, 1987, 1988). . . . NBA All-Defensive second team (1983, 1989, 1990). . . . NBA All-Rookie team (1981).

Season Team	G	Min.	FGM	FGA	Pct.	FTM	FTA	Pct.	Off.	Def.	Tot.	Ast.	PF	Dq.	Stl.	Blk.	TO	Pts.	Avg.
80-81 — Boston	82	1645	355	666	.533	108	159	.679	155	204	359	55	260	3	27	151	110	818	10.0
81-82 — Boston	82	2332	465	875	.531	187	248	.754	191	365	556	91	264	1	30	185	137	1117	13.6
82-83 — Boston	82	2345	483	893	.541	193	269	.717	215	338	553	104	241	3	34	192	159	1511	14.1
83-84 — Boston	82	2577	587	1055	.556	336	439	.765	208	402	610	104	243	5	23	126	150	1511	18.4
84-85 — Boston	79	2653	605	1062	.570	355	467	.760	229	483	712	141	234	3	28	120	157	1565	19.8

M

Season	Team	G	Min.	FGM	FGA	Pct.	FTM	FTA	Pct.	Off.	Def.	Tot.	Ast.	PF	Dq.	Stl.	Blk.	TO	Pts.	Avg.
85-86	Boston	68	2397	561	978	.574	326	420	.776	171	380	551	181	192	2	29	134	149	1448	21.3
86-87	Boston	77	3060	790	1307	*.604	428	512	.836	247	516	763	198	240	1	38	172	197	2008	26.1
87-88	Boston	64	2390	550	911	*.604	346	434	.797	159	377	536	171	179	1	27	92	141	1446	22.6
88-89	Boston	78	2876	661	1211	.546	436	533	.818	223	414	637	172	223	2	26	97	196	1758	22.5
89-90	Boston	82	2722	648	1181	.549	393	440	.893	201	476	677	172	250	3	30	157	183	1712	20.9
90-91	Boston	68	2067	504	912	.553	228	275	.829	145	335	480	126	194	2	25	146	140	1251	18.4
91-92	Boston	56	1398	323	634	.509	134	163	.822	119	211	330	82	112	1	11	59	82	780	13.9
Totals	....	900	28462	6532	11685	.559	3470	4359	.796	2263	4501	6764	1597	2632	27	328	1631	1801	16573	18.4

Three-point field goals: 1980-81, 0-for-2. 1982-83, 0-for-1. 1983-84, 1-for-3 (.333). 1984-85, 0-for-6. 1986-87, 0-for-4. 1988-89, 0-for-4. 1989-90, 23-for-69 (.333). 1990-91, 15-for-37 (.405). 1991-92, 0-for-13. Totals, 39-for-139 (.281).

NBA PLAYOFF RECORD

Season	Team	G	Min.	FGM	FGA	Pct.	FTM	FTA	Pct.	Off.	Def.	Tot.	Ast.	PF	Dq.	Stl.	Blk.	TO	Pts.	Avg.
80-81	Boston	17	296	61	113	.540	23	36	.639	29	30	59	14	51	1	4	25	15	145	8.5
81-82	Boston	12	344	77	134	.575	40	53	.755	41	44	85	11	44	0	5	27	16	194	16.2
82-83	Boston	7	177	34	62	.548	10	18	.556	15	27	42	5	16	0	3	7	10	78	11.1
83-84	Boston	23	702	123	244	.504	94	121	.777	62	81	143	27	75	1	3	35	38	340	14.8
84-85	Boston	21	837	172	303	.568	121	150	.807	74	134	208	32	73	3	13	46	60	465	22.1
85-86	Boston	18	715	168	290	.579	112	141	.794	51	104	155	48	64	0	8	43	48	448	24.9
86-87	Boston	21	827	174	298	.584	96	126	.762	66	128	194	39	71	2	7	30	54	444	21.1
87-88	Boston	17	716	158	262	.603	115	137	.839	55	81	136	40	65	1	7	30	39	432	25.4
88-89	Boston	3	115	20	41	.488	17	23	.739	7	17	24	9	13	0	1	2	4	57	19.0
89-90	Boston	5	192	42	69	.609	25	29	.862	8	31	39	13	17	0	2	10	14	110	22.0
90-91	Boston	11	376	78	148	.527	66	80	.825	18	54	72	20	42	0	5	14	14	228	20.7
91-92	Boston	10	376	65	126	.516	35	44	.795	21	46	67	13	34	0	5	5	9	165	16.5
Totals	....	165	5603	1172	2090	.561	754	958	.787	447	777	1224	271	565	8	63	274	321	3106	18.8

Three-point field goals: 1982-83, 0-for-1. 1983-84, 0-for-3. 1985-86, 0-for-1. 1987-88, 1-for-1. 1989-90, 1-for-3 (.333). 1990-91, 6-for-11 (.545). 1991-92, 0-for-1. Totals, 8-for-21 (.381).

NBA ALL-STAR GAME RECORD

Season	Team	Min.	FGM	FGA	Pct.	FTM	FTA	Pct.	Off.	Def.	Tot.	Ast.	PF	Dq.	Stl.	Blk.	TO	Pts.
1984	Boston	11	3	7	.429	4	6	.667	2	3	5	0	1	0	0	0	2	10
1986	Boston	20	3	8	.375	2	2	1.000	3	7	10	2	4	0	0	4	0	8
1987	Boston	30	7	11	.636	2	2	1.000	4	3	7	2	5	0	0	4	0	16
1988	Boston	14	0	1	.000	2	2	1.000	0	1	1	1	2	0	0	2	2	2
1989	Boston	16	5	7	.714	0	0	...	1	2	3	0	3	0	0	2	1	10
1990	Boston	20	6	11	.545	0	0	...	2	6	8	1	4	0	0	0	0	13
1991	Boston	14	0	3	.000	2	2	1.000	1	2	3	2	2	0	1	0	0	2
Totals	....	125	24	48	.500	12	14	.857	13	24	37	8	21	0	1	12	5	61

Three-point field goals: 1990, 1-for-1. 1991, 0-for-1. Totals, 1-for-2 (.500).

McKEY, DERRICK
F, SUPERSONICS

PERSONAL: Born October 10, 1966, in Meridian, Miss. . . . 6-10/225. . . . Full name: Derrick Wayne McKey.
HIGH SCHOOL: Meridian (Miss.).
COLLEGE: Alabama.
TRANSACTIONS/CAREER NOTES: Selected as undergraduate by Seattle SuperSonics in first round (ninth pick overall) of 1987 NBA Draft.

M

COLLEGIATE RECORD

NOTES: THE SPORTING NEWS All-America second team (1987).

Season	Team	G	Min.	FGM	FGA	Pct.	FTM	FTA	Pct.	Reb.	Pts.	Avg.
84-85	Alabama	33	728	74	155	.477	20	33	.606	134	168	5.1
85-86	Alabama	33	1117	178	280	.636	92	117	.786	262	448	13.6
86-87	Alabama	33	1199	247	425	.581	100	116	.862	247	615	18.6
Totals	....	99	3044	499	860	.580	212	266	.797	643	1231	12.4

Three-point field goals: 1986-87, 21-for-50 (.420).

NBA REGULAR-SEASON RECORD

HONORS: NBA All-Rookie team (1988).

Season	Team	G	Min.	FGM	FGA	Pct.	FTM	FTA	Pct.	Off.	Def.	Tot.	Ast.	PF	Dq.	Stl.	Blk.	TO	Pts.	Avg.
87-88	Seattle.........	82	1706	255	519	.491	173	224	.772	115	213	328	107	237	3	70	63	108	694	8.5
88-89	Seattle.........	82	2804	487	970	.502	301	375	.803	167	297	464	219	264	4	105	70	188	1305	15.9
89-90	Seattle.........	80	2748	468	949	.493	315	403	.782	170	319	489	187	247	2	87	81	192	1254	15.7
90-91	Seattle.........	73	2503	438	847	.517	235	278	.845	172	251	423	169	220	2	91	56	158	1115	15.3
91-92	Seattle.........	52	1757	285	604	.472	188	222	.847	95	173	268	120	142	2	61	47	114	777	14.9
Totals	....	369	11518	1933	3889	.497	1212	1502	.807	719	1253	1972	802	1110	13	414	317	760	5145	13.9

Three-point field goals: 1987-88, 11-for-30 (.367). 1988-89, 30-for-89 (.337). 1989-90, 3-for-23 (.130). 1990-91, 4-for-19 (.211). 1991-92, 19-for-50 (.380). Totals, 67-for-211 (.318).

NBA PLAYOFF RECORD

Season	Team	G	Min.	FGM	FGA	Pct.	FTM	FTA	Pct.	Off.	Def.	Tot.	Ast.	PF	Dq.	Stl.	Blk.	TO	Pts.	Avg.
87-88	Seattle.........	5	109	24	38	.632	10	17	.588	7	13	20	8	12	0	3	5	5	60	12.0
88-89	Seattle.........	8	286	44	89	.494	17	21	.810	21	31	52	18	33	1	6	15	23	106	13.3
90-91	Seattle.........	4	114	16	28	.571	6	11	.545	7	16	23	8	13	0	3	0	6	38	9.5
91-92	Seattle.........	9	315	52	99	.525	38	45	.844	17	27	44	24	37	1	7	12	22	147	16.3
Totals	....	26	824	136	254	.535	71	94	.755	52	87	139	58	95	2	19	32	56	351	13.5

Three-point field goals: 1987-88, 2-for-6 (.333). 1988-89, 1-for-9 (.111). 1990-91, 0-for-1. 1991-92, 5-for-16 (.313). Totals, 8-for-32 (.250).

McKINNEY, CARLTON
F/G

PERSONAL: Born October 21, 1964, in San Diego.... 6-5/ 210.... Full name: Carlton B. McKinney.
HIGH SCHOOL: Nixon (Tex.).
COLLEGE: Tulsa, then Southern Methodist.
TRANSACTIONS/CAREER NOTES: Never drafted by an NBA franchise.... Signed as free agent by Los Angeles Clippers (August 15, 1989).... Waived by Clippers (November 29, 1989).... Played in Continental Basketball Association with Topeka Sizzlers (1988-89), Quad City Thunder and Santa Barbara Islanders (1989-90) and Rapid City Thrillers (1991-92).... Played in Italy (1990-91).... Signed as free agent by New York Knicks (September 30, 1991). ... Waived by Knicks (November 14, 1991).... Played in France (1991-92).

COLLEGIATE RECORD

Season Team	G	Min.	FGM	FGA	Pct.	FTM	FTA	Pct.	Reb.	Pts.	Avg.
83-84 —Tulsa	21	309	43	100	.430	24	30	.800	47	110	5.2
84-85 —Tulsa	31	470	81	173	.468	18	28	.643	52	180	5.8
85-86 —Southern Methodist					Did not play—transfer student.						
86-87 —Southern Methodist	29	1011	193	417	.463	29	41	.707	164	444	15.3
87-88 —Southern Methodist	35	1197	243	483	.503	40	57	.702	128	561	16.0
Totals	116	2987	560	1173	.477	111	156	.712	391	1295	11.2

Three-point field goals: 1986-87, 29-for-76 (.382). 1987-88, 35-for-84 (.417). Totals, 64-for-160 (.400).

CBA REGULAR-SEASON RECORD

| | | | 2-POINT | | | 3-POINT | | | | | | | | |
Season Team	G	Min.	FGM	FGA	Pct.	FGM	FGA	Pct.	FTM	FTA	Pct.	Reb.	Ast.	Pts.	Avg.
88-89 —Topeka	41	1646	399	847	.471	31	92	.337	63	94	.670	219	111	954	23.3
89-90 —Q.C.-S.B.	44	1127	322	661	.487	11	36	.306	48	59	.814	120	86	725	16.5
91-92 —Rapid City	25	598	110	239	.460	16	46	.348	14	23	.609	77	34	282	11.3
Totals	110	3371	831	1747	.476	58	174	.333	125	176	.710	416	231	1961	17.8

NBA REGULAR-SEASON RECORD

| | | | | | | | | | — REBOUNDS — | | | | | | | | |
Season Team	G	Min.	FGM	FGA	Pct.	FTM	FTA	Pct.	Off.	Def.	Tot.	Ast.	PF	Dq.	Stl.	Blk.	TO	Pts.	Avg.
89-90 —L.A. Clippers	7	104	8	32	.250	2	4	.500	4	8	12	7	15	1	6	1	7	18	2.6
91-92 —New York	2	9	2	9	.222	0	0	...	0	1	1	0	1	0	0	0	0	4	2.0
Totals	9	113	10	41	.244	2	4	.500	4	9	13	7	16	1	6	1	7	22	2.4

Three-point field goals: 1989-90, 0-for-1.

McMILLAN, NATE
G/F, SUPERSONICS

M

PERSONAL: Born August 3, 1964, in Raleigh, N.C.... 6-5/197.... Full name: Nathaniel McMillan.
HIGH SCHOOL: Enloe (Raleigh, N.C.).
COLLEGE: Chowan (N.C.), then North Carolina State.
TRANSACTIONS/CAREER NOTES: Selected by Seattle SuperSonics in second round (30th pick overall) of 1986 NBA Draft.

COLLEGIATE RECORD

Season Team	G	Min.	FGM	FGA	Pct.	FTM	FTA	Pct.	Reb.	Pts.	Avg.
82-83 —Chowan College	27	...	101	174	.580	64	92	.696	134	266	9.9
83-84 —Chowan College	35	...	180	331	.544	100	130	.769	342	460	13.1
84-85 —North Carolina State	33	973	94	207	.454	64	95	.674	189	252	7.6
85-86 —North Carolina State	34	1208	127	262	.485	66	90	.733	155	320	9.4
Junior college totals	62	...	281	505	.556	164	222	.739	476	726	11.7
Four-year-college totals	67	2181	221	469	.471	130	185	.703	344	572	8.5

NBA REGULAR-SEASON RECORD

RECORDS: Shares single-game record for most assists by a rookie—25 (February 23, 1987, vs. Los Angeles Clippers).

| | | | | | | | | | — REBOUNDS — | | | | | | | | |
Season Team	G	Min.	FGM	FGA	Pct.	FTM	FTA	Pct.	Off.	Def.	Tot.	Ast.	PF	Dq.	Stl.	Blk.	TO	Pts.	Avg.
86-87 —Seattle	71	1972	143	301	.475	87	141	.617	101	230	331	583	238	4	125	45	155	373	5.3
87-88 —Seattle	82	2453	235	496	.474	145	205	.707	117	221	338	702	238	1	169	47	189	624	7.6
88-89 —Seattle	75	2341	199	485	.410	119	189	.630	143	245	388	696	236	3	156	42	211	532	7.1
89-90 —Seattle	82	2338	207	438	.473	98	153	.641	127	276	403	598	289	7	140	37	187	523	6.4
90-91 —Seattle	78	1434	132	305	.433	57	93	.613	71	180	251	371	211	6	104	20	122	338	4.3
91-92 —Seattle	72	1652	177	405	.437	54	84	.643	92	160	252	359	218	4	129	29	112	435	6.0
Totals	460	12190	1093	2430	.450	560	865	.647	651	1312	1963	3309	1430	25	823	220	976	2825	6.1

Three-point field goals: 1986-87, 0-for-7. 1987-88, 9-for-24 (.375). 1988-89, 15-for-70 (.214). 1989-90, 11-for-31 (.355). 1990-91, 17-for-48 (.354). 1991-92, 27-for-98 (.276). Totals, 79-for-278 (.284).

NBA PLAYOFF RECORD

| | | | | | | | | | — REBOUNDS — | | | | | | | | |
Season Team	G	Min.	FGM	FGA	Pct.	FTM	FTA	Pct.	Off.	Def.	Tot.	Ast.	PF	Dq.	Stl.	Blk.	TO	Pts.	Avg.
86-87 —Seattle	14	356	27	62	.435	17	24	.708	13	41	54	112	42	1	14	10	26	71	5.1
87-88 —Seattle	5	127	12	35	.343	9	14	.643	6	15	21	33	11	0	2	3	8	33	6.6
88-89 —Seattle	8	200	19	40	.475	16	25	.640	9	16	25	63	21	0	10	5	19	54	6.8
90-91 —Seattle	5	95	6	23	.261	2	4	.500	6	12	18	22	15	0	6	1	3	14	2.8
91-92 —Seattle	9	246	35	83	.422	10	14	.714	14	19	33	63	35	1	16	3	22	86	9.6
Totals	41	1024	99	243	.407	54	81	.667	48	103	151	293	124	2	48	22	78	258	6.3

Three-point field goals: 1987-88, 0-for-1. 1988-89, 0-for-2. 1990-91, 0-for-2. 1991-92, 6-for-26 (.231). Totals, 6-for-31 (.194).

MILLER, REGGIE
G, PACERS

PERSONAL: Born August 24, 1965, in Riverside, Calif. . . . 6-7/185. . . . Full name: Reginald Wayne Miller. . . . Brother of Darrell Miller, outfielder/catcher with California Angels (1984-88); and brother of Cheryl Miller, member of gold-medal-winning U.S. Olympic basketball team (1984).
HIGH SCHOOL: Riverside Polytechnic (Calif.).
COLLEGE: UCLA.
TRANSACTIONS/CAREER NOTES: Selected by Indiana Pacers in first round (11th pick overall) of 1987 NBA Draft.

COLLEGIATE RECORD

Season Team	G	Min.	FGM	FGA	Pct.	FTM	FTA	Pct.	Reb.	Pts.	Avg.
83-84 —UCLA	28	384	56	110	.509	18	28	.643	42	130	4.6
84-85 —UCLA	33	1174	192	347	.553	119	148	.804	141	503	15.2
85-86 —UCLA	29	1112	274	493	.556	202	229	.882	153	750	25.9
86-87 —UCLA	32	1166	247	455	.543	149	179	.832	173	712	22.3
Totals	122	3836	769	1405	.547	488	584	.836	509	2095	17.2

Three-point field goals: 1986-87, 69-for-157 (.439).

NBA REGULAR-SEASON RECORD

Season Team	G	Min.	FGM	FGA	Pct.	FTM	FTA	Pct.	REBOUNDS Off.	Def.	Tot.	Ast.	PF	Dq.	Stl.	Blk.	TO	Pts.	Avg.
87-88 —Indiana	82	1840	306	627	.488	149	186	.801	95	95	190	132	157	0	53	19	101	822	10.0
88-89 —Indiana	74	2536	398	831	.479	287	340	.844	73	219	292	227	170	2	93	29	143	1181	16.0
89-90 —Indiana	82	3192	661	1287	.514	544	627	.868	95	200	295	311	175	1	110	18	222	2016	24.6
90-91 —Indiana	82	2972	596	1164	.512	551	600	*.918	81	200	281	331	165	1	109	13	163	1855	22.6
91-92 —Indiana	82	3120	562	1121	.501	442	515	.858	82	236	318	314	210	1	105	26	157	1695	20.7
Totals	402	13660	2523	5030	.502	1973	2268	.870	426	950	1376	1315	877	5	470	105	786	7569	18.8

Three-point field goals: 1987-88, 61-for-172 (.355). 1988-89, 98-for-244 (.402). 1989-90, 150-for-362 (.414). 1990-91, 112-for-322 (.348). 1991-92, 129-for-341 (.378). Totals, 550-for-1441 (.382).

NBA PLAYOFF RECORD

Season Team	G	Min.	FGM	FGA	Pct.	FTM	FTA	Pct.	REBOUNDS Off.	Def.	Tot.	Ast.	PF	Dq.	Stl.	Blk.	TO	Pts.	Avg.
89-90 —Indiana	3	125	20	35	.571	19	21	.905	1	11	12	6	6	0	3	0	3	62	20.7
90-91 —Indiana	5	193	34	70	.486	32	37	.865	5	11	16	14	14	0	8	2	12	108	21.6
91-92 —Indiana	3	130	25	43	.581	24	30	.800	4	3	7	14	12	1	4	0	4	81	27.0
Totals	11	448	79	148	.534	75	88	.852	10	25	35	34	32	1	15	2	19	251	22.8

Three-point field goals: 1989-90, 3-for-7 (.429). 1990-91, 8-for-19 (.421). 1991-92, 7-for-11 (.636). Totals, 18-for-37 (.486).

NBA ALL-STAR GAME RECORD

Season Team	Min.	FGM	FGA	Pct.	FTM	FTA	Pct.	REBOUNDS Off.	Def.	Tot.	Ast.	PF	Dq.	Stl.	Blk.	TO	Pts.
1990 —Indiana	14	2	3	.667	0	0	...	0	1	1	3	1	0	1	0	0	4

Three-point field goals: 1990, 0-for-1.

MILLS, TERRY
F, NETS

PERSONAL: Born December 21, 1967, in Romulus, Mich. . . . 6-10/230. . . . Full name: Terry Richard Mills. . . . Nephew of John Long, guard with Detroit Pistons, Indiana Pacers and Atlanta Hawks (1978-79 through 1990-91).
HIGH SCHOOL: Romulus (Mich.).
COLLEGE: Michigan.
TRANSACTIONS/CAREER NOTES: Selected by Milwaukee Bucks in first round (16th pick overall) of 1990 NBA Draft. . . . Traded by Bucks to Denver Nuggets for Danny Schayes (August 1, 1990). . . . Traded by Nuggets to New Jersey Nets in three-way deal in which Nets sent Greg Anderson to Nuggets, Nuggets sent Walter Davis to Portland Trail Blazers and Trail Blazers sent Drazen Petrovic to Nets (January 23, 1991); Nuggets also received 1992 first-round draft choice from Nets and 1993 second-round draft choice from Trail Blazers, and Trail Blazers received 1992 second-round draft choice from Nuggets.

NOTES: Member of NCAA Division I championship team (1989).

COLLEGIATE RECORD

Season Team	G	Min.	FGM	FGA	Pct.	FTM	FTA	Pct.	Reb.	Pts.	Avg.
86-87 —Michigan					Did not play—ineligible.						
87-88 —Michigan	34	884	181	341	.531	51	70	.729	216	413	12.1
88-89 —Michigan	37	999	180	319	.564	70	91	.769	218	430	11.6
89-90 —Michigan	31	961	237	405	.585	88	116	.759	247	562	18.1
Totals	102	2844	598	1065	.562	209	277	.755	681	1405	13.8

Three-point field goals: 1987-88, 0-for-2. 1988-89, 0-for-2. Totals, 0-for-4.

NBA REGULAR-SEASON RECORD

Season Team	G	Min.	FGM	FGA	Pct.	FTM	FTA	Pct.	REBOUNDS Off.	Def.	Tot.	Ast.	PF	Dq.	Stl.	Blk.	TO	Pts.	Avg.
90-91 —Denver-N.J.	55	819	134	288	.465	47	66	.712	82	147	229	33	100	0	35	29	43	315	5.7
91-92 —New Jersey	82	1714	310	670	.463	114	152	.750	187	266	453	84	200	3	48	41	82	742	9.0
Totals	137	2533	444	958	.463	161	218	.739	269	413	682	117	300	3	83	70	125	1057	7.7

Three-point field goals: 1990-91, 0-for-4. 1991-92, 8-for-23 (.348). Totals, 8-for-27 (.296).

NBA PLAYOFF RECORD

Season Team	G	Min.	FGM	FGA	Pct.	FTM	FTA	Pct.	REBOUNDS Off.	Def.	Tot.	Ast.	PF	Dq.	Stl.	Blk.	TO	Pts.	Avg.
91-92 —New Jersey	4	77	10	27	.370	7	11	.636	9	15	24	8	18	0	1	2	7	27	6.8

Three-point field goals: 1991-92, 0-for-1.

MITCHELL, SAM
F, PACERS

PERSONAL: Born September 2, 1963, in Columbus, Ga. . . . 6-7/210. . . . Full name: Samuel E. Mitchell Jr. **HIGH SCHOOL:** Columbus (Ga.). **COLLEGE:** Mercer (Ga.).

TRANSACTIONS/CAREER NOTES: Selected by Houston Rockets in third round (54th pick overall) of 1985 NBA Draft. . . . Waived by Rockets (October 22, 1985). . . . Played in Continental Basketball Association with Wisconsin Flyers (1985-86 and 1986-87) and Rapid City Thrillers (1986-87). . . . Re-signed as free agent by Rockets (October 7, 1986). . . . Waived by Rockets (October 28, 1986). . . . Played in France (1987-88 and 1988-89). . . . Signed as free agent by Minnesota Timberwolves (July 23, 1989). . . . Traded by Timberwolves with Pooh Richardson to Indiana Pacers for Chuck Person and Micheal Williams (September 8, 1992).

COLLEGIATE RECORD

Season Team	G	Min.	FGM	FGA	Pct.	FTM	FTA	Pct.	Reb.	Pts.	Avg.
81-82 — Mercer	27	...	77	155	.497	38	53	.717	100	192	7.1
82-83 — Mercer	28	964	178	343	.519	105	134	.784	164	461	16.5
83-84 — Mercer	26	935	219	432	.507	121	155	.781	184	559	21.5
84-85 — Mercer	31	1157	294	570	.516	186	248	.750	255	774	25.0
Totals	112	...	768	1500	.512	450	590	.763	703	1986	17.7

CBA REGULAR-SEASON RECORD

Season Team	G	Min.	2-POINT FGM	FGA	Pct.	3-POINT FGM	FGA	Pct.	FTM	FTA	Pct.	Reb.	Ast.	Pts.	Avg.
85-86 — Wisconsin	13	450	106	235	.451	1	3	.333	55	83	.663	95	16	270	20.8
86-87 — Wisc.-R.C.	42	1370	250	542	.461	3	12	.250	154	210	.733	256	31	663	15.8
Totals	55	1820	356	777	.458	4	15	.267	209	293	.713	351	47	933	17.0

NBA REGULAR-SEASON RECORD

Season Team	G	Min.	FGM	FGA	Pct.	FTM	FTA	Pct.	REBOUNDS Off.	Def.	Tot.	Ast.	PF	Dq.	Stl.	Blk.	TO	Pts.	Avg.
89-90 — Minnesota	80	2414	372	834	.446	268	349	.768	180	282	462	89	301	7	66	54	96	1012	12.7
90-91 — Minnesota	82	3121	445	1010	.441	307	396	.775	188	332	520	133	*338	13	66	57	104	1197	14.6
91-92 — Minnesota	82	2151	307	725	.423	209	266	.786	158	315	473	94	230	3	53	39	97	825	10.1
Totals	244	7686	1124	2569	.438	784	1011	.775	526	929	1455	316	869	23	185	150	297	3034	12.4

Three-point field goals: 1989-90, 0-for-9. 1990-91, 0-for-9. 1991-92, 2-for-11 (.182). Totals, 2-for-29 (.069).

MONROE, RODNEY
G, HAWKS

PERSONAL: Born April 16, 1968, in Baltimore. . . . 6-3/185. . . . Full name: Rodney Eugene Monroe. **HIGH SCHOOL:** Saint Maria Goretti (Hagarstown, Md.). **COLLEGE:** North Carolina State.

TRANSACTIONS/CAREER NOTES: Selected by Atlanta Hawks in second round (30th pick overall) of 1991 NBA Draft.

COLLEGIATE RECORD

NOTES: THE SPORTING NEWS All-America first team (1991).

Season Team	G	Min.	FGM	FGA	Pct.	FTM	FTA	Pct.	Reb.	Pts.	Avg.
87-88 — North Carolina State	32	665	132	277	.477	42	51	.824	77	355	11.1
88-89 — North Carolina State	31	1064	240	513	.468	98	123	.797	149	663	21.4
89-90 — North Carolina State	30	1095	228	505	.451	157	192	.818	130	697	23.2
90-91 — North Carolina State	31	1165	285	641	.445	162	183	.885	136	836	27.0
Totals	124	3989	885	1936	.457	459	549	.836	492	2551	20.6

Three-point field goals: 1987-88, 49-for-114 (.430). 1988-89, 85-for-212 (.401). 1989-90, 84-for-174 (.483). 1990-91, 104-for-239 (.435). Totals, 322-for-739 (.436).

NBA REGULAR-SEASON RECORD

Season Team	G	Min.	FGM	FGA	Pct.	FTM	FTA	Pct.	REBOUNDS Off.	Def.	Tot.	Ast.	PF	Dq.	Stl.	Blk.	TO	Pts.	Avg.
91-92 — Atlanta	38	313	53	144	.368	19	23	.826	12	21	33	27	19	0	12	2	23	131	3.4

Three-point field goals: 1991-92, 6-for-27 (.222).

MOORE, TRACY
G, MAVERICKS

PERSONAL: Born December 28, 1965, in Oklahoma City. . . . 6-4/200. . . . Full name: Tracy Lamont Moore. **HIGH SCHOOL:** John Marshall (Oklahoma City). **COLLEGE:** Tulsa.

TRANSACTIONS/CAREER NOTES: Never drafted by an NBA franchise. . . . Played in Continental Basketball Association with Tulsa Fast Breakers (1988-89 and 1989-90), Quad City Thunder and Columbus Horizon (1989-90) and Tulsa Zone (1990-91 and 1991-92). . . . Signed by Dallas Mavericks to first of two consecutive 10-day contracts (January 17, 1992). . . . Signed by Mavericks for remainder of season (February 6, 1992).

COLLEGIATE RECORD

Season Team	G	Min.	FGM	FGA	Pct.	FTM	FTA	Pct.	Reb.	Pts.	Avg.
84-85 — Tulsa	31	423	75	152	.493	33	45	.733	25	183	5.9
85-86 — Tulsa	32	1095	217	453	.479	105	139	.755	114	539	16.8
86-87 — Tulsa	30	984	204	445	.458	88	122	.721	127	506	16.9
87-88 — Tulsa	28	1032	211	483	.437	109	151	.722	128	595	21.3
Totals	121	3534	707	1533	.461	335	457	.733	394	1823	15.1

Three-point field goals: 1986-87, 10-for-26 (.385). 1987-88, 64-for-137 (.467). Totals, 74-for-163 (.454).

CBA REGULAR-SEASON RECORD

Season	Team	G	Min.	2-POINT FGM	FGA	Pct.	3-POINT FGM	FGA	Pct.	FTM	FTA	Pct.	Reb.	Ast.	Pts.	Avg.
88-89	Tulsa...............	46	1074	217	456	.476	18	47	.383	68	105	.648	138	55	556	12.1
89-90	Tul.-Q.C.-Col...	36	731	173	336	.515	7	19	.368	60	75	.800	89	49	427	11.9
90-91	Tulsa...............	50	1583	295	570	.518	38	95	.400	144	192	.750	250	100	848	17.0
91-92	Tulsa...............	27	1054	257	499	.515	25	75	.333	241	283	.852	142	74	830	30.7
	Totals	159	4442	942	1861	.506	88	236	.373	513	655	.783	619	278	2661	16.7

NBA REGULAR-SEASON RECORD

Season	Team	G	Min.	FGM	FGA	Pct.	FTM	FTA	Pct.	REBOUNDS Off.	Def.	Tot.	Ast.	PF	Dq.	Stl.	Blk.	TO	Pts.	Avg.
91-92	Dallas..........	42	782	130	325	.400	65	78	.833	31	51	82	48	97	0	32	4	44	355	8.5

Three-point field goals: 1991-92, 30-for-84 (.357).

MORRIS, CHRIS
F, NETS

PERSONAL: Born January 20, 1966, in Atlanta. . . . 6-8/210. . . . Full name: Christopher Vernard Morris.
HIGH SCHOOL: Douglass (Atlanta).
COLLEGE: Auburn.
TRANSACTIONS/CAREER NOTES: Selected by New Jersey Nets in first round (fourth pick overall) of 1988 NBA Draft.

COLLEGIATE RECORD

Season	Team	G	Min.	FGM	FGA	Pct.	FTM	FTA	Pct.	Reb.	Pts.	Avg.
84-85	Auburn..............................	34	1032	155	325	.477	44	71	.620	169	354	10.4
85-86	Auburn..............................	33	1023	128	256	.500	69	103	.670	171	325	9.8
86-87	Auburn..............................	31	985	170	304	.559	69	97	.711	225	418	13.5
87-88	Auburn..............................	30	1018	241	501	.481	105	132	.795	295	620	20.7
	Totals	128	4058	694	1386	.501	287	403	.712	860	1717	13.4

Three-point field goals: 1986-87, 9-for-27 (.333). 1987-88, 33-for-97 (.340). Totals, 42-for-124 (.339).

HONORS: NBA All-Rookie second team (1989).

NBA REGULAR-SEASON RECORD

Season	Team	G	Min.	FGM	FGA	Pct.	FTM	FTA	Pct.	REBOUNDS Off.	Def.	Tot.	Ast.	PF	Dq.	Stl.	Blk.	TO	Pts.	Avg.
88-89	New Jersey ..	76	2096	414	905	.457	182	254	.717	188	209	397	119	250	4	102	60	190	1074	14.1
89-90	New Jersey ..	80	2449	449	1065	.422	228	316	.722	194	228	422	143	219	1	130	79	185	1187	14.8
90-91	New Jersey ..	79	2553	409	962	.425	179	244	.734	210	311	521	220	248	5	138	96	167	1042	13.2
91-92	New Jersey ..	77	2394	346	726	.477	165	231	.714	199	295	494	197	211	2	129	81	171	879	11.4
	Totals	312	9492	1618	3658	.442	754	1045	.722	791	1043	1834	679	928	12	499	316	713	4182	13.4

Three-point field goals: 1988-89, 64-for-175 (.366). 1989-90, 61-for-193 (.316). 1990-91, 45-for-179 (.251). 1991-92, 22-for-110 (.200). Totals, 192-for-657 (.292).

NBA PLAYOFF RECORD

Season	Team	G	Min.	FGM	FGA	Pct.	FTM	FTA	Pct.	REBOUNDS Off.	Def.	Tot.	Ast.	PF	Dq.	Stl.	Blk.	TO	Pts.	Avg.
91-92	New Jersey ..	4	135	32	58	.552	7	9	.778	11	9	20	5	11	0	7	7	8	75	18.8

Three-point field goals: 1991-92, 4-for-10 (.400).

MORTON, JOHN
G, HEAT

PERSONAL: Born May 18, 1967, in Bronx, N.Y. . . . 6-3/195. . . . Full name: John Morton Jr.
HIGH SCHOOL: Walton (Bronx, N.Y.).
COLLEGE: Seton Hall.
TRANSACTIONS/CAREER NOTES: Selected by Cleveland Cavaliers in first round (25th pick overall) of 1989 NBA Draft. . . . Waived by Cavaliers (November 14, 1991). . . . Signed as free agent by Miami Heat (November 22, 1991).

COLLEGIATE RECORD

Season	Team	G	Min.	FGM	FGA	Pct.	FTM	FTA	Pct.	Reb.	Pts.	Avg.
85-86	Seton Hall	31	611	82	186	.441	68	107	.636	47	232	7.5
86-87	Seton Hall	27	734	90	199	.452	100	137	.730	70	282	10.4
87-88	Seton Hall	35	1008	156	321	.486	132	157	.841	67	449	12.8
88-89	Seton Hall	38	1082	210	482	.436	159	194	.820	129	658	17.3
	Totals	131	3435	538	1188	.453	459	595	.771	313	1621	12.4

Three-point field goals: 1986-87, 2-for-14 (.143). 1987-88, 5-for-17 (.294). 1988-89, 79-for-189 (.418). Totals, 86-for-220 (.391).

NBA REGULAR-SEASON RECORD

Season	Team	G	Min.	FGM	FGA	Pct.	FTM	FTA	Pct.	REBOUNDS Off.	Def.	Tot.	Ast.	PF	Dq.	Stl.	Blk.	TO	Pts.	Avg.
89-90	Cleveland	37	402	48	161	.298	43	62	.694	7	25	32	67	30	0	18	4	51	146	3.9
90-91	Cleveland	66	1207	120	274	.438	113	139	.813	41	62	103	243	112	1	61	18	107	357	5.4
91-92	Clev.-Miami .	25	270	36	93	.387	32	38	.842	6	20	26	32	23	0	13	1	28	106	4.2
	Totals	128	1879	204	528	.386	188	239	.787	54	107	161	342	165	1	92	23	186	609	4.8

Three-point field goals: 1989-90, 7-for-30 (.233). 1990-91, 4-for-12 (.333). 1991-92, 2-for-16 (.125). Totals, 13-for-58 (.224).

NBA PLAYOFF RECORD

Season	Team	G	Min.	FGM	FGA	Pct.	FTM	FTA	Pct.	REBOUNDS Off.	Def.	Tot.	Ast.	PF	Dq.	Stl.	Blk.	TO	Pts.	Avg.
89-90	Cleveland	2	9	2	5	.400	2	2	1.000	0	0	0	1	0	0	0	0	1	6	3.0
91-92	Miami..........	1	2	0	0	...	2	2	1.000	0	0	0	0	0	0	0	0	1	2	2.0
	Totals	3	11	2	5	.400	4	4	1.000	0	0	0	1	0	0	0	0	2	8	2.7

MULLIN, CHRIS
F, WARRIORS

PERSONAL: Born July 30, 1963, in New York. ... 6-7/215. ... Full name: Christopher Paul Mullin.
HIGH SCHOOL: Xaverian (Brooklyn, N.Y.).
COLLEGE: St. John's.
TRANSACTIONS/CAREER NOTES: Selected by Golden State Warriors in first round (seventh pick overall) of 1985 NBA Draft.
MISCELLANEOUS: Member of gold-medal-winning U.S. Olympic teams (1984, 1992).

COLLEGIATE RECORD

NOTES: THE SPORTING NEWS All-America first team (1985). ... THE SPORTING NEWS All-America second team (1984).

Season Team	G	Min.	FGM	FGA	Pct.	FTM	FTA	Pct.	Reb.	Pts.	Avg.
81-82 —St. John's	30	1061	175	328	.534	148	187	.791	97	498	16.6
82-83 —St. John's	33	1210	228	395	.577	173	197	.878	123	629	19.1
83-84 —St. John's	27	1070	225	394	.571	169	187	.904	120	619	22.9
84-85 —St. John's	35	1327	251	482	.521	192	233	.824	169	694	19.8
Totals	125	4668	879	1599	.550	682	804	.848	509	2440	19.5

NBA REGULAR-SEASON RECORD

HONORS: All-NBA first team (1992). ... All-NBA second team (1989, 1991). ... All-NBA third team (1990).

Season Team	G	Min.	FGM	FGA	Pct.	FTM	FTA	Pct.	Off.	Def.	Tot.	Ast.	PF	Dq.	Stl.	Blk.	TO	Pts.	Avg.
85-86 —Golden State	55	1391	287	620	.463	189	211	.896	42	73	115	105	130	1	70	23	75	768	14.0
86-87 —Golden State	82	2377	477	928	.514	269	326	.825	39	142	181	261	217	1	98	36	154	1242	15.1
87-88 —Golden State	60	2033	470	926	.508	239	270	.885	58	147	205	290	136	3	113	32	156	1213	20.2
88-89 —Golden State	82	3093	830	1630	.509	493	553	.892	152	331	483	415	178	1	176	39	296	2176	26.5
89-90 —Golden State	78	2830	682	1272	.536	505	568	.889	130	333	463	319	142	1	123	45	239	1956	25.1
90-91 —Golden State	82	*3315	777	1449	.536	513	580	.884	141	302	443	329	176	2	173	63	245	2107	25.7
91-92 —Golden State	81	*3346	830	1584	.524	350	420	.833	127	323	450	286	171	1	173	62	202	2074	25.6
Totals	520	18385	4353	8409	.518	2558	2928	.874	689	1651	2340	2005	1150	10	926	300	1367	11536	22.2

Three-point field goals: 1985-86, 5-for-27 (.185). 1986-87, 19-for-63 (.302). 1987-88, 34-for-97 (.351). 1988-89, 23-for-100 (.230). 1989-90, 87-for-234 (.372). 1990-91, 40-for-133 (.301). 1991-92, 64-for-175 (.366). Totals, 272-for-829 (.328).

NBA PLAYOFF RECORD

Season Team	G	Min.	FGM	FGA	Pct.	FTM	FTA	Pct.	Off.	Def.	Tot.	Ast.	PF	Dq.	Stl.	Blk.	TO	Pts.	Avg.
86-87 —Golden State	10	262	49	98	.500	12	16	.750	2	13	15	23	31	0	9	2	16	113	11.3
88-89 —Golden State	8	341	88	163	.540	58	67	.866	11	36	47	36	19	0	14	11	32	235	29.4
90-91 —Golden State	8	366	69	131	.527	43	50	.860	9	49	58	23	23	0	15	12	25	190	23.8
91-92 —Golden State	4	168	27	63	.429	13	14	.929	3	9	12	12	8	0	5	2	8	71	17.8
Totals	30	1137	233	455	.512	126	147	.857	25	107	132	94	81	0	43	27	81	609	20.3

Three-point field goals: 1986-87, 3-for-4 (.750). 1988-89, 1-for-8 (.125). 1990-91, 9-for-13 (.692). 1991-92, 4-for-12 (.333). Totals, 17-for-37 (.459).

NBA ALL-STAR GAME RECORD

Season Team	Min.	FGM	FGA	Pct.	FTM	FTA	Pct.	Off.	Def.	Tot.	Ast.	PF	Dq.	Stl.	Blk.	TO	Pts.
1989 —Golden State	14	1	4	.250	2	2	1.000	2	0	2	2	0	0	0	0	1	4
1990 —Golden State	16	1	5	.200	1	2	.500	1	2	3	1	0	0	2	1	1	3
1991 —Golden State	24	4	8	.500	4	4	1.000	0	2	2	2	2	0	2	0	2	13
1992 —Golden State	24	6	7	.857	0	0	...	0	1	1	3	0	0	0	0	1	13
Totals	78	12	24	.500	7	8	.875	3	5	8	8	2	0	4	1	5	33

Three-point field goals: 1991, 1-for-1. 1992, 1-for-1. Totals, 2-for-2.

MURDOCK, ERIC
G, BUCKS

PERSONAL: Born June 14, 1968, in Somerville, N.J. ... 6-1/190. ... Full name: Eric Lloyd Murdock.
HIGH SCHOOL: Bridgewater-Raritan (Raritan, N.J.).
COLLEGE: Providence.
TRANSACTIONS/CAREER NOTES: Selected by Utah Jazz in first round (21st pick overall) of 1991 NBA Draft. ... Traded by Jazz with Blue Edwards and 1992 first-round draft choice to Milwaukee Bucks for Jay Humphries and Larry Krystkowiak (June 24, 1992).

COLLEGIATE RECORD

NOTES: THE SPORTING NEWS All-America second team (1991).

Season Team	G	Min.	FGM	FGA	Pct.	FTM	FTA	Pct.	Reb.	Pts.	Avg.
87-88 —Providence	28	768	114	276	.413	45	61	.738	85	300	10.7
88-89 —Providence	29	936	164	359	.457	99	130	.762	135	471	16.2
89-90 —Providence	28	833	147	351	.419	96	126	.762	116	432	15.4
90-91 —Providence	32	1111	262	589	.445	238	293	.812	168	818	25.6
Totals	117	3648	687	1575	.436	478	610	.784	504	2021	17.3

Three-point field goals: 1987-88, 27-for-76 (.355). 1988-89, 44-for-126 (.349). 1989-90, 42-for-115 (.365). 1990-91, 56-for-160 (.350). Totals, 169-for-477 (.354).

NBA REGULAR-SEASON RECORD

Season Team	G	Min.	FGM	FGA	Pct.	FTM	FTA	Pct.	Off.	Def.	Tot.	Ast.	PF	Dq.	Stl.	Blk.	TO	Pts.	Avg.
91-92 —Utah	50	478	76	183	.415	46	61	.754	21	33	54	92	52	0	30	7	50	203	4.1

Three-point field goals: 1991-92, 5-for-26 (.192).

M

NBA PLAYOFF RECORD

Season	Team	G	Min.	FGM	FGA	Pct.	FTM	FTA	Pct.	REBOUNDS Off.	Def.	Tot.	Ast.	PF	Dq.	Stl.	Blk.	TO	Pts.	Avg.
91-92	—Utah	3	11	3	5	.600	2	2	1.000	0	3	3	1	1	0	1	1	3	8	2.7

Three-point field goals: 1991-92, 0-for-1.

MURPHY, TOD
C/F

PERSONAL: Born December 24, 1963, in Long Beach, Calif. . . . 6-9/220. . . . Full name: Tod James Murphy. **HIGH SCHOOL:** Lakewood (Calif.). **COLLEGE:** UC Irvine.

TRANSACTIONS/CAREER NOTES: Selected by Seattle SuperSonics in third round (53rd pick overall) of 1986 NBA Draft. . . . Played in Italy (1986-87). . . . Draft rights relinquished by SuperSonics (September 17, 1987). . . . Signed as free agent by Los Angeles Clippers (October 6, 1987). . . . Waived by Clippers (November 9, 1987). . . . Played in Continental Basketball Association with Albany Patroons (1987-88). . . . Played in Spain (1988-89). . . . Signed as free agent by Minnesota Timberwolves (August 16, 1989). . . . Waived by Timberwolves (June 16, 1992).

COLLEGIATE RECORD

Season	Team	G	Min.	FGM	FGA	Pct.	FTM	FTA	Pct.	Reb.	Pts.	Avg.
82-83	—UC Irvine	28	704	89	172	.517	66	93	.710	150	244	8.7
83-84	—UC Irvine	29	872	154	268	.575	110	135	.815	203	418	14.4
84-85	—UC Irvine	30	1047	190	340	.559	130	153	.850	268	511	17.0
85-86	—UC Irvine	30	1116	211	378	.558	182	244	.746	216	605	20.2
	Totals	117	3739	644	1158	.556	488	625	.781	837	1778	15.2

Three-point field goals: 1984-85, 1-for-3 (.333). 1985-86, 1-for-1. Totals, 2-for-4 (.500).

NBA REGULAR-SEASON RECORD

Season	Team	G	Min.	FGM	FGA	Pct.	FTM	FTA	Pct.	REBOUNDS Off.	Def.	Tot.	Ast.	PF	Dq.	Stl.	Blk.	TO	Pts.	Avg.
87-88	—L.A. Clippers	1	19	1	1	1.000	3	4	.750	1	1	2	2	2	0	1	0	0	5	5.0
89-90	—Minnesota	82	2493	260	552	.471	144	203	.709	207	357	564	106	229	2	76	60	61	680	8.3
90-91	—Minnesota	52	1063	90	227	.396	70	105	.667	92	163	255	60	101	1	25	20	32	251	4.8
91-92	—Minnesota	47	429	39	80	.488	19	34	.559	36	74	110	11	40	0	9	8	18	98	2.1
	Totals	182	4004	390	860	.453	236	346	.682	336	595	931	179	372	3	111	88	111	1034	5.7

Three-point field goals: 1989-90, 16-for-43 (.372). 1990-91, 1-for-17 (.059). 1991-92, 1-for-2 (.500). Totals, 18-for-62 (.290).

CBA REGULAR-SEASON RECORD

NOTES: CBA Playoff Most Valuable Player (1988).

Season	Team	G	Min.	2-POINT FGM	FGA	Pct.	3-POINT FGM	FGA	Pct.	FTM	FTA	Pct.	Reb.	Ast.	Pts.	Avg.
87-88	—Albany	32	751	104	175	.594	0	2	.000	98	120	.817	214	28	306	9.6

MUSTAF, JERROD
F, SUNS

PERSONAL: Born October 28, 1969, in Whiteville, N.C. . . . 6-10/245. . . . Full name: Terrah Jerrod Mustaf. **HIGH SCHOOL:** DeMatha Catholic (Hyattsville, Md.). **COLLEGE:** Maryland.

TRANSACTIONS/CAREER NOTES: Selected as undergraduate by New York Knicks in first round (17th pick overall) of 1990 NBA Draft. . . . Traded by Knicks with Trent Tucker and 1992 and 1994 second-round draft choices to Phoenix Suns for Xavier McDaniel (October 1, 1991).

COLLEGIATE RECORD

Season	Team	G	Min.	FGM	FGA	Pct.	FTM	FTA	Pct.	Reb.	Pts.	Avg.
88-89	—Maryland	26	847	157	302	.520	53	74	.716	202	371	14.3
89-90	—Maryland	33	1048	236	446	.529	127	164	.774	254	609	18.5
	Totals	59	1895	393	748	.525	180	238	.756	456	980	16.6

Three-point field goals: 1988-89, 4-for-16 (.250). 1989-90, 10-for-20 (.500). Totals, 14-for-36 (.389).

NBA REGULAR-SEASON RECORD

Season	Team	G	Min.	FGM	FGA	Pct.	FTM	FTA	Pct.	REBOUNDS Off.	Def.	Tot.	Ast.	PF	Dq.	Stl.	Blk.	TO	Pts.	Avg.
90-91	—New York	62	825	106	228	.465	56	87	.644	51	118	169	36	109	0	15	14	61	268	4.3
91-92	—Phoenix........	52	545	92	193	.477	49	71	.690	45	100	145	45	59	0	21	16	51	233	4.5
	Totals	114	1370	198	421	.470	105	158	.665	96	218	314	81	168	0	36	30	112	501	4.4

Three-point field goals: 1990-91, 0-for-1.

NBA PLAYOFF RECORD

Season	Team	G	Min.	FGM	FGA	Pct.	FTM	FTA	Pct.	REBOUNDS Off.	Def.	Tot.	Ast.	PF	Dq.	Stl.	Blk.	TO	Pts.	Avg.
90-91	—New York	3	22	4	5	.800	4	5	.800	3	2	5	0	2	0	0	1	1	12	4.0

MUTOMBO, DIKEMBE
C, NUGGETS

PERSONAL: Born June 25, 1966, in Kinshasa, Zaire. . . . 7-2/245. . . . Full name: Dikembe Mutombo Mpolondo Mukamba Jean Jacque Wamutombo. . . . Name pronounced Di-KEM-bay Moo-TUM-bo.

HIGH SCHOOL: Institute Boboto (Kinshasa, Zaire). **COLLEGE:** Georgetown. **TRANSACTIONS/CAREER NOTES:** Selected by Denver Nuggets in first round (fourth pick overall) of 1991 NBA Draft.

COLLEGIATE RECORD

NOTES: The Sporting News All-America third team (1991).

Season Team	G	Min.	FGM	FGA	Pct.	FTM	FTA	Pct.	Reb.	Pts.	Avg.
87-88 —Georgetown						Did not play.					
88-89 —Georgetown	33	374	53	75	.707	23	48	.479	109	129	3.9
89-90 —Georgetown	31	797	129	182	.709	73	122	.598	325	331	10.7
90-91 —Georgetown	32	1090	170	290	.586	147	209	.703	389	487	15.2
Totals	96	2261	352	547	.644	243	379	.641	823	947	9.9

NBA REGULAR-SEASON RECORD

HONORS: NBA All-Rookie first team (1992).

Season Team	G	Min.	FGM	FGA	Pct.	FTM	FTA	Pct.	REBOUNDS Off.	Def.	Tot.	Ast.	PF	Dq.	Stl.	Blk.	TO	Pts.	Avg.
91-92 —Denver	71	2716	428	869	.493	321	500	.642	316	554	870	156	273	1	43	210	252	1177	16.6

NBA ALL-STAR GAME RECORD

Season Team	Min.	FGM	FGA	Pct.	FTM	FTA	Pct.	REBOUNDS Off.	Def.	Tot.	Ast.	PF	Dq.	Stl.	Blk.	TO	Pts.
1992 —Denver	10	2	4	.500	0	0	...	1	1	2	1	0	0	1	0	2	4

NANCE, LARRY
F/C, CAVALIERS

PERSONAL: Born February 12, 1959, in Anderson, S.C. . . . 6-10/235. . . . Full name: Larry Donell Nance.
HIGH SCHOOL: McDuffie (Anderson, S.C.).
COLLEGE: Clemson.
TRANSACTIONS/CAREER NOTES: Selected by Phoenix Suns in first round (20th pick overall) of 1981 NBA Draft. . . . Traded by Suns with Mike Sanders and 1988 first-round draft choice to Cleveland Cavaliers for Tyrone Corbin, Kevin Johnson, Mark West, 1988 first- and second-round draft choices and 1989 second-round draft choice (February 25, 1988).

COLLEGIATE RECORD

Season Team	G	Min.	FGM	FGA	Pct.	FTM	FTA	Pct.	Reb.	Pts.	Avg.
77-78 —Clemson	25	273	35	75	.467	8	17	.471	78	78	3.1
78-79 —Clemson	29	837	137	264	.519	49	77	.636	210	323	11.1
79-80 —Clemson	32	961	174	338	.515	98	164	.598	259	446	13.9
80-81 —Clemson	31	887	207	360	.575	80	116	.690	237	494	15.9
Totals	117	2958	553	1037	.533	235	374	.628	784	1341	11.5

NBA REGULAR-SEASON RECORD

HONORS: NBA All-Defensive first team (1989). . . . NBA All-Defensive second team (1992).

Season Team	G	Min.	FGM	FGA	Pct.	FTM	FTA	Pct.	REBOUNDS Off.	Def.	Tot.	Ast.	PF	Dq.	Stl.	Blk.	TO	Pts.	Avg.
81-82 —Phoenix	80	1186	227	436	.521	75	117	.641	95	161	256	82	169	2	42	71	104	529	6.6
82-83 —Phoenix	82	2914	588	1069	.550	193	287	.672	239	471	710	197	254	4	99	217	190	1370	16.7
83-84 —Phoenix	82	2899	601	1044	.576	249	352	.707	227	451	678	214	274	5	86	174	177	1451	17.7
84-85 —Phoenix	61	2202	515	877	.587	180	254	.709	195	341	536	159	185	2	88	104	136	1211	19.9
85-86 —Phoenix	73	2484	582	1001	.581	310	444	.698	169	449	618	240	247	6	70	130	210	1474	20.2
86-87 —Phoenix	69	2569	585	1062	.551	381	493	.773	188	411	599	233	223	4	86	148	149	1552	22.5
87-88 —Phoe.-Clev.	67	2383	487	920	.529	304	390	.779	193	414	607	207	242	10	63	159	155	1280	19.1
88-89 —Cleveland	73	2526	496	920	.539	267	334	.799	156	425	581	159	186	0	57	206	117	1259	17.2
89-90 —Cleveland	62	2065	412	807	.511	186	239	.778	162	354	516	161	185	3	54	122	110	1011	16.3
90-91 —Cleveland	80	2927	635	1211	.524	265	330	.803	201	485	686	237	219	3	66	200	131	1537	19.2
91-92 —Cleveland	81	2880	556	1032	.539	263	320	.822	213	457	670	232	200	2	80	243	87	1375	17.0
Totals	810	27035	5684	10379	.548	2673	3560	.751	2038	4419	6457	2121	2384	41	791	1774	1566	14049	17.3

Three-point field goals: 1981-82, 0-for-1. 1982-83, 1-for-3 (.333). 1983-84, 0-for-7. 1984-85, 1-for-2 (.500). 1985-86, 0-for-8. 1986-87, 1-for-5 (.200). 1987-88, 2-for-6 (.333). 1988-89, 0-for-4. 1989-90, 1-for-1. 1990-91, 2-for-8 (.250). 1991-92, 0-for-6. Totals, 8-for-51 (.157).

NBA PLAYOFF RECORD

Season Team	G	Min.	FGM	FGA	Pct.	FTM	FTA	Pct.	REBOUNDS Off.	Def.	Tot.	Ast.	PF	Dq.	Stl.	Blk.	TO	Pts.	Avg.
81-82 —Phoenix	7	128	25	41	.610	4	8	.500	13	19	32	7	15	1	10	11	12	54	7.7
82-83 —Phoenix	3	103	14	35	.400	8	10	.800	10	15	25	3	12	1	3	6	6	36	12.0
83-84 —Phoenix	17	633	118	200	.590	51	76	.671	51	97	148	40	59	1	16	34	31	287	16.9
87-88 —Cleveland	5	200	34	64	.531	16	18	.889	10	26	36	18	13	0	2	11	14	84	16.8
88-89 —Cleveland	5	195	38	69	.551	21	32	.656	16	23	39	16	12	0	3	12	9	97	19.4
89-90 —Cleveland	5	159	26	45	.578	9	12	.750	4	20	24	12	20	0	3	10	4	61	12.2
91-92 —Cleveland	17	681	124	251	.494	58	70	.829	45	112	157	43	56	1	14	46	26	306	18.0
Totals	59	2099	379	705	.538	167	226	.739	149	312	461	139	187	4	51	130	102	925	15.7

Three-point field goals: 1991-92, 0-for-1.

NBA ALL-STAR GAME RECORD

Season Team	Min.	FGM	FGA	Pct.	FTM	FTA	Pct.	REBOUNDS Off.	Def.	Tot.	Ast.	PF	Dq.	Stl.	Blk.	TO	Pts.
1985 —Phoenix	15	7	8	.875	2	2	1.000	1	4	5	0	5	0	0	2	2	16
1989 —Cleveland	17	5	9	.556	0	0	...	3	3	6	1	1	0	1	1	0	10
Totals	32	12	17	.706	2	2	1.000	4	7	11	1	6	0	1	3	2	26

DID YOU KNOW. . .

. . . that no guard has been chosen No. 1 overall in an NBA draft since Magic Johnson in 1979?

MN

NEALY, ED
F, SUNS

PERSONAL: Born February 19, 1960, in Pittsburg, Kan. . . . 6-7/240. . . . Full name: Eddie Carl Nealy.
HIGH SCHOOL: Bonner Springs (Kan.).
COLLEGE: Kansas State.
TRANSACTIONS/CAREER NOTES: Selected by Kansas City Kings in eighth round (166th pick overall) of 1982 NBA Draft. . . . Waived by Kings (July 10, 1984). . . . Played in Continental Basketball Association with Sarasota Stingers (1984-85) and Tampa Bay Thrillers (1985-86). . . . Re-signed as free agent by Kings (July 20, 1984). . . . Waived by Kings (October 24, 1984). . . . Re-signed as free agent by Kings (February 27, 1985). . . . Waived by Kings (October 21, 1985). . . . Signed as free agent by San Antonio Spurs (July 15, 1986). . . . Signed as free agent by Chicago Bulls (September 27, 1988). . . . Traded by Bulls with 1989 second-round draft choice to Phoenix Suns for Craig Hodges (December 14, 1988). . . . Traded by Suns to Bulls for 1996 second-round draft choice (October 5, 1989). . . . Signed as veteran free agent by Suns (July 23, 1990).

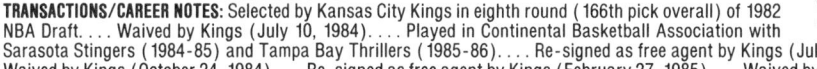

COLLEGIATE RECORD

Season	Team	G	Min.	FGM	FGA	Pct.	FTM	FTA	Pct.	Reb.	Pts.	Avg.
78-79	Kansas State	28	. . .	115	266	.432	56	71	.789	230	286	10.2
79-80	Kansas State	31	. . .	114	242	.471	76	105	.724	272	304	9.8
80-81	Kansas State	33	. . .	152	289	.526	59	82	.720	301	363	11.0
81-82	Kansas State	31	. . .	138	243	.568	75	122	.615	268	351	11.3
	Totals	123	. . .	519	1040	.499	266	380	.700	1071	1304	10.6

NBA REGULAR-SEASON RECORD

Season	Team	G	Min.	FGM	FGA	Pct.	FTM	FTA	Pct.	Off. Reb.	Def. Reb.	Tot. Reb.	Ast.	PF	Dq.	Stl.	Blk.	TO	Pts.	Avg.
82-83	Kansas City	82	1643	147	247	.595	70	114	.614	170	315	485	62	247	4	68	12	51	364	4.4
83-84	Kansas City	71	960	63	126	.500	48	60	.800	73	149	222	50	138	1	41	9	33	174	2.5
84-85	Kansas City	22	225	26	44	.591	10	19	.526	15	29	44	18	26	0	3	1	12	62	2.8
86-87	San Antonio	60	980	84	192	.438	51	69	.739	96	188	284	83	144	1	40	11	36	223	3.7
87-88	San Antonio	68	837	50	109	.459	41	63	.651	82	140	222	49	94	0	29	5	27	142	2.1
88-89	Chi.-Phoe.	43	258	13	36	.361	4	9	.444	22	56	78	14	45	0	7	1	7	30	0.7
89-90	Chicago	46	503	37	70	.529	30	41	.732	46	92	138	28	67	0	16	4	17	104	2.3
90-91	Phoenix	55	573	45	97	.464	28	38	.737	44	107	151	36	46	0	24	4	19	123	2.2
91-92	Phoenix	52	505	62	121	.512	16	24	.667	25	86	111	37	45	0	16	2	17	160	3.1
	Totals	499	6484	527	1042	.506	298	437	.682	573	1162	1735	377	852	6	244	49	219	1382	2.8

Three-point field goals: 1986-87, 4-for-31 (.129). 1987-88, 1-for-2 (.500). 1988-89, 0-for-2. 1989-90, 0-for-2. 1990-91, 5-for-16 (.313). 1991-92, 20-for-50 (.400). Totals, 30-for-103 (.291).

NBA PLAYOFF RECORD

Season	Team	G	Min.	FGM	FGA	Pct.	FTM	FTA	Pct.	Off. Reb.	Def. Reb.	Tot. Reb.	Ast.	PF	Dq.	Stl.	Blk.	TO	Pts.	Avg.
83-84	Kansas City	2	19	2	2	1.000	2	2	1.000	2	4	6	2	1	0	0	1	6	3.0	
87-88	San Antonio	2	36	2	4	.500	0	0	. . .	3	4	7	4	6	0	1	0	1	4	2.0
88-89	Phoenix	4	6	1	3	.333	0	0	. . .	1	2	3	0	0	0	0	0	2	0.5	
89-90	Chicago	15	228	17	36	.472	13	21	.619	16	36	52	5	45	1	10	1	7	47	3.1
90-91	Phoenix	2	20	1	5	.200	0	0	. . .	2	3	5	0	2	0	0	0	1	2	1.0
91-92	Phoenix	8	67	7	18	.389	4	4	1.000	4	14	18	4	12	0	3	0	0	23	2.9
	Totals	33	376	30	68	.441	19	27	.704	28	63	91	15	66	1	14	1	10	84	2.5

Three-point field goals: 1989-90, 0-for-1. 1990-91, 0-for-1. 1991-92, 5-for-13 (.385). Totals, 5-for-15 (.333).

CBA REGULAR-SEASON RECORD

Season	Team	G	Min.	2-POINT FGM	2-POINT FGA	Pct.	3-POINT FGM	3-POINT FGA	Pct.	FTM	FTA	Pct.	Reb.	Ast.	Pts.	Avg.
84-85	Sarasota	39	1350	156	267	.584	1	2	.500	113	142	.796	371	53	428	11.0
85-86	Tampa Bay	29	926	91	169	.538	0	1	.000	59	79	.747	309	34	241	8.3
	Totals	68	2276	247	436	.567	1	3	.333	172	221	.778	680	87	669	9.8

NEVITT, CHUCK
C

PERSONAL: Born June 13, 1959, in Cortez, Colo. . . . 7-5/237. . . . Full name: Charles Goodrich Nevitt.
HIGH SCHOOL: Sprayberry (Marietta, Ga.).
COLLEGE: North Carolina State.
TRANSACTIONS/CAREER NOTES: Selected by Houston Rockets in third round (63rd pick overall) of 1982 NBA Draft. . . . Waived by Rockets (October 22, 1982). . . . Claimed off waivers by Milwaukee Bucks (October 22, 1982). . . . Waived by Bucks (October 28, 1982). . . . Signed as free agent by Rockets (June 1, 1983). . . . Waived by Rockets (November 29, 1983). . . . Signed as free agent by Los Angeles Lakers (September 15, 1984). . . . Waived by Lakers (November 6, 1984). . . . Re-signed by Lakers to first of two consecutive 10-day contracts (March 5, 1985). . . . Re-signed by Lakers (March 25, 1985). . . . Waived by Lakers (November 22, 1985). . . . Signed as free agent by Detroit Pistons (November 29, 1985). . . . Rights relinquished by Pistons (July 25, 1988). . . . Signed as free agent by San Antonio Spurs (September 27, 1988). . . . Waived by Spurs (October 24, 1988). . . . Signed as free agent by Rockets (October 26, 1988). . . . Played in Continental Basketball Association with Rapid City Thrillers (1989-90). . . . Waived by Rockets (January 11, 1990). . . . Did not play in 1990-91 season. . . . Signed as free agent by Chicago Bulls (October 2, 1991). . . . Waived by Bulls (October 30, 1991). . . . Re-signed as free agent by Bulls (November 17, 1991). . . . Waived by Bulls (December 17, 1991).
MISCELLANEOUS: Member of NBA championship team (1985).

COLLEGIATE RECORD

Season	Team	G	Min.	FGM	FGA	Pct.	FTM	FTA	Pct.	Reb.	Pts.	Avg.
77-78	North Carolina State					Did not play—injured.						
78-79	North Carolina State	19	. . .	10	20	.500	4	15	.267	25	24	1.3
79-80	North Carolina State	19	. . .	14	23	.609	2	10	.200	34	30	1.6

Season Team	G	Min.	FGM	FGA	Pct.	FTM	FTA	Pct.	Reb.	Pts.	Avg.
80-81 —North Carolina State	21	...	15	26	.577	10	23	.435	24	40	1.9
81-82 —North Carolina State	31	...	70	119	.588	32	57	.561	137	172	5.5
Totals	90	...	109	188	.580	48	105	.457	220	266	3.0

NBA REGULAR-SEASON RECORD

Season Team	G	Min.	FGM	FGA	Pct.	FTM	FTA	Pct.	REBOUNDS Off.	Def.	Tot.	Ast.	PF	Dq.	Stl.	Blk.	TO	Pts.	Avg.
82-83 —Houston	6	64	11	15	.733	1	4	.250	6	11	17	0	14	0	1	12	7	23	3.8
84-85 —L.A. Lakers	11	59	5	17	.294	2	8	.250	5	15	20	3	20	0	0	15	10	12	1.1
85-86 —LAL-Detroit	29	126	15	43	.349	19	26	.731	13	19	32	7	35	0	4	19	12	49	1.7
86-87 —Detroit	41	267	31	63	.492	14	24	.583	36	47	83	4	73	0	7	30	21	76	1.9
87-88 —Detroit	17	63	7	21	.333	3	6	.500	4	14	18	0	12	0	1	5	2	17	1.0
88-89 —Houston	43	228	27	62	.435	11	16	.688	17	47	64	3	51	1	5	29	22	65	1.5
89-90 —Houston	3	9	2	2	1.000	0	0	...	0	3	3	1	3	0	0	1	2	4	1.3
90-91 —										Did not play.								
91-92 —Chicago	4	9	1	3	.333	0	0	...	0	1	1	1	2	0	0	0	3	2	0.5
Totals	154	825	99	226	.438	50	84	.595	81	157	238	19	210	1	18	111	79	248	1.6

NBA PLAYOFF RECORD

Season Team	G	Min.	FGM	FGA	Pct.	FTM	FTA	Pct.	REBOUNDS Off.	Def.	Tot.	Ast.	PF	Dq.	Stl.	Blk.	TO	Pts.	Avg.
84-85 —L.A. Lakers	7	37	3	9	.333	4	8	.500	3	3	6	1	11	0	4	6	2	10	1.4
85-86 —Detroit	1	1	0	0	...	0	0	...	0	0	0	0	0	0	0	0	0	0	0.0
86-87 —Detroit	3	10	1	5	.200	2	2	1.000	1	5	6	0	1	0	0	3	3	4	1.3
87-88 —Detroit	3	4	1	2	.500	0	0	...	2	1	3	0	1	0	0	0	1	2	0.7
88-89 —Houston	2	3	0	0	...	0	0	...	0	1	1	0	0	0	0	0	0	0	0.0
Totals	16	55	5	16	.313	6	10	.600	6	10	16	1	13	0	4	9	6	16	1.0

CBA REGULAR-SEASON RECORD

Season Team	G	Min.	2-POINT FGM	FGA	Pct.	3-POINT FGM	FGA	Pct.	FTM	FTA	Pct.	Reb.	Ast.	Pts.	Avg.
89-90 —Rapid City	6	125	14	29	.483	0	0	...	9	10	.900	46	6	37	6.2

NEWMAN, JOHNNY
F, HORNETS

PERSONAL: Born November 28, 1963, in Danville, Va. . . . 6-7/190. . . . Full name: John Sylvester Newman Jr.
HIGH SCHOOL: George Washington (Danville, Va.).
COLLEGE: Richmond.
TRANSACTIONS/CAREER NOTES: Selected by Cleveland Cavaliers in second round (29th pick overall) of 1986 NBA Draft. . . . Waived by Cavaliers (November 5, 1987). . . . Signed as free agent by New York Knicks (November 12, 1987). . . . Signed as unrestricted free agent by Charlotte Hornets (July 28, 1990).

COLLEGIATE RECORD

Season Team	G	Min.	FGM	FGA	Pct.	FTM	FTA	Pct.	Reb.	Pts.	Avg.
82-83 —Richmond	28	763	137	259	.529	69	96	.719	87	343	12.3
83-84 —Richmond	32	1189	273	517	.528	155	197	.787	196	701	21.9
84-85 —Richmond	32	1128	270	490	.551	140	181	.773	166	680	21.3
85-86 —Richmond	30	1123	253	489	.517	153	172	.890	219	659	22.0
Totals	122	4203	933	1755	.532	517	646	.800	668	2383	19.5

NBA REGULAR-SEASON RECORD

Season Team	G	Min.	FGM	FGA	Pct.	FTM	FTA	Pct.	REBOUNDS Off.	Def.	Tot.	Ast.	PF	Dq.	Stl.	Blk.	TO	Pts.	Avg.
86-87 —Cleveland	59	630	113	275	.411	66	76	.868	36	34	70	27	67	0	20	7	46	293	5.0
87-88 —New York	77	1589	270	620	.435	207	246	.841	87	72	159	62	204	5	72	11	103	773	10.0
88-89 —New York	81	2336	455	957	.475	286	351	.815	93	113	206	162	259	4	111	23	153	1293	16.0
89-90 —New York	80	2277	374	786	.476	239	299	.799	60	131	191	180	254	3	95	22	143	1032	12.9
90-91 —Charlotte	81	2477	478	1017	.470	385	476	.809	94	160	254	188	278	7	100	17	189	1371	16.9
91-92 —Charlotte	55	1651	295	618	.477	236	308	.766	71	108	179	146	181	4	70	14	129	839	15.3
Totals	433	10960	1985	4273	.465	1419	1756	.808	441	618	1059	765	1243	23	468	94	763	5601	12.9

Three-point field goals: 1986-87, 1-for-22 (.045). 1987-88, 26-for-93 (.280). 1988-89, 97-for-287 (.338). 1989-90, 45-for-142 (.317). 1990-91, 30-for-84 (.357). 1991-92, 13-for-46 (.283). Totals, 212-for-674 (.315).

NBA PLAYOFF RECORD

Season Team	G	Min.	FGM	FGA	Pct.	FTM	FTA	Pct.	REBOUNDS Off.	Def.	Tot.	Ast.	PF	Dq.	Stl.	Blk.	TO	Pts.	Avg.
87-88 —New York	4	113	31	68	.456	14	16	.875	8	3	11	7	16	0	6	1	6	76	19.0
88-89 —New York	9	258	50	107	.467	38	49	.776	13	12	25	17	27	1	8	1	18	145	16.1
89-90 —New York	10	231	38	85	.447	37	49	.755	11	10	21	10	41	1	9	3	17	117	11.7
Totals	23	602	119	260	.458	89	114	.781	32	25	57	34	84	2	23	5	41	338	14.7

Three-point field goals: 1987-88, 0-for-9. 1988-89, 7-for-28 (.250). 1989-90, 4-for-10 (.400). Totals, 11-for-47 (.234).

NORMAN, KEN
F, CLIPPERS

PERSONAL: Born September 5, 1964, in Chicago. . . . 6-8/223. . . . Full name: Kenneth Darnel Norman. . . . Nickname: Snake. . . . Known as Ken Colliers in high school. . . . Half-brother of Bobby Duckworth, wide receiver with San Diego Chargers, Los Angeles Rams and Philadelphia Eagles (1982-86).
HIGH SCHOOL: Richard T. Crane (Chicago).
COLLEGE: Wabash Valley (Ill.), then Illinois.
TRANSACTIONS/CAREER NOTES: Selected by Los Angeles Clippers in first round (19th pick overall) of 1987 NBA Draft.

COLLEGIATE RECORD

NOTES: THE SPORTING NEWS All-America second team (1987).

Season	Team	G	Min.	FGM	FGA	Pct.	FTM	FTA	Pct.	Reb.	Pts.	Avg.
82-83	Wabash Valley	35	...	302	499	.605	111	165	.673	362	715	20.4
83-84	Illinois					Did not play—redshirted.						
84-85	Illinois	29	462	86	136	.632	55	83	.663	107	227	7.8
85-86	Illinois	32	1015	216	337	.641	93	116	.802	226	525	16.4
86-87	Illinois	31	1112	256	443	.578	128	176	.727	303	641	20.7
	Junior college totals	35	...	302	499	.605	111	165	.673	362	715	20.4
	Four-year-college totals	92	2589	558	916	.609	276	375	.736	636	1393	15.1

Three-point field goals: 1986-87, 1-for-4 (.250).

NBA REGULAR-SEASON RECORD

										— REBOUNDS —								
Season	Team	G	Min.	FGM	FGA	Pct.	FTM	FTA	Pct.	Off.	Def.	Tot.	Ast.	PF	Dq.	Stl.	Blk.	TO	Pts.	Avg.
87-88	L.A. Clippers	66	1435	241	500	.482	87	170	.512	100	163	263	78	123	0	44	34	103	569	8.6
88-89	L.A. Clippers	80	3020	638	1271	.502	170	270	.630	245	422	667	277	223	2	106	66	206	1450	18.1
89-90	L.A. Clippers	70	2334	484	949	.510	153	242	.632	143	327	470	160	196	0	78	59	190	1128	16.1
90-91	L.A. Clippers	70	2309	520	1037	.501	173	275	.629	177	320	497	159	192	0	63	63	139	1219	17.4
91-92	L.A. Clippers	77	2009	402	821	.490	121	226	.535	158	290	448	125	145	0	53	66	100	929	12.1
	Totals	363	11107	2285	4578	.499	704	1183	.595	823	1522	2345	799	879	2	344	288	738	5295	14.6

Three-point field goals: 1987-88, 0-for-10. 1988-89, 4-for-21 (.190). 1989-90, 7-for-16 (.438). 1990-91, 6-for-32 (.188). 1991-92, 4-for-28 (.143). Totals, 21-for-107 (.196).

NBA PLAYOFF RECORD

										— REBOUNDS —								
Season	Team	G	Min.	FGM	FGA	Pct.	FTM	FTA	Pct.	Off.	Def.	Tot.	Ast.	PF	Dq.	Stl.	Blk.	TO	Pts.	Avg.
91-92	L.A. Clippers	5	184	27	53	.509	9	17	.529	19	30	49	15	18	0	4	3	6	63	12.6

Three-point field goals: 1991-92, 0-for-2.

OAKLEY, CHARLES
F, KNICKS

PERSONAL: Born December 18, 1963, in Cleveland.... 6-9/245.
HIGH SCHOOL: John Hay (Cleveland).
COLLEGE: Virginia Union.
TRANSACTIONS/CAREER NOTES: Selected by Cleveland Cavaliers in first round (ninth pick overall) of 1985 NBA Draft.... Draft rights traded by Cavaliers with draft rights to Calvin Duncan to Chicago Bulls for Ennis Whatley and draft rights to Keith Lee (June 18, 1985).... Traded by Bulls with 1988 first- and third-round draft choices to New York Knicks for Bill Cartwright and 1988 first- and third-round draft choices (June 27, 1988).

COLLEGIATE RECORD

NOTES: Led NCAA Division II with 17.3 rebounds per game (1985).

Season	Team	G	Min.	FGM	FGA	Pct.	FTM	FTA	Pct.	Reb.	Pts.	Avg.
81-82	Virginia Union	28	...	169	274	.617	106	174	.609	349	444	15.9
82-83	Virginia Union	28	...	220	378	.582	100	170	.588	365	540	19.3
83-84	Virginia Union	30	...	256	418	.612	139	224	.621	393	651	21.7
84-85	Virginia Union	31	...	283	453	.625	178	266	.669	535	744	24.0
	Totals	117	...	928	1523	.609	523	834	.627	1642	2379	20.3

NBA REGULAR-SEASON RECORD

HONORS: NBA All-Rookie team (1986).

										— REBOUNDS —								
Season	Team	G	Min.	FGM	FGA	Pct.	FTM	FTA	Pct.	Off.	Def.	Tot.	Ast.	PF	Dq.	Stl.	Blk.	TO	Pts.	Avg.
85-86	Chicago	77	1772	281	541	.519	178	269	.662	255	409	664	133	250	9	68	30	175	740	9.6
86-87	Chicago	82	2980	468	1052	.445	245	357	.686	299	*775	*1074	296	315	4	85	36	299	1192	14.5
87-88	Chicago	82	2816	375	776	.483	261	359	.727	326	*740	*1066	248	272	2	68	28	241	1014	12.4
88-89	New York	82	2604	426	835	.510	197	255	.773	343	518	861	187	270	1	104	14	248	1061	12.9
89-90	New York	61	2196	336	641	.524	217	285	.761	258	469	727	146	220	3	64	16	165	889	14.6
90-91	New York	76	2739	307	595	.516	239	305	.784	305	615	920	204	288	4	62	17	215	853	11.2
91-92	New York	82	2309	210	402	.522	86	117	.735	256	444	700	133	258	2	67	15	123	506	6.2
	Totals	542	17416	2403	4842	.496	1423	1947	.731	2042	3970	6012	1347	1873	25	518	156	1466	6255	11.5

Three-point field goals: 1985-86, 0-for-3. 1986-87, 11-for-30 (.367). 1987-88, 3-for-12 (.250). 1988-89, 12-for-48 (.250). 1989-90, 0-for-3. 1990-91, 0-for-2. 1991-92, 0-for-3. Totals, 26-for-101 (.257).

NBA PLAYOFF RECORD

										— REBOUNDS —								
Season	Team	G	Min.	FGM	FGA	Pct.	FTM	FTA	Pct.	Off.	Def.	Tot.	Ast.	PF	Dq.	Stl.	Blk.	TO	Pts.	Avg.
85-86	Chicago	3	88	11	21	.524	8	13	.615	10	20	30	3	13	0	6	2	5	30	10.0
86-87	Chicago	3	129	19	50	.380	20	24	.833	17	29	46	6	13	0	4	1	8	60	20.0
87-88	Chicago	10	290	40	91	.440	21	24	.875	39	89	128	32	33	0	6	4	18	101	10.1
88-89	New York	9	299	35	73	.479	16	24	.667	43	58	101	11	31	1	12	1	22	87	9.7
89-90	New York	10	336	43	84	.512	34	52	.654	39	71	110	27	33	1	11	2	22	121	12.1
90-91	New York	3	100	10	21	.476	3	6	.500	15	16	31	3	13	0	2	1	7	23	7.7
91-92	New York	12	354	22	58	.379	20	27	.741	44	64	108	8	36	0	8	5	15	64	5.3
	Totals	50	1679	180	398	.452	122	170	.718	207	347	554	90	172	2	49	16	97	486	9.7

Three-point field goals: 1986-87, 2-for-4 (.500). 1987-88, 0-for-2. 1988-89, 1-for-2 (.500). 1989-90, 1-for-1. Totals, 4-for-9 (.444).

NO

DID YOU KNOW...

... that no one played in all 82 games for the Mavericks, Magic, Kings or Bullets last season?

OGG, ALAN
C, HEAT

PERSONAL: Born July 5, 1967, in Lancaster, O. . . . 7-2/245. . . . Full name: Raymond Alan Ogg.
HIGH SCHOOL: Gardendale (Ala.).
COLLEGE: Alabama-Birmingham.
TRANSACTIONS/CAREER NOTES: Never drafted by an NBA franchise. . . . Signed as free agent by Miami Heat (August 8, 1990). . . . Waived by Heat (December 3, 1990). . . . Re-signed by Heat to first of two consecutive 10-day contracts (January 7, 1991). . . . Re-signed by Heat for remainder of season (January 27, 1991).

COLLEGIATE RECORD

Season Team	G	Min.	FGM	FGA	Pct.	FTM	FTA	Pct.	Reb.	Pts.	Avg.
86-87 — Alabama-Birmingham	31	330	31	68	.456	10	16	.625	75	72	2.3
87-88 — Alabama-Birmingham	27	232	24	50	.480	11	15	.733	49	59	2.2
88-89 — Alabama-Birmingham	34	893	146	255	.573	42	59	.712	206	334	9.8
89-90 — Alabama-Birmingham	31	713	143	242	.591	41	61	.672	191	327	10.5
Totals	123	2168	344	615	.559	104	151	.689	521	792	6.4

Three-point field goals: 1989-90, 0-for-1.

NBA REGULAR-SEASON RECORD

Season Team	G	Min.	FGM	FGA	Pct.	FTM	FTA	Pct.	Off.	Def.	Tot.	Ast.	PF	Dq.	Stl.	Blk.	TO	Pts.	Avg.
90-91 — Miami	31	261	24	55	.436	6	10	.600	15	34	49	2	53	1	6	27	8	54	1.7
91-92 — Miami	43	367	46	84	.548	16	30	.533	30	44	74	7	73	0	5	28	19	108	2.5
Totals	74	628	70	139	.504	22	40	.550	45	78	123	9	126	1	11	55	27	162	2.2

Three-point field goals: 1990-91, 0-for-2.

NBA PLAYOFF RECORD

Season Team	G	Min.	FGM	FGA	Pct.	FTM	FTA	Pct.	Off.	Def.	Tot.	Ast.	PF	Dq.	Stl.	Blk.	TO	Pts.	Avg.
91-92 — Miami	3	15	1	3	.333	1	2	.500	0	1	1	0	3	0	1	3	0	3	1.0

OLAJUWON, HAKEEM
C, ROCKETS

PERSONAL: Born January 21, 1963, in Lagos, Nigeria. . . . 7-0/255. . . . Full name: Hakeem Abdul Olajuwon. . . . Known as Akeem Olajuwon until March 9, 1991.
HIGH SCHOOL: Moslem Teachers College (Lagos, Nigeria).
COLLEGE: Houston.
TRANSACTIONS/CAREER NOTES: Selected by Houston Rockets in first round (first pick overall) of 1984 NBA Draft.

COLLEGIATE RECORD

NOTES: THE SPORTING NEWS All-America first team (1984). . . . NCAA Division I Tournament Most Outstanding Player (1983). . . . Led NCAA Division I with .675 field-goal percentage (1984). . . . Led NCAA Division I with 13.5 rebounds per game (1984). . . . Led NCAA Division I with 5.6 blocked shots per game (1984).

Season Team	G	Min.	FGM	FGA	Pct.	FTM	FTA	Pct.	Reb.	Pts.	Avg.
80-81 — Houston						Did not play.					
81-82 — Houston	29	529	91	150	.607	58	103	.563	179	240	8.3
82-83 — Houston	34	932	192	314	.611	88	148	.595	388	472	13.9
83-84 — Houston	37	1260	249	369	.675	122	232	.526	500	620	16.8
Totals	100	2721	532	833	.639	268	483	.555	1067	1332	13.3

NBA REGULAR-SEASON RECORD

HONORS: All-NBA first team (1987, 1988, 1989). . . . All-NBA second team (1986, 1990). . . . All-NBA third team (1991). . . . NBA All-Defensive first team (1987, 1988, 1990). . . . NBA All-Defensive second team (1985, 1991). . . . NBA All-Rookie team (1985).
NOTES: Led NBA with 13.5 rebounds per game (1989) and 14.0 rebounds per game (1990). . . . Led NBA with 4.59 blocked shots per game (1990) and 3.95 blocked shots per game (1991).

Season Team	G	Min.	FGM	FGA	Pct.	FTM	FTA	Pct.	Off.	Def.	Tot.	Ast.	PF	Dq.	Stl.	Blk.	TO	Pts.	Avg.
84-85 — Houston	82	2914	677	1258	.538	338	551	.613	*440	534	974	111	*344	10	99	220	234	1692	20.6
85-86 — Houston	68	2467	625	1188	.526	347	538	.645	333	448	781	137	271	9	134	231	195	1597	23.5
86-87 — Houston	75	2760	677	1332	.508	400	570	.702	315	543	858	220	294	8	140	254	228	1755	23.4
87-88 — Houston	79	2825	712	1385	.514	381	548	.695	302	657	959	163	324	7	162	214	243	1805	22.8
88-89 — Houston	82	3024	790	1556	.508	454	652	.696	338	*767	*1105	149	329	10	213	282	275	2034	24.8
89-90 — Houston	82	3124	806	1609	.501	382	536	.713	299	*850	*1149	234	314	6	174	*376	316	1995	24.3
90-91 — Houston	56	2062	487	959	.508	213	277	.769	219	551	770	131	221	5	121	221	174	1187	21.2
91-92 — Houston	70	2636	591	1177	.502	328	428	.766	246	599	845	157	263	7	127	304	187	1510	21.6
Totals	594	21812	5365	10464	.513	2843	4100	.693	2492	4949	7441	1302	2360	62	1170	2102	1852	13575	22.9

Three-point field goals: 1986-87, 1-for-5 (.200). 1987-88, 0-for-4. 1988-89, 0-for-10. 1989-90, 1-for-6 (.167). 1990-91, 0-for-4. 1991-92, 0-for-1. Totals, 2-for-30 (.067).

NBA PLAYOFF RECORD

NOTES: Shares NBA Finals single-game record for most blocked shots—8 (June 5, 1986, vs. Boston). . . . Shares single-game record for most blocked shots—10 (April 29, 1990, vs. Los Angeles Lakers).

Season Team	G	Min.	FGM	FGA	Pct.	FTM	FTA	Pct.	Off.	Def.	Tot.	Ast.	PF	Dq.	Stl.	Blk.	TO	Pts.	Avg.
84-85 — Houston	5	187	42	88	.477	22	46	.478	33	32	65	7	22	0	7	13	11	106	21.2
85-86 — Houston	20	766	205	387	.530	127	199	.638	101	135	236	39	87	3	40	69	43	537	26.9
86-87 — Houston	10	389	110	179	.615	72	97	.742	39	74	113	25	44	1	13	43	36	292	29.2

Season Team	G	Min.	FGM	FGA	Pct.	FTM	FTA	Pct.	Off.	Def.	Tot.	Ast.	PF	Dq.	Stl.	Blk.	TO	Pts.	Avg.
									— REBOUNDS —										
87-88 —Houston	4	162	56	98	.571	38	43	.884	20	47	67	7	14	0	9	11	9	150	37.5
88-89 —Houston	4	162	42	81	.519	17	25	.680	14	38	52	12	17	0	10	11	10	101	25.3
89-90 —Houston	4	161	31	70	.443	12	17	.706	15	31	46	8	19	0	10	23	11	74	18.5·
90-91 —Houston	3	129	26	45	.578	14	17	.824	12	32	44	6	11	0	4	8	8	66	22.0
Totals	50	1956	512	948	.540	302	444	.680	234	389	623	104	214	4	93	178	128	1326	26.5

Three-point field goals: 1985-86, 0-for-1. 1986-87, 0-for-1. 1987-88, 0-for-1. 1990-91, 0-for-1. Totals, 0-for-4.

NBA ALL-STAR GAME RECORD

Season Team	Min.	FGM	FGA	Pct.	FTM	FTA	Pct.	Off.	Def.	Tot.	Ast.	PF	Dq.	Stl.	Blk.	TO	Pts.
								— REBOUNDS —									
1985 —Houston	15	2	2	1.000	2	6	.333	2	3	5	1	1	0	0	2	0	6
1986 —Houston	15	1	8	.125	1	2	.500	1	4	5	0	3	0	1	2	1	3
1987 —Houston	26	2	6	.333	6	8	.750	4	9	13	2	6	1	0	3	1	10
1988 —Houston	28	8	13	.615	5	7	.714	7	2	9	2	3	0	2	2	4	21
1989 —Houston	25	5	12	.417	2	3	.667	4	3	7	3	2	0	3	2	3	12
1990 —Houston	31	2	14	.143	4	10	.400	9	7	16	2	1	0	1	1	4	8
1992 —Houston	20	3	6	.500	1	2	.500	0	4	4	2	3	0	2	1	3	7
Totals	160	23	61	.377	21	38	.553	27	32	59	12	19	1	9	13	16	67

OLIVER, BRIAN
G, 76ERS

PERSONAL: Born June 1, 1968, in Chicago. . . . 6-4/210. . . . Full name: Brian Darnell Oliver.
HIGH SCHOOL: Wills (Smyrna, Ga.).
COLLEGE: Georgia Tech.
TRANSACTIONS/CAREER NOTES: Selected by Philadelphia 76ers in second round (32nd pick overall) of 1990 NBA Draft.

COLLEGIATE RECORD

Season Team	G	Min.	FGM	FGA	Pct.	FTM	FTA	Pct.	Reb.	Pts.	Avg.
86-87 —Georgia Tech	29	879	72	158	.456	54	75	.720	91	205	7.1
87-88 —Georgia Tech	32	1106	157	310	.506	76	102	.745	139	403	12.6
88-89 —Georgia Tech	32	1163	191	345	.554	106	135	.785	179	516	16.1
89-90 —Georgia Tech	34	1277	260	504	.516	147	204	.721	204	724	21.3
Totals	127	4425	680	1317	.516	383	516	.742	613	1848	14.6

Three-point field goals: 1986-87, 7-for-18 (.389). 1987-88, 13-for-38 (.342). 1988-89, 28-for-70 (.400). 1989-90, 57-for-147 (.388). Totals, 105-for-273 (.385).

NBA REGULAR-SEASON RECORD

Season Team	G	Min.	FGM	FGA	Pct.	FTM	FTA	Pct.	Off.	Def.	Tot.	Ast.	PF	Dq.	Stl.	Blk.	TO	Pts.	Avg.
									— REBOUNDS —										
90-91 —Philadelphia.	73	800	111	272	.408	52	71	.732	18	62	80	88	76	0	34	4	50	279	3.8
91-92 —Philadelphia.	34	279	33	100	.330	15	22	.682	10	20	30	20	33	0	10	2	24	81	2.4
Totals	107	1079	144	372	.387	67	93	.720	28	82	110	108	109	0	44	6	74	360	3.4

Three-point field goals: 1990-91, 5-for-18 (.278). 1991-92, 0-for-4. Totals, 5-for-22 (.227).

NBA PLAYOFF RECORD

Season Team	G	Min.	FGM	FGA	Pct.	FTM	FTA	Pct.	Off.	Def.	Tot.	Ast.	PF	Dq.	Stl.	Blk.	TO	Pts.	Avg.
									— REBOUNDS —										
90-91 —Philadelphia.	4	15	2	6	.333	2	2	1.000	0	0	0	1	4	0	1	0	0	6	1.5

OLIVER, JIMMY
G/F, CAVALIERS

PERSONAL: Born July 12, 1969, in Menifee, Ark. . . . 6-5/208. . . . Full name: Jimmy Allen Oliver.
HIGH SCHOOL: Morrilton (Ark.).
COLLEGE: Purdue.
TRANSACTIONS/CAREER NOTES: Selected by Cleveland Cavaliers in second round (39th pick overall) of 1991 NBA Draft.

COLLEGIATE RECORD

Season Team	G	Min.	FGM	FGA	Pct.	FTM	FTA	Pct.	Reb.	Pts.	Avg.
87-88 —Purdue					Did not play—ineligible.						
88-89 —Purdue	31	565	60	138	.435	18	31	.581	74	164	5.3
89-90 —Purdue	30	705	88	180	.489	43	67	.642	76	239	8.0
90-91 —Purdue	29	1026	189	406	.466	99	115	.861	133	556	19.2
Totals	90	2296	337	724	.465	160	213	.751	283	959	10.7

Three-point field goals: 1988-89, 26-for-66 (.394). 1989-90, 20-for-58 (.345). 1990-91, 79-for-184 (.429). Totals, 125-for-308 (.406).

NBA REGULAR-SEASON RECORD

Season Team	G	Min.	FGM	FGA	Pct.	FTM	FTA	Pct.	Off.	Def.	Tot.	Ast.	PF	Dq.	Stl.	Blk.	TO	Pts.	Avg.
									— REBOUNDS —										
91-92 —Cleveland.....	27	252	39	98	.398	17	22	.773	9	18	27	20	22	0	9	2	9	96	3.6

Three-point field goals: 1991-92, 1-for-9 (.111).

DID YOU KNOW. . .

. . . that the Sacramento Kings were a combined 0-10 against Portland and Golden State in 1991-92?

OWENS, BILLY
F/G, WARRIORS

PERSONAL: Born May 1, 1969, in Carlisle, Pa. . . . 6-9/220. . . . Full name: Billy E. Owens. **HIGH SCHOOL:** Carlisle (Pa.). **COLLEGE:** Syracuse.

TRANSACTIONS/CAREER NOTES: Selected as undergraduate by Sacramento Kings in first round (third pick overall) of 1991 NBA Draft. . . . Traded by Kings to Golden State Warriors for Mitch Richmond and Les Jepsen (November 1, 1991).

COLLEGIATE RECORD

NOTES: THE SPORTING NEWS All-America second team (1991).

Season Team	G	Min.	FGM	FGA	Pct.	FTM	FTA	Pct.	Reb.	Pts.	Avg.
88-89—Syracuse	38	1215	196	376	.521	94	145	.648	263	494	13.0
89-90—Syracuse	33	1188	228	469	.486	127	176	.722	276	602	18.2
90-91—Syracuse	32	1215	282	554	.509	157	233	.674	371	744	23.3
Totals	103	3618	706	1399	.505	378	554	.682	910	1840	17.9

Three-point field goals: 1988-89, 8-for-36 (.222). 1989-90, 19-for-60 (.317). 1990-91, 23-for-58 (.397). Totals, 50-for-154 (.325).

NBA REGULAR-SEASON RECORD

HONORS: NBA All-Rookie first team (1992).

Season Team	G	Min.	FGM	FGA	Pct.	FTM	FTA	Pct.	Off.	Def.	Tot.	Ast.	PF	Dq.	Stl.	Blk.	TO	Pts.	Avg.
91-92—Golden State	80	2510	468	891	.525	204	312	.654	243	396	639	188	276	4	90	65	179	1141	14.3

Three-point field goals: 1991-92, 1-for-9 (.111).

NBA PLAYOFF RECORD

Season Team	G	Min.	FGM	FGA	Pct.	FTM	FTA	Pct.	Off.	Def.	Tot.	Ast.	PF	Dq.	Stl.	Blk.	TO	Pts.	Avg.
91-92—Golden State	4	157	30	57	.526	17	27	.630	13	20	33	13	14	0	8	2	6	77	19.3

OWENS, KEITH
C/F, LAKERS

PERSONAL: Born May 31, 1969, in San Francisco . . . 6-7/225. . . . Full name: Keith Kensel Owens. **HIGH SCHOOL:** Birmingham (Van Nuys, Calif.). **COLLEGE:** UCLA.

TRANSACTIONS/CAREER NOTES: Never drafted by an NBA franchise. . . . Signed as free agent by Los Angeles Lakers (September 30, 1991).

COLLEGIATE RECORD

Season Team	G	Min.	FGM	FGA	Pct.	FTM	FTA	Pct.	Reb.	Pts.	Avg.
87-88—UCLA	10	17	3	5	.600	0	1	.000	7	6	0.6
88-89—UCLA	29	317	18	29	.621	15	26	.577	58	51	1.8
89-90—UCLA	26	257	23	46	.500	7	11	.636	58	53	2.0
90-91—UCLA	32	686	71	127	.559	58	73	.795	169	200	6.3
Totals	97	1277	115	207	.556	80	111	.721	292	310	3.2

Three-point field goals: 1989-90, 0-for-1. 1990-91, 0-for-1. Totals, 0-for-2.

NBA REGULAR-SEASON RECORD

Season Team	G	Min.	FGM	FGA	Pct.	FTM	FTA	Pct.	Off.	Def.	Tot.	Ast.	PF	Dq.	Stl.	Blk.	TO	Pts.	Avg.
91-92—L.A. Lakers	20	80	9	32	.281	8	10	.800	8	7	15	3	11	0	5	4	2	26	1.3

PACK, ROBERT
G, TRAIL BLAZERS

PERSONAL: Born February 3, 1969, in New Orleans. . . . 6-2/180. . . . Full name: Robert John Pack Jr. **HIGH SCHOOL:** Lawless (New Orleans). **COLLEGE:** Tyler Junior College (Tex.), then Southern California.

TRANSACTIONS/CAREER NOTES: Never drafted by an NBA franchise. . . . Signed as free agent by Portland Trail Blazers (September 16, 1991).

COLLEGIATE RECORD

Season Team	G	Min.	FGM	FGA	Pct.	FTM	FTA	Pct.	Reb.	Pts.	Avg.
87-88—Tyler Junior College					Statistics unavailable.						
88-89—Tyler Junior College					Statistics unavailable.						
89-90—Southern California	28	883	118	250	.472	84	124	.677	67	339	12.1
90-91—Southern California	29	941	145	302	.480	123	155	.794	93	427	14.7
Totals	57	1824	263	552	.476	207	279	.742	160	766	13.4

Three-point field goals: 1989-90, 19-for-57 (.333). 1990-91, 14-for-55 (.255). Totals, 33-for-112 (.295).

NBA REGULAR-SEASON RECORD

Season Team	G	Min.	FGM	FGA	Pct.	FTM	FTA	Pct.	Off.	Def.	Tot.	Ast.	PF	Dq.	Stl.	Blk.	TO	Pts.	Avg.
91-92—Portland	72	894	115	272	.423	102	127	.803	32	65	97	140	101	0	40	4	92	332	4.6

Three-point field goals: 1991-92, 0-for-10.

NBA PLAYOFF RECORD

Season Team	G	Min.	FGM	FGA	Pct.	FTM	FTA	Pct.	Off.	Def.	Tot.	Ast.	PF	Dq.	Stl.	Blk.	TO	Pts.	Avg.
91-92—Portland	14	52	4	18	.222	3	4	.750	2	4	6	7	10	0	5	1	3	11	0.8

OP

PARISH, ROBERT
C, CELTICS

PERSONAL: Born August 30, 1953, in Shreveport, La. . . . 7-0/230. . . . Full name: Robert Lee Parish.
HIGH SCHOOL: Woodlawn (Shreveport, La.).
COLLEGE: Centenary (La.).
TRANSACTIONS/CAREER NOTES: Selected by Golden State Warriors in first round (eighth pick overall) of 1976 NBA Draft. . . . Traded by Warriors with 1980 first-round draft choice to Boston Celtics for two 1980 first-round draft choices (June 9, 1980).
MISCELLANEOUS: Member of NBA championship teams (1981, 1984, 1986).

COLLEGIATE RECORD

NOTES: THE SPORTING NEWS All-America first team (1976).

Season Team	G	Min.	FGM	FGA	Pct.	FTM	FTA	Pct.	Reb.	Pts.	Avg.
72-73 — Centenary	27	885	285	492	.579	50	82	.610	505	620	23.0
73-74 — Centenary	25	841	224	428	.523	49	78	.628	382	497	19.9
74-75 — Centenary	29	900	237	423	.560	74	112	.661	447	548	18.9
75-76 — Centenary	27	939	288	489	.589	93	134	.694	486	669	24.8
Totals	108	3565	1034	1832	.564	266	406	.655	1820	2334	21.6

NBA REGULAR-SEASON RECORD

HONORS: All-NBA second team (1982). . . . All-NBA third team (1989).

Season Team	G	Min.	FGM	FGA	Pct.	FTM	FTA	Pct.	REBOUNDS Off.	Def.	Tot.	Ast.	PF	Dq.	Stl.	Blk.	TO	Pts.	Avg.
76-77 — Golden State	77	1384	288	573	.503	121	171	.708	201	342	543	74	224	7	55	94	. . .	697	9.1
77-78 — Golden State	82	1969	430	911	.472	165	264	.625	211	469	680	95	291	10	79	123	201	1025	12.5
78-79 — Golden State	76	2411	554	1110	.499	196	281	.698	265	651	916	115	303	10	100	217	233	1304	17.2
79-80 — Golden State	72	2119	510	1006	.507	203	284	.715	247	536	783	122	248	6	58	115	225	1223	17.0
80-81 — Boston	82	2298	635	1166	.545	282	397	.710	245	532	777	144	310	9	81	214	191	1552	18.9
81-82 — Boston	80	2534	669	1235	.542	252	355	.710	288	578	866	140	267	5	68	192	221	1590	19.9
82-83 — Boston	78	2459	619	1125	.550	271	388	.698	260	567	827	141	222	4	79	148	185	1509	19.3
83-84 — Boston	80	2867	623	1140	.546	274	368	.745	243	614	857	139	266	7	55	116	184	1520	19.0
84-85 — Boston	79	2850	551	1016	.542	292	393	.743	263	577	840	125	223	2	56	101	186	1394	17.6
85-86 — Boston	81	2567	530	966	.549	245	335	.731	246	524	770	145	215	3	65	116	187	1305	16.1
86-87 — Boston	80	2995	588	1057	.556	227	309	.735	254	597	851	173	266	5	64	144	191	1403	17.5
87-88 — Boston	74	2312	442	750	.589	177	241	.734	173	455	628	115	198	5	55	84	154	1061	14.3
88-89 — Boston	80	2840	596	1045	.570	294	409	.719	342	654	996	175	209	2	79	116	200	1486	18.6
89-90 — Boston	79	2396	505	871	.580	233	312	.747	259	537	796	103	189	2	38	69	169	1243	15.7
90-91 — Boston	81	2441	485	811	.598	237	309	.767	271	585	856	66	197	1	66	103	153	1207	14.9
91-92 — Boston	79	2285	468	874	.535	179	232	.772	219	486	705	70	172	2	68	97	131	1115	14.1
Totals	1260	38727	8493	15656	.542	3648	5048	.723	3987	8704	12691	1942	3800	80	1066	2049	2811	20634	16.4

Three-point field goals: 1979-80, 0-for-1. 1980-81, 0-for-1. 1982-83, 0-for-1. 1986-87, 0-for-1. 1987-88, 0-for-1. 1990-91, 0-for-1. Totals, 0-for-6.

NBA PLAYOFF RECORD

NOTES: Holds career record for most offensive rebounds—552.

Season Team	G	Min.	FGM	FGA	Pct.	FTM	FTA	Pct.	REBOUNDS Off.	Def.	Tot.	Ast.	PF	Dq.	Stl.	Blk.	TO	Pts.	Avg.
76-77 — Golden State	10	239	52	108	.481	17	26	.654	43	60	103	11	42	1	7	11	. . .	121	12.1
80-81 — Boston	17	492	108	219	.493	39	58	.672	50	96	146	19	74	2	21	39	44	255	15.0
81-82 — Boston	12	426	102	209	.488	51	75	.680	43	92	135	18	47	1	5	48	39	255	21.3
82-83 — Boston	7	249	43	89	.483	17	20	.850	21	53	74	9	18	0	5	9	17	103	14.7
83-84 — Boston	23	869	139	291	.478	64	99	.646	76	172	248	27	100	6	23	41	45	342	14.9
84-85 — Boston	21	803	136	276	.493	87	111	.784	57	162	219	31	68	0	21	34	50	359	17.1
85-86 — Boston	18	591	106	225	.471	58	89	.652	52	106	158	25	47	1	9	30	44	270	15.0
86-87 — Boston	21	734	149	263	.567	79	103	.767	59	139	198	28	79	4	18	35	38	377	18.0
87-88 — Boston	17	626	100	188	.532	50	61	.820	51	117	168	21	42	0	11	19	38	250	14.7
88-89 — Boston	3	112	20	44	.455	7	9	.778	6	20	26	6	5	0	4	2	6	47	15.7
89-90 — Boston	5	170	31	54	.574	17	18	.944	23	27	50	13	21	0	5	7	12	79	15.8
90-91 — Boston	10	296	58	97	.598	42	61	.689	33	59	92	6	34	1	8	7	16	158	15.8
91-92 — Boston	10	335	50	101	.495	20	28	.714	38	59	97	14	22	0	7	15	9	120	12.0
Totals	174	5942	1094	2164	.506	548	758	.723	552	1162	1714	228	599	16	144	297	358	2736	15.7

Three-point field goals: 1986-87, 0-for-1.

NBA ALL-STAR GAME RECORD

Season Team	Min.	FGM	FGA	Pct.	FTM	FTA	Pct.	REBOUNDS Off.	Def.	Tot.	Ast.	PF	Dq.	Stl.	Blk.	TO	Pts.
1981 — Boston	25	5	18	.278	6	6	1.000	6	4	10	2	3	0	0	2	1	16
1982 — Boston	20	9	12	.750	3	4	.750	0	7	7	1	2	0	0	2	1	21
1983 — Boston	18	5	6	.833	3	4	.750	0	3	3	0	2	0	1	1	1	13
1984 — Boston	28	5	11	.455	2	4	.500	4	11	15	2	1	0	3	0	4	12
1985 — Boston	10	2	5	.400	0	0	. . .	3	3	6	1	0	0	0	0	0	4
1986 — Boston	7	0	0	. . .	0	2	.000	0	1	1	0	0	0	0	0	1	0
1987 — Boston	8	2	3	.667	0	0	. . .	0	3	3	0	1	0	0	1	0	4
1990 — Boston	21	7	11	.636	0	1	.000	2	2	4	2	4	0	0	1	1	14
1991 — Boston	5	1	2	.500	0	0	. . .	1	3	4	0	2	0	0	0	1	2
Totals	142	36	68	.529	14	21	.667	16	37	53	8	15	0	4	8	10	86

DID YOU KNOW. . .

. . . that Kevin Willis' 1,258 rebounds in 1991-92 were the most ever by an Atlanta player?

P

PAXSON, JOHN

G, BULLS

PERSONAL: Born September 29, 1960, in Dayton, O.... 6-2/185.... Full name: John MacBeth Paxson.... Son of Jim Paxson Sr., forward with Minneapolis Lakers and Cincinnati Royals (1956-57 and 1957-58); and brother of Jim Paxson Jr., guard with Portland Trail Blazers and Boston Celtics (1979-80 through 1989-90).
HIGH SCHOOL: Alter (Kettering, O.).
COLLEGE: Notre Dame.
TRANSACTIONS/CAREER NOTES: Selected by San Antonio Spurs in first round (19th pick overall) of 1983 NBA Draft.... Signed as veteran free agent by Chicago Bulls (October 29, 1985); Spurs relinquished their right of first refusal in exchange for cash.
MISCELLANEOUS: Member of NBA championship teams (1991, 1992).

COLLEGIATE RECORD

NOTES: THE SPORTING NEWS All-America second team (1983).

Season	Team	G	Min.	FGM	FGA	Pct.	FTM	FTA	Pct.	Reb.	Pts.	Avg.
79-80	Notre Dame	27	459	42	87	.483	41	55	.745	34	125	4.6
80-81	Notre Dame	29	1062	113	218	.518	61	89	.685	53	287	9.9
81-82	Notre Dame	27	1055	185	346	.535	72	93	.774	55	442	16.4
82-83	Notre Dame	29	1082	219	411	.533	74	100	.740	63	512	17.7
	Totals	112	3658	559	1062	.526	248	337	.736	205	1366	12.2

NBA REGULAR-SEASON RECORD

Season	Team	G	Min.	FGM	FGA	Pct.	FTM	FTA	Pct.	REBOUNDS Off.	REBOUNDS Def.	REBOUNDS Tot.	Ast.	PF	Dq.	Stl.	Blk.	TO	Pts.	Avg.
83-84	San Antonio	49	458	61	137	.445	16	26	.615	4	29	33	149	47	0	10	2	32	142	2.9
84-85	San Antonio	78	1259	196	385	.509	84	100	.840	19	49	68	215	117	0	45	3	81	486	6.2
85-86	Chicago	75	1570	153	328	.466	74	92	.804	18	76	94	274	172	2	55	2	63	395	5.3
86-87	Chicago	82	2689	386	793	.487	106	131	.809	22	117	139	467	207	1	66	8	105	930	11.3
87-88	Chicago	81	1888	287	582	.493	33	45	.733	16	88	104	303	154	2	49	1	64	640	7.9
88-89	Chicago	78	1738	246	513	.480	31	36	.861	13	81	94	308	162	1	53	6	71	567	7.3
89-90	Chicago	82	2365	365	708	.516	56	68	.824	27	92	119	335	176	1	83	6	85	819	10.0
90-91	Chicago	82	1971	317	578	.548	34	41	.829	15	76	91	297	136	0	62	3	69	710	8.7
91-92	Chicago	79	1946	257	487	.528	29	37	.784	21	75	96	241	142	0	49	9	44	555	7.0
	Totals	686	15884	2268	4511	.503	463	576	.804	155	683	838	2589	1313	7	472	40	614	5244	7.6

Three-point field goals: 1983-84, 4-for-22 (.182). 1984-85, 10-for-34 (.294). 1985-86, 15-for-51 (.294). 1986-87, 52-for-140 (.371). 1987-88, 33-for-95 (.347). 1988-89, 44-for-133 (.331). 1989-90, 33-for-92 (.359). 1990-91, 42-for-96 (.438). 1991-92, 12-for-44 (.273). Totals, 245-for-707 (.347).

NBA PLAYOFF RECORD

NOTES: Shares NBA Finals single-game record for highest field-goal percentage (minimum 8 made) — 1.000 (June 5, 1991, vs. Los Angeles Lakers, 8 for 8).

Season	Team	G	Min.	FGM	FGA	Pct.	FTM	FTA	Pct.	REBOUNDS Off.	REBOUNDS Def.	REBOUNDS Tot.	Ast.	PF	Dq.	Stl.	Blk.	TO	Pts.	Avg.
84-85	San Antonio	5	114	21	42	.500	7	9	.778	0	5	5	21	9	0	5	0	5	51	10.2
85-86	Chicago	3	80	7	15	.467	13	17	.765	0	0	0	5	9	0	3	0	3	27	9.0
86-87	Chicago	3	87	11	22	.500	1	1	1.000	0	3	3	11	9	0	2	0	5	26	8.7
87-88	Chicago	10	165	20	53	.377	4	4	1.000	0	4	4	30	24	1	1	1	5	46	4.6
88-89	Chicago	16	302	37	78	.474	14	16	.875	2	8	10	34	35	1	12	0	15	93	5.8
89-90	Chicago	15	395	37	87	.425	14	14	1.000	2	20	22	54	42	3	9	0	15	92	6.1
90-91	Chicago	17	487	62	117	.530	14	14	1.000	2	21	23	53	32	0	11	0	6	140	8.2
91-92	Chicago	22	598	73	139	.525	16	19	.842	0	22	22	61	53	1	14	1	13	174	7.9
	Totals	91	2228	268	553	.485	83	94	.883	6	83	89	269	213	6	57	2	67	649	7.1

Three-point field goals: 1984-85, 2-for-9 (.222). 1986-87, 3-for-7 (.429). 1987-88, 2-for-12 (.167). 1988-89, 5-for-19 (.263). 1989-90, 4-for-9 (.444). 1990-91, 2-for-14 (.143). 1991-92, 12-for-27 (.444). Totals, 30-for-97 (.309).

PAYNE, KENNY

F, 76ERS

PERSONAL: Born November 25, 1966, in Laurel, Miss.... 6-8/220.... Full name: Kenneth Victor Payne.
HIGH SCHOOL: Northeast Jones (Laurel, Miss.).
COLLEGE: Louisville.
TRANSACTIONS/CAREER NOTES: Selected by Philadelphia 76ers in first round (19th pick overall) of 1989 NBA Draft.

COLLEGIATE RECORD

NOTES: Member of NCAA Division I championship team (1986).

Season	Team	G	Min.	FGM	FGA	Pct.	FTM	FTA	Pct.	Reb.	Pts.	Avg.
85-86	Louisville	34	303	52	119	.437	17	22	.773	58	121	3.6
86-87	Louisville	26	320	43	123	.350	16	23	.696	66	108	4.2
87-88	Louisville	35	1035	156	325	.480	29	38	.763	164	375	10.7
88-89	Louisville	33	987	196	386	.508	42	50	.840	188	479	14.5
	Totals	128	2645	447	953	.469	104	133	.782	476	1083	8.5

Three-point field goals: 1986-87, 6-for-24 (.250). 1987-88, 34-for-83 (.410). 1988-89, 45-for-105 (.429). Totals, 85-for-212 (.401).

NBA REGULAR-SEASON RECORD

Season	Team	G	Min.	FGM	FGA	Pct.	FTM	FTA	Pct.	REBOUNDS Off.	REBOUNDS Def.	REBOUNDS Tot.	Ast.	PF	Dq.	Stl.	Blk.	TO	Pts.	Avg.
89-90	Philadelphia	35	216	47	108	.435	16	18	.889	11	15	26	10	37	0	7	6	20	114	3.3
90-91	Philadelphia	47	444	68	189	.360	26	29	.897	17	49	66	16	43	0	10	6	21	166	3.5
91-92	Philadelphia	49	353	65	145	.448	9	13	.692	13	41	54	17	34	0	16	8	19	144	2.9
	Totals	131	1013	180	442	.407	51	60	.850	41	105	146	43	114	0	33	20	60	424	3.2

Three-point field goals: 1989-90, 4-for-10 (.400). 1990-91, 4-for-18 (.222). 1991-92, 5-for-12 (.417). Totals, 13-for-40 (.325).

P

NBA PLAYOFF RECORD

Season	Team	G	Min.	FGM	FGA	Pct.	FTM	FTA	Pct.	Off.	Def.	Tot.	Ast.	PF	Dq.	Stl.	Blk.	TO	Pts.	Avg.
										— REBOUNDS —										
89-90	Philadelphia.	3	10	2	5	.400	2	2	1.000	1	1	2	0	3	0	0	0	1	6	2.0

Three-point field goals: 1989-90, 0-for-2.

PAYTON, GARY
G, SUPERSONICS

PERSONAL: Born July 23, 1968, in Oakland, Calif. . . . 6-4/190. . . . Full name: Gary Dwayne Payton.
HIGH SCHOOL: Skyline (Oakland, Calif.).
COLLEGE: Oregon State.
TRANSACTIONS/CAREER NOTES: Selected by Seattle SuperSonics in first round (second pick overall) of 1990 NBA Draft.

COLLEGIATE RECORD

NOTES: THE SPORTING NEWS All-America first team (1990).

Season	Team	G	Min.	FGM	FGA	Pct.	FTM	FTA	Pct.	Reb.	Pts.	Avg.
86-87	Oregon State	30	1115	153	333	.459	55	82	.671	120	374	12.5
87-88	Oregon State	31	1178	180	368	.489	58	83	.699	103	449	14.5
88-89	Oregon State	30	1140	208	438	.475	105	155	.677	122	603	20.1
89-90	Oregon State	29	1095	288	571	.504	118	171	.690	135	746	25.7
	Totals	120	4528	829	1710	.485	336	491	.684	480	2172	18.1

Three-point field goals: 1986-87, 13-for-35 (.371). 1987-88, 31-for-78 (.397). 1988-89, 82-for-213 (.385). 1989-90, 52-for-156 (.333). Totals, 178-for-482 (.369).

NBA REGULAR-SEASON RECORD

HONORS: NBA All-Rookie second team (1991).

Season	Team	G	Min.	FGM	FGA	Pct.	FTM	FTA	Pct.	Off.	Def.	Tot.	Ast.	PF	Dq.	Stl.	Blk.	TO	Pts.	Avg.
										— REBOUNDS —										
90-91	Seattle	82	2244	259	575	.450	69	97	.711	108	135	243	528	249	3	165	15	180	588	7.2
91-92	Seattle	81	2549	331	734	.451	99	148	.669	123	172	295	506	248	0	147	21	174	764	9.4
	Totals	163	4793	590	1309	.451	168	245	.686	231	307	538	1034	497	3	312	36	354	1352	8.3

Three-point field goals: 1990-91, 1-for-13 (.077). 1991-92, 3-for-23 (.130). Totals, 4-for-36 (.111).

NBA PLAYOFF RECORD

Season	Team	G	Min.	FGM	FGA	Pct.	FTM	FTA	Pct.	Off.	Def.	Tot.	Ast.	PF	Dq.	Stl.	Blk.	TO	Pts.	Avg.
										— REBOUNDS —										
90-91	Seattle	5	135	11	27	.407	2	2	1.000	5	8	13	32	16	0	8	1	9	24	4.8
91-92	Seattle	8	221	27	58	.466	7	12	.583	6	15	21	38	26	1	8	2	10	61	7.6
	Totals	13	356	38	85	.447	9	14	.643	11	23	34	70	42	1	16	3	19	85	6.5

Three-point field goals: 1990-91, 0-for-1. 1991-92, 0-for-2. Totals, 0-for-3.

PERDUE, WILL
C, BULLS

PERSONAL: Born August 29, 1965, in Melbourne, Fla. . . . 7-0/240. . . . Full name: William Edward Perdue III.
HIGH SCHOOL: Merritt Island (Fla.).
COLLEGE: Vanderbilt.
TRANSACTIONS/CAREER NOTES: Selected by Chicago Bulls in first round (11th pick overall) of 1988 NBA Draft.
MISCELLANEOUS: Member of NBA championship teams (1991, 1992).

COLLEGIATE RECORD

Season	Team	G	Min.	FGM	FGA	Pct.	FTM	FTA	Pct.	Reb.	Pts.	Avg.
83-84	Vanderbilt	17	111	21	45	.467	4	9	.444	38	46	2.7
84-85	Vanderbilt					Did not play—redshirted.						
85-86	Vanderbilt	22	181	31	53	.585	14	32	.438	61	76	3.5
86-87	Vanderbilt	34	1033	233	389	.599	126	204	.618	295	592	17.4
87-88	Vanderbilt	31	1013	234	369	.634	99	147	.673	314	567	18.3
	Totals	104	2338	519	856	.606	243	392	.620	708	1281	12.3

NBA REGULAR-SEASON RECORD

Season	Team	G	Min.	FGM	FGA	Pct.	FTM	FTA	Pct.	Off.	Def.	Tot.	Ast.	PF	Dq.	Stl.	Blk.	TO	Pts.	Avg.
										— REBOUNDS —										
88-89	Chicago	30	190	29	72	.403	8	14	.571	18	27	45	11	38	0	4	6	15	66	2.2
89-90	Chicago	77	884	111	268	.414	72	104	.692	88	126	214	46	150	0	19	26	65	294	3.8
90-91	Chicago	74	972	116	235	.494	75	112	.670	122	214	336	47	147	1	23	57	75	307	4.1
91-92	Chicago	77	1007	152	278	.547	45	91	.495	108	204	312	80	133	1	16	43	72	350	4.5
	Totals	258	3053	408	853	.478	200	321	.623	336	571	907	184	468	2	62	132	227	1017	3.9

Three-point field goals: 1989-90, 0-for-5. 1990-91, 0-for-3. 1991-92, 1-for-2 (.500). Totals, 1-for-10 (.100).

NBA PLAYOFF RECORD

Season	Team	G	Min.	FGM	FGA	Pct.	FTM	FTA	Pct.	Off.	Def.	Tot.	Ast.	PF	Dq.	Stl.	Blk.	TO	Pts.	Avg.
										— REBOUNDS —										
88-89	Chicago	3	22	6	9	.667	2	3	.667	3	3	6	2	4	0	0	0	0	14	4.7
89-90	Chicago	13	78	13	28	.464	13	18	.722	7	12	19	2	13	0	0	5	4	40	3.1
90-91	Chicago	17	198	29	53	.547	12	22	.545	32	33	65	4	41	1	2	8	14	70	4.1
91-92	Chicago	18	157	18	37	.486	9	20	.450	18	22	40	9	34	1	3	10	12	45	2.5
	Totals	51	455	66	127	.520	36	63	.571	60	70	130	17	92	2	5	23	30	169	3.3

Three-point field goals: 1988-89, 0-for-1. 1989-90, 1-for-2 (.500). 1991-92, 0-for-1. Totals, 1-for-4 (.250).

P

— 139 —

PERKINS, SAM
F/C, LAKERS

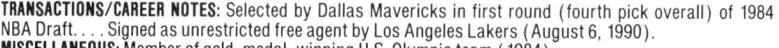

PERSONAL: Born June 14, 1961, in Brooklyn, N.Y. . . . 6-9/257. . . . Full name: Samuel Bruce Perkins.
HIGH SCHOOL: Shaker (Latham, N.Y.).
COLLEGE: North Carolina.
TRANSACTIONS/CAREER NOTES: Selected by Dallas Mavericks in first round (fourth pick overall) of 1984 NBA Draft. . . . Signed as unrestricted free agent by Los Angeles Lakers (August 6, 1990).
MISCELLANEOUS: Member of gold-medal-winning U.S. Olympic team (1984).

COLLEGIATE RECORD

NOTES: THE SPORTING NEWS All-America first team (1984). . . . THE SPORTING NEWS All-America second team (1982, 1983). . . . Member of NCAA Division I championship team (1982).

Season	Team	G	Min.	FGM	FGA	Pct.	FTM	FTA	Pct.	Reb.	Pts.	Avg.
80-81	—North Carolina	37	. . .	199	318	.626	152	205	.741	289	550	14.9
81-82	—North Carolina	32	. . .	174	301	.578	109	142	.768	250	457	14.3
82-83	—North Carolina	35	. . .	218	414	.527	145	177	.819	330	593	16.9
83-84	—North Carolina	31	. . .	195	331	.589	155	181	.856	298	545	17.6
	Totals	135	. . .	786	1364	.576	561	705	.796	1167	2145	15.9

Three-point field goals: 1982-83, 12-for-28 (.429).

NBA REGULAR-SEASON RECORD

HONORS: NBA All-Rookie team (1985).

| | | | | | | | | | | — REBOUNDS — | | | | | | | | | |
Season	Team	G	Min.	FGM	FGA	Pct.	FTM	FTA	Pct.	Off.	Def.	Tot.	Ast.	PF	Dq.	Stl.	Blk.	TO	Pts.	Avg.
84-85	—Dallas	82	2317	347	736	.471	200	244	.820	189	416	605	135	236	1	63	63	102	903	11.0
85-86	—Dallas	80	2626	458	910	.503	307	377	.814	195	490	685	153	212	2	75	94	145	1234	15.4
86-87	—Dallas	80	2687	461	957	.482	245	296	.828	197	419	616	146	269	6	109	77	132	1186	14.8
87-88	—Dallas	75	2499	394	876	.450	273	332	.822	201	400	601	118	227	2	74	54	119	1066	14.2
88-89	—Dallas	78	2860	445	959	.464	274	329	.833	235	453	688	127	224	1	76	92	141	1171	15.0
89-90	—Dallas	76	2668	435	883	.493	330	424	.778	209	363	572	175	225	4	88	64	148	1206	15.9
90-91	—L.A. Lakers	73	2504	368	744	.495	229	279	.821	167	371	538	108	247	2	64	78	103	983	13.5
91-92	—L.A. Lakers	63	2332	361	803	.450	304	372	.817	192	364	556	141	192	1	64	62	83	1041	16.5
	Totals	607	20493	3269	6868	.476	2162	2653	.815	1585	3276	4861	1103	1832	19	613	584	973	8790	14.5

Three-point field goals: 1984-85, 9-for-36 (.250). 1985-86, 11-for-33 (.333). 1986-87, 19-for-54 (.352). 1987-88, 5-for-30 (.167). 1988-89, 7-for-38 (.184). 1989-90, 6-for-28 (.214). 1990-91, 18-for-64 (.281). 1991-92, 15-for-69 (.217). Totals, 90-for-352 (.256).

NBA PLAYOFF RECORD

| | | | | | | | | | | — REBOUNDS — | | | | | | | | | |
Season	Team	G	Min.	FGM	FGA	Pct.	FTM	FTA	Pct.	Off.	Def.	Tot.	Ast.	PF	Dq.	Stl.	Blk.	TO	Pts.	Avg.
84-85	—Dallas	4	169	24	49	.490	26	34	.765	16	35	51	11	13	1	2	1	3	75	18.8
85-86	—Dallas	10	347	57	133	.429	33	43	.767	30	53	83	24	32	0	9	14	16	149	14.9
86-87	—Dallas	4	133	26	52	.500	16	23	.696	12	22	34	5	16	0	4	1	9	68	17.0
87-88	—Dallas	17	572	88	195	.451	53	66	.803	39	73	112	31	51	1	25	17	30	230	13.5
89-90	—Dallas	3	118	16	36	.444	13	17	.765	10	12	22	8	17	2	3	2	7	45	15.0
90-91	—L.A. Lakers	19	752	121	221	.548	83	109	.761	41	116	157	33	69	0	15	27	37	336	17.7
	Totals	57	2091	332	686	.484	224	292	.767	148	311	459	112	198	4	58	62	102	903	15.8

Three-point field goals: 1984-85, 1-for-4 (.250). 1985-86, 2-for-8 (.250). 1986-87, 0-for-4. 1987-88, 1-for-7 (.143). 1989-90, 0-for-1. 1990-91, 11-for-30 (.367). Totals, 15-for-54 (.278).

PERRY, ELLIOT
G, HORNETS

PERSONAL: Born March 28, 1969, in Memphis, Tenn. . . . 6-0/160. . . . Full name: Elliot Lamonte Perry.
HIGH SCHOOL: Treadwell (Memphis, Tenn.).
COLLEGE: Memphis State.
TRANSACTIONS/CAREER NOTES: Selected by Los Angeles Clippers in second round (37th pick overall) of 1991 NBA Draft. . . . Waived by Clippers (November 25, 1991). . . . Played in Continental Basketball Association with La Crosse Catbirds (1991-92). . . . Signed as free agent by Charlotte Hornets (December 9, 1991).

COLLEGIATE RECORD

Season	Team	G	Min.	FGM	FGA	Pct.	FTM	FTA	Pct.	Reb.	Pts.	Avg.
87-88	—Memphis State	32	968	140	336	.417	87	108	.806	113	420	13.1
88-89	—Memphis State	32	1017	202	437	.462	192	234	.821	109	620	19.4
89-90	—Memphis State	30	970	175	419	.418	137	182	.753	110	504	16.8
90-91	—Memphis State	32	1169	235	507	.464	146	184	.793	111	665	20.8
	Totals	126	4124	752	1699	.443	562	708	.794	443	2209	17.5

Three-point field goals: 1987-88, 53-for-136 (.390). 1988-89, 24-for-76 (.316). 1989-90, 17-for-66 (.258). 1990-91, 49-for-136 (.360). Totals, 143-for-414 (.345).

NBA REGULAR-SEASON RECORD

| | | | | | | | | | | — REBOUNDS — | | | | | | | | | |
Season	Team	G	Min.	FGM	FGA	Pct.	FTM	FTA	Pct.	Off.	Def.	Tot.	Ast.	PF	Dq.	Stl.	Blk.	TO	Pts.	Avg.
91-92	—LAC-Char	50	437	49	129	.380	27	41	.659	14	25	39	78	36	0	34	3	50	126	2.5

Three-point field goals: 1991-92, 1-for-7 (.143).

CBA REGULAR-SEASON RECORD

| | | | | — 2-POINT — | | | — 3-POINT — | | | | | | | | |
Season	Team	G	Min.	FGM	FGA	Pct.	FGM	FGA	Pct.	FTM	FTA	Pct.	Reb.	Ast.	Pts.	Avg.
91-92	—La Crosse	2	59	8	15	.533	0	3	.000	11	13	.846	2	9	27	13.5

P

PERRY, TIM

F, 76ERS

PERSONAL: Born June 4, 1965, in Freehold, N.J. . . . 6-9/220. . . . Full name: Timothy D. Perry.
HIGH SCHOOL: Freehold (N.J.).
COLLEGE: Temple.

TRANSACTIONS/CAREER NOTES: Selected by Phoenix Suns in first round (seventh pick overall) of 1988 NBA Draft. . . . Traded by Suns with Jeff Hornacek and Andrew Lang to Philadelphia 76ers for Charles Barkley (June 17, 1992).

COLLEGIATE RECORD

Season Team	G	Min.	FGM	FGA	Pct.	FTM	FTA	Pct.	Reb.	Pts.	Avg.
84-85 — Temple	30	621	29	70	.414	10	20	.500	118	68	2.3
85-86 — Temple	31	1101	141	249	.566	77	134	.575	293	359	11.6
86-87 — Temple	36	1271	180	350	.514	103	166	.620	310	463	12.9
87-88 — Temple	33	1103	203	347	.585	72	113	.637	264	478	14.5
Totals	130	4096	553	1016	.544	262	433	.605	985	1368	10.5

NBA REGULAR-SEASON RECORD

Season Team	G	Min.	FGM	FGA	Pct.	FTM	FTA	Pct.	Off.	Def.	Tot.	Ast.	PF	Dq.	Stl.	Blk.	TO	Pts.	Avg.
88-89 — Phoenix	62	614	108	201	.537	40	65	.615	61	71	132	18	47	0	19	32	37	257	4.1
89-90 — Phoenix	60	612	100	195	.513	53	90	.589	79	73	152	17	76	0	21	22	47	254	4.2
90-91 — Phoenix	46	587	75	144	.521	43	70	.614	53	73	126	27	60	1	23	43	32	193	4.2
91-92 — Phoenix	80	2483	413	789	.523	153	215	.712	204	347	551	134	237	2	44	116	141	982	12.3
Totals	248	4296	696	1329	.524	289	440	.657	397	564	961	196	420	3	107	213	257	1686	6.8

Three-point field goals: 1988-89, 1-for-4 (.250). 1989-90, 1-for-1. 1990-91, 0-for-5. 1991-92, 3-for-8 (.375). Totals, 5-for-18 (.278).

NBA PLAYOFF RECORD

Season Team	G	Min.	FGM	FGA	Pct.	FTM	FTA	Pct.	Off.	Def.	Tot.	Ast.	PF	Dq.	Stl.	Blk.	TO	Pts.	Avg.
88-89 — Phoenix	4	17	2	4	.500	0	2	.000	1	1	2	0	1	0	2	1	1	4	1.0
89-90 — Phoenix	11	100	13	25	.520	8	18	.444	10	11	21	2	19	0	3	6	5	34	3.1
91-92 — Phoenix	8	185	38	63	.603	23	32	.719	12	27	39	11	24	1	3	6	14	99	12.4
Totals	23	302	53	92	.576	31	52	.596	23	39	62	13	44	1	8	13	20	137	6.0

PERSON, CHUCK

F, TIMBERWOLVES

PERSONAL: Born June 27, 1964, in Brantley, Ala. . . . 6-8/225. . . . Full name: Chuck Connors Person.
HIGH SCHOOL: Brantley (Ala.).
COLLEGE: Auburn.

TRANSACTIONS/CAREER NOTES: Selected by Indiana Pacers in first round (fourth pick overall) of 1986 NBA Draft. . . . Traded by Pacers with Micheal Williams to Minnesota Timberwolves for Pooh Richardson and Sam Mitchell (September 8, 1992).

COLLEGIATE RECORD

NOTES: THE SPORTING NEWS All-America second team (1985, 1986).

Season Team	G	Min.	FGM	FGA	Pct.	FTM	FTA	Pct.	Reb.	Pts.	Avg.
82-83 — Auburn	28	636	118	218	.541	25	33	.758	128	261	9.3
83-84 — Auburn	31	1079	255	470	.543	83	114	.728	249	593	19.1
84-85 — Auburn	34	1240	334	614	.544	79	107	.738	303	747	22.0
85-86 — Auburn	33	1178	310	597	.519	90	112	.804	260	710	21.5
Totals	126	4133	1017	1899	.536	277	366	.757	940	2311	18.3

NBA REGULAR-SEASON RECORD

HONORS: NBA Rookie of the Year (1987). . . . NBA All-Rookie team (1987).

Season Team	G	Min.	FGM	FGA	Pct.	FTM	FTA	Pct.	Off.	Def.	Tot.	Ast.	PF	Dq.	Stl.	Blk.	TO	Pts.	Avg.
86-87 — Indiana	82	2956	635	1358	.468	222	297	.747	168	509	677	295	310	4	90	16	211	1541	18.8
87-88 — Indiana	79	2807	575	1252	.459	132	197	.670	171	365	536	309	266	4	73	8	210	1341	17.0
88-89 — Indiana	80	3012	711	1453	.489	243	307	.792	144	372	516	289	280	12	83	18	308	1728	21.6
89-90 — Indiana	77	2714	605	1242	.487	211	270	.781	126	319	445	230	217	1	53	20	170	1515	19.7
90-91 — Indiana	80	2566	620	1231	.504	165	229	.721	121	296	417	238	221	1	56	17	184	1474	18.4
91-92 — Indiana	81	2923	616	1284	.480	133	197	.675	114	312	426	382	247	5	68	18	216	1497	18.5
Totals	479	16978	3762	7820	.481	1106	1497	.739	844	2173	3017	1743	1541	27	423	97	1299	9096	19.0

Three-point field goals: 1986-87, 49-for-138 (.355). 1987-88, 59-for-177 (.333). 1988-89, 63-for-205 (.307). 1989-90, 94-for-253 (.372). 1990-91, 69-for-203 (.340). 1991-92, 132-for-354 (.373). Totals, 466-for-1330 (.350).

NBA PLAYOFF RECORD

NOTES: Holds single-game record for most three-point field goals made—7 (April 28, 1991, vs. Boston).

Season Team	G	Min.	FGM	FGA	Pct.	FTM	FTA	Pct.	Off.	Def.	Tot.	Ast.	PF	Dq.	Stl.	Blk.	TO	Pts.	Avg.
86-87 — Indiana	4	159	38	74	.514	30	39	.769	6	27	33	20	14	0	5	2	15	108	27.0
89-90 — Indiana	3	123	17	45	.378	5	12	.417	6	14	20	12	11	0	1	0	4	40	13.3
90-91 — Indiana	5	192	48	90	.533	17	21	.810	3	25	28	16	15	1	5	0	12	130	26.0
91-92 — Indiana	3	118	19	47	.404	8	12	.667	1	8	9	7	11	0	2	0	6	51	17.0
Totals	15	592	122	256	.477	60	84	.714	16	74	90	55	51	1	13	2	37	329	21.9

DID YOU KNOW. . .

. . . that the Cleveland Cavaliers lost only three of 45 games last season in which they led at halftime?

P

Three-point field goals: 1986-87, 2-for-8 (.250). 1989-90, 1-for-10 (.100). 1990-91, 17-for-31 (.548). 1991-92, 5-for-15 (.333). Totals, 25-for-64 (.391).

PETERSEN, JIM
F/C, WARRIORS

PERSONAL: Born February 22, 1962, in Minneapolis. . . . 6-10/240. . . . Full name: James Richard Petersen.
HIGH SCHOOL: St. Louis Park (Minn.).
COLLEGE: Minnesota.
TRANSACTIONS/CAREER NOTES: Selected by Houston Rockets in third round (51st pick overall) of 1984 NBA Draft. . . . Traded by Rockets with Rodney McCray to Sacramento Kings for Otis Thorpe (October 11, 1988). . . . Traded by Kings to Golden State Warriors for Ralph Sampson (September 27, 1989).

COLLEGIATE RECORD

Season Team	G	Min.	FGM	FGA	Pct.	FTM	FTA	Pct.	Reb.	Pts.	Avg.
80-81—Minnesota	22	...	13	26	.500	1	4	.250	22	27	1.2
81-82—Minnesota	21	...	24	52	.462	14	22	.636	43	62	3.0
82-83—Minnesota	29	...	82	149	.550	18	28	.643	155	182	6.3
83-84—Minnesota	24	...	115	180	.639	39	54	.722	166	269	11.2
Totals	96	...	234	407	.575	72	108	.667	386	540	5.6

NBA REGULAR-SEASON RECORD

Season Team	G	Min.	FGM	FGA	Pct.	FTM	FTA	Pct.	REBOUNDS Off.	Def.	Tot.	Ast.	PF	Dq.	Stl.	Blk.	TO	Pts.	Avg.
84-85—Houston	60	714	70	144	.486	50	66	.758	44	103	147	29	125	1	14	32	71	190	3.2
85-86—Houston	82	1664	196	411	.477	113	160	.706	149	247	396	85	231	2	38	54	84	505	6.2
86-87—Houston	82	2403	386	755	.511	152	209	.727	177	380	557	127	268	5	43	102	152	924	11.3
87-88—Houston	69	1793	249	488	.510	114	153	.745	145	291	436	106	203	3	36	40	119	613	8.9
88-89—Sacramento	66	1633	278	606	.459	115	154	.747	121	292	413	81	236	8	47	68	147	671	10.2
89-90—Golden State	43	592	60	141	.426	52	73	.712	49	111	160	23	103	0	17	20	36	172	4.0
90-91—Golden State	62	834	114	236	.483	50	76	.658	69	131	200	27	153	2	13	41	48	279	4.5
91-92—Golden State	27	169	18	40	.450	7	10	.700	12	33	45	9	35	0	5	6	5	43	1.6
Totals	491	9802	1371	2821	.486	653	901	.725	766	1588	2354	487	1354	21	213	363	662	3397	6.9

Three-point field goals: 1985-86, 0-for-3. 1986-87, 0-for-4. 1987-88, 1-for-6 (.167). 1988-89, 0-for-8. 1989-90, 0-for-1. 1990-91, 1-for-4 (.250). 1991-92, 0-for-2. Totals, 2-for-28 (.071).

NBA PLAYOFF RECORD

Season Team	G	Min.	FGM	FGA	Pct.	FTM	FTA	Pct.	REBOUNDS Off.	Def.	Tot.	Ast.	PF	Dq.	Stl.	Blk.	TO	Pts.	Avg.
84-85—Houston	3	8	1	1	1.000	0	0	...	1	1	2	1	2	0	0	0	1	2	0.7
85-86—Houston	20	378	44	108	.407	23	33	.697	47	64	111	21	58	1	9	9	16	111	5.6
86-87—Houston	10	187	28	51	.549	12	18	.667	14	32	46	6	26	1	5	2	10	68	6.8
87-88—Houston	4	98	12	23	.522	7	12	.583	7	14	21	6	11	1	1	2	4	31	7.8
90-91—Golden State	9	117	12	17	.706	5	8	.625	4	23	27	3	35	1	2	4	2	29	3.2
Totals	46	788	97	200	.485	47	71	.662	73	134	207	37	132	4	17	17	33	241	5.2

PETROVIC, DRAZEN
G, NETS

PERSONAL: Born October 22, 1964, in Sibenik, Yugoslavia. . . . 6-5/208. . . . Name pronounced DRAZ-en PET-tro-vich.
COLLEGE: University of Zagreb (Yugoslavia).
TRANSACTIONS/CAREER NOTES: Selected by Portland Trail Blazers in third round (60th pick overall) of 1986 NBA Draft. . . . Traded by Trail Blazers to New Jersey Nets in three-way deal in which Denver Nuggets sent Walter Davis to Trail Blazers and Terry Mills to Nets, and Nets sent Greg Anderson to Nuggets (January 23, 1991); Nuggets also received 1992 first-round draft choice from Nets and 1993 second-round draft choice from Trail Blazers and Trail Blazers received 1992 second-round draft choice from Nuggets.
MISCELLANEOUS: Member of silver-medal-winning Yugoslavian Olympic team (1988). . . . Member of silver-medal-winning Croatian Olympic team (1992).

NBA REGULAR-SEASON RECORD

Season Team	G	Min.	FGM	FGA	Pct.	FTM	FTA	Pct.	REBOUNDS Off.	Def.	Tot.	Ast.	PF	Dq.	Stl.	Blk.	TO	Pts.	Avg.
89-90—Portland	77	967	207	427	.485	135	160	.844	50	61	111	116	134	0	23	2	96	583	7.6
90-91—Port.-N.J.	61	1015	243	493	.493	114	137	.832	51	59	110	86	132	0	43	1	81	623	10.2
91-92—New Jersey	82	3027	668	1315	.508	232	287	.808	97	161	258	252	248	3	105	11	215	1691	20.6
Totals	220	5009	1118	2235	.500	481	584	.824	198	281	479	454	514	3	171	14	392	2897	13.2

Three-point field goals: 1989-90, 34-for-74 (.459). 1990-91, 23-for-65 (.354). 1991-92, 123-for-277 (.444). Totals, 180-for-416 (.433).

NBA PLAYOFF RECORD

Season Team	G	Min.	FGM	FGA	Pct.	FTM	FTA	Pct.	REBOUNDS Off.	Def.	Tot.	Ast.	PF	Dq.	Stl.	Blk.	TO	Pts.	Avg.
89-90—Portland	20	253	48	109	.440	21	36	.583	10	22	32	20	37	0	6	0	20	122	6.1
91-92—New Jersey	4	163	41	76	.539	11	13	.846	4	6	10	13	13	0	4	1	8	97	24.3
Totals	24	416	89	185	.481	32	49	.653	14	28	42	33	50	0	10	1	28	219	9.1

Three-point field goals: 1989-90, 5-for-16 (.313). 1991-92, 4-for-12 (.333). Totals, 9-for-28 (.321).

PHILLS, BOBBY
G, CAVALIERS

PERSONAL: Born December 20, 1969, in Baton Rouge, La. . . . 6-5/217. . . . Full name: Bobby Ray Phills II.
HIGH SCHOOL: Southern University Lab (Baton Rouge, La.).
COLLEGE: Southern (La.).
TRANSACTIONS/CAREER NOTES: Selected by Milwaukee Bucks in second round (45th pick overall) of 1991 NBA Draft. . . . Waived by Bucks (December 18, 1991). . . . Played in Continental Basketball Association

with Sioux Falls Skyforce (1991-92).... Signed by Cleveland Cavaliers to 10-day contract (March 19, 1992).... Signed by Cavaliers for remainder of season (March 29, 1992).

COLLEGIATE RECORD

NOTES: Led NCAA Division I with 4.39 three-point field-goals made per game (1991).

Season Team	G	Min.	FGM	FGA	Pct.	FTM	FTA	Pct.	Reb.	Pts.	Avg.
87-88 —Southern	23	158	26	53	.491	30	42	.714	41	85	3.7
88-89 —Southern	31	923	166	385	.431	44	60	.733	142	420	13.5
89-90 —Southern	31	937	232	574	.404	46	70	.657	132	622	20.1
90-91 —Southern	28	986	260	641	.406	152	211	.720	132	795	28.4
Totals	113	3004	684	1653	.414	272	383	.710	447	1922	17.0

Three-point field goals: 1987-88, 3-for-7 (.429). 1988-89, 44-for-128 (.344). 1989-90, 112-for-300 (.373). 1990-91, 123-for-353 (.348). Totals, 282-for-788 (.358).

CBA REGULAR-SEASON RECORD

				2-POINT			3-POINT							
Season Team	G	Min.	FGM	FGA	Pct.	FGM	FGA	Pct.	FTM	FTA	Pct.	Reb.	Ast.	Pts.	Avg.
91-92 —Sioux Falls	34	1272	259	518	.500	30	106	.283	177	230	.770	222	92	785	23.1

NBA REGULAR-SEASON RECORD

									— REBOUNDS —								
Season Team	G	Min.	FGM	FGA	Pct.	FTM	FTA	Pct.	Off.	Def.	Tot.	Ast.	PF	Dq.	Stl.	Blk.	TO	Pts.	Avg.
91-92 —Cleveland	10	65	12	28	.429	7	11	.636	4	4	8	4	3	0	3	1	8	31	3.1

Three-point field goals: 1991-92, 0-for-2.

NBA PLAYOFF RECORD

									— REBOUNDS —								
Season Team	G	Min.	FGM	FGA	Pct.	FTM	FTA	Pct.	Off.	Def.	Tot.	Ast.	PF	Dq.	Stl.	Blk.	TO	Pts.	Avg.
91-92 —Cleveland	5	12	4	9	.444	3	4	.750	2	4	6	5	1	0	1	0	2	11	2.2

Three-point field goals: 1991-92, 0-for-1.

PIERCE, RICKY
G, SUPERSONICS

PERSONAL: Born August 19, 1959, in Dallas.... 6-4/215.... Full name: Ricky Charles Pierce.
HIGH SCHOOL: South Garland (Garland, Tex.).
COLLEGE: Walla Walla Community College (Wash.), then Rice.
TRANSACTIONS/CAREER NOTES: Selected by Detroit Pistons in first round (18th pick overall) of 1982 NBA Draft.... Traded by Pistons to San Diego Clippers for 1986 and 1987 second-round draft choices (October 17, 1983).... Traded by Clippers with Terry Cummings and Craig Hodges to Milwaukee Bucks for Marques Johnson, Harvey Catchings, Junior Bridgeman and cash (September 29, 1984).... Traded by Bucks to Seattle SuperSonics for Dale Ellis (February 15, 1991).

COLLEGIATE RECORD

Season Team	G	Min.	FGM	FGA	Pct.	FTM	FTA	Pct.	Reb.	Pts.	Avg.
78-79 —Walla Walla C.C.	...	...	...	...	...	...	...	...	...	...	19.0
79-80 —Rice	26	878	202	421	.480	94	131	.718	214	498	19.2
80-81 —Rice	26	901	230	444	.518	84	119	.706	181	544	20.9
81-82 —Rice	30	1104	314	614	.511	177	223	.794	226	805	26.8
Four-year-college totals	82	2883	746	1479	.504	355	473	.751	621	1847	22.5

NBA REGULAR-SEASON RECORD

HONORS: NBA Sixth Man Award (1987, 1990).

									— REBOUNDS —								
Season Team	G	Min.	FGM	FGA	Pct.	FTM	FTA	Pct.	Off.	Def.	Tot.	Ast.	PF	Dq.	Stl.	Blk.	TO	Pts.	Avg.
82-83 —Detroit	39	265	33	88	.375	18	32	.563	15	20	35	14	42	0	8	4	18	85	2.2
83-84 —San Diego	69	1280	268	570	.470	149	173	.861	59	76	135	60	143	1	27	13	81	685	9.9
84-85 —Milwaukee	44	882	165	307	.537	102	124	.823	49	68	117	94	117	0	34	5	63	433	9.8
85-86 —Milwaukee	81	2147	429	798	.538	266	310	.858	94	137	231	177	252	6	83	6	107	1127	13.9
86-87 —Milwaukee	79	2505	575	1077	.534	387	440	.880	117	149	266	144	222	0	64	24	120	1540	19.5
87-88 —Milwaukee	37	965	248	486	.510	107	122	.877	30	53	83	73	94	0	21	7	57	606	16.4
88-89 —Milwaukee	75	2078	527	1018	.518	255	297	.859	82	115	197	156	193	1	77	19	112	1317	17.6
89-90 —Milwaukee	59	1709	503	987	.510	307	366	.839	64	103	167	133	158	2	50	7	129	1359	23.0
90-91 —Mil.-Seattle	78	2167	561	1156	.485	430	471	.913	67	124	191	168	170	1	60	13	147	1598	20.5
91-92 —Seattle	78	2658	620	1306	.475	417	455	.916	93	140	233	241	213	2	86	20	189	1690	21.7
Totals	639	16656	3929	7793	.504	2438	2790	.874	670	985	1655	1260	1604	13	510	118	1023	10440	16.3

Three-point field goals: 1982-83, 1-for-7 (.143). 1983-84, 0-for-9. 1984-85, 1-for-4 (.250). 1985-86, 3-for-23 (.130). 1986-87, 3-for-28 (.107). 1987-88, 3-for-14 (.214). 1988-89, 8-for-36 (.222). 1989-90, 46-for-133 (.346). 1990-91, 46-for-116 (.397). 1991-92, 33-for-123 (.268). Totals, 144-for-493 (.292).

NBA PLAYOFF RECORD

									— REBOUNDS —								
Season Team	G	Min.	FGM	FGA	Pct.	FTM	FTA	Pct.	Off.	Def.	Tot.	Ast.	PF	Dq.	Stl.	Blk.	TO	Pts.	Avg.
84-85 —Milwaukee	8	198	36	73	.493	7	9	.778	8	10	18	15	26	0	3	1	17	79	9.9
85-86 —Milwaukee	13	322	52	113	.460	40	45	.889	20	16	36	20	42	0	8	3	15	144	11.1
86-87 —Milwaukee	12	317	68	142	.479	55	67	.821	12	16	28	16	39	0	10	5	19	191	15.9
87-88 —Milwaukee	5	105	25	53	.472	8	9	.889	6	8	14	9	9	0	1	2	4	59	11.8
88-89 —Milwaukee	9	292	77	141	.546	41	47	.872	5	20	25	25	31	1	11	2	9	201	22.3
89-90 —Milwaukee	4	122	28	60	.467	28	31	.903	6	3	9	6	14	0	5	0	3	89	22.3
90-91 —Seattle	5	112	19	57	.333	16	17	.941	6	8	14	4	12	1	4	1	11	57	11.4
91-92 —Milwaukee	9	316	63	131	.481	47	54	.870	9	13	22	28	24	0	5	1	24	176	19.6
Totals	65	1784	368	770	.478	242	279	.867	72	94	166	123	197	2	47	15	102	996	15.3

Three-point field goals: 1984-85, 0-for-2. 1985-86, 0-for-2. 1987-88, 1-for-5 (.200). 1988-89, 6-for-8 (.750). 1989-90, 5-for-10 (.500). 1990-91, 3-for-10 (.300). 1991-92, 3-for-11 (.273). Totals, 18-for-48 (.375).

P

NBA ALL-STAR GAME RECORD

Season	Team	Min.	FGM	FGA	Pct.	FTM	FTA	Pct.	REBOUNDS Off.	Def.	Tot.	Ast.	PF	Dq.	Stl.	Blk.	TO	Pts.
1991	—Milwaukee	19	4	8	.500	1	1	1.000	0	2	2	2	2	0	0	0	2	9

PINCKNEY, ED
F, CELTICS

PERSONAL: Born March 27, 1963, in Bronx, N.Y. ... 6-9/215. ... Full name: Edward Lewis Pinckney.
HIGH SCHOOL: Adlai E. Stevenson (Bronx, N.Y.).
COLLEGE: Villanova.
TRANSACTIONS/CAREER NOTES: Selected by Phoenix Suns in first round (10th pick overall) of 1985 NBA Draft. ... Traded by Suns with 1988 second-round draft choice to Sacramento Kings for Eddie Johnson (June 21, 1987). ... Traded by Kings with Joe Kleine to Boston Celtics for Danny Ainge and Brad Lohaus (February 23, 1989).

COLLEGIATE RECORD

NOTES: NCAA Division I Tournament Most Outstanding Player (1985). ... Member of NCAA Division I championship team (1985).

Season	Team	G	Min.	FGM	FGA	Pct.	FTM	FTA	Pct.	Reb.	Pts.	Avg.
81-82	—Villanova..............................	32	1083	169	264	.640	115	161	.714	249	453	14.2
82-83	—Villanova..............................	31	1029	129	227	.568	130	171	.760	301	388	12.5
83-84	—Villanova..............................	31	1068	162	268	.604	154	222	.694	246	478	15.4
84-85	—Villanova..............................	35	1186	177	295	.600	192	263	.730	311	546	15.6
	Totals	129	4366	637	1054	.604	591	817	.723	1107	1865	14.5

NBA REGULAR-SEASON RECORD

Season	Team	G	Min.	FGM	FGA	Pct.	FTM	FTA	Pct.	REBOUNDS Off.	Def.	Tot.	Ast.	PF	Dq.	Stl.	Blk.	TO	Pts.	Avg.
85-86	—Phoenix.......	80	1602	255	457	.558	171	254	.673	95	213	308	90	190	3	71	37	148	681	8.5
86-87	—Phoenix.......	80	2250	290	497	.584	257	348	.739	179	401	580	116	196	1	86	54	135	837	10.5
87-88	—Sacramento .	79	1177	179	343	.522	133	178	.747	94	136	230	66	118	0	39	32	77	491	6.2
88-89	—Sac.-Boston	80	2012	319	622	.513	280	350	.800	166	283	449	118	202	2	83	66	119	918	11.5
89-90	—Boston	77	1082	135	249	.542	92	119	.773	93	132	225	68	126	1	34	42	56	362	4.7
90-91	—Boston	70	1165	131	243	.539	104	116	.897	155	186	341	45	147	0	61	43	45	366	5.2
91-92	—Boston	81	1917	203	378	.537	207	255	.812	252	312	564	62	158	1	70	56	73	613	7.6
	Totals	547	11205	1512	2789	.542	1244	1620	.768	1034	1663	2697	565	1137	8	444	330	653	4268	7.8

Three-point field goals: 1985-86, 0-for-2. 1986-87, 0-for-2. 1987-88, 0-for-2. 1988-89, 0-for-6. 1989-90, 0-for-1. 1990-91, 0-for-1. 1991-92, 0-for-1. Totals, 0-for-15.

NBA PLAYOFF RECORD

Season	Team	G	Min.	FGM	FGA	Pct.	FTM	FTA	Pct.	REBOUNDS Off.	Def.	Tot.	Ast.	PF	Dq.	Stl.	Blk.	TO	Pts.	Avg.
88-89	—Boston	3	45	3	12	.250	2	2	1.000	2	3	5	1	7	0	1	1	4	8	2.7
89-90	—Boston	4	25	6	7	.857	7	9	.778	2	4	6	0	3	0	0	2	19	4.8
90-91	—Boston	11	170	16	21	.762	17	21	.810	23	17	40	2	17	0	6	2	2	49	4.5
91-92	—Boston	10	314	35	58	.603	26	31	.839	36	48	84	7	30	0	12	9	13	96	9.6
	Totals	28	554	60	98	.612	52	63	.825	63	72	135	10	57	0	19	12	21	172	6.1

Three-point field goals: 1991-92, 0-for-1.

PIPPEN, SCOTTIE
F/G, BULLS

PERSONAL: Born September 25, 1965, in Hamburg, Ark. ... 6-7/210.
HIGH SCHOOL: Hamburg (Ark.).
COLLEGE: Central Arkansas.
TRANSACTIONS/CAREER NOTES: Selected by Seattle SuperSonics in first round (fifth pick overall) of 1987 NBA Draft. ... Draft rights traded by SuperSonics to Chicago Bulls for draft rights to Olden Polynice, 1988 or 1989 second-round draft choice and option to exchange 1989 first-round draft choices (June 22, 1987).
MISCELLANEOUS: Member of NBA championship teams (1991, 1992). ... Member of gold-medal-winning U.S. Olympic team (1992).

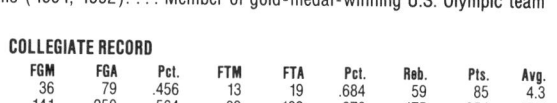

COLLEGIATE RECORD

Season	Team	G	Min.	FGM	FGA	Pct.	FTM	FTA	Pct.	Reb.	Pts.	Avg.
83-84	—Central Arkansas	20	...	36	79	.456	13	19	.684	59	85	4.3
84-85	—Central Arkansas	19	...	141	250	.564	69	102	.676	175	351	18.5
85-86	—Central Arkansas	29	...	229	412	.556	116	169	.686	266	574	19.8
86-87	—Central Arkansas	25	...	231	390	.592	105	146	.719	249	590	23.6
	Totals	93	...	637	1131	.563	303	436	.695	749	1600	17.2

Three-point field goals: 1986-87, 23-for-40 (.575).

NBA REGULAR-SEASON RECORD

HONORS: All-NBA second team (1992). ... NBA All-Defensive first team (1992). ... NBA All-Defensive second team (1991).

Season	Team	G	Min.	FGM	FGA	Pct.	FTM	FTA	Pct.	REBOUNDS Off.	Def.	Tot.	Ast.	PF	Dq.	Stl.	Blk.	TO	Pts.	Avg.
87-88	—Chicago.......	79	1650	261	564	.463	99	172	.576	115	183	298	169	214	3	91	52	131	625	7.9
88-89	—Chicago.......	73	2413	413	867	.476	201	301	.668	138	307	445	256	261	8	139	61	199	1048	14.4
89-90	—Chicago.......	82	3148	562	1150	.489	199	295	.675	150	397	547	444	298	6	211	101	278	1351	16.5
90-91	—Chicago.......	82	3014	600	1153	.520	240	340	.706	163	432	595	511	270	3	193	93	232	1461	17.8
91-92	—Chicago.......	82	3164	687	1359	.506	330	434	.760	185	445	630	572	242	2	155	93	253	1720	21.0
	Totals	398	13389	2523	5093	.495	1069	1542	.693	751	1764	2515	1952	1285	22	789	400	1093	6205	15.6

Three-point field goals: 1987-88, 4-for-23 (.174). 1988-89, 21-for-77 (.273). 1989-90, 28-for-112 (.250). 1990-91, 21-for-68 (.309). 1991-92, 16-for-80 (.200). Totals, 90-for-360 (.250).

NBA PLAYOFF RECORD

Season	Team	G	Min.	FGM	FGA	Pct.	FTM	FTA	Pct.	Off.	Def.	Tot.	Ast.	PF	Dq.	Stl.	Blk.	TO	Pts.	Avg.
87-88	Chicago	10	294	46	99	.465	5	7	.714	24	28	52	24	33	1	8	8	26	100	10.0
88-89	Chicago	17	619	84	182	.462	32	50	.640	34	95	129	67	63	2	23	16	41	222	13.1
89-90	Chicago	15	612	104	210	.495	71	100	.710	33	75	108	83	62	0	31	19	49	289	19.3
90-91	Chicago	17	704	142	282	.504	80	101	.792	37	114	151	99	58	1	42	19	55	368	21.6
91-92	Chicago	22	899	152	325	.468	118	155	.761	59	134	193	147	72	1	41	25	70	428	19.5
	Totals	81	3128	528	1098	.481	306	413	.741	187	446	633	420	288	5	145	87	241	1407	17.4

Three-point field goals: 1987-88, 3-for-6 (.500). 1988-89, 22-for-56 (.393). 1989-90, 10-for-31 (.323). 1990-91, 4-for-17 (.235). 1991-92, 6-for-24 (.250). Totals, 45-for-134 (.336).

NBA ALL-STAR GAME RECORD

Season	Team	Min.	FGM	FGA	Pct.	FTM	FTA	Pct.	Off.	Def.	Tot.	Ast.	PF	Dq.	Stl.	Blk.	TO	Pts.
1990	Chicago	12	2	4	.500	0	0	...	0	1	1	0	1	0	1	1	1	4
1992	Chicago	21	6	13	.462	2	3	.667	4	0	4	1	0	0	2	1	1	14
	Totals	33	8	17	.471	2	3	.667	4	1	5	1	1	0	3	2	2	18

Three-point field goals: 1990, 0-for-1.

POLYNICE, OLDEN
C, PISTONS

PERSONAL: Born November 21, 1964, in Port-au-Prince, Haiti.... 7-0/250.... Name pronounced POL-a-niece.
HIGH SCHOOL: All Hallows Institute (Bronx, N.Y.).
COLLEGE: Virginia.
TRANSACTIONS/CAREER NOTES: Played in Italy (1986-87).... Selected as undergraduate by Chicago Bulls in first round (eighth pick overall) of 1987 NBA Draft.... Draft rights traded by Bulls with 1988 or 1989 second-round draft choice and option to exchange 1989 first-round draft choices to Seattle SuperSonics for draft rights to Scottie Pippen (June 22, 1987).... Traded by SuperSonics with 1991 first-round draft choice and 1993 or 1994 first-round draft choice to Los Angeles Clippers for Benoit Benjamin (February 20, 1991).... Traded by Clippers with 1996 and 1997 second-round draft choices to Detroit Pistons for William Bedford and rights to Don MacLean (June 24, 1992).

COLLEGIATE RECORD

Season	Team	G	Min.	FGM	FGA	Pct.	FTM	FTA	Pct.	Reb.	Pts.	Avg.
83-84	Virginia	33	866	98	178	.551	57	97	.588	184	253	7.7
84-85	Virginia	32	1095	161	267	.603	94	157	.599	243	416	13.0
85-86	Virginia	30	1074	183	320	.572	116	182	.637	240	482	16.1
	Totals	95	3035	442	765	.578	267	436	.612	667	1151	12.1

ITALIAN LEAGUE RECORD

Season	Team	G	Min.	FGM	FGA	Pct.	FTM	FTA	Pct.	Reb.	Pts.	Avg.
86-87	Rimini	30	968	214	378	.566	82	137	.599	330	518	17.3

NBA REGULAR-SEASON RECORD

Season	Team	G	Min.	FGM	FGA	Pct.	FTM	FTA	Pct.	Off.	Def.	Tot.	Ast.	PF	Dq.	Stl.	Blk.	TO	Pts.	Avg.
87-88	Seattle	82	1080	118	254	.465	101	158	.639	122	208	330	33	215	1	32	26	81	337	4.1
88-89	Seattle	80	835	91	180	.506	51	86	.593	98	108	206	21	164	0	37	30	46	233	2.9
89-90	Seattle	79	1085	156	289	.540	47	99	.475	128	172	300	15	187	0	25	21	35	360	4.6
90-91	Seattle-LAC	79	2092	316	564	.560	146	252	.579	220	333	553	42	192	1	43	32	88	778	9.8
91-92	L.A. Clippers	76	1834	244	470	.519	125	201	.622	195	341	536	46	165	0	45	20	83	613	8.1
	Totals	396	6926	925	1757	.526	470	796	.590	763	1162	1925	157	923	2	182	129	333	2321	5.9

Three-point field goals: 1987-88, 0-for-2. 1988-89, 0-for-2. 1989-90, 1-for-2 (.500). 1990-91, 0-for-1. 1991-92, 0-for-1. Totals, 1-for-8 (.125).

NBA PLAYOFF RECORD

Season	Team	G	Min.	FGM	FGA	Pct.	FTM	FTA	Pct.	Off.	Def.	Tot.	Ast.	PF	Dq.	Stl.	Blk.	TO	Pts.	Avg.
87-88	Seattle	5	44	5	11	.455	0	2	.000	2	6	8	0	6	0	3	0	1	10	2.0
88-89	Seattle	8	162	25	41	.610	7	13	.538	27	35	62	1	32	1	6	4	5	57	7.1
91-92	L.A. Clippers	5	63	7	12	.583	2	6	.333	2	16	18	2	11	0	1	1	1	16	3.2
	Totals	18	269	37	64	.578	9	21	.429	31	57	88	3	49	1	10	5	7	83	4.6

POPSON, DAVE
F/C

PERSONAL: Born May 17, 1964, in Kingston, Pa.... 6-10/220.... Full name: David G. Popson.
HIGH SCHOOL: Bishop O'Reilly (Kingston, Pa.).
COLLEGE: North Carolina.
TRANSACTIONS/CAREER NOTES: Selected by Detroit Pistons in fourth round (88th pick overall) of 1987 NBA Draft.... Played in France (1987-88).... Waived by Pistons (November 1, 1988).... Claimed off waivers by Los Angeles Clippers (November 3, 1988).... Waived by Clippers (November 14, 1988).... Re-signed as free agent by Clippers (November 17, 1988).... Waived by Clippers (December 8, 1988).... Played in Continental Basketball Association with Albany Patroons (1988-89, 1989-90 and 1991-92) and Birmingham Bandits (1991-92).... Re-signed by Clippers to 10-day contract (January 8, 1989).... Signed by Miami Heat to first of two consecutive 10-day contracts (March 22, 1989).... Re-signed by Heat for remainder of season (April 12, 1989).... Signed as free agent by Boston Celtics (August 17, 1990).... Waived by Celtics (December 24, 1990).... Re-signed as free agent by Celtics (December 27, 1990).... Rights renounced by Celtics (June 1991).... Signed as free agent by Atlanta Hawks (October 3, 1991).... Waived by Hawks (October 29, 1991). ... Signed by Milwaukee Bucks to first of two consecutive 10-day contracts (March 4, 1992).

P

COLLEGIATE RECORD

Season	Team	G	Min.	FGM	FGA	Pct.	FTM	FTA	Pct.	Reb.	Pts.	Avg.
83-84	North Carolina	29	185	25	58	.431	6	10	.600	35	56	1.9
84-85	North Carolina	35	507	90	170	.529	31	42	.738	87	211	6.0
85-86	North Carolina	34	411	61	121	.504	11	13	.846	88	133	3.9
86-87	North Carolina	36	803	153	283	.541	54	70	.771	172	360	10.0
Totals		134	1906	329	632	.521	102	135	.756	382	760	5.7

Three-point field goals: 1986-87, 0-for-1.

NBA REGULAR-SEASON RECORD

Season	Team	G	Min.	FGM	FGA	Pct.	FTM	FTA	Pct.	Off.	Def.	Tot.	Ast.	PF	Dq.	Stl.	Blk.	TO	Pts.	Avg.
88-89	LAC-Miami..	17	106	16	40	.400	2	4	.500	12	15	27	8	17	0	1	3	10	34	2.0
90-91	Boston	19	64	13	32	.406	9	10	.900	7	7	14	2	12	0	1	2	6	35	1.8
91-92	Milwaukee ...	5	26	3	7	.429	1	2	.500	2	3	5	3	5	0	2	1	4	7	1.4
Totals		41	196	32	79	.405	12	16	.750	21	25	46	13	34	0	4	6	20	76	1.9

Three-point field goals: 1991-92, 0-for-1.

CBA REGULAR-SEASON RECORD

| Season | Team | G | Min. | 2-POINT | | | 3-POINT | | | FTM | FTA | Pct. | Reb. | Ast. | Pts. | Avg. |
				FGM	FGA	Pct.	FGM	FGA	Pct.							
88-89	Albany	14	300	69	127	.543	0	0	...	16	28	.571	85	13	154	11.0
89-90	Albany	10	233	44	94	.468	0	1	.000	10	10	1.000	59	13	98	9.8
91-92	Albany-Birm....	39	1129	177	417	.424	1	5	.200	61	81	.753	250	37	418	10.7
Totals		63	1662	290	638	.455	1	6	.167	87	119	.731	394	63	670	10.6

PORTER, TERRY
G, TRAIL BLAZERS

PERSONAL: Born April 8, 1963, in Milwaukee.... 6-3/195.
HIGH SCHOOL: South Division (Milwaukee).
COLLEGE: Wisconsin-Stevens Point.
TRANSACTIONS/CAREER NOTES: Selected by Portland Trail Blazers in first round (24th pick overall) of 1985 NBA Draft.

COLLEGIATE RECORD

Season	Team	G	Min.	FGM	FGA	Pct.	FTM	FTA	Pct.	Reb.	Pts.	Avg.
81-82	Wisconsin-Stevens Point	25	273	21	57	.368	9	13	.692	13	51	2.0
82-83	Wisconsin-Stevens Point	30	949	140	229	.611	62	89	.697	117	342	11.4
83-84	Wisconsin-Stevens Point	32	1040	244	392	.622	112	135	.830	165	600	18.8
84-85	Wisconsin-Stevens Point	30	1042	233	405	.575	126	151	.834	155	592	19.7
Totals		117	3304	638	1083	.589	309	388	.796	450	1585	13.5

NBA REGULAR-SEASON RECORD

Season	Team	G	Min.	FGM	FGA	Pct.	FTM	FTA	Pct.	Off.	Def.	Tot.	Ast.	PF	Dq.	Stl.	Blk.	TO	Pts.	Avg.
85-86	Portland	79	1214	212	447	.474	125	155	.806	35	82	117	198	136	0	81	1	106	562	7.1
86-87	Portland	80	2714	376	770	.488	280	334	.838	70	267	337	715	192	0	159	9	255	1045	13.1
87-88	Portland	82	2991	462	890	.519	274	324	.846	65	313	378	831	204	0	150	16	244	1222	14.9
88-89	Portland	81	3102	540	1146	.471	272	324	.840	85	282	367	770	187	1	146	8	248	1431	17.7
89-90	Portland	80	2781	448	969	.462	421	472	.892	59	213	272	726	150	0	151	4	245	1406	17.6
90-91	Portland	81	2665	486	944	.515	279	339	.823	52	230	282	649	151	2	158	12	189	1381	17.0
91-92	Portland	82	2784	521	1129	.461	315	368	.856	51	204	255	477	155	1	127	12	188	1485	18.1
Totals		565	18251	3045	6295	.484	1966	2316	.849	417	1591	2008	4366	1175	5	972	62	1475	8532	15.1

Three-point field goals: 1985-86, 13-for-42 (.310). 1986-87, 13-for-60 (.217). 1987-88, 24-for-69 (.348). 1988-89, 72-for-219 (.329). 1989-90, 89-for-238 (.374). 1990-91, 130-for-313 (.415). 1991-92, 128-for-324 (.395). Totals, 469-for-1265 (.371).

NBA PLAYOFF RECORD

NOTES: Shares NBA Finals single-game record for most three-point field goal attempts—9 (June 14, 1990, vs. Detroit).

Season	Team	G	Min.	FGM	FGA	Pct.	FTM	FTA	Pct.	Off.	Def.	Tot.	Ast.	PF	Dq.	Stl.	Blk.	TO	Pts.	Avg.
85-86	Portland	4	68	12	27	.444	2	4	.500	1	4	5	12	10	0	3	2	6	27	6.8
86-87	Portland	4	150	24	50	.480	18	20	.900	1	18	19	40	14	0	10	2	13	68	17.0
87-88	Portland	4	149	29	52	.558	9	13	.692	4	10	14	28	13	0	10	0	13	68	17.0
88-89	Portland	3	124	26	52	.500	10	12	.833	6	10	16	25	8	0	1	1	7	66	22.0
89-90	Portland	21	815	127	274	.464	139	165	.842	9	52	61	155	51	1	28	3	62	433	20.6
90-91	Portland	16	595	102	204	.500	68	79	.861	8	36	44	105	32	0	24	1	32	289	18.1
91-92	Portland	21	870	147	285	.516	119	143	.832	25	72	97	141	49	0	22	3	46	450	21.4
Totals		73	2771	467	944	.495	365	436	.837	54	202	256	506	177	1	98	12	179	1401	19.2

Three-point field goals: 1985-86, 1-for-6 (.167). 1986-87, 2-for-5 (.400). 1987-88, 1-for-3 (.333). 1988-89, 4-for-11 (.364). 1989-90, 40-for-102 (.392). 1990-91, 17-for-47 (.362). 1991-92, 37-for-78 (.474). Totals, 102-for-252 (.405).

NBA ALL-STAR GAME RECORD

Season	Team	Min.	FGM	FGA	Pct.	FTM	FTA	Pct.	Off.	Def.	Tot.	Ast.	PF	Dq.	Stl.	Blk.	TO	Pts.
1991	Portland	15	2	6	.333	0	0	...	1	2	3	4	2	0	2	1	3	4

Three-point field goals: 1991, 0-for-2.

DID YOU KNOW. . .

... that Kurt Rambis has the highest field-goal percentage (150 field goals minimum) in playoff history? Rambis has shot .574 (284 for 495) in 139 games.

PRESSEY, PAUL
G/F

PERSONAL: Born December 24, 1958, in Richmond, Va. . . . 6-5/200. . . . Full name: Paul Matthew Pressey.
HIGH SCHOOL: George Wythe (Richmond, Va.).
COLLEGE: Western Texas, then Tulsa.
TRANSACTIONS/CAREER NOTES: Selected by Milwaukee Bucks in first round (20th pick overall) of 1982 NBA Draft. . . . Traded by Bucks to San Antonio Spurs for Frank Brickowski (August 1, 1990).

COLLEGIATE RECORD

Season Team	G	Min.	FGM	FGA	Pct.	FTM	FTA	Pct.	Reb.	Pts.	Avg.
78-79 — Western Texas	33	. . .	191	286	.668	78	103	.757	262	460	13.9
79-80 — Western Texas	37	. . .	213	327	.651	93	122	.762	291	519	14.0
80-81 — Tulsa	33	1050	137	288	.476	66	114	.579	178	340	10.3
81-82 — Tulsa	30	973	154	275	.560	87	131	.664	192	395	13.2
Junior college totals	70		404	613	.659	171	225	.760	553	979	14.0
Four-year-college totals	63	2023	291	563	.517	153	245	.624	370	735	11.7

NBA REGULAR-SEASON RECORD

HONORS: NBA All-Defensive first team (1985, 1986). . . . NBA All-Defensive second team (1987).

Season Team	G	Min.	FGM	FGA	Pct.	FTM	FTA	Pct.	Off.	Def.	Tot.	Ast.	PF	Dq.	Stl.	Blk.	TO	Pts.	Avg.
82-83 — Milwaukee ...	79	1528	213	466	.457	105	176	.597	83	198	281	207	174	2	99	47	162	532	6.7
83-84 — Milwaukee ...	81	1730	276	528	.523	120	200	.600	102	180	282	252	241	6	86	50	157	674	8.3
84-85 — Milwaukee ...	80	2876	480	928	.517	317	418	.758	149	280	429	543	258	4	129	56	247	1284	16.1
85-86 — Milwaukee ...	80	2704	411	843	.488	316	392	.806	127	272	399	623	247	4	168	71	240	1146	14.3
86-87 — Milwaukee ...	61	2057	294	616	.477	242	328	.738	98	198	296	441	213	4	110	47	186	846	13.9
87-88 — Milwaukee ...	75	2484	345	702	.491	285	357	.798	130	245	375	523	233	6	112	34	198	983	13.1
88-89 — Milwaukee ...	67	2170	307	648	.474	187	241	.776	73	189	262	439	221	2	119	44	184	813	12.1
89-90 — Milwaukee ...	57	1400	239	506	.472	144	190	.758	59	113	172	244	149	3	71	23	109	628	11.0
90-91 — San Antonio .	70	1683	201	426	.472	110	133	.827	50	126	176	271	174	1	63	32	130	528	7.5
91-92 — San Antonio .	56	759	60	161	.373	28	41	.683	22	73	95	142	86	0	29	19	64	151	2.7
Totals	706	19391	2826	5824	.485	1854	2476	.749	893	1874	2767	3685	1996	32	986	423	1677	7585	10.7

Three-point field goals: 1982-83, 1-for-9 (.111). 1983-84, 2-for-9 (.222). 1984-85, 7-for-20 (.350). 1985-86, 8-for-44 (.182). 1986-87, 16-for-55 (.291). 1987-88, 8-for-39 (.205). 1988-89, 12-for-55 (.218). 1989-90, 6-for-43 (.140). 1990-91, 16-for-57 (.281). 1991-92, 3-for-21 (.143). Totals, 79-for-352 (.224).

NBA PLAYOFF RECORD

Season Team	G	Min.	FGM	FGA	Pct.	FTM	FTA	Pct.	Off.	Def.	Tot.	Ast.	PF	Dq.	Stl.	Blk.	TO	Pts.	Avg.
82-83 — Milwaukee ...	9	150	19	47	.404	8	20	.400	14	19	33	14	23	0	9	6	18	46	5.1
83-84 — Milwaukee ...	16	351	52	100	.520	38	56	.679	17	42	59	50	53	1	22	9	38	142	8.9
84-85 — Milwaukee ...	8	296	45	88	.511	31	38	.816	15	33	48	61	27	1	18	5	32	122	15.3
85-86 — Milwaukee ...	14	530	76	157	.484	67	88	.761	19	41	60	110	48	0	18	13	50	225	16.1
86-87 — Milwaukee ...	12	465	68	146	.466	34	46	.739	28	34	62	103	51	3	28	8	35	171	14.3
87-88 — Milwaukee ...	5	178	23	50	.460	23	30	.767	6	13	19	33	21	0	4	3	16	70	14.0
89-90 — Milwaukee ...	4	129	19	44	.432	21	26	.808	8	13	21	30	14	0	6	1	7	59	14.8
90-91 — San Antonio .	4	124	13	32	.406	6	9	.667	5	6	11	16	15	0	8	3	6	33	8.3
91-92 — San Antonio .	3	46	6	18	.333	0	0	. . .	1	2	3	3	9	1	3	1	5	13	4.3
Totals	75	2269	321	682	.471	228	313	.728	113	203	316	420	261	6	116	49	207	881	11.7

Three-point field goals: 1982-83, 0-for-1. 1983-84, 0-for-3. 1984-85, 1-for-3 (.333). 1985-86, 6-for-18 (.333). 1986-87, 1-for-8 (.125). 1987-88, 1-for-3 (.333). 1989-90, 0-for-3. 1990-91, 1-for-4 (.250). 1991-92, 1-for-2 (.500). Totals, 11-for-45 (.244).

PRICE, MARK
G, CAVALIERS

PERSONAL: Born February 15, 1964, in Bartlesville, Okla. . . . 6-0/178. . . . Full name: William Mark Price. . . . Brother of Brent Price, guard with Washington Bullets.
HIGH SCHOOL: Enid (Okla.).
COLLEGE: Georgia Tech.
TRANSACTIONS/CAREER NOTES: Selected by Dallas Mavericks in second round (25th pick overall) of 1986 NBA Draft. . . . Draft rights traded by Mavericks to Cleveland Cavaliers for 1989 second-round draft choice and cash (June 17, 1986).

COLLEGIATE RECORD

Season Team	G	Min.	FGM	FGA	Pct.	FTM	FTA	Pct.	Reb.	Pts.	Avg.
82-83 — Georgia Tech	28	1020	201	462	.435	93	106	.877	105	568	20.3
83-84 — Georgia Tech	29	1078	191	375	.509	70	85	.824	61	452	15.6
84-85 — Georgia Tech	35	1302	223	462	.483	137	163	.840	71	583	16.7
85-86 — Georgia Tech	34	1204	233	441	.528	124	145	.855	94	590	17.4
Totals	126	4604	848	1740	.487	424	499	.850	331	2193	17.4

Three-point field goals: 1982-83, 73-for-166 (.440).

NBA REGULAR-SEASON RECORD

HONORS: All-NBA third team (1989, 1992).

Season Team	G	Min.	FGM	FGA	Pct.	FTM	FTA	Pct.	Off.	Def.	Tot.	Ast.	PF	Dq.	Stl.	Blk.	TO	Pts.	Avg.
86-87 — Cleveland	67	1217	173	424	.408	95	114	.833	33	84	117	202	75	1	43	4	105	464	6.9
87-88 — Cleveland	80	2626	493	974	.506	221	252	.877	54	126	180	480	119	1	99	12	184	1279	16.0
88-89 — Cleveland	75	2728	529	1006	.526	263	292	.901	48	178	226	631	98	0	115	7	212	1414	18.9
89-90 — Cleveland	73	2706	489	1066	.459	300	338	.888	66	185	251	666	89	0	114	5	214	1430	19.6
90-91 — Cleveland	16	571	97	195	.497	59	62	.952	8	37	45	166	23	0	42	2	56	271	16.9
91-92 — Cleveland	72	2138	438	897	.488	270	285	*.947	38	135	173	535	113	0	94	12	159	1247	17.3
Totals	383	11986	2219	4562	.486	1208	1343	.899	247	745	992	2680	517	2	507	42	930	6105	15.9

P

Three-point field goals: 1986-87, 23-for-70 (.329). 1987-88, 72-for-148 (.486). 1988-89, 93-for-211 (.441). 1989-90, 152-for-374 (.406). 1990-91, 18-for-53 (.340). 1991-92, 101-for-261 (.387). Totals, 459-for-1117 (.411).

NBA PLAYOFF RECORD

Season Team	G	Min.	FGM	FGA	Pct.	FTM	FTA	Pct.	REBOUNDS Off.	Def.	Tot.	Ast.	PF	Dq.	Stl.	Blk.	TO	Pts.	Avg.
87-88 — Cleveland.....	5	205	38	67	.567	24	25	.960	3	15	18	38	11	1	3	0	8	105	21.0
88-89 — Cleveland.....	4	158	22	57	.386	14	15	.933	4	9	13	22	3	0	3	0	19	64	16.0
89-90 — Cleveland.....	5	192	32	61	.525	30	30	1.000	0	14	14	44	9	0	9	1	15	100	20.0
91-92 — Cleveland.....	17	603	118	238	.496	66	73	.904	10	32	42	128	34	0	24	4	56	327	19.2
Totals	31	1158	210	423	.496	134	143	.937	17	70	87	232	57	1	39	5	98	596	19.2

Three-point field goals: 1987-88, 5-for-12 (.417). 1988-89, 6-for-16 (.375). 1989-90, 6-for-17 (.353). 1991-92, 25-for-69 (.362). Totals, 42-for-114 (.368).

NBA ALL-STAR GAME RECORD

Season Team	Min.	FGM	FGA	Pct.	FTM	FTA	Pct.	REBOUNDS Off.	Def.	Tot.	Ast.	PF	Dq.	Stl.	Blk.	TO	Pts.
1989 — Cleveland...........	20	3	9	.333	2	2	1.000	1	2	3	1	2	0	2	0	2	9
1992 — Cleveland...........	15	1	5	.200	4	4	1.000	0	0	0	3	1	0	1	0	3	6
Totals	35	4	14	.286	6	6	1.000	1	2	3	4	3	0	3	0	5	15

Three-point field goals: 1989, 1-for-4 (.250). 1992, 0-for-3. Totals, 1-for-7 (.143).

PRITCHARD, KEVIN
G

PERSONAL: Born July 17, 1967, in Bloomington, Ind. ... 6-3/180. ... Full name: Kevin Lee Pritchard.
HIGH SCHOOL: Thomas Edison (Tulsa, Okla.).
COLLEGE: Kansas.

TRANSACTIONS/CAREER NOTES: Selected by Golden State Warriors in second round (34th pick overall) of 1990 NBA Draft. ... Traded by Warriors to San Antonio Spurs for future considerations (May 17, 1991). ... Waived by Spurs (October 28, 1991). ... Signed as free agent by Boston Celtics (October 30, 1991). ... Waived by Celtics (November 25, 1991). ... Signed as free agent by Celtics (November 27, 1991). ... Waived by Celtics (January 7, 1992).

COLLEGIATE RECORD

NOTES: Member of NCAA Division I championship team (1988).

Season Team	G	Min.	FGM	FGA	Pct.	FTM	FTA	Pct.	Reb.	Pts.	Avg.
86-87 — Kansas..................................	36	962	134	294	.456	41	54	.759	77	345	9.6
87-88 — Kansas..................................	37	1100	144	296	.486	88	119	.740	95	393	10.6
88-89 — Kansas..................................	31	944	155	306	.507	83	108	.769	76	448	14.5
89-90 — Kansas..................................	35	976	177	337	.525	106	130	.815	89	506	14.5
Totals	139	3982	610	1233	.495	318	411	.774	337	1692	12.2

Three-point field goals: 1986-87, 36-for-88 (.409). 1987-88, 17-for-54 (.315). 1988-89, 55-for-129 (.426). 1989-90, 46-for-108 (.426). Totals, 154-for-379 (.406).

NBA REGULAR-SEASON RECORD

Season Team	G	Min.	FGM	FGA	Pct.	FTM	FTA	Pct.	REBOUNDS Off.	Def.	Tot.	Ast.	PF	Dq.	Stl.	Blk.	TO	Pts.	Avg.
90-91 — Golden State	62	773	88	229	.384	62	77	.805	16	49	65	81	104	1	30	8	59	243	3.9
91-92 — Boston	11	136	16	34	.471	14	18	.778	1	10	11	30	17	0	3	4	11	46	4.2
Totals	73	909	104	263	.395	76	95	.800	17	59	76	111	121	1	33	12	70	289	4.0

Three-point field goals: 1990-91, 5-for-31 (.161). 1991-92, 0-for-3. Totals, 5-for-34 (.147).

QUINNETT, BRIAN
F

PERSONAL: Born May 30, 1966, in Pullman, Wash. ... 6-8/235. ... Full name: Brian Ralph Quinnett. ... Name pronounced Qui-NETT.
HIGH SCHOOL: Cheney (Wash.).
COLLEGE: Washington State.

TRANSACTIONS/CAREER NOTES: Selected by New York Knicks in second round (50th pick overall) of 1989 NBA Draft. ... Traded by Knicks to Dallas Mavericks for James Donaldson (February 20, 1992).

COLLEGIATE RECORD

NOTES: Suffered broken foot (November 1987); granted additional year of eligibility.

Season Team	G	Min.	FGM	FGA	Pct.	FTM	FTA	Pct.	Reb.	Pts.	Avg.
84-85 — Washington State..................	24	517	63	133	.474	16	21	.762	77	142	5.9
85-86 — Washington State..................	31	815	122	250	.488	29	49	.592	138	273	8.8
86-87 — Washington State..................	28	944	186	373	.499	53	75	.707	145	462	16.5
87-88 — Washington State..................	1	29	6	16	.375	3	4	.750	8	15	15.0
88-89 — Washington State..................	28	917	210	437	.481	76	105	.724	164	516	18.4
Totals	112	3222	587	1209	.486	177	254	.697	532	1408	12.6

Three-point field goals: 1986-87, 37-for-94 (.394). 1987-88, 0-for-1. 1988-89, 20-for-55 (.364). Totals, 57-for-150 (.380).

NBA REGULAR-SEASON RECORD

Season Team	G	Min.	FGM	FGA	Pct.	FTM	FTA	Pct.	REBOUNDS Off.	Def.	Tot.	Ast.	PF	Dq.	Stl.	Blk.	TO	Pts.	Avg.
89-90 — New York	31	193	19	58	.328	2	3	.667	9	19	28	11	27	0	3	4	4	40	1.3
90-91 — New York	68	1011	139	303	.459	26	36	.722	65	80	145	53	100	0	22	13	52	319	4.7
91-92 — N.Y.-Dallas..	39	326	43	124	.347	16	26	.615	16	35	51	12	32	0	16	8	16	115	2.9
Totals	138	1530	201	485	.414	44	65	.677	90	134	224	76	159	0	41	25	72	474	3.4

Three-point field goals: 1989-90, 0-for-2. 1990-91, 15-for-43 (.349). 1991-92, 13-for-41 (.317). Totals, 28-for-86 (.326).

NBA PLAYOFF RECORD

									— REBOUNDS —									
Season Team	G	Min.	FGM	FGA	Pct.	FTM	FTA	Pct.	Off.	Def.	Tot.	Ast.	PF	Dq.	Stl.	Blk.	TO	Pts.	Avg.
89-90 — New York	3	16	2	4	.500	0	0	...	5	3	8	2	2	0	0	0	1	5	1.7
90-91 — New York	3	36	4	8	.500	0	0	...	0	1	1	3	2	0	1	0	2	9	3.0
Totals	6	52	6	12	.500	0	0	...	5	4	9	5	4	0	1	0	3	14	2.3

Three-point field goals: 1989-90, 1-for-1. 1990-91, 1-for-3 (.333). Totals, 2-for-4 (.500).

RAMBIS, KURT
F, SUNS

PERSONAL: Born February 25, 1958, in Cupertino, Calif. . . . 6-8/213. . . . Full name: Darrell Kurt Rambis.
HIGH SCHOOL: Cupertino (Calif.).
COLLEGE: Santa Clara.
TRANSACTIONS/CAREER NOTES: Selected by New York Knicks in third round (58th pick overall) of 1980 NBA Draft. . . . Waived by Knicks (September 18, 1980). . . . Played in Greece (1980-81). . . . Re-signed by Knicks to 10-day contract (January 1981). . . . Signed as free agent by Los Angeles Lakers (September 13, 1981). . . . Signed as unrestricted free agent by Charlotte Hornets (July 28, 1988). . . . Traded by Hornets with two 1990 second-round draft choices to Phoenix Suns for Armon Gilliam (December 13, 1989).
MISCELLANEOUS: Member of NBA championship teams (1982, 1985, 1987, 1988).

COLLEGIATE RECORD

Season Team	G	Min.	FGM	FGA	Pct.	FTM	FTA	Pct.	Reb.	Pts.	Avg.
76-77 — Santa Clara	27	...	167	317	.527	70	125	.560	313	404	15.0
77-78 — Santa Clara	27	...	136	268	.507	99	143	.692	231	371	13.7
78-79 — Santa Clara	27	763	172	336	.512	78	109	.716	226	422	15.6
79-80 — Santa Clara	27	860	211	395	.534	107	168	.637	267	529	19.6
Totals	108	...	686	1316	.521	354	545	.650	1037	1726	16.0

NBA REGULAR-SEASON RECORD

									— REBOUNDS —									
Season Team	G	Min.	FGM	FGA	Pct.	FTM	FTA	Pct.	Off.	Def.	Tot.	Ast.	PF	Dq.	Stl.	Blk.	TO	Pts.	Avg.
81-82 — Los Angeles .	64	1131	118	228	.518	59	117	.504	116	232	348	56	167	2	60	76	77	295	4.6
82-83 — Los Angeles .	78	1806	235	413	.569	114	166	.687	164	367	531	90	233	2	105	63	145	584	7.5
83-84 — Los Angeles .	47	743	63	113	.558	42	66	.636	82	184	266	34	108	0	30	14	56	168	3.6
84-85 — L.A. Lakers ..	82	1617	181	327	.554	68	103	.660	164	364	528	69	211	0	82	47	97	430	5.2
85-86 — L.A. Lakers ..	74	1573	160	269	.595	88	122	.721	156	361	517	69	198	0	66	33	97	408	5.5
86-87 — L.A. Lakers ..	78	1514	163	313	.521	120	157	.764	159	294	453	63	201	1	74	41	104	446	5.7
87-88 — L.A. Lakers ..	70	845	102	186	.548	73	93	.785	103	165	268	54	103	0	39	13	59	277	4.0
88-89 — Charlotte.....	75	2233	325	627	.518	182	248	.734	269	434	703	159	208	4	100	57	148	832	11.1
89-90 — Char.-Phoe..	74	1904	190	373	.509	82	127	.646	156	369	525	135	208	0	100	37	104	462	6.2
90-91 — Phoenix.......	62	900	83	167	.497	60	85	.706	77	189	266	64	107	1	25	11	45	226	3.6
91-92 — Phoenix.......	28	381	38	82	.463	14	18	.778	23	83	106	37	46	0	12	14	25	90	3.2
Totals	732	14647	1658	3098	.535	902	1302	.693	1469	3042	4511	830	1790	10	693	406	957	4218	5.8

Three-point field goals: 1981-82, 0-for-1. 1982-83, 0-for-2. 1988-89, 0-for-3. 1989-90, 0-for-3. 1990-91, 0-for-2. Totals, 0-for-11.

NBA PLAYOFF RECORD

NOTES: Holds career record for highest field-goal percentage (minimum 150 made) — .574.

									— REBOUNDS —									
Season Team	G	Min.	FGM	FGA	Pct.	FTM	FTA	Pct.	Off.	Def.	Tot.	Ast.	PF	Dq.	Stl.	Blk.	TO	Pts.	Avg.
81-82 — Los Angeles .	14	279	33	64	.516	16	26	.615	32	54	86	11	47	0	8	12	17	82	5.9
82-83 — Los Angeles .	15	377	45	79	.570	23	35	.657	27	63	90	19	51	0	13	16	23	113	7.5
83-84 — Los Angeles .	21	428	60	92	.652	21	33	.636	33	88	121	14	57	0	10	10	22	141	6.7
84-85 — L.A. Lakers ..	19	375	48	81	.593	19	28	.679	42	87	129	17	52	0	18	9	19	115	6.1
85-86 — L.A. Lakers ..	14	267	27	45	.600	13	18	.722	26	57	83	14	39	0	10	7	18	67	4.8
86-87 — L.A. Lakers ..	17	215	24	41	.585	31	34	.912	16	51	67	9	42	0	8	3	13	79	4.6
87-88 — L.A. Lakers ..	19	186	21	34	.618	9	13	.692	13	38	51	9	28	0	5	2	8	51	2.7
89-90 — Phoenix.......	16	385	24	54	.444	19	28	.679	39	84	123	22	51	0	8	8	17	67	4.2
90-91 — Phoenix.......	4	53	2	5	.400	0	0	...	8	6	14	4	6	0	5	1	4	4	1.0
Totals	139	2565	284	495	.574	151	215	.702	236	528	764	119	373	0	85	68	141	719	5.2

Three-point field goals: 1989-90, 0-for-1.

RANDALL, MARK
F, TIMBERWOLVES

PERSONAL: Born September 30, 1967, in Edina, Minn. . . . 6-9/235. . . . Full name: Mark Christopher Randall.
HIGH SCHOOL: Cherry Creek (Englewood, Colo.).
COLLEGE: Kansas.
TRANSACTIONS/CAREER NOTES: Selected by Chicago Bulls in first round (26th pick overall) of 1991 NBA Draft. . . . Waived by Bulls (December 30, 1991). . . . Claimed off waivers by Minnesota Timberwolves (January 2, 1992).

COLLEGIATE RECORD

Season Team	G	Min.	FGM	FGA	Pct.	FTM	FTA	Pct.	Reb.	Pts.	Avg.
86-87 — Kansas	31	325	54	102	.529	32	51	.627	83	140	4.5
87-88 — Kansas					Did not play — jaw and sinus surgery.						
88-89 — Kansas	31	844	201	311	.646	95	145	.655	208	497	16.0
89-90 — Kansas	35	902	183	305	.600	100	148	.676	216	466	13.3
90-91 — Kansas	35	1025	205	319	.643	113	178	.635	216	524	15.0
Totals	132	3096	643	1037	.620	340	522	.651	723	1627	12.3

Three-point field goals: 1988-89, 0-for-1. 1989-90, 0-for-1. 1990-91, 1-for-4 (.250). Totals, 1-for-6 (.167).

NBA REGULAR-SEASON RECORD

Season Team	G	Min.	FGM	FGA	Pct.	FTM	FTA	Pct.	Off.	Def.	Tot.	Ast.	PF	Dq.	Stl.	Blk.	TO	Pts.	Avg.
91-92 —Chi.-Min.	54	441	68	149	.456	32	43	.744	39	32	71	33	39	0	12	3	25	171	3.2

Three-point field goals: 1991-92, 3-for-16 (.188).

RASMUSSEN, BLAIR
C, HAWKS

PERSONAL: Born November 13, 1962, in Auburn, Wash. . . . 7-0/260. . . . Full name: Blair Allen Rasmussen. . . . Name pronounced RASS-muss-en.
HIGH SCHOOL: Auburn (Wash.).

COLLEGE: Oregon.
TRANSACTIONS/CAREER NOTES: Selected by Denver Nuggets in first round (15th pick overall) of 1985 NBA Draft. . . . Traded by Nuggets to Atlanta Hawks in three-way deal in which Hawks sent draft rights to Anthony Avent to Milwaukee Bucks and Bucks sent draft rights to Kevin Brooks to Nuggets (July 1, 1991); Nuggets also received Bucks' 1994 second-round draft choice and other considerations.

COLLEGIATE RECORD

Season Team	G	Min.	FGM	FGA	Pct.	FTM	FTA	Pct.	Reb.	Pts.	Avg.
81-82 —Oregon	27	521	67	141	.475	39	53	.736	129	173	6.4
82-83 —Oregon	27	819	160	296	.541	80	116	.690	146	400	14.8
83-84 —Oregon	29	1017	196	377	.520	90	112	.804	176	482	16.6
84-85 —Oregon	31	1081	195	381	.512	109	151	.722	222	499	16.1
Totals	114	3438	618	1195	.517	318	432	.736	673	1554	13.6

NBA REGULAR-SEASON RECORD

Season Team	G	Min.	FGM	FGA	Pct.	FTM	FTA	Pct.	Off.	Def.	Tot.	Ast.	PF	Dq.	Stl.	Blk.	TO	Pts.	Avg.
85-86 —Denver	48	330	61	150	.407	31	39	.795	37	60	97	16	63	0	3	10	40	153	3.2
86-87 —Denver	74	1421	268	570	.470	169	231	.732	183	282	465	60	224	6	24	58	79	705	9.5
87-88 —Denver	79	1779	435	884	.492	132	170	.776	130	307	437	78	241	2	22	81	73	1002	12.7
88-89 —Denver	77	1308	257	577	.445	69	81	.852	105	182	287	49	194	2	29	41	49	583	7.6
89-90 —Denver	81	1995	445	895	.497	111	134	.828	174	420	594	82	300	10	40	104	75	1001	12.4
90-91 —Denver	70	2325	405	885	.458	63	93	.677	170	508	678	70	307	*15	52	132	81	875	12.5
91-92 —Atlanta........	81	1968	347	726	.478	30	40	.750	94	299	393	107	233	1	35	48	51	729	9.0
Totals	510	11126	2218	4687	.473	605	788	.768	893	2058	2951	462	1562	36	205	474	448	5048	9.9

Three-point field goals: 1989-90, 0-for-1. 1990-91, 2-for-5 (.400). 1991-92, 5-for-23 (.217). Totals, 7-for-29 (.241).

NBA PLAYOFF RECORD

Season Team	G	Min.	FGM	FGA	Pct.	FTM	FTA	Pct.	Off.	Def.	Tot.	Ast.	PF	Dq.	Stl.	Blk.	TO	Pts.	Avg.
85-86 —Denver	10	175	39	96	.406	33	41	.805	27	33	60	10	28	1	5	9	7	111	11.1
86-87 —Denver	3	92	22	45	.489	5	10	.500	8	15	23	7	12	0	2	2	5	49	16.3
87-88 —Denver	11	277	60	127	.472	18	20	.900	25	46	71	7	33	0	1	12	6	138	12.5
88-89 —Denver	2	4	0	0	. . .	0	0	. . .	0	0	0	0	1	0	0	0	1	0	0.0
89-90 —Denver	3	84	19	48	.396	9	10	.900	8	18	26	1	10	0	2	4	2	47	15.7
Totals	29	632	140	316	.443	65	81	.802	68	112	180	25	84	1	10	27	21	345	11.9

REID, J.R.
F/C, HORNETS

PERSONAL: Born March 31, 1968, in Virginia Beach, Va. . . . 6-9/256. . . . Full name: Herman Reid Jr.
HIGH SCHOOL: Kempsville (Virginia Beach, Va.).
COLLEGE: North Carolina.
TRANSACTIONS/CAREER NOTES: Selected as undergraduate by Charlotte Hornets in first round (fifth pick overall) of 1989 NBA Draft.
MISCELLANEOUS: Member of bronze-medal-winning U.S. Olympic team (1988).

COLLEGIATE RECORD

NOTES: THE SPORTING NEWS All-America second team (1988).

Season Team	G	Min.	FGM	FGA	Pct.	FTM	FTA	Pct.	Reb.	Pts.	Avg.
86-87 —North Carolina	36	1030	198	339	.584	132	202	.653	268	528	14.7
87-88 —North Carolina	33	1042	222	366	.607	151	222	.680	293	595	18.0
88-89 —North Carolina	27	716	164	267	.614	101	151	.669	170	429	15.9
Totals	96	2788	584	972	.601	384	575	.668	731	1552	16.2

NBA REGULAR-SEASON RECORD

HONORS: NBA All-Rookie second team (1990).

Season Team	G	Min.	FGM	FGA	Pct.	FTM	FTA	Pct.	Off.	Def.	Tot.	Ast.	PF	Dq.	Stl.	Blk.	TO	Pts.	Avg.
89-90 —Charlotte......	82	2757	358	814	.440	192	289	.664	199	492	691	101	292	7	92	54	172	908	11.1
90-91 —Charlotte......	80	2467	360	773	.466	182	259	.703	154	348	502	89	286	6	87	47	153	902	11.3
91-92 —Charlotte......	51	1257	213	435	.490	134	190	.705	96	221	317	81	159	0	49	23	84	560	11.0
Totals	213	6481	931	2022	.460	508	738	.688	449	1061	1510	271	737	13	228	124	409	2370	11.1

Three-point field goals: 1989-90, 0-for-5. 1990-91, 0-for-2. 1991-92, 0-for-3. Totals, 0-for-10.

REYNOLDS, JERRY
G/F, MAGIC

PERSONAL: Born December 23, 1962, in Brooklyn, N.Y. . . . 6-8/206. . . . Nickname: Ice.
HIGH SCHOOL: Alexander Hamilton (Elmsford, N.Y.).
COLLEGE: Madison Area Technical College (Wisc.), then Louisiana State.
TRANSACTIONS/CAREER NOTES: Selected as undergraduate by Milwaukee Bucks in first round (22nd pick

overall) of 1985 NBA Draft. . . . Traded by Bucks to Seattle SuperSonics for 1990 second-round draft choice (October 4, 1988). . . . Selected by Orlando Magic from SuperSonics in NBA expansion draft (June 15, 1989).

COLLEGIATE RECORD

Season Team	G	Min.	FGM	FGA	Pct.	FTM	FTA	Pct.	Reb.	Pts.	Avg.
81-82 —Madison Area Tech..................						Did not play.					
82-83 —Louisiana State	32	888	126	236	.534	88	142	.620	198	340	10.6
83-84 —Louisiana State	29	899	162	307	.528	85	158	.538	239	409	14.1
84-85 —Louisiana State	29	803	128	255	.502	64	107	.598	176	320	11.0
Four-year-college totals	90	2590	416	798	.521	237	407	.582	613	1069	11.9

NBA REGULAR-SEASON RECORD

									— REBOUNDS —									
Season Team	G	Min.	FGM	FGA	Pct.	FTM	FTA	Pct.	Off.	Def.	Tot.	Ast.	PF	Dq.	Stl.	Blk.	TO	Pts.	Avg.
85-86 —Milwaukee ...	55	508	72	162	.444	58	104	.558	37	43	80	86	57	0	43	19	52	203	3.7
86-87 —Milwaukee ...	58	963	140	356	.393	118	184	.641	72	101	173	106	91	0	50	30	82	404	7.0
87-88 —Milwaukee ...	62	1161	188	419	.449	119	154	.773	70	90	160	104	97	0	74	32	104	498	8.0
88-89 —Seattle.........	56	737	149	357	.417	127	167	.760	49	51	100	62	58	0	53	26	57	428	7.6
89-90 —Orlando	67	1817	309	741	.417	239	322	.742	91	232	323	180	162	1	93	64	139	858	12.8
90-91 —Orlando	80	1843	344	793	.434	336	419	.802	88	211	299	203	123	0	95	56	172	1034	12.9
91-92 —Orlando	46	1159	197	518	.380	158	189	.836	47	102	149	151	69	0	63	17	96	555	12.1
Totals	424	8188	1399	3346	.418	1155	1539	.750	454	830	1284	892	657	1	471	244	702	3980	9.4

Three-point field goals: 1985-86, 1-for-2 (.500). 1986-87, 6-for-18 (.333). 1987-88, 3-for-7 (.429). 1988-89, 3-for-15 (.200). 1989-90, 1-for-14 (.071). 1990-91, 10-for-34 (.294). 1991-92, 3-for-24 (.125). Totals, 27-for-114 (.237).

NBA PLAYOFF RECORD

									— REBOUNDS —									
Season Team	G	Min.	FGM	FGA	Pct.	FTM	FTA	Pct.	Off.	Def.	Tot.	Ast.	PF	Dq.	Stl.	Blk.	TO	Pts.	Avg.
85-86 —Milwaukee ...	7	40	7	17	.412	6	11	.545	3	6	9	4	5	0	4	3	4	20	2.9
86-87 —Milwaukee ...	4	5	1	3	.333	1	2	.500	1	0	1	2	0	0	3	0	0	3	0.8
87-88 —Milwaukee ...	3	12	4	6	.667	0	0	. . .	0	1	1	1	1	0	0	0	1	8	2.7
88-89 —Seattle.........	4	40	7	22	.318	7	10	.700	1	4	5	1	6	0	2	6	4	22	5.5
Totals	18	97	19	48	.396	14	23	.609	5	11	16	8	12	0	9	9	9	53	2.9

Three-point field goals: 1985-86, 0-for-1. 1986-87, 0-for-1. 1988-89, 1-for-4 (.250). Totals, 1-for-6 (.167).

RICE, GLEN
F/G, HEAT

PERSONAL: Born May 28, 1967, in Flint, Mich. . . . 6-8/220. . . . Full name: Glen Anthony Rice.
HIGH SCHOOL: Northwestern Community (Flint, Mich.).
COLLEGE: Michigan.
TRANSACTIONS/CAREER NOTES: Selected by Miami Heat in first round (fourth pick overall) of 1989 NBA Draft.

COLLEGIATE RECORD

NOTES: THE SPORTING NEWS All-America second team (1989). . . . Most Outstanding Player in NCAA Division I tournament (1989). . . . Member of NCAA Division I championship team (1989).

Season Team	G	Min.	FGM	FGA	Pct.	FTM	FTA	Pct.	Reb.	Pts.	Avg.
85-86 —Michigan..............................	32	520	105	191	.550	15	25	.600	97	225	7.0
86-87 —Michigan..............................	32	1056	226	402	.562	85	108	.787	294	540	16.9
87-88 —Michigan..............................	33	. . .	308	539	.571	79	98	.806	236	728	22.1
88-89 —Michigan..............................	37	1258	363	629	.577	124	149	.832	232	949	25.6
Totals	134	. . .	1002	1761	.569	303	380	.797	859	2442	18.2

Three-point field goals: 1986-87, 3-for-12 (.250). 1987-88, 33-for-77 (.429). 1988-89, 99-for-192 (.516). Totals, 135-for-281 (.480).

NBA REGULAR-SEASON RECORD

HONORS: NBA All-Rookie second team (1990).

									— REBOUNDS —									
Season Team	G	Min.	FGM	FGA	Pct.	FTM	FTA	Pct.	Off.	Def.	Tot.	Ast.	PF	Dq.	Stl.	Blk.	TO	Pts.	Avg.
89-90 —Miami..........	77	2311	470	1071	.439	91	124	.734	100	252	352	138	198	1	67	27	113	1048	13.6
90-91 —Miami..........	77	2646	550	1193	.461	171	209	.818	85	296	381	189	216	0	101	26	166	1342	17.4
91-92 —Miami..........	79	3007	672	1432	.469	266	318	.836	84	310	394	184	170	0	90	35	145	1765	22.3
Totals	233	7964	1692	3696	.458	528	651	.811	269	858	1127	511	584	1	258	88	424	4155	17.8

Three-point field goals: 1989-90, 17-for-69 (.246). 1990-91, 71-for-184 (.386). 1991-92, 155-for-396 (.391). Totals, 243-for-649 (.374).

NBA PLAYOFF RECORD

									— REBOUNDS —									
Season Team	G	Min.	FGM	FGA	Pct.	FTM	FTA	Pct.	Off.	Def.	Tot.	Ast.	PF	Dq.	Stl.	Blk.	TO	Pts.	Avg.
91-92 —Miami..........	3	119	24	64	.375	6	7	.857	3	7	10	5	7	0	2	0	6	57	19.0

Three-point field goals: 1991-92, 3-for-12 (.250).

RICHARDSON, POOH
G, PACERS

PERSONAL: Born May 14, 1966, in Philadelphia. . . . 6-1/180. . . . Full name: Jerome Richardson Jr.
HIGH SCHOOL: Benjamin Franklin (Philadelphia).
COLLEGE: UCLA.
TRANSACTIONS/CAREER NOTES: Selected by Minnesota Timberwolves in first round (10th pick overall) of 1989 NBA Draft. . . . Traded by Timberwolves with Sam Mitchell to Indiana Pacers for Chuck Person and Micheal Williams (September 8, 1992).

COLLEGIATE RECORD

Season Team	G	Min.	FGM	FGA	Pct.	FTM	FTA	Pct.	Reb.	Pts.	Avg.
85-86 — UCLA	29	983	128	260	.492	51	74	.689	131	307	10.6
86-87 — UCLA	32	1112	144	273	.527	46	79	.582	163	336	10.5
87-88 — UCLA	30	1035	142	302	.470	62	93	.667	153	348	11.6
88-89 — UCLA	31	1167	186	335	.555	50	89	.562	118	470	15.2
Totals	122	4297	600	1170	.513	209	335	.624	565	1461	12.0

Three-point field goals: 1986-87, 2-for-8 (.250). 1987-88, 2-for-7 (.286). 1988-89, 48-for-97 (.495). Totals, 52-for-112 (.464).

NBA REGULAR-SEASON RECORD

HONORS: NBA All-Rookie first team (1990).

Season Team	G	Min.	FGM	FGA	Pct.	FTM	FTA	Pct.	— REBOUNDS — Off.	Def.	Tot.	Ast.	PF	Dq.	Stl.	Blk.	TO	Pts.	Avg.
89-90 — Minnesota....	82	2581	426	925	.461	63	107	.589	55	162	217	554	143	0	133	25	141	938	11.4
90-91 — Minnesota....	82	3154	635	1350	.470	89	165	.539	82	204	286	734	114	0	131	13	174	1401	17.1
91-92 — Minnesota....	82	2922	587	1261	.466	123	178	.691	91	210	301	685	152	0	119	25	204	1350	16.5
Totals	246	8657	1648	3536	.466	275	450	.611	228	576	804	1973	409	0	383	63	519	3689	15.0

Three-point field goals: 1989-90, 23-for-83 (.277). 1990-91, 42-for-128 (.328). 1991-92, 53-for-155 (.342). Totals, 118-for-366 (.322).

RICHMOND, MITCH
G, KINGS

PERSONAL: Born June 30, 1965, in Fort Lauderdale, Fla. . . . 6-5/215. . . . Full name: Mitchell James Richmond.
HIGH SCHOOL: Boyd Anderson (Fort Lauderdale, Fla.).
COLLEGE: Moberly Area Junior College (Mo.), then Kansas State.
TRANSACTIONS/CAREER NOTES: Selected by Golden State Warriors in first round (fifth pick overall) of 1988 NBA Draft. . . . Traded by Warriors with Les Jepsen to Sacramento Kings for Billy Owens (November 1, 1991).
MISCELLANEOUS: Member of bronze-medal-winning U.S. Olympic team (1988).

COLLEGIATE RECORD

NOTES: THE SPORTING NEWS All-America second team (1988).

Season Team	G	Min.	FGM	FGA	Pct.	FTM	FTA	Pct.	Reb.	Pts.	Avg.
84-85 — Moberly Area Junior College ...	40	...	180	375	.480	55	85	.647	185	415	10.4
85-86 — Moberly Area Junior College ...	38	...	242	506	.478	124	180	.689	251	608	16.0
86-87 — Kansas State	30	964	201	450	.447	118	155	.761	170	559	18.6
87-88 — Kansas State	34	1200	268	521	.514	186	240	.775	213	768	22.6
Junior college totals	78		422	881	.479	179	265	.675	436	1023	13.1
Four-year-college totals	64	2164	469	971	.483	304	395	.770	383	1327	20.7

Three-point field goals: 1986-87, 39-for-108 (.361). 1987-88, 46-for-98 (.469). Totals, 85-for-206 (.413).

NBA REGULAR-SEASON RECORD

HONORS: NBA Rookie of the Year (1989). . . . NBA All-Rookie first team (1989).

Season Team	G	Min.	FGM	FGA	Pct.	FTM	FTA	Pct.	— REBOUNDS — Off.	Def.	Tot.	Ast.	PF	Dq.	Stl.	Blk.	TO	Pts.	Avg.
88-89 — Golden State	79	2717	649	1386	.468	410	506	.810	158	310	468	334	223	5	82	13	269	1741	22.0
89-90 — Golden State	78	2799	640	1287	.497	406	469	.866	98	262	360	223	210	3	98	24	201	1720	22.1
90-91 — Golden State	77	3027	703	1424	.494	394	465	.847	147	305	452	238	207	0	126	34	230	1840	23.9
91-92 — Sacramento .	80	3095	685	1465	.468	330	406	.813	62	257	319	411	231	1	92	34	247	1803	22.5
Totals	314	11638	2677	5562	.481	1540	1846	.834	465	1134	1599	1206	871	9	398	105	947	7104	22.6

Three-point field goals: 1988-89, 33-for-90 (.367). 1989-90, 34-for-95 (.358). 1990-91, 40-for-115 (.348). 1991-92, 103-for-268 (.384). Totals, 210-for-568 (.370).

NBA PLAYOFF RECORD

Season Team	G	Min.	FGM	FGA	Pct.	FTM	FTA	Pct.	— REBOUNDS — Off.	Def.	Tot.	Ast.	PF	Dq.	Stl.	Blk.	TO	Pts.	Avg.
88-89 — Golden State	8	314	62	135	.459	34	38	.895	10	48	58	35	25	0	14	1	24	161	20.1
90-91 — Golden State	9	372	85	169	.503	23	24	.958	10	37	47	22	28	1	5	6	17	201	22.3
Totals	17	686	147	304	.484	57	62	.919	20	85	105	57	53	1	19	7	41	362	21.3

Three-point field goals: 1988-89, 3-for-16 (.188). 1990-91, 8-for-24 (.333). Totals, 11-for-40 (.275).

RIVERS, DAVID
G

PERSONAL: Born January 20, 1965, in Jersey City, N.J. . . . 6-0/180. . . . Full name: David Lee Rivers.
HIGH SCHOOL: St. Anthony's (Jersey City, N.J.).
COLLEGE: Notre Dame.
TRANSACTIONS/CAREER NOTES: Selected by Los Angeles Lakers in first round (25th pick overall) of 1988 NBA Draft. . . . Selected by Minnesota Timberwolves from Lakers in NBA expansion draft (June 15, 1989). . . . Waived by Timberwolves (November 2, 1989). . . . Signed as free agent by Los Angeles Clippers (November 14, 1989). . . . Played in Continental Basketball Association with Tulsa Fast Breakers (1990-91) and La Crosse Catbirds (1991-92). . . . Signed as free agent by Clippers (November 23, 1991). . . . Waived by Clippers (January 7, 1992).

COLLEGIATE RECORD

Season Team	G	Min.	FGM	FGA	Pct.	FTM	FTA	Pct.	Reb.	Pts.	Avg.
84-85 — Notre Dame	30	1068	168	398	.422	138	173	.798	78	474	15.8
85-86 — Notre Dame	28	930	159	353	.450	149	186	.801	84	467	16.7
86-87 — Notre Dame	32	1179	172	380	.453	134	159	.843	116	501	15.7
87-88 — Notre Dame	28	1027	205	462	.444	162	199	.814	115	616	22.0
Totals	118	4204	704	1593	.442	583	717	.813	393	2058	17.4

Three-point field goals: 1986-87, 23-for-60 (.383). 1987-88, 44-for-105 (.419). Totals, 67-for-165 (.406).

NBA REGULAR-SEASON RECORD

Season Team	G	Min.	FGM	FGA	Pct.	FTM	FTA	Pct.	Off.	Def.	Tot.	Ast.	PF	Dq.	Stl.	Blk.	TO	Pts.	Avg.
88-89 —L.A. Lakers ..	47	440	49	122	.402	35	42	.833	13	30	43	106	50	0	23	9	61	134	2.9
89-90 —L.A. Clippers	52	724	80	197	.406	59	78	.756	30	55	85	155	53	0	31	0	88	219	4.2
91-92 —L.A. Clippers	15	122	10	30	.333	10	11	.909	10	9	19	21	14	0	7	1	17	30	2.0
Totals	114	1286	139	349	.398	104	131	.794	53	94	147	282	117	0	61	10	166	383	3.4

Three-point field goals: 1988-89, 1-for-6 (.167). 1989-90, 0-for-5. 1991-92, 0-for-1. Totals, 1-for-12 (.083).

NBA PLAYOFF RECORD

Season Team	G	Min.	FGM	FGA	Pct.	FTM	FTA	Pct.	Off.	Def.	Tot.	Ast.	PF	Dq.	Stl.	Blk.	TO	Pts.	Avg.
88-89 —L.A. Lakers ..	6	33	4	12	.333	7	8	.875	1	3	4	6	6	0	0	0	4	15	2.5

Three-point field goals: 1988-89, 0-for-2.

CBA REGULAR-SEASON RECORD

NOTES: Led CBA with 12.9 assists per game (1992).

Season Team	G	Min.	2-POINT FGM	FGA	Pct.	3-POINT FGM	FGA	Pct.	FTM	FTA	Pct.	Reb.	Ast.	Pts.	Avg.
90-91 —Tulsa...............	34	1169	166	335	.496	22	66	.333	146	174	.839	131	257	544	16.0
91-92 —La Crosse........	32	1270	199	419	.475	13	42	.310	161	205	.785	101	414	598	18.7
Totals	66	2439	365	754	.484	35	108	.324	307	379	.810	232	671	1142	17.3

RIVERS, DOC
G, CLIPPERS

PERSONAL: Born October 13, 1961, in Chicago. . . . 6-4/185. . . . Full name: Glenn Anton Rivers. . . . Nephew of Jim Brewer, forward with four NBA teams (1973-74 through 1981-82); cousin of Byron Irvin, guard with Portland Trail Blazers and Washington Bullets (1989-90 and 1990-91); and cousin of Ken Singleton, outfielder/designated hitter with New York Mets, Montreal Expos and Baltimore Orioles (1970-84).

HIGH SCHOOL: Proviso East (Maywood, Ill.).

COLLEGE: Marquette.

TRANSACTIONS/CAREER NOTES: Selected as undergraduate by Atlanta Hawks in second round (31st pick overall) of 1983 NBA Draft. . . . Traded by Hawks to Los Angeles Clippers for 1991 first-round draft choices and 1993 and 1994 second-round draft choices (June 26, 1991).

COLLEGIATE RECORD

Season Team	G	Min.	FGM	FGA	Pct.	FTM	FTA	Pct.	Reb.	Pts.	Avg.
80-81 —Marquette	31	...	182	329	.553	70	119	.588	99	434	14.0
81-82 —Marquette	29	...	173	382	.453	70	108	.648	99	416	14.3
82-83 —Marquette	29	...	163	373	.437	58	95	.611	94	384	13.2
Totals	89	...	518	1084	.478	198	322	.615	292	1234	13.9

NBA REGULAR-SEASON RECORD

Season Team	G	Min.	FGM	FGA	Pct.	FTM	FTA	Pct.	Off.	Def.	Tot.	Ast.	PF	Dq.	Stl.	Blk.	TO	Pts.	Avg.
83-84 —Atlanta........	81	1938	250	541	.462	255	325	.785	72	148	220	314	286	8	127	30	174	757	9.3
84-85 —Atlanta........	69	2126	334	701	.476	291	378	.770	66	148	214	410	250	7	163	53	176	974	14.1
85-86 —Atlanta........	53	1571	220	464	.474	172	283	.608	49	113	162	443	185	2	120	13	141	612	11.5
86-87 —Atlanta........	82	2590	342	758	.451	365	441	.828	83	216	299	823	287	5	171	30	217	1053	12.8
87-88 —Atlanta........	80	2502	403	890	.453	319	421	.758	83	283	366	747	272	3	140	41	210	1134	14.2
88-89 —Atlanta........	76	2462	371	816	.455	247	287	.861	89	197	286	525	263	6	181	40	158	1032	13.6
89-90 —Atlanta........	48	1526	218	480	.454	138	170	.812	47	153	200	264	151	2	116	22	98	598	12.5
90-91 —Atlanta........	79	2586	444	1020	.435	221	262	.844	47	206	253	340	216	2	148	47	125	1197	15.2
91-92 —L.A. Clippers	59	1657	226	533	.424	163	196	.832	23	124	147	233	166	2	111	19	92	641	10.9
Totals	627	18958	2808	6203	.453	2171	2763	.786	559	1588	2147	4099	2076	37	1277	295	1391	7998	12.8

Three-point field goals: 1983-84, 2-for-12 (.167). 1984-85, 15-for-36 (.417). 1985-86, 0-for-16. 1986-87, 4-for-21 (.190). 1987-88, 9-for-33 (.273). 1988-89, 43-for-124 (.347). 1989-90, 24-for-66 (.364). 1990-91, 88-for-262 (.336). 1991-92, 26-for-92 (.283). Totals, 211-for-662 (.319).

NBA PLAYOFF RECORD

NOTES: Shares single-game record for most assists in one half—15 (May 16, 1988, vs. Boston).

Season Team	G	Min.	FGM	FGA	Pct.	FTM	FTA	Pct.	Off.	Def.	Tot.	Ast.	PF	Dq.	Stl.	Blk.	TO	Pts.	Avg.
83-84 —Atlanta........	5	130	16	32	.500	36	41	.878	7	3	10	16	16	0	12	4	9	68	13.6
85-86 —Atlanta........	9	262	40	92	.435	31	42	.738	10	32	42	78	38	2	18	0	26	114	12.7
86-87 —Atlanta........	8	245	18	47	.383	26	52	.500	6	21	27	90	32	0	9	3	25	62	7.8
87-88 —Atlanta........	12	409	71	139	.511	39	43	.907	8	51	59	115	40	1	25	2	25	188	15.7
88-89 —Atlanta........	5	191	22	57	.386	17	24	.708	4	20	24	34	22	2	7	2	12	67	13.4
90-91 —Atlanta........	5	173	30	64	.469	17	19	.895	6	14	20	15	14	0	5	2	4	78	15.6
91-92 —L.A. Clippers	5	187	25	56	.446	22	27	.815	4	15	19	21	16	0	6	0	3	76	15.2
Totals	49	1597	222	487	.456	188	248	.758	45	156	201	369	178	5	82	13	104	653	13.3

Three-point field goals: 1983-84, 0-for-3. 1985-86, 3-for-6 (.500). 1987-88, 7-for-22 (.318). 1988-89, 6-for-19 (.316). 1990-91, 1-for-11 (.091). 1991-92, 4-for-8 (.500). Totals, 21-for-69 (.304).

NBA ALL-STAR GAME RECORD

Season Team	Min.	FGM	FGA	Pct.	FTM	FTA	Pct.	Off.	Def.	Tot.	Ast.	PF	Dq.	Stl.	Blk.	TO	Pts.
1988 —Atlanta...............	16	2	4	.500	5	11	.455	0	3	3	6	3	0	0	0	3	9

ROBERTS, FRED
F, BUCKS

PERSONAL: Born August 14, 1960, in Provo, Utah. . . . 6-10/218. . . . Full name: Frederick Clark Roberts.
HIGH SCHOOL: Bingham (South Jordan, Utah).
COLLEGE: Brigham Young.
TRANSACTIONS/CAREER NOTES: Selected by Milwaukee Bucks in second round (27th pick overall) of 1982 NBA Draft. . . . Draft rights traded by Bucks with Mickey Johnson to New Jersey Nets for Phil Ford and 1983 second-round draft choice (November 10, 1982). . . . Played in Italy (1982-83). . . . Draft rights traded by Nets with 1983 second-round draft choice and cash to San Antonio Spurs in exchange for the Spurs' relinquishing their rights to Coach Stan Albeck (June 7, 1983). . . . Traded by Spurs to Utah Jazz for 1986 and 1988 second-round draft choices (December 18, 1984). . . . Traded by Jazz to Boston Celtics for 1987 third-round draft choice (September 25, 1986). . . . Selected by Miami Heat from Celtics in NBA expansion draft (June 23, 1988). . . . Traded by Heat to Bucks for 1988 second-round draft choice (June 23, 1988).

COLLEGIATE RECORD

Season Team	G	Min.	FGM	FGA	Pct.	FTM	FTA	Pct.	Reb.	Pts.	Avg.
78-79—Brigham Young	28	861	158	291	.543	83	106	.783	191	399	14.3
79-80—Brigham Young	29	891	151	257	.588	71	98	.724	177	373	12.9
80-81—Brigham Young	32	1188	216	373	.579	171	220	.777	255	603	18.8
81-82—Brigham Young	30	1118	162	338	.479	142	178	.798	215	466	15.5
Totals	119	4058	687	1259	.546	467	602	.776	838	1841	15.5

ITALIAN LEAGUE RECORD

Season Team	G	Min.	FGM	FGA	Pct.	FTM	FTA	Pct.	Reb.	Pts.	Avg.
82-83—Fort. Bologna	30	1114	233	462	.504	106	148	.716	258	572	19.1

NBA REGULAR-SEASON RECORD

Season Team	G	Min.	FGM	FGA	Pct.	FTM	FTA	Pct.	Off.	Def.	Tot.	Ast.	PF	Dq.	Stl.	Blk.	TO	Pts.	Avg.
83-84—San Antonio	79	1531	214	399	.536	144	172	.837	102	202	304	98	219	4	52	38	100	573	7.3
84-85—S.A.-Utah	74	1178	208	418	.498	150	182	.824	78	108	186	87	141	0	28	22	89	567	7.7
85-86—Utah	58	469	74	167	.443	67	87	.770	31	49	80	27	72	0	8	6	53	216	3.7
86-87—Boston	73	1079	139	270	.515	124	153	.810	54	136	190	62	129	1	22	20	89	402	5.5
87-88—Boston	74	1032	161	330	.488	128	165	.776	60	102	162	81	118	0	16	15	68	450	6.1
88-89—Milwaukee	71	1251	155	319	.486	104	129	.806	68	141	209	66	126	0	36	23	80	417	5.9
89-90—Milwaukee	82	2235	330	666	.496	195	249	.783	107	204	311	147	210	5	56	25	130	857	10.5
90-91—Milwaukee	82	2114	357	670	.533	170	209	.813	107	174	281	135	190	2	63	29	135	888	10.8
91-92—Milwaukee	80	1746	311	645	.482	128	171	.749	103	154	257	122	177	0	52	40	122	769	9.6
Totals	673	12635	1949	3884	.502	1210	1517	.798	710	1270	1980	825	1382	12	333	218	866	5139	7.6

Three-point field goals: 1983-84, 1-for-4 (.250). 1984-85, 1-for-1. 1985-86, 1-for-2 (.500). 1986-87, 0-for-3. 1987-88, 0-for-6. 1988-89, 3-for-14 (.214). 1989-90, 2-for-11 (.182). 1990-91, 4-for-25 (.160). 1991-92, 19-for-37 (.514). Totals, 31-for-103 (.301).

NBA PLAYOFF RECORD

Season Team	G	Min.	FGM	FGA	Pct.	FTM	FTA	Pct.	Off.	Def.	Tot.	Ast.	PF	Dq.	Stl.	Blk.	TO	Pts.	Avg.
84-85—Utah	10	130	19	43	.442	16	20	.800	6	11	17	9	16	0	7	3	14	54	5.4
85-86—Utah	4	31	7	15	.467	8	9	.889	4	3	7	3	5	0	0	0	6	22	5.5
86-87—Boston	20	265	30	59	.508	31	44	.705	15	18	33	12	47	0	6	3	12	91	4.6
87-88—Boston	15	100	11	21	.524	7	11	.636	8	8	16	3	20	1	3	0	6	29	1.9
88-89—Milwaukee	9	345	49	100	.490	34	40	.850	11	28	39	20	29	1	5	4	13	132	14.7
89-90—Milwaukee	4	79	13	20	.650	13	16	.813	5	3	8	3	9	0	1	1	5	39	9.8
90-91—Milwaukee	3	103	16	35	.457	2	2	1.000	4	11	15	7	5	0	2	1	5	34	11.3
Totals	65	1053	145	293	.495	111	142	.782	53	82	135	57	131	2	23	12	61	401	6.2

Three-point field goals: 1988-89, 0-for-3. 1989-90, 0-for-1. 1990-91, 0-for-1. Totals, 0-for-5.

ROBERTS, STANLEY
C, MAGIC

PERSONAL: Born February 7, 1970, in Hopkins, S.C. . . . 7-0/285. . . . Full name: Stanley Corvet Roberts.
HIGH SCHOOL: Lower Richland (Hopkins, S.C.).
COLLEGE: Louisiana State.
TRANSACTIONS/CAREER NOTES: Played in Spain with Real Madrid (1990-91). . . . Selected by Orlando Magic in first round (23rd pick overall) of 1991 NBA Draft.

COLLEGIATE RECORD

Season Team	G	Min.	FGM	FGA	Pct.	FTM	FTA	Pct.	Reb.	Pts.	Avg.
88-89—Louisiana State					Did not play—ineligible.						
89-90—Louisiana State	32	859	200	347	.576	51	111	.459	315	451	14.1
Totals	32	859	200	347	.576	51	111	.459	315	451	14.1

SPANISH LEAGUE RECORD

Season Team	G	Min.	FGM	FGA	Pct.	FTM	FTA	Pct.	Reb.	Pts.	Avg.
90-91—Real Madrid	34	992	172	286	.601	53	111	.477	296	397	11.7

HONORS: NBA All-Rookie second team (1992).

NBA REGULAR-SEASON RECORD

Season Team	G	Min.	FGM	FGA	Pct.	FTM	FTA	Pct.	Off.	Def.	Tot.	Ast.	PF	Dq.	Stl.	Blk.	TO	Pts.	Avg.
91-92—Orlando	55	1118	236	446	.529	101	196	.515	113	223	336	39	221	7	22	83	78	573	10.4

Three-point field goals: 1991-92, 0-for-1.

ROBERTSON, ALVIN
G, BUCKS

PERSONAL: Born July 22, 1962, in Barberton, O. . . . 6-4/208. . . . Full name: Alvin Cyrrale Robertson.
HIGH SCHOOL: Barberton (O.)
COLLEGE: Crowder Junior College (Mo.), then Arkansas.
TRANSACTIONS/CAREER NOTES: Selected by San Antonio Spurs in first round (seventh pick overall) of 1984 NBA Draft. . . . Traded by Spurs with Greg Anderson and future considerations to Milwaukee Bucks for Terry Cummings and future considerations (May 28, 1989).
MISCELLANEOUS: Member of gold-medal-winning U.S. Olympic team (1984).

COLLEGIATE RECORD

Season Team	G	Min.	FGM	FGA	Pct.	FTM	FTA	Pct.	Reb.	Pts.	Avg.
80-81—Crowder Junior College	34	...	269	470	.572	73	112	.652	284	611	18.0
81-82—Arkansas	28	495	84	159	.528	35	58	.603	62	203	7.3
82-83—Arkansas	28	915	161	294	.548	76	115	.661	137	398	14.2
83-84—Arkansas	32	1109	187	375	.499	122	182	.670	175	496	15.5
Junior college totals	34	...	269	470	.572	73	112	.652	284	611	18.0
Four-year-college totals	88	2519	432	828	.522	233	355	.656	374	1097	12.5

NBA REGULAR-SEASON RECORD

RECORDS: Holds career record for highest steals-per-game average—2.83. . . . Holds single-season record for most steals—301; and highest steals-per-game average—3.67 (1986).
HONORS: NBA Defensive Player of the Year (1986). . . . NBA Most Improved Player (1986). . . . All-NBA second team (1986). . . . NBA All-Defensive first team (1987, 1991). . . . NBA All-Defensive second team (1986, 1988, 1989, 1990).
NOTES: Led NBA with 3.67 steals per game (1986), 3.21 steals per game (1987) and 3.04 steals per game (1991).

									— REBOUNDS —								
Season Team	G	Min.	FGM	FGA	Pct.	FTM	FTA	Pct.	Off.	Def.	Tot.	Ast.	PF	Dq.	Stl.	Blk.	TO	Pts.	Avg.
84-85—San Antonio .	79	1685	299	600	.498	124	169	.734	116	149	265	275	217	1	127	24	167	726	9.2
85-86—San Antonio .	82	2878	562	1093	.514	260	327	.795	184	332	516	448	296	4	*301	40	256	1392	17.0
86-87—San Antonio .	81	2697	589	1264	.466	244	324	.753	186	238	424	421	264	2	*260	35	243	1435	17.7
87-88—San Antonio .	82	2978	655	1408	.465	273	365	.748	165	333	498	557	300	4	243	69	251	1610	19.6
88-89—San Antonio .	65	2287	465	962	.483	183	253	.723	157	227	384	393	259	6	197	36	231	1122	17.3
89-90—Milwaukee ...	81	2599	476	946	.503	197	266	.741	230	329	559	445	280	2	207	17	217	1153	14.2
90-91—Milwaukee ...	81	2598	438	904	.485	199	263	.757	191	268	459	444	273	5	*246	16	212	1098	13.6
91-92—Milwaukee ...	82	2463	396	922	.430	151	198	.763	175	175	350	360	263	5	210	32	223	1010	12.3
Totals	633	20185	3880	8099	.479	1631	2165	.753	1404	2051	3455	3343	2152	29	1791	269	1800	9546	15.1

Three-point field goals: 1984-85, 4-for-11 (.364). 1985-86, 8-for-29 (.276). 1986-87, 13-for-48 (.271). 1987-88, 27-for-95 (.284). 1988-89, 9-for-45 (.200). 1989-90, 4-for-26 (.154). 1990-91, 23-for-63 (.365). 1991-92, 67-for-210 (.319). Totals, 155-for-527 (.294).

NBA PLAYOFF RECORD

									— REBOUNDS —								
Season Team	G	Min.	FGM	FGA	Pct.	FTM	FTA	Pct.	Off.	Def.	Tot.	Ast.	PF	Dq.	Stl.	Blk.	TO	Pts.	Avg.
85-86—San Antonio .	3	98	8	29	.276	11	13	.846	5	9	14	19	10	0	7	1	5	27	9.0
87-88—San Antonio .	3	119	30	53	.566	7	9	.778	5	9	14	28	15	1	12	1	9	70	23.3
89-90—Milwaukee ...	4	155	35	67	.522	24	34	.706	10	13	23	19	16	0	9	0	15	94	23.5
90-91—Milwaukee ...	3	118	29	49	.592	10	13	.769	7	11	18	15	12	0	8	0	10	71	23.7
Totals	13	490	102	198	.515	52	69	.754	27	42	69	81	53	1	36	2	39	262	20.2

Three-point field goals: 1987-88, 3-for-7 (.429). 1989-90, 0-for-1. 1990-91, 3-for-9 (.333). Totals, 6-for-17 (.353).

NBA ALL-STAR GAME RECORD

								— REBOUNDS —							
Season Team	Min.	FGM	FGA	Pct.	FTM	FTA	Pct.	Off.	Def.	Tot.	Ast.	PF	Dq.	Stl.	Blk.	TO	Pts.
1986 —San Antonio	20	2	6	.333	0	0	...	1	8	9	5	1	0	0	0	4	4
1987 —San Antonio	16	2	5	.400	2	2	1.000	2	1	3	1	1	0	2	0	1	6
1988 —San Antonio	12	1	3	.333	0	0	...	0	0	0	1	1	0	0	0	2	2
1991 —Milwaukee	12	2	4	.500	2	2	1.000	0	2	2	0	0	0	0	0	3	6
Totals	60	7	18	.389	4	4	1.000	3	10	13	7	3	0	2	0	10	18

ROBINSON, CLIFF
F, TRAIL BLAZERS

PERSONAL: Born December 16, 1966, in Buffalo, N.Y. . . . 6-10/225. . . . Full name: Clifford Ralph Robinson.
HIGH SCHOOL: Riverside (Buffalo, N.Y.).
COLLEGE: Connecticut.
TRANSACTIONS/CAREER NOTES: Selected by Portland Trail Blazers in second round (36th pick overall) of 1989 NBA Draft.

COLLEGIATE RECORD

Season Team	G	Min.	FGM	FGA	Pct.	FTM	FTA	Pct.	Reb.	Pts.	Avg.
85-86—Connecticut	28	442	60	164	.366	36	59	.610	88	156	5.6
86-87—Connecticut	16	556	107	255	.420	69	121	.570	119	289	18.1
87-88—Connecticut	34	1079	222	463	.479	156	238	.655	233	600	17.6
88-89—Connecticut	31	974	235	500	.470	145	212	.684	228	619	20.0
Totals	109	3051	624	1382	.452	406	630	.644	668	1664	15.3

Three-point field goals: 1986-87, 6-for-18 (.333). 1988-89, 4-for-12 (.333). Totals, 10-for-30 (.333).

NBA REGULAR-SEASON RECORD

									— REBOUNDS —								
Season Team	G	Min.	FGM	FGA	Pct.	FTM	FTA	Pct.	Off.	Def.	Tot.	Ast.	PF	Dq.	Stl.	Blk.	TO	Pts.	Avg.
89-90—Portland	82	1565	298	751	.397	138	251	.550	110	198	308	72	226	4	53	53	129	746	9.1
90-91—Portland	82	1940	373	806	.463	205	314	.653	123	226	349	151	263	2	78	76	133	957	11.7
91-92—Portland	82	2124	398	854	.466	219	330	.664	140	276	416	137	274	11	85	107	154	1016	12.4
Totals	246	5629	1069	2411	.443	562	895	.628	373	700	1073	360	763	17	216	236	416	2719	11.1

Three-point field goals: 1989-90, 12-for-44 (.273). 1990-91, 6-for-19 (.316). 1991-92, 1-for-11 (.091). Totals, 19-for-74 (.257).

Season	Team	G	Min.	FGM	FGA	Pct.	FTM	FTA	Pct.	Off.	Def.	Tot.	Ast.	PF	Dq.	Stl.	Blk.	TO	Pts.	Avg.
										—	REBOUNDS	—								
89-90	—Portland.......	21	391	54	151	.358	29	52	.558	32	55	87	23	71	1	19	24	25	137	6.5
90-91	—Portland.......	16	354	63	117	.538	38	69	.551	24	39	63	18	47	1	7	16	25	165	10.3
91-92	—Portland.......	21	522	91	197	.462	44	77	.571	25	63	88	43	84	3	22	21	28	227	10.8
	Totals	58	1267	208	465	.447	111	198	.561	81	157	238	84	202	5	48	61	78	529	9.1

Three-point field goals: 1989-90, 0-for-4. 1990-91, 1-for-3 (.333). 1991-92, 1-for-6 (.167). Totals, 2-for-13 (.154).

ROBINSON, CLIFF

F, LAKERS

PERSONAL: Born March 13, 1960, in Oakland, Calif.... 6-9/240.... Full name: Clifford Trent Robinson.
HIGH SCHOOL: Castlemont (Oakland, Calif.).
COLLEGE: Southern California.

TRANSACTIONS/CAREER NOTES: Selected as undergraduate by New Jersey Nets in first round (11th pick overall) of 1979 NBA draft.... Traded by Nets to Kansas City Kings for Otis Birdsong and 1981 second-round draft choice (June 8, 1981).... Traded by Kings to Cleveland Cavaliers for Reggie Johnson (February 16, 1982).... Traded by Cavaliers with draft rights to Tim McCormick and cash to Washington Bullets for draft rights to Melvin Turpin (June 19, 1984).... Traded by Bullets with Jeff Ruland to Philadelphia 76ers for Moses Malone, Terry Catledge, 1986 first-round draft choice and 1988 first-round draft choice (June 16, 1986).... Played in Italy (1989-90).... Played in Continental Basketball Association with Rapid City Thrillers (1991-92).... Signed by Los Angeles Lakers to first of two consecutive 10-day contracts (March 29, 1992).... Signed by Lakers for remainder of season (April 8, 1992).

COLLEGIATE RECORD

Season	Team	G	Min.	FGM	FGA	Pct.	FTM	FTA	Pct.	Reb.	Pts.	Avg.
77-78	—Southern California	24	724	191	367	.520	60	100	.600	231	442	18.4
78-79	—Southern California	21	670	159	338	.470	76	107	.710	243	394	18.8
	Totals	45	1394	350	705	.496	136	207	.657	474	836	18.6

NBA REGULAR-SEASON RECORD

Season	Team	G	Min.	FGM	FGA	Pct.	FTM	FTA	Pct.	Off.	Def.	Tot.	Ast.	PF	Dq.	Stl.	Blk.	TO	Pts.	Avg.
										—	REBOUNDS	—								
79-80	—New Jersey ..	70	1661	391	833	.469	168	242	.694	174	332	506	98	178	1	61	34	137	951	13.6
80-81	—New Jersey ..	63	1822	525	1070	.491	178	248	.718	120	361	481	105	216	6	58	52	182	1229	19.5
81-82	—K.C.-Clev.	68	2175	518	1143	.453	222	313	.709	174	435	609	120	222	4	88	103	149	1258	18.5
82-83	—Cleveland.....	77	2601	587	1230	.477	213	301	.708	190	666	856	145	272	7	61	58	224	1387	18.0
83-84	—Cleveland.....	73	2402	533	1185	.450	234	334	.701	156	597	753	185	195	2	51	32	187	1301	17.8
84-85	—Washington .	60	1870	422	896	.471	158	213	.742	141	405	546	149	187	4	51	47	161	1003	16.7
85-86	—Washington .	78	2563	595	1255	.474	269	353	.762	180	500	680	186	217	2	98	44	206	1460	18.7
86-87	—Philadelphia.	55	1586	338	729	.464	139	184	.755	86	221	307	89	150	1	86	30	123	815	14.8
87-88	—Philadelphia.	62	2110	483	1041	.464	210	293	.717	116	289	405	131	192	4	79	39	161	1178	19.0
88-89	—Philadelphia.	14	416	90	187	.481	32	44	.727	19	56	75	32	37	0	17	2	34	212	15.1
90-91	—									Did not play.										
91-92	—L.A. Lakers ..	9	78	11	27	.407	7	8	.875	7	12	19	9	4	0	5	0	7	29	3.2
	Totals	629	19284	4493	9596	.468	1830	2533	.722	1363	3874	5237	1249	1870	31	655	441	1571	10823	17.2

Three-point field goals: 1979-80, 1-for-4 (.250). 1980-81, 1-for-1. 1981-82, 0-for-4. 1982-83, 0-for-5. 1983-84, 1-for-2 (.500). 1984-85, 1-for-2 (.500). 1985-86, 1-for-3 (.333). 1986-87, 0-for-4. 1987-88, 2-for-9 (.222). 1988-89, 0-for-1. 1991-92, 0-for-1. Totals, 7-for-36 (.194).

NBA PLAYOFF RECORD

Season	Team	G	Min.	FGM	FGA	Pct.	FTM	FTA	Pct.	Off.	Def.	Tot.	Ast.	PF	Dq.	Stl.	Blk.	TO	Pts.	Avg.
										—	REBOUNDS	—								
84-85	—Washington .	4	123	25	56	.446	9	12	.750	12	18	30	4	14	0	4	2	3	59	14.8
85-86	—Washington .	5	177	46	93	.495	15	31	.484	17	26	43	17	19	1	10	3	15	107	21.4
86-87	—Philadelphia.	5	138	30	61	.492	13	15	.867	10	33	43	6	15	0	3	7	8	73	14.6
91-92	—L.A. Lakers ..	3	24	3	10	.300	5	8	.625	2	4	6	1	6	0	3	1	2	11	3.7
	Totals	17	462	104	220	.473	42	66	.636	41	81	122	28	54	1	20	13	28	250	14.7

CBA REGULAR-SEASON RECORD

Season	Team	G	Min.	2-POINT			3-POINT			FTM	FTA	Pct.	Reb.	Ast.	Pts.	Avg.
				FGM	FGA	Pct.	FGM	FGA	Pct.							
91-92	—Rapid City	20	608	137	298	.460	2	8	.250	65	89	.730	188	50	345	17.3

ROBINSON, DAVID

C, SPURS

PERSONAL: Born August 6, 1965, in Key West, Fla.... 7-1/235. ... Full name: David Maurice Robinson.... Nickname: The Admiral.
HIGH SCHOOL: Osbourn Park (Manassas, Va.).

COLLEGE: Navy.
TRANSACTIONS/CAREER NOTES: Selected by San Antonio Spurs in first round (first pick overall) of 1987 NBA Draft.... In military service during 1987-88 and 1988-89 seasons.
MISCELLANEOUS: Member of bronze-medal-winning U.S. Olympic team (1988) and gold-medal-winning U.S. Olympic team (1992).

COLLEGIATE RECORD

NOTES: THE SPORTING NEWS College Player of the Year (1987).... THE SPORTING NEWS All-America first team (1986, 1987).... Led NCAA Division I with 13.0 rebounds per game (1986).... Led NCAA Division I with 5.91 blocked shots per game (1986) and 4.50 blocked shots per game (1987).

Season	Team	G	Min.	FGM	FGA	Pct.	FTM	FTA	Pct.	Reb.	Pts.	Avg.
83-84	—Navy	28	...	86	138	.623	42	73	.575	111	214	7.6
84-85	—Navy	32	...	302	469	.644	152	243	.626	370	756	23.6

Season Team	G	Min.	FGM	FGA	Pct.	FTM	FTA	Pct.	Reb.	Pts.	Avg.
85-86 —Navy	35	...	294	484	.607	208	331	.628	455	796	22.7
86-87 —Navy	32	...	350	592	.591	202	317	.637	378	903	28.2
Totals	127	...	1032	1683	.613	604	964	.627	1314	2669	21.0

Three-point field goals: 1986-87, 1-for-1.

NBA REGULAR-SEASON RECORD

HONORS: NBA Defensive Player of the Year (1992).... NBA Rookie of the Year (1990).... Schick Award, for all-around contributions to team's success (1990, 1991).... All-NBA first team (1991, 1992).... All-NBA third team (1990).... NBA All-Defensive first team (1991, 1992).... NBA All-Defensive second team (1990).... NBA All-Rookie first team (1990).

NOTES: Led NBA with 13.0 rebounds per game (1991).... Led NBA with 4.49 blocked shots per game (1992).

Season Team	G	Min.	FGM	FGA	Pct.	FTM	FTA	Pct.	Off.	Def.	Tot.	Ast.	PF	Dq.	Stl.	Blk.	TO	Pts.	Avg.
89-90 —San Antonio	82	3002	690	1300	.531	613	837	.732	303	680	983	164	259	3	138	319	257	1993	24.3
90-91 —San Antonio	82	3095	754	1366	.552	592	777	.762	335	728	*1063	208	264	5	127	*320	270	2101	25.6
91-92 —San Antonio	68	2564	592	1074	.551	393	561	.701	261	568	829	181	219	2	158	*305	182	1578	23.2
Totals	232	8661	2036	3740	.544	1598	2175	.735	899	1976	2875	553	742	10	423	944	709	5672	24.4

Three-point field goals: 1989-90, 0-for-2. 1990-91, 1-for-7 (.143). 1991-92, 1-for-8 (.125). Totals, 2-for-17 (.118).

NBA PLAYOFF RECORD

Season Team	G	Min.	FGM	FGA	Pct.	FTM	FTA	Pct.	Off.	Def.	Tot.	Ast.	PF	Dq.	Stl.	Blk.	TO	Pts.	Avg.
89-90 —San Antonio	10	375	89	167	.533	65	96	.677	36	84	120	23	35	1	11	40	24	243	24.3
90-91 —San Antonio	4	166	35	51	.686	33	38	.868	11	43	54	8	11	0	6	15	15	103	25.8
Totals	14	541	124	218	.569	98	134	.731	47	127	174	31	46	1	17	55	39	346	24.7

Three-point field goals: 1990-91, 0-for-1.

NBA ALL-STAR GAME RECORD

Season Team	Min.	FGM	FGA	Pct.	FTM	FTA	Pct.	Off.	Def.	Tot.	Ast.	PF	Dq.	Stl.	Blk.	TO	Pts.
1990 —San Antonio	25	7	12	.583	1	2	.500	2	8	10	1	1	0	2	1	1	15
1991 —San Antonio	18	6	13	.462	4	5	.800	3	3	6	0	5	0	2	3	2	16
1992 —San Antonio	18	7	9	.778	5	8	.625	1	4	5	2	3	0	3	1	0	19
Totals	61	20	34	.588	10	15	.667	6	15	21	3	9	0	7	5	3	50

ROBINSON, LARRY
G

PERSONAL: Born January 11, 1968, in Bossier City, La.... 6-5/180.... Second cousin of Robert Parish, center with Boston Celtics.

HIGH SCHOOL: Airline (Bossier City, La.).

COLLEGE: Eastern Oklahoma State, then Centenary (La.).

TRANSACTIONS/CAREER NOTES: Never drafted by an NBA franchise.... Signed as free agent by Washington Bullets (September 25, 1990).... Waived by Bullets (December 10, 1990).... Signed by Golden State Warriors to 10-day contract (January 8, 1991).... Re-signed by Warriors for remainder of season (January 11, 1991).... Waived by Warriors (March 19, 1991).... Signed by Bullets for remainder of season (April 18, 1991).... Re-signed by Bullets (September 30, 1991).... Waived by Bullets (October 25, 1991).... Signed as free agent by Boston Celtics (October 29, 1991).... Waived by Celtics (November 11, 1991).... Played in Continental Basketball Association with Rapid City Thrillers (1991-92).

COLLEGIATE RECORD

Season Team	G	Min.	FGM	FGA	Pct.	FTM	FTA	Pct.	Reb.	Pts.	Avg.
86-87 —Eastern Oklahoma State					Statistics unavailable.						
87-88 —Eastern Oklahoma State					Statistics unavailable.						
88-89 —Centenary	30	1038	228	461	.495	87	124	.702	202	558	18.6
89-90 —Centenary	30	1042	280	521	.537	117	168	.696	212	689	23.0
Four-year-college totals	60	2080	508	982	.517	204	292	.699	414	1247	20.8

Three-point field goals: 1988-89, 15-for-48 (.313). 1989-90, 12-for-40 (.300). Totals, 27-for-88 (.307).

NBA REGULAR-SEASON RECORD

Season Team	G	Min.	FGM	FGA	Pct.	FTM	FTA	Pct.	Off.	Def.	Tot.	Ast.	PF	Dq.	Stl.	Blk.	TO	Pts.	Avg.
90-91 —G.S.-Wash.	36	425	62	150	.413	15	27	.556	29	22	51	35	49	0	16	1	27	139	3.9
91-92 —Boston	1	6	1	5	.200	0	0	...	2	0	2	1	3	0	0	0	1	2	2.0
Totals	37	431	63	155	.406	15	27	.556	31	22	53	36	52	0	16	1	28	141	3.8

Three-point field goals: 1990-91, 0-for-1.

CBA REGULAR-SEASON RECORD

Season Team	G	Min.	2-POINT FGM	2-POINT FGA	2-POINT Pct.	3-POINT FGM	3-POINT FGA	3-POINT Pct.	FTM	FTA	Pct.	Reb.	Ast.	Pts.	Avg.
91-92 —Rapid City	52	1372	239	493	.485	52	115	.452	75	117	.641	209	102	709	13.6

ROBINSON, RUMEAL
G, HAWKS

PERSONAL: Born November 13, 1966, in Jamaica.... 6-2/200.... Full name: Rumeal James Robinson.

HIGH SCHOOL: Cambridge Rindge and Latin School (Mass.).

COLLEGE: Michigan.

TRANSACTIONS/CAREER NOTES: Selected by Atlanta Hawks in first round (10th pick overall) of 1990 NBA Draft.

COLLEGIATE RECORD

NOTES: THE SPORTING NEWS All-America third team (1990).... Member of NCAA Division I championship team (1989).

Season Team	G	Min.	FGM	FGA	Pct.	FTM	FTA	Pct.	Reb.	Pts.	Avg.
86-87 —Michigan					Did not play—ineligible.						
87-88 —Michigan	33	858	115	208	.553	84	126	.667	101	321	9.7
88-89 —Michigan	37	1110	199	357	.557	122	186	.656	125	550	14.9
89-90 —Michigan	30	1020	201	410	.490	125	185	.676	127	575	19.2
Totals	100	2988	515	975	.528	331	497	.666	353	1446	14.5

Three-point field goals: 1987-88, 7-for-26 (.269). 1988-89, 30-for-64 (.469). 1989-90, 48-for-117 (.410). Totals, 85-for-207 (.411).

NBA REGULAR-SEASON RECORD

| | | | | | | | | | — REBOUNDS — | | | | | | | | | |
Season Team	G	Min.	FGM	FGA	Pct.	FTM	FTA	Pct.	Off.	Def.	Tot.	Ast.	PF	Dq.	Stl.	Blk.	TO	Pts.	Avg.
90-91 —Atlanta	47	674	108	242	.446	47	80	.588	20	51	71	132	65	0	32	8	76	265	5.6
91-92 —Atlanta	81	2220	423	928	.456	175	275	.636	64	155	219	446	178	0	105	24	206	1055	13.0
Totals	128	2894	531	1170	.454	222	355	.625	84	206	290	578	243	0	137	32	282	1320	10.3

Three-point field goals: 1990-91, 2-for-11 (.182). 1991-92, 34-for-104 (.327). Totals, 36-for-115 (.313).

NBA PLAYOFF RECORD

| | | | | | | | | | — REBOUNDS — | | | | | | | | | |
Season Team	G	Min.	FGM	FGA	Pct.	FTM	FTA	Pct.	Off.	Def.	Tot.	Ast.	PF	Dq.	Stl.	Blk.	TO	Pts.	Avg.
90-91 —Atlanta	2	13	1	4	.250	0	0	...	0	1	1	1	1	0	1	0	4	2	1.0

RODMAN, DENNIS
F, PISTONS

PERSONAL: Born May 13, 1961, in Trenton, N.J.... 6-8/210.... Full name: Dennis Keith Rodman.... Nickname: Worm.
HIGH SCHOOL: South Oak Cliff (Dallas).
COLLEGE: Cooke County Junior College (Tex.), then Southeastern Oklahoma State.
TRANSACTIONS/CAREER NOTES: Did not play high school basketball.... Selected by Detroit Pistons in second round (27th pick overall) of 1986 NBA Draft.
MISCELLANEOUS: Member of NBA championship teams (1989, 1990).

COLLEGIATE RECORD

NOTES: Led NAIA with 16.1 rebounds per game (1985) and 17.8 rebounds per game (1986).

Season Team	G	Min.	FGM	FGA	Pct.	FTM	FTA	Pct.	Reb.	Pts.	Avg.
82-83 —Cooke County Junior College...	16	...	114	185	.616	53	91	.582	212	281	17.6
83-84 —Southeastern Oklahoma State.	30	...	303	490	.618	173	264	.655	392	779	26.0
84-85 —Southeastern Oklahoma State.	32	...	353	545	.648	151	267	.566	510	857	26.8
85-86 —Southeastern Oklahoma State.	34	...	332	515	.645	165	252	.655	605	829	24.4
Junior college totals	16	...	114	185	.616	53	91	.582	212	281	17.6
Four-year-college totals	96	...	988	1550	.637	489	783	.625	1507	2465	25.7

NBA REGULAR-SEASON RECORD

HONORS: NBA Defensive Player of the Year (1990, 1991).... Schick Award, for all-around contributions to team's success (1992).... All-NBA third team (1992).... NBA All-Defensive first team (1989, 1990, 1991, 1992).
NOTES: Led NBA with 18.7 rebounds per game (1992).

| | | | | | | | | | — REBOUNDS — | | | | | | | | | |
Season Team	G	Min.	FGM	FGA	Pct.	FTM	FTA	Pct.	Off.	Def.	Tot.	Ast.	PF	Dq.	Stl.	Blk.	TO	Pts.	Avg.
86-87 —Detroit	77	1155	213	391	.545	74	126	.587	163	169	332	56	166	1	38	48	93	500	6.5
87-88 —Detroit	82	2147	398	709	.561	152	284	.535	318	397	715	110	273	5	75	45	156	953	11.6
88-89 —Detroit	82	2208	316	531	*.595	97	155	.626	327	445	772	99	292	4	55	76	126	735	9.0
89-90 —Detroit	82	2377	288	496	.581	142	217	.654	336	456	792	72	276	2	52	60	90	719	8.8
90-91 —Detroit	82	2747	276	560	.493	111	176	.631	*361	665	1026	85	281	7	65	55	94	669	8.2
91-92 —Detroit	82	3301	342	635	.539	84	140	.600	*523	*1007	*1530	191	248	0	68	70	140	800	9.8
Totals	487	13935	1833	3322	.552	660	1098	.601	2028	3139	5167	613	1536	19	353	354	699	4376	9.0

Three-point field goals: 1986-87, 0-for-1. 1987-88, 5-for-17 (.294). 1988-89, 6-for-26 (.231). 1989-90, 1-for-9 (.111). 1990-91, 6-for-30 (.200). 1991-92, 32-for-101 (.317). Totals, 50-for-184 (.272).

NBA PLAYOFF RECORD

| | | | | | | | | | — REBOUNDS — | | | | | | | | | |
Season Team	G	Min.	FGM	FGA	Pct.	FTM	FTA	Pct.	Off.	Def.	Tot.	Ast.	PF	Dq.	Stl.	Blk.	TO	Pts.	Avg.
86-87 —Detroit	15	245	40	74	.541	18	32	.563	32	39	71	3	48	0	6	17	17	98	6.5
87-88 —Detroit	23	474	71	136	.522	22	54	.407	51	85	136	21	87	1	14	14	31	164	7.1
88-89 —Detroit	17	409	37	70	.529	24	35	.686	56	114	170	16	58	0	6	12	24	98	5.8
89-90 —Detroit	19	560	54	95	.568	18	35	.514	55	106	161	17	62	1	9	13	31	126	6.6
90-91 —Detroit	15	495	41	91	.451	10	24	.417	67	110	177	14	55	1	11	10	13	94	6.3
91-92 —Detroit	5	156	16	27	.593	4	8	.500	16	35	51	9	17	0	4	2	7	36	7.2
Totals	94	2339	259	493	.525	96	188	.511	277	489	766	80	327	3	50	68	123	616	6.6

Three-point field goals: 1987-88, 0-for-2. 1988-89, 0-for-4. 1990-91, 2-for-9 (.222). 1991-92, 0-for-2. Totals, 2-for-17 (.118).

NBA ALL-STAR GAME RECORD

| | | | | | | | | — REBOUNDS — | | | | | | | | |
Season Team	Min.	FGM	FGA	Pct.	FTM	FTA	Pct.	Off.	Def.	Tot.	Ast.	PF	Dq.	Stl.	Blk.	TO	Pts.
1990 —Detroit	11	2	4	.500	0	0	...	3	1	4	1	1	0	0	1	2	4
1992 —Detroit	25	2	7	.286	0	0	...	7	6	13	0	1	0	1	0	2	4
Totals	36	4	11	.364	0	0	...	10	7	17	1	2	0	1	1	4	8

ROLLINS, TREE
C, ROCKETS

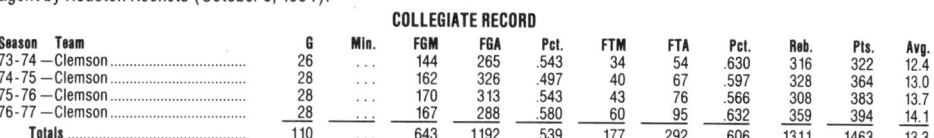

PERSONAL: Born June 16, 1955, in Winter Haven, Fla. . . . 7-1/255. . . . Full name: Wayne Monte Rollins. **HIGH SCHOOL:** Crisp County (Cordele, Ga.). **COLLEGE:** Clemson.

TRANSACTIONS/CAREER NOTES: Selected by Atlanta Hawks in first round (14th pick overall) of 1977 NBA Draft. . . . Signed as unrestricted free agent by Cleveland Cavaliers (August 2, 1988). . . . Signed as unrestricted free agent by Detroit Pistons (September 4, 1990). . . . Rights renounced by Pistons (July 10, 1991). . . . Signed as free agent by Houston Rockets (October 9, 1991).

COLLEGIATE RECORD

Season Team	G	Min.	FGM	FGA	Pct.	FTM	FTA	Pct.	Reb.	Pts.	Avg.
73-74 —Clemson	26	. . .	144	265	.543	34	54	.630	316	322	12.4
74-75 —Clemson	28	. . .	162	326	.497	40	67	.597	328	364	13.0
75-76 —Clemson	28	. . .	170	313	.543	43	76	.566	308	383	13.7
76-77 —Clemson	28	. . .	167	288	.580	60	95	.632	359	394	14.1
Totals	110	. . .	643	1192	.539	177	292	.606	1311	1463	13.3

NBA REGULAR-SEASON RECORD

HONORS: NBA All-Defensive first team (1984). . . . NBA All-Defensive second team (1983).
NOTES: Led NBA with 4.29 blocked shots per game (1983).

Season Team	G	Min.	FGM	FGA	Pct.	FTM	FTA	Pct.	Off.	Def.	Tot.	Ast.	PF	Dq.	Stl.	Blk.	TO	Pts.	Avg.
77-78 —Atlanta	80	1795	253	520	.487	104	148	.703	179	373	552	79	326	16	57	218	121	610	7.6
78-79 —Atlanta	81	1900	297	555	.535	89	141	.631	219	369	588	49	328	19	4	254	87	683	8.4
79-80 —Atlanta	82	2123	287	514	.558	157	220	.714	283	491	774	76	322	12	54	244	99	731	8.9
80-81 —Atlanta	40	1044	116	210	.552	46	57	.807	102	184	286	35	151	7	29	117	57	278	7.0
81-82 —Atlanta	79	2018	202	346	.584	79	129	.612	168	443	611	59	285	4	35	224	79	483	6.1
82-83 —Atlanta	80	2472	261	512	.510	98	135	.726	210	533	743	75	294	7	49	*343	95	620	7.8
83-84 —Atlanta	77	2351	274	529	.518	118	190	.621	200	393	593	62	297	9	35	277	101	666	8.6
84-85 —Atlanta	70	1750	186	339	.549	67	93	.720	113	329	442	52	213	6	35	167	80	439	6.3
85-86 —Atlanta	74	1781	173	347	.499	69	90	.767	131	327	458	41	239	5	38	167	91	415	5.6
86-87 —Atlanta	74	1764	171	313	.546	63	87	.724	155	333	488	22	240	1	43	140	61	405	5.5
87-88 —Atlanta	76	1765	133	260	.512	70	80	.875	142	317	459	20	229	2	31	132	51	336	4.4
88-89 —Cleveland	60	583	62	138	.449	12	19	.632	38	101	139	19	89	0	11	38	22	136	2.3
89-90 —Cleveland	48	674	57	125	.456	11	16	.688	58	95	153	24	83	3	13	53	35	125	2.6
90-91 —Detroit	37	202	14	33	.424	8	14	.571	13	29	42	4	35	0	2	20	15	36	1.0
91-92 —Houston	59	697	46	86	.535	26	30	.867	61	110	171	15	85	0	14	62	18	118	2.0
Totals	1017	22919	2532	4827	.525	1017	1449	.702	2072	4427	6499	632	3216	91	450	2456	1012	6081	6.0

Three-point field goals: 1980-81, 0-for-1. 1982-83, 0-for-1. 1985-86, 0-for-1. 1988-89, 0-for-1. 1989-90, 0-for-1. Totals, 0-for-5.

NBA PLAYOFF RECORD

Season Team	G	Min.	FGM	FGA	Pct.	FTM	FTA	Pct.	Off.	Def.	Tot.	Ast.	PF	Dq.	Stl.	Blk.	TO	Pts.	Avg.
77-78 —Atlanta	2	51	7	12	.583	2	8	.250	3	6	9	1	8	1	1	4	3	16	8.0
78-79 —Atlanta	9	212	21	51	.412	9	13	.692	19	52	71	5	29	1	3	24	14	51	5.7
79-80 —Atlanta	5	134	18	31	.581	6	10	.600	18	20	38	3	25	3	2	14	6	42	8.4
81-82 —Atlanta	2	65	2	6	.333	3	4	.750	5	3	8	2	8	1	0	6	5	7	3.5
82-83 —Atlanta	3	118	13	27	.481	3	9	.333	10	20	30	3	12	1	1	10	6	29	9.7
83-84 —Atlanta	5	152	10	25	.400	5	8	.625	10	24	34	1	23	1	2	10	11	25	5.0
85-86 —Atlanta	9	248	26	47	.553	7	11	.636	18	60	78	3	32	2	2	15	12	59	6.6
86-87 —Atlanta	9	221	15	28	.536	10	14	.714	19	34	53	3	33	0	3	16	7	40	4.4
87-88 —Atlanta	12	333	20	36	.556	13	15	.867	23	48	71	6	46	0	10	19	5	53	4.4
88-89 —Cleveland	5	74	6	8	.750	3	5	.600	5	11	16	1	10	0	3	7	1	15	3.0
89-90 —Cleveland	3	38	1	3	.333	6	8	.750	0	8	8	1	7	0	2	1	3	8	2.7
90-91 —Detroit	6	32	2	2	1.000	0	0	. . .	1	2	3	0	6	0	1	1	2	4	0.7
Totals	70	1678	141	276	.511	67	105	.638	131	288	419	29	239	10	30	127	75	349	5.0

ROYAL, DONALD
F, MAGIC

PERSONAL: Born May 2, 1966, in New Orleans. . . . 6-8/210. . . . Full name: Donald Adam Royal. **HIGH SCHOOL:** Augustine (New Orleans). **COLLEGE:** Notre Dame.

TRANSACTIONS/CAREER NOTES: Selected by Cleveland Cavaliers in third round (52nd pick overall) of 1987 NBA Draft. . . . Waived by Cavaliers (October 23, 1987). . . . Played in Continental Basketball Association with Pensacola Tornados (1987-88), Cedar Rapids Silver Bullets (1988-89) and Tri-City Chinook (1991-92). . . . Signed as free agent by Minnesota Timberwolves (September 12, 1989). . . . Played in Israel (1990-91). . . . Rights renounced by Timberwolves (August 16, 1991). . . . Signed as free agent by Orlando Magic (September 26, 1991). . . . Waived by Magic (October 28, 1991). . . . Signed as free agent by San Antonio Spurs (December 3, 1991). . . . Signed as free agent by Magic (August 24, 1992).

COLLEGIATE RECORD

Season Team	G	Min.	FGM	FGA	Pct.	FTM	FTA	Pct.	Reb.	Pts.	Avg.
83-84 —Notre Dame	31	405	38	64	.594	28	45	.622	72	104	3.4
84-85 —Notre Dame	30	848	75	151	.497	122	156	.782	164	272	9.1
85-86 —Notre Dame	28	777	88	151	.583	121	158	.766	138	297	10.6
86-87 —Notre Dame	28	1028	132	229	.576	178	217	.820	196	442	15.8
Totals	117	3058	333	595	.560	449	576	.780	570	1115	9.5

CBA REGULAR-SEASON RECORD

| Season Team | G | Min. | 2-POINT | | | 3-POINT | | | FTM | FTA | Pct. | Reb. | Ast. | Pts. | Avg. |
			FGM	FGA	Pct.	FGM	FGA	Pct.							
87-88 —Pensacola	48	904	122	233	.524	0	1	.000	104	141	.738	158	44	348	7.3

R

Season Team	G	Min.	FGM	2-POINT FGA	Pct.	3-POINT FGM	FGA	Pct.	FTM	FTA	Pct.	Reb.	Ast.	Pts.	Avg.
88-89 — Cedar Rapids ...	53	1206	216	438	.493	0	2	.000	266	359	.741	252	98	698	13.2
91-92 — Tri-City............	10	368	77	138	.558	0	0	...	69	89	.775	66	27	223	22.3
Totals	111	2478	415	809	.513	0	3	.000	439	589	.745	476	169	1269	11.4

NBA REGULAR-SEASON RECORD

Season Team	G	Min.	FGM	FGA	Pct.	FTM	FTA	Pct.	REBOUNDS Off.	Def.	Tot.	Ast.	PF	Dq.	Stl.	Blk.	TO	Pts.	Avg.
89-90 — Minnesota....	66	746	117	255	.459	153	197	.777	69	68	137	43	107	0	32	8	...	387	5.9
91-92 — San Antonio.	60	718	80	178	.449	92	133	.692	65	59	124	34	73	0	25	7	39	252	4.2
Totals	126	1464	197	433	.455	245	330	.742	134	127	261	77	180	0	57	15	39	639	5.1

Three-point field goals: 1989-90, 0-for-1.

NBA PLAYOFF RECORD

Season Team	G	Min.	FGM	FGA	Pct.	FTM	FTA	Pct.	REBOUNDS Off.	Def.	Tot.	Ast.	PF	Dq.	Stl.	Blk.	TO	Pts.	Avg.
91-92 — San Antonio.	3	57	5	9	.556	5	9	.556	5	7	12	0	7	0	2	2	6	15	5.0

RUDD, DELANEY
G

PERSONAL: Born November 8, 1962, in Halifax, N.C. ... 6-2/195. ... Full name: Edward Delaney Rudd.
HIGH SCHOOL: Eastman (Hollister, N.C.).
COLLEGE: Wake Forest.
TRANSACTIONS/CAREER NOTES: Selected by Utah Jazz in fourth round (83rd pick overall) of 1985 NBA Draft. ... Waived by Jazz (October 21, 1985). ... Played in Continental Basketball Association with Bay State Bombardiers and Maine Windjammers (1985-86). ... Did not play basketball (1986-87). ... Played in Greece (1987-88 and 1988-89). ... Signed as free agent by Milwaukee Bucks (October 6, 1989). ... Waived by Bucks (November 2, 1989). ... Signed as free agent by Jazz (November 6, 1989).

COLLEGIATE RECORD

Season Team	G	Min.	FGM	FGA	Pct.	FTM	FTA	Pct.	Reb.	Pts.	Avg.
81-82 — Wake Forest	22	150	10	30	.333	5	10	.500	4	25	1.1
82-83 — Wake Forest	32	1004	171	324	.528	53	69	.768	63	408	12.8
83-84 — Wake Forest	31	1011	170	328	.518	73	85	.859	55	413	13.3
84-85 — Wake Forest	29	1000	210	452	.465	63	77	.818	74	483	16.7
Totals	114	3165	561	1134	.495	194	241	.805	196	1329	11.7

Three-point field goals: 1982-83, 13-for-29 (.448).

CBA REGULAR-SEASON RECORD

Season Team	G	Min.	FGM	2-POINT FGA	Pct.	3-POINT FGM	FGA	Pct.	FTM	FTA	Pct.	Reb.	Ast.	Pts.	Avg.
85-86 — Bay St.-Maine .	9	122	15	43	.349	0	1	.000	6	9	.667	10	23	36	4.0

NBA REGULAR-SEASON RECORD

Season Team	G	Min.	FGM	FGA	Pct.	FTM	FTA	Pct.	REBOUNDS Off.	Def.	Tot.	Ast.	PF	Dq.	Stl.	Blk.	TO	Pts.	Avg.
89-90 — Utah	77	850	111	259	.429	35	53	.660	12	43	55	177	81	0	22	1	88	273	3.5
90-91 — Utah	82	874	124	285	.435	59	71	.831	14	52	66	216	92	0	36	2	102	324	4.0
91-92 — Utah	65	538	75	188	.399	32	42	.762	15	39	54	109	64	0	15	1	49	193	3.0
Totals	224	2262	310	732	.423	126	166	.759	41	134	175	502	237	0	73	4	239	790	3.5

Three-point field goals: 1989-90, 16-for-56 (.286). 1990-91, 17-for-61 (.279). 1991-92, 11-for-47 (.234). Totals, 44-for-164 (.268).

NBA PLAYOFF RECORD

Season Team	G	Min.	FGM	FGA	Pct.	FTM	FTA	Pct.	REBOUNDS Off.	Def.	Tot.	Ast.	PF	Dq.	Stl.	Blk.	TO	Pts.	Avg.
89-90 — Utah	5	45	8	23	.348	1	2	.500	1	2	3	13	10	0	1	0	3	18	3.6
90-91 — Utah	9	58	9	21	.429	2	4	.500	2	0	2	17	6	0	3	0	3	24	2.7
91-92 — Utah	10	84	10	21	.476	3	4	.750	0	4	4	19	11	0	3	0	4	25	2.5
Totals	24	187	27	65	.415	6	10	.600	3	6	9	49	27	0	7	0	10	67	2.8

Three-point field goals: 1989-90, 1-for-7 (.143). 1990-91, 4-for-12 (.333). 1991-92, 2-for-7 (.286). Totals, 7-for-26 (.269).

RULAND, JEFF
C, 76ERS

PERSONAL: Born December 16, 1958, in Bayshore, N.Y. ... 6-11/275. ... Full name: Jeffrey George Ruland.
HIGH SCHOOL: Sachem (Lake Ronkonkoma, N.Y.).
COLLEGE: Iona.
TRANSACTIONS/CAREER NOTES: Selected as undergraduate by Golden State Warriors in second round (25th pick overall) of 1980 NBA Draft. ... Draft rights traded by Warriors to Washington Bullets for a 1981 second-round draft choice (June 10, 1980). ... Played in Spain (1980-81). ... Traded by Bullets with Cliff Robinson to Philadelphia 76ers for Moses Malone, Terry Catledge and 1986 and 1988 first-round draft choices (June 16, 1986). ... Announced retirement after suffering knee injury during 1986-87 season. ... Signed as free agent by Philadelphia 76ers (January 6, 1992).

COLLEGIATE RECORD

Season Team	G	Min.	FGM	FGA	Pct.	FTM	FTA	Pct.	Reb.	Pts.	Avg.
77-78 — Iona..	26	...	228	384	.594	124	180	.689	332	580	22.3
78-79 — Iona..	29	...	233	347	.671	124	172	.721	328	590	20.3
79-80 — Iona..	34	...	256	399	.642	173	267	.648	407	685	20.1
Totals	89	...	717	1130	.635	421	619	.680	1067	1855	20.8

HONORS: NBA All-Rookie team (1982).

								— REBOUNDS —														
Season	Team	G	Min.	FGM	FGA	Pct.	FTM	FTA	Pct.	Off.	Def.	Tot.	Ast.	PF	Dq.	Stl.	Blk.	TO	Pts.	Avg.
81-82	—Washington .	82	2214	420	749	.561	342	455	.752	253	509	762	134	319	7	44	58	237	1183	14.4
82-83	—Washington .	79	2862	580	1051	.552	375	544	.689	293	578	871	234	312	12	74	77	297	1536	19.4
83-84	—Washington .	75	*3082	599	1035	.579	466	636	.733	265	657	922	296	285	8	68	72	*342	1665	22.2
84-85	—Washington .	37	1436	250	439	.569	200	292	.685	127	283	410	162	128	2	31	27	179	700	18.9
85-86	—Washington .	30	1114	212	383	.554	145	200	.725	107	213	320	159	100	1	23	25	121	569	19.0
86-87	—Philadelphia.	5	116	19	28	.679	9	12	.750	12	16	28	10	13	0	0	4	10	47	9.4
87-88	—								Did not play—retired.												
88-89	—								Did not play—retired.												
89-90	—								Did not play—retired.												
90-91	—								Did not play—retired.												
91-92	—Philadelphia.	13	209	20	38	.526	11	16	.688	16	31	47	5	45	0	7	4	20	51	3.9
Totals	....	321	11033	2100	3723	.564	1548	2155	.718	1073	2287	3360	1000	1202	30	247	267	1206	5751	17.9

Three-point field goals: 1981-82, 1-for-3 (.333). 1982-83, 1-for-3 (.333). 1983-84, 1-for-7 (143). 1984-85, 0-for-2. 1985-86, 0-for-4. Totals, 3-for-19 (.158).

NBA PLAYOFF RECORD

								— REBOUNDS —														
Season	Team	G	Min.	FGM	FGA	Pct.	FTM	FTA	Pct.	Off.	Def.	Tot.	Ast.	PF	Dq.	Stl.	Blk.	TO	Pts.	Avg.
81-82	—Washington .	7	237	38	79	.481	43	56	.768	29	37	66	5	24	1	3	4	23	119	17.0
83-84	—Washington .	4	187	37	71	.521	22	27	.815	16	35	51	31	15	0	2	3	19	96	24.0
84-85	—Washington .	4	162	28	47	.596	14	20	.700	12	22	34	21	15	0	9	4	23	70	17.5
85-86	—Washington .	2	54	7	14	.500	14	17	.824	5	7	12	10	6	0	0	2	6	28	14.0
Totals	....	17	640	110	211	.521	93	120	.775	62	101	163	67	60	1	14	13	71	313	18.4

Three-point field goals: 1981-82, 0-for-1. 1983-84, 0-for-1. 1984-85, 0-for-2. Totals, 0-for-4.

NBA ALL-STAR GAME RECORD

							— REBOUNDS —									
Season	Team	Min.	FGM	FGA	Pct.	FTM	FTA	Pct.	Off.	Def.	Tot.	Ast.	PF	Dq.	Stl.	Blk.	TO	Pts.
1984	—Washington	13	2	3	.667	2	2	1.000	1	3	4	2	2	0	1	0	2	6

SALLEY, JOHN
F/C, HEAT

PERSONAL: Born May 16, 1964, in Brooklyn, N.Y. . . . 6-11/244. . . . Full name: John Thomas Salley.
HIGH SCHOOL: Canarsie (Brooklyn, N.Y.).
COLLEGE: Georgia Tech.
TRANSACTIONS/CAREER NOTES: Selected by Detroit Pistons in first round (11th pick overall) of 1986 NBA Draft. . . . Traded by Pistons to Miami Heat for rights to Isaiah Morris and conditional draft choice (September 8, 1992).
MISCELLANEOUS: Member of NBA championship teams (1989, 1990).

COLLEGIATE RECORD

Season	Team	G	Min.	FGM	FGA	Pct.	FTM	FTA	Pct.	Reb.	Pts.	Avg.
82-83	—Georgia Tech	27	829	104	207	.502	102	160	.638	153	310	11.5
83-84	—Georgia Tech	29	992	126	214	.589	89	132	.674	167	341	11.8
84-85	—Georgia Tech	35	1231	193	308	.627	105	165	.636	250	491	14.0
85-86	—Georgia Tech	34	1145	172	284	.606	101	170	.594	228	445	13.1
Totals	....	125	4197	595	1013	.587	397	627	.633	798	1587	12.7

NBA REGULAR-SEASON RECORD

								— REBOUNDS —														
Season	Team	G	Min.	FGM	FGA	Pct.	FTM	FTA	Pct.	Off.	Def.	Tot.	Ast.	PF	Dq.	Stl.	Blk.	TO	Pts.	Avg.
86-87	—Detroit.........	82	1463	163	290	.562	105	171	.614	108	188	296	54	256	5	44	125	74	431	5.3
87-88	—Detroit.........	82	2003	258	456	.566	185	261	.709	166	236	402	113	294	4	53	137	120	701	8.5
88-89	—Detroit.........	67	1458	166	333	.499	135	195	.692	134	201	335	75	197	3	40	72	100	467	7.0
89-90	—Detroit.........	82	1914	209	408	.512	174	244	.713	154	285	439	67	282	7	51	153	97	593	7.2
90-91	—Detroit.........	74	1649	179	377	.475	186	256	.727	137	190	327	70	240	7	52	112	91	544	7.4
91-92	—Detroit.........	72	1774	249	486	.512	186	260	.715	106	190	296	116	222	1	49	110	102	684	9.5
Totals	....	459	10261	1224	2350	.521	971	1387	.700	805	1290	2095	495	1491	27	289	709	584	3420	7.5

Three-point field goals: 1986-87, 0-for-1. 1988-89, 0-for-2. 1989-90, 1-for-4 (.250). 1990-91, 0-for-1. 1991-92, 0-for-3. Totals, 1-for-11 (.091).

NBA PLAYOFF RECORD

								— REBOUNDS —														
Season	Team	G	Min.	FGM	FGA	Pct.	FTM	FTA	Pct.	Off.	Def.	Tot.	Ast.	PF	Dq.	Stl.	Blk.	TO	Pts.	Avg.
86-87	—Detroit.........	15	311	33	66	.500	27	42	.643	30	42	72	11	60	1	3	17	14	93	6.2
87-88	—Detroit.........	23	623	56	104	.538	49	69	.710	64	91	155	21	88	2	15	37	23	161	7.0
88-89	—Detroit.........	17	392	58	99	.586	36	54	.667	34	45	79	9	58	0	9	25	12	152	8.9
89-90	—Detroit.........	20	547	58	122	.475	74	98	.755	57	60	117	20	76	2	9	33	22	190	9.5
90-91	—Detroit.........	15	308	38	70	.543	36	60	.600	20	42	62	11	58	1	6	20	13	112	7.5
91-92	—Detroit.........	5	149	20	44	.455	23	28	.821	10	20	30	14	18	0	3	14	9	63	12.6
Totals	....	95	2330	263	505	.521	245	351	.698	215	300	515	86	358	6	45	146	93	771	8.1

Three-point field goals: 1987-88, 0-for-1. 1991-92, 0-for-1. Totals, 0-for-2.

SAMPSON, RALPH
C/F

PERSONAL: Born July 7, 1960, in Harrisonburg, Va. . . . 7-4/230. . . . Full name: Ralph Lee Sampson Jr.
HIGH SCHOOL: Harrisonburg (Va.).
COLLEGE: Virginia.
TRANSACTIONS/CAREER NOTES: Selected by Houston Rockets in first round (first pick overall) of 1983 NBA Draft. . . . Traded by Rockets with Steve Harris to Golden State Warriors for Joe Barry Carroll and Eric

Floyd (December 12, 1987).... Traded by Warriors to Sacramento Kings for Jim Petersen (September 27, 1989).... Waived by Kings (October 25, 1991).... Signed as free agent by Washington Bullets (November 19, 1991).... Waived by Bullets (January 6, 1992).... Played in Spain (1991-92).

COLLEGIATE RECORD

NOTES: THE SPORTING NEWS College Player of the Year (1982).... THE SPORTING NEWS All-America first team (1981, 1982, 1983).

Season Team	G	Min.	FGM	FGA	Pct.	FTM	FTA	Pct.	Reb.	Pts.	Avg.
79-80 — Virginia	34	1017	221	404	.547	66	94	.702	381	508	14.9
80-81 — Virginia	33	1056	230	413	.557	125	198	.631	378	585	17.7
81-82 — Virginia	32	1002	198	353	.561	110	179	.615	366	506	15.8
82-83 — Virginia	33	995	250	414	.604	126	179	.704	386	629	19.1
Totals	132	4070	899	1584	.568	427	650	.657	1511	2228	16.9

NBA REGULAR-SEASON RECORD

HONORS: NBA Rookie of the Year (1984).... All-NBA second team (1985).... NBA All-Rookie team (1984).

Season Team	G	Min.	FGM	FGA	Pct.	FTM	FTA	Pct.	Off.	Def.	Tot.	Ast.	PF	Dq.	Stl.	Blk.	TO	Pts.	Avg.
83-84 — Houston	82	2693	716	1369	.523	287	434	.661	293	620	913	163	339	16	70	197	294	1720	21.0
84-85 — Houston	82	3086	753	1499	.502	303	448	.676	227	626	853	224	306	10	81	168	*326	1809	22.1
85-86 — Houston	79	2864	624	1280	.488	241	376	.641	258	621	879	283	308	12	99	129	285	1491	18.9
86-87 — Houston	43	1326	277	566	.489	118	189	.624	88	284	372	120	169	6	40	58	126	672	15.6
87-88 — Hou.-G.S.	48	1663	299	682	.438	149	196	.760	140	322	462	122	164	3	41	8	171	749	15.6
88-89 — Golden State	61	1086	164	365	.449	62	95	.653	105	202	307	77	170	3	31	65	90	393	6.4
89-90 — Sacramento	26	417	48	129	.372	12	23	.522	11	73	84	28	66	1	14	22	34	109	4.2
90-91 — Sacramento	25	348	34	93	.366	5	19	.263	41	70	111	17	54	0	11	17	27	74	3.0
91-92 — Washington	10	108	9	29	.310	4	6	.667	11	19	30	4	14	1	3	8	10	22	2.2
Totals	456	13591	2924	6012	.486	1181	1786	.661	1174	2837	4011	1038	1590	52	390	672	1363	7039	15.4

Three-point field goals: 1983-84, 1-for-4 (.250). 1984-85, 0-for-6. 1985-86, 2-for-15 (.133). 1986-87, 0-for-3. 1987-88, 2-for-11 (.182). 1988-89, 3-for-8 (.375). 1989-90, 1-for-4 (.250). 1990-91, 1-for-5 (.200). 1991-92, 0-for-2. Totals, 10-for-58 (.172).

NBA PLAYOFF RECORD

Season Team	G	Min.	FGM	FGA	Pct.	FTM	FTA	Pct.	Off.	Def.	Tot.	Ast.	PF	Dq.	Stl.	Blk.	TO	Pts.	Avg.
84-85 — Houston	5	193	43	100	.430	19	37	.514	25	58	83	7	23	2	2	8	17	106	21.2
85-86 — Houston	20	741	156	301	.518	86	118	.729	66	149	215	80	79	1	30	35	71	399	20.0
86-87 — Houston	10	330	75	146	.514	35	43	.814	27	61	88	21	47	1	2	12	31	186	18.6
88-89 — Golden State	3	43	9	22	.409	2	4	.500	6	8	14	1	8	0	1	2	4	20	6.7
Totals	38	1307	283	569	.497	142	202	.703	124	276	400	109	157	4	35	57	123	711	18.7

Three-point field goals: 1984-85, 1-for-1. 1985-86, 1-for-1. 1986-87, 1-for-2 (.500). 1988-89, 0-for-4. Totals, 3-for-8 (.375).

NBA ALL-STAR GAME RECORD

NOTES: NBA All-Star Game Most Valuable Player (1985).

Season Team	Min.	FGM	FGA	Pct.	FTM	FTA	Pct.	Off.	Def.	Tot.	Ast.	PF	Dq.	Stl.	Blk.	TO	Pts.
1984 — Houston	16	4	7	.571	1	2	.500	1	4	5	0	4	0	0	0	3	9
1985 — Houston	29	10	15	.667	4	6	.667	3	7	10	1	5	0	0	1	1	24
1986 — Houston	21	7	11	.636	2	2	1.000	1	3	4	1	4	0	0	0	2	16
Totals	66	21	33	.636	7	10	.700	5	14	19	2	13	0	0	1	6	49

SPANISH LEAGUE RECORD

Season Team	G	Min.	FGM	FGA	Pct.	FTM	FTA	Pct.	Reb.	Pts.	Avg.
91-92 — Unicaja Ronda	8	227	21	71	.296	14	22	.636	54	56	7.0

SANDERS, JEFF
F, HAWKS

PERSONAL: Born January 14, 1966, in Augusta, Ga.... 6-8/240....
Full name: Jeffery Raynard Sanders.
HIGH SCHOOL: T.W. Josey (Augusta, Ga.).
COLLEGE: Georgia Southern.

TRANSACTIONS/CAREER NOTES: Selected by Chicago Bulls in first round (20th pick overall) of 1989 NBA Draft.... Traded by Bulls to Miami Heat for a future second-round draft choice (October 2, 1990).... Waived by Heat (October 30, 1990).... Played in Continental Basketball Association with Albany Patroons (1990-91 and 1991-92) and Grand Rapids Hoops and Fort Wayne Fury (1991-92).... Signed by Charlotte Hornets to 10-day contract (January 22, 1991).... Signed as free agent by New York Knicks (October 3, 1991).... Waived by Kincks (October 7, 1991).... Signed by Atlanta Hawks to first of two consecutive 10-day contracts (February 26, 1992).... Signed by Hawks for remainder of season (March 17, 1992).

COLLEGIATE RECORD

Season Team	G	Min.	FGM	FGA	Pct.	FTM	FTA	Pct.	Reb.	Pts.	Avg.
85-86 — Georgia Southern	28	725	106	193	.549	57	94	.606	180	269	9.6
86-87 — Georgia Southern	31	986	150	288	.521	58	88	.659	202	358	11.5
87-88 — Georgia Southern	31	1092	231	419	.551	98	135	.726	255	560	18.1
88-89 — Georgia Southern	29	1031	279	515	.542	116	159	.730	256	674	23.2
Totals	119	3834	766	1415	.541	329	476	.691	893	1861	15.6

NBA REGULAR-SEASON RECORD

Season Team	G	Min.	FGM	FGA	Pct.	FTM	FTA	Pct.	Off.	Def.	Tot.	Ast.	PF	Dq.	Stl.	Blk.	TO	Pts.	Avg.
89-90 — Chicago	31	182	13	40	.325	2	4	.500	17	22	39	9	27	0	4	4	15	28	0.9
90-91 — Charlotte	3	43	6	14	.429	1	2	.500	3	6	9	1	6	0	1	1	1	13	4.3
91-92 — Atlanta	12	117	20	45	.444	7	9	.778	9	17	26	9	15	0	5	3	5	47	3.9
Totals	46	342	39	99	.394	10	15	.667	29	45	74	19	48	0	10	8	21	88	1.9

NBA PLAYOFF RECORD

								— REBOUNDS —										
Season Team	G	Min.	FGM	FGA	Pct.	FTM	FTA	Pct.	Off.	Def.	Tot.	Ast.	PF	Dq.	Stl.	Blk.	TO	Pts.	Avg.
89-90 —Chicago........	3	3	1	1	1.000	0	0	...	0	0	0	0	0	0	0	0	0	2	0.7

CBA REGULAR-SEASON RECORD

			2-POINT			3-POINT									
Season Team	G	Min.	FGM	FGA	Pct.	FGM	FGA	Pct.	FTM	FTA	Pct.	Reb.	Ast.	Pts.	Avg.
90-91 —Albany	38	1032	236	423	.558	0	1	.000	87	117	.744	304	71	559	14.7
91-92 —Al.-G.R.-F.W...	44	1773	356	693	.514	0	0	...	173	223	.776	405	164	885	20.1
Totals	82	2805	592	1116	.530	0	1	.000	260	340	.765	709	235	1444	17.6

SANDERS, MIKE
F, CAVALIERS

PERSONAL: Born May 7, 1960, in Vidalia, La. . . . 6-6/215. . . . Full name: Michael Anthony Sanders.
HIGH SCHOOL: DeRidder (La.).
COLLEGE: UCLA.

TRANSACTIONS/CAREER NOTES: Selected by Kansas City Kings in fourth round (74th pick overall) of 1982 NBA Draft. . . . Waived by Kings (October 4, 1982). . . . Played in Continental Basketball Association with Montana Golden Nuggets (1982-83) and Sarasota Stingers (1983-84). . . . Signed as free agent by San Antonio Spurs (February 9, 1983). . . . Waived by Spurs (October 17, 1983). . . . Signed as free agent by Phoenix Suns (December 19, 1983). . . . Traded by Suns with Larry Nance and 1988 first-round draft choice to Cleveland Cavaliers for Tyrone Corbin, Kevin Johnson, Mark West, 1988 first- and second-round draft choices and 1989 second-round draft choice (February 25, 1988). . . . Signed as unrestricted free agent by Indiana Pacers (September 8, 1989). . . . Waived by Pacers (November 18, 1991). . . . Signed by Cleveland Cavaliers to 10-day contract (March 12, 1992). . . . Signed by Cavaliers for remainder of season (March 22, 1992).

COLLEGIATE RECORD

Season Team	G	Min.	FGM	FGA	Pct.	FTM	FTA	Pct.	Reb.	Pts.	Avg.
78-79 —UCLA....................................	23	138	16	38	.421	11	16	.688	35	43	1.9
79-80 —UCLA....................................	32	805	142	248	.573	76	96	.792	190	360	11.3
80-81 —UCLA....................................	27	814	161	287	.561	95	124	.766	179	417	15.4
81-82 —UCLA....................................	27	943	150	299	.502	90	116	.776	173	390	14.4
Totals	109	2700	469	872	.538	272	352	.773	577	1210	11.1

CBA REGULAR-SEASON RECORD

NOTES: CBA Rookie of the Year (1983). . . . CBA All-Star first team (1983). . . . CBA All-Defensive second team (1983).

			2-POINT			3-POINT									
Season Team	G	Min.	FGM	FGA	Pct.	FGM	FGA	Pct.	FTM	FTA	Pct.	Reb.	Ast.	Pts.	Avg.
82-83 —Montana	30	1036	273	473	.577	0	0	...	123	149	.826	247	42	669	22.3
83-84 —Sarasota	7	295	69	126	.548	0	1	.000	56	65	.862	52	8	194	27.7
Totals	37	1331	342	599	.571	0	1	.000	179	214	.836	299	50	863	23.3

NBA REGULAR-SEASON RECORD

								— REBOUNDS —										
Season Team	G	Min.	FGM	FGA	Pct.	FTM	FTA	Pct.	Off.	Def.	Tot.	Ast.	PF	Dq.	Stl.	Blk.	TO	Pts.	Avg.
82-83 —San Antonio .	26	393	76	157	.484	31	43	.721	31	63	94	19	57	0	18	6	28	183	7.0
83-84 —Phoenix.......	50	586	97	203	.478	29	42	.690	40	63	103	44	101	0	23	12	44	223	4.5
84-85 —Phoenix.......	21	418	85	175	.486	45	59	.763	38	51	89	29	59	0	23	4	34	215	10.2
85-86 —Phoenix.......	82	1644	347	676	.513	208	257	.809	104	169	273	150	236	3	76	31	143	905	11.0
86-87 —Phoenix.......	82	1655	357	722	.494	143	183	.781	101	170	271	126	210	1	61	23	105	859	10.5
87-88 —Phoe.-Clev...	59	883	153	303	.505	59	76	.776	38	71	109	56	131	1	33	9	50	365	6.2
88-89 —Cleveland.....	82	2102	332	733	.453	97	135	.719	98	209	307	133	230	2	89	32	104	764	9.3
89-90 —Indiana........	82	1531	225	479	.470	55	75	.733	78	152	230	89	220	1	43	23	79	510	6.2
90-91 —Indiana........	80	1357	206	494	.417	47	57	.825	73	112	185	106	198	1	37	26	65	463	5.8
91-92 —Ind.-Clev......	31	633	92	161	.571	36	47	.766	27	69	96	53	83	1	24	10	22	221	7.1
Totals	595	11202	1970	4103	.480	750	974	.770	628	1129	1757	805	1525	10	425	176	674	4708	7.9

Three-point field goals: 1982-83, 0-for-2. 1985-86, 3-for-15 (.200). 1986-87, 2-for-17 (.118). 1987-88, 0-for-1. 1988-89, 3-for-10 (.300). 1989-90, 5-for-14 (.357). 1990-91, 4-for-20 (.200). 1991-92, 1-for-3 (.333). Totals, 18-for-82 (.220).

NBA PLAYOFF RECORD

								— REBOUNDS —										
Season Team	G	Min.	FGM	FGA	Pct.	FTM	FTA	Pct.	Off.	Def.	Tot.	Ast.	PF	Dq.	Stl.	Blk.	TO	Pts.	Avg.
82-83 —San Antonio .	6	25	7	13	.538	0	0	...	2	7	9	4	3	0	0	0	0	14	2.3
83-84 —Phoenix.......	15	152	22	46	.478	16	17	.941	10	10	20	7	31	0	6	4	14	60	4.0
84-85 —Phoenix.......	3	91	22	37	.595	8	10	.800	8	7	15	10	8	0	5	0	9	52	17.3
87-88 —Cleveland.....	5	134	28	52	.538	8	10	.800	11	14	25	7	21	0	3	2	11	64	12.8
88-89 —Cleveland.....	5	87	15	30	.500	3	5	.600	6	10	16	4	11	0	2	1	10	33	6.6
89-90 —Indiana........	3	24	5	11	.455	0	0	...	5	1	6	2	4	0	0	0	2	11	3.7
90-91 —Indiana........	5	41	6	10	.600	2	4	.500	0	4	4	4	9	0	4	2	1	15	3.0
91-92 —Cleveland.....	17	418	56	115	.487	17	21	.810	20	35	55	37	62	0	15	12	23	130	7.6
Totals	59	972	161	314	.513	54	67	.806	62	88	150	75	149	0	35	21	70	379	6.4

Three-point field goals: 1987-88, 0-for-1. 1989-90, 1-for-1. 1990-91, 1-for-2 (.500). 1991-92, 1-for-3 (.333). Totals, 3-for-7 (.429).

SCHAYES, DAN
C, BUCKS

PERSONAL: Born May 10, 1959, in Syracuse, N.Y. . . . 6-11/260. . . . Full name: Daniel Leslie Schayes. . . . Name pronounced SHAZE. . . . Son of Dolph Schayes, forward with Syracuse Nationals of National Basketball League (1948-49), Syracuse Nationals and Philadelphia 76ers of NBA (1949-50 through 1963-64), former NBA Supervisor of Referees, and member of Naismith Memorial Basketball Hall of Fame.
HIGH SCHOOL: Jamesville DeWitt (DeWitt, N.Y.).

— 163 —

COLLEGE: Syracuse.
TRANSACTIONS/CAREER NOTES: Selected by Utah Jazz in first round (13th pick overall) of 1981 NBA Draft. . . . Traded by Jazz with other considerations to Denver Nuggets for Rich Kelley (February 7, 1983). . . . Traded by Nuggets to Milwaukee Bucks for draft rights to Terry Mills (August 1, 1990).

COLLEGIATE RECORD

Season Team	G	Min.	FGM	FGA	Pct.	FTM	FTA	Pct.	Reb.	Pts.	Avg.
77-78 —Syracuse	24	. . .	39	69	.565	34	45	.756	96	112	4.7
78-79 —Syracuse	29	. . .	62	117	.530	55	66	.833	121	179	6.2
79-80 —Syracuse	30	. . .	59	116	.509	60	78	.769	134	178	5.9
80-81 —Syracuse	34	. . .	165	285	.579	166	202	.822	284	496	14.6
Totals	117	. . .	325	587	.554	315	391	.806	635	965	8.2

NBA REGULAR-SEASON RECORD

| | | | | | | | | | — REBOUNDS — | | | | | | | | | |
Season Team	G	Min.	FGM	FGA	Pct.	FTM	FTA	Pct.	Off.	Def.	Tot.	Ast.	PF	Dq.	Stl.	Blk.	TO	Pts.	Avg.
81-82 —Utah	82	1623	252	524	.481	140	185	.757	131	296	427	146	292	4	46	72	151	644	7.9
82-83 —Utah-Den.	82	2284	342	749	.457	228	295	.773	200	435	635	205	325	8	54	98	253	912	11.1
83-84 —Denver	82	1420	183	371	.493	215	272	.790	145	288	433	91	308	5	32	60	119	581	7.1
84-85 —Denver	56	542	60	129	.465	79	97	.814	48	96	144	38	98	2	20	25	44	199	3.6
85-86 —Denver	80	1654	221	440	.502	216	278	.777	154	285	439	79	298	7	42	63	105	658	8.2
86-87 —Denver	76	1556	210	405	.519	229	294	.779	120	260	380	85	266	5	20	74	95	649	8.5
87-88 —Denver	81	2166	361	668	.540	407	487	.836	200	462	662	106	323	9	62	92	155	1129	13.9
88-89 —Denver	76	1918	317	607	.522	332	402	.826	142	358	500	105	320	8	42	81	160	969	12.8
89-90 —Denver	53	1194	163	330	.494	225	264	.852	117	225	342	61	200	7	41	45	72	551	10.4
90-91 —Milwaukee	82	2228	298	597	.499	274	328	.835	174	361	535	98	264	4	55	61	106	870	10.6
91-92 —Milwaukee	43	726	83	199	.417	74	96	.771	58	110	168	34	98	0	19	19	41	240	5.6
Totals	793	17311	2490	5019	.496	2419	2998	.807	1489	3176	4665	1048	2792	59	433	690	1301	7402	9.3

Three-point field goals: 1981-82, 0-for-1. 1982-83, 0-for-1. 1983-84, 0-for-2. 1985-86, 0-for-1. 1987-88, 0-for-2. 1988-89, 3-for-9 (.333). 1989-90, 0-for-4. 1990-91, 0-for-5. Totals, 3-for-25 (.120).

NBA PLAYOFF RECORD

| | | | | | | | | | — REBOUNDS — | | | | | | | | | |
Season Team	G	Min.	FGM	FGA	Pct.	FTM	FTA	Pct.	Off.	Def.	Tot.	Ast.	PF	Dq.	Stl.	Blk.	TO	Pts.	Avg.
82-83 —Denver	8	163	21	43	.488	15	15	1.000	11	29	40	14	25	0	2	5	17	57	7.1
83-84 —Denver	5	81	11	18	.611	6	8	.750	3	21	24	4	20	0	4	3	7	28	5.6
84-85 —Denver	9	118	11	26	.423	14	20	.700	8	22	30	12	22	0	3	4	5	36	4.0
85-86 —Denver	10	295	46	86	.535	24	30	.800	34	48	82	9	37	1	4	17	21	116	11.6
86-87 —Denver	3	75	12	17	.706	6	9	.667	6	11	17	2	10	0	1	2	3	30	10.0
87-88 —Denver	11	314	55	88	.625	70	83	.843	30	49	79	18	46	1	3	10	24	180	16.4
88-89 —Denver	2	36	1	7	.143	6	8	.750	2	9	11	1	4	0	1	1	1	8	4.0
90-91 —Milwaukee	3	71	9	23	.391	10	11	.909	4	8	12	3	8	0	3	1	6	28	9.3
Totals	51	1153	166	308	.539	151	184	.821	98	197	295	63	172	2	21	43	84	483	9.5

Three-point field goals: 1990-91, 0-for-1.

SCHEFFLER, STEVE
F/C

PERSONAL: Born September 3, 1967, in Grand Rapids, Mich. . . . 6-9/250. . . . Full name: Stephen Robert Scheffler. . . . Brother of Tom Scheffler, forward with Portland Trail Blazers (1984-85).
HIGH SCHOOL: Forest Hills Northern (Grand Rapids, Mich.).
COLLEGE: Purdue.
TRANSACTIONS/CAREER NOTES: Selected by Charlotte Hornets in second round (39th pick overall) of 1990 NBA Draft. . . . Waived by Hornets (May 31, 1991). . . . Signed as free agent by Boston Celtics (October 2, 1991). . . . Waived by Celtics (October 30, 1991). . . . Played in Continental Basketball Association with Quad City Thunder (1991-92). . . . Signed by Sacramento Kings to 10-day contract (February 13, 1992). . . . Signed by Denver Nuggets to first of two consecutive 10-day contracts (February 27, 1992). . . . Signed by Nuggets for remainder of season (March 17, 1992).

COLLEGIATE RECORD

NOTES: THE SPORTING NEWS All-America second team (1990).

Season Team	G	Min.	FGM	FGA	Pct.	FTM	FTA	Pct.	Reb.	Pts.	Avg.
86-87 —Purdue	16	73	9	16	.563	6	14	.429	24	24	1.5
87-88 —Purdue	33	548	80	113	.708	65	100	.650	144	225	6.8
88-89 —Purdue	31	830	146	219	.667	111	143	.776	187	403	13.0
89-90 —Purdue	30	996	173	248	.698	157	195	.805	183	503	16.8
Totals	110	2447	408	596	.685	339	452	.750	538	1155	10.5

NBA REGULAR-SEASON RECORD

| | | | | | | | | | — REBOUNDS — | | | | | | | | | |
Season Team	G	Min.	FGM	FGA	Pct.	FTM	FTA	Pct.	Off.	Def.	Tot.	Ast.	PF	Dq.	Stl.	Blk.	TO	Pts.	Avg.
90-91 —Charlotte	39	227	20	39	.513	19	21	.905	21	24	45	9	20	0	6	2	4	59	1.5
91-92 —Sac.-Den.	11	61	6	9	.667	9	12	.750	10	4	14	0	10	0	3	1	1	21	1.9
Totals	50	288	26	48	.542	28	33	.848	31	28	59	9	30	0	9	3	5	80	1.6

CBA REGULAR-SEASON RECORD

| | | | 2-POINT | | | 3-POINT | | | | | | | | |
Season Team	G	Min.	FGM	FGA	Pct.	FGM	FGA	Pct.	FTM	FTA	Pct.	Reb.	Ast.	Pts.	Avg.
91-92 —Quad City	41	1335	233	381	.612	0	0	. . .	144	178	.809	309	36	610	14.9

DID YOU KNOW. . .

. . . that Kevin Loughery has coached six NBA teams, the most of any active coach?

SCHINTZIUS, DWAYNE
C

PERSONAL: Born October 14, 1968, in Brandon, Fla. . . . 7-2/260. . . . Name pronounced SHIN-sus.
HIGH SCHOOL: Brandon (Fla.).
COLLEGE: Florida.

TRANSACTIONS/CAREER NOTES: Selected by San Antonio Spurs in first round (24th pick overall) of 1990 NBA Draft. . . . Traded by Spurs with 1994 second-round draft choice to Sacramento Kings for Antoine Carr (September 23, 1991). . . . Waived by Kings (July 20, 1992).

COLLEGIATE RECORD

Season Team	G	Min.	FGM	FGA	Pct.	FTM	FTA	Pct.	Reb.	Pts.	Avg.
86-87—Florida	34	931	161	366	.440	48	65	.738	206	370	10.9
87-88—Florida	35	1069	224	456	.491	54	74	.730	228	503	14.4
88-89—Florida	30	1120	220	422	.521	99	140	.707	290	541	18.0
89-90—Florida	11	355	90	163	.552	30	38	.789	105	210	19.1
Totals	110	3475	695	1407	.494	231	317	.729	829	1624	14.8

Three-point field goals: 1987-88, 1-for-5 (.200). 1988-89, 2-for-6 (.333). 1989-90, 0-for-8. Totals, 3-for-19 (.158).

NBA REGULAR-SEASON RECORD

Season Team	G	Min.	FGM	FGA	Pct.	FTM	FTA	Pct.	Off.	Def.	Tot.	Ast.	PF	Dq.	Stl.	Blk.	TO	Pts.	Avg.
									— REBOUNDS —										
90-91—San Antonio	42	398	68	155	.439	22	40	.550	28	93	121	17	64	0	2	29	34	158	3.8
91-92—Sacramento	33	400	50	117	.427	10	12	.833	43	75	118	20	67	1	6	28	19	110	3.3
Totals	75	798	118	272	.434	32	52	.615	71	168	239	37	131	1	8	57	53	268	3.6

Three-point field goals: 1990-91, 0-for-2. 1991-92, 0-for-4. Totals, 0-for-6.

SCHREMPF, DETLEF
F, PACERS

PERSONAL: Born January 21, 1963, in Leverkusen, West Germany. . . . 6-10/230. . . . Name pronounced DET-lef Shrempf.
HIGH SCHOOL: Centralia (Wash.).
COLLEGE: Washington.

TRANSACTIONS/CAREER NOTES: Selected by Dallas Mavericks in first round (eighth pick overall) of 1985 NBA Draft. . . . Traded by Mavericks with 1990 or 1991 second-round draft choice to Indiana Pacers for Herb Williams (February 21, 1989).
MISCELLANEOUS: Member of West German Olympic team (1984). . . . Member of German Olympic team (1992).

COLLEGIATE RECORD

NOTES: THE SPORTING NEWS All-America second team (1985).

Season Team	G	Min.	FGM	FGA	Pct.	FTM	FTA	Pct.	Reb.	Pts.	Avg.
81-82—Washington	28	314	33	73	.452	26	47	.553	56	92	3.3
82-83—Washington	31	958	124	266	.466	81	113	.717	211	329	10.6
83-84—Washington	31	1186	195	362	.539	131	178	.736	230	521	16.8
84-85—Washington	32	1180	191	342	.558	125	175	.714	255	507	15.8
Totals	122	3638	543	1043	.521	363	513	.708	752	1449	11.9

NBA REGULAR-SEASON RECORD

HONORS: NBA Sixth Man Award (1991, 1992).

Season Team	G	Min.	FGM	FGA	Pct.	FTM	FTA	Pct.	Off.	Def.	Tot.	Ast.	PF	Dq.	Stl.	Blk.	TO	Pts.	Avg.
									— REBOUNDS —										
85-86—Dallas	64	969	142	315	.451	110	152	.724	70	128	198	88	166	1	23	10	84	397	6.2
86-87—Dallas	81	1711	265	561	.472	193	260	.742	87	216	303	161	224	2	50	16	110	756	9.3
87-88—Dallas	82	1587	246	539	.456	201	266	.756	102	177	279	159	189	0	42	32	108	698	8.5
88-89—Dallas-Ind.	69	1850	274	578	.474	273	350	.780	126	269	395	179	220	3	53	19	133	828	12.0
89-90—Indiana	78	2573	424	822	.516	402	490	.820	149	471	620	247	271	6	59	16	180	1267	16.2
90-91—Indiana	82	2632	432	831	.520	441	539	.818	178	482	660	301	262	3	58	22	175	1320	16.1
91-92—Indiana	80	2605	496	925	.536	365	441	.828	202	568	770	312	286	4	62	37	191	1380	17.3
Totals	536	13927	2279	4571	.499	1985	2456	.795	914	2311	3225	1447	1618	19	347	152	981	6646	12.4

Three-point field goals: 1985-86, 3-for-7 (.429). 1986-87, 33-for-69 (.478). 1987-88, 5-for-32 (.156). 1988-89, 7-for-35 (.200). 1989-90, 17-for-48 (.354). 1990-91, 15-for-40 (.375). 1991-92, 23-for-71 (.324). Totals, 103-for-302 (.341).

NBA PLAYOFF RECORD

Season Team	G	Min.	FGM	FGA	Pct.	FTM	FTA	Pct.	Off.	Def.	Tot.	Ast.	PF	Dq.	Stl.	Blk.	TO	Pts.	Avg.
									— REBOUNDS —										
85-86—Dallas	10	120	13	28	.464	11	17	.647	7	16	23	14	24	0	2	1	10	37	3.7
86-87—Dallas	4	97	13	35	.371	5	11	.455	4	8	12	6	13	0	3	2	6	31	7.8
87-88—Dallas	15	274	40	86	.465	36	51	.706	25	30	55	24	29	0	8	7	21	117	7.8
89-90—Indiana	3	125	23	47	.489	15	16	.938	10	26	36	11	17	0	2	0	11	61	20.3
90-91—Indiana	5	179	27	57	.474	25	30	.833	10	26	36	11	17	0	2	1	11	79	15.8
91-92—Indiana	3	120	18	47	.383	25	28	.893	12	27	39	7	10	0	2	1	7	63	21.0
Totals	40	915	134	300	.447	117	153	.765	63	124	187	67	106	0	19	12	65	388	9.7

Three-point field goals: 1985-86, 0-for-1. 1986-87, 0-for-3. 1987-88, 1-for-3 (.333). 1989-90, 0-for-3. 1990-91, 0-for-4. 1991-92, 2-for-4 (.500). Totals, 3-for-18 (.167).

SCOTT, BYRON
G, LAKERS

PERSONAL: Born March 28, 1961, in Ogden, Utah. . . . 6-4/200. . . . Full name: Byron Antom Scott.
HIGH SCHOOL: Morningside (Inglewood, Calif.).
COLLEGE: Arizona State.

TRANSACTIONS/CAREER NOTES: Selected by San Diego Clippers in first round (fourth pick overall) of 1983 NBA Draft. . . . Draft rights traded by Clippers with Swen Nater to Los Angeles Lakers for Norm Nixon,

Eddie Jordan and 1986 and 1987 second-round draft choices (October 10, 1983).
MISCELLANEOUS: Member of NBA championship teams (1985, 1987, 1988).

COLLEGIATE RECORD

Season Team	G	Min.	FGM	FGA	Pct.	FTM	FTA	Pct.	Reb.	Pts.	Avg.
79-80 — Arizona State	29	936	166	332	.500	63	86	.733	79	395	13.6
80-81 — Arizona State	28	1003	197	390	.505	70	101	.693	106	464	16.6
81-82 — Arizona State					Did not play — academic and personal reasons.						
82-83 — Arizona State	33	1206	283	552	.513	147	188	.782	177	713	21.6
Totals	90	3145	646	1274	.507	280	375	.747	362	1572	17.5

NBA REGULAR-SEASON RECORD

HONORS: NBA All-Rookie team (1984).
NOTES: Led NBA with .433 three-point field-goal percentage (1985).

Season Team	G	Min.	FGM	FGA	Pct.	FTM	FTA	Pct.	— REBOUNDS — Off.	Def.	Tot.	Ast.	PF	Dq.	Stl.	Blk.	TO	Pts.	Avg.
83-84 — Los Angeles	74	1637	334	690	.484	112	139	.806	50	114	164	177	174	0	81	19	116	788	10.6
84-85 — L.A. Lakers	81	2305	541	1003	.539	187	228	.820	57	153	210	244	197	1	100	17	138	1295	16.0
85-86 — L.A. Lakers	76	2190	507	989	.513	138	176	.784	55	134	189	164	167	0	85	15	110	1151	15.4
86-87 — L.A. Lakers	82	2729	554	1134	.489	224	251	.892	63	223	286	281	163	0	125	18	144	1397	17.0
87-88 — L.A. Lakers	81	3048	710	1348	.527	272	317	.858	76	257	333	335	204	2	155	27	161	1754	21.7
88-89 — L.A. Lakers	74	2605	588	1198	.491	195	226	.863	72	230	302	231	181	1	114	27	157	1448	19.6
89-90 — L.A. Lakers	77	2593	472	1005	.470	160	209	.766	51	191	242	274	180	2	77	31	122	1197	15.5
90-91 — L.A. Lakers	82	2630	501	1051	.477	118	148	.797	54	192	246	177	146	0	95	21	85	1191	14.5
91-92 — L.A. Lakers	82	2679	460	1005	.458	244	291	.838	74	236	310	226	140	0	105	28	119	1218	14.9
Totals	709	22416	4667	9423	.495	1650	1985	.831	552	1730	2282	2109	1552	6	937	203	1152	11462	16.2

Three-point field goals: 1983-84, 8-for-34 (.235). 1984-85, 26-for-60 (.433). 1985-86, 22-for-61 (.361). 1986-87, 65-for-149 (.436). 1987-88, 62-for-179 (.346). 1988-89, 77-for-193 (.399). 1989-90, 93-for-220 (.423). 1990-91, 71-for-219 (.324). 1991-92, 54-for-157 (.344). Totals, 478-for-1272 (.376).

NBA PLAYOFF RECORD

Season Team	G	Min.	FGM	FGA	Pct.	FTM	FTA	Pct.	— REBOUNDS — Off.	Def.	Tot.	Ast.	PF	Dq.	Stl.	Blk.	TO	Pts.	Avg.
83-84 — Los Angeles	20	404	74	161	.460	21	35	.600	11	26	37	34	39	1	18	2	26	171	8.6
84-85 — L.A. Lakers	19	585	138	267	.517	35	44	.795	16	36	52	50	47	0	41	4	24	321	16.9
85-86 — L.A. Lakers	14	470	90	181	.497	38	42	.905	15	40	55	42	38	0	19	2	30	224	16.0
86-87 — L.A. Lakers	18	608	103	210	.490	53	67	.791	20	42	62	57	52	0	19	4	25	266	14.8
87-88 — L.A. Lakers	24	897	178	357	.499	90	104	.865	26	74	100	60	65	0	34	5	47	470	19.6
88-89 — L.A. Lakers	11	402	79	160	.494	46	55	.836	10	35	45	25	31	0	18	2	20	219	19.9
89-90 — L.A. Lakers	9	325	49	106	.462	10	13	.769	7	30	37	23	32	1	20	3	13	121	13.4
90-91 — L.A. Lakers	18	678	95	186	.511	27	34	.794	13	44	57	29	53	0	23	4	17	237	13.2
91-92 — L.A. Lakers	4	148	22	44	.500	24	27	.889	3	7	10	14	10	0	6	1	5	75	18.8
Totals	137	4517	828	1672	.495	344	421	.817	121	334	455	334	367	2	198	27	207	2104	15.4

Three-point field goals: 1983-84, 2-for-10 (.200). 1984-85, 10-for-21 (.476). 1985-86, 6-for-17 (.353). 1986-87, 7-for-34 (.206). 1987-88, 24-for-55 (.436). 1988-89, 15-for-39 (.385). 1989-90, 13-for-34 (.382). 1990-91, 20-for-38 (.526). 1991-92, 7-for-12 (.583). Totals, 104-for-260 (.400).

SCOTT, DENNIS
G/F, MAGIC

PERSONAL: Born September 5, 1968, in Hagerstown, Md. ... 6-8/229. ... Full name: Dennis Eugene Scott.
HIGH SCHOOL: Flint Hill Prep Academy (Oakton, Va.).
COLLEGE: Georgia Tech.
TRANSACTIONS/CAREER NOTES: Selected as undergraduate by Orlando Magic in first round (fourth pick overall) of 1990 NBA Draft.

COLLEGIATE RECORD

NOTES: THE SPORTING NEWS College Player of the Year (1990). ... THE SPORTING NEWS All-America first team (1990).

Season Team	G	Min.	FGM	FGA	Pct.	FTM	FTA	Pct.	Reb.	Pts.	Avg.
87-88 — Georgia Tech	32	1113	181	411	.440	36	55	.655	161	496	15.5
88-89 — Georgia Tech	32	1205	227	512	.443	79	97	.814	131	649	20.3
89-90 — Georgia Tech	35	1368	336	722	.465	161	203	.793	231	970	27.7
Totals	99	3686	744	1645	.452	276	355	.777	523	2115	21.4

Three-point field goals: 1987-88, 98-for-208 (.471). 1988-89, 116-for-292 (.397). 1989-90, 137-for-331 (.414). Totals, 351-for-831 (.422).

NBA REGULAR-SEASON RECORD

RECORDS: Holds single-season record for most three-point field goals made by a rookie — 125 (1991).
HONORS: NBA All-Rookie first team (1991).

Season Team	G	Min.	FGM	FGA	Pct.	FTM	FTA	Pct.	— REBOUNDS — Off.	Def.	Tot.	Ast.	PF	Dq.	Stl.	Blk.	TO	Pts.	Avg.
90-91 — Orlando	82	2336	503	1183	.425	153	204	.750	62	173	235	134	203	1	62	25	127	1284	15.7
91-92 — Orlando	18	608	133	331	.402	64	71	.901	14	52	66	35	49	1	20	9	31	359	19.9
Totals	100	2944	636	1514	.420	217	275	.789	76	225	301	169	252	2	82	34	158	1643	16.4

Three-point field goals: 1990-91, 125-for-334 (.374). 1991-92, 29-for-89 (.326). Totals, 154-for-423 (.364).

SEIKALY, RONY
C, HEAT

PERSONAL: Born May 10, 1965, in Beirut, Lebanon. ... 6-11/252. ... Full name: Ronald F. Seikaly. ... Name pronounced SIGH-klee.
HIGH SCHOOL: American School (Athens, Greece).
COLLEGE: Syracuse.
TRANSACTIONS/CAREER NOTES: Selected by Miami Heat in first round (ninth pick overall) of 1988 NBA Draft.

NOTES: 1986-87 minutes played totals are missing one game.

Season	Team	G	Min.	FGM	FGA	Pct.	FTM	FTA	Pct.	Reb.	Pts.	Avg.
84-85	Syracuse	31	775	96	177	.542	58	104	.558	198	250	8.1
85-86	Syracuse	32	875	122	223	.547	80	142	.563	250	324	10.1
86-87	Syracuse	38	1032	216	380	.568	141	235	.600	311	573	15.1
87-88	Syracuse	35	1084	218	385	.566	133	234	.568	335	569	16.3
	Totals	136	3766	652	1165	.560	412	715	.576	1094	1716	12.6

Three-point field goals: 1986-87, 0-for-1.

NBA REGULAR-SEASON RECORD

HONORS: NBA Most Improved Player (1990).

Season	Team	G	Min.	FGM	FGA	Pct.	FTM	FTA	Pct.	Off.	Def.	Tot.	Ast.	PF	Dq.	Stl.	Blk.	TO	Pts.	Avg.
88-89	Miami	78	1962	333	744	.448	181	354	.511	204	345	549	55	258	8	46	96	200	848	10.9
89-90	Miami	74	2409	486	968	.502	256	431	.594	253	513	766	78	258	8	78	124	236	1228	16.6
90-91	Miami	64	2171	395	822	.481	258	417	.619	207	502	709	95	213	2	51	86	205	1050	16.4
91-92	Miami	79	2800	463	947	.489	370	505	.733	307	627	934	109	278	2	40	121	216	1296	16.4
	Totals	295	9342	1677	3481	.482	1065	1707	.624	971	1987	2958	337	1007	20	215	427	857	4422	15.0

Three-point field goals: 1988-89, 1-for-4 (.250). 1989-90, 0-for-1. 1990-91, 2-for-6 (.333). 1991-92, 0-for-3. Totals, 3-for-14 (.214).

NBA PLAYOFF RECORD

Season	Team	G	Min.	FGM	FGA	Pct.	FTM	FTA	Pct.	Off.	Def.	Tot.	Ast.	PF	Dq.	Stl.	Blk.	TO	Pts.	Avg.
91-92	Miami	3	117	19	35	.543	24	32	.750	11	19	30	4	15	1	1	5	9	62	20.7

SELLERS, BRAD
F, PISTONS

PERSONAL: Born December 17, 1962, in Warrensville Heights, O. . . . 7-0/227. . . . Full name: Bradley Donn Sellers.
HIGH SCHOOL: Warrensville Heights (O.).
COLLEGE: Wisconsin, then Ohio State.
TRANSACTIONS/CAREER NOTES: Selected by Chicago Bulls in first round (ninth pick overall) of 1986 NBA Draft. . . . Traded by Bulls to Seattle SuperSonics for 1989 first-round draft choice (June 26, 1989). . . . Traded by SuperSonics to Minnesota Timberwolves for Steve Johnson and 1991 second-round draft choice (February 22, 1990). . . . Played in Greece (1990-91). . . . Signed as free agent by Detroit Pistons (August 27, 1991).

COLLEGIATE RECORD

Season	Team	G	Min.	FGM	FGA	Pct.	FTM	FTA	Pct.	Reb.	Pts.	Avg.
81-82	Wisconsin	27	964	167	351	.476	44	67	.657	254	378	14.0
82-83	Wisconsin	28	1009	189	372	.508	82	99	.828	219	460	16.4
83-84	Ohio State					Did not play—transfer student.						
84-85	Ohio State	30	979	186	354	.525	97	125	.776	264	469	15.6
85-86	Ohio State	33	1234	234	492	.476	185	226	.819	416	653	19.8
	Totals	118	4186	776	1569	.495	408	517	.789	1153	1960	16.6

Three-point field goals: 1982-83, 0-for-1.

NBA REGULAR-SEASON RECORD

Season	Team	G	Min.	FGM	FGA	Pct.	FTM	FTA	Pct.	Off.	Def.	Tot.	Ast.	PF	Dq.	Stl.	Blk.	TO	Pts.	Avg.
86-87	Chicago	80	1751	276	606	.455	126	173	.728	155	218	373	102	194	1	44	68	84	680	8.5
87-88	Chicago	82	2212	326	714	.457	124	157	.790	107	143	250	141	174	0	34	66	91	777	9.5
88-89	Chicago	80	1732	231	476	.485	86	101	.851	85	142	227	99	176	2	35	69	72	551	6.9
89-90	Sea.-Min.	59	700	103	254	.406	58	73	.795	39	50	89	33	74	1	17	22	46	264	4.5
91-92	Detroit	43	226	41	88	.466	20	26	.769	15	27	42	14	20	0	1	10	15	102	2.4
	Totals	344	6621	977	2138	.457	414	530	.781	401	580	981	389	638	4	131	235	308	2374	6.9

Three-point field goals: 1986-87, 2-for-10 (.200). 1987-88, 1-for-7 (.143). 1988-89, 3-for-6 (.500). 1989-90, 0-for-5. 1991-92, 0-for-1. Totals, 6-for-29 (.207).

NBA PLAYOFF RECORD

Season	Team	G	Min.	FGM	FGA	Pct.	FTM	FTA	Pct.	Off.	Def.	Tot.	Ast.	PF	Dq.	Stl.	Blk.	TO	Pts.	Avg.
86-87	Chicago	3	68	6	19	.316	3	3	1.000	2	5	7	3	8	0	0	1	1	15	5.0
87-88	Chicago	10	144	15	43	.349	15	17	.882	10	11	21	8	18	0	2	5	5	45	4.5
88-89	Chicago	13	177	22	58	.379	10	12	.833	15	16	31	15	21	0	3	4	6	54	4.2
91-92	Detroit	2	13	2	4	.500	2	2	1.000	0	0	0	2	0	0	0	2	0	6	3.0
	Totals	28	402	45	124	.363	30	34	.882	27	32	59	28	47	0	5	12	12	120	4.3

SHACKLEFORD, CHARLES
C, 76ERS

PERSONAL: Born April 22, 1966, in Kinston, N.C. . . . 6-11/245. . . . Full name: Charles Edward Shackleford.
HIGH SCHOOL: Kinston (N.C.).
COLLEGE: North Carolina State.
TRANSACTIONS/CAREER NOTES: Selected as undergraduate by New Jersey Nets in second round (32nd pick overall) of 1988 NBA Draft. . . . Played in Italy (1990-91). . . . Signed as unrestricted free agent by Philadelphia 76ers (July 10, 1991).

COLLEGIATE RECORD

Season	Team	G	Min.	FGM	FGA	Pct.	FTM	FTA	Pct.	Reb.	Pts.	Avg.
85-86	North Carolina State	29	876	128	244	.525	42	68	.618	178	298	10.3

Season Team	G	Min.	FGM	FGA	Pct.	FTM	FTA	Pct.	Reb.	Pts.	Avg.
86-87 — North Carolina State...............	34	1079	204	429	.476	66	127	.520	260	474	13.9
87-88 — North Carolina State...............	31	942	224	416	.538	68	115	.591	297	516	16.6
Totals	94	2897	556	1089	.511	176	310	.568	735	1288	13.7

Three-point field goals: 1986-87, 0-for-1.

NBA REGULAR-SEASON RECORD

Season Team	G	Min.	FGM	FGA	Pct.	FTM	FTA	Pct.	— REBOUNDS — Off.	Def.	Tot.	Ast.	PF	Dq.	Stl.	Blk.	TO	Pts.	Avg.
88-89 — New Jersey ..	60	484	83	168	.494	21	42	.500	50	103	153	21	71	0	15	18	27	187	3.1
89-90 — New Jersey ..	70	1557	247	535	.462	79	115	.687	180	299	479	56	183	1	40	35	116	573	8.2
91-92 — Philadelphia.	72	1399	205	422	.486	63	95	.663	145	270	415	46	205	3	38	51	62	473	6.6
Totals	202	3440	535	1125	.476	163	252	.647	375	672	1047	123	459	4	93	104	205	1233	6.1

Three-point field goals: 1988-89, 0-for-1. 1989-90, 0-for-1. 1991-92, 0-for-1. Totals, 0-for-3.

ITALIAN LEAGUE RECORD

Season Team	G	Min.	FGM	FGA	Pct.	FTM	FTA	Pct.	Reb.	Pts.	Avg.
90-91 — Phonola Caserta	29	991	246	434	.567	79	114	.693	457	571	19.7

SHAW, BRIAN
G, HEAT

PERSONAL: Born March 22, 1966, in Oakland, Calif. .... 6-6/190. .... Full name: Brian K. Shaw.
HIGH SCHOOL: Bishop O'Dowd (Oakland, Calif.).
COLLEGE: St. Mary's (Calif.), then UC Santa Barbara.
TRANSACTIONS/CAREER NOTES: Selected by Boston Celtics in first round (24th pick overall) of 1988 NBA Draft. .... Played in Italy (1989-90). .... Traded by Celtics to Miami Heat for Sherman Douglas (January 10, 1992).

COLLEGIATE RECORD

Season Team	G	Min.	FGM	FGA	Pct.	FTM	FTA	Pct.	Reb.	Pts.	Avg.
83-84 — St. Mary's (Calif.)	14	129	13	36	.361	14	19	.737	12	40	2.9
84-85 — St. Mary's (Calif.)	27	976	99	246	.402	55	76	.724	144	253	9.4
85-86 — UC Santa Barbara..................					Did not play — transfer student.						
86-87 — UC Santa Barbara..................	29	1013	125	288	.434	47	66	.712	224	315	10.9
87-88 — UC Santa Barbara..................	30	1073	151	324	.466	71	96	.740	260	399	13.3
Totals	100	3191	388	894	.434	187	257	.728	640	1007	10.1

Three-point field goals: 1986-87, 18-for-42 (.429). 1987-88, 26-for-74 (.351). Totals, 44-for-116 (.379).

NBA REGULAR-SEASON RECORD

HONORS: NBA All-Rookie second team (1989).

Season Team	G	Min.	FGM	FGA	Pct.	FTM	FTA	Pct.	— REBOUNDS — Off.	Def.	Tot.	Ast.	PF	Dq.	Stl.	Blk.	TO	Pts.	Avg.
88-89 — Boston	82	2301	297	686	.433	109	132	.826	119	257	376	472	211	1	78	27	188	703	8.6
90-91 — Boston	79	2772	442	942	.469	204	249	.819	104	266	370	602	206	1	105	34	223	1091	13.8
91-92 — Bos.-Miami..	63	1423	209	513	.407	72	91	.791	50	154	204	250	115	0	57	22	99	495	7.9
Totals	224	6496	948	2141	.443	385	472	.816	273	677	950	1324	532	2	240	83	510	2289	10.2

Three-point field goals: 1988-89, 0-for-13. 1990-91, 3-for-27 (.111). 1991-92, 5-for-23 (.217). Totals, 8-for-63 (.127).

NBA PLAYOFF RECORD

Season Team	G	Min.	FGM	FGA	Pct.	FTM	FTA	Pct.	— REBOUNDS — Off.	Def.	Tot.	Ast.	PF	Dq.	Stl.	Blk.	TO	Pts.	Avg.
88-89 — Boston	3	124	22	43	.512	7	9	.778	2	15	17	19	11	0	3	0	6	51	17.0
90-91 — Boston	11	316	47	100	.470	26	30	.867	8	30	38	51	34	0	10	1	25	121	11.0
91-92 — Miami..........	3	85	14	30	.467	5	8	.625	2	11	13	12	13	0	2	0	7	36	12.0
Totals	17	525	83	173	.480	38	47	.809	12	56	68	82	58	0	15	1	38	208	12.2

Three-point field goals: 1988-89, 0-for-1. 1990-91, 1-for-3 (.333). 1991-92, 3-for-5 (.600). Totals, 4-for-9 (.444).

ITALIAN LEAGUE RECORD

Season Team	G	Min.	FGM	FGA	Pct.	FTM	FTA	Pct.	Reb.	Pts.	Avg.
89-90 — Il Messaggero	30	1144	244	418	.584	111	139	.799	274	749	25.0

SIMMONS, LIONEL
F, KINGS

PERSONAL: Born November 14, 1968, in Philadelphia. .... 6-7/210. .... Full name: Lionel James Simmons.
HIGH SCHOOL: South Philadelphia (Philadelphia).
COLLEGE: La Salle.
TRANSACTIONS/CAREER NOTES: Selected by Sacramento Kings in first round (seventh pick overall) of 1990 NBA Draft.

COLLEGIATE RECORD

NOTES: THE SPORTING NEWS All-America first team (1989). .... THE SPORTING NEWS All-America second team (1988, 1990).

Season Team	G	Min.	FGM	FGA	Pct.	FTM	FTA	Pct.	Reb.	Pts.	Avg.
86-87 — La Salle.............................	33	...	263	500	.526	142	186	.763	322	670	20.3
87-88 — La Salle.............................	34	...	297	613	.485	196	259	.757	386	792	23.3
88-89 — La Salle.............................	32	1245	349	716	.487	189	266	.711	365	908	28.4
89-90 — La Salle.............................	32	1220	335	653	.513	146	221	.661	356	847	26.5
Totals	131	...	1244	2482	.501	673	932	.722	1429	3217	24.6

Three-point field goals: 1986-87, 2-for-6 (.333). 1987-88, 2-for-8 (.250). 1988-89, 21-for-56 (.375). 1989-90, 31-for-65 (.477). Totals, 56-for-135 (.415).

HONORS: NBA All-Rookie first team (1991).

Season Team	G	Min.	FGM	FGA	Pct.	FTM	FTA	Pct.	Off.	Def.	Tot.	Ast.	PF	Dq.	Stl.	Blk.	TO	Pts.	Avg.
90-91—Sacramento	79	2978	549	1301	.422	320	435	.736	193	504	697	315	249	0	113	85	230	1421	18.0
91-92—Sacramento	78	2895	527	1162	.454	281	365	.770	149	485	634	337	205	0	135	132	218	1336	17.1
Totals	157	5873	1076	2463	.437	601	800	.751	342	989	1331	652	454	0	248	217	448	2757	17.6

Three-point field goals: 1990-91, 3-for-11 (.273). 1991-92, 1-for-5 (.200). Totals, 4-for-16 (.250).

SKILES, SCOTT
G, MAGIC

PERSONAL: Born March 5, 1964, in LaPorte, Ind. . . . 6-1/180. . . . Full name: Scott Allen Skiles.
HIGH SCHOOL: Plymouth (Ind.).
COLLEGE: Michigan State.
TRANSACTIONS/CAREER NOTES: Selected by Milwaukee Bucks in first round (22nd pick overall) of 1986 NBA Draft. . . . Traded by Bucks to Indiana Pacers for 1989 second-round draft choice (June 22, 1987). . . . Selected by Orlando Magic from Pacers in NBA expansion draft (June 15, 1989).

COLLEGIATE RECORD

NOTES: THE SPORTING NEWS All-America first team (1986).

Season Team	G	Min.	FGM	FGA	Pct.	FTM	FTA	Pct.	Reb.	Pts.	Avg.
82-83—Michigan State	30	1023	141	286	.493	69	83	.831	63	376	12.5
83-84—Michigan State	28	983	153	319	.480	99	119	.832	62	405	14.5
84-85—Michigan State	29	1107	212	420	.505	90	114	.789	93	514	17.7
85-86—Michigan State	31	1172	331	598	.554	188	209	.900	135	850	27.4
Totals	118	4285	837	1623	.516	446	525	.850	353	2145	18.2

Three-point field goals: 1982-83, 25-for-50 (.500).

NBA REGULAR-SEASON RECORD

RECORDS: Holds single-game record for most assists—30 (December 30, 1990, vs. Denver).
HONORS: NBA Most Improved Player (1991).

Season Team	G	Min.	FGM	FGA	Pct.	FTM	FTA	Pct.	Off.	Def.	Tot.	Ast.	PF	Dq.	Stl.	Blk.	TO	Pts.	Avg.
86-87—Milwaukee	13	205	18	62	.290	10	12	.833	6	20	26	45	18	0	5	1	21	49	3.8
87-88—Indiana	51	760	86	209	.411	45	54	.833	11	55	66	180	97	0	22	3	76	223	4.4
88-89—Indiana	80	1571	198	442	.448	130	144	.903	21	128	149	390	151	1	64	2	177	546	6.8
89-90—Orlando	70	1460	190	464	.409	104	119	.874	23	136	159	334	126	0	36	4	90	536	7.7
90-91—Orlando	79	2714	462	1039	.445	340	377	.902	57	213	270	660	192	2	89	4	252	1357	17.2
91-92—Orlando	75	2377	359	868	.414	248	277	.895	36	166	202	544	188	0	74	5	233	1057	14.1
Totals	368	9087	1313	3084	.426	877	983	.892	154	718	872	2153	772	3	290	19	849	3768	10.2

Three-point field goals: 1986-87, 3-for-14 (.214). 1987-88, 6-for-20 (.300). 1988-89, 20-for-67 (.299). 1989-90, 52-for-132 (.394). 1990-91, 93-for-228 (.408). 1991-92, 91-for-250 (.364). Totals, 265-for-711 (.373).

SMITH, CHARLES
C/F, CLIPPERS

PERSONAL: Born July 16, 1965, in Bridgeport, Conn. . . . 6-10/244. . . . Full name: Charles Daniel Smith.
HIGH SCHOOL: Warren Harding (Bridgeport, Conn.).
COLLEGE: Pittsburgh.
TRANSACTIONS/CAREER NOTES: Selected by Philadelphia 76ers in first round (third pick overall) of 1988 NBA Draft. . . . Draft rights traded by 76ers to Los Angeles Clippers for draft rights to Hersey Hawkins and 1989 first-round draft choice (June 28, 1988).
MISCELLANEOUS: Member of bronze-medal-winning U.S. Olympic team (1988).

COLLEGIATE RECORD

Season Team	G	Min.	FGM	FGA	Pct.	FTM	FTA	Pct.	Reb.	Pts.	Avg.
84-85—Pittsburgh	29	956	151	301	.502	133	175	.760	231	435	15.0
85-86—Pittsburgh	29	1077	165	408	.404	131	172	.762	235	461	15.9
86-87—Pittsburgh	33	1050	180	327	.550	202	275	.735	282	562	17.0
87-88—Pittsburgh	31	1020	211	378	.558	162	212	.764	239	587	18.9
Totals	122	4103	707	1414	.500	628	834	.753	987	2045	16.8

Three-point field goals: 1987-88, 3-for-11 (.273).

NBA REGULAR-SEASON RECORD

HONORS: NBA All-Rookie first team (1989).

Season Team	G	Min.	FGM	FGA	Pct.	FTM	FTA	Pct.	Off.	Def.	Tot.	Ast.	PF	Dq.	Stl.	Blk.	TO	Pts.	Avg.
88-89—L.A. Clippers	71	2161	435	878	.495	285	393	.725	173	292	465	103	273	6	68	89	146	1155	16.3
89-90—L.A. Clippers	78	2732	595	1145	.520	454	572	.794	177	347	524	114	294	6	86	119	162	1645	21.1
90-91—L.A. Clippers	74	2703	548	1168	.469	384	484	.793	216	392	608	134	267	4	81	145	165	1480	20.0
91-92—L.A. Clippers	49	1310	251	539	.466	212	270	.785	95	206	301	56	159	2	41	98	69	714	14.6
Totals	272	8906	1829	3730	.490	1335	1719	.777	661	1237	1898	407	993	18	276	451	542	4994	18.4

Three-point field goals: 1988-89, 0-for-3. 1989-90, 1-for-12 (.083). 1990-91, 0-for-7. 1991-92, 0-for-6. Totals, 1-for-28 (.036).

NBA PLAYOFF RECORD

Season Team	G	Min.	FGM	FGA	Pct.	FTM	FTA	Pct.	Off.	Def.	Tot.	Ast.	PF	Dq.	Stl.	Blk.	TO	Pts.	Avg.
91-92—L.A. Clippers	5	148	22	56	.393	14	15	.933	10	18	28	9	24	2	4	12	10	58	11.6

SMITH, DOUG
F, MAVERICKS

PERSONAL: Born September 17, 1969, in Detroit. . . . 6-10/220. . . . Full name: Douglas Smith.
HIGH SCHOOL: MacKenzie (Detroit).
COLLEGE: Missouri.
TRANSACTIONS/CAREER NOTES: Selected by Dallas Mavericks in first round (sixth pick overall) of 1991 NBA Draft.

COLLEGIATE RECORD

NOTES: THE SPORTING NEWS All-America second team (1990, 1991).

Season Team	G	Min.	FGM	FGA	Pct.	FTM	FTA	Pct.	Reb.	Pts.	Avg.
87-88 —Missouri	30	792	145	288	.503	48	75	.640	197	338	11.3
88-89 —Missouri	36	975	217	455	.477	67	91	.736	250	502	13.9
89-90 —Missouri	32	942	260	462	.563	115	161	.714	295	635	19.8
90-91 —Missouri	30	1051	275	553	.497	156	190	.821	311	709	23.6
Totals	128	3760	897	1758	.510	386	517	.747	1053	2184	17.1

Three-point field goals: 1988-89, 1-for-4 (.250). 1989-90, 0-for-1. 1990-91, 3-for-18 (.167). Totals, 4-for-23 (.174).

NBA REGULAR-SEASON RECORD

Season Team	G	Min.	FGM	FGA	Pct.	FTM	FTA	Pct.	REBOUNDS Off.	Def.	Tot.	Ast.	PF	Dq.	Stl.	Blk.	TO	Pts.	Avg.
91-92 —Dallas	76	1707	291	702	.415	89	121	.736	129	262	391	129	259	5	62	34	97	671	8.8

Three-point field goals: 1991-92, 0-for-11.

SMITH, KENNY
G, ROCKETS

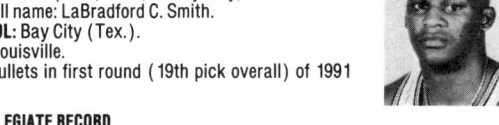

PERSONAL: Born March 8, 1965, in Queens, N.Y. . . . 6-3/170. . . . Full name: Kenneth Smith.
HIGH SCHOOL: Archbishop Molloy (Briarwood, N.Y.).
COLLEGE: North Carolina.
TRANSACTIONS/CAREER NOTES: Selected by Sacramento Kings in first round (sixth pick overall) of 1987 NBA Draft. . . . Traded by Kings with Mike Williams to Atlanta Hawks for Antoine Carr, Sedric Toney and future draft considerations (February 13, 1990). . . . Traded by Hawks with Roy Marble to Houston Rockets for Tim McCormick and John Lucas (September 27, 1990).

COLLEGIATE RECORD

NOTES: THE SPORTING NEWS All-America first team (1987).

Season Team	G	Min.	FGM	FGA	Pct.	FTM	FTA	Pct.	Reb.	Pts.	Avg.
83-84 —North Carolina	23	667	83	160	.519	44	55	.800	40	210	9.1
84-85 —North Carolina	36	1350	173	334	.518	98	114	.860	92	444	12.3
85-86 —North Carolina	34	1109	164	318	.516	80	99	.808	75	408	12.0
86-87 —North Carolina	34	1092	208	414	.502	71	88	.807	76	574	16.9
Totals	127	4218	628	1226	.512	293	356	.823	283	1636	12.9

Three-point field goals: 1986-87, 87-for-213 (.408).

NBA REGULAR-SEASON RECORD

HONORS: NBA All-Rookie team (1988).

Season Team	G	Min.	FGM	FGA	Pct.	FTM	FTA	Pct.	REBOUNDS Off.	Def.	Tot.	Ast.	PF	Dq.	Stl.	Blk.	TO	Pts.	Avg.
87-88 —Sacramento	61	2170	331	694	.477	167	204	.819	40	98	138	434	140	1	92	8	184	841	13.8
88-89 —Sacramento	81	3145	547	1183	.462	263	357	.737	49	177	226	621	173	0	102	7	249	1403	17.3
89-90 —Sac.-Atlanta	79	2421	378	811	.466	161	196	.821	18	139	157	445	143	0	79	8	169	943	11.9
90-91 —Houston	78	2699	522	1003	.520	287	340	.844	36	127	163	554	131	0	106	11	237	1380	17.7
91-92 —Houston	81	2735	432	910	.475	219	253	.866	34	143	177	562	112	0	104	7	227	1137	14.0
Totals	380	13170	2210	4601	.480	1097	1350	.813	177	684	861	2616	699	1	483	41	1066	5704	15.0

Three-point field goals: 1987-88, 12-for-39 (.308). 1988-89, 46-for-128 (.359). 1989-90, 26-for-83 (.313). 1990-91, 49-for-135 (.363). 1991-92, 54-for-137 (.394). Totals, 187-for-522 (.358).

NBA PLAYOFF RECORD

Season Team	G	Min.	FGM	FGA	Pct.	FTM	FTA	Pct.	REBOUNDS Off.	Def.	Tot.	Ast.	PF	Dq.	Stl.	Blk.	TO	Pts.	Avg.
90-91 —Houston	3	113	18	38	.474	8	9	.889	4	4	8	24	5	0	4	1	6	46	15.3

Three-point field goals: 1990-91, 2-for-4 (.500).

SMITH, LaBRADFORD
G, BULLETS

PERSONAL: Born April 3, 1969, in Bay City, Tex. . . . 6-3/200. . . . Full name: LaBradford C. Smith.
HIGH SCHOOL: Bay City (Tex.).
COLLEGE: Louisville.
TRANSACTIONS/CAREER NOTES: Selected by Washington Bullets in first round (19th pick overall) of 1991 NBA Draft.

COLLEGIATE RECORD

Season Team	G	Min.	FGM	FGA	Pct.	FTM	FTA	Pct.	Reb.	Pts.	Avg.
87-88 —Louisville	35	990	136	285	.477	143	158	.905	88	443	12.7
88-89 —Louisville	33	984	125	269	.465	112	129	.868	75	394	11.9
89-90 —Louisville	35	1167	158	318	.497	123	143	.860	117	471	13.5
90-91 —Louisville	30	1031	173	359	.482	113	137	.825	110	498	16.6
Totals	133	4172	592	1231	.481	491	567	.866	390	1806	13.6

Three-point field goals: 1987-88, 28-for-100 (.280). 1988-89, 32-for-86 (.372). 1989-90, 32-for-91 (.352). 1990-91, 39-for-109 (.358). Totals, 131-for-386 (.339).

NBA REGULAR-SEASON RECORD

Season Team	G	Min.	FGM	FGA	Pct.	FTM	FTA	Pct.	REBOUNDS Off.	Def.	Tot.	Ast.	PF	Dq.	Stl.	Blk.	TO	Pts.	Avg.
91-92 —Washington .	48	708	100	246	.407	45	56	.804	30	51	81	99	98	0	44	1	63	247	5.1

Three-point field goals: 1991-92, 2-for-21 (.095).

SMITH, LARRY

F/C, SPURS

PERSONAL: Born January 18, 1958, in Rolling Fork, Miss.... 6-8/251. **HIGH SCHOOL:** Hollandale Simmons (Miss.). **COLLEGE:** Alcorn State. **TRANSACTIONS/CAREER NOTES:** Selected by Golden State Warriors in second round (24th pick overall) of 1980 NBA Draft.... Signed as unrestricted free agent by Houston Rockets (July 11, 1989).... Signed as unrestricted free agent by San Antonio Spurs (August 10, 1992).

COLLEGIATE RECORD

NOTES: Led NCAA Division I with 15.1 rebounds per game (1980).

Season Team	G	Min.	FGM	FGA	Pct.	FTM	FTA	Pct.	Reb.	Pts.	Avg.
76-77 —Alcorn State	34	...	212	402	.527	74	124	.597	222	498	14.6
77-78 —Alcorn State	22	...	137	231	.593	45	74	.608	222	319	14.5
78-79 —Alcorn State	29	...	216	360	.600	81	142	.570	398	513	17.7
79-80 —Alcorn State	26	849	198	342	.579	126	182	.692	392	522	20.1
Totals	111	...	763	1335	.572	326	522	.625	1234	1852	16.7

NBA REGULAR-SEASON RECORD

HONORS: NBA All-Rookie team (1981).

Season Team	G	Min.	FGM	FGA	Pct.	FTM	FTA	Pct.	REBOUNDS Off.	Def.	Tot.	Ast.	PF	Dq.	Stl.	Blk.	TO	Pts.	Avg.
80-81 —Golden State	82	2578	304	594	.512	177	301	.588	433	561	994	93	316	10	70	63	146	785	9.6
81-82 —Golden State	74	2213	220	412	.534	88	159	.553	279	534	813	83	291	7	65	54	105	528	7.1
82-83 —Golden State	49	1433	180	306	.588	53	99	.535	209	276	485	46	186	5	36	20	83	413	8.4
83-84 —Golden State	75	2091	244	436	.560	94	168	.560	282	390	672	72	274	6	61	22	124	582	7.8
84-85 —Golden State	80	2497	366	690	.530	155	256	.605	405	464	869	96	285	5	78	54	160	887	11.1
85-86 —Golden State	77	2441	314	586	.536	112	227	.493	*384	472	856	95	286	7	62	50	135	740	9.6
86-87 —Golden State	80	2374	297	544	.546	113	197	.574	366	551	917	95	295	7	71	56	135	707	8.8
87-88 —Golden State	20	499	58	123	.472	11	27	.407	79	103	182	25	63	1	12	11	36	127	6.4
88-89 —Golden State	80	1897	219	397	.552	18	58	.310	272	380	652	118	248	2	61	54	110	456	5.7
89-90 —Houston	74	1300	101	213	.474	20	55	.364	180	272	452	69	203	3	56	28	70	222	3.0
90-91 —Houston	81	1923	128	263	.487	12	50	.240	302	407	709	88	265	6	83	22	93	268	3.3
91-92 —Houston	45	800	50	92	.543	4	11	.364	107	149	256	33	121	3	21	7	44	104	2.3
Totals	817	22046	2481	4656	.533	857	1608	.533	3298	4559	7857	913	2833	62	676	441	1241	5819	7.1

Three-point field goals: 1981-82, 0-for-1. 1985-86, 0-for-1. 1986-87, 0-for-1. 1987-88, 0-for-1. 1989-90, 0-for-2. 1991-92, 0-for-1. Totals, 0-for-7.

NBA PLAYOFF RECORD

Season Team	G	Min.	FGM	FGA	Pct.	FTM	FTA	Pct.	REBOUNDS Off.	Def.	Tot.	Ast.	PF	Dq.	Stl.	Blk.	TO	Pts.	Avg.
86-87 —Golden State	10	329	43	81	.531	17	24	.708	61	76	137	17	39	0	12	6	14	103	10.3
88-89 —Golden State	8	148	4	16	.250	0	0	...	17	23	40	16	24	0	6	11	6	8	1.0
89-90 —Houston	4	73	6	8	.750	0	0	...	7	6	13	5	11	0	4	0	5	12	3.0
90-91 —Houston	3	57	1	4	.250	0	1	.000	6	7	13	4	11	0	1	1	2	2	0.7
Totals	25	607	54	109	.495	17	25	.680	91	112	203	42	85	0	23	18	27	125	5.0

Three-point field goals: 1990-91, 0-for-1.

SMITH, OTIS

G/F

PERSONAL: Born January 30, 1964, in Jacksonville, Fla.... 6-5/210.... Full name: Otis Fitzgerald Smith. **HIGH SCHOOL:** Forrest (Jacksonville, Fla.). **COLLEGE:** Jacksonville.
TRANSACTIONS/CAREER NOTES: Selected by Denver Nuggets in second round (41st pick overall) of 1986 NBA Draft.... Traded by Nuggets to Golden State Warriors for cash (December 22, 1987).... Selected by Orlando Magic from Warriors in NBA expansion draft (June 15, 1989).

COLLEGIATE RECORD

Season Team	G	Min.	FGM	FGA	Pct.	FTM	FTA	Pct.	Reb.	Pts.	Avg.
82-83 —Jacksonville	29	979	171	362	.472	70	102	.686	251	414	14.3
83-84 —Jacksonville	28	1095	183	375	.488	87	120	.725	215	453	16.2
84-85 —Jacksonville	29	1025	151	313	.482	73	99	.737	197	375	12.9
85-86 —Jacksonville	31	1164	180	387	.465	113	149	.758	248	473	15.3
Totals	117	4263	685	1437	.477	343	470	.730	911	1715	14.7

Three-point field goals: 1982-83, 2-for-7 (.286).

NBA REGULAR-SEASON RECORD

Season Team	G	Min.	FGM	FGA	Pct.	FTM	FTA	Pct.	REBOUNDS Off.	Def.	Tot.	Ast.	PF	Dq.	Stl.	Blk.	TO	Pts.	Avg.
86-87 —Denver	28	168	33	79	.418	12	21	.571	17	17	34	22	30	0	1	1	19	78	2.8
87-88 —Denver-G.S.	72	1549	325	662	.491	178	229	.777	126	121	247	155	160	2	91	42	107	841	11.7
88-89 —Golden State	80	1597	311	715	.435	174	218	.798	128	202	330	140	165	1	88	40	129	803	10.0
89-90 —Orlando	65	1644	348	708	.492	169	222	.761	117	183	300	147	174	0	76	57	102	875	13.5

Season Team	G	Min.	FGM	FGA	Pct.	FTM	FTA	Pct.	Off.	Def.	Tot.	Ast.	PF	Dq.	Stl.	Blk.	TO	Pts.	Avg.
90-91—Orlando	75	1885	407	902	.451	221	301	.734	176	213	389	169	190	1	85	35	140	1044	13.9
91-92—Orlando	55	877	116	318	.365	70	91	.769	40	76	116	57	85	1	36	13	62	310	5.6
Totals	375	7720	1540	3384	.455	824	1082	.762	604	812	1416	690	804	3	377	188	559	3951	10.5

Three-point field goals: 1986-87, 0-for-2. 1987-88, 13-for-41 (.317). 1988-89, 7-for-37 (.189). 1989-90, 10-for-40 (.250). 1990-91, 9-for-46 (.196). 1991-92, 8-for-21 (.381). Totals, 47-for-187 (.251).

NBA PLAYOFF RECORD

Season Team	G	Min.	FGM	FGA	Pct.	FTM	FTA	Pct.	Off.	Def.	Tot.	Ast.	PF	Dq.	Stl.	Blk.	TO	Pts.	Avg.
86-87—Denver	3	19	2	6	.333	6	9	.667	1	4	5	4	1	0	0	2	4	10	3.3
88-89—Golden State	4	49	9	24	.375	1	2	.500	6	7	13	6	5	0	2	1	2	19	4.8
Totals	7	68	11	30	.367	7	11	.636	7	11	18	10	6	0	2	3	6	29	4.1

SMITH, STEVE
G, HEAT

PERSONAL: Born March 31, 1969, in Highland Park, Mich. . . . 6-8/202. . . . Full name: Steven Delano Smith.
HIGH SCHOOL: Pershing (Detroit).
COLLEGE: Michigan State.
TRANSACTIONS/CAREER NOTES: Selected by Miami Heat in first round (fifth pick overall) of 1991 NBA Draft.

COLLEGIATE RECORD

NOTES: THE SPORTING NEWS All-America first team (1990, 1991).

Season Team	G	Min.	FGM	FGA	Pct.	FTM	FTA	Pct.	Reb.	Pts.	Avg.
87-88—Michigan State	28	812	108	232	.466	69	91	.758	112	299	10.7
88-89—Michigan State	33	1168	217	454	.478	129	169	.763	229	585	17.7
89-90—Michigan State	31	1081	233	443	.526	116	167	.695	216	627	20.2
90-91—Michigan State	30	1134	268	566	.474	150	187	.802	183	752	25.1
Totals	122	4195	826	1695	.487	464	614	.756	740	2263	18.5

Three-point field goals: 1987-88, 14-for-30 (.467). 1988-89, 22-for-63 (.349). 1989-90, 45-for-98 (.459). 1990-91, 66-for-162 (.407). Totals, 147-for-353 (.416).

NBA REGULAR-SEASON RECORD

HONORS: NBA All-Rookie first team (1992).

Season Team	G	Min.	FGM	FGA	Pct.	FTM	FTA	Pct.	Off.	Def.	Tot.	Ast.	PF	Dq.	Stl.	Blk.	TO	Pts.	Avg.
91-92—Miami	61	1806	297	654	.454	95	127	.748	81	107	188	278	162	1	59	19	152	729	12.0

Three-point field goals: 1991-92, 40-for-125 (.320).

NBA PLAYOFF RECORD

Season Team	G	Min.	FGM	FGA	Pct.	FTM	FTA	Pct.	Off.	Def.	Tot.	Ast.	PF	Dq.	Stl.	Blk.	TO	Pts.	Avg.
91-92—Miami	3	100	18	34	.529	5	6	.833	3	3	6	15	2	0	4	1	3	48	16.0

Three-point field goals: 1991-92, 7-for-11 (.636).

SMITH, TONY
G, LAKERS

PERSONAL: Born June 14, 1968, in Wauwatosa, Wis. . . . 6-4/205. . . . Full name: Charles Anton Smith.
HIGH SCHOOL: East (Wauwatosa, Wis.).
COLLEGE: Marquette.
TRANSACTIONS/CAREER NOTES: Selected by Los Angeles Lakers in second round (51st pick overall) of 1990 NBA Draft.

COLLEGIATE RECORD

Season Team	G	Min.	FGM	FGA	Pct.	FTM	FTA	Pct.	Reb.	Pts.	Avg.
86-87—Marquette	29	722	86	161	.534	61	81	.753	96	234	8.1
87-88—Marquette	28	894	136	260	.523	88	119	.740	126	367	13.1
88-89—Marquette	28	943	153	275	.556	84	115	.730	109	398	14.2
89-90—Marquette	29	1131	240	485	.495	173	202	.856	137	689	23.8
Totals	114	3690	615	1181	.521	406	517	.785	468	1688	14.8

Three-point field goals: 1986-87, 1-for-3 (.333). 1987-88, 7-for-19 (.368). 1988-89, 8-for-12 (.667). 1989-90, 36-for-87 (.414). Totals, 52-for-121 (.430).

NBA REGULAR-SEASON RECORD

Season Team	G	Min.	FGM	FGA	Pct.	FTM	FTA	Pct.	Off.	Def.	Tot.	Ast.	PF	Dq.	Stl.	Blk.	TO	Pts.	Avg.
90-91—L.A. Lakers	64	695	97	220	.441	40	57	.702	24	47	71	135	80	0	28	12	69	234	3.7
91-92—L.A. Lakers	63	820	113	283	.399	49	75	.653	31	45	76	109	91	0	39	8	50	275	4.4
Totals	127	1515	210	503	.417	89	132	.674	55	92	147	244	171	0	67	20	119	509	4.0

Three-point field goals: 1990-91, 0-for-7. 1991-92, 0-for-11. Totals, 0-for-18.

NBA PLAYOFF RECORD

Season Team	G	Min.	FGM	FGA	Pct.	FTM	FTA	Pct.	Off.	Def.	Tot.	Ast.	PF	Dq.	Stl.	Blk.	TO	Pts.	Avg.
90-91—L.A. Lakers	7	40	6	13	.462	2	3	.667	3	0	3	2	1	1	0	6		14	2.0
91-92—L.A. Lakers	4	40	3	10	.300	1	2	.500	1	1	2	5	5	0	0	3		7	1.8
Totals	11	80	9	23	.391	3	5	.600	4	1	5	7	11	1	5	0	9	21	1.9

Three-point field goals: 1991-92, 0-for-2.

SMITS, RIK

C, PACERS

PERSONAL: Born August 23, 1966, in Eindhoven, Holland. . . . 7-4/265.
HIGH SCHOOL: Almonta (Eindhoven, Holland).
COLLEGE: Marist (N.Y.).
TRANSACTIONS/CAREER NOTES: Selected by Indiana Pacers in first round (second pick overall) of 1988 NBA Draft.

COLLEGIATE RECORD

Season Team	G	Min.	FGM	FGA	Pct.	FTM	FTA	Pct.	Reb.	Pts.	Avg.
84-85 —Marist	29	776	132	233	.567	60	104	.577	162	324	11.2
85-86 —Marist	30	870	216	347	.622	98	144	.681	242	530	17.7
86-87 —Marist	21	634	157	258	.609	109	151	.722	171	423	20.1
87-88 —Marist	27	861	251	403	.623	166	226	.735	236	668	24.7
Totals	107	3141	756	1241	.609	433	625	.693	811	1945	18.2

Three-point field goals: 1987-88, 0-for-2.

NBA REGULAR-SEASON RECORD

HONORS: NBA All-Rookie first team (1989).

Season Team	G	Min.	FGM	FGA	Pct.	FTM	FTA	Pct.	Off.	Def.	Tot.	Ast.	PF	Dq.	Stl.	Blk.	TO	Pts.	Avg.
88-89 —Indiana	82	2041	386	746	.517	184	255	.722	185	315	500	70	310	*14	37	151	130	956	11.7
89-90 —Indiana	82	2404	515	967	.533	241	297	.811	135	377	512	142	*328	11	45	169	143	1271	15.5
90-91 —Indiana	76	1690	342	705	.485	144	189	.762	116	241	357	84	246	3	24	111	86	828	10.9
91-92 —Indiana	74	1772	436	855	.510	152	193	.788	124	293	417	116	231	4	29	100	130	1024	13.8
Totals	314	7907	1679	3273	.513	721	934	.772	560	1226	1786	412	1115	32	135	531	489	4079	13.0

Three-point field goals: 1988-89, 0-for-1. 1989-90, 0-for-1. 1991-92, 0-for-2. Totals, 0-for-4.

NBA PLAYOFF RECORD

Season Team	G	Min.	FGM	FGA	Pct.	FTM	FTA	Pct.	Off.	Def.	Tot.	Ast.	PF	Dq.	Stl.	Blk.	TO	Pts.	Avg.
89-90 —Indiana	3	96	14	28	.500	9	11	.818	4	12	16	3	12	0	2	4	5	37	12.3
90-91 —Indiana	5	88	21	37	.568	7	8	.875	4	14	18	2	23	1	1	7	5	49	9.8
91-92 —Indiana	3	28	4	11	.364	2	2	1.000	3	3	6	0	7	0	2	1	3	10	3.3
Totals	11	212	39	76	.513	18	21	.857	11	29	40	5	42	1	5	12	13	96	8.7

SMREK, MIKE

C

PERSONAL: Born August 31, 1962, in Welland, Ont. . . . 7-0/260. . . . Full name: Michael Frank Smrek.
HIGH SCHOOL: Eastdale Secondary School (Welland, Ont.).
COLLEGE: Canisius.
TRANSACTIONS/CAREER NOTES: Selected by Portland Trail Blazers in second round (25th pick overall) of 1985 NBA Draft. . . . Draft rights traded by Trail Blazers to Chicago Bulls for draft rights to Ben Coleman and Ken Johnson (June 18, 1985). . . . Waived by Bulls (October 30, 1986). . . . Signed as free agent by Los Angeles Lakers (November 7, 1986). . . . Traded by Lakers to San Antonio Spurs for 1990 second-round draft choice (November 2, 1988). . . . Rights relinquished by Spurs (July 19, 1989). . . . Signed by Golden State Warriors for remainder of season (February 27, 1990). . . . Re-signed as unrestricted free agent by Warriors (September 4, 1990). . . . Waived by Warriors (December 21, 1990). . . . Claimed off waivers by Los Angeles Clippers (December 26, 1990). . . . Rights renounced by Clippers (June 26, 1991). . . . Signed as free agent by Utah Jazz (October 3, 1991). . . . Signed by Warriors to 10-day contract (January 28, 1992).
MISCELLANEOUS: Member of NBA championship teams (1987, 1988). . . . Member of Canadian Olympic team (1992).

COLLEGIATE RECORD

Season Team	G	Min.	FGM	FGA	Pct.	FTM	FTA	Pct.	Reb.	Pts.	Avg.
81-82 —Canisius	22	311	24	54	.444	7	14	.500	68	55	2.5
82-83 —Canisius	28	560	49	106	.462	27	52	.519	131	125	4.5
83-84 —Canisius	30	829	153	242	.632	56	96	.583	175	362	12.1
84-85 —Canisius	28	812	172	286	.601	97	148	.655	192	441	15.8
Totals	108	2512	398	688	.578	187	310	.603	566	983	9.1

NBA REGULAR-SEASON RECORD

Season Team	G	Min.	FGM	FGA	Pct.	FTM	FTA	Pct.	Off.	Def.	Tot.	Ast.	PF	Dq.	Stl.	Blk.	TO	Pts.	Avg.
85-86 —Chicago	38	408	46	122	.377	16	29	.552	46	64	110	19	95	0	6	23	29	108	2.8
86-87 —L.A. Lakers	35	233	30	60	.500	16	25	.640	13	24	37	5	70	1	4	13	19	76	2.2
87-88 —L.A. Lakers	48	421	44	103	.427	44	66	.667	27	58	85	8	105	3	7	42	30	132	2.8
88-89 —San Antonio	43	623	72	153	.471	49	76	.645	42	87	129	12	102	2	13	58	48	193	4.5
89-90 —Golden State	13	107	10	24	.417	1	6	.167	11	23	34	1	18	0	4	11	9	21	1.6
90-91 —G.S.-L.A.C.	15	95	9	27	.333	6	12	.500	7	19	26	4	27	1	3	3	3	24	1.6
91-92 —Golden State	2	3	0	0	. . .	0	0	. . .	0	1	1	0	0	0	0	0	0	0	0.0
Totals	194	1890	211	489	.431	132	214	.617	146	276	422	49	417	7	37	150	138	554	2.9

Three-point field goals: 1985-86, 0-for-2.

NBA PLAYOFF RECORD

Season Team	G	Min.	FGM	FGA	Pct.	FTM	FTA	Pct.	Off.	Def.	Tot.	Ast.	PF	Dq.	Stl.	Blk.	TO	Pts.	Avg.
85-86 —Chicago	3	5	0	1	.000	0	0	. . .	0	0	0	0	2	0	0	1	0	0	0.0
86-87 —L.A. Lakers	10	33	2	10	.200	4	6	.667	3	4	7	0	15	0	0	6	1	8	0.8
87-88 —L.A. Lakers	8	34	1	5	.200	1	3	.333	1	5	6	0	4	0	1	3	2	3	0.4
Totals	21	72	3	16	.188	6	9	.556	4	9	13	0	21	0	1	10	3	11	0.5

SPARROW, RORY
G, LAKERS

PERSONAL: Born June 12, 1958, in Suffolk, Va. . . . . 6-2/ 175. . . . Full name: Rory Darnell Sparrow.
HIGH SCHOOL: Eastside (Paterson, N.J.).
COLLEGE: Villanova.

TRANSACTIONS/CAREER NOTES: Selected by New Jersey Nets in fourth round (75th pick overall) of 1980 NBA Draft. . . . Waived by Nets (October 7, 1980). . . . Re-signed by Nets to 10-day contract (December 19, 1980). . . . Played in Continental Basketball Association with Scranton Aces (1980-81). . . . Re-signed as free agent by Nets (February 18, 1981). . . . Traded by Nets to Atlanta Hawks for 1982 fourth-round draft choice (August 12, 1981). . . . Traded by Hawks to New York Knicks for Scott Hastings and cash (February 12, 1983). . . . Traded by Knicks to Chicago Bulls for 1988 second-round draft choice (November 12, 1987). . . . Rights relinquished by Bulls (September 22, 1988). . . . Signed as free agent by Miami Heat (November 3, 1988). . . . Traded by Heat to Sacramento Kings for draft rights to Bimbo Coles (June 27, 1990). . . . Rights renounced by Kings (1991). . . . Signed as free agent by Los Angeles Clippers (October 9, 1991). . . . Waived by Clippers (October 29, 1991). . . . Signed as free agent by Bulls (November 6, 1991). . . . Waived by Bulls (November 25, 1991). . . . Signed as free agent by Los Angeles Lakers (December 6, 1991).

COLLEGIATE RECORD

Season	Team	G	Min.	FGM	FGA	Pct.	FTM	FTA	Pct.	Reb.	Pts.	Avg.
76-77	Villanova	33	. . .	99	193	.513	34	42	.810	69	232	7.0
77-78	Villanova	32	1036	109	213	.512	57	79	.722	74	275	8.6
78-79	Villanova	28	877	145	282	.514	50	61	.820	60	340	12.1
79-80	Villanova	31	937	136	243	.560	64	77	.831	75	336	10.8
	Totals	124	. . .	489	931	.525	205	259	.792	278	1183	9.5

NBA REGULAR-SEASON RECORD

Season	Team	G	Min.	FGM	FGA	Pct.	FTM	FTA	Pct.	Off.	Def.	Tot.	Ast.	PF	Dq.	Stl.	Blk.	TO	Pts.	Avg.
80-81	New Jersey	15	212	22	63	.349	12	16	.750	7	11	18	32	15	0	13	3	18	56	3.7
81-82	Atlanta	82	2610	366	730	.501	124	148	.838	53	171	224	424	240	2	87	13	145	857	10.5
82-83	Atl.-N.Y.	81	2428	392	810	.484	147	199	.739	61	169	230	397	255	4	107	5	197	936	11.6
83-84	New York	79	2436	350	738	.474	108	131	.824	48	141	189	539	230	4	100	8	210	818	10.4
84-85	New York	79	2292	326	662	.492	122	141	.865	38	131	169	557	200	2	81	9	150	781	9.9
85-86	New York	74	2344	345	723	.477	101	127	.795	50	120	170	472	182	1	85	14	154	796	10.8
86-87	New York	80	1951	263	590	.446	71	89	.798	29	86	115	432	160	0	67	6	140	608	7.6
87-88	N.Y.-Chi.	58	1044	117	293	.399	24	33	.727	15	57	72	167	79	1	41	3	58	260	4.5
88-89	Miami	80	2613	444	982	.452	94	107	.879	55	161	216	429	168	0	103	17	204	1000	12.5
89-90	Miami	82	1756	210	510	.412	59	77	.766	37	101	138	298	140	0	49	4	99	487	5.9
90-91	Sacramento	80	2375	371	756	.491	58	83	.699	45	141	186	362	189	1	83	16	126	831	10.4
91-92	Chi.-L.A.L.	46	489	58	151	.384	8	13	.615	3	25	28	83	57	0	12	5	33	127	2.8
	Totals	836	22550	3264	7008	.466	928	1164	.797	441	1314	1755	4192	1915	15	828	103	1534	7557	9.0

Three-point field goals: 1981-82, 1-for-15 (.067). 1982-83, 5-for-22 (.227). 1983-84, 10-for-39 (.256). 1984-85, 7-for-31 (.226). 1985-86, 5-for-20 (.250). 1986-87, 11-for-42 (.262). 1987-88, 2-for-13 (.154). 1988-89, 18-for-74 (.243). 1989-90, 8-for-40 (.200). 1990-91, 31-for-78 (.397). 1991-92, 3-for-15 (.200). Totals, 101-for-389 (.260).

NBA PLAYOFF RECORD

Season	Team	G	Min.	FGM	FGA	Pct.	FTM	FTA	Pct.	Off.	Def.	Tot.	Ast.	PF	Dq.	Stl.	Blk.	TO	Pts.	Avg.
81-82	Atlanta	2	69	5	12	.417	4	4	1.000	2	6	8	11	7	0	2	0	7	14	7.0
82-83	New York	6	202	30	71	.423	17	21	.810	3	10	13	42	18	1	7	0	13	78	13.0
83-84	New York	12	389	54	121	.446	24	30	.800	10	16	26	86	41	2	12	1	30	134	11.2
87-88	Chicago	7	106	10	32	.313	4	6	.667	0	3	3	18	11	0	4	0	4	26	3.7
91-92	L.A. Lakers	3	16	1	4	.250	3	4	.750	1	0	1	4	5	0	1	0	0	5	1.7
	Totals	30	782	100	240	.417	52	65	.800	16	35	51	161	82	3	26	1	54	257	8.6

Three-point field goals: 1981-82, 0-for-1. 1982-83, 1-for-5 (.200). 1983-84, 2-for-6 (.333). 1987-88, 2-for-4 (.500). Totals, 5-for-16 (.313).

CBA REGULAR-SEASON RECORD

				2-POINT			3-POINT							
Season	Team	G	Min.	FGM	FGA	Pct.	FGM	FGA	Pct.	FTM	FTA	Pct.	Reb.	Ast.	Pts.	Avg.
80-81	Scranton	20	827	196	388	.505	2	8	.250	83	107	.776	82	180	481	24.1

SPENCER, FELTON
C, TIMBERWOLVES

PERSONAL: Born January 5, 1968, in Louisville, Ky. . . . 7-0/265. . . . Full name: Felton LaFrance Spencer.
HIGH SCHOOL: Eastern (Middletown, Ky.).
COLLEGE: Louisville.

TRANSACTIONS/CAREER NOTES: Selected by Minnesota Timberwolves in first round (sixth pick overall) of 1990 NBA Draft.

COLLEGIATE RECORD

Season	Team	G	Min.	FGM	FGA	Pct.	FTM	FTA	Pct.	Reb.	Pts.	Avg.
86-87	Louisville	31	356	43	78	.551	32	65	.492	83	118	3.8
87-88	Louisville	35	532	93	157	.592	73	114	.640	146	259	7.4
88-89	Louisville	33	581	85	140	.607	99	135	.733	169	269	8.2
89-90	Louisville	35	995	188	276	.681	146	204	.716	296	522	14.9
	Totals	134	2464	409	651	.628	350	518	.676	694	1168	8.7

NBA REGULAR-SEASON RECORD

HONORS: NBA All-Rookie second team (1991).

Season Team	G	Min.	FGM	FGA	Pct.	FTM	FTA	Pct.	— REBOUNDS — Off.	Def.	Tot.	Ast.	PF	Dq.	Stl.	Blk.	TO	Pts.	Avg.
90-91—Minnesota....	81	2099	195	381	.512	182	252	.722	272	369	641	25	337	14	48	121	77	572	7.1
91-92—Minnesota....	61	1481	141	331	.426	123	178	.691	167	268	435	53	241	7	27	79	70	405	6.6
Totals	142	3580	336	712	.472	305	430	.709	439	637	1076	78	578	21	75	200	147	977	6.9

Three-point field goals: 1990-91, 0-for-1.

STARKS, JOHN
G, KNICKS

PERSONAL: Born August 10, 1965, in Tulsa, Okla. . . . 6-5/185. . . . Full name: John Levell Starks.
HIGH SCHOOL: Tulsa Central (Okla.).
COLLEGE: Northern Oklahoma, then Rogers State (Okla.), then Oklahoma Junior College, then Oklahoma State.
TRANSACTIONS/CAREER NOTES: Never drafted by an NBA franchise. . . . Signed as free agent by Golden State Warriors (September 29, 1988). . . . Played in Continental Basketball Association with Cedar Rapids Silver Bullets (1989-90). . . . Signed as an unrestricted free agent by New York Knicks (October 1, 1990).

COLLEGIATE RECORD

Season Team	G	Min.	FGM	FGA	Pct.	FTM	FTA	Pct.	Reb.	Pts.	Avg.
84-85—Northern Oklahoma	14	. . .	57	123	.463	41	53	.774	33	155	11.1
85-86—Rogers State					Statistics unavailable.						
86-87—Oklahoma Junior College........					Statistics unavailable.						
87-88—Oklahoma State	30	982	154	310	.497	114	136	.838	141	463	15.4
Junior college totals	14	. . .	57	123	.463	41	53	.774	33	155	11.1
Four-year-college totals	30	982	154	310	.497	114	136	.838	141	463	15.4

Three-point field goals: 1987-88, 41-for-108 (.380).

NBA REGULAR-SEASON RECORD

Season Team	G	Min.	FGM	FGA	Pct.	FTM	FTA	Pct.	— REBOUNDS — Off.	Def.	Tot.	Ast.	PF	Dq.	Stl.	Blk.	TO	Pts.	Avg.
88-89—Golden State	36	316	51	125	.408	34	52	.654	15	26	41	27	36	0	23	3	39	146	4.1
90-91—New York	61	1173	180	410	.439	79	105	.752	30	101	131	204	137	1	59	17	74	466	7.6
91-92—New York	82	2118	405	902	.449	235	302	.778	45	146	191	276	231	4	103	18	150	1139	13.9
Totals	179	3607	636	1437	.443	348	459	.758	90	273	363	507	404	5	185	38	263	1751	9.8

Three-point field goals: 1988-89, 10-for-26 (.385). 1990-91, 27-for-93 (.290). 1991-92, 94-for-270 (.348). Totals, 131-for-389 (.337).

NBA PLAYOFF RECORD

Season Team	G	Min.	FGM	FGA	Pct.	FTM	FTA	Pct.	— REBOUNDS — Off.	Def.	Tot.	Ast.	PF	Dq.	Stl.	Blk.	TO	Pts.	Avg.
90-91—New York	3	28	2	5	.400	2	2	1.000	1	2	3	6	4	0	0	0	6	6	2.0
91-92—New York	12	295	46	123	.374	42	52	.808	7	23	30	38	45	1	17	0	22	145	12.1
Totals	15	323	48	128	.375	44	54	.815	8	25	33	44	49	1	17	0	28	151	10.1

Three-point field goals: 1991-92, 11-for-46 (.239).

CBA REGULAR-SEASON RECORD

Season Team	G	Min.	2-POINT FGM	FGA	Pct.	3-POINT FGM	FGA	Pct.	FTM	FTA	Pct.	Reb.	Ast.	Pts.	Avg.
89-90—Cedar Rapids ...	46	1670	337	663	.508	48	138	.348	179	240	.746	246	255	997	21.7

STEWART, LARRY
F, BULLETS

PERSONAL: Born September 21, 1968, in Philadelphia. . . . 6-8/220.
HIGH SCHOOL: Dobbins Tech (Philadelphia).
COLLEGE: Coppin State.
TRANSACTIONS/CAREER NOTES: Never drafted by an NBA franchise. . . . Signed as free agent by Washington Bullets (September 23, 1991).

COLLEGIATE RECORD

Season Team	G	Min.	FGM	FGA	Pct.	FTM	FTA	Pct.	Reb.	Pts.	Avg.
87-88—Coppin State				Did not play—ineligible.							
88-89—Coppin State	28	956	199	302	.659	94	136	.691	280	492	17.6
89-90—Coppin State	33	1221	233	361	.645	150	214	.701	369	616	18.7
90-91—Coppin State	30	1098	244	384	.635	227	289	.785	403	716	23.9
Totals	91	3275	676	1047	.646	471	639	.737	1052	1824	20.0

Three-point field goals: 1988-89, 0-for-1. 1989-90, 0-for-1. 1990-91, 1-for-1. Totals, 1-for-3 (.333).

NBA REGULAR-SEASON RECORD

HONORS: NBA All-Rookie second team (1992).

Season Team	G	Min.	FGM	FGA	Pct.	FTM	FTA	Pct.	— REBOUNDS — Off.	Def.	Tot.	Ast.	PF	Dq.	Stl.	Blk.	TO	Pts.	Avg.
91-92—Washington .	76	2229	303	590	.514	188	233	.807	186	263	449	120	225	3	51	44	112	794	10.4

Three-point field goals: 1991-92, 0-for-3.

STOCKTON, JOHN
G, JAZZ

PERSONAL: Born March 26, 1962, in Spokane, Wash. . . . 6-1/175. . . . Full name: John Houston Stockton.
HIGH SCHOOL: Gonzaga Prep School (Spokane, Wash.).
COLLEGE: Gonzaga.
TRANSACTIONS/CAREER NOTES: Selected by Utah Jazz in first round (16th pick overall) of 1984 NBA Draft.
MISCELLANEOUS: Member of gold-medal-winning U.S. Olympic team (1992).

COLLEGIATE RECORD

Season Team	G	Min.	FGM	FGA	Pct.	FTM	FTA	Pct.	Reb.	Pts.	Avg.
80-81 —Gonzaga	25	235	26	45	.578	26	35	.743	11	78	3.1
81-82 —Gonzaga	27	1054	117	203	.576	69	102	.676	67	303	11.2
82-83 —Gonzaga	27	1036	142	274	.518	91	115	.791	87	375	13.9
83-84 —Gonzaga	28	1053	229	397	.577	126	182	.692	66	584	20.9
Totals	107	3378	514	919	.559	312	434	.719	231	1340	12.5

NBA REGULAR-SEASON RECORD

RECORDS: Holds single-season records for most assists—1,164 (1991); and highest assists-per-game average (minimum 70 games)—14.5 (1990).

HONORS: All-NBA second team (1988, 1989, 1990, 1992).... All-NBA third team (1991).... NBA All-Defensive second team (1989, 1991, 1992).

NOTES: Led NBA with 13.8 assists per game (1988), 13.6 assists per game (1989), 14.5 assists per game (1990), 14.2 assists per game (1991) and 13.7 assists per game (1992).... Led NBA with 3.21 steals per game (1989) and 2.98 steals per game (1992).

Season Team	G	Min.	FGM	FGA	Pct.	FTM	FTA	Pct.	Off.	Def.	Tot.	Ast.	PF	Dq.	Stl.	Blk.	TO	Pts.	Avg.
84-85 —Utah	82	1490	157	333	.471	142	193	.736	26	79	105	415	203	3	109	11	150	458	5.6
85-86 —Utah	82	1935	228	466	.489	172	205	.839	33	146	179	610	227	2	157	10	168	630	7.7
86-87 —Utah	82	1858	231	463	.499	179	229	.782	32	119	151	670	224	1	177	14	164	648	7.9
87-88 —Utah	82	2842	454	791	.574	272	324	.840	54	183	237*1128	247		5	242	16	262	1204	14.7
88-89 —Utah	82	3171	497	923	.538	390	452	.863	83	165	248*1118	241	3	*263	14	308	1400	17.1
89-90 —Utah	78	2915	472	918	.514	354	432	.819	57	149	206*1134	233	3	207	18	272	1345	17.2
90-91 —Utah	82	3103	496	978	.507	363	434	.836	46	191	237*1164	233	1	234	16	298	1413	17.2
91-92 —Utah	82	3002	453	939	.482	308	366	.842	68	202	270*1126	234	3	*244	22	*286	1297	15.8
Totals	652	20316	2988	5811	.514	2180	2635	.827	399	1234	1633	7365	1842	21	1633	121	1908	8395	12.9

Three-point field goals: 1984-85, 2-for-11 (.182). 1985-86, 2-for-15 (.133). 1986-87, 7-for-38 (.184). 1987-88, 24-for-67 (.358). 1988-89, 16-for-66 (.242). 1989-90, 47-for-113 (.416). 1990-91, 58-for-168 (.345). 1991-92, 83-for-204 (.407). Totals, 239-for-682 (.350).

NBA PLAYOFF RECORD

NOTES: Shares single-game record for most assists—24 (May 17, 1988, vs. Los Angeles Lakers).

Season Team	G	Min.	FGM	FGA	Pct.	FTM	FTA	Pct.	Off.	Def.	Tot.	Ast.	PF	Dq.	Stl.	Blk.	TO	Pts.	Avg.
84-85 —Utah	10	186	21	45	.467	26	35	.743	7	21	28	43	30	0	11	2	16	68	6.8
85-86 —Utah	4	73	9	17	.529	8	9	.889	3	3	6	14	10	0	5	0	4	27	6.8
86-87 —Utah	5	157	18	29	.621	10	13	.769	2	9	11	40	18	0	15	1	11	50	10.0
87-88 —Utah	11	478	68	134	.507	75	91	.824	14	31	45	163	36	0	37	3	48	215	19.5
88-89 —Utah	3	139	30	59	.508	19	21	.905	2	8	10	41	15	0	11	5	11	82	27.3
89-90 —Utah	5	194	29	69	.420	16	20	.800	4	12	16	75	20	0	6	0	14	75	15.0
90-91 —Utah	9	373	58	108	.537	37	44	.841	10	32	42	124	33	0	20	2	32	164	18.2
91-92 —Utah	16	623	77	182	.423	65	78	.833	10	37	47	217	38	0	34	5	58	237	14.8
Totals	63	2223	310	643	.482	256	311	.823	52	153	205	717	200	0	139	18	194	918	14.6

Three-point field goals: 1984-85, 0-for-2. 1985-86, 1-for-1. 1986-87, 4-for-5 (.800). 1987-88, 4-for-14 (.286). 1988-89, 3-for-4 (.750). 1989-90, 1-for-13 (.077). 1990-91, 11-for-27 (.407). 1991-92, 18-for-58 (.310). Totals, 42-for-124 (.339).

NBA ALL-STAR GAME RECORD

Season Team	Min.	FGM	FGA	Pct.	FTM	FTA	Pct.	Off.	Def.	Tot.	Ast.	PF	Dq.	Stl.	Blk.	TO	Pts.
1989 —Utah	32	5	6	.833	0	0	...	0	2	2	17	4	0	5	0	12	11
1990 —Utah	15	1	4	.250	0	0	...	0	0	0	6	1	0	1	1	3	2
1991 —Utah	12	1	6	.167	2	4	.500	0	1	1	2	2	0	0	0	0	4
1992 —Utah	18	5	8	.625	0		...	0	1	1	5	2	0	3	0	3	12
Totals	77	12	24	.500	2	4	.500	0	4	4	30	9	0	9	1	18	29

Three-point field goals: 1989, 1-for-1. 1990, 0-for-1. 1992, 2-for-3 (.667). Totals, 3-for-5 (.600).

STRICKLAND, ROD
G, TRAIL BLAZERS

PERSONAL: Born July 11, 1966, in Bronx, N.Y.... 6-3/175.... Full name: Rodney Strickland.

HIGH SCHOOL: Harry S. Truman (Bronx, N.Y.), then Oak Hill Academy (Mouth of Wilson, Va.).

COLLEGE: DePaul.

TRANSACTIONS/CAREER NOTES: Selected as undergraduate by New York Knicks in first round (19th pick overall) of 1988 NBA Draft.... Traded by Knicks to San Antonio Spurs for Maurice Cheeks (February 21, 1990).... Signed as free agent by Portland Trail Blazers (July 3, 1992).

COLLEGIATE RECORD

NOTES: THE SPORTING NEWS All-America first team (1988).

Season Team	G	Min.	FGM	FGA	Pct.	FTM	FTA	Pct.	Reb.	Pts.	Avg.
85-86 —DePaul	31	1063	176	354	.497	85	126	.675	84	437	14.1
86-87 —DePaul	30	980	188	323	.582	106	175	.606	113	490	16.3
87-88 —DePaul	26	837	207	392	.528	83	137	.606	98	521	20.0
Totals	87	2880	571	1069	.534	274	438	.626	295	1448	16.6

Three-point field goals: 1986-87, 8-for-15 (.533). 1987-88, 24-for-54 (.444). Totals, 32-for-69 (.464).

NBA REGULAR-SEASON RECORD

HONORS: NBA All-Rookie second team (1989).

Season Team	G	Min.	FGM	FGA	Pct.	FTM	FTA	Pct.	Off.	Def.	Tot.	Ast.	PF	Dq.	Stl.	Blk.	TO	Pts.	Avg.
88-89 —New York	81	1358	265	567	.467	172	231	.745	51	109	160	319	142	2	98	3	148	721	8.9
89-90 —N.Y.-S.A.	82	2140	343	756	.454	174	278	.626	90	169	259	468	160	3	127	14	170	868	10.6

Season Team	G	Min.	FGM	FGA	Pct.	FTM	FTA	Pct.	Off.	Def.	Tot.	Ast.	PF	Dq.	Stl.	Blk.	TO	Pts.	Avg.
									— REBOUNDS —										
90-91—San Antonio.	58	2076	314	651	.482	161	211	.763	57	162	219	463	125	0	117	11	156	800	13.8
91-92—San Antonio.	57	2053	300	659	.455	182	265	.687	92	173	265	491	122	0	118	17	160	787	13.8
Totals	278	7627	1222	2633	.464	689	985	.699	290	613	903	1741	549	5	460	45	634	3176	11.4

Three-point field goals: 1988-89, 19-for-59 (.322). 1989-90, 8-for-30 (.267). 1990-91, 11-for-33 (.333). 1991-92, 5-for-15 (.333). Totals, 43-for-137 (.314).

NBA PLAYOFF RECORD

Season Team	G	Min.	FGM	FGA	Pct.	FTM	FTA	Pct.	Off.	Def.	Tot.	Ast.	PF	Dq.	Stl.	Blk.	TO	Pts.	Avg.
									— REBOUNDS —										
88-89—New York	9	111	22	49	.449	9	17	.529	6	7	13	25	21	0	4	1	13	54	6.0
89-90—San Antonio.	10	384	54	127	.425	15	27	.556	22	31	53	112	30	2	14	0	34	123	12.3
90-91—San Antonio.	4	168	29	67	.433	17	21	.810	5	16	21	35	14	0	9	0	13	75	18.8
91-92—San Antonio.	2	80	13	22	.591	5	8	.625	0	7	7	19	8	0	3	2	6	31	15.5
Totals	25	743	118	265	.445	46	73	.630	33	61	94	191	73	2	30	3	66	283	11.3

Three-point field goals: 1988-89, 1-for-1. 1989-90, 0-for-7. 1990-91, 0-for-6. Totals, 1-for-14 (.071).

STRONG, DEREK
F

PERSONAL: Born February 9, 1968, in Los Angeles. .... 6-8/220. .... Full name: Derek Lamar Strong.
HIGH SCHOOL: Pacific Palisades, Calif.
COLLEGE: Xavier (Cincinnati, O.).
TRANSACTIONS/CAREER NOTES: Selected by Philadelphia 76ers in second round (47th pick overall) of 1990 NBA Draft. .... Played in Spain (1990-1991). .... Waived by 76ers (March 5, 1992). .... Signed by Washington Bullets to 10-day contract (March 13, 1992).

COLLEGIATE RECORD

Season Team	G	Min.	FGM	FGA	Pct.	FTM	FTA	Pct.	Reb.	Pts.	Avg.
86-87—Xavier				Did not play—ineligible.							
87-88—Xavier	30	668	112	197	.569	94	131	.718	213	318	10.6
88-89—Xavier	33	983	163	264	.617	178	218	.817	264	504	15.3
89-90—Xavier	33	981	146	274	.533	177	211	.839	328	469	14.2
Totals	96	2632	421	735	.573	449	560	.802	805	1291	13.4

NBA REGULAR-SEASON RECORD

Season Team	G	Min.	FGM	FGA	Pct.	FTM	FTA	Pct.	Off.	Def.	Tot.	Ast.	PF	Dq.	Stl.	Blk.	TO	Pts.	Avg.
									— REBOUNDS —										
91-92—Washington .	1	12	0	4	.000	3	4	.750	1	4	5	1	1	0	0	0	1	3	3.0

STROTHERS, LAMONT
G

PERSONAL: Born May 10, 1968, in Nansemond County, Va. .... 6-4/190. .... Full name: William Lamont Strothers.
HIGH SCHOOL: Forest Glen (Suffolk, Va.).
COLLEGE: Christopher Newport (Va.).
TRANSACTIONS/CAREER NOTES: Selected by Golden State Warriors in second round (43rd pick overall) of 1991 NBA Draft. .... Draft rights traded by Warriors to Portland Trail Blazers for 1995 and 1999 second-round draft choices (June 26, 1991).

COLLEGIATE RECORD

Season Team	G	Min.	FGM	FGA	Pct.	FTM	FTA	Pct.	Reb.	Pts.	Avg.
87-88—Christopher Newport	30	...	250	531	.471	125	168	.744	191	652	21.7
88-89—Christopher Newport	29	995	255	549	.464	124	181	.685	158	695	24.0
89-90—Christopher Newport	28	915	232	491	.473	92	129	.713	166	603	21.5
90-91—Christopher Newport	29	955	279	578	.483	146	195	.749	202	759	26.2
Totals	116	...	1016	2149	.473	487	673	.724	717	2709	23.4

Three-point field goals: 1987-88, 27-for-89 (.303). 1988-89, 61-for-194 (.314). 1989-90, 47-for-137 (.343). 1990-91, 55-for-145 (.379). Totals, 190-for-565 (.336).

NBA REGULAR-SEASON RECORD

Season Team	G	Min.	FGM	FGA	Pct.	FTM	FTA	Pct.	Off.	Def.	Tot.	Ast.	PF	Dq.	Stl.	Blk.	TO	Pts.	Avg.
									— REBOUNDS —										
91-92—Portland	4	17	4	12	.333	2	4	.500	1	0	1	1	2	0	1	1	2	10	2.5

Three-point field goals: 1991-92, 0-for-2.

SUNDVOLD, JON
G, HEAT

PERSONAL: Born July 2, 1961, in Sioux Falls, S.D. .... 6-2/175. .... Full name: Jon Thomas Sundvold.
HIGH SCHOOL: Blue Springs (Mo.).
COLLEGE: Missouri.
TRANSACTIONS/CAREER NOTES: Selected by Seattle SuperSonics in first round (16th pick overall) of 1983 NBA Draft. .... Traded by SuperSonics to San Antonio Spurs for 1986 second-round draft choice (October 23, 1985). .... Selected by Miami Heat from Spurs in NBA expansion draft (June 23, 1988).

COLLEGIATE RECORD

Season Team	G	Min.	FGM	FGA	Pct.	FTM	FTA	Pct.	Reb.	Pts.	Avg.
79-80—Missouri.................................	31	790	76	169	.450	44	59	.746	52	196	6.3
80-81—Missouri.................................	32	1134	178	350	.509	85	99	.859	54	441	13.8

Season Team	G	Min.	FGM	FGA	Pct.	FTM	FTA	Pct.	Reb.	Pts.	Avg.
81-82 —Missouri	31	1062	149	307	.485	81	93	.871	66	379	12.2
82-83 —Missouri	34	1303	225	447	.503	131	151	.868	82	581	17.1
Totals	128	4289	628	1273	.493	341	402	.848	254	1597	12.5

NBA REGULAR-SEASON RECORD

NOTES: Led NBA with .522 three-point field-goal percentage (1989).

Season Team	G	Min.	FGM	FGA	Pct.	FTM	FTA	Pct.	REBOUNDS Off.	Def.	Tot.	Ast.	PF	Dq.	Stl.	Blk.	TO	Pts.	Avg.
83-84 —Seattle	73	1284	217	488	.445	64	72	.889	23	68	91	239	81	0	29	1	81	507	6.9
84-85 —Seattle	73	1150	170	400	.425	48	59	.814	17	53	70	206	87	0	36	1	85	400	5.5
85-86 —San Antonio	70	1150	220	476	.462	39	48	.813	22	58	80	261	110	0	34	0	85	500	7.1
86-87 —San Antonio	76	1765	365	751	.486	70	84	.833	20	78	98	315	109	1	35	0	97	850	11.2
87-88 —San Antonio	52	1024	176	379	.464	43	48	.896	14	34	48	183	54	0	27	2	57	421	8.1
88-89 —Miami	68	1338	307	675	.455	47	57	.825	18	69	87	137	78	0	27	1	87	709	10.4
89-90 —Miami	63	867	148	363	.408	44	52	.846	15	56	71	102	69	0	25	0	52	384	6.1
90-91 —Miami	24	225	43	107	.402	11	11	1.000	3	6	9	24	11	0	7	0	16	112	4.7
91-92 —Miami	3	8	1	3	.333	0	0	...	0	0	0	2	2	0	0	0	0	3	1.0
Totals	502	8811	1647	3642	.452	366	431	.849	132	422	554	1469	601	1	220	5	560	3886	7.7

Three-point field goals: 1983-84, 9-for-37 (.243). 1984-85, 12-for-38 (.316). 1985-86, 21-for-60 (.350). 1986-87, 50-for-149 (.336). 1987-88, 26-for-64 (.406). 1988-89, 48-for-92 (.522). 1989-90, 44-for-100 (.440). 1990-91, 15-for-35 (.429). 1991-92, 1-for-1. Totals, 226-for-576 (.392).

NBA PLAYOFF RECORD

Season Team	G	Min.	FGM	FGA	Pct.	FTM	FTA	Pct.	REBOUNDS Off.	Def.	Tot.	Ast.	PF	Dq.	Stl.	Blk.	TO	Pts.	Avg.
83-84 —Seattle	3	22	3	8	.375	2	2	1.000	1	1	2	5	1	0	0	0	1	8	2.7
85-86 —San Antonio	3	43	7	18	.389	1	1	1.000	0	1	1	5	1	0	0	0	5	16	5.3
87-88 —San Antonio	3	90	15	30	.500	2	3	.667	1	3	4	15	3	0	4	0	3	35	11.7
91-92 —Miami	1	2	0	1	.000	0	0	...	0	0	0	0	1	0	0	0	0	0	0.0
Totals	10	157	25	57	.439	5	6	.833	2	5	7	25	6	0	4	0	9	59	5.9

Three-point field goals: 1983-84, 0-for-3. 1985-86, 1-for-6 (.167). 1987-88, 3-for-9 (.333). Totals, 4-for-18 (.222).

SUTTON, GREG
G, SPURS

PERSONAL: Born December 3, 1967, in Santa Cruz, Calif.... 6-2/170.... Full name: Gregory Ray Sutton.
HIGH SCHOOL: Douglass (Oklahoma City).
COLLEGE: Langston (Okla.), then Oral Roberts.
TRANSACTIONS/CAREER NOTES: Selected by San Antonio Spurs in second round (49th pick overall) of 1991 NBA Draft.

COLLEGIATE RECORD

Season Team	G	Min.	FGM	FGA	Pct.	FTM	FTA	Pct.	Reb.	Pts.	Avg.
86-87 —Langston	29	...	198	487	.407	93	124	.750	90	536	18.5
87-88 —Oral Roberts					Did not play—transfer student.						
88-89 —Oral Roberts	28	936	214	564	.379	103	157	.656	121	614	21.9
89-90 —Oral Roberts	41	...	417	976	.427	252	328	.768	205	1256	30.6
90-91 —Oral Roberts	35	...	393	858	.458	229	280	.818	168	1200	34.3
Totals	133	...	1222	2885	.424	677	889	.762	584	3606	27.1

Three-point field goals: 1988-89, 83-for-251 (.331). 1989-90, 170-for-443 (.384). 1990-91, 185-for-463 (.400). Totals, 438-for-1157 (.379).

NBA REGULAR-SEASON RECORD

Season Team	G	Min.	FGM	FGA	Pct.	FTM	FTA	Pct.	REBOUNDS Off.	Def.	Tot.	Ast.	PF	Dq.	Stl.	Blk.	TO	Pts.	Avg.
91-92 —San Antonio	67	601	93	240	.388	34	45	.756	6	41	47	91	111	0	26	9	70	246	3.7

Three-point field goals: 1991-92, 26-for-89 (.292).

NBA PLAYOFF RECORD

Season Team	G	Min.	FGM	FGA	Pct.	FTM	FTA	Pct.	REBOUNDS Off.	Def.	Tot.	Ast.	PF	Dq.	Stl.	Blk.	TO	Pts.	Avg.
91-92 —San Antonio	2	15	2	6	.333	3	3	1.000	0	0	0	2	3	0	1	1	0	7	3.5

Three-point field goals: 1991-92, 0-for-2.

TEAGLE, TERRY
F/G, LAKERS

PERSONAL: Born April 10, 1960, in Broaddus, Tex.... 6-5/200.... Full name: Terry Michael Teagle.
HIGH SCHOOL: Broaddus (Tex.).
COLLEGE: Baylor.
TRANSACTIONS/CAREER NOTES: Selected by Houston Rockets in first round (16th pick overall) of 1982 NBA Draft.... Waived by Rockets (October 23, 1984).... Played in Continental Basketball Association with Detroit Spirits (1984-85).... Signed as free agent by Detroit Pistons (November 7, 1984).... Waived by Pistons (November 20, 1984).... Signed as free agent by Golden State Warriors (March 11, 1985).... Traded by Warriors to Los Angeles Lakers for 1991 first-round draft choice (September 25, 1990).

COLLEGIATE RECORD

Season Team	G	Min.	FGM	FGA	Pct.	FTM	FTA	Pct.	Reb.	Pts.	Avg.
78-79 —Baylor	28	...	164	310	.529	80	113	.708	183	408	14.6
79-80 —Baylor	27	...	239	440	.543	142	171	.830	222	620	23.0
80-81 —Baylor	27	...	214	399	.536	111	151	.735	190	539	20.0
81-82 —Baylor	28	...	259	479	.541	104	144	.722	210	622	22.2
Totals	110	...	876	1628	.538	437	579	.755	805	2189	19.9

NBA REGULAR-SEASON RECORD

Season Team	G	Min.	FGM	FGA	Pct.	FTM	FTA	Pct.	Off.	Def.	Tot.	Ast.	PF	Dq.	Stl.	Blk.	TO	Pts.	Avg.
82-83—Houston	73	1708	332	776	.428	87	125	.696	74	120	194	150	171	0	53	18	137	761	10.4
83-84—Houston	68	616	148	315	.470	37	44	.841	28	50	78	63	81	1	13	4	62	340	5.0
84-85—Detroit-G.S.	21	349	74	137	.540	25	35	.714	22	21	43	14	36	0	13	5	15	175	8.3
85-86—Golden State	82	2158	475	958	.496	211	265	.796	96	139	235	115	241	2	71	34	136	1165	14.2
86-87—Golden State	82	1650	370	808	.458	182	234	.778	68	107	175	105	190	0	68	13	117	922	11.2
87-88—Golden State	47	958	248	546	.454	97	121	.802	41	40	81	61	95	0	32	4	80	594	12.6
88-89—Golden State	66	1569	409	859	.476	182	225	.809	110	153	263	96	173	2	79	17	116	1002	15.2
89-90—Golden State	82	2376	538	1122	.480	244	294	.830	114	253	367	155	231	3	91	15	144	1323	16.1
90-91—L.A. Lakers	82	1498	335	757	.443	145	177	.819	82	99	181	82	165	1	31	8	83	815	9.9
91-92—L.A. Lakers	82	1602	364	805	.452	151	197	.767	91	92	183	113	148	0	66	9	114	880	10.7
Totals	685	14484	3293	7083	.465	1361	1717	.793	726	1074	1800	954	1531	9	517	127	1004	7977	11.6

Three-point field goals: 1982-83, 10-for-29 (.345). 1983-84, 7-for-27 (.259). 1984-85, 2-for-4 (.500). 1985-86, 4-for-25 (.160). 1986-87, 0-for-10. 1987-88, 1-for-9 (.111). 1988-89, 2-for-12 (.167). 1989-90, 3-for-14 (.214). 1990-91, 0-for-9. 1991-92, 1-for-4 (.250). Totals, 30-for-143 (.210).

NBA PLAYOFF RECORD

Season Team	G	Min.	FGM	FGA	Pct.	FTM	FTA	Pct.	Off.	Def.	Tot.	Ast.	PF	Dq.	Stl.	Blk.	TO	Pts.	Avg.
86-87—Golden State	10	233	57	124	.460	30	38	.789	13	7	20	13	27	0	8	1	14	144	14.4
88-89—Golden State	8	240	70	141	.496	18	22	.818	15	22	37	10	27	0	8	3	13	158	19.8
90-91—L.A. Lakers	18	274	47	125	.376	25	32	.781	8	20	28	11	31	0	8	4	16	119	6.6
91-92—L.A. Lakers	4	126	27	55	.491	16	20	.800	3	10	13	8	18	1	5	2	8	70	17.5
Totals	40	873	201	445	.452	89	112	.795	39	59	98	42	103	1	29	10	51	491	12.3

Three-point field goals: 1986-87, 0-for-2. 1988-89, 0-for-2. Totals, 0-for-4.

CBA REGULAR-SEASON RECORD

Season Team	G	Min.	2-POINT			3-POINT			FTM	FTA	Pct.	Reb.	Ast.	Pts.	Avg.
			FGM	FGA	Pct.	FGM	FGA	Pct.							
84-85—Detroit	40	1146	294	532	.553	2	14	.143	187	222	.842	171	67	781	19.5

THOMAS, CARL
G

PERSONAL: Born October 3, 1969, in Dayton, O. . . . 6-4/175. . . . Twin brother of Charles Thomas, guard with Detroit Pistons (1991-92).
HIGH SCHOOL: Everett (Lansing, Mich.).
COLLEGE: Eastern Michigan.
TRANSACTIONS/CAREER NOTES: Never drafted by an NBA franchise. . . . Signed as free agent by Sacramento Kings (October 3, 1991). . . . Waived by Kings (November 4, 1991). . . . Played in Continental Basketball Association with Fort Wayne Fury and Grand Rapids Hoops (1991-92).

COLLEGIATE RECORD

Season Team	G	Min.	FGM	FGA	Pct.	FTM	FTA	Pct.	Reb.	Pts.	Avg.
87-88—Eastern Michigan	20	393	65	126	.516	19	28	.679	55	168	8.4
88-89—Eastern Michigan	29	667	87	215	.405	34	40	.850	121	240	8.3
89-90—Eastern Michigan	31	747	105	213	.493	51	71	.718	126	306	9.9
90-91—Eastern Michigan	33	1096	156	315	.495	64	84	.762	150	465	14.1
Totals	113	2903	413	869	.475	168	223	.753	452	1179	10.4

Three-point field goals: 1987-88, 19-for-45 (.422). 1988-89, 32-for-99 (.323). 1989-90, 45-for-108 (.417). 1990-91, 89-for-191 (.466). Totals, 185-for-443 (.418).

NBA REGULAR-SEASON RECORD

Season Team	G	Min.	FGM	FGA	Pct.	FTM	FTA	Pct.	Off.	Def.	Tot.	Ast.	PF	Dq.	Stl.	Blk.	TO	Pts.	Avg.
91-92—Sacramento	1	31	5	12	.417	1	2	.500	0	0	0	1	3	0	1	0	1	12	12.0

Three-point field goals: 1991-92, 1-for-2 (.500).

CBA REGULAR-SEASON RECORD

Season Team	G	Min.	2-POINT			3-POINT			FTM	FTA	Pct.	Reb.	Ast.	Pts.	Avg.
			FGM	FGA	Pct.	FGM	FGA	Pct.							
91-92—F.W.-Gr. Rap.	56	1895	232	515	.450	35	113	.310	180	224	.804	221	268	749	13.4

THOMAS, CHARLES
G, PISTONS

PERSONAL: Born October 3, 1969, in Dayton, O. . . . 6-3/175. . . . Twin brother of Carl Thomas, guard with Sacramento Kings (1991-92).
HIGH SCHOOL: Everett (Lansing, Mich.).
COLLEGE: Eastern Michigan.
TRANSACTIONS/CAREER NOTES: Never drafted by an NBA franchise. . . . Signed as free agent by Detroit Pistons (July 18, 1991).

COLLEGIATE RECORD

Season Team	G	Min.	FGM	FGA	Pct.	FTM	FTA	Pct.	Reb.	Pts.	Avg.
87-88—Eastern Michigan	15	26	2	5	.400	0	0	. . .	4	4	0.3
88-89—Eastern Michigan	29	551	71	162	.438	25	33	.758	96	203	7.0
89-90—Eastern Michigan	32	545	57	134	.425	24	36	.667	103	163	5.1
90-91—Eastern Michigan	33	1125	121	260	.465	43	55	.782	144	340	10.3
Totals	109	2247	251	561	.447	92	124	.742	347	710	6.5

Three-point field goals: 1987-88, 0-for-1. 1988-89, 36-for-95 (.379). 1989-90, 25-for-77 (.325). 1990-91, 55-for-148 (.372). Totals, 116-for-321 (.361).

NBA REGULAR-SEASON RECORD

Season	Team	G	Min.	FGM	FGA	Pct.	FTM	FTA	Pct.	Off.	Def.	Tot.	Ast.	PF	Dq.	Stl.	Blk.	TO	Pts.	Avg.
91-92	Detroit..........	37	156	18	51	.353	10	15	.667	6	16	22	22	20	0	4	1	17	48	1.3

Three-point field goals: 1991-92, 2-for-17 (.118).

THOMAS, ISIAH

G, PISTONS

PERSONAL: Born April 30, 1961, in Chicago.... 6-1/182.... Full name: Isiah Lord Thomas III.
HIGH SCHOOL: St. Joseph's (Westchester, Ill.).
COLLEGE: Indiana.
TRANSACTIONS/CAREER NOTES: Selected as undergraduate by Detroit Pistons in first round (second pick overall) of 1981 NBA Draft.
MISCELLANEOUS: Member of U.S. Olympic team (1980).... Member of NBA championship teams (1989, 1990).

COLLEGIATE RECORD

NOTES: THE SPORTING NEWS All-America first team (1981).... NCAA Division I Tournament Most Outstanding Player (1981).... Member of NCAA Division I championship team (1981).

Season	Team	G	Min.	FGM	FGA	Pct.	FTM	FTA	Pct.	Reb.	Pts.	Avg.
79-80	Indiana..................................	29	...	154	302	.510	115	149	.772	116	423	14.6
80-81	Indiana..................................	34	...	212	383	.554	121	163	.742	105	545	16.0
	Totals	63	...	366	685	.534	236	312	.756	221	968	15.4

NBA REGULAR-SEASON RECORD

HONORS: All-NBA first team (1984, 1985, 1986).... All-NBA second team (1983, 1987).... NBA All-Rookie team (1982).
NOTES: Led NBA with 13.9 assists per game (1985).

Season	Team	G	Min.	FGM	FGA	Pct.	FTM	FTA	Pct.	Off.	Def.	Tot.	Ast.	PF	Dq.	Stl.	Blk.	TO	Pts.	Avg.
81-82	Detroit........	72	2433	453	1068	.424	302	429	.704	57	152	209	565	253	2	150	17	299	1225	17.0
82-83	Detroit........	81	*3093	725	1537	.472	368	518	.710	105	223	328	634	318	8	199	29	*326	1854	22.9
83-84	Detroit........	82	3007	669	1448	.462	388	529	.733	103	224	327	914	324	8	204	33	307	1748	21.3
84-85	Detroit........	81	3089	646	1410	.458	399	493	.809	114	247	361	*1123	288	8	187	25	302	1720	21.2
85-86	Detroit........	77	2790	609	1248	.488	365	462	.790	83	194	277	830	245	9	171	20	289	1609	20.9
86-87	Detroit........	81	3013	626	1353	.463	400	521	.768	82	237	319	813	251	5	153	20	343	1671	20.6
87-88	Detroit........	81	2927	621	1341	.463	305	394	.774	64	214	278	678	217	0	141	17	273	1577	19.5
88-89	Detroit........	80	2924	569	1227	.464	287	351	.818	49	224	273	663	209	0	133	20	298	1458	18.2
89-90	Detroit........	81	2993	579	1322	.438	292	377	.775	74	234	308	765	206	0	139	19	*322	1492	18.4
90-91	Detroit........	48	1657	289	665	.435	179	229	.782	35	125	160	446	118	4	75	10	185	776	16.2
91-92	Detroit........	78	2918	564	1264	.446	292	378	.772	68	179	247	560	194	2	118	15	252	1445	18.5
	Totals	842	30844	6350	13883	.457	3577	4681	.764	834	2253	3087	7991	2623	46	1670	225	3196	16575	19.7

Three-point field goals: 1981-82, 17-for-59 (.288). 1982-83, 36-for-125 (.288). 1983-84, 22-for-65 (.338). 1984-85, 29-for-113 (.257). 1985-86, 26-for-84 (.310). 1986-87, 19-for-98 (.194). 1987-88, 30-for-97 (.309). 1988-89, 33-for-121 (.273). 1989-90, 42-for-136 (.309). 1990-91, 19-for-65 (.292). 1991-92, 25-for-86 (.291). Totals, 298-for-1049 (.284).

NBA PLAYOFF RECORD

NOTES: NBA Finals Most Valuable Player (1990).... Holds NBA Finals single-game records for most points in one quarter—25 (June 19, 1988, vs. Los Angeles Lakers); and most field goals in one quarter—11 (June 19, 1988, vs. Los Angeles Lakers).... Shares NBA Finals single-game records for most field goals in one half—14; and most steals—6 (June 19, 1988, vs. Los Angeles Lakers).

Season	Team	G	Min.	FGM	FGA	Pct.	FTM	FTA	Pct.	Off.	Def.	Tot.	Ast.	PF	Dq.	Stl.	Blk.	TO	Pts.	Avg.
83-84	Detroit........	5	198	39	83	.470	27	35	.771	7	12	19	55	22	1	13	6	23	107	21.4
84-85	Detroit........	9	355	83	166	.500	47	62	.758	11	36	47	101	39	2	19	4	30	219	24.3
85-86	Detroit........	4	163	41	91	.451	24	36	.667	8	14	22	48	17	0	9	3	17	106	26.5
86-87	Detroit........	15	562	134	297	.451	83	110	.755	21	46	67	130	51	1	39	4	42	361	24.1
87-88	Detroit........	23	911	183	419	.437	125	151	.828	26	81	107	201	71	2	66	8	85	504	21.9
88-89	Detroit........	17	633	115	279	.412	71	96	.740	24	49	73	141	39	0	27	4	43	309	18.2
89-90	Detroit........	20	758	148	320	.463	81	102	.794	21	88	109	163	65	1	43	7	72	409	20.5
90-91	Detroit........	13	436	60	149	.403	50	69	.725	13	41	54	111	41	1	13	2	41	176	13.5
91-92	Detroit........	5	200	22	65	.338	22	28	.786	3	23	26	37	18	0	5	0	16	70	14.0
	Totals	111	4216	825	1869	.441	530	689	.769	134	390	524	987	363	8	234	38	369	2261	20.4

Three-point field goals: 1983-84, 2-for-6 (.333). 1984-85, 6-for-15 (.400). 1985-86, 0-for-5. 1986-87, 10-for-33 (.303). 1987-88, 13-for-44 (.295). 1988-89, 8-for-30 (.267). 1989-90, 32-for-68 (.471). 1990-91, 6-for-22 (.273). 1991-92, 4-for-11 (.364). Totals, 81-for-234 (.346).

NBA ALL-STAR GAME RECORD

NOTES: NBA All-Star Game Most Valuable Player (1984, 1986).... Holds career record for most steals—29.

Season	Team	Min.	FGM	FGA	Pct.	FTM	FTA	Pct.	Off.	Def.	Tot.	Ast.	PF	Dq.	Stl.	Blk.	TO	Pts.
1982	Detroit...............	17	5	7	.714	2	4	.500	1	0	1	4	1	0	3	0	1	12
1983	Detroit...............	29	9	14	.643	1	1	1.000	3	1	4	7	0	0	4	0	5	19
1984	Detroit...............	39	9	17	.529	3	3	1.000	3	2	5	15	4	0	4	0	6	21
1985	Detroit...............	25	9	14	.643	1	1	1.000	1	1	2	5	2	0	2	0	1	22
1986	Detroit...............	36	11	19	.579	8	9	.889	0	1	1	10	2	0	5	0	5	30
1987	Detroit...............	24	4	6	.667	8	9	.889	2	1	3	9	3	0	0	0	1	16
1988	Detroit...............	28	4	10	.400	0		...	1	1	2	15	1	0	1	0	0	8
1989	Detroit...............	33	7	13	.538	4	6	.667	1	1	2	14	2	0	4	0	6	19
1990	Detroit...............	27	7	12	.583	0		...	1	3	4	9	0	0	3	0	1	15
1991	Detroit...............					Selected, did not play—injured.													
1992	Detroit...............	28	7	14	.500	0	0	...	1	1	2	5	0	0	3	0	3	15
	Totals	286	72	126	.571	27	33	.818	13	12	25	93	15	0	29	0	39	177

Three-point field goals: 1984, 0-for-2. 1985, 3-for-4 (.750). 1986, 0-for-1. 1989, 1-for-3 (.333). 1990, 1-for-1. 1992, 1-for-3 (.333). Totals, 6-for-14 (.429).

THOMPSON, BILLY

F

PERSONAL: Born December 1, 1963, in Camden, N.J. . . . 6-7/220. . . . Full name: William Stansbury Thompson.
HIGH SCHOOL: Camden (N.J.).
COLLEGE: Louisville.
TRANSACTIONS/CAREER NOTES: Selected by Atlanta Hawks in first round (19th pick overall) of 1986 NBA Draft. . . . Draft rights traded by Hawks with draft rights to Ron Kellogg to Los Angeles Lakers for Mike McGee and draft rights to Ken Barlow (June 17, 1986). . . . Selected by Miami Heat from Lakers in NBA expansion draft (June 23, 1988). . . . Rights renounced by Heat (July 1, 1991). . . . Signed as free agent by Milwaukee Bucks (October 5, 1991). . . . Waived by Bucks (October 31, 1991). . . . Signed by Golden State Warriors to 10-day contract (March 4, 1992). . . . Released by Warriors (March 9, 1992).
MISCELLANEOUS: Member of NBA championship teams (1987, 1988).

COLLEGIATE RECORD

NOTES: Member of NCAA Division I championship team (1986).

Season Team	G	Min.	FGM	FGA	Pct.	FTM	FTA	Pct.	Reb.	Pts.	Avg.
82-83 —Louisville	36	710	104	213	.488	53	81	.654	140	261	7.3
83-84 —Louisville	31	877	106	209	.507	72	98	.735	173	284	9.2
84-85 —Louisville	37	1262	220	427	.515	118	158	.747	311	558	15.1
85-86 —Louisville	39	1216	221	384	.576	140	196	.714	304	582	14.9
Totals	143	4065	651	1233	.528	383	533	.719	928	1685	11.8

NBA REGULAR-SEASON RECORD

Season Team	G	Min.	FGM	FGA	Pct.	FTM	FTA	Pct.	REBOUNDS Off.	Def.	Tot.	Ast.	PF	Dq.	Stl.	Blk.	TO	Pts.	Avg.
86-87 —L.A. Lakers ..	59	762	142	261	.544	48	74	.649	69	102	171	60	148	1	15	30	61	332	5.6
87-88 —L.A. Lakers ..	9	38	3	13	.231	8	10	.800	2	7	9	1	11	0	1	0	6	14	1.6
88-89 —Miami..........	79	2273	349	716	.487	156	224	.696	241	331	572	176	260	8	56	105	189	854	10.8
89-90 —Miami..........	79	2142	375	727	.516	115	185	.622	238	313	551	166	237	1	54	89	156	867	11.0
90-91 —Miami..........	73	1481	205	411	.499	89	124	.718	120	192	312	111	161	3	32	48	117	499	6.8
91-92 —Golden State	1	1	0	0	0	0	0	0	0	0	0	0	0	0	0	0	0	0	0.0
Totals	300	6697	1074	2128	.505	416	617	.674	670	945	1615	514	817	13	158	272	529	2566	8.6

Three-point field goals: 1986-87, 0-for-1. 1988-89, 0-for-4. 1989-90, 2-for-4 (.500). 1990-91, 0-for-4. Totals, 2-for-13 (.154).

NBA PLAYOFF RECORD

Season Team	G	Min.	FGM	FGA	Pct.	FTM	FTA	Pct.	REBOUNDS Off.	Def.	Tot.	Ast.	PF	Dq.	Stl.	Blk.	TO	Pts.	Avg.
86-87 —L.A. Lakers ..	3	27	6	11	.545	2	2	1.000	3	3	6	2	2	0	4	0	0	14	4.7

THOMPSON, LaSALLE

F/C, PACERS

PERSONAL: Born June 23, 1961, in Cincinnati. . . . 6-10/260. . . . Full name: LaSalle Thompson III.
HIGH SCHOOL: Withrow (Cincinnati).
COLLEGE: Texas.
TRANSACTIONS/CAREER NOTES: Selected by Kansas City Kings in first round (fifth pick overall) of 1982 NBA Draft. . . . Kings franchise moved from Kansas City to Sacramento for 1985-86 season. . . . Traded by Kings with Randy Wittman to Indiana Pacers for Wayman Tisdale and 1990 or 1991 second-round draft choice (February 20, 1989).

COLLEGIATE RECORD

NOTES: Led NCAA Division I with 13.5 rebounds per game (1982).

Season Team	G	Min.	FGM	FGA	Pct.	FTM	FTA	Pct.	Reb.	Pts.	Avg.
79-80 —Texas	30	971	153	274	.558	77	103	.748	292	383	12.8
80-81 —Texas	30	1106	235	411	.572	107	147	.728	370	577	19.2
81-82 —Texas	27	1042	196	371	.528	111	164	.677	365	503	18.6
Totals	87	3119	584	1056	.553	295	414	.713	1027	1463	16.8

NBA REGULAR-SEASON RECORD

Season Team	G	Min.	FGM	FGA	Pct.	FTM	FTA	Pct.	REBOUNDS Off.	Def.	Tot.	Ast.	PF	Dq.	Stl.	Blk.	TO	Pts.	Avg.
82-83 —Kansas City .	71	987	147	287	.512	89	137	.650	133	242	375	33	186	1	40	61	96	383	5.4
83-84 —Kansas City .	80	1915	333	637	.523	160	223	.717	260	449	709	86	327	8	71	145	168	826	10.3
84-85 —Kansas City .	82	2458	369	695	.531	227	315	.721	274	580	854	130	328	4	98	128	202	965	11.8
85-86 —Sacramento .	80	2377	411	794	.518	202	276	.732	252	518	770	168	295	8	71	109	184	1024	12.8
86-87 —Sacramento .	82	2166	362	752	.481	188	255	.737	237	450	687	122	290	6	69	126	143	912	11.1
87-88 —Sacramento .	69	1257	215	456	.471	118	164	.720	138	289	427	68	217	1	54	73	109	550	8.0
88-89 —Sac.-Ind.	76	2329	416	850	.489	227	281	.808	224	494	718	81	285	12	79	94	179	1059	13.9
89-90 —Indiana........	82	2126	223	471	.473	107	134	.799	175	455	630	106	313	11	65	71	150	554	6.8
90-91 —Indiana........	82	1946	276	565	.489	72	104	.692	154	409	563	147	265	4	63	63	168	625	7.6
91-92 —Indiana........	80	1299	168	359	.468	58	71	.817	98	283	381	102	207	0	52	34	98	394	4.9
Totals	784	18860	2920	5866	.498	1448	1960	.739	1945	4169	6114	1043	2713	55	662	904	1497	7292	9.3

Three-point field goals: 1982-83, 0-for-1. 1985-86, 0-for-1. 1986-87, 0-for-5. 1987-88, 2-for-5 (.400). 1988-89, 0-for-1. 1989-90, 1-for-5 (.200). 1990-91, 1-for-5 (.200). 1991-92, 0-for-2. Totals, 4-for-25 (.160).

NBA PLAYOFF RECORD

Season Team	G	Min.	FGM	FGA	Pct.	FTM	FTA	Pct.	REBOUNDS Off.	Def.	Tot.	Ast.	PF	Dq.	Stl.	Blk.	TO	Pts.	Avg.
83-84 —Kansas City .	3	93	18	40	.450	9	11	.818	11	19	30	4	14	0	3	4	5	45	15.0
85-86 —Sacramento .	3	99	11	32	.344	7	12	.583	14	21	35	2	8	0	2	6	4	29	9.7
89-90 —Indiana........	3	54	7	15	.467	4	4	1.000	6	9	15	2	13	0	0	1	7	18	6.0

Season Team	G	Min.	FGM	FGA	Pct.	FTM	FTA	Pct.	Off.	Def.	Tot.	Ast.	PF	Dq.	Stl.	Blk.	TO	Pts.	Avg.
90-91—Indiana.........	5	126	19	39	.487	7	7	1.000	6	25	31	8	15	0	4	7	10	45	9.0
91-92—Indiana.........	3	63	7	11	.636	2	2	1.000	2	11	13	4	11	0	1	4	3	16	5.3
Totals	17	435	62	137	.453	29	36	.806	39	85	124	20	61	0	10	22	29	153	9.0

THOMPSON, STEPHEN
G

PERSONAL: Born December 2, 1968, in Los Angeles. ... 6-4/185.
HIGH SCHOOL: Crenshaw (Los Angeles).
COLLEGE: Syracuse.
TRANSACTIONS/CAREER NOTES: Never drafted by an NBA franchise. ... Played in Continental Basketball Association with Rapid City Thrillers (1990-91) and Oklahoma City Cavalry (1991-92). ... Signed as free agent by Sacramento Kings (October 4, 1991). ... Waived by Kings (October 29, 1991). ... Signed as free agent by Orlando Magic (January 2, 1992). ... Waived by Magic (January 7, 1992). ... Signed by Kings to first of two consecutive 10-day contracts (February 27, 1992). ... Signed by Kings for remainder of season (March 17, 1992).

COLLEGIATE RECORD

NOTES: 1986-87 minutes played totals are missing one game.

Season Team	G	Min.	FGM	FGA	Pct.	FTM	FTA	Pct.	Reb.	Pts.	Avg.
86-87—Syracuse.............................	38	464	72	155	.465	46	86	.535	70	192	5.1
87-88—Syracuse.............................	35	1072	196	348	.563	98	168	.583	171	492	14.1
88-89—Syracuse.............................	38	1257	297	465	.639	83	167	.497	190	683	18.0
89-90—Syracuse.............................	33	1141	236	463	.510	101	201	.502	171	589	17.8
Totals	144	3934	801	1431	.560	328	622	.527	602	1956	13.6

Three-point field goals: 1986-87, 2-for-3 (.667). 1987-88, 2-for-4 (.500). 1988-89, 6-for-21 (.286). 1989-90, 16-for-58 (.276). Totals, 26-for-86 (.302).

CBA REGULAR-SEASON RECORD

NOTES: CBA Rookie of the Year (1991). ... CBA All-Star second team (1991, 1992). ... CBA All-Rookie team (1991).

			2-POINT			3-POINT							
Season Team	G	Min.	FGM	FGA	Pct.	FGM	FGA	Pct.	FTM	FTA	Pct.	Reb.	Ast.	Pts.	Avg.
90-91—Rapid City	50	2010	542	935	.580	16	36	.444	304	430	.707	319	154	*1436	28.7
91-92—Oklahoma City .	39	1511	386	713	.541	8	32	.250	208	325	.640	226	88	1004	*25.7
Totals	89	3521	928	1648	.563	24	68	.353	512	755	.678	545	242	2440	27.4

NBA REGULAR-SEASON RECORD

									— REBOUNDS —									
Season Team	G	Min.	FGM	FGA	Pct.	FTM	FTA	Pct.	Off.	Def.	Tot.	Ast.	PF	Dq.	Stl.	Blk.	TO	Pts.	Avg.
91-92—Orl.-Sac.	19	91	14	37	.378	3	8	.375	11	8	19	8	9	0	6	3	5	31	1.6

Three-point field goals: 1991-92, 0-for-1.

THORNTON, BOB
F/C, JAZZ

PERSONAL: Born July 10, 1962, in Los Angeles. ... 6-10/225. ... Full name: Robert George Thornton.
HIGH SCHOOL: Mission Viejo (Calif.).
COLLEGE: Saddleback Community College (Calif.), then UC Irvine.
TRANSACTIONS/CAREER NOTES: Selected by New York Knicks in fourth round (87th pick overall) of 1984 NBA Draft. ... Played in Spanish National League with Madrid Caja (1984-85). ... Waived by Knicks (December 16, 1987). ... Signed as free agent by Philadelphia 76ers (December 19, 1987). ... Traded by 76ers to Minnesota Timberwolves for 1991 second-round draft choice (November 10, 1990). ... Signed as free agent by Utah Jazz (April 15, 1992). ... Played in Continental Basketball Association with Sioux Falls Skyforce (1991-92).

COLLEGIATE RECORD

Season Team	G	Min.	FGM	FGA	Pct.	FTM	FTA	Pct.	Reb.	Pts.	Avg.
80-81—Saddleback C.C........................	28	...	70	136	.515	31	50	.620	149	171	6.1
81-82—UC Irvine	29	452	44	88	.500	33	45	.733	93	121	4.2
82-83—UC Irvine	27	639	125	216	.579	75	117	.641	161	325	12.0
83-84—UC Irvine	29	817	151	236	.640	65	118	.551	236	367	12.7
Junior college totals	28		70	136	.515	31	50	.620	149	171	6.1
Four-year-college totals	85	1908	320	540	.593	173	280	.618	490	813	9.6

NBA REGULAR-SEASON RECORD

									— REBOUNDS —									
Season Team	G	Min.	FGM	FGA	Pct.	FTM	FTA	Pct.	Off.	Def.	Tot.	Ast.	PF	Dq.	Stl.	Blk.	TO	Pts.	Avg.
85-86—New York	71	1323	125	274	.456	86	162	.531	113	177	290	43	209	5	30	7	83	336	4.7
86-87—New York	33	282	29	67	.433	13	20	.650	18	38	56	8	48	0	4	3	24	71	2.2
87-88—N.Y.-Phil........	48	593	65	130	.500	34	55	.618	46	66	112	15	103	1	11	3	35	164	3.4
88-89—Philadelphia.	54	449	47	111	.423	32	60	.533	36	56	92	15	87	0	8	7	23	127	2.4
89-90—Philadelphia.	56	592	48	112	.429	26	51	.510	45	88	133	17	105	1	20	12	35	123	2.2
90-91—Minnesota ...	12	110	4	13	.308	8	10	.800	1	14	15	1	18	0	0	3	9	16	1.3
91-92—Utah	2	6	1	7	.143	2	2	1.000	2	0	2	0	1	0	0	0	0	4	2.0
Totals	276	3355	319	714	.447	201	360	.558	261	439	700	99	571	7	73	35	209	841	3.0

Three-point field goals: 1986-87, 0-for-1. 1987-88, 0-for-2. 1988-89, 1-for-3 (.333). 1989-90, 1-for-3 (.333). Totals, 2-for-9 (.222).

NBA PLAYOFF RECORD

									— REBOUNDS —									
Season Team	G	Min.	FGM	FGA	Pct.	FTM	FTA	Pct.	Off.	Def.	Tot.	Ast.	PF	Dq.	Stl.	Blk.	TO	Pts.	Avg.
89-90—Philadelphia.	9	89	7	18	.389	5	10	.500	11	4	15	4	22	0	2	1	2	19	2.1
91-92—Utah	7	32	2	5	.400	3	4	.750	4	5	9	1	3	0	0	0	1	7	1.0
Totals	16	121	9	23	.391	8	14	.571	15	9	24	5	25	0	2	1	3	26	1.6

CBA REGULAR-SEASON RECORD

Season	Team	G	Min.	2-POINT FGM	2-POINT FGA	Pct.	3-POINT FGM	3-POINT FGA	Pct.	FTM	FTA	Pct.	Reb.	Ast.	Pts.	Avg.
91-92	Sioux Falls.......	13	394	64	108	.593	0	0	...	40	58	.690	127	22	168	12.9

THORPE, OTIS
F, ROCKETS

PERSONAL: Born August 5, 1962, in Boynton Beach, Fla.... 6-10/246....
Full name: Otis Henry Thorpe.
HIGH SCHOOL: Lake Worth Community (Fla.).
COLLEGE: Providence.
TRANSACTIONS/CAREER NOTES: Selected by Kansas City Kings in first round (ninth pick overall) of 1984 NBA Draft.... Kings franchise moved from Kansas City to Sacramento for 1985-86 season.... Traded by Kings to Houston Rockets for Rodney McCray and Jim Petersen (October 11, 1988).

COLLEGIATE RECORD

Season	Team	G	Min.	FGM	FGA	Pct.	FTM	FTA	Pct.	Reb.	Pts.	Avg.
80-81	Providence..............................	26	668	100	194	.515	50	76	.658	137	250	9.6
81-82	Providence..............................	27	942	153	283	.541	74	115	.643	216	380	14.1
82-83	Providence..............................	31	1041	204	321	.636	91	138	.659	249	499	16.1
83-84	Providence..............................	29	1051	167	288	.580	162	248	.653	300	496	17.1
	Totals	113	3702	624	1086	.575	377	577	.653	902	1625	14.4

NBA REGULAR-SEASON RECORD

Season	Team	G	Min.	FGM	FGA	Pct.	FTM	FTA	Pct.	Off.	Def.	Tot.	Ast.	PF	Dq.	Stl.	Blk.	TO	Pts.	Avg.
84-85	Kansas City .	82	1918	411	685	.600	230	371	.620	187	369	556	111	256	2	34	37	187	1052	12.8
85-86	Sacramento .	75	1675	289	492	.587	164	248	.661	137	283	420	84	233	3	35	34	123	742	9.9
86-87	Sacramento .	82	2956	567	1050	.540	413	543	.761	259	560	819	201	292	11	46	60	189	1547	18.9
87-88	Sacramento .	82	3072	622	1226	.507	460	609	.755	279	558	837	266	264	3	62	56	228	1704	20.8
88-89	Houston	82	3135	521	961	.542	328	450	.729	272	515	787	202	259	6	82	37	225	1370	16.7
89-90	Houston	82	2947	547	998	.548	307	446	.688	258	476	734	261	270	5	66	24	229	1401	17.1
90-91	Houston	82	3039	549	988	.556	334	480	.696	287	559	846	197	278	10	73	20	217	1435	17.5
91-92	Houston	82	3056	558	943	.592	304	463	.657	285	577	862	250	307	7	52	37	237	1420	17.3
	Totals	649	21798	4064	7343	.553	2540	3610	.704	1964	3897	5861	1572	2159	47	450	305	1635	10671	16.4

Three-point field goals: 1984-85, 0-for-2. 1986-87, 0-for-3. 1987-88, 0-for-6. 1988-89, 0-for-2. 1989-90, 0-for-10. 1990-91, 3-for-7 (.429). 1991-92, 0-for-7. Totals, 3-for-37 (.081).

NBA PLAYOFF RECORD

Season	Team	G	Min.	FGM	FGA	Pct.	FTM	FTA	Pct.	Off.	Def.	Tot.	Ast.	PF	Dq.	Stl.	Blk.	TO	Pts.	Avg.
85-86	Sacramento .	3	35	3	13	.231	6	13	.462	8	4	12	0	4	0	0	1	1	12	4.0
88-89	Houston	4	152	24	37	.649	16	21	.762	6	14	20	12	17	1	5	1	15	64	16.0
89-90	Houston	4	164	27	45	.600	26	38	.684	14	19	33	7	12	0	5	0	9	80	20.0
90-91	Houston	3	116	22	38	.579	3	6	.500	7	18	25	8	8	0	2	0	6	47	15.7
	Totals	14	467	76	133	.571	51	78	.654	35	55	90	27	41	1	12	2	31	203	14.5

NBA ALL-STAR GAME RECORD

Season	Team	Min.	FGM	FGA	Pct.	FTM	FTA	Pct.	Off.	Def.	Tot.	Ast.	PF	Dq.	Stl.	Blk.	TO	Pts.
1992	Houston	4	1	1	1.000	0	0	...	0	0	0	0	0	0	0	0	0	2

THREATT, SEDALE
G, LAKERS

PERSONAL: Born September 10, 1961, in Atlanta.... 6-2/185....
Full name: Sedale Eugene Threatt. ... Name pronounced Suh-DALE THREET.
HIGH SCHOOL: Therrell (Atlanta).
COLLEGE: West Virginia Tech.
TRANSACTIONS/CAREER NOTES: Selected by Philadelphia 76ers in sixth round (139th pick overall) of 1983 NBA Draft.... Traded by 76ers to Chicago Bulls for Steve Colter and future second-round draft choice (December 31, 1986). ... Traded by Bulls to Seattle SuperSonics for Sam Vincent (February 25, 1988).... Traded by SuperSonics to Los Angeles Lakers for 1994, 1995 and 1996 second-round draft choices (October 2, 1991).

COLLEGIATE RECORD

Season	Team	G	Min.	FGM	FGA	Pct.	FTM	FTA	Pct.	Reb.	Pts.	Avg.
79-80	West Virginia Tech	28	...	204	424	.481	90	126	.714	97	498	17.8
80-81	West Virginia Tech	31	...	237	524	.452	74	104	.712	122	548	17.7
81-82	West Virginia Tech	34	...	299	598	.500	156	214	.729	118	754	22.2
82-83	West Virginia Tech	27	951	284	510	.557	120	164	.732	104	688	25.5
	Totals	120	...	1024	2056	.498	440	608	.724	441	2488	20.7

NBA REGULAR-SEASON RECORD

Season	Team	G	Min.	FGM	FGA	Pct.	FTM	FTA	Pct.	Off.	Def.	Tot.	Ast.	PF	Dq.	Stl.	Blk.	TO	Pts.	Avg.
83-84	Philadelphia.	45	464	62	148	.419	23	28	.821	17	23	40	41	65	1	13	2	33	147	3.3
84-85	Philadelphia.	82	1304	188	416	.452	66	90	.733	21	78	99	175	171	2	80	16	99	446	5.4
85-86	Philadelphia.	70	1754	310	684	.453	75	90	.833	21	100	121	193	157	1	93	5	102	696	9.9
86-87	Phil.-Chi.	68	1446	239	534	.448	95	119	.798	26	82	108	259	164	0	74	13	89	580	8.5
87-88	Chi.-Seattle.	71	1055	216	425	.508	57	71	.803	23	65	88	160	100	0	60	8	63	492	6.9
88-89	Seattle.........	63	1220	235	476	.494	63	77	.818	31	86	117	238	155	0	83	4	77	544	8.6
89-90	Seattle.........	65	1481	303	599	.506	130	157	.828	43	72	115	216	164	0	65	8	77	744	11.4
90-91	Seattle.........	80	2066	433	835	.519	137	173	.792	25	74	99	273	191	0	113	8	138	1013	12.7
91-92	L.A. Lakers ..	82	3070	509	1041	.489	202	243	.831	43	210	253	593	231	1	168	16	182	1240	15.1
	Totals	626	13860	2495	5158	.484	848	1048	.809	250	790	1040	2148	1398	5	749	80	860	5903	9.4

Three-point field goals: 1983-84, 1-for-8 (.125). 1984-85, 4-for-22 (.182). 1985-86, 1-for-24 (.042). 1986-87, 7-for-32 (.219). 1987-88, 3-for-27 (.111). 1988-89, 11-for-30 (.367). 1989-90, 8-for-32 (.250). 1990-91, 10-for-35 (.286). 1991-92, 20-for-62 (.323). Totals, 65-for-272 (.239).

NBA PLAYOFF RECORD

| | | | | | | | | | — REBOUNDS — | | | | | | | | |
Season	Team	G	Min.	FGM	FGA	Pct.	FTM	FTA	Pct.	Off.	Def.	Tot.	Ast.	PF	Dq.	Stl.	Blk.	TO	Pts.	Avg.
83-84	—Philadelphia.	3	6	1	3	.333	0	0	...	1	1	2	1	0	0	1	0	2	2	0.7
84-85	—Philadelphia.	4	28	2	7	.286	0	0	...	1	0	1	5	2	0	1	0	3	4	1.0
85-86	—Philadelphia.	12	312	67	143	.469	26	33	.788	6	19	25	42	35	0	23	2	15	160	13.3
86-87	—Chicago........	3	70	8	17	.471	4	4	1.000	2	3	5	16	11	0	1	0	2	20	6.7
87-88	—Seattle.........	5	80	14	34	.412	4	4	1.000	2	9	11	11	7	0	1	0	5	32	6.4
88-89	—Seattle.........	8	201	39	82	.476	17	20	.850	3	10	13	49	22	0	17	0	11	96	12.0
90-91	—Seattle.........	5	136	30	56	.536	9	10	.900	1	7	8	17	14	0	5	0	8	73	14.6
91-92	—L.A. Lakers ..	4	162	24	46	.522	9	12	.750	0	8	8	17	11	0	2	0	11	59	14.8
	Totals	44	995	185	388	.477	69	83	.831	16	57	73	158	102	0	51	2	57	446	10.1

Three-point field goals: 1983-84, 0-for-2. 1985-86, 0-for-2. 1987-88, 0-for-1. 1988-89, 1-for-4 (.250). 1990-91, 4-for-11 (.364). 1991-92, 2-for-3 (.667). Totals, 7-for-23 (.304).

TISDALE, WAYMAN
F, KINGS

PERSONAL: Born June 9, 1964, in Tulsa, Okla.... 6-9/260....
Full name: Wayman Lawrence Tisdale.
HIGH SCHOOL: Booker T. Washington (Tulsa, Okla.).
COLLEGE: Oklahoma.

TRANSACTIONS/CAREER NOTES: Selected as undergraduate by Indiana Pacers in first round (second pick overall) of 1985 NBA Draft.... Traded by Pacers with 1990 or 1991 second-round draft choice to Sacramento Kings for LaSalle Thompson and Randy Wittman (February 20, 1989).
MISCELLANEOUS: Member of gold-medal-winning U.S. Olympic team (1984).

COLLEGIATE RECORD

NOTES: THE SPORTING NEWS All-America first team (1984, 1985).... THE SPORTING NEWS All-America second team (1983).

Season	Team	G	Min.	FGM	FGA	Pct.	FTM	FTA	Pct.	Reb.	Pts.	Avg.
82-83	—Oklahoma..............................	33	1138	338	583	.580	134	211	.635	341	810	24.5
83-84	—Oklahoma..............................	34	1232	369	639	.577	181	283	.640	329	919	27.0
84-85	—Oklahoma..............................	37	1283	370	640	.578	192	273	.703	378	932	25.2
	Totals	104	3653	1077	1862	.578	507	767	.661	1048	2661	25.6

NBA REGULAR-SEASON RECORD

| | | | | | | | | | — REBOUNDS — | | | | | | | | |
Season	Team	G	Min.	FGM	FGA	Pct.	FTM	FTA	Pct.	Off.	Def.	Tot.	Ast.	PF	Dq.	Stl.	Blk.	TO	Pts.	Avg.
85-86	—Indiana........	81	2277	516	1002	.515	160	234	.684	191	393	584	79	290	3	32	44	188	1192	14.7
86-87	—Indiana........	81	2159	458	892	.513	258	364	.709	217	258	475	117	293	9	50	26	139	1174	14.5
87-88	—Indiana........	79	2378	511	998	.512	246	314	.783	168	323	491	103	274	5	54	34	145	1268	16.1
88-89	—Ind.-Sac.......	79	2434	532	1036	.514	317	410	.773	187	422	609	128	290	7	55	52	172	1381	17.5
89-90	—Sacramento.	79	2937	726	1383	.525	306	391	.783	185	410	595	108	251	3	54	54	153	1758	22.3
90-91	—Sacramento.	33	1116	262	542	.483	136	170	.800	75	178	253	66	99	0	23	28	82	660	20.0
91-92	—Sacramento .	72	2521	522	1043	.500	151	198	.763	135	334	469	106	248	3	55	79	124	1195	16.6
	Totals	504	15822	3527	6896	.511	1574	2081	.756	1158	2318	3476	707	1745	30	323	317	1003	8628	17.1

Three-point field goals: 1985-86, 0-for-2. 1986-87, 0-for-2. 1987-88, 0-for-2. 1988-89, 0-for-4. 1989-90, 0-for-6. 1990-91, 0-for-1. 1991-92, 0-for-2. Totals, 0-for-19.

NBA PLAYOFF RECORD

| | | | | | | | | | — REBOUNDS — | | | | | | | | |
Season	Team	G	Min.	FGM	FGA	Pct.	FTM	FTA	Pct.	Off.	Def.	Tot.	Ast.	PF	Dq.	Stl.	Blk.	TO	Pts.	Avg.
86-87	—Indiana........	4	108	19	31	.613	13	23	.565	5	11	16	9	17	1	1	0	5	51	12.8

TOLBERT, TOM
F, WARRIORS

PERSONAL: Born October 16, 1965, in Long Beach, Calif.... 6-7/240....
Full name: Byron Thomas Tolbert.
HIGH SCHOOL: Lakewood (Calif.).
COLLEGE: UC Irvine, then Cerritos (Calif.), then Arizona.

TRANSACTIONS/CAREER NOTES: Selected by Charlotte Hornets in second round (34th pick overall) of 1988 NBA Draft.... Waived by Hornets (December 30, 1988).... Signed as free agent by Golden State Warriors (October 5, 1989).... Waived by Warriors (November 2, 1989).... Re-signed as free agent by Warriors (November 9, 1989).

COLLEGIATE RECORD

NOTES: Suffered shoulder injury (1983-84); granted extra year of eligibility.

Season	Team	G	Min.	FGM	FGA	Pct.	FTM	FTA	Pct.	Reb.	Pts.	Avg.
83-84	—UC Irvine	4	15	3	4	.750	0	0	...	1	6	1.5
84-85	—UC Irvine	6	53	6	19	.316	4	5	.800	12	16	2.7
85-86	—Cerritos...............................	32	...	217	354	.613	85	125	.680	251	519	16.2
86-87	—Arizona...............................	30	803	156	305	.511	98	139	.705	186	418	13.9
87-88	—Arizona...............................	38	1034	192	351	.547	151	186	.812	220	536	14.1
	Junior college totals	32	...	217	354	.613	85	125	.680	251	519	16.2
	Four-year-college totals	78	1905	357	679	.526	253	330	.767	419	976	12.5

Three-point field goals: 1986-87, 8-for-18 (.444). 1987-88, 1-for-2 (.500). Totals, 9-for-20 (.450).

NBA REGULAR-SEASON RECORD

Season	Team	G	Min.	FGM	FGA	Pct.	FTM	FTA	Pct.	Off.	Def.	Tot.	Ast.	PF	Dq.	Stl.	Blk.	TO	Pts.	Avg.
										— REBOUNDS —										
88-89	Charlotte......	14	117	17	37	.459	6	12	.500	7	14	21	7	20	0	2	4	2	40	2.9
89-90	Golden State	70	1347	218	442	.493	175	241	.726	122	241	363	58	191	0	23	25	79	616	8.8
90-91	Golden State	62	1371	183	433	.423	127	172	.738	87	188	275	76	195	4	35	38	80	500	8.1
91-92	Golden State	35	310	33	86	.384	22	40	.550	14	41	55	21	73	0	10	6	20	90	2.6
	Totals	181	3145	451	998	.452	330	465	.710	230	484	714	162	479	4	70	73	181	1246	6.9

Three-point field goals: 1988-89, 0-for-3. 1989-90, 5-for-18 (.278). 1990-91, 7-for-21 (.333). 1991-92, 2-for-8 (.250). Totals, 14-for-50 (.280).

NBA PLAYOFF RECORD

Season	Team	G	Min.	FGM	FGA	Pct.	FTM	FTA	Pct.	Off.	Def.	Tot.	Ast.	PF	Dq.	Stl.	Blk.	TO	Pts.	Avg.
										— REBOUNDS —										
90-91	Golden State	9	116	14	33	.424	3	11	.273	0	18	18	8	29	0	3	4	4	32	3.6

Three-point field goals: 1990-91, 1-for-3 (.333).

TRIPUCKA, KELLY
F/G

PERSONAL: Born February 16, 1959, in Glen Ridge, N.J. . . . 6-6/225. . . . Full name: Peter Kelly Tripucka.
HIGH SCHOOL: Bloomfield Senior (N.J.).
COLLEGE: Notre Dame.
TRANSACTIONS/CAREER NOTES: Selected by Detroit Pistons in first round (12th pick overall) of 1981 NBA Draft. . . . Traded by Pistons with Kent Benson to Utah Jazz for Adrian Dantley and 1987 and 1990 second-round draft choices (August 21, 1986). . . . Traded by Jazz to Charlotte Hornets for Mike Brown (June 23, 1988). . . . Contract expired (July 1991). . . . Played in France (1991-92).

COLLEGIATE RECORD

Season	Team	G	Min.	FGM	FGA	Pct.	FTM	FTA	Pct.	Reb.	Pts.	Avg.
77-78	Notre Dame.............................	31	643	141	247	.571	80	108	.741	161	362	11.7
78-79	Notre Dame.............................	29	807	143	277	.516	129	151	.854	125	415	14.3
79-80	Notre Dame.............................	23	691	150	270	.556	115	151	.762	151	415	18.0
80-81	Notre Dame.............................	29	919	195	354	.551	137	168	.815	169	527	18.2
	Totals	112	3060	629	1148	.548	461	578	.798	606	1719	15.3

NBA REGULAR-SEASON RECORD

HONORS: NBA All-Rookie team (1982).

Season	Team	G	Min.	FGM	FGA	Pct.	FTM	FTA	Pct.	Off.	Def.	Tot.	Ast.	PF	Dq.	Stl.	Blk.	TO	Pts.	Avg.
										— REBOUNDS —										
81-82	Detroit.........	82	3077	636	1281	.496	495	621	.797	219	224	443	270	241	0	89	16	280	1772	21.6
82-83	Detroit.........	58	2252	565	1156	.489	392	464	.845	126	138	264	237	157	0	67	20	187	1536	26.5
83-84	Detroit.........	76	2493	595	1296	.459	426	523	.815	119	187	306	228	190	0	65	17	190	1618	21.3
84-85	Detroit.........	55	1675	396	831	.477	255	288	.885	66	152	218	135	118	1	49	14	118	1049	19.1
85-86	Detroit.........	81	2626	615	1236	.498	380	444	.856	116	232	348	265	167	0	93	10	183	1622	20.0
86-87	Utah	79	1865	291	621	.469	197	226	.872	54	188	242	243	147	0	85	11	167	798	10.1
87-88	Utah	49	976	139	303	.459	59	68	.868	30	87	117	105	68	1	34	4	68	368	7.5
88-89	Charlotte......	71	2302	568	1215	.467	440	508	.866	79	188	267	224	196	0	88	16	236	1606	22.6
89-90	Charlotte......	79	2404	442	1029	.430	310	351	.883	82	240	322	224	220	1	75	16	176	1232	15.6
90-91	Charlotte......	77	1289	187	412	.454	152	167	.910	46	130	176	159	130	0	33	13	92	541	7.0
	Totals	707	20959	4434	9380	.473	3106	3660	.849	937	1766	2703	2090	1634	3	678	137	1697	12142	17.2

Three-point field goals: 1981-82, 5-for-22 (.227). 1982-83, 14-for-37 (.378). 1983-84, 2-for-17 (.118). 1984-85, 2-for-5 (.400). 1985-86, 12-for-25 (.480). 1986-87, 19-for-52 (.365). 1987-88, 31-for-74 (.419). 1988-89, 30-for-84 (.357). 1989-90, 38-for-104 (.365). 1990-91, 15-for-45 (.333). Totals, 168-for-465 (.361).

NBA PLAYOFF RECORD

Season	Team	G	Min.	FGM	FGA	Pct.	FTM	FTA	Pct.	Off.	Def.	Tot.	Ast.	PF	Dq.	Stl.	Blk.	TO	Pts.	Avg.
										— REBOUNDS —										
83-84	Detroit.........	5	208	48	102	.471	41	51	.804	10	13	23	15	22	1	11	0	18	137	27.4
84-85	Detroit.........	9	288	49	118	.415	35	40	.875	19	20	39	29	22	0	4	3	19	133	14.8
85-86	Detroit.........	4	175	33	71	.465	21	23	.913	10	13	23	9	14	1	3	2	16	87	21.8
86-87	Utah	5	70	14	20	.700	4	4	1.000	1	6	7	3	6	0	4	0	7	32	6.4
87-88	Utah	2	9	1	3	.333	0	0	...	1	0	1	1	1	0	0	0	1	2	1.0
	Totals	25	750	145	314	.462	101	118	.856	41	52	93	57	65	2	22	5	61	391	15.6

Three-point field goals: 1983-84, 0-for-1. 1984-85, 0-for-1. 1986-87, 0-for-3. Totals, 0-for-5.

NBA ALL-STAR GAME RECORD

Season	Team	Min.	FGM	FGA	Pct.	FTM	FTA	Pct.	Off.	Def.	Tot.	Ast.	PF	Dq.	Stl.	Blk.	TO	Pts.
									— REBOUNDS —									
1982	Detroit...............	15	3	7	.429	0	0	...	0	1	1	2	0	0	0	0	1	6
1984	Detroit...............	6	0	0	...	1	2	.500	0	0	0	2	1	0	1	0	2	1
	Totals	21	3	7	.429	1	2	.500	0	1	1	4	1	0	1	0	3	7

FRENCH LEAGUE

Season	Team	G	Min.	FGM	FGA	Pct.	FTM	FTA	Pct.	Reb.	Pts.	Avg.
91-92	Limoges	7	218	40	72	.556	28	31	.903	12	108	15.4

TUCKER, TRENT
G

PERSONAL: Born December 20, 1959, in Tarboro, N.C. . . . 6-5/193. . . . Full name: Kelvin Trent Tucker.
HIGH SCHOOL: Northwestern Community (Flint, Mich.).
COLLEGE: Minnesota.
TRANSACTIONS/CAREER NOTES: Selected by New York Knicks in first round (sixth pick overall) of 1982 NBA Draft. . . . Traded by Knicks with Jerrod Mustaf and 1992 and 1994 second-round draft choices to Phoenix

Suns for Xavier McDaniel (October 1, 1991).... Waived by Suns (November 15, 1991).... Signed by San Antonio Spurs to first of two consecutive 10-day contracts (February 29, 1992).... Signed by Spurs for remainder of season (March 18, 1992).

COLLEGIATE RECORD

NOTES: THE SPORTING NEWS All-America first team (1982).

Season Team	G	Min.	FGM	FGA	Pct.	FTM	FTA	Pct.	Reb.	Pts.	Avg.
78-79 — Minnesota	25	...	114	239	.477	19	32	.594	85	247	9.9
79-80 — Minnesota	32	...	152	310	.490	34	46	.739	103	338	10.6
80-81 — Minnesota	29	...	187	362	.517	56	69	.812	102	430	14.8
81-82 — Minnesota	29	...	178	353	.504	74	90	.822	103	430	14.8
Totals	115	...	631	1264	.499	183	237	.772	393	1445	12.6

NBA REGULAR-SEASON RECORD

Season Team	G	Min.	FGM	FGA	Pct.	FTM	FTA	Pct.	Off.	Def.	Tot.	Ast.	PF	Dq.	Stl.	Blk.	TO	Pts.	Avg.
82-83 — New York	78	1830	299	647	.462	43	64	.672	75	141	216	195	235	1	56	6	70	655	8.4
83-84 — New York	63	1228	225	450	.500	25	33	.758	43	87	130	138	124	0	63	8	54	481	7.6
84-85 — New York	77	1819	293	606	.484	38	48	.792	74	114	188	199	195	0	75	15	64	653	8.5
85-86 — New York	77	1788	349	740	.472	79	100	.790	70	99	169	192	167	0	65	8	70	818	10.6
86-87 — New York	70	1691	325	691	.470	77	101	.762	49	86	135	166	169	1	116	13	78	795	11.4
87-88 — New York	71	1248	193	455	.424	51	71	.718	32	87	119	117	158	3	53	6	47	506	7.1
88-89 — New York	81	1824	263	579	.454	43	55	.782	55	121	176	132	163	0	88	6	59	687	8.5
89-90 — New York	81	1725	253	606	.417	66	86	.767	57	117	174	173	159	0	74	8	73	667	8.2
90-91 — New York	65	1194	191	434	.440	17	27	.630	33	72	105	111	120	0	44	9	46	463	7.1
91-92 — San Antonio	24	415	60	129	.465	16	20	.800	8	29	37	27	39	0	21	3	14	155	6.5
Totals	687	14762	2451	5337	.459	455	605	.752	496	953	1449	1450	1529	5	655	82	575	5880	8.6

Three-point field goals: 1982-83, 14-for-30 (.467). 1983-84, 6-for-16 (.375). 1984-85, 29-for-72 (.403). 1985-86, 41-for-91 (.451). 1986-87, 68-for-161 (.422). 1987-88, 69-for-167 (.413). 1988-89, 118-for-296 (.399). 1989-90, 95-for-245 (.388). 1990-91, 64-for-153 (.418). 1991-92, 19-for-48 (.396). Totals, 523-for-1279 (.409).

NBA PLAYOFF RECORD

Season Team	G	Min.	FGM	FGA	Pct.	FTM	FTA	Pct.	Off.	Def.	Tot.	Ast.	PF	Dq.	Stl.	Blk.	TO	Pts.	Avg.
82-83 — New York	6	85	9	15	.600	7	10	.700	2	7	9	5	7	0	2	0	2	26	4.3
83-84 — New York	12	254	42	84	.500	6	10	.600	6	12	18	27	32	0	11	3	12	91	7.6
87-88 — New York	4	71	8	19	.421	3	4	.750	0	2	2	4	4	0	3	0	1	25	6.3
88-89 — New York	9	159	27	58	.466	2	4	.500	9	10	19	14	20	0	10	2	6	71	7.9
89-90 — New York	10	178	22	55	.400	6	6	1.000	5	9	14	20	19	0	10	0	6	60	6.0
90-91 — New York	3	66	9	25	.360	2	2	1.000	3	9	12	9	7	0	1	0	1	24	8.0
91-92 — San Antonio	3	38	6	14	.429	1	1	1.000	1	2	3	2	3	0	0	0	3	14	4.7
Totals	47	851	123	270	.456	27	37	.730	26	51	77	81	92	0	37	5	31	311	6.6

Three-point field goals: 1982-83, 1-for-2 (.500). 1983-84, 1-for-5 (.200). 1987-88, 6-for-13 (.462). 1988-89, 15-for-32 (.469). 1989-90, 10-for-27 (.370). 1990-91, 4-for-10 (.400). 1991-92, 1-for-5 (.200). Totals, 38-for-94 (.404).

TURNER, ANDRE
G, BULLETS

PERSONAL: Born December 13, 1964, in Memphis, Tenn.... 5-11/160.
HIGH SCHOOL: Mitchell (Memphis, Tenn.).
COLLEGE: Memphis State.
TRANSACTIONS/CAREER NOTES: Selected by Los Angeles Lakers in third round (69th pick overall) of 1986 NBA Draft.... Waived by Lakers (October 28, 1986).... Signed as free agent by Boston Celtics (November 6, 1986).... Waived by Celtics (November 25, 1986).... Played in Continental Basketball Association with Rockford Lightning (1986-87) and La Crosse Catbirds (1986-87, 1988-89, 1989-90 and 1990-91).... Signed as free agent by Houston Rockets (October 9, 1987).... Selected by Miami Heat from Rockets in NBA expansion draft (June 23, 1988).... Waived by Heat (November 3, 1988).... Signed by Milwaukee Bucks to 10-day contract (January 3, 1989).... Signed as free agent by Charlotte Hornets (October 5, 1989).... Waived by Hornets (October 31, 1989).... Claimed off waivers by Los Angeles Clippers (November 1, 1989).... Waived by Clippers (November 14, 1989).... Signed as free agent by Hornets (November 23, 1989).... Waived by Hornets (December 13, 1989).... Re-signed as free agent by Hornets (October 2, 1990).... Waived by Hornets (October 24, 1990).... Signed as free agent by Philadelphia 76ers (November 20, 1990).... Signed as unrestricted free agent by Washington Bullets (October 31, 1991).

COLLEGIATE RECORD

Season Team	G	Min.	FGM	FGA	Pct.	FTM	FTA	Pct.	Reb.	Pts.	Avg.
82-83 — Memphis State	31	1006	127	245	.518	54	67	.806	35	308	9.9
83-84 — Memphis State	33	1052	107	234	.457	58	87	.667	45	272	8.2
84-85 — Memphis State	34	1157	154	309	.498	80	112	.714	79	388	11.4
85-86 — Memphis State	34	1137	196	410	.478	82	96	.854	67	474	13.9
Totals	132	4352	584	1198	.487	274	362	.757	226	1442	10.9

NBA REGULAR-SEASON RECORD

Season Team	G	Min.	FGM	FGA	Pct.	FTM	FTA	Pct.	Off.	Def.	Tot.	Ast.	PF	Dq.	Stl.	Blk.	TO	Pts.	Avg.
86-87 — Boston	3	18	2	5	.400	0	0	...	1	1	2	1	1	0	0	0	5	4	1.3
87-88 — Houston	12	99	12	34	.353	10	14	.714	4	4	8	23	13	0	7	1	12	35	2.9
88-89 — Milwaukee	4	13	3	6	.500	0	0	...	0	3	3	0	2	0	2	0	4	6	1.5
89-90 — LAC-Char	11	115	11	38	.289	4	4	1.000	4	4	8	23	6	0	8	0	12	26	2.4
90-91 — Philadelphia	70	1407	168	383	.439	64	87	.736	36	116	152	311	124	0	63	0	95	412	5.9
91-92 — Washington	70	871	111	261	.425	61	77	.792	17	73	90	177	59	0	57	2	84	284	4.1
Totals	170	2523	307	727	.422	139	182	.764	62	201	263	535	205	0	137	3	212	767	4.5

Three-point field goals: 1986-87, 0-for-1. 1987-88, 1-for-7 (.143). 1989-90, 0-for-2. 1990-91, 12-for-33 (.364). 1991-92, 1-for-16 (.063). Totals, 14-for-59 (.237).

NBA PLAYOFF RECORD

Season Team	G	Min.	FGM	FGA	Pct.	FTM	FTA	Pct.	Off.	Def.	Tot.	Ast.	PF	Dq.	Stl.	Blk.	TO	Pts.	Avg.
									— REBOUNDS —										
90-91 — Philadelphia.	8	189	21	48	.438	13	16	.813	2	11	13	35	12	0	11	0	8	58	7.3

Three-point field goals: 1990-91, 3-for-9 (.333).

CBA REGULAR-SEASON RECORD

Season Team	G	Min.	2-POINT			3-POINT			FTM	FTA	Pct.	Reb.	Ast.	Pts.	Avg.
			FGM	FGA	Pct.	FGM	FGA	Pct.							
86-87 — Rock.-La Cr.	47	1329	228	475	.480	5	35	.143	117	142	.824	110	240	588	12.5
88-89 — La Crosse	38	1378	222	474	.468	19	84	.226	169	204	.828	102	220	670	17.6
89-90 — La Crosse........	34	1343	255	509	.501	13	50	.260	151	182	.830	115	308	700	20.6
90-91 — La Crosse........	2	92	17	40	.425	0	1	.000	10	10	1.000	6	12	44	22.0
Totals	121	4142	722	1498	.482	37	170	.218	447	538	.831	333	780	2002	16.5

TURNER, JEFF
F, MAGIC

PERSONAL: Born April 9, 1962, in Bangor, Me. . . . 6-9/240. . . . Full name: Jeffrey Steven Turner.
HIGH SCHOOL: Brandon (Fla.).
COLLEGE: Vanderbilt.
TRANSACTIONS/CAREER NOTES: Selected by New Jersey Nets in first round (17th pick overall) of 1984 NBA Draft. . . . Played in Italy (1987-88 and 1988-89). . . . Signed as unrestricted free agent by Orlando Magic (July 11, 1989).
MISCELLANEOUS: Member of gold-medal-winning U.S. Olympic team (1984).

COLLEGIATE RECORD

Season Team	G	Min.	FGM	FGA	Pct.	FTM	FTA	Pct.	Reb.	Pts.	Avg.
80-81 — Vanderbilt..........................	28	586	40	96	.417	20	31	.645	84	100	3.6
81-82 — Vanderbilt..........................	27	772	99	189	.524	52	71	.732	145	250	9.3
82-83 — Vanderbilt..........................	33	1008	180	366	.492	75	98	.765	182	435	13.2
83-84 — Vanderbilt..........................	29	953	200	375	.533	86	102	.843	213	486	16.8
Totals	117	3319	519	1026	.506	233	302	.772	624	1271	10.9

NBA REGULAR-SEASON RECORD

Season Team	G	Min.	FGM	FGA	Pct.	FTM	FTA	Pct.	Off.	Def.	Tot.	Ast.	PF	Dq.	Stl.	Blk.	TO	Pts.	Avg.
									— REBOUNDS —										
84-85 — New Jersey ..	72	1429	171	377	.454	79	92	.859	88	130	218	108	243	8	29	7	90	421	5.8
85-86 — New Jersey ..	53	650	84	171	.491	58	78	.744	45	92	137	14	125	4	21	3	49	226	4.3
86-87 — New Jersey ..	76	1003	151	325	.465	76	104	.731	80	117	197	60	200	6	33	13	81	378	5.0
89-90 — Orlando	60	1105	132	308	.429	42	54	.778	52	175	227	53	161	4	23	12	61	308	5.1
90-91 — Orlando	71	1683	259	532	.487	85	112	.759	108	255	363	97	234	5	29	10	126	609	8.6
91-92 — Orlando	75	1591	225	499	.451	79	114	.693	62	184	246	92	229	6	24	16	106	530	7.1
Totals	407	7461	1022	2212	.462	419	554	.756	435	953	1388	424	1192	33	159	61	513	2472	6.1

Three-point field goals: 1984-85, 0-for-3. 1985-86, 0-for-1. 1986-87, 0-for-1. 1989-90, 2-for-10 (.200). 1990-91, 6-for-15 (.400). 1991-92, 1-for-8 (.125). Totals, 9-for-38 (.237).

NBA PLAYOFF RECORD

Season Team	G	Min.	FGM	FGA	Pct.	FTM	FTA	Pct.	Off.	Def.	Tot.	Ast.	PF	Dq.	Stl.	Blk.	TO	Pts.	Avg.
									— REBOUNDS —										
84-85 — New Jersey ..	3	21	2	5	.400	0	0	...	2	2	4	2	6	0	0	0	0	4	1.3
85-86 — New Jersey ..	3	18	1	3	.333	1	1	1.000	0	3	3	3	7	0	0	0	4	3	1.0
Totals	6	39	3	8	.375	1	1	1.000	2	5	7	5	13	0	0	0	4	7	1.2

ITALIAN LEAGUE RECORD

Season Team	G	Min.	FGM	FGA	Pct.	FTM	FTA	Pct.	Reb.	Pts.	Avg.
87-88 — Arexons Cantu.......................	35	1271	216	417	.518	137	150	.913	187	641	18.3
88-89 — Vis. Cantu	33	1104	186	318	.585	124	148	.838	249	562	17.0
Totals	68	2375	402	735	.547	261	298	.876	436	1203	17.7

TURNER, JOHN
F

PERSONAL: Born November 30, 1967, in Washington, D.C. . . . 6-8/245. . . . Full name: John L. Turner.
HIGH SCHOOL: Eleanor Roosevelt (Greenbelt, Md.).
COLLEGE: Allegany Community College (Md.), then Georgetown, then Phillips (Okla.).
TRANSACTIONS/CAREER NOTES: Selected by Houston Rockets in first round (20th pick overall) of 1991 NBA Draft. . . . Signed to play in Spain (August 21, 1992). . . . Waived by Rockets (August 26, 1992).

COLLEGIATE RECORD

Season Team	G	Min.	FGM	FGA	Pct.	FTM	FTA	Pct.	Reb.	Pts.	Avg.
86-87 — Allegany Community College...	39	...	336	587	.572	162	231	.701	510	835	21.4
87-88 — Georgetown					Did not play — ineligible.						
88-89 — Georgetown	32	682	73	156	.468	64	116	.552	199	210	6.6
89-90 — Phillips	18	...	162	341	.475	80	142	.563	243	414	23.0
90-91 — Phillips	27	...	259	489	.530	119	190	.626	370	654	24.2
Junior college totals	39	...	336	587	.572	162	231	.701	510	835	21.4
Four-year-college totals	77	...	494	986	.501	263	448	.587	812	1278	16.6

Three-point field goals: 1989-90, 10-for-31 (.323). 1990-91, 17-for-47 (.362). Totals, 27-for-78 (.346).

NBA REGULAR-SEASON RECORD

Season Team	G	Min.	FGM	FGA	Pct.	FTM	FTA	Pct.	Off.	Def.	Tot.	Ast.	PF	Dq.	Stl.	Blk.	TO	Pts.	Avg.
									— REBOUNDS —										
91-92 — Houston	42	345	43	98	.439	31	59	.525	38	40	78	12	40	0	6	4	32	117	2.8

VANDEWEGHE, KIKI
F

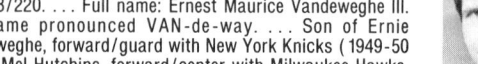

PERSONAL: Born August 1, 1958, in Weisbaden, West Germany. . . . 6-8/220. . . . Full name: Ernest Maurice Vandeweghe III. . . . Name pronounced VAN-de-way. . . . Son of Ernie Vandeweghe, forward/guard with New York Knicks (1949-50 through 1952-53 and 1955-56); and nephew of Mel Hutchins, forward/center with Milwaukee Hawks, Fort Wayne Pistons and New York Knicks (1951-52 through 1957-58).
HIGH SCHOOL: Pacific Palisades (Calif.).
COLLEGE: UCLA.
TRANSACTIONS/CAREER NOTES: Selected by Dallas Mavericks in first round (11th pick overall) of 1980 NBA Draft. . . . Traded by Mavericks with 1986 first-round draft choice to Denver Nuggets for 1981 and 1985 first-round draft choices (December 3, 1980). . . . Traded by Nuggets to Portland Trail Blazers for Fat Lever, Calvin Natt, Wayne Cooper, 1985 first-round draft choice and 1984 second-round draft choice (June 7, 1984). . . . Traded by Trail Blazers to New York Knicks for 1989 first-round draft choice (February 23, 1989). . . . Waived by Knicks (June 24, 1992).

COLLEGIATE RECORD

Season	Team	G	Min.	FGM	FGA	Pct.	FTM	FTA	Pct.	Reb.	Pts.	Avg.
76-77	—UCLA	23	230	35	70	.500	12	17	.706	41	82	3.6
77-78	—UCLA	28	592	101	184	.549	46	67	.687	123	248	8.9
78-79	—UCLA	30	916	166	267	.622	95	117	.812	189	427	14.2
79-80	—UCLA	32	1081	234	420	.557	155	196	.791	216	623	19.5
	Totals	113	2819	536	941	.570	308	397	.776	569	1380	12.2

NBA REGULAR-SEASON RECORD

NOTES: Led NBA with .481 three-point field-goal percentage (1987).

Season	Team	G	Min.	FGM	FGA	Pct.	FTM	FTA	Pct.	Off.	Def.	Tot.	Ast.	PF	Dq.	Stl.	Blk.	TO	Pts.	Avg.
80-81	—Denver	51	1376	229	537	.426	130	159	.818	86	184	270	94	116	0	29	24	86	588	11.5
81-82	—Denver	82	2775	706	1260	.560	347	405	.857	149	312	461	247	217	1	52	29	189	1760	21.5
82-83	—Denver	82	2909	841	1537	.547	489	559	.875	124	313	437	203	198	0	66	38	177	2186	26.7
83-84	—Denver	78	2734	895	1603	.558	494	580	.852	84	289	373	238	187	1	53	50	156	2295	29.4
84-85	—Portland	72	2502	618	1158	.534	369	412	.896	74	154	228	106	116	0	37	22	116	1616	22.4
85-86	—Portland	79	2791	719	1332	.540	523	602	.869	92	124	216	187	161	0	54	17	177	1962	24.8
86-87	—Portland	79	3029	808	1545	.523	467	527	.886	86	165	251	220	137	0	52	17	139	2122	26.9
87-88	—Portland	37	1038	283	557	.508	159	181	.878	36	73	109	71	68	0	21	7	48	747	20.2
88-89	—Port.-N.Y.	45	934	200	426	.469	80	89	.899	26	45	71	69	78	0	19	11	41	499	11.1
89-90	—New York	22	563	102	231	.442	44	48	.917	15	38	53	41	28	0	15	3	26	258	11.7
90-91	—New York	75	2420	458	927	.494	259	288	.899	78	102	180	110	122	0	42	10	108	1226	16.3
91-92	—New York	67	956	188	383	.491	65	81	.802	31	57	88	57	87	0	15	8	27	467	7.0
	Totals	769	24027	6047	11496	.526	3426	3931	.872	881	1856	2737	1643	1515	2	455	236	1290	15726	20.4

Three-point field goals: 1980-81, 0-for-7. 1981-82, 1-for-13 (.077). 1982-83, 15-for-51 (.294). 1983-84, 11-for-30 (.367). 1984-85, 11-for-33 (.333). 1985-86, 1-for-8 (.125). 1986-87, 39-for-81 (.481). 1987-88, 22-for-58 (.379). 1988-89, 19-for-48 (.396). 1989-90, 10-for-19 (.526). 1990-91, 51-for-141 (.362). 1991-92, 26-for-66 (.394). Totals, 206-for-555 (.371).

NBA PLAYOFF RECORD

Season	Team	G	Min.	FGM	FGA	Pct.	FTM	FTA	Pct.	Off.	Def.	Tot.	Ast.	PF	Dq.	Stl.	Blk.	TO	Pts.	Avg.
81-82	—Denver	3	109	25	43	.581	18	18	1.000	4	14	18	9	7	0	2	4	6	68	22.7
82-83	—Denver	8	317	87	160	.544	40	50	.800	6	46	52	32	16	0	4	7	12	214	26.8
83-84	—Denver	5	180	49	96	.510	27	28	.964	6	17	23	20	14	1	9	5	10	127	25.4
84-85	—Portland	9	311	85	158	.538	31	33	.939	14	13	27	17	23	0	8	3	12	202	22.4
85-86	—Portland	4	149	40	69	.580	32	32	1.000	2	3	5	8	12	0	2	2	9	112	28.0
86-87	—Portland	4	174	38	71	.535	22	26	.846	5	8	13	11	10	0	1	1	11	99	24.8
87-88	—Portland	4	72	11	40	.275	9	9	1.000	3	10	13	7	8	0	1	0	3	31	7.8
88-89	—New York	9	159	25	49	.510	20	21	.952	2	9	11	7	10	0	3	2	5	73	8.1
89-90	—New York	10	236	31	74	.419	8	10	.800	7	5	12	14	14	0	5	2	7	76	7.6
90-91	—New York	3	99	13	32	.406	22	25	.880	1	7	8	4	8	0	1	0	12	51	17.0
91-92	—New York	8	75	13	24	.542	6	7	.857	3	3	6	4	10	0	2	1	1	36	4.5
	Totals	67	1881	417	816	.511	235	259	.907	53	135	188	133	132	1	38	27	88	1089	16.3

Three-point field goals: 1982-83, 0-for-4. 1983-84, 2-for-5 (.400). 1984-85, 1-for-7 (.143). 1985-86, 0-for-2. 1986-87, 1-for-4 (.250). 1987-88, 0-for-5. 1988-89, 3-for-8 (.375). 1989-90, 6-for-13 (.462). 1990-91, 3-for-5 (.600). 1991-92, 4-for-5 (.800). Totals, 20-for-58 (.345).

NBA ALL-STAR GAME RECORD

Season	Team	Min.	FGM	FGA	Pct.	FTM	FTA	Pct.	Off.	Def.	Tot.	Ast.	PF	Dq.	Stl.	Blk.	TO	Pts.
1983	—Denver	14	3	4	.750	1	2	.500	0	3	3	1	0	0	1	0	0	7
1984	—Denver	26	7	13	.538	0	0	. . .	1	2	3	1	2	0	0	0	0	14
	Totals	40	10	17	.588	1	2	.500	1	5	6	2	2	0	1	0	0	21

VAUGHT, LOY
F, CLIPPERS

PERSONAL: Born February 27, 1967, in Grand Rapids, Mich. . . . 6-9/240. . . . Full name: Loy Stephen Vaught. . . . Name pronounced VAWT.
HIGH SCHOOL: East Kentwood (Kentwood, Mich.).
COLLEGE: Michigan.
TRANSACTIONS/CAREER NOTES: Selected by Los Angeles Clippers in first round (13th pick overall) of 1990 NBA Draft.

NOTES: Member of NCAA Division I championship team (1989).

Season	Team	G	Min.	FGM	FGA	Pct.	FTM	FTA	Pct.	Reb.	Pts.	Avg.
86-87	Michigan	32	416	68	122	.557	11	22	.500	125	147	4.6
87-88	Michigan	34	748	151	243	.621	55	76	.724	150	357	10.5
88-89	Michigan	37	851	201	304	.661	63	81	.778	296	467	12.6
89-90	Michigan	31	930	197	331	.595	86	107	.804	346	480	15.5
	Totals	134	2945	617	1000	.617	215	286	.752	917	1451	10.8

Three-point field goals: 1988-89, 2-for-5 (.400). 1989-90, 0-for-1. Totals, 2-for-6 (.333).

NBA REGULAR-SEASON RECORD

Season	Team	G	Min.	FGM	FGA	Pct.	FTM	FTA	Pct.	Off.	Def.	Tot.	Ast.	PF	Dq.	Stl.	Blk.	TO	Pts.	Avg.
90-91	L.A. Clippers	73	1178	175	359	.487	49	74	.662	124	225	349	40	135	2	20	23	49	399	5.5
91-92	L.A. Clippers	79	1687	271	551	.492	55	69	.797	160	352	512	71	165	1	37	31	66	601	7.6
	Totals	152	2865	446	910	.490	104	143	.727	284	577	861	111	300	3	57	54	115	1000	6.6

Three-point field goals: 1990-91, 0-for-2. 1991-92, 4-for-5 (.800). Totals, 4-for-7 (.571).

NBA PLAYOFF RECORD

Season	Team	G	Min.	FGM	FGA	Pct.	FTM	FTA	Pct.	Off.	Def.	Tot.	Ast.	PF	Dq.	Stl.	Blk.	TO	Pts.	Avg.
91-92	L.A. Clippers	5	36	7	11	.636	2	2	1.000	2	10	12	4	3	0	1	1	1	17	3.4

Three-point field goals: 1991-92, 1-for-1.

VIANNA, JOAO
F

PERSONAL: Born November 15, 1966, in Trabajara, Brazil. . . . 6-9/220.
TRANSACTIONS/CAREER NOTES: Never drafted by an NBA franchise. . . . Played in Puerto Rico (1990-91). . . . Signed as free agent by Dallas Mavericks (October 2, 1991). . . . Waived by Mavericks (November 12, 1991).
MISCELLANEOUS: Member of Brazilian Olympic team (1992).

NBA REGULAR-SEASON RECORD

Season	Team	G	Min.	FGM	FGA	Pct.	FTM	FTA	Pct.	Off.	Def.	Tot.	Ast.	PF	Dq.	Stl.	Blk.	TO	Pts.	Avg.
91-92	Dallas	1	9	1	2	.500	0	0	...	0	0	0	2	3	0	0	0	1	2	2.0

VINCENT, SAM
G, BUCKS

PERSONAL: Born May 18, 1963, in Lansing, Mich. . . . 6-2/185. . . . Full name: James Samuel Vincent. . . . Brother of Jay Vincent, forward with six NBA teams (1981-82 through 1989-90).
HIGH SCHOOL: Eastern (Lansing, Mich.).
COLLEGE: Michigan State.
TRANSACTIONS/CAREER NOTES: Selected by Boston Celtics in first round (20th pick overall) of 1985 NBA Draft. . . . Traded by Celtics with Scott Wedman to Seattle SuperSonics for 1989 second-round draft choice (October 16, 1987). . . . Traded by SuperSonics to Chicago Bulls for Sedale Threatt (February 25, 1988). . . . Selected by Orlando Magic from Bulls in NBA expansion draft (June 15, 1989). . . . Traded by Magic with 1994 second-round draft choice to Milwaukee Bucks for Lester Conner (August 4, 1992).
MISCELLANEOUS: Member of NBA championship team (1986).

COLLEGIATE RECORD

NOTES: THE SPORTING NEWS All-America first team (1985).

Season	Team	G	Min.	FGM	FGA	Pct.	FTM	FTA	Pct.	Reb.	Pts.	Avg.
81-82	Michigan State	28	965	130	282	.461	68	91	.747	78	328	11.7
82-83	Michigan State	30	1066	180	401	.449	133	172	.773	79	498	16.6
83-84	Michigan State	23	740	130	261	.498	99	122	.811	62	359	15.6
84-85	Michigan State	29	1093	245	450	.544	176	208	.846	112	666	23.0
	Totals	110	3864	685	1394	.491	476	593	.803	331	1851	16.8

Three-point field goals: 1982-83, 5-for-11 (.455).

NBA REGULAR-SEASON RECORD

Season	Team	G	Min.	FGM	FGA	Pct.	FTM	FTA	Pct.	Off.	Def.	Tot.	Ast.	PF	Dq.	Stl.	Blk.	TO	Pts.	Avg.
85-86	Boston	57	432	59	162	.364	65	70	.929	11	37	48	69	59	0	17	4	49	184	3.2
86-87	Boston	46	374	60	136	.441	51	55	.927	5	22	27	59	33	0	13	1	33	171	3.7
87-88	Seattle-Chi..	72	1501	210	461	.456	145	167	.868	35	117	152	381	145	0	55	16	136	573	8.0
88-89	Chicago	70	1703	274	566	.484	106	129	.822	34	156	190	335	124	0	53	10	142	656	9.4
89-90	Orlando	63	1657	258	564	.457	188	214	.879	37	157	194	354	108	1	65	20	132	705	11.2
90-91	Orlando	49	975	152	353	.431	99	120	.825	17	90	107	197	74	0	30	5	91	406	8.3
91-92	Orlando	39	885	150	349	.430	110	130	.846	19	82	101	148	55	1	35	4	72	411	10.5
	Totals	396	7527	1163	2591	.449	764	885	.863	158	661	819	1543	598	2	268	60	655	3106	7.8

Three-point field goals: 1985-86, 1-for-4 (.250). 1987-88, 8-for-21 (.381). 1988-89, 2-for-17 (.118). 1989-90, 1-for-14 (.071). 1990-91, 3-for-19 (.158). 1991-92, 1-for-13 (.077). Totals, 16-for-88 (.182).

NBA PLAYOFF RECORD

Season	Team	G	Min.	FGM	FGA	Pct.	FTM	FTA	Pct.	Off.	Def.	Tot.	Ast.	PF	Dq.	Stl.	Blk.	TO	Pts.	Avg.
85-86	Boston	9	41	8	28	.286	6	6	1.000	1	6	7	5	9	0	2	0	4	22	2.4
86-87	Boston	17	141	23	56	.411	27	35	.771	3	9	12	19	13	0	3	2	10	74	4.4
87-88	Chicago	10	251	41	110	.373	20	25	.800	6	13	19	44	23	0	8	1	27	102	10.2
88-89	Chicago	16	113	10	33	.303	9	12	.750	4	4	8	19	9	0	3	1	6	29	1.8
	Totals	52	546	82	227	.361	62	78	.795	14	32	46	87	54	0	16	4	47	227	4.4

Three-point field goals: 1985-86, 0-for-1. 1986-87, 1-for-2 (.500). 1987-88, 0-for-3. 1988-89, 0-for-2. Totals, 1-for-8 (.125).

VOLKOV, ALEXANDER
F, HAWKS

PERSONAL: Born March 28, 1964, in Omsk, U.S.S.R. . . . 6-10/235. . . . Name pronounced VOHL-kov.
COLLEGE: Kiev Institute (Kiev, U.S.S.R.).
TRANSACTIONS/CAREER NOTES: Selected by Atlanta Hawks in sixth round (134th pick overall) of 1986 NBA Draft. . . . Played on Soviet national team (1985-86 through 1988-89).
MISCELLANEOUS: Member of gold-medal-winning Soviet Olympic team (1988). . . . Member of Unified Olympic team (1992).

NBA REGULAR-SEASON RECORD

Season Team	G	Min.	FGM	FGA	Pct.	FTM	FTA	Pct.	Off.	Def.	Tot.	Ast.	PF	Dq.	Stl.	Blk.	TO	Pts.	Avg.
89-90 —Atlanta.........	72	937	137	284	.482	70	120	.583	52	67	119	83	166	3	36	22	52	357	5.0
90-91 —Atlanta.........								Did not play—injured.											
91-92 —Atlanta.........	77	1516	251	569	.441	125	198	.631	103	162	265	250	178	2	66	30	102	662	8.6
Totals	149	2453	388	853	.455	195	318	.613	155	229	384	333	344	5	102	52	154	1019	6.8

Three-point field goals: 1989-90, 13-for-34 (.382). 1991-92, 35-for-110 (.318). Totals, 48-for-144 (.333).

VRANKOVIC, STOJAN
C, CELTICS

PERSONAL: Born January 22, 1964, in Drnis, Yugoslavia. . . . 7-2/260. . . . Name pronounced Stoy-yan Vrank-o-vic.
TRANSACTIONS/CAREER NOTES: Never drafted by an NBA franchise. . . . Member of Yugoslavian national team (1985-86 through 1988-89). . . . Played in Greece (1989-90). . . . Signed as free agent by Boston Celtics (October 2, 1990).
MISCELLANEOUS: Member of silver-medal-winning Yugoslavian Olympic team (1988). . . . Member of silver-medal-winning Croatian Olympic team (1992).

NBA REGULAR-SEASON RECORD

Season Team	G	Min.	FGM	FGA	Pct.	FTM	FTA	Pct.	Off.	Def.	Tot.	Ast.	PF	Dq.	Stl.	Blk.	TO	Pts.	Avg.
90-91 —Boston	31	166	24	52	.462	10	18	.556	15	36	51	4	43	1	1	29	24	58	1.9
91-92 —Boston	19	110	15	32	.469	7	12	.583	8	20	28	5	22	0	0	17	10	37	1.9
Totals	50	276	39	84	.464	17	30	.567	23	56	79	9	65	1	1	46	34	95	1.9

NBA PLAYOFF RECORD

Season Team	G	Min.	FGM	FGA	Pct.	FTM	FTA	Pct.	Off.	Def.	Tot.	Ast.	PF	Dq.	Stl.	Blk.	TO	Pts.	Avg.
90-91 —Boston	1	4	1	1	1.000	0	1	.000	0	2	2	0	2	0	0	0	1	2	2.0
91-92 —Boston	1	3	1	1	1.000	0	0	...	0	0	0	1	0	0	0	0	0	2	2.0
Totals	2	7	2	2	1.000	0	1	.000	0	2	2	1	2	0	0	0	1	4	2.0

WALKER, DARRELL
G, PISTONS

PERSONAL: Born March 9, 1961, in Chicago. . . . 6-4/180.
HIGH SCHOOL: Corliss (Chicago).
COLLEGE: Westark Community College (Ark.), then Arkansas.
TRANSACTIONS/CAREER NOTES: Selected by New York Knicks in first round (12th pick overall) of 1983 NBA Draft. . . . Traded by Knicks to Denver Nuggets for 1987 first-round draft choice (October 2, 1986). . . . Traded by Nuggets with Mark Alarie to Washington Bullets for Michael Adams and Jay Vincent (November 2, 1987). . . . Traded by Bullets to Detroit Pistons for draft considerations (September 5, 1991).

COLLEGIATE RECORD

Season Team	G	Min.	FGM	FGA	Pct.	FTM	FTA	Pct.	Reb.	Pts.	Avg.
79-80 —Westark Community College ...	37	1332	255	472	.540	117	178	.657	259	627	16.9
80-81 —Arkansas	31	926	137	269	.509	75	125	.600	139	349	11.3
81-82 —Arkansas	29	1039	162	316	.513	106	161	.658	152	430	14.8
82-83 —Arkansas	30	1105	197	374	.527	152	238	.639	172	546	18.2
Junior college totals	37	1332	255	472	.540	117	178	.657	259	627	16.9
Four-year-college totals	90	3070	496	959	.517	333	524	.635	463	1325	14.7

NBA REGULAR-SEASON RECORD

HONORS: NBA All-Rookie team (1984).

Season Team	G	Min.	FGM	FGA	Pct.	FTM	FTA	Pct.	Off.	Def.	Tot.	Ast.	PF	Dq.	Stl.	Blk.	TO	Pts.	Avg.
83-84 —New York	82	1324	216	518	.417	208	263	.791	74	93	167	284	202	1	127	15	194	644	7.9
84-85 —New York	82	2489	430	989	.435	243	347	.700	128	150	278	408	244	2	167	21	204	1103	13.5
85-86 —New York	81	2023	324	753	.430	190	277	.686	100	120	220	337	216	1	146	36	192	838	10.3
86-87 —Denver	81	2020	358	742	.482	272	365	.745	157	170	327	282	229	0	120	37	187	988	12.2
87-88 —Washington .	52	940	114	291	.392	82	105	.781	43	84	127	100	105	2	62	10	69	310	6.0
88-89 —Washington .	79	2565	286	681	.420	142	184	.772	135	372	507	496	215	2	155	23	184	714	9.0
89-90 —Washington .	81	2883	316	696	.454	138	201	.687	173	541	714	652	220	1	139	30	173	772	9.5
90-91 —Washington .	71	2305	230	535	.430	93	154	.604	140	358	498	459	199	2	78	33	154	553	7.8
91-92 —Detroit.........	74	1541	161	381	.423	65	105	.619	85	153	238	205	134	0	63	18	79	387	5.2
Totals	683	18090	2435	5586	.436	1433	2001	.716	1035	2041	3076	3223	1764	11	1057	223	1436	6309	9.2

Three-point field goals: 1983-84, 4-for-15 (.267). 1984-85, 0-for-17. 1985-86, 0-for-10. 1986-87, 0-for-4. 1987-88, 0-for-6. 1988-89, 0-for-9. 1989-90, 2-for-21 (.095). 1990-91, 0-for-9. 1991-92, 0-for-10. Totals, 6-for-101 (.059).

NBA PLAYOFF RECORD

Season Team	G	Min.	FGM	FGA	Pct.	FTM	FTA	Pct.	REBOUNDS Off.	Def.	Tot.	Ast.	PF	Dq.	Stl.	Blk.	TO	Pts.	Avg.
83-84 — New York	12	195	27	73	.370	28	46	.609	20	15	35	20	29	0	24	2	32	82	6.8
86-87 — Denver	3	68	11	34	.324	4	7	.571	3	7	10	5	4	0	2	0	4	26	8.7
87-88 — Washington .	5	155	22	54	.407	11	16	.688	9	15	24	14	18	0	7	4	9	55	11.0
91-92 — Detroit.........	5	68	3	9	.333	4	4	1.000	5	7	12	4	7	0	1	0	5	10	2.0
Totals	25	486	63	170	.371	47	73	.644	37	44	81	43	58	0	34	6	50	173	6.9

Three-point field goals: 1987-88, 0-for-1.

WEBB, SPUD
G, KINGS

PERSONAL: Born July 13, 1963, in Dallas.... 5-7/135.... Full name: Anthony Jerome Webb.
HIGH SCHOOL: Wilmer-Hutchins (Dallas).
COLLEGE: Midland (Tex.), then North Carolina State.
TRANSACTIONS/CAREER NOTES: Selected by Detroit Pistons in fourth round (87th pick overall) of 1985 NBA Draft.... Draft rights relinquished by Pistons (September 24, 1985).... Signed as free agent by Atlanta Hawks (September 26, 1985).... Traded by Hawks with 1994 second-round draft choice to Sacramento Kings for Travis Mays (July 1, 1991).

COLLEGIATE RECORD

Season Team	G	Min.	FGM	FGA	Pct.	FTM	FTA	Pct.	Reb.	Pts.	Avg.
81-82 — Midland...................................	38	...	277	538	.515	235	301	.781	77	789	20.8
82-83 — Midland...................................	35	...	196	440	.445	120	155	.774	106	512	14.6
83-84 — North Carolina State...............	33	980	128	279	.459	67	88	.761	59	323	9.8
84-85 — North Carolina State...............	33	919	140	291	.481	86	113	.761	66	366	11.1
Junior college totals........................	73		473	978	.484	355	456	.779	183	1301	17.8
Four-year-college totals	66	1899	268	570	.470	153	201	.761	125	689	10.4

NBA REGULAR-SEASON RECORD

Season Team	G	Min.	FGM	FGA	Pct.	FTM	FTA	Pct.	REBOUNDS Off.	Def.	Tot.	Ast.	PF	Dq.	Stl.	Blk.	TO	Pts.	Avg.
85-86 — Atlanta........	79	1229	199	412	.483	216	275	.785	27	96	123	337	164	1	82	5	159	616	7.8
86-87 — Atlanta........	33	532	71	162	.438	80	105	.762	6	54	60	167	65	1	34	2	70	223	6.8
87-88 — Atlanta........	82	1347	191	402	.475	107	131	.817	16	130	146	337	125	0	63	11	131	490	6.0
88-89 — Atlanta........	81	1219	133	290	.459	52	60	.867	21	102	123	284	104	0	70	6	83	319	3.9
89-90 — Atlanta........	82	2184	294	616	.477	162	186	.871	38	163	201	477	185	0	105	12	141	751	9.2
90-91 — Atlanta........	75	2197	359	803	.447	231	266	.868	41	133	174	417	180	0	118	6	146	1003	13.4
91-92 — Sacramento .	77	2724	448	1006	.445	262	305	.859	30	193	223	547	193	1	125	24	229	1231	16.0
Totals	509	11432	1695	3691	.459	1110	1328	.836	179	871	1050	2566	1016	3	597	66	959	4633	9.1

Three-point field goals: 1985-86, 2-for-11 (.182). 1986-87, 1-for-6 (.167). 1987-88, 1-for-19 (.053). 1988-89, 1-for-22 (.045). 1989-90, 1-for-19 (.053). 1990-91, 54-for-168 (.321). 1991-92, 73-for-199 (.367). Totals, 133-for-444 (.300).

NBA PLAYOFF RECORD

Season Team	G	Min.	FGM	FGA	Pct.	FTM	FTA	Pct.	REBOUNDS Off.	Def.	Tot.	Ast.	PF	Dq.	Stl.	Blk.	TO	Pts.	Avg.
85-86 — Atlanta........	9	183	42	81	.519	26	33	.788	6	25	31	65	13	0	4	1	10	110	12.2
86-87 — Atlanta........	8	122	9	19	.474	13	17	.765	1	7	8	38	10	0	6	0	18	31	3.9
87-88 — Atlanta........	12	211	35	81	.432	34	37	.919	4	16	20	56	22	0	9	0	10	106	8.8
88-89 — Atlanta........	5	55	3	11	.273	2	2	1.000	0	4	4	15	6	0	4	0	0	8	1.6
90-91 — Atlanta........	5	154	25	57	.439	11	16	.688	8	14	22	24	13	0	7	1	13	66	13.2
Totals	39	725	114	249	.458	86	105	.819	19	66	85	198	64	0	30	2	51	321	8.2

Three-point field goals: 1985-86, 0-for-2. 1986-87, 0-for-1. 1987-88, 2-for-8 (.250). 1990-91, 5-for-12 (.417). Totals, 7-for-23 (.304).

WEST, DOUG
G, TIMBERWOLVES

PERSONAL: Born May 27, 1967, in Altoona, Pa. ... 6-6/200. ... Full name: Jeffery Douglas West.
HIGH SCHOOL: Altoona Area (Pa.).
COLLEGE: Villanova.
TRANSACTIONS/CAREER NOTES: Selected by Minnesota Timberwolves in second round (38th pick overall) of 1989 NBA Draft.

COLLEGIATE RECORD

Season Team	G	Min.	FGM	FGA	Pct.	FTM	FTA	Pct.	Reb.	Pts.	Avg.
85-86 — Villanova...............................	37	995	158	307	.515	60	88	.682	136	376	10.2
86-87 — Villanova...............................	31	1022	180	376	.479	94	129	.729	151	470	15.2
87-88 — Villanova...............................	37	1281	215	433	.497	92	127	.724	181	583	15.8
88-89 — Villanova...............................	33	1137	226	488	.463	90	125	.720	162	608	18.4
Totals	138	4435	779	1604	.486	336	469	.716	630	2037	14.8

Three-point field goals: 1986-87, 16-for-43 (.372). 1987-88, 61-for-143 (.427). 1988-89, 66-for-177 (.373). Totals, 143-for-363 (.394).

NBA REGULAR-SEASON RECORD

Season Team	G	Min.	FGM	FGA	Pct.	FTM	FTA	Pct.	REBOUNDS Off.	Def.	Tot.	Ast.	PF	Dq.	Stl.	Blk.	TO	Pts.	Avg.
89-90 — Minnesota....	52	378	53	135	.393	26	32	.813	24	46	70	18	61	0	10	6	31	135	2.6
90-91 — Minnesota....	75	824	118	246	.480	58	84	.690	56	80	136	48	115	0	35	23	41	294	3.9
91-92 — Minnesota....	80	2540	463	894	.518	186	231	.805	107	150	257	281	239	1	66	26	120	1116	14.0
Totals	207	3742	634	1275	.497	270	347	.778	187	276	463	347	415	1	111	55	192	1545	7.5

Three-point field goals: 1989-90, 3-for-11 (.273). 1990-91, 0-for-1. 1991-92, 4-for-23 (.174). Totals, 7-for-35 (.200).

W

WEST, MARK
C, SUNS

PERSONAL: Born November 5, 1960, in Petersburg, Va. . . . 6-10/246. . . . Full name: Mark Andre West.
HIGH SCHOOL: Petersburg (Va.).
COLLEGE: Old Dominion.

TRANSACTIONS/CAREER NOTES: Selected by Dallas Mavericks in second round (30th pick overall) of 1983 NBA Draft. . . . Waived by Mavericks (October 23, 1984). . . . Signed as free agent by Milwaukee Bucks (November 6, 1984). . . . Waived by Bucks (November 12, 1984). . . . Signed as free agent by Cleveland Cavaliers (November 23, 1984). . . . Traded by Cavaliers with Tyrone Corbin, Kevin Johnson, 1988 first- and second-round draft choices and 1989 second-round draft choice to Phoenix Suns for Larry Nance, Mike Sanders and 1988 first-round draft choice (February 25, 1988).

COLLEGIATE RECORD

NOTES: Led NCAA Division I with 4.04 blocked shots per game (1981) and 4.1 blocked shots per game (1982).

Season Team	G	Min.	FGM	FGA	Pct.	FTM	FTA	Pct.	Reb.	Pts.	Avg.
79-80 —Old Dominion	30	679	67	141	.475	10	27	.370	212	144	4.8
80-81 —Old Dominion	28	845	128	243	.527	48	83	.578	287	304	10.9
81-82 —Old Dominion	30	1007	197	323	.610	78	147	.531	300	472	15.7
82-83 —Old Dominion	29	1005	169	297	.569	80	163	.491	314	418	14.4
Totals	117	3536	561	1004	.559	216	420	.514	1113	1338	11.4

NBA REGULAR-SEASON RECORD

Season Team	G	Min.	FGM	FGA	Pct.	FTM	FTA	Pct.	Off.	Def.	Tot.	Ast.	PF	Dq.	Stl.	Blk.	TO	Pts.	Avg.
83-84 —Dallas	34	202	15	42	.357	7	22	.318	19	27	46	13	55	0	1	15	12	37	1.1
84-85 —Mil.-Clev.	66	888	106	194	.546	43	87	.494	90	161	251	15	197	7	13	49	59	255	3.9
85-86 —Cleveland	67	1172	113	209	.541	54	103	.524	97	225	322	20	235	6	27	62	91	280	4.2
86-87 —Cleveland	78	1333	209	385	.543	89	173	.514	126	213	339	41	229	5	22	81	106	507	6.5
87-88 —Clev.-Phoe.	83	2098	316	573	.551	170	285	.596	165	358	523	74	265	4	47	147	173	802	9.7
88-89 —Phoenix	82	2019	243	372	.653	108	202	.535	167	384	551	39	273	4	35	187	103	594	7.2
89-90 —Phoenix	82	2399	331	530	*.625	199	288	.691	212	516	728	45	277	5	36	184	126	861	10.5
90-91 —Phoenix	82	1957	247	382	.647	135	206	.655	171	393	564	37	266	2	32	161	86	629	7.7
91-92 —Phoenix	82	1436	196	310	.632	109	171	.637	134	238	372	22	239	2	14	81	82	501	6.1
Totals	656	13504	1776	2997	.593	914	1537	.595	1181	2515	3696	306	2036	35	227	967	838	4466	6.8

Three-point field goals: 1984-85, 0-for-1. 1986-87, 0-for-2. 1987-88, 0-for-1. Totals, 0-for-4.

NBA PLAYOFF RECORD

Season Team	G	Min.	FGM	FGA	Pct.	FTM	FTA	Pct.	Off.	Def.	Tot.	Ast.	PF	Dq.	Stl.	Blk.	TO	Pts.	Avg.
83-84 —Dallas	4	32	5	9	.556	2	3	.667	0	7	7	3	11	1	0	3	3	12	3.0
84-85 —Cleveland	4	68	3	5	.600	2	5	.400	5	13	18	4	19	0	2	0	5	8	2.0
88-89 —Phoenix	12	227	32	50	.640	10	14	.714	21	32	53	6	36	1	7	19	13	74	6.2
89-90 —Phoenix	16	544	75	130	.577	27	50	.540	53	111	164	5	73	3	4	41	26	177	11.1
90-91 —Phoenix	4	93	9	15	.600	5	7	.714	8	10	18	2	15	0	2	10	3	23	5.8
91-92 —Phoenix	8	96	14	19	.737	4	8	.500	8	9	17	2	21	1	2	4	2	32	4.0
Totals	48	1060	138	228	.605	50	87	.575	95	182	277	22	175	6	17	77	52	326	6.8

WHATLEY, ENNIS
G, TRAIL BLAZERS

PERSONAL: Born August 11, 1962, in Birmingham, Ala. . . . 6-3/180.
HIGH SCHOOL: Phillips (Birmingham, Ala.).
COLLEGE: Alabama.

TRANSACTIONS/CAREER NOTES: Selected as undergraduate by Kansas City Kings in first round (13th pick overall) of 1983 NBA Draft. . . . Draft rights traded by Kings with draft rights to Chris McNealy and 1984 second-round draft choice to Chicago Bulls for Mark Olberding and draft rights to Larry Micheaux (June 28, 1983). . . . Traded by Bulls with draft rights to Keith Lee to Cleveland Cavaliers for draft rights to Charles Oakley and Calvin Duncan (June 18, 1985). . . . Waived by Cavaliers (December 16, 1985). . . . Signed by Washington Bullets to 10-day contract (January 2, 1986). . . . Signed by San Antonio Spurs to 10-day contract (February 1, 1986). . . . Signed as free agent by Bullets (September 4, 1986). . . . Waived by Bullets (November 3, 1987). . . . Played in Continental Basketball Association with Mississippi Jets (1987-88) and Wichita Falls Texans (1988-89 and 1990-91). . . . Signed by Atlanta Hawks to first of two consecutive 10-day contracts (February 11, 1988). . . . Signed as free agent by Boston Celtics (September 14, 1988). . . . Waived by Celtics (October 31, 1988). . . . Signed by Los Angeles Clippers to first of two consecutive 10-day contracts (March 20, 1989). . . . Signed as free agent by Portland Trail Blazers (October 4, 1991).

COLLEGIATE RECORD

NOTES: THE SPORTING NEWS All-America second team (1983).

Season Team	G	Min.	FGM	FGA	Pct.	FTM	FTA	Pct.	Reb.	Pts.	Avg.
81-82 —Alabama	31	996	141	285	.495	93	129	.721	76	375	12.1
82-83 —Alabama	32	1109	183	366	.500	121	157	.771	128	487	15.2
Totals	63	2105	324	651	.498	214	286	.748	204	862	13.7

NBA REGULAR-SEASON RECORD

Season Team	G	Min.	FGM	FGA	Pct.	FTM	FTA	Pct.	Off.	Def.	Tot.	Ast.	PF	Dq.	Stl.	Blk.	TO	Pts.	Avg.
83-84 —Chicago	80	2159	261	556	.469	146	200	.730	63	134	197	662	223	4	119	17	268	668	8.4
84-85 —Chicago	70	1385	140	313	.447	68	86	.791	34	67	101	381	141	1	66	10	144	349	5.0
85-86 —Cl-Was-SA.	14	107	15	35	.429	5	10	.500	4	10	14	23	10	0	5	1	10	35	2.5
86-87 —Washington	73	1816	246	515	.478	126	165	.764	58	136	194	392	172	0	92	10	138	618	8.5
87-88 —Atlanta	5	24	4	9	.444	3	4	.750	0	4	4	2	3	0	2	0	4	11	2.2
88-89 —L.A. Clippers	8	90	12	33	.364	10	11	.909	2	14	16	22	15	0	7	1	11	34	4.3
91-92 —Portland	23	209	21	51	.412	27	31	.871	6	15	21	34	12	0	14	3	14	69	3.0
Totals	273	5790	699	1512	.462	385	507	.759	167	380	547	1516	576	5	305	42	589	1784	6.5

Three-point field goals: 1983-84, 0-for-2. 1984-85, 1-for-9 (.111). 1986-87, 0-for-2. 1991-92, 0-for-4. Totals, 1-for-17 (.059).

								— REBOUNDS —									
Season	Team	G	Min.	FGM	FGA	Pct.	FTM	FTA	Pct.	Off.	Def.	Tot.	Ast.	PF	Dq.	Stl.	Blk.	TO	Pts.	Avg.
86-87	—Washington .	2	32	3	12	.250	0	0	...	1	2	3	6	2	0	2	0	8	6	3.0
91-92	—Portland.......	15	96	6	20	.300	4	4	1.000	0	10	10	13	11	0	7	0	4	16	1.1
	Totals	17	128	9	32	.281	4	4	1.000	1	12	13	19	13	0	9	0	12	22	1.3

Three-point field goals: 1991-92, 0-for-1.

CBA REGULAR-SEASON RECORD

NOTES: CBA All-Star second team (1989).

				2-POINT			3-POINT								
Season	Team	G	Min.	FGM	FGA	Pct.	FGM	FGA	Pct.	FTM	FTA	Pct.	Reb.	Ast.	Pts.	Avg.
87-88	—Mississippi.......	29	1070	207	365	.567	2	16	.125	150	189	.794	116	218	570	19.7
88-89	—Wichita Falls ...	47	1869	395	770	.513	0	11	.000	195	234	.833	268	289	985	21.0
90-91	—Wichita Falls ...	40	1588	311	619	.502	6	24	.250	141	173	.815	216	362	781	19.5
	Totals	116	4527	913	1754	.521	8	51	.157	486	596	.815	600	869	2336	20.1

WHITE, RANDY
F, MAVERICKS

PERSONAL: Born November 4, 1967, in Shreveport, La.... 6-8/244.
HIGH SCHOOL: Huntington (Shreveport, La.).
COLLEGE: Louisiana Tech.
TRANSACTIONS/CAREER NOTES: Selected by Dallas Mavericks in first round (eighth pick overall) of 1989 NBA Draft.

COLLEGIATE RECORD

Season	Team	G	Min.	FGM	FGA	Pct.	FTM	FTA	Pct.	Reb.	Pts.	Avg.
85-86	—Louisiana Tech	34	697	115	221	.520	82	123	.667	156	312	9.2
86-87	—Louisiana Tech	30	782	145	252	.575	88	130	.677	196	379	12.6
87-88	—Louisiana Tech	31	1009	226	354	.638	121	189	.640	359	578	18.6
88-89	—Louisiana Tech	32	1026	245	408	.600	171	229	.747	337	678	21.2
	Totals	127	3514	731	1235	.592	462	671	.689	1048	1947	15.3

Three-point field goals: 1986-87, 1-for-1. 1987-88, 5-for-15 (.333). 1988-89, 17-for-38 (.447). Totals, 23-for-54 (.426).

NBA REGULAR-SEASON RECORD

										— REBOUNDS —								
Season	Team	G	Min.	FGM	FGA	Pct.	FTM	FTA	Pct.	Off.	Def.	Tot.	Ast.	PF	Dq.	Stl.	Blk.	TO	Pts.	Avg.
89-90	—Dallas...........	55	707	93	252	.369	50	89	.562	78	95	173	21	124	0	24	6	47	237	4.3
90-91	—Dallas...........	79	1901	265	665	.399	159	225	.707	173	331	504	63	308	6	81	44	131	695	8.8
91-92	—Dallas...........	65	1021	145	382	.380	124	162	.765	96	140	236	31	157	1	31	22	68	418	6.4
	Totals	199	3629	503	1299	.387	333	476	.700	347	566	913	115	589	7	136	72	246	1350	6.8

Three-point field goals: 1989-90, 1-for-14 (.071). 1990-91, 6-for-37 (.162). 1991-92, 4-for-27 (.148). Totals, 11-for-78 (.141).

NBA PLAYOFF RECORD

										— REBOUNDS —								
Season	Team	G	Min.	FGM	FGA	Pct.	FTM	FTA	Pct.	Off.	Def.	Tot.	Ast.	PF	Dq.	Stl.	Blk.	TO	Pts.	Avg.
89-90	—Dallas...........	1	2	0	0	...	0	0	...	0	0	0	0	0	0	0	0	0	0	0.0

WIGGINS, MITCHELL
G, 76ERS

PERSONAL: Born September 28, 1959, in Lenoir County, N.C. ...6-4/185.
HIGH SCHOOL: North Lenoir (La Grange, N.C.).
COLLEGE: Truett-McConnell (Ga.), then Clemson, then Florida State.
TRANSACTIONS/CAREER NOTES: Selected by Indiana Pacers in first round (23rd pick overall) of 1983 NBA Draft.... Draft rights traded by Pacers to Chicago Bulls for draft rights to Sidney Lowe and 1984 second-round draft choice (June 28, 1983).... Traded by Bulls with 1985 second- and third-round draft choices to Houston Rockets for Caldwell Jones (August 10, 1984).... Played in Continental Basketball Association with Mississippi Jets (1986-87) and Quad City Thunder (1987-88).... Disqualified from the NBA under rules of the league's Anti-Drug Program (January 13, 1987).... Reinstated by the NBA (July 27, 1989).... Did not play basketball (1990-91).... Signed as free agent by Philadelphia 76ers (July 16, 1991).

COLLEGIATE RECORD

Season	Team	G	Min.	FGM	FGA	Pct.	FTM	FTA	Pct.	Reb.	Pts.	Avg.
78-79	—Truett-McConnell..................	...	...	...	...	...	...	...	...	...	...	25.2
79-80	—Clemson	32	537	76	162	.469	25	45	.556	96	177	5.5
80-81	—Florida State					Did not play—transfer student.						
81-82	—Florida State	22	808	223	388	.575	77	102	.755	213	523	23.8
82-83	—Florida State	24	873	216	410	.527	112	147	.762	196	544	22.7
	Junior college totals	...	...	...	...	...	...	...	...	...	...	25.2
	Four-year-college totals	78	2218	515	960	.536	214	294	.728	505	1244	15.9

NBA REGULAR-SEASON RECORD

										— REBOUNDS —								
Season	Team	G	Min.	FGM	FGA	Pct.	FTM	FTA	Pct.	Off.	Def.	Tot.	Ast.	PF	Dq.	Stl.	Blk.	TO	Pts.	Avg.
83-84	—Chicago........	82	2123	399	890	.448	213	287	.742	138	190	328	187	278	8	106	11	139	1018	12.4
84-85	—Houston	82	1575	318	657	.484	96	131	.733	110	125	235	119	195	1	83	13	90	738	9.0
85-86	—Houston	78	1198	222	489	.454	86	118	.729	87	72	159	101	155	1	59	5	62	531	6.8
86-87	—Houston	32	822	153	350	.437	49	65	.754	74	59	133	76	82	1	44	3	59	355	11.1
89-90	—Houston	66	1852	416	853	.488	192	237	.810	133	153	286	104	165	0	85	1	87	1024	15.5
91-92	—Philadelphia.	49	569	88	229	.384	35	51	.686	43	51	94	22	67	0	20	1	25	211	4.3
	Totals	389	8105	1596	3468	.460	671	889	.755	585	650	1235	609	942	11	397	34	453	3877	10.0

W

Three-point field goals: 1983-84, 7-for-29 (.241). 1984-85, 6-for-23 (.261). 1985-86, 1-for-12 (.083). 1986-87, 0-for-5. 1989-90, 0-for-3. 1991-92, 0-for-1. Totals, 14-for-73 (.192).

NBA PLAYOFF RECORD

Season Team	G	Min.	FGM	FGA	Pct.	FTM	FTA	Pct.	Off.	Def.	Tot.	Ast.	PF	Dq.	Stl.	Blk.	TO	Pts.	Avg.
84-85 —Houston	5	45	9	18	.500	0	0	...	3	1	4	1	6	0	4	0	3	18	3.6
85-86 —Houston	20	443	89	179	.497	21	28	.750	38	38	76	31	44	0	14	3	27	199	10.0
89-90 —Houston	4	51	7	15	.467	2	3	.667	4	9	13	2	5	0	1	0	4	16	4.0
Totals	29	539	105	212	.495	23	31	.742	45	48	93	34	55	0	19	3	34	233	8.0

Three-point field goals: 1985-86, 0-for-3.

CBA REGULAR-SEASON RECORD

Season Team	G	Min.	2-POINT			3-POINT			FTM	FTA	Pct.	Reb.	Ast.	Pts.	Avg.
			FGM	FGA	Pct.	FGM	FGA	Pct.							
86-87 —Mississippi.......	6	175	55	128	.430	0	3	.000	16	22	.727	38	24	126	21.0
87-88 —Quad City	5	204	53	116	.457	0	3	.000	30	40	.750	41	15	136	27.2
Totals	11	379	108	244	.443	0	6	.000	46	62	.742	79	39	262	23.8

WILEY, MORLON
G, HAWKS

PERSONAL: Born September 24, 1966, in New Orleans. . . . 6-4/192. . . . Full name: Morlon David Wiley. . . . Name pronounced MORE-lin WHY-lee. . . . Brother of Michael Wiley, forward with San Antonio Spurs and San Diego Clippers (1980-81 and 1981-82).

HIGH SCHOOL: Long Beach Polytechnic (Calif.).
COLLEGE: Long Beach State.
TRANSACTIONS/CAREER NOTES: Selected by Dallas Mavericks in second round (46th pick overall) of 1988 NBA Draft. . . . Selected by Orlando Magic from Mavericks in NBA expansion draft (June 15, 1989). . . . Waived by Magic (November 30, 1990). . . . Re-signed by Magic (December 4, 1990). . . . Waived by Magic (December 4, 1991). . . . Signed as free agent by San Antonio Spurs (December 17, 1991). . . . Waived by Spurs (December 23, 1991). . . . Signed as free agent by Atlanta Hawks (January 2, 1992). . . . Played in Continental Basketball Association with Rapid City Thrillers (1991-92).

COLLEGIATE RECORD

Season Team	G	Min.	FGM	FGA	Pct.	FTM	FTA	Pct.	Reb.	Pts.	Avg.
84-85 —Long Beach State	27	641	58	152	.382	24	32	.750	50	157	5.8
85-86 —Long Beach State	29	802	137	299	.458	54	68	.794	76	338	11.7
86-87 —Long Beach State	28	783	125	324	.386	64	80	.800	80	357	12.8
87-88 —Long Beach State	29	977	218	425	.513	85	111	.766	116	578	19.9
Totals	113	3203	538	1200	.448	227	291	.780	322	1430	12.7

Three-point field goals: 1984-85, 17-for-41 (.415). 1985-86, 10-for-39 (.256). 1986-87, 43-for-109 (.394). 1987-88, 57-for-137 (.416). Totals, 127-for-326 (.390).

NBA REGULAR-SEASON RECORD

Season Team	G	Min.	FGM	FGA	Pct.	FTM	FTA	Pct.	Off.	Def.	Tot.	Ast.	PF	Dq.	Stl.	Blk.	TO	Pts.	Avg.
88-89 —Dallas..........	51	408	46	114	.404	13	16	.813	13	34	47	76	61	0	25	6	34	111	2.2
89-90 —Orlando	40	638	92	208	.442	28	38	.737	13	39	52	114	65	0	45	3	63	229	5.7
90-91 —Orlando	34	350	45	108	.417	17	25	.680	4	13	17	73	37	1	24	0	34	113	3.3
91-92 —Orl-SA-Atl...	53	870	83	193	.430	24	35	.686	24	57	81	180	89	0	47	3	60	204	3.8
Totals	178	2266	266	623	.427	82	114	.719	54	143	197	443	252	1	141	12	191	657	3.7

Three-point field goals: 1988-89, 6-for-24 (.250). 1989-90, 17-for-46 (.370). 1990-91, 6-for-12 (.500). 1991-92, 14-for-42 (.333). Totals, 43-for-124 (.347).

CBA REGULAR-SEASON RECORD

Season Team	G	Min.	2-POINT			3-POINT			FTM	FTA	Pct.	Reb.	Ast.	Pts.	Avg.
			FGM	FGA	Pct.	FGM	FGA	Pct.							
91-92 —Rapid City	5	99	11	31	.355	1	5	.200	3	4	.750	9	18	28	5.6

WILKINS, DOMINIQUE
F, HAWKS

PERSONAL: Born January 12, 1960, in Paris, France. . . . 6-8/215. . . . Full name: Jacques Dominique Wilkins. . . . Brother of Gerald Wilkins, forward with New York Knicks.
HIGH SCHOOL: Washington (N.C.).

COLLEGE: Georgia.
TRANSACTIONS/CAREER NOTES: Selected as undergraduate by Utah Jazz in first round (third pick overall) of 1982 NBA Draft. . . . Draft rights traded by Jazz to Atlanta Hawks for John Drew, Freeman Williams and cash (September 2, 1982).

COLLEGIATE RECORD

NOTES: THE SPORTING NEWS All-America second team (1981, 1982).

Season Team	G	Min.	FGM	FGA	Pct.	FTM	FTA	Pct.	Reb.	Pts.	Avg.
79-80 —Georgia	16	508	135	257	.525	27	37	.730	104	297	18.6
80-81 —Georgia	31	1157	310	582	.533	112	149	.752	234	732	23.6
81-82 —Georgia	31	1083	278	526	.529	103	160	.644	250	659	21.3
Totals	78	2748	723	1365	.530	242	346	.699	588	1688	21.6

NBA REGULAR-SEASON RECORD

HONORS: All-NBA first team (1986). . . . All-NBA second team (1987, 1988, 1991). . . . All-NBA third team (1989). . . . NBA All-Rookie team (1983).

Season	Team	G	Min.	FGM	FGA	Pct.	FTM	FTA	Pct.	Off.	Def.	Tot.	Ast.	PF	Dq.	Stl.	Blk.	TO	Pts.	Avg.
82-83	Atlanta	82	2697	601	1220	.493	230	337	.682	226	252	478	129	210	1	84	63	180	1434	17.5
83-84	Atlanta	81	2961	684	1429	.479	382	496	.770	254	328	582	126	197	1	117	87	215	1750	21.6
84-85	Atlanta	81	3023	853	*1891	.451	486	603	.806	226	331	557	200	170	0	135	54	225	2217	27.4
85-86	Atlanta	78	3049	888	*1897	.468	577	705	.818	261	357	618	206	170	0	138	49	251	2366	*30.3
86-87	Atlanta	79	2969	828	1787	.463	607	742	.818	210	284	494	261	149	0	117	51	215	2294	29.0
87-88	Atlanta	78	2948	909	1957	.464	541	655	.826	211	291	502	224	162	0	103	47	218	2397	30.7
88-89	Atlanta	80	2997	814	1756	.464	442	524	.844	256	297	553	211	138	0	117	52	181	2099	26.2
89-90	Atlanta	80	2888	810	1672	.484	459	569	.807	217	304	521	200	141	0	126	47	174	2138	26.7
90-91	Atlanta	81	3078	770	1640	.470	476	574	.829	261	471	732	265	156	0	123	65	201	2101	25.9
91-92	Atlanta	42	1601	424	914	.464	294	352	.835	103	192	295	158	77	0	52	24	122	1179	28.1
Totals		762	28211	7581	16163	.469	4494	5557	.809	2225	3107	5332	1980	1570	2	1112	539	1982	19975	26.2

Three-point field goals: 1982-83, 2-for-11 (.182). 1983-84, 0-for-11. 1984-85, 25-for-81 (.309). 1985-86, 13-for-70 (.186). 1986-87, 31-for-106 (.292). 1987-88, 38-for-129 (.295). 1988-89, 29-for-105 (.276). 1989-90, 59-for-183 (.322). 1990-91, 85-for-249 (.341). 1991-92, 37-for-128 (.289). Totals, 319-for-1073 (.297).

NBA PLAYOFF RECORD

Season	Team	G	Min.	FGM	FGA	Pct.	FTM	FTA	Pct.	Off.	Def.	Tot.	Ast.	PF	Dq.	Stl.	Blk.	TO	Pts.	Avg.
82-83	Atlanta	3	109	17	42	.405	12	14	.857	8	7	15	1	9	0	2	1	10	47	15.7
83-84	Atlanta	5	197	35	84	.417	26	31	.839	21	20	41	11	13	0	12	1	15	96	19.2
85-86	Atlanta	9	360	94	217	.433	68	79	.861	20	34	54	25	24	0	9	2	30	257	28.6
86-87	Atlanta	9	360	86	210	.410	66	74	.892	27	43	70	25	25	0	16	8	26	241	26.8
87-88	Atlanta	12	473	137	300	.457	96	125	.768	37	40	77	34	24	0	16	6	30	374	31.2
88-89	Atlanta	5	212	52	116	.448	27	38	.711	10	17	27	17	5	0	4	8	12	136	27.2
90-91	Atlanta	5	195	35	94	.372	32	35	.914	6	26	32	13	8	0	9	5	11	104	20.8
Totals		48	1906	456	1063	.429	327	396	.826	129	187	316	126	108	0	68	31	134	1255	26.1

Three-point field goals: 1982-83, 1-for-1. 1983-84, 0-for-1. 1985-86, 1-for-5 (.200). 1986-87, 3-for-10 (.300). 1987-88, 4-for-18 (.222). 1988-89, 5-for-17 (.294). 1990-91, 2-for-15 (.133). Totals, 16-for-67 (.239).

NBA ALL-STAR GAME RECORD

Season	Team	Min.	FGM	FGA	Pct.	FTM	FTA	Pct.	Off.	Def.	Tot.	Ast.	PF	Dq.	Stl.	Blk.	TO	Pts.
1986	Atlanta	17	6	15	.400	1	2	.500	2	1	3	2	2	0	0	1	1	13
1987	Atlanta	24	3	9	.333	4	7	.571	3	2	5	1	2	0	1	2	0	10
1988	Atlanta	30	12	22	.545	5	6	.833	1	4	5	0	3	0	0	1	0	29
1989	Atlanta	15	3	8	.375	3	3	1.000	1	1	2	0	0	0	3	0	2	9
1990	Atlanta	16	5	10	.500	2	2	1.000	0	0	0	4	1	0	1	0	0	13
1991	Atlanta	22	3	11	.273	6	8	.750	3	0	3	4	2	0	1	1	2	12
Totals		124	32	75	.427	21	28	.750	10	8	18	11	10	0	5	4	7	86

Three-point field goals: 1990, 1-for-1. 1991, 0-for-2. Totals, 1-for-3 (.333).

WILKINS, GERALD
G, KNICKS

PERSONAL: Born September 11, 1963, in Atlanta.... 6-6/210.... Full name: Gerald Bernard Wilkins.... Brother of Dominique Wilkins, forward with Atlanta Hawks.
HIGH SCHOOL: Mays (Atlanta).
COLLEGE: Moberly Area Junior College (Mo.), then Tennessee-Chattanooga.
TRANSACTIONS/CAREER NOTES: Selected by New York Knicks in second round (47th pick overall) of 1985 NBA Draft.

COLLEGIATE RECORD

Season	Team	G	Min.	FGM	FGA	Pct.	FTM	FTA	Pct.	Reb.	Pts.	Avg.
81-82	Moberly Area Junior College	39	1340	312	566	.551	97	126	.770	229	721	18.5
82-83	UT-Chattanooga	30	...	169	350	.483	41	62	.661	113	379	12.6
83-84	UT-Chattanooga	23	737	161	297	.542	73	105	.695	92	398	17.3
84-85	UT-Chattanooga	32	1188	276	532	.519	120	190	.632	147	672	21.0
Junior college totals		39	1340	312	566	.551	97	126	.770	229	721	18.5
Four-year-college totals		85	...	606	1179	.514	234	357	.655	352	1449	17.0

Three-point field goals: 1982-83, 0-for-2. 1983-84, 3-for-10 (.300). Totals, 3-for-12 (.250).

NBA REGULAR-SEASON RECORD

Season	Team	G	Min.	FGM	FGA	Pct.	FTM	FTA	Pct.	Off.	Def.	Tot.	Ast.	PF	Dq.	Stl.	Blk.	TO	Pts.	Avg.
85-86	New York	81	2025	437	934	.468	132	237	.557	92	116	208	161	155	0	68	9	157	1013	12.5
86-87	New York	80	2758	633	1302	.486	235	335	.701	120	174	294	354	165	0	88	18	214	1527	19.1
87-88	New York	81	2703	591	1324	.446	191	243	.786	106	164	270	326	183	1	90	22	212	1412	17.4
88-89	New York	81	2414	462	1025	.451	186	246	.756	95	149	244	274	166	1	115	22	169	1161	14.3
89-90	New York	82	2609	472	1032	.457	208	259	.803	133	238	371	330	188	0	95	21	194	1191	14.5
90-91	New York	68	2164	380	804	.473	169	206	.820	78	129	207	275	181	0	82	23	161	938	13.8
91-92	New York	82	2344	431	964	.447	116	159	.730	74	132	206	219	195	4	76	17	113	1016	12.4
Totals		555	17017	3406	7385	.461	1237	1685	.734	698	1102	1800	1939	1233	6	614	132	1220	8258	14.9

Three-point field goals: 1985-86, 7-for-25 (.280). 1986-87, 26-for-74 (.351). 1987-88, 39-for-129 (.302). 1988-89, 51-for-172 (.297). 1989-90, 39-for-125 (.312). 1990-91, 9-for-43 (.209). 1991-92, 38-for-108 (.352). Totals, 209-for-676 (.309).

NBA PLAYOFF RECORD

Season	Team	G	Min.	FGM	FGA	Pct.	FTM	FTA	Pct.	Off.	Def.	Tot.	Ast.	PF	Dq.	Stl.	Blk.	TO	Pts.	Avg.
87-88	New York	4	149	33	69	.478	12	14	.857	1	7	8	19	12	0	4	0	11	80	20.0
88-89	New York	9	290	63	131	.481	18	23	.783	9	24	33	42	27	1	12	3	22	145	16.1
89-90	New York	10	319	63	137	.460	18	22	.818	14	22	36	52	23	0	14	1	18	146	14.6

Season Team	G	Min.	FGM	FGA	Pct.	FTM	FTA	Pct.	Off.	Def.	Tot.	Ast.	PF	Dq.	Stl.	Blk.	TO	Pts.	Avg.
									— REBOUNDS —										
90-91—New York	3	78	14	38	.368	2	2	1.000	2	6	8	5	11	0	5	1	8	32	10.7
91-92—New York	12	344	45	109	.413	16	23	.696	12	18	30	34	35	0	5	1	15	107	8.9
Totals	38	1180	218	484	.450	66	84	.786	38	77	115	152	108	1	40	6	74	510	13.4

Three-point field goals: 1987-88, 2-for-4 (.500). 1988-89, 1-for-10 (.100). 1989-90, 2-for-8 (.250). 1990-91, 2-for-7 (.286). 1991-92, 1-for-13 (.077). Totals, 8-for-42 (.190).

WILLIAMS, BRIAN
F/C, MAGIC

PERSONAL: Born April 6, 1969, in Fresno, Calif. . . . 6-11/242. . . . Full name: Brian Carson Williams.
HIGH SCHOOL: Bishop Gorman (Las Vegas), then Santa Monica (Calif.).
COLLEGE: Maryland, then Arizona.
TRANSACTIONS/CAREER NOTES: Selected by Orlando Magic in first round (10th pick overall) of 1991 NBA Draft.

COLLEGIATE RECORD

Season Team	G	Min.	FGM	FGA	Pct.	FTM	FTA	Pct.	Reb.	Pts.	Avg.
87-88—Maryland	29	813	156	260	.600	51	76	.671	173	363	12.5
88-89—Arizona					Did not play—transfer student.						
89-90—Arizona	32	693	130	235	.553	80	110	.727	181	340	10.6
90-91—Arizona	35	878	195	315	.619	99	147	.673	273	489	14.0
Totals	96	2384	481	810	.594	230	333	.691	627	1192	12.4

Three-point field goals: 1989-90, 0-for-1.

NBA REGULAR-SEASON RECORD

Season Team	G	Min.	FGM	FGA	Pct.	FTM	FTA	Pct.	Off.	Def.	Tot.	Ast.	PF	Dq.	Stl.	Blk.	TO	Pts.	Avg.
									— REBOUNDS —										
91-92—Orlando	48	905	171	324	.528	95	142	.669	115	157	272	33	139	2	41	53	86	437	9.1

WILLIAMS, BUCK
F, TRAIL BLAZERS

PERSONAL: Born March 8, 1960, in Rocky Mount, N.C. . . . 6-8/225. . . . Full name: Charles Linwood Williams.
HIGH SCHOOL: Rocky Mount (N.C.).
COLLEGE: Maryland.
TRANSACTIONS/CAREER NOTES: Selected as undergraduate by New Jersey Nets in first round (third pick overall) of 1981 NBA Draft. . . . Traded by Nets to Portland Trail Blazers for Sam Bowie and 1989 first-round draft choice (June 24, 1989).
MISCELLANEOUS: Member of U.S. Olympic team (1980).

COLLEGIATE RECORD

Season Team	G	Min.	FGM	FGA	Pct.	FTM	FTA	Pct.	Reb.	Pts.	Avg.
78-79—Maryland	30	. . .	120	206	.583	60	109	.550	323	300	10.0
79-80—Maryland	24	. . .	143	236	.606	85	128	.664	242	371	15.5
80-81—Maryland	31	1080	183	283	.647	116	182	.637	363	482	15.5
Totals	85	. . .	446	725	.615	261	419	.623	928	1153	13.6

NBA REGULAR-SEASON RECORD

HONORS: NBA Rookie of the Year (1982). . . . All-NBA second team (1983). . . . NBA All-Defensive first team (1990, 1991). . . . NBA All-Defensive second team (1988, 1992). . . . NBA All-Rookie team (1982).

Season Team	G	Min.	FGM	FGA	Pct.	FTM	FTA	Pct.	Off.	Def.	Tot.	Ast.	PF	Dq.	Stl.	Blk.	TO	Pts.	Avg.
									— REBOUNDS —										
81-82—New Jersey ..	82	2825	513	881	.582	242	388	.624	347	658	1005	107	285	5	84	84	235	1268	15.5
82-83—New Jersey ..	82	2961	536	912	.588	324	523	.620	365	662	1027	125	270	4	91	110	246	1396	17.0
83-84—New Jersey ..	81	3003	495	926	.535	284	498	.570	*355	645	1000	130	298	3	81	125	237	1274	15.7
84-85—New Jersey ..	82	*3182	577	1089	.530	336	538	.625	323	682	1005	167	293	7	63	110	238	1491	18.2
85-86—New Jersey ..	82	3070	500	956	.523	301	445	.676	329	657	986	131	294	9	73	96	244	1301	15.9
86-87—New Jersey ..	82	2976	521	936	.557	430	588	.731	322	701	1023	129	315	8	78	91	280	1472	18.0
87-88—New Jersey ..	70	2637	466	832	.560	346	518	.668	298	536	834	109	266	5	68	44	189	1279	18.3
88-89—New Jersey ..	74	2446	373	702	.531	213	320	.666	249	447	696	78	223	0	61	36	142	959	13.0
89-90—Portland	82	2801	413	754	.548	288	408	.706	250	550	800	116	285	4	69	39	168	1114	13.6
90-91—Portland	80	2582	358	595	*.602	217	308	.705	227	524	751	97	247	2	47	47	137	933	11.7
91-92—Portland	80	2519	340	563	*.604	221	293	.754	260	444	704	108	244	4	62	41	130	901	11.3
Totals	877	31002	5092	9146	.557	3202	4827	.663	3325	6506	9831	1297	3020	51	777	823	2246	13388	15.3

Three-point field goals: 1981-82, 0-for-1. 1982-83, 0-for-4. 1983-84, 0-for-4. 1984-85, 1-for-4 (.250). 1985-86, 0-for-2. 1986-87, 0-for-1. 1987-88, 1-for-1. 1988-89, 0-for-3. 1989-90, 0-for-1. 1991-92, 0-for-1. Totals, 2-for-22 (.091).

NBA PLAYOFF RECORD

Season Team	G	Min.	FGM	FGA	Pct.	FTM	FTA	Pct.	Off.	Def.	Tot.	Ast.	PF	Dq.	Stl.	Blk.	TO	Pts.	Avg.
									— REBOUNDS —										
81-82—New Jersey ..	2	79	14	26	.538	7	15	.467	11	10	21	3	7	0	1	2	4	35	17.5
82-83—New Jersey ..	2	85	11	22	.500	16	20	.800	9	14	23	4	12	2	2	5	38	19.0
83-84—New Jersey ..	11	473	63	130	.485	45	81	.556	57	98	155	16	44	2	15	17	29	171	15.5
84-85—New Jersey ..	3	123	26	40	.650	22	30	.733	14	18	32	1	12	0	3	5	6	74	24.7
85-86—New Jersey ..	3	126	21	29	.724	20	26	.769	12	19	31	2	15	1	6	1	6	62	20.7
89-90—Portland	21	776	101	199	.508	71	105	.676	67	126	193	39	74	1	13	6	41	273	13.0
90-91—Portland	16	572	65	130	.500	35	58	.603	53	90	143	14	55	1	10	4	24	165	10.3
91-92—Portland	21	758	66	130	.508	69	91	.758	61	118	179	22	73	1	27	17	45	201	9.6
Totals	79	2992	367	706	.520	285	426	.669	284	493	777	101	292	8	77	54	160	1019	12.9

W

NBA ALL-STAR GAME RECORD

								— REBOUNDS —									
Season	Team	Min.	FGM	FGA	Pct.	FTM	FTA	Pct.	Off.	Def.	Tot.	Ast.	PF	Dq.	Stl.	Blk.	TO	Pts.
1982	—New Jersey	22	2	7	.286	0	2	.000	1	9	10	1	3	0	0	2	3	4
1983	—New Jersey	19	3	4	.750	2	4	.500	3	4	7	1	0	0	1	0	0	8
1986	—New Jersey	20	5	8	.625	3	5	.600	3	4	7	4	0	0	0	0	1	13
	Totals	61	10	19	.526	5	11	.455	7	17	24	6	3	0	1	2	4	25

WILLIAMS, HERB
C/F, MAVERICKS

PERSONAL: Born February 16, 1958, in Columbus, O. . . . 6-11/260. . . . Full name: Herbert L. Williams.
HIGH SCHOOL: Marion Franklin (Columbus, O.).
COLLEGE: Ohio State.
TRANSACTIONS/CAREER NOTES: Selected by Indiana Pacers in first round (14th pick overall) of 1981 NBA Draft. . . . Traded by Pacers to Dallas Mavericks for Detlef Schrempf and 1990 or 1991 second-round draft choice (February 21, 1989).

COLLEGIATE RECORD

Season	Team	G	Min.	FGM	FGA	Pct.	FTM	FTA	Pct.	Reb.	Pts.	Avg.
77-78	—Ohio State	27	992	196	407	.482	60	91	.659	308	452	16.7
78-79	—Ohio State	31	1212	253	483	.524	111	166	.669	325	617	19.9
79-80	—Ohio State	29	1069	206	415	.496	97	147	.660	263	509	17.6
80-81	—Ohio State	27	1020	179	368	.486	75	109	.688	215	433	16.0
	Totals	114	4293	834	1673	.499	343	513	.669	1111	2011	17.6

NBA REGULAR-SEASON RECORD

									— REBOUNDS —										
Season	Team	G	Min.	FGM	FGA	Pct.	FTM	FTA	Pct.	Off.	Def.	Tot.	Ast.	PF	Dq.	Stl.	Blk.	TO	Pts.	Avg.
81-82	—Indiana........	82	2277	407	854	.477	126	188	.670	175	430	605	139	200	0	53	178	137	942	11.5
82-83	—Indiana........	78	2513	580	1163	.499	155	220	.705	151	432	583	262	230	4	54	171	229	1315	16.9
83-84	—Indiana........	69	2279	411	860	.478	207	295	.702	154	400	554	215	193	4	60	108	207	1029	14.9
84-85	—Indiana........	75	2557	575	1211	.475	224	341	.657	154	480	634	252	218	1	54	134	265	1375	18.3
85-86	—Indiana........	78	2770	627	1275	.492	294	403	.730	172	538	710	174	244	2	50	184	210	1549	19.9
86-87	—Indiana........	74	2526	451	939	.480	199	269	.740	143	400	543	174	255	9	59	93	145	1101	14.9
87-88	—Indiana........	75	1966	311	732	.425	126	171	.737	116	353	469	98	244	1	37	146	119	748	10.0
88-89	—Ind.-Dallas ...	76	2470	322	739	.436	133	194	.686	135	458	593	124	236	5	46	134	149	777	10.2
89-90	—Dallas........	81	2199	295	665	.444	108	159	.670	76	315	391	119	243	4	51	106	106	700	8.6
90-91	—Dallas........	60	1832	332	655	.507	83	130	.638	86	271	357	95	197	3	30	88	113	747	12.5
91-92	—Dallas...........	75	2040	367	851	.431	124	171	.725	106	348	454	94	189	2	35	98	114	859	11.5
	Totals	823	25429	4678	9944	.470	1779	2541	.700	1468	4425	5893	1746	2449	35	529	1440	1794	11142	13.5

Three-point field goals: 1981-82, 2-for-7 (.286). 1982-83, 0-for-7. 1983-84, 0-for-4. 1984-85, 1-for-9 (.111). 1985-86, 1-for-12 (.083). 1986-87, 0-for-9. 1987-88, 0-for-6. 1988-89, 0-for-5. 1989-90, 2-for-9 (.222). 1990-91, 0-for-4. 1991-92, 1-for-6 (.167). Totals, 7-for-78 (.090).

NBA PLAYOFF RECORD

									— REBOUNDS —										
Season	Team	G	Min.	FGM	FGA	Pct.	FTM	FTA	Pct.	Off.	Def.	Tot.	Ast.	PF	Dq.	Stl.	Blk.	TO	Pts.	Avg.
86-87	—Indiana........	4	134	20	34	.588	7	13	.538	3	17	20	7	12	0	0	1	11	47	11.8
89-90	—Dallas..........	3	81	14	23	.609	13	16	.813	4	9	13	5	16	1	1	2	3	41	13.7
	Totals	7	215	34	57	.596	20	29	.690	7	26	33	12	28	1	1	3	14	88	12.6

WILLIAMS, JAYSON
F, 76ERS

PERSONAL: Born February 22, 1968, in Ritter, S.C. . . . 6-10/240.
HIGH SCHOOL: Christ The King (Queens, N.Y.).
COLLEGE: St. John's.
TRANSACTIONS/CAREER NOTES: Selected by Phoenix Suns in first round (21st pick overall) of 1990 NBA Draft. . . . Draft rights traded by Suns to Philadelphia 76ers for 1993 first-round draft choice (October 28, 1990).

W

COLLEGIATE RECORD

Season	Team	G	Min.	FGM	FGA	Pct.	FTM	FTA	Pct.	Reb.	Pts.	Avg.
86-87	—St. John's...............................					Did not play—ineligible.						
87-88	—St. John's...............................	28	662	102	199	.513	72	120	.600	143	276	9.9
88-89	—St. John's...............................	31	1036	236	412	.573	134	191	.702	246	606	19.5
89-90	—St. John's...............................	13	377	70	131	.534	49	80	.613	101	190	14.6
	Totals	72	2075	408	742	.550	255	391	.652	490	1072	14.9

Three-point field goals: 1988-89, 0-for-2. 1989-90, 1-for-2 (.500). Totals, 1-for-4 (.250).

NBA REGULAR-SEASON RECORD

									— REBOUNDS —										
Season	Team	G	Min.	FGM	FGA	Pct.	FTM	FTA	Pct.	Off.	Def.	Tot.	Ast.	PF	Dq.	Stl.	Blk.	TO	Pts.	Avg.
90-91	—Philadelphia.	52	508	72	161	.447	37	56	.661	41	70	111	16	92	1	9	6	40	182	3.5
91-92	—Philadelphia.	50	646	75	206	.364	56	88	.636	62	83	145	12	110	1	20	20	44	206	4.1
	Totals	102	1154	147	367	.401	93	144	.646	103	153	256	28	202	2	29	26	84	388	3.8

Three-point field goals: 1990-91, 1-for-2 (.500).

NBA PLAYOFF RECORD

									— REBOUNDS —										
Season	Team	G	Min.	FGM	FGA	Pct.	FTM	FTA	Pct.	Off.	Def.	Tot.	Ast.	PF	Dq.	Stl.	Blk.	TO	Pts.	Avg.
90-91	—Philadelphia.	4	10	4	5	.800	0	0	. . .	2	2	4	0	1	0	0	0	1	8	2.0

WILLIAMS, JOHN
F/C, CAVALIERS

PERSONAL: Born August 9, 1962, in Sorrento, La. . . . 6-11/245. . . . Nickname: Hot Rod.
HIGH SCHOOL: St. Amant (La.).
COLLEGE: Tulane.

TRANSACTIONS/CAREER NOTES: Selected by Cleveland Cavaliers in second round (45th pick overall) of 1985 NBA Draft. . . . Played in United States Basketball League with Rhode Island (1985) and Staten Island (1986).

COLLEGIATE RECORD

Season Team	G	Min.	FGM	FGA	Pct.	FTM	FTA	Pct.	Reb.	Pts.	Avg.
81-82 — Tulane	28	932	163	279	.584	88	133	.662	202	414	14.8
82-83 — Tulane	31	996	151	317	.476	83	118	.703	166	385	12.4
83-84 — Tulane	28	1038	202	355	.569	140	184	.761	222	544	19.4
84-85 — Tulane	28	1006	189	334	.566	120	155	.774	219	498	17.8
Totals	115	3972	705	1285	.549	431	590	.731	809	1841	16.0

NBA REGULAR-SEASON RECORD

HONORS: NBA All-Rookie team (1987).

Season Team	G	Min.	FGM	FGA	Pct.	FTM	FTA	Pct.	Off.	Def.	Tot.	Ast.	PF	Dq.	Stl.	Blk.	TO	Pts.	Avg.
86-87 — Cleveland	80	2714	435	897	.485	298	400	.745	222	407	629	154	197	0	58	167	139	1168	14.6
87-88 — Cleveland	77	2106	316	663	.477	211	279	.756	159	347	506	103	203	2	61	145	104	843	10.9
88-89 — Cleveland	82	2125	356	700	.509	235	314	.748	173	304	477	108	188	1	77	134	102	948	11.6
89-90 — Cleveland	82	2776	528	1070	.493	325	440	.739	220	443	663	168	214	2	86	167	143	1381	16.8
90-91 — Cleveland	43	1293	199	430	.463	107	164	.652	111	179	290	100	126	2	36	69	63	505	11.7
91-92 — Cleveland	80	2432	341	678	.503	270	359	.752	228	379	607	196	191	2	60	182	83	952	11.9
Totals	444	13446	2175	4438	.490	1446	1956	.739	1113	2059	3172	829	1119	9	378	864	634	5797	13.1

Three-point field goals: 1986-87, 0-for-1. 1987-88, 0-for-1. 1988-89, 1-for-4 (.250). 1990-91, 0-for-1. 1991-92, 0-for-4. Totals, 1-for-11 (.091).

NBA PLAYOFF RECORD

Season Team	G	Min.	FGM	FGA	Pct.	FTM	FTA	Pct.	Off.	Def.	Tot.	Ast.	PF	Dq.	Stl.	Blk.	TO	Pts.	Avg.
87-88 — Cleveland	5	133	20	40	.500	6	13	.462	13	16	29	4	13	0	3	7	4	46	9.2
88-89 — Cleveland	5	161	21	45	.467	13	18	.722	7	27	34	10	12	0	2	7	11	55	11.0
89-90 — Cleveland	5	174	39	70	.557	17	22	.773	14	32	46	11	23	1	2	5	7	95	19.0
91-92 — Cleveland	17	567	84	154	.545	87	109	.798	50	80	130	42	58	2	24	17	31	255	15.0
Totals	32	1035	164	309	.531	123	162	.759	84	155	239	67	106	3	31	36	53	451	14.1

WILLIAMS, JOHN
F, BULLETS

PERSONAL: Born October 26, 1966, in Los Angeles. . . . 6-9/260. . . . Full name: John Sam Williams.
HIGH SCHOOL: Crenshaw (Los Angeles).
COLLEGE: Louisiana State.

TRANSACTIONS/CAREER NOTES: Selected as undergraduate by Washington Bullets in first round (12th pick overall) of 1986 NBA Draft. . . . Suspended by Bullets for 1991-92 season.

COLLEGIATE RECORD

Season Team	G	Min.	FGM	FGA	Pct.	FTM	FTA	Pct.	Reb.	Pts.	Avg.
84-85 — Louisiana State	29	935	163	305	.534	62	81	.765	190	388	13.4
85-86 — Louisiana State	37	1277	269	540	.498	120	155	.774	313	658	17.8
Totals	66	2212	432	845	.511	182	236	.771	503	1046	15.8

NBA REGULAR-SEASON RECORD

Season Team	G	Min.	FGM	FGA	Pct.	FTM	FTA	Pct.	Off.	Def.	Tot.	Ast.	PF	Dq.	Stl.	Blk.	TO	Pts.	Avg.
86-87 — Washington	78	1773	283	624	.454	144	223	.646	130	236	366	191	173	1	129	30	122	718	9.2
87-88 — Washington	82	2428	427	910	.469	188	256	.734	127	317	444	232	217	3	117	34	145	1047	12.8
88-89 — Washington	82	2413	438	940	.466	225	290	.776	158	415	573	356	213	1	142	70	157	1120	13.7
89-90 — Washington	18	632	130	274	.474	65	84	.774	27	109	136	84	33	0	21	9	43	327	18.2
90-91 — Washington	33	941	164	393	.417	73	97	.753	42	135	177	133	63	0	39	6	68	411	12.5
91-92 — Washington								Did not play — suspended.											
Totals	293	8187	1442	3141	.459	695	950	.732	484	1212	1696	996	699	5	448	149	535	3623	12.4

Three-point field goals: 1986-87, 8-for-36 (.222). 1987-88, 5-for-38 (.132). 1988-89, 19-for-71 (.268). 1989-90, 2-for-18 (.111). 1990-91, 10-for-41 (.244). Totals, 44-for-204 (.216).

NBA PLAYOFF RECORD

Season Team	G	Min.	FGM	FGA	Pct.	FTM	FTA	Pct.	Off.	Def.	Tot.	Ast.	PF	Dq.	Stl.	Blk.	TO	Pts.	Avg.
86-87 — Washington	3	49	8	14	.571	4	7	.571	4	7	11	2	3	0	2	0	2	20	6.7
87-88 — Washington	5	185	23	48	.479	19	32	.594	11	18	29	21	18	1	8	4	12	65	13.0
Totals	8	234	31	62	.500	23	39	.590	15	25	40	23	21	1	10	4	14	85	10.6

Three-point field goals: 1986-87, 0-for-1. 1987-88, 0-for-1. Totals, 0-for-2.

DID YOU KNOW. . .

. . . that Chris Mullin has led the NBA in minutes played in each of the last two seasons?

WILLIAMS, KENNY
F, PACERS

PERSONAL: Born June 9, 1969, in Elizabeth City, N.C. .... 6-9/ 205.... Full name: Kenneth Ray Williams.
HIGH SCHOOL: Northeastern (Elizabeth City, N.C.).
COLLEGE: Barton County Community College (Kan.), then Elizabeth City State (N.C.).
TRANSACTIONS/CAREER NOTES: Selected by Indiana Pacers in second round (46th pick overall) of 1990 NBA Draft.

COLLEGIATE RECORD

Season Team	G	Min.	FGM	FGA	Pct.	FTM	FTA	Pct.	Reb.	Pts.	Avg.
88-89 —Barton County C.C.	31	...	...	...	...	...	...	...	278	636	20.5
89-90 —Elizabeth City State					Did not play.						
Junior college totals	31	...	...	...	...	...	...	...	278	636	20.5
Four-year-college totals											

NBA REGULAR-SEASON RECORD

Season Team	G	Min.	FGM	FGA	Pct.	FTM	FTA	Pct.	Off.	Def.	Tot.	Ast.	PF	Dq.	Stl.	Blk.	TO	Pts.	Avg.
90-91 —Indiana	75	527	93	179	.520	34	50	.680	56	75	131	31	81	0	11	31	41	220	2.9
91-92 —Indiana	60	565	113	218	.518	26	43	.605	64	65	129	40	99	0	20	41	22	252	4.2
Totals	135	1092	206	397	.519	60	93	.645	120	140	260	71	180	0	31	72	63	472	3.5

Three-point field goals: 1990-91, 0-for-3. 1991-92, 0-for-4. Totals, 0-for-7.

NBA PLAYOFF RECORD

Season Team	G	Min.	FGM	FGA	Pct.	FTM	FTA	Pct.	Off.	Def.	Tot.	Ast.	PF	Dq.	Stl.	Blk.	TO	Pts.	Avg.
90-91 —Indiana	2	2	0	0	...	0	2	.000	0	0	0	0	1	0	0	0	0	0	0.0
91-92 —Indiana	1	1	0	0	...	0	0	...	0	0	0	0	0	0	1	0	0	0	0.0
Totals	3	3	0	0	...	0	2	.000	0	0	0	0	1	0	1	0	0	0	0.0

WILLIAMS, MICHEAL
G, TIMBERWOLVES

PERSONAL: Born July 23, 1966, in Dallas. .... 6-2/175. .... Full name: Micheal Douglas Williams.
HIGH SCHOOL: David Carter (Dallas).
COLLEGE: Baylor.
TRANSACTIONS/CAREER NOTES: Selected by Detroit Pistons in second round (48th pick overall) of 1988 NBA Draft. ... Traded by Pistons with draft rights to Kenny Battle to Phoenix Suns for draft rights to Anthony Cook (June 27, 1989). ... Waived by Suns (December 12, 1989). ... Signed as free agent by Dallas Mavericks (December 14, 1989). ... Waived by Mavericks (December 26, 1989). ... Played in Continental Basketball Association with Rapid City Thrillers (1989-90). ... Signed by Charlotte Hornets to first of two consecutive 10-day contracts (March 13, 1990). ... Re-signed by Hornets for remainder of season (April 2, 1990). ... Signed as free agent by Indiana Pacers (August 7, 1990). ... Traded by Pacers with Chuck Person to Minnesota Timberwolves for Pooh Richardson and Sam Mitchell (September 8, 1992).
MISCELLANEOUS: Member of NBA championship team (1989).

COLLEGIATE RECORD

Season Team	G	Min.	FGM	FGA	Pct.	FTM	FTA	Pct.	Reb.	Pts.	Avg.
84-85 —Baylor	28	787	149	306	.487	111	140	.793	66	409	14.6
85-86 —Baylor	22	...	104	225	.462	79	98	.806	63	287	13.0
86-87 —Baylor	31	1112	188	396	.475	137	192	.714	94	534	17.2
87-88 —Baylor	34	1262	216	428	.505	161	231	.697	108	625	18.4
Totals	115	...	657	1355	.485	488	661	.738	331	1855	16.1

Three-point field goals: 1986-87, 21-for-67 (.313). 1987-88, 32-for-85 (.376). Totals, 53-for-152 (.349).

NBA REGULAR-SEASON RECORD

HONORS: NBA All-Defensive second team (1992).

Season Team	G	Min.	FGM	FGA	Pct.	FTM	FTA	Pct.	Off.	Def.	Tot.	Ast.	PF	Dq.	Stl.	Blk.	TO	Pts.	Avg.
88-89 —Detroit	49	358	47	129	.364	31	47	.660	9	18	27	70	44	0	13	3	42	127	2.6
89-90 —Phoe.-Char..	28	329	60	119	.504	36	46	.783	12	20	32	81	39	0	22	1	33	156	5.6
90-91 —Indiana	73	1706	261	523	.499	290	330	.879	49	127	176	348	202	1	150	17	150	813	11.1
91-92 —Indiana	79	2750	404	824	.490	372	427	.871	73	209	282	647	262	7	233	22	240	1188	15.0
Totals	229	5143	772	1595	.484	729	850	.858	143	374	517	1146	547	8	418	43	465	2284	10.0

Three-point field goals: 1988-89, 2-for-9 (.222). 1989-90, 0-for-3. 1990-91, 1-for-7 (.143). 1991-92, 8-for-33 (.242). Totals, 11-for-52 (.212).

NBA PLAYOFF RECORD

Season Team	G	Min.	FGM	FGA	Pct.	FTM	FTA	Pct.	Off.	Def.	Tot.	Ast.	PF	Dq.	Stl.	Blk.	TO	Pts.	Avg.
88-89 —Detroit	4	6	0	0	...	2	2	1.000	1	1	2	2	1	0	1	0	0	2	0.5
90-91 —Indiana	5	183	30	65	.462	43	48	.896	7	9	16	42	23	2	14	0	12	103	20.6
91-92 —Indiana	3	106	18	43	.419	11	15	.733	1	7	8	24	12	0	9	0	7	50	16.7
Totals	12	295	48	108	.444	56	65	.862	9	17	26	68	36	2	24	0	19	155	12.9

Three-point field goals: 1990-91, 0-for-1. 1991-92, 3-for-9 (.333). Totals, 3-for-10 (.300).

CBA REGULAR-SEASON RECORD

Season Team	G	Min.	2-POINT FGM	FGA	Pct.	3-POINT FGM	FGA	Pct.	FTM	FTA	Pct.	Reb.	Ast.	Pts.	Avg.
89-90 —Rapid City	23	817	152	265	.574	0	7	.000	119	146	.815	94	184	423	18.4

W

WILLIAMS, REGGIE
F/G, NUGGETS

PERSONAL: Born March 5, 1964, in Baltimore. . . . 6-7/195.
HIGH SCHOOL: Dunbar (Baltimore).
COLLEGE: Georgetown.
TRANSACTIONS/CAREER NOTES: Selected by Los Angeles Clippers in first round (fourth pick overall) of 1987 NBA Draft. . . . Traded by Clippers with draft rights to Danny Ferry to Cleveland Cavaliers for Ron Harper, 1990 and 1992 first-round draft choices and 1991 second-round draft choice (November 16, 1989). . . . Waived by Cavaliers (February 26, 1990). . . . Signed by San Antonio Spurs for remainder of season (March 5, 1990). . . . Re-signed as free agent by Spurs (October 5, 1990). . . . Waived by Spurs (December 24, 1990). . . . Signed as free agent by Denver Nuggets (January 4, 1991).

COLLEGIATE RECORD

NOTES: THE SPORTING NEWS All-America first team (1987). . . . Member of NCAA Division I championship team (1984).

Season	Team	G	Min.	FGM	FGA	Pct.	FTM	FTA	Pct.	Reb.	Pts.	Avg.
83-84	Georgetown	37	764	130	300	.433	76	99	.768	131	336	9.1
84-85	Georgetown	35	1043	168	332	.506	80	106	.755	200	416	11.9
85-86	Georgetown	32	1013	227	430	.528	109	149	.732	261	563	17.6
86-87	Georgetown	34	1205	284	589	.482	156	194	.804	294	802	23.6
	Totals	138	4025	809	1651	.490	421	548	.768	886	2117	15.3

Three-point field goals: 1986-87, 78-for-202 (.386).

NBA REGULAR-SEASON RECORD

Season	Team	G	Min.	FGM	FGA	Pct.	FTM	FTA	Pct.	Off.	Def.	Tot.	Ast.	PF	Dq.	Stl.	Blk.	TO	Pts.	Avg.
87-88	L.A. Clippers	35	857	152	427	.356	48	66	.727	55	63	118	58	108	1	29	21	63	365	10.4
88-89	L.A. Clippers	63	1303	260	594	.438	92	122	.754	70	109	179	103	181	1	81	29	114	642	10.2
89-90	LAC-CI-SA..	47	743	131	338	.388	52	68	.765	28	55	83	53	102	2	32	14	45	320	6.8
90-91	S.A.-Denver	73	1896	384	855	.449	166	197	.843	133	173	306	133	253	9	113	41	112	991	13.6
91-92	Denver	81	2623	601	1277	.471	216	269	.803	145	260	405	235	270	4	148	68	173	1474	18.2
	Totals	299	7422	1528	3491	.438	574	722	.795	431	660	1091	582	914	17	403	173	507	3792	12.7

Three-point field goals: 1987-88, 13-for-58 (.224). 1988-89, 30-for-104 (.288). 1989-90, 6-for-37 (.162). 1990-91, 57-for-157 (.363). 1991-92, 56-for-156 (.359). Totals, 162-for-512 (.316).

NBA PLAYOFF RECORD

Season	Team	G	Min.	FGM	FGA	Pct.	FTM	FTA	Pct.	Off.	Def.	Tot.	Ast.	PF	Dq.	Stl.	Blk.	TO	Pts.	Avg.
89-90	San Antonio	9	49	9	27	.333	2	2	1.000	5	6	11	3	8	0	2	0	5	20	2.2

Three-point field goals: 1989-90, 0-for-2.

WILLIAMS, SCOTT
C, BULLS

PERSONAL: Born March 21, 1968, in Hacienda Heights, Calif. . . . 6-10/230.
HIGH SCHOOL: Woodrow Wilson (Los Angeles).
COLLEGE: North Carolina.
TRANSACTIONS/CAREER NOTES: Never drafted by an NBA franchise. . . . Signed as free agent by Chicago Bulls (July 20, 1990).
MISCELLANEOUS: Member of NBA championship teams (1991, 1992).

COLLEGIATE RECORD

Season	Team	G	Min.	FGM	FGA	Pct.	FTM	FTA	Pct.	Reb.	Pts.	Avg.
86-87	North Carolina	36	540	78	157	.497	43	77	.558	150	199	5.5
87-88	North Carolina	34	900	162	283	.572	107	159	.673	217	434	12.8
88-89	North Carolina	35	802	165	297	.556	68	104	.654	254	398	11.4
89-90	North Carolina	33	813	190	343	.554	96	156	.615	240	477	14.5
	Totals	138	3055	595	1080	.551	314	496	.633	861	1508	10.9

Three-point field goals: 1986-87, 0-for-1. 1987-88, 3-for-7 (.429). 1988-89, 0-for-2. 1989-90, 1-for-7 (.143). Totals, 4-for-17 (.235).

NBA REGULAR-SEASON RECORD

Season	Team	G	Min.	FGM	FGA	Pct.	FTM	FTA	Pct.	Off.	Def.	Tot.	Ast.	PF	Dq.	Stl.	Blk.	TO	Pts.	Avg.
90-91	Chicago	51	337	53	104	.510	20	28	.714	42	56	98	16	51	0	12	13	23	127	2.5
91-92	Chicago	63	690	83	172	.483	48	74	.649	90	157	247	50	122	0	13	36	35	214	3.4
	Totals	114	1027	136	276	.493	68	102	.667	132	213	345	66	173	0	25	49	58	341	3.0

Three-point field goals: 1990-91, 1-for-2 (.500). 1991-92, 0-for-3. Totals, 1-for-5 (.200).

NBA PLAYOFF RECORD

Season	Team	G	Min.	FGM	FGA	Pct.	FTM	FTA	Pct.	Off.	Def.	Tot.	Ast.	PF	Dq.	Stl.	Blk.	TO	Pts.	Avg.
90-91	Chicago	12	72	6	13	.462	11	20	.550	4	16	20	3	15	0	1	3	4	23	1.9
91-92	Chicago	22	321	34	70	.486	20	28	.714	33	62	95	7	65	0	6	18	15	88	4.0
	Totals	34	393	40	83	.482	31	48	.646	37	78	115	10	80	0	7	21	19	111	3.3

Three-point field goals: 1990-91, 0-for-1. 1991-92, 0-for-1. Totals, 0-for-2.

WILLIS, KEVIN
F/C, HAWKS

PERSONAL: Born September 6, 1962, in Los Angeles. . . . 7-0/240. . . . Full name: Kevin Alvin Willis.
HIGH SCHOOL: Pershing (Detroit).
COLLEGE: Jackson Community College (Mich.), then Michigan State.
TRANSACTIONS/CAREER NOTES: Selected by Atlanta Hawks in first round (11th pick overall) of 1984 NBA Draft.

COLLEGIATE RECORD

Season	Team	G	Min.	FGM	FGA	Pct.	FTM	FTA	Pct.	Reb.	Pts.	Avg.
80-81	Jackson Community College ...	...	...	...	...	...	...	...	...	...	...	19.0
81-82	Michigan State	27	518	73	154	.474	17	30	.567	113	163	6.0
82-83	Michigan State	27	865	162	272	.596	36	70	.514	258	360	13.3
83-84	Michigan State	25	738	118	240	.492	39	59	.661	192	275	11.0
	Junior college totals	...	...	...	...	...	...	...	...	...	...	19.0
	Four-year-college totals	79	2121	353	666	.530	92	159	.579	563	798	10.1

Three-point field goals: 1982-83, 0-for-1.

NBA REGULAR-SEASON RECORD

Season	Team	G	Min.	FGM	FGA	Pct.	FTM	FTA	Pct.	Off.	Def.	Tot.	Ast.	PF	Dq.	Stl.	Blk.	TO	Pts.	Avg.
84-85	Atlanta	82	1785	322	690	.467	119	181	.657	177	345	522	36	226	4	31	49	104	765	9.3
85-86	Atlanta	82	2300	419	511	.820	172	263	.654	243	461	704	45	294	6	66	44	177	1010	12.3
86-87	Atlanta	81	2626	538	1003	.536	227	320	.709	321	528	849	62	313	4	65	61	173	1304	16.1
87-88	Atlanta	75	2091	356	687	.518	159	245	.649	235	312	547	28	240	2	68	42	138	871	11.6
88-89	Atlanta						Did not play—injured.													12.4
89-90	Atlanta	81	2273	418	805	.519	168	246	.683	253	392	645	57	259	4	63	47	144	1006	12.4
90-91	Atlanta	80	2373	444	881	.504	159	238	.668	259	445	704	99	235	2	60	40	153	1051	13.1
91-92	Atlanta	81	2962	591	1224	.483	292	363	.804	418	840	1258	173	223	0	72	54	197	1480	18.3
	Totals	562	16410	3088	5801	.532	1296	1856	.698	1906	3323	5229	500	1790	22	425	337	1086	7487	13.3

Three-point field goals: 1984-85, 2-for-9 (.222). 1985-86, 0-for-6. 1986-87, 1-for-4 (.250). 1987-88, 0-for-2. 1989-90, 2-for-7 (.286). 1990-91, 4-for-10 (.400). 1991-92, 6-for-37 (.162). Totals, 15-for-75 (.200).

NBA PLAYOFF RECORD

Season	Team	G	Min.	FGM	FGA	Pct.	FTM	FTA	Pct.	Off.	Def.	Tot.	Ast.	PF	Dq.	Stl.	Blk.	TO	Pts.	Avg.
85-86	Atlanta	9	280	55	98	.561	15	23	.652	31	34	65	5	38	2	7	8	15	125	13.9
86-87	Atlanta	9	356	60	115	.522	21	31	.677	33	50	83	6	33	0	9	7	17	141	15.7
87-88	Atlanta	12	462	80	138	.580	34	50	.680	36	72	108	11	51	1	10	10	25	194	16.2
90-91	Atlanta	5	159	27	67	.403	21	30	.700	18	27	45	5	22	0	3	1	2	77	15.4
	Totals	35	1257	222	418	.531	91	134	.679	118	183	301	27	144	3	29	26	59	537	15.3

Three-point field goals: 1987-88, 0-for-1. 1990-91, 2-for-3 (.667). Totals, 2-for-4 (.500).

NBA ALL-STAR GAME RECORD

Season	Team	Min.	FGM	FGA	Pct.	FTM	FTA	Pct.	Off.	Def.	Tot.	Ast.	PF	Dq.	Stl.	Blk.	TO	Pts.
1992	Atlanta	14	4	10	.400	0	0	...	4	0	4	0	1	0	0	0	0	8

WINCHESTER, KENNARD
G

PERSONAL: Born September 3, 1966, in Chestertown, Md. ... 6-5/212. ... Full name: Kennard Norman Winchester Jr.
HIGH SCHOOL: Queen Anne's County (Centreville, Md.).
COLLEGE: James Madison, then Averett (Va.).
TRANSACTIONS/CAREER NOTES: Never drafted by an NBA franchise. ... Played with Club Atenas in Argentina (1989-90). ... Signed as free agent by Houston Rockets (September 11, 1990). ... Re-signed as restricted free agent by Rockets (June 28, 1991). ... Waived by Rockets (August 27, 1991). ... Signed as free agent by Boston Celtics (September 25, 1991). ... Waived by Celtics (October 30, 1991). ... Signed as free agent by Rockets (November 1, 1991). ... Waived by Rockets (November 11, 1991). ... Signed as free agent by New York Knicks (November 14, 1991).

COLLEGIATE RECORD

Season	Team	G	Min.	FGM	FGA	Pct.	FTM	FTA	Pct.	Reb.	Pts.	Avg.
85-86	James Madison	20	189	30	66	.455	5	18	.278	20	65	3.3
86-87	James Madison	30	896	167	329	.508	71	93	.763	171	407	13.6
87-88	James Madison	28	893	181	393	.461	66	86	.767	180	451	16.1
88-89	Averett	17	...	144	253	.569	53	74	.716	155	347	20.4
	Totals	95	...	522	1041	.501	195	271	.720	526	1270	13.4

Three-point field goals: 1986-87, 2-for-11 (.182). 1987-88, 23-for-79 (.291). 1988-89, 6-for-21 (.286). Totals, 31-for-111 (.279).

NBA REGULAR-SEASON RECORD

Season	Team	G	Min.	FGM	FGA	Pct.	FTM	FTA	Pct.	Off.	Def.	Tot.	Ast.	PF	Dq.	Stl.	Blk.	TO	Pts.	Avg.
90-91	Houston	64	607	98	245	.400	35	45	.778	34	33	67	25	70	0	16	13	30	239	3.7
91-92	Hou.-N.Y.	19	81	13	30	.433	8	10	.800	6	9	15	8	5	0	2	2	2	35	1.8
	Totals	83	688	111	275	.404	43	55	.782	40	42	82	33	75	0	18	15	32	274	3.3

Three-point field goals: 1990-91, 8-for-20 (.400). 1991-92, 1-for-2 (.500). Totals, 9-for-22 (.409).

NBA PLAYOFF RECORD

Season	Team	G	Min.	FGM	FGA	Pct.	FTM	FTA	Pct.	Off.	Def.	Tot.	Ast.	PF	Dq.	Stl.	Blk.	TO	Pts.	Avg.
91-92	New York	3	11	3	5	.600	0	1	.000	0	0	0	2	0	0	0	0	1	6	2.0

WINGATE, DAVID
G, BULLETS

PERSONAL: Born December 15, 1963, in Baltimore. ... 6-5/185. ... Full name: David Grover Stacey Wingate Jr.
HIGH SCHOOL: Dunbar (Baltimore).
COLLEGE: Georgetown.
TRANSACTIONS/CAREER NOTES: Selected by Philadelphia 76ers in second round (44th pick overall) of 1986 NBA Draft. ... Traded by 76ers with Maurice Cheeks and Christian Welp to San Antonio Spurs for Johnny

Dawkins and Jay Vincent (August 28, 1989). . . . Waived by Spurs (June 28, 1991). . . . Signed as free agent by Washington Bullets (September 30, 1991).

COLLEGIATE RECORD

NOTES: Member of NCAA Division I championship team (1984).

Season Team	G	Min.	FGM	FGA	Pct.	FTM	FTA	Pct.	Reb.	Pts.	Avg.
82-83 — Georgetown	32	855	149	335	.445	87	124	.702	95	385	12.0
83-84 — Georgetown	37	1005	161	370	.435	93	129	.721	135	415	11.2
84-85 — Georgetown	38	1128	191	395	.484	91	132	.689	135	473	12.4
85-86 — Georgetown	32	956	196	394	.497	117	155	.755	129	509	15.9
Totals	139	3944	697	1494	.467	388	540	.719	494	1782	12.8

NBA REGULAR-SEASON RECORD

Season Team	G	Min.	FGM	FGA	Pct.	FTM	FTA	Pct.	Off.	Def.	Tot.	Ast.	PF	Dq.	Stl.	Blk.	TO	Pts.	Avg.
86-87 — Philadelphia.	77	1612	259	602	.430	149	201	.741	70	86	156	155	169	1	93	19	128	680	8.8
87-88 — Philadelphia.	61	1419	218	545	.400	99	132	.750	44	57	101	119	125	0	47	22	104	545	8.9
88-89 — Philadelphia.	33	372	54	115	.470	27	34	.794	12	25	37	73	43	0	9	2	35	137	4.2
89-90 — San Antonio.	78	1856	220	491	.448	87	112	.777	62	133	195	208	154	2	89	18	127	527	6.8
90-91 — San Antonio.	25	563	53	138	.384	29	41	.707	24	51	75	46	66	0	19	5	42	136	5.4
91-92 — Washington .	81	2127	266	572	.465	105	146	.719	80	189	269	247	162	1	123	21	124	638	7.9
Totals	355	7949	1070	2463	.434	496	666	.745	292	541	833	848	719	4	380	87	560	2663	7.5

Three-point field goals: 1986-87, 13-for-52 (.250). 1987-88, 10-for-40 (.250). 1988-89, 2-for-6 (.333). 1989-90, 0-for-13. 1990-91, 1-for-9 (.111). 1991-92, 1-for-18 (.056). Totals, 27-for-138 (.196).

NBA PLAYOFF RECORD

Season Team	G	Min.	FGM	FGA	Pct.	FTM	FTA	Pct.	Off.	Def.	Tot.	Ast.	PF	Dq.	Stl.	Blk.	TO	Pts.	Avg.
86-87 — Philadelphia.	5	90	15	37	.405	9	14	.643	5	7	12	9	11	1	5	1	9	41	8.2
89-90 — San Antonio.	10	293	40	77	.519	9	12	.750	9	28	37	38	34	1	18	3	14	91	9.1
90-91 — San Antonio.	3	38	6	12	.500	2	3	.667	1	2	3	1	8	1	1	0	1	14	4.7
Totals	18	421	61	126	.484	20	29	.690	15	37	52	48	53	3	24	4	24	146	8.1

Three-point field goals: 1986-87, 2-for-2. 1989-90, 2-for-3 (.667). Totals, 4-for-5 (.800).

WITTMAN, RANDY
G, PACERS

PERSONAL: Born October 28, 1959, in Indianapolis. . . . 6-6/210. . . . Full name: Randy Scott Wittman.
HIGH SCHOOL: Ben Davis (Indianapolis).
COLLEGE: Indiana.

TRANSACTIONS/CAREER NOTES: Selected by Washington Bullets in first round (22nd pick overall) of 1983 NBA Draft. . . . Draft rights traded by Bullets to Atlanta Hawks for Tom McMillen and 1984 second-round draft choice (July 5, 1983). . . . Traded by Hawks with 1988 first-round draft choice to Sacramento Kings for Reggie Theus, 1988 third-round draft choice and future considerations (June 27, 1988). . . . Traded by Kings with LaSalle Thompson to Indiana Pacers for Wayman Tisdale and 1990 or 1991 second-round draft choice (February 20, 1989).

COLLEGIATE RECORD

NOTES: Suffered stress fracture of right ankle during 1979-80 season; granted extra year of eligibility. . . . Member of NCAA Division I championship team (1981).

Season Team	G	Min.	FGM	FGA	Pct.	FTM	FTA	Pct.	Reb.	Pts.	Avg.
78-79 — Indiana	34	...	101	190	.532	39	53	.736	90	241	7.1
79-80 — Indiana	5	...	13	28	.464	3	4	.750	7	29	5.8
80-81 — Indiana	35	...	155	286	.542	53	69	.768	79	363	10.4
81-82 — Indiana	29	...	144	299	.482	59	78	.756	94	347	12.0
82-83 — Indiana	30	...	236	435	.543	89	108	.824	135	569	19.0
Totals	133	...	649	1238	.524	243	312	.779	405	1549	11.6

Three-point field goals: 1982-83, 8-for-18 (.444).

NBA REGULAR-SEASON RECORD

Season Team	G	Min.	FGM	FGA	Pct.	FTM	FTA	Pct.	Off.	Def.	Tot.	Ast.	PF	Dq.	Stl.	Blk.	TO	Pts.	Avg.
83-84 — Atlanta	78	1071	160	318	.503	28	46	.609	14	57	71	71	82	0	17	0	32	350	4.5
84-85 — Atlanta	41	1168	187	352	.531	30	41	.732	16	57	73	125	58	0	28	7	57	406	9.9
85-86 — Atlanta	81	2760	467	881	.530	104	135	.770	51	119	170	306	118	0	81	14	114	1043	12.9
86-87 — Atlanta	71	2049	398	792	.503	100	127	.787	30	94	124	211	107	0	39	16	88	900	12.7
87-88 — Atlanta	82	2412	376	787	.478	71	89	.798	39	131	170	302	117	0	50	18	82	823	10.0
88-89 — Sac.-Ind.	64	1120	130	286	.455	28	41	.683	26	54	80	111	43	0	23	2	32	291	4.5
89-90 — Indiana	61	544	62	122	.508	5	6	.833	4	26	30	44	39	0	7	4	23	130	2.1
90-91 — Indiana	41	355	35	79	.443	4	6	.667	6	27	33	25	9	0	10	4	10	74	1.8
91-92 — Indiana	24	115	8	19	.421	1	2	.500	1	8	9	4	4	0	2	0	3	17	0.7
Totals	543	11594	1823	3636	.501	371	493	.753	187	573	760	1201	559	0	257	65	441	4034	7.4

Three-point field goals: 1983-84, 2-for-5 (.400). 1984-85, 2-for-7 (.286). 1985-86, 5-for-16 (.313). 1986-87, 4-for-12 (.333). 1988-89, 3-for-6 (.500). 1989-90, 1-for-2 (.500). 1990-91, 0-for-5. Totals, 17-for-53 (.321).

NBA PLAYOFF RECORD

Season Team	G	Min.	FGM	FGA	Pct.	FTM	FTA	Pct.	Off.	Def.	Tot.	Ast.	PF	Dq.	Stl.	Blk.	TO	Pts.	Avg.
83-84 — Atlanta	5	96	20	37	.541	0	0	...	5	4	9	11	5	0	1	0	4	40	8.0
85-86 — Atlanta	9	348	71	135	.526	18	26	.692	4	20	24	30	16	0	10	1	13	160	17.8
86-87 — Atlanta	9	300	67	121	.554	14	17	.824	3	15	18	30	22	0	4	4	12	148	16.4
87-88 — Atlanta	12	344	66	122	.541	5	7	.714	9	17	26	43	24	0	7	1	13	137	11.4
89-90 — Indiana	2	11	0	1	.000	0	0	...	0	1	1	0	0	0	0	0	0	0	0.0
90-91 — Indiana	1	6	1	1	1.000	0	0	...	0	0	0	1	1	0	0	0	0	2	2.0
Totals	38	1105	225	417	.540	37	50	.740	21	57	78	115	68	0	22	6	42	487	12.8

Three-point field goals: 1985-86, 0-for-2.

WOLF, JOE
F/C

PERSONAL: Born December 17, 1964, in Kohler, Wis. . . . 6-11/230. . . . Full name: Joseph James Wolf.
HIGH SCHOOL: Kohler (Wis.).
COLLEGE: North Carolina.
TRANSACTIONS/CAREER NOTES: Selected by Los Angeles Clippers in first round (13th pick overall) of 1987 NBA Draft. . . . Signed as unrestricted free agent by Denver Nuggets (October 5, 1990).

COLLEGIATE RECORD

Season Team	G	Min.	FGM	FGA	Pct.	FTM	FTA	Pct.	Reb.	Pts.	Avg.
83-84 —North Carolina	30	412	38	79	.481	25	33	.758	85	101	3.4
84-85 —North Carolina	30	914	112	198	.566	50	64	.781	158	274	9.1
85-86 —North Carolina	34	854	149	280	.532	42	59	.712	224	340	10.0
86-87 —North Carolina	34	1005	212	371	.571	69	87	.793	240	516	15.2
Totals	128	3185	511	928	.551	186	243	.765	707	1231	9.6

Three-point field goals: 1986-87, 23-for-40 (.575).

NBA REGULAR-SEASON RECORD

Season Team	G	Min.	FGM	FGA	Pct.	FTM	FTA	Pct.	Off.	Def.	Tot.	Ast.	PF	Dq.	Stl.	Blk.	TO	Pts.	Avg.
87-88 —L.A. Clippers	42	1137	136	334	.407	45	54	.833	51	136	187	98	139	8	38	16	76	320	7.6
88-89 —L.A. Clippers	66	1450	170	402	.423	44	64	.688	83	188	271	113	152	1	32	16	94	386	5.8
89-90 —L.A. Clippers	77	1325	155	392	.395	55	71	.775	63	169	232	62	129	0	30	24	77	370	4.8
90-91 —Denver	74	1593	234	519	.451	69	83	.831	136	264	400	107	244	8	60	31	95	539	7.3
91-92 —Denver	67	1160	100	277	.361	53	66	.803	97	143	240	61	124	1	32	14	60	254	3.8
Totals	326	6665	795	1924	.413	266	338	.787	430	900	1330	441	788	18	192	101	402	1869	5.7

Three-point field goals: 1987-88, 3-for-15 (.200). 1988-89, 2-for-14 (.143). 1989-90, 5-for-25 (.200). 1990-91, 2-for-15 (.133). 1991-92, 1-for-11 (.091). Totals, 13-for-80 (.163).

WOOLRIDGE, ORLANDO
F, PISTONS

PERSONAL: Born December 16, 1959, in Bernice, La. . . . 6-9/215. . . . Full name: Orlando Vernada Woolridge.
HIGH SCHOOL: All Saints (Pelican, La.), then Mansfield (La.).
COLLEGE: Notre Dame.
TRANSACTIONS/CAREER NOTES: Selected by Chicago Bulls in first round (sixth pick overall) of 1981 NBA Draft. . . . Signed as veteran free agent by New Jersey Nets (October 2, 1986); Bulls agreed not to exercise their right of first refusal in exchange for 1987 first-round draft choice and 1988 and 1990 second-round draft choices. . . . Signed as unrestricted free agent by Los Angeles Lakers (August 10, 1988). . . . Traded by Lakers to Denver Nuggets for 1993 and 1995 second-round draft choices (August 3, 1990). . . . Traded by Nuggets to Detroit Pistons for Scott Hastings and 1992 second-round draft choice (August 13, 1992).

COLLEGIATE RECORD

NOTES: THE SPORTING NEWS All-America second team (1981).

Season Team	G	Min.	FGM	FGA	Pct.	FTM	FTA	Pct.	Reb.	Pts.	Avg.
77-78 —Notre Dame	24	230	41	78	.526	16	33	.485	51	98	4.1
78-79 —Notre Dame	30	752	145	253	.573	41	56	.732	145	331	11.0
79-80 —Notre Dame	27	835	124	212	.585	81	117	.692	186	329	12.2
80-81 —Notre Dame	28	924	156	240	.650	90	135	.667	168	402	14.4
Totals	109	2741	466	783	.595	228	341	.669	550	1160	10.6

NBA REGULAR-SEASON RECORD

Season Team	G	Min.	FGM	FGA	Pct.	FTM	FTA	Pct.	Off.	Def.	Tot.	Ast.	PF	Dq.	Stl.	Blk.	TO	Pts.	Avg.
81-82 —Chicago	75	1188	202	394	.513	144	206	.699	82	145	227	81	152	1	23	24	107	548	7.3
82-83 —Chicago	57	1627	361	622	.580	217	340	.638	122	176	298	97	177	1	38	44	157	939	16.5
83-84 —Chicago	75	2544	570	1086	.525	303	424	.715	130	239	369	136	253	6	71	60	188	1444	19.3
84-85 —Chicago	77	2816	679	1225	.554	409	521	.785	158	277	435	135	185	0	58	38	178	1767	22.9
85-86 —Chicago	70	2248	540	1090	.495	364	462	.788	150	200	350	213	186	2	49	47	174	1448	20.7
86-87 —New Jersey	75	2638	556	1067	.521	438	564	.777	118	249	367	261	243	4	54	86	213	1551	20.7
87-88 —New Jersey	19	622	110	247	.445	92	130	.708	31	60	91	71	73	2	13	20	48	312	16.4
88-89 —L.A. Lakers	74	1491	231	494	.468	253	343	.738	81	189	270	58	130	0	30	65	103	715	9.7
89-90 —L.A. Lakers	62	1421	306	550	.556	176	240	.733	49	136	185	96	160	2	39	46	73	788	12.7
90-91 —Denver	53	1823	490	983	.498	350	439	.797	141	220	361	119	145	2	69	23	152	1330	25.1
91-92 —Detroit	82	2113	452	907	.498	241	353	.683	109	151	260	88	154	0	41	33	133	1146	14.0
Totals	719	20531	4497	8665	.519	2987	4022	.743	1171	2042	3213	1355	1858	20	485	486	1526	11988	16.7

Three-point field goals: 1981-82, 0-for-3. 1982-83, 0-for-3. 1983-84, 1-for-2 (.500). 1984-85, 0-for-5. 1985-86, 4-for-23 (.174). 1986-87, 1-for-8 (.125). 1987-88, 0-for-2. 1988-89, 0-for-1. 1989-90, 0-for-5. 1990-91, 0-for-4. 1991-92, 1-for-9 (.111). Totals, 7-for-65 (.108).

NBA PLAYOFF RECORD

Season Team	G	Min.	FGM	FGA	Pct.	FTM	FTA	Pct.	Off.	Def.	Tot.	Ast.	PF	Dq.	Stl.	Blk.	TO	Pts.	Avg.
84-85 —Chicago	4	167	34	68	.500	14	18	.778	6	7	13	8	19	1	6	1	12	82	20.5
85-86 —Chicago	3	135	25	62	.403	13	15	.867	6	8	14	4	12	0	3	1	4	63	21.0
88-89 —L.A. Lakers	15	276	39	75	.520	44	62	.710	20	50	70	17	35	0	2	15	22	122	8.1
89-90 —L.A. Lakers	9	199	40	70	.571	26	37	.703	6	17	23	10	25	1	8	8	11	106	11.8
91-92 —Detroit	5	128	23	52	.442	9	16	.563	5	5	10	3	14	0	1	1	6	55	11.0
Totals	36	905	161	327	.492	106	148	.716	43	87	130	42	105	2	20	26	55	428	11.9

Three-point field goals: 1985-86, 0-for-1. 1989-90, 0-for-1. Totals, 0-for-2.

W

WORTHY, JAMES

F, LAKERS

PERSONAL: Born February 27, 1961, in Gastonia, N.C. . . . . 6-9/225. . . . Full name: James Ager Worthy.
HIGH SCHOOL: Ashbrook (Gastonia, N.C.).
COLLEGE: North Carolina.
TRANSACTIONS/CAREER NOTES: Selected as undergraduate by Los Angeles Lakers in first round (first pick overall) of 1982 NBA Draft.
MISCELLANEOUS: Member of NBA championship teams (1985, 1987, 1988).

COLLEGIATE RECORD

NOTES: THE SPORTING NEWS All-America first team (1982). . . . NCAA Division I Tournament Most Outstanding Player (1982). . . . Member of NCAA Division I championship team (1982).

Season Team	G	Min.	FGM	FGA	Pct.	FTM	FTA	Pct.	Reb.	Pts.	Avg.
79-80 —North Carolina	14	...	74	126	.587	27	45	.600	104	175	12.5
80-81 —North Carolina	36	...	208	416	.500	96	150	.640	301	512	14.2
81-82 —North Carolina	34	...	203	354	.573	126	187	.674	215	532	15.6
Totals	84		485	896	.541	249	382	.652	620	1219	14.5

NBA REGULAR-SEASON RECORD

HONORS: All-NBA third team (1990, 1991). . . . NBA All-Rookie team (1983).

Season Team	G	Min.	FGM	FGA	Pct.	FTM	FTA	Pct.	REBOUNDS Off.	Def.	Tot.	Ast.	PF	Dq.	Stl.	Blk.	TO	Pts.	Avg.
82-83 —Los Angeles	77	1970	447	772	.579	138	221	.624	157	242	399	132	221	2	91	64	178	1033	13.4
83-84 —Los Angeles	82	2415	495	890	.556	195	257	.759	157	358	515	207	244	5	77	70	181	1185	14.5
84-85 —L.A. Lakers	80	2696	610	1066	.572	190	245	.776	169	342	511	201	196	0	87	67	198	1410	17.6
85-86 —L.A. Lakers	75	2454	629	1086	.579	242	314	.771	136	251	387	201	195	0	82	77	149	1500	20.0
86-87 —L.A. Lakers	82	2819	651	1207	.539	292	389	.751	158	308	466	226	206	0	108	83	168	1594	19.4
87-88 —L.A. Lakers	75	2655	617	1161	.531	242	304	.796	129	245	374	289	175	1	72	55	155	1478	19.7
88-89 —L.A. Lakers	81	2960	702	1282	.548	251	321	.782	169	320	489	288	175	0	108	56	182	1657	20.5
89-90 —L.A. Lakers	80	2960	711	1298	.548	248	317	.782	160	318	478	288	190	0	99	49	160	1685	21.1
90-91 —L.A. Lakers	78	3008	716	1455	.492	212	266	.797	107	249	356	275	117	0	104	35	127	1670	21.4
91-92 —L.A. Lakers	54	2108	450	1007	.447	166	204	.814	98	207	305	252	89	0	76	23	127	1075	19.9
Totals	764	26045	6028	11224	.537	2176	2838	.767	1440	2840	4280	2359	1808	8	904	579	1625	14287	18.7

Three-point field goals: 1982-83, 1-for-4 (.250). 1983-84, 0-for-6. 1984-85, 0-for-7. 1985-86, 0-for-13. 1986-87, 0-for-13. 1987-88, 2-for-16 (.125). 1988-89, 2-for-23 (.087). 1989-90, 15-for-49 (.306). 1990-91, 26-for-90 (.289). 1991-92, 9-for-43 (.209). Totals, 55-for-264 (.208).

NBA PLAYOFF RECORD

NOTES: NBA Finals Most Valuable Player (1988).

Season Team	G	Min.	FGM	FGA	Pct.	FTM	FTA	Pct.	REBOUNDS Off.	Def.	Tot.	Ast.	PF	Dq.	Stl.	Blk.	TO	Pts.	Avg.
83-84 —Los Angeles	21	708	164	274	.599	42	69	.609	36	69	105	56	57	0	27	11	39	371	17.7
84-85 —L.A. Lakers	19	626	166	267	.622	75	111	.676	35	61	96	41	53	1	17	13	26	408	21.5
85-86 —L.A. Lakers	14	539	121	217	.558	32	47	.681	22	43	65	45	43	0	16	10	36	274	19.6
86-87 —L.A. Lakers	18	681	176	298	.591	73	97	.753	31	70	101	63	42	0	28	22	40	425	23.6
87-88 —L.A. Lakers	24	896	204	390	.523	97	128	.758	53	86	139	106	58	0	33	19	55	506	21.1
88-89 —L.A. Lakers	15	600	153	270	.567	63	80	.788	37	64	101	42	36	0	18	16	33	372	24.8
89-90 —L.A. Lakers	9	366	90	181	.497	36	43	.837	11	39	50	27	18	0	14	3	22	218	24.2
90-91 —L.A. Lakers	18	733	161	346	.465	53	72	.736	25	48	73	70	34	0	19	2	40	379	21.1
Totals	138	5149	1235	2243	.551	471	647	.728	250	480	730	450	341	2	172	96	291	2953	21.4

Three-point field goals: 1983-84, 1-for-2 (.500). 1984-85, 1-for-2 (.500). 1985-86, 0-for-4. 1986-87, 0-for-2. 1987-88, 1-for-9 (.111). 1988-89, 3-for-8 (.375). 1989-90, 2-for-8 (.250). 1990-91, 4-for-24 (.167). Totals, 12-for-59 (.203).

NBA ALL-STAR GAME RECORD

Season Team	Min.	FGM	FGA	Pct.	FTM	FTA	Pct.	REBOUNDS Off.	Def.	Tot.	Ast.	PF	Dq.	Stl.	Blk.	TO	Pts.
1986 —L.A. Lakers	28	10	19	.526	0	0	...	2	1	3	2	3	0	0	2	1	20
1987 —L.A. Lakers	29	10	14	.714	2	2	1.000	6	2	8	3	3	0	1	0	2	22
1988 —L.A. Lakers	13	2	8	.250	0	1	.000	1	2	3	1	0	0	1	0	0	4
1989 —L.A. Lakers	18	4	7	.571	0	0	...	0	2	2	2	0	0	0	0	0	8
1990 —L.A. Lakers	19	1	11	.091	0	0	...	3	1	4	0	1	0	1	0	0	2
1991 —L.A. Lakers	21	3	11	.273	3	4	.750	0	2	2	0	1	0	3	0	1	9
1992 —L.A. Lakers	14	4	7	.571	1	2	.500	0	4	4	1	0	0	1	0	0	9
Totals	142	34	77	.442	6	9	.667	12	14	26	9	10	0	7	4	4	74

Three-point field goals: 1986, 0-for-2. 1989, 0-for-1. Totals, 0-for-3.

WY

YOUNG, DANNY

G, CLIPPERS

PERSONAL: Born July 26, 1962, in Raleigh, N.C. . . . . Full name: Danny Richardson Young.
HIGH SCHOOL: Enloe (Raleigh, N.C.).
COLLEGE: Wake Forest.
TRANSACTIONS/CAREER NOTES: Selected by Seattle SuperSonics in second round (39th pick overall) of 1984 NBA Draft. . . . Waived by SuperSonics (November 13, 1984). . . . Played in Continental Basketball Association with Wyoming Wildcatters (1984-85). . . . Re-signed as free agent by SuperSonics (August 9, 1985). . . . Waived by SuperSonics (October 31, 1988). . . . Signed as free agent by Portland Trail Blazers (November 2, 1988). . . . Waived by Trail Blazers (January 7, 1992). . . . Signed as free agent by Los Angeles Clippers (January 9, 1992).

COLLEGIATE RECORD

Season Team	G	Min.	FGM	FGA	Pct.	FTM	FTA	Pct.	Reb.	Pts.	Avg.
80-81 —Wake Forest	29	491	58	117	.496	33	48	.688	38	149	5.1

Season	Team	G	Min.	FGM	FGA	Pct.	FTM	FTA	Pct.	Reb.	Pts.	Avg.
81-82	—Wake Forest	30	946	129	254	.508	60	84	.714	74	318	10.6
82-83	—Wake Forest	31	999	144	315	.457	82	115	.713	66	397	12.8
83-84	—Wake Forest	32	1043	124	272	.456	58	82	.707	59	306	9.6
	Totals	122	3479	455	958	.475	233	329	.708	237	1170	9.6

Three-point field goals: 1982-83, 27-for-73 (.370).

NBA REGULAR-SEASON RECORD

Season	Team	G	Min.	FGM	FGA	Pct.	FTM	FTA	Pct.	Off.	Def.	Tot.	Ast.	PF	Dq.	Stl.	Blk.	TO	Pts.	Avg.
84-85	—Seattle	3	26	2	10	.200	0	0	...	0	3	3	2	2	0	3	0	2	4	1.3
85-86	—Seattle	82	1901	227	449	.506	90	106	.849	29	91	120	303	113	0	110	9	92	568	6.9
86-87	—Seattle	73	1482	132	288	.458	59	71	.831	23	90	113	353	72	0	74	3	85	352	4.8
87-88	—Seattle	77	949	89	218	.408	43	53	.811	18	57	75	218	69	0	52	2	37	243	3.2
88-89	—Portland	48	952	115	250	.460	50	64	.781	17	57	74	123	50	0	55	3	45	297	6.2
89-90	—Portland	82	1393	138	328	.421	91	112	.813	29	93	122	231	84	0	82	4	80	383	4.7
90-91	—Portland	75	897	103	271	.380	41	45	.911	22	53	75	141	49	0	50	7	50	283	3.8
91-92	—Port.-L.A.C.	62	1023	100	255	.392	57	67	.851	16	59	75	172	53	0	46	4	47	280	4.5
	Totals	502	8623	906	2069	.438	431	518	.832	154	503	657	1543	492	0	472	32	438	2410	4.8

Three-point field goals: 1984-85, 0-for-1. 1985-86, 24-for-74 (.324). 1986-87, 29-for-79 (.367). 1987-88, 22-for-77 (.286). 1988-89, 17-for-50 (.340). 1989-90, 16-for-59 (.271). 1990-91, 36-for-104 (.346). 1991-92, 23-for-70 (.329). Totals, 167-for-514 (.325).

NBA PLAYOFF RECORD

Season	Team	G	Min.	FGM	FGA	Pct.	FTM	FTA	Pct.	Off.	Def.	Tot.	Ast.	PF	Dq.	Stl.	Blk.	TO	Pts.	Avg.
86-87	—Seattle	14	208	21	52	.404	10	10	1.000	4	12	16	48	21	1	15	0	7	57	4.1
87-88	—Seattle	5	95	11	21	.524	10	10	1.000	3	7	10	19	7	0	2	2	7	32	6.4
88-89	—Portland	3	66	12	26	.462	1	2	.500	2	6	8	12	2	0	1	0	2	28	9.3
89-90	—Portland	21	294	28	72	.389	19	27	.704	11	19	30	32	29	0	14	2	17	86	4.1
90-91	—Portland	7	36	6	11	.545	0	0	...	0	0	0	7	0	0	0	0	2	12	1.7
91-92	—L.A. Clippers	3	11	2	4	.500	0	0	...	0	0	0	1	0	0	0	0	2	4	1.3
	Totals	53	710	80	186	.430	40	49	.816	20	44	64	119	59	1	32	4	37	219	4.1

Three-point field goals: 1986-87, 5-for-16 (.313). 1987-88, 0-for-3. 1988-89, 3-for-8 (.375). 1989-90, 11-for-29 (.379). 1990-91, 0-for-1. 1991-92, 0-for-2. Totals, 19-for-59 (.322).

CBA REGULAR-SEASON RECORD

| Season | Team | G | Min. | 2-POINT | | | 3-POINT | | | FTM | FTA | Pct. | Reb. | Ast. | Pts. | Avg. |
				FGM	FGA	Pct.	FGM	FGA	Pct.							
84-85	—Wyoming	26	489	77	156	.494	4	12	.333	59	61	.967	34	95	225	8.7

Y

INDIVIDUAL CAREER HIGHS

REGULAR SEASON

Player	FGM	FGA	FTM	FTA	Reb.	Ast.	Pts.
Alaa Abdelnaby	10	21	7	10	13	2	20
Mark Acres	8	11	7	10	17	4	19
Michael Adams	17	34	17	19	11	19	54
Rafael Addison	10	15	5	8	11	5	22
Mark Aguirre	21	40	14	20	15	17	49
Danny Ainge	20	29	13	13	11	15	45
Mark Alarie	10	18	6	6	13	5	22
Victor Alexander	10	15	8	9	16	3	28
Greg Anderson	13	19	11	16	22	6	31
Kenny Anderson	9	21	6	8	7	12	18
Nick Anderson	16	28	10	13	14	10	37
Ron Anderson	15	26	12	12	15	8	36
Willie Anderson	18	26	12	14	12	12	36
Michael Ansley	11	23	9	11	16	4	26
Greg Anthony	8	14	8	10	10	13	20
B.J. Armstrong	10	17	10	10	6	10	22
Vincent Askew	6	11	8	9	8	8	16
Keith Askins	7	11	6	6	9	6	18
Stacey Augmon	14	23	13	16	11	7	32
Isaac Austin	3	6	4	4	4	2	7
Milos Babic	2	4	4	4	5	2	6
John Bagley	16	21	10	12	11	19	35
Thurl Bailey	17	27	13	16	17	9	41
Stephen Bardo	0	0	0	0	1	0	0
Charles Barkley	18	30	21	26	25	14	47
Dana Barros	11	22	8	8	6	10	28
John Battle	12	23	12	14	7	14	28
Kenny Battle	8	14	9	12	10	5	23
William Bedford	8	18	9	9	13	4	20
Benoit Benjamin	15	23	12	15	23	9	34
Winston Bennett	9	13	9	10	14	5	23
David Benoit	7	11	6	6	11	3	15
Larry Bird	22	36	16	17	21	17	60
Rolando Blackman	19	32	22	23	11	10	46
Lance Blanks	6	6	4	6	5	4	12
Mookie Blaylock	12	23	8	11	12	15	27
Muggsy Bogues	10	17	7	8	8	19	22
Manute Bol	7	14	8	14	19	3	18
Anthony Bonner	8	17	7	10	15	8	21
Anthony Bowie	13	22	8	8	10	7	31
Sam Bowie	15	26	14	18	21	8	38
Terrell Brandon	7	17	9	12	7	13	19
Randy Breuer	14	28	12	17	17	6	40
Frank Brickowski	12	28	14	20	17	10	34
Kevin Brooks	5	7	3	4	6	3	13
Scott Brooks	8	15	9	9	5	13	21
Tony Brown	11	19	11	14	11	9	29
Chucky Brown	12	17	8	8	9	5	30
Dee Brown	10	19	8	9	10	14	23
Myron Brown	2	2	0	0	2	3	4
Mike Brown	8	16	10	12	16	5	24
Randy Brown	6	9	6	6	4	7	12
Mark Bryant	7	12	8	10	15	4	20
Jud Buechler	5	8	5	8	7	4	12
Matt Bullard	9	15	3	5	9	4	20
Willie Burton	11	23	11	14	12	6	28
Steve Burtt	10	18	9	10	5	11	23
Michael Cage	12	19	15	19	30	6	29
Demetrius Calip	1	6	1	2	2	6	3
Rick Calloway	7	11	4	5	5	6	16
Tony Campbell	15	31	16	23	14	8	44
Elden Campbell	9	15	7	8	14	3	25
Antoine Carr	18	29	14	18	14	8	41
Bill Cartwright	16	26	19	19	18	8	38
Terry Catledge	18	29	14	19	22	5	49
Duane Causwell	9	17	8	12	16	5	22
Cedric Ceballos	13	22	9	12	13	5	34
Tom Chambers	22	32	18	22	18	9	60
Rex Chapman	17	32	13	13	11	11	38
Maurice Cheeks	15	23	11	14	10	21	32

Player	FGM	FGA	FTM	FTA	Reb.	Ast.	Pts.
Pete Chilcutt	8	16	2	2	9	5	19
Derrick Coleman	15	28	15	20	23	11	42
Bimbo Coles	9	16	10	11	8	12	22
Steve Colter	14	21	12	14	10	12	35
Marty Conlon	5	8	8	8	6	2	14
Lester Conner	10	17	11	13	13	18	24
Anthony Cook	7	15	7	10	18	2	14
Wayne Cooper	13	22	12	14	19	7	32
Tom Copa	2	5	1	3	4	2	5
Lanard Copeland	4	10	2	2	4	3	8
Tyrone Corbin	15	27	9	10	19	10	36
Chris Corchiani	4	9	6	6	8	9	11
Corey Crowder	4	8	2	2	3	3	10
Terry Cummings	19	32	14	20	24	10	52
Dell Curry	14	26	7	8	8	10	31
Quintin Dailey	17	29	15	18	10	12	44
Brad Daugherty	15	25	15	18	24	13	44
Brad Davis	14	17	11	14	8	17	32
Dale Davis	9	10	6	10	13	3	19
Terry Davis	9	16	8	12	21	3	20
Walter Davis	19	33	19	21	13	12	45
Johnny Dawkins	13	25	13	14	8	15	30
Vinny Del Negro	13	19	12	15	8	13	28
Vlade Divac	13	18	10	13	17	6	32
James Donaldson	12	19	13	17	27	7	29
Sherman Douglas	15	26	13	17	7	17	42
Greg Dreiling	5	8	7	10	11	4	15
Clyde Drexler	20	33	15	17	16	16	50
Kevin Duckworth	14	27	14	16	18	5	32
Chris Dudley	7	16	9	18	21	4	20
Joe Dumars	19	33	18	19	10	14	45
Ledell Eackles	17	33	12	14	9	9	40
Mark Eaton	8	18	10	12	25	7	20
Patrick Eddie	1	5	0	0	1	0	2
James Edwards	16	29	18	19	18	7	39
Kevin Edwards	14	26	12	12	10	12	34
Blue Edwards	14	19	8	10	9	7	30
Craig Ehlo	12	25	8	11	14	12	31
Mario Elie	10	17	9	9	8	8	27
Sean Elliott	14	22	14	15	17	12	34
Dale Ellis	20	39	17	19	12	9	53
LeRon Ellis	3	9	2	6	6	1	6
Pervis Ellison	14	28	10	11	22	7	31
A.J. English	13	22	9	11	8	11	31
Patrick Ewing	22	37	18	22	24	7	51
Dave Feitl	8	16	10	10	17	4	20
Duane Ferrell	11	22	8	9	10	7	27
Danny Ferry	8	16	9	10	16	6	21
Vern Fleming	15	23	14	18	13	18	31
Sleepy Floyd	16	28	22	27	13	19	41
Greg Foster	7	12	5	6	10	4	17
Rick Fox	13	23	6	10	9	6	31
Tellis Frank	11	22	8	11	15	6	24
Anthony Frederick	9	17	9	10	10	5	22
Kevin Gamble	16	25	9	12	12	10	34
Winston Garland	12	23	10	12	12	16	31
Tom Garrick	10	14	8	9	8	18	23
Chris Gatling	6	10	6	7	15	2	18
Kenny Gattison	14	21	9	11	18	5	29
Tate George	10	20	10	11	8	10	22
Kendall Gill	13	27	11	13	13	11	32
Armon Gilliam	18	26	11	14	21	9	41
Gerald Glass	14	27	6	7	13	7	32
Mike Gminski	15	23	15	16	22	9	41
Dan Godfread	2	3	2	2	1	0	4
Paul Graham	11	22	7	8	7	9	24
Ron Grandison	5	9	9	10	8	5	15
Gary Grant	13	23	9	10	11	21	31
Greg Grant	7	14	5	6	6	14	15
Harvey Grant	15	26	9	11	16	8	34
Horace Grant	11	21	13	14	20	9	28
Jeff Grayer	12	21	8	9	13	6	27
A.C. Green	13	23	17	21	18	6	33
Rickey Green	16	25	13	17	9	20	45
Sean Green	7	15	3	4	5	5	15
Sidney Green	16	27	13	14	23	8	36

Player	FGM	FGA	FTM	FTA	Reb.	Ast.	Pts.
Jack Haley	8	16	7	11	18	3	19
Tom Hammonds	14	24	6	7	12	5	31
Bob Hansen	12	20	9	11	11	9	28
Tim Hardaway	17	33	13	15	10	19	43
Derek Harper	16	29	14	16	11	18	42
Ron Harper	19	29	15	19	16	15	40
Scott Hastings	8	16	9	10	17	6	17
Hersey Hawkins	14	25	15	17	12	9	43
Gerald Henderson	12	20	9	12	9	17	31
Steve Henson	6	13	4	4	5	8	17
Carl Herrera	6	10	4	6	8	2	14
Rod Higgins	15	20	14	16	12	9	41
Sean Higgins	13	19	4	5	8	4	29
Tyrone Hill	10	13	6	9	17	4	20
Donald Hodge	9	15	7	9	14	5	24
Craig Hodges	13	23	8	8	9	12	29
Dave Hoppen	7	14	6	6	14	4	17
Dennis Hopson	12	24	12	14	9	6	32
Jeff Hornacek	14	25	12	12	14	18	35
Brian Howard	5	9	4	6	6	3	14
Jay Humphries	14	23	12	15	10	16	36
Cedric Hunter	0	0	0	0	0	0	0
Byron Irvin	10	15	8	11	8	6	23
Mike Iuzzolino	7	15	10	12	7	11	23
Chris Jackson	16	32	6	6	7	8	35
Jaren Jackson	5	9	3	5	4	3	13
Mark Jackson	14	27	12	15	11	19	34
Dave Jamerson	7	17	6	6	5	8	16
Henry James	10	16	6	8	8	5	25
Les Jepsen	2	6	3	5	6	1	5
Buck Johnson	14	22	10	11	13	10	32
Avery Johnson	9	17	7	10	6	18	22
Magic Johnson	18	36	19	22	18	24	46
Eddie A. Johnson	18	32	16	18	15	10	45
Kevin Johnson	17	29	23	24	13	21	44
Larry Johnson	16	25	13	13	23	10	34
Vinnie Johnson	15	25	11	12	11	15	35
Charles Jones	7	13	6	9	16	7	17
Michael Jordan	24	43	26	27	18	17	69
Shawn Kemp	13	23	14	17	21	5	31
Steve Kerr	9	16	6	7	6	11	24
Jerome Kersey	15	26	15	16	20	10	36
Alec Kessler	9	15	8	9	15	3	21
Bo Kimble	9	18	8	10	8	5	27
Albert King	17	29	12	12	14	11	34
Bernard King	20	38	22	26	18	14	60
Rich King	4	10	6	6	5	4	10
Stacey King	10	16	10	13	14	6	24
Greg Kite	7	13	6	8	16	6	16
Joe Kleine	10	17	8	10	18	8	23
Negele Knight	12	25	8	15	7	19	27
Bart Kofoed	5	7	4	6	5	9	15
Jon Koncak	9	19	9	16	20	7	25
Larry Krystkowiak	11	18	15	17	18	7	31
Bill Laimbeer	16	27	12	13	24	11	35
Jerome Lane	10	21	5	11	25	7	22
Andrew Lang	9	15	7	9	19	4	21
Eric Leckner	8	15	7	10	12	4	21
Doug Lee	4	10	4	7	7	4	9
Kurk Lee	3	5	5	6	4	6	8
Gary Leonard	3	6	2	4	4	1	6
Jim Les	6	13	8	9	7	17	20
Fat Lever	16	28	13	14	22	23	38
Cliff Levingston	11	20	11	14	17	7	29
Reggie Lewis	17	30	12	15	12	9	42
Marcus Liberty	11	22	9	12	13	5	25
Todd Lichti	12	22	10	12	9	6	29
Alton Lister	13	17	8	12	21	6	30
Brad Lohaus	11	24	7	10	16	7	29
Grant Long	12	21	12	15	20	6	30
Luc Longley	7	13	6	8	11	4	20
Kevin Lynch	6	10	4	4	5	6	12
Mark Macon	10	19	8	14	10	8	23
Dan Majerle	15	25	12	13	13	13	37
Jeff Malone	19	35	14	15	11	10	48
Karl Malone	22	34	20	24	22	9	61

Player	FGM	FGA	FTM	FTA	Reb.	Ast.	Pts
Moses Malone	20	35	21	26	37	7	53
Danny Manning	16	26	11	15	16	9	39
Sarunas Marciulionis	13	21	13	18	9	10	35
Jeff Martin	9	18	8	10	12	5	25
Anthony Mason	8	13	7	12	17	5	17
Tony Massenburg	9	11	10	11	9	1	19
Vernon Maxwell	15	26	19	22	9	13	51
Tharon Mayes	4	9	5	9	3	5	12
Travis Mays	11	19	17	18	6	13	36
Bob McCann	5	7	4	4	6	3	10
George McCloud	8	15	6	6	9	9	20
Tim McCormick	13	19	11	15	16	8	29
Rodney McCray	12	21	12	14	18	14	30
Xavier McDaniel	18	36	13	20	19	8	41
Kevin McHale	22	30	15	19	18	10	56
Derrick McKey	15	25	15	15	17	9	34
Carlton McKinney	3	8	1	2	4	4	7
Nate McMillan	8	13	10	13	14	25	21
Reggie Miller	15	28	15	17	10	11	44
Terry Mills	10	18	7	11	19	4	25
Sam Mitchell	14	24	13	14	17	7	37
Rodney Monroe	5	13	4	4	3	4	13
Tracy Moore	8	16	6	8	6	4	19
Chris Morris	14	25	11	14	18	10	33
John Morton	8	15	11	14	7	11	21
Chris Mullin	16	28	17	19	18	14	47
Eric Murdock	5	10	6	6	5	5	12
Tod Murphy	10	18	9	10	20	4	24
Jerrod Mustaf	7	18	6	7	12	5	19
Dikembe Mutombo	12	22	15	21	22	7	39
Larry Nance	19	29	13	18	21	14	45
Ed Nealy	9	15	8	10	16	5	23
Chuck Nevitt	5	6	4	4	10	2	12
Johnny Newman	14	25	18	22	11	8	41
Ken Norman	18	31	12	15	20	12	38
Charles Oakley	14	27	13	15	35	15	35
Alan Ogg	5	9	2	5	7	2	11
Hakeem Olajuwon	21	34	14	20	25	10	52
Brian Oliver	7	15	6	7	5	7	19
Jimmy Oliver	5	9	4	4	3	5	11
Billy Owens	11	22	9	11	14	7	30
Keith Owens	3	7	2	2	4	1	8
Robert Pack	7	11	7	7	5	7	16
Robert Parish	16	31	13	18	32	10	40
John Paxson	12	20	9	10	6	14	28
Kenny Payne	10	21	5	6	7	3	24
Gary Payton	8	18	8	10	11	16	22
Will Perdue	8	11	9	12	14	5	16
Sam Perkins	19	29	14	16	20	7	45
Elliot Perry	4	8	5	6	4	6	12
Tim Perry	12	21	7	10	16	7	27
Chuck Person	19	32	12	13	18	11	47
Jim Petersen	11	19	12	16	16	6	28
Drazen Petrovic	17	26	10	11	8	8	39
Bobby Phills	5	9	3	4	4	1	11
Ricky Pierce	17	28	16	17	12	9	45
Ed Pinckney	11	17	12	15	18	6	27
Scottie Pippen	17	28	11	15	18	15	43
Olden Polynice	12	15	9	12	18	4	30
Dave Popson	4	13	3	4	4	2	10
Terry Porter	14	26	14	15	13	19	40
Paul Pressey	13	23	17	19	15	16	30
Mark Price	13	24	18	20	11	20	37
Kevin Pritchard	7	14	7	10	4	8	15
Brian Quinnett	8	14	4	5	9	3	20
Kurt Rambis	11	16	8	12	22	8	23
Mark Randall	6	11	4	4	6	4	14
Blair Rasmussen	16	28	10	11	16	7	35
J.R. Reid	11	22	11	12	20	6	26
Jerry Reynolds	13	25	14	17	14	11	34
Glen Rice	19	32	12	13	14	8	46
Pooh Richardson	16	27	12	14	10	17	35
Mitch Richmond	17	28	16	19	12	12	47
David Rivers	5	11	5	8	8	10	15
Doc Rivers	14	24	17	17	14	21	37
Fred Roberts	14	20	13	14	15	8	34

Player	FGM	FGA	FTM	FTA	Reb.	Ast.	Pts.
Stanley Roberts	11	18	8	14	15	4	24
Alvin Robertson	17	29	14	15	16	17	41
Cliff R. Robinson	10	21	13	16	11	8	22
Cliff T. Robinson	19	29	15	20	23	10	40
David Robinson	16	30	17	22	24	11	43
Larry Robinson	6	14	2	2	6	5	13
Rumeal Robinson	12	22	11	14	9	15	31
Dennis Rodman	15	21	9	12	34	8	34
Tree Rollins	13	18	8	9	23	6	26
Donald Royal	8	16	11	13	11	4	23
Delaney Rudd	7	12	5	6	5	8	18
Jeff Ruland	16	27	18	22	24	12	38
John Salley	10	18	11	12	13	6	28
Ralph Sampson	19	33	15	17	25	9	43
Jeff Sanders	4	11	3	4	7	2	9
Mike Sanders	14	20	11	14	13	7	30
Danny Schayes	12	23	18	18	24	11	37
Steve Scheffler	3	5	4	6	6	2	7
Dwayne Schintzius	7	14	4	8	11	5	16
Detlef Schrempf	13	21	14	14	23	12	35
Byron Scott	15	27	13	14	11	11	38
Dennis Scott	16	33	10	12	9	7	40
Rony Seikaly	15	24	14	26	24	6	40
Brad Sellers	14	25	9	12	13	8	32
Charles Shackleford	9	17	7	11	26	5	23
Brian Shaw	14	24	10	12	15	17	31
Lionel Simmons	16	31	14	16	19	12	42
Scott Skiles	14	25	13	14	12	30	41
Tony Smith	7	12	5	6	5	8	18
Charles D. Smith	17	28	18	21	17	6	52
Doug Smith	11	20	6	8	14	8	26
Kenny Smith	15	23	13	15	8	17	38
LaBradford Smith	7	16	4	4	6	9	17
Larry Smith	11	19	9	14	31	6	25
Michael Smith	11	18	5	6	10	8	24
Otis Smith	14	27	12	12	16	8	33
Steve Smith	10	19	7	10	8	9	24
Rik Smits	14	26	10	13	16	5	34
Mike Smrek	7	12	5	8	11	4	15
Rory Sparrow	13	23	11	12	10	17	32
Felton Spencer	8	14	9	11	19	4	23
John Starks	12	22	12	15	9	11	30
Larry Stewart	9	15	10	11	12	6	23
John Stockton	14	22	15	16	9	28	34
Rod Strickland	11	21	10	14	10	19	28
Derek Strong	0	4	3	4	5	1	3
Lamont Strothers	3	4	1	2	1	1	7
Jon Sundvold	12	22	8	9	7	14	28
Greg Sutton	6	10	4	6	4	5	14
Roy Tarpley	15	25	11	13	25	7	35
Terry Teagle	16	26	16	18	12	7	44
Carl Thomas	5	12	1	2	0	1	12
Charles Thomas	4	11	2	4	6	6	11
Isiah Thomas	19	34	16	20	12	25	47
LaSalle Thompson	13	20	13	14	22	8	31
Mychal Thompson	17	28	12	20	21	11	38
Stephen Thompson	2	5	3	3	4	2	5
Billy Thompson	13	20	11	14	18	7	30
Bob Thornton	7	13	6	8	14	5	17
Otis Thorpe	15	27	14	19	26	11	37
Sedale Threatt	16	29	12	14	10	15	42
Wayman Tisdale	19	28	13	17	18	7	40
Tom Tolbert	10	14	10	12	15	9	27
Kelly Tripucka	19	30	20	22	14	11	56
Trent Tucker	13	21	8	10	9	11	34
Andre Turner	6	14	6	8	8	13	18
Jeff Turner	10	19	8	9	13	6	28
John Turner	7	11	7	8	7	2	15
Kiki Vandeweghe	21	31	18	22	13	10	51
Loy Vaught	10	19	6	7	20	7	23
Joao Vianna	1	2	0	0	0	2	2
Sam Vincent	13	21	17	18	11	17	35
Alexander Volkov	11	17	9	11	10	10	25
Stojan Vrankovic	3	6	2	4	7	2	7
Darrell Walker	14	25	13	16	17	17	39
Spud Webb	13	21	13	14	8	15	32

Player	FGM	FGA	FTM	FTA	Reb.	Ast.	Pts.
Doug West	12	20	9	11	10	9	28
Mark West	11	17	12	14	24	5	27
Ennis Whatley	9	16	9	11	8	22	21
Randy White	11	20	8	12	15	3	24
Mitchell Wiggins	15	26	12	12	10	9	34
Morlon Wiley	11	17	8	8	7	14	24
Gerald Wilkins	18	30	13	14	14	13	43
Dominique Wilkins	21	42	20	22	19	10	57
Brian Williams	11	18	7	11	17	4	24
Buck Williams	14	22	18	19	27	7	35
Herb Williams	17	32	17	20	29	8	40
Jayson Williams	6	14	7	10	11	4	17
John Williams	13	23	13	15	18	7	33
John S. Williams	12	24	11	13	14	13	30
Kenny Williams	11	15	4	6	10	4	23
Micheal Williams	10	16	16	17	11	18	29
Reggie Williams	15	27	9	11	13	9	34
Scott Williams	4	9	5	6	16	4	12
Kevin Willis	16	27	12	15	33	7	39
Kennard Winchester	8	15	6	7	5	2	18
David Wingate	11	24	11	13	11	15	28
Randy Wittman	14	22	9	9	7	12	30
Joe Wolf	9	17	6	7	16	7	23
Orlando Woolridge	18	28	15	20	16	10	44
James Worthy	17	29	14	18	17	14	38
Danny Young	9	13	7	7	6	13	21

PLAYOFFS

Player	FGM	FGA	FTM	FTA	Reb.	Ast.	Pts.
Alaa Abdelnaby	2	4	1	2	2	1	5
Mark Acres	3	5	4	4	7	1	6
Michael Adams	8	19	7	8	12	9	25
Rafael Addison	2	7	0	0	0	1	5
Mark Aguirre	19	30	11	13	17	10	39
Danny Ainge	12	22	7	9	10	14	30
Mark Alarie	4	7	2	2	3	1	8
Victor Alexander	2	4	1	1	4	1	4
Greg Anderson	8	14	3	4	10	2	18
Kenny Anderson	2	6	2	2	3	2	6
Ron Anderson	13	20	10	11	7	6	26
Willie Anderson	18	25	7	9	10	7	38
Greg Anthony	4	9	4	7	5	8	14
B.J. Armstrong	7	11	8	8	4	10	18
Vincent Askew	3	8	2	4	4	2	8
Keith Askins	3	6	0	2	5	2	8
John Bagley	11	21	12	12	7	15	35
Thurl Bailey	15	29	12	15	14	6	39
Charles Barkley	15	25	15	21	22	12	39
Dana Barros	5	9	3	4	2	4	12
John Battle	7	13	9	10	6	5	19
Kenny Battle	2	7	1	1	2	0	5
William Bedford	3	9	4	4	9	2	7
Benoit Benjamin	6	13	14	14	9	1	26
Winston Bennett	10	13	2	4	8	2	22
David Benoit	6	13	2	2	7	2	16
Larry Bird	17	33	14	15	21	16	43
Rolando Blackman	19	33	13	14	10	11	43
Lance Blanks	1	2	0	0	1	3	2
Mookie Blaylock	5	16	2	2	5	12	12
Muggsy Bogues	0	0	0	0	0	2	0
Manute Bol	3	7	4	6	12	1	10
Anthony Bowie	0	1	0	0	0	0	0
Sam Bowie	6	14	6	12	20	5	16
Terrell Brandon	3	10	2	2	3	6	6
Randy Breuer	9	14	7	8	12	3	21
Frank Brickowski	10	18	6	10	12	5	23
Scott Brooks	3	4	2	3	2	3	10
Tony Brown	4	5	2	2	4	2	9
Chucky Brown	4	8	2	4	5	1	8
Dee Brown	9	14	8	10	9	10	22
Mike Brown	6	10	6	7	12	2	15
Mark Bryant	5	8	4	4	7	1	10
Matt Bullard	0	0	0	0	0	0	0
Steve Burtt	5	7	6	6	2	4	14
Michael Cage	7	10	5	7	11	2	16
Tony Campbell	6	12	5	7	4	2	15
Elden Campbell	9	12	5	6	12	3	21
Antoine Carr	9	16	6	9	12	3	20
Bill Cartwright	10	19	11	13	14	7	29
Terry Catledge	13	22	6	9	12	2	27
Cedric Ceballos	9	14	6	8	9	4	20
Tom Chambers	17	29	16	16	17	7	41
Maurice Cheeks	12	20	11	14	10	16	33
Derrick Coleman	11	22	8	11	14	9	24
Bimbo Coles	3	6	5	7	4	4	9
Steve Colter	11	15	3	5	6	8	26
Marty Conlon	0	1	2	2	1	0	2
Lester Conner	1	1	2	2	1	2	2
Wayne Cooper	10	18	4	8	14	7	23
Tom Copa	0	0	0	0	0	0	0
Lanard Copeland	1	3	0	0	1	0	2
Tyrone Corbin	11	15	8	8	14	4	28
Corey Crowder	2	3	0	1	1	1	4
Terry Cummings	16	26	13	16	18	6	41
Dell Curry	1	3	0	0	1	2	2
Quintin Dailey	12	20	4	4	5	5	25
Brad Daugherty	12	22	16	17	17	9	40
Brad Davis	8	10	6	7	6	10	26
Dale Davis	2	6	0	0	13	2	4
Walter Davis	15	29	11	13	10	13	34
Johnny Dawkins	9	17	7	10	5	15	18
Vlade Divac	12	20	7	8	14	5	27
James Donaldson	8	12	9	10	20	3	18

Player	FGM	FGA	FTM	FTA	Reb.	Ast.	Pts.
Sherman Douglas	2	6	1	2	2	6	5
Greg Dreiling	3	4	2	2	7	0	6
Clyde Drexler	15	30	12	15	15	15	42
Kevin Duckworth	14	22	9	11	16	5	33
Chris Dudley	2	5	3	6	8	2	5
Joe Dumars	15	26	13	17	7	11	35
Mark Eaton	10	17	8	10	15	5	20
James Edwards	13	23	9	10	9	4	32
Kevin Edwards	3	6	2	4	3	3	8
Blue Edwards	7	13	8	8	10	3	22
Craig Ehlo	9	18	5	7	10	13	25
Mario Elie	11	15	5	6	9	5	22
Sean Elliott	9	16	12	14	8	5	24
Dale Ellis	18	30	8	11	14	6	43
LeRon Ellis	0	0	0	0	0	0	0
Patrick Ewing	18	34	17	18	20	10	45
Dave Feitl	1	2	2	2	1	0	2
Duane Ferrell	4	6	4	4	8	2	9
Danny Ferry	2	6	3	3	5	1	8
Vern Fleming	9	14	9	11	11	8	19
Sleepy Floyd	18	26	13	14	8	18	51
Rick Fox	3	9	2	2	2	2	8
Kevin Gamble	10	21	4	4	8	6	22
Winston Garland	6	15	6	7	7	8	18
Chris Gatling	7	9	6	9	12	0	16
Tate George	2	10	1	3	0	4	5
Armon Gilliam	8	16	9	10	15	3	25
Mike Gminski	12	19	12	12	13	5	28
Gary Grant	3	6	2	2	2	6	6
Greg Grant	4	7	0	0	3	3	9
Horace Grant	10	17	7	8	20	7	22
Jeff Grayer	4	7	2	2	3	3	10
A.C. Green	9	13	10	13	18	7	21
Rickey Green	12	24	8	10	10	16	32
Sean Green	0	0	0	0	0	0	0
Sidney Green	7	14	3	6	12	3	17
Jack Haley	1	2	1	2	1	1	3
Bob Hansen	10	19	8	10	9	7	25
Tim Hardaway	15	29	8	15	8	20	33
Derek Harper	12	21	9	12	6	16	35
Ron Harper	12	24	7	10	12	7	31
Scott Hastings	4	5	4	5	4	2	10
Hersey Hawkins	14	26	15	15	10	8	39
Gerald Henderson	10	17	5	7	6	9	22
Steve Henson	4	6	3	4	2	1	12
Rod Higgins	7	14	8	10	14	6	21
Sean Higgins	0	1	0	0	0	1	0
Tyrone Hill	4	4	2	2	6	1	9
Craig Hodges	10	18	5	5	5	9	25
Dave Hoppen	2	2	0	2	1	0	4
Dennis Hopson	1	3	3	4	1	1	3
Jeff Hornacek	13	22	14	14	11	12	36
Jay Humphries	9	15	7	8	6	15	24
Byron Irvin	3	11	4	4	6	3	10
Mark Jackson	11	24	9	11	7	16	28
Dave Jamerson	3	8	6	6	3	2	12
Henry James	1	4	2	4	1	1	4
Buck Johnson	6	15	6	6	8	6	16
Avery Johnson	3	5	2	2	2	3	6
Magic Johnson	15	26	20	22	18	24	44
Eddie A. Johnson	13	27	10	10	11	6	35
Kevin Johnson	14	27	18	19	9	19	37
Vinnie Johnson	16	21	10	13	12	13	34
Charles Jones	5	9	4	6	9	2	11
Michael Jordan	24	45	23	28	19	13	63
Shawn Kemp	10	16	12	15	20	2	28
Steve Kerr	4	8	2	2	3	5	9
Jerome Kersey	14	23	12	15	16	8	34
Alec Kessler	0	2	2	2	1	0	2
Bo Kimble	0	1	0	0	0	1	0
Albert King	12	22	5	8	9	4	28
Bernard King	19	35	12	15	12	5	46
Rich King	0	0	0	0	0	0	0
Stacey King	9	15	7	8	9	2	21
Greg Kite	4	5	2	3	9	2	8
Joe Kleine	6	10	6	7	11	1	12

Player	FGM	FGA	FTM	FTA	Reb.	Ast.	Pts.
Negele Knight	8	13	3	4	2	5	18
Bart Kofoed	3	6	2	2	3	4	7
Jon Koncak	5	7	11	11	13	4	19
Larry Krystkowiak	8	15	14	16	13	5	22
Bill Laimbeer	10	23	13	13	19	6	31
Jerome Lane	2	5	2	2	3	2	4
Andrew Lang	6	9	8	11	10	2	20
Eric Leckner	3	7	3	4	6	2	8
Doug Lee	0	2	0	0	0	1	0
Gary Leonard	1	1	0	0	2	0	2
Jim Les	0	0	0	0	0	1	0
Fat Lever	12	24	12	12	16	18	30
Cliff Levingston	6	9	6	8	9	2	17
Reggie Lewis	17	32	9	12	11	9	42
Todd Lichti	9	15	7	7	13	8	22
Alton Lister	9	14	9	13	17	3	22
Brad Lohaus	6	14	1	2	8	2	15
Grant Long	7	15	4	6	9	4	17
Dan Majerle	10	24	10	12	11	6	25
Jeff Malone	15	24	14	15	8	8	35
Karl Malone	17	31	22	24	22	7	44
Moses Malone	16	34	18	20	26	6	42
Danny Manning	12	20	9	13	10	5	33
Sarunas Marciulionis	8	14	15	15	4	9	27
Anthony Mason	5	8	5	8	11	4	13
Tony Massenburg	0	0	0	0	0	0	0
Vernon Maxwell	12	25	5	8	5	5	31
Bob McCann	3	6	0	0	2	0	6
George McCloud	5	7	4	7	1	4	17
Tim McCormick	5	7	3	4	9	3	12
Rodney McCray	10	19	10	10	12	11	24
Xavier McDaniel	20	29	8	12	17	8	42
Kevin McHale	15	25	14	16	17	7	34
Derrick McKey	12	17	7	9	11	5	27
Nate McMillan	7	17	7	8	8	16	17
Reggie Miller	11	19	12	18	5	6	32
Terry Mills	4	9	4	6	7	3	9
Chris Morris	12	20	5	6	8	3	28
John Morton	2	3	2	2	0	0	6
Chris Mullin	16	30	16	19	11	7	41
Eric Murdock	2	3	2	2	2	1	6
Jerrod Mustaf	2	2	4	5	2	0	8
Larry Nance	13	22	10	13	16	8	32
Ed Nealy	4	7	4	6	9	3	10
Chuck Nevitt	2	5	2	2	5	1	6
Johnny Newman	14	25	10	14	6	5	34
Ken Norman	6	13	3	4	14	6	14
Charles Oakley	8	20	10	12	20	7	26
Alan Ogg	1	2	1	2	1	0	3
Hakeem Olajuwon	19	33	13	20	26	6	49
Brian Oliver	2	2	2	2	0	1	4
Billy Owens	10	18	5	9	12	6	25
Robert Pack	3	6	2	2	2	2	6
Robert Parish	14	25	11	15	19	6	33
John Paxson	9	16	11	15	5	9	23
Kenny Payne	2	4	2	2	1	0	4
Gary Payton	6	13	4	8	5	12	15
Will Perdue	6	10	6	9	10	3	16
Sam Perkins	13	22	11	13	19	5	29
Tim Perry	12	17	7	9	10	3	31
Chuck Person	16	27	12	15	17	7	40
Jim Petersen	7	12	9	11	13	4	15
Drazen Petrovic	17	31	6	6	5	6	40
Bobby Phills	2	4	2	2	2	2	4
Ricky Pierce	13	21	14	17	7	7	35
Ed Pinckney	6	9	8	8	14	2	17
Scottie Pippen	13	23	11	14	15	13	32
Olden Polynice	5	7	5	5	11	1	13
Terry Porter	13	19	15	16	8	15	41
Paul Pressey	12	20	15	17	10	16	28
Mark Price	11	19	9	9	6	18	35
Brian Quinnett	3	5	0	0	7	2	7
Kurt Rambis	8	11	5	7	15	5	19
Blair Rasmussen	13	23	6	8	13	4	28
Jerry Reynolds	4	10	5	6	4	2	14
Glen Rice	10	26	4	5	6	3	25

Player	FGM	FGA	FTM	FTA	Reb.	Ast.	Pts.
Mitch Richmond	13	29	8	9	13	8	30
David Rivers	2	6	3	3	1	2	6
Doc Rivers	14	19	15	16	13	22	34
Fred Roberts	12	19	9	11	7	5	33
Alvin Robertson	15	23	10	11	8	12	38
Cliff R. Robinson	9	15	6	13	9	6	24
Cliff T. Robinson	15	27	6	9	11	6	31
David Robinson	11	21	12	15	16	6	31
Rumeal Robinson	1	4	0	0	1	1	2
Dennis Rodman	10	16	6	10	20	3	23
Tree Rollins	8	14	6	10	17	3	18
Donald Royal	2	4	2	5	8	0	6
Delaney Rudd	3	7	2	2	1	9	8
Jeff Ruland	13	22	15	17	20	10	33
John Salley	10	17	9	12	13	4	23
Ralph Sampson	13	25	10	14	24	10	33
Jeff Sanders	1	1	0	0	0	0	2
Mike Sanders	8	17	6	6	8	6	20
Danny Schayes	11	16	13	15	14	5	33
Detlef Schrempf	9	22	10	11	16	5	26
Byron Scott	14	24	10	12	11	7	35
Rony Seikaly	9	15	14	16	12	2	26
Brad Sellers	8	14	8	8	7	3	22
Brian Shaw	9	21	7	8	8	9	22
Tony Smith	5	6	2	3	2	2	12
Charles D. Smith	7	13	8	8	9	4	16
Kenny Smith	7	16	4	4	3	12	19
Larry Smith	8	15	4	5	23	6	18
Michael Smith	4	5	4	4	0	1	9
Otis Smith	6	9	4	5	8	2	12
Steve Smith	7	14	3	3	5	7	19
Rik Smits	9	10	5	6	7	2	23
Mike Smrek	1	4	4	6	2	0	4
Rory Sparrow	8	16	8	8	8	11	22
John Starks	9	14	8	9	4	5	27
John Stockton	13	21	16	19	9	24	34
Rod Strickland	12	20	6	10	9	17	30
Jon Sundvold	6	11	2	2	2	7	14
Greg Sutton	1	5	3	3	0	1	5
Roy Tarpley	12	24	9	15	20	6	27
Terry Teagle	14	24	8	8	6	5	30
Isiah Thomas	18	33	14	17	12	16	43
LaSalle Thompson	9	19	5	6	17	3	23
Mychal Thompson	15	23	10	12	17	8	40
Billy Thompson	4	7	2	2	4	2	8
Bob Thornton	3	4	2	4	7	2	6
Otis Thorpe	9	17	11	14	10	4	27
Sedale Threatt	12	20	6	9	7	9	29
Wayman Tisdale	8	13	5	8	5	3	20
Tom Tolbert	3	5	2	4	4	3	7
Kelly Tripucka	15	27	11	14	11	6	40
Trent Tucker	9	13	4	4	6	7	18
Andre Turner	4	9	7	8	4	7	11
Jeff Turner	2	4	1	1	4	2	4
Kiki Vandeweghe	17	24	12	13	14	7	37
Loy Vaught	4	5	2	2	5	2	8
Sam Vincent	11	17	9	11	4	14	31
Stojan Vrankovic	1	1	0	1	2	1	2
Darrell Walker	8	17	7	10	9	7	20
Spud Webb	10	19	13	16	7	18	21
Mark West	10	17	6	8	21	2	24
Ennis Whatley	3	8	2	2	2	5	6
Randy White	0	0	0	0	0	0	0
Mitchell Wiggins	10	16	4	4	7	4	24
Gerald Wilkins	16	22	7	9	11	10	34
Dominique Wilkins	19	37	15	17	14	6	50
Buck Williams	12	17	11	16	18	5	28
Herb Williams	9	12	6	8	8	4	19
Jayson Williams	3	4	0	0	3	0	6
John Williams	10	17	10	12	13	5	23
John S. Williams	7	14	6	10	7	9	19
Kenny Williams	0	0	0	2	0	0	0
Micheal Williams	8	16	12	14	6	11	24
Reggie Williams	3	13	1	1	5	1	7
Scott Williams	6	7	4	6	9	3	12
Kevin Willis	12	20	8	11	14	3	27

Player	FGM	FGA	FTM	FTA	Reb.	Ast.	Pts.
Kennard Winchester	2	3	0	1	0	2	4
David Wingate	6	14	5	6	8	6	16
Randy Wittman	16	25	9	12	7	8	35
Orlando Woolridge	11	27	8	8	9	5	28
James Worthy	17	26	10	12	16	10	40
Danny Young	5	11	6	6	4	8	12

ANDERSON, ERIC
F

PERSONAL: Born May 26, 1970, in Chicago.... 6-9/220.... Full name: Eric Walfred Anderson.
HIGH SCHOOL: St. Francis De Sales (Chicago).
COLLEGE: Indiana.
TRANSACTIONS/CAREER NOTES: Never drafted by an NBA franchise.

COLLEGIATE RECORD

Season Team	G	Min.	FGM	FGA	Pct.	FTM	FTA	Pct.	Reb.	Pts.	Avg.
88-89 —Indiana	34	964	145	266	.545	114	157	.726	208	404	11.9
89-90 —Indiana	29	957	182	339	.537	107	147	.728	202	473	16.3
90-91 —Indiana	34	1039	175	345	.507	115	165	.697	243	466	13.7
91-92 —Indiana	34	948	133	282	.472	88	109	.807	173	372	10.9
Totals	131	3908	635	1232	.515	424	578	.734	826	1715	13.1

Three-point field goals: 1989-90, 2-for-7 (.286). 1990-91, 1-for-4 (.250). 1991-92, 18-for-42 (.429). Totals, 21-for-53 (.396).

AVENT, ANTHONY
F, BUCKS

PERSONAL: Born October 18, 1969, in Rocky Mount, N.C.... 6-10/235.
HIGH SCHOOL: M.X. Shabbaz (Newark, N.J.).
COLLEGE: Seton Hall.
TRANSACTIONS/CAREER NOTES: Selected by Atlanta Hawks in first round (15th pick overall) of 1991 NBA Draft.... Draft rights traded by Hawks to Milwaukee Bucks in three-way deal in which Denver Nuggets sent Blair Rasmussen to Hawks and Bucks sent draft rights to Kevin Brooks to Nuggets (July 1, 1991); Nuggets also received 1994 second-round draft choice and other considerations from Bucks.... Played in Italy (1991-92).

COLLEGIATE RECORD

Season Team	G	Min.	FGM	FGA	Pct.	FTM	FTA	Pct.	Reb.	Pts.	Avg.
87-88 —Seton Hall					Did not play—ineligible.						
88-89 —Seton Hall	38	395	68	149	.456	32	49	.653	114	168	4.4
89-90 —Seton Hall	28	842	119	244	.488	55	89	.618	262	293	10.5
90-91 —Seton Hall	34	1114	228	395	.577	150	200	.750	335	606	17.8
Totals	100	2351	415	788	.527	237	338	.701	711	1067	10.7

ITALIAN LEAGUE RECORD

Season Team	G	Min.	FGM	FGA	Pct.	FTM	FTA	Pct.	Reb.	Pts.	Avg.
91-92 —Phonola Caserta	15	450	84	158	.532	29	41	.707	154	197	13.1

BARRY, JON
G, CELTICS

PERSONAL: Born July 25, 1969, in Oakland, Calif.... 6-5/195.... Full name: Jon Alan Barry.... Son of Rick Barry, forward with San Francisco Warriors, Golden State Warriors and Houston Rockets of NBA (1965-66, 1966-67 and 1972-73 through 1979-80), and Oakland Oaks, Washington Capitols and New York Nets of American Basketball Association (1968-69 through 1971-72), and member of Naismith Memorial Basketball Hall of Fame.
HIGH SCHOOL: De La Salle Catholic (Concord, Calif.).
COLLEGE: Pacific, then Paris Junior College (Tex.), then Georgia Tech.
TRANSACTIONS/CAREER NOTES: Selected by Boston Celtics in first round (21st pick overall) of 1992 NBA Draft.

COLLEGIATE RECORD

Season Team	G	Min.	FGM	FGA	Pct.	FTM	FTA	Pct.	Reb.	Pts.	Avg.
87-88 —Pacific	29	809	100	269	.372	53	71	.746	74	275	9.5
88-89 —Paris Junior College					Did not play.						
89-90 —Paris Junior College	30	...	204	358	.570	58	73	.795	108	513	17.1
90-91 —Georgia Tech	30	1088	180	405	.444	41	56	.732	110	478	15.9
91-92 —Georgia Tech	35	1231	201	468	.429	101	145	.697	152	602	17.2
Junior college totals	30	...	204	358	.570	58	73	.795	108	513	17.1
Four-year-college totals	94	3128	481	1142	.421	195	272	.717	336	1355	14.4

Three-point field goals: 1987-88, 22-for-59 (.373). 1990-91, 77-for-209 (.368). 1991-92, 99-for-265 (.374). Totals, 198-for-533 (.371).

BENNETT, ELMER
G, HAWKS

PERSONAL: Born February 13, 1970, in Evanston, Ill.... 6-0/171.... Full name: Elmer James Bennett.
HIGH SCHOOL: Bellaire (Tex.).
COLLEGE: Notre Dame.
TRANSACTIONS/CAREER NOTES: Selected by Atlanta Hawks in second round (38th pick overall) of 1992 NBA Draft.

COLLEGIATE RECORD

Season Team	G	Min.	FGM	FGA	Pct.	FTM	FTA	Pct.	Reb.	Pts.	Avg.
88-89 —Notre Dame	30	436	67	146	.459	25	39	.641	36	165	5.5
89-90 —Notre Dame	29	716	112	233	.481	84	114	.737	45	317	10.9

Season Team	G	Min.	FGM	FGA	Pct.	FTM	FTA	Pct.	Reb.	Pts.	Avg.
90-91 —Notre Dame	32	1127	161	389	.414	106	144	.736	95	460	14.4
91-92 —Notre Dame	33	1187	195	441	.442	112	159	.704	119	546	16.5
Totals	124	3466	535	1209	.443	327	456	.717	295	1488	12.0

Three-point field goals: 1988-89, 5-for-14 (.357). 1989-90, 9-for-25 (.360). 1990-91, 32-for-87 (.368). 1991-92, 44-for-133 (.331). Totals, 90-for-259 (.347).

BENNETT, TONY
G, HORNETS

PERSONAL: Born June 1, 1969, in Green Bay, Wisc.... 6-0/175.
HIGH SCHOOL: Preble (Green Bay, Wisc.).
COLLEGE: Wisconsin-Green Bay.
TRANSACTIONS/CAREER NOTES: Selected by Charlotte Hornets in second round (35th pick overall) of 1992 NBA Draft.

COLLEGIATE RECORD

NOTES: THE SPORTING NEWS All-America second team (1992).

Season Team	G	Min.	FGM	FGA	Pct.	FTM	FTA	Pct.	Reb.	Pts.	Avg.
88-89 —Wisconsin-Green Bay	27	930	179	343	.522	111	131	.847	54	516	19.1
89-90 —Wisconsin-Green Bay	30	1079	179	355	.504	73	85	.859	66	499	16.6
90-91 —Wisconsin-Green Bay	31	1118	229	419	.547	127	152	.836	73	665	21.5
91-92 —Wisconsin-Green Bay	30	995	205	384	.534	100	121	.826	86	605	20.2
Totals	118	4122	792	1501	.528	411	489	.840	279	2285	19.4

Three-point field goals: 1988-89, 47-for-107 (.439). 1989-90, 68-for-141 (.482). 1990-91, 80-for-150 (.533). 1991-92, 95-for-186 (.511). Totals, 290-for-584 (.497).

BLAIR, CURTIS
G, ROCKETS

PERSONAL: Born September 24, 1970, in Roanoke, Va.... 6-3/187.
HIGH SCHOOL: Patrick Henry (Roanoke, Va.).
COLLEGE: Richmond.
TRANSACTIONS/CAREER NOTES: Selected by Houston Rockets in second round (53rd pick overall) of 1992 NBA Draft.

COLLEGIATE RECORD

Season Team	G	Min.	FGM	FGA	Pct.	FTM	FTA	Pct.	Reb.	Pts.	Avg.
88-89 —Richmond	31	344	42	98	.429	24	34	.706	51	115	3.7
89-90 —Richmond	32	1156	139	329	.422	71	99	.717	141	391	12.2
90-91 —Richmond	32	1151	193	429	.450	97	131	.740	130	516	16.1
91-92 —Richmond	30	1118	212	453	.468	125	158	.791	137	608	20.3
Totals	125	3769	586	1309	.448	317	422	.751	459	1630	13.0

Three-point field goals: 1988-89, 7-for-24 (.292). 1989-90, 42-for-110 (.382). 1990-91, 33-for-96 (.344). 1991-92, 59-for-141 (.418). Totals, 141-for-371 (.380).

BOOTH, DAVID
F

PERSONAL: Born May 28, 1970, in Peoria, Ill.... 6-7/200.
HIGH SCHOOL: Manual (Peoria, Ill.).
COLLEGE: DePaul.
TRANSACTIONS/CAREER NOTES: Never drafted by an NBA franchise.

COLLEGIATE RECORD

Season Team	G	Min.	FGM	FGA	Pct.	FTM	FTA	Pct.	Reb.	Pts.	Avg.
88-89 —DePaul	33	719	131	278	.471	63	86	.733	145	328	9.9
89-90 —DePaul	35	1140	221	501	.441	125	163	.767	213	592	16.9
90-91 —DePaul	29	908	198	388	.510	140	185	.757	196	543	18.7
91-92 —DePaul	27	798	163	319	.511	116	150	.773	144	470	17.4
Totals	124	3565	713	1486	.480	444	584	.760	698	1933	15.6

Three-point field goals: 1988-89, 3-for-16 (.188). 1989-90, 25-for-72 (.347). 1990-91, 7-for-26 (.269). 1991-92, 28-for-68 (.412). Totals, 63-for-182 (.346).

BROWN, P.J.
C, NETS

PERSONAL: Born October 14, 1968, in Detroit.... 6-11/225.... Full name: Collier Brown Jr.
HIGH SCHOOL: Winnfield Senior (La.).
COLLEGE: Louisiana Tech.
TRANSACTIONS/CAREER NOTES: Selected by New Jersey Nets in second round (29th pick overall) of 1992 NBA Draft.

COLLEGIATE RECORD

Season Team	G	Min.	FGM	FGA	Pct.	FTM	FTA	Pct.	Reb.	Pts.	Avg.
88-89 —Louisiana Tech	32	569	61	147	.415	25	44	.568	178	149	4.7
89-90 —Louisiana Tech	27	672	94	204	.461	48	81	.593	230	239	8.9
90-91 —Louisiana Tech	31	936	170	315	.540	98	150	.653	301	445	14.4
91-92 —Louisiana Tech	31	931	151	309	.489	84	115	.730	308	395	12.7
Totals	121	3108	476	975	.488	255	390	.654	1017	1228	10.1

Three-point field goals: 1988-89, 2-for-3 (.667). 1989-90, 3-for-5 (.600). 1990-91, 7-for-20 (.350). 1991-92, 9-for-25 (.360). Totals, 21-for-53 (.396).

BURROUGHS, TIM

F, TIMBERWOLVES

PERSONAL: Born October 14, 1969, in Hopkins, S.C. . . . 6-8/250. . . . Full name: Timothy Burroughs.
HIGH SCHOOL: Lower Richland (Hopkins, S.C.).
COLLEGE: Independence Junior College (Kan.), then Delgado (La.), then Jacksonville.
TRANSACTIONS/CAREER NOTES: Selected by Minnesota Timberwolves in second round (51st pick overall) of 1992 NBA Draft.

COLLEGIATE RECORD

Season Team	G	Min.	FGM	FGA	Pct.	FTM	FTA	Pct.	Reb.	Pts.	Avg.
88-89 —Independence Junior College...	29	. . .	121	218	.555	. . .	. . .	. . .	212	. . .	. . .
89-90 —Delgado..................................	34	. . .	248	459	.540	196	288	.681	466	694	20.4
90-91 —Jacksonville...........................	27	806	167	310	.539	80	130	.615	350	414	15.3
91-92 —Jacksonville...........................	28	800	152	303	.502	128	181	.707	370	436	15.6
Junior college totals.........................	63	. . .	369	677	.545	. . .	. . .	. . .	678	. . .	. . .
Four-year-college totals	55	1606	319	613	.520	208	311	.669	720	850	15.5

Three-point field goals: 1990-91, 0-for-2. 1991-92, 4-for-8 (.500). Totals, 4-for-10 (.400).

CAMBRIDGE, DEXTER

F, MAVERICKS

PERSONAL: Born January 29, 1970, in Eleuthra, Bahamas. . . . 6-7/225. . . . Full name: Dexter Ryan Cambridge.
HIGH SCHOOL: A.F. Adderly (Nassau, Bahamas).
COLLEGE: Lon Morris (Tex.), then Texas.
TRANSACTIONS/CAREER NOTES: Never drafted by an NBA franchise. . . . Signed as free agent by Dallas Mavericks (August 24, 1992).

COLLEGIATE RECORD

NOTES: Led Division I Junior Colleges in points-per-game average—33.1 (1990).

Season Team	G	Min.	FGM	FGA	Pct.	FTM	FTA	Pct.	Reb.	Pts.	Avg.
88-89 — Lon Morris	. . .	. . .	. . .	. . .	. . .	. . .	. . .	. . .	. . .	. . .	20.4
89-90 — Lon Morris	30	. . .	391	. . .	. . .	165	. . .	. . .	. . .	993	33.1
90-91 — Texas.......................................	32	599	136	292	.466	91	119	.765	125	389	12.2
91-92 — Texas.......................................	19	540	168	290	.579	76	116	.655	166	413	21.7
Four-year-college Totals	51	1139	304	582	.522	167	235	.711	291	802	15.7

Three-point field goals: 1990-91, 26-for-81 (.321). 1991-92, 1-for-11 (.091). Totals, 27-for-92 (.293).

CHRISTIE, DOUG

G, SUPERSONICS

PERSONAL: Born May 9, 1970, in Seattle. . . . 6-6/200. . . . Full name: Douglas Dale Christie.
HIGH SCHOOL: Rainier Beach (Seattle).
COLLEGE: Pepperdine.
TRANSACTIONS/CAREER NOTES: Selected by Seattle SuperSonics in first round (17th pick overall) of 1992 NBA Draft.

COLLEGIATE RECORD

Season Team	G	Min.	FGM	FGA	Pct.	FTM	FTA	Pct.	Reb.	Pts.	Avg.
88-89 — Pepperdine...............................					Did not play—ineligible.						
89-90 — Pepperdine...............................	28	687	84	167	.503	70	98	.714	115	250	8.9
90-91 — Pepperdine...............................	28	913	188	401	.469	143	187	.765	145	536	19.1
91-92 — Pepperdine...............................	31	1058	211	453	.466	144	193	.746	183	606	19.5
Totals	87	2658	483	1021	.473	357	478	.747	443	1392	16.0

Three-point field goals: 1989-90, 12-for-47 (.255). 1990-91, 17-for-65 (.262). 1991-92, 40-for-120 (.333). Totals, 69-for-232 (.297).

COOPER, DUANE

G, LAKERS

PERSONAL: Born June 25, 1969, in Benton Harbor, Mich. . . . 6-1/185. . . . Full name: Samuel Duane Cooper.
HIGH SCHOOL: Lakewood (Calif.).
COLLEGE: Southern California.
TRANSACTIONS/CAREER NOTES: Selected by Los Angeles Lakers in second round (36th pick overall) of 1992 NBA Draft.

COLLEGIATE RECORD

Season Team	G	Min.	FGM	FGA	Pct.	FTM	FTA	Pct.	Reb.	Pts.	Avg.
87-88 —Southern California	27	180	10	32	.313	10	15	.667	16	31	1.1
88-89 —Southern California	32	535	48	114	.421	20	43	.465	59	130	4.1
89-90 —Southern California					Did not play—broken foot.						
90-91 —Southern California	29	889	74	164	.451	19	30	.633	102	206	7.1
91-92 —Southern California	30	1012	119	240	.496	67	104	.644	78	365	12.2
Totals	118	2616	251	550	.456	116	192	.604	255	732	6.2

Three-point field goals: 1987-88, 1-for-9 (.111). 1988-89, 14-for-41 (.341). 1990-91, 39-for-92 (.424). 1991-92, 60-for-141 (.426). Totals, 114-for-283 (.403).

DID YOU KNOW. . .

. . . that Dennis Rodman had 12 of the NBA's top 14 single-game rebounding performances in 1991-92?

DANIELS, LLOYD
G, SPURS

PERSONAL: Born September 4, 1967, in Brooklyn, N.Y. . . . . 6-7/210. **HIGH SCHOOL:** Andrew Jackson (Queens, N.Y.). **COLLEGE:** Did not attend college. **TRANSACTIONS/CAREER NOTES:** Never drafted by an NBA franchise. . . . Played in Continental Basketball Association with Topeka Sizzlers (1987-88) and Quad City Thunder (1989-90). . . . Played in New Zealand (1988-89). . . . Played in United States Basketball League with Miami Tropics (1990-91) and Long Island Surf (1991-92). . . . Played in Global Basketball Association with Greensboro City Gaters (1991-92). . . . Signed as free agent by San Antonio Spurs (July 21, 1992).

CBA REGULAR-SEASON RECORD

Season Team	G	Min.	2-POINT FGM	FGA	Pct.	3-POINT FGM	FGA	Pct.	FTM	FTA	Pct.	Reb.	Ast.	Pts.	Avg.
87-88 — Topeka	28	749	170	337	.504	8	32	.250	84	124	.677	98	114	448	16.0
89-90 — Quad City	4	63	4	16	.250	2	4	.500	1	2	.500	9	5	15	3.8
Totals	32	812	174	353	.493	10	36	.278	85	126	.675	107	119	463	14.5

DAVIS, BRIAN
F, SUNS

PERSONAL: Born June 21, 1970, in Atlantic City, N.J. . . . . 6-7/200. **HIGH SCHOOL:** Bladensburg (Md.). **COLLEGE:** Duke. **TRANSACTIONS/CAREER NOTES:** Selected by Phoenix Suns in second round (48th pick overall) of 1992 NBA Draft.

COLLEGIATE RECORD

NOTES: Member of NCAA Division I championship teams (1991, 1992).

Season Team	G	Min.	FGM	FGA	Pct.	FTM	FTA	Pct.	Reb.	Pts.	Avg.
88-89 — Duke	29	245	20	52	.385	27	53	.509	33	67	2.3
89-90 — Duke	37	531	62	130	.477	61	95	.642	80	185	5.0
90-91 — Duke	39	903	104	228	.456	89	122	.730	158	298	7.6
91-92 — Duke	36	1111	140	291	.481	114	154	.740	163	402	11.2
Totals	141	2790	326	701	.465	291	424	.686	434	952	6.8

Three-point field goals: 1990-91, 1-for-5 (.200). 1991-92, 8-for-39 (.205). Totals, 9-for-44 (.205).

DAVIS, HUBERT
G, KNICKS

PERSONAL: Born May 17, 1970, in Winston-Salem, N.C. . . . . 6-5/183. . . . Full name: Hubert Ira Davis Jr. . . . Nephew of Walter Davis, forward with Denver Nuggets. **HIGH SCHOOL:** Lake Braddock Secondary School (Burke, Va.). **COLLEGE:** North Carolina. **TRANSACTIONS/CAREER NOTES:** Selected by New York Knicks in first round (20th pick overall) of 1992 NBA Draft.

COLLEGIATE RECORD

Season Team	G	Min.	FGM	FGA	Pct.	FTM	FTA	Pct.	Reb.	Pts.	Avg.
88-89 — North Carolina	35	248	44	86	.512	24	31	.774	27	116	3.3
89-90 — North Carolina	34	725	111	249	.446	59	74	.797	60	325	9.6
90-91 — North Carolina	35	851	161	309	.521	81	97	.835	85	467	13.3
91-92 — North Carolina	33	1095	241	474	.508	140	169	.828	76	707	21.4
Totals	137	2919	557	1118	.498	304	371	.819	248	1615	11.8

Three-point field goals: 1988-89, 4-for-13 (.308). 1989-90, 44-for-111 (.396). 1990-91, 64-for-131 (.489). 1991-92, 85-for-198 (.429). Totals, 197-for-453 (.435).

DAY, TODD
G/F, BUCKS

PERSONAL: Born January 7, 1970, in Decatur, Ill. . . . 6-8/200. . . . Full name: Todd F. Day. **HIGH SCHOOL:** Hamilton (Memphis, Tenn.). **COLLEGE:** Arkansas. **TRANSACTIONS/CAREER NOTES:** Selected by Milwaukee Bucks in first round (eighth pick overall) of 1992 NBA Draft.

COLLEGIATE RECORD

NOTES: THE SPORTING NEWS All-America second team (1992).

Season Team	G	Min.	FGM	FGA	Pct.	FTM	FTA	Pct.	Reb.	Pts.	Avg.
88-89 — Arkansas	32	741	148	328	.451	98	137	.715	129	425	13.3
89-90 — Arkansas	35	1008	237	483	.491	139	183	.760	188	684	19.5
90-91 — Arkansas	38	1121	277	586	.473	165	221	.747	201	786	20.7
91-92 — Arkansas	22	711	173	347	.499	97	127	.764	155	500	22.7
Totals	127	3581	835	1744	.479	499	668	.747	673	2395	18.9

Three-point field goals: 1988-89, 31-for-90 (.344). 1989-90, 71-for-176 (.403). 1990-91, 67-for-189 (.354). 1991-92, 57-for-133 (.429). Totals, 226-for-588 (.384).

DID YOU KNOW. . .

. . . that Houston's Otis Thorpe has played in 542 consecutive games, the NBA's longest current streak?

DUMAS, RICHARD
F, SUNS

PERSONAL: Born May 19, 1969, in Tulsa, Okla. . . . 6-7/204. . . . Full name: Richard Wayne Dumas. . . . Son of Richard Dumas, guard with Houston Mavericks of the American Basketball Association (1968-69).
HIGH SCHOOL: Booker T. Washington (Tulsa, Okla.).
COLLEGE: Oklahoma State.
TRANSACTIONS/CAREER NOTES: Played in Israel (1990-91). . . . Selected by Phoenix Suns in second round (46th pick overall) of 1991 NBA Draft. . . . Suspended for season for failing random drug test (October 31, 1991). . . . Played in Continental Basketball Association with Oklahoma City Cavalry (1991-92).

COLLEGIATE RECORD

Season Team	G	Min.	FGM	FGA	Pct.	FTM	FTA	Pct.	Reb.	Pts.	Avg.
87-88 — Oklahoma State	30	937	203	372	.546	115	154	.747	193	521	17.4
88-89 — Oklahoma State	28	850	184	411	.448	66	107	.617	197	439	15.7
89-90 — Oklahoma State	12	276	62	113	.549	28	44	.636	65	152	12.7
Totals	70	2063	449	896	.501	209	305	.685	455	1112	15.9

Three-point field goals: 1987-88, 0-for-2. 1988-89, 5-for-21 (.238). 1989-90, 0-for-3. Totals, 5-for-26 (.192).

CBA REGULAR-SEASON RECORD

Season Team	G	Min.	2-POINT			3-POINT			FTM	FTA	Pct.	Reb.	Ast.	Pts.	Avg.
			FGM	FGA	Pct.	FGM	FGA	Pct.							
91-92 — Oklahoma City .	9	349	102	180	.567	0	0	. . .	60	75	.800	78	24	264	29.3

ELLIS, LaPHONSO
F, NUGGETS

PERSONAL: Born May 5, 1970, in East St. Louis, Ill. . . . 6-8/240.
HIGH SCHOOL: Lincoln (East St. Louis, Ill.).
COLLEGE: Notre Dame.
TRANSACTIONS/CAREER NOTES: Selected by Denver Nuggets in first round (fifth pick overall) of 1992 NBA Draft.

COLLEGIATE RECORD

Season Team	G	Min.	FGM	FGA	Pct.	FTM	FTA	Pct.	Reb.	Pts.	Avg.
88-89 — Notre Dame	27	819	156	277	.563	52	76	.684	254	365	13.5
89-90 — Notre Dame	22	712	114	223	.511	79	117	.675	278	309	14.0
90-91 — Notre Dame	15	495	90	157	.573	58	81	.716	158	246	16.4
91-92 — Notre Dame	33	1194	227	360	.631	127	194	.655	385	585	17.7
Totals	97	3220	587	1017	.577	316	468	.675	1075	1505	15.5

Three-point field goals: 1988-89, 1-for-1. 1989-90, 2-for-6 (.333). 1990-91, 8-for-17 (.471). 1991-92, 4-for-9 (.444). Totals, 15-for-33 (.455).

ELLIS, RON
F, SUNS

PERSONAL: Born September 18, 1968, in Monroe, La. . . . 6-7/215. . . . Full name: Ronald Ellis.
HIGH SCHOOL: Rayville (La.).
COLLEGE: Tyler Junior College (Tex.), then Louisiana Tech.
TRANSACTIONS/CAREER NOTES: Selected by Phoenix Suns in second round (49th pick overall) of 1992 NBA Draft.

COLLEGIATE RECORD

Season Team	G	Min.	FGM	FGA	Pct.	FTM	FTA	Pct.	Reb.	Pts.	Avg.
88-89 — Tyler Junior College					Statistics unavailable.						
89-90 — Tyler Junior College	34	. . .	. . .	. . .	. . .	. . .	. . .	. . .	364	622	18.3
90-91 — Louisiana Tech	31	820	157	296	.530	92	123	.748	228	416	13.4
91-92 — Louisiana Tech	31	896	189	351	.538	104	129	.806	240	486	15.7
Junior college totals	34	. . .	. . .	. . .	. . .	. . .	. . .	. . .	364	622	18.3
Four-year-college totals	62	1716	346	647	.535	196	252	.778	468	902	14.5

Three-point field goals: 1990-91, 10-for-24 (.417). 1991-92, 4-for-17 (.235). Totals, 14-for-41 (.341).

FISH, MATT
C, WARRIORS

PERSONAL: Born November 18, 1969, in Washington, Ia. . . . 6-11/235.
HIGH SCHOOL: Washington (Ia.).
COLLEGE: UNC Wilmington.
TRANSACTIONS/CAREER NOTES: Selected by Golden State Warriors in second round (50th pick overall) of 1992 NBA Draft.

COLLEGIATE RECORD

Season Team	G	Min.	FGM	FGA	Pct.	FTM	FTA	Pct.	Reb.	Pts.	Avg.
88-89 — UNC Wilmington	6	50	7	12	.583	1	4	.250	7	15	2.5
89-90 — UNC Wilmington	28	525	100	176	.568	38	77	.494	157	238	8.5
90-91 — UNC Wilmington	28	647	114	207	.551	53	84	.631	190	281	10.0
91-92 — UNC Wilmington	28	865	206	319	.646	82	130	.631	262	494	17.6
Totals	90	2087	427	714	.598	174	295	.590	616	1028	11.4

GEIGER, MATT
C, HEAT

PERSONAL: Born September 10, 1969, in Salem, Mass. . . . 7-1/251. . . . Full name: Matthew Allen Geiger.
HIGH SCHOOL: Countryside Senior (Clearwater, Fla.).
COLLEGE: Auburn, then Georgia Tech.
TRANSACTIONS/CAREER NOTES: Selected by Miami Heat in second round (42nd pick overall) of 1992 NBA Draft.

COLLEGIATE RECORD

Season Team	G	Min.	FGM	FGA	Pct.	FTM	FTA	Pct.	Reb.	Pts.	Avg.
87-88 —Auburn	30	597	80	156	.513	33	50	.660	124	193	6.4
88-89 —Auburn	28	807	170	337	.504	106	154	.688	186	446	15.9
89-90 —Georgia Tech					Did not play—transfer student.						
90-91 —Georgia Tech	27	711	130	237	.549	49	73	.671	172	309	11.4
91-92 —Georgia Tech	35	952	165	270	.611	84	119	.706	254	414	11.8
Totals	120	3067	545	1000	.545	272	396	.687	736	1362	11.4

Three-point field goals: 1988-89, 0-for-4. 1990-91, 0-for-3. 1991-92, 0-for-2. Totals, 0-for-9.

GREEN, LITTERIAL
G, MAGIC

PERSONAL: Born March 7, 1970, in Pascagoula, Miss. . . . 6-1/185.
HIGH SCHOOL: Moss Point (Miss.).
COLLEGE: Georgia.
TRANSACTIONS/CAREER NOTES: Selected by Chicago Bulls in second round (39th pick overall) of 1992 NBA Draft. . . . Rights traded by Bulls to Orlando Magic for 1993 second-round draft choice (July 7, 1992).

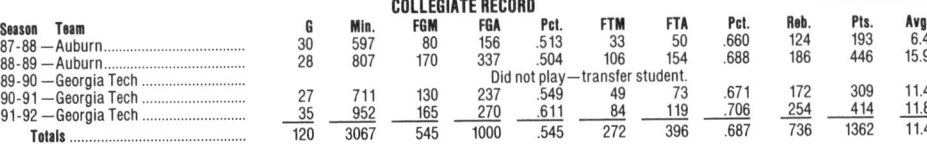

COLLEGIATE RECORD

Season Team	G	Min.	FGM	FGA	Pct.	FTM	FTA	Pct.	Reb.	Pts.	Avg.
88-89 —Georgia	31	998	144	356	.404	145	187	.775	57	481	15.5
89-90 —Georgia	28	889	160	384	.417	121	171	.708	75	490	17.5
90-91 —Georgia	28	839	187	423	.442	146	188	.777	72	576	20.6
91-92 —Georgia	29	976	183	448	.408	136	198	.687	87	564	19.4
Totals	116	3702	674	1611	.418	548	744	.737	291	2111	18.2

Three-point field goals: 1988-89, 48-for-122 (.393). 1989-90, 49-for-128 (.383). 1990-91, 56-for-151 (.371). 1991-92, 62-for-143 (.434). Totals, 215-for-544 (.395).

GUGLIOTTA, TOM
F, BULLETS

PERSONAL: Born December 19, 1969, in Huntington Station, N.Y. . . . 6-10/240. . . . Full name: Thomas James Gugliotta.
HIGH SCHOOL: Walt Whitman (Huntington Station, N.Y.).
COLLEGE: North Carolina State.
TRANSACTIONS/CAREER NOTES: Selected by Washington Bullets in first round (sixth pick overall) of 1992 NBA Draft.

COLLEGIATE RECORD

Season Team	G	Min.	FGM	FGA	Pct.	FTM	FTA	Pct.	Reb.	Pts.	Avg.
88-89 —North Carolina State	21	171	18	42	.429	19	29	.655	35	56	2.7
89-90 —North Carolina State	30	886	135	268	.504	41	61	.672	211	334	11.1
90-91 —North Carolina State	31	1123	170	340	.500	65	101	.644	281	471	15.2
91-92 —North Carolina State	30	1107	240	534	.449	102	149	.685	293	675	22.5
Totals	112	3287	563	1184	.476	227	340	.668	820	1536	13.7

Three-point field goals: 1988-89, 1-for-2 (.500). 1989-90, 23-for-47 (.489). 1990-91, 66-for-166 (.398). 1991-92, 93-for-233 (.399). Totals, 183-for-448 (.408).

HORRY, ROBERT
F, ROCKETS

PERSONAL: Born August 25, 1970, in Andalusia, Ala. . . . 6-9/220.
HIGH SCHOOL: Andalusia (Ala.).
COLLEGE: Alabama.
TRANSACTIONS/CAREER NOTES: Selected by Houston Rockets in first round (11th pick overall) of 1992 NBA Draft.

COLLEGIATE RECORD

Season Team	G	Min.	FGM	FGA	Pct.	FTM	FTA	Pct.	Reb.	Pts.	Avg.
88-89 —Alabama	31	590	79	185	.427	38	59	.644	156	200	6.5
89-90 —Alabama	35	1022	164	351	.467	79	104	.760	217	457	13.1
90-91 —Alabama	32	959	133	296	.449	82	102	.804	260	381	11.9
91-92 —Alabama	35	1185	196	417	.470	120	165	.727	296	554	15.8
Totals	133	3756	572	1249	.458	319	430	.742	929	1592	12.0

Three-point field goals: 1988-89, 4-for-13 (.308). 1989-90, 50-for-117 (.427). 1990-91, 33-for-98 (.337). 1991-92, 42-for-120 (.350). Totals, 129-for-348 (.371).

HOUSTON, BYRON
F, BULLS

PERSONAL: Born November 22, 1969, in Watonga, Kan. . . . 6-7/250.
HIGH SCHOOL: Star-Spencer (Oklahoma City).
COLLEGE: Oklahoma State.
TRANSACTIONS/CAREER NOTES: Selected by Chicago Bulls in first round (27th pick overall) of 1992 NBA Draft.

COLLEGIATE RECORD

Season Team	G	Min.	FGM	FGA	Pct.	FTM	FTA	Pct.	Reb.	Pts.	Avg.
88-89 —Oklahoma State	30	842	140	240	.583	111	149	.745	251	391	13.0
89-90 —Oklahoma State	31	1030	189	358	.528	196	268	.731	309	574	18.5
90-91 —Oklahoma State	32	1084	250	436	.573	223	300	.743	336	726	22.7
91-92 —Oklahoma State	34	1157	249	467	.533	168	240	.700	294	688	20.2
Totals	127	4113	828	1501	.552	698	957	.729	1190	2379	18.7

Three-point field goals: 1989-90, 0-for-6. 1990-91, 3-for-4 (.750). 1991-92, 22-for-79 (.278). Totals, 25-for-89 (.281).

JACKSON, JIM
G, MAVERICKS

PERSONAL: Born October 14, 1970, in Toledo, O. . . . 6-6/220. . . . Full name: James Arthur Jackson.
HIGH SCHOOL: Macomber-Whitney (Toledo, O.).
COLLEGE: Ohio State.
TRANSACTIONS/CAREER NOTES: Selected as undergraduate by Dallas Mavericks in first round (fourth pick overall) of 1992 NBA Draft.

COLLEGIATE RECORD

NOTES: THE SPORTING NEWS All-America first team (1992). . . . THE SPORTING NEWS All-America third team (1991).

Season Team	G	Min.	FGM	FGA	Pct.	FTM	FTA	Pct.	Reb.	Pts.	Avg.
89-90 —Ohio State	30	1035	194	389	.499	73	93	.785	166	482	16.1
90-91 —Ohio State	31	997	228	441	.517	112	149	.752	169	585	18.9
91-92 —Ohio State	32	1133	264	535	.493	146	180	.811	217	718	22.4
Totals	93	3165	686	1365	.503	331	422	.784	552	1785	19.2

Three-point field goals: 1989-90, 21-for-59 (.356). 1990-91, 17-for-51 (.333). 1991-92, 44-for-108 (.407). Totals, 82-for-218 (.376).

JOHNSON, DAVE
G/F, TRAIL BLAZERS

PERSONAL: Born November 16, 1970, in Morgan City, La. . . . 6-7/210.
HIGH SCHOOL: Morgan City (La.), then Maine Central Institute (Pittsfield, Me.).
COLLEGE: Syracuse.
TRANSACTIONS/CAREER NOTES: Selected by Portland Trail Blazers in first round (26th pick overall) of 1992 NBA Draft.

COLLEGIATE RECORD

Season Team	G	Min.	FGM	FGA	Pct.	FTM	FTA	Pct.	Reb.	Pts.	Avg.
88-89 —Syracuse	37	541	59	129	.457	35	68	.515	74	156	4.2
89-90 —Syracuse	31	558	76	190	.400	44	72	.611	73	203	6.5
90-91 —Syracuse	32	1118	226	453	.499	131	199	.658	201	621	19.4
91-92 —Syracuse	32	1212	208	501	.415	150	212	.708	223	634	19.8
Totals	132	3429	569	1273	.447	360	551	.653	571	1614	12.2

Three-point field goals: 1988-89, 3-for-20 (.150). 1989-90, 7-for-25 (.280). 1990-91, 38-for-100 (.380). 1991-92, 68-for-199 (.342). Totals, 116-for-344 (.337).

JONES, POPEYE
F, ROCKETS

PERSONAL: Born June 17, 1970, in Dresden, Tenn. . . . 6-8/270. . . . Full name: Ronald Jerome Jones.
HIGH SCHOOL: Dresden (Tenn.).
COLLEGE: Murray State.
TRANSACTIONS/CAREER NOTES: Selected by Houston Rockets in second round (41st pick overall) of 1992 NBA Draft.

COLLEGIATE RECORD

NOTES: Led NCAA Division I with 14.4 rebounds per game (1992).

Season Team	G	Min.	FGM	FGA	Pct.	FTM	FTA	Pct.	Reb.	Pts.	Avg.
88-89 —Murray State	30	518	65	133	.489	43	57	.754	138	173	5.8
89-90 —Murray State	30	1038	217	434	.500	137	181	.757	336	586	19.5
90-91 —Murray State	33	1052	268	544	.493	123	173	.711	469	666	20.2
91-92 —Murray State	30	994	232	475	.488	161	207	.778	431	632	21.1
Totals	123	3602	782	1586	.493	464	618	.751	1374	2057	16.7

Three-point field goals: 1989-90, 15-for-34 (.441). 1990-91, 7-for-32 (.219). 1991-92, 7-for-18 (.389). Totals, 29-for-84 (.345).

KEEFE, ADAM
F, HAWKS

PERSONAL: Born February 22, 1970, in Irvine, Calif. . . . 6-9/241. . . . Full name: Adam T. Keefe.
HIGH SCHOOL: Woodbridge (Irvine, Calif.).
COLLEGE: Stanford.
TRANSACTIONS/CAREER NOTES: Selected by Atlanta Hawks in first round (10th pick overall) of 1992 NBA Draft.

COLLEGIATE RECORD

Season Team	G	Min.	FGM	FGA	Pct.	FTM	FTA	Pct.	Reb.	Pts.	Avg.
88-89 —Stanford	33	653	93	147	.633	91	132	.689	179	277	8.4
89-90 —Stanford	30	1065	210	335	.627	179	247	.725	272	599	20.0
90-91 —Stanford	33	1204	252	414	.609	203	267	.760	313	709	21.5
91-92 —Stanford	29	1080	275	488	.564	179	240	.746	355	734	25.3
Totals	125	4002	830	1384	.600	652	886	.736	1119	2319	18.6

Three-point field goals: 1990-91, 2-for-4 (.500). 1991-92, 5-for-11 (.455). Totals, 7-for-15 (.467).

KING, CHRIS
F

PERSONAL: Born July 24, 1969, in Newton Grove, N.C. . . . . 6-8/215. . . . Full name: Christopher Donnell King.
HIGH SCHOOL: Hobbton (Newton Grove, N.C.).
COLLEGE: Wake Forest.
TRANSACTIONS/CAREER NOTES: Selected by Seattle SuperSonics in second round (45th pick overall) of 1992 NBA Draft. . . . Signed to play in Spain (August 18, 1992).

COLLEGIATE RECORD

Season Team	G	Min.	FGM	FGA	Pct.	FTM	FTA	Pct.	Reb.	Pts.	Avg.
88-89 —Wake Forest	28	788	168	311	.540	68	104	.654	171	404	14.4
89-90 —Wake Forest	28	939	189	346	.546	73	124	.589	208	452	16.1
90-91 —Wake Forest	30	950	179	366	.489	77	121	.636	172	452	15.1
91-92 —Wake Forest	27	845	166	329	.505	70	101	.693	139	413	15.3
Totals	113	3522	702	1352	.519	288	450	.640	690	1721	15.2

Three-point field goals: 1988-89, 0-for-2. 1989-90, 1-for-2 (.500). 1990-91, 17-for-41 (.415). 1991-92, 11-for-32 (.344). Totals, 29-for-77 (.377).

LAETTNER, CHRISTIAN
F, TIMBERWOLVES

PERSONAL: Born August 17, 1969, in Angola, N.Y. . . . 6-11/235. . . . Full name: Christian Donald Laettner. . . . Name pronounced LATE-ner.
HIGH SCHOOL: Nichols School (Buffalo, N.Y.).
COLLEGE: Duke.
TRANSACTIONS/CAREER NOTES: Selected by Minnesota Timberwolves in first round (third pick overall) of 1992 NBA Draft.
MISCELLANEOUS: Member of gold-medal-winning U.S. Olympic team (1992).

COLLEGIATE RECORD

NOTES: THE SPORTING NEWS College Player of the Year (1992). . . . THE SPORTING NEWS college All-America first team (1992). . . . THE SPORTING NEWS college All-America second team (1991). . . . THE SPORTING NEWS college All-America third team (1990). . . . Most Outstanding Player in NCAA Division I tournament (1991). . . . Member of NCAA Division I championship teams (1991, 1992).

Season Team	G	Min.	FGM	FGA	Pct.	FTM	FTA	Pct.	Reb.	Pts.	Avg.
88-89 —Duke	36	607	115	159	.723	88	121	.727	170	319	8.9
89-90 —Duke	38	1135	194	380	.511	225	269	.836	364	619	16.3
90-91 —Duke	39	1178	271	471	.575	211	263	.802	340	771	19.8
91-92 —Duke	35	1128	254	442	.575	189	232	.815	275	751	21.5
Totals	148	4048	834	1452	.574	713	885	.806	1149	2460	16.6

Three-point field goals: 1988-89, 1-for-1. 1989-90, 6-for-12 (.500). 1990-91, 18-for-53 (.340). 1991-92, 54-for-97 (.557). Totals, 79-for-163 (.485).

MacLEAN, DON
F, CLIPPERS

PERSONAL: Born January 16, 1970, in Palo Alto, Calif. . . . 6-10/240. . . . Full name: Donald James MacLean.
HIGH SCHOOL: Simi Valley (Calif.).
COLLEGE: UCLA.
TRANSACTIONS/CAREER NOTES: Selected by Detroit Pistons in first round (19th pick overall) of 1992 NBA Draft. . . . Rights traded by Pistons with William Bedford to Los Angeles Clippers for Olden Polynice and 1996 and 1997 second-round draft choices (June 24, 1992).

COLLEGIATE RECORD

NOTES: THE SPORTING NEWS All-America second team (1992). . . . Led NCAA Division I with .921 free-throw percentage (1992).

Season Team	G	Min.	FGM	FGA	Pct.	FTM	FTA	Pct.	Reb.	Pts.	Avg.
88-89 —UCLA	31	999	217	391	.555	142	174	.816	231	577	18.6
89-90 —UCLA	33	1111	238	461	.516	179	211	.848	287	656	19.9
90-91 —UCLA	31	1008	259	470	.551	193	228	.846	226	714	23.0
91-92 —UCLA	32	1033	229	454	.504	197	214	.921	248	661	20.7
Totals	127	4151	943	1776	.531	711	827	.860	992	2608	20.5

Three-point field goals: 1988-89, 1-for-3 (.333). 1989-90, 1-for-2 (.500). 1990-91, 3-for-13 (.231). 1991-92, 6-for-17 (.353). Totals, 11-for-35 (.314).

MAXEY, MARLON
F, TIMBERWOLVES

PERSONAL: Born February 19, 1969, in Chicago. . . . 6-8/250. . . . Full name: Marlon Lee Maxey.
HIGH SCHOOL: Percy L. Julian (Chicago).
COLLEGE: Minnesota, then Texas-El Paso.
TRANSACTIONS/CAREER NOTES: Selected by Minnesota Timberwolves in second round (28th pick overall) of 1992 NBA Draft.

COLLEGIATE RECORD

Season Team	G	Min.	FGM	FGA	Pct.	FTM	FTA	Pct.	Reb.	Pts.	Avg.
87-88 —Minnesota	13	108	9	32	.281	13	21	.619	42	31	2.4
88-89 —Texas-El Paso					Did not play—transfer student.						
89-90 —Texas-El Paso	30	797	140	256	.547	92	133	.692	235	372	12.4

Season Team	G	Min.	FGM	FGA	Pct.	FTM	FTA	Pct.	Reb.	Pts.	Avg.
90-91 —Texas-El Paso	17	450	81	158	.513	82	114	.719	120	244	14.4
91-92 —Texas-El Paso	25	710	135	259	.521	109	150	.727	184	379	15.2
Totals	85	2065	365	705	.518	296	418	.708	581	1026	12.1

MAYBERRY, LEE
G, BUCKS

PERSONAL: Born June 12, 1970, in Tulsa, Okla. . . . 6-2/175. . . . Full name: Orva Lee Mayberry Jr.
HIGH SCHOOL: Rogers (Tulsa, Okla.).
COLLEGE: Arkansas.
TRANSACTIONS/CAREER NOTES: Selected by Milwaukee Bucks in first round (23rd pick overall) of 1992 NBA Draft.

COLLEGIATE RECORD

Season Team	G	Min.	FGM	FGA	Pct.	FTM	FTA	Pct.	Reb.	Pts.	Avg.
88-89 —Arkansas	32	1001	157	314	.500	67	91	.736	102	414	12.9
89-90 —Arkansas	35	1131	193	381	.507	57	72	.792	100	508	14.5
90-91 —Arkansas	38	1216	192	397	.484	59	93	.634	129	500	13.2
91-92 —Arkansas	34	1167	181	368	.492	93	125	.744	78	518	15.2
Totals	139	4515	723	1460	.495	276	381	.724	409	1940	14.0

Three-point field goals: 1988-89, 33-for-74 (.446). 1989-90, 65-for-129 (.504). 1990-91, 57-for-149 (.383). 1991-92, 63-for-162 (.389). Totals, 218-for-514 (.424).

MILLER, OLIVER
F/C, SUNS

PERSONAL: Born April 6, 1970, in Fort Worth, Tex. . . . 6-9/290. . . . Full name: Oliver J. Miller.
HIGH SCHOOL: Southwest (Fort Worth, Tex.).
COLLEGE: Arkansas.
TRANSACTIONS/CAREER NOTES: Selected by Phoenix Suns in first round (22nd pick overall) of 1992 NBA Draft.

COLLEGIATE RECORD

NOTES: Led NCAA Division I with .704 field-goal percentage (1991).

Season Team	G	Min.	FGM	FGA	Pct.	FTM	FTA	Pct.	Reb.	Pts.	Avg.
88-89 —Arkansas	30	599	88	161	.547	50	78	.641	112	230	7.7
89-90 —Arkansas	35	757	152	238	.639	86	132	.652	219	390	11.1
90-91 —Arkansas	38	931	254	361	.704	87	135	.644	294	596	15.7
91-92 —Arkansas	34	956	186	309	.602	86	133	.647	261	458	13.5
Totals	137	3243	680	1069	.636	309	478	.646	886	1674	12.2

Three-point field goals: 1988-89, 4-for-12 (.333). 1989-90, 0-for-4. 1990-91, 1-for-3 (.333). 1991-92, 0-for-11. Totals, 5-for-30 (.167).

MINER, HAROLD
G, HEAT

PERSONAL: Born May 5, 1971, in Inglewood, Calif. . . . 6-5/210. . . . Full name: Harold David Miner.
HIGH SCHOOL: Inglewood (Calif.).
COLLEGE: Southern California.
TRANSACTIONS/CAREER NOTES: Selected as undergraduate by Miami Heat in first round (12th pick overall) of 1992 NBA Draft.

COLLEGIATE RECORD

NOTES: THE SPORTING NEWS college All-America second team (1992).

Season Team	G	Min.	FGM	FGA	Pct.	FTM	FTA	Pct.	Reb.	Pts.	Avg.
89-90 —Southern California	28	978	206	436	.472	106	126	.841	101	578	20.6
90-91 —Southern California	29	1049	235	519	.453	152	190	.800	159	681	23.5
91-92 —Southern California	30	1042	250	571	.438	232	286	.811	211	789	26.3
Totals	87	3069	691	1526	.453	490	602	.814	471	2048	23.5

Three-point field goals: 1989-90, 60-for-142 (.423). 1990-91, 59-for-175 (.337). 1991-92, 57-for-162 (.352). Totals, 176-for-479 (.367).

MORNINGSTAR, DARREN
C, CELTICS

PERSONAL: Born April 22, 1969, in Stevenson, Wash. . . . 6-10/235.
HIGH SCHOOL: Stevenson (Wash.).
COLLEGE: Navy, then Pittsburgh.
TRANSACTIONS/CAREER NOTES: Selected by Boston Celtics in second round (47th pick overall) of 1992 NBA Draft.

COLLEGIATE RECORD

Season Team	G	Min.	FGM	FGA	Pct.	FTM	FTA	Pct.	Reb.	Pts.	Avg.
87-88 —Navy	5	127	23	60	.383	15	24	.625	30	61	12.2
88-89 —Pittsburgh					Did not play—transfer student.						
89-90 —Pittsburgh	29	375	39	85	.459	33	54	.611	82	111	3.8
90-91 —Pittsburgh	33	549	84	179	.469	58	90	.644	134	226	6.8
91-92 —Pittsburgh	34	863	164	326	.503	90	166	.542	210	418	12.3
Totals	101	1914	310	650	.477	196	334	.587	456	816	8.1

MORRIS, ISAIAH
F, PISTONS

PERSONAL: Born April 2, 1969, in Richmond, Va. . . . 6-8/228. . . . Full name: Isaiah Butch Morris.
HIGH SCHOOL: Huguenot (Richmond, Va.).
COLLEGE: San Jacinto (Tex.), then Arkansas.

TRANSACTIONS/CAREER NOTES: Selected by Miami Heat in second round (37th pick overall) of 1992 NBA draft. . . . Rights traded by Heat with conditional draft choice to Detroit Pistons for John Salley (September 8, 1992).

COLLEGIATE RECORD

Season Team	G	Min.	FGM	FGA	Pct.	FTM	FTA	Pct.	Reb.	Pts.	Avg.
88-89 — San Jacinto	40	781	202	344	.587	70	85	.824	273	477	11.9
89-90 — San Jacinto	38	795	194	304	.638	87	119	.731	282	475	12.5
90-91 — Arkansas	38	649	117	235	.498	51	64	.797	157	286	7.5
91-92 — Arkansas	34	712	133	277	.480	81	98	.827	169	348	10.2
Junior college totals	78	1576	396	648	.611	157	204	.770	555	952	12.2
Four-year-college totals	72	1361	250	512	.488	132	162	.815	326	634	8.8

Three-point field goals: 1990-91, 1-for-2 (.500). 1991-92, 1-for-7 (.143). Totals, 2-for-9 (.222).

MOURNING, ALONZO
C, HORNETS

PERSONAL: Born February 8, 1970, in Chesapeake, Va. . . . 6-10/240.
HIGH SCHOOL: Indian River (Chesapeake, Va.)
COLLEGE: Georgetown.

TRANSACTIONS/CAREER NOTES: Selected by Charlotte Hornets in first round (second pick overall) of 1992 NBA Draft.

COLLEGIATE RECORD

NOTES: THE SPORTING NEWS All-America second team (1990, 1992) . . . Led NCAA Division I with 4.97 blocked shots per game (1989).

Season Team	G	Min.	FGM	FGA	Pct.	FTM	FTA	Pct.	Reb.	Pts.	Avg.
88-89 — Georgetown	34	962	158	262	.603	130	195	.667	248	447	13.1
89-90 — Georgetown	31	937	145	276	.525	220	281	.783	265	510	16.5
90-91 — Georgetown	23	682	105	201	.522	149	188	.793	176	363	15.8
91-92 — Georgetown	32	1051	204	343	.595	272	359	.758	343	681	21.3
Totals	120	3632	612	1082	.566	771	1023	.754	1032	2001	16.7

Three-point field goals: 1988-89, 1-for-4 (.250). 1989-90, 0-for-2. 1990-91, 4-for-13 (.308). 1991-92, 6-for-23 (.261). Totals, 11-for-42 (.262).

MURRAY, TRACY
F, TRAIL BLAZERS

PERSONAL: Born July 25, 1971, in Los Angeles. . . . 6-8/225.
HIGH SCHOOL: Glendora (Calif.).
COLLEGE: UCLA.
TRANSACTIONS/CAREER NOTES: Selected as undergraduate by San Antonio Spurs in first round (18th pick overall) of 1992 NBA Draft. . . . Rights traded by Spurs to Milwaukee Bucks for Dale Ellis (July 1, 1992). . . . Rights traded by Bucks to Portland Trail Blazers for Alaa Abdelnaby (July 1, 1992).

COLLEGIATE RECORD

Season Team	G	Min.	FGM	FGA	Pct.	FTM	FTA	Pct.	Reb.	Pts.	Avg.
89-90 — UCLA	33	863	146	330	.442	69	90	.767	182	407	12.3
90-91 — UCLA	32	1003	247	491	.503	112	141	.794	213	679	21.2
91-92 — UCLA	33	1083	240	446	.538	148	185	.800	232	706	21.4
Totals	98	2949	633	1267	.500	329	416	.791	627	1792	18.3

Three-point field goals: 1989-90, 46-for-134 (.343). 1990-91, 73-for-189 (.386). 1991-92, 78-for-156 (.500). Totals, 197-for-479 (.411).

O'NEAL, SHAQUILLE
C, MAGIC

PERSONAL: Born March 6, 1972, in Newark, N.J. . . . 7-1/301. . . . Full name: Shaquille Rashaun O'Neal.
HIGH SCHOOL: Cole (San Antonio).
COLLEGE: Louisiana State.

TRANSACTIONS/CAREER NOTES: Selected as undergraduate by Orlando Magic in first round (first pick overall) of 1992 NBA Draft.

COLLEGIATE RECORD

NOTES: THE SPORTING NEWS All-America first team (1990, 1991). . . . Led NCAA Division I with 14.7 rebounds per game (1991). . . . Led NCAA Division I with 5.2 blocked shots per game (1992).

Season Team	G	Min.	FGM	FGA	Pct.	FTM	FTA	Pct.	Reb.	Pts.	Avg.
89-90 — Louisiana State	32	901	180	314	.573	85	153	.556	385	445	13.9
90-91 — Louisiana State	28	881	312	497	.628	150	235	.638	411	774	27.6
91-92 — Louisiana State	30	959	294	478	.615	134	254	.528	421	722	24.1
Totals	90	2741	786	1289	.610	369	642	.575	1217	1941	21.6

DID YOU KNOW. . .

. . . that the Miami Heat has never beaten the Bulls, Suns, Trail Blazers or Lakers?

OTHICK, MATT
G, SPURS

PERSONAL: Born March 16, 1969, in Clovis, N.M. . . . 6-2/165. . . . Full name: Matthew Brian Othick. . . . Name pronounced AH-thick.
HIGH SCHOOL: Bishop Gorman.
COLLEGE: Arizona.

TRANSACTIONS/CAREER NOTES: Never drafted by an NBA franchise. . . . Signed as free agent by San Antonio Spurs (August 19, 1992).

COLLEGIATE RECORD

Season Team	G	Min.	FGM	FGA	Pct.	FTM	FTA	Pct.	Reb.	Pts.	Avg.
88-89 — Arizona	31	446	49	108	.454	56	68	.824	37	179	5.8
89-90 — Arizona	32	824	72	178	.404	86	110	.782	68	277	8.7
90-91 — Arizona	35	935	74	193	.383	77	98	.786	84	273	7.8
91-92 — Arizona	31	936	103	221	.466	49	74	.662	77	326	10.5
Totals	129	3141	298	700	.426	268	350	.766	266	1055	8.2

Three-point field goals: 1988-89, 25-for-65 (.385). 1989-90, 47-for-128 (.367). 1990-91, 48-for-134 (.358). 1991-92, 71-for-158 (.449). Totals, 191-for-485 (.394).

PEELER, ANTHONY
G, LAKERS

PERSONAL: Born November 25, 1969, in Kansas City, Mo. . . . 6-4/215. . . . Full name: Anthony Eugene Peeler.
HIGH SCHOOL: Paseo (Kansas City, Mo.).
COLLEGE: Missouri.

TRANSACTIONS/CAREER NOTES: Selected by Los Angeles Lakers in first round (15th pick overall) of 1992 NBA Draft.

COLLEGIATE RECORD

Season Team	G	Min.	FGM	FGA	Pct.	FTM	FTA	Pct.	Reb.	Pts.	Avg.
88-89 — Missouri	36	801	130	258	.504	89	118	.754	134	362	10.1
89-90 — Missouri	31	1031	184	413	.446	130	169	.769	168	522	16.8
90-91 — Missouri	21	725	134	282	.475	116	151	.768	131	408	19.4
91-92 — Missouri	29	1026	218	475	.459	187	232	.806	160	678	23.4
Totals	117	3583	666	1428	.466	522	670	.779	593	1970	16.8

Three-point field goals: 1988-89, 13-for-37 (.351). 1989-90, 24-for-68 (.353). 1990-91, 24-for-58 (.414). 1991-92, 55-for-132 (.417). Totals, 116-for-295 (.393).

PRICE, BRENT
G, BULLETS

PERSONAL: Born December 9, 1968, in Shawnee, Okla. . . . 6-1/165. . . . Full name: Hartley Brent Price. . . . Brother of Mark Price, guard with Cleveland Cavaliers.
HIGH SCHOOL: Enid (Okla.).

COLLEGE: South Carolina, then Oklahoma.
TRANSACTIONS/CAREER NOTES: Selected by Washington Bullets in second round (32nd pick overall) of 1992 NBA Draft.

COLLEGIATE RECORD

Season Team	G	Min.	FGM	FGA	Pct.	FTM	FTA	Pct.	Reb.	Pts.	Avg.
87-88 — South Carolina	29	643	98	213	.460	66	77	.857	47	311	10.7
88-89 — South Carolina	30	952	144	294	.490	76	90	.844	75	432	14.4
89-90 — Oklahoma					Did not play—transfer student.						
90-91 — Oklahoma	35	1197	178	428	.416	166	198	.838	127	613	17.5
91-92 — Oklahoma	30	1064	182	391	.465	120	152	.789	111	560	18.7
Totals	124	3856	602	1326	.454	428	517	.828	360	1916	15.5

Three-point field goals: 1987-88, 49-for-112 (.438). 1988-89, 68-for-139 (.489). 1990-91, 91-for-244 (.373). 1991-92, 76-for-194 (.392). Totals, 284-for-689 (.412).

ROBERTS, BRETT
F, KINGS

PERSONAL: Born March 24, 1970, in Portsmouth, O. . . . 6-8/230. . . . Full name: Brett Joseph Roberts.
HIGH SCHOOL: South Webster (O.).
COLLEGE: Morehead State.

TRANSACTIONS/CAREER NOTES: Selected by Sacramento Kings in second round (54th pick overall) of 1992 NBA Draft.

COLLEGIATE RECORD

NOTES: Led NCAA Division I with 28.1 points per game (1992).

Season Team	G	Min.	FGM	FGA	Pct.	FTM	FTA	Pct.	Reb.	Pts.	Avg.
88-89 — Morehead State	27	695	88	196	.449	57	79	.722	179	244	9.0
89-90 — Morehead State	29	945	150	283	.530	95	127	.748	264	409	14.1
90-91 — Morehead State	22	760	124	268	.463	57	73	.781	198	320	14.5
91-92 — Morehead State	29	1044	278	580	.479	193	219	.881	256	815	28.1
Totals	107	3444	640	1327	.482	402	498	.807	897	1788	16.7

Three-point field goals: 1988-89, 11-for-32 (.344). 1989-90, 14-for-37 (.378). 1990-91, 15-for-45 (.333). 1991-92, 66-for-170 (.388). Totals, 106-for-284 (.373).

RECORD AS BASEBALL PLAYER

TRANSACTIONS/CAREER NOTES: Selected by Cincinnati Reds organization in 33rd round of free-agent draft (June 1, 1988). . . .

Selected by Minnesota Twins organization in fourth round of free-agent draft (June 1, 1991).

Year Team (League)	G	W	L	Pct.	ERA	Sv.	IP	H	R	ER	BB	SO
1991 — Elizabethton (Appalachian)	6	3	0	1.000	2.25	0	28	21	8	7	10	27

ROGERS, STEVE
G, NETS

PERSONAL: Born July 30, 1968, in Montgomery, Ala. . . . 6-5/190. . . . Full name: Steven Maurice Rogers.
HIGH SCHOOL: Lanier (Montgomery, Ala.).
COLLEGE: Middle Tennessee State, then Alabama State.
TRANSACTIONS/CAREER NOTES: Selected by New Jersey Nets in second round (40th pick overall) of 1992 NBA Draft.

COLLEGIATE RECORD

Season Team	G	Min.	FGM	FGA	Pct.	FTM	FTA	Pct.	Reb.	Pts.	Avg.
87-88 — Middle Tennessee State...........	28	258	25	50	.500	35	58	.603	49	87	3.1
88-89 — Alabama State..........................					Did not play—transfer student.						
89-90 — Alabama State.........................	28	985	286	548	.522	213	291	.732	185	831	29.7
90-91 — Alabama State.........................	29	1060	273	546	.500	250	332	.753	206	852	29.4
91-92 — Alabama State.........................	28	1026	233	505	.461	215	274	.785	182	764	27.3
Totals	113	3329	817	1649	.495	713	955	.747	622	2534	22.4

Three-point field goals: 1987-88, 2-for-11 (.182). 1989-90, 46-for-132 (.348). 1990-91, 56-for-147 (.381). 1991-92, 83-for-197 (.421). Totals, 187-for-487 (.384).

ROOKS, SEAN
C, MAVERICKS

PERSONAL: Born September 9, 1969, in New York. . . . 6-10/250. . . . Full name: Sean Lester Rooks.
HIGH SCHOOL: Fontana (Calif.).
COLLEGE: Arizona.
TRANSACTIONS/CAREER NOTES: Selected by Dallas Mavericks in second round (30th pick overall) of 1992 NBA Draft.

COLLEGIATE RECORD

Season Team	G	Min.	FGM	FGA	Pct.	FTM	FTA	Pct.	Reb.	Pts.	Avg.
87-88 — Arizona					Did not play—redshirted.						
88-89 — Arizona	32	362	70	117	.598	40	65	.615	88	180	5.6
89-90 — Arizona	31	684	140	263	.532	114	161	.708	151	394	12.7
90-91 — Arizona	35	800	159	283	.562	98	149	.658	198	418	11.9
91-92 — Arizona	31	878	181	323	.560	140	215	.651	214	505	16.3
Totals	129	2724	550	986	.558	392	590	.664	651	1497	11.6

Three-point field goals: 1990-91, 2-for-4 (.500). 1991-92, 3-for-5 (.600). Totals, 5-for-9 (.556).

SEALY, MALIK
F, PACERS

PERSONAL: Born February 1, 1970, in Bronx, N.Y. . . . 6-8/192.
HIGH SCHOOL: St. Nicholas of Tolentine (Bronx, N.Y.).
COLLEGE: St. John's.
TRANSACTIONS/CAREER NOTES: Selected by Indiana Pacers in first round (14th pick overall) of 1992 NBA Draft.

COLLEGIATE RECORD

Season Team	G	Min.	FGM	FGA	Pct.	FTM	FTA	Pct.	Reb.	Pts.	Avg.
88-89 — St. John's............................	31	1172	163	333	.489	67	120	.558	197	400	12.9
89-90 — St. John's............................	34	1304	227	432	.525	159	213	.746	233	615	18.1
90-91 — St. John's............................	32	1203	263	535	.492	165	222	.743	247	707	22.1
91-92 — St. John's............................	30	1162	247	523	.472	169	213	.793	203	679	22.6
Totals	127	4841	900	1823	.494	560	768	.729	880	2401	18.9

Three-point field goals: 1988-89, 7-for-33 (.212). 1989-90, 2-for-27 (.074). 1990-91, 16-for-53 (.302). 1991-92, 16-for-53 (.302). Totals, 41-for-166 (.247).

SMITH, CHRIS
G, TIMBERWOLVES

PERSONAL: Born May 17, 1970, in Bridgeport, Conn. . . . 6-3/191. . . . Full name: Chris G. Smith.
HIGH SCHOOL: Kolbe Cathedral (Bridgeport, Conn.).
COLLEGE: Connecticut.
TRANSACTIONS/CAREER NOTES: Selected by Minnesota Timberwolves in second round (34th pick overall) of 1992 NBA Draft.

COLLEGIATE RECORD

Season Team	G	Min.	FGM	FGA	Pct.	FTM	FTA	Pct.	Reb.	Pts.	Avg.
88-89 — Connecticut	29	829	111	274	.405	26	46	.565	82	288	9.9
89-90 — Connecticut	37	1221	207	496	.417	146	180	.811	92	635	17.2
90-91 — Connecticut	31	1130	208	474	.439	123	171	.719	90	585	18.9
91-92 — Connecticut	30	1090	202	487	.415	152	190	.800	98	637	21.2
Totals	127	4270	728	1731	.421	447	587	.761	362	2145	16.9

Three-point field goals: 1988-89, 40-for-104 (.385). 1989-90, 75-for-191 (.393). 1990-91, 46-for-117 (.393). 1991-92, 81-for-193 (.420). Totals, 242-for-605 (.400).

SMITH, REGGIE
C, TRAIL BLAZERS

PERSONAL: Born August 21, 1970, in San Jose, Calif. . . . 6-10/240. **HIGH SCHOOL:** Leland (San Jose, Calif.). **COLLEGE:** Texas Christian. **TRANSACTIONS/CAREER NOTES:** Selected by Portland Trail Blazers in second round (31st pick overall) of 1992 NBA Draft.

COLLEGIATE RECORD

Season	Team	G	Min.	FGM	FGA	Pct.	FTM	FTA	Pct.	Reb.	Pts.	Avg.
88-89	—Texas Christian	30	613	88	187	.471	52	98	.531	127	228	7.6
89-90	—Texas Christian	29	763	115	260	.442	74	117	.632	179	304	10.5
90-91	—Texas Christian	28	1004	192	377	.509	106	207	.512	274	490	17.5
91-92	—Texas Christian	34	1135	225	426	.528	158	257	.615	386	608	17.9
	Totals	121	3515	620	1250	.496	390	679	.574	966	1630	13.5

Three-point field goals: 1991-92, 0-for-2.

SPENCER, ELMORE
C, CLIPPERS

PERSONAL: Born December 6, 1969, in Atlanta. . . . 7-0/270. **HIGH SCHOOL:** Booker T. Washington (Atlanta). **COLLEGE:** Georgia, then Connors State Junior College (Okla.), then Clark County Community College (Nev.), then UNLV. **TRANSACTIONS/CAREER NOTES:** Selected by Los Angeles Clippers in first round (25th pick overall) of 1992 NBA Draft.

COLLEGIATE RECORD

Season	Team	G	Min.	FGM	FGA	Pct.	FTM	FTA	Pct.	Reb.	Pts.	Avg.
87-88	—Georgia					Did not play.						
88-89	—Georgia	11	304	59	92	.641	14	28	.500	58	132	12.0
89-90	—Connors State					Statistics unavailable.						
90-91	—UNLV	31	535	82	157	.522	33	70	.471	124	197	6.4
91-92	—UNLV	28	855	174	273	.637	65	119	.546	228	413	14.8
	Totals	70	1694	315	522	.603	112	217	.516	410	742	10.6

Three-point field goals: 1988-89, 0-for-1. 1991-92, 0-for-2. Totals, 0-for-3.

SPREWELL, LATRELL
G, WARRIORS

PERSONAL: Born September 8, 1970, in Milwaukee. . . . 6-5/190. . . . Name pronounced SPREE-well. **HIGH SCHOOL:** Washington (Milwaukee). **COLLEGE:** Three Rivers Community College (Mo.), then Alabama. **TRANSACTIONS/CAREER NOTES:** Selected by Golden State Warriors in first round (24th pick overall) of 1992 NBA Draft.

COLLEGIATE RECORD

Season	Team	G	Min.	FGM	FGA	Pct.	FTM	FTA	Pct.	Reb.	Pts.	Avg.
88-89	—Three Rivers C.C.	26	. . .	169	327	.517	88	133	.662	218	429	16.5
89-90	—Three Rivers C.C.	40	. . .	421	827	.509	217	281	.772	365	1064	26.6
90-91	—Alabama	33	865	116	217	.535	58	84	.690	165	295	8.9
91-92	—Alabama	35	1266	227	460	.493	101	131	.771	183	623	17.8
	Junior college totals	66	. . .	590	1154	.511	305	414	.737	583	1493	22.6
	Four-year-college totals	68	2131	343	677	.507	159	215	.740	348	918	13.5

Three-point field goals: 1990-91, 5-for-12 (.417). 1991-92, 68-for-171 (.398). Totals, 73-for-183 (.399).

STEIGENGA, MATT
F, BULLS

PERSONAL: Born March 27, 1970, in Grand Rapids, Mich. . . . 6-7/225. . . . Full name: Matthew Todd Steigenga. **HIGH SCHOOL:** South Christian (Grand Rapids, Mich.). **COLLEGE:** Michigan State. **TRANSACTIONS/CAREER NOTES:** Selected by Chicago Bulls in second round (52nd pick overall) of 1992 NBA Draft.

COLLEGIATE RECORD

Season	Team	G	Min.	FGM	FGA	Pct.	FTM	FTA	Pct.	Reb.	Pts.	Avg.
88-89	—Michigan State	33	866	115	206	.558	57	77	.740	149	287	8.7
89-90	—Michigan State	34	879	138	235	.587	74	95	.779	119	355	10.4
90-91	—Michigan State	30	913	148	282	.525	70	100	.700	148	379	12.6
91-92	—Michigan State	27	674	103	211	.488	55	81	.679	121	275	10.2
	Totals	124	3332	504	934	.540	256	353	.725	537	1296	10.5

Three-point field goals: 1989-90, 5-for-9 (.556). 1990-91, 13-for-26 (.500). 1991-92, 14-for-43 (.326). Totals, 32-for-78 (.410).

STITH, BRYANT
G, NUGGETS

PERSONAL: Born December 10, 1970, in Emporia, Va. . . . 6-5/208. . . . Full name: Bryant Lamonica Stith. **HIGH SCHOOL:** Brunswick (Lawrenceville, Va.) **COLLEGE:** Virginia. **TRANSACTIONS/CAREER NOTES:** Selected by Denver Nuggets in first round (13th pick overall) of 1992 NBA Draft.

COLLEGIATE RECORD

Season Team	G	Min.	FGM	FGA	Pct.	FTM	FTA	Pct.	Reb.	Pts.	Avg.
88-89 — Virginia	33	942	181	330	.548	150	195	.769	216	513	15.5
89-90 — Virginia	32	1127	217	451	.481	192	247	.777	221	666	20.8
90-91 — Virginia	33	1120	228	484	.471	159	201	.791	203	653	19.8
91-92 — Virginia	33	1202	230	509	.452	189	232	.815	219	684	20.7
Totals	131	4391	856	1774	.483	690	875	.789	859	2516	19.2

Three-point field goals: 1988-89, 1-for-1. 1989-90, 40-for-102 (.392). 1990-91, 38-for-125 (.304). 1991-92, 35-for-95 (.368). Totals, 114-for-323 (.353).

TOWER, KEITH
C

PERSONAL: Born May 15, 1970, in Libby, Mont. . . . 6-11/250. . . . Full name: Keith Raymond Tower.
HIGH SCHOOL: Moon (Coraopolis, Pa.).
COLLEGE: Notre Dame.
TRANSACTIONS/CAREER NOTES: Never drafted by an NBA franchise.

COLLEGIATE RECORD

Season Team	G	Min.	FGM	FGA	Pct.	FTM	FTA	Pct.	Reb.	Pts.	Avg.
88-89 — Notre Dame	29	329	28	50	.560	15	33	.455	81	71	2.4
89-90 — Notre Dame	25	275	19	61	.311	15	25	.600	67	53	2.1
90-91 — Notre Dame	32	971	103	222	.464	48	76	.632	223	254	7.9
91-92 — Notre Dame	31	774	55	139	.396	24	44	.545	165	134	4.3
Totals	117	2349	205	472	.434	102	178	.573	536	512	4.4

Three-point field goals: 1991-92, 0-for-2.

UPCHURCH, CRAIG
F

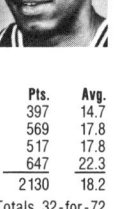

PERSONAL: Born November 18, 1967, in St. Louis. . . . 6-8/210.
HIGH SCHOOL: Beaumont (St. Louis).
COLLEGE: Houston.
TRANSACTIONS/CAREER NOTES: Never drafted by an NBA franchise.

COLLEGIATE RECORD

Season Team	G	Min.	FGM	FGA	Pct.	FTM	FTA	Pct.	Reb.	Pts.	Avg.
87-88 — Houston	31	897	148	262	.565	79	125	.632	163	376	12.1
88-89 — Houston	31	1023	232	398	.583	119	185	.643	203	583	18.8
89-90 — Houston	33	1018	182	338	.538	69	113	.611	231	433	13.1
90-91 — Houston					Did not play—redshirt (back injury).						
91-92 — Houston	31	978	191	357	.535	105	164	.640	200	488	15.7
Totals	126	3916	753	1355	.556	372	587	.634	797	1880	14.9

Three-point field goals: 1987-88, 1-for-11 (.091). 1988-89, 0-for-6. 1989-90, 0-for-2. 1991-92, 1-for-8 (.125). Totals, 2-for-27 (.074).

WEATHERSPOON, CLARENCE
F, 76ERS

PERSONAL: Born September 8, 1970, in Crawford, Miss. . . . 6-6/240.
HIGH SCHOOL: Motley (Columbus, Miss.).
COLLEGE: Southern Mississippi.
TRANSACTIONS/CAREER NOTES: Selected by Philadelphia 76ers in first round (ninth pick overall) of 1992 NBA Draft.

COLLEGIATE RECORD

Season Team	G	Min.	FGM	FGA	Pct.	FTM	FTA	Pct.	Reb.	Pts.	Avg.
88-89 — Southern Mississippi	27	915	152	279	.545	92	156	.590	289	397	14.7
89-90 — Southern Mississippi	32	1166	205	339	.605	159	230	.691	371	569	17.8
90-91 — Southern Mississippi	29	1019	195	331	.589	120	161	.745	355	517	17.8
91-92 — Southern Mississippi	29	1057	246	437	.563	131	194	.675	305	647	22.3
Totals	117	4157	798	1386	.576	502	741	.677	1320	2130	18.2

Three-point field goals: 1988-89, 1-for-3 (.333). 1989-90, 0-for-2. 1990-91, 7-for-14 (.500). 1991-92, 24-for-53 (.453). Totals, 32-for-72 (.444).

WERDANN, ROBERT
C, NUGGETS

PERSONAL: Born September 12, 1970, in Sunnyside, N.Y. . . . 6-11/250.
HIGH SCHOOL: Archbishop Molloy (Queens, N.Y.).
COLLEGE: St. John's.
TRANSACTIONS/CAREER NOTES: Selected by Denver Nuggets in second round (46th pick overall) of 1992 NBA Draft.

COLLEGIATE RECORD

Season Team	G	Min.	FGM	FGA	Pct.	FTM	FTA	Pct.	Reb.	Pts.	Avg.
88-89 — St. John's	29	774	94	190	.495	40	60	.667	191	228	7.9
89-90 — St. John's	34	990	124	246	.504	82	123	.667	250	330	9.7
90-91 — St. John's	32	943	128	259	.494	105	145	.724	226	362	11.3
91-92 — St. John's	12	286	40	87	.460	36	52	.692	69	116	9.7
Totals	107	2993	386	782	.494	263	380	.692	736	1036	9.7

Three-point field goals: 1988-89, 0-for-2. 1990-91, 1-for-1. Totals, 1-for-3 (.333).

WILLIAMS, COREY
G, BULLS

PERSONAL: Born April 24, 1970, in Twiggs, Ga. . . . 6-2/190.
HIGH SCHOOL: Northeast (Macon, Ga.).
COLLEGE: Oklahoma State.
TRANSACTIONS/CAREER NOTES: Selected by Chicago Bulls in second round (33rd pick overall) of 1992 NBA Draft.
MISCELLANEOUS: Selected by Kansas City Chiefs in 12th round (325th pick overall) of 1992 National Football League draft.

COLLEGIATE RECORD

Season	Team	G	Min.	FGM	FGA	Pct.	FTM	FTA	Pct.	Reb.	Pts.	Avg.
88-89	Oklahoma State	30	951	135	305	.443	66	96	.688	106	371	12.4
89-90	Oklahoma State	31	769	114	267	.427	40	53	.755	99	290	9.4
90-91	Oklahoma State	32	714	99	187	.529	53	76	.697	68	267	8.3
91-92	Oklahoma State	35	1059	125	299	.418	97	126	.770	133	392	11.2
	Totals	128	3493	473	1058	.447	256	351	.729	406	1320	10.3

Three-point field goals: 1988-89, 35-for-98 (.357). 1989-90, 22-for-76 (.289). 1990-91, 16-for-40 (.400). 1991-92, 45-for-127 (.354). Totals, 118-for-341 (.346).

WILLIAMS, HENRY
G, SPURS

PERSONAL: Born June 6, 1970, in Indianapolis. . . . 6-1/170. . . .
Full name: Henry Williams Jr.
HIGH SCHOOL: Ben Davis (Indianapolis, Ind.).
COLLEGE: UNC Charlotte.
TRANSACTIONS/CAREER NOTES: Selected by San Antonio Spurs in second round (44th pick overall) of 1992 NBA Draft.

COLLEGIATE RECORD

Season	Team	G	Min.	FGM	FGA	Pct.	FTM	FTA	Pct.	Reb.	Pts.	Avg.
88-89	UNC Charlotte	29	928	188	380	.495	82	103	.796	105	505	17.4
89-90	UNC Charlotte	30	1054	209	505	.414	128	154	.831	106	630	21.0
90-91	UNC Charlotte	27	891	193	453	.426	125	150	.833	85	583	21.6
91-92	UNC Charlotte	32	1123	207	447	.463	146	178	.820	108	665	20.8
	Totals	118	3996	797	1785	.446	481	585	.822	404	2383	20.2

Three-point field goals: 1988-89, 47-for-116 (.405). 1989-90, 84-for-210 (.400). 1990-91, 72-for-212 (.340). 1991-92, 105-for-244 (.430). Totals, 308-for-782 (.394).

WILLIAMS, WALT
F, KINGS

PERSONAL: Born April 16, 1970, in Washington, D.C. . . . 6-8/220. . . . Full name: Walter Ander Williams.
HIGH SCHOOL: Crossland (Temple Hills, Md.).
COLLEGE: Maryland.
TRANSACTIONS/CAREER NOTES: Selected by Sacramento Kings in first round (seventh pick overall) of 1992 NBA Draft.

COLLEGIATE RECORD

NOTES: THE SPORTING NEWS All-America first team (1992).

Season	Team	G	Min.	FGM	FGA	Pct.	FTM	FTA	Pct.	Reb.	Pts.	Avg.
88-89	Maryland	26	617	75	170	.441	33	53	.623	92	190	7.3
89-90	Maryland	33	993	143	296	.483	104	134	.776	138	420	12.7
90-91	Maryland	17	537	109	243	.449	72	86	.837	86	318	18.7
91-92	Maryland	29	1042	256	542	.472	175	231	.758	162	776	26.8
	Totals	105	3189	583	1251	.466	384	504	.762	478	1704	16.2

Three-point field goals: 1988-89, 7-for-27 (.259). 1989-90, 30-for-67 (.448). 1990-91, 28-for-95 (.295). 1991-92, 89-for-240 (.371). Totals, 154-for-429 (.359).

WOODS, RANDY
G, CLIPPERS

PERSONAL: Born September 23, 1970, in Philadelphia. . . . 6-0/185.
HIGH SCHOOL: Ben Franklin (Philadelphia)
COLLEGE: La Salle.
TRANSACTIONS/CAREER NOTES: Selected by Los Angeles Clippers in first round (16th pick overall) of 1992 NBA Draft.

COLLEGIATE RECORD

Season	Team	G	Min.	FGM	FGA	Pct.	FTM	FTA	Pct.	Reb.	Pts.	Avg.
88-89	La Salle					Did not play—ineligible.						
89-90	La Salle	32	1138	146	371	.394	56	76	.737	101	425	13.3
90-91	La Salle	25	875	177	415	.427	105	132	.795	123	539	21.6
91-92	La Salle	31	1183	272	653	.417	182	224	.813	194	847	27.3
	Totals	88	3196	595	1439	.413	343	432	.794	418	1811	20.6

Three-point field goals: 1989-90, 77-for-221 (.348). 1990-91, 80-for-227 (.352). 1991-92, 121-for-341 (.355). Totals, 278-for-789 (.352).

PROMISING NEWCOMERS

HEAD COACHES

ADELMAN, RICK
TRAIL BLAZERS

PERSONAL: Born June 16, 1946, in Lynwood, Calif. . . . 6-2/180. . . . Full name: Richard Leonard Adelman. **HIGH SCHOOL:** St. Pius X (Downey, Calif.). **COLLEGE:** Loyola (Calif.); now Loyola Marymount.

TRANSACTIONS/CAREER NOTES: Selected by San Diego Rockets in seventh round (79th pick overall) of 1968 NBA Draft. . . . Selected by Portland Trail Blazers from Rockets in NBA expansion draft (May 11, 1970). . . . Traded by Trail Blazers to Chicago Bulls for cash and 1974 second-round draft choice (September 14, 1973). . . . Traded by Bulls to New Orleans Jazz for John Block (November 11, 1974). . . . Traded by Jazz with Ollie Johnson to Kansas City-Omaha Kings for Nate Williams (February 1, 1975). . . . Kings franchise moved from Kansas City-Omaha to Kansas City for 1975-76 season. . . . Released by Kings (October 21, 1975).

COLLEGIATE RECORD

Season Team	G	Min.	FGM	FGA	Pct.	FTM	FTA	Pct.	Reb.	Pts.	Avg.
64-65 —Loyola (Calif.)‡				Freshman team statistics unavailable.							
65-66 —Loyola (Calif.)	26	. . .	149	376	.396	129	152	.849	113	427	16.4
66-67 —Loyola (Calif.)	25	. . .	151	349	.433	171	214	.799	124	473	18.9
67-68 —Loyola (Calif.)	25	. . .	177	420	.421	171	216	.792	127	525	21.0
Varsity totals	76	. . .	477	1145	.417	471	582	.809	364	1425	18.8

NBA REGULAR-SEASON RECORD

Season Team	G	Min.	FGM	FGA	Pct.	FTM	FTA	Pct.	Reb.	Ast.	PF	Dq.	Pts.	Avg.
68-69 —San Diego	77	1448	177	449	.394	131	204	.642	216	238	158	1	485	6.3
69-70 —San Diego	35	717	96	247	.389	68	91	.747	81	113	90	0	260	7.4
70-71 —Portland	81	2303	378	895	.422	267	369	.724	282	380	214	2	1023	12.6
71-72 —Portland	80	2445	329	753	.437	151	201	.751	229	413	209	2	808	10.1
72-73 —Portland	76	1822	214	525	.408	73	102	.716	157	294	155	2	591	7.8

Season Team	G	Min.	FGM	FGA	Pct.	FTM	FTA	Pct.	Off.	Def.	Tot.	Ast.	PF	Dq.	Stl.	Blk.	TO	Pts.	Avg.
73-74 —Chicago	55	618	64	170	.376	54	76	.711	16	53	69	56	63	0	36	1	. . .	182	3.3
74-75 —Ch-NO-KC/O.	58	1074	123	291	.423	73	103	.709	25	70	95	112	101	1	70	8	. . .	319	5.5
Totals	462	10427	1381	3330	.415	817	1146	.713	. . .	. . .	1129	1606	990	8	106	9	. . .	3668	7.9

NBA PLAYOFF RECORD

Season Team	G	Min.	FGM	FGA	Pct.	FTM	FTA	Pct.	Reb.	Ast.	PF	Dq.	Pts.	Avg.
68-69 —San Diego	6	187	24	53	.453	22	37	.595	15	29	18	0	70	11.7

Season Team	G	Min.	FGM	FGA	Pct.	FTM	FTA	Pct.	Off.	Def.	Tot.	Ast.	PF	Dq.	Stl.	Blk.	TO	Pts.	Avg.
73-74 —Chicago	9	108	16	34	.471	7	11	.636	1	9	10	7	5	0	7	0	. . .	39	4.3
74-75 —K.C./Omaha	6	34	3	9	.333	6	8	.750	1	1	2	3	9	0	1	0	. . .	12	2.0
Totals	21	329	43	96	.448	35	56	.625	. . .	. . .	27	39	32	0	8	0	. . .	121	5.8

HEAD COACHING RECORD

BACKGROUND: Head coach, Chemeketa Community College, Ore. (1977-1983; record: 141-39, .783). . . . Assistant coach, Portland Trail Blazers (1983-84 to February 18, 1989).

NBA COACHING RECORD

Season Team	REGULAR SEASON				PLAYOFFS		
	W	L	Pct.	Finish	W	L	Pct.
88-89 —Portland	14	21	.400	5th/Pacific Division	0	3	.000
89-90 —Portland	59	23	.720	2nd/Pacific Division	12	9	.571
90-91 —Portland	63	19	.768	1st/Pacific Division	9	7	.563
91-92 —Portland	57	25	.695	1st/Pacific Division	13	8	.619
Totals (4 years)	193	88	.687	Totals (4 years)	34	27	.557

NOTES:
1989— Replaced Mike Schuler as Portland head coach (February 18), with record of 25-22. Lost to Los Angeles Lakers in Western Conference first round.
1990— Defeated Dallas, 3-0, in Western Conference first round; defeated San Antonio, 4-3, in Western Conference semifinals; defeated Phoenix, 4-2, in Western Conference finals; lost to Detroit, 4-1, in NBA Finals.
1991— Defeated Seattle, 3-2, in Western Conference first round; defeated Utah, 4-1, in Western Conference semifinals; lost to Los Angeles Lakers, 4-2, in Western Conference finals.
1992— Defeated Los Angeles Lakers, 3-1, in Western Conference first round; defeated Phoenix, 4-1, in Western Conference semifinals; defeated Utah, 4-2, in Western Conference finals; lost to Chicago, 4-2, in NBA Finals.

ADUBATO, RICHIE
MAVERICKS

PERSONAL: Born November 23, 1937, in East Orange, N.J. . . . 5-10/175. . . . Full name: Richard Adam Adubato. . . . Name pronounced Ah-duh-bah-doe. **HIGH SCHOOL:** East Orange (N.J.).
COLLEGE: William Paterson College, N.J. (did not play college basketball).

HEAD COACHING RECORD

BACKGROUND: Junior varsity coach, Our Lady of the Valley High School, N.J. . . . Head coach, Our Lady of the Valley High School (record: 76-14, .844). . . . Assistant coach, Upsala College, N.J. (1969-70 through 1971-72). . . . Assistant coach, Detroit Pistons (1978-79 to November 1979). . . . Assistant coach, New York Knicks (1982-83 through 1985-86). . . . Assistant coach, Dallas Mavericks (1986-87 to November 29, 1989).

COLLEGIATE COACHING RECORD

Season Team	W	L	Pct.	Finish
72-73 —Upsala College	15	9	.625	5th/Middle Atlantic Conference College Division Northern Section
73-74 —Upsala College	17	10	.630	5th/Middle Atlantic Conference College Division Northern Section
74-75 —Upsala College	18	11	.621	T3rd/Middle Atlantic Conference College Division Northern Section
75-76 —Upsala College	20	9	.690	3rd/Middle Atlantic Conference College Division Northern Section
76-77 —Upsala College	11	14	.440	T5th/Middle Atlantic Conference College Division Northern Section
77-78 —Upsala College	19	9	.679	
Totals (6 years)	100	62	.617	

NBA COACHING RECORD

Season Team	REGULAR SEASON W	L	Pct.	Finish	PLAYOFFS W	L	Pct.
79-80 —Detroit	12	58	.171	6th/Central Division	—	—	—
89-90 —Dallas	42	29	.592	3rd/Midwest Division	0	3	.000
90-91 —Dallas	28	54	.341	6th/Midwest Division	—	—	—
91-92 —Dallas	22	60	.268	5th/Midwest Division	—	—	—
Totals (4 years)	104	201	.341	Totals (1 year)	0	3	.000

NOTES:
1979— Replaced Dick Vitale as Detroit head coach (November 8), with record of 4-8.
1989— Replaced John MacLeod as Dallas head coach (November 29), with record of 5-6.
1990— Lost to Portland in Western Conference first round.

BRISTOW, ALLAN
HORNETS

PERSONAL: Born August 23, 1951, in Richmond, Va. . . . 6-7/210.
. . . Full name: Allan Mercer Bristow Jr.
HIGH SCHOOL: Henrico (Richmond, Va.).
COLLEGE: Virginia Tech.
TRANSACTIONS/CAREER NOTES: Selected by Philadelphia 76ers in second round (21st pick overall) of 1973 NBA Draft. . . . Waived by 76ers (October 22, 1975). . . . Signed as free agent by San Antonio Spurs of American Basketball Association (November 8, 1975). . . . Spurs franchise became part of NBA upon merger of ABA and NBA for 1976-77 season. . . . Signed as veteran free agent by Utah Jazz (June 28, 1979); Spurs received Paul Griffin as compensation. . . . Traded by Jazz with Wayne Cooper to Dallas Mavericks for Bill Robinzine (August 20, 1981).

COLLEGIATE RECORD

Season Team	G	Min.	FGM	FGA	Pct.	FTM	FTA	Pct.	Reb.	Pts.	Avg.
69-70 —Virginia Tech‡	13	. . .	138	261	.529	79	124	.637	222	355	27.3
70-71 —Virginia Tech	25	. . .	185	382	.484	140	175	.800	327	510	20.4
71-72 —Virginia Tech	26	. . .	246	524	.469	158	229	.690	348	650	25.0
72-73 —Virginia Tech	27	. . .	261	549	.475	122	192	.635	312	644	23.9
Varsity totals	78	. . .	692	1455	.476	420	596	.705	987	1804	23.1

NBA REGULAR-SEASON RECORD

Season Team	G	Min.	FGM	FGA	Pct.	FTM	FTA	Pct.	REBOUNDS Off.	Def.	Tot.	Ast.	PF	Dq.	Stl.	Blk.	TO	Pts.	Avg.
73-74 —Philadelphia	55	643	108	270	.400	42	57	.737	68	99	167	92	68	1	29	1	. . .	258	4.7
74-75 —Philadelphia	72	1101	163	393	.415	121	153	.791	111	143	254	99	101	1	25	2	. . .	447	6.2
76-77 —San Antonio	82	2017	365	747	.489	206	258	.798	119	229	348	240	195	1	89	2	. . .	936	11.4
77-78 —San Antonio	82	1481	257	558	.478	152	208	.731	99	158	257	194	150	0	69	4	146	666	8.1
78-79 —San Antonio	74	1324	174	354	.492	124	149	.832	80	167	247	231	154	0	56	15	108	472	6.4
79-80 —Utah	82	2304	377	785	.480	197	243	.811	170	342	512	341	211	2	88	6	119	953	11.6
80-81 —Utah	82	2001	271	611	.444	166	198	.838	103	327	430	383	190	0	63	3	171	713	8.7
81-82 —Dallas	82	2035	218	499	.437	134	164	.817	119	220	339	448	222	2	65	6	165	573	7.0
82-83 —Dallas	37	371	44	99	.444	10	14	.714	24	35	59	70	46	0	6	1	31	104	2.8
Totals	648	13277	1977	4296	.460	1152	1444	.798	893	1720	2613	2098	1337	7	490	40	800	5122	7.9

Three-point field goals: 1979-80, 2-for-7 (.286). 1980-81, 5-for-18 (.278). 1981-82, 3-for-18 (.167). 1982-83, 6-for-13 (.462). Totals, 16-for-56 (.286).

NBA PLAYOFF RECORD

Season Team	G	Min.	FGM	FGA	Pct.	FTM	FTA	Pct.	REBOUNDS Off.	Def.	Tot.	Ast.	PF	Dq.	Stl.	Blk.	TO	Pts.	Avg.
76-77 —San Antonio	2	28	3	9	.333	2	9	.222	3	1	4	7	6	0	2	0	. . .	8	4.0
77-78 —San Antonio	5	51	9	15	.600	4	6	.667	4	7	11	7	10	0	2	0	5	22	4.4
78-79 —San Antonio	13	163	20	49	.408	16	21	.762	12	15	27	28	17	0	9	5	11	56	4.3
Totals	20	242	32	73	.438	22	36	.611	19	23	42	42	33	0	13	5	16	86	4.3

ABA REGULAR-SEASON RECORD

Season Team	G	Min.	2-POINT FGM	FGA	Pct.	3-POINT FGM	FGA	Pct.	FTM	FTA	Pct.	Reb.	Ast.	Pts.	Avg.
75-76 —San Antonio	47	882	125	270	.463	0	1	.000	78	92	.848	174	121	328	7.0

ABA PLAYOFF RECORD

Season Team	G	Min.	2-POINT FGM	FGA	Pct.	3-POINT FGM	FGA	Pct.	FTM	FTA	Pct.	Reb.	Ast.	Pts.	Avg.
75-76 —San Antonio	7	97	13	34	.382	0	1	.000	19	24	.792	14	12	45	6.4

HEAD COACHING RECORD

BACKGROUND: Assistant coach, San Antonio Spurs (1983-84). . . . Assistant coach, Denver Nuggets (1984-85 through 1989-90). . . . Vice president of basketball, Charlotte Hornets (1990-91).

NBA COACHING RECORD

Season Team	REGULAR SEASON W	L	Pct.	Finish	PLAYOFFS W	L	Pct.
91-92 —Charlotte	31	51	.378	T6th/Central Division	—	—	—
Totals (1 year)	31	51	.378				

BROWN, LARRY
CLIPPERS

PERSONAL: Born September 14, 1940, in Brooklyn, N.Y. . . . 5-9/160. . . . Full name: Lawrence Harvey Brown.
HIGH SCHOOL: Long Beach (N.Y.).
COLLEGE: North Carolina.

TRANSACTIONS/CAREER NOTES: Signed by New Orleans Buccaneers of American Basketball Association (1967). . . . Traded by Buccaneers with Doug Moe to Oakland Oaks for Steve Jones, Ron Franz and Barry Leibowitz (June 18, 1968). . . . Oaks franchise moved from Oakland to Washington and renamed Capitols for 1969-70 season. . . . Capitols franchise moved from Washington to Virginia and renamed Squires for 1970-71 season. . . . Sold by Squires to Denver Rockets (January 23, 1971).
MISCELLANEOUS: Member of gold-medal-winning U.S. Olympic team (1964).

COLLEGIATE RECORD

Season Team	G	Min.	FGM	FGA	Pct.	FTM	FTA	Pct.	Reb.	Pts.	Avg.
59-60 — North Carolina†	15	. . .	88	. . .	. . .	100	143	.699	. . .	276	18.4
60-61 — North Carolina	18	. . .	28	54	.519	25	34	.735	28	81	4.5
61-62 — North Carolina	17	. . .	90	204	.441	101	127	.795	52	281	16.5
62-63 — North Carolina	21	. . .	102	231	.442	95	122	.779	50	299	14.2
Varsity totals	56	. . .	220	489	.450	221	283	.781	130	661	11.8

AMATEUR PLAYING RECORD

Season Team	G	Min.	FGM	FGA	Pct.	FTM	FTA	Pct.	Reb.	Pts.	Avg.
63-64 — Akron (Ohio)	. . .	. . .	. . .	. . .	. . .	. . .	. . .	. . .	. . .	398	. . .
64-65 — Akron (Ohio)	32	. . .	144	297	.485	139	167	.832	90	427	13.3
Totals	. . .	. . .	. . .	. . .	. . .	. . .	. . .	. . .	. . .	825	. . .

ABA REGULAR-SEASON RECORD

NOTES: ABA All-Star second team (1968). . . . Member of ABA championship team (1969). . . . Holds single-game record for most assists — 23 (February 20, 1972, vs. Pittsburgh). . . . Led ABA with 6.5 assists per game (1968) and 7.1 assists per game (1969, 1970).

Season Team	G	Min.	2-POINT FGM	FGA	Pct.	3-POINT FGM	FGA	Pct.	FTM	FTA	Pct.	Reb.	Ast.	Pts.	Avg.
67-68 — New Orleans	78	2807	311	812	.383	19	89	.213	366	450	.813	249	*506	1045	13.4
68-69 — Oakland	77	2381	300	671	.447	8	35	.229	301	379	.794	235	*544	925	12.0
69-70 — Washington	82	2766	366	815	.449	10	39	.256	362	439	.825	246	*580	1124	13.7
70-71 — Va.-Denver	63	1343	121	319	.379	6	21	.286	186	225	.827	109	330	446	7.1
71-72 — Denver	76	2012	238	531	.448	5	25	.200	198	244	.811	166	549	689	9.1
Totals	376	11309	1336	3148	.424	48	209	.230	1413	1737	.813	1005	2509	4229	11.2

ABA PLAYOFF RECORD

Season Team	G	Min.	2-POINT FGM	FGA	Pct.	3-POINT FGM	FGA	Pct.	FTM	FTA	Pct.	Reb.	Ast.	Pts.	Avg.
67-68 — New Orleans	17	696	86	194	.443	4	18	.222	100	122	.820	59	129	284	16.7
68-69 — Oakland	16	534	74	170	.435	0	3	.000	76	90	.844	52	87	224	14.0
69-70 — Washington	7	269	32	68	.471	1	5	.200	30	34	.882	35	68	97	13.9
71-72 — Denver	7	211	21	47	.447	0	3	.000	23	24	.958	10	36	65	9.3
Totals	47	1710	213	479	.445	5	29	.172	229	270	.848	156	320	670	14.3

ABA ALL-STAR GAME RECORD

NOTES: ABA All-Star Game Most Valuable Player (1968).

Season Team	Min.	2-POINT FGM	FGA	Pct.	3-POINT FGM	FGA	Pct.	FTM	FTA	Pct.	Reb.	Ast.	Pts.
1968 — New Orleans	22	5	7	.714	2	2	1.000	1	1	1.000	3	5	17
1969 — Oakland	25	1	6	.167	0	1	.000	3	5	.600	0	7	5
1970 — Washington	15	0	2	.000	0	0	. . .	3	3	1.000	3	3	3
Totals	62	6	15	.400	2	3	.667	7	9	.778	6	15	25

HEAD COACHING RECORD

BACKGROUND: Assistant coach, University of North Carolina (1965-66 and 1966-67).
HONORS: ABA Coach of the Year (1973, 1975, 1976).

ABA COACHING RECORD

Season Team	REGULAR SEASON W	L	Pct.	Finish	PLAYOFFS W	L	Pct.
72-73 — Carolina	57	27	.679	1st/Eastern Division	7	5	.583
73-74 — Carolina	47	37	.560	3rd/Eastern Division	0	4	.000
74-75 — Denver	65	19	.774	1st/Western Division	7	6	.538
75-76 — Denver	60	24	.714	1st	6	7	.462
Totals (4 years)	229	107	.682	Totals (4 years)	20	22	.476

NBA COACHING RECORD

Season Team	REGULAR SEASON W	L	Pct.	Finish	PLAYOFFS W	L	Pct.
76-77 — Denver	50	32	.610	1st/Midwest Division	2	4	.500
77-78 — Denver	48	34	.585	1st/Midwest Division	6	7	.462
78-79 — Denver	28	25	.528		—	—	—
81-82 — New Jersey	44	38	.537	3rd/Atlantic Division	0	2	.000
82-83 — New Jersey	47	29	.618		—	—	—
88-89 — San Antonio	21	61	.256	5th/Midwest Division	—	—	—
89-90 — San Antonio	56	26	.683	1st/Midwest Division	6	4	.600
90-91 — San Antonio	55	27	.671	1st/Midwest Division	1	3	.250
91-92 — San Antonio	21	17	.553		—	—	—
— Los Angeles Clippers	23	12	.657	5th/Pacific Division	2	3	.400
Totals (9 years)	393	301	.566	Totals (6 years)	17	23	.425

COLLEGIATE COACHING RECORD

Season	Team	W	L	Pct.	Finish
79-80	UCLA	22	10	.688	4th/Pacific-10 Conference
80-81	UCLA	20	7	.741	3rd/Pacific-10 Conference
83-84	Kansas	22	10	.688	2nd/Big Eight Conference
84-85	Kansas	26	8	.765	2nd/Big Eight Conference
85-86	Kansas	35	4	.897	1st/Big Eight Conference
86-87	Kansas	25	11	.694	T2nd/Big Eight Conference
87-88	Kansas	27	11	.711	3rd/Big Eight Conference
	Totals (7 years)	177	61	.744	

NOTES:

1973— Defeated New York, 4-1, in Eastern Division semifinals; lost to Kentucky, 4-3, in Eastern Division finals.
1974— Lost to Kentucky in Eastern Division semifinals.
1975— Defeated Utah, 4-2, in Western Division semifinals; lost to Indiana, 4-3, in Western Division finals.
1976— Defeated Kentucky, 4-3, in semifinals; lost to New York, 4-2, in ABA Finals.
1977— Lost to Portland in Western Conference semifinals.
1978— Defeated Milwaukee, 4-3, in Western Conference semifinals; lost to Seattle, 4-2, in Western Conference finals.
1979— Resigned as Denver head coach (February 1); replaced by Donnie Walsh.
1980— Defeated Old Dominion, 87-74, in NCAA Tournament first round; defeated DePaul, 77-71, in second round; defeated Ohio State, 72-68, in regional semifinals; defeated Clemson, 85-74, in regional finals; defeated Purdue, 67-62, in semifinals; lost to Louisville, 59-54, in championship game.
1981— Lost to Brigham Young, 78-55, in NCAA Tournament second round.
1982— Lost to Washington in Eastern Conference first round.
1983— Resigned as New Jersey head coach (April 7); replaced by Bill Blair.
1984— Defeated Alcorn State, 57-56, in NCAA Tournament first round; lost to Wake Forest, 69-59, in second round.
1985— Defeated Ohio University, 49-38, in NCAA Tournament first round; lost to Auburn, 66-64, in second round.
1986— Defeated North Carolina A&T, 71-46, in NCAA Tournament first round; defeated Temple, 65-43, in second round; defeated Michigan State, 96-86 (OT), in regional semifinals; defeated North Carolina State, 75-67, in regional finals; lost to Duke, 71-67, in semifinals.
1987— Defeated Houston, 66-55, in NCAA Tournament first round; defeated Southwest Missouri State, 67-63, in second round; lost to Georgetown, 70-57, in regional semifinals.
1988— Defeated Xavier, 85-72, in NCAA Tournament first round; defeated Murray State, 61-58, in second round; defeated Vanderbilt, 77-64, in regional semifinals; defeated Kansas State, 71-58, in regional finals; defeated Duke, 66-59, in semifinals; defeated Oklahoma, 83-79, in championship game.
1990— Defeated Denver, 3-0, in Western Conference first round; lost to Portland, 4-3, in Western Conference semifinals.
1991— Lost to Golden State in Western Conference first round.
1992— Replaced as San Antonio head coach by Bob Bass (January 21); replaced Mike Schuler (21-24) and Mack Calvin (interim head coach, 1-1) as Los Angeles Clippers head coach (February 6), with record of 22-25 and in sixth place. Lost to Utah in Western Conference first round.

DALY, CHUCK
NETS

PERSONAL: Born July 20, 1930, in St. Mary's, Pa. . . . 6-2/180. . . . Full name: Charles Joseph Daly.
HIGH SCHOOL: Kane Area (Pa.).
COLLEGE: St. Bonaventure, then Bloomsburg State (Pa.).

COLLEGIATE RECORD

Season	Team	G	Min.	FGM	FGA	Pct.	FTM	FTA	Pct.	Reb.	Pts.	Avg.
48-49	St. Bonaventure‡					Freshman team statistics unavailable.						
49-50	Bloomsburg State					Did not play—transfer student.						
50-51	Bloomsburg State	16	...	...	...	...	...	...	...	...	215	13.4
51-52	Bloomsburg State	16	...	...	...	...	...	...	...	...	203	12.7
	Varsity totals	32	...	...	...	...	...	...	...	...	418	13.1

HEAD COACHING RECORD

BACKGROUND: Head coach, Punxsutawney High School, Pa. (1955-56 through 1962-63; record: 111-70, .613). . . . Assistant coach, Duke University (1963-64 through 1968-69). . . . Assistant coach, Philadelphia 76ers (1978-December 4, 1981). . . . Broadcaster, Philadelphia 76ers (1982-83). . . . Head coach, U.S. Olympic team (1992).

COLLEGIATE COACHING RECORD

Season	Team	W	L	Pct.	Finish
69-70	Boston College	11	13	.458	Independent
70-71	Boston College	15	11	.577	Independent
71-72	Pennsylvania	25	3	.893	1st/Ivy League
72-73	Pennsylvania	21	7	.750	1st/Ivy League
73-74	Pennsylvania	21	6	.778	1st/Ivy League
74-75	Pennsylvania	23	5	.821	1st/Ivy League
75-76	Pennsylvania	17	9	.654	2nd/Ivy League
76-77	Pennsylvania	18	8	.692	2nd/Ivy League
	Totals (8 years)	151	62	.709	

NBA COACHING RECORD

		REGULAR SEASON				PLAYOFFS		
Season	Team	W	L	Pct.	Finish	W	L	Pct.
81-82	Cleveland	9	32	.220		—	—	—
83-84	Detroit	49	33	.598	2nd/Central Division	2	3	.400
84-85	Detroit	46	36	.561	2nd/Central Division	5	4	.556
85-86	Detroit	46	36	.561	3rd/Central Division	1	3	.250
86-87	Detroit	52	30	.634	2nd/Central Division	10	5	.667
87-88	Detroit	54	28	.659	1st/Central Division	14	9	.609
88-89	Detroit	63	19	.768	1st/Central Division	15	2	.882

Season	Team	W	L	Pct.	REGULAR SEASON Finish	PLAYOFFS W	L	Pct.
89-90	—Detroit	59	23	.720	1st/Central Division	15	5	.750
90-91	—Detroit	50	32	.610	2nd/Central Division	7	8	.467
91-92	—Detroit	48	34	.585	3rd/Central Division	2	3	.400
	Totals (10 years)	476	303	.611	Totals (9 years)	71	42	.628

OLYMPIC RECORD

Season	Team	W	L	Pct.	REGULAR SEASON Finish	PLAYOFFS W	L	Pct.
1992	—Team USA	8	0	1.000	Gold medal	—	—	—

NOTES:

1972— Defeated Providence, 76-60, in NCAA Tournament first round; defeated Villanova, 78-67, in second round; lost to North Carolina, 73-59, in regional final.

1973— Defeated St. John's, 62-61, in NCAA Tournament first round; lost to Providence, 87-65, in second round; lost to Syracuse, 69-68, in regional consolation game.

1974— Lost to Providence, 84-69, in NCAA Tournament first round.

1975— Lost to Kansas State, 69-62, in NCAA Tournament first round.

1981— Replaced Don Delaney (4-13) and Bob Kloppenburg (0-1) as Cleveland head coach (December 4), with record of 4-14.

1982— Replaced by Bill Musselman as Cleveland head coach (February), with record of 13-46.

1984— Lost to New York in Eastern Conference first round.

1985— Defeated New Jersey, 3-0, in Eastern Conference first round; lost to Boston, 4-2, in Eastern Conference semifinals.

1986— Lost to Atlanta in Eastern Conference first round.

1987— Defeated Washington, 3-0, in Eastern Conference first round; defeated Atlanta, 4-1, in Eastern Conference semifinals; lost to Boston, 4-3, in Eastern Conference finals.

1988— Defeated Washington, 3-2, in Eastern Conference first round; defeated Chicago, 4-1, in Eastern Conference semifinals; defeated Boston, 4-2, in Eastern Conference finals; lost to Los Angeles Lakers, 4-3, in NBA Finals.

1989— Defeated Boston, 3-0, in Eastern Conference first round; defeated Milwaukee, 4-0, in Eastern Conference semifinals; defeated Chicago, 4-2, in Eastern Conference finals; defeated Los Angeles Lakers, 4-0, in NBA Finals.

1990— Defeated Indiana, 3-0, in Eastern Conference first round; defeated New York, 4-1, in Eastern Conference semifinals; defeated Chicago, 4-3, in Eastern Conference finals; defeated Portland, 4-1, in NBA Finals.

1991— Defeated Atlanta, 3-2, in Eastern Conference first round; defeated Boston, 4-2, in Eastern Conference semifinals; lost to Chicago, 4-0, in Eastern Conference finals.

1992— Lost to New York in Eastern Conference first round.

Team USA defeated Angola, 116-48; Croatia, 103-70; Germany, 111-68; Brazil, 127-83; and Spain, 122-81, in preliminary round. Defeated Puerto Rico, 115-77, in medal round quarterfinals; defeated Lithuania, 127-76, in semifinals; defeated Croatia, 117-85, in gold medal game.

DUNLEAVY, MIKE
BUCKS

PERSONAL: Born March 21, 1954, in Brooklyn, N.Y.... 6-3/180.... Full name: Michael Joseph Dunleavy.

HIGH SCHOOL: Nazareth Regional (Brooklyn, N.Y.).

COLLEGE: South Carolina.

TRANSACTIONS/CAREER NOTES: Selected by Philadelphia 76ers in sixth round (99th pick overall) of 1976 NBA Draft.... Waived by 76ers (November 14, 1977).... Player/head coach with Carolina Lightning of All-America Basketball Alliance (1977-78).... Signed as free agent by Houston Rockets (March 10, 1978).... Signed as veteran free agent by San Antonio Spurs (October 16, 1982); Rockets agreed not to exercise its right of first refusal in exchange for 1983 third-round draft choice.... Signed as veteran free agent by Milwaukee Bucks (March 8, 1984); Spurs agreed not to exercise its right of first refusal in exchange for 1984 fourth-round draft choice and cash.... Waived by Bucks (October 24, 1985).... Re-signed by Bucks to 10-day contract (February 19, 1989).... Waived by Bucks (February 24, 1989).... Re-signed as free agent by Bucks (December 10, 1989).... Waived by Bucks (December 15, 1989).... Re-signed by Bucks to 10-day contract (March 2, 1990).... Waived by Bucks (March 9, 1990).

COLLEGIATE RECORD

Season	Team	G	Min.	FGM	FGA	Pct.	FTM	FTA	Pct.	Reb.	Pts.	Avg.
72-73	—South Carolina	29	803	122	236	.517	59	72	.819	60	303	10.4
73-74	—South Carolina	27	983	167	369	.453	97	116	.836	85	431	16.0
74-75	—South Carolina	28	1016	182	368	.495	91	119	.765	110	455	16.3
75-76	—South Carolina	27	962	144	297	.485	109	139	.784	87	397	14.7
	Totals	111	3764	615	1270	.484	356	446	.798	342	1586	14.3

NBA REGULAR-SEASON RECORD

NOTES: Led NBA with .345 three-point field-goal percentage (1983).

Season	Team	G	Min.	FGM	FGA	Pct.	FTM	FTA	Pct.	REBOUNDS Off.	Def.	Tot.	Ast.	PF	Dq.	Stl.	Blk.	TO	Pts.	Avg.
76-77	—Philadelphia	32	359	60	145	.414	34	45	.756	10	24	34	56	64	1	13	2	...	154	4.8
77-78	—Phil.-Hou.	15	119	20	50	.400	13	18	.722	1	9	10	28	12	0	9	1	12	53	3.5
78-79	—Houston	74	1486	215	425	.506	159	184	.864	28	100	128	324	168	2	56	5	130	589	8.0
79-80	—Houston	51	1036	148	319	.464	111	134	.828	26	74	100	210	120	2	40	4	110	410	8.0
80-81	—Houston	74	1609	310	632	.491	156	186	.839	28	90	118	268	165	1	64	2	137	777	10.5
81-82	—Houston	70	1315	206	450	.458	75	106	.708	24	80	104	227	161	0	45	3	80	520	7.4
82-83	—San Antonio	79	1619	213	510	.418	120	154	.779	18	116	134	437	210	2	74	4	160	613	7.8
83-84	—Milwaukee	17	404	70	127	.551	32	40	.800	6	22	28	78	51	0	12	1	36	191	11.2
84-85	—Milwaukee	19	433	64	135	.474	25	29	.862	6	25	31	85	55	1	15	3	40	169	8.9
85-86								Did not play.												
86-87								Did not play.												
87-88								Did not play.												
88-89	—Milwaukee	2	5	1	2	.500	0	0	...	0	0	0	0	0	0	0	0	0	3	1.5
89-90	—Milwaukee	5	43	4	14	.286	7	8	.875	0	2	2	10	7	0	1	0	8	17	3.4
	Totals	438	8428	1311	2809	.467	732	904	.810	147	542	689	1723	1013	8	329	25	713	3496	8.0

Three-point field goals: 1979-80, 3-for-20 (.150). 1980-81, 1-for-16 (.063). 1981-82, 33-for-86 (.384). 1982-83, 67-for-194 (.345). 1983-84, 19-for-45 (.422). 1984-85, 16-for-47 (.340). 1988-89, 1-for-2 (.500). 1989-90, 2-for-9 (.222). Totals, 142-for-419 (.339).

NBA PLAYOFF RECORD

									— REBOUNDS —										
Season	Team	G	Min.	FGM	FGA	Pct.	FTM	FTA	Pct.	Off.	Def.	Tot.	Ast.	PF	Dq.	Stl.	Blk.	TO	Pts.	Avg.
76-77	Philadelphia.	11	68	9	25	.360	4	5	.800	1	3	4	9	14	0	3	0	...	22	2.0
78-79	Houston	1	10	0	2	.000	0	0	...	0	1	1	0	1	0	0	0	0	0	0.0
79-80	Houston	6	45	6	12	.500	5	6	.833	2	3	5	13	11	0	5	0	6	17	2.8
80-81	Houston	20	472	69	152	.454	33	38	.868	9	33	42	68	59	1	15	1	30	177	8.9
81-82	Houston	3	66	9	22	.409	5	6	.833	0	3	3	9	7	0	2	0	1	23	7.7
82-83	San Antonio.	11	174	22	65	.338	9	13	.692	3	10	13	49	22	0	9	1	14	61	5.5
83-84	Milwaukee ...	15	393	59	129	.457	33	36	.917	10	25	35	46	59	2	17	0	35	169	11.3
	Totals	67	1228	174	407	.428	89	104	.856	25	78	103	194	173	3	51	2	86	469	7.0

Three-point field goals: 1979-80, 0-for-2. 1980-81, 6-for-15 (.400). 1981-82, 0-for-4. 1982-83, 8-for-30 (.267). 1983-84, 18-for-50 (.360). Totals, 32-for-101 (.317).

AABA REGULAR-SEASON RECORD

				2-POINT			3-POINT								
Season	Team	G	Min.	FGM	FGA	Pct.	FGM	FGA	Pct.	FTM	FTA	Pct.	Reb.	Ast.	Pts.	Avg.
77-78	Carolina	10	332	66	123	.537	2	5	.400	53	60	.883	52	50	191	19.1

HEAD COACHING RECORD

BACKGROUND: Player/head coach, Carolina Lightning of All-America Basketball Alliance (1977-78).... Assistant coach, Milwaukee Bucks (1987-88 through 1989-90).

AABA COACHING RECORD

					REGULAR SEASON		PLAYOFFS		
Season	Team	W	L	Pct.	Finish		W	L	Pct.
77-78	Carolina	8	2	.800	1st/South Division		—	—	—

NBA COACHING RECORD

					REGULAR SEASON		PLAYOFFS		
Season	Team	W	L	Pct.	Finish		W	L	Pct.
90-91	Los Angeles Lakers	58	24	.707	2nd/Pacific Division		12	7	.632
91-92	Los Angeles Lakers	43	39	.524	6th/Pacific Division		—	—	—
	Totals (2 years)	101	63	.616	Totals (1 year)		12	7	.632

NOTES:
1991— Defeated Houston, 3-0, in Western Conference first round; defeated Golden State, 4-1, in Western Conference semifinals; defeated Portland, 4-2, in Western Conference finals; lost to Chicago, 4-1, in NBA Finals.

FORD, CHRIS
CELTICS

PERSONAL: Born January 11, 1949, in Atlantic City, N.J.... 6-5/190.... Full name: Christopher Joseph Ford.
HIGH SCHOOL: Holy Spirit (Absecon, N.J.).
COLLEGE: Villanova.
TRANSACTIONS/CAREER NOTES: Selected by Detroit Pistons in second round (17th pick overall) of 1972 NBA Draft.... Traded by Pistons with 1981 second-round draft choice to Boston Celtics for Earl Tatum (October 19, 1978).
MISCELLANEOUS: Member of NBA championship team (1981).

COLLEGIATE RECORD

Season	Team	G	Min.	FGM	FGA	Pct.	FTM	FTA	Pct.	Reb.	Pts.	Avg.
68-69	Villanova‡	18	...	118	...	...	87	...	...	...	323	17.9
69-70	Villanova.................................	29	...	188	396	.475	89	124	.718	168	465	16.0
70-71	Villanova.................................	34	...	180	400	.450	108	176	.614	200	468	13.8
71-72	Villanova.................................	28	...	206	399	.516	88	146	.603	180	500	17.9
	Varsity totals	91	...	574	1195	.480	285	446	.639	548	1433	15.7

NBA REGULAR-SEASON RECORD

											— REBOUNDS —										
Season	Team	G	Min.	FGM	FGA	Pct.	FTM	FTA	Pct.	Off.	Def.	Tot.	Ast.	PF	Dq.	Stl.	Blk.	TO	Pts.	Avg.
72-73	Detroit..........	74	1537	208	434	.479	60	93	.645	...	...	...	266	194	133	1	...	...	...	476	6.4
73-74	Detroit..........	82	2059	264	595	.444	57	77	.740	109	195	304	279	159	1	148	14	...	585	7.1
74-75	Detroit..........	80	1962	206	435	.474	63	95	.663	93	176	269	230	187	0	113	26	...	475	5.9
75-76	Detroit..........	82	2198	301	707	.426	83	115	.722	80	211	291	272	222	0	178	24	...	685	8.4
76-77	Detroit..........	82	2539	437	918	.476	131	170	.771	96	174	270	337	192	1	179	26	...	1005	12.3
77-78	Detroit..........	82	2582	374	777	.481	113	154	.734	117	151	268	381	182	2	166	17	232	861	10.5
78-79	Detroit-Bos..	81	2737	538	1142	.471	172	227	.758	124	150	274	374	209	3	115	25	210	1248	15.4
79-80	Boston	73	2115	330	709	.465	86	114	.754	77	104	181	215	178	0	111	27	105	816	11.2
80-81	Boston	82	2723	314	707	.444	64	87	.736	72	91	163	295	212	2	100	23	127	728	8.9
81-82	Boston	76	1591	188	450	.418	39	56	.696	52	56	108	142	143	0	42	10	52	435	5.7
	Totals	794	22043	3160	6874	.460	868	1188	.731	...	...	2394	2719	1817	10	1152	192	726	7314	9.2

Three-point field goals: 1979-80, 70-for-164 (.427). 1980-81, 36-for-109 (.330). 1981-82, 20-for-63 (.317). Totals, 126-for-336 (.375).

NBA PLAYOFF RECORD

											— REBOUNDS —										
Season	Team	G	Min.	FGM	FGA	Pct.	FTM	FTA	Pct.	Off.	Def.	Tot.	Ast.	PF	Dq.	Stl.	Blk.	TO	Pts.	Avg.
73-74	Detroit..........	5	94	8	17	.471	4	6	.667	4	11	15	7	10	0	2	2	...	20	4.0
74-75	Detroit..........	3	82	6	11	.545	0	0	...	2	11	13	10	8	0	1	0	...	12	4.0
75-76	Detroit..........	9	276	33	81	.407	12	15	.800	6	30	36	40	33	1	11	5	...	78	8.7
76-77	Detroit..........	3	101	18	44	.409	5	9	.556	8	11	19	12	11	0	7	0	...	41	13.7
79-80	Boston	9	279	34	79	.430	12	15	.800	9	16	25	21	35	1	14	6	13	82	9.1

Season Team	G	Min.	FGM	FGA	Pct.	FTM	FTA	Pct.	REBOUNDS Off.	Def.	Tot.	Ast.	PF	Dq.	Stl.	Blk.	TO	Pts.	Avg.
80-81 — Boston	17	507	66	146	.452	15	25	.600	13	32	45	46	47	0	14	1	19	154	9.1
81-82 — Boston	12	138	20	42	.476	5	7	.714	6	9	15	15	15	0	1	3	3	47	3.9
Totals	58	1477	185	420	.440	53	77	.688	48	120	168	151	159	2	50	17	35	434	7.5

Three-point field goals: 1979-80, 2-for-13 (.154). 1980-81, 7-for-25 (.280). 1981-82, 2-for-7 (.286). Totals, 11-for-45 (.244).

HEAD COACHING RECORD

BACKGROUND: Broadcaster, Boston Celtics (1982-83).... Assistant coach, Celtics (1983-84 through 1989-90).

NBA COACHING RECORD

Season Team	W	L	Pct.	REGULAR SEASON Finish	PLAYOFFS W	L	Pct.
90-91 — Boston	56	26	.683	1st/Atlantic Division	5	6	.455
91-92 — Boston	51	31	.622	T1st/Atlantic Division	6	4	.600
Totals (2 years)	107	57	.652	Totals (2 years)	11	10	.524

NOTES:
1991— Defeated Indiana, 3-2, in Eastern Conference first round; lost to Detroit, 4-2, in Eastern Conference semifinals.
1992— Defeated Indiana, 3-0, in Eastern Conference first round; lost to Cleveland, 4-3, in Eastern Conference semifinals.

GUOKAS, MATT
MAGIC

PERSONAL: Born February 25, 1944, in Philadelphia.... 6-6/195.... Full name: Matthew George Guokas Jr.... Name pronounced GOO-kiss.... Son of Matt Guokas Sr., forward with Philadelphia Warriors of Basketball Association of America (1946-47); and nephew of Al Guokas, forward/guard with Denver Nuggets of National Basketball League (1948-49) and Philadelphia Warriors of NBA (1949-50).
HIGH SCHOOL: St. Joseph's (Philadelphia).
COLLEGE: Miami (Fla.), then St. Joseph's.
TRANSACTIONS/CAREER NOTES: Selected by Philadelphia 76ers in first round of 1966 NBA Draft.... Traded by 76ers to Chicago Bulls for future draft choice (October 16, 1970).... Traded by Bulls with draft choice to Cincinnati Royals for Charlie Paulk (May 14, 1971).... Royals franchise moved from Cincinnati to Kansas City-Omaha and renamed Kings for 1972-73 season. ... Traded by Kings to Houston Rockets for Jimmy Walker (October 29, 1973).... Traded by Rockets with Jack Marin to Buffalo Braves for Kevin Kunnert and Dave Wohl (February 1, 1974).... Traded by Braves with draft choice to Bulls for Bob Weiss (September 4, 1974).... Traded by Bulls to Kansas City Kings for draft choices (December 8, 1975).... Waived by Kings (July 29, 1976).
MISCELLANEOUS: Member of NBA championsip team (1967).

COLLEGIATE RECORD

Season Team	G	Min.	FGM	FGA	Pct.	FTM	FTA	Pct.	Reb.	Pts.	Avg.
62-63 — Miami (Fla.)‡					Freshman team statistics unavailable.						
63-64 — St. Joseph's					Did not play—transfer student.						
64-65 — St. Joseph's	29	...	157	342	.459	71	98	.724	195	385	13.3
65-66 — St. Joseph's	29	...	207	413	.501	94	122	.770	72	508	17.5
Varsity totals	58	...	364	755	.482	165	220	.750	267	893	15.4

NBA REGULAR-SEASON RECORD

Season Team	G	Min.	FGM	FGA	Pct.	FTM	FTA	Pct.	Reb.	Ast.	PF	Dq.	Pts.	Avg.
66-67 — Philadelphia	69	808	79	203	.389	49	81	.605	83	105	82	0	207	3.0
67-68 — Philadelphia	82	1612	190	393	.483	118	152	.776	185	191	172	0	498	6.1
68-69 — Philadelphia	72	838	92	216	.426	54	81	.667	94	104	121	1	238	3.3
69-70 — Philadelphia	80	1558	189	416	.454	106	149	.711	216	222	201	0	484	6.1
70-71 — Philadelphia-Chicago	79	2213	206	418	.493	101	138	.732	158	342	189	1	513	6.5
71-72 — Cincinnati	61	1975	191	385	.496	64	83	.771	142	321	150	0	446	7.3
72-73 — Kansas City/Omaha	79	2846	322	565	.570	74	90	.822	245	403	190	0	718	9.1

Season Team	G	Min.	FGM	FGA	Pct.	FTM	FTA	Pct.	REBOUNDS Off.	Def.	Tot.	Ast.	PF	Dq.	Stl.	Blk.	TO	Pts.	Avg.
73-74 — KCO-Ho-Bu.	75	1871	195	396	.492	39	60	.650	31	90	121	238	150	3	54	21	...	429	5.7
74-75 — Chicago	82	2089	255	500	.510	78	103	.757	24	115	139	178	154	1	45	17	...	588	7.2
75-76 — Chi.-K.C.	56	793	73	173	.422	18	27	.667	22	41	63	70	76	0	18	3	...	164	2.9
Totals	735	16603	1792	3665	.489	701	964	.727	...	...	1446	2174	1485	6	117	41	...	4285	5.8

NBA PLAYOFF RECORD

Season Team	G	Min.	FGM	FGA	Pct.	FTM	FTA	Pct.	Reb.	Ast.	PF	Dq.	Pts.	Avg.
66-67 — Philadelphia	15	252	26	64	.406	13	17	.765	30	23	33	0	65	4.3
67-68 — Philadelphia	13	327	30	79	.380	20	27	.741	43	30	39	0	80	6.2
68-69 — Philadelphia	5	100	11	27	.407	4	5	.800	12	8	12	0	26	5.2
69-70 — Philadelphia	2	23	6	8	.750	1	1	1.000	3	1	1	0	13	6.5
70-71 — Chicago	6	83	8	14	.571	4	5	.800	8	12	8	0	20	3.3

Season Team	G	Min.	FGM	FGA	Pct.	FTM	FTA	Pct.	REBOUNDS Off.	Def.	Tot.	Ast.	PF	Dq.	Stl.	Blk.	TO	Pts.	Avg.
73-74 — Buffalo	6	85	8	15	.533	3	4	.750	3	5	8	13	8	0	0	1	...	19	3.2
74-75 — Chicago	13	202	12	35	.343	7	8	.875	4	10	14	11	20	0	7	1	...	31	2.4
Totals	60	1072	101	242	.417	52	67	.776	...	...	118	98	121	0	7	2	...	254	4.2

COACHING RECORD

BACKGROUND: Broadcaster, Philadelphia 76ers (1977-78 to December 1981).... Assistant coach, 76ers (December 1981 through 1984-85).

NBA COACHING RECORD

Season Team	W	L	Pct.	REGULAR SEASON Finish	PLAYOFFS W	L	Pct.
85-86 — Philadelphia	54	28	.659	2nd/Atlantic Division	6	6	.500
86-87 — Philadelphia	45	37	.549	2nd/Atlantic Division	2	3	.400

Season	Team		W	L	Pct.	Finish		W	L	Pct.
						REGULAR SEASON			PLAYOFFS	
87-88	—Philadelphia		20	23	.465			—	—	—
89-90	—Orlando		18	64	.220	7th/Central Division		—	—	—
90-91	—Orlando		31	51	.378	4th/Midwest Division		—	—	—
91-92	—Orlando		21	61	.256	7th/Atlantic Division		—	—	—
	Totals (6 years)		189	264	.417	Totals (2 years)		8	9	.471

NOTES:
1986— Defeated Washington, 3-2, in Eastern Conference first round; lost to Milwaukee, 4-3, in Eastern Conference semifinals.
1987— Lost to Milwaukee in Eastern Conference first round.
1988— Replaced as Philadelphia head coach by Jim Lynam (February 8).

HILL, BOB
PACERS

PERSONAL: Born November 24, 1948, in Columbus, O. . . . 6-5/200. . . . Full name: Robert W. Hill.
HIGH SCHOOL: Worthington (O.).
COLLEGE: Bowling Green State.

COLLEGIATE RECORD

Season	Team	G	Min.	FGM	FGA	Pct.	FTM	FTA	Pct.	Reb.	Pts.	Avg.
67-68	—Bowling Green State‡	14	. . .	108	215	.502	41	57	.719	127	257	18.4
68-69	—Bowling Green State	20	. . .	22	54	.407	12	22	.545	21	56	2.8
69-70	—Bowling Green State	16	. . .	5	23	.217	6	12	.500	14	16	1.0
70-71	—Bowling Green State	21	. . .	22	49	.449	9	16	.563	31	53	2.5
	Varsity totals	57	. . .	49	126	.389	27	50	.540	66	125	2.2

HEAD COACHING RECORD

BACKGROUND: Assistant coach, Bowling Green State University (1971-1975). . . . Assistant coach, University of Pittsburgh (1975-1977). . . . Assistant coach, University of Kansas (1977-1985). . . . Assistant coach, New York Knicks (1985-86). . . . Scout, Charlotte Hornets (1987-88). . . . Broadcaster, New Jersey Nets (1987-88). . . . Head coach, Vitrus Knorr of Italian League (1988-89). . . . Assistant coach, Indiana Pacers (1989-90 to December 20, 1990).

NBA COACHING RECORD

Season	Team		W	L	Pct.	Finish		W	L	Pct.
						REGULAR SEASON			PLAYOFFS	
86-87	—New York		20	46	.303	T4th/Atlantic Division		—	—	—
90-91	—Indiana		32	25	.561	5th/Central Division		2	3	.400
91-92	—Indiana		40	42	.488	4th/Central Division		0	3	.000
	Totals (3 years)		92	113	.449	Totals (2 years)		2	6	.250

CBA COACHING RECORD

Season	Team		W	L	Pct.	Finish		W	L	Pct.
						REGULAR SEASON			PLAYOFFS	
87-88	—Topeka		5	12	.294	5th/Eastern Division		—	—	—
	Totals (1 year)		5	12	.294					

NOTES:
1986— Replaced Hubie Brown as New York head coach, with record of 4-12.
1988— Replaced John Killilea (13-17) and John Darr (3-4) as Topeka head coach (February), with record of 16-21 and in third place.
1990— Replaced Dick Versace as Indiana head coach (December 20), with record of 9-16.
1991— Lost to Boston in Eastern Conference first round.
1992— Lost to Boston in Eastern Conference first round.

RECORD AS BASEBALL PLAYER

TRANSACTIONS/CAREER NOTES: Selected by San Diego Padres organization in 14th round of free-agent draft (June 8, 1971). . . . Released by Padres organization (July 27, 1971).

Year	Team (League)	G	W	L	Pct.	ERA	Sv.	IP	H	R	ER	BB	SO
1971	—Tri-City (Northwest)	2	0	0	.000	12.00	0	3	5	4	4	2	1

ISSEL, DAN
NUGGETS

PERSONAL: Born October 25, 1948, in Batavia, Ill. . . . 6-9/240. . . . Full name: Daniel Paul Issel.
HIGH SCHOOL: Batavia (Ill.).
COLLEGE: Kentucky.
TRANSACTIONS/CAREER NOTES: Selected by Detroit Pistons in eighth round (122nd pick overall) of 1970 NBA Draft. . . . Selected by Kentucky Colonels in first round of American Basketball Association draft (1970). . . . Traded by Colonels to Baltimore Claws for Tom Owens and cash (September 19, 1975). . . . Traded by Claws to Denver Nuggets for Dave Robisch and cash (October 8, 1975). . . . Nuggets franchise became part of NBA upon merger of ABA and NBA for 1976-77 season.

COLLEGIATE RECORD

NOTES: THE SPORTING NEWS All-America first team (1970). . . . THE SPORTING NEWS All-America second team (1969).

Season	Team	G	Min.	FGM	FGA	Pct.	FTM	FTA	Pct.	Reb.	Pts.	Avg.
66-67	—Kentucky‡	20	. . .	168	332	.506	80	111	.721	355	416	20.8
67-68	—Kentucky	27	836	171	390	.438	102	154	.662	328	444	16.4
68-69	—Kentucky	28	1063	285	534	.534	176	232	.759	381	746	26.6
69-70	—Kentucky	28	1044	369	667	.553	210	275	.764	369	948	33.9
	Varsity totals	83	2943	825	1591	.519	488	661	.738	1078	2138	25.8

HEAD COACHES

ABA REGULAR-SEASON RECORD

ABA co-Rookie of the Year (1971).... ABA All-Star first team (1972).... ABA All-Star second team (1971, 1973, 1974, 1976).... ABA All-Rookie team (1971).... Member of ABA championship team (1975).... Holds single-season record for most points—2,538 (1972).

Season Team	G	Min.	2-POINT FGM	FGA	Pct.	3-POINT FGM	FGA	Pct.	FTM	FTA	Pct.	Reb.	Ast.	Pts.	Avg.
70-71 — Kentucky	83	3274	938	1989	.472	0	5	.000	604	748	.807	1093	162	*2480	*29.9
71-72 — Kentucky	83	3570	969	1990	.487	3	11	.273	591	*753	.785	931	195	*2538	30.6
72-73 — Kentucky	84	*3531	899	1742	.516	3	15	.200	485	635	.764	922	220	*2292	27.3
73-74 — Kentucky	83	3347	826	1709	.483	3	17	.176	457	581	.787	847	137	2118	25.5
74-75 — Kentucky	83	2864	614	1298	.473	0	5	.000	237	321	.738	710	188	1465	17.7
75-76 — Denver	84	2858	751	1468	.512	1	4	.250	425	521	.816	923	201	1930	23.0
Totals	500	19444	4997	10196	.490	10	57	.175	2799	3559	.786	5426	1103	12823	25.6

ABA PLAYOFF RECORD

Season Team	G	Min.	2-POINT FGM	FGA	Pct.	3-POINT FGM	FGA	Pct.	FTM	FTA	Pct.	Reb.	Ast.	Pts.	Avg.
70-71 — Kentucky	19	670	207	408	.507	0	0	...	123	141	.872	221	28	536	28.2
71-72 — Kentucky	6	269	47	113	.416	0	1	.000	38	50	.760	54	5	132	22.0
72-73 — Kentucky	19	821	197	392	.503	1	6	.167	124	156	.795	225	28	521	27.4
73-74 — Kentucky	8	311	60	135	.444	0	0	...	28	33	.848	87	14	148	18.5
74-75 — Kentucky	15	578	122	261	.467	0	0	...	60	74	.811	119	29	304	20.3
75-76 — Denver	13	470	111	226	.491	0	1	.000	44	56	.786	156	32	266	20.5
Totals	80	3119	744	1535	.485	1	8	.125	417	510	.818	862	136	1907	23.8

ABA ALL-STAR GAME RECORD

NOTES: ABA All-Star Game Most Valuable Player (1972).

Season Team	Min.	2-POINT FGM	FGA	Pct.	3-POINT FGM	FGA	Pct.	FTM	FTA	Pct.	Reb.	Ast.	Pts.
1971 — Kentucky	34	8	15	.533	0	0	...	5	8	.625	11	0	21
1972 — Kentucky	23	9	13	.692	0	0	...	3	4	.750	9	5	21
1973 — Kentucky	29	6	14	.429	0	0	...	2	2	1.000	7	4	14
1974 — Kentucky	26	10	15	.667	0	0	...	1	1	1.000	4	1	21
1975 — Denver	20	3	6	.500	0	0	...	1	2	.500	7	1	7
1976 — Denver	31	6	16	.375	0	0	...	7	9	.778	9	5	19
Totals	163	42	79	.532	0	0	...	19	26	.731	47	16	103

NBA REGULAR-SEASON RECORD

Season Team	G	Min.	FGM	FGA	Pct.	FTM	FTA	Pct.	REBOUNDS Off.	Def.	Tot.	Ast.	PF	Dq.	Stl.	Blk.	TO	Pts.	Avg.
76-77 — Denver	79	2507	660	1282	.515	445	558	.797	211	485	696	177	246	7	91	29	...	1765	22.3
77-78 — Denver	82	2851	659	1287	.512	428	547	.782	253	577	830	304	279	5	100	41	259	1746	21.3
78-79 — Denver	81	2742	532	1030	.517	316	419	.754	240	498	738	255	233	6	61	46	171	1380	17.0
79-80 — Denver	82	2938	715	1416	.505	517	667	.775	236	483	719	198	190	1	88	54	163	1951	23.8
80-81 — Denver	80	2641	614	1220	.503	519	684	.759	229	447	676	158	249	6	83	53	130	1749	21.9
81-82 — Denver	81	2472	651	1236	.527	546	655	.834	174	434	608	179	245	4	67	55	169	1852	22.9
82-83 — Denver	80	2431	661	1296	.510	400	479	.835	151	445	596	223	227	0	83	43	174	1726	21.6
83-84 — Denver	76	2076	569	1153	.494	364	428	.850	112	401	513	173	182	2	60	44	122	1506	19.8
84-85 — Denver	77	1684	363	791	.459	257	319	.806	80	251	331	137	171	1	65	31	93	984	12.8
Totals	718	22342	5424	10711	.506	3792	4756	.797	1686	4021	5707	1804	2022	32	698	396	1281	14659	20.4

Three-point field goals: 1979-80, 4-for-12 (.333). 1980-81, 2-for-12 (.167). 1981-82, 4-for-6 (.667). 1982-83, 4-for-19 (.211). 1983-84, 4-for-19 (.211). 1984-85, 1-for-7 (.143). Totals, 19-for-75 (.253).

NBA PLAYOFF RECORD

Season Team	G	Min.	FGM	FGA	Pct.	FTM	FTA	Pct.	REBOUNDS Off.	Def.	Tot.	Ast.	PF	Dq.	Stl.	Blk.	TO	Pts.	Avg.
76-77 — Denver	6	222	49	96	.510	34	45	.756	18	40	58	17	20	0	5	4	...	132	22.0
77-78 — Denver	13	460	103	212	.486	56	65	.862	41	93	134	53	43	1	7	3	39	262	20.2
78-79 — Denver	3	109	24	45	.533	25	31	.806	7	21	28	10	15	0	0	0	9	73	24.3
81-82 — Denver	3	103	32	60	.533	12	12	1.000	8	13	21	5	10	0	3	1	7	76	25.3
82-83 — Denver	8	227	69	136	.507	25	29	.862	13	45	58	25	18	0	9	5	10	163	20.4
83-84 — Denver	5	153	52	102	.510	30	39	.821	10	30	40	8	15	0	6	6	15	137	27.4
84-85 — Denver	15	325	73	159	.459	39	48	.813	14	40	54	27	36	0	12	5	13	186	12.4
Totals	53	1599	402	810	.496	223	269	.829	111	282	393	145	157	1	42	24	93	1029	19.4

Three-point field goals: 1982-83, 0-for-1. 1983-84, 1-for-2 (.500). 1984-85, 1-for-1. Totals, 2-for-4 (.500).

NBA ALL-STAR GAME RECORD

Season Team	Min.	FGM	FGA	Pct.	FTM	FTA	Pct.	REBOUNDS Off.	Def.	Tot.	Ast.	PF	Dq.	Stl.	Blk.	TO	Pts.
1977 — Denver	10	0	3	.000	0	0	...	1	0	1	0	0	0	0	0	...	0

HEAD COACHING RECORD

BACKGROUND: Broadcaster, Denver Nuggets (1988-92).

JACKSON, PHIL
BULLS

PERSONAL: Born September 17, 1945, in Deer Lodge, Mont.... 6-8/ 230.... Full name: Philip D. Jackson.
HIGH SCHOOL: Williston (N.D.).
COLLEGE: North Dakota.
TRANSACTIONS/CAREER NOTES: Selected by New York Knicks in second round (17th pick overall) of 1967 NBA Draft.... Traded by Knicks with a future draft choice to New Jersey Nets for future draft choices (June 8, 1978).... Waived by Nets (October 11, 1978).... Re-signed by Nets (November 10, 1978).... Waived by Nets (Oc-

tober 12, 1979). . . . Re-signed by Nets (February 15, 1980).
MISCELLANEOUS: Member of NBA championship team (1973).

COLLEGIATE RECORD

Season Team	G	Min.	FGM	FGA	Pct.	FTM	FTA	Pct.	Reb.	Pts.	Avg.
63-64 —North Dakota‡	...	...	...	...	...	...	156	.686	361	365	24.3
64-65 —North Dakota	31	...	129	307	.420	107	203	.764	374	631	11.8
65-66 —North Dakota	29	...	238	439	.542	155	278	.748	374	712	21.8
66-67 —North Dakota	26	...	252	468	.538	208	278	.748	374	712	27.4
Varsity totals	86	...	619	1214	.510	470	637	.738	1109	1708	19.9

NBA REGULAR-SEASON RECORD

HONORS: NBA All-Rookie team (1968).

Season Team	G	Min.	FGM	FGA	Pct.	FTM	FTA	Pct.	Reb.	Ast.	PF	Dq.	Pts.	Avg.
67-68 —New York	75	1093	182	455	.400	99	168	.589	338	55	212	3	463	6.2
68-69 —New York	47	924	126	294	.429	80	119	.672	246	43	168	6	332	7.1
69-70 —New York						Did not play—injured.								
70-71 —New York	71	771	118	263	.449	95	133	.714	238	31	169	4	331	4.7
71-72 —New York	80	1273	205	466	.440	167	228	.732	326	72	224	4	577	7.2
72-73 —New York	80	1393	245	553	.443	154	195	.790	344	94	218	2	644	8.1

									— REBOUNDS —								
Season Team	G	Min.	FGM	FGA	Pct.	FTM	FTA	Pct.	Off.	Def.	Tot.	Ast.	PF	Dq.	Stl.	Blk.	TO	Pts.	Avg.
73-74 —New York	82	2050	361	757	.477	191	246	.776	123	355	478	134	277	7	42	67	...	913	11.1
74-75 —New York	78	2285	324	712	.455	193	253	.763	137	463	600	136	330	10	84	53	...	841	10.8
75-76 —New York	80	1461	185	387	.478	110	150	.733	80	263	343	105	275	3	41	20	...	480	6.0
76-77 —N.Y. Knicks	76	1033	102	232	.440	51	71	.718	75	154	229	85	184	4	33	18	...	255	3.4
77-78 —New York	63	654	55	115	.478	43	56	.768	29	81	110	46	106	0	31	15	47	153	2.4
78-79 —New Jersey	59	1070	144	303	.475	86	105	.819	59	119	178	85	168	7	45	22	78	374	6.3
79-80 —New Jersey	16	194	29	46	.630	7	10	.700	12	12	24	12	35	1	5	4	9	65	4.1
Totals	807	14201	2076	4583	.453	1276	1734	.736	...	...	3454	898	2366	51	281	199	134	5428	6.7

Three-point field goals: 1979-80, 0-for-2.

NBA PLAYOFF RECORD

Season Team	G	Min.	FGM	FGA	Pct.	FTM	FTA	Pct.	Reb.	Ast.	PF	Dq.	Pts.	Avg.
67-68 —New York	6	90	10	35	.286	4	5	.800	25	2	23	0	24	4.0
68-69 —New York						Did not play—injured.								
70-71 —New York	5	30	4	14	.286	1	1	1.000	10	2	8	0	9	1.8
71-72 —New York	16	320	57	120	.475	42	57	.737	82	15	51	1	156	9.8
72-73 —New York	17	338	60	120	.500	28	38	.737	72	24	59	3	148	8.7

									— REBOUNDS —								
Season Team	G	Min.	FGM	FGA	Pct.	FTM	FTA	Pct.	Off.	Def.	Tot.	Ast.	PF	Dq.	Stl.	Blk.	TO	Pts.	Avg.
73-74 —New York	12	297	54	116	.466	27	30	.900	15	42	57	15	40	0	10	5	...	135	11.3
74-75 —New York	3	78	10	21	.476	7	8	.875	5	20	25	2	15	0	4	3	...	27	9.0
77-78 —New York	6	50	4	8	.500	4	6	.667	4	6	10	3	11	0	3	0	4	12	2.0
78-79 —New Jersey	2	20	1	3	.333	2	2	1.000	2	1	3	0	1	0	1	0	0	4	2.0
Totals	67	1223	200	437	.458	115	147	.782	...	...	284	63	208	4	18	8	4	515	7.7

HEAD COACHING RECORD

BACKGROUND: Player/assistant coach, New Jersey Nets (1978-79 and 1979-80). . . . Assistant coach, Nets (1980-81). . . . Broadcaster, Nets (1981-82). . . . Assistant coach, Chicago Bulls (1987-88 and 1988-89).
HONORS: CBA Coach of the Year (1985).

CBA COACHING RECORD

	REGULAR SEASON				PLAYOFFS		
Season Team	W	L	Pct.	Finish	W	L	Pct.
82-83 —Albany	8	11	.421	4th/Eastern Division	—	—	—
83-84 —Albany	25	19	.568	2nd/Eastern Division	9	5	.643
84-85 —Albany	34	14	.708	1st/Eastern Division	5	5	.500
85-86 —Albany	24	24	.500	4th/Eastern Division	3	4	.429
86-87 —Albany	26	22	.542	T2nd/Eastern Division	4	4	.500
Totals (5 years)	117	90	.565	Totals (4 years)	21	18	.538

NBA COACHING RECORD

	REGULAR SEASON				PLAYOFFS		
Season Team	W	L	Pct.	Finish	W	L	Pct.
89-90 —Chicago	55	27	.671	2nd/Central Division	10	6	.625
90-91 —Chicago	61	21	.744	1st/Central Division	15	2	.882
91-92 —Chicago	67	15	.817	1st/Central Division	15	7	.682
Totals (3 years)	183	63	.744	Totals (3 years)	40	15	.727

NOTES:
1983— Replaced Dean Meminger (8-15) and player/interim coach Sam Worthen (0-2) as Albany Patroons head coach (January 29), with record of 8-17.
1984— Defeated Bay State, 3-2, in Eastern semifinals; defeated Puerto Rico, 3-1, in Eastern finals; defeated Wyoming, 3-2, in CBA Championship Series.
1985— Defeated Toronto, 3-2, in Eastern semifinals; lost to Tampa Bay, 3-2, in Eastern finals.
1986— Lost to Tampa Bay in Eastern semifinals.
1987— Defeated Mississippi, 4-0, in Eastern semifinals; lost to Rapid City, 4-0, in Eastern final.
1990— Defeated Milwaukee, 3-1, in Eastern Conference first round; defeated Philadelphia, 4-1, in Eastern Conference semifinals; lost to Detroit, 4-3, in Eastern Conference finals.
1991— Defeated New York, 3-0, in Eastern Conference first round; defeated Philadelphia, 4-1, in Eastern Conference semifinals; defeated Detroit, 4-0, in Eastern Conference finals; defeated Los Angeles Lakers, 4-1, in NBA Finals.
1992— Defeated Miami, 3-0, in Eastern Conference first round; defeated New York, 4-3, in Eastern Conference semifinals; defeated Cleveland, 4-2, in Eastern Conference finals; defeated Portland, 4-2, in NBA Finals.

KARL, GEORGE

SUPERSONICS

PERSONAL: Born May 12, 1951, in Penn Hills, Pa. . . . 6-2/190. . . . Full name: George Matthew Karl.
HIGH SCHOOL: Penn Hills (Pa.).
COLLEGE: North Carolina.
TRANSACTIONS/CAREER NOTES: Signed as free agent by San Antonio Spurs of American Basketball Association (1973). . . . Spurs franchise became part of NBA upon merger of NBA and ABA for 1976-77 season.

COLLEGIATE RECORD

Season Team	G	Min.	FGM	FGA	Pct.	FTM	FTA	Pct.	Reb.	Pts.	Avg.
69-70 —North Carolina†	6	...	56	97	.577	20	23	.870	29	132	22.0
70-71 —North Carolina	32	...	150	286	.524	92	115	.800	104	392	12.3
71-72 —North Carolina	29	...	125	241	.519	89	113	.788	72	339	11.7
72-73 —North Carolina	33	...	219	437	.501	124	163	.761	103	562	17.0
Varsity totals	94	...	494	964	.512	305	391	.780	279	1293	13.8

ABA REGULAR-SEASON RECORD

Season Team	G	Min.	2-POINT FGM	FGA	Pct.	3-POINT FGM	FGA	Pct.	FTM	FTA	Pct.	Reb.	Ast.	Pts.	Avg.
73-74 —San Antonio	74	1339	228	480	.475	8	22	.364	94	113	.832	126	160	574	7.8
74-75 —San Antonio	82	1629	257	511	.503	4	23	.174	137	177	.774	155	334	663	8.1
75-76 —San Antonio	75	1200	150	325	.462	0	9	.000	81	106	.764	66	250	381	5.1
Totals	231	4168	635	1316	.483	12	54	.222	312	396	.788	347	744	1618	7.0

ABA PLAYOFF RECORD

Season Team	G	Min.	2-POINT FGM	FGA	Pct.	3-POINT FGM	FGA	Pct.	FTM	FTA	Pct.	Reb.	Ast.	Pts.	Avg.
73-74 —San Antonio	7	141	13	27	.481	0	1	.000	2	5	.400	15	23	28	4.0
74-75 —San Antonio	4	40	1	7	.143	0	1	.000	3	4	.750	3	5	5	1.3
75-76 —San Antonio	6	64	10	21	.476	0	1	.000	6	9	.667	4	17	26	4.3
Totals	17	245	24	55	.436	0	3	.000	11	18	.611	22	45	59	3.5

NBA REGULAR-SEASON RECORD

Season Team	G	Min.	FGM	FGA	Pct.	FTM	FTA	Pct.	REBOUNDS Off.	Def.	Tot.	Ast.	PF	Dq.	Stl.	Blk.	TO	Pts.	Avg.
76-77 —San Antonio	29	251	26	73	.342	29	42	.690	4	13	17	46	36	0	10	0	...	79	2.7
77-78 —San Antonio	4	30	2	6	.333	2	2	1.000	0	5	5	5	6	0	1	0	4	6	1.5
Totals	33	281	27	79	.342	31	44	.705	4	18	22	51	42	0	11	0	4	85	2.6

NBA PLAYOFF RECORD

Season Team	G	Min.	FGM	FGA	Pct.	FTM	FTA	Pct.	REBOUNDS Off.	Def.	Tot.	Ast.	PF	Dq.	Stl.	Blk.	TO	Pts.	Avg.
76-77 —San Antonio	1	1	0	0	...	0	0	...	0	0	0	0	0	0	0	0	...	0	0.0

HEAD COACHING RECORD

BACKGROUND: Assistant coach, San Antonio Spurs (1978-79 and 1979-80). . . . Director of player acquisition, Cleveland Cavaliers (1983-84). . . . Head coach, Real Madrid of Spanish League (1989-90 and 1991-January 1992).
HONORS: CBA Coach of the Year (1981, 1983, 1991).

CBA COACHING RECORD

Season Team	REGULAR SEASON W	L	Pct.	Finish	PLAYOFFS W	L	Pct.
80-81 —Montana	27	15	.643	1st/Western Division	5	5	.500
81-82 —Montana	30	16	.652	2nd/Western Division	2	3	.400
82-83 —Montana	33	11	.750	1st/Western Division	6	5	.545
88-89 —Albany	36	18	.667	1st/Eastern Division	2	4	.333
90-91 —Albany	50	6	.893	1st/Eastern Division	5	6	.455
Totals (5 years)	176	66	.727	Totals (5 years)	20	23	.465

NBA COACHING RECORD

Season Team	REGULAR SEASON W	L	Pct.	Finish	PLAYOFFS W	L	Pct.
84-85 —Cleveland	36	46	.439	4th/Central Division	1	3	.250
85-86 —Cleveland	25	42	.373	—	—	—	—
86-87 —Golden State	42	40	.512	3rd/Pacific Division	4	6	.400
87-88 —Golden State	16	48	.250	—	—	—	—
91-92 —Seattle	27	15	.643	4th/Pacific Division	4	5	.444
Totals (5 years)	146	191	.433	Totals (3 years)	9	14	.391

NOTES:
1981— Defeated Alberta, 2-0, in Western semifinals; defeated Billings, 3-1, in Western finals; lost to Rochester, 4-0, in CBA Championship Series.
1982— Lost to Billings in Western finals.
1983— Defeated Wyoming, 3-1, in Western finals; lost to Detroit, 4-3, in CBA Championship Series.
1985— Lost to Boston in Eastern Conference first round.
1986— Replaced by Gene Littles as Cleveland head coach (March 16).
1987— Defeated Utah, 3-2, in Western Conference first round; lost to Los Angeles Lakers, 4-1, in Western Conference semifinals.
1988— Resigned as Golden State head coach (March 23).
1989— Lost to Wichita Falls in Eastern semifinals.
1991— Defeated Grand Rapids, 3-2, in National Conference first round; lost to Wichita Falls, 4-2, in National Conference finals.
1992— Replaced K.C. Jones (18-18) and Bob Kloppenburg (2-2) as Seattle head coach (January 23), with record of 20-20

and in fifth place. Defeated Golden State, 3-1, in Western Conference first round; lost to Utah, 4-1, in Western Conference semifinals.

LOUGHERY, KEVIN
HEAT

PERSONAL: Born March 28, 1940, in Brooklyn, N.Y. . . . 6-3/190. . . . Full name: Kevin Michael Loughery.
HIGH SCHOOL: Cardinal Hayes (Bronx, N.Y.).
COLLEGE: Boston College, then St. John's.

TRANSACTIONS/CAREER NOTES: Selected by Detroit Pistons in second round (13th pick overall) of 1962 NBA Draft. . . . Traded by Pistons to Baltimore Bullets for Larry Staverman (October 28, 1963). . . . Traded by Bullets with Fred Carter to Philadelphia 76ers for Archie Clark and future draft choice (October 18, 1971).

COLLEGIATE RECORD

Season	Team	G	Min.	FGM	FGA	Pct.	FTM	FTA	Pct.	Reb.	Pts.	Avg.
57-58	Boston College‡	19	. . .	133	. . .	. . .	55	. . .	. . .	. . .	321	16.9
58-59	Boston College	19	. . .	128	. . .	. . .	55	. . .	. . .	. . .	321	16.9
59-60	St. John's					Did not play—transfer student.						
60-61	St. John's	25	. . .	106	252	.421	54	77	.701	116	266	10.6
61-62	St. John's	26	. . .	169	378	.447	65	76	.855	151	403	15.5
	Varsity totals	70	. . .	403	. . .	. . .	184	. . .	. . .	. . .	990	14.1

NBA REGULAR-SEASON RECORD

Season	Team	G	Min.	FGM	FGA	Pct.	FTM	FTA	Pct.	Reb.	Ast.	PF	Dq.	Pts.	Avg.
62-63	Detroit	57	845	146	397	.368	71	100	.710	109	104	135	1	363	6.4
63-64	Detroit-Baltimore	66	1459	236	631	.374	126	177	.712	138	182	175	2	598	9.1
64-65	Baltimore	80	2417	406	957	.424	212	281	.754	235	296	320	13	1024	12.8
65-66	Baltimore	74	2455	526	1264	.416	297	358	.830	227	356	273	8	1349	18.2
66-67	Baltimore	76	2577	520	1306	.398	340	412	.825	349	288	294	10	1380	18.2
67-68	Baltimore	77	2297	458	1127	.406	305	392	.778	247	256	301	13	1221	15.9
68-69	Baltimore	80	3135	717	1636	.438	372	463	.803	266	384	299	3	1806	22.6
69-70	Baltimore	55	2037	477	1082	.441	253	298	.849	168	292	183	3	1207	21.9
70-71	Baltimore	82	2260	481	1193	.403	275	331	.831	219	301	246	2	1237	15.1
71-72	Baltimore-Philadelphia	76	1771	341	809	.422	263	320	.822	183	196	213	3	945	12.4
72-73	Philadelphia	32	955	169	427	.396	107	130	.823	113	148	104	0	445	13.9
	Totals	755	22208	4477	10829	.413	2621	3262	.803	2254	2803	2543	58	11575	15.3

NBA PLAYOFF RECORD

Season	Team	G	Min.	FGM	FGA	Pct.	FTM	FTA	Pct.	Reb.	Ast.	PF	Dq.	Pts.	Avg.
62-63	Detroit	2	26	1	10	.100	1	1	1.000	0	4	3	0	3	1.5
64-65	Baltimore	10	297	53	137	.387	34	38	.895	34	30	36	0	140	14.0
65-66	Baltimore	3	27	3	7	.429	3	6	.500	1	1	4	0	9	3.0
68-69	Baltimore	4	173	29	79	.367	23	35	.657	18	21	16	0	81	20.3
69-70	Baltimore	7	153	26	77	.338	15	21	.714	16	8	24	0	67	9.6
70-71	Baltimore	17	500	84	212	.396	64	85	.753	38	52	57	2	232	13.6
	Totals	43	1176	196	522	.375	140	186	.753	107	116	140	2	532	12.4

HEAD COACHING RECORD

BACKGROUND: Player/head coach, Philadelphia 76ers (February 1973-remainder of 1972-73 season). . . . Broadcaster (1988-89 and 1989-90). . . . Scout, Miami Heat (1988-89 and 1989-90). . . . Assistant coach, Atlanta Hawks (1990-91).

NBA COACHING RECORD

		REGULAR SEASON				PLAYOFFS		
Season	Team	W	L	Pct.	Finish	W	L	Pct.
72-73	Philadelphia	5	26	.161	4th/Atlantic Division	—	—	—
76-77	New York Nets	22	60	.268	5th/Atlantic Division	—	—	—
77-78	New Jersey	24	58	.293	5th/Atlantic Division	—	—	—
78-79	New Jersey	37	45	.451	3rd/Atlantic Division	0	2	.000
79-80	New Jersey	34	48	.415	5th/Atlantic Division	—	—	—
80-81	New Jersey	12	23	.343		—	—	—
81-82	Atlanta	42	40	.512	2nd/Central Division	0	2	.000
82-83	Atlanta	43	39	.524	2nd/Central Division	1	2	.333
83-84	Chicago	27	55	.329	5th/Central Division	—	—	—
84-85	Chicago	38	44	.463	3rd/Central Division	1	3	.250
85-86	Washington	7	6	.538	T3rd/Atlantic Division	2	3	.400
86-87	Washington	42	40	.512	3rd/Atlantic Division	0	3	.000
87-88	Washington	8	19	.296		—	—	—
91-92	Miami	38	44	.463	4th/Atlantic Division	0	3	.000
	Totals (14 years)	379	547	.409	Totals (7 years)	4	18	.182

ABA COACHING RECORD

		REGULAR SEASON				PLAYOFFS		
Season	Team	W	L	Pct.	Finish	W	L	Pct.
73-74	New York Nets	55	29	.655	1st/Eastern Division	12	2	.857
74-75	New York Nets	58	26	.690	T1st/Eastern Division	1	4	.200
75-76	New York Nets	55	29	.655	2nd/Eastern Division	8	5	.615
	Totals (3 years)	168	84	.667	Totals (3 years)	21	11	.656

NOTES:
1973— Replaced Roy Rubin as Philadelphia head coach (February), with record of 4-47.
1974— Defeated Virginia, 4-1, in Eastern Division semifinals; defeated Kentucky, 4-0, in Eastern Division finals; defeated Utah, 4-1, in ABA Finals.
1975— Lost to St. Louis in Eastern Division semifinals.
1976— Defeated San Antonio, 4-3, in semifinals; defeated Denver, 4-2, in ABA Finals.
1979— Lost to Philadelphia in Eastern Conference first round.

HEAD COACHES

1980— Resigned as New Jersey head coach (December); replaced by Bob MacKinnon.
1982— Lost to Philadelphia in Eastern Conference first round.
1983— Lost to Boston in Eastern Conference first round.
1985— Lost to Milwaukee in Eastern Conference first round.
1986— Replaced Gene Shue as Washington head coach (March 19), with record of 32-37. Lost to Philadelphia in Eastern Conference first round.
1987— Lost to Detroit in Eastern Conference first round.
1988— Replaced by Wes Unseld as Washington head coach (January 3).

MOE, DOUG
76ERS

PERSONAL: Born September 21, 1938, in Brooklyn, N.Y. . . . 6-5/220. . . . Full name: Douglas Edwin Moe.
HIGH SCHOOL: Erasmus Hall (Brooklyn, N.Y.), then Bullis Prep School (Silver Springs, Md.).
COLLEGE: North Carolina, then Elon College (N.C.).
TRANSACTIONS/CAREER NOTES: Selected by Chicago Packers in second round (22nd pick overall) of 1961 NBA Draft. . . . Signed by Packers (1961); Packers later refused to honor contract when Moe was implicated in college point-shaving scandal; Moe was exonerated but did not play basketball for four seasons (1961-62 through 1964-65). . . . Played with Padua, Italy (1965-66 and 1966-67). . . . Signed by New Orleans Buccaneers of American Basketball Association (1967). . . . Traded by Buccaneers with Larry Brown to Oakland Oaks for Steve Jones, Ron Franz and Barry Leibowitz (June 18, 1968). . . . Traded by Oaks to Carolina Cougars in three-team deal in which Cougars sent Stew Johnson to Pittsburgh Pipers and Pipers sent Frank Card to Oaks (June 12, 1969). . . . Traded by Cougars to Washington Capitols for Gary Bradds and Ira Harge (July 24, 1970). . . . Capitols franchise moved from Washington to Virginia and renamed Squires for 1970-71 season.

COLLEGIATE RECORD

NOTES: THE SPORTING NEWS All-America second team (1959, 1961).

Season	Team	G	Min.	FGM	FGA	Pct.	FTM	FTA	Pct.	Reb.	Pts.	Avg.
57-58	North Carolina‡					Statistics unavailable.						
58-59	North Carolina	25	. . .	106	265	.400	104	164	.634	179	316	12.6
59-60	North Carolina	12	. . .	60	144	.417	82	113	.726	135	202	16.8
60-61	North Carolina	23	. . .	163	401	.406	143	207	.691	321	469	20.4
	Totals	60	. . .	329	810	.406	329	484	.680	635	987	16.5

ABA REGULAR-SEASON RECORD

NOTES: ABA All-Star first team (1968). . . . ABA All-Star second team (1969). . . . Member of ABA championship team (1969).

				2-POINT			3-POINT								
Season	Team	G	Min.	FGM	FGA	Pct.	FGM	FGA	Pct.	FTM	FTA	Pct.	Reb.	Ast.	Pts.	Avg.
67-68	New Orleans	78	3113	662	1588	.417	3	22	.136	551	693	.795	795	202	1884	24.2
68-69	Oakland	75	2528	524	1213	.432	5	14	.357	360	444	.811	614	151	1423	19.0
69-70	Carolina	80	2671	527	1220	.432	8	34	.235	304	399	.762	437	425	1382	17.3
70-71	Virginia	78	2297	395	861	.459	2	10	.200	221	259	.853	473	270	1017	13.0
71-72	Virginia	67	1472	174	406	.429	1	9	.111	104	129	.806	241	149	455	6.8
	Totals	378	12081	2282	5288	.432	19	89	.213	1540	1924	.800	2560	1197	6161	16.3

ABA PLAYOFF RECORD

				2-POINT			3-POINT								
Season	Team	G	Min.	FGM	FGA	Pct.	FGM	FGA	Pct.	FTM	FTA	Pct.	Reb.	Ast.	Pts.	Avg.
67-68	New Orleans	17	715	140	335	.418	4	11	.364	107	149	.718	169	40	399	23.5
68-69	Oakland	16	593	115	280	.411	0	4	.000	87	111	.784	124	31	317	19.8
69-70	Carolina	4	168	25	72	.347	0	4	.000	12	16	.750	26	25	62	15.5
70-71	Virginia	12	421	89	174	.511	1	3	.333	31	41	.756	57	37	212	17.7
71-72	Virginia	11	245	37	84	.440	0	1	.000	22	25	.880	43	27	96	8.7
	Totals	60	2142	406	945	.430	5	23	.217	259	342	.757	419	160	1086	18.1

ABA ALL-STAR GAME RECORD

			2-POINT			3-POINT								
Season	Team	Min.	FGM	FGA	Pct.	FGM	FGA	Pct.	FTM	FTA	Pct.	Reb.	Ast.	Pts.
1968	New Orleans	29	7	12	.583	0	1	.000	3	5	.600	7	5	17
1969	Oakland	26	6	13	.462	0	0	. . .	5	8	.625	6	6	17
1970	Carolina	36	0	5	.000	0	0	. . .	2	3	.667	8	6	2
	Totals	91	13	30	.433	0	1	.000	10	16	.625	21	17	36

HEAD COACHING RECORD

BACKGROUND: Assistant coach, Elon College, N.C. (1963-64 and 1964-65). . . . Assistant coach/director of player personnel, Carolina Cougars of ABA (1972-73 and 1973-74). . . . Assistant coach/director of player personnel, Denver Nuggets of ABA (1974-75 and 1975-76). . . . Assistant coach, Nuggets (1980).
HONORS: NBA Coach of the Year (1988).

NBA COACHING RECORD

		REGULAR SEASON				PLAYOFFS		
Season	Team	W	L	Pct.	Finish	W	L	Pct.
76-77	San Antonio	44	38	.537	3rd/Central Division	0	2	.000
77-78	San Antonio	52	30	.634	1st/Central Division	2	4	.333
78-79	San Antonio	48	34	.585	1st/Central Division	7	7	.500
79-80	San Antonio	33	33	.500		—	—	—
80-81	Denver	26	25	.510	4th/Midwest Division	—	—	—
81-82	Denver	46	36	.561	T2nd/Midwest Division	1	2	.333
82-83	Denver	45	37	.549	T2nd/Midwest Division	3	5	.375
83-84	Denver	38	44	.463	T3rd/Midwest Division	2	3	.400
84-85	Denver	52	30	.634	1st/Midwest Division	8	7	.533
85-86	Denver	47	35	.573	2nd/Midwest Division	5	5	.500
86-87	Denver	37	45	.451	4th/Midwest Division	0	3	.000

Season	Team	W	L	Pct.	REGULAR SEASON Finish	W	L	PLAYOFFS Pct.
87-88	—Denver	54	28	.659	1st/Midwest Division	5	6	.455
88-89	—Denver	44	38	.537	3rd/Midwest Division	0	3	.000
89-90	—Denver	43	39	.524	4th/Midwest Division	0	3	.000
	Totals (14 years)	609	492	.553	Totals (12 years)	33	50	.398

NOTES:
1977— Lost to Boston in Eastern Conference first round.
1978— Lost to Washington in Eastern Conference semifinals.
1979— Defeated Philadelphia, 4-3, in Eastern Conference semifinals; lost to Washington, 4-3, in Eastern Conference finals.
1980— Replaced as San Antonio head coach by Bob Bass (March 1). Replaced Donnie Walsh as Denver head coach (December), with record of 11-20.
1982— Lost to Phoenix in Western Conference first round.
1983— Defeated Phoenix, 2-1, in Western Conference first round; lost to San Antonio, 4-1, in Western Conference semifinals.
1984— Lost to Utah in Western Conference first round.
1985— Defeated San Antonio, 3-2, in Western Conference first round; defeated Utah, 4-1, in Western Conference semifinals; lost to Los Angeles Lakers, 4-1, in Western Conference finals.
1986— Defeated Portland, 3-1, in Western Conference first round; lost to Houston, 4-2, in Western Conference semifinals.
1987— Lost to Los Angeles Lakers in Western Conference first round.
1988— Defeated Seattle, 3-2, in Western Conference first round; lost to Dallas, 4-2, in Western Conference semifinals.
1989— Lost to Phoenix in Western Conference first round.
1990— Lost to San Antonio, 3-0, in Western Conference first round.

NELSON, DON
WARRIORS

PERSONAL: Born May 15, 1940, in Muskegon, Mich. . . . 6-6/210. . . . Full name: Donald Arvid Nelson.
HIGH SCHOOL: Rock Island (Ill.).
COLLEGE: Iowa.
TRANSACTIONS/CAREER NOTES: Selected by Chicago Zephyrs in third round (19th pick overall) of 1962 NBA Draft. . . . Zephyrs franchise moved from Chicago to Baltimore and renamed Bullets for 1963-64 season. . . . Sold by Bullets to Los Angeles Lakers (September 6, 1963). . . . Waived by Lakers (October 21, 1965). . . . Signed as free agent by Boston Celtics (October 28, 1965).
MISCELLANEOUS: Member of NBA championship teams (1966, 1968, 1969, 1974, 1976).

COLLEGIATE RECORD

Season	Team	G	Min.	FGM	FGA	Pct.	FTM	FTA	Pct.	Reb.	Pts.	Avg.
58-59	—Iowa†			Freshman team did not play intercollegiate schedule.								
59-60	—Iowa	24	. . .	140	320	.438	100	155	.645	241	380	15.8
60-61	—Iowa	24	. . .	197	377	.523	176	268	.657	258	570	23.8
61-62	—Iowa	24	. . .	193	348	.555	186	264	.705	285	572	23.8
	Varsity totals	72	. . .	530	1045	.507	462	687	.672	784	1522	21.1

NBA REGULAR-SEASON RECORD

Season	Team	G	Min.	FGM	FGA	Pct.	FTM	FTA	Pct.	Reb.	Ast.	PF	Dq.	Pts.	Avg.
62-63	—Chicago	62	1071	129	293	.440	161	221	.729	279	72	136	3	419	6.8
63-64	—Los Angeles	80	1406	135	323	.418	149	201	.741	323	76	181	1	419	5.2
64-65	—Los Angeles	39	238	36	85	.424	20	26	.769	73	24	40	1	92	2.4
65-66	—Boston	75	1765	271	618	.439	223	326	.684	403	79	187	1	765	10.2
66-67	—Boston	79	1202	227	509	.446	141	190	.742	295	65	143	0	595	7.5
67-68	—Boston	82	1498	312	632	.494	195	268	.728	431	103	178	1	819	10.0
68-69	—Boston	82	1773	374	771	.485	201	259	.776	458	92	198	2	949	11.6
69-70	—Boston	82	2224	461	920	.501	337	435	.775	601	148	238	3	1259	15.4
70-71	—Boston	82	2254	412	881	.468	317	426	.744	565	153	232	2	1141	13.9
71-72	—Boston	82	2086	389	811	.480	356	452	.788	453	192	220	3	1134	13.8
72-73	—Boston	72	1425	309	649	.476	159	188	.846	315	102	155	1	777	10.8

Season	Team	G	Min.	FGM	FGA	Pct.	FTM	FTA	Pct.	REBOUNDS Off.	Def.	Tot.	Ast.	PF	Dq.	Stl.	Blk.	TO	Pts.	Avg.
73-74	—Boston	82	1748	364	717	.508	215	273	.788	90	255	345	162	189	1	19	13	. . .	943	11.5
74-75	—Boston	79	2052	423	785	*.539	263	318	.827	127	342	469	181	239	2	32	15	. . .	1109	14.0
75-76	—Boston	75	943	175	379	.462	127	161	.789	56	126	182	77	115	0	14	7	. . .	477	6.4
	Totals	1053	21685	4017	8373	.480	2864	3744	.765	. . .	. . .	5192	1526	2451	21	65	35	. . .	10898	10.3

NBA PLAYOFF RECORD

Season	Team	G	Min.	FGM	FGA	Pct.	FTM	FTA	Pct.	Reb.	Ast.	PF	Dq.	Pts.	Avg.
63-64	—Los Angeles	5	56	7	13	.538	3	3	1.000	13	2	11	1	17	3.4
64-65	—Los Angeles	11	212	24	53	.453	19	25	.760	59	19	31	0	67	6.1
65-66	—Boston	17	316	50	118	.424	42	52	.808	85	13	50	0	142	8.4
66-67	—Boston	9	142	27	59	.458	10	17	.588	42	9	12	0	64	7.1
67-68	—Boston	19	468	91	175	.520	55	74	.743	143	32	49	0	237	12.5
68-69	—Boston	18	348	87	168	.518	50	60	.833	83	21	51	0	224	12.4
71-72	—Boston	11	308	52	99	.525	41	48	.854	61	21	30	0	145	13.2
72-73	—Boston	13	303	47	101	.465	49	56	.875	38	15	29	0	143	11.0

Season	Team	G	Min.	FGM	FGA	Pct.	FTM	FTA	Pct.	REBOUNDS Off.	Def.	Tot.	Ast.	PF	Dq.	Stl.	Blk.	TO	Pts.	Avg.
73-74	—Boston	18	467	82	164	.500	41	53	.774	25	72	97	35	54	2	8	3	. . .	205	11.4
74-75	—Boston	11	274	66	117	.564	37	41	.902	18	27	45	26	36	1	2	2	. . .	169	15.4
75-76	—Boston	18	315	52	108	.481	60	69	.870	17	36	53	17	46	1	3	2	. . .	164	9.1
	Totals	150	3209	585	1175	.498	407	498	.817	. . .	. . .	719	210	399	5	13	7	. . .	1577	10.5

HEAD COACHING RECORD

BACKGROUND: Assistant coach, Milwaukee Bucks (September 9-November 22, 1976). . . . Head coach/director of player personnel, Bucks (November 22, 1976-1985). . . . Head coach/vice president of basketball operations, Bucks (1985-May 27,

1987).... Executive vice president, Golden State Warriors (1987-88).... Head coach/general manager, Warriors (1988-89 to present).
HONORS: NBA Coach of the Year (1983, 1985, 1992).

NBA COACHING RECORD

				REGULAR SEASON		PLAYOFFS	
Season Team	W	L	Pct.	Finish	W	L	Pct.
76-77 —Milwaukee	27	37	.422	6th/Midwest Division	—	—	—
77-78 —Milwaukee	44	38	.537	2nd/Midwest Division	5	4	.556
78-79 —Milwaukee	38	44	.463	4th/Midwest Division	—	—	—
79-80 —Milwaukee	49	33	.598	1st/Midwest Division	3	4	.429
80-81 —Milwaukee	60	22	.732	1st/Central Division	3	4	.429
81-82 —Milwaukee	55	27	.671	1st/Central Division	2	4	.333
82-83 —Milwaukee	51	31	.622	1st/Central Division	5	4	.556
83-84 —Milwaukee	50	32	.610	1st/Central Division	8	8	.500
84-85 —Milwaukee	59	23	.720	1st/Central Division	3	5	.375
85-86 —Milwaukee	57	25	.695	1st/Central Division	7	7	.500
86-87 —Milwaukee	50	32	.610	3rd/Central Division	6	6	.500
88-89 —Golden State	43	39	.524	4th/Pacific Division	4	4	.500
89-90 —Golden State	37	45	.451	5th/Pacific Division	—	—	—
90-91 —Golden State	44	38	.537	4th/Pacific Division	4	5	.444
91-92 —Golden State	55	27	.671	2nd/Pacific Division	1	3	.250
Totals (15 years)	719	493	.593	Totals (12 years)	51	58	.468

NOTES:
1976— Replaced Larry Costello as Milwaukee head coach (November 22), with record of 3-15 and in sixth place.
1978— Defeated Phoenix, 2-0, in Western Conference first round; lost to Denver, 4-3, in Western Conference semifinals.
1980— Lost to Seattle in Western Conference semifinals.
1981— Lost to Philadelphia in Eastern Conference semifinals.
1982— Lost to Philadelphia in Eastern Conference semifinals.
1983— Defeated Boston, 4-0, in Eastern Conference semifinals; lost to Philadelphia, 4-1, in Eastern Conference finals.
1984— Defeated Atlanta, 3-2, in Eastern Conference first round; defeated New Jersey, 4-2, in Eastern Conference semifinals; lost to Boston, 4-1, in Eastern Conference finals.
1985— Defeated Chicago, 3-1, in Eastern Conference first round; lost to Philadelphia, 4-0, in Eastern Conference semifinals.
1986— Defeated New Jersey, 3-0, in Eastern Conference first round; defeated Philadelphia, 4-3, in Eastern Conference semifinals; lost to Boston, 4-0, in Eastern Conference finals.
1987— Defeated Philadelphia, 3-2, in Eastern Conference first round; lost to Boston, 4-3, in Eastern Conference semifinals.
1989— Defeated Utah, 3-0, in Western Conference first round; lost to Phoenix, 4-1, in Western Conference semifinals.
1991— Defeated San Antonio, 3-1, in Western Conference first round; lost to Los Angeles Lakers, 4-1, in Western Conference semifinals.
1992— Lost to Seattle in Western Conference first round.

PFUND, RANDY
LAKERS

PERSONAL: Born December 29, 1951, in Oak Park, Ill. ... 6-0/180. ... Full name: Randell Pfund. ... Son of Lee Pfund, pitcher with Brooklyn Dodgers (1945).
HIGH SCHOOL: Wheaton North (Ill.).
COLLEGE: Wheaton College (Ill.).

COLLEGIATE RECORD

Season Team	G	Min.	FGM	FGA	Pct.	FTM	FTA	Pct.	Reb.	Pts.	Avg.
70-71 —Wheaton	26	...	67	155	.432	63	87	.724	80	197	7.6
71-72 —Wheaton	25	...	199	452	.440	121	177	.684	76	519	20.8
72-73 —Wheaton	24	...	163	385	.423	51	78	.654	70	377	15.7
73-74 —Wheaton	25	...	245	582	.421	127	200	.635	58	617	24.7
Totals	100	...	674	1574	.428	362	542	.668	284	1710	17.1

HEAD COACHING RECORD

BACKGROUND: Assistant coach, Glenbard South High School, Ill. (1974-1977). ... Assistant coach, Westmont College, Calif. (1977-78 through 1984-85). ... Assistant coach, Los Angeles Lakers (1985-86 through 1991-92).

RILEY, PAT
KNICKS

PERSONAL: Born March 20, 1945, in Rome, N.Y. ... 6-4/205. ... Full name: Patrick James Riley. ... Son of Leon Riley, outfielder/catcher with Philadelphia Phillies (1944) and minor league manager; and brother of Lee Riley, defensive back with Detroit Lions, Philadelphia Eagles and New York Giants of National Football League (1955-60) and New York Titans of American Football League (1961-62).
HIGH SCHOOL: Linton (Schenectady, N.Y.).
COLLEGE: Kentucky.
TRANSACTIONS/CAREER NOTES: Selected by San Diego Rockets in first round (seventh pick overall) of 1967 NBA Draft. ... Selected by Portland Trail Blazers from Rockets in expansion draft (May 11, 1970). ... Sold by Trail Blazers to Los Angeles Lakers (October 9, 1970). ... Traded by Lakers to Phoenix Suns for draft rights to John Roche and 1976 second-round draft choice (November 3, 1975).
MISCELLANEOUS: Member of NBA championship team (1972). ... Selected by Dallas Cowboys in 11th round of 1967 National Football League draft.

COLLEGIATE RECORD

Season Team	G	Min.	FGM	FGA	Pct.	FTM	FTA	Pct.	Reb.	Pts.	Avg.
63-64 —Kentucky‡	16	...	120	259	.463	93	146	.637	235	333	20.8
64-65 —Kentucky	25	825	160	370	.432	55	89	.618	212	375	15.0

Season	Team	G	Min.	FGM	FGA	Pct.	FTM	FTA	Pct.	Reb.	Pts.	Avg.
65-66	—Kentucky	29	1078	265	514	.516	107	153	.699	259	637	22.0
66-67	—Kentucky	26	953	165	373	.442	122	156	.782	201	452	17.4
	Varsity totals	80	2856	590	1257	.469	284	398	.714	672	1464	18.3

NBA REGULAR-SEASON RECORD

Season	Team	G	Min.	FGM	FGA	Pct.	FTM	FTA	Pct.	Reb.	Ast.	PF	Dq.	Pts.	Avg.
67-68	—San Diego	80	1263	250	660	.379	128	202	.634	177	138	205	1	628	7.9
68-69	—San Diego	56	1027	202	498	.406	90	134	.672	112	136	146	1	494	8.8
69-70	—San Diego	36	474	75	180	.417	40	55	.727	57	85	68	0	190	5.3
70-71	—Los Angeles	54	506	105	254	.413	56	87	.644	54	72	84	0	266	4.9
71-72	—Los Angeles	67	926	197	441	.447	55	74	.743	127	75	110	0	449	6.7
72-73	—Los Angeles	55	801	167	390	.428	65	82	.793	65	81	126	0	399	7.3

										— REBOUNDS —								
Season	Team	G	Min.	FGM	FGA	Pct.	FTM	FTA	Pct.	Off.	Def.	Tot.	Ast.	PF	Dq.	Stl.	Blk.	TO	Pts.	Avg.
73-74	—Los Angeles.	72	1361	287	667	.430	110	144	.764	38	90	128	148	173	1	54	3	...	684	9.5
74-75	—Los Angeles.	46	1016	219	523	.419	69	93	.742	25	60	85	121	128	0	36	4	...	507	11.0
75-76	—L.A.-Phoe. ...	62	813	117	301	.389	55	77	.714	16	34	50	57	112	0	22	6	...	289	4.7
	Totals	528	8187	1619	3914	.414	668	948	.705	...	...	855	913	1152	3	112	13	...	3906	7.4

NBA PLAYOFF RECORD

Season	Team	G	Min.	FGM	FGA	Pct.	FTM	FTA	Pct.	Reb.	Ast.	PF	Dq.	Pts.	Avg.
68-69	—San Diego	5	76	16	37	.432	5	6	.833	11	2	13	0	37	7.4
70-71	—Los Angeles	7	135	29	69	.420	8	11	.727	15	14	12	0	66	9.4
71-72	—Los Angeles	15	244	33	99	.333	12	16	.750	29	14	37	0	78	5.2
72-73	—Los Angeles	7	53	9	27	.333	0	0	...	5	7	10	0	18	2.6

										— REBOUNDS —								
Season	Team	G	Min.	FGM	FGA	Pct.	FTM	FTA	Pct.	Off.	Def.	Tot.	Ast.	PF	Dq.	Stl.	Blk.	TO	Pts.	Avg.
73-74	—Los Angeles.	5	106	18	50	.360	3	4	.750	3	3	6	10	11	0	4	0	...	39	7.8
75-76	—Phoenix.......	5	27	6	15	.400	1	1	1.000	0	0	0	5	3	0	0	0	...	13	2.6
	Totals	44	641	111	297	.374	29	38	.763	...	...	66	52	86	0	4	0	...	251	5.7

HEAD COACHING RECORD

BACKGROUND: Broadcaster, Los Angeles Lakers (1977-79).... Assistant coach, Lakers (1979-80 to November 19, 1981). ... Broadcaster, NBC television (1990-91).

HONORS: NBA Coach of the Year (1990).

NBA COACHING RECORD

		REGULAR SEASON				PLAYOFFS		
Season	Team	W	L	Pct.	Finish	W	L	Pct.
81-82	—Los Angeles	50	21	.704	1st/Pacific Division	12	2	.857
82-83	—Los Angeles	58	24	.707	1st/Pacific Division	8	7	.533
83-84	—Los Angeles	54	28	.659	1st/Pacific Division	14	7	.667
84-85	—Los Angeles Lakers	62	20	.756	1st/Pacific Division	15	4	.789
85-86	—Los Angeles Lakers	62	20	.756	1st/Pacific Division	8	6	.571
86-87	—Los Angeles Lakers	65	17	.793	1st/Pacific Division	15	3	.833
87-88	—Los Angeles Lakers	62	20	.756	1st/Pacific Division	15	9	.625
88-89	—Los Angeles Lakers	57	25	.695	1st/Pacific Division	11	4	.733
89-90	—Los Angeles Lakers	63	19	.768	1st/Pacific Division	4	5	.444
91-92	—New York	51	31	.622	T1st/Atlantic Division	6	6	.500
	Totals (10 years)	584	225	.722	Totals (10 years)	108	53	.671

NOTES:

1981— Replaced Paul Westhead as Los Angeles head coach (November 19), with record of 7-4 and in second place.

1982— Defeated Phoenix, 4-0, in Western Conference semifinals; defeated San Antonio, 4-0, in Western Conference finals; defeated Philadelphia, 4-2, in World Championship Series.

1983— Defeated Portland, 4-1, in Western Conference semifinals; defeated San Antonio, 4-2, in Western Conference finals; lost to Philadelphia, 4-0, in World Championship Series.

1984— Defeated Kansas City, 3-0, in Western Conference first round; defeated Dallas, 4-1, in Western Conference semifinals; defeated Phoenix, 4-2, in Western Conference finals; lost to Boston, 4-3, in World Championship Series.

1985— Defeated Phoenix, 3-0, in Western Conference first round; defeated Portland, 4-1, in Western Conference semifinals; defeated Denver, 4-1, in Western Conference finals; defeated Boston, 4-2, in World Championship Series.

1986— Defeated San Antonio, 3-0, in Western Conference first round; defeated Dallas, 4-2, in Western Conference semifinals; lost to Houston, 4-1, in Western Conference finals.

1987— Defeated Denver, 3-0, in Western Conference first round; defeated Golden State, 4-1, in Western Conference semifinals; defeated Seattle, 4-0, in Western Conference finals; defeated Boston, 4-2, in NBA Finals.

1988— Defeated San Antonio, 3-0, in Western Conference first round; defeated Utah, 4-3, in Western Conference semifinals; defeated Dallas, 4-3, in Western Conference finals; defeated Detroit, 4-3, in NBA Finals.

1989— Defeated Portland, 3-0, in Western Conference first round; defeated Seattle, 4-0, in Western Conference semifinals; defeated Phoenix, 4-0, in Western Conference finals; lost to Detroit, 4-0, in NBA Finals.

1990— Defeated Houston, 3-1, in Western Conference first round; lost to Phoenix, 4-1, in Western Conference finals.

1992— Defeated Detroit, 3-2, in Eastern Conference first round; lost to Chicago, 4-3, in Eastern Conference semifinals.

RODGERS, JIMMY
TIMBERWOLVES

PERSONAL: Born March 12, 1943, in Oak Park, Ill.... 6-3/190.... Full name: James Donald Rodgers.

HIGH SCHOOL: East Leyden (Franklin Park, Ill.).

COLLEGE: Iowa.

COLLEGIATE RECORD

Season	Team	G	Min.	FGM	FGA	Pct.	FTM	FTA	Pct.	Reb.	Pts.	Avg.
61-62	—Iowa†				Freshman team did not play intercollegiate schedule.							
62-63	—Iowa	24	...	89	265	.336	92	115	.800	120	270	11.3

Season	Team	G	Min.	FGM	FGA	Pct.	FTM	FTA	Pct.	Reb.	Pts.	Avg.
63-64	— Iowa	23	...	105	271	.387	87	105	.829	103	297	12.9
64-65	— Iowa	24	...	102	234	.436	93	110	.845	68	297	12.4
Varsity totals		71	...	296	770	.384	272	330	.824	291	864	12.2

HEAD COACHING RECORD

BACKGROUND: Assistant coach, University of North Dakota (1965-66 and 1966-67).... Assistant coach, University of Arkansas (1970-71).... Assistant coach, Cleveland Cavaliers (1971-72 through 1978-79).... Director of player personnel, Cavaliers (1979-80).... Assistant coach, Boston Celtics (1980-81 through 1983-84).... Assistant coach/director of player personnel, Celtics (1984-85 through 1987-88).

COLLEGIATE COACHING RECORD

Season	Team	W	L	Pct.	Finish
67-68	— North Dakota	15	9	.625	T2nd/North Central Conference
68-69	— North Dakota	11	14	.440	T3rd/North Central Conference
69-70	— North Dakota	13	12	.520	T5th/North Central Conference
Totals (3 years)		39	35	.527	

NBA COACHING RECORD

Season	Team	REGULAR SEASON W	L	Pct.	Finish	PLAYOFFS W	L	Pct.
88-89	— Boston	42	40	.512	3rd/Atlantic Division	0	3	.000
89-90	— Boston	52	30	.634	2nd/Atlantic Division	2	3	.400
91-92	— Minnesota	15	67	.183	6th/Midwest Division	—	—	—
Totals (3 years)		109	137	.443	**Totals (2 years)**	2	6	.333

NOTES:
1989— Lost to Detroit in Eastern Conference first round.
1990— Lost to New York in Eastern Conference first round.

ROTHSTEIN, RON
PISTONS

PERSONAL: Born December 27, 1942, in Bronxville, N.Y.... 5-8/165. ... Full name: Ronald Rothstein.
HIGH SCHOOL: Roosevelt (Yonkers, N.Y.).
COLLEGE: Rhode Island.

COLLEGIATE RECORD

Season	Team	G	Min.	FGM	FGA	Pct.	FTM	FTA	Pct.	Reb.	Pts.	Avg.
60-61	— Rhode Island‡					Statistics unavailable.						
61-62	— Rhode Island	25	...	37	85	.435	34	40	.850	35	108	4.3
62-63	— Rhode Island	26	...	45	138	.326	52	68	.765	68	142	5.5
63-64	— Rhode Island	24	...	48	107	.449	32	48	.667	75	128	5.3
Varsity totals		75	...	130	330	.394	118	156	.756	178	378	5.0

HEAD COACHING RECORD

BACKGROUND: Head Coach, Eastchester High School, N.Y.... Assistant coach, Upsala College, N.J. (1974-75).... Head coach, New Rochelle High School, N.Y. (1976-78).... Scout, Atlanta Hawks (1979-82).... Scout, New York Knicks (1982-83).... Assistant coach, Hawks (1983-84 through 1985-86).... Assistant coach, Detroit Pistons (1986-87 and 1987-88).... Broadcaster, Pistons (1991-92).

NBA COACHING RECORD

Season	Team	REGULAR SEASON W	L	Pct.	Finish	PLAYOFFS W	L	Pct.
88-89	— Miami	15	67	.183	6th/Midwest Division	—	—	—
89-90	— Miami	18	64	.220	5th/Atlantic Division	—	—	—
90-91	— Miami	24	58	.293	6th/Atlantic Division	—	—	—
Totals (3 years)		57	189	.232				

SLOAN, JERRY
JAZZ

PERSONAL: Born March 28, 1942, in McLeansboro, Ill.... 6-5/200.... Full name: Gerald Eugene Sloan.
HIGH SCHOOL: McLeansboro (Ill.).
COLLEGE: Illinois, then Evansville College (Ind.).
TRANSACTIONS/CAREER NOTES: Selected by Baltimore Bullets in second round of 1964 NBA Draft.... Selected by Bullets in first round (first pick overall) of 1965 NBA Draft.... Selected by Chicago Bulls from Bullets in NBA expansion draft (April 30, 1966).

COLLEGIATE RECORD

NOTES: Left Illinois before 1961 basketball season.... Outstanding Player in NCAA College Division Tournament (1964, 1965). ... THE SPORTING NEWS All-America second team (1965).

Season	Team	G	Min.	FGM	FGA	Pct.	FTM	FTA	Pct.	Reb.	Pts.	Avg.
61-62	— Evansville					Did not play—transfer student.						
62-63	— Evansville	27	...	152	446	.341	103	151	.682	293	407	15.1
63-64	— Evansville	29	...	160	385	.416	84	114	.737	335	404	13.9
64-65	— Evansville	29	...	207	458	.452	95	126	.754	425	509	17.6
Totals		85	...	519	1289	.403	282	391	.721	1053	1320	15.5

NBA REGULAR-SEASON RECORD

HONORS: NBA All-Defensive first team (1969, 1972, 1974, 1975).... NBA All-Defensive second team (1970, 1971).

Season	Team	G	Min.	FGM	FGA	Pct.	FTM	FTA	Pct.	Reb.	Ast.	PF	Dq.	Pts.	Avg.
65-66	— Baltimore	59	952	120	289	.415	98	139	.705	230	110	176	7	338	5.7
66-67	— Chicago	80	2942	525	1214	.432	340	427	.796	726	170	293	7	1390	17.4

Season	Team	G	Min.	FGM	FGA	Pct.	FTM	FTA	Pct.	Reb.	Ast.	PF	Dq.	Pts.	Avg.
67-68	Chicago	77	2454	369	959	.385	280	386	.725	591	229	291	11	1027	13.3
68-69	Chicago	78	2939	488	1179	.414	333	447	.745	619	276	313	6	1309	16.8
69-70	Chicago	53	1822	310	737	.421	207	318	.651	372	165	179	3	827	15.6
70-71	Chicago	80	3140	592	1342	.441	278	389	.715	701	281	289	5	1462	18.3
71-72	Chicago	82	3035	535	1206	.444	258	391	.660	691	211	309	8	1328	16.2
72-73	Chicago	69	2412	301	733	.411	94	133	.707	475	151	235	5	696	10.1

Season	Team	G	Min.	FGM	FGA	Pct.	FTM	FTA	Pct.	Off.	Def.	Tot.	Ast.	PF	Dq.	Stl.	Blk.	TO	Pts.	Avg.
										— REBOUNDS —										
73-74	Chicago	77	2860	412	921	.447	194	273	.711	150	406	556	149	273	3	183	10	...	1018	13.2
74-75	Chicago	78	2577	380	865	.439	193	258	.748	177	361	538	161	265	5	171	17	...	953	12.2
75-76	Chicago	22	617	84	210	.400	55	78	.705	40	76	116	22	77	1	27	5	...	223	10.1
Totals		755	25750	4116	9655	.426	2330	3239	.719	...	...	5615	1925	2700	61	381	32	...	10571	14.0

NBA PLAYOFF RECORD

Season	Team	G	Min.	FGM	FGA	Pct.	FTM	FTA	Pct.	Reb.	Ast.	PF	Dq.	Pts.	Avg.
65-66	Baltimore	2	34	5	12	.417	3	4	.750	16	6	6	1	13	6.5
66-67	Chicago	3	71	12	31	.387	6	9	.667	10	1	7	0	30	10.0
67-68	Chicago	5	137	12	37	.324	19	25	.760	32	12	19	0	43	8.6
69-70	Chicago	5	190	29	74	.392	16	25	.640	39	11	18	0	74	14.8
70-71	Chicago	7	284	51	117	.436	17	23	.739	63	17	25	1	119	17.0
71-72	Chicago	4	170	26	64	.406	11	19	.579	35	10	18	1	63	15.8
72-73	Chicago	7	292	45	103	.437	14	19	.737	59	14	31	1	104	14.9

Season	Team	G	Min.	FGM	FGA	Pct.	FTM	FTA	Pct.	Off.	Def.	Tot.	Ast.	PF	Dq.	Stl.	Blk.	TO	Pts.	Avg.
										— REBOUNDS —										
73-74	Chicago	6	240	39	88	.443	22	29	.759	18	44	62	12	17	0	7	1	...	100	16.7
74-75	Chicago	13	470	75	163	.460	20	36	.556	24	72	96	26	46	0	20	0	...	170	13.1
Totals		52	1888	294	689	.427	128	189	.677	...	...	412	109	187	4	27	1	...	716	13.8

NBA ALL-STAR GAME RECORD

Season	Team	Min.	FGM	FGA	Pct.	FTM	FTA	Pct.	Reb.	Ast.	PF	Dq.	Pts.
1967	Chicago	22	4	9	.444	0	0	...	4	4	5	0	8
1969	Chicago	18	2	8	.250	0	1	.000	3	0	5	0	4
Totals		40	6	17	.353	0	1	.000	7	4	10	0	12

BACKGROUND: Scout, Chicago Bulls (1976-77).... Assistant coach, Bulls (1977-78 and 1978-79).... Scout, Utah Jazz (1983-84).... Head coach, Evansville Thunder of CBA (1984-November 19, 1984; no record).... Assistant coach, Jazz (November 19, 1984-December 9, 1988).

NBA COACHING RECORD

Season	Team		REGULAR SEASON				PLAYOFFS	
		W	L	Pct.	Finish	W	L	Pct.
79-80	Chicago	30	52	.366	4th/Midwest Division	—	—	—
80-81	Chicago	45	37	.549	2nd/Central Division	2	4	.333
81-82	Chicago	19	32	.373		—	—	—
88-89	Utah	40	25	.615	1st/Midwest Division	0	3	.000
89-90	Utah	55	27	.671	2nd/Midwest Division	2	3	.400
90-91	Utah	54	28	.659	2nd/Midwest Division	4	5	.444
91-92	Utah	55	27	.671	1st/Midwest Division	9	7	.563
Totals (7 years)		298	228	.567	Totals (5 years)	17	22	.436

NOTES:
1981— Defeated New York, 2-0, in Eastern Conference first round; lost to Boston, 4-0, in Eastern Conference semifinals.
1982— Replaced as Chicago head coach by Rod Thorn (February 17).
1988— Replaced retiring Utah head coach Frank Layden (December 9), with record of 11-6.
1989— Lost to Golden State in Western Conference first round.
1990— Lost to Phoenix in Western Conference first round.
1991— Defeated Phoenix, 3-1, in Western Conference first round; lost to Portland, 4-1, in Western Conference semifinals.
1992— Defeated Los Angeles Clippers, 3-2, in Western Conference first round; defeated Seattle, 4-1, in Western Conference semifinals; lost to Portland, 4-2, in Western Conference finals.

ST. JEAN, GARRY

KINGS

PERSONAL: Born February 10, 1942, in Chicopee, Mass. ... 6-4/210.
HIGH SCHOOL: Chicopee (Mass.).
COLLEGE: Springfield (Mass.) College.

COLLEGIATE RECORD

NOTES: Did not play varsity basketball.

Season	Team	G	Min.	FGM	FGA	Pct.	FTM	FTA	Pct.	Reb.	Pts.	Avg.
69-70	Springfield‡	...	...	...	...	...	...	...	...	...	...	13.1

HEAD COACHING RECORD

BACKGROUND: Head coach, Chicopee High School, Mass. (1973-80; record: 122-65, .652).... Assistant coach, Milwaukee Bucks (1980-81 through 1984-85).... Assistant coach, New Jersey Nets (1985-86).... Assistant coach/assistant director of player personnel, Nets (1986-87 and 1987-88).... Assistant coach, Golden State Warriors (1988-89 through 1991-92).

DID YOU KNOW. . .

... that the Washington Bullets were a combined 0-10 against Miami and Philadelphia in 1991-92?

TARKANIAN, JERRY
SPURS

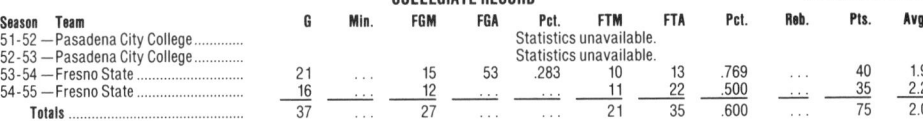

PERSONAL: Born August 8, 1930, in Euclid, O.... 5-9/195.... Full name Jerry Tarkanian.
HIGH SCHOOL: Pasadena (Calif.).
COLLEGE: Pasadena City College (Calif.), then Fresno State.

COLLEGIATE RECORD

Season Team	G	Min.	FGM	FGA	Pct.	FTM	FTA	Pct.	Reb.	Pts.	Avg.
51-52 —Pasadena City College............					Statistics unavailable.						
52-53 —Pasadena City College............					Statistics unavailable.						
53-54 —Fresno State	21	...	15	53	.283	10	13	.769	...	40	1.9
54-55 —Fresno State	16	...	12	...	...	11	22	.500	...	35	2.2
Totals	37	...	27	...	...	21	35	.600	...	75	2.0

HEAD COACHING RECORD

BACKGROUND: Head coach, San Joaquin Memorial High School, Calif. (1956 and 1957).... Head coach, Antelope Valley High School, Calif. (1958).... Head coach, Redlands High School, Calif. (1959 and 1960).

COLLEGIATE COACHING RECORD

Season Team	W	L	Pct.	Finish
61-62 —Riverside City College (Calif.).	14	13	.519	T3rd/Eastern Conference
62-63 —Riverside City College (Calif.).	32	3	.914	1st/Eastern Conference
63-64 —Riverside City College (Calif.).	35	0	1.000	1st/Eastern Conference
64-65 —Riverside City College (Calif.).	31	5	.861	1st/Eastern Conference
65-66 —Riverside City College (Calif.).	33	1	.971	1st/Eastern Conference
66-67 —Pasadena City College............	35	1	.972	
67-68 —Pasadena City College............	32	3	.914	
68-69 —Long Beach State	23	3	.885	1st/California Collegiate Athletics Association
69-70 —Long Beach State	24	5	.828	1st/Pacific Coast Athletic Association
70-71 —Long Beach State	22	4	.846	1st/Pacific Coast Athletic Association
71-72 —Long Beach State	23	3	.885	1st/Pacific Coast Athletic Association
72-73 —Long Beach State	24	2	.923	1st/Pacific Coast Athletic Association
73-74 —UNLV	20	6	.769	3rd/West Coast Athletic Conference
74-75 —UNLV	24	5	.828	1st/West Coast Athletic Conference
75-76 —UNLV	29	2	.935	Independent
76-77 —UNLV	29	3	.906	Independent
77-78 —UNLV	20	8	.714	Independent
78-79 —UNLV	21	8	.724	Independent
79-80 —UNLV	23	9	.719	Independent
80-81 —UNLV	16	12	.571	Independent
81-82 —UNLV	20	10	.667	Independent
82-83 —UNLV	28	3	.903	1st/Pacific Coast Athletic Association
83-84 —UNLV	29	6	.829	1st/Pacific Coast Athletic Association
84-85 —UNLV	28	4	.875	1st/Pacific Coast Athletic Association
85-86 —UNLV	33	5	.868	1st/Pacific Coast Athletic Association
86-87 —UNLV	37	2	.949	1st/Pacific Coast Athletic Association
87-88 —UNLV	28	6	.824	1st/Pacific Coast Athletic Association
88-89 —UNLV	29	8	.784	1st/Big West Conference
89-90 —UNLV	35	5	.875	T1st/Big West Conference
90-91 —UNLV	34	1	.971	1st/Big West Conference
91-92 —UNLV	26	2	.929	1st/Big West Conference
Junior College totals (12 years)	212	26	.891	
Four-year-college totals (24 years) ..	625	122	.837	

NOTES:
1963— Won California Junior College Championship.
1964— Won California Junior College Championship.
1965— Won California Junior College Championship.
1966— Won California Junior College Championship.
1967— Won California Junior College Championship.
1970— Defeated Weber State, 92-73, in NCAA Tournament first round; lost to UCLA, 88-65, in regional semifinal; lost to Santa Clara, 89-66, in regional consolation game.
1971— Defeated Weber State, 77-66, in NCAA Tournament first round; defeated Pacific, 78-65, in regional semifinal; lost to UCLA, 57-55, in regional final. Long Beach State's participation in tournament later voided due to rules infractions.
1972— Defeated Brigham Young, 95-90 (OT), in NCAA Tournament first round; defeated San Francisco, 75-55, in regional semifinal; lost to UCLA, 73-57, in regional final. Long Beach State's participation in tournament later voided due to rules infractions.
1973— Defeated Weber State, 88-75, in NCAA Tournament first round; lost to San Francisco, 77-67, in regional semifinal; defeated Arizona State, 84-80, in regional consolation game. Long Beach State's participation in tournament later voided due to rules infractions.
1975— Defeated San Diego State, 90-80, in NCAA Tournament first round; lost to Arizona State, 84-81, in regional semifinal; defeated Montana, 75-67, in regional consolation game.
1976— Defeated Boise State, 103-78, in NCAA Tournament first round; lost to Arizona, 114-109 (OT), in regional semifinal.
1977— Defeated San Francisco, 121-95, in NCAA Tournament first round; defeated Utah, 88-83, in regional semifinal; defeated Idaho, 107-90, in regional final; lost to North Carolina, 84-83, in national semifinal; defeated UNC Charlotte, 106-94, in consolation game.
1980— Defeated Washington, 93-73, in NIT first round; defeated Long Beach State, 90-81, in second round; defeated St. Peter's, 67-62, in quarterfinals; lost to Virginia, 90-71, in semifinals; lost to Illinois, 84-74, in consolation game.
1982— Defeated Murray State, 87-61, in NIT first round; lost to Tulane, 56-51, in second round.
1983— Lost to North Carolina State, 71-70, in NCAA Tournament second round.
1984— Defeated Princeton, 68-56, in NCAA Tournament first round; defeated Texas-El Paso, 73-60, in second round; lost to Georgetown, 62-48, in regional semifinal.

1985— Defeated San Diego State, 85-80, in NCAA Tournament first round; lost to Kentucky, 64-61, in second round.
1986— Defeated Northeast Louisiana, 74-51, in NCAA Tournament first round; defeated Maryland, 70-64, in second round; lost to Auburn, 70-63, in regional semifinal.
1987— Defeated Idaho State, 95-70, in NCAA Tournament first round; defeated Kansas State, 80-61, in second round; defeated Wyoming, 92-78, in regional semifinal; defeated Iowa, 84-81, in regional final; lost to Indiana, 97-93, in national semifinal.
1988— Defeated Southwest Missouri State, 54-50, in NCAA Tournament first round; lost to Iowa, 104-86, in second round.
1989— Defeated Idaho, 68-56, in NCAA Tournament first round; defeated DePaul, 85-70, in second round; defeated Arizona, 68-67, in regional semifinal; lost to Seton Hall, 84-61, in regional final.
1990— Defeated Arkansas-Little Rock, 102-72, in NCAA Tournament first round; defeated Ohio State, 76-65, in second round; defeated Ball State, 69-67, in regional semifinal; defeated Loyola Marymount, 131-101, in regional final; defeated Georgia Tech, 90-81, in national semifinal; defeated Duke, 103-73, in championship game.
1991— Defeated Montana, 99-65, in NCAA Tournament first round; defeated Georgetown, 62-54, in second round; defeated Utah, 83-66, in regional semifinal; defeated Seton Hall, 77-65, in regional final; lost to Duke, 79-77, in national semifinal.

TOMJANOVICH, RUDY
ROCKETS

PERSONAL: Born November 24, 1948, in Hamtramck, Mich.... 6-8/220.... Full name: Rudolph Tomjanovich.
HIGH SCHOOL: Hamtramck (Mich.).
COLLEGE: Michigan.

TRANSACTIONS/CAREER NOTES: Selected by San Diego Clippers in first round (second pick overall) of 1970 NBA Draft.

COLLEGIATE RECORD

NOTES: THE SPORTING NEWS All-America first team (1970).... THE SPORTING NEWS All-America second team (1969).

Season	Team	G	Min.	FGM	FGA	Pct.	FTM	FTA	Pct.	Reb.	Pts.	Avg.
66-67	—Michigan‡	3	...	28	...	...	6	15	.400	...	62	20.7
67-68	—Michigan	24	...	210	446	.471	49	78	.628	323	469	19.5
68-69	—Michigan	24	...	269	541	.497	79	131	.603	340	617	25.7
69-70	—Michigan	24	...	286	604	.474	150	200	.750	376	722	30.1
	Varsity totals	72		765	1591	.481	278	409	.680	1039	1808	25.1

NBA REGULAR-SEASON RECORD

Season	Team	G	Min.	FGM	FGA	Pct.	FTM	FTA	Pct.	Reb.	Ast.	PF	Dq.	Pts.	Avg.
70-71	—San Diego	77	1062	168	439	.383	73	112	.652	381	73	124	0	409	5.3
71-72	—Houston	78	2689	500	1010	.495	172	238	.723	923	117	193	2	1172	15.0
72-73	—Houston	81	2972	655	1371	.478	250	335	.746	938	178	225	1	1560	19.3

| | | | | | | | | | | — REBOUNDS — | | | | | | | | | |
Season	Team	G	Min.	FGM	FGA	Pct.	FTM	FTA	Pct.	Off.	Def.	Tot.	Ast.	PF	Dq.	Stl.	Blk.	TO	Pts.	Avg.
73-74	—Houston	80	3227	788	1470	.536	385	454	.848	230	487	717	250	230	0	89	66	...	1961	24.5
74-75	—Houston	81	3134	694	1323	.525	289	366	.790	184	429	613	236	230	1	76	24	...	1677	20.7
75-76	—Houston	79	2912	622	1202	.517	221	288	.767	167	499	666	188	206	1	42	19	...	1465	18.5
76-77	—Houston	81	3130	733	1437	.510	287	342	.839	172	512	684	172	198	1	57	27	...	1753	21.6
77-78	—Houston	23	849	217	447	.485	61	81	.753	40	98	138	32	63	0	15	5	38	495	21.5
78-79	—Houston	74	2641	620	1200	.517	168	221	.760	170	402	572	137	186	0	44	18	138	1408	19.0
79-80	—Houston	62	1834	370	778	.476	118	147	.803	132	226	358	109	161	2	32	10	98	880	14.2
80-81	—Houston	52	1264	263	563	.467	65	82	.793	78	130	208	81	121	0	19	6	58	603	11.6
	Totals	768	25714	5630	11240	.501	2089	2666	.784	...	...	6198	1573	1937	8	374	175	332	13383	17.4

Three-point field goals: 1979-80, 22-for-79 (.278). 1980-81, 12-for-51 (.235). Totals, 34-for-130 (.262).

NBA PLAYOFF RECORD

| | | | | | | | | | | — REBOUNDS — | | | | | | | | | |
Season	Team	G	Min.	FGM	FGA	Pct.	FTM	FTA	Pct.	Off.	Def.	Tot.	Ast.	PF	Dq.	Stl.	Blk.	TO	Pts.	Avg.
74-75	—Houston	8	304	72	128	.563	40	48	.833	22	42	64	23	17	0	1	4	...	184	23.0
76-77	—Houston	12	457	107	212	.505	29	37	.784	24	41	65	24	36	0	7	3	...	243	20.3
78-79	—Houston	2	64	9	23	.391	2	5	.400	7	7	14	2	1	0	1	1	1	20	10.0
79-80	—Houston	7	185	24	64	.375	9	13	.692	12	28	40	10	21	1	2	0	14	58	8.3
80-81	—Houston	8	31	1	9	.111	4	6	.667	2	4	6	0	3	0	0	0	2	6	0.8
	Totals	37	1041	213	436	.489	84	109	.771	67	122	189	59	78	1	11	8	17	511	13.8

Three-point field goals: 1979-80, 1-for-7 (.143). 1980-81, 0-for-3. Totals, 1-for-10 (.100).

NBA ALL-STAR GAME RECORD

| | | | | | | | | | — REBOUNDS — | | | | | | | |
Season	Team	Min.	FGM	FGA	Pct.	FTM	FTA	Pct.	Off.	Def.	Tot.	Ast.	PF	Dq.	Stl.	Blk.	TO	Pts.
1974	—Houston	17	2	5	.400	0	0	...	2	3	5	0	1	0	0	0	...	4
1975	—Houston	14	0	3	.000	0	0	...	1	2	3	0	3	0	0	0	...	0
1976	—Houston	12	1	2	.500	0	0	...	1	2	3	0	2	0	0	0	...	2
1977	—Houston	22	3	9	.333	0	0	...	2	8	10	1	1	0	1	1	...	6
1979	—Houston	24	6	13	.462	0	0	...	4	2	6	1	2	0	0	0	0	12
	Totals	89	12	32	.375	0	0	...	10	17	27	2	9	0	1	1	0	24

HEAD COACHING RECORD

BACKGROUND: Scout, Houston Rockets (1981-82 and 1982-83).... Assistant coach, Rockets (1983-84 to February 18, 1992).

NBA COACHING RECORD

| | | | REGULAR SEASON | | | | PLAYOFFS | | |
Season	Team	W	L	Pct.	Finish		W	L	Pct.
91-92	—Houston	16	14	.533	3rd/Midwest Division		—	—	—
	Totals (1 year)	16	14	.533					

NOTES:
1992— Replaced Don Chaney as Houston head coach (February 18), with record of 26-26 and in third place.

UNSELD, WES
BULLETS

PERSONAL: Born March 14, 1946, in Louisville, Ky. . . . 6-7/245. . . . Full name: Westley Sissel Unseld.
HIGH SCHOOL: Seneca (Louisville, Ky.).
COLLEGE: Louisville.
TRANSACTIONS/CAREER NOTES: Selected by Baltimore Bullets in first round (second pick overall) of 1968 NBA Draft. . . . Bullets franchise moved from Baltimore to Washington and renamed Capital Bullets for 1973-74 season. . . . Bullets franchise renamed Washington Bullets for 1974-75 season.
CAREER HONORS: Elected to Naismith Memorial Basketball Hall of Fame (1987).
MISCELLANEOUS: Member of NBA championship team (1978).

COLLEGIATE RECORD

NOTES: THE SPORTING NEWS All-America second team (1967, 1968).

Season Team	G	Min.	FGM	FGA	Pct.	FTM	FTA	Pct.	Reb.	Pts.	Avg.
64-65 — Louisville‡	14	. . .	214	312	.686	73	124	.589	331	501	35.8
65-66 — Louisville	26	. . .	195	374	.521	128	202	.634	505	518	19.9
66-67 — Louisville	28	. . .	201	374	.537	121	177	.684	533	523	18.7
67-68 — Louisville	28	. . .	234	382	.613	177	275	.644	513	645	23.0
Varsity totals	82	. . .	630	1130	.558	426	654	.651	1551	1686	20.6

NBA REGULAR-SEASON RECORD

HONORS: NBA Most Valuable Player (1969). . . . NBA Rookie of the Year (1969). . . . All-NBA first team (1969). . . . NBA All-Rookie team (1969).
NOTES: Led NBA with 14.8 rebounds per game (1975). . . . Led NBA with .56085 field-goal percentage (1976).

Season Team	G	Min.	FGM	FGA	Pct.	FTM	FTA	Pct.	Reb.	Ast.	PF	Dq.	Pts.	Avg.
68-69 — Baltimore	82	2970	427	897	.476	277	458	.605	1491	213	276	4	1131	13.8
69-70 — Baltimore	82	3234	526	1015	.518	273	428	.638	1370	291	250	2	1325	16.2
70-71 — Baltimore	74	2904	424	846	.501	199	303	.657	1253	293	235	2	1047	14.1
71-72 — Baltimore	76	3171	409	822	.498	171	272	.629	1336	278	218	1	989	13.0
72-73 — Baltimore	79	3085	421	854	.493	149	212	.703	1260	347	168	0	991	12.5

								— REBOUNDS —										
Season Team	G	Min.	FGM	FGA	Pct.	FTM	FTA	Pct.	Off.	Def.	Tot.	Ast.	PF	Dq.	Stl.	Blk.	TO	Pts.	Avg.
73-74 — Capital	56	1727	146	333	.438	36	55	.655	152	365	517	159	121	1	56	16	. . .	328	5.9
74-75 — Washington	73	2904	273	544	.502	126	184	.685	318	759	1077	297	180	1	115	68	. . .	672	9.2
75-76 — Washington	78	2922	318	567 *| .561	114	195	.585	271	765	1036	404	203	3	84	59	. . .	750	9.6
76-77 — Washington	82	2860	270	551	.490	100	166	.602	243	634	877	363	253	5	87	45	. . .	640	7.8
77-78 — Washington	80	2644	257	491	.523	93	173	.538	286	669	955	326	234	2	98	45	173	607	7.6
78-79 — Washington	77	2406	346	600	.577	151	235	.643	274	556	830	315	204	2	71	37	156	843	10.9
79-80 — Washington	82	2973	327	637	.513	139	209	.665	334	760	1094	366	249	5	65	61	153	794	9.7
80-81 — Washington	63	2032	225	429	.524	55	86	.640	207	466	673	170	171	1	52	36	97	507	8.0
Totals	984	35832	4369	8586	.509	1883	2976	.633	. . .	. . .	13769	3822	2762	29	628	367	579	10624	10.8

Three-point field goals: 1979-80, 1-for-2 (.500). 1980-81, 2-for-4 (.500). Totals, 3-for-6 (.500).

NBA PLAYOFF RECORD

NOTES: NBA Finals Most Valuable Player (1978).

Season Team	G	Min.	FGM	FGA	Pct.	FTM	FTA	Pct.	Reb.	Ast.	PF	Dq.	Pts.	Avg.
68-69 — Baltimore	4	165	30	57	.526	15	19	.789	74	5	14	0	75	18.8
69-70 — Baltimore	7	289	29	70	.414	15	19	.789	165	24	25	1	73	10.4
70-71 — Baltimore	18	759	96	208	.462	46	81	.568	339	69	60	0	238	13.2
71-72 — Baltimore	6	266	32	65	.492	10	19	.526	75	25	22	0	74	12.3
72-73 — Baltimore	5	201	20	48	.417	9	19	.474	76	17	12	0	49	9.8

								— REBOUNDS —										
Season Team	G	Min.	FGM	FGA	Pct.	FTM	FTA	Pct.	Off.	Def.	Tot.	Ast.	PF	Dq.	Stl.	Blk.	TO	Pts.	Avg.
73-74 — Capital	7	297	31	63	.492	9	15	.600	22	63	85	27	15	0	4	1	. . .	71	10.1
74-75 — Washington	17	734	71	130	.546	40	61	.656	65	211	276	64	39	0	15	20	. . .	182	10.7
75-76 — Washington	7	310	18	39	.462	13	24	.542	26	59	85	28	19	0	6	4	. . .	49	7.0
76-77 — Washington	9	368	30	54	.556	7	12	.583	24	81	105	44	32	0	8	6	. . .	67	7.4
77-78 — Washington	18	677	71	134	.530	27	46	.587	72	144	216	79	62	2	17	7	36	169	9.4
78-79 — Washington	19	736	78	158	.494	39	64	.609	90	163	253	64	66	2	17	14	30	195	10.3
79-80 — Washington	2	87	7	14	.500	4	6	.667	7	21	28	7	5	0	0	3	3	18	9.0
Totals	119	4889	513	1040	.493	234	385	.608	. . .	. . .	1777	453	371	5	67	55	69	1260	10.6

Three-point field goals: 1979-80, 0-for-1.

NBA ALL-STAR GAME RECORD

Season Team	Min.	FGM	FGA	Pct.	FTM	FTA	Pct.	Reb.	Ast.	PF	Dq.	Pts.
1969 — Baltimore	14	5	7	.714	1	3	.333	8	1	3	0	11
1971 — Baltimore	21	4	9	.444	0	0	. . .	10	2	2	0	8
1972 — Baltimore	16	1	5	.200	0	0	. . .	7	1	3	0	2
1973 — Baltimore	11	2	4	.500	0	0	. . .	5	1	0	0	4

								— REBOUNDS —								
Season Team	Min.	FGM	FGA	Pct.	FTM	FTA	Pct.	Off.	Def.	Tot.	Ast.	PF	Dq.	Stl.	Blk.	TO	Pts.
1975 — Washington	15	2	3	.667	2	2	1.000	2	4	6	1	2	0	2	0	. . .	6
Totals	77	14	28	.500	3	5	.600	. . .	. . .	36	6	10	0	2	0	. . .	31

HEAD COACHING RECORD

BACKGROUND: Vice president, Washington Bullets (1981-82 through 1986-87). . . . Vice president/assistant coach, Bullets (1987-January 3, 1988). . . . Vice president/head coach, Bullets (January 3, 1988-present).

NBA COACHING RECORD

			REGULAR SEASON				PLAYOFFS	
Season Team	W	L	Pct.	Finish		W	L	Pct.
87-88 — Washington	30	25	.545	T2nd/Atlantic Division		2	3	.400
88-89 — Washington	40	42	.488	4th/Atlantic Division		—	—	—

Season	Team		REGULAR SEASON				PLAYOFFS	
		W	L	Pct.	Finish	W	L	Pct.
89-90	—Washington	31	51	.378	4th/Atlantic Division	—	—	—
90-91	—Washington	30	52	.366	4th/Atlantic Division	—	—	—
91-92	—Washington	25	57	.305	6th/Atlantic Division	—	—	—
	Totals (5 years)	156	227	.407	Totals (1 year)	2	3	.400

NOTES:
1988— Replaced Kevin Loughery as Washington head coach (January 3), with record of 8-19. Lost to Detroit in Eastern Conference first round.

WEISS, BOB
HAWKS

PERSONAL: Born May 7, 1942, in Easton, Pa.... 6-3/185.... Full name: Robert William Weiss.
HIGH SCHOOL: Athens Area (Pa.).
COLLEGE: Penn State.
TRANSACTIONS/CAREER NOTES: Selected by Philadelphia 76ers in third round (25th pick overall) of 1965 NBA Draft.... Played with Wilmington Blue Bombers in Eastern Basketball League (1965-66 and 1966-67).... Selected by Seattle SuperSonics from 76ers in expansion draft (May 1, 1967).... Selected by Milwaukee Bucks from SuperSonics in expansion draft (May 6, 1968).... Traded by Bucks with Bob Love to Chicago Bulls for Flynn Robinson (November 23, 1968).... Traded by Bulls to Buffalo Braves for Matt Guokas and future draft choice (September 4, 1974).... Waived by Braves (September 29, 1976).... Signed as free agent by Washington Bullets (November 15, 1976).
MISCELLANEOUS: Member of NBA championship team (1967).

COLLEGIATE RECORD

Season	Team	G	Min.	FGM	FGA	Pct.	FTM	FTA	Pct.	Reb.	Pts.	Avg.
61-62	—Penn State†					Freshman team statistics unavailable.						
62-63	—Penn State	20	...	124	293	.423	57	81	.704	90	305	15.3
63-64	—Penn State	23	...	154	353	.436	84	105	.800	90	392	17.0
64-65	—Penn State	24	...	152	362	.420	90	117	.769	114	394	16.4
	Varsity totals	67	...	430	1008	.427	231	303	.762	294	1091	16.3

EBL REGULAR-SEASON RECORD

Notes: Eastern Basketball League All-Star first team (1967).

Season	Team	G	Min.	FGM	FGA	Pct.	FTM	FTA	Pct.	Reb.	Ast.	PF	Dq.	Pts.	Avg.
65-66	—Wilmington	19	...	56	...	...	32	44	.727	55	83	...	...	146	7.7
66-67	—Wilmington	27	...	151	...	...	100	118	.847	103	*238	...	...	403	14.9
	Totals	46	...	207	...	...	132	162	.815	158	321	...	...	549	11.9

NBA REGULAR-SEASON RECORD

Season	Team	G	Min.	FGM	FGA	Pct.	FTM	FTA	Pct.	Reb.	Ast.	PF	Dq.	Pts.	Avg.
65-66	—Philadelphia	7	30	3	9	.333	0	0	...	7	4	10	0	6	0.9
66-67	—Philadelphia	6	29	5	10	.500	2	5	.400	3	10	8	0	12	2.0
67-68	—Seattle	82	1614	295	686	.430	213	254	.839	150	342	137	0	803	9.8
68-69	—Milwaukee-Chicago	77	1478	189	499	.379	128	160	.800	162	199	174	1	506	6.6
69-70	—Chicago	82	2544	365	855	.427	213	253	.842	227	474	206	0	943	11.5
70-71	—Chicago	82	2237	278	659	.422	226	269	.840	189	387	216	1	782	9.5
71-72	—Chicago	82	2450	358	832	.430	212	254	.835	170	377	212	1	928	11.3
72-73	—Chicago	82	2086	279	655	.426	159	189	.841	148	295	151	1	717	8.7

										—REBOUNDS—								
Season	Team	G	Min.	FGM	FGA	Pct.	FTM	FTA	Pct.	Off.	Def.	Tot.	Ast.	PF	Dq.	Stl.	Blk.	TO	Pts.	Avg.
73-74	—Chicago	79	1708	263	564	.466	142	170	.835	32	71	103	303	156	0	104	12	...	668	8.5
74-75	—Buffalo	76	1338	102	261	.391	54	67	.806	21	83	104	260	146	0	82	19	...	258	3.4
75-76	—Buffalo	66	995	89	183	.486	35	48	.729	13	53	66	150	94	0	48	14	...	213	3.2
76-77	—Washington	62	768	62	133	.466	29	37	.784	15	54	69	130	66	0	53	7	...	153	2.5
	Totals	783	17277	2288	5346	.428	1413	1706	.828	...	...	1398	2931	1576	4	287	52	...	5989	7.6

NBA PLAYOFF RECORD

Season	Team	G	Min.	FGM	FGA	Pct.	FTM	FTA	Pct.	Reb.	Ast.	PF	Dq.	Pts.	Avg.
66-67	—Philadelphia	1	4	2	3	.667	0	0	...	2	2	1	0	4	4.0
69-70	—Chicago	5	121	25	59	.424	8	10	.800	6	24	11	0	58	11.6
70-71	—Chicago	7	250	42	92	.457	26	30	.867	18	57	19	0	110	15.7
71-72	—Chicago	4	119	24	49	.490	7	8	.875	13	12	15	1	55	13.8
72-73	—Chicago	7	175	34	79	.430	16	21	.762	16	15	20	0	84	12.0

										—REBOUNDS—								
Season	Team	G	Min.	FGM	FGA	Pct.	FTM	FTA	Pct.	Off.	Def.	Tot.	Ast.	PF	Dq.	Stl.	Blk.	TO	Pts.	Avg.
73-74	—Chicago	11	251	23	74	.311	6	6	1.000	5	15	20	32	20	0	7	1	...	52	4.7
74-75	—Buffalo	7	113	11	23	.478	8	12	.667	2	5	7	17	15	0	4	1	...	30	4.3
75-76	—Buffalo	7	36	3	8	.375	2	3	.667	0	4	4	3	5	0	2	0	...	8	1.1
76-77	—Washington	4	34	3	5	.600	0	1	.000	1	2	3	2	5	0	1	0	...	6	1.5
	Totals	53	1103	167	392	.426	73	91	.802	...	...	89	164	111	1	14	2	...	407	7.7

HEAD COACHING RECORD

BACKGROUND: Assistant coach, San Diego Clippers (1977-78 and 1978-79).... Assistant coach, Dallas Mavericks (1980-81 through 1985-86).... Assistant coach, Orlando Magic (1989-90).

NBA COACHING RECORD

Season	Team		REGULAR SEASON				PLAYOFFS	
		W	L	Pct.	Finish	W	L	Pct.
86-87	—San Antonio	28	54	.341	6th/Midwest Division	—	—	—
87-88	—San Antonio	31	51	.378	5th/Midwest Division	0	3	.000
90-91	—Atlanta	43	39	.524	4th/Central Division	2	3	.400
91-92	—Atlanta	38	44	.463	5th/Central Division	—	—	—
	Totals (4 years)	140	188	.427	Totals (2 years)	2	6	.333

NOTES:
1988— Lost to Los Angeles Lakers in Western Conference first round.
1991— Lost to Detroit in Eastern Conference first round.

WESTPHAL, PAUL
SUNS

PERSONAL: Born November 30, 1950, in Torrance, Calif.... 6-4/ 195.... Full name: Paul Douglas Westphal.
HIGH SCHOOL: Aviation (Redondo Beach, Calif.).
COLLEGE: Southern California.
TRANSACTIONS/CAREER NOTES: Selected by Boston Celtics in first round (10th pick overall) of 1972 NBA Draft.... Traded by Celtics with 1975 and 1976 second-round draft choices to Phoenix Suns for Charlie Scott (May 23, 1975).... Traded by Suns to Seattle SuperSonics for Dennis Johnson (June 4, 1980).... Signed as veteran free agent by New York Knicks (March 12, 1982).... Waived by Knicks (June 20, 1983).... Signed as free agent by Suns (September 27, 1983).... Waived by Suns (October 12, 1984).
MISCELLANEOUS: Member of NBA championship team (1974).

COLLEGIATE RECORD

NOTES: THE SPORTING NEWS All-America second team (1972).

Season	Team	G	Min.	FGM	FGA	Pct.	FTM	FTA	Pct.	Reb.	Pts.	Avg.
68-69	Southern California‡	19	...	134	262	.511	87	119	.731	106	355	18.7
69-70	Southern California	26	...	147	277	.531	84	110	.764	68	378	14.5
70-71	Southern California	26	...	157	328	.479	109	150	.727	84	423	16.3
71-72	Southern California	14	...	106	219	.484	72	95	.758	74	284	20.3
	Varsity totals	66		410	824	.498	265	355	.746	226	1085	16.4

NBA REGULAR-SEASON RECORD

HONORS: All-NBA first team (1977, 1979, 1980).... All-NBA second team (1978).... NBA Comeback Player of the Year (1983).

										— REBOUNDS —									
Season	Team	G	Min.	FGM	FGA	Pct.	FTM	FTA	Pct.	Off.	Def.	Tot.	Ast.	PF	Dq.	Stl.	Blk.	TO	Pts.	Avg.
72-73	Boston	60	482	89	212	.420	67	86	.779	...	...	67	69	88	0	...	...	...	245	4.1
73-74	Boston	82	1165	238	475	.501	112	153	.732	49	94	143	171	173	1	39	34	...	588	7.2
74-75	Boston	82	1581	342	670	.510	119	156	.763	44	119	163	235	192	0	78	33	...	803	9.8
75-76	Phoenix	82	2960	657	1329	.494	365	440	.830	74	185	259	440	218	3	210	38	...	1679	20.5
76-77	Phoenix	81	2600	682	1317	.518	362	439	.825	57	133	190	459	171	1	134	21	...	1726	21.3
77-78	Phoenix	80	2481	809	1568	.516	396	487	.813	41	123	164	437	162	0	138	31	280	2014	25.2
78-79	Phoenix	81	2641	801	1496	.535	339	405	.837	35	124	159	529	159	1	111	26	232	1941	24.0
79-80	Phoenix	82	2665	692	1317	.525	382	443	.862	46	141	187	416	162	0	119	35	207	1792	21.9
80-81	Seattle	36	1078	221	500	.442	153	184	.832	11	57	68	148	70	0	46	14	78	601	16.7
81-82	New York	18	451	86	194	.443	36	47	.766	9	13	22	100	61	1	19	8	47	210	11.7
82-83	New York	80	1978	318	693	.459	148	184	.804	19	96	115	439	180	1	87	16	196	798	10.0
83-84	Phoenix	59	865	144	313	.460	117	142	.824	8	35	43	148	69	0	41	6	77	412	7.0
	Totals	823	20947	5079	10084	.504	2596	3166	.820	...	...	1580	3591	1705	8	1022	262	1117	12809	15.6

Three-point field goals: 1979-80, 26-for-93 (.280). 1980-81, 6-for-25 (.240). 1981-82, 2-for-8 (.250). 1982-83, 14-for-48 (.292). 1983-84, 7-for-26 (.269). Totals, 55-for-200 (.275).

NBA PLAYOFF RECORD

										— REBOUNDS —									
Season	Team	G	Min.	FGM	FGA	Pct.	FTM	FTA	Pct.	Off.	Def.	Tot.	Ast.	PF	Dq.	Stl.	Blk.	TO	Pts.	Avg.
72-73	Boston	11	109	19	39	.487	5	7	.714	...	...	7	9	24	1	...	...	...	43	3.9
73-74	Boston	18	241	46	100	.460	11	15	.733	6	15	21	31	37	0	8	2	...	103	5.7
74-75	Boston	11	183	38	81	.469	12	18	.667	5	8	13	32	21	0	6	2	...	88	8.0
75-76	Phoenix	19	685	165	323	.511	71	93	.763	14	33	47	96	61	1	34	9	...	401	21.1
77-78	Phoenix	2	66	22	47	.468	8	9	.889	3	3	6	19	4	0	1	0	5	52	26.0
78-79	Phoenix	15	534	142	287	.495	52	66	.788	7	26	33	64	38	0	15	5	38	336	22.4
79-80	Phoenix	8	253	69	142	.486	28	32	.875	2	8	10	31	20	0	11	3	13	167	20.9
82-83	New York	6	156	22	50	.440	10	13	.769	0	8	8	34	13	0	2	2	9	57	9.5
83-84	Phoenix	17	222	30	80	.375	28	32	.875	3	5	8	37	23	0	12	0	24	90	5.3
	Totals	107	2449	553	1149	.481	225	285	.789	...	...	153	353	241	2	89	23	89	1337	12.5

Three-point field goals: 1979-80, 1-for-12 (.083). 1982-83, 3-for-8 (.375). 1983-84, 2-for-9 (.222). Totals, 6-for-29 (.207).

NBA ALL-STAR GAME RECORD

									— REBOUNDS —								
Season	Team	Min.	FGM	FGA	Pct.	FTM	FTA	Pct.	Off.	Def.	Tot.	Ast.	PF	Dq.	Stl.	Blk.	TO	Pts.
1977	Phoenix	31	10	16	.625	0	0	...	0	1	1	6	2	0	3	2	...	20
1978	Phoenix	24	9	14	.643	2	5	.400	0	0	0	5	4	0	1	1	3	20
1979	Phoenix	21	8	12	.667	1	2	.500	0	1	1	5	0	0	0	1	1	17
1980	Phoenix	27	8	14	.571	5	6	.833	1	0	1	5	5	0	2	1	3	21
1981	Seattle	25	8	12	.667	3	3	1.000	2	2	4	3	3	0	0	1	4	19
	Totals	128	43	68	.632	11	16	.688	3	4	7	24	14	0	6	5	11	97

Three-point field goals: 1980, 0-for-2.

HEAD COACHING RECORD

BACKGROUND: Assistant coach, Phoenix Suns (1988-89 through 1991-92).

COLLEGIATE COACHING RECORD

Season	Team	W	L	Pct.	Finish
85-86	S'western Baptist Bible Coll. ...	21	9	.700	
86-87	Grand Canyon College (Ariz.).	26	12	.684	NAIA Independent
87-88	Grand Canyon College (Ariz.).	37	6	.860	NAIA Independent
	Totals (3 years)	84	27	.757	

NOTES:
1987— Defeated Fort Lewis College (Colo.), 94-87, in NAIA District 7 first round; lost to Western State College (Colo.), 74-69, in NAIA District 7 championship.
1988— Defeated Southern Colorado, 68-62, in NAIA District 7 first round; defeated Colorado School of Mines, 113-79, in district 7 championship; defeated Hastings College (Neb.), 103-75, in NAIA Tournament first round; defeated Fort Hays State (Kan.), 101-95, in second round; defeated College of Idaho, 99-96 (OT), in third round; defeated Waynesburg State (Pa.), 108-106, in fourth round; defeated Auburn-Montgomery (Ala.), 88-86 (OT), in NAIA championship game.

WILKENS, LENNY
CAVALIERS

PERSONAL: Born October 28, 1937, in Brooklyn, N.Y. . . . 6-1/180. . . . Full name: Leonard Randolph Wilkens.
HIGH SCHOOL: Boys (Brooklyn, N.Y.).
COLLEGE: Providence.
TRANSACTIONS/CAREER NOTES: Selected by St. Louis Hawks in first round of 1960 NBA Draft. . . . Hawks franchise moved from St. Louis to Atlanta for 1968-69 season. . . . Traded by Hawks to Seattle SuperSonics for Walt Hazzard (October 12, 1968). . . . Player/head coach, SuperSonics (1969-70 through 1971-72). . . . Traded by SuperSonics with Barry Clemens to Cleveland Cavaliers for Butch Beard (August 23, 1972). . . . Playing rights transferred from Cavaliers to Portland Trail Blazers for cash (October 7, 1974).
CAREER HONORS: Elected to Naismith Memorial Basketball Hall of Fame (1988).

COLLEGIATE RECORD

NOTES: THE SPORTING NEWS All-America second team (1960).

Season Team	G	Min.	FGM	FGA	Pct.	FTM	FTA	Pct.	Reb.	Pts.	Avg.
56-57 —Providence†	23	. . .	. . .	. . .	. . .	. . .	. . .	. . .	. . .	488	21.2
57-58 —Providence	24	. . .	137	316	.434	84	130	.646	190	358	14.9
58-59 —Providence	27	. . .	167	390	.428	89	144	.618	188	423	15.7
59-60 —Providence	29	. . .	157	362	.434	98	140	.700	205	412	14.2
Varsity totals	80	. . .	461	1068	.432	271	414	.655	583	1193	14.9

NBA REGULAR-SEASON RECORD

NOTES: Led NBA with 9.1 assists per game (1970).

Season Team	G	Min.	FGM	FGA	Pct.	FTM	FTA	Pct.	Reb.	Ast.	PF	Dq.	Pts.	Avg.
60-61 —St. Louis	75	1898	333	783	.425	214	300	.713	335	212	215	5	880	11.7
61-62 —St. Louis	20	870	140	364	.385	84	110	.764	131	116	63	0	364	18.2
62-63 —St. Louis	75	2569	333	834	.399	222	319	.696	403	381	256	6	888	11.8
63-64 —St. Louis	78	2526	334	808	.413	270	365	.740	335	359	287	7	938	12.0
64-65 —St. Louis	78	2854	434	1048	.414	416	558	.746	365	431	283	7	1284	16.5
65-66 —St. Louis	69	2692	411	954	.431	422	532	.793	322	429	248	4	1244	18.0
66-67 —St. Louis	78	2974	448	1036	.432	459	583	.787	412	442	280	6	1355	17.4
67-68 —St. Louis	82	3169	546	1246	.438	546	711	.768	438	679	255	3	1638	20.0
68-69 —Seattle	82	3463	644	1462	.440	547	710	.770	511	674	294	8	1835	22.4
69-70 —Seattle	75	2802	448	1066	.420	438	556	.788	378	*683	212	5	1334	17.8
70-71 —Seattle	71	2641	471	1125	.419	461	574	.803	319	654	201	3	1403	19.8
71-72 —Seattle	80	2989	479	1027	.466	480	620	.774	338	*766	209	4	1438	18.0
72-73 —Cleveland	75	2973	572	1275	.449	394	476	.828	346	628	221	2	1538	20.5

Season Team	G	Min.	FGM	FGA	Pct.	FTM	FTA	Pct.	Off.	Def.	Tot.	Ast.	PF	Dq.	Stl.	Blk.	TO	Pts.	Avg.
73-74 —Cleveland	74	2483	462	994	.465	289	361	.801	80	197	277	522	165	2	97	17	. . .	1213	16.4
74-75 —Portland	65	1161	134	305	.439	152	198	.768	38	82	120	235	96	1	77	9	. . .	420	6.5
Totals	1077	38064	6189	14327	.432	5394	6973	.774	. . .	. . .	5030	7211	3285	63	174	26	. . .	17772	16.5

NBA PLAYOFF RECORD

Season Team	G	Min.	FGM	FGA	Pct.	FTM	FTA	Pct.	Reb.	Ast.	PF	Dq.	Pts.	Avg.
60-61 —St. Louis	12	437	63	166	.380	44	58	.759	72	42	51	4	170	14.2
62-63 —St. Louis	11	400	57	154	.370	37	49	.755	69	69	51	2	151	13.7
63-64 —St. Louis	12	413	64	143	.448	44	58	.759	60	64	42	0	172	14.3
64-65 —St. Louis	4	147	20	57	.351	24	29	.828	12	15	14	0	64	16.0
65-66 —St. Louis	10	391	57	143	.399	57	83	.687	54	70	43	0	171	17.1
66-67 —St. Louis	9	378	58	145	.400	77	90	.856	68	65	34	0	193	21.4
67-68 —St. Louis	6	237	40	91	.440	30	40	.750	38	47	23	1	110	18.3
Totals	64	2403	359	899	.399	313	407	.769	373	372	258	7	1031	16.1

NBA ALL-STAR GAME RECORD

NOTES: NBA All-Star Game Most Valuable Player (1971).

Season Team	Min.	FGM	FGA	Pct.	FTM	FTA	Pct.	Reb.	Ast.	PF	Dq.	Pts.
1963 —St. Louis	25	2	7	.286	0	1	.000	2	3	0	0	4
1964 —St. Louis	14	1	5	.200	1	1	1.000	0	0	3	0	3
1965 —St. Louis	20	2	6	.333	4	4	1.000	3	3	3	0	8
1967 —St. Louis	16	2	6	.333	2	3	.667	2	6	2	0	6
1968 —St. Louis	22	4	10	.400	6	8	.750	3	3	1	0	14
1969 —Seattle	24	3	15	.200	4	5	.800	7	5	3	0	10
1970 —Seattle	17	5	7	.714	2	3	.667	2	4	1	0	12
1971 —Seattle	20	8	11	.727	5	5	1.000	1	1	1	0	21
1973 —Cleveland	24	3	8	.375	1	2	.500	2	1	1	0	7
Totals	182	30	75	.400	25	32	.781	22	26	15	0	85

HEAD COACHING RECORD

BACKGROUND: Player/head coach, Seattle SuperSonics (1969-70 through 1971-72). . . . Player/head coach, Portland Trail Blazers (1974-75). . . . Director of player personnel, SuperSonics (May 13, 1977-November 1977). . . . Head coach/director of player personnel, SuperSonics (November 1977 through 1984-85). . . . Vice president/general manager, SuperSonics (1985-86). . . . Assistant coach, U.S. Olympic team (1992).

NBA COACHING RECORD

Season	Team	W	L	Pct.	Finish	W	L	Pct.
				REGULAR SEASON			**PLAYOFFS**	
69-70	Seattle	36	46	.439	5th/Western Division	—	—	—
70-71	Seattle	38	44	.463	4th/Pacific Division	—	—	—
71-72	Seattle	47	35	.573	3rd/Pacific Division	—	—	—
74-75	Portland	38	44	.463	3rd/Pacific Division	—	—	—
75-76	Portland	37	45	.451	5th/Pacific Division	—	—	—
77-78	Seattle	42	18	.700	3rd/Pacific Division	13	9	.591
78-79	Seattle	52	30	.634	1st/Pacific Division	12	5	.706
79-80	Seattle	56	26	.683	2nd/Pacific Division	7	8	.467
80-81	Seattle	34	48	.415	6th/Pacific Division	—	—	—
81-82	Seattle	52	30	.634	2nd/Pacific Division	3	5	.375
82-83	Seattle	48	34	.585	3rd/Pacific Division	0	2	.000
83-84	Seattle	42	40	.512	3rd/Pacific Division	2	3	.400
84-85	Seattle	31	51	.378	4th/Pacific Division	—	—	—
86-87	Cleveland	31	51	.378	6th/Central Division	—	—	—
87-88	Cleveland	42	40	.512	T4th/Central Division	2	3	.400
88-89	Cleveland	57	25	.695	2nd/Central Division	2	3	.400
89-90	Cleveland	42	40	.512	T4th/Central Division	2	3	.400
90-91	Cleveland	33	49	.402	6th/Central Division	—	—	—
91-92	Cleveland	57	25	.695	2nd/Central Division	9	8	.529
Totals (19 years)		**815**	**721**	**.531**	**Totals (10 years)**	**52**	**49**	**.515**

NOTES:

1977— Replaced Bob Hopkins as Seattle head coach (November), with record of 5-17.

1978— Defeated Los Angeles Lakers, 2-1, in Western Conference first round; defeated Portland, 4-2, in Western Conference semifinals; defeated Denver, 4-2, in Western Conference finals; lost to Washington, 4-3, in World Championship Series.

1979— Defeated Los Angeles Lakers, 4-1, in Western Conference semifinals; defeated Phoenix, 4-3, in Western Conference finals; defeated Washington, 4-1, in World Championship Series.

1980— Defeated Portland, 2-1, in Western Conference first round; defeated Milwaukee, 4-3, in Western Conference semifinals; lost to Los Angeles Lakers, 4-1, in Western Conference finals.

1982— Defeated Houston, 2-1, in Western Conference first round; lost to San Antonio, 4-1, in Western Conference semifinals.

1983— Lost to Portland in Western Conference first round.

1984— Lost to Dallas in Western Conference first round.

1988— Lost to Chicago in Eastern Conference first round.

1989— Lost to Chicago in Eastern Conference first round.

1990— Lost to Philadelphia in Eastern Conference first round.

1992— Defeated New Jersey, 3-1, in Eastern Conference first round; defeated Boston, 4-3, in Eastern Conference semifinals; lost to Chicago, 4-2, in Eastern Conference finals.

ABDUL-JABBAR, KAREEM
C

PERSONAL: Born April 16, 1947, in New York.... 7-2/267.... Formerly known as Lew Alcindor.
HIGH SCHOOL: Power Memorial (New York).
COLLEGE: UCLA.

TRANSACTIONS/CAREER NOTES: Selected by Milwaukee Bucks in first round (first pick overall) of 1969 NBA Draft.... Traded by Bucks with Walt Wesley to Los Angeles Lakers for Elmore Smith, Brian Winters, Dave Meyers and Junior Bridgeman (June 16, 1975).
CAREER HONORS: NBA 35th Anniversary All-Time team (1980).
MISCELLANEOUS: Member of NBA championship teams (1971, 1980, 1982, 1985, 1987, 1988).

COLLEGIATE RECORD

NOTES: THE SPORTING NEWS College Player of the Year (1967, 1969).... THE SPORTING NEWS All-America first team (1967, 1968, 1969).... NCAA Tournament Most Outstanding Player (1967, 1968, 1969).... Member of NCAA championship teams (1967, 1968, 1969).... Led NCAA Division I with .667 field-goal percentage (1967) and .635 field-goal percentage (1969).

Season Team	G	Min.	FGM	FGA	Pct.	FTM	FTA	Pct.	Reb.	Pts.	Avg.
65-66—UCLA‡	21	...	295	432	.683	106	179	.592	452	696	33.1
66-67—UCLA	30	...	346	519	.667	178	274	.650	466	870	29.0
67-68—UCLA	28	...	294	480	.613	146	237	.616	461	734	26.2
68-69—UCLA	30	...	303	477	.635	115	188	.612	440	721	24.0
Varsity totals	88	...	943	1476	.639	439	699	.628	1367	2325	26.4

NBA REGULAR-SEASON RECORD

RECORDS: Holds career records for most seasons played—20; most games played—1,560; most minutes played—57,446; most points—38,387; most field goals made—15,837; most field goals attempted—28,307; most defensive rebounds—9,394; most blocked shots—3,189; and most personal fouls—4,657.... Holds single-season record for most defensive rebounds—1,111 (1976).... Holds single-game record for most defensive rebounds—29 (December 14, 1975, vs. Detroit).
HONORS: NBA Most Valuable Player (1971, 1972, 1974, 1976, 1977, 1980).... NBA Rookie of the Year (1970).... All-NBA first team (1971, 1972, 1973, 1974, 1976, 1977, 1980, 1981, 1984, 1986).... All-NBA second team (1970, 1978, 1979, 1983, 1985). ...NBA All-Defensive first team (1974, 1975, 1979, 1980, 1981).... NBA All-Defensive second team (1970, 1971, 1976, 1977, 1978, 1984).... NBA All-Rookie team (1970).
NOTES: Led NBA with 16.9 rebounds per game (1976).... Led NBA with 3.26 blocked shots per game (1975), 4.12 blocked shots per game (1976), 3.95 blocked shots per game (1979) and 3.41 blocked shots per game (1980).

Season Team	G	Min.	FGM	FGA	Pct.	FTM	FTA	Pct.	Reb.	Ast.	PF	Dq.	Pts.	Avg.
69-70—Milwaukee	82	3534	*938	1810	.518	485	743	.653	1190	337	283	8	*2361	28.8
70-71—Milwaukee	82	3288	*1063	1843	.577	470	681	.690	1311	272	264	4	*2596	*31.7
71-72—Milwaukee	81	3583	*1159	*2019	.574	504	732	.689	1346	370	235	1	*2822	*34.8
72-73—Milwaukee	76	3254	982	1772	.554	328	460	.713	1224	379	208	0	2292	30.2

									— REBOUNDS —									
Season Team	G	Min.	FGM	FGA	Pct.	FTM	FTA	Pct.	Off.	Def.	Tot.	Ast.	PF	Dq.	Stl.	Blk.	TO	Pts.	Avg.
73-74—Milwaukee	81	3548	*948	1759	.539	295	420	.702	287	891	1178	386	238	2	112	283	...	2191	27.0
74-75—Milwaukee	65	2747	812	1584	.513	325	426	.763	194	718	912	264	205	2	65	212	...	1949	30.0
75-76—Los Angeles	82	*3379	914	1728	.529	447	636	.703	272	*1111	*1383	413	292	6	119	*338	...	2275	27.7
76-77—Los Angeles	82	3016	*888	1533	*.579	376	536	.701	266	*824	*1090	319	262	4	101	*261	...	2152	26.2
77-78—Los Angeles	62	2265	663	1205	.550	274	350	.783	186	615	801	269	182	1	103	185	208	1600	25.8
78-79—Los Angeles	80	3157	777	1347	.577	349	474	.736	207	818	1025	431	230	3	76	*316	282	1903	23.8
79-80—Los Angeles	82	3143	835	1383	.604	364	476	.765	190	696	886	371	216	2	81	*280	297	2034	24.8
80-81—Los Angeles	80	2976	836	1457	.574	423	552	.766	197	624	821	272	244	4	59	228	249	2095	26.2
81-82—Los Angeles	76	2677	753	1301	.579	312	442	.706	172	487	659	225	224	0	63	207	230	1818	23.9
82-83—Los Angeles	79	2554	722	1228	.588	278	371	.749	167	425	592	200	220	1	61	170	200	1722	21.8
83-84—Los Angeles	80	2622	716	1238	.578	285	394	.723	169	418	587	211	211	0	55	143	221	1717	21.5
84-85—L.A. Lakers	79	2630	723	1207	.599	289	395	.732	162	460	622	249	238	3	63	162	197	1735	22.0
85-86—L.A. Lakers	79	2629	755	1338	.564	336	439	.765	133	345	478	280	248	2	67	130	203	1846	23.4
86-87—L.A. Lakers	78	2441	560	993	.564	245	343	.714	152	371	523	203	245	2	49	97	186	1366	17.5
87-88—L.A. Lakers	80	2308	480	903	.532	205	269	.762	118	360	478	135	216	1	48	92	159	1165	14.6
88-89—L.A. Lakers	74	1695	313	659	.475	122	165	.739	103	231	334	74	196	1	38	85	95	748	10.1
Totals	1560	57446	15837	28307	.559	6712	9304	.721	...	...	17440	5660	4657	48	1160	3189	2527	38387	24.6

Three-point field goals: 1979-80, 0-for-1. 1980-81, 0-for-1. 1981-82, 0-for-3. 1982-83, 0-for-2. 1983-84, 0-for-1. 1984-85, 0-for-1. 1985-86, 0-for-2. 1986-87, 1-for-3 (.333). 1987-88, 0-for-1. 1988-89, 0-for-3. Totals, 1-for-18 (.056).

NBA PLAYOFF RECORD

NOTES: NBA Finals Most Valuable Player (1971, 1985).... Holds career records for most seasons played—18; most games played—237; most minutes played—8,851; most field goals made—2,356; most field goals attempted—4,422; most points—5,762; most blocked shots—476; and most personal fouls—797.

Season Team	G	Min.	FGM	FGA	Pct.	FTM	FTA	Pct.	Reb.	Ast.	PF	Dq.	Pts.	Avg.
69-70—Milwaukee	10	435	139	245	.567	74	101	.733	168	41	25	1	352	35.2
70-71—Milwaukee	14	577	152	295	.515	68	101	.673	238	35	45	0	372	26.6
71-72—Milwaukee	11	510	139	318	.437	38	54	.704	200	56	35	0	316	28.7
72-73—Milwaukee	6	276	59	138	.428	19	35	.543	97	17	26	0	137	22.8

									— REBOUNDS —									
Season Team	G	Min.	FGM	FGA	Pct.	FTM	FTA	Pct.	Off.	Def.	Tot.	Ast.	PF	Dq.	Stl.	Blk.	TO	Pts.	Avg.
73-74—Milwaukee	16	758	224	402	.557	67	91	.736	67	186	253	78	41	0	20	39	...	515	32.2
76-77—Los Angeles	11	467	147	242	.607	87	120	.725	51	144	195	45	42	0	19	38	...	381	34.6
77-78—Los Angeles	3	134	38	73	.521	5	9	.556	14	27	41	11	14	1	2	12	14	81	27.0
78-79—Los Angeles	8	367	88	152	.579	52	62	.839	18	83	101	38	26	0	8	33	29	228	28.5

Season	Team	G	Min.	FGM	FGA	Pct.	FTM	FTA	Pct.	Off.	Def.	Tot.	Ast.	PF	Dq.	Stl.	Blk.	TO	Pts.	Avg.
79-80	Los Angeles	15	618	198	346	.572	83	105	.790	51	130	181	46	51	0	17	58	55	479	31.9
80-81	Los Angeles	3	134	30	65	.462	20	28	.714	13	37	50	12	14	0	3	8	11	80	26.7
81-82	Los Angeles	14	493	115	221	.520	55	87	.632	33	86	119	51	45	0	14	45	41	285	20.4
82-83	Los Angeles	15	588	163	287	.568	80	106	.755	25	90	115	42	61	1	17	55	50	406	27.1
83-84	Los Angeles	21	767	206	371	.555	90	120	.750	56	117	173	79	71	2	23	45	45	502	23.9
84-85	L.A. Lakers	19	610	168	300	.560	80	103	.777	50	104	154	76	67	0	23	36	52	416	21.9
85-86	L.A. Lakers	14	489	157	282	.557	48	61	.787	26	57	83	49	54	0	15	24	42	362	25.9
86-87	L.A. Lakers	18	559	124	234	.530	97	122	.795	39	84	123	36	56	0	8	35	40	345	19.2
87-88	L.A. Lakers	24	718	141	304	.464	56	71	.789	49	82	131	36	81	1	15	37	46	338	14.1
88-89	L.A. Lakers	15	351	68	147	.463	31	43	.721	13	46	59	19	43	0	5	11	22	167	11.1
	Totals	237	8851	2356	4422	.533	1050	1419	.740			2481	767	797	7	189	476	447	5762	24.3

Three-point field goals: 1982-83, 0-for-1. 1986-87, 0-for-1. 1987-88, 0-for-2. 1988-89, 0-for-1. Totals, 0-for-5.

NBA ALL-STAR GAME RECORD

NOTES: Holds career records for most games played—18; most minutes played—449; most field goals made—105; most field goals attempted—213; most points—251; most blocked shots—31; and most personal fouls—57.

Season	Team	Min.	FGM	FGA	Pct.	FTM	FTA	Pct.	Reb.	Ast.	PF	Dq.	Pts.
1970	Milwaukee	18	4	8	.500	2	2	1.000	11	4	6	1	10
1971	Milwaukee	30	8	16	.500	3	4	.750	14	1	2	0	19
1972	Milwaukee	19	5	10	.500	2	2	1.000	7	2	0	0	12
1973	Milwaukee							Selected, did not play.					

Season	Team	Min.	FGM	FGA	Pct.	FTM	FTA	Pct.	Off.	Def.	Tot.	Ast.	PF	Dq.	Stl.	Blk.	TO	Pts.
1974	Milwaukee	23	7	11	.636	0	0	...	1	7	8	6	2	0	1	1	...	14
1975	Milwaukee	19	3	10	.300	1	2	.500	5	5	10	3	2	0	0	1	...	7
1976	Los Angeles	36	9	16	.563	4	4	1.000	2	13	15	3	3	0	0	3	...	22
1977	Los Angeles	23	8	14	.571	5	6	.833	3	1	4	2	1	0	0	1	...	21
1979	Los Angeles	28	5	12	.417	1	2	.500	1	7	8	3	4	0	1	1	3	11
1980	Los Angeles	30	6	17	.353	5	6	.833	5	11	16	9	5	0	0	6	9	17
1981	Los Angeles	23	6	9	.667	3	3	1.000	2	4	6	4	3	0	0	4	3	15
1982	Los Angeles	22	1	10	.100	0	0	...	1	2	3	1	3	0	0	2	1	2
1983	Los Angeles	32	9	12	.750	2	3	.667	2	4	6	5	1	0	1	4	1	20
1984	Los Angeles	37	11	19	.579	3	4	.750	5	8	13	2	5	0	0	1	4	25
1985	L.A. Lakers	23	5	10	.500	1	2	.500	0	6	6	1	5	0	1	1	1	11
1986	L.A. Lakers	32	9	15	.600	3	4	.750	2	5	7	2	4	0	2	2	5	21
1987	L.A. Lakers	27	4	9	.444	2	2	1.000	2	6	8	3	5	0	0	2	1	10
1988	L.A. Lakers	14	4	9	.444	2	2	1.000	2	2	4	0	3	0	0	0	0	10
1989	L.A. Lakers	13	1	6	.167	2	2	1.000	0	3	3	0	3	0	0	2	0	4
	Totals	449	105	213	.493	41	50	.820	...	...	149	51	57	1	6	31	28	251

Three-point field goals: 1989, 0-for-1.

ARCHIBALD, NATE
G

PERSONAL: Born September 2, 1948, in New York. . . . 6-1/160. . . . Full name: Nathaniel Archibald. . . . Nickname: Tiny.
HIGH SCHOOL: DeWitt Clinton (Bronx, N.Y.).
COLLEGE: Arizona Western, then Texas-El Paso.

TRANSACTIONS/CAREER NOTES: Selected by Cincinnati Royals in second round (19th pick overall) of 1970 NBA Draft. . . . Royals franchise moved from Cincinnati to Kansas City-Omaha and renamed Kings for 1972-73 season. . . . Kings franchise moved from Kansas City-Omaha to Kansas City for 1975-76 season. . . . Traded by Kings to New York Nets for Brian Taylor, Jim Eakins and 1977 and 1978 first-round draft choices (September 10, 1976). . . . Nets franchise moved from New York to New Jersey for 1977-78 season. . . . Traded by Nets to Buffalo Braves for George Johnson and 1979 first-round draft choice (September 1, 1977). . . . Braves franchise moved from Buffalo to San Diego and renamed Clippers for 1978-79 season. . . . Traded by Clippers with Marvin Barnes, Billy Knight and 1981 and 1983 second-round draft choices to Boston Celtics for Kermit Washington, Kevin Kunnert, Sidney Wicks and draft rights to Freeman Williams (August 4, 1978). . . . Waived by Celtics (July 22, 1983). . . . Signed as free agent by Milwaukee Bucks (August 1, 1983).
CAREER HONORS: Elected to Naismith Memorial Basketball Hall of Fame (1990).
MISCELLANEOUS: Member of NBA championship team (1981).

COLLEGIATE RECORD

Season	Team	G	Min.	FGM	FGA	Pct.	FTM	FTA	Pct.	Reb.	Pts.	Avg.
66-67	Arizona Western	27	...	303	...	...	190	...	...	...	796	29.5
67-68	Texas-El Paso	23	...	131	281	.466	102	140	.729	81	364	15.8
68-69	Texas-El Paso	25	...	199	374	.532	161	194	.830	69	559	22.4
69-70	Texas-El Paso	25	...	180	351	.513	176	225	.782	66	536	21.4
	Junior college totals	27	...	303	...	...	190	...	...	...	796	29.5
	Four-year-college totals	73	...	510	1006	.507	439	559	.785	216	1459	20.0

NBA REGULAR-SEASON RECORD

HONORS: All-NBA first team (1973, 1975, 1976). . . . All-NBA second team (1972, 1981).
NOTES: Led NBA with 11.4 assists per game (1973).

Season	Team	G	Min.	FGM	FGA	Pct.	FTM	FTA	Pct.	Reb.	Ast.	PF	Dq.	Pts.	Avg.
70-71	Cincinnati	82	2867	486	1095	.444	336	444	.757	242	450	218	2	1308	16.0
71-72	Cincinnati	76	3272	734	1511	.486	*677	*824	.822	222	701	198	2	2145	28.2
72-73	Kansas City/Omaha	80	*3681	*1028	*2106	.488	*663	*783	.847	223	*910	207	2	*2719	*34.0

Season	Team	G	Min.	FGM	FGA	Pct.	FTM	FTA	Pct.	Off.	Def.	Tot.	Ast.	PF	Dq.	Stl.	Blk.	TO	Pts.	Avg.
73-74	K.C./Omaha	35	1272	222	492	.451	173	211	.820	21	64	85	266	76	0	56	7	...	617	17.6
74-75	K.C./Omaha	82	3244	759	1664	.456	*652	748	.872	48	174	222	557	187	0	119	7	...	2170	26.5
75-76	Kansas City	78	3184	717	1583	.453	501	625	.802	67	146	213	615	169	0	126	15	...	1935	24.8
76-77	N.Y. Nets	34	1277	250	560	.446	197	251	.785	22	58	80	254	77	1	59	11	...	697	20.5
77-78	Buffalo							Selected, did not play—torn achilles tendon.												

Season	Team	G	Min.	FGM	FGA	Pct.	FTM	FTA	Pct.	Off.	Def.	Tot.	Ast.	PF	Dq.	Stl.	Blk.	TO	Pts.	Avg.
										— REBOUNDS —										
78-79 — Boston		69	1662	259	573	.452	242	307	.788	25	78	103	324	132	2	55	6	197	760	11.0
79-80 — Boston		80	2864	383	794	.482	361	435	.830	59	138	197	671	218	2	106	10	242	1131	14.1
80-81 — Boston		80	2820	382	766	.499	342	419	.816	36	140	176	618	201	1	75	18	265	1106	13.8
81-82 — Boston		68	2167	308	652	.472	236	316	.747	25	91	116	541	131	1	52	3	178	858	12.6
82-83 — Boston		66	1811	235	553	.425	220	296	.743	25	66	91	409	110	1	38	4	163	695	10.5
83-84 — Milwaukee ...		46	1038	136	279	.487	64	101	.634	16	60	76	160	78	0	33	0	78	340	7.4
Totals		876	31159	5899	12628	.467	4664	5760	.810	...	...	2046	6476	2002	15	719	81	1123	16481	18.8

Three-point field goals: 1979-80, 4-for-18 (.222). 1980-81, 0-for-9. 1981-82, 6-for-16 (.375). 1982-83, 5-for-24 (.208). 1983-84, 4-for-18 (.222). Totals, 19-for-85 (.224).

NBA PLAYOFF RECORD

Season	Team	G	Min.	FGM	FGA	Pct.	FTM	FTA	Pct.	Off.	Def.	Tot.	Ast.	PF	Dq.	Stl.	Blk.	TO	Pts.	Avg.
										— REBOUNDS —										
74-75 — K.C./Omaha ...		6	242	43	118	.364	35	43	.814	2	9	11	32	18	0	4	0	...	121	20.2
79-80 — Boston		9	332	45	89	.506	37	42	.881	3	8	11	71	28	1	10	0	38	128	14.2
80-81 — Boston		17	630	95	211	.450	76	94	.809	6	22	28	107	39	0	13	0	50	266	15.6
81-82 — Boston		8	277	30	70	.429	25	28	.893	1	16	17	52	21	0	5	2	23	85	10.6
82-83 — Boston		7	161	22	68	.324	22	29	.759	3	7	10	44	12	0	2	0	11	67	9.6
Totals		47	1642	235	556	.423	195	236	.826	15	62	77	306	118	1	34	2	122	667	14.2

Three-point field goals: 1979-80, 1-for-2 (.500). 1980-81, 0-for-5. 1981-82, 0-for-4. 1982-83, 1-for-6 (.167). Totals, 2-for-17 (.118).

NBA ALL-STAR GAME RECORD

NOTES: NBA All-Star Game Most Valuable Player (1981).

Season	Team	Min.	FGM	FGA	Pct.	FTM	FTA	Pct.	Reb.	Ast.	PF	Dq.	Pts.
1973 — Kansas City/Omaha		27	6	12	.500	5	5	1.000	1	5	1	0	17

Season	Team	Min.	FGM	FGA	Pct.	FTM	FTA	Pct.	Off.	Def.	Tot.	Ast.	PF	Dq.	Stl.	Blk.	TO	Pts.
									— REBOUNDS —									
1975 — K.C./Omaha		36	10	15	.667	7	8	.875	1	1	2	6	2	0	3	1	...	27
1976 — Kansas City		30	5	13	.385	3	3	1.000	2	3	5	7	0	0	2	0	...	13
1980 — Boston		21	0	8	.000	2	3	.667	1	2	3	6	1	0	2	0	2	2
1981 — Boston		25	4	7	.571	1	3	.333	0	5	5	9	3	0	3	0	2	9
1982 — Boston		23	2	5	.400	2	2	1.000	1	1	2	7	3	0	1	0	2	6
Totals		162	27	60	.450	20	24	.833	...	...	18	40	10	0	11	1	6	74

ARIZIN, PAUL
F/G

PERSONAL: Born April 9, 1928, in Philadelphia.... 6-4/200.... Full name: Paul Joseph Arizin.
HIGH SCHOOL: La Salle (Philadelphia).
COLLEGE: Villanova.
TRANSACTIONS/CAREER NOTES: Selected by Philadelphia Warriors in first round of 1950 NBA Draft.... Played in Eastern Basketball League with Camden Bullets (1962-63 through 1964-65).
CAREER HONORS: Elected to Naismith Memorial Basketball Hall of Fame (1977).... NBA 25th Anniversary All-Time team (1970).
MISCELLANEOUS: Member of NBA championship team (1956).

COLLEGIATE RECORD

NOTES: THE SPORTING NEWS College Player of the Year (1950).... THE SPORTING NEWS All-America first team (1950).... Led NCAA Division I with 25.3 points per game (1950).

Season	Team	G	Min.	FGM	FGA	Pct.	FTM	FTA	Pct.	Reb.	Pts.	Avg.
46-47 — Villanova							Did not play.					
47-48 — Villanova		24	...	101	...	...	65	...	...	...	267	11.1
48-49 — Villanova		27	...	210	...	...	174	233	.747	...	594	22.0
49-50 — Villanova		29	...	260	527	.493	215	277	.776	...	735	25.3
Totals		80	...	571	...	...	454	...	...	...	1596	20.0

NBA REGULAR-SEASON RECORD

HONORS: All-NBA first team (1952, 1956, 1957).... All-NBA second team (1959).

Season	Team	G	Min.	FGM	FGA	Pct.	FTM	FTA	Pct.	Reb.	Ast.	PF	Dq.	Pts.	Avg.
50-51 — Philadelphia		65	...	352	864	.407	417	526	.793	640	138	284	18	1121	17.2
51-52 — Philadelphia		66	*2939	*548	1222	*.448	*578	707	.818	745	170	250	5	*1674	*25.4
52-53 — Philadelphia						Did not play—in military service.									
53-54 — Philadelphia						Did not play—in military service.									
54-55 — Philadelphia		72	*2953	*529	*1325	.399	454	585	.776	675	210	270	5	1512	21.0
55-56 — Philadelphia		72	2724	617	1378	.448	507	626	.810	539	189	282	11	1741	24.2
56-57 — Philadelphia		71	2767	613	1451	.422	591	*713	.829	561	150	274	13	*1817	*25.6
57-58 — Philadelphia		68	2377	483	1229	.393	440	544	.809	503	135	235	7	1406	20.7
58-59 — Philadelphia		70	2799	632	1466	.431	587	722	.813	637	119	264	7	1851	26.4
59-60 — Philadelphia		72	2618	593	1400	.424	420	526	.798	621	165	263	6	1606	22.3
60-61 — Philadelphia		79	2905	650	1529	.425	532	639	.833	681	188	*335	11	1832	23.2
61-62 — Philadelphia		78	2785	611	1490	.410	484	601	.805	527	201	307	18	1706	21.9
Totals		713	...	5628	13354	.421	5010	6189	.810	6129	1665	2764	101	16266	22.8

NBA PLAYOFF RECORD

Season	Team	G	Min.	FGM	FGA	Pct.	FTM	FTA	Pct.	Reb.	Ast.	PF	Dq.	Pts.	Avg.
50-51 — Philadelphia		2	...	14	27	.519	13	16	.813	20	3	10	1	41	20.5
51-52 — Philadelphia		3	120	24	53	.453	29	33	.879	38	8	17	2	77	25.7
55-56 — Philadelphia		10	409	103	229	.450	83	99	.838	84	29	31	1	289	28.9
56-57 — Philadelphia		2	22	3	8	.375	3	5	.600	8	1	3	0	9	4.5
57-58 — Philadelphia		8	309	66	169	.391	56	72	.778	62	16	26	1	188	23.5
59-60 — Philadelphia		9	371	84	195	.431	69	79	.873	86	33	29	0	237	26.3

Season Team	G	Min.	FGM	FGA	Pct.	FTM	FTA	Pct.	Reb.	Ast.	PF	Dq.	Pts.	Avg.
60-61 —Philadelphia	3	125	22	67	.328	23	33	.697	26	12	17	2	67	22.3
61-62 —Philadelphia	12	459	95	253	.375	88	102	.863	80	26	44	1	278	23.2
Totals	49	...	411	1001	.411	364	439	.829	404	128	177	8	1186	24.2

NBA ALL-STAR GAME RECORD

NOTES: NBA All-Star Game Most Valuable Player (1952).

Season Team	Min.	FGM	FGA	Pct.	FTM	FTA	Pct.	Reb.	Ast.	PF	Dq.	Pts.
1951 —Philadelphia	...	7	12	.583	1	2	.500	7	0	2	0	15
1952 —Philadelphia	32	9	13	.692	8	8	1.000	6	0	1	0	26
1955 —Philadelphia	23	4	9	.444	1	2	.500	2	2	5	0	9
1956 —Philadelphia	28	5	13	.385	3	5	.600	7	1	6	1	13
1957 —Philadelphia	26	6	13	.462	1	2	.500	5	0	2	0	13
1958 —Philadelphia	29	11	17	.647	2	2	1.000	8	2	3	0	24
1959 —Philadelphia	30	4	15	.267	8	9	.889	8	0	2	0	16
1960 —Philadelphia					Selected, did not play—injured.							
1961 —Philadelphia	17	6	12	.500	5	5	1.000	2	1	4	0	17
1962 —Philadelphia	21	2	12	.167	0	0	...	2	0	4	0	4
Totals	...	54	116	.466	29	35	.829	47	6	29	1	137

EBL REGULAR-SEASON RECORD

NOTES: Eastern Basketball League Most Valuable Player (1963).... EBL All-Star first team (1963, 1964).... EBL All-Star second team (1965).

Season Team	G	Min.	FGM	FGA	Pct.	FTM	FTA	Pct.	Reb.	Ast.	PF	Dq.	Pts.	Avg.
62-63 —Camden	28	...	264	...	...	196	249	.787	203	42	...	...	724	25.9
63-64 —Camden	27	...	261	...	...	174	218	.798	226	52	...	...	696	25.8
64-65 —Camden	28	...	226	...	...	196	244	.803	164	50	...	...	657	23.5
Totals	83	...	751	...	...	566	711	.796	593	144	...	...	2077	25.0

BARRY, RICK
F

PERSONAL: Born March 28, 1944, in Elizabeth, N.J. ... 6-7/220. ... Full name: Richard Francis Dennis Barry III.
HIGH SCHOOL: Roselle Park (N.J.).
COLLEGE: Miami (Fla.).
TRANSACTIONS/CAREER NOTES: Selected by San Francisco Warriors in first round of 1965 NBA Draft.... Signed as free agent by Oakland Oaks of American Basketball Association (1967); court order required him to sit out option season with Warriors (1967-68).... Oaks franchise moved to Washington and renamed Capitols for 1969-70 season.... Capitols franchise moved from Washington to Virginia and renamed Squires for 1970-71 season.... Traded by Squires to New York Nets for first-round draft choice and cash (August 1970).... Returned to NBA with Golden State Warriors for 1972-73 season.... Signed as veteran free agent by Houston Rockets (June 17, 1978); Warriors waived their right of first refusal in exchange for John Lucas and cash.
CAREER HONORS: Elected to Naismith Memorial Basketball Hall of Fame (1986).
MISCELLANEOUS: Member of NBA championship team (1975).

COLLEGIATE RECORD

NOTES: THE SPORTING NEWS All-America second team (1965).... Led NCAA Division I with 37.4 points per game (1965).

Season Team	G	Min.	FGM	FGA	Pct.	FTM	FTA	Pct.	Reb.	Pts.	Avg.
61-62 —Miami (Fla.)‡	17	...	208	...	...	73	...	...	...	489	28.8
62-63 —Miami (Fla.)	24	...	162	341	.475	131	158	.829	351	455	19.0
63-64 —Miami (Fla.)	27	...	314	572	.549	242	287	.843	448	870	32.2
64-65 —Miami (Fla.)	26	...	340	651	.522	293	341	.859	475	973	37.4
Varsity totals	77	...	816	1564	.522	666	786	.847	1274	2298	29.8

NBA REGULAR-SEASON RECORD

RECORDS: Holds career record for highest free-throw percentage (minimum 1,200 made)—.900.... Shares single-game record for most free throws made in one quarter—14 (December 6, 1966, vs. New York).
HONORS: NBA Rookie of the Year (1966).... All-NBA first team (1966, 1967, 1974, 1975, 1976).... All-NBA second team (1973).... NBA All-Rookie team (1966).
NOTES: Led NBA with 2.85 steals per game (1975).

Season Team	G	Min.	FGM	FGA	Pct.	FTM	FTA	Pct.	Reb.	Ast.	PF	Dq.	Pts.	Avg.
65-66 —San Francisco	80	2990	745	1698	.439	569	660	.862	850	173	297	2	2059	25.7
66-67 —San Francisco	78	3175	*1011	*2240	.451	*753	852	.884	714	282	258	1	*2775	*35.6
72-73 —Golden State	82	3075	737	1630	.452	358	397	*.902	728	399	245	2	1832	22.3

									REBOUNDS										
Season Team	G	Min.	FGM	FGA	Pct.	FTM	FTA	Pct.	Off.	Def.	Tot.	Ast.	PF	Dq.	Stl.	Blk.	TO	Pts.	Avg.
73-74 —Golden State	80	2918	796	1746	.456	417	464	.899	103	437	540	484	265	4	169	40	...	2009	25.1
74-75 —Golden State	80	3235	1028	*2217	.464	394	436	*.904	92	364	456	492	225	0	*228	33	...	2450	30.6
75-76 —Golden State	81	3122	707	1624	.435	287	311	*.923	74	422	496	496	215	1	202	27	...	1701	21.0
76-77 —Golden State	79	2904	682	1551	.440	359	392	.916	73	349	422	475	194	2	172	58	...	1723	21.8
77-78 —Golden State	82	3024	760	1686	.451	378	409	*.924	75	374	449	446	188	1	158	45	224	1898	23.1
78-79 —Houston	80	2566	461	1000	.461	160	169	*.947	40	237	277	502	195	0	95	38	198	1082	13.5
79-80 —Houston	72	1816	325	771	.422	143	153	*.935	53	183	236	268	182	0	80	28	152	866	12.0
Totals	794	28825	7252	16163	.449	3818	4243	.900	...	...	5168	4017	2264	13	1104	269	574	18395	23.2

Three-point field goals: 1979-80, 73-for-221 (.330).

NBA PLAYOFF RECORD

NOTES: NBA Finals Most Valuable Player (1975). ... Holds NBA Finals record for highest points-per-game average—40.8 (1967).... Holds NBA Finals single-game record for most field goals attempted—48 (April 18, 1967, vs. Philadelphia); and most field goals attempted in one quarter—17 (April 14, 1967, vs. Philadelphia).... Shares NBA Finals single-game records for most field goals made—22 (April 18, 1967, vs. Philadelphia); and most free throws made in one half—12 (April 24, 1967, vs. Philadelphia).... Holds single-game record for most field goals attempted in one quarter—17 (April 14, 1967, vs. Philadelphia).... Shares single-game record for most steals—8 (April 14, 1975, vs. Seattle).

Season	Team	G	Min.	FGM	FGA	Pct.	FTM	FTA	Pct.	Reb.	Ast.	PF	Dq.	Pts.	Avg.
66-67	—San Francisco	15	614	197	489	.403	127	157	.809	113	58	49	0	521	34.7
72-73	—Golden State	11	292	65	164	.396	50	55	.909	54	24	41	1	180	16.4

REBOUNDS

Season	Team	G	Min.	FGM	FGA	Pct.	FTM	FTA	Pct.	Off.	Def.	Tot.	Ast.	PF	Dq.	Stl.	Blk.	TO	Pts.	Avg.
74-75	—Golden State	17	726	189	426	.444	101	110	.918	22	72	94	103	51	1	50	15	...	479	28.2
75-76	—Golden State	13	532	126	289	.436	60	68	.882	20	64	84	84	40	1	38	14	...	312	24.0
76-77	—Golden State	10	415	122	262	.466	40	44	.909	25	34	59	47	32	0	17	7	...	284	28.4
78-79	—Houston	2	65	8	25	.320	8	8	1.000	2	6	8	9	8	0	0	2	2	24	12.0
79-80	—Houston	6	79	12	33	.364	6	6	1.000	0	6	6	15	11	0	1	1	10	33	5.5
Totals		74	2723	719	1688	.426	392	448	.875	...	...	418	340	232	3	106	39	12	1833	24.8

Three-point field goals: 1979-80, 3-for-12 (.250).

NBA ALL-STAR GAME RECORD

NOTES: NBA All-Star Game Most Valuable Player (1967).... Holds single-game record for most field goals attempted—27 (1967).

Season	Team	Min.	FGM	FGA	Pct.	FTM	FTA	Pct.	Reb.	Ast.	PF	Dq.	Pts.
1966	—San Francisco	17	4	10	.400	2	4	.500	2	2	6	1	10
1967	—San Francisco	34	16	27	.593	6	8	.750	6	3	5	0	38
1973	—Golden State						Did not play—injured.						

REBOUNDS

Season	Team	Min.	FGM	FGA	Pct.	FTM	FTA	Pct.	Off.	Def.	Tot.	Ast.	PF	Dq.	Stl.	Blk.	TO	Pts.
1974	—Golden State	19	3	6	.500	2	2	1.000	1	3	4	3	3	0	1	0	...	8
1975	—Golden State	38	11	20	.550	0	0	...	1	4	5	8	4	0	8	1	...	22
1976	—Golden State	28	6	15	.400	5	5	1.000	2	2	4	2	5	0	2	0	...	17
1977	—Golden State	29	7	16	.438	4	4	1.000	1	3	4	8	1	0	2	0	...	18
1978	—Golden State	30	7	17	.412	1	1	1.000	2	2	4	5	6	1	3	0	5	15
Totals		195	54	111	.486	20	24	.833	...	...	29	31	30	2	16	1	5	128

ABA REGULAR-SEASON RECORD

NOTES: ABA All-Star first team (1969, 1970, 1971, 1972).

Season	Team	G	Min.	2-POINT			3-POINT			FTM	FTA	Pct.	Reb.	Ast.	Pts.	Avg.
				FGM	FGA	Pct.	FGM	FGA	Pct.							
67-68	—					Did not play—sat out option year.										
68-69	—Oakland	35	1361	389	757	.514	3	10	.300	403	454	*.888	329	136	*1190	*34.0
69-70	—Washington	52	1849	509	907	.561	8	39	.205	400	463	.864	363	178	1442	27.7
70-71	—New York	59	2502	613	1262	.486	19	86	.221	451	507	*.890	401	294	1734	29.4
71-72	—New York	80	3616	829	1732	.479	73	237	.308	*641	730	*.878	602	327	2518	31.5
Totals		226	9328	2340	4658	.502	103	372	.277	1895	2154	.880	1695	935	6884	30.5

ABA PLAYOFF RECORD

Season	Team	G	Min.	2-POINT			3-POINT			FTM	FTA	Pct.	Reb.	Ast.	Pts.	Avg.
				FGM	FGA	Pct.	FGM	FGA	Pct.							
69-70	—Washington	7	302	105	194	.541	3	9	.333	62	68	.912	70	23	281	40.1
70-71	—New York	6	287	46	108	.426	14	27	.519	48	59	.814	66	17	202	33.7
71-72	—New York	18	749	180	368	.489	23	66	.348	125	146	.856	117	69	554	30.8
Totals		31	1338	331	670	.494	40	102	.392	235	273	.861	253	109	1037	33.5

ABA ALL-STAR GAME RECORD

Season	Team	Min.	2-POINT			3-POINT			FTM	FTA	Pct.	Reb.	Ast.	Pts.
			FGM	FGA	Pct.	FGM	FGA	Pct.						
1968	—Oakland	12	3	9	.333	0	0	...	4	5	.800	3	1	10
1969	—Washington	27	7	12	.583	0	0	...	2	2	1.000	7	7	16
1970	—New York	17	4	6	.667	0	0	...	6	6	1.000	2	2	14
1971	—New York	26	2	10	.200	0	0	...	0	1	.000	12	8	4
Totals		82	16	37	.432	0	0	...	12	14	.857	24	18	44

BAYLOR, ELGIN

F

PERSONAL: Born September 16, 1934, in Washington, D.C.... 6-5/225. ... Full name: Elgin Gay Baylor.
HIGH SCHOOL: Phelps Vocational (Washington, D.C.), then Spingarn (Washington, D.C.).
COLLEGE: The College of Idaho, then Seattle.
TRANSACTIONS/CAREER NOTES: Selected as eligible junior by Minneapolis Lakers in first round (first pick overall) of 1958 NBA Draft.... Lakers franchise moved to Los Angeles for 1960-61 season.
CAREER HONORS: Elected to Naismith Memorial Basketball Hall of Fame (1976).... NBA 35th Anniversary All-Time team (1980).

COLLEGIATE RECORD

NOTES: THE SPORTING NEWS All-America first team (1958).... NCAA University Division Tournament Most Valuable Player (1958).... Led NCAA Division I with .235 rebound average (1957), when championship was determined by highest individual recoveries as percentage of total recoveries by both teams in all games.... Played for Westside Ford (AAU team in Seattle) averaging 34 points per game (1955-56).

Season	Team	G	Min.	FGM	FGA	Pct.	FTM	FTA	Pct.	Reb.	Pts.	Avg.
54-55	—College of Idaho	26	...	332	651	.510	150	232	.647	492	814	31.3
55-56	—Seattle					Did not play—transfer student.						
56-57	—Seattle	25	...	271	555	.488	201	251	.801	508	743	29.7
57-58	—Seattle	29	...	353	697	.506	237	308	.769	559	943	32.5
Totals		80	...	956	1903	.502	588	791	.743	1559	2500	31.3

NBA REGULAR-SEASON RECORD

HONORS: NBA Rookie of the Year (1959).... All-NBA first team (1959, 1960, 1961, 1962, 1963, 1964, 1965, 1967, 1968, 1969).

Season	Team	G	Min.	FGM	FGA	Pct.	FTM	FTA	Pct.	Reb.	Ast.	PF	Dq.	Pts.	Avg.
58-59	Minneapolis	70	2855	605	1482	.408	532	685	.777	1050	287	270	4	1742	24.9
59-60	Minneapolis	70	2873	755	1781	.424	564	770	.732	1150	243	234	2	2074	29.6
60-61	Los Angeles	73	3133	931	2166	.430	676	863	.783	1447	371	279	3	2538	34.8
61-62	Los Angeles	48	2129	680	1588	.428	476	631	.754	892	222	155	1	1836	38.3
62-63	Los Angeles	80	3370	1029	2273	.453	661	790	.837	1146	386	226	1	2719	34.0
63-64	Los Angeles	78	3164	756	1778	.425	471	586	.804	936	347	235	1	1983	25.4
64-65	Los Angeles	74	3056	763	1903	.401	483	610	.792	950	280	235	0	2009	27.1
65-66	Los Angeles	65	1975	415	1034	.401	249	337	.739	621	224	157	0	1079	16.6
66-67	Los Angeles	70	2706	711	1658	.429	440	541	.813	898	215	211	1	1862	26.6
67-68	Los Angeles	77	3029	757	1709	.443	488	621	.786	941	355	232	0	2002	26.0
68-69	Los Angeles	76	3064	730	1632	.447	421	567	.743	805	408	204	0	1881	24.8
69-70	Los Angeles	54	2213	511	1051	.486	276	357	.773	559	292	132	1	1298	24.0
70-71	Los Angeles	2	57	8	19	.421	4	6	.667	11	2	6	0	20	10.0
71-72	Los Angeles	9	239	42	97	.433	22	27	.815	57	18	20	0	106	11.8
Totals		846	33863	8693	20171	.431	5763	7391	.780	11463	3650	2596	14	23149	27.4

NBA PLAYOFF RECORD

NOTES: Holds NBA Finals single-game records for most points—61; and most field goals attempted in one half—25 (April 14, 1962, vs. Boston).... Shares NBA Finals single-game record for most field goals made—22 (April 14, 1962, vs. Boston).... Shares single-game record for most field goals attempted in one half—25 (April 14, 1962, vs. Boston).

Season	Team	G	Min.	FGM	FGA	Pct.	FTM	FTA	Pct.	Reb.	Ast.	PF	Dq.	Pts.	Avg.
58-59	Minneapolis	13	556	122	303	.403	87	113	.770	156	43	52	0	331	25.5
59-60	Minneapolis	9	408	111	234	.474	79	94	.840	128	31	38	0	301	33.4
60-61	Los Angeles	12	540	170	362	.470	117	142	.824	183	55	44	1	457	38.1
61-62	Los Angeles	13	571	186	425	.438	130	168	.774	230	47	45	1	502	38.6
62-63	Los Angeles	13	562	160	362	.442	104	126	.825	177	58	58	0	424	32.6
63-64	Los Angeles	5	221	45	119	.378	31	40	.775	58	28	17	0	121	24.2
64-65	Los Angeles	1	5	0	2	.000	0	0	...	0	1	0	0	0	0.0
65-66	Los Angeles	14	586	145	328	.442	85	105	.810	197	52	38	0	375	26.8
66-67	Los Angeles	3	121	28	76	.368	15	20	.750	39	9	6	0	71	23.7
67-68	Los Angeles	15	633	176	376	.468	76	112	.679	218	60	41	0	428	28.5
68-69	Los Angeles	18	640	107	278	.385	63	100	.630	166	74	56	0	277	15.4
69-70	Los Angeles	18	667	138	296	.466	60	81	.741	173	83	50	1	336	18.7
Totals		134	5510	1388	3161	.439	847	1101	.769	1725	541	445	3	3623	27.0

NBA ALL-STAR GAME RECORD

NOTES: NBA All-Star Game co-Most Valuable Player (1959).... Holds career record for most free throws made—78.... Shares career record for most free throws attempted—98.... Shares single-game record for most free throws made—12 (1962).

Season	Team	Min.	FGM	FGA	Pct.	FTM	FTA	Pct.	Reb.	Ast.	PF	Dq.	Pts.
1959	Minneapolis	32	10	20	.500	4	5	.800	11	1	3	0	24
1960	Minneapolis	28	10	18	.556	5	7	.714	13	3	4	0	25
1961	Los Angeles	27	3	11	.273	9	10	.900	10	4	5	0	15
1962	Los Angeles	37	10	23	.435	12	14	.857	9	4	2	0	32
1963	Los Angeles	36	4	15	.267	9	13	.692	14	7	0	0	17
1964	Los Angeles	29	5	15	.333	5	11	.455	8	5	1	0	15
1965	Los Angeles	27	5	13	.385	8	8	1.000	7	0	4	0	18
1967	Los Angeles	20	8	14	.571	4	4	1.000	5	5	2	0	20
1968	Los Angeles	27	8	13	.615	6	7	.857	6	1	5	0	22
1969	Los Angeles	32	5	13	.385	11	12	.917	9	5	2	0	21
1970	Los Angeles	26	2	9	.222	5	7	.714	7	3	3	0	9
Totals		321	70	164	.427	78	98	.796	99	38	31	0	218

NBA COACHING RECORD

Season	Team	REGULAR SEASON W	L	Pct.	Finish	PLAYOFFS W	L	Pct.
74-75	New Orleans	0	1	.000		—	—	—
76-77	New Orleans	21	35	.375	5th/Central Division	—	—	—
77-78	New Orleans	39	43	.476	5th/Central Division	—	—	—
78-79	New Orleans	26	56	.317	6th/Central Division	—	—	—
Totals (4 years)		86	135	.389		—	—	—

NOTES:

1974— Replaced Scotty Robertson as New Orleans head coach (November), with record of 1-14; replaced as New Orleans head coach by Bill van Breda Kolff (November).

1976— Replaced Bill van Breda Kolff as New Orleans head coach (December), with record of 14-12.

BELLAMY, WALT
C

PERSONAL: Born July 24, 1939, in New Bern, N.C.... 6-11/245.... Full name: Walter Jones Bellamy.... Nickname: Bells.
HIGH SCHOOL: J.T. Barber (New Bern, N.C.).
COLLEGE: Indiana.

TRANSACTIONS/CAREER NOTES: Selected by Chicago Packers in first round (first pick overall) of 1961 NBA Draft.... Packers franchise renamed Zephyrs for 1962-63 season.... Zephyrs franchise moved to Baltimore and changed name to Bullets (1963).... Traded by Bullets to New York Knicks for John Green, John Egan, Jim Barnes and cash (November 2, 1965).... Traded by Knicks with Howard Komives to Detroit Pistons for Dave DeBusschere (December 19, 1968).... Traded by Pistons to Atlanta Hawks for a player to be designated (February 1, 1970); Pistons received John Arthurs from Milwaukee Bucks as part of deal.... Selected by New Orleans Jazz from Hawks in expansion draft (May 20, 1974).... Waived by Jazz (October 18, 1974).
MISCELLANEOUS: Member of gold-medal-winning U.S. Olympic Team (1960).

COLLEGIATE RECORD

NOTES: THE SPORTING NEWS All-America second team (1961).

Season Team	G	Min.	FGM	FGA	Pct.	FTM	FTA	Pct.	Reb.	Pts.	Avg.
57-58 —Indiana‡					Freshman team did not play intercollegiate schedule.						
58-59 —Indiana	22	...	148	289	.512	86	141	.610	335	382	17.4
59-60 —Indiana	24	...	212	396	.535	113	161	.702	324	537	22.4
60-61 —Indiana	24	...	195	389	.501	132	204	.647	428	522	21.8
Varsity totals	70	...	555	1074	.517	331	506	.654	1087	1441	20.6

NBA REGULAR-SEASON RECORD

RECORDS: Holds single-season record for most games played—88 (1969).
HONORS: NBA Rookie of the Year (1962).

Season Team	G	Min.	FGM	FGA	Pct.	FTM	FTA	Pct.	Reb.	Ast.	PF	Dq.	Pts.	Avg.
61-62 —Chicago	79	3344	973	1875	*.519	549	853	.644	1500	210	281	6	2495	31.6
62-63 —Chicago	80	3306	840	1595	.527	553	821	.674	1309	233	283	7	2233	27.9
63-64 —Baltimore	80	3394	811	1582	.513	537	825	.651	1361	126	300	7	2159	27.0
64-65 —Baltimore	80	3301	733	1441	.509	515	752	.685	1166	191	260	2	1981	24.8
65-66 —Baltimore-New York	80	3352	695	1373	.506	430	689	.624	1254	235	294	9	1820	22.8
66-67 —New York	79	3010	565	1084	.521	369	580	.636	1064	206	275	5	1499	19.0
67-68 —New York	82	2695	511	944	.541	350	529	.662	961	164	259	3	1372	16.7
68-69 —New York-Detroit	88	3159	563	1103	.510	401	618	.649	1101	176	320	5	1527	17.4
69-70 —Detroit-Atlanta	79	2028	351	671	.523	215	373	.576	707	143	260	5	917	11.6
70-71 —Atlanta	82	2908	433	879	.493	336	556	.604	1060	230	271	4	1202	14.7
71-72 —Atlanta	82	3187	593	1089	.545	340	581	.585	1049	262	255	2	1526	18.6
72-73 —Atlanta	74	2802	455	901	.505	283	526	.538	964	179	244	1	1193	16.1

— REBOUNDS —

Season Team	G	Min.	FGM	FGA	Pct.	FTM	FTA	Pct.	Off.	Def.	Tot.	Ast.	PF	Dq.	Stl.	Blk.	TO	Pts.	Avg.
73-74 —Atlanta	77	2440	389	801	.486	233	383	.608	264	476	740	189	232	2	52	48	...	1011	13.1
74-75 —New Orleans	1	14	2	2	1.000	2	2	1.000	0	5	5	0	2	0	0	0	...	6	6.0
Totals	1043	38940	7914	15340	.516	5113	8088	.632	...	...	14241	2544	3536	58	52	48	...	20941	20.1

NBA PLAYOFF RECORD

Season Team	G	Min.	FGM	FGA	Pct.	FTM	FTA	Pct.	Reb.	Ast.	PF	Dq.	Pts.	Avg.
64-65 —Baltimore	10	427	74	158	.468	61	92	.663	151	34	38	0	209	20.9
66-67 —New York	4	157	28	54	.519	17	29	.586	66	12	15	0	73	18.3
67-68 —New York	6	277	45	107	.421	30	48	.625	96	21	22	0	120	20.0
69-70 —Atlanta	9	368	59	126	.468	33	46	.717	140	35	32	0	151	16.8
70-71 —Atlanta	5	216	41	69	.594	22	29	.759	72	10	16	0	104	20.8
71-72 —Atlanta	6	247	42	86	.488	27	43	.628	82	11	20	0	111	18.5
72-73 —Atlanta	6	247	34	86	.395	14	31	.452	73	13	17	0	82	13.7
Totals	46	1939	323	686	.471	204	318	.642	680	136	160	0	850	18.5

NBA ALL-STAR GAME RECORD

Season Team	Min.	FGM	FGA	Pct.	FTM	FTA	Pct.	Reb.	Ast.	PF	Dq.	Pts.
1962 —Chicago	29	10	18	.556	3	8	.375	17	1	6	1	23
1963 —Chicago	14	1	4	.250	0	2	.000	1	2	3	0	2
1964 —Baltimore	23	4	11	.364	3	5	.600	7	0	3	0	11
1965 —Baltimore	17	4	5	.800	4	4	1.000	5	1	3	0	12
Totals	83	19	38	.500	10	19	.526	30	4	15	1	48

BING, DAVE

G

PERSONAL: Born November 24, 1943, in Washington, D.C. . . . 6-3/185. . . . Full name: David Bing.
HIGH SCHOOL: Spingarn (Washington, D.C.).
COLLEGE: Syracuse.
TRANSACTIONS/CAREER NOTES: Selected by Detroit Pistons in first round (second pick overall) of 1966 NBA Draft. . . . Traded by Pistons with 1977 first-round draft choice to Washington Bullets for Kevin Porter (August 28, 1975). . . . Waived by Bullets (September 20, 1977). . . . Signed as free agent by Boston Celtics (September 28, 1977).
CAREER HONORS: Elected to Naismith Memorial Basketball Hall of Fame (1989).

COLLEGIATE RECORD

NOTES: THE SPORTING NEWS All-America first team (1965).

Season Team	G	Min.	FGM	FGA	Pct.	FTM	FTA	Pct.	Reb.	Pts.	Avg.
62-63 —Syracuse‡	17	...	170	341	.499	97	131	.740	192	437	25.7
63-64 —Syracuse	25	...	215	460	.467	126	172	.733	206	556	22.2
64-65 —Syracuse	23	...	206	444	.464	121	162	.747	277	533	23.2
65-66 —Syracuse	28	...	308	569	.541	178	222	.802	303	794	28.4
Varsity totals	76	...	729	1473	.495	425	556	.764	786	1883	24.8

NBA REGULAR-SEASON RECORD

HONORS: NBA Rookie of the Year (1967). . . . All-NBA first team (1968, 1971). . . . All-NBA second team (1974). . . . NBA All-Rookie team (1967).

Season Team	G	Min.	FGM	FGA	Pct.	FTM	FTA	Pct.	Reb.	Ast.	PF	Dq.	Pts.	Avg.
66-67 —Detroit	80	2762	664	1522	.436	273	370	.738	359	330	217	2	1601	20.0
67-68 —Detroit	79	3209	*835	*1893	.441	472	668	.707	373	509	254	2	*2142	27.1
68-69 —Detroit	77	3039	678	1594	.425	444	623	.713	382	546	256	3	1800	23.4
69-70 —Detroit	70	2334	575	1295	.444	454	580	.783	299	418	196	0	1604	22.9
70-71 —Detroit	82	3065	799	1710	.467	*615	*772	.797	364	408	228	4	2213	27.0
71-72 —Detroit	45	1936	369	891	.414	278	354	.785	186	317	138	3	1016	22.6
72-73 —Detroit	82	3361	692	1545	.448	456	560	.814	298	637	229	1	1840	22.4

Season	Team	G	Min.	FGM	FGA	Pct.	FTM	FTA	Pct.	REBOUNDS Off.	Def.	Tot.	Ast.	PF	Dq.	Stl.	Blk.	TO	Pts.	Avg.
73-74	—Detroit	81	3124	582	1336	.436	356	438	.813	108	173	281	555	216	1	109	17	...	1520	18.8
74-75	—Detroit	79	3222	578	1333	.434	343	424	.809	86	200	286	610	222	3	116	26	...	1499	19.0
75-76	—Washington	82	2945	497	1113	.447	332	422	.787	94	143	237	492	262	0	118	23	...	1326	16.2
76-77	—Washington	64	1516	271	597	.454	136	176	.773	54	89	143	275	150	1	61	5	...	678	10.6
77-78	—Boston	80	2256	422	940	.449	244	296	.824	76	136	212	300	247	2	79	18	216	1088	13.6
Totals		901	32769	6962	15769	.441	4403	5683	.775	...	...	3420	5397	2615	22	483	89	216	18327	20.3

NBA PLAYOFF RECORD

Season	Team	G	Min.	FGM	FGA	Pct.	FTM	FTA	Pct.	REBOUNDS Off.	Def.	Tot.	Ast.	PF	Dq.	Stl.	Blk.	TO	Pts.	Avg.
67-68	—Detroit	6	254	68	166	.410	33	45	.733	...	...	24	29	21	0	...	...	...	169	28.2
73-74	—Detroit	7	312	55	131	.420	22	30	.733	6	20	26	42	20	0	3	1	...	132	18.9
74-75	—Detroit	3	134	20	47	.426	8	13	.615	3	8	11	29	12	0	5	0	...	48	16.0
75-76	—Washington	7	209	34	76	.447	28	35	.800	6	12	18	28	18	0	7	2	...	96	13.7
76-77	—Washington	8	55	14	32	.438	4	4	1.000	3	3	6	5	5	0	0	1	...	32	4.0
Totals		31	964	191	452	.423	95	127	.748	...	...	85	133	76	0	15	4	...	477	15.4

NBA ALL-STAR GAME RECORD

NOTES: NBA All-Star Game Most Valuable Player (1976).

Season	Team	Min.	FGM	FGA	Pct.	FTM	FTA	Pct.	Reb.	Ast.	PF	Dq.	Pts.
1968	—Detroit	20	4	7	.571	1	1	1.000	2	4	3	0	9
1969	—Detroit	13	1	3	.333	1	1	1.000	0	3	0	0	3
1971	—Detroit	19	2	7	.286	0	0	...	2	2	1	0	4
1973	—Detroit	19	0	4	.000	2	2	1.000	3	0	1	0	2

Season	Team	Min.	FGM	FGA	Pct.	FTM	FTA	Pct.	REBOUNDS Off.	Def.	Tot.	Ast.	PF	Dq.	Stl.	Blk.	TO	Pts.
1974	—Detroit	16	2	9	.222	1	1	1.000	1	5	6	2	1	0	0	0	...	5
1975	—Detroit	12	0	2	.000	2	2	1.000	0	0	0	1	0	0	0	0	...	2
1976	—Washington	26	7	11	.636	2	2	1.000	1	2	3	4	1	0	0	0	...	16
Totals		125	16	43	.372	9	9	1.000	...	...	16	16	7	0	0	0	...	41

BIRD, LARRY

F

PERSONAL: Born December 7, 1956, in West Baden, Ind. . . . 6-9/220. . . . Full name: Larry Joe Bird.
HIGH SCHOOL: Springs Valley (French Lick, Ind.).
COLLEGE: Indiana, then Northwood Institute (Ind.), then Indiana State.
TRANSACTIONS/CAREER NOTES: Selected as eligible junior by Boston Celtics in first round (sixth pick overall) of 1978 NBA Draft.
MISCELLANEOUS: Member of NBA championship teams (1981, 1984, 1986). . . . Member of gold-medal-winning U.S. Olympic team (1992).

COLLEGIATE RECORD

NOTES: THE SPORTING NEWS College Player of the Year (1979). . . . THE SPORTING NEWS All-America first team (1978, 1979).

Season	Team	G	Min.	FGM	FGA	Pct.	FTM	FTA	Pct.	Reb.	Pts.	Avg.
74-75	—Indiana					Did not play.						
75-76	—Indiana State					Did not play—transfer student.						
76-77	—Indiana State	28	1033	375	689	.544	168	200	.840	373	918	32.8
77-78	—Indiana State	32	...	403	769	.524	153	193	.793	369	959	30.0
78-79	—Indiana State	34	...	376	707	.532	221	266	.831	505	973	28.6
Totals		94	...	1154	2165	.533	542	659	.822	1247	2850	30.3

NBA REGULAR-SEASON RECORD

HONORS: NBA Most Valuable Player (1984, 1985, 1986). . . . NBA Rookie of the Year (1980). . . . All-NBA first team (1980, 1981, 1982, 1983, 1984, 1985, 1986, 1987, 1988). . . . All-NBA second team (1990). . . . NBA All-Defensive second team (1982, 1983, 1984). . . . NBA All-Rookie team (1980).

Season	Team	G	Min.	FGM	FGA	Pct.	FTM	FTA	Pct.	REBOUNDS Off.	Def.	Tot.	Ast.	PF	Dq.	Stl.	Blk.	TO	Pts.	Avg.
79-80	—Boston	82	2955	693	1463	.474	301	360	.836	216	636	852	370	279	4	143	53	263	1745	21.3
80-81	—Boston	82	3239	719	1503	.478	283	328	.863	191	704	895	451	239	2	161	63	289	1741	21.2
81-82	—Boston	77	2923	711	1414	.503	328	380	.863	200	637	837	447	244	0	143	66	254	1761	22.9
82-83	—Boston	79	2982	747	1481	.504	351	418	.840	193	677	870	458	197	0	148	71	240	1867	23.6
83-84	—Boston	79	3028	758	1542	.492	374	421	*.888	181	615	796	520	197	0	144	69	237	1908	24.2
84-85	—Boston	80	3161	918	1760	.522	403	457	.882	164	678	842	531	208	0	129	98	248	2295	28.7
85-86	—Boston	82	3113	796	1606	.496	441	492	*.896	190	615	805	557	182	0	166	51	266	2115	25.8
86-87	—Boston	74	3005	786	1497	.525	414	455	*.910	124	558	682	566	185	3	135	70	240	2076	28.1
87-88	—Boston	76	2965	881	1672	.527	415	453	.916	108	595	703	467	157	0	125	57	213	2275	29.9
88-89	—Boston	6	189	49	104	.471	18	19	.947	1	36	37	29	18	0	6	5	11	116	19.3
89-90	—Boston	75	2944	718	1517	.473	319	343	*.930	90	622	712	562	173	2	106	61	243	1820	24.3
90-91	—Boston	60	2277	462	1017	.454	163	183	.891	53	456	509	431	118	0	108	58	187	1164	19.4
91-92	—Boston	45	1662	353	758	.466	150	162	.926	46	388	434	306	82	0	42	33	125	908	20.2
Totals		897	34443	8591	17334	.496	3960	4471	.886	1757	7217	8974	5695	2279	11	1556	755	2816	21791	24.3

Three-point field goals: 1979-80, 58-for-143 (.406). 1980-81, 20-for-74 (.270). 1981-82, 11-for-52 (.212). 1982-83, 22-for-77 (.286). 1983-84, 18-for-73 (.247). 1984-85, 56-for-131 (.427). 1985-86, 82-for-194 (.423). 1986-87, 90-for-225 (.400). 1987-88, 98-for-237 (.414). 1989-90, 65-for-195 (.333). 1990-91, 77-for-198 (.389). 1991-92, 52-for-128 (.406). Totals, 649-for-1727 (.376).

NBA PLAYOFF RECORD

NOTES: NBA Finals Most Valuable Player (1984, 1986). . . . Holds career record for most defensive rebounds—1,323.

Season	Team	G	Min.	FGM	FGA	Pct.	FTM	FTA	Pct.	Off.	Def.	Tot.	Ast.	PF	Dq.	Stl.	Blk.	TO	Pts.	Avg.
79-80 —Boston		9	372	83	177	.469	22	25	.880	22	79	101	42	30	0	14	8	33	192	21.3
80-81 —Boston		17	750	147	313	.470	76	85	.894	49	189	238	103	53	0	39	17	62	373	21.9
81-82 —Boston		12	490	88	206	.427	37	45	.822	33	117	150	67	43	0	23	17	38	214	17.8
82-83 —Boston		6	240	49	116	.422	24	29	.828	20	55	75	41	15	0	13	3	19	123	20.5
83-84 —Boston		23	961	229	437	.524	167	190	.879	62	190	252	136	71	0	54	27	87	632	27.5
84-85 —Boston		20	815	196	425	.461	121	136	.890	53	129	182	115	54	0	34	19	57	520	26.0
85-86 —Boston		18	770	171	331	.517	101	109	.927	34	134	168	148	55	0	37	11	47	466	25.9
86-87 —Boston		23	1015	216	454	.476	176	193	.912	41	190	231	165	55	1	27	19	71	622	27.0
87-88 —Boston		17	763	152	338	.450	101	113	.894	29	121	150	115	45	0	36	14	49	417	24.5
89-90 —Boston		5	207	44	99	.444	29	32	.906	7	39	46	44	10	0	5	5	18	122	24.4
90-91 —Boston		10	396	62	152	.408	44	51	.863	8	64	72	65	28	0	13	3	19	171	17.1
91-92 —Boston		4	107	21	42	.500	3	4	.750	2	16	18	21	7	0	1	2	6	45	11.3
Totals		164	6886	1458	3090	.472	901	1012	.890	360	1323	1683	1062	466	1	296	145	506	3897	23.8

Three-point field goals: 1979-80, 4-for-15 (.267). 1980-81, 3-for-8 (.375). 1981-82, 1-for-6 (.167). 1982-83, 1-for-4 (.250). 1983-84, 7-for-17 (.412). 1984-85, 7-for-25 (.280). 1985-86, 23-for-56 (.411). 1986-87, 14-for-41 (.341). 1987-88, 12-for-32 (.375). 1989-90, 5-for-19 (.263). 1990-91, 3-for-21 (.143). 1991-92, 0-for-5. Totals, 80-for-249 (.321).

NBA ALL-STAR GAME RECORD

NOTES: NBA All-Star Game Most Valuable Player (1982).

Season	Team	Min.	FGM	FGA	Pct.	FTM	FTA	Pct.	Off.	Def.	Tot.	Ast.	PF	Dq.	Stl.	Blk.	TO	Pts.
1980	—Boston	23	3	6	.500	0	0	...	3	3	6	7	1	0	1	0	3	7
1981	—Boston	18	1	5	.200	0	0	...	1	3	4	3	1	0	1	0	2	2
1982	—Boston	28	7	12	.583	5	8	.625	0	12	12	5	3	0	1	1	4	19
1983	—Boston	29	7	14	.500	0	0	...	3	10	13	7	4	0	2	0	5	14
1984	—Boston	33	6	18	.333	4	4	1.000	1	6	7	3	1	0	2	0	2	16
1985	—Boston	31	8	16	.500	5	6	.833	5	3	8	2	3	0	0	1	4	21
1986	—Boston	35	8	18	.444	5	6	.833	2	6	8	5	5	0	7	0	4	23
1987	—Boston	35	7	18	.389	4	4	1.000	0	7	7	1	4	0	4	1	2	18
1988	—Boston	32	2	8	.250	2	2	1.000	0	7	7	1	4	0	4	1	2	6
1990	—Boston	23	3	8	.375	2	2	1.000	2	6	8	3	1	0	3	0	3	8
1991	—Boston					Selected, did not play—injured.													
1992	—Boston					Selected, did not play—injured.													
Totals		287	52	123	.423	27	32	.844	19	60	79	41	28	0	23	3	31	134

Three-point field goals: 1980, 1-for-2 (.500). 1983, 0-for-1. 1985, 0-for-1. 1986, 2-for-4 (.500). 1987, 0-for-3. 1988, 0-for-1. 1990, 0-for-1. Totals, 3-for-13 (.231).

BOONE, RON
G

PERSONAL: Born September 6, 1946, in Oklahoma City.... 6-2/200.... Full name: Ronald Bruce Boone.
HIGH SCHOOL: Tech (Omaha, Neb.).
COLLEGE: Iowa Western Community College, then Idaho State.
TRANSACTIONS/CAREER NOTES: Selected by Phoenix Suns in 11th round (147th pick overall) of 1968 NBA Draft.... Selected by Dallas Chaparrals in eighth round of 1968 ABA Draft.... Traded by Chaparrals with Glen Combs to Utah Stars for Donnie Freeman and Wayne Hightower (January 8, 1971).... Sold by Stars to Spirits of St. Louis (December 2, 1975).... Selected by Kansas City Kings (NBA) from Spirits for $250,000 in ABA dispersal draft (August 5, 1976).... Traded by Kings with 1979 second-round draft choice to Denver Nuggets for Darnell Hillman and draft rights to Mike Evans (June 26, 1978).... Traded by Nuggets with two 1979 second-round draft choices to Los Angeles Lakers for Charlie Scott (June 26, 1978).... Traded by Lakers to Utah Jazz for 1981 third-round draft choice (October 25, 1979).... Waived by Jazz (January 26, 1981).
MISCELLANEOUS: Set professional basketball record by playing in most consecutive games—1041.

COLLEGIATE RECORD

Season	Team	G	Min.	FGM	FGA	Pct.	FTM	FTA	Pct.	Reb.	Pts.	Avg.
64-65 —Iowa Western C.C.		9	...	...	...	...	...	...	...	...	227	25.2
65-66 —Idaho State		10	...	46	119	.387	17	26	.654	95	109	10.9
66-67 —Idaho State		25	...	199	416	.478	160	215	.744	128	558	22.3
67-68 —Idaho State		26	...	223	519	.430	108	159	.679	110	554	21.3
Junior college totals		9	...	...	...	...	...	...	...	...	227	25.2
Four-year-college totals		61	...	468	1054	.444	285	400	.713	333	1221	20.0

ABA REGULAR-SEASON RECORD

NOTES: ABA All-Star first team (1975).... ABA All-Star second team (1974).... ABA All-Rookie team (1969).... Member of ABA championship team (1971).

Season	Team	G	Min.	2-POINT FGM	FGA	Pct.	3-POINT FGM	FGA	Pct.	FTM	FTA	Pct.	Reb.	Ast.	Pts.	Avg.
68-69 —Dallas		78	2682	518	1182	.438	2	15	.133	436	537	.812	394	279	1478	18.9
69-70 —Dallas		84	2340	406	925	.439	17	55	.309	300	382	.785	366	272	1163	13.8
70-71 —Dallas-Utah		86	2476	561	1257	.446	49	138	.355	278	357	.779	564	256	1547	18.0
71-72 —Utah		84	2040	391	897	.436	13	65	.200	271	341	.795	393	233	1092	13.0
72-73 —Utah		84	2585	556	1096	.507	10	40	.250	415	479	.866	423	353	1557	18.5
73-74 —Utah		84	3098	581	1162	.500	6	26	.231	300	343	.875	406	417	1480	17.6
74-75 —Utah		84	3414	862	1743	.495	10	33	.303	363	422	.860	435	372	2117	25.2
75-76 —Utah-St. Louis		78	2961	697	1424	.489	16	43	.372	277	318	.871	319	387	1719	22.0
Totals		662	21596	4572	9686	.472	123	415	.296	2640	3179	.830	3300	2569	12153	18.4

ABA PLAYOFF RECORD

Season	Team	G	Min.	2-POINT FGM	FGA	Pct.	3-POINT FGM	FGA	Pct.	FTM	FTA	Pct.	Reb.	Ast.	Pts.	Avg.
68-69 —Dallas		7	196	38	81	.469	0	4	.000	21	25	.840	22	27	97	13.9
69-70 —Dallas		6	193	43	89	.483	3	8	.375	15	21	.714	27	27	110	18.3

ALL-TIME GREAT PLAYERS

Season Team	G	Min.	2-POINT FGM	FGA	Pct.	3-POINT FGM	FGA	Pct.	FTM	FTA	Pct.	Reb.	Ast.	Pts.	Avg.
70-71—Utah	18	569	104	229	.454	9	27	.333	74	86	.860	110	94	309	17.2
71-72—Utah	11	209	49	100	.490	1	5	.200	25	29	.862	24	26	126	11.5
72-73—Utah	10	360	68	132	.515	0	3	.000	33	34	.971	43	47	169	16.9
73-74—Utah	18	747	137	282	.486	0	7	.000	34	37	.919	108	109	308	17.1
74-75—Utah	6	219	54	127	.425	0	0	...	34	38	.895	24	41	142	23.7
Totals	76	2493	493	1040	.474	13	54	.241	236	270	.874	358	371	1261	16.6

ABA ALL-STAR GAME RECORD

Season Team	Min.	2-POINT FGM	FGA	Pct.	3-POINT FGM	FGA	Pct.	FTM	FTA	Pct.	Reb.	Ast.	Pts.
1971 —Utah	4	2	4	.500	0	0	...	2	3	.667	2	0	6
1974 —Utah	24	6	11	.545	1	2	.500	0	0	...	3	5	15
1975 —Utah	23	4	8	.500	0	0	...	2	2	1.000	2	2	10
1976 —St. Louis	16	5	11	.455	0	0	...	0	0	...	3	2	10
Totals	67	17	34	.500	1	2	.500	4	5	.800	10	9	41

NBA REGULAR-SEASON RECORD

Season Team	G	Min.	FGM	FGA	Pct.	FTM	FTA	Pct.	REBOUNDS Off.	Def.	Tot.	Ast.	PF	Dq.	Stl.	Blk.	TO	Pts.	Avg.
76-77—Kansas City	82	3021	747	1577	.474	324	384	.844	128	193	321	338	258	1	119	19	...	1818	22.2
77-78—Kansas City	82	2653	563	1271	.443	322	377	.854	112	157	269	311	233	3	105	11	303	1448	17.7
78-79—Los Angeles	82	1583	259	569	.455	90	104	.865	53	92	145	154	171	1	66	11	147	608	7.4
79-80—L.A.-Utah	81	2392	405	915	.443	175	196	.893	54	173	227	309	232	3	97	3	197	1004	12.4
80-81—Utah	52	1146	160	371	.431	75	94	.798	17	67	84	161	126	0	33	8	111	406	7.8
Totals	379	10795	2134	4703	.454	986	1155	.854	364	682	1046	1273	1020	8	420	52	758	5284	13.9

Three-point field goals: 1979-80, 19-for-50 (.380). 1980-81, 11-for-39 (.282). Totals, 30-for-89 (.337).

NBA PLAYOFF RECORD

Season Team	G	Min.	FGM	FGA	Pct.	FTM	FTA	Pct.	REBOUNDS Off.	Def.	Tot.	Ast.	PF	Dq.	Stl.	Blk.	TO	Pts.	Avg.
78-79—Los Angeles	8	226	37	77	.481	20	21	.952	7	8	15	14	28	0	9	0	14	94	11.8

BRIAN, FRANK
G

PERSONAL: Born May 1, 1923, in Zachary, La.... 6-1/180.... Full name: Frank Sands Brian.... Nickname: Flash.
HIGH SCHOOL: Zachary (La.).
COLLEGE: Louisiana State.
MISCELLANEOUS: Member of NBL championship team (1949).

COLLEGIATE RECORD

Season Team	G	Min.	FGM	FGA	Pct.	FTM	FTA	Pct.	Reb.	Pts.	Avg.
42-43—Louisiana State					Statistics unavailable.						
45-46—Louisiana State					Statistics unavailable.						
46-47—Louisiana State					Statistics unavailable.						

NBL AND NBA REGULAR-SEASON RECORD

HONORS: All-NBA second team (1950, 1951).... All-NBL first team (1949).... All-NBL second team (1948).

Season Team	G	Min.	FGM	FGA	Pct.	FTM	FTA	Pct.	Reb.	Ast.	PF	Dq.	Pts.	Avg.
47-48—Anderson (NBL)	59	...	248	...	...	155	210	.738	...	...	148	...	651	11.0
48-49—Anderson (NBL)	64	...	216	...	...	201	256	.785	...	...	144	...	633	9.9
49-50—Anderson	64	...	368	1156	.318	402	488	*.824	...	189	192	...	1138	17.8
50-51—Tri-Cities	68	...	363	1127	.322	418	508	.823	244	266	215	4	1144	16.8
51-52—Fort Wayne	66	2672	342	972	.352	367	433	.848	232	233	220	6	1051	15.9
52-53—Fort Wayne	68	1910	245	699	.351	236	297	.795	133	142	205	8	726	10.7
53-54—Fort Wayne	64	973	132	352	.375	137	182	.753	79	92	100	2	401	6.3
54-55—Fort Wayne	71	1381	237	623	.380	217	255	.851	127	142	133	0	691	9.7
55-56—Fort Wayne	37	680	78	263	.297	72	88	.818	88	74	62	0	228	6.2
Totals	561	...	2229	...	...	2205	2717	.812	...	...	1419	...	6663	11.9

NBL AND NBA PLAYOFF RECORD

Season Team	G	Min.	FGM	FGA	Pct.	FTM	FTA	Pct.	Reb.	Ast.	PF	Dq.	Pts.	Avg.
47-48—Anderson (NBL)	6	...	18	...	...	11	16	.688	...	...	...	...	47	7.8
48-49—Anderson (NBL)	7	...	26	...	...	27	32	.844	...	...	...	...	79	11.3
49-50—Anderson	8	...	26	96	.271	43	48	.896	...	19	24	...	95	11.9
51-52—Fort Wayne	2	81	6	24	.250	5	6	.833	6	9	10	0	17	8.5
52-53—Fort Wayne	8	146	13	42	.310	19	25	.760	9	11	23	1	45	5.6
53-54—Fort Wayne	4	106	15	36	.417	11	16	.688	12	10	7	0	41	10.3
54-55—Fort Wayne	11	269	48	120	.400	31	38	.816	22	27	26	0	127	11.5
55-56—Fort Wayne	10	166	26	68	.382	17	21	.810	12	17	15	0	69	6.9
Totals	56	...	178	...	...	164	202	.812	...	...	...	...	520	9.3

NBA ALL-STAR GAME RECORD

Season Team	Min.	FGM	FGA	Pct.	FTM	FTA	Pct.	Reb.	Ast.	PF	Dq.	Pts.
1951 —Tri-Cities	...	5	14	.357	4	5	.800	6	3	2	...	14
1952 —Fort Wayne	25	4	10	.400	5	6	.833	7	4	2	...	13
Totals	...	9	24	.375	9	11	.818	13	7	4	...	27

DID YOU KNOW...

...that the Orlando Magic (1-0) were the only team not to lose an overtime game in 1991-92?

BRIDGES, BILL
F

PERSONAL: Born April 4, 1939, in Hobbs, N.M. . . . 6-6/235. . . . Full name: William C. Bridges.
HIGH SCHOOL: Hobbs (N.M.).
COLLEGE: Kansas.
TRANSACTIONS/CAREER NOTES: Selected by Chicago Packers in third round (32nd pick overall) of 1961 NBA Draft. . . . Played in American Basketball League with Kansas City Steers (1961-62 and 1962-63). . . . Draft rights traded by Packers with Ralph Davis to St. Louis Hawks for Al Ferrari and Shellie McMillion (June 14, 1962). . . . Hawks franchise transfered to Atlanta for 1968-69 season. . . . Traded by Atlanta Hawks to Philadelphia 76ers for Jim Washington (November 19, 1971). . . . Traded by 76ers with Mel Counts to Los Angeles Lakers for Leroy Ellis and John Q. Trapp (November 2, 1972). . . . Waived by Lakers (December 6, 1974). . . . Signed as free agent by Golden State Warriors (March 1, 1975).
MISCELLANEOUS: Member of NBA championship team (1975).

COLLEGIATE RECORD

Season Team	G	Min.	FGM	FGA	Pct.	FTM	FTA	Pct.	Reb.	Pts.	Avg.
			Freshman team did not play intercollegiate schedule.								
57-58 —Kansas‡			117	307	.381	74	129	.574	343	308	12.3
58-59 —Kansas	25	...	112	293	.382	94	142	.662	385	318	11.4
59-60 —Kansas	28	...	146	334	.437	110	155	.710	353	402	16.1
60-61 —Kansas	25	...									
Varsity totals	78	...	375	934	.401	278	426	.653	1081	1028	13.2

ABL REGULAR-SEASON RECORD

NOTES: ABL All-Star first team (1962). . . . Member of ABL championship team (1963). . . . Holds single-game record for most points—55 (December 9, 1962, vs. Oakland).

Season Team	G	Min.	FGM	FGA	Pct.	FTM	FTA	Pct.	Reb.	Ast.	Pts.	Avg.
61-62 —Kansas City	79	3259	638	1400	.456	412	587	.702	*1059	181	1697	21.5
62-63 —Kansas City	29	1185	312	606	.515	225	289	.779	*437	87	*849	29.3
Totals	108	4444	950	2006	.474	637	876	.727	1496	268	2546	23.6

NBA REGULAR-SEASON RECORD

HONORS: NBA All-Defensive second team (1969, 1970).

Season Team	G	Min.	FGM	FGA	Pct.	FTM	FTA	Pct.	Reb.	Ast.	PF	Dq.	Pts.	Avg.
62-63 —St. Louis	27	374	66	160	.413	32	51	.627	144	23	58	0	164	6.1
63-64 —St. Louis	80	1949	268	675	.397	146	224	.652	680	181	269	6	682	8.5
64-65 —St. Louis	79	2362	362	938	.386	186	275	.676	853	187	276	3	910	11.5
65-66 —St. Louis	78	2677	377	927	.407	257	364	.706	951	208	333	11	1011	13.0
66-67 —St. Louis	79	3130	503	1106	.455	367	523	.702	1190	222	325	12	1373	17.4
67-68 —St. Louis	82	3197	466	1009	.462	347	484	.717	1102	253	*366	12	1279	15.6
68-69 —Atlanta	80	2930	351	775	.453	239	353	.677	1132	298	290	3	941	11.8
69-70 —Atlanta	82	3269	443	932	.475	331	451	.734	1145	345	292	6	1217	14.8
70-71 —Atlanta	82	3140	382	834	.458	211	330	.639	1233	240	317	7	975	11.9
71-72 —Atlanta-Philadelphia	78	2756	379	779	.487	222	316	.703	1051	198	269	6	980	12.6
72-73 —Philadelphia-Los Ang.	82	2867	333	722	.461	179	255	.702	904	219	296	3	845	10.3

Season Team	G	Min.	FGM	FGA	Pct.	FTM	FTA	Pct.	Off.	Def.	Tot.	Ast.	PF	Dq.	Stl.	Blk.	TO	Pts.	Avg.
										REBOUNDS									
73-74 —Los Angeles	65	1812	216	513	.421	116	164	.707	193	306	499	148	219	3	58	31	...	548	8.4
74-75 —L.A.-G.S.	32	415	35	93	.376	17	34	.500	64	70	134	31	65	1	11	5	...	87	2.7
Totals	926	30878	4181	9463	.442	2650	3824	.693	...	...	11054	2553	3375	73	69	36	...	11012	11.9

NBA PLAYOFF RECORD

Season Team	G	Min.	FGM	FGA	Pct.	FTM	FTA	Pct.	Reb.	Ast.	PF	Dq.	Pts.	Avg.
62-63 —St. Louis	11	204	41	96	.427	20	27	.741	86	9	31	0	102	9.3
63-64 —St. Louis	12	240	26	83	.313	12	19	.632	84	24	40	0	64	5.3
64-65 —St. Louis	4	145	21	59	.356	10	15	.667	67	9	19	1	52	13.0
65-66 —St. Louis	10	421	86	170	.506	31	43	.721	149	28	47	2	203	20.3
66-67 —St. Louis	9	369	48	128	.375	45	67	.672	169	22	36	2	141	15.7
67-68 —St. Louis	6	216	38	75	.507	18	25	.720	77	14	23	0	94	15.7
68-69 —Atlanta	11	442	69	156	.442	34	48	.708	178	37	48	2	172	15.6
69-70 —Atlanta	9	381	44	110	.400	16	27	.593	154	29	37	1	104	11.6
70-71 —Atlanta	5	229	23	58	.397	3	9	.333	104	5	17	0	49	9.8
72-73 —Los Angeles	17	582	57	136	.419	38	49	.776	158	29	68	2	152	8.9

Season Team	G	Min.	FGM	FGA	Pct.	FTM	FTA	Pct.	Off.	Def.	Tot.	Ast.	PF	Dq.	Stl.	Blk.	TO	Pts.	Avg.
										REBOUNDS									
73-74 —Los Angeles	5	144	12	41	.293	6	13	.462	14	16	30	6	19	0	7	0	...	30	6.0
74-75 —Golden State	14	148	10	23	.435	2	7	.286	13	36	49	7	23	0	9	4	...	22	1.6
Totals	113	3521	475	1135	.419	235	349	.673	...	...	1305	219	408	10	16	4	...	1185	10.5

NBA ALL-STAR GAME RECORD

Season Team	Min.	FGM	FGA	Pct.	FTM	FTA	Pct.	Reb.	Ast.	PF	Dq.	Pts.
1967 —St. Louis	17	4	5	.800	0	2	.000	3	3	1	0	8
1968 —St. Louis	21	7	9	.778	1	4	.250	7	1	4	0	15
1970 —Atlanta	15	2	2	1.000	1	5	.200	4	2	1	0	5
Totals	53	13	16	.813	2	11	.182	14	6	6	0	28

CERVI, AL
G

PERSONAL: Born February 12, 1917, in Buffalo, N.Y. . . . 5-11/185. . . . Full name: Alfred Nicholas Cervi. . . . Nickname: Digger.
HIGH SCHOOL: East (Buffalo, N.Y.).
COLLEGE: None.
TRANSACTIONS/CAREER NOTES: Played with independent teams (1935-36, 1936-37 and 1938-39 through 1944-45 seasons). . . . Syracuse Nationals franchise became part of NBA upon merger of Basketball As-

sociation of America and National Basketball League for 1949-50 season.
CAREER HONORS: Elected to Naismith Memorial Basketball Hall of Fame (1984).
MISCELLANEOUS: Member of NBL championship team (1946).

NBL AND NBA REGULAR-SEASON RECORD

HONORS: All-NBA second team (1950).... All-NBL first team (1947, 1948, 1949).... All-NBL second team (1946).

Season Team	G	Min.	FGM	FGA	Pct.	FTM	FTA	Pct.	Reb.	Ast.	PF	Dq.	Pts.	Avg.
37-38 —Buffalo (NBL)	9	...	19	...	...	6	...	...	...	...	...	...	44	4.9
45-46 —Rochester (NBL)	28	...	112	...	...	76	108	.704	...	...	21	...	300	10.7
46-47 —Rochester (NBL)	44	...	228	...	...	176	236	.746	...	...	127	...	*632	14.4
47-48 —Rochester (NBL)	49	...	234	...	...	187	242	.773	...	...	118	...	655	13.4
48-49 —Syracuse (NBL)	57	...	204	...	...	287	382	.751	...	...	170	...	695	12.2
49-50 —Syracuse	56	...	143	431	.332	287	346	.829	...	264	223	...	573	10.2
50-51 —Syracuse	53	...	132	346	.382	194	237	.819	152	208	180	9	458	8.6
51-52 —Syracuse	55	850	99	280	.354	219	248	.883	87	148	176	7	417	7.6
52-53 —Syracuse	38	301	31	71	.437	81	100	.810	22	28	90	2	143	3.8
Totals	389	...	1202	...	...	1513	...	...	...	...	...	...	3917	10.1

NBL AND NBA PLAYOFF RECORD

Season Team	G	Min.	FGM	FGA	Pct.	FTM	FTA	Pct.	Reb.	Ast.	PF	Dq.	Pts.	Avg.
45-46 —Rochester (NBL)	7	...	23	...	...	24	30	.800	...	...	...	...	70	10.0
46-47 —Rochester (NBL)	11	...	49	...	...	50	68	.735	...	...	...	...	148	13.5
47-48 —Rochester (NBL)	6	...	18	...	...	14	19	.737	...	...	...	...	50	8.3
48-49 —Syracuse (NBL)	6	...	12	...	...	22	30	.733	...	...	...	...	46	7.7
49-50 —Syracuse	11	...	23	68	.338	38	46	.826	...	52	36	...	84	7.6
50-51 —Syracuse	7	...	17	56	.304	44	50	.880	33	38	31	1	78	11.1
51-52 —Syracuse	7	88	7	30	.233	22	23	.957	10	15	23	1	36	5.1
52-53 —Syracuse	2	28	3	5	.600	12	15	.800	0	1	12	1	18	9.0
Totals	57	...	152	...	...	226	281	.804	...	...	...	...	530	9.3

HEAD COACHING RECORD

HONORS: NBL Coach of the Year (1949).

NBL AND NBA COACHING RECORD

Season Team		REGULAR SEASON					PLAYOFFS		
	W	L	Pct.	Finish		W	L	Pct.	
48-49 —Syracuse (NBL)	40	23	.635	2nd/Eastern Division		3	3	.500	
49-50 —Syracuse	51	13	.797	1st/Eastern Division		6	5	.545	
50-51 —Syracuse	32	34	.485	4th/Eastern Division		4	3	.571	
51-52 —Syracuse	40	26	.606	1st/Eastern Division		3	4	.429	
52-53 —Syracuse	47	24	.662	2nd/Eastern Division		0	2	.000	
53-54 —Syracuse	42	30	.583	3rd/Eastern Division		9	4	.692	
54-55 —Syracuse	43	29	.597	1st/Eastern Division		7	4	.636	
55-56 —Syracuse	35	37	.493	3rd/Eastern Division		5	4	.555	
56-57 —Syracuse	4	8	.333			—	—	—	
58-59 —Philadelphia	32	40	.444	4th/Eastern Division		—	—	—	
Totals (10 years)	366	264	.581	Totals (8 years)		37	29	.561	

NOTES:
1949— Defeated Hammond, 2-0, in Eastern Division first round; lost to Anderson, 3-1, in Eastern Division finals.
1950— Defeated Philadelphia, 2-0, in Eastern Division semifinals; defeated New York, 2-1, in Eastern Division finals; lost to Minneapolis, 4-2, in World Championship Series.
1951— Defeated Philadelphia, 2-0, in Eastern Division semifinals; lost to New York, 3-2, in Eastern Division finals.
1952— Defeated Philadelphia, 2-1, in Eastern Division semifinals; lost to New York, 3-1, in Eastern Division finals.
1953— Lost to Boston in Eastern Division semifinals.
1954— Defeated Boston, 96-95 (OT); defeated New York, 75-68; defeated New York, 103-99; and defeated Boston, 98-85, in Eastern Division round robin; defeated Boston, 2-0, in Eastern Division finals; lost to Minneapolis, 4-3, in World Championship Series.
1955— Defeated Boston, 3-1, in Eastern Division finals; defeated Fort Wayne, 4-3, in World Championship Series.
1956— Defeated New York, 82-77, in Eastern Division third-place game; Defeated Boston, 2-1, in Eastern Division semifinals; lost to Philadelphia, 3-2, in Eastern Divsion finals. Replaced as Syracuse head coach by Paul Seymour (November).

CHAMBERLAIN, WILT
C

PERSONAL: Born August 21, 1936, in Philadelphia. ...
7-1/275. ... Full name: Wilton Norman Chamberlain. ...
Nickname: Wilt the Stilt and The Big Dipper.
HIGH SCHOOL: Overbrook (Philadelphia).

COLLEGE: Kansas.
TRANSACTIONS/CAREER NOTES: Played with Harlem Globetrotters during 1958-59 season. ... Selected by Philadelphia Warriors in 1959 NBA Draft (territorial pick). ... Warriors franchise moved from Philadelphia to San Francisco for 1962-63 season. ... Traded by Warriors to Philadelphia 76ers for Paul Neumann, Connie Dierking, Lee Shaffer and cash (January 15, 1965). ... Traded by 76ers to Los Angeles Lakers for Jerry Chambers, Archie Clark and Darrall Imhoff (July 9, 1968).
CAREER HONORS: Elected to Naismith Memorial Basketball Hall of Fame (1978). ... NBA 35th Anniversary All-Time team (1980).
MISCELLANEOUS: Member of NBA championship teams (1967, 1972).

COLLEGIATE RECORD

NOTES: THE SPORTING NEWS All-America first team (1958).

Season Team	G	Min.	FGM	FGA	Pct.	FTM	FTA	Pct.	Reb.	Pts.	Avg.
55-56 —Kansas‡			Freshman team did not play intercollegiate schedule.								
56-57 —Kansas	27	...	275	588	.468	250	399	.627	510	800	29.6
57-58 —Kansas	21	...	228	482	.473	177	291	.608	367	633	30.1
Varsity totals	48	...	503	1070	.470	427	690	.619	877	1433	29.9

NBA REGULAR-SEASON RECORD

RECORDS: Holds career records for most free throws attempted—11,862; most rebounds—23,924; and highest rebounds-per-game average (minimum 400 games)—22.9. . . . Holds single-season records for most minutes played—3,882 (1962); most points—4,029 (1962); highest points-per-game average—50.4 (1962); most points by a rookie—2,707 (1960); most field goals made—1,597 (1962); most consecutive field goals made—35 (February 17 through February 28, 1967); most field goals attempted—3,159 (1962); highest field goal percentage—.727 (1973); most free throws attempted—1,363 (1962); most rebounds—2,149 (1961); most rebounds by a rookie—1,941 (1960); and highest rebounds-per-game average—27.2 (1961). . . . Holds single-game records for most points—100; most points in one half—59; most field goals made—36; most field goals made in one half—22; most field goals attempted—63; most field goals attempted in one half—37; and most field goals attempted in one quarter—21 (March 2, 1962, vs. New York at Hershey, Pa.). . . . Holds single-game records for most points by a rookie—58 (January 25, 1960, vs. Detroit); highest field-goal percentage (minimum 15 made)—1.000 (January 20, 1967, vs. Los Angeles, 15/15; February 24, 1967, vs. Baltimore, 18/18; and March 19, 1967, vs. Baltimore, 16/16); most rebounds—55 (November 24, 1960, vs. Boston); and most rebounds by a rookie—45 (February 6, 1960, vs. Syracuse). . . . Shares single-game record for most free throws made—28 (March 2, 1962, vs. New York at Hershey, Pa.).

HONORS: NBA Most Valuable Player (1960, 1966, 1967, 1968). . . . NBA Rookie of the Year (1960). . . . All-NBA first team (1960, 1961, 1962, 1964, 1966, 1967, 1968). . . . All-NBA second team (1963, 1965, 1972). . . . NBA All-Defensive first team (1972, 1973).

NOTES: Led NBA with 27 rebounds per game (1960), 27.2 rebounds per game (1961), 25.7 rebounds per game (1962), 24.3 rebounds per game (1963), 24.6 rebounds per game (1966), 24.2 rebounds per game (1967), 23.8 rebounds per game (1968), 21.1 rebounds per game (1969), 18.2 rebounds per game (1971), 19.2 rebounds per game (1972) and 18.6 rebounds per game (1973). . . . Led NBA with 8.6 assists per game (1968).

Season	Team	G	Min.	FGM	FGA	Pct.	FTM	FTA	Pct.	Reb.	Ast.	PF	Dq.	Pts.	Avg.
59-60	Philadelphia	72	3338	*1065	*2311	.461	577	*991	.582	*1941	168	150	0	*2707	*37.6
60-61	Philadelphia	79	*3773	*1251	*2457	.509	531	*1054	.504	*2149	148	130	0	*3033	*38.4
61-62	Philadelphia	80	*3882	*1597	*3159	.506	*835	*1363	.613	*2052	192	123	0	*4029	*50.4
62-63	San Francisco	80	*3806	*1463	*2770	.528	660	*1113	.593	*1946	275	136	0	*3586	*44.8
63-64	San Francisco	80	*3689	*1204	*2298	.524	540	*1016	.532	1787	403	182	0	*2948	*36.9
64-65	San Fran.-Philadelphia	73	3301	*1063	*2083	*.510	408	*880	.464	1673	250	146	0	*2534	*34.7
65-66	Philadelphia	79	*3737	*1074	*1990	*.540	501	976	.513	*1943	414	171	0	*2649	*33.5
66-67	Philadelphia	81	*3682	785	1150	*.683	386	*875	.441	*1957	630	143	0	1956	24.1
67-68	Philadelphia	82	*3836	819	1377	.595	354	*932	.380	*1952	*702	160	0	1992	24.3
68-69	Los Angeles	81	3669	641	1099	*.583	382	*857	.446	*1712	366	142	0	1664	20.5
69-70	Los Angeles	12	505	129	227	.568	70	157	.446	221	49	31	0	328	27.3
70-71	Los Angeles	82	3630	668	1226	.545	360	669	.538	*1493	352	174	0	1696	20.7
71-72	Los Angeles	82	3469	496	764	*.649	221	524	.422	*1572	329	196	0	1213	14.8
72-73	Los Angeles	82	3542	426	586	*.727	232	455	.510	*1526	365	191	0	1084	13.2
Totals		1045	47859	12681	23497	.540	6057	11862	.511	23924	4643	2075	0	31419	30.1

NBA PLAYOFF RECORD

NOTES: NBA Finals Most Valuable Player (1972). . . . Holds career record for most free throws attempted—1,627. . . . Holds NBA Finals single-game record for most rebounds in one half—26 (April 16, 1967, vs. San Francisco). . . . Shares NBA Finals single-game record for most free throws attempted in one quarter—11 (April 16, 1967, vs. San Francisco). . . . Holds single-series record for highest rebounds-per-game average—32.0 (1967). . . . Holds single-game records for most rebounds—41 (April 5, 1967, vs. Boston); most rebounds in one half—26 (April 16, 1967, vs. San Francisco); and most points by a rookie—53 (March 14, 1960, vs. Syracuse). . . . Shares single-game records for most field-goals made—24 (March 14, 1960, vs. Syracuse); most field goals attempted—48 (March 22, 1962, vs. Syracuse); and most field goals attempted in one half—25 (March 22, 1962, vs. Syracuse).

Season	Team	G	Min.	FGM	FGA	Pct.	FTM	FTA	Pct.	Reb.	Ast.	PF	Dq.	Pts.	Avg.
59-60	Philadelphia	9	415	125	252	.496	49	110	.445	232	19	17	0	299	33.2
60-61	Philadelphia	3	144	45	96	.469	21	38	.553	69	6	10	0	111	37.0
61-62	Philadelphia	12	576	162	347	.467	96	151	.636	319	37	27	0	420	35.0
63-64	San Francisco	12	558	175	322	.543	66	139	.475	302	39	27	0	416	34.7
64-65	Philadelphia	11	536	123	232	.530	76	136	.559	299	48	29	0	322	29.3
65-66	Philadelphia	5	240	56	110	.509	28	68	.412	151	15	10	0	140	28.0
66-67	Philadelphia	15	718	132	228	.579	62	160	.388	437	135	37	0	326	21.7
67-68	Philadelphia	13	631	124	232	.534	60	158	.380	321	85	29	0	308	23.7
68-69	Los Angeles	18	832	96	176	.545	58	148	.392	444	46	56	0	250	13.9
69-70	Los Angeles	18	851	158	288	.549	82	202	.406	399	81	42	0	398	22.1
70-71	Los Angeles	12	554	85	187	.455	50	97	.515	242	53	33	0	220	18.3
71-72	Los Angeles	15	703	80	142	.563	60	122	.492	315	49	47	0	220	14.7
72-73	Los Angeles	17	801	64	116	.552	49	98	.500	383	60	48	0	177	10.4
Totals		160	7559	1425	2728	.522	757	1627	.465	3913	673	412	0	3607	22.5

NBA ALL-STAR GAME RECORD

NOTES: NBA All-Star Game Most Valuable Player (1960). . . . Holds career record for most rebounds—197. . . . Holds single-game records for most points—42 (1962); most free throws attempted—16 (1962); and most field goals made in one half—10 (1962). . . . Shares single-game records for most points in one half—23 (1962); most field goals made—17 (1962); and most rebounds in one half—16 (1960).

Season	Team	Min.	FGM	FGA	Pct.	FTM	FTA	Pct.	Reb.	Ast.	PF	Dq.	Pts.
1960	Philadelphia	30	9	20	.450	5	7	.714	25	2	1	0	23
1961	Philadelphia	38	2	8	.250	8	15	.533	18	5	1	0	12
1962	Philadelphia	37	17	23	.739	8	16	.500	24	1	4	0	42
1963	San Francisco	35	7	11	.636	3	7	.429	19	0	2	0	17
1964	San Francisco	37	4	14	.286	11	14	.786	20	1	2	0	19
1965	San Francisco	31	9	15	.600	2	8	.250	16	1	4	0	20
1966	Philadelphia	25	8	11	.727	5	9	.556	21	2	2	0	21
1967	Philadelphia	39	6	7	.857	2	5	.400	22	4	1	0	14
1968	Philadelphia	25	3	4	.750	1	4	.250	7	6	2	0	7
1969	Los Angeles	27	2	3	.667	0	1	.000	12	2	2	0	4
1971	Los Angeles	18	1	1	1.000	0	0	. . .	8	5	0	0	2
1972	Los Angeles	24	3	3	1.000	2	8	.250	10	3	2	0	8
1973	Los Angeles	22	1	2	.500	0	0	. . .	7	3	3	0	2
Totals		388	72	122	.590	47	94	.500	197	36	23	0	191

ABA COACHING RECORD

Season Team								PLAYOFFS		
	W	L	Pct.	Finish				W	L	Pct.
73-74 — San Diego	37	47	.440	T4th/Western Division				2	4	.333
Totals (1 year)	37	47	.440	Totals (1 year)				2	4	.333

NOTES:
1974— Lost to Utah in Western Division semifinals.

COUSY, BOB
G

PERSONAL: Born August 9, 1928, in New York. . . . 6-1/175. . . . Full name: Robert Joseph Cousy. . . . Nickname: Houdini of the Hardwood.
HIGH SCHOOL: Andrew Jackson (Queens, N.Y.).
COLLEGE: Holy Cross.

TRANSACTIONS/CAREER NOTES: Selected by Tri-Cities Blackhawks in first round of 1950 NBA Draft. . . . Traded by Blackhawks to Chicago Stags for Gene Vance (1950). . . . NBA rights drawn out of a hat by Boston Celtics for $8,500 in dispersal of Chicago Stags franchise (1950). . . . Traded by Celtics to Cincinnati Royals for Bill Dinwiddie (November 18, 1969).
CAREER HONORS: Elected to Naismith Memorial Basketball Hall of Fame (1970). . . . NBA 25th Anniversary All-Time team (1970) and 35th Anniversary All-Time team (1980).
MISCELLANEOUS: Member of NBA championship teams (1957, 1959, 1960, 1961, 1962, 1963). . . . Commissioner of American Soccer League (1975 through mid-1980 season).

COLLEGIATE RECORD

NOTES: THE SPORTING NEWS All-America first team (1950). . . . THE SPORTING NEWS All-America second team (1949). . . . Member of NCAA championship team (1947).

Season Team	G	Min.	FGM	FGA	Pct.	FTM	FTA	Pct.	Reb.	Pts.	Avg.
46-47 — Holy Cross	30	...	91	...	...	45	...	...	...	227	7.6
47-48 — Holy Cross	30	...	207	...	...	72	108	.667	...	486	16.2
48-49 — Holy Cross	27	...	195	...	...	90	134	.672	...	480	17.8
49-50 — Holy Cross	30	...	216	659	.328	150	199	.754	...	582	19.4
Totals	117	...	709	...	...	357	...	...	...	1775	15.2

NBA REGULAR-SEASON RECORD

RECORDS: Holds single-game record for most assists in one half—19 (February 27, 1959, vs. Minneapolis).
HONORS: NBA Most Valuable Player (1957). . . . All-NBA first team (1952, 1953, 1954, 1955, 1956, 1957, 1958, 1959, 1960, 1961). . . . All-NBA second team (1962, 1963).
NOTES: Led NBA with 7.7 assists per game (1953), 7.2 assists per game (1954), 7.8 assists per game (1955), 8.9 assists per game (1956), 7.5 assists per game (1957), 7.1 assists per game (1958), 8.6 assists per game (1959) and 9.5 assists per game (1960).

Season Team	G	Min.	FGM	FGA	Pct.	FTM	FTA	Pct.	Reb.	Ast.	PF	Dq.	Pts.	Avg.
50-51 — Boston	69	...	401	1138	.352	276	365	.756	474	341	185	2	1078	15.6
51-52 — Boston	66	2681	512	1388	.369	409	506	.808	421	441	190	5	1433	21.7
52-53 — Boston	71	2945	464	*1320	.352	479	587	.816	449	*547	227	4	1407	19.8
53-54 — Boston	72	2857	486	1262	.385	411	522	.787	394	*518	201	3	1383	19.2
54-55 — Boston	71	2747	522	1316	.397	460	570	.807	424	*557	165	1	1504	21.2
55-56 — Boston	72	2767	440	1223	.360	476	564	.844	492	*642	206	2	1356	18.8
56-57 — Boston	64	2364	478	1264	.378	363	442	.821	309	*478	134	0	1319	20.6
57-58 — Boston	65	2222	445	1262	.353	277	326	.850	322	*463	136	1	1167	18.0
58-59 — Boston	65	2403	484	1260	.384	329	385	.855	359	*557	135	0	1297	20.0
59-60 — Boston	75	2588	568	1481	.384	319	403	.792	352	*715	146	2	1455	19.4
60-61 — Boston	76	2468	513	1382	.371	352	452	.779	331	587	196	0	1378	18.1
61-62 — Boston	75	2114	462	1181	.391	251	333	.754	261	584	135	0	1175	15.7
62-63 — Boston	76	1975	392	988	.397	219	298	.735	193	515	175	0	1003	13.2
69-70 — Cincinnati	7	34	1	3	.333	3	3	1.000	5	10	11	0	5	0.7
Totals	924	...	6168	16468	.375	4624	5756	.803	4786	6955	2242	20	16960	18.4

NBA PLAYOFF RECORD

NOTES: Shares NBA Finals single-game record for most assists in one quarter—8 (April 9, 1957, vs. St. Louis). . . . Holds single-game records for most free throws made—30; and most free throws attempted—32 (March 21, 1953, vs. Syracuse).

Season Team	G	Min.	FGM	FGA	Pct.	FTM	FTA	Pct.	Reb.	Ast.	PF	Dq.	Pts.	Avg.
50-51 — Boston	2	...	9	42	.214	10	12	.833	15	12	8	...	28	14.0
51-52 — Boston	3	138	26	65	.400	41	44	.932	12	19	13	1	93	31.0
52-53 — Boston	6	270	46	120	.383	61	73	.836	25	37	21	0	153	25.5
53-54 — Boston	6	260	33	116	.284	60	75	.800	32	38	20	0	126	21.0
54-55 — Boston	7	299	53	139	.381	46	48	.958	43	65	26	0	152	21.7
55-56 — Boston	3	124	28	56	.500	23	25	.920	24	26	4	0	79	26.3
56-57 — Boston	10	440	67	207	.324	68	91	.747	61	93	27	0	202	20.2
57-58 — Boston	11	457	67	196	.342	64	75	.853	71	82	20	0	198	18.0
58-59 — Boston	11	460	72	221	.326	70	94	.745	76	119	28	0	214	19.5
59-60 — Boston	13	468	80	262	.305	39	51	.765	48	116	27	0	199	15.3
60-61 — Boston	10	337	50	147	.340	67	88	.761	43	91	33	1	167	16.7
61-62 — Boston	14	474	86	241	.357	52	76	.684	64	123	43	0	224	16.0
62-63 — Boston	13	413	72	204	.353	39	47	.830	32	116	44	2	183	14.1
Totals	109	...	689	2016	.342	640	799	.801	546	937	314	...	2018	18.5

NBA ALL-STAR GAME RECORD

NOTES: NBA All-Star Game Most Valuable Player (1954, 1957).

Season Team	Min.	FGM	FGA	Pct.	FTM	FTA	Pct.	Reb.	Ast.	PF	Dq.	Pts.
1951 — Boston	...	2	12	.167	4	5	.800	9	8	3	0	8
1952 — Boston	33	4	14	.286	1	2	.500	4	13	3	0	9
1953 — Boston	36	4	11	.364	7	7	1.000	5	3	1	0	15

ALL-TIME GREAT PLAYERS

Season	Team	Min.	FGM	FGA	Pct.	FTM	FTA	Pct.	Reb.	Ast.	PF	Dq.	Pts.
1954	—Boston	34	6	15	.400	8	8	1.000	11	4	1	0	20
1955	—Boston	35	7	14	.500	6	7	.857	9	5	1	0	20
1956	—Boston	24	2	8	.250	3	4	.750	7	2	6	1	7
1957	—Boston	28	4	14	.286	2	2	1.000	5	7	0	0	10
1958	—Boston	31	8	20	.400	4	6	.667	5	10	0	0	20
1959	—Boston	32	4	8	.500	5	6	.833	5	4	0	0	13
1960	—Boston	26	1	7	.143	0	0	. . .	5	8	2	0	2
1961	—Boston	33	2	11	.182	0	0	. . .	3	8	6	1	4
1962	—Boston	31	4	13	.308	3	4	.750	6	8	2	0	11
1963	—Boston	25	4	11	.364	0	0	. . .	4	6	2	0	8
Totals		. . .	52	158	.329	43	51	.843	78	86	27	2	147

COLLEGIATE COACHING RECORD

Season	Team	W	L	Pct.	Finish
63-64	—Boston College	10	11	.476	
64-65	—Boston College	22	7	.759	
65-66	—Boston College	21	5	.808	
66-67	—Boston College	23	3	.885	
67-68	—Boston College	17	8	.680	
68-69	—Boston College	24	4	.857	
Totals (6 years)		117	38	.755	

NBA COACHING RECORD

Season	Team	REGULAR SEASON				PLAYOFFS		
		W	L	Pct.	Finish	W	L	Pct.
69-70	—Cincinnati	36	46	.439	5th/Eastern Division	—	—	—
70-71	—Cincinnati	33	49	.402	3rd/Central Division	—	—	—
71-72	—Cincinnati	30	52	.366	3rd/Central Division	—	—	—
72-73	—Kansas City/Omaha	36	46	.439	4th/Midwest Division	—	—	—
73-74	—Kansas City/Omaha	6	16	.273		—	—	—
Totals (5 years)		141	209	.403		—	—	—

NOTES:
1965— Lost to St. John's, 114-92, in NIT first round.
1966— Defeated Louisville, 96-90 (3 OT), in NIT first round; lost to Villanova, 86-85, in quarterfinals.
1967— Defeated Connecticut, 48-42, in NCAA Tournament first round; defeated St. John's, 63-62, in regional semifinal; lost to North Carolina, 96-80, in regional final.
1968— Lost to St. Bonaventure, 102-93, in NCAA Tournament first round.
1969— Defeated Kansas, 78-62, in NIT first round; defeated Louisville, 88-83, in quarterfinals; defeated Army, 73-61, in semifinals; lost to Temple 89-76, in championship game.
1973— Replaced as Kansas City/Omaha head coach by Draff Young (November).

COWENS, DAVE
C/F

PERSONAL: Born October 25, 1948, in Newport, Ky. . . . 6-9/230. . . . Full name: David William Cowens.
HIGH SCHOOL: Newport Central Catholic (Ky.).
COLLEGE: Florida State.
TRANSACTIONS/CAREER NOTES: Selected by Boston Celtics in first round (fourth pick overall) of 1970 NBA Draft. . . . Traded by Celtics to Milwaukee Bucks for Quinn Buckner (September 9, 1982).
CAREER HONORS: Elected to Naismith Memorial Basketball Hall of Fame (1990).
MISCELLANEOUS: Member of NBA championship teams (1974, 1976).

COLLEGIATE RECORD

NOTES: THE SPORTING NEWS All-America second team (1970).

Season	Team	G	Min.	FGM	FGA	Pct.	FTM	FTA	Pct.	Reb.	Pts.	Avg.
66-67	—Florida State‡	18	. . .	105	208	.505	49	90	.544	357	259	14.4
67-68	—Florida State	27	. . .	206	383	.538	96	131	.733	456	508	18.8
68-69	—Florida State	25	. . .	202	384	.526	104	164	.634	437	508	20.3
69-70	—Florida State	26	. . .	174	355	.490	115	169	.680	447	463	17.8
Varsity totals		78	. . .	582	1122	.519	315	464	.679	1340	1479	19.0

NBA REGULAR-SEASON RECORD

HONORS: NBA Most Valuable Player (1973). . . . NBA co-Rookie of the Year (1971). . . . All-NBA second team (1973, 1975, 1976). . . . NBA All-Defensive first team (1976). . . . NBA All-Defensive second team (1975, 1980). . . . NBA All-Rookie team (1971).

Season	Team	G	Min.	FGM	FGA	Pct.	FTM	FTA	Pct.	Reb.	Ast.	PF	Dq.	Pts.	Avg.
70-71	—Boston	81	3076	550	1302	.422	273	373	.732	1216	228	*350	15	1373	17.0
71-72	—Boston	79	3186	657	1357	.484	175	243	.720	1203	245	*314	10	1489	18.8
72-73	—Boston	82	3425	740	1637	.452	204	262	.779	1329	333	311	7	1684	20.5

Season	Team	G	Min.	FGM	FGA	Pct.	FTM	FTA	Pct.	REBOUNDS			Ast.	PF	Dq.	Stl.	Blk.	TO	Pts.	Avg.
										Off.	Def.	Tot.								
73-74	—Boston	80	3352	645	1475	.437	228	274	.832	264	993	1257	354	294	7	95	101	. . .	1518	19.0
74-75	—Boston	65	2632	569	1199	.475	191	244	.783	229	729	958	296	243	7	87	73	. . .	1329	20.4
75-76	—Boston	78	3101	611	1305	.468	257	340	.756	335	911	1246	325	314	10	94	71	. . .	1479	19.0
76-77	—Boston	50	1888	328	756	.434	162	198	.818	147	550	697	248	181	7	46	49	. . .	818	16.4
77-78	—Boston	77	3215	598	1220	.490	239	284	.842	248	830	1078	351	297	5	102	67	217	1435	18.6
78-79	—Boston	68	2517	488	1010	.483	151	187	.807	152	500	652	242	263	16	76	51	174	1127	16.6
79-80	—Boston	66	2159	422	932	.453	95	122	.779	126	408	534	206	216	2	69	61	108	940	14.2
80-81	—								Did not play—retired.											
81-82	—								Did not play—retired.											
82-83	—Milwaukee	40	1014	136	306	.444	52	63	.825	73	201	274	82	137	4	30	15	44	324	8.1
Totals		766	29565	5744	12499	.460	2027	2590	.783	. . .	. . .	10444	2910	2920	90	599	488	543	13516	17.6

Three-point field goals: 1979-80, 1-for-12 (.083). 1982-83, 0-for-2. Totals, 1-for-14 (.071).

NBA PLAYOFF RECORD

NOTES: Shares single-game record for most defensive rebounds—20 (April 22, 1975, vs. Houston; and May 1, 1977, vs. Philadelphia).

Season Team	G	Min.	FGM	FGA	Pct.	FTM	FTA	Pct.	Reb.	Ast.	PF	Dq.	Pts.	Avg.
71-72 —Boston	11	441	71	156	.455	28	47	.596	152	33	50	2	170	15.5
72-73 —Boston	13	598	129	273	.473	27	41	.659	216	48	54	2	285	21.9

| | | | | | | | | — REBOUNDS — | | | | | | | | |

Season Team	G	Min.	FGM	FGA	Pct.	FTM	FTA	Pct.	Off.	Def.	Tot.	Ast.	PF	Dq.	Stl.	Blk.	TO	Pts.	Avg.
73-74 —Boston	18	772	161	370	.435	47	59	.797	60	180	240	66	85	2	21	17	...	369	20.5
74-75 —Boston	11	479	101	236	.428	23	26	.885	49	132	181	46	50	2	18	6	...	225	20.5
75-76 —Boston	18	798	156	341	.457	66	87	.759	87	209	296	85	84	4	22	13	...	378	21.0
76-77 —Boston	9	379	66	148	.446	17	22	.773	29	105	134	36	37	3	8	13	...	149	16.6
79-80 —Boston	9	301	49	103	.476	10	11	.909	18	48	66	21	37	0	9	7	8	108	12.0
Totals	89	3768	733	1627	.451	218	293	.744	...	...	1285	333	398	15	78	56	8	1684	18.9

Three-point field goals: 1979-80, 0-for-2.

NBA ALL-STAR GAME RECORD

NOTES: NBA All-Star Game Most Valuable Player (1973).

Season Team	Min.	FGM	FGA	Pct.	FTM	FTA	Pct.	Reb.	Ast.	PF	Dq.	Pts.
1972 —Boston	32	5	12	.417	4	5	.800	20	1	4	0	14
1973 —Boston	30	7	15	.467	1	1	1.000	13	1	2	0	15

| | | | | | | | — REBOUNDS — | | | | | | | |

Season Team	Min.	FGM	FGA	Pct.	FTM	FTA	Pct.	Off.	Def.	Tot.	Ast.	PF	Dq.	Stl.	Blk.	TO	Pts.
1974 —Boston	26	5	10	.500	1	3	.333	6	6	12	1	3	0	0	1	...	11
1975 —Boston	15	3	7	.429	0	0	...	0	6	6	3	4	0	1	0	...	6
1976 —Boston	23	6	13	.462	4	5	.800	8	8	16	1	3	0	1	0	...	16
1977 —Boston							Selected, did not play—injured.										
1978 —Boston	28	7	9	.778	0	0	...	6	8	14	5	5	0	2	0	2	14
Totals	154	33	66	.500	10	14	.714	...	...	81	12	21	0	4	1	2	76

NBA COACHING RECORD

		REGULAR SEASON				PLAYOFFS		
Season Team	W	L	Pct.	Finish		W	L	Pct.
78-79 —Boston	27	41	.397	5th/Atlantic Division		—	—	—
Totals (1 year)	27	41	.397					

CBA COACHING RECORD

		REGULAR SEASON				PLAYOFFS		
Season Team	W	L	Pct.	Finish		W	L	Pct.
84-85 —Bay State	20	28	.417	6th/Atlantic Division		—	—	—
Totals (1 year)	20	28	.417					

NOTES:
1978— Replaced Satch Sanders as Boston head coach (November), with record of 2-12.

DANTLEY, ADRIAN
F/G

PERSONAL: Born February 28, 1956, in Washington, D.C. ... 6-5/210. ... Full name: Adrian Delano Dantley.
HIGH SCHOOL: DeMatha Catholic (Hyattsville, Md.).
COLLEGE: Notre Dame.

TRANSACTIONS/CAREER NOTES: Selected by Buffalo Braves in first round (sixth pick overall) of 1976 NBA Draft. ... Traded by Braves with Mike Bantom to Indiana Pacers for Billy Knight (September 1, 1977). ... Traded by Pacers with Dave Robisch to Los Angeles Lakers for James Edwards, Earl Tatum and cash (December 13, 1977). ... Traded by Lakers to Utah Jazz for Spencer Haywood (September 13, 1979). ... Traded by Jazz with 1987 and 1990 second-round draft choices to Detroit Pistons for Kelly Tripucka and Kent Benson (August 21, 1986). ... Traded by Pistons with 1991 first-round draft choice to Dallas Mavericks for Mark Aguirre (February 15, 1989). ... Waived by Mavericks (April 2, 1990). ... Signed as free agent by Milwaukee Bucks (April 2, 1991). ... Played in Italy (1991-92).
MISCELLANEOUS: Member of gold-medal-winning U.S. Olympic team (1976).

COLLEGIATE RECORD

NOTES: THE SPORTING NEWS All-America first team (1975, 1976).

Season Team	G	Min.	FGM	FGA	Pct.	FTM	FTA	Pct.	Reb.	Pts.	Avg.
73-74 —Notre Dame	28	795	189	339	.558	133	161	.826	255	511	18.3
74-75 —Notre Dame	29	1091	315	581	.542	253	314	.806	296	883	30.4
75-76 —Notre Dame	29	1056	300	510	.588	229	294	.779	292	829	28.6
Totals	86	2942	804	1430	.562	615	769	.800	843	2223	25.8

NBA REGULAR-SEASON RECORD

RECORDS: Shares single-game record for most free throws made—28 (January 4, 1984, vs. Houston); and most free throws made in one quarter—14 (December 10, 1986, vs. Sacramento).
HONORS: NBA Rookie of the Year (1977). ... All-NBA second team (1981, 1984). ... NBA All-Rookie team (1977). ... NBA Comeback Player of the Year (1984).

| | | | | | | | | | — REBOUNDS — | | | | | | | | |

Season Team	G	Min.	FGM	FGA	Pct.	FTM	FTA	Pct.	Off.	Def.	Tot.	Ast.	PF	Dq.	Stl.	Blk.	TO	Pts.	Avg.
76-77 —Buffalo	77	2816	544	1046	.520	476	582	.818	251	336	587	144	215	2	91	15	...	1564	20.3
77-78 —Ind.-L.A.	79	2933	578	1128	.512	541	680	.796	265	355	620	253	233	2	118	24	228	1697	21.5
78-79 —Los Angeles .	60	1775	374	733	.510	292	342	.854	131	211	342	138	162	0	63	12	155	1040	17.3
79-80 —Utah	68	2674	730	1267	.576	443	526	.842	183	333	516	191	211	2	96	14	233	1903	28.0
80-81 —Utah	80	*3417	*909	1627	.559	*632	784	.806	192	317	509	322	245	1	109	18	282	*2452	*30.7
81-82 —Utah	81	3222	904	1586	.570	*648	818	.792	231	283	514	324	252	1	95	14	299	2457	30.3
82-83 —Utah	22	887	233	402	.580	210	248	.847	58	82	140	105	62	2	20	0	81	676	30.7
83-84 —Utah	79	2984	802	1438	.558	*813	*946	.859	179	269	448	310	201	0	61	4	263	*2418	*30.6

Season Team	G	Min.	FGM	FGA	Pct.	FTM	FTA	Pct.	REBOUNDS Off.	Def.	Tot.	Ast.	PF	Dq.	Stl.	Blk.	TO	Pts.	Avg.
84-85 —Utah	55	1971	512	964	.531	438	545	.804	148	175	323	186	133	0	57	8	171	1462	26.6
85-86 —Utah	76	2744	818	1453	.563	630	796	.791	178	217	395	264	206	2	64	4	231	2267	29.8
86-87 —Detroit	81	2736	601	1126	.534	539	664	.812	104	228	332	162	193	1	63	7	181	1742	21.5
87-88 —Detroit	69	2144	444	863	.514	492	572	.860	84	143	227	171	144	0	39	10	135	1380	20.0
88-89 —Detroit-Dal..	73	2422	470	954	.493	460	568	.810	117	200	317	171	186	1	43	13	163	1400	19.2
89-90 —Dallas	45	1300	231	484	.477	200	254	.787	78	94	172	80	99	0	20	7	75	662	14.7
90-91 —Milwaukee ...	10	126	19	50	.380	18	26	.692	8	5	13	9	8	0	5	0	6	57	5.7
Totals	955	34151	8169	15121	.540	6832	8351	.818	2207	3248	5455	2830	2550	14	944	150	2503	23177	24.3

Three-point field goals: 1979-80, 0-for-2. 1980-81, 2-for-7 (.286). 1981-82, 1-for-3 (.333). 1983-84, 1-for-4 (.250). 1985-86, 1-for-11 (.091). 1986-87, 1-for-6 (.167). 1987-88, 0-for-2. 1988-89, 0-for-1. 1989-90, 0-for-2. 1990-91, 1-for-3 (.333). Totals, 7-for-41 (.171).

NBA PLAYOFF RECORD

Season Team	G	Min.	FGM	FGA	Pct.	FTM	FTA	Pct.	REBOUNDS Off.	Def.	Tot.	Ast.	PF	Dq.	Stl.	Blk.	TO	Pts.	Avg.
77-78 —Los Angeles .	3	104	20	35	.571	11	17	.647	9	16	25	11	9	0	5	3	6	51	17.0
78-79 —Los Angeles .	8	236	50	89	.562	41	52	.788	10	23	33	11	24	0	6	1	19	141	17.6
83-84 —Utah	11	454	117	232	.504	120	139	.863	37	46	83	46	30	0	10	1	38	354	32.2
84-85 —Utah	10	398	79	151	.523	95	122	.779	25	50	75	20	39	1	16	0	36	253	25.3
85-86 —Utah							Did not play—injured.												
86-87 —Detroit	15	500	111	206	.539	86	111	.775	29	39	68	35	36	0	13	0	33	308	20.5
87-88 —Detroit	23	804	153	292	.524	140	178	.787	37	70	107	46	50	0	19	1	51	446	19.4
90-91 —Milwaukee ...	3	19	1	7	.143	3	4	.750	2	2	4	0	0	0	0	2	5	1.7
Totals	73	2515	531	1012	.525	496	623	.796	149	246	395	169	188	1	69	6	185	1558	21.3

Three-point field goals: 1984-85, 0-for-1. 1987-88, 0-for-2. Totals, 0-for-3.

NBA ALL-STAR GAME RECORD

Season Team	Min.	FGM	FGA	Pct.	FTM	FTA	Pct.	REBOUNDS Off.	Def.	Tot.	Ast.	PF	Dq.	Stl.	Blk.	TO	Pts.
1980 —Utah	30	8	15	.533	7	8	.875	4	1	5	2	1	0	2	0	2	23
1981 —Utah	21	3	9	.333	2	2	1.000	2	3	5	0	1	0	1	0	1	8
1982 —Utah	21	6	8	.750	0	1	.000	1	1	2	0	2	0	0	0	1	12
1984 —Utah	18	1	8	.125	0	0		0	2	2	1	4	0	1	0	1	2
1985 —Utah	23	2	6	.333	6	6	1.000	0	2	2	1	4	0	1	0	2	10
1986 —Utah	17	3	8	.375	2	2	1.000	1	6	7	3	1	0	1	0	0	8
Totals	130	23	54	.426	17	19	.895	8	15	23	7	13	0	6	0	6	63

ITALIAN LEAGUE RECORD

Season Team	G	Min.	FGM	FGA	Pct.	FTM	FTA	Pct.	Reb.	Pts.	Avg.
91-92 —Breeze Milano	26	874	246	413	.596	168	208	.808	144	695	26.7

DAVIES, BOB
G

PERSONAL: Born January 15, 1920, in Harrisburg, Pa. . . . Died April 22, 1990. . . . 6-1/175. . . . Full name: Robert Edris Davies. . . . Nickname: The Harrisburg Houdini.
HIGH SCHOOL: John Harris (Harrisburg, Pa.).
COLLEGE: Franklin & Marshall (Pa.), then Seton Hall.
TRANSACTIONS/CAREER NOTES: Played with Great Lakes (Ill.) Naval Training Station during 1942-43 season (led team in scoring—269 points, 114 field goals and 41 free throws). . . . In military service during 1942-43, 1943-44 and 1944-45 seasons. . . . Played in American Basketball League with Brooklyn Indians (1943-44) and New York Gothams (1944-45). . . . Signed as free agent by Rochester Royals of National Basketball League (1945). . . . Royals franchise transferred to Basketball Assocation of America for 1948-49 season. . . . Royals franchise became part of NBA upon merger of BAA and NBL for 1949-50 season.
CAREER HONORS: Elected to Naismith Memorial Basketball Hall of Fame (1969). . . . NBA 25th Anniversary All-Time team (1970).
MISCELLANEOUS: Member of NBA championship team (1951). . . . Member of NBL championship team (1946).

COLLEGIATE RECORD

Season Team	G	Min.	FGM	FGA	Pct.	FTM	FTA	Pct.	Reb.	Pts.	Avg.
37-38 —Franklin & Marshall‡			Freshman team statistics unavailable.								
38-39 —Seton Hall‡			Freshman team statistics unavailable.								
39-40 —Seton Hall	18	...	78	...		56	...	...	...	212	11.8
40-41 —Seton Hall	22	...	91	...		42	...	...	...	224	10.2
41-42 —Seton Hall	19	...	81	...		63	...	...	...	225	11.8
Varsity totals	59	...	250	...		161	...	...	...	661	11.2

NBL AND NBA REGULAR-SEASON RECORD

HONORS: All-NBA first team (1950, 1951, 1952). . . . All-NBA second team (1953). . . . All-BAA first team (1949). . . . NBL Most Valuable Player (1947). . . . All-NBL first team (1947). . . . All-NBL second team (1948).
NOTES: Led BAA with 5.4 assists per game (1949).

Season Team	G	Min.	FGM	FGA	Pct.	FTM	FTA	Pct.	Reb.	Ast.	PF	Dq.	Pts.	Avg.
45-46 —Rochester (NBL)	27	...	86	...	...	70	103	.680	...	...	85	...	242	9.0
46-47 —Rochester (NBL)	32	...	166	...	...	130	166	.783	...	...	90	...	462	14.4
47-48 —Rochester (NBL)	48	...	176	...	...	121	161	.752	...	...	111	...	473	9.9
48-49 —Rochester (BAA)	60	...	317	871	.364	270	348	.776	...	*321	197	...	904	15.1
49-50 —Rochester	64	...	317	887	.357	261	347	.752	...	294	187	...	895	14.0
50-51 —Rochester	63	...	326	877	.372	303	381	.795	197	287	208	7	955	15.2
51-52 —Rochester	65	2394	379	990	.383	294	379	.776	189	390	269	10	1052	16.2
52-53 —Rochester	66	2216	339	880	.385	351	466	.753	195	280	261	7	1029	15.6
53-54 —Rochester	72	2137	288	777	.371	311	433	.718	194	323	224	4	887	12.3
54-55 —Rochester	72	1870	326	785	.415	220	293	.751	205	355	220	2	872	12.1
Totals	569	...	2720	...	...	2331	3077	.758	...	...	1852	...	7771	13.7

NBL AND NBA PLAYOFF RECORD

Season Team	G	Min.	FGM	FGA	Pct.	FTM	FTA	Pct.	Reb.	Ast.	PF	Dq.	Pts.	Avg.
45-46 —Rochester (NBL)	7	...	28	...	...	30	41	.732	...	...	13	...	86	12.3
46-47 —Rochester (NBL)	11	...	54	...	...	43	63	.683	...	...	30	...	151	13.7
47-48 —Rochester (NBL)	11	...	56	...	...	49	64	.766	...	...	26	...	161	14.6
48-49 —Rochester (BAA)	4	...	19	51	.373	10	13	.769	...	13	12	...	48	12.0
49-50 —Rochester	2	...	4	17	.235	7	8	.875	...	9	11	...	15	7.5
50-51 —Rochester	14	...	79	234	.338	64	80	.800	43	75	45	1	222	15.9
51-52 —Rochester	6	233	37	92	.402	45	55	.818	13	28	18	0	119	19.8
52-53 —Rochester	3	91	6	29	.207	14	20	.700	4	14	11	0	26	8.7
53-54 —Rochester	6	172	17	52	.327	17	23	.739	12	14	16	0	51	8.5
54-55 —Rochester	3	75	11	33	.333	3	4	.750	6	9	11	0	25	8.3
Totals	67	...	311	...	...	282	371	.760	...	...	193	...	904	13.5

NBA ALL-STAR GAME RECORD

Season Team	Min.	FGM	FGA	Pct.	FTM	FTA	Pct.	Reb.	Ast.	PF	Dq.	Pts.
1951 —Rochester	...	4	6	.667	5	5	1.000	5	5	3	0	13
1952 —Rochester	27	4	11	.364	0	0	...	0	5	4	0	8
1953 —Rochester	17	3	7	.429	3	6	.500	3	2	2	0	9
1954 —Rochester	31	8	16	.500	2	3	.667	5	5	4	0	18
Totals	...	19	40	.475	10	14	.714	13	17	13	0	48

COLLEGIATE COACHING RECORD

Season Team	W	L	Pct.	Finish
46-47 —Seton Hall	24	3	.889	
55-56 —Gettysburg	11	17	.393	
56-57 —Gettysburg	7	18	.280	
Totals (3 years)	42	38	.525	

DeBUSSCHERE, DAVE
F/G

PERSONAL: Born October 16, 1940, in Detroit. . . . 6-6/235. . . . Full name: David Albert DeBusschere.
HIGH SCHOOL: Austin Catholic (Detroit).
COLLEGE: Detroit.
TRANSACTIONS/CAREER NOTES: Selected by Detroit Pistons in 1962 NBA Draft (territorial pick). . . . Traded by Pistons to New York Knicks for Walt Bellamy and Howard Komives (December 19, 1968).
CAREER HONORS: Elected to Naismith Memorial Basketball Hall of Fame (1982).
MISCELLANEOUS: Member of NBA championship teams (1970, 1973).

COLLEGIATE RECORD

Season Team	G	Min.	FGM	FGA	Pct.	FTM	FTA	Pct.	Reb.	Pts.	Avg.
58-59 —Detroit‡	15	...	144	306	.471	68	101	.673	305	356	23.7
59-60 —Detroit	27	...	288	665	.433	115	196	.587	540	691	25.6
60-61 —Detroit	27	...	256	636	.403	86	155	.555	514	598	22.1
61-62 —Detroit	26	...	267	616	.433	162	242	.669	498	696	26.8
Varsity totals	80		811	1917	.423	363	593	.612	1552	1985	24.8

NBA REGULAR-SEASON RECORD

HONORS: All-NBA second team (1969). . . . NBA All-Defensive first team (1969, 1970, 1971, 1972, 1973, 1974).

Season Team	G	Min.	FGM	FGA	Pct.	FTM	FTA	Pct.	Reb.	Ast.	PF	Dq.	Pts.	Avg.
62-63 —Detroit	80	2352	406	944	.430	206	287	.718	694	207	247	2	1018	12.7
63-64 —Detroit	15	304	52	133	.391	25	43	.581	105	23	32	1	129	8.6
64-65 —Detroit	79	2769	508	1196	.425	306	437	.700	874	253	242	5	1322	16.7
65-66 —Detroit	79	2696	524	1284	.408	249	378	.659	916	209	252	5	1297	16.4
66-67 —Detroit	78	2897	531	1278	.415	361	512	.705	924	216	297	7	1423	18.2
67-68 —Detroit	80	3125	573	1295	.442	289	435	.664	1081	181	304	3	1435	17.9
68-69 —Detroit-New York	76	2943	506	1140	.444	229	328	.698	888	191	290	6	1241	16.3
69-70 —New York	79	2627	488	1082	.451	176	256	.688	790	194	244	2	1152	14.6
70-71 —New York	81	2891	523	1243	.421	217	312	.696	901	220	237	2	1263	15.6
71-72 —New York	80	3072	520	1218	.427	193	265	.728	901	291	219	1	1233	15.4
72-73 —New York	77	2827	532	1224	.435	194	260	.746	787	259	215	1	1258	16.3

| | | | | | | | | | — REBOUNDS — | | | | | | | | |
Season Team	G	Min.	FGM	FGA	Pct.	FTM	FTA	Pct.	Off.	Def.	Tot.	Ast.	PF	Dq.	Stl.	Blk.	TO	Pts.	Avg.
73-74 —New York	71	2699	559	1212	.461	164	217	.756	134	623	757	253	222	2	67	39	...	1282	18.1
Totals	875	31202	5722	13249	.432	2609	3730	.699	...	...	9618	2497	2801	37	67	39	...	14053	16.1

NBA PLAYOFF RECORD

Season Team	G	Min.	FGM	FGA	Pct.	FTM	FTA	Pct.	Reb.	Ast.	PF	Dq.	Pts.	Avg.
62-63 —Detroit	4	159	25	59	.424	30	44	.682	63	6	14	1	80	20.0
67-68 —Detroit	6	263	45	106	.425	26	45	.578	97	13	23	0	116	19.3
68-69 —New York	10	419	61	174	.351	41	50	.820	148	33	43	0	163	16.3
69-70 —New York	19	701	130	309	.421	45	68	.662	220	46	63	1	305	16.1
70-71 —New York	12	488	84	202	.416	29	44	.659	156	22	40	1	197	16.4
71-72 —New York	16	616	109	242	.450	48	64	.750	193	37	51	2	266	16.6
72-73 —New York	17	632	117	265	.442	31	40	.775	179	58	57	0	265	15.6

| | | | | | | | | | — REBOUNDS — | | | | | | | | |
Season Team	G	Min.	FGM	FGA	Pct.	FTM	FTA	Pct.	Off.	Def.	Tot.	Ast.	PF	Dq.	Stl.	Blk.	TO	Pts.	Avg.
73-74 —New York	12	404	63	166	.380	18	29	.621	25	74	99	38	36	0	7	4	...	144	12.0
Totals	96	3682	634	1523	.416	268	384	.698	...	...	1155	253	327	5	7	4	...	1536	16.0

NBA ALL-STAR GAME RECORD

NOTES: Holds single-game record for most field goals made in one quarter—8 (1967).

Season	Team	Min.	FGM	FGA	Pct.	FTM	FTA	Pct.	Reb.	Ast.	PF	Dq.	Pts.
1966	—Detroit	22	1	14	.071	2	2	1.000	6	1	1	0	4
1967	—Detroit	25	11	17	.647	0	0	...	6	0	1	0	22
1968	—Detroit	12	0	3	.000	0	0	...	4	0	1	0	0
1970	—New York	14	5	10	.500	0	0	...	7	2	1	0	10
1971	—New York	19	4	7	.571	0	0	...	7	3	3	0	8
1972	—New York	26	4	8	.500	0	0	...	11	0	2	0	8
1973	—New York	25	4	8	.500	1	2	.500	7	2	1	0	9

Season	Team	Min.	FGM	FGA	Pct.	FTM	FTA	Pct.	Off.	Def.	Tot.	Ast.	PF	Dq.	Stl.	Blk.	TO	Pts.
1974	—New York	24	8	14	.571	0	0	...	2	1	3	3	2	0	1	0	...	16
	Totals	167	37	81	.457	3	4	.750	...	...	51	11	12	0	1	0	...	77

HEAD COACHING RECORD

BACKGROUND: Player/head coach, Detroit Pistons (November 1964 to March 1967).
RECORDS: Youngest coach in the history of the NBA.

NBA COACHING RECORD

Season	Team		REGULAR SEASON				PLAYOFFS	
		W	L	Pct.	Finish	W	L	Pct.
64-65	—Detroit	29	40	.420	4th/Western Division	—	—	—
65-66	—Detroit	22	58	.275	5th/Western Division	—	—	—
66-67	—Detroit	28	45	.384		—	—	—
	Totals (3 years)	79	143	.356				

NOTES:
1964— Replaced Charles Wolf as Detroit head coach (November), with record of 2-9.
1967— Replaced as Detroit head coach by Donnis Butcher (March).

RECORD AS BASEBALL PLAYER

TRANSACTIONS/CAREER NOTES: Signed by Chicago White Sox (April 1, 1962).... On disabled list (June 4-20, 1964).... On restricted list (September 7, 1965-December 19, 1968).... Released by White Sox organization (December 23, 1968).
STATISTICAL NOTES: Led Pacific Coast League in games started by pitcher with 34 in 1965.

Year	Team (League)	G	W	L	Pct.	ERA	Sv.	IP	H	R	ER	BB	SO
1962	—Chicago (A.L.)	12	0	0	...	2.00	...	18	5	7	4	23	8
	—Savannah (South Atlantic)	15	10	1	.909	2.49	...	94	62	35	26	53	93
1963	—Chicago (A.L.)	24	3	4	.429	3.11	...	84	80	35	29	34	53
1964	—Indianapolis (Pacific Coast)	32	15	8	.652	3.93	...	174	173	88	76	66	126
1965	—Indianapolis (Pacific Coast)	35	15	12	.556	3.65	...	*244	*255	120	99	66	176
	Major league totals (2 years)	36	3	4	.429	2.91	...	102	85	42	33	66	126

ENGLISH, ALEX

F

PERSONAL: Born January 5, 1954, in Columbia, S.C. ... 6-7/190. ...
Full name: Alexander English.
HIGH SCHOOL: Dreher (Columbia, S.C.).
COLLEGE: South Carolina.

TRANSACTIONS/CAREER NOTES: Selected by Milwaukee Bucks in second round (23rd pick overall) of 1976 NBA Draft.... Signed as veteran free agent by Indiana Pacers (June 8, 1978); Bucks waived their right of first refusal in exchange for 1979 first-round draft choice (October 3, 1978).... Traded by Pacers with 1980 first-round draft choice to Denver Nuggets for George McGinnis (February 1, 1980).... Signed as unrestricted free agent by Dallas Mavericks (August 15, 1990).... Played in Italy (1991-92).

COLLEGIATE RECORD

Season	Team	G	Min.	FGM	FGA	Pct.	FTM	FTA	Pct.	Reb.	Pts.	Avg.
72-73	—South Carolina	29	1037	189	368	.514	44	70	.629	306	422	14.6
73-74	—South Carolina	27	1007	209	395	.529	75	112	.670	237	493	18.3
74-75	—South Carolina	28	1024	199	359	.554	49	77	.636	244	447	16.0
75-76	—South Carolina	27	1045	258	468	.551	94	134	.701	277	610	22.6
	Totals	111	4113	855	1590	.538	262	393	.667	1064	1972	17.8

NBA REGULAR-SEASON RECORD

HONORS: All-NBA second team (1982, 1983, 1986).

Season	Team	G	Min.	FGM	FGA	Pct.	FTM	FTA	Pct.	Off.	Def.	Tot.	Ast.	PF	Dq.	Stl.	Blk.	TO	Pts.	Avg.
76-77	—Milwaukee	60	648	132	277	.477	46	60	.767	68	100	168	25	78	0	17	18	...	310	5.2
77-78	—Milwaukee	82	1552	343	633	.542	104	143	.727	144	251	395	129	178	1	41	55	137	790	9.6
78-79	—Indiana	81	2696	563	1102	.511	173	230	.752	253	402	655	271	214	3	70	78	196	1299	16.0
79-80	—Ind.-Denver	78	2401	553	1113	.497	210	266	.789	269	336	605	224	206	0	73	62	214	1318	16.9
80-81	—Denver	81	3093	768	1555	.494	390	459	.850	273	373	646	290	255	2	106	100	241	1929	23.8
81-82	—Denver	82	3015	855	1553	.551	372	443	.840	210	348	558	433	261	2	87	120	261	2082	25.4
82-83	—Denver	82	2988	*959	*1857	.516	406	490	.829	263	338	601	397	235	1	116	126	263	*2326	*28.4
83-84	—Denver	82	2870	907	1714	.529	352	427	.824	216	248	464	406	252	3	83	95	222	2167	26.4
84-85	—Denver	81	2924	*939	1812	.518	383	462	.829	203	255	458	344	259	1	101	46	251	2262	27.9
85-86	—Denver	81	3024	*951	1888	.504	511	593	.862	192	213	405	320	235	1	73	29	249	*2414	29.8
86-87	—Denver	82	3085	965	1920	.503	411	487	.844	146	198	344	422	216	0	73	21	214	2345	28.6
87-88	—Denver	80	2818	843	1704	.495	314	379	.829	166	207	373	377	193	1	70	23	181	2000	25.0
88-89	—Denver	82	2990	924	1881	.491	325	379	.858	148	178	326	383	174	0	66	12	198	2175	26.5
89-90	—Denver	80	2211	635	1293	.491	161	183	.880	119	167	286	225	130	0	51	23	93	1433	17.9
90-91	—Dallas	79	1748	322	734	.439	119	140	.850	108	146	254	105	141	0	40	25	101	763	9.7
	Totals	1193	38063	10659	21036	.507	4277	5141	.832	2778	3760	6538	4351	3027	15	1067	833	2821	25613	21.5

Three-point field goals: 1979-80, 2-for-6 (.333). 1980-81, 3-for-5 (.600). 1981-82, 0-for-8. 1982-83, 2-for-12 (.167). 1983-84, 1-for-7 (.143). 1984-85, 1-for-5 (.200). 1985-86, 1-for-5 (.200). 1986-87, 4-for-15 (.267). 1987-88, 0-for-6. 1988-89, 2-for-8 (.250). 1989-90, 2-for-5 (.400). 1990-91, 0-for-1. Totals, 18-for-83 (.217).

NBA PLAYOFF RECORD

Season	Team	G	Min.	FGM	FGA	Pct.	FTM	FTA	Pct.	Off.	Def.	Tot.	Ast.	PF	Dq.	Stl.	Blk.	TO	Pts.	Avg.
77-78	Milwaukee ...	9	208	48	78	.615	25	32	.781	16	26	42	13	20	0	6	7	12	121	13.4
81-82	Denver	3	118	26	55	.473	6	7	.857	8	15	23	17	6	0	3	3	4	58	19.3
82-83	Denver	7	270	67	150	.447	47	53	.887	20	24	44	42	21	0	4	7	21	181	25.9
83-84	Denver	5	203	60	102	.588	25	28	.893	16	24	40	28	17	0	3	2	7	145	29.0
84-85	Denver	14	536	163	304	.536	97	109	.890	36	56	92	63	40	1	17	5	30	423	30.2
85-86	Denver	10	394	106	229	.463	61	71	.859	18	17	35	52	29	0	4	4	28	273	27.3
86-87	Denver	3	76	25	49	.510	6	7	.857	10	4	14	10	9	1	0	0	8	56	18.7
87-88	Denver	11	438	116	255	.455	35	43	.814	31	28	59	48	34	0	7	3	16	267	24.3
88-89	Denver	3	108	32	62	.516	14	16	.875	8	5	13	11	6	0	1	0	14	78	26.0
89-90	Denver	3	76	25	44	.568	9	11	.818	3	6	9	9	6	0	2	1	2	59	19.7
Totals	....	68	2427	668	1328	.503	325	377	.862	166	205	371	293	188	2	47	32	142	1661	24.4

Three-point field goals: 1982-83, 0-for-2. 1983-84, 0-for-1. 1984-85, 0-for-1. 1985-86, 0-for-1. 1987-88, 0-for-3. Totals, 0-for-8.

NBA ALL-STAR GAME RECORD

Season	Team	Min.	FGM	FGA	Pct.	FTM	FTA	Pct.	Off.	Def.	Tot.	Ast.	PF	Dq.	Stl.	Blk.	TO	Pts.
1982	Denver	12	2	6	.333	0	0	...	2	3	5	1	2	0	1	0	1	4
1983	Denver	23	7	14	.500	0	1	.000	2	2	4	0	2	0	1	2	2	14
1984	Denver	19	6	8	.750	1	1	1.000	0	0	0	2	2	0	1	1	3	13
1985	Denver	14	0	3	.000	0	0	...	1	1	2	1	1	0	0	0	2	0
1986	Denver	16	8	12	.667	0	0	...	1	0	1	2	0	0	0	1	1	16
1987	Denver	13	0	6	.000	0	0	...	0	0	0	1	1	0	0	0	2	0
1988	Denver	22	5	10	.500	0	0	...	2	1	3	4	0	0	1	0	0	10
1989	Denver	29	8	13	.615	0	0	...	1	2	3	4	0	0	2	0	3	16
Totals	....	148	36	72	.500	1	2	.500	9	9	18	15	8	0	6	4	14	73

ITALIAN LEAGUE RECORD

Season	Team	G	Min.	FGM	FGA	Pct.	FTM	FTA	Pct.	Reb.	Pts.	Avg.
91-92	Depi Napoli	15	474	87	178	.489	39	48	.813	71	213	14.2

ERVING, JULIUS
F

PERSONAL: Born February 22, 1950, in Roosevelt, N.Y. . . . . 6-7/210. . . . Full name: Julius Winfield Erving II. . . . Nickname: Dr. J.
HIGH SCHOOL: Roosevelt (N.Y.).
COLLEGE: Massachusetts.

TRANSACTIONS/CAREER NOTES: Signed as undergraduate free agent by Virginia Squires of American Basketball Association (April 6, 1971). . . . Selected by Milwaukee Bucks in first round (12th pick overall) of 1972 NBA Draft. . . . Traded by Squires with Willie Sojourner to New York Nets for George Carter, draft rights to Kermit Washington and cash (August 1, 1973). . . . Nets franchise became part of NBA upon merger with ABA for 1976-77 season. . . . Sold by Nets to Philadelphia 76ers (October 20, 1976).
CAREER HONORS: NBA 35th Anniversary All-Time team (1980).
MISCELLANEOUS: Member of NBA championship team (1983).

COLLEGIATE RECORD

Season	Team	G	Min.	FGM	FGA	Pct.	FTM	FTA	Pct.	Reb.	Pts.	Avg.
68-69	Massachusetts‡	15	...	112	216	.519	49	81	.605	214	273	18.2
69-70	Massachusetts	25	969	238	468	.509	167	230	.726	522	643	25.7
70-71	Massachusetts	27	1029	286	609	.470	155	206	.752	527	727	26.9
Varsity totals	....	52	1998	524	1077	.487	322	436	.739	1049	1370	26.3

ABA REGULAR-SEASON RECORD

NOTES: ABA Most Valuable Player (1974, 1976). . . . ABA co-Most Valuable Player (1975). . . . ABA All-Star first team (1973, 1974, 1975, 1976). . . . ABA All-Star second team (1972). . . . ABA All-Defensive team (1976). . . . ABA All-Rookie team (1972). . . . Member of ABA championship teams (1974, 1976). . . . Holds career record for highest points-per-game average (minimum 250 games) —28.7.

Season	Team	G	Min.	FGM	FGA	Pct.	FGM	FGA	Pct.	FTM	FTA	Pct.	Reb.	Ast.	Pts.	Avg.
				2-POINT			**3-POINT**									
71-72	Virginia	84	3513	907	1810	.501	3	16	.188	467	627	.745	1319	335	2290	27.3
72-73	Virginia	71	2993	889	1780	.499	5	24	.208	475	612	.776	867	298	*2268	*31.9
73-74	New York	84	3398	897	1742	.515	17	43	.395	454	593	.766	899	434	*2299	*27.4
74-75	New York	84	3402	885	1719	.515	29	87	.333	486	608	.799	914	462	2343	27.9
75-76	New York	84	3244	915	1770	.517	34	103	.330	530	662	.801	925	423	*2462	*29.3
Totals	....	407	16550	4493	8821	.509	88	273	.322	2412	3102	.778	4924	1952	11662	28.7

ABA PLAYOFF RECORD

NOTES: ABA Playoff Most Valuable Player (1974, 1976).

Season	Team	G	Min.	FGM	FGA	Pct.	FGM	FGA	Pct.	FTM	FTA	Pct.	Reb.	Ast.	Pts.	Avg.
				2-POINT			**3-POINT**									
71-72	Virginia	11	504	146	280	.521	1	4	.250	71	85	.835	224	72	366	33.3
72-73	Virginia	5	219	59	109	.541	0	3	.000	30	40	.750	45	16	148	29.6
73-74	New York	14	579	156	294	.531	5	11	.455	63	85	.741	135	67	390	27.9
74-75	New York	5	211	55	113	.487	0	8	.000	27	32	.844	49	28	137	27.4
75-76	New York	13	551	156	286	.545	4	14	.286	127	158	.804	164	64	451	34.7
Totals	....	48	2064	572	1082	.529	10	40	.250	318	400	.795	617	247	1492	31.1

ABA ALL-STAR GAME RECORD

Season	Team	Min.	FGM	2-POINT FGA	Pct.	FGM	3-POINT FGA	Pct.	FTM	FTA	Pct.	Reb.	Ast.	Pts.
1972	—Virginia	25	9	15	.600	0	0	...	2	2	1.000	6	3	20
1973	—Virginia	30	8	16	.500	0	0	...	6	8	.750	5	1	22
1974	—New York	27	6	15	.400	0	0	...	2	2	1.000	11	8	14
1975	—New York	27	5	11	.455	1	1	1.000	8	10	.800	7	7	21
1976	—New York	25	9	12	.750	0	1	.000	5	7	.714	7	5	23
	Totals	134	37	69	.536	1	2	.500	23	29	.793	36	24	100

NBA REGULAR-SEASON RECORD

HONORS: NBA Most Valuable Player (1981).... All-NBA first team (1978, 1980, 1981, 1982, 1983).... All-NBA second team (1977, 1984).

Season	Team	G	Min.	FGM	FGA	Pct.	FTM	FTA	Pct.	Off.	Def.	Tot.	Ast.	PF	Dq.	Stl.	Blk.	TO	Pts.	Avg.
76-77	—Philadelphia.	82	2940	685	1373	.499	400	515	.777	192	503	695	306	251	1	159	113	...	1770	21.6
77-78	—Philadelphia.	74	2429	611	1217	.502	306	362	.845	179	302	481	279	207	0	135	97	238	1528	20.6
78-79	—Philadelphia.	78	2802	715	1455	.491	373	501	.745	198	366	564	357	207	0	133	100	315	1803	23.1
79-80	—Philadelphia.	78	2812	838	1614	.519	420	534	.787	215	361	576	355	208	0	170	140	284	2100	26.9
80-81	—Philadelphia.	82	2874	794	1524	.521	422	536	.787	244	413	657	364	233	0	173	147	266	2014	24.6
81-82	—Philadelphia.	81	2789	780	1428	.546	411	539	.763	220	337	557	319	229	1	161	141	214	1974	24.4
82-83	—Philadelphia.	72	2421	605	1170	.517	330	435	.759	173	318	491	263	202	1	112	131	196	1542	21.4
83-84	—Philadelphia.	77	2683	678	1324	.512	364	483	.754	190	342	532	309	217	3	141	139	230	1727	22.4
84-85	—Philadelphia.	78	2535	610	1236	.494	338	442	.765	172	242	414	233	199	0	135	109	208	1561	20.0
85-86	—Philadelphia.	74	2474	521	1085	.480	289	368	.785	169	201	370	248	196	3	113	82	214	1340	18.1
86-87	—Philadelphia.	60	1918	400	850	.471	191	235	.813	115	149	264	191	137	0	76	94	158	1005	16.8
	Totals	836	28677	7237	14276	.507	3844	4950	.777	2067	3534	5601	3224	2286	9	1508	1293	2323	18364	22.0

Three-point field goals: 1979-80, 4-for-20 (.200). 1980-81, 4-for-18 (.222). 1981-82, 3-for-11 (.273). 1982-83, 2-for-7 (.286). 1983-84, 7-for-21 (.333). 1984-85, 3-for-14 (.214). 1985-86, 9-for-32 (.281). 1986-87, 14-for-53 (.264). Totals, 46-for-176 (.261).

NBA PLAYOFF RECORD

Season	Team	G	Min.	FGM	FGA	Pct.	FTM	FTA	Pct.	Off.	Def.	Tot.	Ast.	PF	Dq.	Stl.	Blk.	TO	Pts.	Avg.
76-77	—Philadelphia.	19	758	204	390	.523	110	134	.821	41	81	122	85	45	0	41	23	...	518	27.3
77-78	—Philadelphia.	10	358	88	180	.489	42	56	.750	40	57	97	40	30	0	15	18	35	218	21.8
78-79	—Philadelphia.	9	372	89	172	.517	51	67	.761	29	41	70	53	22	0	18	17	38	229	25.4
79-80	—Philadelphia.	18	694	165	338	.488	108	136	.794	31	105	136	79	56	0	36	37	56	440	24.4
80-81	—Philadelphia.	16	592	143	301	.475	81	107	.757	52	62	114	54	54	0	22	41	55	367	22.9
81-82	—Philadelphia.	21	780	168	324	.519	124	165	.752	57	99	156	99	55	0	37	37	67	461	22.0
82-83	—Philadelphia.	13	493	95	211	.450	49	68	.721	32	67	99	44	42	1	15	27	39	239	18.4
83-84	—Philadelphia.	5	194	36	76	.474	19	22	.864	9	23	32	25	14	0	8	6	21	91	18.2
84-85	—Philadelphia.	13	434	84	187	.449	54	63	.857	29	44	73	48	34	0	25	11	37	222	17.1
85-86	—Philadelphia.	12	433	81	180	.450	48	65	.738	26	44	70	50	32	0	11	16	39	212	17.7
86-87	—Philadelphia.	5	180	34	82	.415	21	25	.840	14	11	25	17	19	0	7	6	9	91	18.2
	Totals	141	5288	1187	2441	.486	707	908	.779	360	634	994	594	403	1	235	239	396	3088	21.9

Three-point field goals: 1979-80, 2-for-9 (.222). 1980-81, 0-for-1. 1981-82, 1-for-6 (.167). 1982-83, 0-for-1. 1983-84, 0-for-1. 1984-85, 0-for-1. 1985-86, 2-for-11 (.182). Totals, 5-for-30 (.167).

NBA ALL-STAR GAME RECORD

NOTES: NBA All-Star Game Most Valuable Player (1977, 1983).... Holds single-game record for most free throws attempted in one quarter—11 (1978).... Shares single-game record for most free throws made in one quarter—9 (1978).

Season	Team	Min.	FGM	FGA	Pct.	FTM	FTA	Pct.	Off.	Def.	Tot.	Ast.	PF	Dq.	Stl.	Blk.	TO	Pts.
1977	—Philadelphia.......	30	12	20	.600	6	6	1.000	5	7	12	3	2	0	4	1	...	30
1978	—Philadelphia.......	27	3	14	.214	10	12	.833	2	6	8	3	1	0	0	1	2	16
1979	—Philadelphia.......	39	10	22	.455	9	12	.750	6	2	8	5	4	0	2	0	1	29
1980	—Philadelphia.......	20	4	12	.333	3	4	.750	2	3	5	2	5	0	2	1	2	11
1981	—Philadelphia.......	29	6	15	.400	6	7	.857	3	0	3	2	2	0	2	1	2	18
1982	—Philadelphia.......	32	7	16	.438	2	4	.500	3	5	8	2	4	0	1	2	4	16
1983	—Philadelphia.......	28	11	19	.579	3	3	1.000	3	3	6	3	1	0	1	2	2	25
1984	—Philadelphia.......	36	14	22	.636	6	8	.750	4	4	8	5	4	0	2	2	1	34
1985	—Philadelphia.......	23	5	15	.333	2	2	1.000	2	2	4	3	3	0	1	0	1	12
1986	—Philadelphia.......	19	4	10	.400	0	2	.000	1	3	4	2	2	0	2	0	2	8
1987	—Philadelphia.......	33	9	13	.692	3	3	1.000	3	1	4	5	3	0	1	1	2	22
	Totals	316	85	178	.478	50	63	.794	34	36	70	35	31	0	18	11	19	221

Three-point field goals: 1987, 1-for-1.

FOUST, LARRY
C/F

PERSONAL: Born June 24, 1928, in Painesville, O.... Died October 27, 1984.... 6-9/250.... Full name: Lawrence Michael Foust.
HIGH SCHOOL: South Catholic (Philadelphia).
COLLEGE: La Salle.
TRANSACTIONS/CAREER NOTES: Selected by Chicago Stags in first round of 1950 NBA Draft.... Draft rights selected by Fort Wayne Pistons in dispersal of Stags franchise (1950).... Pistons franchise moved from Fort Wayne to Detroit for 1957-58 season.... Traded by Detroit Pistons with cash to Minneapolis Lakers for Walt Dukes (September 12, 1957).... Traded by Lakers to St. Louis Hawks for Charlie Share, cash and draft rights to Nick Mantis and Willie Merriweather (February 1, 1960).

COLLEGIATE RECORD

NOTES: THE SPORTING NEWS All-America fifth team (1950).

Season	Team	G	Min.	FGM	FGA	Pct.	FTM	FTA	Pct.	Reb.	Pts.	Avg.
46-47	—La Salle	26	...	103	...	...	49	...	...	...	255	9.8
47-48	—La Salle	24	...	157	...	...	87	...	...	...	401	16.7

Season Team	G	Min.	FGM	FGA	Pct.	FTM	FTA	Pct.	Reb.	Pts.	Avg.
48-49 —La Salle	28	...	177	...	...	99	164	.604	...	453	16.2
49-50 —La Salle	25	...	136	...	...	83	122	.680	...	355	14.2
Totals	103	...	573	...	...	318	...	...	...	1464	14.2

NBA REGULAR-SEASON RECORD

HONORS: All-NBA first team (1955).... All-NBA second team (1952).

Season Team	G	Min.	FGM	FGA	Pct.	FTM	FTA	Pct.	Reb.	Ast.	PF	Dq.	Pts.	Avg.
50-51 —Fort Wayne	68	...	327	944	.346	261	396	.659	681	90	247	6	915	13.5
51-52 —Fort Wayne	66	2615	390	989	.394	267	394	.678	†880	200	245	10	1047	15.9
52-53 —Fort Wayne	67	2303	311	865	.360	336	465	.723	769	151	267	16	958	14.3
53-54 —Fort Wayne	72	2693	376	919	.409	338	475	.712	967	161	258	4	1090	15.1
54-55 —Fort Wayne	70	2264	398	818	*.487	393	513	.766	700	118	264	9	1189	17.0
55-56 —Fort Wayne	72	2024	367	821	.447	432	555	.778	648	127	263	7	1166	16.2
56-57 —Fort Wayne	61	1533	243	617	.394	273	380	.718	555	71	221	7	759	12.4
57-58 —Minneapolis	72	2200	391	982	.398	428	566	.756	876	108	299	11	1210	16.8
58-59 —Minneapolis	72	1933	301	771	.390	280	366	.765	627	91	233	5	882	12.3
59-60 —Minneapolis-St. Louis	72	1964	312	766	.407	253	320	.791	621	96	241	7	877	12.2
60-61 —St. Louis	68	1208	194	489	.397	164	208	.788	389	77	165	0	552	8.1
61-62 —St. Louis	57	1153	204	433	.471	145	178	.815	328	78	186	2	553	9.7
Totals	817	...	3814	9414	.405	3570	4816	.741	8041	1368	2889	84	11198	13.7

NBA PLAYOFF RECORD

Season Team	G	Min.	FGM	FGA	Pct.	FTM	FTA	Pct.	Reb.	Ast.	PF	Dq.	Pts.	Avg.
50-51 —Fort Wayne	3	...	14	45	.311	8	10	.800	37	5	5	...	36	12.0
51-52 —Fort Wayne	2	77	12	23	.522	6	7	.857	30	5	8	1	30	15.0
52-53 —Fort Wayne	8	332	48	121	.397	57	68	.838	111	6	34	2	153	19.1
53-54 —Fort Wayne	4	129	11	41	.268	19	25	.760	38	7	21	2	41	10.3
54-55 —Fort Wayne	11	331	60	152	.395	52	73	.712	107	26	43	0	172	15.6
55-56 —Fort Wayne	10	289	49	130	.377	70	89	.787	127	14	38	2	168	16.8
56-57 —Fort Wayne	2	64	13	23	.565	19	23	.826	25	6	10	0	45	22.5
58-59 —Minneapolis	13	404	56	134	.418	41	50	.820	136	12	47	2	153	11.8
59-60 —St. Louis	12	205	29	74	.392	20	25	.800	68	11	36	0	78	6.5
60-61 —St. Louis	8	89	9	20	.450	8	14	.571	28	2	13	0	26	3.3
Totals	73	...	301	763	.394	300	384	.781	707	94	255	...	902	12.4

NBA ALL-STAR GAME RECORD

Season Team	Min.	FGM	FGA	Pct.	FTM	FTA	Pct.	Reb.	Ast.	PF	Dq.	Pts.
1951 —Fort Wayne	...	1	6	.167	0	0	...	5	2	3	0	2
1952 —Fort Wayne					Did not play—injured.							
1953 —Fort Wayne	18	5	7	.714	0	0	...	6	0	4	0	10
1954 —Fort Wayne	27	1	9	.111	1	1	1.000	15	0	1	0	3
1955 —Fort Wayne	24	3	10	.300	1	1	1.000	7	1	1	0	7
1956 —Fort Wayne	20	3	9	.333	3	4	.750	4	0	1	0	9
1958 —Minneapolis	13	1	4	.250	8	8	1.000	3	0	3	0	10
1959 —Minneapolis	16	3	9	.333	2	2	1.000	9	0	3	0	8
Totals	...	17	54	.315	15	16	.938	49	3	16	0	49

FRAZIER, WALT

G

PERSONAL: Born March 29, 1945, in Atlanta. ... 6-4/205. ... Full name: Walter Frazier Jr. ... Nickname: Clyde.
HIGH SCHOOL: David Howard (Atlanta).
COLLEGE: Southern Illinois.
TRANSACTIONS/CAREER NOTES: Selected by New York Knicks in first round (fifth pick overall) of 1967 NBA Draft. ... Acquired from Knicks by Cleveland Cavaliers as compensation for anticipated signing of veteran free agent Jim Cleamons (October 7, 1977). ... Waived by Cavaliers (October 19, 1979).
CAREER HONORS: Elected to Naismith Memorial Basketball Hall of Fame (1986).
MISCELLANEOUS: Member of NBA championship teams (1970, 1973).

COLLEGIATE RECORD

NOTES: THE SPORTING NEWS All-America second team (1967).

Season Team	G	Min.	FGM	FGA	Pct.	FTM	FTA	Pct.	Reb.	Pts.	Avg.
63-64 —Southern Illinois‡	14	...	133	225	.591	52	85	.612	129	318	22.7
64-65 —Southern Illinois	24	...	161	353	.456	88	111	.793	221	410	17.1
65-66 —Southern Illinois						Did not play—ineligible.					
66-67 —Southern Illinois	26	...	192	397	.484	90	126	.714	310	474	18.2
Varsity totals	50	...	353	750	.471	178	237	.751	531	884	17.7

NBA REGULAR-SEASON RECORD

HONORS: All-NBA first team (1970, 1972, 1974, 1975). ... All-NBA second team (1971, 1973). ... NBA All-Defensive first team (1969, 1970, 1971, 1972, 1973, 1974, 1975). ... NBA All-Rookie team (1968).

Season Team	G	Min.	FGM	FGA	Pct.	FTM	FTA	Pct.	Reb.	Ast.	PF	Dq.	Pts.	Avg.
67-68 —New York	74	1588	256	568	.451	154	235	.655	313	305	199	2	666	9.0
68-69 —New York	80	2949	531	1052	.505	341	457	.746	499	635	245	2	1403	17.5
69-70 —New York	77	3040	600	1158	.518	409	547	.748	465	629	203	1	1609	20.9
70-71 —New York	80	3455	651	1317	.494	434	557	.779	544	536	240	1	1736	21.7
71-72 —New York	77	3126	669	1307	.512	450	557	.808	513	446	185	0	1788	23.2
72-73 —New York	78	3181	681	1389	.490	286	350	.817	570	461	186	0	1648	21.1

Season Team	G	Min.	FGM	FGA	Pct.	FTM	FTA	Pct.	— REBOUNDS —			Ast.	PF	Dq.	Stl.	Blk.	TO	Pts.	Avg.
									Off.	Def.	Tot.								
73-74 —New York	80	3338	674	1429	.472	295	352	.838	120	416	536	551	212	2	161	15	...	1643	20.5
74-75 —New York	78	3204	672	1391	.483	331	400	.828	90	375	465	474	205	2	190	14	...	1675	21.5
75-76 —New York	59	2427	470	969	.485	186	226	.823	79	321	400	351	163	1	106	9	...	1126	19.1

Season	Team	G	Min.	FGM	FGA	Pct.	FTM	FTA	Pct.	Off.	Def.	Tot.	Ast.	PF	Dq.	Stl.	Blk.	TO	Pts.	Avg.
										— REBOUNDS —										
76-77	N.Y. Knicks ..	76	2687	532	1089	.489	259	336	.771	52	241	293	403	194	0	132	9	...	1323	17.4
77-78	Cleveland	51	1664	336	714	.471	153	180	.850	54	155	209	209	124	1	77	9	113	825	16.2
78-79	Cleveland	12	279	54	122	.443	21	27	.778	7	13	20	32	22	0	13	2	22	129	10.8
79-80	Cleveland	3	27	4	11	.364	2	2	1.000	1	2	3	8	2	0	2	1	4	10	3.3
	Totals	825	30965	6130	12516	.490	3321	4226	.786	...	...	4830	5040	2180	12	681	59	139	15581	18.9

Three-point field goals: 1979-80, 0-for-1.

NBA PLAYOFF RECORD

Season	Team	G	Min.	FGM	FGA	Pct.	FTM	FTA	Pct.	Reb.	Ast.	PF	Dq.	Pts.	Avg.
67-68	New York	4	119	12	33	.364	14	18	.778	22	25	12	0	38	9.5
68-69	New York	10	415	89	177	.503	34	57	.596	74	91	30	0	212	21.2
69-70	New York	19	834	118	247	.478	68	89	.764	149	156	53	0	304	16.0
70-71	New York	12	501	108	204	.529	55	75	.733	70	54	45	0	271	22.6
71-72	New York	16	704	148	276	.536	92	125	.736	112	98	48	0	388	24.3
72-73	New York	17	765	150	292	.514	73	94	.777	124	106	52	1	373	21.9

Season	Team	G	Min.	FGM	FGA	Pct.	FTM	FTA	Pct.	Off.	Def.	Tot.	Ast.	PF	Dq.	Stl.	Blk.	TO	Pts.	Avg.
										— REBOUNDS —										
73-74	New York	12	491	113	225	.502	44	49	.898	21	74	95	48	41	1	21	4	...	270	22.5
74-75	New York	3	124	29	46	.630	13	16	.813	3	17	20	21	4	0	11	0	...	71	23.7
	Totals	93	3953	767	1500	.511	393	523	.751	...	...	666	599	285	2	32	4	...	1927	20.7

NBA ALL-STAR GAME RECORD

NOTES: NBA All-Star Game Most Valuable Player (1975).

Season	Team	Min.	FGM	FGA	Pct.	FTM	FTA	Pct.	Reb.	Ast.	PF	Dq.	Pts.
1970	New York	24	3	7	.429	1	2	.500	3	4	2	0	7
1971	New York	26	3	9	.333	0	0	...	6	5	2	0	6
1972	New York	25	7	11	.636	1	2	.500	3	5	2	0	15
1973	New York	26	5	15	.333	0	0	...	6	2	1	0	10

Season	Team	Min.	FGM	FGA	Pct.	FTM	FTA	Pct.	Off.	Def.	Tot.	Ast.	PF	Dq.	Stl.	Blk.	TO	Pts.
									— REBOUNDS —									
1974	New York	28	5	12	.417	2	2	1.000	1	1	2	5	1	0	3	0	...	12
1975	New York	35	10	17	.588	10	11	.909	0	5	5	2	2	0	4	0	...	30
1976	New York	19	2	7	.286	4	4	1.000	0	2	2	3	0	0	2	0	...	8
	Totals	183	35	78	.449	18	21	.857	...	...	27	26	10	0	9	0	...	88

FREE, WORLD B.
G

PERSONAL: Born December 9, 1953, in Atlanta. . . . 6-3/190. . . . Formerly known as Lloyd Free.
HIGH SCHOOL: Canarsie (Brooklyn, N.Y.).
COLLEGE: Guilford (N.C.).

TRANSACTIONS/CAREER NOTES: Selected as undergraduate by Philadelphia 76ers in second round (23rd pick overall) of 1975 NBA Draft. . . . Traded by 76ers to San Diego Clippers for 1984 first-round draft choice (October 12, 1978). . . . Traded by Clippers to Golden State Warriors for Phil Smith and 1984 first-round draft choice (August 28, 1980). . . . Traded by Warriors to Cleveland Cavaliers for Ron Brewer (December 15, 1982). . . . Signed as veteran free agent by 76ers (December 30, 1986); Cavaliers agreed not to exercise their right of first refusal in exchange for 1990 second-round draft choice. . . . Waived by 76ers (March 4, 1987). . . . Signed as free agent by Houston Rockets (October 1, 1987).

COLLEGIATE RECORD

NOTES: Most Valuable Player in NAIA tournament (1973). . . . Member of NAIA championship team (1973).

Season	Team	G	Min.	FGM	FGA	Pct.	FTM	FTA	Pct.	Reb.	Pts.	Avg.
72-73	Guilford	33	...	272	572	.476	153	217	.705	191	697	21.1
73-74	Guilford	24	...	216	456	.474	165	225	.733	200	597	24.9
74-75	Guilford	28	...	247	486	.508	218	291	.749	163	712	25.4
	Totals	85	...	735	1514	.485	536	733	.731	554	2006	23.6

HONORS: All-NBA second team (1979).

NBA REGULAR-SEASON RECORD

Season	Team	G	Min.	FGM	FGA	Pct.	FTM	FTA	Pct.	Off.	Def.	Tot.	Ast.	PF	Dq.	Stl.	Blk.	TO	Pts.	Avg.
										— REBOUNDS —										
75-76	Philadelphia.	71	1121	239	533	.448	112	186	.602	64	61	125	104	107	0	37	6	...	590	8.3
76-77	Philadelphia.	78	2253	467	1022	.457	334	464	.720	97	140	237	266	207	2	75	25	...	1268	16.3
77-78	Philadelphia.	76	2050	390	857	.455	411	562	.731	92	120	212	306	199	0	68	41	200	1191	15.7
78-79	San Diego	78	2954	795	1653	.481	*654	*865	.756	127	174	301	340	253	8	111	35	297	2244	28.8
79-80	San Diego	68	2585	737	1556	.474	*572	760	.753	129	109	238	283	195	0	81	32	228	2055	30.2
80-81	Golden State	65	2370	516	1157	.446	528	649	.814	48	111	159	361	183	1	85	11	195	1565	24.1
81-82	Golden State	78	2796	650	1452	.448	479	647	.740	118	130	248	419	222	1	71	8	208	1789	22.9
82-83	G.S.-Clev.	73	2638	649	1423	.456	430	583	.738	92	109	201	290	241	4	97	15	209	1743	23.9
83-84	Cleveland	75	2375	626	1407	.445	395	504	.784	89	128	217	226	214	2	94	8	154	1669	22.3
84-85	Cleveland	71	2249	609	1328	.459	308	411	.749	61	150	211	320	163	0	75	16	139	1597	22.5
85-86	Cleveland	75	2535	652	1433	.455	379	486	.780	72	146	218	314	186	1	91	19	172	1754	23.4
86-87	Philadelphia.	20	285	39	123	.317	36	47	.766	5	14	19	30	26	0	5	4	18	116	5.8
87-88	Houston	58	682	143	350	.409	80	100	.800	14	30	44	60	74	2	20	3	49	374	6.4
	Totals	886	26893	6512	14294	.456	4718	6264	.753	1008	1422	2430	3319	2270	21	910	223	1869	17955	20.3

Three-point field goals: 1979-80, 9-for-25 (.360). 1980-81, 5-for-31 (.161). 1981-82, 10-for-56 (.179). 1982-83, 15-for-45 (.333). 1983-84, 22-for-69 (.319). 1984-85, 71-for-193 (.368). 1985-86, 71-for-169 (.420). 1986-87, 2-for-9 (.222). 1987-88, 8-for-35 (.229). Totals, 213-for-632 (.337).

NBA PLAYOFF RECORD

Season	Team	G	Min.	FGM	FGA	Pct.	FTM	FTA	Pct.	Off.	Def.	Tot.	Ast.	PF	Dq.	Stl.	Blk.	TO	Pts.	Avg.
										— REBOUNDS —										
75-76	Philadelphia.	3	62	11	28	.393	10	13	.769	1	0	1	5	6	0	3	0	...	32	10.7
76-77	Philadelphia.	15	281	63	170	.371	53	77	.688	10	22	32	29	33	0	12	8	...	179	11.9

Season Team	G	Min.	FGM	FGA	Pct.	FTM	FTA	Pct.	Off.	Def.	Tot.	Ast.	PF	Dq.	Stl.	Blk.	TO	Pts.	Avg.
77-78 —Philadelphia.	10	268	51	124	.411	59	81	.728	10	21	31	37	26	0	4	6	26	161	16.1
84-85 —Cleveland	4	150	41	93	.441	23	25	.920	4	6	10	31	12	0	6	0	6	105	26.3
87-88 —Houston	2	12	0	2	.000	0	0	...	1	1	2	1	2	0	0	0	3	0	0.0
Totals	34	773	166	417	.398	145	196	.740	26	50	76	103	79	0	25	14	35	477	14.0

Three-point field goals: 1984-85, 0-for-4. 1987-88, 0-for-1. Totals, 0-for-5.

NBA ALL-STAR GAME RECORD

Season Team	Min.	FGM	FGA	Pct.	FTM	FTA	Pct.	— REBOUNDS — Off.	Def.	Tot.	Ast.	PF	Dq.	Stl.	Blk.	TO	Pts.
1980 —San Diego	21	7	13	.538	0	1	.000	1	2	3	5	1	0	0	1	5	14

FULKS, JOE
F/C

PERSONAL: Born October 26, 1921, in Birmingham, Ky. . . . Died March 21, 1976. . . . 6-5/190. . . . Full name: Joseph Franklin Fulks. . . . Nickname: Jumpin' Joe.
HIGH SCHOOL: Birmingham (Ky.), then Kuttawa (Ky.).
COLLEGE: Murray State.
TRANSACTIONS/CAREER NOTES: In military service during 1943-44, 1944-45 and 1945-46 seasons. . . . Signed by Philadelphia Warriors of Basketball Association of America (1946). . . . Warriors franchise became part of NBA upon merger of BAA and National Basketball League for 1949-50 season.
CAREER HONORS: Elected to Naismith Memorial Basketball Hall of Fame (1977). . . . NBA 25th Anniversary All-Time team (1970).
MISCELLANEOUS: Member of NBA championship team (1947).

COLLEGIATE RECORD

NOTES: Elected to NAIA Basketball Hall of Fame (1952).

Season Team	G	Min.	FGM	FGA	Pct.	FTM	FTA	Pct.	Reb.	Pts.	Avg.
41-42 —Murray State	22	...	117	...	...	50	76	.658	...	284	12.9
42-43 —Murray State	25	...	135	...	...	67	100	.670	...	337	13.5
Totals	47	...	252	...	...	117	176	.665	...	621	13.2

NBA REGULAR-SEASON RECORD

HONORS: All-NBA first team (1947, 1948, 1949). . . . All-NBA second team (1951).

Season Team	G	Min.	FGM	FGA	Pct.	FTM	FTA	Pct.	Reb.	Ast.	PF	Dq.	Pts.	Avg.
46-47 —Philadelphia (BAA)	60	...	*475	*1557	.305	*439	*601	.730	...	25	199	...	*1389	*23.2
47-48 —Philadelphia (BAA)	43	...	326	*1258	.259	*297	390	.762	...	26	162	...	949	*22.1
48-49 —Philadelphia (BAA)	60	...	529	*1689	.313	502	638	.787	...	74	262	...	1560	26.0
49-50 —Philadelphia	68	...	336	1209	.278	293	421	.696	...	56	240	...	965	14.2
50-51 —Philadelphia	66	...	429	1358	.316	378	442	*.855	523	117	247	8	1236	18.7
51-52 —Philadelphia	61	1904	336	1078	.312	250	303	.825	368	123	255	13	922	15.1
52-53 —Philadelphia	70	2085	332	960	.346	168	231	.727	387	138	319	20	832	11.9
53-54 —Philadelphia	61	501	61	229	.266	28	49	.571	101	28	90	0	150	2.5
Totals	489	...	2824	9338	.302	2355	3075	.766	...	587	1774	...	8003	16.4

NBA PLAYOFF RECORD

Season Team	G	Min.	FGM	FGA	Pct.	FTM	FTA	Pct.	Reb.	Ast.	PF	Dq.	Pts.	Avg.
46-47 —Philadelphia (BAA)	10	...	74	257	.288	74	94	.787	...	3	32	...	222	22.2
47-48 —Philadelphia (BAA)	13	...	92	380	.242	98	121	.810	...	3	55	...	282	21.7
48-49 —Philadelphia (BAA)	1	...	0	0	...	0	0	...	...	0	1	...	0	0.0
49-50 —Philadelphia	2	...	5	26	.192	5	10	.500	...	2	10	...	15	7.5
50-51 —Philadelphia	2	...	16	49	.327	20	27	.741	16	1	9	0	52	26.0
51-52 —Philadelphia	3	70	5	33	.152	7	9	.778	12	2	13	1	17	5.7
Totals	31	...	192	745	.258	204	261	.782	...	11	120	...	588	19.0

NBA ALL-STAR GAME RECORD

Season Team	Min.	FGM	FGA	Pct.	FTM	FTA	Pct.	Reb.	Ast.	PF	Dq.	Pts.
1951 —Philadelphia	...	6	15	.400	7	9	.778	7	3	5	0	19
1952 —Philadelphia	9	3	7	.429	0	1	.000	5	2	2	0	6
Totals	9	9	22	.409	7	10	.700	12	5	7	0	25

GALLATIN, HARRY
F/C

PERSONAL: Born April 26, 1927, in Roxana, Ill. . . . 6-6/215. . . . Full name: Harry J. Gallatin. . . . Nickname: The Horse.
HIGH SCHOOL: Roxana (Ill.).
COLLEGE: Northeast Missouri State Teachers College.
TRANSACTIONS/CAREER NOTES: Selected by New York Knicks in first round of 1948 BAA Draft. . . . Knicks franchise became part of NBA upon merger of BAA and NBL for 1949-50 season. . . . Traded by Knicks with Dick Atha and Nat Clifton to Detroit Pistons for Mel Hutchins and first-round draft choice (April 3, 1957).
CAREER HONORS: Elected to Naismith Memorial Basketball Hall of Fame (1990).

COLLEGIATE RECORD

NOTES: Elected to NAIA Basketball Hall of Fame (1957).

Season Team	G	Min.	FGM	FGA	Pct.	FTM	FTA	Pct.	Reb.	Pts.	Avg.
46-47 —Northeast Missouri State	31	...	149	...	...	53	89	.596	...	351	11.3
47-48 —Northeast Missouri State	31	...	178	465	.383	109	162	.673	...	465	15.0
Totals	62	...	327	...	...	162	251	.645	...	816	13.2

NBA REGULAR-SEASON RECORD

HONORS: All-NBA first team (1954)....All-NBA second team (1955).
NOTES: Led NBA with 15.3 rebounds per game (1954).

Season Team	G	Min.	FGM	FGA	Pct.	FTM	FTA	Pct.	Reb.	Ast.	PF	Dq.	Pts.	Avg.
48-49—New York (BAA)	52	...	157	479	.328	120	169	.710	...	63	127	...	434	8.3
49-50—New York	68	...	263	664	.396	277	366	.757	...	56	215	...	803	11.8
50-51—New York	66	...	293	705	.416	259	354	.732	800	180	244	4	845	12.8
51-52—New York	66	1931	233	527	.442	275	341	.806	661	115	223	5	741	11.2
52-53—New York	70	2333	282	635	.444	301	430	.700	916	126	224	6	865	12.4
53-54—New York	72	2690	258	639	.404	433	552	.784	*1098	153	208	2	949	13.2
54-55—New York	72	2548	330	859	.384	393	483	.814	995	176	206	5	1053	14.6
55-56—New York	72	2378	322	834	.386	358	455	.787	740	168	220	6	1002	13.9
56-57—New York	72	1943	332	817	.406	415	519	.800	725	85	202	1	1079	15.0
57-58—Detroit	72	1990	340	898	.379	392	498	.787	749	86	217	5	1072	14.9
Totals	682	...	2810	7057	.398	3223	4167	.773	...	1208	2086	...	8843	13.0

NBA PLAYOFF RECORD

Season Team	G	Min.	FGM	FGA	Pct.	FTM	FTA	Pct.	Reb.	Ast.	PF	Dq.	Pts.	Avg.
48-49—New York (BAA)	6	...	20	56	.357	32	39	.821	...	10	31	...	72	12.0
49-50—New York	5	...	20	52	.385	25	32	.781	...	6	23	...	65	13.0
50-51—New York	14	...	49	140	.350	67	87	.770	163	26	57	3	165	11.8
51-52—New York	14	471	50	122	.410	51	66	.773	134	19	45	1	151	10.8
52-53—New York	11	303	36	86	.419	44	59	.746	120	15	29	0	116	10.5
53-54—New York	4	151	16	35	.457	22	31	.710	61	6	12	0	54	13.5
54-55—New York	3	108	19	42	.452	17	22	.773	44	7	11	0	55	18.3
57-58—Detroit	7	182	32	87	.368	26	37	.703	70	11	27	1	90	12.9
Totals	64	...	242	620	.390	284	373	.761	...	100	235	...	768	12.0

NBA ALL-STAR GAME RECORD

Season Team	Min.	FGM	FGA	Pct.	FTM	FTA	Pct.	Reb.	Ast.	PF	Dq.	Pts.
1951 —New York	...	2	4	.500	1	1	1.000	5	2	4	0	5
1952 —New York	22	3	5	.600	1	4	.250	9	3	3	0	7
1953 —New York	19	1	4	.250	1	2	.500	3	2	1	0	3
1954 —New York	28	0	2	.000	5	6	.833	18	3	0	0	5
1955 —New York	36	4	7	.571	5	5	1.000	14	3	2	0	13
1956 —New York	30	5	12	.417	6	7	.857	5	2	4	0	16
1957 —New York	24	4	7	.571	0	2	.000	11	1	3	0	8
Totals	...	19	41	.463	19	27	.704	65	16	17	0	57

HEAD COACHING RECORD

HONORS: NBA Coach of the Year (1963).

COLLEGIATE COACHING RECORD

Season Team	W	L	Pct.	Finish
58-59—Southern Illinois-Carbondale	17	10	.630	2nd/Interstate Intercollegiate Athletic Conference
59-60—Southern Illinois-Carbondale	20	9	.690	T1st/Interstate Intercollegiate Athletic Conference
60-61—Southern Illinois-Carbondale	21	6	.778	1st/Interstate Intercollegiate Athletic Conference
61-62—Southern Illinois-Carbondale	21	10	.677	1st/Interstate Intercollegiate Athletic Conference
67-68—Southern Ill.-Edwardsville	5	5	.500	
68-69—Southern Ill.-Edwardsville	7	10	.412	
69-70—Southern Ill.-Edwardsville	7	16	.304	
Totals (7 years)	98	66	.598	

NBA COACHING RECORD

Season Team	REGULAR SEASON				PLAYOFFS		
	W	L	Pct.	Finish	W	L	Pct.
62-63—St. Louis	48	32	.600	2nd/Western Division	6	5	.545
63-64—St. Louis	46	34	.575	2nd/Western Division	6	6	.500
64-65—St. Louis	17	16	.515		—	—	—
—New York	19	23	.452	4th/Eastern Division	—	—	—
65-66—New York	6	15	.286		—	—	—
Totals (4 years)	136	120	.531	Totals (2 years)	12	11	.522

NOTES:

1959— Defeated Wittenberg, 90-80, in NCAA College Division Tournament regional semifinal; lost to Belmont Academy, 79-70, in regional final.

1960— Defeated McKendree, 97-71, in NCAA College Division Tournament regional; lost to Oklahoma Baptist, 75-71, in semifinal.

1961— Defeated Trinity (Tex.), 96-84, in NCAA College Division Tournament regional semifinal; lost to Southeast Missouri, 87-84, in regional final.

1962— Defeated Union, 78-56, in NCAA College Division Tournament regional semifinal; defeated Evansville, 88-83, in regional final; defeated Northeastern, 73-57, in quarterfinal; lost to Mount St. Mary's, 58-57, in semifinals; defeated Nebraska Wesleyan 98-81, in third-place game.

1963— Defeated Detroit, 3-1, in Western Division semifinals; lost to Los Angeles, 4-3, in Western Division finals.

1964— Defeated Los Angeles, 3-2, in Western Division semifinals; lost to San Francisco, 4-3, in Western Division finals. Replaced as St. Louis head coach by Richie Guerin (November).

1965— Replaced Eddie Donovan as New York head coach (January), with record of 12-26. Replaced as New York head coach by Dick McGuire (November 29).

RECORD AS BASEBALL PLAYER

TRANSACTION/CAREER NOTES: Signed by Erwin (Tenn.) of Appalachian League (January 1945)....On military service list (July 1945-February 24, 1949)....Placed on suspended list (July 13, 1950)....Released (September 29, 1950).

Year Team (League)	G	W	L	Pct.	ERA	Sv.	IP	H	R	ER	BB	SO
1949—Decatur (Three I)	32	7	9	.438	4.28	...	166	171	88	79	85	78

GERVIN, GEORGE
G/F

PERSONAL: Born April 27, 1952, in Detroit.... 6-7/185.... Nickname: Iceman.... Brother of Derrick Gervin, guard with New Jersey Nets (1989-90 and 1990-91).
HIGH SCHOOL: Martin Luther King (Detroit).
COLLEGE: Long Beach State, then Eastern Michigan.
TRANSACTIONS/CAREER NOTES: Selected as undergraduate by Virginia Squires in first round of 1973 ABA special circumstance draft. ... Selected by Phoenix Suns in third round (40th pick overall) of 1974 NBA Draft. ... Sold by Squires to San Antonio Spurs (January 30, 1974).... Spurs franchise became part of NBA upon merger of ABA and NBA for 1976-77 season.... Traded by Spurs to Chicago Bulls for David Greenwood (October 24, 1985).... Played in Italy (1986-87). ... Played with Quad City Thunder of Continental Basketball Association (1989-90).

COLLEGIATE RECORD

NOTES: Left Long Beach State before the start of 1969-70 season.

Season Team	G	Min.	FGM	FGA	Pct.	FTM	FTA	Pct.	Reb.	Pts.	Avg.
70-71—Eastern Michigan	9	300	65	123	.528	28	39	.718	104	158	17.6
71-72—Eastern Michigan	30	1098	339	571	.594	208	265	.785	458	886	29.5
Totals	39	1398	404	694	.582	236	304	.776	562	1044	26.8

ABA REGULAR-SEASON RECORD

NOTES: ABA All-Star second team (1975, 1976).... ABA All-Rookie team (1973).

Season Team	G	Min.	2-POINT FGM	FGA	Pct.	3-POINT FGM	FGA	Pct.	FTM	FTA	Pct.	Reb.	Ast.	Pts.	Avg.
72-73—Virginia	30	689	155	315	.492	6	26	.231	96	118	.814	128	34	424	14.1
73-74—Va.-San Ant.	74	2511	664	1370	.485	8	56	.143	378	464	.815	624	142	1730	23.4
74-75—San Antonio	84	3113	767	1600	.479	17	55	.309	380	458	.830	697	207	1965	23.4
75-76—San Antonio	81	2748	692	1359	.509	14	55	.255	342	399	.857	546	201	1768	21.8
Totals	269	9061	2278	4644	.491	45	192	.234	1196	1439	.831	1995	584	5887	21.9

ABA PLAYOFF RECORD

Season Team	G	Min.	2-POINT FGM	FGA	Pct.	3-POINT FGM	FGA	Pct.	FTM	FTA	Pct.	Reb.	Ast.	Pts.	Avg.
72-73—Virginia	5	200	33	72	.458	1	5	.200	23	34	.676	38	8	93	18.6
73-74—San Antonio	7	226	56	114	.491	1	1	1.000	29	31	.935	52	19	144	20.6
74-75—San Antonio	6	276	76	159	.478	3	12	.250	43	52	.827	84	8	204	34.0
75-76—San Antonio	7	288	67	125	.536	0	3	.000	56	69	.812	64	19	190	27.1
Totals	25	990	232	470	.494	5	21	.238	151	186	.812	238	54	631	25.2

ABA ALL-STAR GAME RECORD

Season Team	Min.	2-POINT FGM	FGA	Pct.	3-POINT FGM	FGA	Pct.	FTM	FTA	Pct.	Reb.	Ast.	Pts.
1974—Virginia	21	3	8	.375	0	1	.000	3	4	.750	5	3	9
1975—San Antonio	30	8	14	.571	0	1	.000	7	8	.875	6	3	23
1976—San Antonio	16	3	13	.231	0	0	...	1	2	.500	6	1	8
Totals	67	14	35	.400	0	2	.000	11	14	.786	17	7	40

NBA REGULAR-SEASON RECORD

RECORDS: Holds single-game record for most points in one quarter—33 (April 9, 1978, vs. New Orleans).
HONORS: All-NBA first team (1978, 1979, 1980, 1981, 1982).... All-NBA second team (1977, 1983).

Season Team	G	Min.	FGM	FGA	Pct.	FTM	FTA	Pct.	REBOUNDS Off.	Def.	Tot.	Ast.	PF	Dq.	Stl.	Blk.	TO	Pts.	Avg.
76-77—San Antonio	82	2705	726	1335	.544	443	532	.833	134	320	454	238	286	12	105	104	...	1895	23.1
77-78—San Antonio	82	2857	*864	1611	.536	504	607	.830	118	302	420	302	255	3	136	110	306	*2232	*27.2
78-79—San Antonio	80	2888	*947	*1749	.541	471	570	.826	142	258	400	219	275	5	137	91	286	*2365	*29.6
79-80—San Antonio	78	2934	*1024	*1940	.528	505	593	.852	154	249	403	202	208	0	110	79	254	*2585	*33.1
80-81—San Antonio	82	2765	850	1729	.492	512	620	.826	126	293	419	260	212	4	94	56	251	2221	27.1
81-82—San Antonio	79	2817	*993	*1987	.500	555	642	.864	138	254	392	187	215	2	77	45	210	*2551	*32.3
82-83—San Antonio	78	2830	757	1553	.487	517	606	.853	111	246	357	264	243	5	88	67	247	2043	26.2
83-84—San Antonio	76	2584	765	1561	.490	427	507	.842	106	207	313	220	219	3	79	47	224	1967	25.9
84-85—San Antonio	72	2091	600	1182	.508	324	384	.844	79	155	234	178	208	2	66	48	198	1524	21.2
85-86—Chicago	82	2065	519	1100	.472	283	322	.879	78	137	215	144	210	4	49	23	161	1325	16.2
Totals	791	26536	8045	15747	.511	4541	5383	.844	1186	2421	3607	2214	2331	40	941	670	2137	20708	26.2

Three-point field goals: 1979-80, 32-for-102 (.314). 1980-81, 9-for-35 (.257). 1981-82, 10-for-36 (.278). 1982-83, 12-for-33 (.364). 1983-84, 10-for-24 (.417). 1984-85, 0-for-10. 1985-86, 4-for-19 (.211). Totals, 77-for-259 (.297).

NBA PLAYOFF RECORD

Season Team	G	Min.	FGM	FGA	Pct.	FTM	FTA	Pct.	REBOUNDS Off.	Def.	Tot.	Ast.	PF	Dq.	Stl.	Blk.	TO	Pts.	Avg.
76-77—San Antonio	2	62	19	44	.432	12	15	.800	5	6	11	3	9	1	1	2	...	50	25.0
77-78—San Antonio	6	227	78	142	.549	43	56	.768	11	23	34	19	23	0	6	16	19	199	33.2
78-79—San Antonio	14	513	158	295	.536	84	104	.808	33	49	82	35	51	1	27	14	40	400	28.6
79-80—San Antonio	3	122	37	74	.500	26	30	.867	9	11	20	12	8	0	5	3	9	100	33.3
80-81—San Antonio	7	274	77	154	.500	36	45	.800	9	26	35	24	19	1	5	5	20	190	27.1
81-82—San Antonio	9	373	103	228	.452	59	71	.831	19	47	66	41	36	1	10	4	31	265	29.4
82-83—San Antonio	11	437	108	208	.519	61	69	.884	21	53	74	37	39	1	12	4	46	277	25.2
84-85—San Antonio	5	183	42	79	.532	27	34	.794	3	15	18	14	19	0	3	3	20	111	22.2
85-86—Chicago	2	11	0	1	.000	0	0	...	0	1	1	1	3	0	0	0	2	0	0.0
Totals	59	2202	622	1225	.508	348	424	.821	110	231	341	186	207	5	69	51	187	1592	27.0

Three-point field goals: 1979-80, 0-for-2. 1980-81, 0-for-3. 1981-82, 0-for-3. 1982-83, 0-for-2. 1984-85, 0-for-3. Totals, 0-for-13.

NBA ALL-STAR GAME RECORD

NOTES: NBA All-Star Game Most Valuable Player (1980).

Season	Team	Min.	FGM	FGA	Pct.	FTM	FTA	Pct.	REBOUNDS Off.	Def.	Tot.	Ast.	PF	Dq.	Stl.	Blk.	TO	Pts.
1977	—San Antonio	12	0	6	.000	0	0	...	0	1	1	0	1	0	0	1	...	0
1978	—San Antonio	18	4	11	.364	1	3	.333	1	1	2	1	2	0	2	1	2	9
1979	—San Antonio	34	8	16	.500	10	11	.909	2	4	6	2	4	0	1	1	3	26
1980	—San Antonio	40	14	26	.538	6	9	.667	4	6	10	3	2	0	3	0	3	34
1981	—San Antonio	24	5	9	.556	1	2	.500	1	2	3	0	3	0	2	1	2	11
1982	—San Antonio	27	5	14	.357	2	2	1.000	1	5	6	1	3	0	3	3	0	12
1983	—San Antonio	14	3	8	.375	2	2	1.000	0	0	0	3	3	0	2	0	0	9
1984	—San Antonio	21	5	6	.833	3	3	1.000	0	2	2	1	5	0	1	1	6	13
1985	—San Antonio	25	10	12	.833	3	4	.750	0	3	3	1	2	0	3	1	4	23
	Totals	215	54	108	.500	28	36	.778	9	24	33	12	25	0	16	9	20	137

ITALIAN LEAGUE RECORD

Season	Team	G	Min.	FGM	FGA	Pct.	FTM	FTA	Pct.	Reb.	Pts.	Avg.
86-87	—Banco Roma	27	893	263	525	.501	159	190	.837	134	704	26.1

CBA REGULAR-SEASON RECORD

Season	Team	G	Min.	2-POINT FGM	FGA	Pct.	3-POINT FGM	FGA	Pct.	FTM	FTA	Pct.	Reb.	Ast.	Pts.	Avg.
89-90	—Quad City	14	391	115	235	.489	0	0	...	54	73	.740	91	20	284	20.3

GILMORE, ARTIS
C

PERSONAL: Born September 21, 1949, in Chipley, Fla. . . . 7-2/265.
HIGH SCHOOL: Roulhac (Chipley, Fla.), then Carver (Dothan, Ala.)
COLLEGE: Gardner-Webb Junior College (N.C.), then Jacksonville.
TRANSACTIONS/CAREER NOTES: Selected by Chicago Bulls in seventh
round (117th pick overall) of 1971 NBA Draft. . . . Selected by Kentucky Colonels in first round of 1971
ABA draft. . . . Selected by Bulls from Colonels for $1,100,000 in ABA dispersal draft (August 5, 1976). . . .
Traded by Bulls to San Antonio Spurs for Dave Corzine, Mark Olberding and cash (July 22, 1982). . . . Traded by Spurs to Bulls
for 1988 second-round draft choice (June 22, 1987). . . . Waived by Bulls (December 26, 1987). . . . Signed as free agent by
Boston Celtics (January 8, 1988). . . . Played in Italy (1988-89).

COLLEGIATE RECORD

NOTES: THE SPORTING NEWS All-America first team (1971). . . . THE SPORTING NEWS All-America second team (1970). . . .
Holds NCAA career record for rebounds per game—22.7. . . . Led NCAA Division I with 22.2 rebounds per game (1970) and 23.2
rebounds per game (1971).

Season	Team	G	Min.	FGM	FGA	Pct.	FTM	FTA	Pct.	Reb.	Pts.	Avg.
67-68	—Gardner-Webb	31	...	296	...	...	121	...	...	...	713	23.0
68-69	—Gardner-Webb	36	...	326	...	...	140	...	...	...	792	22.0
69-70	—Jacksonville	28	...	307	529	.580	128	202	.634	621	742	26.5
70-71	—Jacksonville	26	...	229	405	.565	112	188	.596	603	570	21.9
	Junior college totals	67	...	622			261	...	...	...	1505	22.5
	Four-year-college totals	54	...	536	934	.574	240	390	.615	1224	1312	24.3

ABA REGULAR-SEASON RECORD

NOTES: ABA Most Valuable Player (1972). . . . ABA Rookie of the Year (1972). . . . ABA All-Star first team (1972, 1973, 1974,
1975, 1976). . . . ABA All-Defensive team (1973, 1974, 1975, 1976). . . . ABA All-Rookie Team (1972). . . . Member of ABA
championship team (1975). . . . Holds single-game record for most rebounds—40 (February 3, 1974, vs. New York). . . . Holds
single-season record for most blocked shots—422 (1972). . . . Led ABA with 17.8 rebounds per game (1972), 17.5 rebounds
per game (1973), 18.3 rebounds per game (1974) and 15.5 rebounds per game (1976).

Season	Team	G	Min.	2-POINT FGM	FGA	Pct.	3-POINT FGM	FGA	Pct.	FTM	FTA	Pct.	Reb.	Ast.	Pts.	Avg.
71-72	—Kentucky	84	*3666	806	1348	*.598	0	0	...	391	605	.646	*1491	230	2003	23.8
72-73	—Kentucky	84	3502	686	1226	*.560	1	2	.500	368	572	.643	*1476	295	1743	20.8
73-74	—Kentucky	84	*3502	621	1257	.494	0	3	.000	326	489	.667	*1538	329	1568	18.7
74-75	—Kentucky	84	*3493	783	1349	.580	1	2	.500	412	592	.696	*1361	208	1081	12.9
75-76	—Kentucky	84	3286	773	1401	.552	0	0	...	521	*764	.682	*1303	211	2067	24.6
	Totals	420	17449	3669	6581	.558	2	7	.286	2018	3022	.668	7169	1273	8462	20.1

ABA PLAYOFF RECORD

NOTES: ABA Playoff Most Valuable Player (1975).

Season	Team	G	Min.	2-POINT FGM	FGA	Pct.	3-POINT FGM	FGA	Pct.	FTM	FTA	Pct.	Reb.	Ast.	Pts.	Avg.
71-72	—Kentucky	6	285	52	90	.578	0	0	...	27	38	.711	106	25	131	21.8
72-73	—Kentucky	19	780	142	261	.544	0	0	...	77	123	.626	260	75	361	19.0
73-74	—Kentucky	8	344	71	127	.559	0	0	...	38	66	.576	149	28	180	22.5
74-75	—Kentucky	15	679	132	245	.539	0	0	...	98	127	.772	264	38	362	24.1
75-76	—Kentucky	10	390	93	153	.608	0	0	...	56	75	.747	152	19	242	24.2
	Totals	58	2478	490	876	.559	0	0	...	296	429	.690	931	185	1276	22.0

ABA ALL-STAR GAME RECORD

NOTES: ABA All-Star Game Most Valuable Player (1974).

Season	Team	Min.	2-POINT FGM	FGA	Pct.	3-POINT FGM	FGA	Pct.	FTM	FTA	Pct.	Reb.	Ast.	Pts.
1972	—Kentucky	27	4	5	.800	0	0	...	6	10	.600	10	2	14
1973	—Kentucky	31	3	8	.375	0	0	...	4	8	.500	16	0	10
1974	—Kentucky	27	8	12	.667	0	0	...	2	3	.667	13	1	18
1975	—Kentucky	28	4	8	.500	0	0	...	3	7	.429	13	2	11
1976	—Kentucky	27	5	7	.714	0	0	...	6	7	.857	7	1	14
	Totals	140	24	40	.600	0	0	...	21	35	.600	59	6	67

NBA REGULAR-SEASON RECORD

RECORDS: Holds career record for highest field-goal percentage (minimum 2,000 made) — .599.
HONORS: NBA All-Defensive second team (1978).

Season Team	G	Min.	FGM	FGA	Pct.	FTM	FTA	Pct.	Off.	Def.	Tot.	Ast.	PF	Dq.	Stl.	Blk.	TO	Pts.	Avg.
76-77—Chicago.......	82	2877	570	1091	.522	387	586	.660	313	757	1070	199	266	4	44	203	...	1527	18.6
77-78—Chicago.......	82	3067	704	1260	.559	471	*669	.704	318	753	1071	263	261	4	42	181	*366	1879	22.9
78-79—Chicago.......	82	3265	753	1310	.575	434	587	.739	293	750	1043	274	280	2	50	156	310	1940	23.7
79-80—Chicago.......	48	1568	305	513	.595	245	344	.712	108	324	432	133	167	5	29	59	133	855	17.8
80-81—Chicago.......	82	2832	547	816	*.670	375	532	.705	220	608	828	172	295	2	47	198	236	1469	17.9
81-82—Chicago.......	82	2796	546	837	*.652	424	552	.768	224	611	835	136	287	4	49	220	227	1517	18.5
82-83—San Antonio.	82	2797	556	888	*.626	367	496	.740	299	685	984	126	273	4	40	192	254	1479	18.0
83-84—San Antonio.	64	2034	351	556	*.631	280	390	.718	213	449	662	70	229	4	36	132	149	982	15.3
84-85—San Antonio.	81	2756	532	854	.623	484	646	.749	231	615	846	131	306	4	40	173	241	1548	19.1
85-86—San Antonio.	71	2395	423	684	.618	338	482	.701	166	434	600	102	239	3	39	108	186	1184	16.7
86-87—San Antonio.	82	2405	346	580	.597	242	356	.680	185	394	579	150	235	2	39	95	178	934	11.4
87-88—Chi.-Boston.	71	893	99	181	.547	67	128	.523	69	142	211	21	148	0	15	30	67	265	3.7
Totals	909	29685	5732	9570	.599	4114	5768	.713	2639	6522	9161	1777	2986	38	470	1747	2347	15579	17.1

Three-point field goals: 1981-82, 1-for-1. 1982-83, 0-for-6. 1983-84, 0-for-3. 1984-85, 0-for-2. 1985-86, 0-for-1. Totals, 1-for-13 (.077).

NBA PLAYOFF RECORD

Season Team	G	Min.	FGM	FGA	Pct.	FTM	FTA	Pct.	Off.	Def.	Tot.	Ast.	PF	Dq.	Stl.	Blk.	TO	Pts.	Avg.
76-77—Chicago.......	3	126	19	40	.475	18	23	.783	15	24	39	6	9	0	3	8	...	56	18.7
80-81—Chicago.......	6	247	35	60	.583	38	55	.691	24	43	67	12	15	0	6	17	17	108	18.0
82-83—San Antonio.	11	401	76	132	.576	32	46	.696	37	105	142	18	46	1	9	34	27	184	16.7
84-85—San Antonio.	5	185	29	52	.558	31	45	.689	10	40	50	7	18	0	2	7	23	89	17.8
85-86—San Antonio.	3	107	16	24	.667	8	14	.571	7	11	18	3	11	0	7	1	10	40	13.3
87-88—Boston	14	86	4	8	.500	7	14	.500	4	16	20	1	14	0	0	4	4	15	1.1
Totals	42	1152	179	316	.566	134	197	.680	97	239	336	47	113	1	27	71	81	492	11.7

NBA ALL-STAR GAME RECORD

Season Team	Min.	FGM	FGA	Pct.	FTM	FTA	Pct.	Off.	Def.	Tot.	Ast.	PF	Dq.	Stl.	Blk.	TO	Pts.
1978 —Chicago..............	13	2	4	.500	6	8	.750	0	2	2	0	1	0	1	2	1	10
1979 —Chicago..............	15	3	4	.750	2	2	1.000	1	0	1	2	1	0	0	0	1	8
1981 —Chicago..............	22	5	7	.714	1	2	.500	1	5	6	2	4	0	0	1	0	11
1982 —Chicago..............	16	3	6	.500	1	1	1.000	1	2	3	2	4	0	0	1	2	7
1983 —San Antonio....	16	2	4	.500	1	2	.500	1	4	5	1	4	0	1	0	1	5
1986 —San Antonio.......	13	3	4	.750	4	4	1.000	1	1	2	1	4	0	2	0	0	10
Totals	95	18	29	.621	15	19	.789	5	14	19	8	18	0	4	4	5	51

ITALIAN LEAGUE RECORD

Season Team	G	Min.	FGM	FGA	Pct.	FTM	FTA	Pct.	Reb.	Pts.	Avg.
88-89 —Bologna Arimo	35	1101	166	270	.615	97	147	.660	386	429	12.3

GOODRICH, GAIL
G

PERSONAL: Born April 23, 1943, in Los Angeles.... 6-1/175.... Full name: Gail Charles Goodrich Jr.
HIGH SCHOOL: Polytechnic (Pasadena, Calif.).
COLLEGE: UCLA.
TRANSACTIONS/CAREER NOTES: Selected by Los Angeles Lakers 1965 NBA Draft (territorial pick).... Selected by Phoenix Suns from Lakers in expansion draft (May 6, 1968).... Traded by Suns to Lakers for Mel Counts (May 20, 1970).... Played out option with Lakers.... Signed as veteran free agent by New Orleans Jazz (July 19, 1976).... Lakers received 1977 and 1979 first-round draft choices and 1980 second-round draft choice as compensation; Jazz received 1977 second-round draft choice to complete transaction (October 6, 1976).
MISCELLANEOUS: Member of NBA championship team (1972).

COLLEGIATE RECORD

NOTES: THE SPORTING NEWS All-America first team (1964).... Member of NCAA Division I championship teams (1964, 1965).

Season Team	G	Min.	FGM	FGA	Pct.	FTM	FTA	Pct.	Reb.	Pts.	Avg.
61-62—UCLA‡..................................	20	...	189	385	.491	110	155	.710	122	488	24.4
62-63—UCLA.................................	29	...	117	280	.418	66	103	.641	101	300	10.3
63-64—UCLA.................................	30	...	243	530	.458	160	225	.711	156	646	21.5
64-65—UCLA.................................	30	...	277	528	.525	190	265	.717	158	744	24.8
Varsity totals	89	...	637	1338	.476	416	593	.702	415	1690	19.0

NBA REGULAR-SEASON RECORD

HONORS: All-NBA first team (1974).

Season Team	G	Min.	FGM	FGA	Pct.	FTM	FTA	Pct.	Reb.	Ast.	PF	Dq.	Pts.	Avg.
65-66—Los Angeles	65	1008	203	503	.404	103	149	.691	130	103	103	1	509	7.8
66-67—Los Angeles	77	1780	352	776	.454	253	337	.751	251	210	194	3	957	12.4
67-68—Los Angeles	79	2057	395	812	.486	302	392	.770	199	205	228	2	1092	13.8
68-69—Phoenix.........................	81	3236	718	1746	.411	495	663	.747	437	518	253	3	1931	23.8
69-70—Phoenix.........................	81	3234	568	1251	.454	488	604	.808	340	605	251	3	1624	20.0
70-71—Los Angeles	79	2808	558	1174	.475	264	343	.770	260	380	258	3	1380	17.5
71-72—Los Angeles	82	3040	826	1695	.487	475	559	.850	295	365	210	0	2127	25.9
72-73—Los Angeles	76	2697	750	1615	.464	314	374	.840	263	332	193	1	1814	23.9

Season Team	G	Min.	FGM	FGA	Pct.	FTM	FTA	Pct.	Off.	Def.	Tot.	Ast.	PF	Dq.	Stl.	Blk.	TO	Pts.	Avg.
73-74—Los Angeles.	82	3061	784	1773	.442	*508	*588	.864	95	155	250	427	227	3	126	12	...	2076	25.3
74-75—Los Angeles.	72	2668	656	1429	.459	318	378	.841	96	123	219	420	214	1	102	6	...	1630	22.6

Season Team	G	Min.	FGM	FGA	Pct.	FTM	FTA	Pct.	Off.	Def.	Tot.	Ast.	PF	Dq.	Stl.	Blk.	TO	Pts.	Avg.
75-76 —Los Angeles .	75	2646	583	1321	.441	293	346	.847	94	120	214	421	238	3	123	17	...	1459	19.5
76-77 —New Orleans.	27	609	136	305	.446	68	85	.800	25	36	61	74	43	0	22	2	...	340	12.6
77-78 —New Orleans.	81	2553	520	1050	.495	264	332	.795	75	102	177	388	186	0	82	22	205	1304	16.1
78-79 —New Orleans.	74	2130	382	850	.449	174	204	.853	68	115	183	357	177	1	90	13	185	938	12.7
Totals	1031	33527	7431	16300	.456	4319	5354	.807	...	...	3279	4805	2775	24	545	72	390	19181	18.6

NBA PLAYOFF RECORD

Season Team	G	Min.	FGM	FGA	Pct.	FTM	FTA	Pct.	Reb.	Ast.	PF	Dq.	Pts.	Avg.
65-66 —Los Angeles	11	290	43	92	.467	29	43	.674	42	33	35	0	115	10.5
66-67 —Los Angeles	3	81	11	31	.355	11	18	.611	9	10	5	0	33	11.0
67-68 —Los Angeles	10	100	23	47	.489	14	18	.778	14	14	10	0	60	6.0
69-70 —Phoenix	7	265	56	118	.475	30	35	.857	32	38	21	0	142	20.3
70-71 —Los Angeles	12	518	105	247	.425	95	113	.841	38	91	38	0	305	25.4
71-72 —Los Angeles	15	575	130	292	.445	97	108	.898	38	50	50	0	357	23.8
72-73 —Los Angeles	17	604	139	310	.448	62	79	.785	61	67	53	1	340	20.0

Season Team	G	Min.	FGM	FGA	Pct.	FTM	FTA	Pct.	Off.	Def.	Tot.	Ast.	PF	Dq.	Stl.	Blk.	TO	Pts.	Avg.
73-74 —Los Angeles .	5	189	35	90	.389	28	33	.848	7	9	16	30	7	0	7	1	...	98	19.6
Totals	80	2622	542	1227	.442	366	447	.819	...	...	250	333	219	1	7	1	...	1450	18.1

NBA ALL-STAR GAME RECORD

Season Team	Min.	FGM	FGA	Pct.	FTM	FTA	Pct.	Reb.	Ast.	PF	Dq.	Pts.
1969 —Phoenix	6	2	4	.500	1	2	.500	1	1	1	0	5
1972 —Los Angeles	14	2	7	.286	0	0	...	1	2	2	0	4
1973 —Los Angeles	16	1	7	.143	0	0	...	2	1	2	0	2

Season Team	Min.	FGM	FGA	Pct.	FTM	FTA	Pct.	Off.	Def.	Tot.	Ast.	PF	Dq.	Stl.	Blk.	TO	Pts.
1974 —Los Angeles	26	9	16	.563	0	0	...	1	3	4	6	2	0	1	0	...	18
1975 —Los Angeles	15	2	4	.500	0	0	...	0	1	1	4	1	0	0	0	...	4
Totals	77	16	38	.421	1	2	.500	...	...	9	14	8	0	1	0	...	33

GREER, HAL
G

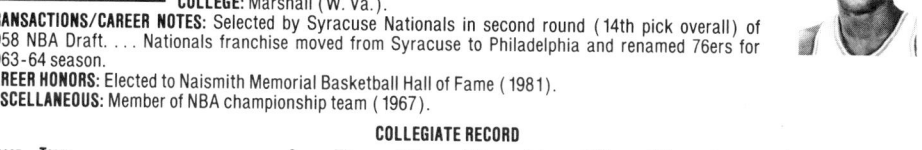

PERSONAL: Born June 26, 1936, in Huntington, W. Va. ... 6-2/175. ... Full name: Harold Everett Greer.
HIGH SCHOOL: Douglass (Huntington, W. Va.)
COLLEGE: Marshall (W. Va.).
TRANSACTIONS/CAREER NOTES: Selected by Syracuse Nationals in second round (14th pick overall) of 1958 NBA Draft. ... Nationals franchise moved from Syracuse to Philadelphia and renamed 76ers for 1963-64 season.
CAREER HONORS: Elected to Naismith Memorial Basketball Hall of Fame (1981).
MISCELLANEOUS: Member of NBA championship team (1967).

COLLEGIATE RECORD

Season Team	G	Min.	FGM	FGA	Pct.	FTM	FTA	Pct.	Reb.	Pts.	Avg.
54-55 —Marshall‡	...	...	...	...	...	...	...	...	...	...	18.0
55-56 —Marshall	23	...	128	213	.601	101	145	.697	153	357	15.5
56-57 —Marshall	24	...	167	329	.508	119	156	.763	332	453	18.9
57-58 —Marshall	24	...	236	432	.546	95	114	.833	280	567	23.6
Varsity totals	71	...	531	974	.545	315	415	.759	765	1377	19.4

NBA REGULAR-SEASON RECORD

HONORS: All-NBA second team (1963, 1964, 1965, 1966, 1967, 1968, 1969).

Season Team	G	Min.	FGM	FGA	Pct.	FTM	FTA	Pct.	Reb.	Ast.	PF	Dq.	Pts.	Avg.
58-59 —Syracuse	68	1625	308	679	.454	137	176	.778	196	101	189	1	753	11.1
59-60 —Syracuse	70	1979	388	815	.476	148	189	.783	303	188	208	4	924	13.2
60-61 —Syracuse	79	2763	623	1381	.451	305	394	.774	455	302	212	0	1551	19.6
61-62 —Syracuse	71	2705	644	1442	.447	331	404	.819	524	313	252	2	1619	22.8
62-63 —Syracuse	80	2631	600	1293	.464	362	434	.834	457	275	286	4	1562	19.5
63-64 —Philadelphia	80	3157	715	1611	.444	435	525	.829	484	374	291	6	1865	23.3
64-65 —Philadelphia	70	2600	539	1245	.433	335	413	.811	355	313	254	7	1413	20.2
65-66 —Philadelphia	80	3326	703	1580	.445	413	514	.804	473	384	315	6	1819	22.7
66-67 —Philadelphia	80	3086	699	1524	.459	367	466	.788	422	303	302	5	1765	22.1
67-68 —Philadelphia	82	3263	777	1626	.478	422	549	.769	444	372	289	6	1976	24.1
68-69 —Philadelphia	82	3311	732	1595	.459	432	543	.796	435	414	294	8	1896	23.1
69-70 —Philadelphia	80	3024	705	1551	.455	352	432	.815	376	405	300	8	1762	22.0
70-71 —Philadelphia	81	3060	591	1371	.431	326	405	.805	364	369	289	4	1508	18.6
71-72 —Philadelphia	81	2410	389	866	.449	181	234	.774	271	316	268	10	959	11.8
72-73 —Philadelphia	38	848	91	232	.392	32	39	.821	106	111	76	1	214	5.6
Totals	1122	39788	8504	18811	.452	4578	5717	.801	5665	4540	3825	72	21586	19.2

NBA PLAYOFF RECORD

Season Team	G	Min.	FGM	FGA	Pct.	FTM	FTA	Pct.	Reb.	Ast.	PF	Dq.	Pts.	Avg.
58-59 —Syracuse	9	277	39	93	.419	26	32	.813	47	20	35	2	104	11.6
59-60 —Syracuse	3	84	22	43	.512	3	4	.750	14	10	5	0	47	15.7
60-61 —Syracuse	8	232	41	106	.387	33	40	.825	33	19	32	1	115	14.4
61-62 —Syracuse	1	5	0	0	...	0	0	...	0	0	1	0	0	0.0
62-63 —Syracuse	5	214	44	87	.506	29	35	.829	27	21	21	1	117	23.4
63-64 —Philadelphia	5	211	37	95	.389	33	39	.846	28	30	19	1	107	21.4
64-65 —Philadelphia	11	505	101	222	.455	69	87	.793	81	55	45	2	271	24.6
65-66 —Philadelphia	5	226	32	91	.352	18	23	.783	36	21	21	0	82	16.4
66-67 —Philadelphia	15	688	161	375	.429	94	118	.797	88	79	55	1	416	27.7
67-68 —Philadelphia	13	553	120	278	.432	95	111	.856	79	55	49	1	335	25.8
68-69 —Philadelphia	5	204	26	81	.321	28	36	.778	30	23	23	0	80	16.0

Season Team	G	Min.	FGM	FGA	Pct.	FTM	FTA	Pct.	Reb.	Ast.	PF	Dq.	Pts.	Avg.
69-70—Philadelphia	5	178	33	74	.446	11	13	.846	17	27	16	0	77	15.4
70-71—Philadelphia	7	265	49	112	.438	27	36	.750	25	33	35	4	125	17.9
Totals	92	3642	705	1657	.425	466	574	.812	505	393	357	13	1876	20.4

NBA ALL-STAR GAME RECORD

NOTES: NBA All-Star Game Most Valuable Player (1968).... Holds single-game record for most points in one quarter—19 (1968).

Season Team	Min.	FGM	FGA	Pct.	FTM	FTA	Pct.	Reb.	Ast.	PF	Dq.	Pts.
1961 —Syracuse	18	7	11	.636	0	0	...	6	2	2	0	14
1962 —Syracuse	24	3	14	.214	2	7	.286	10	9	3	0	8
1963 —Syracuse	15	3	7	.429	0	0	...	3	2	4	0	6
1964 —Philadelphia	20	5	10	.500	3	4	.750	3	4	1	0	13
1965 —Philadelphia	21	5	11	.455	3	4	.750	4	1	2	0	13
1966 —Philadelphia	23	4	13	.308	1	1	1.000	5	1	4	0	9
1967 —Philadelphia	31	5	16	.313	7	8	.875	4	1	5	0	17
1968 —Philadelphia	17	8	8	1.000	5	7	.714	3	3	2	0	21
1969 —Philadelphia	17	0	1	.000	4	5	.800	3	2	2	0	4
1970 —Philadelphia	21	7	11	.636	1	1	1.000	4	3	4	0	15
Totals	207	47	102	.461	26	37	.703	45	28	29	0	120

CBA COACHING RECORD

		REGULAR SEASON			PLAYOFFS		
Season Team	W	L	Pct.	Finish	W	L	Pct.
80-81—Philadelphia	17	23	.425	3rd/Eastern Division	3	3	.500
Totals (1 year)	17	23	.425	Totals (1 year)	3	3	.500

NOTES:
1981— Defeated Atlantic City, 2-1, in Eastern semifinals; lost to Rochester, 2-1, in Eastern finals.

GUERIN, RICHIE
G

PERSONAL: Born May 29, 1932, in New York.... 6-4/210.... Full name: Richard V. Guerin.
HIGH SCHOOL: Mt. St. Michael Academy (Bronx, N.Y.).
COLLEGE: Iona.
TRANSACTIONS/CAREER NOTES: Selected by New York Knicks in second round of 1954 NBA Draft.... In military service during 1954-55 and 1955-56 seasons; played with Quantico Marines and Marine All-Star teams.... Traded by Knicks to St. Louis Hawks for cash and second-round draft choice (October 18, 1963).

COLLEGIATE RECORD

Season Team	G	Min.	FGM	FGA	Pct.	FTM	FTA	Pct.	Reb.	Pts.	Avg.
					Freshman team statistics unavailable.						
50-51—Iona‡											
51-52—Iona	27	...	159	...	...	146	...	...	...	464	17.2
52-53—Iona	21	...	139	283	.491	114	172	.663	...	392	18.7
53-54—Iona	21	...	171	405	.422	177	249	.711	...	519	24.7
Varsity totals	69	...	469	...	...	437	...	...	...	1375	19.9

NBA REGULAR-SEASON RECORD

HONORS: All-NBA second team (1959, 1960, 1962).

Season Team	G	Min.	FGM	FGA	Pct.	FTM	FTA	Pct.	Reb.	Ast.	PF	Dq.	Pts.	Avg.
56-57—New York	72	1793	257	699	.368	181	292	.620	334	182	186	3	695	9.7
57-58—New York	63	2368	344	973	.354	353	511	.691	489	317	202	3	1041	16.5
58-59—New York	71	2558	443	1046	.424	405	505	.802	518	364	255	1	1291	18.2
59-60—New York	74	2429	579	1379	.420	457	591	.773	505	468	242	3	1615	21.8
60-61—New York	79	3023	612	1545	.396	496	626	.792	628	503	310	3	1720	21.8
61-62—New York	78	3346	839	1897	.442	625	762	.820	501	539	299	3	2303	29.5
62-63—New York	79	2712	596	1380	.432	509	600	.848	331	348	228	2	1701	21.5
63-64—New York-St. Louis	80	2366	351	846	.415	347	424	.818	256	375	276	4	1049	13.1
64-65—St. Louis	57	1678	295	662	.446	231	301	.767	149	271	193	1	821	14.4
65-66—St. Louis	80	2363	414	998	.415	362	446	.812	314	388	256	4	1190	14.9
66-67—St. Louis	79	2275	394	904	.436	304	416	.731	192	345	247	2	1092	13.8
67-68—					Did not play—retired.									
68-69—Atlanta	27	472	47	111	.423	57	74	.770	59	99	66	0	151	5.6
69-70—Atlanta	8	64	3	11	.273	1	1	1.000	2	12	9	0	7	0.9
Totals	847	27447	5174	12451	.416	4328	5549	.780	4278	4211	2769	29	14676	17.3

NBA PLAYOFF RECORD

Season Team	G	Min.	FGM	FGA	Pct.	FTM	FTA	Pct.	Reb.	Ast.	PF	Dq.	Pts.	Avg.
58-59—New York	2	77	9	35	.257	12	14	.857	18	15	11	1	30	15.0
63-64—St. Louis	12	428	75	169	.444	67	85	.788	50	49	54	1	217	18.1
64-65—St. Louis	4	125	25	65	.385	19	25	.760	8	21	14	0	69	17.3
65-66—St. Louis	10	399	72	159	.453	62	76	.816	37	79	41	0	206	20.6
66-67—St. Louis	9	228	36	86	.419	24	30	.800	23	39	23	0	96	10.7
68-69—Atlanta	3	32	1	4	.250	1	2	.500	5	7	8	0	3	1.0
69-70—Atlanta	2	56	13	21	.619	7	7	1.000	8	4	6	0	33	16.5
Totals	42	1345	231	539	.429	192	239	.803	149	214	157	2	654	15.6

NBA ALL-STAR GAME RECORD

Season Team	Min.	FGM	FGA	Pct.	FTM	FTA	Pct.	Reb.	Ast.	PF	Dq.	Pts.
1958 —New York	22	2	10	.200	3	4	.750	8	7	3	0	7
1959 —New York	22	1	7	.143	3	5	.600	3	3	1	0	5
1960 —New York	22	5	11	.455	2	2	1.000	4	4	4	0	12
1961 —New York	15	3	8	.375	5	6	.833	0	2	1	0	11
1962 —New York	27	10	17	.588	3	6	.500	3	1	6	1	23
1963 —New York	14	2	3	.667	1	3	.333	1	1	2	0	5
Totals	122	23	56	.411	17	26	.654	19	18	17	1	63

HONORS: NBA Coach of the Year (1968).

NBA COACHING RECORD

Season Team		W	L	Pct.	REGULAR SEASON Finish	W	L	Pct.
64-65 — St. Louis		28	19	.596	2nd/Western Division	1	3	.250
65-66 — St. Louis		36	44	.450	3rd/Western Division	6	4	.600
66-67 — St. Louis		39	42	.481	2nd/Western Division	5	4	.556
67-68 — St. Louis		56	26	.683	1st/Western Division	2	4	.333
68-69 — Atlanta		48	34	.585	2nd/Western Division	5	6	.455
69-70 — Atlanta		48	34	.585	1st/Western Division	4	5	.444
70-71 — Atlanta		36	46	.439	2nd/Central Division	1	4	.200
71-72 — Atlanta		36	46	.439	2nd/Central Division	2	4	.333
Totals (8 years)		327	291	.529	Totals (8 years)	26	34	.433

NOTES:

1964— Replaced Harry Gallatin as St. Louis head coach (November), with record of 17-16.
1965— Lost to Baltimore in Western Division semifinals.
1966— Defeated Baltimore, 3-0, in Western Division semifinals; lost to Los Angeles, 4-3, in Western Division finals.
1967— Defeated Chicago, 3-0, in Western Division semifinals; lost to San Francisco, 4-2, in Western Division finals.
1968— Lost to San Francisco in Western Division semifinals. Hawks franchise moved to Atlanta for 1968-69 season.
1969— Defeated San Diego, 4-2, in Western Division semifinals; lost to Los Angeles, 4-1, in Western Division finals.
1970— Defeated Chicago, 4-1, in Western Division semifinals; lost to Los Angeles, 4-0, in Western Division finals.
1971— Lost to New York in Eastern Conference semifinals.
1972— Lost to Boston in Eastern Conference semifinals.

HAGAN, CLIFF
F/G

PERSONAL: Born December 9, 1931, in Owensboro, Ky. . . . 6-4/215. . . . Full name: Clifford Oldham Hagan. . . . Nickname: Li'l Abner.
HIGH SCHOOL: Owensboro (Ky.).
COLLEGE: Kentucky.
TRANSACTIONS/CAREER NOTES: Selected by Boston Celtics in third round of 1953 NBA Draft. . . . In military service during 1954-55 and 1955-56 seasons; played at Andrews Air Force Base. . . . Draft rights traded by Celtics with Ed Macauley to St. Louis Hawks for first-round draft choice (April 30, 1956). . . . Signed as player/head coach by Dallas Chaparrals of American Basketball Association (June 1967).
CAREER HONORS: Elected to Naismith Memorial Basketball Hall of Fame (1977).
MISCELLANEOUS: Member of NBA championship team (1958).

COLLEGIATE RECORD

NOTES: Member of NCAA championship team (1951).

Season Team	G	Min.	FGM	FGA	Pct.	FTM	FTA	Pct.	Reb.	Pts.	Avg.
49-50 — Kentucky‡	12	. . .	114	244	.467	42	58	.724	. . .	270	22.5
50-51 — Kentucky	20	. . .	69	188	.367	45	61	.738	169	183	9.2
51-52 — Kentucky	32	. . .	264	633	.417	245	351	.698	528	692	21.6
52-53 — Kentucky					Did not play—team suspended for season.						
53-54 — Kentucky	25	. . .	234	514	.455	132	191	.691	338	600	24.0
Varsity totals	77	. . .	567	1335	.425	341	487	.700	1035	1475	19.2

NBA REGULAR-SEASON RECORD

HONORS: All-NBA second team (1958, 1959).

Season Team	G	Min.	FGM	FGA	Pct.	FTM	FTA	Pct.	Reb.	Ast.	PF	Dq.	Pts.	Avg.
56-57 — St. Louis	67	971	134	371	.361	100	145	.690	247	86	165	3	368	5.5
57-58 — St. Louis	70	2190	503	1135	.443	385	501	.768	707	175	267	9	1391	19.9
58-59 — St. Louis	72	2702	646	1417	.456	415	536	.774	783	245	275	10	1707	23.7
59-60 — St. Louis	75	2798	719	1549	.464	421	524	.803	803	299	270	4	1859	24.8
60-61 — St. Louis	78	2701	661	1490	.444	383	467	.820	718	381	286	9	1705	21.9
61-62 — St. Louis	77	2784	701	1490	.470	362	439	.825	533	370	282	8	1764	22.9
62-63 — St. Louis	79	1716	491	1055	.465	244	305	.800	341	191	221	2	1226	15.5
63-64 — St. Louis	77	2279	572	1280	.447	269	331	.813	377	189	272	4	1413	18.4
64-65 — St. Louis	77	1739	393	901	.436	214	268	.799	276	136	182	0	1000	13.0
65-66 — St. Louis	74	1851	419	942	.445	176	206	.854	234	164	177	1	1014	13.7
Totals	746	21731	5239	11630	.450	2969	3722	.798	5019	2236	2397	50	13447	18.0

NBA PLAYOFF RECORD

Season Team	G	Min.	FGM	FGA	Pct.	FTM	FTA	Pct.	Reb.	Ast.	PF	Dq.	Pts.	Avg.
56-57 — St. Louis	10	419	62	143	.434	46	63	.730	112	28	47	3	170	17.0
57-58 — St. Louis	11	418	111	221	.502	83	99	.838	115	37	48	3	305	27.7
58-59 — St. Louis	6	259	63	123	.512	45	54	.833	72	16	21	0	171	28.5
59-60 — St. Louis	14	544	125	296	.422	89	109	.817	138	54	54	1	339	24.2
60-61 — St. Louis	12	455	104	235	.443	56	69	.812	118	54	45	1	264	22.0
62-63 — St. Louis	11	255	83	179	.464	37	53	.698	55	34	42	4	203	18.5
63-64 — St. Louis	12	392	75	175	.429	45	54	.833	74	57	34	0	195	16.3
64-65 — St. Louis	4	123	34	75	.453	6	12	.500	26	7	14	0	74	18.5
65-66 — St. Louis	10	200	44	97	.454	25	27	.926	34	18	15	0	113	11.3
Totals	90	3065	701	1544	.454	432	540	.800	744	305	320	12	1834	20.4

NBA ALL-STAR GAME RECORD

Season Team	Min.	FGM	FGA	Pct.	FTM	FTA	Pct.	Reb.	Ast.	PF	Dq.	Pts.
1958 — St. Louis					Did not play—injured.							
1959 — St. Louis	22	6	12	.500	3	3	1.000	8	3	5	0	15
1960 — St. Louis	21	1	9	.111	0	0	. . .	3	2	1	0	2

Season Team	Min.	FGM	FGA	Pct.	FTM	FTA	Pct.	Reb.	Ast.	PF	Dq.	Pts.
1961 —St. Louis	13	2	9	.222	2	2	1.000	2	0	1	0	2
1962 —St. Louis	9	1	3	.333	0	0	...	2	1	1	0	2
Totals	65	10	33	.303	5	5	1.000	15	6	8	0	21

ABA REGULAR-SEASON RECORD

Season Team	G	Min.	2-POINT			3-POINT			FTM	FTA	Pct.	Reb.	Ast.	Pts.	Avg.
			FGM	FGA	Pct.	FGM	FGA	Pct.							
67-68 —Dallas	56	1737	371	756	.491	0	3	.000	277	351	.789	334	276	1019	18.2
68-69 —Dallas	35	579	132	258	.512	0	1	.000	123	144	.854	102	122	387	11.1
69-70 —Dallas	3	27	8	12	.667	0	1	.000	1	2	.500	...	...	17	5.7
Totals	94	2343	511	1026	.498	0	5	.000	401	497	.807	...	...	1423	15.1

ABA PLAYOFF RECORD

Season Team	G	Min.	2-POINT			3-POINT			FTM	FTA	Pct.	Reb.	Ast.	Pts.	Avg.
			FGM	FGA	Pct.	FGM	FGA	Pct.							
67-68 —Dallas	3	70	14	37	.378	0	0	...	9	13	.692	13	9	37	12.3
68-69 —Dallas	2	45	5	14	.357	0	0	...	8	10	.800	6	14	18	9.0
Totals	5	115	19	51	.373	0	0	...	17	23	.739	19	23	55	11.0

ABA ALL-STAR GAME RECORD

Season Team	Min.	2-POINT			3-POINT			FTM	FTA	Pct.	Reb.	Ast.	Pts.
		FGM	FGA	Pct.	FGM	FGA	Pct.						
1968 —Dallas	24	4	11	.364	0	0	...	2	2	1.000	0	5	10

HEAD COACHING RECORD

BACKGROUND: Player/head coach, Dallas Chaparrals of American Basketball Association (1967-68 to January 1970).

ABA COACHING RECORD

Season Team	REGULAR SEASON				PLAYOFFS		
	W	L	Pct.	Finish	W	L	Pct.
67-68 —Dallas	46	32	.590	2nd/Western Division	4	4	.500
68-69 —Dallas	41	37	.526	4th/Western Division	3	4	.426
69-70 —Dallas	22	21	.512		—	—	—
Totals (3 years)	109	90	.548	Totals (2 years)	7	8	.467

NOTES:
1968— Defeated Houston, 3-0, in Western Division semifinals; lost to New Orleans, 4-1, in Western Division finals.
1969— Lost to New Orleans in Western Division semifinal.
1970— Replaced as Dallas head coach by Max Williams (January).

HAVLICEK, JOHN
F/G

PERSONAL: Born April 8, 1940, in Martins Ferry, O. . . . 6-5/205. . . . Full name: John J. Havlicek. . . . Nickname: Hondo.
HIGH SCHOOL: Bridgeport (O.).
COLLEGE: Ohio State.
TRANSACTIONS/CAREER NOTES: Selected by Boston Celtics in first round of 1962 NBA Draft.
CAREER HONORS: Elected to Naismith Memorial Basketball Hall of Fame (1983). . . . NBA 35th Anniversary All-Time team (1980).
MISCELLANEOUS: Member of NBA championship teams (1963, 1964, 1965, 1966, 1968, 1969, 1974, 1976). . . . Selected as wide receiver by Cleveland Browns in seventh round of 1962 National Football League draft.

COLLEGIATE RECORD

NOTES: THE SPORTING NEWS All-America second team (1962). . . . Member of NCAA championship team (1960).

Season Team	G	Min.	FGM	FGA	Pct.	FTM	FTA	Pct.	Reb.	Pts.	Avg.
58-59 —Ohio State‡			Freshman team did not play intercollegiate schedule.								
59-60 —Ohio State	28	...	144	312	.462	53	74	.716	205	341	12.2
60-61 —Ohio State	28	...	173	321	.539	61	87	.701	244	407	14.5
61-62 —Ohio State	28	...	196	377	.520	83	109	.761	271	475	17.0
Varsity totals	84	...	513	1010	.508	197	270	.730	720	1223	14.6

NBA REGULAR-SEASON RECORD

HONORS: All-NBA first team (1971, 1972, 1973, 1974). . . . All-NBA second team (1964, 1966, 1968, 1969, 1970, 1975, 1976). . . . NBA All-Defensive first team (1972, 1973, 1974, 1975, 1976). . . . NBA All-Defensive second team (1969, 1970, 1971).

Season Team	G	Min.	FGM	FGA	Pct.	FTM	FTA	Pct.	Reb.	Ast.	PF	Dq.	Pts.	Avg.
62-63 —Boston	80	2200	483	1085	.445	174	239	.728	534	179	189	2	1140	14.3
63-64 —Boston	80	2587	640	1535	.417	315	422	.746	428	238	227	1	1595	19.9
64-65 —Boston	75	2169	570	1420	.401	235	316	.744	371	199	200	2	1375	18.3
65-66 —Boston	71	2175	530	1328	.399	274	349	.785	423	210	158	1	1334	18.8
66-67 —Boston	81	2602	684	1540	.444	365	441	.828	532	278	210	0	1733	21.4
67-68 —Boston	82	2921	666	1551	.429	368	453	.812	546	384	237	2	1700	20.7
68-69 —Boston	82	3174	692	1709	.405	387	496	.780	570	441	247	0	1771	21.6
69-70 —Boston	81	3369	736	1585	.464	488	578	.844	635	550	211	1	1960	24.2
70-71 —Boston	81	*3678	892	1982	.450	554	677	.818	730	607	200	0	2338	28.9
71-72 —Boston	82	*3698	897	1957	.458	458	549	.834	672	614	183	1	2252	27.5
72-73 —Boston	80	3367	766	1704	.450	370	431	.858	567	529	195	1	1902	23.8

Season Team	G	Min.	FGM	FGA	Pct.	FTM	FTA	Pct.	REBOUNDS			Ast.	PF	Dq.	Stl.	Blk.	TO	Pts.	Avg.
									Off.	Def.	Tot.								
73-74 —Boston	76	3091	685	1502	.456	346	416	.832	138	349	487	447	196	1	95	32	...	1716	22.6
74-75 —Boston	82	3132	642	1411	.455	289	332	.870	154	330	484	432	231	2	110	16	...	1573	19.2
75-76 —Boston	76	2598	504	1121	.450	281	333	.844	116	198	314	278	204	1	97	29	...	1289	17.0
76-77 —Boston	79	2913	580	1283	.452	235	288	.816	109	273	382	400	208	4	84	18	...	1395	17.7
77-78 —Boston	82	2797	546	1217	.449	230	269	.855	93	239	332	328	185	2	90	22	204	1322	16.1
Totals	1270	46471	10513	23930	.439	5369	6589	.815	...	...	8007	6114	3281	21	476	117	204	26395	20.8

NBA PLAYOFF RECORD

NOTES: NBA Finals Most Valuable Player (1974).... Shares NBA Finals single-game records for most points in an overtime period—9 (May 10, 1974, vs. Milwaukee); and most steals—6 (May 3, 1974, vs. Milwaukee).... Shares single-game record for most field goals made—24 (April 1, 1973, vs. Atlanta).

Season Team	G	Min.	FGM	FGA	Pct.	FTM	FTA	Pct.	Reb.	Ast.	PF	Dq.	Pts.	Avg.
62-63 — Boston	11	254	56	125	.448	18	27	.667	53	17	28	1	130	11.8
63-64 — Boston	10	289	61	159	.384	35	44	.795	43	32	26	0	157	15.7
64-65 — Boston	12	405	88	250	.352	46	55	.836	88	29	44	1	222	18.5
65-66 — Boston	17	719	153	374	.409	95	113	.841	154	70	69	2	401	23.6
66-67 — Boston	9	330	95	212	.448	57	71	.803	73	28	30	0	247	27.4
67-68 — Boston	19	862	184	407	.452	125	151	.828	164	142	67	1	493	25.9
68-69 — Boston	18	850	170	382	.445	118	138	.855	179	100	58	2	458	25.4
71-72 — Boston	11	517	108	235	.460	85	99	.859	92	70	35	1	301	27.4
72-73 — Boston	12	479	112	235	.477	61	74	.824	62	65	24	0	285	23.8

| | | | | | | | | — REBOUNDS — | | | | | | |

Season Team	G	Min.	FGM	FGA	Pct.	FTM	FTA	Pct.	Off.	Def.	Tot.	Ast.	PF	Dq.	Stl.	Blk.	TO	Pts.	Avg.
73-74 — Boston	18	811	199	411	.484	89	101	.881	28	88	116	108	43	0	24	6	...	487	27.1
74-75 — Boston	11	464	83	192	.432	66	76	.868	18	39	57	51	38	1	16	1	...	232	21.1
75-76 — Boston	15	505	80	180	.444	38	47	.809	18	38	56	51	22	0	12	5	...	198	13.2
76-77 — Boston	9	375	62	167	.371	41	50	.820	15	34	49	62	33	0	8	4	...	165	18.3
Totals	172	6860	1451	3329	.436	874	1046	.836	...	...	1186	825	517	9	60	16	...	3776	22.0

NBA ALL-STAR GAME RECORD

Season Team	Min.	FGM	FGA	Pct.	FTM	FTA	Pct.	Reb.	Ast.	PF	Dq.	Pts.
1966 — Boston	25	6	16	.375	6	6	1.000	6	1	2	0	18
1967 — Boston	17	7	14	.500	0	0	...	2	1	1	0	14
1968 — Boston	22	9	15	.600	8	11	.727	5	4	0	0	26
1969 — Boston	31	6	14	.429	2	2	1.000	7	2	2	0	14
1970 — Boston	29	7	15	.467	3	3	1.000	5	7	2	0	17
1971 — Boston	24	6	12	.500	0	2	.000	3	2	3	0	12
1972 — Boston	24	5	13	.385	5	5	1.000	3	2	2	0	15
1973 — Boston	22	6	10	.600	2	5	.400	3	5	1	0	14

| | | | | | | | — REBOUNDS — | | | | | | |

Season Team	Min.	FGM	FGA	Pct.	FTM	FTA	Pct.	Off.	Def.	Tot.	Ast.	PF	Dq.	Stl.	Blk.	TO	Pts.
1974 — Boston	18	5	10	.500	0	2	.000	0	0	2	2	0	1	0	...	10
1975 — Boston	31	7	12	.583	2	2	1.000	1	5	6	1	2	0	2	0	...	16
1976 — Boston	21	3	10	.300	3	3	1.000	1	1	2	2	0	0	1	0	...	9
1977 — Boston	17	2	5	.400	0	0	...	0	1	1	1	1	0	0	0	...	4
1978 — Boston	22	5	8	.625	0	0	...	0	3	3	1	2	0	0	0	4	10
Totals	303	74	154	.481	31	41	.756	...	...	46	31	20	0	4	0	4	179

HAYES, ELVIN
F/C

PERSONAL: Born November 17, 1945, in Rayville, La.... 6-9/235.... Full name: Elvin Ernest Hayes.
HIGH SCHOOL: Eula D. Britton (Rayville, La.).
COLLEGE: Houston.
TRANSACTIONS/CAREER NOTES: Selected by San Diego Rockets in first round (first pick overall) of 1968 NBA Draft.... Rockets franchise moved from San Diego to Houston for 1971-72 season.... Traded by Rockets to Baltimore Bullets for Jack Marin and future considerations (June 23, 1972).... Bullets franchise moved from Baltimore to Washington and renamed Capital Bullets for 1973-74 season.... Bullets franchise renamed Washington Bullets for 1974-75 season.... Traded by Bullets to Rockets for second-round draft choices in 1981 and 1983 (June 8, 1981).
CAREER HONORS: Elected to Naismith Memorial Basketball Hall of Fame (1989).
MISCELLANEOUS: Member of NBA championship team (1978).

COLLEGIATE RECORD

NOTES: THE SPORTING NEWS College Player of the Year (1968).... THE SPORTING NEWS All-America first team (1967, 1968).... THE SPORTING NEWS All-America second team (1966).

Season Team	G	Min.	FGM	FGA	Pct.	FTM	FTA	Pct.	Reb.	Pts.	Avg.
64-65 — Houston†	21	...	217	478	.454	93	176	.528	500	527	25.1
65-66 — Houston	29	946	323	570	.567	143	257	.556	490	789	27.2
66-67 — Houston	31	1119	373	750	.497	135	227	.595	488	881	28.4
67-68 — Houston	33	1270	519	945	.549	176	285	.618	624	1214	36.8
Varsity totals	93	3335	1215	2265	.536	454	769	.590	1602	2884	31.0

NBA REGULAR-SEASON RECORD

RECORDS: Holds single-season record for most minutes played by a rookie—3,695 (1969).
HONORS: All-NBA first team (1975, 1977, 1979).... All-NBA second team (1973, 1974, 1976).... NBA All-Defensive second team (1974, 1975).... NBA All-Rookie team (1969).
NOTES: Led NBA with 16.9 rebounds per game (1970) and 18.1 rebounds per game (1974).

Season Team	G	Min.	FGM	FGA	Pct.	FTM	FTA	Pct.	Reb.	Ast.	PF	Dq.	Pts.	Avg.
68-69 — San Diego	82	*3695	*930	*2082	.447	467	746	.626	1406	113	266	2	*2327	*28.4
69-70 — San Diego	82	*3665	914	*2020	.452	428	622	.688	*1386	162	270	5	2256	27.5
70-71 — San Diego	82	3633	948	*2215	.428	454	676	.672	1362	186	225	1	2350	28.7
71-72 — Houston	82	3461	832	1918	.434	399	615	.649	1197	270	233	1	2063	25.2
72-73 — Baltimore	81	3347	713	1607	.444	291	434	.671	1177	127	232	3	1717	21.2

| | | | | | | | | — REBOUNDS — | | | | | | |

Season Team	G	Min.	FGM	FGA	Pct.	FTM	FTA	Pct.	Off.	Def.	Tot.	Ast.	PF	Dq.	Stl.	Blk.	TO	Pts.	Avg.
73-74 — Capital	81	*3602	689	1627	.423	357	495	.721	*354	*1109	*1463	163	252	...	86	240	...	1735	21.4
74-75 — Washington	82	3465	739	1668	.443	409	534	.766	221	783	1004	206	238	0	158	187	...	1887	23.0
75-76 — Washington	80	2975	649	1381	.470	287	457	.628	210	668	878	121	293	5	104	202	...	1585	19.8
76-77 — Washington	82	*3364	760	1516	.501	422	614	.687	289	740	1029	158	312	6	87	220	...	1942	23.7
77-78 — Washington	81	3246	636	1409	.451	326	514	.634	335	740	1075	149	313	7	96	159	229	1598	19.7

Season Team	G	Min.	FGM	FGA	Pct.	FTM	FTA	Pct.	Off.	Def.	Tot.	Ast.	PF	Dq.	Stl.	Blk.	TO	Pts.	Avg.
									— REBOUNDS —										
78-79—Washington.	82	3105	720	1477	.487	349	534	.654	312	682	994	143	308	5	75	190	235	1789	21.8
79-80—Washington.	81	3183	761	1677	.454	334	478	.699	269	627	896	129	309	9	62	189	215	1859	23.0
80-81—Washington.	81	2931	584	1296	.451	271	439	.617	235	554	789	98	300	6	68	171	189	1439	17.8
81-82—Houston	82	3032	519	1100	.472	280	422	.664	267	480	747	144	287	4	62	104	208	1318	16.1
82-83—Houston	81	2302	424	890	.476	196	287	.683	199	417	616	158	232	2	50	81	200	1046	12.9
83-84—Houston	81	994	158	389	.406	86	132	.652	87	173	260	71	123	1	16	28	82	402	5.0
Totals	1303	50000	10976	24272	.452	5356	7999	.670	...	...	16279	2398	4193	53	864	1771	1358	27313	21.0

Three-point field goals: 1979-80, 3-for-13 (.231). 1980-81, 0-for-10. 1981-82, 0-for-5. 1982-83, 2-for-4 (.500). 1983-84, 0-for-2. Totals, 5-for-34 (.147).

NBA PLAYOFF RECORD

NOTES: Holds NBA Finals single-game record for most offensive rebounds—11 (May 27, 1979, vs. Seattle).

Season Team	G	Min.	FGM	FGA	Pct.	FTM	FTA	Pct.	Reb.	Ast.	PF	Dq.	Pts.	Avg.
68-69—San Diego..................	6	278	60	114	.526	35	53	.660	83	5	21	0	155	25.8
72-73—Baltimore	5	228	53	105	.505	23	33	.697	57	5	16	0	129	25.8

Season Team	G	Min.	FGM	FGA	Pct.	FTM	FTA	Pct.	Off.	Def.	Tot.	Ast.	PF	Dq.	Stl.	Blk.	TO	Pts.	Avg.
									— REBOUNDS —										
73-74—Capital	7	323	76	143	.531	29	41	.707	31	80	111	21	23	0	5	15	...	181	25.9
74-75—Washington.	17	751	174	372	.468	86	127	.677	46	140	186	37	70	3	26	39	...	434	25.5
75-76—Washington.	7	305	54	122	.443	32	55	.582	16	72	88	10	24	0	5	28	...	140	20.0
76-77—Washington.	9	405	74	173	.428	41	59	.695	29	93	122	17	39	0	10	22	...	189	21.0
77-78—Washington.	21	868	189	385	.491	79	133	.594	103	176	279	43	86	2	32	52	57	457	21.8
78-79—Washington.	19	786	170	396	.429	87	130	.669	94	172	266	38	79	3	17	52	56	427	22.5
79-80—Washington.	2	92	16	41	.390	8	10	.800	10	12	22	6	8	0	0	4	4	40	20.0
81-82—Houston	3	124	17	50	.340	8	15	.533	7	23	30	3	12	0	2	10	6	42	14.0
Totals	96	4160	883	1901	.464	428	656	.652	...	...	1244	185	378	8	97	222	123	2194	22.9

NBA ALL-STAR GAME RECORD

Season Team	Min.	FGM	FGA	Pct.	FTM	FTA	Pct.	Reb.	Ast.	PF	Dq.	Pts.
1969 —San Diego..................	21	4	9	.444	3	3	1.000	5	0	4	0	11
1970 —San Diego..................	35	9	21	.429	6	12	.500	15	1	1	0	24
1971 —San Diego..................	19	4	13	.308	2	3	.667	4	2	1	0	10
1972 —Houston	11	1	6	.167	2	2	1.000	2	0	2	0	4
1973 —Baltimore	16	4	13	.308	2	2	1.000	12	0	0	0	10

Season Team	Min.	FGM	FGA	Pct.	FTM	FTA	Pct.	Off.	Def.	Tot.	Ast.	PF	Dq.	Stl.	Blk.	TO	Pts.
								— REBOUNDS —									
1974 —Capital	35	5	13	.385	2	3	.667	4	11	15	6	4	0	0	1	...	12
1975 —Washington	17	2	6	.333	0	0	...	0	5	5	2	1	0	1	0	...	4
1976 —Washington	31	6	14	.429	0	2	.000	3	7	10	1	5	0	1	0	...	12
1977 —Washington	11	6	6	1.000	0	10	.000	0	2	2	1	5	0	0	0	...	12
1978 —Washington	11	1	7	.143	0	0	...	3	1	4	0	4	0	1	0	1	2
1979 —Washington	28	5	11	.455	3	5	.600	4	9	13	0	5	0	1	1	1	13
1980 —Washington	29	5	10	.500	2	2	1.000	2	3	5	4	5	0	1	4	3	12
Totals	264	52	129	.403	22	44	.500	...	...	92	17	37	0	5	6	5	126

HAYWOOD, SPENCER
F/C

PERSONAL: Born April 22, 1949, in Silver City, Miss.... 6-9/225.
HIGH SCHOOL: Pershing (Detroit).
COLLEGE: Trinidad State Junior College (Colo.), then Detroit.
TRANSACTIONS/CAREER NOTES: Signed as undergraduate free agent by Denver Rockets of American Basketball Association (August 16, 1969).... Selected by Buffalo Braves in second round (30th pick overall) of 1971 NBA Draft. ... Terminated contract with Rockets and signed by Seattle SuperSonics (1971).... Traded by SuperSonics to New York Knicks for cash and the option of Eugene Short or future draft choice (October 24, 1975).... Traded by Knicks to New Orleans Jazz for Joe C. Meriweather (January 5, 1979).... Jazz franchise moved from New Orleans to Utah for 1979-80 season.... Traded by Jazz to Los Angeles Lakers for Adrian Dantley (September 13, 1979).... Waived by Lakers (August 19, 1980).... Played in Italy (1980-81 and 1981-82).... Signed as free agent by Washington Bullets (October 24, 1981).... Waived by Bullets (March 9, 1983).
MISCELLANEOUS: Member of NBA championship team (1980).... Member of gold-medal-winning U.S. Olympic team (1968).

COLLEGIATE RECORD

NOTES: THE SPORTING NEWS All-America first team (1969).... Led NCAA Division I with 21.5 rebounds per game (1969).

Season Team	G	Min.	FGM	FGA	Pct.	FTM	FTA	Pct.	Reb.	Pts.	Avg.
67-68—Trinidad State Junior College..	30	...	358	675	.530	129	195	.662	663	845	28.2
68-69—Detroit..........................	24	...	288	508	.567	195	254	.768	530	771	32.1
Junior college totals..........................	30	...	358	675	.530	129	195	.662	663	845	28.2
Four-year-college totals	24	...	288	508	.567	195	254	.768	530	771	32.1

ABA REGULAR-SEASON RECORD

NOTES: ABA Most Valuable Player (1970).... ABA Rookie of the Year (1970).... ABA All-Star first team (1970).... ABA All-Rookie team (1970).... Holds single-season records for most minutes played—3808 (1970); most field goals made—986 (1970); most rebounds—1637 (1970); and highest rebounds-per-game average—19.5 (1970).... Led ABA with 19.5 rebounds per game (1970).

Season Team	G	Min.	2-POINT			3-POINT			FTM	FTA	Pct.	Reb.	Ast.	Pts.	Avg.
			FGM	FGA	Pct.	FGM	FGA	Pct.							
69-70—Denver	84	*3808	*986	1987	.496	0	11	.000	547	705	.776	*1637	190	*2519	*30.0

NBA REGULAR-SEASON RECORD

HONORS: All-NBA first team (1972, 1973).... All-NBA second team (1974, 1975).

Season Team	G	Min.	FGM	FGA	Pct.	FTM	FTA	Pct.	Reb.	Ast.	PF	Dq.	Pts.	Avg.
70-71 —Seattle..............................	33	1162	260	579	.449	160	218	.734	396	48	84	1	680	20.6
71-72 —Seattle..............................	73	3167	717	1557	.461	480	586	.819	926	148	208	0	1914	26.2
72-73 —Seattle..............................	77	3259	889	1868	.476	473	564	.839	995	196	213	2	2251	29.2

| Season Team | G | Min. | FGM | FGA | Pct. | FTM | FTA | Pct. | — REBOUNDS — | | | Ast. | PF | Dq. | Stl. | Blk. | TO | Pts. | Avg. |
									Off.	Def.	Tot.								
73-74 —Seattle.........	75	3039	694	1520	.457	373	458	.814	318	689	1007	240	198	2	65	106	...	1761	23.5
74-75 —Seattle.........	68	2529	608	1325	.459	309	381	.811	198	432	630	137	173	1	54	108	...	1525	22.4
75-76 —New York	78	2892	605	1360	.445	339	448	.757	234	644	878	92	255	1	53	80	...	1549	19.9
76-77 —N.Y. Knicks..	31	1021	202	449	.450	109	131	.832	77	203	280	50	72	0	14	29	...	513	16.5
77-78 —New York	67	1765	412	852	.484	96	135	.711	141	301	442	126	188	1	37	72	140	920	13.7
78-79 —N.Y.-N.O.	68	2361	595	1205	.494	231	292	.791	172	361	533	127	236	8	40	82	200	1421	20.9
79-80 —Los Angeles .	76	1544	288	591	.487	159	206	.772	132	214	346	93	197	2	35	57	134	736	9.7
81-82 —Washington .	76	2086	395	829	.476	219	260	.842	144	278	422	64	249	6	45	68	175	1009	13.3
82-83 —Washington .	38	775	125	312	.401	63	87	.724	77	106	183	30	94	2	12	27	67	313	8.2
Totals	760	25600	5790	12447	.465	3011	3766	.800	...	...	7038	1351	2167	26	355	629	716	14592	19.2

Three-point field goals: 1979-80, 1-for-4 (.250). 1981-82, 0-for-3. 1982-83, 0-for-1. Totals, 1-for-8 (.125).

NBA PLAYOFF RECORD

| Season Team | G | Min. | FGM | FGA | Pct. | FTM | FTA | Pct. | — REBOUNDS — | | | Ast. | PF | Dq. | Stl. | Blk. | TO | Pts. | Avg. |
									Off.	Def.	Tot.								
74-75 —Seattle.........	9	337	47	131	.359	47	61	.770	20	61	81	18	29	0	7	11	...	141	15.7
77-78 —New York	6	177	43	85	.506	11	11	1.000	19	23	42	12	24	1	2	5	10	97	16.2
79-80 —Los Angeles .	11	145	25	53	.472	13	16	.813	14	12	26	4	17	0	0	6	20	63	5.7
81-82 —Washington .	7	231	57	115	.496	26	35	.743	16	23	39	7	28	0	4	14	15	140	20.0
Totals	33	890	172	384	.448	97	123	.789	69	119	188	41	98	1	13	36	45	441	13.4

Three-point field goals: 1979-80, 0-for-1.

NBA ALL-STAR GAME RECORD

Season Team	Min.	FGM	FGA	Pct.	FTM	FTA	Pct.	Reb.	Ast.	PF	Dq.	Pts.
1972 —Seattle..............................	25	4	10	.400	3	4	.750	7	1	2	0	11
1973 —Seattle..............................	22	5	10	.500	2	2	1.000	10	0	5	0	12

| Season Team | Min. | FGM | FGA | Pct. | FTM | FTA | Pct. | — REBOUNDS — | | | Ast. | PF | Dq. | Stl. | Blk. | TO | Pts. |
								Off.	Def.	Tot.							
1974 —Seattle...............	33	10	17	.588	3	3	1.000	2	9	11	5	5	0	0	3	...	23
1975 —Seattle...............	17	1	9	.111	0	0	...	1	2	3	0	1	0	0	0	...	2
Totals	97	20	46	.435	8	9	.889	...	...	31	6	13	0	0	3	...	48

ITALIAN LEAGUE RECORD

Season Team	G	Min.	FGM	FGA	Pct.	FTM	FTA	Pct.	Reb.	Pts.	Avg.
80-81 —Venezia	34	...	334	601	.556	132	179	.737	354	800	23.5
81-82 —Carrera	5	175	63	100	.630	24	32	.750	37	150	30.0
Totals	39	...	397	701	.566	156	211	.739	391	950	24.4

HOWELL, BAILEY
F

PERSONAL: Born January 20, 1937, in Middleton, Tenn.... 6-7/220. ... Full name: Bailey E. Howell.
HIGH SCHOOL: Middleton (Tenn.).
COLLEGE: Mississippi State.
TRANSACTIONS/CAREER NOTES: Selected by Detroit Pistons in first round of 1959 NBA Draft.... Traded by Pistons with Bob Ferry, Don Ohl, Wally Jones and Les Hunter to Baltimore Bullets for Terry Dischinger, Don Kojis and Rod Thorn (June 18, 1964).... Traded by Bullets to Boston Celtics for Mel Counts (September 1, 1966).... Selected by Buffalo Braves from Celtics in NBA expansion draft (May 11, 1970).... Traded by Braves to Philadelphia 76ers for Bob Kauffman and cash or future draft choice (May 11, 1970).
MISCELLANEOUS: Member of NBA championship teams (1968, 1969).

COLLEGIATE RECORD

NOTES: THE SPORTING NEWS All-America first team (1959).... Led NCAA major college division with .568 field-goal percentage (1957).

Season Team	G	Min.	FGM	FGA	Pct.	FTM	FTA	Pct.	Reb.	Pts.	Avg.
55-56 —Mississippi State‡				Freshman team statistics unavailable.							
56-57 —Mississippi State	25	...	217	382	.568	213	285	.747	492	647	25.9
57-58 —Mississippi State	25	...	226	439	.515	243	315	.771	406	695	27.8
58-59 —Mississippi State	25	...	231	464	.498	226	292	.774	379	688	27.5
Varsity totals	75	...	674	1285	.525	682	892	.765	1277	2030	27.1

NBA REGULAR-SEASON RECORD

HONORS: All-NBA second team (1963).

Season Team	G	Min.	FGM	FGA	Pct.	FTM	FTA	Pct.	Reb.	Ast.	PF	Dq.	Pts.	Avg.
59-60 —Detroit.............................	75	2346	510	1119	.456	312	422	.739	790	63	282	13	1332	17.8
60-61 —Detroit.............................	77	2752	607	1293	.469	601	798	.753	1111	196	297	10	1815	23.6
61-62 —Detroit.............................	79	2857	553	1193	.464	470	612	.768	996	186	317	10	1576	19.9
62-63 —Detroit.............................	79	2971	637	1235	.516	519	650	.798	910	232	301	9	1793	22.7
63-64 —Detroit.............................	77	2700	598	1267	.472	470	581	.809	776	205	290	9	1666	21.6
64-65 —Baltimore	80	2975	515	1040	.495	504	629	.801	869	208	*345	10	1534	19.2
65-66 —Baltimore	79	2328	481	986	.488	402	551	.730	773	155	306	12	1364	17.3
66-67 —Boston	81	2503	636	1242	.512	349	471	.741	677	103	296	4	1621	20.0
67-68 —Boston	82	2801	643	1336	.481	335	461	.727	805	133	285	4	1621	19.8
68-69 —Boston	78	2527	612	1257	.487	313	426	.735	685	137	285	3	1537	19.7
69-70 —Boston	82	2078	399	931	.429	235	308	.763	550	120	261	4	1033	12.6
70-71 —Philadelphia....................	82	1589	324	686	.472	230	315	.730	441	115	234	2	878	10.7
Totals	951	30427	6515	13585	.480	4740	6224	.762	9383	1853	3499	90	17770	18.7

NBA PLAYOFF RECORD

Season	Team	G	Min.	FGM	FGA	Pct.	FTM	FTA	Pct.	Reb.	Ast.	PF	Dq.	Pts.	Avg.
59-60	Detroit	2	72	14	41	.341	6	8	.750	17	3	8	0	34	17.0
60-61	Detroit	5	144	20	57	.351	16	23	.696	46	22	22	1	56	11.2
61-62	Detroit	10	378	69	163	.423	62	75	.827	96	23	48	3	200	20.0
62-63	Detroit	4	163	24	64	.375	23	27	.852	42	11	19	1	71	17.8
64-65	Baltimore	9	350	67	130	.515	53	70	.757	105	19	38	3	187	20.8
65-66	Baltimore	3	94	23	50	.460	8	11	.727	30	2	13	1	54	18.0
66-67	Boston	9	241	59	122	.484	20	30	.667	66	5	35	2	138	15.3
67-68	Boston	19	597	135	264	.511	74	107	.692	146	22	84	6	344	18.1
68-69	Boston	18	551	112	229	.489	46	64	.719	118	19	84	3	270	15.0
70-71	Philadelphia	7	122	19	45	.422	9	18	.500	31	4	25	1	47	6.7
	Totals	86	2712	542	1165	.465	317	433	.732	697	130	376	21	1401	16.3

NBA ALL-STAR GAME RECORD

Season	Team	Min.	FGM	FGA	Pct.	FTM	FTA	Pct.	Reb.	Ast.	PF	Dq.	Pts.
1961	Detroit	16	5	10	.500	3	4	.750	3	3	4	0	13
1962	Detroit	8	1	2	.500	0	0	...	0	1	1	0	2
1963	Detroit	11	2	3	.667	0	0	...	1	1	2	0	4
1964	Detroit	6	1	3	.333	0	0	...	2	0	0	0	2
1966	Baltimore	26	3	11	.273	1	2	.500	2	2	4	0	7
1967	Boston	14	1	4	.250	2	2	1.000	2	1	1	0	4
	Totals	81	13	33	.394	6	8	.750	10	8	12	0	32

HUDSON, LOU
F/G

PERSONAL: Born July 11, 1944, in Greensboro, N.C. . . . 6-5/210. . . . Full name: Louis Clyde Hudson. . . . Nickname: Sweet Lou.
HIGH SCHOOL: Dudley Senior (Greensboro, N.C.).
COLLEGE: Minnesota.
TRANSACTIONS/CAREER NOTES: Selected by St. Louis Hawks in first round (fourth pick overall) of 1966 NBA Draft. . . . Hawks franchise moved from St. Louis to Atlanta for 1968-69 season. . . . Traded by Hawks to Los Angeles Lakers for Ollie Johnson (September 30, 1977).

COLLEGIATE RECORD

Season	Team	G	Min.	FGM	FGA	Pct.	FTM	FTA	Pct.	Reb.	Pts.	Avg.
62-63	Minnesota†			Freshman team did not play intercollegiate schedule.								
63-64	Minnesota	24	...	191	435	.439	53	85	.624	191	435	18.1
64-65	Minnesota	24	...	231	463	.499	96	123	.780	247	558	23.3
65-66	Minnesota	17	...	143	303	.472	50	77	.649	138	336	19.8
	Varsity totals	65	...	565	1201	.470	199	285	.698	576	1329	20.4

NBA REGULAR-SEASON RECORD

HONORS: All-NBA second team (1970). . . . NBA All-Rookie team (1967).

Season	Team	G	Min.	FGM	FGA	Pct.	FTM	FTA	Pct.	Reb.	Ast.	PF	Dq.	Pts.	Avg.
66-67	St. Louis	80	2446	620	1328	.467	231	327	.706	435	95	277	3	1471	18.4
67-68	St. Louis	46	966	227	500	.454	120	164	.732	193	65	113	2	574	12.5
68-69	Atlanta	81	2869	716	1455	.492	338	435	.777	533	216	248	0	1770	21.9
69-70	Atlanta	80	3091	830	1564	.531	371	450	.824	373	276	225	1	2031	25.4
70-71	Atlanta	76	3113	829	1713	.484	381	502	.759	386	257	186	0	2039	26.8
71-72	Atlanta	77	3042	775	1540	.503	349	430	.812	385	309	225	0	1899	24.7
72-73	Atlanta	75	3027	816	1710	.477	397	481	.825	467	258	197	1	2029	27.1

Season	Team	G	Min.	FGM	FGA	Pct.	FTM	FTA	Pct.	REBOUNDS			Ast.	PF	Dq.	Stl.	Blk.	TO	Pts.	Avg.
										Off.	Def.	Tot.								
73-74	Atlanta	65	2588	678	1356	.500	295	353	.836	126	224	350	216	205	3	160	29	...	1651	25.4
74-75	Atlanta	11	380	97	225	.431	48	57	.842	14	33	47	40	33	1	13	2	...	242	22.0
75-76	Atlanta	81	2558	569	1205	.472	237	291	.814	104	196	300	214	241	3	124	17	...	1375	17.0
76-77	Atlanta	58	1745	413	905	.456	142	169	.840	48	81	129	155	160	2	67	19	...	968	16.7
77-78	Los Angeles	82	2283	493	992	.497	137	177	.774	80	108	188	193	196	0	94	14	150	1123	13.7
78-79	Los Angeles	78	1686	329	636	.517	110	124	.887	64	76	140	141	133	1	58	17	99	768	9.8
	Totals	890	29794	7392	15129	.489	3156	3960	.797	...	...	3926	2435	2439	17	516	98	249	17940	20.2

NBA PLAYOFF RECORD

Season	Team	G	Min.	FGM	FGA	Pct.	FTM	FTA	Pct.	Reb.	Ast.	PF	Dq.	Pts.	Avg.
66-67	St. Louis	9	317	77	179	.430	49	68	.721	48	15	35	1	203	22.6
67-68	St. Louis	6	181	44	99	.444	42	47	.894	43	14	21	0	130	21.7
68-69	Atlanta	11	424	101	216	.468	40	52	.769	59	32	43	1	242	22.0
69-70	Atlanta	9	360	78	187	.417	41	50	.820	40	33	34	2	197	21.9
70-71	Atlanta	5	213	49	108	.454	29	39	.744	35	15	19	0	127	25.4
71-72	Atlanta	6	266	63	139	.453	24	29	.828	33	21	13	0	150	25.0
72-73	Atlanta	6	255	76	166	.458	26	29	.897	47	17	16	0	178	29.7

Season	Team	G	Min.	FGM	FGA	Pct.	FTM	FTA	Pct.	REBOUNDS			Ast.	PF	Dq.	Stl.	Blk.	TO	Pts.	Avg.
										Off.	Def.	Tot.								
77-78	Los Angeles	3	93	14	38	.368	7	8	.875	7	2	9	9	9	0	5	0	5	35	11.7
78-79	Los Angeles	6	90	17	32	.531	4	4	1.000	1	3	4	8	6	0	1	0	5	38	6.3
	Totals	61	2199	519	1164	.446	262	326	.804	...	...	318	164	196	4	6	0	10	1300	21.3

NBA ALL-STAR GAME RECORD

Season	Team	Min.	FGM	FGA	Pct.	FTM	FTA	Pct.	Reb.	Ast.	PF	Dq.	Pts.
1969	Atlanta	20	6	13	.462	1	1	1.000	1	1	0	0	13
1970	Atlanta	18	5	12	.417	5	5	1.000	1	0	1	0	15
1971	Atlanta	17	6	13	.462	2	3	.667	3	1	3	0	14
1972	Atlanta	18	2	7	.286	2	2	1.000	3	3	3	0	6
1973	Atlanta	9	2	8	.250	2	2	1.000	2	0	2	0	6

Season	Team	Min.	FGM	FGA	Pct.	FTM	FTA	Pct.	REBOUNDS Off.	Def.	Tot.	Ast.	PF	Dq.	Stl.	Blk.	TO	Pts.
1974	—Atlanta	17	5	8	.625	2	2	1.000	1	2	3	1	2	0	0	1	...	12
	Totals	99	26	61	.426	14	15	.933	...	...	13	6	11	0	0	1	...	66

JEANNETTE, BUDDY
G

PERSONAL: Born September 15, 1917, in New Kensington, Pa. . . . 5-11/175. . . . Full name: Harry Edward Jeannette.
HIGH SCHOOL: New Kensington (Pa.).
COLLEGE: Washington & Jefferson (Pa.).
TRANSACTIONS/CAREER NOTES: Warren Penns franchise transferred to Cleveland and renamed White Horses (February 10, 1939). . . . Played in New York-Penn League with Elmira in 1939 and New York State League with Saratoga in 1942.
MISCELLANEOUS: Member of BAA championship team (1948). . . . Member of NBL championship teams (1943, 1944, 1945).

COLLEGIATE RECORD

Season	Team	G	Min.	FGM	FGA	Pct.	FTM	FTA	Pct.	Reb.	Pts.	Avg.
34-35	—Washington and Jefferson	14	...	62	...	...	...	35	.000	...	159	11.4
35-36	—Washington and Jefferson	20	...	92	...	...	...	42	.000	...	226	11.3
36-37	—Washington and Jefferson	18	...	92	...	...	...	56	.000	...	240	13.3
37-38	—Washington and Jefferson	20	...	...	...	...	...	...	...	...	240	12.0
	Totals	72	...	...	...	...	...	...	...	...	865	12.0

NBL AND NBA REGULAR-SEASON RECORD

HONORS: All-BAA second team (1948). . . . All-NBL first team (1941, 1944, 1945, 1946). . . . All-NBL second team (1943).

Season	Team	G	Min.	FGM	FGA	Pct.	FTM	FTA	Pct.	Reb.	Ast.	PF	Dq.	Pts.	Avg.
38-39	—Warren-Clev. (NBL)	26	...	54	...	...	65	...	...	...	...	57	...	173	6.7
39-40	—Detroit (NBL)	25	...	45	...	...	52	76	.684	...	...	62	...	142	5.7
40-41	—Detroit (NBL)	23	...	75	...	...	54	86	.628	...	...	56	...	204	8.9
42-43	—Sheboygan (NBL)	4	...	24	...	...	14	17	.824	...	...	8	...	62	15.5
43-44	—Fort Wayne (NBL)	22	...	68	...	...	48	64	.750	...	...	46	...	184	8.4
44-45	—Fort Wayne (NBL)	27	...	85	...	...	82	111	*.739	...	...	67	...	252	9.3
45-46	—Fort Wayne (NBL)	34	...	99	...	...	105	136	.772	...	...	184	...	303	8.9
47-48	—Baltimore (BAA)	46	...	150	430	.349	191	252	.758	...	70	147	...	491	10.7
48-49	—Baltimore (BAA)	56	...	73	199	.367	167	213	.784	...	124	157	...	313	5.6
49-50	—Baltimore	37	...	42	148	.284	109	133	.820	...	93	82	...	193	5.2
	Totals	300	...	715	...	...	887	...	...	...	...	866	...	2317	7.7

NBL AND NBA PLAYOFF RECORD

Season	Team	G	Min.	FGM	FGA	Pct.	FTM	FTA	Pct.	Reb.	Ast.	PF	Dq.	Pts.	Avg.
39-40	—Detroit (NBL)	3	...	6	...	...	8	...	...	...	...	...	...	20	6.7
40-41	—Detroit (NBL)	3	...	8	...	...	5	...	...	...	...	...	...	21	7.0
42-43	—Sheboygan (NBL)	5	...	16	...	...	17	...	...	...	...	...	...	49	9.8
43-44	—Fort Wayne (NBL)	5	...	12	...	...	10	...	...	...	...	...	...	34	6.8
44-45	—Fort Wayne (NBL)	7	...	22	...	...	23	...	...	...	...	...	...	67	9.6
45-46	—Fort Wayne (NBL)	4	...	7	...	...	5	6	.833	...	...	...	...	19	4.8
47-48	—Baltimore (BAA)	11	...	30	61	.492	37	42	.881	...	12	45	...	97	8.8
48-49	—Baltimore (BAA)	3	...	2	13	.154	4	4	1.000	...	5	11	...	8	2.7
	Totals	41	...	103	...	...	109	...	...	...	...	...	...	315	7.7

ABL REGULAR-SEASON RECORD

Season	Team	G	Min.	FGM	FGA	Pct.	FTM	FTA	Pct.	Reb.	Ast.	Pts.	Avg.
46-47	—Baltimore	29	...	113	...	...	118	...	...	...	...	344	11.9

HEAD COACHING RECORD

BACKGROUND: Player/head coach, Baltimore Bullets of ABL (1946-47). . . . Assistant coach, Pittsburgh Condors of ABA (1970-71).

ABL COACHING RECORD

Season	Team	REGULAR SEASON W	L	Pct.	Finish	PLAYOFFS W	L	Pct.
46-47	—Baltimore	31	3	.912	1st/Southern Division	2	1	.667
	Totals (1 year)	31	3	.912	Totals (1 year)	2	1	.667

COLLEGIATE COACHING RECORD

Season	Team	W	L	Pct.	Finish
52-53	—Georgetown	13	7	.650	
53-54	—Georgetown	11	18	.379	
54-55	—Georgetown	12	13	.480	
55-56	—Georgetown	13	11	.542	
	Totals (4 years)	49	49	.500	

NBA COACHING RECORD

Season	Team	REGULAR SEASON W	L	Pct.	Finish	PLAYOFFS W	L	Pct.
47-48	—Baltimore (BAA)	28	20	.583	2nd/Western Division	9	3	.750
48-49	—Baltimore (BAA)	29	31	.483	3rd/Eastern Division	1	2	.333
49-50	—Baltimore	25	43	.368	5th/Eastern Division	—	—	—
50-51	—Baltimore	14	23	.378		—	—	—
64-65	—Baltimore	37	43	.463	3rd/Western Division	5	5	.500
66-67	—Baltimore	3	13	.188		—	—	—
	Totals (6 years)	136	173	.440	Totals (3 years)	15	10	.600

Season Team	W	L	Pct.	Finish		W	L	Pct.
			REGULAR SEASON			**PLAYOFFS**		
59-60 — Baltimore	20	8	.714	2nd		2	2	.500
60-61 — Baltimore	19	9	.679	1st		2	0	1.000
Totals (2 years)	39	17	.696	Totals (2 years)		4	2	.667

ABA COACHING RECORD

Season Team	W	L	Pct.	Finish		W	L	Pct.
			REGULAR SEASON			**PLAYOFFS**		
69-70 — Pittsburgh	15	30	.333	5th/Eastern Division		—	—	—
Totals (1 year)	15	30	.333					

NOTES:

1948— Defeated Chicago, 75-72, in Western Division tie-breaker; defeated New York, 2-1, in Quarterfinals; defeated Chicago, 2-0, in Semifinals; defeated Philadelphia, 4-2, in World Championship Series.

1949— Lost to New York in Eastern Division semifinals.

1951— Replaced as Baltimore head coach by Walt Budko (January).

1960— Defeated Allentown, 103-89, in Semifinal; lost to Easton, 2-1, in EBL Finals.

1961— Defeated Scranton, 132-107, in Semifinal; defeated Allentown, 119-104, in EBL Final.

1965— Defeated St. Louis, 3-1, in Western Division semifinals; lost to Los Angeles, 4-2, in Western Division finals.

1966— Replaced Michael Farmer as Baltimore head coach, with record of 1-8 (November). Replaced as Baltimore head coach by Gene Shue (December).

JOHNSON, DENNIS
G

PERSONAL: Born September 18, 1954, in San Pedro, Calif. . . . 6-4/202. . . . Full name: Dennis Wayne Johnson. . . . Nickname: D.J.

HIGH SCHOOL: Dominguez (Compton, Calif.).

COLLEGE: Los Angeles Harbor Junior College, then Pepperdine.

TRANSACTIONS/CAREER NOTES: Selected as hardship case by Seattle SuperSonics in second round (29th pick overall) of 1976 NBA Draft. . . . Traded by SuperSonics to Phoenix Suns for Paul Westphal (June 4, 1980). . . . Traded by Suns with 1983 first- and third-round draft choices to Boston Celtics for Rick Robey and two 1983 second-round draft choices (June 27, 1983).

MISCELLANEOUS: Member of NBA championship teams (1979, 1984, 1986).

COLLEGIATE RECORD

Season Team	G	Min.	FGM	FGA	Pct.	FTM	FTA	Pct.	Reb.	Pts.	Avg.
73-74 — Los Angeles Harbor J.C.	...	699	103	191	.539	45	82	.549	230	251	...
74-75 — Los Angeles Harbor J.C.	28	967	...	...	...	...	...	...	336	511	18.3
75-76 — Pepperdine	27	930	181	378	.479	63	112	.563	156	425	15.7
Junior college totals	...	1666	...	...	...	...	...	...	566	762	27.2
Four-year-college totals	27	930	181	378	.479	63	112	.563	156	425	15.7

NBA REGULAR-SEASON RECORD

HONORS: All-NBA first team (1981). . . . All-NBA second team (1980). . . . NBA All-Defensive first team (1979, 1980, 1981, 1982, 1983, 1987). . . . NBA All-Defensive second team (1984, 1985, 1986).

Season Team	G	Min.	FGM	FGA	Pct.	FTM	FTA	Pct.	REBOUNDS Off.	Def.	Tot.	Ast.	PF	Dq.	Stl.	Blk.	TO	Pts.	Avg.
76-77 — Seattle	81	1667	285	566	.504	179	287	.624	161	141	302	123	221	3	123	57	...	749	9.2
77-78 — Seattle	81	2209	367	881	.417	297	406	.732	152	142	294	230	213	2	118	51	164	1031	12.7
78-79 — Seattle	80	2717	482	1110	.434	306	392	.781	146	228	374	280	209	2	100	97	191	1270	15.9
79-80 — Seattle	81	2937	574	1361	.422	380	487	.780	173	241	414	332	267	6	144	82	227	1540	19.0
80-81 — Phoenix	79	2615	532	1220	.436	411	501	.820	160	203	363	291	244	2	136	61	208	1486	18.8
81-82 — Phoenix	80	2937	577	1228	.470	399	495	.806	142	268	410	369	253	6	105	55	233	1561	19.5
82-83 — Phoenix	77	2551	398	861	.462	292	369	.791	92	243	335	388	204	1	97	39	204	1093	14.2
83-84 — Boston	80	2665	384	878	.437	281	330	.852	87	193	280	338	251	6	93	57	172	1053	13.2
84-85 — Boston	80	2976	493	1066	.462	261	306	.853	91	226	317	543	224	2	96	39	212	1254	15.7
85-86 — Boston	78	2732	482	1060	.455	243	297	.818	69	199	268	456	206	3	110	35	173	1213	15.6
86-87 — Boston	79	2933	423	953	.444	209	251	.833	45	216	261	594	201	0	87	38	177	1062	13.4
87-88 — Boston	77	2670	352	803	.438	255	298	.856	62	178	240	598	204	0	93	29	195	971	12.6
88-89 — Boston	72	2309	277	638	.434	160	195	.821	31	159	190	472	211	3	94	21	175	721	10.0
89-90 — Boston	75	2036	206	475	.434	118	140	.843	48	153	201	485	179	2	81	14	117	531	7.1
Totals	1100	35954	5832	13100	.445	3791	4754	.797	1459	2790	4249	5499	3087	38	1477	675	2448	15535	14.1

Three-point field goals: 1979-80, 12-for-58 (.207). 1980-81, 11-for-51 (.216). 1981-82, 8-for-42 (.190). 1982-83, 5-for-31 (.161). 1983-84, 4-for-32 (.125). 1984-85, 7-for-26 (.269). 1985-86, 6-for-42 (.143). 1986-87, 7-for-62 (.113). 1987-88, 12-for-46 (.261). 1988-89, 7-for-50 (.140). 1989-90, 1-for-24 (.042). Totals, 80-for-464 (.172).

NBA PLAYOFF RECORD

NOTES: NBA Finals Most Valuable Player (1979). . . . Shares NBA Finals single-game record for most free throws made in one half— 12 (June 12, 1984, vs. Los Angeles).

Season Team	G	Min.	FGM	FGA	Pct.	FTM	FTA	Pct.	REBOUNDS Off.	Def.	Tot.	Ast.	PF	Dq.	Stl.	Blk.	TO	Pts.	Avg.
77-78 — Seattle	22	827	121	294	.412	112	159	.704	47	54	101	72	63	0	23	23	53	354	16.1
78-79 — Seattle	17	691	136	302	.450	84	109	.771	44	60	104	69	63	0	28	26	51	356	20.9
79-80 — Seattle	15	582	100	244	.410	52	62	.839	25	39	64	57	48	2	27	10	43	257	17.1
80-81 — Phoenix	7	267	52	110	.473	32	42	.762	7	26	33	20	18	0	9	9	19	137	19.6
81-82 — Phoenix	7	271	63	132	.477	30	39	.769	13	18	31	32	28	2	15	4	25	156	22.3
82-83 — Phoenix	3	108	22	48	.458	10	12	.833	6	17	23	17	9	0	5	2	8	54	18.0
83-84 — Boston	22	808	129	319	.404	104	120	.867	30	49	79	97	75	1	25	7	53	365	16.6
84-85 — Boston	21	848	142	319	.445	80	93	.860	24	60	84	154	66	0	31	9	72	364	17.3
85-86 — Boston	18	715	109	245	.445	67	84	.798	23	53	76	107	58	2	39	5	51	291	16.2

Season	Team	G	Min.	FGM	FGA	Pct.	FTM	FTA	Pct.	Off.	Def.	Tot.	Ast.	PF	Dq.	Stl.	Blk.	TO	Pts.	Avg.
86-87 —Boston		23	964	168	361	.465	96	113	.850	24	67	91	205	71	0	16	8	44	435	18.9
87-88 —Boston		17	702	91	210	.433	82	103	.796	15	62	77	139	51	0	24	8	45	270	15.9
88-89 —Boston		3	59	4	15	.267	0	0	....	2	2	4	9	8	0	3	0	3	8	2.7
89-90 —Boston		5	162	30	62	.484	7	7	1.000	2	12	14	28	17	1	2	2	10	69	13.8
Totals		180	7004	1167	2661	.439	756	943	.802	262	519	781	1006	575	8	247	113	477	3116	17.3

Three-point field goals: 1979-80, 5-for-15 (.333). 1980-81, 1-for-5 (.200). 1981-82, 0-for-3. 1982-83, 0-for-1. 1983-84, 3-for-7 (.429). 1984-85, 0-for-14. 1985-86, 6-for-16 (.375). 1986-87, 3-for-26 (.115). 1987-88, 6-for-16 (.375). 1989-90, 2-for-6 (.333). Totals, 26-for-109 (.239).

NBA ALL-STAR GAME RECORD

Season	Team	Min.	FGM	FGA	Pct.	FTM	FTA	Pct.	Off.	Def.	Tot.	Ast.	PF	Dq.	Stl.	Blk.	TO	Pts.
1979	—Seattle...............	27	5	7	.714	2	2	1.000	1	0	1	3	3	0	0	1	1	12
1980	—Seattle...............	20	7	13	.538	5	6	.833	2	2	4	1	3	0	2	1	2	19
1981	—Phoenix...............	24	5	8	.625	9	10	.900	1	1	2	1	1	0	3	0	2	19
1982	—Phoenix...............	15	0	2	.000	1	2	.500	2	3	5	1	1	0	0	2	3	1
1985	—Boston	12	3	7	.429	2	2	1.000	1	5	6	3	2	0	0	0	1	8
	Totals	98	20	37	.541	19	22	.864	7	11	18	9	10	0	5	4	9	59

JOHNSON, GUS
F

PERSONAL: Born December 13, 1938, in Akron, O. . . . Died April 29, 1987. . . . 6-6/235. . . . Full name: Gus Johnson Jr. . . . Nickname: Honeycomb.
HIGH SCHOOL: Central Hower (Akron, O.).
COLLEGE: Akron, then Boise Junior College (Idaho), then Idaho.
TRANSACTIONS/CAREER NOTES: Selected by Baltimore Bullets in second round (11th pick overall) of 1963 NBA Draft. . . . Traded by Bullets to Phoenix Suns for second-round draft choice (April 10, 1972). . . . Waived by Suns (December 1, 1972). . . . Signed as free agent by Indiana Pacers of American Basketball Association (December 15, 1972).

COLLEGIATE RECORD

NOTES: Left Akron before start of 1959-60 basketball season.

Season	Team	G	Min.	FGM	FGA	Pct.	FTM	FTA	Pct.	Reb.	Pts.	Avg.
62-63	—Idaho..................	23	...	188	438	.429	62	105	.590	466	438	19.0

NBA REGULAR-SEASON RECORD

HONORS: All-NBA second team (1965, 1966, 1970, 1971). . . . NBA All-Defensive first team (1970, 1971). . . . NBA All-Rookie team (1964).

Season	Team	G	Min.	FGM	FGA	Pct.	FTM	FTA	Pct.	Reb.	Ast.	PF	Dq.	Pts.	Avg.
63-64 —Baltimore		78	2847	571	1329	.430	210	319	.658	1064	169	321	11	1352	17.3
64-65 —Baltimore		76	2899	577	1379	.418	261	386	.676	988	270	258	4	1415	18.6
65-66 —Baltimore		42	1284	273	661	.413	131	178	.736	546	114	136	3	677	16.1
66-67 —Baltimore		73	2626	620	1377	.450	271	383	.708	855	194	281	7	1511	20.7
67-68 —Baltimore		60	2271	482	1033	.467	180	270	.667	782	159	223	7	1144	19.1
68-69 —Baltimore		49	1671	359	782	.459	160	223	.717	568	97	176	1	878	17.9
69-70 —Baltimore		78	2919	578	1282	.451	197	272	.724	1086	264	269	6	1353	17.3
70-71 —Baltimore		66	2538	494	1090	.453	214	290	.738	1128	192	227	4	1202	18.2
71-72 —Baltimore		39	668	103	269	.383	43	63	.683	226	51	91	0	249	6.4
72-73 —Phoenix		21	417	69	181	.381	25	36	.694	136	31	55	0	163	7.8
Totals		582	20140	4126	9383	.440	1692	2420	.699	7379	1541	2037	43	9944	17.1

NBA PLAYOFF RECORD

Season	Team	G	Min.	FGM	FGA	Pct.	FTM	FTA	Pct.	Reb.	Ast.	PF	Dq.	Pts.	Avg.
64-65 —Baltimore		10	377	62	173	.358	34	46	.739	111	34	38	1	158	15.8
65-66 —Baltimore		1	8	1	4	.250	0	0	...	0	0	1	0	2	2.0
69-70 —Baltimore		7	298	51	111	.459	27	34	.794	80	9	20	0	129	18.4
70-71 —Baltimore		11	365	54	128	.422	35	47	.745	114	30	34	0	143	13.0
71-72 —Baltimore		5	77	9	30	.300	2	2	1.000	25	3	17	0	20	4.0
Totals		34	1125	177	446	.397	98	129	.760	330	76	110	1	452	13.3

NBA ALL-STAR GAME RECORD

Season	Team	Min.	FGM	FGA	Pct.	FTM	FTA	Pct.	Reb.	Ast.	PF	Dq.	Pts.
1965	—Baltimore	25	7	13	.538	11	13	.846	8	2	2	0	25
1968	—Baltimore	16	3	9	.333	1	2	.500	6	1	2	0	7
1969	—Baltimore	18	4	10	.400	5	8	.625	10	0	3	0	13
1970	—Baltimore	17	5	12	.417	0	0	...	7	1	2	0	10
1971	—Baltimore	23	5	12	.417	2	2	1.000	4	2	3	0	12
	Totals	99	24	56	.429	19	25	.760	35	6	12	0	67

ABA REGULAR-SEASON RECORD

NOTES: Member of ABA championship team (1973).

Season	Team	G	Min.	2-POINT FGM	2-POINT FGA	2-POINT Pct.	3-POINT FGM	3-POINT FGA	3-POINT Pct.	FTM	FTA	Pct.	Reb.	Ast.	Pts.	Avg.
72-73 —Indiana.............		50	753	128	278	.460	4	21	.190	31	42	.738	245	62	299	6.0

ABA PLAYOFF RECORD

Season	Team	G	Min.	2-POINT FGM	2-POINT FGA	2-POINT Pct.	3-POINT FGM	3-POINT FGA	3-POINT Pct.	FTM	FTA	Pct.	Reb.	Ast.	Pts.	Avg.
72-73 —Indiana.............		17	184	15	56	.268	0	3	.000	3	4	.750	69	15	42	2.5

JOHNSTON, NEIL

C

PERSONAL: Born February 4, 1929, in Chillicothe, O. . . . Died September 27, 1978. . . . 6-8/210. . . . Full name: Donald Neil Johnston. . . . Nickname: Gabby.
HIGH SCHOOL: Chillicothe (O.).
COLLEGE: Ohio State.
TRANSACTIONS/CAREER NOTES: Signed as free agent by Philadelphia Warriors (1951). . . . Signed as player/head coach by Pittsburgh Rens of Amercian Basketball League (1961).
CAREER HONORS: Elected to Naismith Memorial Basketball Hall of Fame (1989).
MISCELLANEOUS: Member of NBA championship team (1956).

COLLEGIATE RECORD

NOTES: Signed pro baseball contract in 1948 and became ineligible for his final two years at Ohio State.

Season Team	G	Min.	FGM	FGA	Pct.	FTM	FTA	Pct.	Reb.	Pts.	Avg.
46-47 —Ohio State	7	...	5	...	...	3	8	.375	...	13	1.9
47-48 —Ohio State	20	...	67	219	.306	46	87	.529	...	180	9.0
Totals	27		72			49	95	.516	...	193	7.1

NBA REGULAR-SEASON RECORD

HONORS: All-NBA first team (1953, 1954, 1955, 1956). . . . All-NBA second team (1957).
NOTES: Led NBA with 15.1 rebounds per game (1955).

Season Team	G	Min.	FGM	FGA	Pct.	FTM	FTA	Pct.	Reb.	Ast.	PF	Dq.	Pts.	Avg.
51-52 —Philadelphia	64	993	141	299	.472	100	151	.662	342	39	154	5	382	6.0
52-53 —Philadelphia	70	*3166	*504	1114	*.452	*556	*794	.700	976	197	248	6	*1564	*22.3
53-54 —Philadelphia	72	*3296	*591	*1317	.449	*577	*772	.747	797	203	259	7	*1759	*24.4
54-55 —Philadelphia	72	2917	521	1184	.440	*589	*769	.766	*1085	215	255	4	*1631	*22.7
55-56 —Philadelphia	70	2594	499	1092	*.457	549	685	.801	872	225	251	8	1547	22.1
56-57 —Philadelphia	69	2531	520	1163	*.447	535	648	.826	855	203	231	2	1575	22.8
57-58 —Philadelphia	71	2408	473	1102	.429	442	540	.819	790	166	233	4	1388	19.5
58-59 —Philadelphia	28	393	54	164	.329	69	88	.784	139	21	50	0	177	6.3
Totals	516	18298	3303	7435	.444	3417	4447	.768	5856	1269	1681	36	10023	19.4

NBA PLAYOFF RECORD

Season Team	G	Min.	FGM	FGA	Pct.	FTM	FTA	Pct.	Reb.	Ast.	PF	Dq.	Pts.	Avg.
51-52 —Philadelphia	3	32	5	10	.500	6	8	.750	10	1	8	0	16	5.3
55-56 —Philadelphia	10	397	69	169	.408	65	92	.707	143	51	41	0	203	20.3
56-57 —Philadelphia	2	84	17	53	.321	4	6	.667	35	9	9	0	38	19.0
57-58 —Philadelphia	8	189	30	78	.385	27	33	.818	69	14	18	0	87	10.9
Totals	23	702	121	310	.390	102	139	.734	257	75	76	0	344	15.0

NBA ALL-STAR GAME RECORD

Season Team	Min.	FGM	FGA	Pct.	FTM	FTA	Pct.	Reb.	Ast.	PF	Dq.	Pts.
1953 —Philadelphia	27	5	13	.385	1	2	.500	12	0	2	0	11
1954 —Philadelphia	20	2	9	.222	2	4	.500	7	2	1	0	6
1955 —Philadelphia	15	1	7	.143	1	1	1.000	6	1	0	0	3
1956 —Philadelphia	25	5	9	.556	7	11	.636	10	1	3	0	17
1957 —Philadelphia	23	8	12	.667	3	3	1.000	9	1	2	0	19
1958 —Philadelphia	22	6	13	.462	2	2	1.000	8	1	5	0	14
Totals	132	27	63	.429	16	23	.696	52	6	13	0	70

ABL REGULAR-SEASON RECORD

Season Team	G	Min.	FGM	FGA	Pct.	FTM	FTA	Pct.	Reb.	Ast.	Pts.	Avg.
61-62 —Pittsburgh	5	106	15	37	.405	24	16	1.500	18	10	49	9.8

HEAD COACHING RECORD

BACKGROUND: Player/head coach, Pittsburgh Rens of American Basketball League (1961-62).

NBA COACHING RECORD

Season Team	W	L	Pct.	REGULAR SEASON Finish	W	L	PLAYOFFS Pct.
59-60 —Philadelphia	49	26	.653	2nd/Eastern Division	4	5	.444
60-61 —Philadelphia	46	33	.582	2nd/Eastern Division	0	3	.000
Totals (2 years)	95	59	.617	Totals (2 years)	4	8	.333

ABL COACHING RECORD

Season Team	W	L	Pct.	REGULAR SEASON Finish	W	L	PLAYOFFS Pct.
61-62 —Pittsburgh	41	40	.506	2nd/Eastern Division	0	1	.000
62-63 —Pittsburgh	12	10	.545	3rd	—	—	—
Totals (2 years)	53	50	.515	Totals (1 year)	0	1	.000

EBL COACHING RECORD

Season Team	W	L	Pct.	REGULAR SEASON Finish	W	L	PLAYOFFS Pct.
64-65 —Wilmington	12	16	.429	5th	—	—	—
65-66 —Wilmington	20	8	.714	1st/Eastern Division	4	2	.667
Totals (2 years)	32	24	.571	Totals (1 year)	4	2	.667

NOTES:
1960— Defeated Syracuse, 2-1, in Eastern Division semifinals; lost to Boston, 4-2, in Eastern Division finals.
1961— Lost to Syracuse in Eastern Division semifinals.
1962— ABL disbanded (December 31).
1966— Defeated Trenton, 2-1, in Eastern Finals; defeated Wilkes-Barre, 2-1, in EBL Finals.

RECORD AS BASEBALL PLAYER

TRANSACTION/CAREER NOTES: Signed by Philadelphia Phillies organization (August 1948).... Released by Phillies organization (June 1, 1952).

Year	Team (League)	G	W	L	Pct.	ERA	Sv.	IP	H	R	ER	BB	SO
1949 — Terre Haute (Three I)		29	10	12	.455	3.14	...	166	159	85	58	73	129
1950 — Terre Haute (Three I)		28	11	12	.478	2.89	...	168	132	78	54	102	126
1951 — Wilmington (Inter-State)		27	3	9	.250	5.40	...	115	126	76	69	79	104

JONES, SAM
G

PERSONAL: Born June 24, 1933, in Wilmington, N.C. ... 6-4/205. ... Full name: Samuel Jones.
HIGH SCHOOL: Laurinburg Institute (N.C.).
COLLEGE: North Carolina Central.
TRANSACTIONS/CAREER NOTES: Selected by Boston Celtics in first round of 1957 NBA Draft.
CAREER HONORS: Elected to Naismith Memorial Basketball Hall of Fame (1983).... NBA 25th Anniversary All-Time team (1970).
MISCELLANEOUS: Member of NBA championship teams (1959, 1960, 1961, 1962, 1963, 1964, 1965, 1966, 1968, 1969).

COLLEGIATE RECORD

NOTES: Elected to NAIA Basketball Hall of Fame (1962).

Season Team	G	Min.	FGM	FGA	Pct.	FTM	FTA	Pct.	Reb.	Pts.	Avg.
51-52 — North Carolina Central	22	...	126	263	.479	48	78	.615	150	300	13.6
52-53 — North Carolina Central	24	...	169	370	.457	115	180	.639	248	453	18.9
53-54 — North Carolina Central	27	...	208	432	.481	98	137	.715	223	514	19.0
54-55 —			Did not play—in military service.								
55-56 —			Did not play—in military service.								
56-57 — North Carolina Central	27	...	174	398	.437	155	202	.767	288	503	18.6
Totals	100	...	677	1463	.463	416	597	.697	909	1770	17.7

NBA REGULAR-SEASON RECORD

HONORS: All-NBA second team (1965, 1966, 1967).

Season Team	G	Min.	FGM	FGA	Pct.	FTM	FTA	Pct.	Reb.	Ast.	PF	Dq.	Pts.	Avg.
57-58 — Boston	56	594	100	233	.429	60	84	.714	160	37	42	0	260	4.6
58-59 — Boston	71	1466	305	703	.434	151	196	.770	428	101	102	0	761	10.7
59-60 — Boston	74	1512	355	782	.454	168	220	.764	375	125	101	1	878	11.9
60-61 — Boston	78	2028	480	1069	.449	211	268	.787	421	217	148	1	1171	15.0
61-62 — Boston	78	2388	596	1284	.464	243	297	.818	458	232	149	0	1435	18.4
62-63 — Boston	76	2323	621	1305	.476	257	324	.793	396	241	162	1	1499	19.7
63-64 — Boston	76	2381	612	1359	.450	249	318	.783	349	202	192	1	1473	19.4
64-65 — Boston	80	2885	821	1818	.452	428	522	.820	411	223	176	0	2070	25.9
65-66 — Boston	67	2155	626	1335	.469	325	407	.799	347	216	170	0	1577	23.5
66-67 — Boston	72	2325	638	1406	.454	318	371	.857	338	217	191	1	1594	22.1
67-68 — Boston	73	2408	621	1348	.461	311	376	.827	357	216	181	0	1553	21.3
68-69 — Boston	70	1820	496	1103	.450	148	189	.783	265	182	121	0	1140	16.3
Totals	871	24285	6271	13745	.456	2869	3572	.803	4305	2209	1735	5	15411	17.7

NBA PLAYOFF RECORD

Season Team	G	Min.	FGM	FGA	Pct.	FTM	FTA	Pct.	Reb.	Ast.	PF	Dq.	Pts.	Avg.
57-58 — Boston	8	75	10	22	.455	11	16	.688	24	4	7	0	31	3.9
58-59 — Boston	11	192	40	108	.370	33	39	.846	63	17	14	0	113	10.3
59-60 — Boston	13	197	45	117	.385	17	21	.810	41	18	15	0	107	8.2
60-61 — Boston	10	258	50	112	.446	31	35	.886	54	22	22	0	131	13.1
61-62 — Boston	14	504	123	277	.444	42	60	.700	99	44	30	0	288	20.6
62-63 — Boston	13	450	120	248	.484	69	83	.831	81	32	42	1	309	23.8
63-64 — Boston	10	356	91	180	.506	50	68	.735	47	23	24	0	232	23.2
64-65 — Boston	12	495	135	294	.459	73	84	.869	55	30	39	1	343	28.6
65-66 — Boston	17	602	154	343	.449	114	136	.838	86	53	65	1	422	24.8
66-67 — Boston	9	326	95	207	.459	50	58	.862	46	28	30	1	240	26.7
67-68 — Boston	19	685	162	367	.441	66	84	.786	64	50	58	0	390	20.5
68-69 — Boston	18	514	124	296	.419	55	69	.797	58	37	45	1	303	16.8
Totals	154	4654	1149	2571	.447	611	753	.811	718	358	391	5	2909	18.9

NBA ALL-STAR GAME RECORD

Season Team	Min.	FGM	FGA	Pct.	FTM	FTA	Pct.	Reb.	Ast.	PF	Dq.	Pts.
1962 — Boston	14	1	8	.125	0	1	.000	1	0	1	0	2
1964 — Boston	27	8	20	.400	0	0	...	4	3	2	0	16
1965 — Boston	24	2	12	.167	2	2	1.000	5	3	2	0	6
1966 — Boston	22	5	11	.455	2	2	1.000	2	5	0	0	12
1968 — Boston	15	2	5	.400	1	1	1.000	2	4	1	0	5
Totals	102	18	56	.321	5	6	.833	14	15	6	0	41

HEAD COACHING RECORD

BACKGROUND: Athletic director/head coach, Federal City College, Washington, D.C. (1969-1973).... Assistant coach, New Orleans NBA (1974-75).

COLLEGIATE COACHING RECORD

Season Team	W	L	Pct.	Finish
69-70 — Federal City College	5	8	.385	
70-71 — Federal City College	12	9	.571	
71-72 — Federal City College	11	9	.550	
72-73 — Federal City College	11	13	.458	
73-74 — North Carolina Central	5	16	.238	7th/Mid-Eastern Athletic Conference.
Totals (5 years)	44	55	.444	

KERR, RED

C

PERSONAL: Born August 17, 1932, in Chicago. . . . 6-9/230. . . . Full name: John G. Kerr.
HIGH SCHOOL: Tilden Technical School (Chicago).
COLLEGE: Illinois.
TRANSACTIONS/CAREER NOTES: Selected by Syracuse Nationals in first round (sixth pick overall) of 1954 NBA Draft. . . . Nationals franchise moved from Syracuse to Philadelphia and renamed 76ers for 1963-64 season. . . . Traded by 76ers to Baltimore Bullets for Wally Jones (September 22, 1965). . . . Selected by Chicago Bulls from Bullets in expansion draft (April 30, 1966).
MISCELLANEOUS: Member of NBA championship team (1955).

COLLEGIATE RECORD

Season	Team	G	Min.	FGM	FGA	Pct.	FTM	FTA	Pct.	Reb.	Pts.	Avg.
50-51	—Illinois‡			Freshman team did not play intercollegiate schedule.								
51-52	—Illinois	26	...	143	365	.392	71	124	.573	...	357	13.7
52-53	—Illinois	22	...	153	397	.385	80	123	.650	...	386	17.5
53-54	—Illinois	22	...	210	520	.404	136	214	.636	...	556	25.3
	Varsity totals	70	...	506	1282	.395	287	461	.623	...	1299	18.6

NBA REGULAR-SEASON RECORD

Season	Team	G	Min.	FGM	FGA	Pct.	FTM	FTA	Pct.	Reb.	Ast.	PF	Dq.	Pts.	Avg.
54-55	—Syracuse	72	1529	301	718	.419	152	223	.682	474	80	165	2	754	10.5
55-56	—Syracuse	72	2114	377	935	.403	207	316	.655	607	84	168	3	961	13.3
56-57	—Syracuse	72	2191	333	827	.403	225	313	.719	807	90	190	3	891	12.4
57-58	—Syracuse	72	2384	407	1020	.399	280	422	.664	963	88	197	4	1094	15.2
58-59	—Syracuse	72	2671	502	1139	.441	281	367	.766	1008	142	183	1	1285	17.8
59-60	—Syracuse	75	2361	436	1111	.392	233	310	.752	913	168	207	4	1105	14.7
60-61	—Syracuse	79	2676	419	1056	.397	218	299	.729	951	199	230	4	1056	13.4
61-62	—Syracuse	80	2767	541	1220	.443	222	302	.735	1176	243	282	7	1304	16.3
62-63	—Syracuse	80	2561	507	1069	.474	241	320	.753	1049	214	208	3	1255	15.7
63-64	—Philadelphia	80	2938	536	1250	.429	268	357	.751	1018	275	187	2	1340	16.8
64-65	—Philadelphia	80	1810	264	714	.370	126	181	.696	551	197	132	1	654	8.2
65-66	—Baltimore	71	1770	286	692	.413	209	272	.768	586	225	148	0	781	11.0
	Totals	905	27772	4909	11751	.418	2662	3682	.723	10103	2005	2297	34	12480	13.8

NBA PLAYOFF RECORD

Season	Team	G	Min.	FGM	FGA	Pct.	FTM	FTA	Pct.	Reb.	Ast.	PF	Dq.	Pts.	Avg.
54-55	—Syracuse	11	363	59	151	.391	34	61	.557	118	13	27	0	152	13.8
55-56	—Syracuse	8	213	37	77	.481	15	33	.455	68	10	23	0	89	11.1
56-57	—Syracuse	5	162	28	65	.431	20	29	.690	69	6	7	0	76	15.2
57-58	—Syracuse	3	116	18	55	.327	14	18	.778	61	3	5	0	50	16.7
58-59	—Syracuse	9	312	50	142	.352	30	33	.909	108	24	20	0	130	14.4
59-60	—Syracuse	3	104	15	51	.294	11	12	.917	25	9	9	0	41	13.7
60-61	—Syracuse	8	210	30	88	.341	16	23	.696	99	20	18	0	76	9.5
61-62	—Syracuse	5	193	41	109	.376	6	8	.750	80	10	15	0	88	17.6
62-63	—Syracuse	5	187	26	60	.433	16	21	.762	75	9	12	0	68	13.6
63-64	—Philadelphia	5	185	40	83	.482	15	20	.750	69	16	12	0	95	19.0
64-65	—Philadelphia	11	181	24	67	.358	15	21	.714	38	28	20	0	63	5.7
65-66	—Baltimore	3	49	2	11	.182	1	2	.500	17	4	5	0	5	1.7
	Totals	76	2275	370	959	.386	193	281	.687	827	152	173	0	933	12.3

NBA ALL-STAR GAME RECORD

Season	Team	Min.	FGM	FGA	Pct.	FTM	FTA	Pct.	Reb.	Ast.	PF	Dq.	Pts.
1956	—Syracuse	16	2	4	.500	0	1	.000	8	0	2	0	4
1959	—Syracuse	21	3	14	.214	1	2	.500	9	2	0	0	7
1963	—Syracuse	11	0	4	.000	2	2	1.000	2	1	3	0	2
	Totals	48	5	22	.227	3	5	.600	19	3	5	0	13

HEAD COACHING RECORD

HONORS: NBA Coach of the Year (1967).

NBA COACHING RECORD

		REGULAR SEASON				PLAYOFFS		
Season	Team	W	L	Pct.	Finish	W	L	Pct.
66-67	—Chicago	33	48	.407	4th/Western Division	0	3	.000
67-68	—Chicago	29	53	.354	4th/Western Division	1	4	.200
68-69	—Phoenix	16	66	.195	7th/Western Division	—	—	—
69-70	—Phoenix	15	23	.395		—	—	—
	Totals (4 years)	93	190	.329	**Totals (2 years)**	1	7	.125

NOTES:
1967— Lost to St. Louis in Western Division semifinals.
1968— Lost to Los Angeles in Western Division semifinals.
1970— Resigned as Phoenix head coach (January 2); replaced by Jerry Colangelo.

LANIER, BOB

C

PERSONAL: Born September 10, 1948, in Buffalo, N.Y. . . . 6-11/265. . . . Full name: Robert Jerry Lanier Jr.
HIGH SCHOOL: Bennett (Buffalo, N.Y.).
COLLEGE: St. Bonaventure.
TRANSACTIONS/CAREER NOTES: Selected by Detroit Pistons in first round (first pick overall) of 1970 NBA Draft. . . . Traded by Pistons to Milwaukee Bucks for Kent Benson and 1980 first-round draft choice (February 4, 1980).

COLLEGIATE RECORD

NOTES: THE SPORTING NEWS All-America first team (1970).

Season	Team	G	Min.	FGM	FGA	Pct.	FTM	FTA	Pct.	Reb.	Pts.	Avg.
66-67	St. Bonaventure†	15	...	...	...	...	...	...	...	...	450	30.0
67-68	St. Bonaventure	25	...	272	466	.584	112	175	.640	390	656	26.2
68-69	St. Bonaventure	24	...	270	460	.587	114	181	.630	374	654	27.3
69-70	St. Bonaventure	26	...	308	549	.561	141	194	.727	416	757	29.1
	Varsity totals	75	...	850	1475	.576	367	550	.667	1180	2067	27.6

NBA REGULAR-SEASON RECORD

HONORS: NBA All-Rookie team (1971).

Season	Team	G	Min.	FGM	FGA	Pct.	FTM	FTA	Pct.	Reb.	Ast.	PF	Dq.	Pts.	Avg.
70-71	Detroit	82	2017	504	1108	.455	273	376	.726	665	146	272	4	1281	15.6
71-72	Detroit	80	3092	834	1690	.493	388	505	.768	1205	248	297	6	2056	25.7
72-73	Detroit	81	3150	810	1654	.490	307	397	.773	1205	260	278	4	1927	23.8

Season	Team	G	Min.	FGM	FGA	Pct.	FTM	FTA	Pct.	Off.	Def.	Tot.	Ast.	PF	Dq.	Stl.	Blk.	TO	Pts.	Avg.
73-74	Detroit	81	3047	748	1483	.504	326	409	.797	269	805	1074	343	273	7	110	247	...	1822	22.5
74-75	Detroit	76	2987	731	1433	.510	361	450	.802	225	689	914	350	237	1	75	172	...	1823	24.0
75-76	Detroit	64	2363	541	1017	.532	284	370	.768	217	529	746	217	203	2	79	86	...	1366	21.3
76-77	Detroit	64	2446	678	1269	.534	260	318	.818	200	545	745	214	174	0	70	126	...	1616	25.3
77-78	Detroit	63	2311	622	1159	.537	298	386	.772	197	518	715	216	185	2	82	93	225	1542	24.5
78-79	Detroit	53	1835	489	950	.515	275	367	.749	164	330	494	140	181	5	50	75	175	1253	23.6
79-80	Detroit-Mil.	63	2131	466	867	.537	277	354	.782	152	400	552	184	200	3	74	89	162	1210	19.2
80-81	Milwaukee	67	1753	376	716	.525	208	277	.751	128	285	413	179	184	0	73	81	139	961	14.3
81-82	Milwaukee	74	1986	407	729	.558	182	242	.752	92	296	388	219	211	3	72	56	166	996	13.5
82-83	Milwaukee	39	978	163	332	.491	91	133	.684	58	142	200	105	125	2	34	24	82	417	10.7
83-84	Milwaukee	72	2007	392	685	.572	194	274	.708	141	314	455	186	228	8	58	51	163	978	13.6
	Totals	959	32103	7761	15092	.514	3724	4858	.767	...	...	9698	3007	3048	47	777	1100	1112	19248	20.1

Three-point field goals: 1979-80, 1-for-6 (.167). 1980-81, 1-for-1. 1981-82, 0-for-2. 1982-83, 0-for-1. 1983-84, 0-for-3. Totals, 2-for-13 (.154).

NBA PLAYOFF RECORD

Season	Team	G	Min.	FGM	FGA	Pct.	FTM	FTA	Pct.	Off.	Def.	Tot.	Ast.	PF	Dq.	Stl.	Blk.	TO	Pts.	Avg.
73-74	Detroit	7	303	77	152	.507	30	38	.789	26	81	107	21	28	1	4	14	...	184	26.3
74-75	Detroit	3	128	26	51	.510	9	12	.750	5	27	32	19	10	0	4	12	...	61	20.3
75-76	Detroit	9	359	95	172	.552	45	50	.900	39	75	114	30	34	1	8	21	...	235	26.1
76-77	Detroit	3	118	34	54	.630	16	19	.842	13	37	50	6	10	0	3	7	...	84	28.0
79-80	Milwaukee	7	256	52	101	.515	31	42	.738	17	48	65	31	23	0	7	8	17	135	19.3
80-81	Milwaukee	7	236	50	85	.588	23	32	.719	12	40	52	28	18	0	12	8	15	123	17.6
81-82	Milwaukee	6	212	41	80	.513	14	25	.560	18	27	45	22	21	2	8	5	14	96	16.0
82-83	Milwaukee	9	250	51	89	.573	21	35	.600	17	46	63	23	32	2	5	14	21	123	13.7
83-84	Milwaukee	16	499	82	171	.480	39	44	.886	32	85	117	55	57	1	11	10	38	203	12.7
	Totals	67	2361	508	955	.532	228	297	.768	179	466	645	235	233	7	62	99	105	1244	18.6

Three-point field goals: 1981-82, 0-for-1.

NBA ALL-STAR GAME RECORD

NOTES: NBA All-Star Game Most Valuable Player (1974).

Season	Team	Min.	FGM	FGA	Pct.	FTM	FTA	Pct.	Reb.	Ast.	PF	Dq.	Pts.
1972	Detroit	5	0	2	.000	2	3	.667	3	0	0	0	2
1973	Detroit	12	5	9	.556	0	0	...	6	0	1	0	10

Season	Team	Min.	FGM	FGA	Pct.	FTM	FTA	Pct.	Off.	Def.	Tot.	Ast.	PF	Dq.	Stl.	Blk.	TO	Pts.
1974	Detroit	26	11	15	.733	2	2	1.000	2	8	10	2	1	0	0	2	...	24
1975	Detroit	12	1	4	.250	0	0	...	2	5	7	2	3	0	2	0	...	2
1977	Detroit	20	7	8	.875	3	3	1.000	5	5	10	4	3	0	1	1	...	17
1978	Detroit	4	0	0	...	1	2	.500	2	0	2	0	0	0	0	1		1
1979	Detroit	31	5	10	.500	0	0	...	1	3	4	4	4	0	1	1	0	10
1982	Milwaukee	11	3	7	.429	2	2	1.000	2	1	3	0	3	0	0	0	1	8
	Totals	121	32	55	.582	10	12	.833	...	...	45	12	15	0	4	4	2	74

LUCAS, JERRY
F/C

PERSONAL: Born March 30, 1940, in Middletown, O.... 6-8/235.... Full name: Jerry Ray Lucas.... Nickname: Luke.
HIGH SCHOOL: Middletown (O.).
COLLEGE: Ohio State.
TRANSACTIONS/CAREER NOTES: Selected by Cincinnati Royals in 1962 NBA Draft (territorial pick).... Signed by Cleveland Pipers of American Basketball League (1962); Pipers dropped out of ABL prior to 1962-63 season.... Did not play pro basketball (1962-63).... Traded by Royals to San Francisco Warriors for Jim King and Bill Turner (October 25, 1969).... Traded by Warriors to New York Knicks for Cazzie Russell (May 7, 1971).
CAREER HONORS: Elected to Naismith Memorial Basketball Hall of Fame (1979).
MISCELLANEOUS: Member of NBA championship team (1973).... Member of gold-medal-winning U.S. Olympic team (1960).

COLLEGIATE RECORD

NOTES: THE SPORTING NEWS College Player of the Year (1961, 1962).... THE SPORTING NEWS All-America first team (1960, 1961, 1962).... Member of NCAA championship team (1960).... Led NCAA Division I with .637 field-goal percentage (1960), .623 field-goal percentage (1961) and .611 field-goal percentage (1962).... Led NCAA Division I with .198 rebound average (1960-61) and .211 rebound average (1961-62), when championship was determined by highest individual recoveries as percentage of total recoveries by both teams in all games.

Season Team	G	Min.	FGM	FGA	Pct.	FTM	FTA	Pct.	Reb.	Pts.	Avg.
58-59 —Ohio State‡			Freshman team did not play intercollegiate schedule.								
59-60 —Ohio State	27	...	283	444	.637	144	187	.770	442	710	26.3
60-61 —Ohio State	27	...	256	411	.623	159	208	.764	470	671	24.9
61-62 —Ohio State	28	...	237	388	.611	135	169	.799	499	609	21.8
Varsity totals	82		776	1243	.624	438	564	.777	1411	1990	24.3

NBA REGULAR-SEASON RECORD

HONORS: NBA Rookie of the Year (1964).... All-NBA first team (1965, 1966, 1968).... All-NBA second team (1964, 1967). ... NBA All-Rookie team (1964).

Season Team	G	Min.	FGM	FGA	Pct.	FTM	FTA	Pct.	Reb.	Ast.	PF	Dq.	Pts.	Avg.
63-64 —Cincinnati	79	3273	545	1035	*.527	310	398	.779	1375	204	300	6	1400	17.7
64-65 —Cincinnati	66	2864	558	1121	.498	298	366	.814	1321	157	214	1	1414	21.4
65-66 —Cincinnati	79	3517	690	1523	.453	317	403	.787	1668	213	274	5	1697	21.5
66-67 —Cincinnati	81	3558	577	1257	.459	284	359	.791	1547	268	280	2	1438	17.8
67-68 —Cincinnati	82	3619	707	1361	.519	346	445	.778	1560	251	243	3	1760	21.5
68-69 —Cincinnati	74	3075	555	1007	.551	247	327	.755	1360	306	206	0	1357	18.3
69-70 —Cincinnati-San Fran.	67	2420	405	799	.507	200	255	.784	951	173	166	2	1010	15.1
70-71 —San Francisco	80	3251	623	1250	.498	289	367	.787	1265	293	197	0	1535	19.2
71-72 —New York	77	2926	543	1060	.512	197	249	.791	1011	318	218	1	1283	16.7
72-73 —New York	71	2001	312	608	.513	80	100	.800	510	317	157	0	704	9.9

Season Team	G	Min.	FGM	FGA	Pct.	FTM	FTA	Pct.	Off.	Def.	Tot.	Ast.	PF	Dq.	Stl.	Blk.	TO	Pts.	Avg.
									— REBOUNDS —										
73-74 —New York	73	1627	194	420	.462	67	96	.698	62	312	374	230	134	0	28	24	...	455	6.2
Totals	829	32131	5709	11441	.499	2635	3365	.783	...	...	12942	2730	2389	20	28	24	...	14053	17.0

NBA PLAYOFF RECORD

Season Team	G	Min.	FGM	FGA	Pct.	FTM	FTA	Pct.	Reb.	Ast.	PF	Dq.	Pts.	Avg.
63-64 —Cincinnati	10	370	48	123	.390	26	37	.703	125	34	37	1	122	12.2
64-65 —Cincinnati	4	195	38	75	.507	17	22	.773	84	9	12	0	93	23.3
65-66 —Cincinnati	5	231	40	85	.471	27	35	.771	101	14	14	0	107	21.4
66-67 —Cincinnati	4	183	24	55	.436	2	2	1.000	77	8	15	0	50	12.5
70-71 —San Francisco	5	171	39	77	.506	11	16	.688	50	16	14	0	89	17.8
71-72 —New York	16	737	119	238	.500	59	71	.831	173	85	49	1	297	18.6
72-73 —New York	17	368	54	112	.482	20	23	.870	85	39	47	0	128	7.5

Season Team	G	Min.	FGM	FGA	Pct.	FTM	FTA	Pct.	Off.	Def.	Tot.	Ast.	PF	Dq.	Stl.	Blk.	TO	Pts.	Avg.
									— REBOUNDS —										
73-74 —New York	11	115	5	21	.238	0	0	...	6	16	22	9	9	0	4	0	...	10	0.9
Totals	72	2370	367	786	.467	162	206	.786	...	...	717	214	197	2	4	0	...	896	12.4

NBA ALL-STAR GAME RECORD

NOTES: NBA All-Star Game Most Valuable Player (1965).

Season Team	Min.	FGM	FGA	Pct.	FTM	FTA	Pct.	Reb.	Ast.	PF	Dq.	Pts.
1964 —Cincinnati	36	3	6	.500	5	6	.833	8	0	5	0	11
1965 —Cincinnati	35	12	19	.632	1	1	1.000	10	1	2	0	25
1966 —Cincinnati	23	4	11	.364	2	2	1.000	19	0	2	0	10
1967 —Cincinnati	22	3	5	.600	1	1	1.000	7	2	3	0	7
1968 —Cincinnati	21	6	9	.667	4	4	1.000	5	4	3	0	16
1969 —Cincinnati	17	2	5	.400	4	5	.800	6	1	3	0	8
1971 —San Francisco	29	5	9	.556	2	2	1.000	9	4	2	0	12
Totals	183	35	64	.547	19	21	.905	64	12	20	0	89

MACAULEY, ED

C/F

PERSONAL: Born March 22, 1928, in St. Louis. ... 6-8/190. ... Full name: Charles Edward Macauley Jr. ... Nickname: Easy Ed.
HIGH SCHOOL: St. Louis University High School (St. Louis).
COLLEGE: St. Louis.
TRANSACTIONS/CAREER NOTES: Selected by St. Louis Bombers in 1949 Basketball Association of America Draft (territorial pick).... Selected by Boston Celtics in NBA Dispersal Draft (April 25, 1950).... Traded by Celtics with draft rights to Cliff Hagan to St. Louis Hawks for first-round draft choice (April 29, 1956).
CAREER HONORS: Elected to Naismith Memorial Basketball Hall of Fame (1960).
MISCELLANEOUS: Member of NBA championship team (1958).

COLLEGIATE RECORD

NOTES: THE SPORTING NEWS All-America first team (1949).... Led NCAA Division I with .524 field-goal percentage (1949).

Season Team	G	Min.	FGM	FGA	Pct.	FTM	FTA	Pct.	Reb.	Pts.	Avg.
45-46 —St. Louis	23	...	94	...	...	71	...	...	...	259	11.3
46-47 —St. Louis	28	...	141	...	...	104	...	...	...	386	13.8
47-48 —St. Louis	27	...	132	324	.407	104	159	.654	...	368	13.6
48-49 —St. Louis	26	...	144	275	.524	116	153	.758	...	404	15.5
Totals	104	...	511	...	...	395	...	...	...	1417	13.6

NBA REGULAR-SEASON RECORD

HONORS: All-NBA first team (1951, 1952, 1953).... All-NBA second team (1954).

Season Team	G	Min.	FGM	FGA	Pct.	FTM	FTA	Pct.	Reb.	Ast.	PF	Dq.	Pts.	Avg.
49-50 —St. Louis	67	...	351	882	.398	379	528	.718	...	200	221	...	1081	16.1
50-51 —Boston	68	...	459	985	.466	466	614	.759	616	252	205	4	1384	20.4
51-52 —Boston	66	2631	384	888	.432	496	621	.799	529	232	174	0	1264	19.2
52-53 —Boston	69	2902	451	997	.452	500	667	.750	629	280	188	0	1402	20.3
53-54 —Boston	71	2792	462	950	*.486	420	554	.758	571	271	168	1	1344	18.9
54-55 —Boston	71	2706	403	951	.424	442	558	.792	600	275	171	0	1248	17.6
55-56 —Boston	71	2354	420	995	.422	400	504	.794	422	211	158	2	1240	17.5
56-57 —St. Louis	72	2582	414	987	.419	359	479	.749	440	202	206	2	1187	16.5

Season	Team	G	Min.	FGM	FGA	Pct.	FTM	FTA	Pct.	Reb.	Ast.	PF	Dq.	Pts.	Avg.
57-58	—St. Louis	72	1908	376	879	.428	267	369	.724	478	143	156	2	1019	14.2
58-59	—St. Louis	14	196	22	75	.293	21	35	.600	40	13	20	1	65	4.6
	Totals	641	...	3742	8589	.436	3750	4929	.761	...	2079	1667	...	11234	17.5

NBA PLAYOFF RECORD

Season	Team	G	Min.	FGM	FGA	Pct.	FTM	FTA	Pct.	Reb.	Ast.	PF	Dq.	Pts.	Avg.
50-51	—Boston	2	...	17	36	.472	10	16	.625	18	8	4	0	44	22.0
51-52	—Boston	3	129	27	49	.551	16	19	.842	33	11	11	1	70	23.3
52-53	—Boston	6	278	31	71	.437	39	54	.722	58	21	23	2	101	16.8
53-54	—Boston	5	127	8	22	.364	9	13	.692	21	21	14	0	25	5.0
54-55	—Boston	7	283	43	93	.462	41	54	.759	52	32	21	0	127	18.1
55-56	—Boston	3	73	12	30	.400	7	11	.636	15	5	6	0	31	10.3
56-57	—St. Louis	10	297	44	109	.404	54	74	.730	62	22	39	3	142	14.2
57-58	—St. Louis	11	227	36	89	.404	36	50	.720	62	18	23	0	108	9.8
	Totals	47	...	218	499	.437	212	291	.729	321	138	141	6	648	13.8

NBA ALL-STAR GAME RECORD

NOTES: NBA All-Star Game Most Valuable Player (1951).

Season	Team	Min.	FGM	FGA	Pct.	FTM	FTA	Pct.	Reb.	Ast.	PF	Dq.	Pts.
1951	—Boston	...	7	12	.583	6	7	.857	6	1	3	0	20
1952	—Boston	28	3	7	.429	9	9	1.000	7	3	2	0	15
1953	—Boston	35	5	12	.417	8	8	1.000	7	3	2	0	18
1954	—Boston	25	4	11	.364	5	6	.833	1	3	2	0	13
1955	—Boston	27	1	5	.200	4	5	.800	4	2	1	0	6
1956	—Boston	20	1	9	.111	2	4	.500	2	3	3	0	4
1957	—St. Louis	19	3	6	.500	1	2	.500	5	3	0	0	7
	Totals	...	24	62	.387	35	41	.854	32	18	13	0	83

NBA COACHING RECORD

		REGULAR SEASON				PLAYOFFS		
Season	Team	W	L	Pct.	Finish	W	L	Pct.
58-59	—St. Louis	43	19	.694	1st/Western Division	2	4	.333
59-60	—St. Louis	46	29	.613	1st/Western Divison	7	7	.500
	Totals (2 years)	89	48	.650	Totals (2 years)	9	11	.450

NOTES:
1958— Replaced Andy Phillip as St. Louis head coach (November), with record of 6-4.
1959— Lost to Minneapolis in Western Division finals.
1960— Defeated Minneapolis, 4-3, in Western Division finals; lost to Boston, 4-3, in World Championship Series.

MARAVICH, PETE

G

PERSONAL: Born June 22, 1947, in Aliquippa, Pa.... Died January 5, 1988.... 6-5/200.... Full name: Peter Press Maravich.... Nickname: Pistol Pete.... Son of Press Maravich, former college coach, guard with Youngstown Bears of National Basketball League (1945-46) and Pittsburgh Ironmen of Basketball Association of America (1946-47).
HIGH SCHOOL: Daniels (Clemson, S.C.), then Needham Broughton (Raleigh, N.C.), then Edwards Military Institute (Salemburg, N.C.).
COLLEGE: Louisiana State.
TRANSACTIONS/CAREER NOTES: Selected by Atlanta Hawks in first round (third pick overall) of 1970 NBA Draft.... Traded by Hawks to New Orleans Jazz for Dean Meminger, Bob Kauffman, 1974 and 1975 first-round draft choices and 1975 and 1976 second-round draft choices (May 3, 1974).... Jazz franchise moved from New Orleans to Utah for 1979-80 season.... Waived by Jazz (January 17, 1980).... Signed as free agent by Boston Celtics (January 22, 1980).
CAREER HONORS: Elected to Naismith Memorial Basketball Hall of Fame (1986).

COLLEGIATE RECORD

NOTES: THE SPORTING NEWS College Player of the Year (1970).... THE SPORTING NEWS All-America first team (1968, 1969, 1970).... Holds NCAA career records for most points—3667; highest points-per-game average—44.2; most field goals made—1387; most field goals attempted—3166; most free throws made (three-year career)—893; most free throws attempted (three-year career)—1152; and most games scoring at least 50 points—28.... Holds NCAA single-season records for most points—1381; highest points-per-game average—44.5; most field goals made—522; most field goals attempted—1168; and most games scoring at least 50 points—10 (1970).... Holds NCAA single-game record for most free throws made—30 (December 22, 1969, vs. Oregon State in 31 attempts).... Led NCAA Division I with 43.8 points per game (1968), 44.2 points per game (1969) and 44.5 points per game (1970).

Season	Team	G	Min.	FGM	FGA	Pct.	FTM	FTA	Pct.	Reb.	Pts.	Avg.
66-67	—Louisiana State†	17	...	273	604	.452	195	234	.833	176	741	43.6
67-68	—Louisiana State	26	...	432	1022	.423	274	338	.811	195	1138	43.8
68-69	—Louisiana State	26	...	433	976	.444	282	378	.746	169	1148	44.2
69-70	—Louisiana State	31	...	522	1168	.447	337	436	.773	164	1381	44.5
	Varsity totals	83	...	1387	3166	.438	893	1152	.775	528	3667	44.2

NBA REGULAR-SEASON RECORD

RECORDS: Shares single-game records for most free throws made in one quarter—14 (November 28, 1973, vs. Buffalo); and most free throws attempted in one quarter—16 (January 2, 1973, vs. Chicago).
HONORS: All-NBA first team (1976, 1977).... All-NBA second team (1973, 1978).... NBA All-Rookie team (1971).

Season	Team	G	Min.	FGM	FGA	Pct.	FTM	FTA	Pct.	Reb.	Ast.	PF	Dq.	Pts.	Avg.
70-71	—Atlanta	81	2926	738	1613	.458	404	505	.800	298	355	238	1	1880	23.2
71-72	—Atlanta	66	2302	460	1077	.427	355	438	.811	256	393	207	0	1275	19.3
72-73	—Atlanta	79	3089	789	1789	.441	485	606	.800	346	546	245	1	2063	26.1

Season Team	G	Min.	FGM	FGA	Pct.	FTM	FTA	Pct.	REBOUNDS Off.	Def.	Tot.	Ast.	PF	Dq.	Stl.	Blk.	TO	Pts.	Avg.
73-74 —Atlanta	76	2903	819	*1791	.457	469	568	.826	98	276	374	396	261	4	111	13	...	2107	27.7
74-75 —New Orleans	79	2853	655	1562	.419	390	481	.811	93	329	422	488	227	4	120	18	...	1700	21.5
75-76 —New Orleans	62	2373	604	1316	.459	396	488	.811	46	254	300	332	197	3	87	23	...	1604	25.9
76-77 —New Orleans	73	3041	886	*2047	.433	*501	600	.835	90	284	374	392	191	1	84	22	...	*2273	*31.1
77-78 —New Orleans	50	2041	556	1253	.444	240	276	.870	49	129	178	335	116	1	101	8	248	1352	27.0
78-79 —New Orleans	49	1824	436	1035	.421	233	277	.841	33	88	121	243	104	2	60	18	200	1105	22.6
79-80 —Utah-Boston	43	964	244	543	.449	91	105	.867	17	61	78	83	79	1	24	6	82	589	13.7
Totals	658	24316	6187	14026	.441	3564	4344	.820	...	...	2747	3563	1865	18	587	108	530	15948	24.2

Three-point field goals: 1979-80, 10-for-15 (.667).

NBA PLAYOFF RECORD

Season Team	G	Min.	FGM	FGA	Pct.	FTM	FTA	Pct.	Reb.	Ast.	PF	Dq.	Pts.	Avg.
70-71 —Atlanta	5	199	46	122	.377	18	26	.692	26	24	14	0	110	22.0
71-72 —Atlanta	6	219	54	121	.446	58	71	.817	32	28	24	0	166	27.7
72-73 —Atlanta	6	234	65	155	.419	27	34	.794	29	40	24	1	157	26.2

Season Team	G	Min.	FGM	FGA	Pct.	FTM	FTA	Pct.	REBOUNDS Off.	Def.	Tot.	Ast.	PF	Dq.	Stl.	Blk.	TO	Pts.	Avg.
79-80 —Boston	9	104	25	51	.490	2	3	.667	0	8	8	6	12	0	3	0	9	54	6.0
Totals	26	756	190	449	.423	105	134	.784	...	...	95	98	74	1	3	0	9	487	18.7

Three-point field goals: 1979-80, 2-for-6 (.333).

NBA ALL-STAR GAME RECORD

Season Team	Min.	FGM	FGA	Pct.	FTM	FTA	Pct.	Reb.	Ast.	PF	Dq.	Pts.
1973 —Atlanta	22	4	8	.500	0	0	...	3	5	4	0	8

Season Team	Min.	FGM	FGA	Pct.	FTM	FTA	Pct.	REBOUNDS Off.	Def.	Tot.	Ast.	PF	Dq.	Stl.	Blk.	TO	Pts.
1974 —Atlanta	22	4	15	.267	7	9	.778	1	2	3	4	2	0	0	0	...	15
1977 —New Orleans	21	5	13	.385	0	0	...	0	0	0	4	1	0	4	0	...	10
1978 —New Orleans							Selected, did not play—injured.										
1979 —New Orleans	14	5	8	.625	0	0	...	0	2	2	1	0	0	0	0	4	10
Totals	79	18	44	.409	7	9	.778	...	...	8	15	8	0	4	0	4	43

MARTIN, SLATER
G

PERSONAL: Born October 22, 1925, in Houston. ... 5-10/170. ... Full name: Slater N. Martin Jr. ... Nickname: Dugie.
HIGH SCHOOL: Thomas Jefferson (Houston).
COLLEGE: Texas.
TRANSACTIONS/CAREER NOTES: Selected by Minneapolis Lakers in 1949 Basketball Association of America Draft. ... Lakers franchise became part of NBA upon merger of BAA and National Basketball League for 1949-50 season. ... Traded by Lakers with Jerry Bird and player to be named later to New York Knicks for Walter Dukes and draft rights to Burdette Haldorson (October 26, 1956). ... Traded by Knicks to St. Louis Hawks for Willie Naulls (December 10, 1956).
CAREER HONORS: Elected to Naismith Memorial Basketball Hall of Fame (1981).
MISCELLANEOUS: Member of NBA championship teams (1950, 1952, 1953, 1954, 1958).

COLLEGIATE RECORD

NOTES: THE SPORTING NEWS All-America fifth team (1949).

Season Team	G	Min.	FGM	FGA	Pct.	FTM	FTA	Pct.	Reb.	Pts.	Avg.
43-44 —Texas	14	...	75	...	...	...	34	...	...	184	13.1
44-45 —						Did not play—in military service.					
45-46 —						Did not play—in military service.					
46-47 —Texas	27	...	109	...	...	37	...	...	...	255	9.4
47-48 —Texas	25	...	126	...	...	65	85	.765	...	317	12.7
48-49 —Texas	24	...	165	...	...	54	...	...	...	384	16.0
Totals	90	...	475	...	...	190	...	...	...	1140	12.7

NBA REGULAR-SEASON RECORD

HONORS: All-NBA second team (1954, 1956, 1957, 1958, 1959).

Season Team	G	Min.	FGM	FGA	Pct.	FTM	FTA	Pct.	Reb.	Ast.	PF	Dq.	Pts.	Avg.
49-50 —Minneapolis	67	...	106	302	.351	59	93	.634	...	148	162	...	271	4.0
50-51 —Minneapolis	68	...	227	627	.362	121	177	.684	246	235	199	3	575	8.5
51-52 —Minneapolis	66	2480	237	632	.375	142	190	.747	228	249	226	9	616	9.3
52-53 —Minneapolis	70	2556	260	634	.410	224	287	.780	186	250	246	4	744	10.6
53-54 —Minneapolis	69	2472	254	654	.388	176	243	.724	166	253	198	3	684	9.9
54-55 —Minneapolis	72	2784	350	919	.381	276	359	.769	260	427	221	7	976	13.6
55-56 —Minneapolis	72	*2838	309	863	.358	329	395	.833	260	445	202	2	947	13.2
56-57 —New York-St. Louis	66	2401	244	736	.332	230	291	.790	288	269	193	1	718	10.9
57-58 —St. Louis	60	2098	258	768	.336	206	276	.746	228	218	187	0	722	12.0
58-59 —St. Louis	71	2504	245	706	.347	197	254	.776	253	336	230	8	687	9.7
59-60 —St. Louis	64	1756	142	383	.371	113	155	.729	187	330	174	2	397	6.2
Totals	745	...	2632	7224	.364	2073	2720	.762	...	3160	2238	...	7337	9.8

NBA PLAYOFF RECORD

Season Team	G	Min.	FGM	FGA	Pct.	FTM	FTA	Pct.	Reb.	Ast.	PF	Dq.	Pts.	Avg.
49-50 —Minneapolis	12	...	21	50	.420	14	24	.583	...	25	35	...	56	4.7
50-51 —Minneapolis	7	...	18	51	.353	14	27	.519	42	25	20	...	50	7.1
51-52 —Minneapolis	13	523	38	110	.345	41	56	.732	37	56	64	4	117	9.0
52-53 —Minneapolis	12	453	41	103	.398	39	51	.765	31	43	49	1	121	10.1
53-54 —Minneapolis	13	533	37	112	.330	52	70	.743	29	60	52	1	126	9.7
54-55 —Minneapolis	7	315	28	94	.298	40	49	.816	28	31	23	0	96	13.7
55-56 —Minneapolis	3	121	17	37	.459	20	24	.833	7	15	9	0	54	18.0

Season Team	G	Min.	FGM	FGA	Pct.	FTM	FTA	Pct.	Reb.	Ast.	PF	Dq.	Pts.	Avg.
56-57 —St. Louis	10	439	55	155	.355	56	74	.757	42	49	39	2	166	16.6
57-58 —St. Louis	11	416	44	137	.321	39	63	.619	48	40	40	1	127	11.5
58-59 —St. Louis	1	18	4	5	.800	0	0	...	3	2	2	0	8	8.0
59-60 —St. Louis	3	58	1	13	.077	1	4	.250	3	8	9	0	3	1.0
Totals	92	...	304	867	.351	316	442	.715	...	354	342	...	924	10.0

NBA ALL-STAR GAME RECORD

Season Team	Min.	FGM	FGA	Pct.	FTM	FTA	Pct.	Reb.	Ast.	PF	Dq.	Pts.
1953 —Minneapolis	26	2	10	.200	1	1	1.000	2	1	2	0	5
1954 —Minneapolis	23	1	5	.200	0	0	...	0	3	3	0	2
1955 —Minneapolis	23	2	5	.400	1	2	.500	2	5	3	0	5
1956 —Minneapolis	29	3	7	.429	3	3	1.000	1	7	5	0	9
1957 —St. Louis	31	4	11	.364	0	0	...	2	3	1	0	8
1958 —St. Louis	26	2	9	.222	2	4	.500	2	8	3	0	6
1959 —St. Louis	22	2	6	.333	1	2	.500	6	1	2	0	5
Totals	180	16	53	.302	8	12	.667	15	28	19	0	40

HEAD COACHING RECORD

BACKGROUND: Player/head coach, St. Louis Hawks (1957). . . . Head coach/general manager, Houston Mavericks of ABA (1967-68).

NBA COACHING RECORD

Season Team	REGULAR SEASON				PLAYOFFS		
	W	L	Pct.	Finish	W	L	Pct.
56-57 —St. Louis	5	3	.625		—	—	—
Totals (1 year)	5	3	.625		—	—	—

ABA COACHING RECORD

Season Team	REGULAR SEASON				PLAYOFFS		
	W	L	Pct.	Finish	W	L	Pct.
67-68 —Houston	29	49	.372	4th/Western Division	0	3	.000
68-69 —Houston	3	9	.250		—	—	—
Totals (2 years)	32	58	.356		0	3	.000

NOTES:
1957— Replaced Red Holzman as St. Louis head coach (January), with record of 14-19; replaced as St. Louis head coach by Alex Hannum (January).
1968— Lost to Dallas in Western Division semifinals. Replaced as Houston head coach by Jim Weaver (November).

McADOO, BOB
C/F

PERSONAL: Born September 25, 1951, in Greensboro, N.C. . . . 6-9/225. . . . Full name: Robert Allen McAdoo Jr.
HIGH SCHOOL: Ben Smith (Greensboro, N.C.).
COLLEGE: Vincennes (Ind.), then North Carolina.
TRANSACTIONS/CAREER NOTES: Selected as hardship case by Buffalo Braves in first round (second pick overall) of 1972 NBA Draft. . . . Traded by Braves with Tom McMillen to New York Knicks for John Gianelli and cash (December 9, 1976). . . . Traded by Knicks to Boston Celtics for three 1979 first-round draft choices and player to be named later (February 12, 1979); Knicks acquired Tom Barker to complete the deal (February 14, 1979). . . . Acquired by Detroit Pistons for two 1980 first-round draft choices to complete compensation for Celtics earlier signing of veteran free agent M.L. Carr (September 6, 1979). . . . Waived by Pistons (March 11, 1981). . . . Signed as free agent by New Jersey Nets (March 13, 1981). . . . Traded by Nets to Los Angeles Lakers for 1983 second-round draft choice and cash (December 24, 1981). . . . Signed as veteran free agent by Philadelphia 76ers (January 31, 1986); Lakers relinquished their right of first refusal. . . . Played in Italy (1986-87 through 1991-92).
MISCELLANEOUS: Member of NBA championship teams (1982, 1985).

COLLEGIATE RECORD

NOTES: THE SPORTING NEWS All-America first team (1972).

Season Team	G	Min.	FGM	FGA	Pct.	FTM	FTA	Pct.	Reb.	Pts.	Avg.
69-70 —Vincennes	32	...	258	...	...	101	134	.754	320	617	19.3
70-71 —Vincennes	27	...	273	...	...	129	164	.787	297	675	25.0
71-72 —North Carolina	31	...	243	471	.516	118	167	.707	312	604	19.5
Junior college totals	59	...	531	...	...	230	298	.772	617	1292	21.9
Four-year-college totals	31	...	243	471	...	118	167	.707	312	604	19.5

NBA REGULAR-SEASON RECORD

HONORS: NBA Most Valuable Player (1975). . . . NBA Rookie of the Year (1973). . . . All-NBA first team (1975). . . . All-NBA second team (1974). . . . NBA All-Rookie team (1973).

Season Team	G	Min.	FGM	FGA	Pct.	FTM	FTA	Pct.	Reb.	Ast.	PF	Dq.	Pts.	Avg.
72-73 —Buffalo	80	2562	585	1293	.452	271	350	.774	728	139	256	6	1441	18.0

									— REBOUNDS —								
Season Team	G	Min.	FGM	FGA	Pct.	FTM	FTA	Pct.	Off.	Def.	Tot.	Ast.	PF	Dq.	Stl.	Blk.	TO	Pts.	Avg.
73-74 —Buffalo	74	3185	901	1647	*.547	459	579	.793	281	836	1117	170	252	3	88	246	...	*2261	*30.6
74-75 —Buffalo	82	*3539	*1095	2138	.512	641	*796	.805	307	848	*1155	179	278	3	92	174	...	*2831	*34.5
75-76 —Buffalo	78	3328	*934	*1918	.487	*559	*734	.762	241	724	965	315	298	5	93	160	...	*2427	*31.1
76-77 —Buff.-Knicks	72	2798	740	1445	.512	381	516	.738	199	727	926	205	262	3	77	99	...	1861	25.8
77-78 —New York	79	3182	814	1564	.520	469	645	.727	236	774	1010	298	297	6	105	126	346	2097	26.5
78-79 —N.Y.-Boston	60	2231	596	1127	.529	295	450	.656	130	390	520	168	189	3	74	67	217	1487	24.8
79-80 —Detroit	58	2097	492	1025	.480	235	322	.730	100	367	467	200	178	3	73	65	238	1222	21.1
80-81 —Detroit-N.J.	16	321	68	157	.433	29	41	.707	17	50	67	30	38	0	17	13	32	165	10.3
81-82 —Los Angeles	41	746	151	330	.458	90	126	.714	45	114	159	32	109	1	22	36	51	392	9.6
82-83 —Los Angeles	47	1019	292	562	.520	119	163	.730	76	171	247	39	153	2	40	40	68	703	15.0
83-84 —Los Angeles	70	1456	352	748	.471	212	264	.803	82	207	289	74	182	0	42	50	127	916	13.1

Season	Team	G	Min.	FGM	FGA	Pct.	FTM	FTA	Pct.	Off.	Def.	Tot.	Ast.	PF	Dq.	Stl.	Blk.	TO	Pts.	Avg.
										— REBOUNDS —										
84-85	L.A. Lakers ..	66	1254	284	546	.520	122	162	.753	79	216	295	67	170	0	18	53	95	690	10.5
85-86	Philadelphia.	29	609	116	251	.462	62	81	.765	25	78	103	35	64	0	10	18	49	294	10.1
	Totals	852	28327	7420	14751	.503	3944	5229	.754	...	...	8048	1951	2726	35	751	1147	1223	18787	22.1

Three-point field goals: 1979-80, 3-for-24 (.125). 1980-81, 0-for-1. 1981-82, 0-for-5. 1982-83, 0-for-1. 1983-84, 0-for-5. 1984-85, 0-for-1. Totals, 3-for-37 (.081).

NBA PLAYOFF RECORD

Season	Team	G	Min.	FGM	FGA	Pct.	FTM	FTA	Pct.	Off.	Def.	Tot.	Ast.	PF	Dq.	Stl.	Blk.	TO	Pts.	Avg.
										— REBOUNDS —										
73-74	Buffalo	6	271	76	159	.478	38	47	.809	14	68	82	9	25	1	6	13	...	190	31.7
74-75	Buffalo	7	327	104	216	.481	54	73	.740	25	69	94	10	29	1	6	19	...	262	37.4
75-76	Buffalo	9	406	97	215	.451	58	82	.707	31	97	128	29	37	3	7	18	...	252	28.0
77-78	New York	6	238	61	126	.484	21	35	.600	11	47	58	23	19	0	7	12	23	143	23.8
81-82	Los Angeles .	14	388	101	179	.564	32	47	.681	21	74	95	22	43	2	10	21	35	234	16.7
82-83	Los Angeles .	8	166	37	84	.440	11	14	.786	15	31	46	5	23	0	11	10	14	87	10.9
83-84	Los Angeles .	20	447	111	215	.516	57	81	.704	30	78	108	12	63	0	12	27	39	279	14.0
84-85	L.A. Lakers ..	19	398	91	193	.472	35	47	.745	25	61	86	15	66	2	9	26	32	217	11.4
85-86	Philadelphia.	5	73	20	36	.556	14	16	.875	8	6	14	2	13	0	4	5	2	54	10.8
	Totals	94	2714	698	1423	.491	320	442	.724	180	531	711	127	318	9	72	151	145	1718	18.3

Three-point field goals: 1982-83, 2-for-6 (.333). 1983-84, 0-for-1. 1984-85, 0-for-1. Totals, 2-for-8 (.250).

NBA ALL-STAR GAME RECORD

Season	Team	Min.	FGM	FGA	Pct.	FTM	FTA	Pct.	Off.	Def.	Tot.	Ast.	PF	Dq.	Stl.	Blk.	TO	Pts.
									— REBOUNDS —									
1974	Buffalo	13	3	4	.750	5	8	.625	1	2	3	1	4	0	0	1	...	11
1975	Buffalo	26	4	9	.444	3	3	1.000	4	2	6	2	4	0	0	1	...	11
1976	Buffalo	29	10	14	.714	2	4	.500	2	5	7	1	5	0	0	0	...	22
1977	N.Y. Knicks	38	13	23	.565	4	4	1.000	3	7	10	2	3	0	3	1	...	30
1978	New York	20	7	14	.500	0	0	...	3	1	4	0	2	0	1	0	3	14
	Totals	126	37	64	.578	14	19	.737	13	17	30	6	18	0	4	2	3	88

ITALIAN LEAGUE RECORD

Season	Team	G	Min.	FGM	FGA	Pct.	FTM	FTA	Pct.	Reb.	Pts.	Avg.
86-87	Tracer Milan	38	1320	387	730	.530	205	268	.765	388	991	26.1
87-88	Tracer Milan	39	1398	422	730	.578	236	293	.805	333	1097	28.1
88-89	Philips Milan	38	1195	334	610	.548	161	200	.805	299	861	22.7
89-90	Philips Milan	33	1014	329	587	.560	178	215	.828	248	851	25.8
90-91	Filanto	23	858	278	490	.567	179	225	.796	219	759	33.0
91-92	Filanti Fori	20	700	199	399	.499	129	159	.811	188	538	26.9
	Totals	191	6485	1949	3546	.550	1088	1360	.800	1675	5097	26.7

McGINNIS, GEORGE
F

PERSONAL: Born August 12, 1950, in Indianapolis. . . . 6-8/235. . . . Full name: George F. McGinnis.
HIGH SCHOOL: George Washington (Indianapolis).
COLLEGE: Indiana.

TRANSACTIONS/CAREER NOTES: Selected by Philadelphia 76ers in second round (22nd pick overall) of 1973 NBA Draft. . . . Signed as undergraduate free agent by Indiana Pacers of American Basketball Assocation in lieu of 1972 first-round draft choice (1971). . . . Invoked proviso under which he could buy his way out of contract with Pacers. . . . Signed by 76ers (July 10, 1975) after Commissioner Larry O'Brien revoked contract McGinnis had signed with New York Knicks (May 30, 1975). . . . Traded by 76ers to Denver Nuggets for Bobby Jones and Ralph Simpson (August 16, 1978). . . . Traded by Nuggets to Pacers for Alex English and 1980 first-round draft choice (February 1, 1980). . . . Waived by Pacers (October 27, 1982).

COLLEGIATE RECORD

Season	Team	G	Min.	FGM	FGA	Pct.	FTM	FTA	Pct.	Reb.	Pts.	Avg.
69-70	Indiana†					Did not play—ineligible.						
70-71	Indiana....................................	24	...	283	615	.460	153	249	.614	352	719	30.0
	Varsity totals	24	...	283	615	.460	153	249	.614	352	719	30.0

ABA REGULAR-SEASON RECORD

NOTES: ABA co-Most Valuable Player (1975). . . . ABA All-Star first team (1974, 1975). . . . ABA All-Star second team (1973). . . . ABA All-Rookie team (1972). . . . Member of ABA championship teams (1972, 1973).

Season	Team	G	Min.	FGM	FGA	Pct.	FGM	FGA	Pct.	FTM	FTA	Pct.	Reb.	Ast.	Pts.	Avg.
				— 2-POINT —			— 3-POINT —									
71-72	Indiana.............	78	2179	459	961	.478	6	38	.158	298	462	.645	711	137	1234	15.8
72-73	Indiana.............	82	3347	860	1723	.499	8	32	.250	517	*778	.665	1022	205	2261	27.6
73-74	Indiana.............	80	3266	784	1652	.475	5	34	.147	488	*715	.683	1197	267	2071	25.9
74-75	Indiana.............	79	3193	811	1759	.461	62	175	.354	*545	*753	.724	1126	495	*2353	*29.8
	Totals	319	11985	2914	6095	.478	81	279	.290	1848	2708	.682	4056	1104	7919	24.8

ABA PLAYOFF RECORD

NOTES: ABA Playoff Most Valuable Player (1973).

Season	Team	G	Min.	FGM	FGA	Pct.	FGM	FGA	Pct.	FTM	FTA	Pct.	Reb.	Ast.	Pts.	Avg.
				— 2-POINT —			— 3-POINT —									
71-72	Indiana.............	20	633	102	246	.415	4	15	.267	94	150	.627	277	52	310	15.5
72-73	Indiana.............	18	732	161	352	.457	0	5	.000	109	149	.732	222	39	431	23.9
73-74	Indiana.............	14	585	117	254	.461	2	7	.286	96	129	.744	166	47	336	24.0
74-75	Indiana.............	18	731	190	382	.497	23	73	.315	132	192	.688	286	148	581	32.3
	Totals	70	2681	570	1234	.462	29	100	.290	431	620	.695	951	286	1658	23.7

ABA ALL-STAR GAME RECORD

Season	Team	Min.	FGM	FGA	Pct.	FGM	FGA	Pct.	FTM	FTA	Pct.	Reb.	Ast.	Pts.
			2-POINT			3-POINT								
1972	—Indiana	34	10	14	.714	0	1	.000	3	6	.500	15	2	23
1973	—Indiana	30	7	21	.333	0	0	...	0	0	...	11	1	14
1974	—Indiana	32	6	13	.462	0	1	.000	6	11	.545	12	5	18
	Totals	96	23	48	.479	0	2	.000	9	17	.529	38	8	55

NBA REGULAR-SEASON RECORD

HONORS: All-NBA first team (1976).... All-NBA second team (1977).

Season	Team	G	Min.	FGM	FGA	Pct.	FTM	FTA	Pct.	Off.	Def.	Tot.	Ast.	PF	Dq.	Stl.	Blk.	TO	Pts.	Avg.
										— REBOUNDS —										
75-76	—Philadelphia.	77	2946	647	1552	.417	475	642	.740	260	707	967	359	334	13	198	41	...	1769	23.0
76-77	—Philadelphia.	79	2769	659	1439	.458	372	546	.681	324	587	911	302	299	4	163	37	...	1690	21.4
77-78	—Philadelphia.	78	2533	588	1270	.463	411	574	.716	282	528	810	294	287	6	137	27	312	1587	20.3
78-79	—Denver	76	2552	603	1273	.474	509	765	.665	256	608	864	283	321	16	129	52	*346	1715	22.6
79-80	—Denver-Ind..	73	2208	400	886	.451	270	488	.553	222	477	699	333	303	12	101	23	281	1072	14.7
80-81	—Indiana........	69	1845	348	768	.453	207	385	.538	164	364	528	210	242	3	99	28	221	903	13.1
81-82	—Indiana........	76	1341	141	378	.373	72	159	.453	93	305	398	204	98	4	96	28	131	354	4.7
	Totals	528	16194	3386	7566	.448	2316	3559	.651	1601	3576	5177	1985	1884	58	923	236	1291	9090	17.2

Three-point field goals: 1979-80, 2-for-15 (.133). 1980-81, 0-for-7. 1981-82, 0-for-3. Totals, 2-for-25 (.080).

NBA PLAYOFF RECORD

Season	Team	G	Min.	FGM	FGA	Pct.	FTM	FTA	Pct.	Off.	Def.	Tot.	Ast.	PF	Dq.	Stl.	Blk.	TO	Pts.	Avg.
										— REBOUNDS —										
75-76	—Philadelphia.	3	120	29	61	.475	11	18	.611	9	32	41	12	14	1	1	4	...	69	23.0
76-77	—Philadelphia.	19	603	102	273	.374	65	114	.570	62	136	198	69	83	2	23	6	...	269	14.2
77-78	—Philadelphia.	10	273	53	125	.424	41	49	.837	24	54	78	30	40	1	15	1	38	147	14.7
80-81	—Indiana........	2	39	3	15	.200	4	8	.500	2	8	10	7	6	0	2	0	5	10	5.0
	Totals	34	1035	187	474	.395	121	189	.640	97	230	327	118	143	4	41	11	43	495	14.6

NBA ALL-STAR GAME RECORD

Season	Team	Min.	FGM	FGA	Pct.	FTM	FTA	Pct.	Off.	Def.	Tot.	Ast.	PF	Dq.	Stl.	Blk.	TO	Pts.
									— REBOUNDS —									
1976	—Philadelphia.......	19	4	9	.444	2	4	.500	1	6	7	2	2	0	0	0	...	10
1977	—Philadelphia.......	26	2	9	.222	0	2	.000	5	2	7	2	3	0	4	0	...	4
1979	—Denver	25	5	12	.417	6	11	.545	2	4	6	3	4	0	5	0	...	16
	Totals	70	11	30	.367	8	17	.471	8	12	20	7	9	0	9	0	...	30

McGUIRE, DICK
G

PERSONAL: Born January 25, 1926, in Huntington, N.Y.... 6-0/180....
Full name: Richard J. McGuire. ... Nickname: Tricky Dick.
HIGH SCHOOL: LaSalle Academy (New York).
COLLEGE: St. John's, then Dartmouth.

TRANSACTIONS/CAREER NOTES: Selected by New York Knicks in first round of 1949 Basketball Association of America Draft. ... Knicks franchise became part of NBA upon merger of BAA and National Basketball League for 1949-50 season.... Traded by Knicks to Detroit Pistons for 1958 first-round draft choice (April 3, 1957).

COLLEGIATE RECORD

NOTES: THE SPORTING NEWS All-America second team (1944).

Season	Team	G	Min.	FGM	FGA	Pct.	FTM	FTA	Pct.	Reb.	Pts.	Avg.
43-44	—St. John's	16	...	43	...	...	20	...	...	...	106	6.6
43-44	—Dartmouth	5	...	17	...	...	9	10	.900	...	43	8.6
44-45	—				Did not play — in military service.							
45-46	—				Did not play — in military service.							
46-47	—St. John's	21	...	63	...	...	37	...	...	...	163	7.8
47-48	—St. John's	22	...	75	...	...	72	115	.626	...	222	10.1
48-49	—St. John's	25	...	121	...	...	72	125	.576	...	314	12.6
	Totals	84	...	302	...	...	201	...	...	...	805	9.6

NBA REGULAR-SEASON RECORD

HONORS: All-NBA second team (1951).

Season	Team	G	Min.	FGM	FGA	Pct.	FTM	FTA	Pct.	Reb.	Ast.	PF	Dq.	Pts.	Avg.
49-50	—New York	68	...	190	563	.337	204	313	.652	...	*386	160	...	584	8.6
50-51	—New York	64	...	179	482	.371	179	276	.649	334	400	154	2	537	8.4
51-52	—New York	64	2018	204	474	.430	183	290	.631	332	388	181	4	591	9.2
52-53	—New York	61	1783	142	373	.381	153	269	.569	280	296	172	3	437	7.2
53-54	—New York	68	2343	201	493	.408	220	345	.638	310	354	199	3	622	9.1
54-55	—New York	71	2310	226	581	.389	195	303	.644	322	542	143	0	647	9.1
55-56	—New York	62	1685	152	438	.347	121	193	.627	220	362	146	0	425	6.9
56-57	—New York	72	1191	140	366	.383	105	163	.644	146	222	103	0	385	5.3
57-58	—Detroit	69	2311	203	544	.373	150	225	.667	291	454	178	0	556	8.1
58-59	—Detroit	71	2063	232	543	.427	191	258	.740	285	443	147	1	655	9.2
59-60	—Detroit	68	1466	179	402	.445	124	201	.617	264	358	112	0	482	7.1
	Totals	738	...	2048	5259	.389	1825	2836	.644	...	4205	1695	...	5921	8.0

NBA PLAYOFF RECORD

Season	Team	G	Min.	FGM	FGA	Pct.	FTM	FTA	Pct.	Reb.	Ast.	PF	Dq.	Pts.	Avg.
49-50	—New York	5	...	22	52	.423	19	26	.731	...	27	21	...	63	12.6
50-51	—New York	14	...	25	80	.313	24	53	.453	83	78	50	1	74	5.3
51-52	—New York	14	546	48	107	.449	49	86	.570	71	90	46	1	145	10.4
52-53	—New York	11	360	24	59	.407	35	55	.636	63	70	25	0	83	7.5
53-54	—New York	4	68	4	16	.250	3	5	.600	4	5	12	0	11	2.8

Season Team	G	Min.	FGM	FGA	Pct.	FTM	FTA	Pct.	Reb.	Ast.	PF	Dq.	Pts.	Avg.
54-55 — New York	3	75	6	19	.316	8	12	.667	9	12	7	0	20	6.7
57-58 — Detroit	7	236	25	60	.417	17	24	.708	33	40	13	0	67	9.6
58-59 — Detroit	3	109	20	32	.625	7	11	.636	17	19	10	0	47	15.7
59-60 — Detroit	2	42	5	12	.417	1	3	.333	4	9	3	0	11	5.5
Totals	63	...	179	437	.410	163	275	.593	...	350	187	...	521	8.3

NBA ALL-STAR GAME RECORD

Season Team	Min.	FGM	FGA	Pct.	FTM	FTA	Pct.	Reb.	Ast.	PF	Dq.	Pts.
1951 — New York	...	3	4	.750	0	0	...	5	10	2	0	6
1952 — New York	18	0	0	...	1	3	.333	1	4	0	0	1
1954 — New York	24	2	5	.400	0	0	...	4	2	1	0	4
1955 — New York	25	1	2	.500	1	2	.500	3	6	1	0	3
1956 — New York	29	2	9	.222	2	5	.400	0	3	1	0	6
1958 — Detroit	31	2	4	.500	0	0	...	7	10	4	0	4
1959 — Detroit	24	2	7	.286	1	2	.500	3	3	2	0	5
Totals	...	12	31	.387	5	12	.417	23	38	11	0	29

HEAD COACHING RECORD

BACKGROUND: Player/head coach, Detroit Pistons (December 28, 1959-remainder of season).

NBA COACHING RECORD

	REGULAR SEASON				PLAYOFFS		
Season Team	W	L	Pct.	Finish	W	L	Pct.
59-60 — Detroit	17	24	.415	2nd/Western Division	0	2	.000
60-61 — Detroit	34	45	.430	3rd/Western Division	2	3	.400
61-62 — Detroit	37	43	.463	3rd/Western Division	5	5	.500
62-63 — Detroit	34	46	.425	3rd/Western Division	1	3	.250
65-66 — New York	24	35	.407	4th/Eastern Division	—	—	—
66-67 — New York	36	45	.444	4th/Eastern Division	1	3	.250
67-68 — New York	15	22	.405		—	—	—
Totals (7 years)	197	260	.431	Totals (5 years)	9	16	.360

NOTES:
1959— Replaced Detroit head coach Red Rocha (December 28), with record of 13-21.
1960— Lost to Minneapolis in Western Division semifinals.
1961— Lost to Los Angeles in Western Division semifinals.
1962— Defeated Cincinnati, 3-1, in Western Division semifinals; lost to Los Angeles, 4-2, in Western Division finals.
1963— Lost to St. Louis in Western Division semifinals.
1965— Replaced Harry Gallatin as New York head coach (November 29), with record of 6-15 and in fourth place.
1967— Lost to Boston in Eastern Division semifinals. Replaced as New York head coach by Red Holzman (December).

MIKAN, GEORGE
C

PERSONAL: Born June 18, 1924, in Joliet, Ill. ... 6-10/245. ... Full name: George Lawrence Mikan Jr. ... Brother of Ed Mikan, forward/center with Chicago Stags of Basketball Association of America (1948-49) and six NBA teams (1949-50 through 1953-54); and father of Larry Mikan, forward with Cleveland Cavaliers (1970-71).

HIGH SCHOOL: Joliet Catholic (Ill.), then Quigley Prep (Chicago).

COLLEGE: DePaul.

TRANSACTIONS/CAREER NOTES: Signed by Chicago Stags of National Basketball League (March 16, 1946). ... Stags dropped out of NBL and entered Professional Basketball League of America for 1947-48 season. ... PBLA disbanded (November 13, 1947); Chicago was refused a franchise in the NBL and Mikan was awarded to Minneapolis Lakers at NBL meeting (November 17, 1947); Mikan scored 193 points in the eight PBLA games played by Stags before the league folded and led the league in total points and scoring average. ... Signed by Minneapolis Lakers of NBL (November 1947). ... Lakers franchise transferred to Basketball Association of America for 1948-49 season. ... Lakers franchise became part of NBA upon merger of BAA and NBL for 1949-50 season.

CAREER HONORS: Elected to Naismith Memorial Basketball Hall of Fame (1959). ... NBA 25th Anniversary All-Time team (1970) and 35th Anniversary All-Time team (1980).

MISCELLANEOUS: Member of NBA championship teams (1950, 1952, 1953, 1954). ... Member of BAA championship team (1949). ... Member of NBL championship teams (1947, 1948).

COLLEGIATE RECORD

NOTES: THE SPORTING NEWS All-America first team (1944, 1945).

Season Team	G	Min.	FGM	FGA	Pct.	FTM	FTA	Pct.	Reb.	Pts.	Avg.
41-42 — DePaul‡				Freshman team statistics unavailable.							
42-43 — DePaul	24	...	97	...	...	77	111	.694	...	271	11.3
43-44 — DePaul	26	...	188	...	...	110	169	.651	...	486	18.7
44-45 — DePaul	24	...	218	...	...	122	199	.613	...	558	23.3
45-46 — DePaul	24	...	206	...	...	143	186	.769	...	555	23.1
Varsity totals	98	...	709	...	...	452	665	.680	...	1870	19.1

NBL AND NBA REGULAR-SEASON RECORD

HONORS: All-NBA first team (1950, 1951, 1952, 1953, 1954). ... All-BAA first team (1949).
NOTES: Led NBA with 13.5 rebounds per game (1952) and 14.4 rebounds per game (1953).

Season Team	G	Min.	FGM	FGA	Pct.	FTM	FTA	Pct.	Reb.	Ast.	PF	Dq.	Pts.	Avg.
46-47 — Chicago (NBL)	25	...	147	...	...	119	164	.726	...	...	90	...	*413	*16.5
47-48 — Minneapolis (NBL)	56	...	*406	...	...	*383	*500	.766	...	...	210	...	*1195	*21.3
48-49 — Minneapolis (BAA)	60	...	*583	1403	.416	*532	*689	.772	...	218	260	...	*1698	*28.3
49-50 — Minneapolis	68	...	*649	*1595	.407	*567	*728	.779	...	197	*297	...	*1865	*27.4
50-51 — Minneapolis	68	...	*678	*1584	.428	*576	*717	.803	958	208	*308	14	*1932	*28.4
51-52 — Minneapolis	64	2572	545	*1414	.385	433	555	.780	866	194	*286	14	*1523	*23.8

Season Team	G	Min.	FGM	FGA	Pct.	FTM	FTA	Pct.	Reb.	Ast.	PF	Dq.	Pts.	Avg.
52-53 —Minneapolis	70	2651	500	1252	.399	442	567	.780	*1007	201	290	12	1442	20.6
53-54 —Minneapolis	72	2362	441	1160	.380	424	546	.777	1028	174	268	4	1306	18.1
54-55 —						Did not play—retired.								
55-56 —Minneapolis	37	765	148	375	.395	94	122	.770	308	53	153	6	390	10.5
Totals	520	...	4097	...	...	3570	4588	.778	...	...	2162	...	11764	22.6

NBL AND NBA PLAYOFF RECORD

Season Team	G	Min.	FGM	FGA	Pct.	FTM	FTA	Pct.	Reb.	Ast.	PF	Dq.	Pts.	Avg.
46-47 —Chicago (NBL)	11	...	72	...	...	73	104	.702	...	...	48	...	217	19.7
47-48 —Minneapolis (NBL)	10	...	88	...	...	68	97	.701	...	...	37	...	244	24.4
48-49 —Minneapolis (BAA)	10	...	103	227	.454	97	121	.802	...	21	44	...	303	30.3
49-50 —Minneapolis	12	...	121	316	.383	134	170	.788	...	36	47	...	376	31.3
50-51 —Minneapolis	7	...	62	152	.408	44	55	.800	74	9	25	1	168	24.0
51-52 —Minneapolis	13	553	99	261	.379	109	138	.790	207	36	63	3	307	23.6
52-53 —Minneapolis	12	463	78	213	.366	82	112	.732	185	23	56	5	238	19.8
53-54 —Minneapolis	13	424	87	190	.458	78	96	.813	171	25	56	1	252	19.4
55-56 —Minneapolis	3	60	13	35	.371	10	13	.769	28	5	14	0	36	12.0
Totals	91	...	723	...	...	695	906	.767	...	...	390	...	2141	23.5

NBA ALL-STAR GAME RECORD

NOTES: NBA All-Star Game Most Valuable Player (1953).

Season Team	Min.	FGM	FGA	Pct.	FTM	FTA	Pct.	Reb.	Ast.	PF	Dq.	Pts.
1951 —Minneapolis	...	4	17	.235	4	6	.667	11	3	2	0	12
1952 —Minneapolis	29	9	19	.474	8	9	.889	15	1	5	0	26
1953 —Minneapolis	40	9	26	.346	4	4	1.000	16	2	2	0	22
1954 —Minneapolis	31	6	18	.333	6	8	.750	9	1	5	0	18
Totals	...	28	80	.350	22	27	.815	51	7	14	0	78

NBA COACHING RECORD

		REGULAR SEASON				PLAYOFFS		
Season Team	W	L	Pct.	Finish		W	L	Pct.
57-58 —Minneapolis	9	30	.231			—	—	—
Totals (1 year)	9	30	.231					

NOTES:
1958— Resigned as Minneapolis head coach and replaced by John Kundla (January).

MIKKELSEN, VERN
F/C

PERSONAL: Born October 21, 1928, in Fresno, Calif.... 6-7/230.... Full name: Arild Verner Agerskov Mikkelsen.
HIGH SCHOOL: Askov (Minn.).
COLLEGE: Hamline (Minn.).
TRANSACTIONS/CAREER NOTES: Selected by Minneapolis Lakers in first round of 1949 NBA Draft.
MISCELLANEOUS: Member of NBA championship teams (1950, 1952, 1953, 1954).

COLLEGIATE RECORD

NOTES: THE SPORTING NEWS All-America fourth team (1949).... Inducted into NAIA Basketball Hall of Fame (1956).... Led NCAA Division II with .538 field-goal percentage (1949).

Season Team	G	Min.	FGM	FGA	Pct.	FTM	FTA	Pct.	Reb.	Pts.	Avg.
45-46 —Hamline					Statistics unavailable.						
46-47 —Hamline	26	...	102	...	...	52	...	...	...	256	9.8
47-48 —Hamline	31	...	199	...	...	119	...	...	...	517	16.7
48-49 —Hamline	30	...	203	377	.538	113	177	.638	...	519	17.3
Totals	87	...	504	...	...	284	...	...	...	1292	14.9

NBA REGULAR-SEASON RECORD

RECORDS: Holds career record for most disqualifications—127.
HONORS: All-NBA second team (1951, 1952, 1953, 1955).

Season Team	G	Min.	FGM	FGA	Pct.	FTM	FTA	Pct.	Reb.	Ast.	PF	Dq.	Pts.	Avg.
49-50 —Minneapolis	68	...	288	722	.399	215	286	.752	...	123	222	...	791	11.6
50-51 —Minneapolis	64	...	359	893	.402	186	275	.676	655	181	260	13	904	14.1
51-52 —Minneapolis	66	2345	363	866	.419	283	372	.761	681	180	282	16	1009	15.3
52-53 —Minneapolis	70	2465	378	868	.435	291	387	.752	654	148	289	14	1047	15.0
53-54 —Minneapolis	72	2247	288	771	.374	221	298	.742	615	119	264	7	797	11.1
54-55 —Minneapolis	71	2559	440	1043	.422	447	598	.747	722	145	*319	14	1327	18.7
55-56 —Minneapolis	72	2100	317	821	.386	328	408	.804	608	173	*319	17	962	13.4
56-57 —Minneapolis	72	2198	322	854	.377	342	424	.807	630	121	*312	*18	986	13.7
57-58 —Minneapolis	72	2390	439	1070	.410	370	471	.786	805	166	299	*20	1248	17.3
58-59 —Minneapolis	72	2139	353	904	.390	286	355	.806	570	159	246	8	992	13.8
Totals	699	...	3547	8812	.403	2969	3874	.766	...	1515	2812	...	10063	14.4

NBA PLAYOFF RECORD

Season Team	G	Min.	FGM	FGA	Pct.	FTM	FTA	Pct.	Reb.	Ast.	PF	Dq.	Pts.	Avg.
49-50 —Minneapolis	12	...	55	149	.369	46	60	.767	...	18	32	...	156	13.0
50-51 —Minneapolis	7	...	39	96	.406	31	47	.660	67	17	35	3	109	15.6
51-52 —Minneapolis	13	496	60	139	.432	53	64	.828	110	20	66	4	173	13.3
52-53 —Minneapolis	12	400	44	133	.331	56	66	.848	104	24	59	3	144	12.0
53-54 —Minneapolis	13	375	51	111	.459	31	36	.861	73	17	52	1	133	10.2
54-55 —Minneapolis	7	209	30	85	.353	36	46	.783	78	13	36	4	96	13.7
55-56 —Minneapolis	3	90	11	26	.423	18	20	.900	17	2	14	2	40	13.3
56-57 —Minneapolis	5	162	33	83	.398	22	34	.647	43	17	29	4	88	17.6
58-59 —Minneapolis	13	371	73	177	.412	56	73	.767	93	24	54	3	202	15.5
Totals	85	...	396	999	.397	349	446	.783	...	152	377	...	1141	13.4

Season	Team	Min.	FGM	FGA	Pct.	FTM	FTA	Pct.	Reb.	Ast.	PF	Dq.	Pts.
1951	—Minneapolis	...	4	11	.364	3	4	.750	9	1	3	0	11
1952	—Minneapolis	23	5	8	.625	2	2	1.000	10	0	2	0	12
1953	—Minneapolis	19	3	13	.231	0	0	...	6	3	3	0	6
1955	—Minneapolis	25	7	15	.467	2	3	.667	9	1	5	0	16
1956	—Minneapolis	22	5	13	.385	6	7	.857	9	2	4	0	16
1957	—Minneapolis	21	3	10	.300	0	4	.000	9	1	3	0	6
Totals		...	27	70	.386	13	20	.650	52	8	20	0	67

HEAD COACHING RECORD

BACKGROUND: General manager, Minnesota Pipers of ABA (1968-69).

ABA COACHING RECORD

			REGULAR SEASON			PLAYOFFS	
Season	Team	W	L	Pct.	Finish	W	L	Pct.
68-69	—Minnesota	6	7	.462		—	—	—
Totals (1 year)		6	7	.462		—	—	—

NOTES:
1969— Replaced Jim Harding as Minnesota head coach (January), with record of 20-12; later replaced by Gus Young.

MONCRIEF, SIDNEY
G

PERSONAL: Born September 21, 1957, in Little Rock, Ark. . . . 6-3/183. . . . Full name: Sidney A. Moncrief. . . . Nickname: The Squid.
HIGH SCHOOL: Hall (Little Rock, Ark.).
COLLEGE: Arkansas.
TRANSACTIONS/CAREER NOTES: Selected by Milwaukee Bucks in first round (fifth pick overall) of 1979 NBA Draft. . . . Signed as unrestricted free agent by Atlanta Hawks (October 4, 1990). . . . Rights renounced by Hawks (September 29, 1991).

COLLEGIATE RECORD

NOTES: THE SPORTING NEWS All-America second team (1979). . . . Led NCAA Division I with .665 field-goal percentage (1976).

Season	Team	G	Min.	FGM	FGA	Pct.	FTM	FTA	Pct.	Reb.	Pts.	Avg.
75-76	—Arkansas	28	...	149	224	.665	56	77	.727	213	354	12.6
76-77	—Arkansas	28	997	157	242	.649	117	171	.684	235	431	15.4
77-78	—Arkansas	36	1293	209	354	.590	203	256	.793	278	621	17.3
78-79	—Arkansas	30	1157	224	400	.560	212	248	.855	289	660	22.0
Totals		122	...	739	1220	.606	588	752	.782	1015	2066	16.9

NBA REGULAR-SEASON RECORD

HONORS: NBA Defensive Player of the Year (1983, 1984). . . . All-NBA first team (1983). . . . All-NBA second team (1982, 1984, 1985, 1986). . . . NBA All-Defensive first team (1983, 1984, 1985, 1986). . . . NBA All-Defensive second team (1982).

Season	Team	G	Min.	FGM	FGA	Pct.	FTM	FTA	Pct.	Off.	Def.	Tot.	Ast.	PF	Dq.	Stl.	Blk.	TO	Pts.	Avg.
79-80	—Milwaukee	77	1557	211	451	.468	232	292	.795	154	184	338	133	106	0	72	16	117	654	8.5
80-81	—Milwaukee	80	2417	400	739	.541	320	398	.804	186	220	406	264	156	1	90	37	145	1122	14.0
81-82	—Milwaukee	80	2980	556	1063	.523	468	573	.817	221	313	534	382	206	3	138	22	208	1581	19.8
82-83	—Milwaukee	76	2710	606	1156	.524	499	604	.826	192	245	437	300	180	1	113	23	197	1712	22.5
83-84	—Milwaukee	79	3075	560	1125	.498	529	624	.848	215	313	528	358	204	2	108	27	217	1654	20.9
84-85	—Milwaukee	73	2734	561	1162	.483	454	548	.828	149	242	391	382	197	1	117	39	184	1585	21.7
85-86	—Milwaukee	73	2567	470	962	.489	498	580	.859	115	219	334	357	178	1	103	18	174	1471	20.2
86-87	—Milwaukee	39	992	158	324	.488	136	162	.840	57	70	127	121	73	0	27	10	63	460	11.8
87-88	—Milwaukee	56	1428	217	444	.489	164	196	.837	58	122	180	204	109	0	41	12	86	603	10.8
88-89	—Milwaukee	62	1594	261	532	.491	205	237	.865	46	126	172	188	114	1	65	13	94	752	12.1
89-90	—						Did not play—retired.													
90-91	—Atlanta	72	1096	117	240	.488	82	105	.781	31	97	128	104	112	0	50	9	66	337	4.7
Totals		767	23150	4117	8198	.502	3587	4319	.831	1424	2151	3575	2793	1635	10	924	226	1551	11931	15.6

Three-point field goals: 1979-80, 0-for-1. 1980-81, 2-for-9 (.222). 1981-82, 1-for-14 (.071). 1982-83, 1-for-10 (.100). 1983-84, 5-for-18 (.278). 1984-85, 9-for-33 (.273). 1985-86, 33-for-103 (.320). 1986-87, 8-for-31 (.258). 1987-88, 5-for-31 (.161). 1988-89, 25-for-73 (.342). 1990-91, 21-for-64 (.328). Totals, 110-for-387 (.284).

NBA PLAYOFF RECORD

Season	Team	G	Min.	FGM	FGA	Pct.	FTM	FTA	Pct.	Off.	Def.	Tot.	Ast.	PF	Dq.	Stl.	Blk.	TO	Pts.	Avg.
79-80	—Milwaukee	7	182	30	51	.588	27	31	.871	17	14	31	11	14	0	5	1	14	87	12.4
80-81	—Milwaukee	7	277	30	69	.435	38	51	.745	19	28	47	20	24	0	12	3	21	98	14.0
81-82	—Milwaukee	6	252	31	74	.419	30	38	.789	15	15	30	24	22	1	9	2	12	92	15.3
82-83	—Milwaukee	9	377	62	142	.437	46	61	.754	28	32	60	33	25	1	18	3	27	170	18.9
83-84	—Milwaukee	16	618	99	191	.518	106	134	.791	44	67	111	68	54	1	28	9	61	305	19.1
84-85	—Milwaukee	8	319	55	99	.556	70	75	.933	10	24	34	40	26	0	5	4	20	184	23.0
85-86	—Milwaukee	9	327	52	122	.426	44	63	.698	15	26	41	44	30	0	5	5	21	152	16.9
86-87	—Milwaukee	12	426	78	165	.473	73	90	.811	21	33	54	36	43	0	13	6	24	233	19.4
87-88	—Milwaukee	5	173	24	50	.480	26	27	.963	6	13	19	26	14	0	3	1	11	75	15.0
88-89	—Milwaukee	9	184	19	48	.396	15	16	.938	8	18	26	13	17	0	5	2	11	55	6.1
90-91	—Atlanta	5	91	11	22	.500	13	16	.813	6	10	16	2	16	0	3	0	3	36	7.2
Totals		93	3226	491	1033	.475	488	602	.811	189	280	469	317	285	3	106	36	225	1487	16.0

Three-point field goals: 1981-82, 0-for-1. 1982-83, 0-for-1. 1983-84, 1-for-4 (.250). 1984-85, 4-for-10 (.400). 1985-86, 4-for-14 (.286). 1986-87, 4-for-14 (.286). 1987-88, 1-for-1. 1988-89, 2-for-7 (.286). 1990-91, 1-for-6 (.167). Totals, 17-for-58 (.293).

Season	Team	Min.	FGM	FGA	Pct.	FTM	FTA	Pct.	REBOUNDS Off.	Def.	Tot.	Ast.	PF	Dq.	Stl.	Blk.	TO	Pts.
1982	—Milwaukee	22	3	11	.273	0	2	.000	3	1	4	1	2	0	1	0	1	6
1983	—Milwaukee	23	8	14	.571	4	5	.800	3	2	5	4	1	0	6	1	1	20
1984	—Milwaukee	26	3	6	.500	2	2	1.000	1	4	5	2	3	0	5	0	4	8
1985	—Milwaukee	22	1	5	.200	6	6	1.000	2	3	5	4	1	0	0	0	2	8
1986	—Milwaukee	26	4	11	.364	7	7	1.000	3	0	3	1	0	0	0	1	0	16
	Totals	119	19	47	.404	19	22	.864	12	10	22	12	7	0	12	2	8	58

Three-point field goals: 1986, 1-for-1.

MONROE, EARL

G

PERSONAL: Born November 21, 1944, in Philadelphia. . . . 6-3/ 190. . . . Full name: Vernon Earl Monroe. . . . Nickname: The Pearl.
HIGH SCHOOL: John Bartram (Philadelphia).
COLLEGE: Winston-Salem State (N.C.).
TRANSACTIONS/CAREER NOTES: Selected by Baltimore Bullets in first round (second pick overall) of 1967 NBA Draft. . . . Traded by Bullets to New York Knicks for Dave Stallworth, Mike Riordan and cash (November 10, 1971).
CAREER HONORS: Elected to Naismith Memorial Basketball Hall of Fame (1989).
MISCELLANEOUS: Member of NBA championship team (1973).

COLLEGIATE RECORD

NOTES: THE SPORTING NEWS All-America first team (1966). . . . Holds NCAA Division II single-season record for most points—1329 (1967). . . . Inducted into NAIA Basketball Hall of Fame (1975). . . . Named Outstanding Player in NCAA College Division Tournament (1967). . . . Member of NCAA College Division Tournament championship team (1967).

Season	Team	G	Min.	FGM	FGA	Pct.	FTM	FTA	Pct.	Reb.	Pts.	Avg.
63-64	—Winston-Salem State	23	...	71	...	...	21	...	...	...	163	7.1
64-65	—Winston-Salem State	30	...	286	...	...	125	176	.710	211	697	23.2
65-66	—Winston-Salem State	25	...	292	519	.563	162	187	.866	167	746	29.8
66-67	—Winston-Salem State	32	...	509	839	.607	311	391	.795	218	1329	41.5
	Totals	110	...	1158	...	...	619	...	...	...	2935	26.7

NBA REGULAR-SEASON RECORD

HONORS: NBA Rookie of the Year (1968). . . . All-NBA first team (1969). . . . NBA All-Rookie team (1968).

Season	Team	G	Min.	FGM	FGA	Pct.	FTM	FTA	Pct.	Reb.	Ast.	PF	Dq.	Pts.	Avg.
67-68	—Baltimore	82	3012	742	1637	.453	507	649	.781	465	349	282	3	1991	24.3
68-69	—Baltimore	80	3075	809	1837	.440	447	582	.768	280	392	261	1	2065	25.8
69-70	—Baltimore	82	3051	695	1557	.446	532	641	.830	257	402	258	3	1922	23.4
70-71	—Baltimore	81	2843	663	1501	.442	406	506	.802	213	354	220	3	1732	21.4
71-72	—Baltimore-New York	63	1337	287	662	.434	175	224	.781	100	142	139	1	749	11.9
72-73	—New York	75	2370	496	1016	.488	171	208	.822	245	288	195	1	1163	15.5

Season	Team	G	Min.	FGM	FGA	Pct.	FTM	FTA	Pct.	REBOUNDS Off.	Def.	Tot.	Ast.	PF	Dq.	Stl.	Blk.	TO	Pts.	Avg.
73-74	—New York	41	1194	240	513	.468	93	113	.823	22	99	121	110	97	0	34	19	...	573	14.0
74-75	—New York	78	2814	668	1462	.457	297	359	.827	56	271	327	270	200	0	108	29	...	1633	20.9
75-76	—New York	76	2889	647	1354	.478	280	356	.787	48	225	273	304	209	1	111	22	...	1574	20.7
76-77	—N.Y. Knicks	77	2656	613	1185	.517	307	366	.839	45	178	223	366	197	0	91	23	...	1533	19.9
77-78	—New York	76	2369	556	1123	.495	242	291	.832	47	135	182	361	189	0	60	19	179	1354	17.8
78-79	—New York	64	1393	329	699	.471	129	154	.838	26	48	74	189	123	0	48	6	98	787	12.3
79-80	—New York	51	633	161	352	.457	56	64	.875	16	20	36	67	46	0	21	3	28	378	7.4
	Totals	926	29636	6906	14898	.464	3642	4513	.807	...	...	2796	3594	2416	13	473	121	305	17454	18.8

NBA PLAYOFF RECORD

Season	Team	G	Min.	FGM	FGA	Pct.	FTM	FTA	Pct.	Reb.	Ast.	PF	Dq.	Pts.	Avg.
68-69	—Baltimore	4	171	44	114	.386	25	31	.806	21	16	10	0	113	28.3
69-70	—Baltimore	7	299	74	154	.481	48	60	.800	23	28	23	0	196	28.0
70-71	—Baltimore	18	671	145	356	.407	107	135	.793	64	74	56	0	397	22.1
71-72	—New York	16	429	76	185	.411	45	57	.789	45	47	41	0	197	12.3
72-73	—New York	16	504	111	211	.526	36	48	.750	51	51	39	0	258	16.1

Season	Team	G	Min.	FGM	FGA	Pct.	FTM	FTA	Pct.	REBOUNDS Off.	Def.	Tot.	Ast.	PF	Dq.	Stl.	Blk.	TO	Pts.	Avg.
73-74	—New York	12	407	81	165	.491	47	55	.855	8	40	48	25	26	0	8	9	...	209	17.4
74-75	—New York	3	89	12	45	.267	18	22	.818	1	8	9	6	6	0	4	2	...	42	14.0
77-78	—New York	6	145	24	62	.387	11	18	.611	1	4	5	17	15	0	6	0	6	59	9.8
	Totals	82	2715	567	1292	.439	337	426	.791	...	...	266	264	216	0	18	11	6	1471	17.9

NBA ALL-STAR GAME RECORD

Season	Team	Min.	FGM	FGA	Pct.	FTM	FTA	Pct.	Reb.	Ast.	PF	Dq.	Pts.
1969	—Baltimore	27	6	15	.400	9	12	.750	4	4	4	0	21
1971	—Baltimore	18	3	9	.333	0	0	...	5	2	3	0	6

Season	Team	Min.	FGM	FGA	Pct.	FTM	FTA	Pct.	REBOUNDS Off.	Def.	Tot.	Ast.	PF	Dq.	Stl.	Blk.	TO	Pts.
1975	—New York	25	3	8	.375	3	5	.600	0	3	3	2	2	0	1	0	...	9
1977	—N.Y. Knicks	15	2	7	.286	0	0	...	0	0	0	3	1	0	0	0	...	4
	Totals	85	14	39	.359	12	17	.706	...	...	12	11	10	0	1	0	...	40

DID YOU KNOW. . .

. . . that Don Nelson is the only man to have appeared in over 2,500 NBA games as a player and coach?

MURPHY, CALVIN
G

PERSONAL: Born May 9, 1948, in Norwalk, Conn. . . . 5-9/165. . . . Full name: Calvin Jerome Murphy. **HIGH SCHOOL:** Norwalk (Conn.). **COLLEGE:** Niagara.

TRANSACTIONS/CAREER NOTES: Selected by San Diego Rockets in second round (18th pick overall) of 1970 NBA Draft. . . . Rockets franchise moved from San Diego to Houston for 1971-72 season.

COLLEGIATE RECORD

NOTES: THE SPORTING NEWS All-America second team (1969, 1970).

Season Team	G	Min.	FGM	FGA	Pct.	FTM	FTA	Pct.	Reb.	Pts.	Avg.
66-67 —Niagara‡	19	...	364	719	.506	201	239	.841	102	929	48.9
67-68 —Niagara	24	...	337	772	.437	242	288	.840	118	916	38.2
68-69 —Niagara	24	...	294	700	.420	190	230	.826	87	778	32.4
69-70 —Niagara	29	...	316	692	.457	222	252	.881	103	854	29.4
Varsity totals	77		947	2164	.438	654	770	.849	308	2548	33.1

NBA REGULAR-SEASON RECORD

RECORDS: Holds single-season records for highest free-throw percentage—.958 (1981); and most consecutive free throws made—78 (December 27, 1980, through February 28, 1981).
HONORS: NBA All-Rookie team (1971).

Season Team	G	Min.	FGM	FGA	Pct.	FTM	FTA	Pct.	Reb.	Ast.	PF	Dq.	Pts.	Avg.
70-71 —San Diego	82	2020	471	1029	.458	356	434	.820	245	329	263	4	1298	15.8
71-72 —Houston	82	2538	571	1255	.455	349	392	.890	258	393	298	6	1491	18.2
72-73 —Houston	77	1697	381	820	.465	239	269	.888	149	262	211	3	1001	13.0

Season Team	G	Min.	FGM	FGA	Pct.	FTM	FTA	Pct.	Off.	Def.	Tot.	Ast.	PF	Dq.	Stl.	Blk.	TO	Pts.	Avg.
73-74 —Houston	81	2922	671	1285	.522	310	357	.868	51	137	188	603	310	8	157	4	...	1652	20.4
74-75 —Houston	78	2513	557	1152	.484	341	386	.883	52	121	173	381	281	8	128	4	...	1455	18.7
75-76 —Houston	82	2995	675	1369	.493	372	410	.907	52	157	209	596	294	3	151	6	...	1722	21.0
76-77 —Houston	82	2764	596	1216	.490	272	307	.886	54	118	172	386	281	6	144	8	...	1464	17.9
77-78 —Houston	76	2900	852	*1737	.491	245	267	.918	57	107	164	259	241	4	112	3	173	1949	25.6
78-79 —Houston	82	2941	707	1424	.496	246	265	.928	78	95	173	351	288	5	117	6	187	1660	20.2
79-80 —Houston	76	2676	624	1267	.493	271	302	.897	68	82	150	299	269	3	143	9	162	1520	20.0
80-81 —Houston	76	2014	528	1074	.492	206	215	*.958	33	54	87	222	209	0	111	6	129	1266	16.7
81-82 —Houston	64	1204	277	648	.427	100	110	.909	20	41	61	163	142	0	43	1	82	655	10.2
82-83 —Houston	64	1423	337	754	.447	138	150	*.920	34	40	74	158	163	3	59	4	89	816	12.8
Totals	1002	30607	7247	15030	.482	3445	3864	.892	...	...	2103	4402	3250	53	1165	51	822	17949	17.9

Three-point field goals: 1979-80, 1-for-25 (.040). 1980-81, 4-for-17 (.235). 1981-82, 1-for-16 (.063). 1982-83, 4-for-14 (.286). Totals, 10-for-72 (.139).

NBA PLAYOFF RECORD

Season Team	G	Min.	FGM	FGA	Pct.	FTM	FTA	Pct.	Off.	Def.	Tot.	Ast.	PF	Dq.	Stl.	Blk.	TO	Pts.	Avg.
74-75 —Houston	8	305	72	156	.462	51	57	.895	9	10	19	45	36	2	14	1	...	195	24.4
76-77 —Houston	12	420	102	213	.479	28	30	.933	7	12	19	75	47	1	19	2	...	232	19.3
78-79 —Houston	2	73	9	31	.290	8	9	.889	2	1	3	6	9	0	8	1	2	26	13.0
79-80 —Houston	7	265	58	108	.537	13	13	1.000	4	6	10	26	29	1	11	0	16	131	18.7
80-81 —Houston	19	540	142	287	.495	58	60	.967	7	17	24	57	69	0	26	0	42	344	18.1
81-82 —Houston	3	57	5	22	.227	7	8	.875	2	1	3	4	7	0	1	0	4	17	5.7
Totals	51	1660	388	817	.475	165	177	.932	31	47	78	213	197	4	79	4	64	945	18.5

Three-point field goals: 1979-80, 2-for-4 (.500). 1980-81, 2-for-7 (.286). 1981-82, 0-for-3. Totals, 4-for-14 (.286).

NBA ALL-STAR GAME RECORD

Season Team	Min.	FGM	FGA	Pct.	FTM	FTA	Pct.	Off.	Def.	Tot.	Ast.	PF	Dq.	Stl.	Blk.	TO	Pts.
1979 —Houston	15	3	5	.600	0	0	...	0	1	1	5	4	0	2	0	4	6

PETTIT, BOB
F/C

PERSONAL: Born December 12, 1932, in Baton Rouge, La. . . . 6-9/215. . . . Full name: Robert Lee Pettit Jr. **HIGH SCHOOL:** Baton Rouge (La.). **COLLEGE:** Louisiana State.

TRANSACTIONS/CAREER NOTES: Selected by Milwaukee Hawks in first round of 1954 NBA Draft. . . . Hawks franchise moved from Milwaukee to St. Louis for 1955-56 season.
CAREER HONORS: Elected to Naismith Memorial Basketball Hall of Fame (1970). . . . NBA 25th Anniversary All-Time team (1970) and 35th Anniversary All-Time team (1980). **MISCELLANEOUS:** Member of NBA championship team (1958).

COLLEGIATE RECORD

Season Team	G	Min.	FGM	FGA	Pct.	FTM	FTA	Pct.	Reb.	Pts.	Avg.
50-51 —Louisiana State‡	10	...	...	...	...	...	...	...	...	270	27.0
51-52 —Louisiana State	23	...	237	549	.432	115	192	.599	315	589	25.6
52-53 —Louisiana State	21	...	193	394	.490	133	215	.619	263	519	24.7
53-54 —Louisiana State	25	...	281	573	.490	223	308	.724	432	785	31.4
Varsity totals	69	...	711	1516	.469	471	715	.659	1010	1893	27.4

NBA REGULAR-SEASON RECORD

HONORS: NBA Most Valuable Player (1956, 1959). . . . NBA Rookie of the Year (1955). . . . All-NBA first team (1955, 1956, 1957, 1958, 1959, 1960, 1961, 1962, 1963, 1964). . . . All-NBA second team (1965).

Season Team	G	Min.	FGM	FGA	Pct.	FTM	FTA	Pct.	Reb.	Ast.	PF	Dq.	Pts.	Avg.
54-55 —Milwaukee	72	2659	520	1279	.407	426	567	.751	994	229	258	5	1466	20.4
55-56 —St. Louis	72	2794	*646	*1507	.429	*557	*757	.736	*1164	189	202	1	*1849	*25.7

Season	Team	G	Min.	FGM	FGA	Pct.	FTM	FTA	Pct.	Reb.	Ast.	PF	Dq.	Pts.	Avg.
56-57	—St. Louis	71	2491	*613	*1477	.415	529	684	.773	1037	133	181	1	1755	24.7
57-58	—St. Louis	70	2528	581	1418	.410	557	744	.749	1216	157	222	6	1719	24.6
58-59	—St. Louis	72	2873	*719	1640	.438	*667	*879	.759	1182	221	200	3	*2105	*29.2
59-60	—St. Louis	72	2896	669	1526	.438	544	722	.753	1221	257	204	0	1882	26.1
60-61	—St. Louis	76	3027	769	1720	.447	582	804	.724	1540	262	217	1	2120	27.9
61-62	—St. Louis	78	3282	867	1928	.450	695	901	.771	1459	289	296	4	2429	31.1
62-63	—St. Louis	79	3090	778	1746	.446	*685	885	.774	1191	245	282	9	2241	28.4
63-64	—St. Louis	80	3296	791	1708	.463	608	771	.789	1224	259	300	3	2190	27.4
64-65	—St. Louis	50	1754	396	923	.429	332	405	.820	621	128	167	0	1124	22.5
	Totals	792	30690	7349	16872	.436	6182	8119	.761	12849	2369	2529	33	20880	26.4

NBA PLAYOFF RECORD

NOTES: Holds NBA Finals single-game records for most free throws made— 19; and most free throws attempted— 24 (April 9, 1958, vs. Boston). . . . Shares NBA Finals single-game record for most free throws attempted in one quarter— 11 (April 9, 1958, vs. Boston).

Season	Team	G	Min.	FGM	FGA	Pct.	FTM	FTA	Pct.	Reb.	Ast.	PF	Dq.	Pts.	Avg.
55-56	—St. Louis	8	274	47	128	.367	59	70	.843	84	18	20	0	153	19.1
56-57	—St. Louis	10	430	98	237	.414	102	133	.767	168	25	33	0	298	29.8
57-58	—St. Louis	11	430	90	230	.391	86	118	.729	181	20	31	0	266	24.2
58-59	—St. Louis	6	257	58	137	.423	51	65	.785	75	14	20	0	167	27.8
59-60	—St. Louis	14	576	129	292	.442	107	142	.754	221	52	43	1	365	26.1
60-61	—St. Louis	12	526	117	284	.412	109	144	.757	211	38	42	0	343	28.6
62-63	—St. Louis	11	463	119	259	.459	112	144	.778	166	33	34	0	350	31.8
63-64	—St. Louis	12	494	93	226	.412	66	79	.835	174	33	44	0	252	21.0
64-65	—St. Louis	4	95	15	41	.366	16	20	.800	24	8	10	0	46	11.5
	Totals	88	3545	766	1834	.418	708	915	.774	1304	241	277	1	2240	25.5

NBA ALL-STAR GAME RECORD

NOTES: NBA All-Star Game Most Valuable Player (1956, 1958, 1962). . . . NBA All-Star Game co-Most Valuable Player (1959). . . . Holds single-game records for most rebounds— 27; and most rebounds in one quarter— 10 (1962). . . . Shares single-game record for most rebounds in one half— 16 (1962).

Season	Team	Min.	FGM	FGA	Pct.	FTM	FTA	Pct.	Reb.	Ast.	PF	Dq.	Pts.
1955	—Milwaukee	27	3	14	.214	2	4	.500	9	2	0	0	8
1956	—St. Louis	31	7	17	.412	6	7	.857	24	7	4	0	20
1957	—St. Louis	31	8	18	.444	5	6	.833	11	2	2	0	21
1958	—St. Louis	38	10	21	.476	8	10	.800	26	1	1	0	28
1959	—St. Louis	34	8	21	.381	9	9	1.000	16	5	1	0	25
1960	—St. Louis	28	4	15	.267	3	6	.500	14	2	2	0	11
1961	—St. Louis	32	13	22	.591	3	7	.429	9	0	2	0	29
1962	—St. Louis	37	10	20	.500	5	5	1.000	27	2	5	0	25
1963	—St. Louis	32	7	16	.438	11	12	.917	13	0	1	0	25
1964	—St. Louis	36	6	15	.400	7	9	.778	17	2	3	0	19
1965	—St. Louis	34	5	14	.357	3	5	.600	12	0	4	0	13
	Totals	360	81	193	.420	62	80	.775	178	23	25	0	224

NBA COACHING RECORD

		REGULAR SEASON				PLAYOFFS		
Season	Team	W	L	Pct.	Finish	W	L	Pct.
61-62	—St. Louis	4	2	.667	4th/Western Division	—	—	—
	Totals (1 year)	4	2	.667				

NOTES:
1962— Replaced Paul Seymour (5-9) and Andrew Levane (20-40) as St. Louis head coach (March), with record of 25-49.

POLLARD, JIM
F

PERSONAL: Born July 9, 1922, in Oakland, Calif. . . . 6-5/185. . . . Full name: James Clifford Pollard. . . . Nickname: The Kangaroo Kid.
HIGH SCHOOL: Oakland Technical (Calif.).
COLLEGE: Stanford.
TRANSACTIONS/CAREER NOTES: Signed by Minneapolis Lakers of National Basketball League (1947). . . . Lakers franchise transferred to Basketball Association of America for 1948-49 season. . . . Lakers franchise became part of NBA upon merger of BAA and NBL for 1949-50 season.
CAREER HONORS: Elected to Naismith Memorial Basketball Hall of Fame (1977).
MISCELLANEOUS: Member of NBA championship teams (1950, 1952, 1953, 1954). . . . Member of BAA championship team (1949). . . . Member of NBL championship team (1948).

COLLEGIATE RECORD

NOTES: Member of NCAA Division I championship team (1942). . . . In military service during 1942-43, 1943-44 and 1944-45 seasons; played with Alameda, Calif. Coast Guard team.

Season	Team	G	Min.	FGM	FGA	Pct.	FTM	FTA	Pct.	Reb.	Pts.	Avg.
40-41	—Stanford‡				Freshman team statistics unavailable.							
41-42	—Stanford	23	. . .	103	. . .	. . .	35	48	.729	. . .	241	10.5
	Varsity totals	23	. . .	103	. . .	. . .	35	48	.729	. . .	241	10.5

ABL REGULAR-SEASON RECORD

Season	Team	G	Min.	FGM	FGA	Pct.	FTM	FTA	Pct.	Reb.	Ast.	Pts.	Avg.
45-46	—San Diego Dons	15	. . .	84	. . .	. . .	55	. . .	. . .	. . .	. . .	*223	14.9
46-47	—Oakland Bittners	20	. . .	. . .	. . .	. . .	. . .	. . .	. . .	. . .	. . .	*279	14.0
	Totals	35	. . .	. . .	. . .	. . .	. . .	. . .	. . .	. . .	. . .	502	14.3

NBL AND NBA REGULAR-SEASON RECORD

HONORS: All-NBA first team (1950). . . . All-NBA second team (1952, 1954). . . . All-BAA first team (1949).

Season Team	G	Min.	FGM	FGA	Pct.	FTM	FTA	Pct.	Reb.	Ast.	PF	Dq.	Pts.	Avg.
47-48 —Minneapolis (NBL)	59	...	310	...	...	140	207	.676	...	...	147	...	760	12.9
48-49 —Minneapolis (BAA)	53	...	314	792	.396	156	227	.687	...	142	144	...	784	14.8
49-50 —Minneapolis	66	...	394	1140	.346	185	242	.764	...	252	143	...	973	14.7
50-51 —Minneapolis	54	...	256	728	.352	117	156	.750	484	184	157	4	629	11.6
51-52 —Minneapolis	65	2545	411	1155	.356	183	260	.704	593	234	199	4	1005	15.5
52-53 —Minneapolis	66	2403	333	933	.357	193	251	.769	452	231	194	3	859	13.0
53-54 —Minneapolis	71	2483	326	882	.370	179	230	.778	500	214	161	0	831	11.7
54-55 —Minneapolis	63	1960	265	749	.354	151	186	.812	458	160	147	3	681	10.8
Totals	497	...	2609	...	...	1304	1759	.741	...	...	1292	...	6522	13.1

NBL AND NBA PLAYOFF RECORD

Season Team	G	Min.	FGM	FGA	Pct.	FTM	FTA	Pct.	Reb.	Ast.	PF	Dq.	Pts.	Avg.
47-48 —Minneapolis (NBL)	10	...	48	...	...	27	41	.659	...	...	...	...	123	12.3
48-49 —Minneapolis (BAA)	10	...	43	147	.293	44	62	.710	...	39	31	...	130	13.0
49-50 —Minneapolis semifinals ...	12	...	50	175	.286	44	62	.710	...	56	36	...	144	12.0
50-51 —Minneapolis	7	...	35	108	.324	25	30	.833	62	27	27	1	95	13.6
51-52 —Minneapolis	11	469	70	173	.405	37	50	.740	71	33	34	1	177	16.1
52-53 —Minneapolis	12	455	62	167	.371	48	62	.774	86	49	37	2	172	14.3
53-54 —Minneapolis	13	543	56	155	.361	48	60	.800	110	41	27	0	160	12.3
54-55 —Minneapolis	7	257	33	104	.317	33	46	.717	78	14	13	0	99	14.1
Totals	82	...	397	...	...	306	413	.741	...	...	...	...	1100	13.4

NBA ALL-STAR GAME RECORD

Season Team	Min.	FGM	FGA	Pct.	FTM	FTA	Pct.	Reb.	Ast.	PF	Dq.	Pts.
1951 —Minneapolis	...	2	11	.182	0	0	...	4	5	1	0	4
1952 —Minneapolis	29	2	17	.118	0	0	...	11	5	3	0	4
1954 —Minneapolis	41	10	22	.455	3	5	.600	3	3	3	0	23
1955 —Minneapolis	27	7	19	.368	3	3	1.000	4	0	1	0	17
Totals	...	21	69	.304	6	8	.750	22	13	8	0	48

COLLEGIATE COACHING RECORD

Season Team	W	L	Pct.	Finish
55-56 —LaSalle.................................	15	10	.600	
56-57 —LaSalle.................................	17	9	.654	
57-58 —LaSalle.................................	16	9	.640	
Totals (3 years)	48	28	.632	

NBA COACHING RECORD

Season Team	REGULAR SEASON				PLAYOFFS		
	W	L	Pct.	Finish	W	L	Pct.
59-60 —Minneapolis	14	25	.359	3rd/Western Division	5	4	.556
61-62 —Chicago.................................	18	62	.225	5th/Western Division	—	—	—
Totals (2 years)	32	87	.269	Totals (1 year)	5	4	.556

ABA COACHING RECORD

Season Team	REGULAR SEASON				PLAYOFFS		
	W	L	Pct.	Finish	W	L	Pct.
67-68 —Minnesota..............................	50	28	.641	2nd/Eastern Division	4	6	.400
68-69 —Miami....................................	43	35	.551	2nd/Eastern Division	5	7	.417
69-70 —Miami....................................	5	15	.250		—	—	—
Totals (3 years)	98	78	.557	Totals (2 years)	9	13	.409

NOTES:

1960— Replaced John Castellani as Minneapolis head coach (January 2), with 11-25 record. Defeated Detroit, 2-0, in Western Division semifinals; lost to St. Louis, 4-3, in Western Division finals.

1968— Defeated Kentucky, 3-2, in Eastern Division semifinals; lost to Pittsburgh, 4-1, in Eastern Division finals. Minnesota Muskies franchise moved to Miami and were renamed the Floridians for 1968-69 season.

1969— Defeated Minnesota, 4-3, in Eastern Division semifinals; lost to Indiana, 4-1, in Eastern Division finals. Replaced as Miami head coach by Hal Blitman (November).

REED, WILLIS

C/F

PERSONAL: Born June 25, 1942, in Hico, La. ... 6-10/240. ... Full name: Willis Reed Jr.

HIGH SCHOOL: West Side (Lillie, La.).

COLLEGE: Grambling State.

TRANSACTIONS/CAREER NOTES: Selected by New York Knicks in second round (10th pick overall) of 1964 NBA Draft.

CAREER HONORS: Elected to Naismith Memorial Basketball Hall of Fame (1981).

MISCELLANEOUS: Member of NBA championship teams (1970, 1973).

COLLEGIATE RECORD

NOTES: Member of NAIA championship team (1961).... Elected to NAIA Basketball Hall of Fame (1970).

Season Team	G	Min.	FGM	FGA	Pct.	FTM	FTA	Pct.	Reb.	Pts.	Avg.
60-61 —Grambling State.....................	35	...	146	239	.611	86	122	.705	312	378	10.8
61-62 —Grambling State.....................	26	...	189	323	.585	80	102	.784	380	458	17.6
62-63 —Grambling State.....................	33	...	282	489	.577	135	177	.763	563	699	21.2
63-64 —Grambling State.....................	28	...	301	486	.619	143	199	.719	596	745	26.6
Totals	122	...	918	1537	.597	444	600	.740	1851	2280	18.7

NBA REGULAR-SEASON RECORD

HONORS: NBA Most Valuable Player (1970).... NBA Rookie of the Year (1965).... All-NBA first team (1970).... All-NBA second team (1967, 1968, 1969, 1971).... NBA All-Defensive first team (1970).... NBA All-Rookie team (1965).

Season	Team	G	Min.	FGM	FGA	Pct.	FTM	FTA	Pct.	Reb.	Ast.	PF	Dq.	Pts.	Avg.
64-65	— New York	80	3042	629	1457	.432	302	407	.742	1175	133	339	14	1560	19.5
65-66	— New York	76	2537	438	1009	.434	302	399	.757	883	91	323	13	1178	15.5
66-67	— New York	78	2824	635	1298	.489	358	487	.735	1136	126	293	9	1628	20.9
67-68	— New York	81	2879	659	1346	.490	367	509	.721	1073	159	343	12	1685	20.8
68-69	— New York	82	3108	704	1351	.521	325	435	.747	1191	190	314	7	1733	21.1
69-70	— New York	81	3089	702	1385	.507	351	464	.756	1126	161	287	2	1755	21.7
70-71	— New York	73	2855	614	1330	.462	299	381	.785	1003	148	228	1	1527	20.9
71-72	— New York	11	363	60	137	.438	27	39	.692	96	22	30	0	147	13.4
72-73	— New York	69	1876	334	705	.474	92	124	.742	590	126	205	0	760	11.0

Season	Team	G	Min.	FGM	FGA	Pct.	FTM	FTA	Pct.	Off.	Def.	Tot.	Ast.	PF	Dq.	Stl.	Blk.	TO	Pts.	Avg.
										— REBOUNDS —										
73-74	— New York	19	500	84	184	.457	42	53	.792	47	94	141	30	49	0	12	21	...	210	11.1
Totals		650	23073	4859	10202	.476	2465	3298	.747	...	...	8414	1186	2411	58	12	21	...	12183	18.7

NBA PLAYOFF RECORD

NOTES: NBA Finals Most Valuable Player (1970, 1973).

Season	Team	G	Min.	FGM	FGA	Pct.	FTM	FTA	Pct.	Reb.	Ast.	PF	Dq.	Pts.	Avg.
66-67	— New York	4	148	43	80	.538	24	25	.960	55	7	19	1	110	27.5
67-68	— New York	6	210	53	98	.541	22	30	.733	62	11	24	1	128	21.3
68-69	— New York	10	429	101	198	.510	55	70	.786	141	19	40	1	257	25.7
69-70	— New York	18	732	178	378	.471	70	95	.737	248	51	60	0	426	23.7
70-71	— New York	12	504	81	196	.413	26	39	.667	144	27	41	0	188	15.7
72-73	— New York	17	486	97	208	.466	18	21	.857	129	30	65	1	212	12.5

Season	Team	G	Min.	FGM	FGA	Pct.	FTM	FTA	Pct.	Off.	Def.	Tot.	Ast.	PF	Dq.	Stl.	Blk.	TO	Pts.	Avg.
										— REBOUNDS —										
73-74	— New York	11	132	17	45	.378	3	5	.600	4	18	22	4	26	0	2	0	...	37	3.4
Totals		78	2641	570	1203	.474	218	285	.765	...	...	801	149	275	4	2	0	...	1358	17.4

NBA ALL-STAR GAME RECORD

NOTES: NBA All-Star Game Most Valuable Player (1970).

Season	Team	Min.	FGM	FGA	Pct.	FTM	FTA	Pct.	Reb.	Ast.	PF	Dq.	Pts.
1965	— New York	25	3	11	.273	1	2	.500	5	1	2	0	7
1966	— New York	23	7	11	.636	2	2	1.000	8	1	3	0	16
1967	— New York	17	2	6	.333	0	0	...	9	1	0	0	4
1968	— New York	25	7	14	.500	2	3	.667	8	1	4	0	16
1969	— New York	14	5	8	.625	0	0	...	4	2	2	0	10
1970	— New York	30	9	18	.500	3	3	1.000	11	0	6	1	21
1971	— New York	27	5	16	.313	4	6	.667	13	1	3	0	14
Totals		161	38	84	.452	12	16	.750	58	7	20	1	88

HEAD COACHING RECORD

BACKGROUND: Volunteer assistant, St. John's University (1980-81).... Assistant coach, Atlanta Hawks (1985-86 and 1986-87).... Assistant coach, Sacramento Kings (1987-88).

NBA COACHING RECORD

			REGULAR SEASON				PLAYOFFS	
Season	Team	W	L	Pct.	Finish	W	L	Pct.
77-78	— New York	43	39	.524	2nd/Atlantic Division	2	4	.333
78-79	— New York	6	8	.429		—	—	—
87-88	— New Jersey	7	21	.250	5th/Atlantic Division	—	—	—
88-89	— New Jersey	26	56	.317	5th/Atlantic Division	—	—	—
Totals (4 years)		82	124	.398	Totals (1 year)	2	4	.333

COLLEGIATE COACHING RECORD

Season	Team	W	L	Pct.	Finish
81-82	— Creighton	7	20	.259	8th/Missouri Valley Conference
82-83	— Creighton	8	19	.296	10th/Missouri Valley Conference
83-84	— Creighton	17	14	.548	4th/Missouri Valley Conference
84-85	— Creighton	20	11	.645	4th/Missouri Valley Conference
Totals (4 years)		52	64	.448	

NOTES:
1978— Defeated Cleveland, 2-0, in Eastern Conference first round; lost to Philadelphia, 4-0, in Eastern Conference semifinals. Replaced as New York head coach by Red Holzman (November).
1984— Lost to Nebraska, 56-54, in NIT first round.
1988— Replaced interim head coach Bob MacKinnon as New Jersey head coach (February 29), with record of 12-42.

ROBERTSON, OSCAR
G

PERSONAL: Born November 24, 1938, in Charlotte, Tenn. ... 6-5/220. ... Full name: Oscar Palmer Robertson. ... Nickname: Big O.
HIGH SCHOOL: Crispus Attucks (Indianapolis).

COLLEGE: Cincinnati.
TRANSACTIONS/CAREER NOTES: Selected by Cincinnati Royals in 1960 NBA Draft (territorial pick). ... Traded by Royals to Milwaukee Bucks for Flynn Robinson and Charlie Paulk (April 21, 1970).
CAREER HONORS: Elected to Naismith Memorial Basketball Hall of Fame (1979). ... NBA 35th Anniversary All-Time team (1980).
MISCELLANEOUS: Member of NBA championship team (1971).... Member of gold-medal-winning U.S. Olympic team (1960).

COLLEGIATE RECORD

NOTES: THE SPORTING NEWS College Player of the Year (1958, 1959, 1960).... THE SPORTING NEWS All-America first team

(1958, 1959, 1960).... Led NCAA Division I with 35.1 points per game (1958), 32.6 points per game (1959) and 33.7 points per game (1960).

Season Team	G	Min.	FGM	FGA	Pct.	FTM	FTA	Pct.	Reb.	Pts.	Avg.
56-57 —Cincinnati‡	13	...	151	...	...	127	178	.713	...	429	33.0
57-58 —Cincinnati	28	1085	352	617	.571	280	355	.789	425	984	35.1
58-59 —Cincinnati	30	1172	331	650	.509	316	398	.794	489	978	32.6
59-60 —Cincinnati	30	1155	369	701	.526	273	361	.756	424	1011	33.7
Varsity totals	88	3412	1052	1968	.535	869	1114	.780	1338	2973	33.8

NBA REGULAR-SEASON RECORD

RECORDS: Holds single-game record for most free throws made in one half—19 (December 27, 1964, vs. Baltimore).... Shares single-game records for most free throws attempted in one half—22; and most free throws attempted in one quarter—16 (December 27, 1964, vs. Baltimore).

HONORS: NBA Most Valuable Player (1964).... NBA Rookie of the Year (1961).... All-NBA first team (1961, 1962, 1963, 1964, 1965, 1966, 1967, 1968, 1969).... All-NBA second team (1970, 1971).

NOTES: Led NBA with 9.7 assists per game (1961), 11.4 assists per game (1962), 11.0 assists per game (1964), 11.5 assists per game (1965), 11.1 assists per game (1966) and 9.8 assists per game (1969).

Season Team	G	Min.	FGM	FGA	Pct.	FTM	FTA	Pct.	Reb.	Ast.	PF	Dq.	Pts.	Avg.
60-61 —Cincinnati	71	3012	756	1600	.473	653	794	.822	716	*690	219	3	2165	30.5
61-62 —Cincinnati	79	3503	866	1810	.478	700	872	.803	985	*899	258	1	2432	30.8
62-63 —Cincinnati	80	3521	825	1593	.518	614	758	.810	835	758	293	1	2264	28.3
63-64 —Cincinnati	79	3559	840	1740	.483	*800	938	*.853	783	*868	280	3	2480	31.4
64-65 —Cincinnati	75	3421	807	1681	.480	*665	793	.839	674	*861	205	2	2279	30.4
65-66 —Cincinnati	76	3493	818	1723	.475	742	881	.842	586	*847	227	1	2378	31.3
66-67 —Cincinnati	79	3468	838	1699	.493	736	843	.873	486	845	226	2	2412	30.5
67-68 —Cincinnati	65	2765	660	1321	.500	*576	660	*.873	391	633	199	2	1896	*29.2
68-69 —Cincinnati	79	3461	656	1351	.486	*643	767	.838	502	*772	231	2	1955	24.7
69-70 —Cincinnati	69	2865	647	1267	.511	454	561	.809	422	558	175	1	1748	25.3
70-71 —Milwaukee	81	3194	592	1193	.496	385	453	.850	462	668	203	0	1569	19.4
71-72 —Milwaukee	64	2390	419	887	.472	276	330	.836	323	491	116	0	1114	17.4
72-73 —Milwaukee	73	2737	446	983	.454	238	281	.847	360	551	167	0	1130	15.5

									— REBOUNDS —								
Season Team	G	Min.	FGM	FGA	Pct.	FTM	FTA	Pct.	Off.	Def.	Tot.	Ast.	PF	Dq.	Stl.	Blk.	TO	Pts.	Avg.
73-74 —Milwaukee	70	2477	338	772	.438	212	254	.835	71	208	279	446	132	0	77	4	...	888	12.7
Totals	1040	43866	9508	19620	.485	7694	9185	.838	...	...	7804	9887	2931	18	77	4	...	26710	25.7

NBA PLAYOFF RECORD

Season Team	G	Min.	FGM	FGA	Pct.	FTM	FTA	Pct.	Reb.	Ast.	PF	Dq.	Pts.	Avg.
61-62 —Cincinnati	4	185	42	81	.519	31	39	.795	44	44	18	1	115	28.8
62-63 —Cincinnati	12	570	124	264	.470	133	154	.864	156	108	41	0	381	31.8
63-64 —Cincinnati	10	471	92	202	.455	109	127	.858	89	84	30	0	293	29.3
64-65 —Cincinnati	4	195	38	89	.427	36	39	.923	19	48	14	0	112	28.0
65-66 —Cincinnati	5	224	49	120	.408	61	68	.897	38	39	20	1	159	31.8
66-67 —Cincinnati	4	183	33	64	.516	33	37	.892	16	45	9	0	99	24.8
70-71 —Milwaukee	14	520	102	210	.486	52	69	.754	70	124	39	0	256	18.3
71-72 —Milwaukee	11	380	57	140	.407	30	36	.833	64	83	29	0	144	13.1
72-73 —Milwaukee	6	256	48	96	.500	31	34	.912	28	45	21	1	127	21.2

									— REBOUNDS —								
Season Team	G	Min.	FGM	FGA	Pct.	FTM	FTA	Pct.	Off.	Def.	Tot.	Ast.	PF	Dq.	Stl.	Blk.	TO	Pts.	Avg.
73-74 —Milwaukee	16	689	90	200	.450	44	52	.846	15	39	54	149	46	0	15	4	...	224	14.0
Totals	86	3673	675	1466	.460	560	655	.855	...	...	578	769	267	3	15	4	...	1910	22.2

NBA ALL-STAR GAME RECORD

NOTES: NBA All-Star Game Most Valuable Player (1961, 1964, 1969).... Shares career record for most free throws attempted—98.... Shares single-game record for most free throws made—12 (1965).

Season Team	Min.	FGM	FGA	Pct.	FTM	FTA	Pct.	Reb.	Ast.	PF	Dq.	Pts.
1961 —Cincinnati	34	8	13	.615	7	9	.778	9	14	5	0	23
1962 —Cincinnati	37	9	20	.450	8	14	.571	7	13	3	0	26
1963 —Cincinnati	37	9	15	.600	3	4	.750	3	6	5	0	21
1964 —Cincinnati	42	10	23	.435	6	10	.600	14	8	4	0	26
1965 —Cincinnati	40	8	18	.444	12	13	.923	6	8	5	0	28
1966 —Cincinnati	25	6	12	.500	5	6	.833	10	8	0	0	17
1967 —Cincinnati	34	9	20	.450	8	10	.800	2	5	4	0	26
1968 —Cincinnati	22	7	9	.778	4	7	.571	1	5	2	0	18
1969 —Cincinnati	32	8	16	.500	8	8	1.000	6	5	3	0	24
1970 —Cincinnati	29	9	11	.818	3	4	.750	6	4	3	0	21
1971 —Milwaukee	24	2	6	.333	1	3	.333	2	2	3	0	5
1972 —Milwaukee	24	3	9	.333	5	10	.500	3	3	4	0	11
Totals	380	88	172	.512	70	98	.714	69	81	41	0	246

RODGERS, GUY
G

PERSONAL: Born September 1, 1935, in Philadelphia.... 6-0/185.... Full name: Guy William Rodgers Jr.
HIGH SCHOOL: Northeast (Philadelphia).
COLLEGE: Temple.

TRANSACTIONS/CAREER NOTES: Selected by Philadelphia Warriors in 1958 NBA Draft (territorial pick).... Warriors franchise moved from Philadelphia to San Francisco for 1962-63 season.... Traded by Warriors to Chicago Bulls for draft choice, cash and two players to be named later (September 7, 1966); Jim King and Jeff Mullins sent to Warriors to complete deal.... Traded by Bulls to Cincinnati Royals for Flynn Robinson, cash and two future draft choices (October 20, 1967).... Selected by Milwaukee Bucks from Royals in expansion draft (May 6, 1968).

COLLEGIATE RECORD

NOTES: THE SPORTING NEWS All-America first team (1958).

Season	Team	G	Min.	FGM	FGA	Pct.	FTM	FTA	Pct.	Reb.	Pts.	Avg.
54-55	—Temple†	15	...	...	...	...	...	...	...	...	278	18.5
55-56	—Temple	31	...	243	552	.440	87	155	.561	186	573	18.5
56-57	—Temple	29	...	216	565	.382	159	224	.710	202	591	20.4
57-58	—Temple	30	...	249	564	.441	105	171	.614	199	603	20.1
	Varsity totals	90	...	708	1681	.421	351	550	.638	587	1767	19.6

NBA REGULAR-SEASON RECORD

NOTES: Led NBA with 10.4 assists per game (1963) and 11.2 assists per game (1967).

Season	Team	G	Min.	FGM	FGA	Pct.	FTM	FTA	Pct.	Reb.	Ast.	PF	Dq.	Pts.	Avg.
58-59	—Philadelphia	45	1565	211	535	.394	61	112	.545	281	261	132	1	483	10.7
59-60	—Philadelphia	68	2483	338	870	.389	111	181	.613	391	482	196	3	787	11.6
60-61	—Philadelphia	78	2905	397	1029	.386	206	300	.687	509	677	262	3	1000	12.8
61-62	—Philadelphia	80	2650	267	749	.356	121	182	.665	348	643	312	12	655	8.2
62-63	—San Francisco	79	3249	445	1150	.387	208	286	.727	394	*825	296	7	1098	13.9
63-64	—San Francisco	79	2695	337	923	.365	198	280	.707	328	556	245	4	872	11.0
64-65	—San Francisco	79	2699	465	1225	.380	223	325	.686	323	565	256	4	1153	14.6
65-66	—San Francisco	79	2902	586	1571	.373	296	407	.727	421	846	241	6	1468	18.6
66-67	—Chicago	81	3063	538	1377	.391	383	475	.806	346	*908	243	1	1459	18.0
67-68	—Chicago-Cincinnati	79	1546	148	426	.347	107	133	.805	150	380	167	1	403	5.1
68-69	—Milwaukee	81	2157	325	862	.377	184	232	.793	226	561	207	2	834	10.3
69-70	—Milwaukee	64	749	68	191	.356	67	90	.744	74	213	73	1	203	3.2
	Totals	892	28663	4125	10908	.378	2165	3003	.721	3791	6917	2630	45	10415	11.7

NBA PLAYOFF RECORD

Season	Team	G	Min.	FGM	FGA	Pct.	FTM	FTA	Pct.	Reb.	Ast.	PF	Dq.	Pts.	Avg.
59-60	—Philadelphia	9	370	49	136	.360	20	36	.556	77	54	39	3	118	13.1
60-61	—Philadelphia	3	121	21	57	.368	11	20	.550	21	15	16	2	53	17.7
61-62	—Philadelphia	13	482	52	145	.359	35	55	.636	7	88	57	3	139	10.7
63-64	—San Francisco	12	419	57	173	.329	33	47	.702	58	90	46	1	147	12.3
66-67	—Chicago	3	97	15	40	.375	4	5	.800	6	18	11	0	34	11.3
69-70	—Milwaukee	7	68	4	14	.286	9	12	.750	4	21	7	0	17	2.4
	Totals	47	1557	198	565	.350	112	175	.640	173	286	176	9	508	10.8

NBA ALL-STAR GAME RECORD

Season	Team	Min.	FGM	FGA	Pct.	FTM	FTA	Pct.	Reb.	Ast.	PF	Dq.	Pts.
1963	—San Francisco	17	3	6	.500	1	2	.500	2	4	2	0	7
1964	—San Francisco	22	3	6	.500	0	0	...	2	2	4	0	6
1966	—San Francisco	34	4	11	.364	0	0	...	7	11	4	0	8
1967	—Chicago	28	0	4	.000	1	1	1.000	2	8	3	0	1
	Totals	101	10	27	.370	2	3	.667	13	25	13	0	22

RUSSELL, BILL
C

PERSONAL: Born February 12, 1934, in Monroe, La. ... 6-10/220. ... Full name: William Felton Russell.
HIGH SCHOOL: McClymond (Oakland, Calif.).
COLLEGE: San Francisco.
TRANSACTIONS/CAREER NOTES: Selected by Boston Celtics in first round (third pick overall) of 1956 NBA Draft (Celtics traded Ed Macauley and Cliff Hagan to St. Louis Hawks for its first-round choice, April 29, 1956).
CAREER HONORS: Elected to Naismith Memorial Basketball Hall of Fame (1974). ... Declared Greatest Player in the History of the NBA by Professional Basketball Writers' Association of America (1980). ... NBA 25th Anniversary All-Time Team (1970) and 35th Anniversary All-Time Team (1980).
MISCELLANEOUS: Member of NBA championship teams (1957, 1959, 1960, 1961, 1962, 1963, 1964, 1965, 1966, 1968 (also coach), 1969 (also coach). ... Member of gold-medal-winning U.S. Olympic team (1956).

COLLEGIATE RECORD

NOTES: NCAA Tournament Most Outstanding Player (1955). ... Member of NCAA championship teams (1955, 1956).

Season	Team	G	Min.	FGM	FGA	Pct.	FTM	FTA	Pct.	Reb.	Pts.	Avg.
52-53	—San Francisco†	23	...	...	...	...	...	...	...	...	461	20.0
53-54	—San Francisco	21	...	150	309	.485	117	212	.552	403	417	19.9
54-55	—San Francisco	29	...	229	423	.541	164	278	.590	594	622	21.4
55-56	—San Francisco	29	...	246	480	.513	105	212	.495	609	597	20.6
	Varsity totals	79	...	625	1212	.516	386	702	.550	1606	1636	20.7

NBA REGULAR-SEASON RECORD

RECORDS: Holds single-game record for most rebounds in one half—32 (November 16, 1957, vs. Philadelphia).
HONORS: NBA Most Valuable Player (1958, 1961, 1962, 1963, 1965). ... All-NBA first team (1959, 1963, 1965). ... All-NBA second team (1958, 1960, 1961, 1962, 1964, 1966, 1967, 1968). ... NBA All-Defensive first team (1969).
NOTES: Led NBA with 19.6 rebounds per game (1957), 22.7 rebounds per game (1958), 23.0 rebounds per game (1959), 24.7 rebounds per game (1964) and 24.1 rebounds per game (1965).

Season	Team	G	Min.	FGM	FGA	Pct.	FTM	FTA	Pct.	Reb.	Ast.	PF	Dq.	Pts.	Avg.
56-57	—Boston	48	1695	277	649	.427	152	309	.492	943	88	143	2	706	14.7
57-58	—Boston	69	2640	456	1032	.442	230	443	.519	*1564	202	181	2	1142	16.6
58-59	—Boston	70	*2979	456	997	.457	256	428	.598	*1612	222	161	3	1168	16.7
59-60	—Boston	74	3146	555	1189	.467	240	392	.612	1778	277	210	0	1350	18.2
60-61	—Boston	78	3458	532	1250	.426	258	469	.550	1868	268	155	0	1322	16.9
61-62	—Boston	76	3433	575	1258	.457	286	481	.595	1790	341	207	3	1436	18.9
62-63	—Boston	78	3500	511	1182	.432	287	517	.555	1843	348	189	1	1309	16.8

Season	Team	G	Min.	FGM	FGA	Pct.	FTM	FTA	Pct.	Reb.	Ast.	PF	Dq.	Pts.	Avg.
63-64	—Boston	78	3482	466	1077	.433	236	429	.550	*1930	370	190	0	1168	15.0
64-65	—Boston	78	*3466	429	980	.438	244	426	.573	*1878	410	204	1	1102	14.1
65-66	—Boston	78	3386	391	943	.415	223	405	.551	1779	371	221	4	1005	12.9
66-67	—Boston	81	3297	395	870	.454	285	467	.610	1700	472	258	4	1075	13.3
67-68	—Boston	78	2953	365	858	.425	247	460	.537	1451	357	242	2	977	12.5
68-69	—Boston	77	3291	279	645	.433	204	388	.526	1484	374	231	2	762	9.9
Totals		963	40726	5687	12930	.440	3148	5614	.561	21620	4100	2592	24	14522	15.1

NBA PLAYOFF RECORD

NOTES: Holds career record for most rebounds—4,104. . . . Holds NBA Finals records for highest rebounds-per-game average—29.5 (1959); and highest rebounds-per-game average by a rookie—22.9 (1957). . . . Holds NBA Finals single-game records for most free throws attempted in one half—15 (April 11, 1961, vs. St. Louis); most rebounds—40 (March 29, 1960, vs. St. Louis and April 18, 1962, vs. Los Angeles); most rebounds by a rookie—32 (April 13, 1957, vs. St. Louis); and most rebounds in one quarter—19 (April 18, 1962, vs. Los Angeles).

Season	Team	G	Min.	FGM	FGA	Pct.	FTM	FTA	Pct.	Reb.	Ast.	PF	Dq.	Pts.	Avg.
56-57	—Boston	10	409	54	148	.365	31	61	.508	244	32	41	1	139	13.9
57-58	—Boston	9	355	48	133	.361	40	66	.606	221	24	24	0	136	15.1
58-59	—Boston	11	496	65	159	.409	41	67	.612	305	40	28	1	171	15.5
59-60	—Boston	13	572	94	206	.456	53	75	.707	336	38	38	1	241	18.5
60-61	—Boston	10	462	73	171	.427	45	86	.523	299	48	24	0	191	19.1
61-62	—Boston	14	672	116	253	.459	82	113	.726	370	70	49	0	314	22.4
62-63	—Boston	13	617	96	212	.453	72	109	.661	326	66	36	0	264	20.3
63-64	—Boston	10	451	47	132	.356	37	67	.552	272	44	33	0	131	13.1
64-65	—Boston	12	561	79	150	.527	40	76	.526	302	76	43	2	198	16.5
65-66	—Boston	17	814	124	261	.475	76	123	.618	428	85	60	0	324	19.1
66-67	—Boston	9	390	31	86	.360	33	52	.635	198	50	32	1	95	10.6
67-68	—Boston	19	869	99	242	.409	76	130	.585	434	99	73	1	274	14.4
68-69	—Boston	18	829	77	182	.423	41	81	.506	369	98	65	1	195	10.8
Totals		165	7497	1003	2335	.430	667	1106	.603	4104	770	546	8	2673	16.2

NBA ALL-STAR GAME RECORD

NOTES: NBA All-Star Game Most Valuable Player (1963).

Season	Team	Min.	FGM	FGA	Pct.	FTM	FTA	Pct.	Reb.	Ast.	PF	Dq.	Pts.
1958	—Boston	26	5	12	.417	1	3	.333	11	2	5	0	11
1959	—Boston	27	3	10	.300	1	1	1.000	9	1	4	0	7
1960	—Boston	27	3	7	.429	0	2	.000	8	3	1	0	6
1961	—Boston	28	9	15	.600	6	8	.750	11	1	2	0	24
1962	—Boston	27	5	12	.417	2	3	.667	12	2	2	0	12
1963	—Boston	37	8	14	.571	3	4	.750	24	5	3	0	19
1964	—Boston	42	6	13	.462	1	2	.500	21	2	4	0	13
1965	—Boston	33	7	12	.583	3	9	.333	13	5	6	1	17
1966	—Boston	23	1	6	.167	0	0	. . .	10	2	2	0	2
1967	—Boston	22	1	2	.500	0	0	. . .	5	5	2	0	2
1968	—Boston	23	2	4	.500	0	0	. . .	9	8	5	0	4
1969	—Boston	28	1	4	.250	1	2	.500	6	3	1	0	3
Totals		343	51	111	.459	18	34	.529	139	39	37	1	120

HEAD COACHING RECORD

BACKGROUND: Player/head coach, Boston Celtics (1966-67 through 1968-69). . . . Head coach/general manager, Seattle Supersonics (1973-74 through 1976-77).

NBA COACHING RECORD

Season	Team	W	L	Pct.	Finish	W	L	Pct.
						— PLAYOFFS —		
		— REGULAR SEASON —						
66-67	—Boston	60	21	.741	2nd/Eastern Division	4	5	.444
67-68	—Boston	54	28	.659	2nd/Eastern Division	12	7	.632
68-69	—Boston	48	34	.585	4th/Eastern Division	12	6	.667
73-74	—Seattle	36	46	.439	3rd/Pacific Division	—	—	—
74-75	—Seattle	43	39	.524	2nd/Pacific Division	4	5	.444
75-76	—Seattle	43	39	.524	2nd/Pacific Division	2	4	.333
76-77	—Seattle	40	42	.488	4th/Pacific Division	—	—	—
87-88	—Sacramento	17	41	.293		—	—	—
Totals (8 years)		341	290	.540	Totals (5 years)	34	27	.557

NOTES:

1967— Defeated New York, 3-1, in Eastern Division semifinals; lost to Philadelphia, 4-1, in Eastern Division finals.
1968— Defeated Detroit, 4-2, in Eastern Division semifinals; defeated Philadelphia, 4-3, in Eastern Division finals; defeated Los Angeles, 4-2, in World Championship Series.
1969— Defeated Philadelphia, 4-1, in Eastern Division semifinals; defeated New York, 4-2, in Eastern Division finals; defeated Los Angeles, 4-3, in World Championship Series.
1975— Defeated Detroit, 2-1, in Western Conference first round; lost to Golden State, 4-2, in Western Conference semifinals.
1976— Lost to Phoenix in Western Conference semifinals.
1988— Replaced as Sacramento head coach by Jerry Reynolds (March 7).

SCHAYES, DOLPH
F/C

PERSONAL: Born May 19, 1928, in New York. . . . 6-8/220. . . . Full name: Adolph Schayes. . . . Father of Dan Schayes, center with Milwaukee Bucks.
HIGH SCHOOL: DeWitt Clinton (Bronx, N.Y.).
COLLEGE: New York University.
TRANSACTIONS/CAREER NOTES: Selected by Tri-Cities Hawks in 1948 National Basketball League Draft. . . . NBL draft rights obtained from Hawks by Syracuse Nationals (1948). . . . Nationals franchise became part of NBA upon merger

of Basketball Association of America and NBL for 1949-50. . . . Nationals franchise moved from Syracuse to Philadelphia and renamed 76ers for 1963-64.

CAREER HONORS: Elected to Naismith Memorial Basketball Hall of Fame (1972). . . . NBA 25th Anniversary All-Time Team (1970).

MISCELLANEOUS: Member of NBA championship team (1955).

COLLEGIATE RECORD

Season Team	G	Min.	FGM	FGA	Pct.	FTM	FTA	Pct.	Reb.	Pts.	Avg.
44-45 —New York University	11	...	46	...	...	23	...	...	...	115	10.5
45-46 —New York University	22	...	54	...	...	41	...	...	...	149	6.8
46-47 —New York University	21	...	66	...	...	63	...	...	...	195	9.3
47-48 —New York University	26	...	124	...	...	108	...	...	...	356	13.7
Totals	80	...	290	...	...	235	...	...	...	815	10.2

NBL AND NBA REGULAR-SEASON RECORD

HONORS: All-NBA first team (1952, 1953, 1954, 1955, 1957, 1958). . . . All-NBA second team (1950, 1951, 1956, 1959, 1960, 1961).

NOTES: Led NBA with 16.4 rebounds per game (1951).

Season Team	G	Min.	FGM	FGA	Pct.	FTM	FTA	Pct.	Reb.	Ast.	PF	Dq.	Pts.	Avg.
48-49 —Syracuse (NBL)	63	...	272	...	...	267	369	.724	...	...	232	...	811	12.9
49-50 —Syracuse	64	...	348	903	.385	376	486	.774	...	259	225	...	1072	16.8
50-51 —Syracuse	66	...	332	930	.357	457	608	.752	*1080	251	271	9	1121	17.0
51-52 —Syracuse	63	2004	263	740	.355	342	424	.807	773	182	213	5	868	13.8
52-53 —Syracuse	71	2668	375	1002	.374	512	619	.827	920	227	271	9	1262	17.8
53-54 —Syracuse	72	2655	370	973	.380	488	590	.827	870	214	232	4	1228	17.1
54-55 —Syracuse	72	2526	422	1103	.383	489	587	.833	887	213	247	6	1333	18.5
55-56 —Syracuse	72	2517	465	1202	.387	542	632	.858	891	200	251	9	1472	20.4
56-57 —Syracuse	72	*2851	496	1308	.379	*625	691	.904	1008	229	219	5	1617	22.5
57-58 —Syracuse	72	*2918	581	1458	.398	629	696	*.904	1022	224	244	6	1791	24.9
58-59 —Syracuse	72	2645	504	1304	.387	526	609	.864	962	178	280	9	1534	21.3
59-60 —Syracuse	75	2741	578	1440	.401	533	597	*.893	959	256	263	10	1689	22.5
60-61 —Syracuse	79	3007	594	1595	.372	*680	783	.868	960	296	296	9	1868	23.6
61-62 —Syracuse	56	1480	268	751	.357	286	319	*.897	439	120	167	4	822	14.7
62-63 —Syracuse	66	1438	223	575	.388	181	206	.879	375	175	177	2	627	9.5
63-64 —Philadelphia	24	350	44	143	.308	46	57	.807	110	48	76	3	134	5.6
Totals	1059	...	6135	...	...	6979	8273	.844	...	...	3664	...	19249	18.2

NBL AND NBA PLAYOFF RECORD

Season Team	G	Min.	FGM	FGA	Pct.	FTM	FTA	Pct.	Reb.	Ast.	PF	Dq.	Pts.	Avg.
48-49 —Syracuse (NBL)	6	...	27	...	...	32	42	.762	...	...	26	...	86	14.3
49-50 —Syracuse	11	...	57	148	.385	74	101	.733	...	28	43	...	188	17.1
50-51 —Syracuse	7	...	47	105	.448	49	64	.766	102	20	28	2	143	20.4
51-52 —Syracuse	7	248	41	91	.451	60	78	.769	90	15	34	2	142	20.3
52-53 —Syracuse	2	58	4	16	.250	10	13	.769	17	1	7	0	18	9.0
53-54 —Syracuse	13	374	64	140	.457	80	108	.741	136	24	40	1	208	16.0
54-55 —Syracuse	11	363	60	167	.359	89	106	.840	141	40	48	3	209	19.0
55-56 —Syracuse	8	310	52	142	.366	73	83	.880	111	27	27	0	177	22.1
56-57 —Syracuse	5	215	29	95	.305	49	55	.891	90	14	18	0	107	21.4
57-58 —Syracuse	3	131	25	64	.391	30	36	.833	45	6	10	0	80	26.7
58-59 —Syracuse	9	351	78	195	.400	98	107	.916	117	41	36	0	254	28.2
59-60 —Syracuse	3	126	30	66	.455	28	30	.933	48	8	10	0	88	29.3
60-61 —Syracuse	8	308	51	152	.336	63	70	.900	91	21	32	2	165	20.6
61-62 —Syracuse	5	95	24	66	.364	9	13	.692	35	5	21	0	57	11.4
62-63 —Syracuse	5	108	20	44	.455	11	12	.917	28	7	17	0	51	10.2
Totals	103	...	609	...	...	755	918	.822	...	...	397	...	1973	19.2

NBA ALL-STAR GAME RECORD

Season Team	Min.	FGM	FGA	Pct.	FTM	FTA	Pct.	Reb.	Ast.	PF	Dq.	Pts.
1951 —Syracuse	...	7	10	.700	1	2	.500	14	3	1	0	15
1952 —Syracuse					Did not play—injured.							
1953 —Syracuse	26	2	7	.286	4	4	1.000	13	3	3	0	8
1954 —Syracuse	24	1	3	.333	4	6	.667	12	1	1	0	6
1955 —Syracuse	29	6	12	.500	3	3	1.000	13	1	4	0	15
1956 —Syracuse	25	4	8	.500	6	10	.600	4	2	2	0	14
1957 —Syracuse	25	4	6	.667	1	1	1.000	10	1	1	0	9
1958 —Syracuse	39	6	15	.400	6	6	1.000	9	2	4	0	18
1959 —Syracuse	22	3	14	.214	7	8	.875	13	1	6	1	13
1960 —Syracuse	27	8	19	.421	3	3	1.000	10	0	3	0	19
1961 —Syracuse	27	7	15	.467	7	7	1.000	6	3	4	0	21
1962 —Syracuse	4	0	0	...	0	0	...	1	0	3	0	0
Totals	...	48	109	.440	42	50	.840	105	17	32	1	138

HEAD COACHING RECORD

BACKGROUND: Player/head coach, Philadelphia 76ers (1963-64).

HONORS: NBA Coach of the Year (1966).

NBA COACHING RECORD

Season Team	REGULAR SEASON				PLAYOFFS		
	W	L	Pct.	Finish	W	L	Pct.
63-64 —Philadelphia	34	46	.425	3rd/Eastern Division	2	3	.400
64-65 —Philadelphia	40	40	.500	3rd/Eastern Division	6	5	.545
65-66 —Philadelphia	55	25	.688	1st/Eastern Division	1	4	.200
70-71 —Buffalo	22	60	.268	4th/Atlantic Division	—	—	—
71-72 —Buffalo	0	1	.000		—	—	—
Totals (5 years)	151	172	.467	Totals (3 years)	9	12	.429

NOTES:
1964— Lost to Cincinnati in Eastern Division semifinals.
1965— Defeated Cincinnati, 3-1, in Eastern Division semifinals; lost to Boston, 4-3, in Eastern Division finals.
1966— Lost to Boston in Eastern Division finals.
1971— Replaced as Buffalo head coach by John McCarthy (October).

SHARMAN, BILL
G

PERSONAL: Born May 25, 1926, in Abilene, Tex. . . . 6-1/190. . . . Full name: William Walton Sharman.
HIGH SCHOOL: Narbonne (Lomita, Calif.), then Porterville (Calif.).
COLLEGE: Southern California.
TRANSACTIONS/CAREER NOTES: Selected by Washington Capitols in second round of 1950 NBA Draft. . . . Selected by Fort Wayne Pistons in 1951 NBA Dispersal Draft of Capitols franchise (did not report to Fort Wayne). . . . Traded by Pistons with Bob Brannum to Boston Celtics for NBA rights to Charlie Share (1951). . . . Signed as player/head coach by Los Angeles Jets of American Basketball League (1961).
CAREER HONORS: Elected to Naismith Memorial Basketball Hall of Fame (1975). . . . NBA 25th Anniversary All-Time Team (1970).
MISCELLANEOUS: Member of NBA championship teams (1957, 1959, 1960, 1961).

COLLEGIATE RECORD

NOTES: THE SPORTING NEWS All-America first team (1950). . . . THE SPORTING NEWS All-America third team (1949). . . . In military service during 1944-45 and 1945-46 seasons.

Season Team	G	Min.	FGM	FGA	Pct.	FTM	FTA	Pct.	Reb.	Pts.	Avg.
46-47 —Southern California	10	...	16	...	...	9	12	.750	...	41	4.1
47-48 —Southern California	24	...	100	...	...	38	44	.864	...	238	9.9
48-49 —Southern California	24	...	142	...	...	98	125	.784	...	382	15.9
49-50 —Southern California	24	...	171	421	.406	104	129	.806	...	446	18.6
Totals	82	...	429	...	...	249	310	.803	...	1107	13.5

NBA REGULAR-SEASON RECORD

HONORS: All-NBA first team (1956, 1957, 1958, 1959). . . . All-NBA second team (1953, 1955, 1960).

Season Team	G	Min.	FGM	FGA	Pct.	FTM	FTA	Pct.	Reb.	Ast.	PF	Dq.	Pts.	Avg.
50-51 —Washington	31	...	141	361	.391	96	108	.889	96	39	86	3	378	12.2
51-52 —Boston	63	1389	244	628	.389	183	213	.859	221	151	181	3	671	10.7
52-53 —Boston	71	2333	403	925	.436	341	401	*.850	288	191	240	7	1147	16.2
53-54 —Boston	72	2467	412	915	.450	331	392	*.844	255	229	211	4	1155	16.0
54-55 —Boston	68	2453	453	1062	.427	347	387	*.897	302	280	212	2	1253	18.4
55-56 —Boston	72	2698	538	1229	.438	358	413	*.867	259	339	197	1	1434	19.9
56-57 —Boston	67	2403	516	1241	.416	381	421	*.905	286	236	188	1	1413	21.1
57-58 —Boston	63	2214	550	1297	.424	302	338	.893	295	167	156	3	1402	22.3
58-59 —Boston	72	2382	562	1377	.408	342	367	*.932	292	179	173	1	1466	20.4
59-60 —Boston	71	1916	559	1225	.456	252	291	.866	262	144	154	2	1370	19.3
60-61 —Boston	61	1538	383	908	.422	210	228	*.921	223	146	127	0	976	16.0
Totals	711	...	4761	11168	.426	3143	3559	.883	2779	2101	1925	27	12665	17.8

NBA PLAYOFF RECORD

Season Team	G	Min.	FGM	FGA	Pct.	FTM	FTA	Pct.	Reb.	Ast.	PF	Dq.	Pts.	Avg.
51-52 —Boston	1	27	7	12	.583	1	1	1.000	3	7	4	0	15	15.0
52-53 —Boston	6	201	20	60	.333	30	32	.938	15	15	26	1	70	11.7
53-54 —Boston	6	206	35	81	.432	43	50	.860	25	10	29	2	113	18.8
54-55 —Boston	7	290	55	110	.500	35	38	.921	38	38	24	1	145	20.7
55-56 —Boston	3	119	18	46	.391	16	17	.941	7	12	7	0	52	17.3
56-57 —Boston	10	377	75	197	.381	61	64	.953	35	29	23	1	211	21.1
57-58 —Boston	11	406	90	221	.407	52	56	.929	54	25	28	0	232	21.1
58-59 —Boston	11	322	82	193	.425	57	59	.966	36	28	35	0	221	20.1
59-60 —Boston	13	364	88	209	.421	43	53	.811	45	20	22	1	219	16.8
60-61 —Boston	10	261	68	133	.511	32	36	.889	27	17	22	0	168	16.8
Totals	78	2573	538	1262	.426	370	406	.911	285	201	220	6	1446	18.5

NBA ALL-STAR GAME RECORD

NOTES: NBA All-Star Game Most Valuable Player (1955). . . . Holds single-game record for most field goals attempted in one quarter— 12 (1960).

Season Team	Min.	FGM	FGA	Pct.	FTM	FTA	Pct.	Reb.	Ast.	PF	Dq.	Pts.
1953 —Boston	26	5	8	.625	1	1	1.000	4	0	2	0	11
1954 —Boston	30	6	9	.667	2	4	.500	2	3	3	0	14
1955 —Boston	18	5	10	.500	5	5	1.000	4	2	4	0	15
1956 —Boston	24	2	8	.250	3	4	.750	7	2	6	1	7
1957 —Boston	23	5	17	.294	2	2	1.000	3	2	2	0	10
1958 —Boston	25	6	19	.316	3	3	1.000	4	3	2	0	15
1959 —Boston	24	3	12	.250	5	6	.833	2	0	1	0	11
1960 —Boston	26	8	21	.381	1	1	1.000	6	2	1	0	17
Totals	196	40	104	.385	22	26	.846	32	14	21	1	100

ABL REGULAR-SEASON RECORD

Season Team	G	Min.	FGM	FGA	Pct.	FTM	FTA	Pct.	Reb.	Ast.	Pts.	Avg.
61-62 —Los Angeles	19	346	35	80	.438	37	34	1.088	43	37	107	5.6

HEAD COACHING RECORD

BACKGROUND: Player/head coach, Los Angeles Jets of American Basketball League (1961-62).
HONORS: ABA co-Coach of the Year (1970). . . . NBA Coach of the Year (1972).

COLLEGIATE COACHING RECORD

Season	Team	W	L	Pct.	Finish
62-63	Cal State - Los Angeles	10	12	.455	4th/California Collegiate Athletic Association
63-64	Cal State - Los Angeles	17	8	.680	2nd/California Collegiate Athletic Association
	Totals (2 years)	27	20	.574	

ABL COACHING RECORD

Season	Team	REGULAR SEASON W	L	Pct.	Finish	PLAYOFFS W	L	Pct.
61-62	Los Angeles - Cleveland	43	26	.615		5	2	.714
	Totals (1 year)	43	26	.615		5	2	.714

NBA COACHING RECORD

Season	Team	REGULAR SEASON W	L	Pct.	Finish	PLAYOFFS W	L	Pct.
66-67	San Francisco	44	37	.543	1st/Western Division	9	6	.600
67-68	San Francisco	43	39	.524	3rd/Western Division	4	6	.400
71-72	Los Angeles	69	13	.841	1st/Pacific Division	12	3	.800
72-73	Los Angeles	60	22	.732	1st/Pacific Division	9	8	.529
73-74	Los Angeles	47	35	.573	1st/Pacific Division	1	4	.200
74-75	Los Angeles	30	52	.366	5th/Pacific Division	—	—	—
75-76	Los Angeles	40	42	.488	4th/Pacific Division	—	—	—
	Totals (7 years)	333	240	.581	Totals (5 years)	35	27	.565

ABA COACHING RECORD

Season	Team	REGULAR SEASON W	L	Pct.	Finish	PLAYOFFS W	L	Pct.
68-69	Los Angeles ABA	33	45	.423	5th/Western Division	—	—	—
69-70	Los Angeles ABA	43	41	.512	4th/Western Division	10	7	.588
70-71	Utah ABA	57	27	.679	2nd/Western Division	12	6	.667
	Totals (3 years)	133	113	.541	Totals (2 years)	22	13	.629

NOTES:

1962— Los Angeles Jets had 24-15 record when they folded after first half of season (January 10); Sharman then replaced John McLendon, who resigned as Cleveland Pipers head coach (January 28), and guided Pipers to ABL Championship.

1967— Defeated Los Angeles, 3-0, in Western Division semifinals; defeated St. Louis, 4-2, in Western Division finals; lost to Philadelphia, 4-2, in World Championship Series.

1968— Defeated St. Louis, 4-2, in Western Division semifinals; lost to Los Angeles, 4-0, in Western Division finals.

1970— Defeated Dallas, 4-2, in Western Division semifinals; defeated Denver, 4-1, in Western Division finals; lost to Indiana, 4-2, in ABA Finals.

1971— Defeated Texas, 4-0, in Western Division semifinals; defeated Indiana, 4-3, in Western Division finals; defeated Kentucky, 4-3, in ABA Finals.

1972— Defeated Chicago, 4-0, in Western Conference semifinals; defeated Milwaukee, 4-2, in Western Conference finals; defeated New York, 4-1, in World Championship Series.

1973— Defeated Chicago, 4-3, in Western Conference semifinals; defeated Golden State, 4-1, in Western Conference finals; lost to New York, 4-1, in World Championship Series.

1974— Lost to Milwaukee in Western Conference first round.

RECORD AS BASEBALL PLAYER

Year	Team (League)	Pos.	BATTING G	AB	R	H	2B	3B	HR	RBI	Avg.	SB	FIELDING PO	A	E	Avg.
1950	Elmira (East.)	OF	10	38	5	11	2	0	1	11	.289	0	17	0	1	.944
	Pueblo (Western)	OF	111	427	65	123	22	8	11	70	.288	11	214	16	10	.958
1951	Fort Worth (Texas)	OF	157	570	84	163	18	5	8	53	.286	23	254	11	2	.993
1952	St. Paul (Am. Assoc.)	OF	137	411	63	121	16	4	16	77	.294	2	215	15	3	.987
1953	Mobile (Southern Assoc.)	OF	90	228	21	48	8	1	5	17	.211	0	136	6	2	.986
1954						Out of Organized Baseball.										
1955	St. Paul (Am. Assoc.)	OF-3B	133	424	59	124	15	0	11	58	.292	3	183	100	11	.963

SIKMA, JACK
C/F

PERSONAL: Born November 14, 1955, in Kankakee, Ill. . . . 7-0/250. . . . Full name: Jack Wayne Sikma.
HIGH SCHOOL: St. Anne (Ill.).
COLLEGE: Illinois Wesleyan.
TRANSACTIONS/CAREER NOTES: Selected by Seattle SuperSonics in first round (eighth pick overall) of 1977 NBA Draft. . . . Traded by SuperSonics with 1987 and 1989 second-round draft choices to Milwaukee Bucks for Alton Lister and 1987 and 1989 first-round draft choices (July 1, 1986).
MISCELLANEOUS: Member of NBA championship team (1979).

COLLEGIATE RECORD

Season	Team	G	Min.	FGM	FGA	Pct.	FTM	FTA	Pct.	Reb.	Pts.	Avg.
73-74	Illinois Wesleyan	21	. . .	148	306	.484	28	37	.757	223	324	15.4
74-75	Illinois Wesleyan	30	. . .	265	537	.493	80	112	.714	415	610	20.3
75-76	Illinois Wesleyan	25	. . .	204	385	.530	93	126	.738	290	501	20.0
76-77	Illinois Wesleyan	31	. . .	302	324	.932	189	235	.804	477	837	27.0
	Totals	107	. . .	919	1552	.592	390	510	.765	1405	2272	21.2

NBA REGULAR-SEASON RECORD

HONORS: NBA All-Defensive second team (1982). . . . NBA All-Rookie team (1978).

Season	Team	G	Min.	FGM	FGA	Pct.	FTM	FTA	Pct.	REBOUNDS Off.	Def.	Tot.	Ast.	PF	Dq.	Stl.	Blk.	TO	Pts.	Avg.
77-78	Seattle	82	2238	342	752	.455	192	247	.777	196	482	678	134	300	6	68	40	186	876	10.7
78-79	Seattle	82	2958	476	1034	.460	329	404	.814	232	781	1013	261	295	4	82	67	253	1281	15.6

Season Team	G	Min.	FGM	FGA	Pct.	FTM	FTA	Pct.	Off.	Def.	Tot.	Ast.	PF	Dq.	Stl.	Blk.	TO	Pts.	Avg.
79-80 —Seattle.........	82	2793	470	989	.475	235	292	.805	198	710	908	279	232	5	68	77	202	1175	14.3
80-81 —Seattle.........	82	2920	595	1311	.454	340	413	.823	184	668	852	248	282	5	78	93	201	1530	18.7
81-82 —Seattle.........	82	3049	581	1212	.479	447	523	.855	223	*815	1038	277	268	5	102	107	213	1611	19.6
82-83 —Seattle.........	75	2564	484	1043	.464	400	478	.837	213	645	858	233	263	4	87	65	190	1368	18.2
83-84 —Seattle.........	82	2993	576	1155	.499	411	480	.856	225	*686	911	327	301	6	95	92	236	1563	19.1
84-85 —Seattle.........	68	2402	461	943	.489	335	393	.852	164	559	723	285	239	1	83	91	160	1259	18.5
85-86 —Seattle.........	80	2790	508	1100	.462	355	411	.864	146	602	748	301	293	4	92	73	214	1371	17.1
86-87 —Milwaukee ...	82	2536	390	842	.463	265	313	.847	208	614	822	203	328	14	88	90	160	1045	12.7
87-88 —Milwaukee ...	82	2923	514	1058	.486	321	348	*.922	195	514	709	279	316	11	93	80	157	1352	16.5
88-89 —Milwaukee ...	80	2587	360	835	.431	266	294	.905	141	482	623	289	300	6	85	61	145	1068	13.4
89-90 —Milwaukee ...	71	2250	344	827	.416	230	260	.885	109	383	492	229	244	5	76	48	139	986	13.9
90-91 —Milwaukee ...	77	1940	295	691	.427	166	197	.843	108	333	441	143	218	4	65	64	130	802	10.4
Totals	1107	36943	6396	13792	.464	4292	5053	.849	2542	8274	10816	3488	3879	80	1162	1048	2586	17287	15.6

Three-point field goals: 1979-80, 0-for-1. 1980-81, 0-for-5. 1981-82, 2-for-13 (.154). 1982-83, 0-for-8. 1983-84, 0-for-2. 1984-85, 2-for-10 (.200). 1985-86, 0-for-13. 1986-87, 0-for-2. 1987-88, 3-for-14 (.214). 1988-89, 82-for-216 (.380). 1989-90, 68-for-199 (.342). 1990-91, 46-for-135 (.341). Totals, 203-for-618 (.328).

NBA PLAYOFF RECORD

Season Team	G	Min.	FGM	FGA	Pct.	FTM	FTA	Pct.	Off.	Def.	Tot.	Ast.	PF	Dq.	Stl.	Blk.	TO	Pts.	Avg.
77-78 —Seattle.........	22	701	115	247	.466	71	91	.780	50	128	178	27	101	7	18	11	35	301	13.7
78-79 —Seattle.........	17	655	103	224	.460	48	61	.787	39	160	199	43	70	2	16	24	40	254	14.9
79-80 —Seattle.........	15	534	65	163	.399	46	54	.852	30	96	126	55	55	1	17	5	35	176	11.7
81-82 —Seattle.........	8	315	57	128	.445	50	58	.862	21	76	97	24	34	1	9	8	16	164	20.5
82-83 —Seattle.........	2	75	11	31	.355	8	12	.667	6	20	26	11	7	0	2	2	5	30	15.0
83-84 —Seattle.........	5	193	49	98	.500	12	14	.857	11	40	51	5	22	1	3	7	9	10	2.0
86-87 —Milwaukee ...	12	426	73	150	.487	48	49	.980	33	97	130	23	56	3	15	10	18	194	16.2
87-88 —Milwaukee ...	5	190	35	76	.461	25	30	.833	24	38	62	13	23	0	2	4	15	95	19.0
88-89 —Milwaukee ...	9	301	37	94	.394	23	28	.821	9	41	50	30	41	2	8	4	21	105	11.7
89-90 —Milwaukee ...	4	117	6	23	.261	6	8	.750	0	14	14	7	19	0	2	4	12	20	5.0
90-91 —Milwaukee ...	3	51	6	15	.400	1	2	.500	3	9	12	6	4	0	5	1	3	14	4.7
Totals	102	3558	557	1249	.446	338	407	.830	226	719	945	244	432	17	97	80	209	1363	13.4

Three-point field goals: 1979-80, 0-for-2. 1982-83, 0-for-1. 1983-84, 0-for-1. 1986-87, 0-for-1. 1987-88, 0-for-3. 1988-89, 8-for-28 (.286). 1989-90, 2-for-7 (.286). 1990-91, 1-for-2 (.500). Totals, 11-for-45 (.244).

NBA ALL-STAR GAME RECORD

Season Team	Min.	FGM	FGA	Pct.	FTM	FTA	Pct.	Off.	Def.	Tot.	Ast.	PF	Dq.	Stl.	Blk.	TO	Pts.
1979 —Seattle...............	18	4	5	.800	0	0	...	1	3	4	0	1	0	0	0	0	8
1980 —Seattle...............	28	4	10	.400	0	0	...	2	6	8	4	5	0	2	3	3	8
1981 —Seattle...............	21	2	5	.400	2	2	1.000	1	3	4	4	5	0	1	1	1	6
1982 —Seattle...............	21	5	11	.455	0	0	...	2	7	9	1	2	0	2	1	1	10
1983 —Seattle...............	17	4	6	.667	0	0	...	1	2	3	1	2	0	1	1	1	5
1984 —Seattle...............	30	5	12	.417	5	6	.833	5	7	12	1	4	0	3	0	0	15
1985 —Seattle...............	12	0	2	.000	0	0	...	0	2	2	0	1	0	0	1	1	0
Totals	147	24	51	.471	7	8	.875	12	30	42	11	20	0	9	7	7	52

Three-point field goals: 1980, 0-for-1. 1981, 0-for-1. 1983, 0-for-1. Totals, 0-for-3.

SILAS, PAUL

F/C

PERSONAL: Born July 12, 1943, in Prescott, Ariz.... 6-7/230.... Full name: Paul Theron Silas.
HIGH SCHOOL: McClymond (Oakland, Calif.).
COLLEGE: Creighton.

TRANSACTIONS/CAREER NOTES: Selected by St. Louis Hawks in second round (12th pick overall) of 1964 NBA Draft.... Played in Eastern Basketball League with Wilkes-Barre Barons (1965-66).... Hawks franchise moved from St. Louis to Atlanta for 1968-69 season.... Traded by Hawks to Phoenix Suns for Gary Gregor (May 8, 1969).... Traded by Suns to Boston Celtics (September 19, 1972) to complete deal in which Suns acquired draft rights to Charlie Scott (March 14, 1972).... Traded by Celtics to Denver Nuggets in three-way deal, in which Curtis Rowe was traded by Detroit Pistons to Celtics, and Ralph Simpson was traded by Nuggets to Pistons (October 20, 1976).... Traded by Nuggets with Willie Wise and Marvin Webster to Seattle SuperSonics for Tom Burleson, Bob Wilkerson and 1977 second-round draft choice (May 24, 1977).... Signed as veteran free agent by San Diego Clippers (May 21, 1980); SuperSonics received 1985 second-round draft choice as compensation.
MISCELLANEOUS: Member of NBA championship teams (1974, 1976, 1979).

COLLEGIATE RECORD

NOTES: Led NCAA Division I with 20.6 rebounds per game (1963).... Holds NCAA record for most rebounds in 3-year career—1,751.

Season Team	G	Min.	FGM	FGA	Pct.	FTM	FTA	Pct.	Reb.	Pts.	Avg.
60-61 —Creighton‡	21	...	225	...	...	96	119	.807	568	546	26.0
61-62 —Creighton	25	...	213	524	.406	125	215	.581	563	551	22.0
62-63 —Creighton	27	...	220	531	.414	133	228	.583	557	573	21.2
63-64 —Creighton	29	...	210	529	.397	117	194	.603	631	537	18.5
Varsity totals	81	...	643	1584	.406	375	637	.589	1751	1661	20.5

NBA REGULAR-SEASON RECORD

HONORS: NBA All-Defensive first team (1975, 1976).... NBA All-Defensive second team (1971, 1972, 1973).

Season Team	G	Min.	FGM	FGA	Pct.	FTM	FTA	Pct.	Reb.	Ast.	PF	Dq.	Pts.	Avg.
64-65 —St. Louis..........................	79	1243	140	375	.373	83	164	.506	576	48	161	1	363	4.6
65-66 —St. Louis..........................	46	586	70	173	.405	35	61	.574	236	22	72	0	175	3.8
66-67 —St. Louis..........................	77	1570	207	482	.429	113	213	.531	669	74	208	4	527	6.8

Season Team	G	Min.	FGM	FGA	Pct.	FTM	FTA	Pct.	Reb.	Ast.	PF	Dq.	Pts.	Avg.
67-68 —St. Louis..........	82	2652	399	871	.458	299	424	.705	958	162	243	4	1097	13.4
68-69 —Atlanta..........	79	1853	241	575	.419	204	333	.613	745	140	166	0	686	8.7
69-70 —Phoenix..........	78	2836	373	804	.464	250	412	.607	916	214	266	5	996	12.8
70-71 —Phoenix..........	81	2944	338	789	.428	285	416	.685	1015	247	227	3	961	11.9
71-72 —Phoenix..........	80	3082	485	1031	.470	433	560	.773	955	343	201	2	1403	17.5
72-73 —Boston..........	80	2618	400	851	.470	266	380	.700	1039	251	197	1	1066	13.3

Season Team	G	Min.	FGM	FGA	Pct.	FTM	FTA	Pct.	Off.	Def.	Tot.	Ast.	PF	Dq.	Stl.	Blk.	TO	Pts.	Avg.
									— REBOUNDS —										
73-74 —Boston	82	2599	340	772	.440	264	337	.783	334	581	915	186	246	3	63	20	...	944	11.5
74-75 —Boston	82	2661	312	749	.417	244	344	.709	348	677	1025	224	229	3	60	22	...	868	10.6
75-76 —Boston	81	2662	315	740	.426	236	333	.709	*365	660	1025	203	227	3	56	33	...	866	10.7
76-77 —Denver	81	1959	206	572	.360	170	255	.667	236	370	606	132	183	0	58	23	...	582	7.2
77-78 —Seattle........	82	2172	184	464	.397	109	186	.586	289	377	666	145	182	0	65	16	152	477	5.8
78-79 —Seattle........	82	1957	170	402	.423	116	194	.598	259	316	575	115	177	3	31	19	98	456	5.6
79-80 —Seattle........	82	1595	113	299	.378	89	136	.654	204	232	436	66	120	0	25	5	83	315	3.8
Totals	1254	34989	4293	9949	.432	3196	4748	.673	...	...	12357	2572	3105	32	358	138	333	11782	9.4

NBA PLAYOFF RECORD

Season Team	G	Min.	FGM	FGA	Pct.	FTM	FTA	Pct.	Reb.	Ast.	PF	Dq.	Pts.	Avg.
64-65 —St. Louis..........	4	42	4	10	.400	3	4	.750	18	1	6	0	11	2.8
65-66 —St. Louis..........	7	80	5	18	.278	8	11	.727	34	2	11	0	18	2.6
66-67 —St. Louis..........	8	122	9	36	.250	11	18	.611	52	6	17	0	29	3.6
67-68 —St. Louis..........	6	178	22	51	.431	27	38	.711	57	21	17	0	71	11.8
68-69 —Atlanta..........	11	258	21	58	.362	19	37	.514	92	21	32	0	61	5.5
69-70 —Phoenix..........	7	286	46	109	.422	21	32	.656	111	30	29	1	113	16.1
72-73 —Boston..........	13	512	47	120	.392	31	50	.620	196	39	39	0	125	9.6

Season Team	G	Min.	FGM	FGA	Pct.	FTM	FTA	Pct.	Off.	Def.	Tot.	Ast.	PF	Dq.	Stl.	Blk.	TO	Pts.	Avg.
									— REBOUNDS —										
73-74 —Boston	18	574	50	126	.397	44	53	.830	53	138	191	47	51	2	13	9	...	144	8.0
74-75 —Boston	11	405	42	92	.457	16	25	.640	46	84	130	40	45	1	12	2	...	100	9.1
75-76 —Boston	18	741	69	154	.448	56	69	.812	78	168	246	42	67	1	24	6	...	194	10.8
76-77 —Denver	6	141	14	33	.424	13	24	.542	16	24	40	16	23	1	2	4	...	41	6.8
77-78 —Seattle........	22	605	33	94	.351	41	60	.683	73	114	187	36	59	0	12	6	28	107	4.9
78-79 —Seattle........	17	418	21	54	.389	31	46	.674	40	58	98	19	44	1	9	5	34	73	4.3
79-80 —Seattle........	15	257	13	43	.302	11	13	.846	33	42	75	15	29	0	9	2	9	37	2.5
Totals	163	4619	396	998	.397	332	480	.692	...	...	1527	335	469	7	81	34	71	1124	6.9

NBA ALL-STAR GAME RECORD

Season Team	Min.	FGM	FGA	Pct.	FTM	FTA	Pct.	Reb.	Ast.	PF	Dq.	Pts.
1972 —Phoenix..........	15	0	6	.000	2	3	.667	9	1	1	0	2

Season Team	Min.	FGM	FGA	Pct.	FTM	FTA	Pct.	Off.	Def.	Tot.	Ast.	PF	Dq.	Stl.	Blk.	TO	Pts.
								— REBOUNDS —									
1975 —Boston..........	15	2	4	.500	2	2	1.000	0	2	2	2	0	4	0	...	6
Totals	30	2	10	.200	4	5	.800	...	...	11	3	3	0	4	0	...	8

EBL REGULAR-SEASON RECORD

Season Team	G	Min.	FGM	FGA	Pct.	FTM	FTA	Pct.	Reb.	Ast.	PF	Dq.	Pts.	Avg.
65-66 —Wilkes-Barre..........	5	...	25	...	...	13	21	.619	85	9	...	...	63	12.6

NBA COACHING RECORD

		REGULAR SEASON				PLAYOFFS		
Season Team	W	L	Pct.	Finish		W	L	Pct.
80-81 —San Diego..........	36	46	.439	5th/Pacific Division		—	—	—
81-82 —San Diego..........	17	65	.207	6th/Pacific Division		—	—	—
82-83 —San Diego..........	25	57	.305	6th/Pacific Division		—	—	—
Totals (3 years)	78	168	.317					

THEUS, REGGIE
G

PERSONAL: Born October 13, 1957, in Inglewood, Calif.... 6-7/213....
Full name: Reggie Wayne Theus.
HIGH SCHOOL: Inglewood (Calif.).
COLLEGE: UNLV.

TRANSACTIONS/CAREER NOTES: Selected as undergraduate by Chicago Bulls in first round (ninth pick overall) of 1978 NBA Draft.... Traded by Bulls to Kansas City Kings for Steve Johnson, 1984 second-round draft choice and two 1985 second-round draft choices (February 15, 1984).... Kings franchise moved from Kansas City to Sacramento for 1985-86 season.... Traded by Kings with 1988 third-round draft choice and future considerations to Atlanta Hawks for Randy Wittman and 1988 first-round draft choice (June 27, 1988).... Selected by Orlando Magic from Hawks in NBA expansion draft (June 15, 1989).... Traded by Magic to New Jersey Nets for 1993 and 1995 second-round draft choices (June 25, 1990).... Waived by Nets (August 15, 1991).

COLLEGIATE RECORD

Season Team	G	Min.	FGM	FGA	Pct.	FTM	FTA	Pct.	Reb.	Pts.	Avg.
75-76 —UNLV	31	...	68	163	.417	48	60	.800	53	184	5.9
76-77 —UNLV	32	...	178	358	.497	108	132	.818	145	464	14.5
77-78 —UNLV	28	...	181	389	.465	167	207	.807	191	529	18.9
Totals	91	...	427	910	.469	323	399	.810	389	1177	12.9

NBA REGULAR-SEASON RECORD

HONORS: NBA All-Rookie team (1979).

Season Team	G	Min.	FGM	FGA	Pct.	FTM	FTA	Pct.	Off.	Def.	Tot.	Ast.	PF	Dq.	Stl.	Blk.	TO	Pts.	Avg.
									— REBOUNDS —										
78-79 —Chicago........	82	2753	537	1119	.480	264	347	.761	92	136	228	429	270	2	93	18	303	1338	16.3
79-80 —Chicago........	82	3029	566	1172	.483	500	597	.838	143	186	329	515	262	4	114	20	348	1660	20.2

Season	Team	G	Min.	FGM	FGA	Pct.	FTM	FTA	Pct.	Off.	Def.	Tot.	Ast.	PF	Dq.	Stl.	Blk.	TO	Pts.	Avg.
										— REBOUNDS —										
80-81	Chicago	82	2820	543	1097	.495	445	550	.809	124	163	287	426	258	1	122	20	259	1549	18.9
81-82	Chicago	82	2838	560	1194	.469	363	449	.808	115	197	312	476	243	1	87	16	277	1508	18.4
82-83	Chicago	82	2856	749	1567	.478	434	542	.801	91	209	300	484	281	6	143	17	321	1953	23.8
83-84	Chi.-K.C.	61	1498	262	625	.419	214	281	.762	50	79	129	352	171	3	50	12	156	745	12.2
84-85	Kansas City	82	2543	501	1029	.487	334	387	.863	106	164	270	656	250	0	95	18	307	1341	16.4
85-86	Sacramento	82	2919	546	1137	.480	405	490	.827	73	231	304	788	231	3	112	20	327	1503	18.3
86-87	Sacramento	79	2872	577	1223	.472	429	495	.867	86	180	266	692	208	3	78	16	289	1600	20.3
87-88	Sacramento	73	2653	619	1318	.470	320	385	.831	72	160	232	463	173	0	59	16	234	1574	21.6
88-89	Atlanta	82	2517	497	1067	.466	285	335	.851	86	156	242	387	236	0	108	16	194	1296	15.8
89-90	Orlando	76	2350	517	1178	.439	378	443	.853	75	146	221	407	194	1	60	12	226	1438	18.9
90-91	New Jersey	81	2955	583	1247	.468	292	343	.851	69	160	229	378	231	0	85	35	252	1510	18.6
Totals		1026	34603	7057	14973	.471	4663	5644	.826	1182	2167	3349	6453	3008	24	1206	236	3493	19015	18.5

Three-point field goals: 1979-80, 28-for-105 (.267). 1980-81, 18-for-90 (.200). 1981-82, 25-for-100 (.250). 1982-83, 21-for-91 (.231). 1983-84, 7-for-42 (.167). 1984-85, 5-for-38 (.132). 1985-86, 6-for-35 (.171). 1986-87, 17-for-78 (.218). 1987-88, 16-for-59 (.271). 1988-89, 17-for-58 (.293). 1989-90, 26-for-105 (.248). 1990-91, 52-for-144 (.361). Totals, 238-for-945 (.252).

NBA PLAYOFF RECORD

Season	Team	G	Min.	FGM	FGA	Pct.	FTM	FTA	Pct.	Off.	Def.	Tot.	Ast.	PF	Dq.	Stl.	Blk.	TO	Pts.	Avg.
										— REBOUNDS —										
80-81	Chicago	6	232	40	90	.444	37	43	.860	7	14	21	38	22	0	9	0	15	119	19.8
83-84	Kansas City	3	81	17	43	.395	9	10	.900	4	7	11	16	9	0	5	0	9	43	14.3
85-86	Sacramento	3	102	18	46	.391	9	12	.750	3	5	8	19	9	0	3	2	14	45	15.0
88-89	Atlanta	5	127	14	38	.368	9	12	.750	3	4	7	24	18	1	1	0	10	37	7.4
Totals		17	542	89	217	.410	64	77	.831	17	30	47	97	58	1	18	2	48	244	14.4

Three-point field goals: 1980-81, 2-for-9 (.222). 1983-84, 0-for-3. 1985-86, 0-for-1. 1988-89, 0-for-2. Totals, 2-for-15 (.133).

NBA ALL-STAR GAME RECORD

Season	Team	Min.	FGM	FGA	Pct.	FTM	FTA	Pct.	Off.	Def.	Tot.	Ast.	PF	Dq.	Stl.	Blk.	TO	Pts.
									— REBOUNDS —									
1981	Chicago	19	4	7	.571	0	0	...	0	1	1	3	0	0	2	0	4	8
1983	Chicago	8	0	5	.000	0	0	...	1	0	1	1	1	0	0	0	0	0
Totals		27	4	12	.333	0	0	...	1	1	2	4	1	0	2	0	4	8

THURMOND, NATE

C/F

PERSONAL: Born July 25, 1941, in Akron, O. . . . 6-11/235. . . . Full name: Nathaniel Thurmond.

HIGH SCHOOL: Central Hower (Akron, O.).

COLLEGE: Bowling Green State.

TRANSACTIONS/CAREER NOTES: Selected by San Francisco Warriors in first round of 1963 NBA Draft. . . . Warriors franchise renamed Golden State Warriors for 1971-72 season. . . . Traded by Warrriors to Chicago Bulls for Clifford Ray, cash and 1975 first-round draft choice (September 3, 1974). . . . Traded by Bulls with Rowland Garrett to Cleveland Cavaliers for Steve Patterson and Eric Fernsten (November 27, 1975).

CAREER HONORS: Elected to Naismith Memorial Basketball Hall of Fame (1984).

COLLEGIATE RECORD

NOTES: Holds NCAA Tournament single-game record for most rebounds—31 (1963, vs. Mississippi State). . . . THE SPORTING NEWS All-America first team (1963).

Season	Team	G	Min.	FGM	FGA	Pct.	FTM	FTA	Pct.	Reb.	Pts.	Avg.
59-60	Bowling Green State‡	17	...	...	...	...	...	...	...	208	225	13.2
60-61	Bowling Green State	24	...	170	427	.398	87	129	.674	449	427	17.8
61-62	Bowling Green State	25	...	163	358	.455	67	113	.593	394	393	15.7
62-63	Bowling Green State	27	...	206	466	.442	124	197	.629	452	536	19.9
Varsity totals		76		539	1251	.431	278	439	.633	1295	1356	17.8

NBA REGULAR-SEASON RECORD

RECORDS: Holds single-game record for most rebounds in one quarter—18 (February 28, 1965, vs. Baltimore).

HONORS: NBA All-Defensive first team (1969, 1971). . . . NBA All-Defensive second team (1972, 1973, 1974). . . . NBA All-Rookie team (1964).

Season	Team	G	Min.	FGM	FGA	Pct.	FTM	FTA	Pct.	Reb.	Ast.	PF	Dq.	Pts.	Avg.
63-64	San Francisco	76	1966	219	554	.395	95	173	.549	790	86	184	2	533	7.0
64-65	San Francisco	77	3173	519	1240	.419	235	357	.658	1395	157	232	3	1273	16.5
65-66	San Francisco	73	2891	454	1119	.406	280	428	.654	1312	111	223	7	1188	16.3
66-67	San Francisco	65	2755	467	1068	.437	280	445	.629	1382	166	183	3	1214	18.7
67-68	San Francisco	51	2222	382	929	.411	282	438	.644	1121	215	137	1	1046	20.5
68-69	San Francisco	71	3208	571	1394	.410	382	621	.615	1402	253	171	0	1524	21.5
69-70	San Francisco	43	1919	341	824	.414	261	346	.754	762	150	110	1	943	21.9
70-71	San Francisco	82	3351	623	1401	.445	395	541	.730	1128	257	192	1	1641	20.0
71-72	Golden State	78	3362	628	1454	.432	417	561	.743	1252	230	214	1	1673	21.4
72-73	Golden State	79	3419	517	1159	.446	315	439	.718	1349	280	240	2	1349	17.1

Season	Team	G	Min.	FGM	FGA	Pct.	FTM	FTA	Pct.	Off.	Def.	Tot.	Ast.	PF	Dq.	Stl.	Blk.	TO	Pts.	Avg.
										— REBOUNDS —										
73-74	Golden State	62	2463	308	694	.444	191	287	.666	249	629	878	165	179	4	41	179	...	807	13.0
74-75	Chicago	80	2756	250	686	.364	132	224	.589	259	645	904	328	271	6	46	195	...	632	7.9
75-76	Chi.-Clev.	78	1393	142	337	.421	62	123	.504	115	300	415	94	160	1	22	98	...	346	4.4
76-77	Cleveland	49	997	100	246	.407	68	106	.642	121	253	374	83	128	2	16	81	...	268	5.5
Totals		964	35875	5521	13105	.421	3395	5089	.667	...	...	14464	2575	2624	34	125	553	...	14437	15.0

NBA PLAYOFF RECORD

Season	Team	G	Min.	FGM	FGA	Pct.	FTM	FTA	Pct.	Reb.	Ast.	PF	Dq.	Pts.	Avg.
63-64	San Francisco	12	410	42	98	.429	36	53	.679	148	12	46	0	120	10.0
66-67	San Francisco	15	690	93	215	.433	52	91	.571	346	47	52	1	238	15.9

Season Team	G	Min.	FGM	FGA	Pct.	FTM	FTA	Pct.	Reb.	Ast.	PF	Dq.	Pts.	Avg.
68-69 —San Francisco	6	263	40	102	.392	20	34	.588	117	28	18	0	100	16.7
70-71 —San Francisco	5	192	36	97	.371	16	20	.800	51	15	20	0	88	17.6
71-72 —Golden State	5	230	53	122	.434	21	28	.750	89	26	12	0	127	25.4
72-73 —Golden State	11	460	64	161	.398	32	40	.800	145	40	30	1	160	14.5

Season Team	G	Min.	FGM	FGA	Pct.	FTM	FTA	Pct.	— REBOUNDS — Off.	Def.	Tot.	Ast.	PF	Dq.	Stl.	Blk.	TO	Pts.	Avg.
74-75 —Chicago	13	254	14	38	.368	18	37	.486	24	63	87	31	36	0	5	21	...	46	3.5
75-76 —Cleveland	13	375	37	79	.468	13	32	.406	38	79	117	28	52	2	6	29	...	87	6.7
76-77 —Cleveland	1	1	0	0	...	0	0	...	0	1	1	0	0	0	0	1	...	0	0.0
Totals	81	2875	379	912	.416	208	335	.621	...	...	1101	227	266	4	11	51	...	966	11.9

NBA ALL-STAR GAME RECORD

Season Team	Min.	FGM	FGA	Pct.	FTM	FTA	Pct.	Reb.	Ast.	PF	Dq.	Pts.
1965 —San Francisco	10	0	2	.000	0	0	...	3	0	1	0	0
1966 —San Francisco	33	3	16	.188	1	3	.333	16	1	1	0	7
1967 —San Francisco	42	7	16	.438	2	4	.500	18	0	1	0	16
1968 —San Francisco	Selected, did not play—injured.											
1970 —San Francisco	Selected, did not play—injured.											
1973 —Golden State	14	2	5	.400	0	0	...	4	1	2	0	4

Season Team	Min.	FGM	FGA	Pct.	FTM	FTA	Pct.	— REBOUNDS — Off.	Def.	Tot.	Ast.	PF	Dq.	Stl.	Blk.	TO	Pts.
1974 —Golden State	5	2	4	.500	0	1	.000	1	2	3	0	0	0	0	0	...	4
Totals	104	14	43	.326	3	8	.375	...	...	44	2	5	0	0	0	...	31

TWYMAN, JACK
F/G

PERSONAL: Born May 11, 1934, in Pittsburgh. ... 6-6/210. ... Full name: John Kennedy Twyman.
HIGH SCHOOL: Pittsburgh Central Catholic.
COLLEGE: Cincinnati.
TRANSACTIONS/CAREER NOTES: Selected by Rochester Royals in second round (10th pick overall) of 1955 NBA Draft. ... Royals franchise moved from Rochester to Cincinnati for 1957-58 season.
CAREER HONORS: Elected to Naismith Memorial Basketball Hall of Fame (1982).

COLLEGIATE RECORD

Season Team	G	Min.	FGM	FGA	Pct.	FTM	FTA	Pct.	Reb.	Pts.	Avg.
51-52 —Cincinnati	16	...	27	83	.325	13	27	.481	55	67	4.2
52-53 —Cincinnati	24	716	136	323	.421	89	143	.622	362	361	15.0
53-54 —Cincinnati	21	777	174	443	.393	110	145	.759	347	458	21.8
54-55 —Cincinnati	29	1097	285	628	.454	142	192	.740	478	712	24.6
Totals	90	...	622	1477	.421	354	507	.698	1242	1598	17.8

NBA REGULAR-SEASON RECORD

HONORS: All-NBA second team (1960, 1962).

Season Team	G	Min.	FGM	FGA	Pct.	FTM	FTA	Pct.	Reb.	Ast.	PF	Dq.	Pts.	Avg.
55-56 —Rochester	72	2186	417	987	.422	204	298	.685	466	171	239	4	1038	14.4
56-57 —Rochester	72	2338	449	1023	.439	276	363	.760	354	123	251	4	1174	16.3
57-58 —Cincinnati	72	2178	465	1028	*.452	307	396	.775	464	110	224	3	1237	17.2
58-59 —Cincinnati	72	2713	710	*1691	.420	437	558	.783	653	209	277	6	1857	25.8
59-60 —Cincinnati	75	3023	870	2063	.422	*598	762	.785	664	260	275	10	2338	31.2
60-61 —Cincinnati	79	2920	796	1632	.488	405	554	.731	669	225	279	5	1997	25.3
61-62 —Cincinnati	80	2991	739	1542	.479	353	435	.811	638	323	315	5	1831	22.9
62-63 —Cincinnati	80	2523	641	1335	.480	304	375	.811	598	214	286	7	1586	19.8
63-64 —Cincinnati	68	2004	447	993	.450	189	228	.829	364	137	267	7	1083	15.9
64-65 —Cincinnati	80	2236	479	1081	.443	198	239	.828	383	137	239	4	1156	14.5
65-66 —Cincinnati	73	943	224	498	.450	95	117	.812	168	60	122	1	543	7.4
Totals	823	26055	6237	13873	.450	3366	4325	.778	5421	1969	2774	56	15840	19.2

NBA PLAYOFF RECORD

Season Team	G	Min.	FGM	FGA	Pct.	FTM	FTA	Pct.	Reb.	Ast.	PF	Dq.	Pts.	Avg.
57-58 —Cincinnati	2	74	15	45	.333	7	12	.583	22	1	6	0	37	18.5
61-62 —Cincinnati	4	149	34	78	.436	8	8	1.000	29	12	18	0	76	19.0
62-63 —Cincinnati	12	410	92	205	.449	65	77	.844	98	30	47	1	249	20.8
63-64 —Cincinnati	10	354	83	176	.472	29	49	.592	87	16	41	1	205	20.5
64-65 —Cincinnati	4	97	19	48	.396	11	11	1.000	17	3	16	0	49	12.3
65-66 —Cincinnati	2	11	2	4	.500	1	2	.500	2	0	3	0	5	2.5
Totals	34	1095	245	556	.441	121	159	.761	255	62	131	2	621	18.3

NBA ALL-STAR GAME RECORD

Season Team	Min.	FGM	FGA	Pct.	FTM	FTA	Pct.	Reb.	Ast.	PF	Dq.	Pts.
1957 —Rochester	17	1	8	.125	1	3	.333	0	1	1	0	3
1958 —Cincinnati	25	8	13	.615	2	2	1.000	3	0	3	0	18
1959 —Cincinnati	23	8	12	.667	2	4	.500	8	3	4	0	18
1960 —Cincinnati	28	11	17	.647	5	8	.625	5	1	4	0	27
1962 —Cincinnati	8	4	6	.667	3	3	1.000	1	2	0	0	11
1963 —Cincinnati	16	6	12	.500	0	0	...	4	1	2	0	12
Totals	117	38	68	.559	13	20	.650	21	8	14	0	89

WALKER, CHET
F/G

PERSONAL: Born February 22, 1940, in Benton Harbor, Mich. ... 6-7/220. ... Full name: Chester Walker. ... Nickname: The Jet.
HIGH SCHOOL: Benton Harbor (Mich.).
COLLEGE: Bradley.
TRANSACTIONS/CAREER NOTES: Selected by Syracuse Nationals in second round (14th pick overall) of 1962 NBA Draft. ... Nationals franchise moved from Syracuse to Philadelphia and renamed 76ers for

1963-64 season. . . . Traded by 76ers with Shaler Halimon to Chicago Bulls for Jim Washington and player to be named later (September 2, 1969).
MISCELLANEOUS: Member of NBA championship team (1967).

COLLEGIATE RECORD

NOTES: THE SPORTING NEWS All-America first team (1962). . . . THE SPORTING NEWS All-America second team (1961).

Season Team	G	Min.	FGM	FGA	Pct.	FTM	FTA	Pct.	Reb.	Pts.	Avg.
58-59 —Bradley‡	15	...	146	264	.553	56	93	.602	246	348	23.2
59-60 —Bradley	29	...	244	436	.560	144	234	.615	388	632	21.8
60-61 —Bradley	26	...	238	423	.563	180	250	.720	327	656	25.2
61-62 —Bradley	26	...	268	500	.536	151	236	.640	321	687	26.4
Varsity totals	81	...	750	1359	.552	475	720	.660	1036	1975	24.4

NBA REGULAR-SEASON RECORD

HONORS: NBA All-Rookie team (1963).

Season Team	G	Min.	FGM	FGA	Pct.	FTM	FTA	Pct.	Reb.	Ast.	PF	Dq.	Pts.	Avg.
62-63 —Syracuse	78	1992	352	751	.469	253	362	.699	561	83	220	3	957	12.3
63-64 —Philadelphia	76	2775	492	1118	.440	330	464	.711	784	124	232	3	1314	17.3
64-65 —Philadelphia	79	2187	377	936	.403	288	388	.742	528	132	200	2	1042	13.2
65-66 —Philadelphia	80	2603	443	982	.451	335	468	.716	636	201	238	3	1221	15.3
66-67 —Philadelphia	81	2691	561	1150	.488	445	581	.766	660	188	232	4	1567	19.3
67-68 —Philadelphia	82	2623	539	1172	.460	387	533	.726	607	157	252	3	1465	17.9
68-69 —Philadelphia	82	2753	554	1145	.484	369	459	.804	640	144	244	0	1477	18.0
69-70 —Chicago	78	2726	596	1249	.477	483	568	.850	604	192	203	1	1675	21.5
70-71 —Chicago	81	2927	650	1398	.465	480	559	*.859	588	179	187	2	1780	22.0
71-72 —Chicago	78	2588	619	1225	.505	481	568	.847	473	178	171	0	1719	22.0
72-73 —Chicago	79	2455	597	1248	.478	376	452	.832	395	179	166	1	1570	19.9

Season Team	G	Min.	FGM	FGA	Pct.	FTM	FTA	Pct.	Off.	Def.	Tot.	Ast.	PF	Dq.	Stl.	Blk.	TO	Pts.	Avg.
73-74 —Chicago	82	2661	572	1178	.486	439	502	.875	131	275	406	200	201	1	68	4	...	1583	19.3
74-75 —Chicago	76	2452	524	1076	.487	413	480	.860	114	318	432	169	181	0	49	6	...	1461	19.2
Totals	1032	33433	6876	14628	.470	5079	6384	.796	...	...	7314	2126	2727	23	117	10	...	18831	18.2

NBA PLAYOFF RECORD

Season Team	G	Min.	FGM	FGA	Pct.	FTM	FTA	Pct.	Reb.	Ast.	PF	Dq.	Pts.	Avg.
62-63 —Syracuse	5	130	27	53	.509	22	30	.733	47	9	8	0	76	15.2
63-64 —Philadelphia	5	190	30	77	.390	34	46	.739	52	13	15	0	94	18.8
64-65 —Philadelphia	11	469	83	173	.480	57	75	.760	79	18	38	0	223	20.3
65-66 —Philadelphia	5	181	24	64	.375	25	31	.806	37	15	18	0	73	14.6
66-67 —Philadelphia	15	551	115	246	.467	96	119	.807	114	32	44	0	326	21.7
67-68 —Philadelphia	13	485	86	210	.410	76	112	.679	96	24	44	1	248	19.1
68-69 —Philadelphia	4	109	23	43	.535	8	12	.667	23	8	5	0	54	13.5
69-70 —Chicago	5	178	35	83	.422	27	33	.818	42	11	14	0	97	19.4
70-71 —Chicago	7	234	44	100	.440	17	24	.708	50	22	20	0	105	15.0
71-72 —Chicago	4	97	16	38	.421	13	16	.813	14	4	7	0	45	11.3
72-73 —Chicago	7	229	42	121	.347	33	37	.892	62	14	15	0	117	16.7

Season Team	G	Min.	FGM	FGA	Pct.	FTM	FTA	Pct.	Off.	Def.	Tot.	Ast.	PF	Dq.	Stl.	Blk.	TO	Pts.	Avg.
73-74 —Chicago	11	403	81	159	.509	68	79	.861	26	35	61	18	26	0	10	1	...	230	20.9
74-75 —Chicago	13	432	81	164	.494	66	75	.880	10	50	60	24	32	2	13	1	...	228	17.5
Totals	105	3688	687	1531	.449	542	689	.787	...	...	737	212	286	3	23	2	...	1916	18.2

NBA ALL-STAR GAME RECORD

Season Team	Min.	FGM	FGA	Pct.	FTM	FTA	Pct.	Reb.	Ast.	PF	Dq.	Pts.
1964 —Philadelphia	12	2	5	.400	0	0	...	0	0	1	0	4
1966 —Philadelphia	25	3	10	.300	2	3	.667	6	4	2	0	8
1967 —Philadelphia	22	6	9	.667	3	4	.750	4	1	2	0	15
1970 —Chicago	17	1	3	.333	2	2	1.000	2	1	2	0	4
1971 —Chicago	19	3	9	.333	4	5	.800	3	1	1	0	10
1973 —Chicago	16	1	5	.200	2	2	1.000	1	0	2	0	4

Season Team	Min.	FGM	FGA	Pct.	FTM	FTA	Pct.	Off.	Def.	Tot.	Ast.	PF	Dq.	Stl.	Blk.	TO	Pts.
1974 —Chicago	14	4	5	.800	4	4	1.000	0	2	2	1	1	0	0	0	...	12
Totals	125	20	46	.435	17	20	.850	...	...	18	8	11	0	0	0	...	57

WALTON, BILL

C/F

PERSONAL: Born November 5, 1952, in La Mesa, Calif. . . . 6-11/235. . . . Full name: William Theodore Walton III. . . . Brother of Bruce Walton, offensive tackle/offensive guard/center with Dallas Cowboys (1973-75).
HIGH SCHOOL: Helix (La Mesa, Calif.).
COLLEGE: UCLA.
TRANSACTIONS/CAREER NOTES: Selected by Portland Trail Blazers in first round (first pick overall) of 1974 NBA Draft. . . . Signed as veteran free agent by San Diego Clippers (May 13, 1979); Trail Blazers received Kevin Kunnert, Kermit Washington, 1980 first-round draft choice and cash as compensation (September 18, 1979). . . . Clippers franchise moved from San Diego to Los Angeles for 1984-85 season. . . . Traded by Clippers to Boston Celtics for Cedric Maxwell, 1986 first-round draft choice and cash (September 6, 1985).
MISCELLANEOUS: Member of NBA championship teams (1977, 1986).

COLLEGIATE RECORD

NOTES: THE SPORTING NEWS College Player of the Year (1972, 1973, 1974). . . . THE SPORTING NEWS All-America first team (1972, 1973, 1974). . . . NCAA Division I Tournament Most Outstanding Player (1972, 1973). . . . Member of NCAA Division I championship teams (1972, 1973). . . . Holds NCAA tournament single-season record for highest field-goal percentage (minimum of 40 made)—76.3 percent, 45-of-59 (1973)....Holds NCAA tournament record for highest field-goal percentage in career (minimum of 60 made)—68.6 percent, 109-of-159 (1972 through 1974).

Season Team	G	Min.	FGM	FGA	Pct.	FTM	FTA	Pct.	Reb.	Pts.	Avg.
70-71—UCLA‡	20	...	155	266	.583	52	82	.634	321	362	18.1
71-72—UCLA	30	...	238	372	.640	157	223	.704	466	633	21.1
72-73—UCLA	30	...	277	426	.650	59	102	.578	506	612	20.4
73-74—UCLA	27	...	232	349	.665	58	100	.580	398	522	19.3
Varsity totals	87	...	747	1147	.651	274	425	.645	1370	1767	20.3

NBA REGULAR-SEASON RECORD

HONORS: NBA Most Valuable Player (1978)....NBA Sixth Man Award (1986)....All-NBA first team (1978)....All-NBA second team (1977)....NBA All-Defensive first team (1977, 1978).
NOTES: Led NBA with 14.4 rebounds per game (1977)....Led NBA with 3.25 blocked shots per game (1977).

Season Team	G	Min.	FGM	FGA	Pct.	FTM	FTA	Pct.	REBOUNDS Off.	Def.	Tot.	Ast.	PF	Dq.	Stl.	Blk.	TO	Pts.	Avg.
74-75—Portland	35	1153	177	345	.513	94	137	.686	92	349	441	167	115	4	29	94	...	448	12.8
75-76—Portland	51	1687	345	732	.471	133	228	.583	132	549	681	220	144	3	49	82	...	823	16.1
76-77—Portland	65	2264	491	930	.528	228	327	.697	211	723	934	245	174	5	66	211	...	1210	18.6
77-78—Portland	58	1929	460	882	.522	177	246	.720	118	648	766	291	145	3	60	146	206	1097	18.9
78-79—Portland								Did not play—injured.											
79-80—San Diego	14	337	81	161	.503	32	54	.593	28	98	126	34	37	0	8	38	37	194	13.9
80-81—San Diego								Did not play—injured.											
81-82—San Diego								Did not play—injured.											
82-83—San Diego	33	1099	200	379	.528	65	117	.556	75	248	323	120	113	0	34	119	105	465	14.1
83-84—San Diego	55	1476	288	518	.556	92	154	.597	132	345	477	183	153	1	45	88	177	668	12.1
84-85—L.A. Clippers	67	1647	269	516	.521	138	203	.680	168	432	600	156	184	0	50	140	174	676	10.1
85-86—Boston	80	1546	231	411	.562	144	202	.713	136	408	544	165	210	1	38	106	151	606	7.6
86-87—Boston	10	112	10	26	.385	8	15	.533	11	20	31	9	23	0	1	10	15	28	2.8
87-88—								Did not play—injured.											
Totals	468	13250	2552	4900	.521	1111	1683	.660	1103	3820	4923	1590	1298	17	380	1034	865	6215	13.3

Three-point field goals: 1983-84, 0-for-2. 1984-85, 0-for-2. Totals, 0-for-4.

NBA PLAYOFF RECORD

NOTES: NBA Finals Most Valuable Player (1977)....Holds NBA Finals single-game record for most defensive rebounds—20 (June 3, 1977, vs. Philadelphia; and June 5, 1977, vs. Philadelphia)....Shares NBA Finals single-game record for most blocked shots—8 (June 5, 1977, vs. Philadelphia)....Shares single-game record for most defensive rebounds—20 (June 3, 1977, vs. Philadelphia; and June 5, 1977, vs. Philadelphia).

Season Team	G	Min.	FGM	FGA	Pct.	FTM	FTA	Pct.	REBOUNDS Off.	Def.	Tot.	Ast.	PF	Dq.	Stl.	Blk.	TO	Pts.	Avg.
76-77—Portland	19	755	153	302	.507	39	57	.684	56	232	288	104	80	3	20	64	...	345	18.2
77-78—Portland	2	49	11	18	.611	5	7	.714	5	17	22	4	1	0	3	3	6	27	13.5
85-86—Boston	16	291	54	93	.581	19	23	.826	25	78	103	27	45	1	6	12	22	127	7.9
86-87—Boston	12	102	12	25	.480	5	14	.357	9	22	31	10	23	0	3	4	8	29	2.4
Totals	49	1197	230	438	.525	68	101	.673	95	349	444	145	149	4	32	83	36	528	10.8

Three-point field goals: 1985-86, 0-for-1.

NBA ALL-STAR GAME RECORD

Season Team	Min.	FGM	FGA	Pct.	FTM	FTA	Pct.	REBOUNDS Off.	Def.	Tot.	Ast.	PF	Dq.	Stl.	Blk.	TO	Pts.
1977—Portland							Selected, did not play—injured.										
1978—Portland	31	6	14	.429	3	3	1.000	2	8	10	2	3	0	3	2	4	15
Totals	31	6	14	.429	3	3	1.000	2	8	10	2	3	0	3	2	4	15

WEST, JERRY
G

PERSONAL: Born May 28, 1938, in Cheylan, W. Va....6-2/185....Full name: Jerry Alan West.
HIGH SCHOOL: East Bank (W. Va.).
COLLEGE: West Virginia.
TRANSACTIONS/CAREER NOTES: Selected by Minneapolis Lakers in first round (second pick overall) of 1960 NBA Draft....Lakers franchise moved from Minneapolis to Los Angeles for 1960-61 season.
CAREER HONORS: Elected to Naismith Memorial Basketball Hall of Fame (1979)....NBA 35th Anniversary All-Time team (1980).
MISCELLANEOUS: Member of NBA championship team (1972)....Member of gold-medal-winning U.S. Olympic team (1960).

COLLEGIATE RECORD

NOTES: THE SPORTING NEWS All-America first team (1959, 1960)....NCAA Tournament Most Outstanding Player (1959).

Season Team	G	Min.	FGM	FGA	Pct.	FTM	FTA	Pct.	Reb.	Pts.	Avg.
56-57—West Virginia‡	17	...	114	...	...	104	...	...	...	332	19.5
57-58—West Virginia	28	799	178	359	.496	142	194	.732	311	498	17.8
58-59—West Virginia	34	1210	340	656	.518	223	320	.697	419	903	26.6
59-60—West Virginia	31	1129	325	645	.504	258	337	.766	510	908	29.3
Varsity totals	93	3138	843	1660	.508	623	851	.732	1240	2309	24.8

NBA REGULAR-SEASON RECORD

RECORDS: Holds single-season record for most free throws made—840 (1966).
HONORS: All-NBA first team (1962, 1963, 1964, 1965, 1966, 1967, 1970, 1971, 1972, 1973)....All-NBA second team (1968, 1969)....NBA All-Defensive first team (1970, 1971, 1972, 1973)....NBA All-Defensive second team (1969).
NOTES: Led NBA with 9.7 assists per game (1972).

Season Team	G	Min.	FGM	FGA	Pct.	FTM	FTA	Pct.	Reb.	Ast.	PF	Dq.	Pts.	Avg.
60-61—Los Angeles	79	2797	529	1264	.419	331	497	.666	611	333	213	1	1389	17.6
61-62—Los Angeles	75	3087	799	1795	.445	712	926	.769	591	402	173	4	2310	30.8

Season	Team	G	Min.	FGM	FGA	Pct.	FTM	FTA	Pct.	Reb.	Ast.	PF	Dq.	Pts.	Avg.
62-63	Los Angeles	55	2163	559	1213	.461	371	477	.778	384	307	150	1	1489	27.1
63-64	Los Angeles	72	2906	740	1529	.484	584	702	.832	443	403	200	2	2064	28.7
64-65	Los Angeles	74	3066	822	1655	.497	648	789	.821	447	364	221	2	2292	31.0
65-66	Los Angeles	79	3218	818	1731	.473	*840	*977	.860	562	480	243	1	2476	31.3
66-67	Los Angeles	66	2670	645	1389	.464	602	686	.878	392	447	160	1	1892	28.7
67-68	Los Angeles	51	1919	476	926	.514	391	482	.811	294	310	152	1	1343	26.3
68-69	Los Angeles	61	2394	545	1156	.471	490	597	.821	262	423	156	1	1580	25.9
69-70	Los Angeles	74	3106	831	1673	.497	*647	*785	.824	338	554	160	3	2309	*31.2
70-71	Los Angeles	69	2845	667	1351	.494	525	631	.832	320	655	180	0	1859	26.9
71-72	Los Angeles	77	2973	735	1540	.477	515	633	.814	327	747	209	0	1985	25.8
72-73	Los Angeles	69	2460	618	1291	.479	339	421	.805	289	607	138	0	1575	22.8

Season	Team	G	Min.	FGM	FGA	Pct.	FTM	FTA	Pct.	Off.	Def.	Tot.	Ast.	PF	Dq.	Stl.	Blk.	TO	Pts.	Avg.
										— REBOUNDS —										
73-74	Los Angeles	31	967	232	519	.447	165	198	.833	30	86	116	206	80	0	81	23	...	629	20.3
Totals		932	36571	9016	19032	.474	7160	8801	.814	...	...	5376	6238	2435	17	81	23	...	25192	27.0

NBA PLAYOFF RECORD

NOTES: NBA Finals Most Valuable Player (1969).... Holds career record for most free throws made—1,213.... Holds single-series record for highest points-per-game average—46.3 (1965).

Season	Team	G	Min.	FGM	FGA	Pct.	FTM	FTA	Pct.	Reb.	Ast.	PF	Dq.	Pts.	Avg.
60-61	Los Angeles	12	461	99	202	.490	77	106	.726	104	63	39	0	275	22.9
61-62	Los Angeles	13	557	144	310	.465	121	150	.807	88	57	38	0	409	31.5
62-63	Los Angeles	13	538	144	286	.504	74	100	.740	106	61	34	0	362	27.8
63-64	Los Angeles	5	206	57	115	.496	42	53	.792	36	17	20	0	156	31.2
64-65	Los Angeles	11	470	155	351	.442	137	155	.884	63	58	37	0	447	40.6
65-66	Los Angeles	14	619	185	357	.518	109	125	.872	88	79	40	0	479	34.2
66-67	Los Angeles	1	1	0	0	...	0	0	...	1	0	0	0	0	0.0
67-68	Los Angeles	15	622	165	313	.527	132	169	.781	81	82	47	0	462	30.8
68-69	Los Angeles	18	757	196	423	.463	164	204	.804	71	135	52	1	556	30.9
69-70	Los Angeles	18	830	196	418	.469	170	212	.802	66	151	55	1	562	31.2
71-72	Los Angeles	15	608	128	340	.376	88	106	.830	73	134	39	0	344	22.9
72-73	Los Angeles	17	638	151	336	.449	99	127	.780	76	132	49	1	401	23.6

Season	Team	G	Min.	FGM	FGA	Pct.	FTM	FTA	Pct.	Off.	Def.	Tot.	Ast.	PF	Dq.	Stl.	Blk.	TO	Pts.	Avg.
										— REBOUNDS —										
73-74	Los Angeles	1	14	2	9	.222	0	0	...	0	2	2	1	1	0	0	0	...	4	4.0
Totals		153	6321	1622	3460	.469	1213	1507	.805	...	...	855	970	451	3	0	0	...	4457	29.1

NBA ALL-STAR GAME RECORD

NOTES: NBA All-Star Game Most Valuable Player (1972).

Season	Team	Min.	FGM	FGA	Pct.	FTM	FTA	Pct.	Reb.	Ast.	PF	Dq.	Pts.
1961	Los Angeles	25	2	8	.250	5	6	.833	2	4	3	0	9
1962	Los Angeles	31	7	14	.500	4	6	.667	3	1	2	0	18
1963	Los Angeles	32	5	15	.333	3	4	.750	7	5	1	0	13
1964	Los Angeles	42	8	20	.400	1	1	1.000	4	5	3	0	17
1965	Los Angeles	40	8	16	.500	4	6	.667	5	6	2	0	20
1966	Los Angeles	11	1	5	.200	2	2	1.000	1	0	2	0	4
1967	Los Angeles	30	6	11	.545	4	4	1.000	3	6	3	0	16
1968	Los Angeles	32	7	17	.412	3	4	.750	6	6	4	0	17
1969						Selected, did not play—injured.							
1970	Los Angeles	31	7	12	.583	8	12	.667	5	5	3	0	22
1971	Los Angeles	20	2	4	.500	1	3	.333	1	9	1	0	5
1972	Los Angeles	27	6	9	.667	1	2	.500	4	5	2	0	13
1973	Los Angeles	20	3	6	.500	0	0	...	4	3	2	0	6
1974						Selected, did not play—injured.							
Totals		341	62	137	.453	36	50	.720	47	55	28	0	160

NBA COACHING RECORD

		REGULAR SEASON				PLAYOFFS		
Season	Team	W	L	Pct.	Finish	W	L	Pct.
76-77	Los Angeles	53	29	.646	1st/Pacific Division	4	7	.364
77-78	Los Angeles	45	37	.549	4th/Pacific Division	1	2	.333
78-79	Los Angeles	47	35	.573	3rd/Pacific Division	3	5	.375
Totals (3 years)		145	101	.589	Totals (3 years)	8	14	.364

NOTES:

1977— Defeated Golden State, 4-3, in Western Conference semifinals; lost to Portland, 4-0, in Western Conference finals.
1978— Lost to Seattle in Western Conference first round.
1979— Defeated Denver, 2-1, in Western Conference first round; lost to Seattle, 4-1, in Western Conference semifinals.

WHITE, JO JO

G

PERSONAL: Born November 16, 1946, in St. Louis. ... 6-3/190. ... Full name: Joseph Henry White.

HIGH SCHOOL: Vashon (St. Louis), then McKinley (St. Louis).

COLLEGE: Kansas.

TRANSACTIONS/CAREER NOTES: Selected by Boston Celtics in first round (ninth pick overall) of 1969 NBA Draft. ... Traded by Celtics to Golden State Warriors for 1979 first-round draft choice (January 30, 1979).... Sold by Warriors to Kansas City Kings (September 10, 1980).... Played in Continental Basketball Association with Topeka Sizzlers (1987-88).

MISCELLANEOUS: Member of NBA championship teams (1974, 1976).... Member of gold-medal-winning U.S. Olympic team (1968).

COLLEGIATE RECORD

NOTES: THE SPORTING NEWS All-America first team (1968, 1969).

Season Team	G	Min.	FGM	FGA	Pct.	FTM	FTA	Pct.	Reb.	Pts.	Avg.
64-65—Kansas†	2	...	11	34	.324	11	15	.733	25	33	16.5
65-66—Kansas†	6	...	35	88	.398	18	27	.667	32	88	14.7
65-66—Kansas	9	...	44	112	.393	14	26	.538	68	102	11.3
66-67—Kansas	27	...	170	416	.409	59	72	.819	150	399	14.8
67-68—Kansas	30	...	188	462	.407	83	115	.722	107	459	15.3
68-69—Kansas	18	...	134	286	.469	58	79	.734	84	326	18.1
Varsity totals	84	...	536	1276	.420	214	292	.733	409	1286	15.3

NBA REGULAR-SEASON RECORD

HONORS: All-NBA second team (1975, 1977).... NBA All-Rookie team (1970).

Season Team	G	Min.	FGM	FGA	Pct.	FTM	FTA	Pct.	Reb.	Ast.	PF	Dq.	Pts.	Avg.
69-70—Boston	60	1328	309	684	.452	111	135	.822	169	145	132	1	729	12.2
70-71—Boston	75	2787	693	1494	.464	215	269	.799	376	361	255	5	1601	21.3
71-72—Boston	79	3261	770	1788	.431	285	343	.831	446	416	227	1	1825	23.1
72-73—Boston	82	3250	717	1665	.431	178	228	.781	414	498	185	2	1612	19.7

Season Team	G	Min.	FGM	FGA	Pct.	FTM	FTA	Pct.	REBOUNDS Off.	Def.	Tot.	Ast.	PF	Dq.	Stl.	Blk.	TO	Pts.	Avg.
73-74—Boston	82	3238	649	1445	.449	190	227	.837	100	251	351	448	185	1	105	25	...	1488	18.1
74-75—Boston	82	3220	658	1440	.457	186	223	.834	84	227	311	458	207	1	128	17	...	1502	18.3
75-76—Boston	82	3257	670	1492	.449	212	253	.838	61	252	313	445	183	2	107	20	...	1552	18.9
76-77—Boston	82	3333	638	1488	.429	333	383	.869	87	296	383	492	193	5	118	22	...	1609	19.6
77-78—Boston	46	1641	289	690	.419	103	120	.858	53	127	180	209	109	2	49	7	117	681	14.8
78-79—Boston-G.S.	76	2338	404	910	.444	139	158	.880	42	158	200	347	173	1	80	7	212	947	12.5
79-80—Golden State	78	2052	336	706	.476	97	114	.851	42	139	181	239	186	0	88	13	157	770	9.9
80-81—Kansas City	13	236	36	82	.439	11	18	.611	3	18	21	37	21	0	11	1	18	83	6.4
Totals	837	29941	6169	13884	.444	2060	2471	.834	...	...	3345	4095	2056	21	686	112	504	14399	17.2

Three-point field goals: 1979-80, 1-for-6 (.167).

NBA PLAYOFF RECORD

NOTES: NBA Finals Most Valuable Player (1976).

Season Team	G	Min.	FGM	FGA	Pct.	FTM	FTA	Pct.	Reb.	Ast.	PF	Dq.	Pts.	Avg.
71-72—Boston	11	432	109	220	.495	40	48	.833	59	58	31	0	258	23.5
72-73—Boston	13	583	135	300	.450	49	54	.907	54	83	44	2	319	24.5

Season Team	G	Min.	FGM	FGA	Pct.	FTM	FTA	Pct.	REBOUNDS Off.	Def.	Tot.	Ast.	PF	Dq.	Stl.	Blk.	TO	Pts.	Avg.
73-74—Boston	18	765	132	310	.426	34	46	.739	17	58	75	98	56	1	15	2	...	298	16.6
74-75—Boston	11	462	100	227	.441	27	33	.818	18	32	50	63	32	0	11	4	...	227	20.6
75-76—Boston	18	791	165	371	.445	78	95	.821	12	59	71	98	51	0	23	1	...	408	22.7
76-77—Boston	9	395	91	201	.453	28	33	.848	10	29	39	52	27	0	14	0	...	210	23.3
Totals	80	3428	732	1629	.449	256	309	.828	...	...	348	452	241	3	63	7	...	1720	21.5

NBA ALL-STAR GAME RECORD

Season Team	Min.	FGM	FGA	Pct.	FTM	FTA	Pct.	Reb.	Ast.	PF	Dq.	Pts.
1971—Boston	22	5	10	.500	0	0	...	9	2	2	0	10
1972—Boston	18	6	15	.400	0	2	.000	4	3	1	0	12
1973—Boston	18	3	7	.429	0	0	...	5	5	0	0	6

Season Team	Min.	FGM	FGA	Pct.	FTM	FTA	Pct.	REBOUNDS Off.	Def.	Tot.	Ast.	PF	Dq.	Stl.	Blk.	TO	Pts.
1974—Boston	22	6	12	.500	1	3	.333	2	4	6	4	1	0	2	1	...	13
1975—Boston	13	1	2	.500	5	6	.833	0	1	1	4	1	0	0	0	...	7
1976—Boston	16	3	7	.429	0	0	...	0	1	1	1	1	0	2	0	...	6
1977—Boston	15	5	7	.714	0	0	...	0	1	1	2	0	0	0	0	...	10
Totals	124	29	60	.483	6	11	.545	...	...	27	21	6	0	4	1	...	64

CBA REGULAR-SEASON RECORD

Season Team	G	Min.	2-POINT FGM	FGA	Pct.	3-POINT FGM	FGA	Pct.	FTM	FTA	Pct.	Reb.	Ast.	Pts.	Avg.
87-88—Topeka	5	122	12	27	.444	0	3	.000	4	6	.667	6	21	28	5.6

YARDLEY, GEORGE
F

PERSONAL: Born November 23, 1928, in Hollywood, Calif.... 6-5/195.... Full name: George Harry Yardley III.
HIGH SCHOOL: Balboa (San Francisco).
COLLEGE: Stanford.

TRANSACTIONS/CAREER NOTES: Selected by Fort Wayne Pistons in first round of 1950 NBA Draft.... Played with the San Francisco Stewart Chevrolets in the National Industrial Basketball League, an Amateur Athletic Union League, during 1950-51 season (finished third in the league in scoring with a 13.1 point average on 104 field goals and 53 free throws for 261 points in 20 games).... In military service during 1951-52 and 1952-53 seasons.... Signed by Pistons (1953).... Pistons franchise moved from Fort Wayne to Detroit for 1957-58 season.... Traded by Pistons to Syracuse Nationals for Ed Conlin (February 13, 1959).... Played in American Basketball League with Los Angeles Jets (1961-62).

COLLEGIATE RECORD

Season Team	G	Min.	FGM	FGA	Pct.	FTM	FTA	Pct.	Reb.	Pts.	Avg.
46-47—Stanford†				Freshman team statistics unavailable.							
47-48—Stanford	18	...	22	...	...	8	20	.400	...	52	2.9
48-49—Stanford	28	...	126	377	.334	93	131	.710	...	345	12.3
49-50—Stanford	25	...	164	452	.363	95	130	.731	...	423	16.9
Varsity totals	71	...	312	...	...	196	281	.698	...	820	11.5

NBA REGULAR-SEASON RECORD

HONORS: All-NBA first team (1958).... All-NBA second team (1957).

Season	Team	G	Min.	FGM	FGA	Pct.	FTM	FTA	Pct.	Reb.	Ast.	PF	Dq.	Pts.	Avg.
53-54	—Fort Wayne	63	1489	209	492	.425	146	205	.712	407	99	166	3	564	9.0
54-55	—Fort Wayne	60	2150	363	869	.418	310	416	.745	594	126	205	7	1036	17.3
55-56	—Fort Wayne	71	2353	434	1067	.407	365	492	.742	686	159	212	2	1233	17.4
56-57	—Fort Wayne	72	2691	522	1273	.410	503	639	.787	755	147	231	2	1547	21.5
57-58	—Detroit	72	2843	673	*1624	.414	*655	*808	.811	768	97	226	3	*2001	*27.8
58-59	—Detroit-Syracuse	61	1839	446	1042	.428	317	407	.779	431	65	159	2	1209	19.8
59-60	—Syracuse	73	2390	549	1214	.452	377	462	.816	570	123	227	3	1475	20.2
	Totals	472	15755	3196	7581	.422	2673	3429	.780	4211	816	1426	22	9065	19.2

NBA PLAYOFF RECORD

Season	Team	G	Min.	FGM	FGA	Pct.	FTM	FTA	Pct.	Reb.	Ast.	PF	Dq.	Pts.	Avg.
53-54	—Fort Wayne	4	107	16	33	.485	10	12	.833	24	3	10	0	42	10.5
54-55	—Fort Wayne	11	420	57	143	.399	60	79	.759	99	36	37	2	174	15.8
55-56	—Fort Wayne	10	406	77	183	.421	76	98	.776	139	26	25	0	230	23.0
56-57	—Fort Wayne	2	85	24	53	.453	9	11	.818	19	8	7	0	57	28.5
57-58	—Detroit	7	254	52	127	.409	60	67	.896	72	17	26	0	164	23.4
58-59	—Syracuse	9	333	83	189	.439	60	70	.857	87	21	29	0	226	25.1
59-60	—Syracuse	3	88	15	39	.385	10	12	.833	17	1	9	0	40	13.3
	Totals	46	1693	324	767	.422	285	349	.817	457	112	143	2	933	20.3

NBA ALL-STAR GAME RECORD

Season	Team	Min.	FGM	FGA	Pct.	FTM	FTA	Pct.	Reb.	Ast.	PF	Dq.	Pts.
1955	—Fort Wayne	22	4	11	.364	3	4	.750	4	2	2	0	11
1956	—Fort Wayne	19	3	7	.429	2	3	.667	6	1	1	0	8
1957	—Fort Wayne	25	4	10	.400	1	1	1.000	9	0	2	0	9
1958	—Detroit	32	8	15	.533	3	5	.600	9	1	1	0	19
1959	—Detroit	17	2	8	.250	2	2	1.000	4	0	3	0	6
1960	—Syracuse	16	5	9	.556	1	2	.500	3	0	4	0	11
	Totals	131	26	60	.433	12	17	.706	35	4	13	0	64

ABL REGULAR-SEASON RECORD

Season	Team	G	Min.	FGM	FGA	Pct.	FTM	FTA	Pct.	Reb.	Ast.	Pts.	Avg.
61-62	—Los Angeles	25	948	159	378	.421	148	122	1.213	172	65	482	19.3

ZASLOFSKY, MAX

G/F

PERSONAL: Born December 7, 1925, in Brooklyn, N.Y.... Died October 15, 1985.... 6-2/170.
HIGH SCHOOL: Thomas Jefferson (Brooklyn, N.Y.).
COLLEGE: St. John's.
TRANSACTIONS/CAREER NOTES: Signed as free agent by Chicago Stags of Basketball Association of America (1946).... Stags franchise became part of NBA upon merger of BAA and National Basketball League for 1949-50 season.... Name drawn out of hat by New York Knicks for $15,000 in dispersal of Stags franchise (1950).... Traded by Knicks to Baltimore Bullets for Jim Baechtold (1953).... Traded by Bullets to Milwaukee Hawks (November 1953). ... Traded by Hawks to Fort Wayne Pistons (December 1953).

COLLEGIATE RECORD

NOTES: Played only one year of college basketball; in military service during 1944-45 season.

Season	Team	G	Min.	FGM	FGA	Pct.	FTM	FTA	Pct.	Reb.	Pts.	Avg.
45-46	—St. John's	18	...		59	...	22	38	.579	...	140	7.8

NBA REGULAR-SEASON RECORD

HONORS: All-NBA first team (1950).... All-BAA first team (1947, 1948, 1949).

Season	Team	G	Min.	FGM	FGA	Pct.	FTM	FTA	Pct.	Reb.	Ast.	PF	Dq.	Pts.	Avg.
46-47	—Chicago (BAA)	61	...	336	1020	.329	205	278	.737	...	40	121	...	877	14.4
47-48	—Chicago (BAA)	48	...	*373	1156	.323	261	333	.784	...	29	125	...	*1007	*21.0
48-49	—Chicago (BAA)	58	...	425	1216	.350	347	413	.840	...	149	156	...	1197	20.6
49-50	—Chicago	68	...	397	1132	.351	321	381	*.843	...	155	185	...	1115	16.4
50-51	—New York	66	...	302	853	.354	231	298	.775	228	136	150	...	835	12.7
51-52	—New York	66	...	322	958	.336	287	380	.755	194	156	183	...	931	14.1
52-53	—New York	29	...	123	320	.384	98	142	.690	75	55	81	...	344	11.9
53-54	—Balt.-Mil.-Fort Wayne	65	...	278	756	.368	255	357	.714	160	154	142	...	811	12.5
54-55	—Fort Wayne	70	...	269	821	.328	247	352	.702	191	203	130	...	785	11.2
55-56	—Fort Wayne	9	...	29	81	.358	30	35	.857	16	16	18	...	88	9.8
	Totals	540	...	2854	8313	.343	2282	2969	.769	...	1093	1291	...	7990	14.8

NBA PLAYOFF RECORD

Season	Team	G	Min.	FGM	FGA	Pct.	FTM	FTA	Pct.	Reb.	Ast.	PF	Dq.	Pts.	Avg.
46-47	—Chicago (BAA)	11	...	60	199	.302	29	44	.659	...	4	26	...	149	13.5
47-48	—Chicago (BAA)	5	...	30	88	.341	37	47	.787	...	0	17	...	97	19.4
48-49	—Chicago (BAA)	2	...	15	49	.306	14	18	.778	...	6	3	...	44	22.0
49-50	—Chicago	2	...	15	32	.469	15	18	.833	...	6	7	...	45	22.5
50-51	—New York	14	...	88	217	.406	74	100	.740	58	38	43	...	250	17.9
51-52	—New York	14	...	69	185	.373	89	110	.809	44	23	51	...	227	16.2
53-54	—Fort Wayne	4	...	11	36	.306	13	15	.867	3	6	7	...	35	8.8
54-55	—Fort Wayne	11	...	18	44	.409	16	20	.800	16	18	20	...	52	4.7
	Totals	63	...	306	850	.360	287	372	.772	...	101	174	...	899	14.3

NBA ALL-STAR GAME RECORD

Season	Team	Min.	FGM	FGA	Pct.	FTM	FTA	Pct.	Reb.	Ast.	PF	Dq.	Pts.
1952	—New York	...	3	7	.429	5	5	1.000	4	2	0	0	11

ABA COACHING RECORD

Season	Team	W	L	Pct.	REGULAR SEASON Finish	PLAYOFFS W	L	Pct.
67-68 — New Jersey		36	42	.462	T4th/Eastern Division	—	—	—
68-69 — New York		17	61	.218	5th/Eastern Division	—	—	—
Totals (2 years)		53	103	.340				

ALL-TIME GREAT COACHES

ATTLES, AL

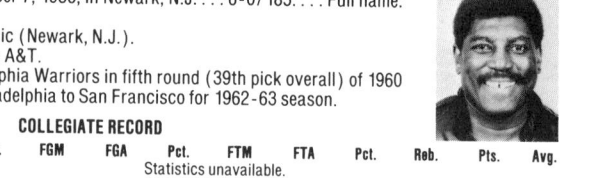

PERSONAL: Born November 7, 1936, in Newark, N.J. . . . 6-0/185. . . . Full name: Alvin A. Attles.
HIGH SCHOOL: Weequachic (Newark, N.J.).
COLLEGE: North Carolina A&T.
TRANSACTIONS/CAREER NOTES: Selected by Philadelphia Warriors in fifth round (39th pick overall) of 1960 NBA Draft. . . . Warriors franchise moved from Philadelphia to San Francisco for 1962-63 season.

COLLEGIATE RECORD

Season Team	G	Min.	FGM	FGA	Pct.	FTM	FTA	Pct.	Reb.	Pts.	Avg.
56-57 —North Carolina A&T					Statistics unavailable.						
57-58 —North Carolina A&T					Statistics unavailable.						
58-59 —North Carolina A&T	29	. . .	105	225	.467	56	91	.615	. . .	266	9.2
59-60 —North Carolina A&T	24	. . .	190	301	.631	47	71	.662	80	427	17.8
Totals	53	. . .	295	526	.561	103	162	.636	. . .	693	13.1

NBA REGULAR-SEASON RECORD

Season Team	G	Min.	FGM	FGA	Pct.	FTM	FTA	Pct.	Reb.	Ast.	PF	Dq.	Pts.	Avg.
60-61 —Philadelphia	77	1544	222	543	.409	97	162	.599	214	174	235	5	541	7.0
61-62 —Philadelphia	75	2468	343	724	.474	158	267	.592	355	333	279	8	844	11.3
62-63 —San Francisco	71	1876	301	630	.478	133	206	.646	205	184	253	7	735	10.4
63-64 —San Francisco	70	1883	289	640	.452	185	275	.673	236	197	249	4	763	10.9
64-65 —San Francisco	73	1733	254	662	.384	171	274	.624	239	205	242	7	679	9.3
65-66 —San Francisco	79	2053	364	724	.503	154	252	.611	322	225	265	7	882	11.2
66-67 —San Francisco	70	1764	212	467	.454	88	151	.583	321	269	265	13	512	7.3
67-68 —San Francisco	67	1992	252	540	.467	150	216	.694	276	390	284	9	654	9.8
68-69 —San Francisco	51	1516	162	359	.451	95	149	.638	181	306	183	3	419	8.2
69-70 —San Francisco	45	676	78	202	.386	75	113	.664	74	142	103	0	231	5.1
70-71 —San Francisco	34	321	22	54	.407	24	41	.585	40	58	59	2	68	2.0
Totals	712	17826	2499	5545	.451	1330	2106	.632	2463	2483	2417	65	6328	8.9

NBA PLAYOFF RECORD

Season Team	G	Min.	FGM	FGA	Pct.	FTM	FTA	Pct.	Reb.	Ast.	PF	Dq.	Pts.	Avg.
60-61 —Philadelphia	3	110	12	26	.462	5	14	.357	12	9	14	0	29	9.7
61-62 —Philadelphia	12	338	28	76	.368	17	31	.548	55	27	54	4	73	6.1
63-64 —San Francisco	12	386	58	144	.403	30	56	.536	37	30	54	5	146	12.2
66-67 —San Francisco	15	237	20	46	.435	6	16	.375	62	38	45	1	46	3.1
67-68 —San Francisco	10	277	25	62	.403	23	30	.767	53	70	49	2	73	7.3
68-69 —San Francisco	6	109	7	21	.333	1	4	.250	18	21	17	0	15	2.5
70-71 —San Francisco	4	47	4	7	.571	4	7	.571	8	11	13	0	12	3.0
Totals	62	1504	154	382	.403	86	158	.544	245	206	246	12	394	6.4

NBA COACHING RECORD

		REGULAR SEASON				PLAYOFFS		
Season Team	W	L	Pct.	Finish		W	L	Pct.
69-70 —San Francisco	8	22	.267	6th/Western Division		—	—	—
70-71 —San Francisco	41	41	.500	2nd/Pacific Division		1	4	.200
71-72 —Golden State	51	31	.622	2nd/Pacific Division		1	4	.200
72-73 —Golden State	47	35	.573	2nd/Pacific Division		5	6	.455
73-74 —Golden State	44	38	.537	2nd/Pacific Division		—	—	—
74-75 —Golden State	48	34	.585	1st/Pacific Division		12	5	.706
75-76 —Golden State	59	23	.720	1st/Pacific Division		7	6	.538
76-77 —Golden State	46	36	.561	3rd/Pacific Division		5	5	.500
77-78 —Golden State	43	39	.524	5th/Pacific Division		—	—	—
78-79 —Golden State	38	44	.463	6th/Pacific Division		—	—	—
79-80 —Golden State	18	43	.295	6th/Pacific Division		—	—	—
80-81 —Golden State	39	43	.476	4th/Pacific Division		—	—	—
81-82 —Golden State	45	37	.549	4th/Pacific Division		—	—	—
82-83 —Golden State	30	52	.366	5th/Pacific Division		—	—	—
Totals (14 years)	557	518	.518	Totals (6 years)		31	30	.508

NOTES:
1971— Lost to Milwaukee in Western Conference semifinals.
1972— Lost to Milwaukee in Western Conference semifinals.
1973— Defeated Milwaukee, 4-2, in Western Conference semifinals; lost to Los Angeles, 4-1, in Western Conference finals.
1975— Defeated Seattle, 4-2, in Western Conference semifinals; defeated Chicago, 4-3, in Western Conference finals; defeated Washington, 4-0, in World Championship Series.
1976— Defeated Detroit, 4-2, in Western Conference semifinals; lost to Phoenix, 4-3, in Western Conference finals.
1977— Defeated Detroit, 2-1, in Western Conference first round; lost to Los Angeles, 4-3, in Western Conference semifinals.
1980— Missed final 21 games of season due to injury; replaced by assistant coach John Bach (6-15) for remainder of season.

AUERBACH, RED

PERSONAL: Born September 20, 1917, in Brooklyn, N.Y. . . . 5-10/170. . . . Full name: Arnold Jacob Auerbach. . . . Name pronounced HOUR-back.
HIGH SCHOOL: Eastern District (Brooklyn, N.Y.).
COLLEGE: Seth Low Junior College (N.Y.), then George Washington.

COLLEGIATE RECORD

Season Team	G	Min.	FGM	FGA	Pct.	FTM	FTA	Pct.	Reb.	Pts.	Avg.
36-37 — Seth Low Junior College				Statistics unavailable.							
37-38 — George Washington	17	...	22	...	...	8	12	.667	...	52	3.1
38-39 — George Washington	20	...	54	...	...	12	19	.632	...	120	6.0
39-40 — George Washington	19	...	69	...	...	24	39	.615	...	162	8.5
Four-year-college totals	56	...	145	...	...	44	70	.629	...	334	6.0

HEAD COACHING RECORD

BACKGROUND: Head coach, St. Alban's Prep (Washington, D.C.).... Head coach, Roosevelt High School (Washington, D.C.). ... Assistant coach, Duke University (1949-50).
HONORS: NBA Coach of the Year (1965).... Elected to Naismith Memorial Basketball Hall of Fame (1968).... NBA 25th Anniversary All-Time team coach (1970).... NBA Executive of the Year (1980).... Selected as the "Greatest Coach in the History of the NBA" by the Professional Basketball Writers' Association of America (1980).
RECORDS: Holds NBA career record for most wins—938.

NBA COACHING RECORD

		REGULAR SEASON				PLAYOFFS		
Season Team	W	L	Pct.	Finish	W	L	Pct.
46-47 — Washington (BAA)	49	11	.817	1st/Eastern Division	2	4	.333
47-48 — Washington (BAA)	28	20	.583	4th/Eastern Division	—	—	—
48-49 — Washington (BAA)	38	22	.633	1st/Eastern Division	6	5	.545
49-50 — Tri-Cities	28	29	.491	3rd/Western Division	1	2	.333
50-51 — Boston	39	30	.565	2nd/Eastern Division	0	2	.000
51-52 — Boston	39	27	.591	2nd/Eastern Division	1	2	.333
52-53 — Boston	46	25	.648	3rd/Eastern Division	3	3	.500
53-54 — Boston	42	30	.583	T2nd/Eastern Division	2	4	.333
54-55 — Boston	36	36	.500	3rd/Eastern Division	3	4	.429
55-56 — Boston	39	33	.542	2nd/Eastern Division	1	2	.333
56-57 — Boston	44	28	.611	1st/Eastern Division	7	3	.700
57-58 — Boston	49	23	.681	1st/Eastern Division	6	5	.545
58-59 — Boston	52	20	.722	1st/Eastern Division	8	3	.727
59-60 — Boston	59	16	.787	1st/Eastern Division	8	5	.615
60-61 — Boston	57	22	.722	1st/Eastern Division	8	2	.800
61-62 — Boston	60	20	.750	1st/Eastern Division	8	6	.571
62-63 — Boston	58	22	.725	1st/Eastern Division	8	5	.615
63-64 — Boston	59	21	.738	1st/Eastern Division	8	2	.800
64-65 — Boston	62	18	.775	1st/Eastern Division	8	4	.667
65-66 — Boston	54	26	.675	1st/Eastern Division	11	6	.647
Totals (20 years)	938	479	.662	Totals (19 years)	99	69	.589

NOTES:
1947— Lost to Chicago, 4-2, in BAA semifinals.
1949— Defeated Philadelphia, 2-0, in Eastern Division semifinals; defeated New York, 2-1, in Eastern Division finals; lost to Minneapolis, 4-2, in World Championship Series.
1950— Lost to Anderson in Western Division semifinals.
1951— Lost to New York in Eastern Division semifinals.
1952— Lost to New York in Eastern Division semifinals.
1953— Defeated Syracuse, 2-0, in Eastern Division semifinals; lost to New York, 3-1, in Eastern Division finals.
1954— Defeated New York, 93-71; lost to Syracuse, 96-95 (OT); defeated New York, 79-78; and lost to Syracuse, 98-85, in Eastern Division round robin. Lost to Syracuse, 2-0, in Eastern Division finals.
1955— Defeated New York, 2-1, in Eastern Division semifinals; lost to Syracuse, 3-1, in Eastern Division finals.
1956— Lost to Syracuse in Eastern Division semifinals.
1957— Defeated Syracuse, 3-0, in Eastern Division finals; defeated St. Louis, 4-3, in World Championship Series.
1958— Defeated Philadelphia, 4-1, in Eastern Division finals; lost to St. Louis, 4-2, in World Championship Series.
1959— Defeated Syracuse, 4-3, in Eastern Division finals; defeated Minneapolis, 4-0, in World Championship Series.
1960— Defeated Philadelphia, 4-2, in Eastern Division finals; defeated St. Louis, 4-3, in World Championship Series.
1961— Defeated Syracuse, 4-1, in Eastern Division finals; defeated St. Louis, 4-1, in World Championship Series.
1962— Defeated Philadelphia, 4-3, in Eastern Division finals; defeated Los Angeles, 4-3, in World Championship Series.
1963— Defeated Cincinnati, 4-3, in Eastern Division finals; defeated Los Angeles, 4-2, in World Championship Series.
1964— Defeated Cincinnati, 4-1, in Eastern Division finals; defeated San Francisco, 4-1, in World Championship Series.
1965— Defeated Philadelphia, 4-3, in Eastern Division finals; defeated Los Angeles, 4-1, in World Championship Series.
1966— Defeated Cincinnati, 3-2 in Eastern Division semifinals; defeated Philadelphia, 4-1, in Eastern Division finals, defeated Los Angeles, 4-3, in World Championship Series.

COSTELLO, LARRY

PERSONAL: Born July 2, 1931, in Minoa, N.Y.... 6-1/188.... Full name: Lawrence Ronald Costello.
HIGH SCHOOL: Minoa (N.Y.).
COLLEGE: Niagara.
TRANSACTIONS/CAREER NOTES: Selected by Philadelphia Warriors in second round of 1954 NBA Draft.... Sold by Warriors to Syracuse Nationals (October 10, 1957).... Nationals franchise moved from Syracuse to Philadelphia and renamed 76ers for 1963-64 season.... Played in Eastern Basketball League with Wilkes-Barre Barons (1965-66).... Drafted by Milwaukee Bucks from 76ers in expansion draft (May 6, 1968).
MISCELLANEOUS: Member of NBA championship team (1967).

COLLEGIATE RECORD

Season Team	G	Min.	FGM	FGA	Pct.	FTM	FTA	Pct.	Reb.	Pts.	Avg.
50-51 — Niagara‡				Freshman team statistics unavailable.							
51-52 — Niagara	28	...	131	...	...	58	87	.667	...	320	11.4
52-53 — Niagara	28	...	185	...	...	140	194	.722	...	510	18.2
53-54 — Niagara	29	...	160	...	...	125	152	.822	...	445	15.3
Varsity totals	85	...	476	...	...	323	433	.746	...	1275	15.0

NBA REGULAR-SEASON RECORD

HONORS: All-NBA second team (1961).

Season Team	G	Min.	FGM	FGA	Pct.	FTM	FTA	Pct.	Reb.	Ast.	PF	Dq.	Pts.	Avg.
54-55 — Philadelphia	19	463	46	139	.331	26	32	.813	49	78	37	0	118	6.2
55-56 — Philadelphia					Did not play—in military service.									
56-57 — Philadelphia	72	2111	186	497	.374	175	222	.788	323	236	182	2	547	7.6
57-58 — Syracuse	72	2746	378	888	.426	320	378	.847	378	317	246	3	1076	14.9
58-59 — Syracuse	70	2750	414	948	.437	280	349	.802	365	379	263	7	1108	15.8
59-60 — Syracuse	71	2469	372	822	.453	249	289	.862	388	449	234	4	993	14.0
60-61 — Syracuse	75	2167	407	844	.482	270	338	.799	292	413	286	9	1084	14.5
61-62 — Syracuse	63	1854	310	726	.427	247	295	.837	245	359	220	5	867	13.8
62-63 — Syracuse	78	2066	285	660	.432	288	327	*.881	237	334	263	4	858	11.0
63-64 — Philadelphia	45	1137	191	408	.468	147	170	.865	105	167	150	3	529	11.8
64-65 — Philadelphia	64	1967	309	695	.445	243	277	*.877	169	275	242	10	861	13.5
66-67 — Philadelphia	49	976	130	293	.444	120	133	.902	103	140	141	2	380	7.8
67-68 — Philadelphia	28	492	67	148	.453	67	81	.827	51	68	62	0	201	7.2
Totals	706	21198	3095	7068	.438	2432	2891	.841	2705	3215	2326	49	8622	12.2

NBA PLAYOFF RECORD

Season Team	G	Min.	FGM	FGA	Pct.	FTM	FTA	Pct.	Reb.	Ast.	PF	Dq.	Pts.	Avg.
56-57 — Philadelphia	2	16	3	8	.375	0	1	.000	5	2	3	0	6	3.0
57-58 — Syracuse	3	134	10	34	.294	14	14	1.000	25	12	6	0	34	11.3
58-59 — Syracuse	9	361	54	121	.446	51	61	.836	53	54	40	2	159	17.7
59-60 — Syracuse	3	122	20	47	.426	10	12	.833	14	20	15	1	50	16.7
60-61 — Syracuse	8	269	42	103	.408	47	55	.855	35	52	39	3	131	16.4
61-62 — Syracuse	5	167	22	51	.431	29	33	.879	16	28	21	0	73	14.6
62-63 — Syracuse	5	134	16	37	.432	19	23	.826	4	23	27	2	51	10.2
63-64 — Philadelphia	5	36	3	14	.214	10	10	1.000	3	4	14	1	16	3.2
64-65 — Philadelphia	10	207	22	53	.415	11	16	.688	12	20	43	2	55	5.5
66-67 — Philadelphia	2	25	6	8	.750	5	5	1.000	4	3	2	0	17	8.5
Totals	52	1471	198	476	.416	196	230	.852	171	218	210	11	592	11.4

NBA ALL-STAR GAME RECORD

Season Team	Min.	FGM	FGA	Pct.	FTM	FTA	Pct.	Reb.	Ast.	PF	Dq.	Pts.
1958 — Syracuse	17	0	6	.000	1	1	1.000	1	4	2	0	1
1959 — Syracuse	18	3	8	.375	1	1	1.000	3	3	1	0	7
1960 — Syracuse	20	5	9	.556	0	0	...	4	2	1	0	10
1961 — Syracuse	5	1	2	.500	0	0	...	0	0	2	0	2
1962 — Syracuse					Did not play—injured.							
1965 — Philadelphia	11	2	7	.286	0	0	...	1	2	2	0	4
Totals	71	11	32	.344	2	2	1.000	9	11	8	0	24

EBL REGULAR-SEASON RECORD

Season Team	G	Min.	FGM	FGA	Pct.	FTM	FTA	Pct.	Reb.	Ast.	PF	Dq.	Pts.	Avg.
65-66 — Wilkes-Barre	12	...	54			53	59	.898	22	83	...	...	167	13.9

HEAD COACHING RECORD

BACKGROUND: Head coach, Minoa High School, N.Y. (1965-66).... Head coach, Milwaukee Does of Women's Professional Basketball League (1979-80).

NBA COACHING RECORD

Season Team	REGULAR SEASON W	L	Pct.	Finish	PLAYOFFS W	L	Pct.
68-69 — Milwaukee	27	55	.329	7th/Eastern Division	—	—	—
69-70 — Milwaukee	56	26	.683	2nd/Eastern Division	5	5	.500
70-71 — Milwaukee	66	16	.805	1st/Eastern Division	12	2	.857
71-72 — Milwaukee	63	19	.768	1st/Midwest Division	6	5	.545
72-73 — Milwaukee	60	22	.732	1st/Midwest Division	2	4	.333
73-74 — Milwaukee	59	23	.720	1st/Midwest Division	11	5	.688
74-75 — Milwaukee	38	44	.463	4th/Midwest Division	—	—	—
75-76 — Milwaukee	38	44	.463	1st/Midwest Division	1	2	.333
76-77 — Milwaukee	3	15	.167		—	—	—
78-79 — Chicago	20	36	.357		—	—	—
Totals (10 years)	430	300	.589		Totals (6 years) 37	23	.617

COLLEGIATE COACHING RECORD

Season Team	W	L	Pct.	Finish
80-81 — Utica	13	12	.520	Independent
81-82 — Utica	4	22	.154	Independent
82-83 — Utica	11	15	.423	Independent
83-84 — Utica	11	15	.423	Independent
84-85 — Utica	15	12	.556	Independent
85-86 — Utica	13	14	.481	Independent
86-87 — Utica	10	16	.385	Independent
Totals (7 years)	77	106	.421	

NOTES:

1970— Defeated Philadelphia, 4-3, in Eastern Division semifinals; lost to New York, 4-1, in Eastern Division finals.

1971— Defeated San Francisco, 4-1, in Western Conference semifinals; defeated Los Angeles, 4-1, in Western Conference finals; defeated Baltimore, 4-0, in World Championship Series.

1972— Defeated Golden State, 4-1, in Western Conference semifinals; lost to Los Angeles, 4-2, in Western Conference finals.

1973— Lost to Golden State in Western Conference semifinals.

1974— Defeated Los Angeles, 4-1, in Western Conference Semifinals; defeated Chicago, 4-0, in Western Conference finals; lost to Boston, 4-3, in World Championship Series.

1976— Lost to Detroit in Western Conference first round. Resigned as Milwaukee head coach and replaced by Don Nelson (No-

vember 22).
1979— Replaced as Chicago head coach by Scotty Robertson (February 16).

CUNNINGHAM, BILLY

PERSONAL: Born June 3, 1943, in Brooklyn, N.Y. . . . 6-7/
210. . . . Full name: William John Cunningham.
HIGH SCHOOL: Erasmus Hall (Brooklyn, N.Y.).
COLLEGE: North Carolina.

TRANSACTIONS/CAREER NOTES: Selected by Philadelphia 76ers in first round of 1965 NBA Draft. . . . Signed as free agent by Carolina Cougars of American Basketball Association (August 1969). . . . Signed as free agent by 76ers (1969). . . . Suspended by NBA (1972). . . . Restored by NBA (1974) . . . Returned to 76ers (1974).
CAREER HONORS: Elected to Naismith Memorial Basketball Hall of Fame (1985).
MISCELLANEOUS: Member of NBA championship team (1967).

COLLEGIATE RECORD

NOTES: THE SPORTING NEWS All-America second team (1965).

Season Team	G	Min.	FGM	FGA	Pct.	FTM	FTA	Pct.	Reb.	Pts.	Avg.
61-62 — North Carolina‡	10	. . .	81	162	.500	45	78	.577	127	207	20.7
62-63 — North Carolina	21	. . .	186	380	.489	105	170	.618	339	477	22.7
63-64 — North Carolina	24	. . .	233	526	.443	157	249	.631	379	623	26.0
64-65 — North Carolina	24	. . .	237	481	.493	135	213	.634	344	609	25.4
Varsity totals	69		656	1387	.473	397	632	.628	1062	1709	24.8

NBA REGULAR-SEASON RECORD

HONORS: All-NBA first team (1969, 1970, 1971). . . . All-NBA second team (1972). . . . NBA All-Rookie team (1966).

Season Team	G	Min.	FGM	FGA	Pct.	FTM	FTA	Pct.	Reb.	Ast.	PF	Dq.	Pts.	Avg.
65-66 — Philadelphia	80	2134	431	1011	.426	281	443	.634	599	207	301	12	1143	14.3
66-67 — Philadelphia	81	2168	556	1211	.459	383	558	.686	589	205	260	2	1495	18.5
67-68 — Philadelphia	74	2076	516	1178	.438	368	509	.723	562	187	260	3	1400	18.9
68-69 — Philadelphia	82	3345	739	1736	.426	556	754	.737	1050	287	*329	10	2034	24.8
69-70 — Philadelphia	81	3194	802	1710	.469	510	700	.729	1101	352	331	15	2114	26.1
70-71 — Philadelphia	81	3090	702	1519	.462	455	620	.734	946	395	328	5	1859	23.0
71-72 — Philadelphia	75	2900	658	1428	.461	428	601	.712	918	443	295	12	1744	23.3

									— REBOUNDS —								
Season Team	G	Min.	FGM	FGA	Pct.	FTM	FTA	Pct.	Off.	Def.	Tot.	Ast.	PF	Dq.	Stl.	Blk.	TO	Pts.	Avg.
74-75 — Philadelphia	80	2859	609	1423	.428	345	444	.777	130	596	726	442	270	4	91	35	. . .	1563	19.5
75-76 — Philadelphia	20	640	103	251	.410	68	88	.773	29	118	147	107	57	1	24	10	. . .	274	13.7
Totals	654	22406	5116	11467	.446	3394	4717	.720	. . .	. . .	6638	2625	2431	64	115	45	. . .	13626	20.8

NBA PLAYOFF RECORD

Season Team	G	Min.	FGM	FGA	Pct.	FTM	FTA	Pct.	Reb.	Ast.	PF	Dq.	Pts.	Avg.
65-66 — Philadelphia	4	69	5	31	.161	11	13	.846	18	10	11	0	21	5.3
66-67 — Philadelphia	15	339	83	221	.376	59	90	.656	93	33	53	1	225	15.0
67-68 — Philadelphia	3	86	24	43	.558	14	17	.824	22	10	16	1	62	20.7
68-69 — Philadelphia	5	217	49	117	.419	24	38	.632	63	12	24	1	122	24.4
69-70 — Philadelphia	5	205	61	123	.496	24	36	.667	52	20	19	0	146	29.2
70-71 — Philadelphia	7	301	67	142	.472	47	67	.701	108	40	28	0	181	25.9
Totals	39	1217	289	677	.427	179	261	.686	356	125	151	3	757	19.4

NBA ALL-STAR GAME RECORD

Season Team	Min.	FGM	FGA	Pct.	FTM	FTA	Pct.	Reb.	Ast.	PF	Dq.	Pts.
1969 — Philadelphia	22	5	10	.500	0	0	. . .	5	1	3	0	10
1970 — Philadelphia	28	7	13	.538	5	5	1.000	4	2	3	0	19
1971 — Philadelphia	19	2	8	.250	1	2	.500	4	3	1	0	5
1972 — Philadelphia	24	4	13	.308	6	8	.750	10	3	4	0	14
Totals	93	18	44	.409	12	15	.800	23	9	11	0	48

ABA REGULAR-SEASON RECORD

NOTES: ABA Most Valuable Player (1973). . . . ABA All-Star first team (1973).

			— 2-POINT —			— 3-POINT —									
Season Team	G	Min.	FGM	FGA	Pct.	FGM	FGA	Pct.	FTM	FTA	Pct.	Reb.	Ast.	Pts.	Avg.
72-73 — Carolina	84	3248	757	1534	.493	14	49	.286	472	598	.789	1012	530	2028	24.1
73-74 — Carolina	32	1190	252	529	.476	1	8	.125	149	187	.797	331	150	656	20.5
Totals	116	4438	1009	2063	.489	15	57	.263	621	785	.791	1343	680	2684	23.1

ABA PLAYOFF RECORD

			— 2-POINT —			— 3-POINT —									
Season Team	G	Min.	FGM	FGA	Pct.	FGM	FGA	Pct.	FTM	FTA	Pct.	Reb.	Ast.	Pts.	Avg.
72-73 — Carolina	12	472	111	219	.507	1	4	.250	57	83	.687	142	61	282	23.5
73-74 — Carolina	3	61	9	29	.310	0	2	.000	4	5	.800	16	6	22	7.3
Totals	15	533	120	248	.484	1	6	.167	61	88	.693	158	67	304	20.3

ABA ALL-STAR GAME RECORD

		— 2-POINT —			— 3-POINT —								
Season Team	Min.	FGM	FGA	Pct.	FGM	FGA	Pct.	FTM	FTA	Pct.	Reb.	Ast.	Pts.
1973 — Carolina	20	9	11	.818	0	1	.000	0	0	. . .	6	4	18

NBA COACHING RECORD

		— REGULAR SEASON —				— PLAYOFFS —	
Season Team	W	L	Pct.	Finish	W	L	Pct.
77-78 — Philadelphia	53	23	.697	1st/Atlantic Division	6	4	.600
78-79 — Philadelphia	47	35	.573	2nd/Atlantic Division	5	4	.556
79-80 — Philadelphia	59	23	.720	2nd/Atlantic Division	12	6	.667

Season	Team	W	L	Pct.	REGULAR SEASON Finish	PLAYOFFS W	L	Pct.
80-81	Philadelphia	62	20	.756	T 1st/Atlantic Division	9	7	.563
81-82	Philadelphia	58	24	.707	2nd/Atlantic Division	12	9	.571
82-83	Philadelphia	65	17	.793	1st/Atlantic Division	12	1	.923
83-84	Philadelphia	52	30	.634	2nd/Atlantic Division	2	3	.400
84-85	Philadelphia	58	24	.707	2nd/Atlantic Division	8	5	.615
	Totals (8 years)	454	196	.698	Totals (8 years)	66	39	.629

NOTES:

1977— Replaced Gene Shue as Philadelphia head coach (November 4), with record of 2-4.

1978— Defeated New York, 4-0, in Eastern Conference semifinals; lost to Washington, 4-2, in Eastern Conference finals.

1979— Defeated New Jersey, 2-0, in Eastern Conference first round; lost to San Antonio, 4-3, in Eastern Conference semifinals.

1980— Defeated Washington, 2-0, in Eastern Conference first round; defeated Atlanta, 4-1, in Eastern Conference semifinals; defeated Boston, 4-1, in Eastern Conference finals; lost to Los Angeles, 4-2, in World Championship Series.

1981— Defeated Indiana, 2-0, in Eastern Conference first round; defeated Milwaukee, 4-3, in Eastern Conference semifinals; lost to Boston, 4-3, in Eastern Conference finals.

1982— Defeated Atlanta, 2-0, in Eastern Conference first round; defeated Milwaukee, 4-2, in Eastern Conference semifinals; defeated Boston, 4-3, in Eastern Conference finals; lost to Los Angeles, 4-2, in World Championship Series.

1983— Defeated New York, 4-0, in Eastern Conference semifinals; defeated Boston, 4-1, in Eastern Conference finals; defeated Los Angeles, 4-0, in World Championship series.

1984— Lost to New Jersey in Eastern Conference first round.

1985— Defeated Washington, 3-1, in Eastern Conference first round; defeated Milwaukee, 4-0, in Eastern Conference semifinals; lost to Boston, 4-1, in Eastern Conference finals.

FITZSIMMONS, COTTON

PERSONAL: Born October 7, 1931, in Hannibal, Mo.... 5-7/160.... Full name: Lowell Fitzsimmons.... Father of Gary Fitzsimmons, director of player personnel with Cleveland Cavaliers.

HIGH SCHOOL: Bowling Green (Mo.).

COLLEGE: Hannibal-LaGrange (Mo.), then Midwestern State (Tex.).

COLLEGIATE RECORD

Season	Team	G	Min.	FGM	FGA	Pct.	FTM	FTA	Pct.	Reb.	Pts.	Avg.
52-53	Hannibal-LaGrange‡	33	...	...	...	...	...	...	...	...	838	25.4
53-54	Midwestern State	27	...	53	161	.329	128	173	.740	...	234	8.7
54-55	Midwestern State	27	...	118	258	.457	162	210	.771	...	398	14.7
55-56	Midwestern State	28	...	148	319	.464	164	223	.735	...	460	16.4
	Varsity totals	82	...	319	738	.432	454	606	.749	...	1092	13.3

HEAD COACHING RECORD

BACKGROUND: Assistant coach, Kansas State University (1967-68).... Director of player personnel, Golden State Warriors (1976-77).... Director of player personnel, Phoenix Suns (1987-88).... Head coach/director of player personnel, Suns (1988-89 through 1991-92).

HONORS: NBA Coach of the Year (1979, 1989).

COLLEGE COACHING RECORD

Season	Team	W	L	Pct.	Finish
58-59	Moberly J.C. (Mo.)	16	15	.516	
59-60	Moberly J.C. (Mo.)	19	8	.704	
60-61	Moberly J.C. (Mo.)	26	5	.839	
61-62	Moberly J.C. (Mo.)	26	9	.743	
62-63	Moberly J.C. (Mo.)	26	6	.813	
63-64	Moberly J.C. (Mo.)	24	5	.828	
64-65	Moberly J.C. (Mo.)	25	5	.833	
65-66	Moberly J.C. (Mo.)	29	5	.853	
66-67	Moberly J.C. (Mo.)	31	2	.939	
68-69	Kansas State	14	12	.538	T2nd/Big Eight Conference
69-70	Kansas State	20	8	.714	1st/Big Eight Conference
	Junior college totals (9 years)	222	60	.787	
	Four-year college totals (2 years)	34	20	.630	

NBA COACHING RECORD

Season	Team	W	L	Pct.	REGULAR SEASON Finish	PLAYOFFS W	L	Pct.
70-71	Phoenix	48	34	.585	3rd/Midwest Division	—	—	—
71-72	Phoenix	49	33	.598	3rd/Midwest Division	—	—	—
72-73	Atlanta	46	36	.561	2nd/Central Division	2	4	.333
73-74	Atlanta	35	47	.427	2nd/Central Division	—	—	—
74-75	Atlanta	31	51	.378	4th/Central Division	—	—	—
75-76	Atlanta	28	46	.378		—	—	—
77-78	Buffalo	27	55	.329	4th/Atlantic Division	—	—	—
78-79	Kansas City	48	34	.585	1st/Midwest Division	1	4	.200
79-80	Kansas City	47	35	.573	2nd/Midwest Division	1	2	.333
80-81	Kansas City	40	42	.488	T2nd/Midwest Division	7	8	.467
81-82	Kansas City	30	52	.366	4th/Midwest Division	—	—	—
82-83	Kansas City	45	37	.549	T2nd/Midwest Division	—	—	—
83-84	Kansas City	38	44	.463	T3rd/Midwest Division	0	3	.000
84-85	San Antonio	41	41	.500	T4th/Midwest Division	2	3	.400
85-86	San Antonio	35	47	.427	6th/Midwest Division	0	3	.000
88-89	Phoenix	55	27	.671	2nd/Pacific Division	7	5	.583
89-90	Phoenix	54	28	.659	3rd/Pacific Division	9	7	.563
90-91	Phoenix	55	27	.671	3rd/Pacific Division	1	3	.250

Season	Team	W	L	Pct.	REGULAR SEASON Finish		W	L	PLAYOFFS Pct.
91-92	—Phoenix..............................	53	29	.646	3rd/Pacific Division		4	4	.500
	Totals (19 years)............................	805	745	.519	Totals (10 years)		34	46	.425

NOTES:
1966— Won National Junior College Athletic Association national tournament.
1967— Won National Junior College Athletic Association national tournament.
1970— Lost to New Mexico, 70-66, in NCAA Tournament regional semifinal.
1973— Lost to Boston in Eastern Conference semifinals.
1976— Replaced as Atlanta head coach by Gene Tormohlen (March).
1979— Lost to Phoenix in Western Conference semifinals.
1980— Lost to Phoenix in Western Conference first round.
1981— Defeated Portland, 2-1, in Western Conference first round; defeated Phoenix, 4-3, in Western Conference semifinals; lost to Houston, 4-1, in Western Conference finals.
1984— Lost to Los Angeles Lakers in Western Conference first round.
1985— Lost to Denver in Western Conference first round.
1986— Lost to Los Angeles Lakers in Western Conference first round.
1989— Defeated Denver, 3-0, in Western Conference first round; defeated Golden State, 4-1, in Western Conference semifinals; lost to Los Angeles Lakers, 4-0, in Western Conference finals.
1990— Defeated Utah, 3-2, in Western Conference first round; defeated Los Angeles Lakers, 4-1, in Western Conference semi-finals; lost to Portland, 4-2, in Western Conference finals.
1991— Lost to Utah in Western Conference first round.
1992— Defeated San Antonio, 3-0, in Western Conference first round; lost to Portland, 4-1, in Western Conference semifinals.

HANNUM, ALEX

PERSONAL: Born July 19, 1923, in Los Angeles. . . . 6-7/225. . . . Full name: Alexander Murray Hannum.
HIGH SCHOOL: Hamilton (Los Angeles).
COLLEGE: Southern California.
TRANSACTIONS/CAREER NOTES: Played for Los Angeles Shamrocks, an Amateur Athletic Union team and averaged 9.8 points per game (1945-46). . . . Signed by Oshkosh All-Stars of National Basketball League (1948). . . . Sold by Oshkosh of NBL to Syracuse Nationals of NBA (1949). . . . Traded by Nationals with Fred Scolari to Baltimore Bullets for Red Rocha (1951). . . . Sold by Bullets to Rochester Royals during 1951-52 season. . . . Sold by Royals to Milwaukee Hawks (1954). . . . Hawks franchise moved from Milwaukee to St. Louis for 1955-56 season. . . . Released by Hawks (1956). . . . Signed by Fort Wayne Pistons (1956). . . . Released by Pistons (December 12, 1956). . . . Signed by Hawks (December 17, 1956).

COLLEGIATE RECORD

NOTES: In military service (1943-44 through 1945-46).

Season	Team	G	Min.	FGM	FGA	Pct.	FTM	FTA	Pct.	Reb.	Pts.	Avg.
41-42	—Southern California‡..............					Freshman team statistics unavailable.						
42-43	—Southern California	15	...	23	...	...	9	20	.450	...	55	3.7
46-47	—Southern California	24	...	...	...	...	...	...	...	...	251	10.5
47-48	—Southern California	23	...	108	...	...	...	...	...	...	263	11.4
	Varsity totals	62	...	...	...	...	...	...	...	...	569	9.2

NBL AND NBA REGULAR-SEASON RECORD

Season	Team	G	Min.	FGM	FGA	Pct.	FTM	FTA	Pct.	Reb.	Ast.	PF	Dq.	Pts.	Avg.
48-49	—Oshkosh (NBL)	62	...	126	...	...	113	191	.592	...	...	188	...	365	5.9
49-50	—Syracuse......................	64	...	177	488	.363	128	186	.688	...	129	264	...	482	7.5
50-51	—Syracuse......................	63	...	182	494	.368	107	197	.543	301	119	271	16	471	7.5
51-52	—Baltimore-Rochester......	66	1508	170	462	.368	98	138	.710	336	133	271	16	438	6.6
52-53	—Rochester	68	1288	129	360	.358	88	133	.662	279	81	258	18	346	5.1
53-54	—Rochester	72	1707	175	503	.348	102	164	.622	350	105	279	11	452	6.3
54-55	—Milwaukee	53	1088	126	358	.352	61	107	.570	245	105	206	9	313	5.9
55-56	—St. Louis......................	71	1480	146	453	.322	93	154	.604	344	157	271	10	385	5.4
56-57	—Fort Wayne-St. Louis......	59	642	77	223	.345	37	56	.661	158	28	135	2	191	3.2
	Totals	578	...	1308	...	...	827	1326	.624	...	...	2143	...	3443	6.0

NBL AND NBA PLAYOFF RECORD

Season	Team	G	Min.	FGM	FGA	Pct.	FTM	FTA	Pct.	Reb.	Ast.	PF	Dq.	Pts.	Avg.
48-49	—Oshkosh (NBL)	7	...	12	...	...	16	26	.615	...	...	...	...	40	5.7
49-50	—Syracuse......................	11	...	38	86	.442	17	34	.500	...	10	50	...	93	8.5
50-51	—Syracuse......................	7	...	17	39	.436	8	10	.800	47	17	37	3	42	6.0
51-52	—Rochester	6	146	16	42	.381	8	13	.615	26	8	30	3	40	6.7
52-53	—Rochester	3	52	4	10	.400	3	8	.375	4	2	16	1	11	3.7
53-54	—Rochester	6	107	12	29	.414	15	24	.625	22	5	28	3	39	6.5
55-56	—St. Louis......................	8	159	21	66	.318	19	35	.543	29	10	36	3	61	7.6
56-57	—St. Louis......................	2	6	0	2	.000	0	0	...	0	0	2	...	0	0.0
	Totals	50	...	120	...	...	86	150	.573	...	...	...	...	326	6.5

HEAD COACHING RECORD

HONORS: NBA Coach of the Year (1965). . . . ABA Coach of the Year (1969).

NBA COACHING RECORD

Season	Team	W	L	Pct.	REGULAR SEASON Finish		W	L	PLAYOFFS Pct.
56-57	—St. Louis..............................	15	16	.484	T1st/Western Division		6	4	.600
57-58	—St. Louis..............................	41	31	.569	1st/Western Division		8	3	.727
60-61	—Syracuse..............................	38	41	.481	3rd/Eastern Division		4	4	.500

Season	Team	W	L	Pct.	REGULAR SEASON Finish	PLAYOFFS W	L	Pct.
61-62	—Syracuse	41	39	.513	3rd/Eastern Division	2	3	.400
62-63	—Syracuse	48	32	.600	2nd/Eastern Division	2	3	.400
63-64	—San Francisco	48	32	.600	1st/Western Division	5	7	.417
64-65	—San Francisco	17	63	.215	5th/Western Division	—	—	—
65-66	—San Francisco	35	45	.438	4th/Western Division	—	—	—
66-67	—Philadelphia	68	13	.840	1st/Eastern Division	11	4	.733
67-68	—Philadelphia	62	20	.756	1st/Eastern Division	7	6	.538
69-70	—San Diego	18	38	.321	7th/Western Division	—	—	—
70-71	—San Diego	40	42	.488	3rd/Pacific Division	—	—	—
	Totals (12 years)	471	412	.533	Totals (8 years)	45	34	.570

ABA COACHING RECORD

Season	Team	W	L	Pct.	REGULAR SEASON Finish	PLAYOFFS W	L	Pct.
68-69	—Oakland	60	18	.769	1st/Western Division	12	4	.750
71-72	—Denver	34	50	.405	4th/Western Division	3	4	.429
72-73	—Denver	47	37	.560	3rd/Western Division	1	4	.200
73-74	—Denver	37	47	.440	T4th/Western Division	—	—	—
	Totals (4 years)	178	152	.539	Totals (3 years)	16	12	.571

NOTES:

1957— Replaced Red Holzman (14-19) and Slater Martin (5-3) as St. Louis head coach (January), with record of 19-22. Defeated Fort Wayne, 115-103, and Minneapolis, 114-111, in Western Division tiebreakers; defeated Minneapolis, 3-0, in Western Division finals; lost to Boston, 4-3, in World Championship series.

1958— Defeated Detroit, 4-1, in Western Division finals; defeated Boston, 4-2, in World Championship Series.

1961— Defeated Philadelphia, 3-0, in Eastern Division semifinals; lost to Boston, 4-1, in Eastern Division finals.

1962— Lost to Philadelphia in Eastern Division semifinals.

1963— Lost to Cincinnati in Eastern Division semifinals.

1964— Defeated St. Louis, 4-3, in Western Division finals; lost to Boston, 4-1, in World Championship Series.

1967— Defeated Cincinnati, 3-1, in Eastern Division semifinals; defeated Boston, 4-1, in Eastern Division finals; defeated San Francisco, 4-2, in World Championship Series.

1968— Defeated New York, 4-2, in Eastern Divison semifinals; lost to Boston, 4-3, in Eastern Division finals.

1969— Defeated Denver, 4-3, in Western Division semifinals; defeated New Orleans, 4-0, in Western Division finals; defeated Indiana, 4-1, in ABA Finals. Replaced Jack McMahon as San Diego head coach (December), with record of 9-17.

1972— Lost to Indiana in Western Division semifinals.

1973— Lost to Indiana in Western Division semifinals.

HEINSOHN, TOM

PERSONAL: Born August 26, 1934, in Jersey City, N.J. . . . 6-7/218. . . . Full name: Thomas William Heinsohn.
HIGH SCHOOL: St. Michael's (Union City, N.J.).
COLLEGE: Holy Cross.
TRANSACTIONS/CAREER NOTES: Selected by Boston Celtics in 1956 NBA Draft (territorial pick).
CAREER HONORS: Elected to Naismith Memorial Basketball Hall of Fame (1985).
MISCELLANEOUS: Member of NBA championship teams (1957, 1959, 1960, 1961, 1962, 1963, 1964, 1965).

COLLEGIATE RECORD

Season	Team	G	Min.	FGM	FGA	Pct.	FTM	FTA	Pct.	Reb.	Pts.	Avg.
52-53	—Holy Cross†	15	. . .	97	. . .	. . .	70	. . .	. . .	. . .	264	17.6
53-54	—Holy Cross	28	. . .	175	364	.481	94	142	.662	300	444	15.9
54-55	—Holy Cross	26	. . .	232	499	.465	141	215	.656	385	605	23.3
55-56	—Holy Cross	27	. . .	254	630	.403	232	304	.763	569	740	27.4
	Varsity totals	81	. . .	661	1493	.443	467	661	.707	1254	1789	22.1

NBA REGULAR-SEASON RECORD

HONORS: NBA Rookie of the Year (1957). . . . All-NBA second team (1961, 1962, 1963, 1964).

Season	Team	G	Min.	FGM	FGA	Pct.	FTM	FTA	Pct.	Reb.	Ast.	PF	Dq.	Pts.	Avg.
56-57	—Boston	72	2150	446	1123	.397	271	343	.790	705	117	304	12	1163	16.2
57-58	—Boston	69	2206	468	1226	.382	294	394	.746	705	125	274	6	1230	17.8
58-59	—Boston	66	2089	465	1192	.390	312	391	.798	638	164	271	11	1242	18.8
59-60	—Boston	75	2420	673	1590	.423	283	386	.733	794	171	275	8	1629	21.7
60-61	—Boston	74	2256	627	1566	.400	325	424	.767	732	141	260	7	1579	21.3
61-62	—Boston	79	2383	692	1613	.429	358	437	.819	747	165	280	2	1742	22.1
62-63	—Boston	76	2004	550	1300	.423	340	407	.835	569	95	270	4	1440	18.9
63-64	—Boston	76	2040	487	1223	.398	283	342	.827	460	183	268	3	1257	16.5
64-65	—Boston	67	1706	365	954	.383	182	229	.795	399	157	252	5	912	13.6
	Totals	654	19254	4773	11787	.405	2648	3353	.790	5749	1318	2454	58	12194	18.6

NBA PLAYOFF RECORD

Season	Team	G	Min.	FGM	FGA	Pct.	FTM	FTA	Pct.	Reb.	Ast.	PF	Dq.	Pts.	Avg.
56-57	—Boston	10	370	90	231	.390	49	69	.710	117	20	40	1	229	22.9
57-58	—Boston	11	349	68	194	.351	56	72	.778	119	18	52	3	192	17.5
58-59	—Boston	11	348	91	220	.414	37	56	.661	98	32	41	0	219	19.9
59-60	—Boston	13	423	112	267	.419	60	80	.750	126	27	53	2	284	21.8
60-61	—Boston	10	291	82	201	.408	33	43	.767	99	20	36	1	197	19.7
61-62	—Boston	14	445	116	291	.399	58	76	.763	115	34	58	4	290	20.7
62-63	—Boston	13	413	123	270	.456	75	98	.765	116	15	55	2	321	24.7
63-64	—Boston	10	308	70	180	.389	34	42	.810	80	26	36	0	174	17.4
64-65	—Boston	12	276	66	181	.365	20	32	.625	84	23	46	1	152	12.7
	Totals	104	3223	818	2035	.402	422	568	.743	954	215	417	14	2058	19.8

NBA ALL-STAR GAME RECORD

Season	Team	Min.	FGM	FGA	Pct.	FTM	FTA	Pct.	Reb.	Ast.	PF	Dq.	Pts.
1957	—Boston	23	5	17	.294	2	2	1.000	7	0	3	0	12
1961	—Boston	19	2	16	.125	0	0	...	6	1	4	0	4
1962	—Boston	13	4	11	.364	2	2	1.000	2	1	4	0	10
1963	—Boston	21	6	11	.545	3	4	.750	2	1	4	0	15
1964	—Boston	21	5	12	.417	0	0	...	3	0	5	0	10
1965	—Boston							Selected, did not play—injured.					
	Totals	97	22	67	.328	7	8	.875	20	3	20	0	51

HEAD COACHING RECORD

HONORS: NBA Coach of the Year (1973).

NBA COACHING RECORD

		REGULAR SEASON				PLAYOFFS		
Season	Team	W	L	Pct.	Finish	W	L	Pct.
69-70	—Boston	34	48	.415	6th/Eastern Division	—	—	—
70-71	—Boston	44	38	.537	3rd/Atlantic Division	—	—	—
71-72	—Boston	56	26	.683	1st/Atlantic Division	5	6	.455
72-73	—Boston	68	14	.829	1st/Atlantic Division	7	6	.538
73-74	—Boston	56	26	.683	1st/Atlantic Division	12	6	.667
74-75	—Boston	60	22	.732	1st/Atlantic Division	6	5	.545
75-76	—Boston	54	28	.659	1st/Atlantic Division	12	6	.667
76-77	—Boston	44	38	.537	2nd/Atlantic Division	5	4	.556
77-78	—Boston	11	23	.324		—	—	—
	Totals (9 years)	427	263	.619	Totals (6 years)	47	33	.588

NOTES:

1972— Defeated Atlanta, 4-2, in Eastern Conference semifinals; lost to New York, 4-1, in Eastern Conference finals.

1973— Defeated Atlanta, 4-2, in Eastern Conference semifinals; lost to New York, 4-3, in Eastern Conference finals.

1974— Defeated Buffalo, 4-2, in Eastern Conference semifinals; defeated New York, 4-1, in Eastern Conference finals; defeated Milwaukee, 4-3, in World Championship Series.

1975— Defeated Houston, 4-1, in Eastern Conference semifinals; lost to Washington, 4-2, in Eastern Conference finals.

1976— Defeated Buffalo, 4-2, in Eastern Conference semifinals; defeated Cleveland, 4-2, in Eastern Conference finals; defeated Phoenix, 4-2, in World Championship Series.

1977— Defeated San Antonio, 2-0, in Eastern Conference first round; lost to Philadelphia, 4-3, in Eastern Conference semifinals.

1978— Replaced as Boston head coach by Satch Sanders (January 3).

HOLZMAN, RED

PERSONAL: Born August 10, 1920, in Brooklyn, N.Y. . . . 5-10/175. . . . Full name: William Holzman.

HIGH SCHOOL: Franklin K. Lane (Brooklyn, N.Y.).

COLLEGE: Baltimore, then City College of New York.

TRANSACTIONS/CAREER NOTES: Played in New York State League with Albany (1941-42). . . . In military service during 1942-43, 1943-44 and 1944-45 seasons; played at Norfolk, Va., Naval Training Station and scored 305 points in 1942-43 and 258 points in 1943-44. . . . Signed by Rochester Royals of National Basketball League (1945). . . . Played in American Basketball League with New York (1945-46). . . . Royals franchise transferred to Basketball Association of America for 1948-49 season. . . . Royals franchise became part of NBA upon merger of BAA and NBL for 1949-50 season. . . . Acquired from Royals by Milwaukee Hawks (1953).

MISCELLANEOUS: Member of NBL championship team (1946). . . . Member of NBA championship team (1951).

COLLEGIATE RECORD

Season	Team	G	Min.	FGM	FGA	Pct.	FTM	FTA	Pct.	Reb.	Pts.	Avg.
38-39	—Baltimore					Statistics unavailable.						
39-40	—City College of New York					Did not play—transfer student.						
40-41	—City College of New York	21	...	96	...	...	37	...	...	...	229	10.9
41-42	—City College of New York	18	...	87	...	...	51	...	...	...	225	12.5
	Totals	39	...	183	...	...	88	...	...	...	454	11.6

ABL REGULAR-SEASON RECORD

Season	Team	G	Min.	FGM	FGA	Pct.	FTM	FTA	Pct.	Reb.	Ast.	Pts.	Avg.
45-46	—New York	4	...	18	...	...	...	...	...	...	...	48	12.0

NBL AND NBA REGULAR-SEASON RECORD

HONORS: All-NBL first team (1946, 1948). . . . All-NBL second team (1947).

Season	Team	G	Min.	FGM	FGA	Pct.	FTM	FTA	Pct.	Reb.	Ast.	PF	Dq.	Pts.	Avg.
45-46	—Rochester (NBL)	34	...	144	...	...	77	115	.670	...	...	54	...	365	10.7
46-47	—Rochester (NBL)	44	...	227	...	...	74	139	.532	...	...	68	...	528	12.0
47-48	—Rochester (NBL)	60	...	246	...	...	117	182	.643	...	...	58	...	609	10.2
48-49	—Rochester (BAA)	60	...	225	691	.326	96	157	.611	...	149	93	...	546	9.1
49-50	—Rochester	68	...	206	625	.330	144	210	.686	...	200	67	...	556	8.2
50-51	—Rochester	68	...	183	561	.326	130	179	.726	152	147	94	0	496	7.3
51-52	—Rochester	65	1065	104	372	.280	61	85	.718	106	115	95	1	269	4.1
52-53	—Rochester	46	392	38	149	.255	27	38	.711	40	35	56	2	103	2.2
53-54	—Milwaukee	51	649	74	224	.330	48	73	.658	46	75	73	1	196	3.8
	Totals	496	...	1447	...	...	774	1178	.657	...	...	658	...	3668	7.4

NBL AND NBA PLAYOFF RECORD

Season	Team	G	Min.	FGM	FGA	Pct.	FTM	FTA	Pct.	Reb.	Ast.	PF	Dq.	Pts.	Avg.
45-46	—Rochester (NBL)	7	...	30	...	...	21	31	.677	...	...	10	...	81	11.6
46-47	—Rochester (NBL)	11	...	42	...	...	22	29	.759	...	...	22	...	106	9.6
47-48	—Rochester (NBL)	10	...	35	...	...	10	15	.667	...	...	6	...	80	8.0

Season Team	G	Min.	FGM	FGA	Pct.	FTM	FTA	Pct.	Reb.	Ast.	PF	Dq.	Pts.	Avg.
48-49 —Rochester (BAA)	4	...	18	40	.450	5	6	.833	...	13	3	...	41	10.3
49-50 —Rochester	2	...	3	9	.333	1	2	.500	...	0	3	...	7	3.5
50-51 —Rochester	14	...	31	76	.408	23	34	.676	19	20	14	0	85	6.1
51-52 —Rochester	6	65	3	15	.200	1	6	.167	6	2	3	0	7	1.2
52-53 —Rochester	2	14	1	5	.200	1	4	.250	1	1	4	0	3	1.5
Totals	56	...	163	...	...	84	127	.661	...	...	65	...	410	7.3

HEAD COACHING RECORD

HONORS: NBA Coach of the Year (1970).... Elected to Naismith Memorial Basketball Hall of Fame (1985).

NBA COACHING RECORD

	REGULAR SEASON				PLAYOFFS		
Season Team	W	L	Pct.	Finish	W	L	Pct.
53-54 —Milwaukee	10	16	.385	4th/Western Division	—	—	—
54-55 —Milwaukee	26	46	.361	4th/Western Division	—	—	—
55-56 —St. Louis.............................	33	39	.458	T2nd/Western Division	4	5	.444
56-57 —St. Louis.............................	14	19	.424		—	—	—
67-68 —New York	28	17	.622	3rd/Eastern Division	2	4	.333
68-69 —New York	54	28	.659	3rd/Eastern Division	6	4	.600
69-70 —New York	60	22	.732	1st/Eastern Division	12	7	.632
70-71 —New York	52	30	.634	1st/Atlantic Division	7	5	.583
71-72 —New York	48	34	.585	2nd/Atlantic Division	9	7	.563
72-73 —New York	57	25	.695	2nd/Atlantic Division	12	5	.706
73-74 —New York	49	33	.598	2nd/Atlantic Division	5	7	.417
74-75 —New York	40	42	.488	3rd/Atlantic Division	1	2	.333
75-76 —New York	38	44	.463	4th/Atlantic Division	—	—	—
76-77 —New York	40	42	.488	3rd/Atlantic Division	—	—	—
78-79 —New York	25	43	.368	4th/Atlantic Division	—	—	—
79-80 —New York	39	43	.476	T3rd/Atlantic Division	—	—	—
80-81 —New York	50	32	.610	3rd/Atlantic Division	0	2	.000
81-82 —New York	33	49	.402	5th/Atlantic Division	—	—	—
Totals (18 years)	696	604	.535	Totals (10 years)	58	48	.547

NOTES:
1954— Replaced Andrew Levane as Milwaukee head coach with record of 11-35.
1955— Milwaukee franchise transferred to St. Louis.
1956— Lost to Minneapolis, 103-97, in Western Division 2nd place game; defeated Minneapolis, 2-1, in Western Division semi-finals; lost to Fort Wayne, 3-2, in Western Division finals.
1957— Replaced as St. Louis head coach by Slater Martin (January).
1967— Replaced Dick McGuire as New York head coach (December), with record of 15-22 and in fifth place.
1968— Lost to Philadelphia in Eastern Division semifinals.
1969— Defeated Baltimore, 4-0, in Eastern Division semifinals; lost to Boston, 4-2, in Eastern Division finals.
1970— Defeated Baltimore, 4-3, in Eastern Division semifinals; defeated Milwaukee, 4-1, in Eastern Division finals; defeated Los Angeles, 4-3, in World Championship Series.
1971— Defeated Atlanta, 4-1, in Eastern Conference semifinals; lost to Baltimore, 4-3, in Eastern Conference finals.
1972— Defeated Baltimore, 4-2, in Eastern Conference semifinals; defeated Boston, 4-1, in Eastern Conference finals; lost to Los Angeles, 4-1, in World Championship Series.
1973— Defeated Baltimore, 4-1, in Eastern Conference semifinals; defeated Boston, 4-3, in Eastern Conference finals; defeated Los Angeles, 4-1, in World Championship Series.
1974— Defeated Capital, 4-3, in Eastern Conference semifinals; lost to Boston, 4-1, in Eastern Conference Finals.
1975— Lost to Houston in Eastern Conference first round.
1978— Replaced Willis Reed as New York head coach (November), with record of 6-8.
1981— Lost to Chicago in Eastern Conference first round.

JONES, K.C.

PERSONAL: Born May 25, 1932, in Taylor, Tex.... 6-1/200.
HIGH SCHOOL: Commerce (San Francisco).
COLLEGE: San Francisco.
TRANSACTIONS/CAREER NOTES: Selected by Boston Celtics in second round of 1956 NBA Draft.... In military service (1956-57 and 1957-58); played at Fort Leonard Wood, Mo.; named to Amateur Athletic Union All-America team as a member of 1957-58 Fort Leonard Wood team.... Played in Eastern Basketball League with Hartford Capitols (1967-68).
CAREER HONORS: Elected to Naismith Memorial Basketball Hall of Fame (1988).
MISCELLANEOUS: Member of NBA championship teams (1959, 1960, 1961, 1962, 1963, 1964, 1965, 1966).... Selected by Los Angeles Rams in 30th round of 1955 National Football League draft.... Member of gold-medal-winning U.S. Olympic team (1956).

COLLEGIATE RECORD

NOTES: Underwent appendectomy after one game of the 1953-54 season and was granted an extra year of eligibility by the University of San Francisco; however, he was ineligible for the 1955-56 NCAA tournament because he was playing his fifth season of college basketball.... Member of NCAA championship team (1955).

Season Team	G	Min.	FGM	FGA	Pct.	FTM	FTA	Pct.	Reb.	Pts.	Avg.
51-52 —San Francisco.........................	24	...	44	128	.344	46	64	.719	...	134	5.6
52-53 —San Francisco.........................	23	...	63	159	.396	81	149	.544	...	207	9.0
53-54 —San Francisco.........................	1	...	3	12	.250	2	2	1.000	3	8	8.0
54-55 —San Francisco.........................	29	...	105	293	.358	97	144	.674	148	307	10.6
55-56 —San Francisco.........................	25	...	76	208	.365	93	142	.655	130	245	9.8
Totals	102	...	291	800	.364	319	501	.637	...	901	8.8

NBA REGULAR-SEASON RECORD

Season	Team	G	Min.	FGM	FGA	Pct.	FTM	FTA	Pct.	Reb.	Ast.	PF	Dq.	Pts.	Avg.
58-59	Boston	49	609	65	192	.339	41	68	.603	127	70	58	0	171	3.5
59-60	Boston	74	1274	169	414	.408	128	170	.753	199	189	109	1	466	6.3
60-61	Boston	78	1607	203	601	.338	186	320	.581	279	253	200	3	592	7.6
61-62	Boston	79	2023	289	707	.409	145	231	.628	291	339	204	2	723	9.2
62-63	Boston	79	1945	230	591	.389	112	177	.633	263	317	221	3	572	7.2
63-64	Boston	80	2424	283	722	.392	88	168	.524	372	407	253	0	654	8.2
64-65	Boston	78	2434	253	639	.396	143	227	.630	318	437	263	5	649	8.3
65-66	Boston	80	2710	240	619	.388	209	303	.690	304	503	243	4	689	8.6
66-67	Boston	78	2446	182	459	.397	119	189	.630	240	389	273	7	483	6.2
	Totals	675	17472	1914	4944	.387	1171	1853	.632	2392	2904	1824	25	4999	7.4

NBA PLAYOFF RECORD

Season	Team	G	Min.	FGM	FGA	Pct.	FTM	FTA	Pct.	Reb.	Ast.	PF	Dq.	Pts.	Avg.
58-59	Boston	8	75	5	20	.250	5	5	1.000	12	10	8	0	15	1.9
59-60	Boston	13	232	27	80	.338	17	22	.773	45	14	28	0	71	5.5
60-61	Boston	9	103	9	30	.300	7	14	.500	19	15	17	0	25	2.8
61-62	Boston	14	329	44	102	.431	38	53	.717	56	55	50	1	126	9.0
62-63	Boston	13	250	19	64	.297	21	30	.700	36	37	42	1	59	4.5
63-64	Boston	10	312	25	72	.347	13	25	.520	37	68	40	0	63	6.3
64-65	Boston	12	396	43	104	.413	35	45	.778	39	74	49	1	121	10.1
65-66	Boston	17	543	45	109	.413	39	57	.684	52	75	65	0	129	7.6
66-67	Boston	9	254	24	75	.320	11	18	.611	24	48	36	1	59	6.6
	Totals	105	2494	241	656	.367	186	269	.691	320	396	335	4	668	6.4

EBL REGULAR-SEASON RECORD

Season	Team	G	Min.	FGM	FGA	Pct.	FTM	FTA	Pct.	Reb.	Ast.	PF	Dq.	Pts.	Avg.
67-68	Hartford	6	. . .	15	. . .	. . .	9	18	.500	24	41	. . .	. . .	39	6.5

HEAD COACHING RECORD

BACKGROUND: Assistant coach, Harvard University (1970-71).... Assistant coach, Los Angeles Lakers (1971-72).... Assistant coach, Milwaukee Bucks (1976-77).... Assistant coach, Boston Celtics (1978-79 through 1982-83).... Vice president/basketball operations, Celtics (1988-89).... Assistant coach, Seattle Supersonics (1989-90).

COLLEGIATE COACHING RECORD

Season	Team	W	L	Pct.	Finish
67-68	Brandeis	11	10	.524	
68-69	Brandeis	12	9	.571	
69-70	Brandeis	11	13	.458	
	Totals (3 years)	34	32	.515	

ABA COACHING RECORD

Season	Team	REGULAR SEASON W	L	Pct.	Finish	PLAYOFFS W	L	Pct.
72-73	San Diego	30	54	.357	4th/Western Division	0	4	.000
	Totals (1 year)	30	54	.357		0	4	.000

NBA COACHING RECORD

Season	Team	REGULAR SEASON W	L	Pct.	Finish	PLAYOFFS W	L	Pct.
73-74	Capital	47	35	.573	1st/Central Division	3	4	.429
74-75	Washington	60	22	.732	1st/Central Division	8	9	.471
75-76	Washington	48	34	.585	2nd/Central Division	3	4	.429
83-84	Boston	62	20	.756	1st/Atlantic Division	15	8	.652
84-85	Boston	63	19	.768	1st/Atlantic Division	13	8	.619
85-86	Boston	67	15	.817	1st/Atlantic Division	15	3	.833
86-87	Boston	59	23	.720	1st/Atlantic Division	13	10	.565
87-88	Boston	57	25	.695	1st/Atlantic Division	9	8	.529
90-91	Seattle	41	41	.500	5th/Pacific Division	2	3	.400
91-92	Seattle	18	18	.500		—	—	—
	Totals (10 years)	522	252	.674	Totals (9 years)	81	57	.587

NOTES:
1973 — Lost to Utah in Western Division semifinals.
1974 — Lost to New York in Eastern Conference semifinals.
1975 — Defeated Buffalo, 4-3, in Eastern Conference semifinals; defeated Boston, 4-2, in Eastern Conference finals; lost to Golden State, 4-0, in World Championship Series.
1976 — Lost to Cleveland in Eastern Conference semifinals.
1984 — Defeated Washington, 3-1, in Eastern Conference first round; defeated New York, 4-3, in Eastern Conference semifinals; defeated Milwaukee, 4-1, in Eastern Conference finals; defeated Los Angeles, 4-3, in World Championship Series.
1985 — Defeated Cleveland, 3-1, in Eastern Conference first round; defeated Detroit, 4-2, in Eastern Conference semifinals; defeated Philadelphia, 4-1, in Eastern Conference finals; lost to Los Angeles Lakers, 4-2, in World Championship Series.
1986 — Defeated Chicago, 3-0, in Eastern Conference first round; defeated Atlanta, 4-1, in Eastern Conference semifinals; defeated Milwaukee, 4-0, in Eastern Conference finals; defeated Houston, 4-2, in NBA Finals.
1987 — Defeated Chicago, 3-0, in Eastern Conference first round; defeated Milwaukee, 4-3, in Eastern Conference semifinals; defeated Detroit, 4-3, in Eastern Conference finals; lost to Los Angeles Lakers, 4-2, in NBA Finals.
1988 — Defeated New York, 3-1, in Eastern Conference first round; defeated Atlanta, 4-3, in Eastern Conference semifinals; lost to Detroit, 4-2, in Eastern Conference finals.
1991 — Lost to Portland in Western Conference first round.
1992 — Replaced as Seattle head coach by interim coach Bob Kloppenburg (January 15).

KUNDLA, JOHN

PERSONAL: Born July 3, 1916, in Star Junction, Pa. . . . 6-2/180. . . . Full name: John Albert Kundla.
HIGH SCHOOL: Central (Minneapolis).
COLLEGE: Minnesota.

COLLEGIATE RECORD

Season Team	G	Min.	FGM	FGA	Pct.	FTM	FTA	Pct.	Reb.	Pts.	Avg.
35-36 —Minnesota†				Freshman team statistics unavailable.							
36-37 —Minnesota	15	...	53	...	...	34	53	.642	...	140	9.3
37-38 —Minnesota	20	...	62	...	...	41	77	.532	...	165	8.3
38-39 —Minnesota	17	...	71	...	...	40	63	.635	...	182	10.7
Varsity totals	52	...	186	...	...	115	193	.596	...	487	9.4

HEAD COACHING RECORD

BACKGROUND: Head coach, De La Salle High School (Minn.).

COLLEGIATE COACHING RECORD

Season Team	W	L	Pct.	Finish
46-47 —St. Thomas (Minn.)	11	11	.500	
59-60 —Minnesota	12	12	.500	T3rd/Big Ten Conference
60-61 —Minnesota	10	13	.435	T4th/Big Ten Conference
61-62 —Minnesota	10	14	.417	7th/Big Ten Conference
62-63 —Minnesota	12	12	.500	T4th/Big Ten Conference
63-64 —Minnesota	17	7	.708	3rd/Big Ten Conference
64-65 —Minnesota	19	5	.792	2nd/Big Ten Conference
65-66 —Minnesota	14	10	.583	T5th/Big Ten Conference
66-67 —Minnesota	9	15	.375	9th/Big Ten Conference
67-68 —Minnesota	7	17	.292	T9th/Big Ten Conference
Totals (10 years)	121	116	.511	

NBL COACHING RECORD

Season Team	REGULAR SEASON				PLAYOFFS		
	W	L	Pct.	Finish	W	L	Pct.
47-48 —Minneapolis	43	17	.717	1st/Western Division	8	2	.800
Totals (1 year)	43	17	.717	Totals (1 year)	8	2	.800

NBA COACHING RECORD

Season Team	REGULAR SEASON				PLAYOFFS		
	W	L	Pct.	Finish	W	L	Pct.
48-49 —Minneapolis	44	16	.733	2nd/Western Division	8	2	.800
49-50 —Minneapolis	51	17	.750	T1st/Central Division	11	2	.833
50-51 —Minneapolis	44	24	.647	1st/Western Division	3	4	.429
51-52 —Minneapolis	40	26	.606	2nd/Western Division	9	4	.692
52-53 —Minneapolis	48	22	.686	1st/Western Division	9	3	.750
53-54 —Minneapolis	46	26	.639	1st/Western Division	9	4	.692
54-55 —Minneapolis	40	32	.556	2nd/Western Division	3	4	.429
55-56 —Minneapolis	33	39	.458	T2nd/Western Division	1	3	.333
56-57 —Minneapolis	34	38	.472	T1st/Western Division	2	4	.400
57-58 —Minneapolis	10	23	.303	4th/Western Division	—	—	—
58-59 —Minneapolis	33	39	.458	2nd/Western Division	6	7	.462
Totals (11 years)	423	302	.583	Totals (10 years)	61	37	.622

NOTES:
1948— Defeated Oshkosh, 3-1, in NBL playoffs; defeated Tri-Cities, 2-0; defeated Rochester, 3-1, in NBL championship series.
1949— Defeated Chicago, 2-0, in Western Division semifinals; defeated Rochester, 2-0, in Western Division finals; defeated Washington, 4-2, in World Championship Series.
1950— Defeated Rochester, 78-76, in Central Division first place game; defeated Chicago, 2-0, in Central Division semifinals; defeated Fort Wayne, 2-0, in Central Division finals; defeated Anderson, 2-0, in NBA semifinals; defeated Syracuse, 4-2, in World Championship Series.
1951— Defeated Indianapolis, 2-1, in Western Division semifinals; lost to Rochester, 3-1, in Western Division finals.
1952— Defeated Indianapolis, 2-0, in Western Division semifinals; defeated Rochester, 3-1, in Western Division finals; defeated New York, 4-3, in World Championship Series.
1953— Defeated Indianapolis, 2-0, in Western Division semifinals; defeated Fort Wayne, 3-2, in Western Division finals; defeated New York, 4-1, in World Championship Series.
1954— Defeated Rochester, 109-88; Fort Wayne, 90-85; and Fort Wayne, 78-73, in Western Division round robin; defeated Rochester, 2-1, in Western Division semifinals; defeated Syracuse, 4-3, in World Championship Series.
1955— Defeated Rochester, 2-1, in Western Division semifinals; lost to Fort Wayne, 3-1, in Western Division finals.
1956— Defeated St. Louis, 103-97, in Western Division second place game; lost to St. Louis, 2-1, in Western Division semifinals.
1957— Defeated Fort Wayne, 2-0, in Western Division semifinals; lost to St. Louis, 114-111, in Western Division tiebreaker; lost to St. Louis, 3-0, in Western Division finals.
1958— Replaced George Mikan as Minneapolis head coach (January 14), with record of 9-30 and in fourth place.
1959— Defeated Detroit, 2-1, in Western Division semifinals; defeated St. Louis, 4-2, in Western Division finals; lost to Boston, 4-0, in World Championship Series.

DID YOU KNOW. . .

. . . that the 1992 NBA Draft in Portland was the first ever held outside of New York City?

LAPCHICK, JOE

PERSONAL: Born April 12, 1900, in Yonkers, N.Y. . . . Died August 10, 1970. . . . 6-5/185. . . . Full name: Joseph Bohomiel Lapchick.
TRANSACTIONS/CAREER NOTES: Played with independent teams, including the original Celtics (1918-1920, 1924-1926, 1932-1936).
CAREER HONORS: Elected to Naismith Memorial Basketball Hall of Fame (1966).
MISCELLANEOUS: Did not play high school or college basketball.

PRO RECORD

Season	Team	League	G	FGM	FTM	Pts.	Avg.
20-21	—Holyoke	IL	11	14	40	68	6.2
	—Schenectady	NYSL	5	2	10	14	2.8
21-22	—Schenectady-Troy	NYSL	32	12	95	119	3.7
	—Brooklyn	MBL	10	6	20	32	3.2
	—Holyoke	IL	16	13	40	66	4.1
22-23	—Brooklyn	MBL	33	34	109	177	5.4
	—Troy	NYSL	24	13	59	85	3.5
	—Holyoke	IL			Statistics unavailable.		
26-27	—Brooklyn	ABL	32	35	131	201	6.3
	—New York	NBL	16	19	57	95	5.9
27-28	—New York	ABL	47	103	110	316	6.7
28-29	—Cleveland	ABL	39	51	86	188	4.8
29-30	—Cleveland	ABL	52	47	92	186	3.6
30-31	—Cleveland-Toledo	ABL	30	22	49	93	3.1
32-33	—Yonkers	MBL	1	0	0	0	0.0
ABL Pro totals			238	292	575	1159	4.9

COLLEGIATE COACHING RECORD

Season	Team	W	L	Pct.	Finish
36-37	—St. John's	12	7	.632	Independent
37-38	—St. John's	15	4	.789	Independent
38-39	—St. John's	18	4	.818	Independent
39-40	—St. John's	15	5	.750	Independent
40-41	—St. John's	11	6	.647	Independent
41-42	—St. John's	16	5	.762	Independent
42-43	—St. John's	21	3	.875	Independent
43-44	—St. John's	18	5	.783	Independent
44-45	—St. John's	21	3	.875	Independent
45-46	—St. John's	17	6	.739	Independent
46-47	—St. John's	16	7	.696	Independent
56-57	—St. John's	14	9	.609	Independent
57-58	—St. John's	18	8	.692	Independent
58-59	—St. John's	20	6	.769	Independent
59-60	—St. John's	17	8	.680	Independent
60-61	—St. John's	20	5	.800	Independent
61-62	—St. John's	21	5	.808	Independent
62-63	—St. John's	9	15	.375	Independent
63-64	—St. John's	14	11	.560	Independent
64-65	—St. John's	21	8	.724	Independent
Totals (20 years)		334	130	.720	

NBA COACHING RECORD

		REGULAR SEASON				PLAYOFFS		
Season	Team	W	L	Pct.	Finish	W	L	Pct.
47-48	—New York (BAA)	26	22	.542	2nd/Eastern Division	1	2	.333
48-49	—New York (BAA)	32	28	.533	2nd/Eastern Division	3	3	.500
49-50	—New York	40	28	.588	2nd/Eastern Division	3	2	.600
50-51	—New York	36	30	.545	3rd/Eastern Division	8	6	.571
51-52	—New York	37	29	.561	3rd/Eastern Division	8	6	.571
52-53	—New York	47	23	.671	1st/Eastern Division	6	5	.545
53-54	—New York	44	28	.611	1st/Eastern Division	0	4	.000
54-55	—New York	38	34	.528	2nd/Eastern Division	1	2	.333
55-56	—New York	26	25	.510		—	—	—
Totals (9 years)		326	247	.569	**Totals (8 years)**	30	30	.500

NOTES:
1939— Defeated Roanoke, 71-47, NIT quarterfinals; lost to Loyola, 51-46, in semifinals; lost to Bradley, 40-35, in third-place game.
1940— Lost to Duquesne, 38-31, in NIT quarterfinals.
1943— Defeated Rice, 51-49, in NIT quarterfinals; defeated Fordham, 69-43, in semifinals; defeated Toledo, 48-27, in final.
1944— Defeated Bowling Green, 44-40, in NIT quarterfinals; defeated Kentucky, 48-45, in semifinals; defeated DePaul, 47-39, in final.
1945— Defeated Muhlenberg, 34-33, in NIT quarterfinals; lost to Bowling Green, 57-44, in semifinals; lost to Rhode Island, 64-57, in third-place game.
1946— Lost to West Virginia, 70-58, in NIT quarterfinals.
1947— Lost to North Carolina State, 61-55, in NIT quarterfinals.
1948— Lost to Baltimore in quarterfinals.
1949— Defeated Baltimore, 2-1, in Eastern Division semifinals; lost to Washington, 2-1, in Eastern Division finals.
1950— Defeated Washington, 2-0, in Eastern Division semifinals; lost to Syracuse, 2-1, in Eastern Division finals.
1951— Defeated Boston, 2-0, in Eastern Division semifinals; defeated Syracuse, 3-2, in Eastern Division finals; lost to Rochester, 4-3, in World Championship Series.
1952— Defeated Boston, 2-1, in Eastern Division semifinals; defeated Syracuse, 3-1, in Eastern Division finals; lost to Minneapolis, 4-3, in World Championship Series.
1953— Defeated Baltimore, 2-0, in Eastern Division semifinals; defeated Boston, 3-1, in Eastern Division finals; lost to Minneapolis, 4-1, in World Championship Series.

1954— Lost to Boston, 93-71; Syracuse, 75-68; Boston, 79-78; and Syracuse, 103-99, in Eastern Division round robin.
1955— Lost to Boston in Eastern Division semifinals.
1956— Resigned as New York head coach.
1958— Defeated Butler, 76-69, in NIT first round; defeated Utah, 71-70, in quarterfinals; lost to Dayton, 80-56, in semifinals; lost to St. Bonaventure, 84-69, in third-place game.
1959— Defeated Villanova, 75-67, in NIT first round; defeated St. Bonaventure, 82-74, in quarterfinals; defeated Providence, 76-55, in semifinals; defeated Bradley, 76-71 (OT), in final.
1960— Lost to St. Bonaventure, 106-71, in NIT quarterfinals.
1961— Lost to Wake Forest, 97-74, in NCAA Tournament first round.
1962— Defeated Holy Cross, 80-74, in NIT quarterfinals; defeated Duquesne, 76-65, in semifinals; lost to Dayton, 73-67, in final.
1965— Defeated Boston College, 114-92, in NIT first round; defeated New Mexico, 61-54, in quarterfinals; defeated Army, 67-60, in semifinals; defeated Villanova, 55-51, in final.

MacLEOD, JOHN

PERSONAL: Born October 3, 1937, in New Albany, Ind. . . . 6-0/170.
. . . Full name: John Matthew MacLeod.
HIGH SCHOOL: New Providence (Clarksville, Ind.).
COLLEGE: Bellarmine (Ky.).

COLLEGIATE RECORD

Season Team	G	Min.	FGM	FGA	Pct.	FTM	FTA	Pct.	Reb.	Pts.	Avg.
55-56 —Bellarmine					Statistics unavailable.						
56-57 —Bellarmine	10	...	0	...	...	1	...	...	...	1	0.1
57-58 —Bellarmine	8	...	2	...	...	3	10	.300	...	7	0.9
58-59 —Bellarmine	5	...	2	...	...	4	...	...	...	8	1.6
Totals	23	...	4	...	...	8	...	...	...	16	0.7

HEAD COACHING RECORD

BACKGROUND: Assistant coach, DeSales High School, Ky. (1959-60 through 1961-62). . . . Head coach, Smithville High School, Ind. (1963-64 and 1964-65; record: 16-24). . . . Assistant coach, Cathedral High School, Ind. (1965-66). . . . Assistant coach, University of Oklahoma (1966-67).

COLLEGIATE COACHING RECORD

Season Team	W	L	Pct.	Finish
67-68 —Oklahoma	13	13	.500	T3rd/Big Eight Conference
68-69 —Oklahoma	7	19	.269	8th/Big Eight Conference
69-70 —Oklahoma	19	9	.679	3rd/Big Eight Conference
70-71 —Oklahoma	19	8	.704	2nd/Big Eight Conference
71-72 —Oklahoma	14	12	.538	3rd/Big Eight Conference
72-73 —Oklahoma	18	8	.692	4th/Big Eight Conference
91-92 —Notre Dame	18	15	.545	Independent
Totals (7 years)	110	84	.567	

NBA COACHING RECORD

Season Team	REGULAR SEASON W	L	Pct.	Finish	PLAYOFFS W	L	Pct.
73-74 —Phoenix	30	52	.396	4th/Pacific Division	—	—	—
74-75 —Phoenix	32	50	.390	4th/Pacific Division	—	—	—
75-76 —Phoenix	42	40	.512	3rd/Pacific Division	10	9	.526
76-77 —Phoenix	34	48	.415	5th/Pacific Division	—	—	—
77-78 —Phoenix	49	33	.598	2nd/Pacific Division	0	2	.000
78-79 —Phoenix	50	32	.610	2nd/Pacific Division	9	6	.600
79-80 —Phoenix	55	27	.671	3rd/Pacific Division	3	5	.375
80-81 —Phoenix	57	25	.695	1st/Pacific Division	3	4	.429
81-82 —Phoenix	46	36	.561	3rd/Pacific Division	2	5	.286
82-83 —Phoenix	53	29	.646	2nd/Pacific Division	1	2	.333
83-84 —Phoenix	41	41	.500	4th/Pacific Division	9	8	.529
84-85 —Phoenix	36	46	.439	3rd/Pacific Division	0	3	.000
85-86 —Phoenix	32	50	.390	T3rd/Pacific Division	—	—	—
86-87 —Phoenix	22	34	.393		—	—	—
87-88 —Dallas	53	29	.646	2nd/Midwest Division	10	7	.588
88-89 —Dallas	38	44	.463	4th/Midwest Division	—	—	—
89-90 —Dallas	5	6	.455		—	—	—
90-91 —New York	32	35	.478	3rd/Atlantic Division	0	3	.000
Totals (18 years)	707	657	.518	Totals (10 years)	47	54	.465

NOTES:
1970— Defeated Louisville, 74-73, in NIT first round; lost to Louisiana State, 97-94, in quarterfinals.
1971— Lost to Hawaii, 87-86 (2 OT), in NIT first round.
1976— Defeated Seattle, 4-2, in Western Conference semifinals; defeated Golden State, 4-3, in Western Conference finals; lost to Boston, 4-2, in World Championship Series.
1978— Lost to Milwaukee in Western Conference first round.
1979— Defeated Portland, 2-1, in Western Conference first round; defeated Kansas City, 4-1, in Western Conference semifinals; lost to Seattle, 4-3, in Western Conference finals.
1980— Defeated Kansas City, 2-1, in Western Conference first round; lost to Los Angeles Lakers, 4-1, in Western Conference semifinals.
1981— Lost to Kansas City in Western Conference semifinals.
1982— Defeated Denver, 2-1, in Western Conference semifinals; lost to Los Angeles Lakers, 4-0, in Western Conference semifinals.
1983— Lost to Denver in Western Conference first round.

1984— Defeated Portland, 3-2, in Western Conference first round; defeated Utah, 4-2, in Western Conference semifinals; lost to
Los Angeles Lakers, 4-2, in Western Conference finals.
1985— Lost to Los Angeles Lakers in Western Conference first round.
1987— Replaced as Phoenix head coach by Dick Van Arsdale (February 26).
1988— Defeated Houston, 3-1, in Western Conference first round; defeated Denver, 4-2, in Western Conference semifinals; lost
to Los Angeles Lakers, 4-3, in Western Conference finals.
1989— Replaced as Dallas head coach by Richie Adubato (November 29).
1990— Replaced Stu Jackson as New York head coach (December 3), with record of 7-8.
1991— Lost to Chicago in Eastern Conference first round.
1992— Defeated Western Michigan, 63-56, in NIT first round; defeated Kansas State, 64-47, in second round; defeated Manhattan, 74-58, in quarterfinals; defeated Utah, 58-55, in semifinals; lost to Virginia, 81-76, in final.

RAMSAY, JACK

PERSONAL: Born February 21, 1925, in Philadelphia. . . . 6-1/180. . . .
Full name: John T. Ramsay.
HIGH SCHOOL: Upper Darby Senior (Pa.).
COLLEGE: St. Joseph's, then Villanova.

TRANSACTIONS/CAREER NOTES: Played with San Diego Dons, an Amateur Athletic Union team (1945-46).
. . . Played in Eastern Basketball League with Harrisburg and Sudbury (1949-50 through 1954-55).

COLLEGIATE RECORD

Season	Team	G	Min.	FGM	FGA	Pct.	FTM	FTA	Pct.	Reb.	Pts.	Avg.
42-43	St. Joseph's‡					Freshman team statistics unavailable.						
43-44						Did not play—in military service.						
44-45						Did not play—in military service.						
45-46						Did not play—in military service.						
46-47	St. Joseph's	21	...	72	214	.336	20	32	.625	...	164	7.8
47-48	St. Joseph's	14	...	60	...	...	38	...	...	...	158	11.3
48-49	St. Joseph's	23	...	75	...	...	52	...	...	...	202	8.8
	Varsity totals	58	...	207			110			...	524	9.0

EBL REGULAR-SEASON RECORD

Season	Team	G	Min.	FGM	FGA	Pct.	FTM	FTA	Pct.	Reb.	Ast.	PF	Dq.	Pts.	Avg.
49-50	Harrisburg	25	...	134	...	...	68	...	...	...	...	...	...	336	13.4
51-52	Sunbury	26	...	159	...	...	86	...	...	...	...	...	...	404	15.5
52-53	Sunbury	21	...	116	...	...	97	...	...	...	...	...	...	329	15.7
53-54	Sunbury	28	...	112	...	...	101	...	...	...	...	...	...	325	11.6
54-55	Sunbury	30	...	164	...	...	155	...	...	...	...	...	...	483	16.1
	Totals	130	...	685	...	...	507	...	...	...	...	...	...	1877	14.4

HEAD COACHING RECORD

BACKGROUND: Head coach, St. James High School (Pa.) and later head coach, Mount Pleasant High School, Del. (1949-1955).
. . . General manager, Philadelphia 76ers (1966-67 and 1967-68). . . . Head coach/general manager, 76ers (1968-69 and
1969-70).

COLLEGIATE COACHING RECORD

Season	Team	W	L	Pct.	Finish
55-56	St. Joseph's	23	6	.793	Independent
56-57	St. Joseph's	17	7	.708	Independent
57-58	St. Joseph's	18	9	.667	2nd/Middle Atlantic Conference
58-59	St. Joseph's	22	5	.815	1st/Middle Atlantic Conference
59-60	St. Joseph's	20	7	.741	1st/Middle Atlantic Conference
60-61	St. Joseph's	25	5	.833	1st/Middle Atlantic Conference
61-62	St. Joseph's	18	10	.643	1st/Middle Atlantic Conference
62-63	St. Joseph's	23	5	.821	1st/Middle Atlantic Conference
63-64	St. Joseph's	18	10	.643	T2nd/Middle Atlantic Conference
64-65	St. Joseph's	26	3	.897	1st/Middle Atlantic Conference
65-66	St. Joseph's	24	5	.828	1st/Middle Atlantic Conference
	Totals (11 years)	234	72	.765	

NBA COACHING RECORD

		REGULAR SEASON				PLAYOFFS		
Season	Team	W	L	Pct.	Finish	W	L	Pct.
68-69	Philadelphia	55	27	.671	2nd/Eastern Division	1	4	.200
69-70	Philadelphia	42	40	.512	4th/Eastern Division	1	4	.200
70-71	Philadelphia	47	35	.573	2nd/Atlantic Division	3	4	.429
71-72	Philadelphia	30	52	.366	3rd/Atlantic Division	—	—	—
72-73	Buffalo	21	61	.256	3rd/Atlantic Division	—	—	—
73-74	Buffalo	42	40	.512	3rd/Atlantic Division	2	4	.333
74-75	Buffalo	49	33	.598	2nd/Atlantic Division	3	4	.429
75-76	Buffalo	46	36	.561	T2nd/Atlantic Division	4	5	.444
76-77	Portland	49	33	.598	2nd/Pacific Division	14	5	.737
77-78	Portland	58	24	.707	1st/Pacific Division	2	4	.333
78-79	Portland	45	37	.549	4th/Pacific Division	1	2	.333
79-80	Portland	38	44	.463	4th/Pacific Division	1	2	.333
80-81	Portland	45	37	.549	3rd/Pacific Division	1	2	.333
81-82	Portland	42	40	.512	5th/Pacific Division	—	—	—
82-83	Portland	46	36	.561	4th/Pacific Division	3	4	.429
83-84	Portland	48	34	.585	2nd/Pacific Division	2	3	.400
84-85	Portland	42	40	.512	2nd/Pacific Division	4	5	.444
85-86	Portland	40	42	.488	2nd/Pacific Division	1	3	.250
86-87	Indiana	41	41	.500	4th/Central Division	1	3	.250
87-88	Indiana	38	44	.463	6th/Central Division	—	—	—
88-89	Indiana	0	7	.000		—	—	—
	Totals (21 years)	864	783	.525	Totals (16 years)	44	58	.431

ALL-TIME GREAT COACHES

NOTES:

1956— Defeated Seton Hall, 74-65, in NIT quarterfinals; lost to Louisville, 89-79, in semifinals; defeated St. Francis-New York, 93-82, in third-place game.
1958— Defeated St. Peter's, 83-72, in NIT first round; lost to St. Bonaventure, 79-75, in quarterfinals.
1959— Lost to West Virginia, 95-92, in NCAA Tournament first round; lost to Navy, 70-59, in regional consolation game.
1960— Lost to Duke, 58-56, in NCAA Tournament first round; lost to West Virginia, 106-100, in regional consolation game.
1961— Defeated Princeton, 72-67, in NCAA Tournament regional final; defeated Wake Forest, 96-86, in regional final; lost to Ohio State, 95-69, in national semifinal; defeated Utah, 127-120 (4 OT), in consolation game.
1962— Lost to Wake Forest, 96-85 (OT), in NCAA Tournament regional semifinal; lost to New York University, 94-85, in regional consolation game.
1963— Defeated Princeton, 82-81, in NCAA Tournament first round; defeated West Virginia, 97-88, in regional semifinal; lost to Duke, 73-59, in regional final.
1964— Defeated Miami (Fla.), 86-76, in NIT first round; lost to Bradley, 83-81, in quarterfinals.
1965— Defeated Connecticut, 67-61, in NCAA Tournament first round; lost to Providence, 81-73 (OT), in regional semifinal; lost to North Carolina State, 103-81, in regional consolation game.
1966— Defeated Providence, 65-48, in NCAA Tournament first round; lost to Duke, 76-74, in regional semifinal; defeated Davidson, 92-76, in regional consolation game.
1969— Lost to Boston in Eastern Division semifinals.
1970— Lost to Milwaukee in Eastern Division semifinals.
1971— Lost to Baltimore in Eastern Conference semifinals.
1974— Lost to Boston in Eastern Conference semifinals.
1975— Lost to Washington in Eastern Conference semifinals.
1976— Defeated Philadelphia, 2-1, in Eastern Conference first round; lost to Boston, 4-2, in Eastern Conference semifinals.
1977— Defeated Chicago, 2-1, in Western Conference first round; defeated Denver, 4-2, in Western Conference semifinals; defeated Los Angeles Lakers, 4-0, in Western Conference finals; defeated Philadelphia, 4-2, in World Championship Series.
1978— Lost to Seattle in Western Conference semifinals.
1979— Lost to Phoenix in Western Conference first round.
1980— Lost to Seattle in Western Conference first round.
1981— Lost to Kansas City in Western Conference first round.
1983— Defeated Seattle, 2-0, in Western Conference first round; lost to Los Angeles Lakers, 4-1, in Western Conference semifinals.
1984— Lost to Phoenix in Western Conference first round.
1985— Defeated Dallas, 3-1, in Western Conference first round; lost to Los Angeles Lakers, 4-1, in Western Conference semifinals.
1986— Lost to Denver in Western Conference first round.
1987— Lost to Atlanta in Eastern Conference first round.
1988— Resigned as Indiana head coach (November 17); replaced by Mel Daniels.